SCHOOL AND SOCIETY

EDITED BY J. McKEEN CATTELL

VOLUME XXXIV
JULY-DECEMBER, 1931

WITH WHICH HAS BEEN COMBINED THE
EDUCATIONAL REVIEW
Edited by WILLIAM McANDREW

NEW YORK
THE SCIENCE PRESS
1931

THE SCIENCE PRESS PRINTING COMPANY
LANCASTER, PA.

CONTENTS AND INDEX

VOLUME XXXIV—JULY-DECEMBER, 1931

NAMES OF CONTRIBUTORS ARE PRINTED IN SMALL CAPITALS

ACHILLES, P. S., Nation-wide Surveys in Reading, English Usage and Vocabulary, 233
ADAMS, J., Teachers by the Grace of God, 303
Administrator, College, Goes to School, A. M. PALMER, 704
Adult Education, 312
Advisory Committee on Education, National, 325, 393, 461, Report, 740, Recommendations, 760
Age of College Students, 620
Alexander, C., Educational Finance, 38
Allegany School of Natural History, 365
Allen, H., The Airship, 38
American Univ. Center in Paris, Site, 220
Andrews, F. F., The Holy Land Under Mandate, 782
ANGELL, R. C., Influence of the Economic Depression on Student Life at Univ. of Michigan, 649
Anti-Semitic Disorders at Vienna, 49
Arkansas, Public Education in, 118
Art Judgment, A. C. EURICH and H. A. CARROLL, 204
Athens College, 691
Athletics and Alumni Education, W. B. SHAW, 278
ATHLETICS, COLLEGE DIRECTOR OF, Varsity Football, 699
Atlanta Univ., Library, 87; New Buildings, 693
Attendance, School, in United States, 526
Australia, Closing of Country Schools, 618

B., L. C., Employment of Cornell Graduates, 264
BAGLEY, W. C., The Profession of Teaching, 105
Bagley, W. C., Education, Crime and Social Progress, 28
Balkan Universities, Student Unrest in, 657
BALLOU, F. W., Training and Advancement, 187
Bankes, W. J., Your Complete Life, 482
Bartholomew, W., and F. Hurlbut, The Business Man's English, 782
BARTON, W. A., The True-False Examination, 544
BAYLOR, A. S., National Council of Education, 154
Becker, C. L., Modern History, 164
BELLEAU, W. E., Regulation of Private Schools, 436
Bennington College, 223
BENNION, M., Teacher-Training Curricula, 551
Berens, H. A., High-school Awards, 478
Berry, Martha, 314
Bible, Reading in Public Schools, 627; at Oxford, 842
BLANCHARD, H., International Student Service, 628
Blanche, W. W., and J. Speck, A Gateway to Music, 37
Bliss, H. E., Organization of Knowledge, 347
Bolton, F. E., Adolescent Education, 31, 775
Bonser, Frederick Gordon, H. HARAP, 796
Books, for Children, 255; Reviews, 25, 164, 340, 471, 638, 770
Bookshelves, Seven Hundred Miles of, 232
BOUTWELL, W. D., National Education Assoc., 109
BOYER, C. F., Reading for Honors, 214
Breslich, E. R., Teaching Secondary School Mathematics, 346
BREWSTER, E. H., A Liberal Education, 432
BRIGGS, T. H., Cooperating in Economy, 718
British, Universities and the Land Tax, 6; Museum Library, 283; Students, Empire Travel for, 220; Education, 324, in 1930, 557; Effect of Industry on, 671; Educational Broadcasting, 361; Children at the Seaside, 440; Assoc., for the Advancement of Science, Education at, 257, Educational Development, 1831–1931, A Centenary Survey, C. G. ROBERTSON, 445
Broadcast Program of National Advisory Council, 461
Broadcasting, Educational, 117; British, 361
Broadhurst, J., and M. O. Lerrigo, Health Horizons, 647
BROOME, E. C., The Superintendent and the White House Conference, 135
Bryn Mawr Summer School, 588
Budget, School, 265
Business, Crisis, and the College, W. J. MATHERLY, 369; School, Purposes of, C. S. MARSH, 811
Butler, Nicholas Murray, Celebration in Honor of, 830
Caldwell, O. W., C. E. Skinner and J. W. Tietz, Biological Foundations of Education, 36
CAMPBELL, E. C., and L. P. KIRBY, Educational Organization in New Mexico, 59
Campbell, W., Amateur Acting and Production, 172
Carnegie, United Kingdom Trust, 252; Foundation for the Advancement of Teaching, 312
Carpenter, W. W., and J. Rufi, 166
Carr, W. G., and J. Waage, The Lesson Assignment, 642
Case, C. M., Social Process and Human Progress, 639
Case, R. D., The Platoon School in America, 36
Casner, M. G., and R. H. Gabriel, Exploring American History, 342
CASON, H., Essay Examination and Test, 413
Catholic Educational Association, R. WALTERS, 17
CATTELL, J. McK., Education under the National Government, 325
Cestre, C., and Others, French Books, 776
CHAMBERS, M. M., State University, 64
CHAMBERS, S., The Project Preeminent, 465
Charter, W. W., M. F. Rice and E. W. Beck, Conduct Problem, 478
CHASE, H. W., New Statutes of the University of Illinois, 874
CHATTERJEE, R., Poet Tagore's University, 681
Chautauqua Institution, 51
Chemistry, Teachers of, at Buffalo, 256
Chicago, Schools, 15; Experimental School, 120, 145; Administration Debâcle, 841; Univ. of, International House, 51
Child, Labor, in India, 129; Sunday, 499; Guidance in London, 525
Chile's Students, 153
China, The Schools of, 6
Chinese, Ten Million in School, 724; Students, Riots of, 825
Christian Colleges, Evangelical, Undergraduates in a Group of, J. H. FURBAY, 813

9340

Chrysalis Club, L. PIERCE, 231
Church College and Character, C. A. MANEY, 576
Cigarettes and Coeducation, C. HOOPER, 322
Cincinnati, Univ. Teachers College, 828
Cinematographic Institute, 84
CLARK, E. L., Predicting College Grades, 765
Classics, and the Modern Magazine, M. L. GUBERLET, 599; A Moral Equivalent for, J. S. CLELAND, 873
CLELAND, J. S., A Moral Equivalent for the Classics, 873
Coddling, Surcease of, W. MCANDREW, 767
COFFMAN, L. D., Challenge to the College Graduate, 1
Cole, R. D., Modern Foreign Languages, 343
College, Graduate, Challenge to, L. D. COFFMAN, 1; Success, C. F. ROSS, 20; Entrance Examination Board, R. WALTERS, 672
Colleges, Attack on, G. WAKEHAM, 125; and Secondary Schools of Middle States, R. WALTERS, 837
COLLIER, H. G., Vineland Laboratory, 426
Colombia, Elementary Education in, H. C. LANKS, 631
Columbia Univ., Summer Session, 223; Post-Graduate Medical School and Hospital, 285; Edward S. Harkness Library, 559; Officers, A Quarter of a Century of Learning, 644
COMISH, A., Contract Plan, 95
Community Planning and the Problem Child, N. FENTON, 387
Consolidating the Colleges, J. A. POLLARD, 404
Contract Plan, A. COMISH, 95
Cooper, Jacob, Greek Prize, 528
Cornell Univ., Graduates, Employment of, L. C. B., 264; Registration Statistics, 659
Correspondence Courses for Public High Schools, 590
Cost of Education in Oregon, 363
Costs, per Child in Schools of N. Y. City, 313; Per Capita, H. L. HUMKE, 743
Cotter, A. C., Logic and Epistemology, 171
Country Life Conference, Amer., 192
Course-crabbing, N. ISRAELI, 540
Crawford, J. and P., Greek Tales, 348
Crawford, R. P., The Magazine Article, 777
Cunningham, A. S., Presidents, 342
Curme, G. O., Syntax, 345

D., E. H., American Library Association, 202
DARSIE, M. L., David Starr Jordan, 822
Davis, S. E., The Teacher's Relationships, 32; Teaching the Elementary Curriculum, 640
Deaf, Education of, 751; Instructors of, M. F. MEYER, 235
DEAN, A COLLEGE, Concerning Marks, 504
Delayen, G., Cicero, 772
DEMIASHKEVICH, M. J., French and German Academic Examinations and Degrees, 515
Depreciation in Public School Buildings, H. R. WOODWARD, 870
DEWEY, J., Modern Education, 579
Dewey, J., Educational Confusion, 640
Dictionary, English, and Invention, H. G. GOOD, 492
Directive Aims in Education, D. SNEDDEN, 745
Discussion Technique, A. O. HANSEN, 93; H. B. SMITH and L. R. DELONG, 533
Doughton, I., Philosophy of Education, 646

Eby, F., Early Protestant Educators, 774
Economic, Depression and Education, J. K. NORTON, 271; Situation and the Schools, 876; Association, American, Detroit Meeting, 99
Economy, Cooperating in, T. H. BRIGGS, 718
Edgerton, A. C., A Speech for Every Occasion, 172
Editorial Comment, W. MCANDREW, 23, 159, 337, 469, 635
Edmonson, J. B., and A. Dondineau, Citizenship and Occupations through Problems, 638
Education, Some Problems in, W. A. SUTTON, 103; Secretary of, 739; Office of, Report, 750; and the Eighteenth Amendment, H. HARAP, 758
Educational Conference, P. A. WITTY and H. C. LEHMAN, 807
Eells, W. C., The Junior College, 781
Eggleston, M. W., Stories for Bedtime, 778
Eighteenth Amendment, H. HARAP, 758; and the National Education Association, J. E. MORGAN, 834
Elementary School Teachers, F. W. BALLOU, 187
Eliot, T. D., Standards of Living, 165
ELLIS, E., Graduate Work for Teachers of the Social Studies, 322
Emmet, W. LeR., Autobiography of an Engineer, 779
Engelhardt, F., Public-School Organization and Administration, 167
England, Teaching by Moving Pictures in, 749
English, Children Living in Basements, 392; School Child, Health of, 826
Enrolment in September, 1931, 510
EURICH, A. C., and H. A. CARROLL, Art Judgment, 204
Evolution, E. LINTON, 76
Examination, of School Children, 116; True-False, W. A. BARTON, 544
Examinations and Degrees, Academic, French and German, M. J. DEMIASHKEVICH, 515
EXPERIMENTER, The Market for Scholarly and Competent Teachers, 732
Eye Strain, Plans for Survey on, 221

FACADE, R., Literature of Education, 401
FARWELL, H. W., What am I really Doing?, 686
Federal, Relations to Schools, 737; Government, Education in, 325, 812
FENTON, N., Community Planning, 387
Films, Sound, 7
Finance, School, National Survey, 193; and the State, 286
Financial Status of the Small College, 315
First Things in Education, W. H. KILPATRICK, 847
Florida, Public School Appropriations, 589
Football, COLLEGE DIRECTOR OF ATHLETICS, 699
Foreign Fellowship Students, Orientation of, 500
Franklin Institute Building, 619
Frasier, G. W., and W. D. Armentrout, Literature of Education, 646
Free Education in College, C. J. TURCK, 435
Freedom, Intellectual, A. STROHM, 71
FREEMAN, H. A., First Graders' Religious Ideas, 733
Freshmen, in the Lowest Tenth in Reading, F. P. ROBINSON, 843; Aptitude of, E. G. WILLIAMSON, 874
FURBAY, J. H., Undergraduates in a Group of Evangelical Christian Colleges, 813

9340

Gallagher, E. J., Vocational Guidance and Success, 779
Garvan Scholarships, Award, 50
GARVER, P. N., Married Women Teachers, 571
Gates, A. I., Interest and Ability in Reading, 172
Gates, A. L., Reading for Administrators, 34
GERBERICH, J. R., Educational Guidance Program, 606
Germany, A New School in, 617
Gerwig, G. W., Editor, School Betterment, 474
Gifts and Bequests, 8
GILLIS, F. M., Intelligence in College Students, 266
GOOD, H. G., Invention and the English Dictionary, 492
Good, I. C., and J. M. Crow, Home Room Activities, 37
GOODSELL, W., Women's Education, 774
Goucher College, Tenure of Office at, 829
Grades, G. MORLAN, 321; Humanizing, G. WAKEHAM, 596
Graduate Schools, Instruction in, G. MORLAN, 58
GRAHAM, F. P., The University To-day, 815, 854
Grammar, A Purpose in, H. RAND, 403
GRAY, O., A Teachers' Convention, 809
Greenawalt, L., School-Press Management, 35
GRIFFIN, G. H. Y., Checking Reading Contracts, 513
GRINNELL, J. E., School News, 566
Growth of College and University Education, 86
GUBERLET, M. L., The Classics and the Modern Magazine, 599
Guidance Program, J. R. GERBERICH, 606
GUMMERE, R. M., Humanity Reinforced, 664

Hall, F. S., Social Work Year Book, 27
HANCE, R. T., Publication, 625
Handicapped Children in Illinois, 84
HANSEN, A. O., Discussion Technique, 93
Hansome, M., World Workers' Educational Movements, 776
HARAP, H., Education and the Eighteenth Amendment, 758; Frederick Gordon Bonser, 796
Hatfield, W. W., and H. D. Roberts, The Spirit of America in Literature, 34
Hawaii, Univ. of, Summer Session, 591
Hebrew Education in Palestine, L. I. RIKLIS, 293
HEDGES, C. C., The Triangle of Life, 197
Herring, C. C., and K. Terrill, The Genius of Mexico, 479
HERTZBERG, O. E., Entrance Requirements for Teacher-training Institutions, 702
HICKS, C. R., Bonuses for Pets, 834
High-school, Students in New York City, 85; Curriculum, 153; Teachers of the Social Studies, Graduate Work for, E. ELLIS, 322
Hill, C. M., and R. D. Mosher, Making the Most of High School, 775
Hillegas, M. B., Classroom Supervision, 641
HITCH, E., Scholarships of Culver Military Academy, 229
Honesty and Examinations, J. R. PATRICK, 320
Honeywell, R. J., Educational Work of Thomas Jefferson, 341
HOOPER, C., Coeducation and Cigarettes, 322
Humanity Reinforced, R. M. GUMMERE, 664
HUMKE, H. L., Equality of Opportunity, 743
Hunkins, R. V., The Superintendent at Work, 642
HURD, A. W., Remedial Instruction, 467
Huse, H. R., Psychology of Foreign Language Study, 344
Hyatt, A. L., Index to Children's Plays, 781
Hygiene, Mental, for Schools, P. M. SYMONDS, 39; and Vocational Guidance, J. MILLER, 125; at New School for Social Research, 396

Illinois, Handicapped Children, 34; Univ. of, New Statutes, H. W. CHASE, 874
Illiteracy, Decrease in, 49, 394; in Virginia, 526
India, Child Labor in, 129; Educational Journals, 375; Education, 424
Indian, Education, W. C. RYAN, JR., 418; and Unemployment, 461; Service, Educational Appointments, 658, Superintendents, Educational Conference of, W. C. RYAN, JR., 764
Individual Differences, H. B. REED, 100
Instruction in Graduate Schools, J. JACK, 535
Intelligence in College Students, F. M. GILLIS, 266
International Student Service, Conference of, H. BLANCHARD, 628
Irish Free State, Free Meals for School Children, 190; Education in, 459; School Attendance, 864
ISRAELI, N., Course-crabbing, 540

JACK, J., Instruction in Graduate Schools, 535
Japan, English Teaching in, 141; Liberal Education in, 466
Japanese Ainu, Schools for, 598
Jastrow, J., Effective Thinking, 479
Jeans, J., The Mysterious Universe, 170
JEFFERSON. B. L., H. H. PECKHAM and H. R. WILSON, Freshman Rhetoric and Practice Book, 173
Jolting the Colleges, G. WAKEHAM, 262
Jordan, David Starr, M. L. DARSIE, 822
Jordan, R. H., Education as a Life Work, 29

Kane, E. A., Your Speech, 776
Katz, D., and Others, Students' Attitudes, 646
KELTY, M. C., Growth of the American People, 34
Kentucky, Univ. of, Library of, 121
KILPATRICK, W. H., First Things in Education, 847
KleinSmid, R. B. von, Anniversary, 727
Koos, L. V., Secondary Education, 29
Kyte, G. C., School Supervision, 781

Labor and Education, 539
LANCELOT, W. H., Measurement of Teaching Ability, 236
LANGDON, H. G., A College President, 249
LANKS, H. C., Elementary Education in Colombia, 631
Lawrence College, Picture Rental Service, 460
Lewis, W. D., E. M. Gehres and A. L. Rowland, New Silent Readers, 471
LEWIS, W. M., Mediocrity and the College, 713
Liberal, Arts, College, Movement, 425; Education, E. H. BREWSTER, 432; Broadcast, 693, 704; Students, V. L. MANGUN, 442; Control of, I. J. LUBBERS, 877
Libraries of the World, 393
Library, Grants, Federal, 14; of Congress, 190; College, L. R. WILSON, 483; Assoc., Amer., Endowment Funds, 50; New Haven Meeting, 202
Life, Triangle of, C. C. HEDGES, 197
Linguistic Atlas of the U. S., 143
Linnell, A., The School Festival, 780
LINTON, E., Evolution, 76
Literature of Education, R. FACADE, 401
Littlefield, H. W., Europe of 1500–1848, 773
London, Child Guidance in, 525; Science Museum, Children's Gallery, 863

Lorimor, F., The Making of Adult Minds, 776
Lowth, F. J., The Country Teacher, 167
LUBBERS, I. J., Who Controls the Liberal Arts College?, 877
LUDEMAN, W. W., Teaching Experience, 537
Lynde, C. J., A Laboratory Course in Everyday Physics, 779
Lyon, L. S., Education for Business, 779

MCANDREW, W., Editorial Comment, 23, 159, 337, 469, 635, 767; Book Reviews, 25, 164, 340, 471, 638, 770
McGowan, E. B., and C. A. Waite, Textiles and Clothing, 481
McKeon, R., Medieval Philosophers, 171
MacLatchey, J. H., Education on the Air, 647
McLester, A., Character Traits in Children, 171
MANEY, C. A., Church College and Character, 576
MANGUN, V. L., Liberal Arts Students, 442
Marks, Concerning, A COLLEGE DEAN, 504
Married Teachers and Multiple Positions in N. Y. City, 621
Marriott, J. A. R., How England Lives, 640
MARSH, C. S., The School of Business, 811
Massachusetts State College, 130
Mathematical Encyclopedia, G. A. MILLER, 756
MATHERLY, W. J., The College and the Current Business Crisis, 369
Matthews, M. L., Elementary Home Economics, 776
Mays, A. B., Vocational Education, 38
Meade, R. E., G. Cochran and H. M. Eddy, Malot's Sans Famille, 174
Medical Inspection, Expenditures on, 558
Mediocrity and the College, W. M. LEWIS, 713
Mental Health, Courses, 118
Messenger, J. F., History of Education, 773
Metropolitan Museum of Art, Lectures, 426
Mexican Children, Art Ability of, A. STOLZ and H. T. MANUEL, 379
MEYER, M. F., Instructors of the Deaf, 235
Mezes, Sidney E., 408
Michigan, Univ. of, Alumni University, 52; Economic Depression and Student Life, R. C. ANGELL, 649
MIDDLEBROOK, L. R., A Modest Proposal, 507
Miller, Professor, and Ohio State Univ., 224; C. G., Argumentation and Debate, 777
MILLER, G. A., A Mathematical Encyclopedia, 756
MILLER, J., Vocational Guidance and Mental Hygiene, 125
Minnesota, Teacher Retirement Fund, 286
Missouri, Univ. of, Extension Division, 254
Modern Education, J. DEWEY, 579
MOORE, F. E., Adult Vocational Education, 291
MORGAN, J. E., National Education Association and the Eighteenth Amendment, 834
Morgan, M. E., and E. C. Cline, Systematizing the Work of School Principals, 37
MORLAN, G., Instruction in Graduate Schools, 58; Grades, 321
Morrill, A. A., M. A. Bessey and J. V. Walsh, Applied Office Practice, 170
Morrison, H. C., Teaching in Secondary School, 33
Moscow, Education in, 525
Moss, F. A., Medical Aptitude Tests, 132
Moss, F. A., Psychology for Nurses, 169
Mower, E. C., International Government, 480
Munro, W. B., Democracy and Its Problems, 165
Mursell, J. L., and M. Glenn, The Psychology of School Music Teaching, 348

National, Council of Education, A. S. BAYLOR, 154; Government, Education Under, J. MCK. CATTELL, 325; Educ. Assoc., Los Angeles Meeting, 103; W. D. BOUTWELL, 109, 135
Nelson, J. F., Personality and Intelligence, 347
New, England College, A. L. LOWELL, 547; Mexico, Educational Organization in, C. C. CAMPBELL and L. P. KIRBY, 59; York, City, Playgrounds, 7; Budget, 254, for Recreation, 85; Increase of High-School Students, 85; Prison Education in, 144; Expenditures for Education, 497; Schools, Sites and Supplies, 119; Part-time in, 192; Costs per Child, 313; Secondary School, Building, 459, 570; Married Teachers and Multiple Positions, 621; Child Welfare, 659; Children, Savings, 866; State, Education of Teachers, 364; Schools, Investigation, 801
News, Review, 471; School, J. E. GRINNELL, 566
NICHOLS, M. L., Tests in Science, 409
North Carolina, Schools, Appropriation, 191; Univ. of, Appropriations, 62; Installation of President Graham, 727, 815, 854
Northwestern Univ., The Austin Foundation at, W. D. SCOTT, 735
NORTON, J. K., Education and the Economic Depression, 271

Ohio, State Colleges and Universities, Decline in Appropriations, 142; Univ. and Professor Miller, 224
O'Neill, J. M., and R. L. Cortright, Debate and Oral Discussion, 34
One-room Schools, 9
Oregon, Cost of Education in, 363; Univ. of, Reading for Honors, C. V. BOYER, 214
Osburn, W. J., and B. J. Rohan, Gifted Children, 35
Overman, J. R., Transfer of Training, 346
Oxford, H. P. PERKINS, 175

PALMER, A. M., The College Administrator Goes to School, 704
PALMER, C. W., Absences, Lateness and Drop-outs in the Northeast High School, Philadelphia, 68
Parents, and the Schools, 15; In Defense of, W. E. SLATER, 700
Parker, B. M., Science for Intermediate Grades, 779
Patri, A., The Questioning Child, 31
PATRICK, J. R., Examinations and Honesty, 320
PEARSON, P. H., Reducing Waste in the Work of Students, 371
Pennsylvania, Superintendent of Public Instruction, 9; Educational Problems of, J. N. RULE, 98
People's University, J. S. ROUCEK, 199
PERKINS, H. P., Oxford, 175
PERKINS, L., The Study of Spanish, 626
Personality Adjustment, I. S. WILE, 584
Pets, Bonuses for, C. R. HICKS, 834
Philadelphia, Northeast High School, Absences, Lateness and Drop-outs in, C. W. PALMER, 68
Philanthropic Foundations, Expenditures, 619
Phillips, C. A., The Elementary Curriculum, 169
PIERCE, L., Chrysalis Club, 231
Pipkin, C. W., Social Politics and Modern Democracies, 638
Pitkin, W. B., How We Learn, 476
Placement, After, I. M. YATES, 568
Playgrounds, Supervised, of N. Y. City, Survey, 7
Political Applications and Educational Appointments, J. R. SHANNON, 301

POLLARD, J. A., Consolidating the Colleges, 404
Porter, M. P., The Teacher in the New School, 32
Porto Rico, Teachers at Summer Schools, 284
Portugal, Homeless Children in, 423
POTEAT, W. L., In Defense of Scholarship, 611
Predicting College Grades, E. L. CLARK, 765
President, College, H. G. LANGDON, 249
Pressey, S. L., and L. C. Pressey, Standard Tests, 482
Primary Pupils, First and Second Semester, F. L. WHITNEY and C. G. SWANSON, 377
Princeton Univ., Fine Memorial Hall, 314, 527
Prison Education in N. Y. City, 144
Private Schools, Regulation of, W. E. BELLEAU, 436
Problem Child and Community Planning, N. FENTON, 387
Professions, Education for, M. W. WALLACE, 239
Project Preeminent, S. CHAMBERS, 465
Proposal, Modest, L. R. MIDDLEBROOK, 507
Protesting too Much, 539
Prussia, Closing of Normal Schools in, 749
Psychological Tests for Art Students, 590
Publication, R. T. HANCE, 625

Radio, Council on, Lectures, 725; Broadcasting, 117, 361, 461, 758
Ralston, A., and C. T. Gage, Present-day Psychology, 168
RAND, H., Purpose in Grammar, 403
Read, H. S., and E. Lee, Social Science Readers, 482
Reading, Remedial, W. H. THOMPSON, 156; Surveys in, P. S. ACHILLES, 233; Contracts in a College Course, Checking, G. H. Y. GRIFFIN, 513
Reavis, W. C., P. R. Pierce and E. H. Stullken, The Elementary School, 643
Records Bureau, Educational, B. D. WOODS, 835
Recreation, N. Y. City Budget for, 85; Conference, International, 88
REED, H. B., Individual Differences, 100
Registration in American Universities and Colleges, Statistics of, 1931, R. WALTERS, 783
Registrations, School, 361
Religious, Education, P. H. VIETH, 357; Ideas, First Graders', H. A. FREEMAN, 733
RELLER, T. L., A Student Views the Yale Experiment in the Graduate Study of Education, 667
Remedial Instruction, A. W. HURD, 465
RIBBER, OLE MAN, Wisconsin Experiment, 150
Richards, I., Our California Home, 481
Richards, L. E., Florence Nightingale, 477
RIKLIS, L. I., Hebrew Education in Palestine, 293
ROBERTSON, C. G., Educational Development, 1831–1931; A Centenary Survey and a Forecast, 445
Robinson, D. S., Principles of Reasoning, 171
ROBINSON, F. P., College Freshmen in the Lowest Tenth in Reading, 843
ROSS, C. F., College Success, 20
ROSS, J., The Heart of Democracy, 770
ROUCEK, J. S., The People's University, 199; Roumanian Educational System, 373
ROWELL, A. L., The New England College, 547
Rugg, H., Democracy, 25, Culture and Education, 26, American Culture, 475
RULE, J. N., Educational Problems of Pennsylvania, 98
Rural High Schools, Small, 498
Russell, C., Classroom Scaler and Grader, 642
Russell, M. M., Producing Your Own Plays, 777
Russia, Soviet, Compulsory Education in, 311
Russian Universities, Governance of Students, 799
Rutgers Univ., New President of, 867
RYAN, W. C., JR., Indian Education, 418; Educational Conferences of Indian Service Superintendents, 764

SABINE, G. H., State Universities, 349
Safety Council, National, Child Education Section, 287
Salaries of Teachers, 253
Samoa, Educational Endowment for, 588
Saskatchewan, Education in the Province of, 692
Savings, School, 827
Schaaf, W. L., Mathematics for Junior High School Teachers, 170
Scheidemann, N. V., Psychology of Exceptional Children, 782
Schilpp, P. A., Editor, Higher Education, 28
Scholarship, In Defense of, W. L. POTEAT, 611
Scholarships, Garvan, Award, 50; at Culver Military Acad., E. HITCH, 229
School-leaving Age and Unemployment, 570
Science Fair for Children, 724
Scotland, Cost of Education, 496
SCOTT, W. D., The Austin Foundation at Northwestern University, 735
Secondary Education, Conference on, J. H. SHAW, 511
Seely, H. F., Enjoying Poetry, 173
Selbert, N., Child Health, 31
SHANNON, J. R., Educational Appointments and Political Applications, 301
SHAW, J. H., Secondary Education, 511
SHAW, W. B., Athletics and Alumni Education, 278
Shirley, M. M., The First Two Years, 774
SHUMWAY, W., Survey Courses and the Junior College, 207
SLATER, W. E., in Defense of Parents, 700
Small College, Financial Status of, 315
SMITH, H. B., and L. R. DELONG, Discussion Technique, 533
Smith, H. L., and L. McK. Krueger, Psychology of Human Relationships, 638; and Harold Littell, Philosophy of Human Relations, 638
Smith, P. J., Editor, Philophaster of Robert Burton, 174
Smith College Endowment Fund, 660
SNEDDEN, D., Directive Aims in Education, 745; Towards Better Education, 771
Social Usage in High Schools, R. STRANG, 709
Southern California, University of, Experimental Entrance Program at, 222
Spanish, The Study of, L. PERKINS, 626
State, Universities, G. H. SABINE, 349; M. M. CHAMBERS, 64
Stevens, M. P., The Activities Curriculum in the Primary Grades, 169
Stevenson, I., Safety Education, 476
Stokes, A., The Open Door to Poetry, 648
STOLZ, A., and H. T. MANUEL, Art Ability of Mexican Children, 379
STRANG, R., Social Usage in Junior and Senior High Schools, 709
STRAYER, G. D., The Contribution of Public Education to the Welfare of the Nation, 307
STROHM, A., Intellectual Freedom, 71
Student Service, Internat. Conference, 395
Students, National Funds for, 395
Sullivan, Dr. James, The Late, Tribute to, 728
Summer Session, Columbia, 223; Bryn Mawr, 588; Univ. of Hawaii, 591

Superintendent and White House Conference, E. C. BROOME, 135
Survey Courses and the Junior College, W. SHUMWAY, 207
SUTTON, W. A., Problems in Education, 103
SWIFT, F. H., Women's Education, T. Woody, 15; Public School Finance, 346
SYMONDS, P. M., Mental Hygiene for Schools, 39

Tagore's University, R. CHATTERJEE, 681
Talbot, M., and L. Rosenberry, History of the Amer. Assoc. of Univ. Women, 645
Teacher Selection, 232
Teacher Training Institutions, 285; Commercial, Nat. Assoc. of, 376; for Large Cities, G. F. ZOOK, 381; Curricula for Understanding, M. BENNION, 551; Entrance Requirements for, O. E. HERTZBERG, 702
Teacher's Turn to be Helped, 201
Teachers' Convention, O. GRAY, 809
Teachers, by the Grace of God, J. ADAMS, 303; College, Columbia Univ., 528; Scholarly and Competent, Market for, EXPERIMENTER, 732
Teaching, The Profession of, W. C. BAGLEY, 105; Ability, Measurement of, W. H. LANCELOT, 236
Testing the Examiners, 298
Tests, Medical Aptitude, 1931–32, F. A. MOSS, 132; in Science, M. L. NICHOLS, 409; Essay Examination, H. CASON, 413
Text-books, Requests for Free Copies, 97
Theisen, W. W., and S. A. Leonard, Real Life Stories, Heroic Deeds, 481
THOMPSON, W. H., Remedial Reading, 156
Thorndike, E. L., Human Learning, 168; A Teacher's Word Book, 173
Todd, J. M., Learning to Draw, 782
Trade Training for Small Towns, 866
Transvaal, Education in, 799
Tressler, J. C., Grammar in Action, 648
Trow, W. C., Educational Psychology, 647
TURCK, C. J., Free Education in College, 435
Tyson, L., Application of Radio to Education, 781

Ullman, R. R., Success, 166
Unemployed, Youthful, Educational Needs of, 827
Unemployment and Schooling, 224; and School Attendance, 365
Universities, American Assoc. of, R. W., 741
University, To-day, F. P. GRAHAM, 815, 854; Amer. Assoc. of, Graduate Fellowships, 726; Training for National Service, 67; Professors, Amer. Assoc., Chicago Meeting of, 726

Vienna, Anti-Semitic Disorders at, 49
VIETH, P. H., Religious Education, 357
Vineland Laboratory, H. G. COLLIER, 426
Virginia, Illiteracy in, 526
Vocational Schools, Enrolment, 800; Education and Economic Depression, 144; Adult, F. E. MOORE, 291; College Credit for, 362

W., R., Association of American Universities, 741
WAKEHAM, G., Attack on Colleges, 125; Jolting the Colleges, 262; Humanizing Grades, 596
Wales, Salary Reductions in, 691
Wallace, A., Mothers of Famous Men, 481
WALLACE, M. W., Education for Professions, 239
WALTERS, R., Catholic Education Association, 17; College Entrance Examination Board, 672; Middle States Assoc. of Colleges and Secondary Schools, 837; Statistics of Registration in American Universities and Colleges, 1931, 783
Waples, D., and R. W. Tyler, What People Want to Read About, 343
Waste in Work of Students, P. H. PEARSON, 371
Watkins, R. K., and R. C. Bedell, Learning and Test Activities in General Science, 779
Webb, W. P., The Great Plains, 471
Week, American Education, 299; Education, 561
Week-end School, 200
Welfare of the Nation, Contribution of Public Education to, G. D. STRAYER, 307
Wesleyan Univ., Centennial Celebration, 498; Salary Increases, 560
Wheat, H. G., Psychology in the Elementary School, 30
White House Conference on Child Protection, 30
WHITNEY, F. L., and C. G. SWANSON, Progress of Primary Pupils, 377
Whitney, F. L., Methods in Educational Research, 641
WILE, I. S., Personality Adjustment, 584
Wilkins, L. A., and M. A. Luria, "Lecturas Faciles," 343
Williams, B. C., A Book of Essays, 777
Williams College, Institute of Politics, 88
WILLIAMSON, E. G., Scholastic Aptitude of Freshmen, 674
WILSON, L. R., The College Library, 483
Winship, Dr., In Honor of, 621
Winston, S., Illiteracy in the U. S., 35
Wisconsin, Univ. of, "University City," 87; Tent Colony, 120; Experiment, OLE MAN RIBBER, 150; College Course in Radio, 801; Self-supporting Students, 829
Witmer, Lightner, Volume in Honor of, 802
WITTY, P. A., and H. C. LEHMAN, The Educational Conference, 807
Women Teachers, Married, P. N. GARVER, 571
Women's College, New, 297
WOOD, D. B., Educational Records Bureau, 835
Woodhouse, W. J., The Fight for an Empire, 773
WOODWARD, H. R., Depreciation in Public School Buildings, 870
Woodworth, R. S., Contemporary Psychology, 646
Woody, T., History of Women's Education in the United States, F. H. SWIFT, 15; Educational Views of Benjamin Franklin, 340
World, Federation of Education Associations, 146, 605, 865; Regional Conference, 865

Yale Univ., Masters of Colleges, 52; Summer Educational Conference, 255; Appointments, 427; Residential Colleges, 560; Dedication of Dwight Hall, 591; Experiment in the Graduate Study of Education, A Student Views, T. L. RELLER, 667; Finances of, 752
Yale-in-China, Twenty-fifth Anniversary, 694
Yardley, M., Newman's Idea of a University, 780
YATES, I. M., After Placement, 568
Yeager, W. A., Training of Elementary Teachers, 478
Yes and No Report, 738
Youth, Criticism of, 875

ZOOK, G. F., Teacher Training for Large Cities, 381

SCHOOL AND SOCIETY

EDITED BY J. McKEEN CATTELL

WITH WHICH IS COMBINED THE

EDUCATIONAL REVIEW

EDITED BY WILLIAM McANDREW

Volume 34 Saturday, July 4, 1931 Number 862

TO-DAY'S CHALLENGE TO THE COLLEGE GRADUATE[1]

By LOTUS D. COFFMAN

PRESIDENT OF THE UNIVERSITY OF MINNESOTA

All commencement addresses are supposed to begin by declaring that we are living in a new world. I do not propose to break with that tradition. I have seen life transformed during my lifetime. My boyhood was spent on a farm and in a small town. I can remember seeing my own grandmother dip tallow candles; I have seen her card the wool, spin the yarn, knit the socks. My own mother quilted quilts; made clothing for the family, did the baking; while on the farm the reaping was done with the sickle, the cradle and the dropper; we cut our own wood, split our own rails, cleaned our grain, and in a thousand ways found employment from sun-up until dark. There were no telephones, no good roads, no automobiles, no chain stores (in fact, the country peddler drove by our farm every week and exchanged coffee, sugar and gingham for our eggs and butter and my game).

The community in which I grew up was typical of the rest of the United States. It was characterized by personal initiative, individual enterprise, community pride and the disposition on the part of every one to work. These are the social forces that have built America.

Now in that same community modern machinery is found on the farms, men work fewer hours per day, macadam roads lead in every direction, automobiles and telephones are found in every home, the radios in most of them; chain stores and the chain creamery occupy permanent sites in the town, and soon the banks will be a part of a chain banking system. There is more activity, more moving of materials, more organization of forces and processes. The community thinks it is a progressive community, and it is.

These changes have come, of course, with the development of mechanical power, which emancipated man from much of his ancient drudgery. Men differ enormously in their views as to what this means to mankind. Certain it is that machines have increased man's productive power on the one hand and apparently multiplied his wants on the other. The luxuries and superluxuries of yesterday are ordinary commodities of to-day. New occupations and new trades have been created. The more we produce the more the advertiser insists we need. It seems that everything,

[1] An address at the commencement exercises of the University of Michigan, June 22, 1931.

when once made, must be sold and used—radios must be listened to, movies seen, chewing gum chewed, cigarettes smoked, and cosmetics spread on the cheeks and lips. Not thrift but greater spending, not saving but more selling, are ideals that have displaced those of my boyhood days.

The coming of the machine has been accompanied by a disappearance of craftsmanship. Strange things are happening in America. Oriental rugs are manufactured in Philadelphia; Sicilian, Grecian and Turkestan art is being duplicated at various places in this country; antique furniture will be made for you while you wait; the linens, laces, luncheon cloths and the like, formerly produced in the Russian and Belgian households with artistic accuracy and beauty, are now being produced in manufacturing plants. Hand production is so slow that we are unwilling to wait for it. We want everything and we want it now. Now we have mass production, which crystallizes things in single designs and puts a brake on experiment and personal initiative. It speeds up the processes of production but slows down the creative effort of the common man.

The spirit of the machine, with its tendency toward mass output and standardization, has invaded every field. Mergers and vast organizations of capital and enterprise abound everywhere. Even the professions have not escaped. The doctors have organized for diagnosis and treatment—that old-fashioned family physician, with his deep understanding of human nature and his comforting smile, has almost disappeared; the independent editor is being absorbed by the syndicate paper; lawyers have organized themselves to fit in with the new scheme of life; even professors have become members of protective associations. The rural merchant is disappearing, and the farmer he serves is being drawn into a vast social organization.

As Mr. Beard and others in "Whither Mankind" declare, the most striking characteristic of modern times is the omnipotence of the collective man as contrasted with the feebleness of the individual man. And yet the forces that have shaped history in the past have had to do with the worth of the individual, with his knowledge, his aspirations, his dreams, with his self-expression for achievement, for liberty to live his own life, to shape his own thought, to express his own opinions, to be the center of his own personal world. More recently the tide of human interests has been away from the creative things of art, poetry, philosophy and religion, in the direction of great organizations of capital and industry.

Youth seldom establish themselves in business any more. Instead they get jobs where their success often depends on their speed rather than on their knowledge and creative ability. Indeed initiative may be regarded as a sign of inefficiency. The danger is that increasing thousands will fall victim to routine types of work and develop routine types of mind. Efficiency is the modern pagan god before whom we bow in order that dividends may be paid. There are millions of us just now who are wondering if we have not been worshipping too blindly at the shrine of this modern deity; at any rate, we have suddenly discovered that he is no longer able to pay us our dividends.

It was the late Dr. E. E. Slosson, director of *Science Service,* who declared that in our civilization the mechanical forces have got ahead of the moral and intellectual forces. He said that modern man is like the Arabian fisherman who liberated from the bottle genii he did not know how to control.

Stuart Chase comes forward with this provoking statement: "This is the last great adventure—the boldest, most exhilarating, most dangerous adventure that ever challenged the intelligence and spirit of mankind. From our brains have sprung a billion wild horses, now running wild and almost certain sooner or later to run amuck. Where are the riders with the whirling rope; where are the light-hearted youth to mount, be thrown, and rise to mount again?''

How difficult this will be for youth, for its view of the world is different from that of its immediate ancestors. The older generation is dwelling in thought in one area and acting in another, while the younger generation finds itself facing the new wilderness which science has produced without many of the traditions of the older generation.

What shall happen in America and throughout the world seems to be largely a matter of psychology. The gods never sense danger so long as man aspires to divinity by the spiritual route, but they begin to raise their Olympic eyebrows when material prosperity is counted upon to blaze a new path to heaven.

And that I fear has been the ambition of most of the human race in recent years and what a price we are now paying for it! The people of the earth find it difficult to turn from a life of gambling to one of toil, and to make matters worse they find less toil to engage in. Poverty and misery and unemployment stalk abroad in the midst of plenty. The bedtime story of many of the captains of industry whose feet have suddenly become mired in the clay they themselves have produced is a story that sends mankind after ever-disappearing and constantly recurring economic rainbows. Fitful spurts of artificial prosperity, without the development of a constructive program based upon sound policies, will only involve us the more deeply in the approaching maelstroms of to-morrow.

When one views the world situation he finds little hope in it. Apparently the political leaders are interested in preserving and in developing still further the spirit of nationalism. No government has been willing to make any vital changes in its policies in the interest of international good will. Political instability and national insecurity prevail everywhere. With revolutions in Spain, Portugal, Argentine, Nicaragua, Bolivia, Peru, Brazil, turmoil in China, unrest in India, a dictatorship in Italy, Hitlerism in Germany, Communism in Russia, the diplomats and statesmen have little to show for their efforts. Major tensions exist between France and Germany, Germany and Poland, France and Italy, Russia and the rest of the world. Men talk less happily about peace than they did a few years ago. More money is being spent for armament, except by Great Britain, than was spent in 1925 and this, some one has said, is the barometer of international temptation.

The governments of the world are at the crossroads. Government by expedient rather than principle based upon a well-ordered program is the order of the day. The people in their frantic anxiety are seeking relief and help for an intolerable situation through government action. Their despair expresses itself in desperation. And governments do not know how to deal with many of the questions with which they are faced.

The things men want are protection for their homes, security of position, education for their children and the comforts that science can bring to them. These things they are willing to work for; these things they will undertake to have even if they have to obtain them in some other way. Communism in its various forms will not be held at bay by negative actions and attempts at government regulation; instead there must be positive action and constructive program if we are to be spared the consequences of outbreaks of violence.

In the dark days of October, 1929, when the era of illusive prosperity came to an end, and economic disaster and unemployment settled down over the nations of the earth, we began to appreciate more vividly than before how deeply and intimately our welfare is involved with that of the rest of the world. We Americans sometimes delude ourselves with the pleasant thought that we are secure in our isolation when the most patent fact of current history is the interdependence of the nations of the earth.

Now we are giving hasty and superficial consideration to the causes of the debacle. The machine order of civilization, over-production, under-consumption and a dozen other shibboleths were at once raised into bolder relief in our discussions. No satisfactory explanation or solution has been offered as yet. We are still dealing with these vital issues on the basis of emotion. We are impatient with and intolerant of the methods of the intellect. Whim and caprice and the phantasies of the moment often control our actions more than solid facts and demonstrated procedures. We prefer to trust to "hunches" rather than informed opinion.

When our emotion becomes militant then we hear the voice of the crusader vociferating against everything with which he does not agree. Militant intolerance is the kind that invites the world to consume our goods but tells it to consume its own at home. It inveighs against Russia's lack of religion and certain moral standards but smiles deprecatingly and sardonically at Reno where there are now so many prospective divorcees that they must live in tents. It frowns upon nationalism but practices it with a vengeance here at home. Thinking men maintain that nothing will ever arouse us to the necessity of larger allegiances except a challenge to democracy itself. And that challenge may be coming.

How important it is that we give special attention to this thought just now, for America walks in uncertainty and fear and yet holds a key position among the nations of the earth. The danger of position resides in the misuse of power. The more strength we have the more we are tempted. This is as true of nations as of individuals. If nations go to pieces, indeed if a civilization goes to pieces, it will not be because of weakness but of abused strength. The disasters of history have been caused by the strong rather than by the weak nations. Ultimate victory to a nation never comes from prestige, power, wealth or empire. These are the forces that produce disintegration. Not swagger, superciliousness, arrogance or aloofness, but rather the quality which St. Paul meant when he said, "I know how to abound," is the quality essential to success. The practice of it is the practice of the highest of the arts. America needs to cultivate it. In her strength lies greatest danger.

At a time when we are facing the greatest of crises Americans are seeking substitutes for intelligence. They are compromising with the future and dealing with the things nearest at hand. They are following or trying to follow the paths that are most attractive and alluring. They are modifying their conceptions of the values of life with the shifting winds of expediency. The truth is the chief weakness of a democratic people is its unwillingness or inability to set up remote goals and to strive to attain them. In a country where you have one hundred and twenty million persons, each exercising his kingly qualities, special training, expert service and common sense find it hard to get a hearing. The only solution we have for most of our problems is to wait for time, the tide of affairs and some fortuitous combination of circumstances.

The most popular American substitute for intelligence is the appointment of committees. Let a group of Americans be together long enough, talk long enough, reach a certain state of exhaustion and they will appoint a committee to consider the thing they are talking about. They always place on their committee a number of persons who are not expected to know anything about the thing they are expected to report upon. They insist that the committee shall be open-minded. Its members start in with open minds and usually finish with their minds still open.

If there was ever a time when we needed to pay a duty to intelligence that time is now. With the methods we have used thus far we have not been able to avert war, to free ourselves from superstition and fear, to banish hatred and prejudice, nor to eliminate poverty. And we are facing a new kind of slavery. It is the slavery that grows out of a surplus of leisure for which we are not prepared biologically or by education. Man was meant for a life of activity; in an environment of leisure he begins to degenerate. L. P. Jacks recently said, "The evils of enforced leisure are almost as bad as the evils of enforced labor, and it really is a new form of slavery."

It is possible that the universities may have been partly responsible for the overemphasis which the substitutes for intelligence have received. At any rate they can not claim that they taught the graduates of yesterday what they now need to know about economics and international relations. Perhaps they did not know themselves. But in that failure lies a partial explanation of our present world situation. A university that is mortgaged to the past and reaches aimlessly to the future serves no useful purpose, nor can it be condoned for its failure to provide the leaders it claimed it was training.

There is no good reason why our universities should stand helpless at such times. Others may seek to prevent the recurrence of the plague that hangs like a pall over us by legislation or the use of some other substitute for intelligence, but educated men and educational institutions may do much by gathering the facts and courageously imparting the information relating to such problems, to drive fear and terror from the hearts of those who do not know how to emancipate themselves. Now is a time to consider hard realities. One of the ablest business leaders stated the matter well the other day when he said: "The need is for leadership, sympathetic in its understanding, tolerant in its view-point, and dynamic in its courage."

The subject of this address is "To-day's Challenge to the College Graduate." Thus far I have made no reference to it. Outside the cloistered walls of universities and colleges there are hunger and want and distress; throughout the earth there are insurrection and misunderstanding; prosperity, universal peace, tolerance, international good will, are still dreams to be realized; the conflict between freedom and initiative on the one hand, and submission and control on the other, between personal liberty and some form of human slavery, has been raised to a new magnitude and power. We are faced with a challenge that is peremptory and ominous. The time has arrived when faith needs to be testified to in works. The performance of these works calls for broadmindedness, an openmindedness, a progressive and enlightened liberalism. A distinguished leader of American thought recently declared "that stubborn resistance to betterment may well be the first step toward catastrophe." The world's problems now imperiously crying out for solution are the challenge to the college graduate. It is he presumably who has been prepared for the coming hour.

EDUCATIONAL EVENTS

BRITISH UNIVERSITIES AND THE LAND TAX

A MEMORIAL in support of the claim for exemption from the proposed land tax has been submitted to the chancellor of the exchequer by the standing committee of the universities. Sir Charles Grant Robertson, vice-chancellor of Birmingham University, and chairman of the committee, in writing to Mr. Snowden, stated:

As we are public institutions we propose to publish this memorandum in order that it may be quite clear that in the universities we approach this question on purely educational grounds and are in no way concerned with the general political, social or economic issues raised by the land tax proposals.

The memorial recalled that less than two years ago Mr. Snowden received a deputation which asked for an increase in the treasury grant in aid of universities, and decided to add £250,000 to the grant for the new quinquennium, and to bring the total amount of that grant up to £1,800,000. In a letter to Viscount Cecil of Chelwood Mr. Snowden observed: "It is quite reasonable that the state should contribute in substantial measure to the cost of maintaining our universities and colleges as active centers of education and research, and few, if any, items of public expenditure can be of clearer national value."

Successive governments have shown by their action that they recognize it to be in the national interest to deal generously with the universities, to strengthen their capacity to advance knowledge in all its branches, and to provide an unfailing supply of men and women with a thorough training in the arts and sciences on which the intellectual and material welfare of the people must be based. If this country is to hold its place in the fiercely competitive modern world of commerce and industry, and is to preserve a high standard of living for its inhabitants, it will need to draw more and more freely upon the knowledge and abilities which it is the special purpose of the universities to develop. In providing an annual grant of £1,800,000 for the universities and university colleges of this country, the government was presumably satisfied that no less a sum would serve to keep them in that state of efficiency which the national interest seemed to demand. The universities can not believe that it is the real wish of the government that a part of that necessary grant should now be withdrawn under the operation of a tax.

It is accordingly with deep concern that the universities have observed the apparent intention that the tax on land values embodied in the finance bill should be applied to land belonging to university institutions. The universities venture respectfully to submit that they are as genuinely deserving of favorable treatment in this matter at the hands of the state as the hospitals, which are specifically exempted under clause 19 (*f*) of the bill. The disinterested promotion of higher education and research which is the function of the universities you have recognized to be of clear national value; and it would be difficult to maintain that this service is not fully comparable in importance with the relief and cure of disease. Indeed, the medical treatment which the hospitals are able to give to the sick is throughout based upon the results of research work of which the bulk has been, and is being, conducted in the scientific departments of universities.

On these grounds it is claimed that for the purposes of the proposed tax it is neither equitable nor expedient to draw any distinction between hospitals and university institutions.

THE SCHOOLS OF CHINA

MISS MARY SMITH MARTIN, of Tientsin, China, contributes to *The Christian Science Monitor* an account of the methods now used in the schools of China. She says in part that the most recent development in the history of Chinese education is the adoption of the French administration system with its university units, which is being worked out at the present time. Their schools are divided by the six-three-three system. The primary school is composed of the first six grades; the junior middle school corresponds to the American junior high school, and includes the seventh, eighth and ninth grades, and the senior middle school the last three grades.

In the schools there is now a definite program of physical education, including formal exercises and games of every sort. A series of interscholastic meets took place a short time ago, wherein all the schools of north China, Manchuria and Korea met in competition. In the schools of modern China, civics is a living, vital and exciting subject to the Chinese student. The interest in economic problems also is intense.

The curriculum in the middle schools is similar to that of American high schools. The classical language, Wen Li, in which all learning was formerly pursued, now corresponds in a way to the western world's study of Latin or Greek. A sufficient knowledge of Wen Li is required to insure a genuine appreciation and knowledge of China's great literary heritage. The children must practice changing Wen Li into Pei Hua, or Mandarin, the official language of China, and *vice versa*. The school library movement has taken great strides forward in recent years and browsing among Chinese books and taking notes on their reading is encouraged.

Theoretically the method of lecturing by the teacher and memorizing by the pupil is done away with. In actual facts this method is still being used, which is to be expected, as the educational system in force for centuries could not be entirely eliminated. However, an effort is being made to lay less stress on the memorizing of text-book materials and more on the actual use of the material.

A TEST ON THE VALUE OF SOUND FILMS

THE letter which has been made public at the White House follows:

The president has been requested by an impressive number of city and state superintendents of schools to lend his good offices to the organization of a test of the purpose and place of sound films in public school instruction.

These gentlemen suggest that the governors of the states of the union should request their respective state superintendents of schools to select a boy or a girl of at least grammar school age and mentally adapted to such a test, together with one of your educational officials, to come to Washington where tests will be applied to the group from all the states under the direction of a committee of experts chosen by the Office of Education in the Department of the Interior. George Washington University has offered to furnish facilities and to interest itself in these tests.

At the intercession of the representative public school authorities, Mr. Clarke, of the Fox Film Company, has agreed to prepare a number of educational films for this purpose. It is not proposed that it shall lead to exclusive privileges for any particular film company either in the tests or in the subsequent preparation of films, if it should be found that a definite educational value can be introduced into the schools through the use of such films.

It is my understanding that traveling and other expenses will be taken care of. It is proposed that the tests should take place beginning July 6. If the matter meets with your approval, the president would be pleased to have your state superintendent of schools advise the Office of Education here promptly as to participation in the fashion above set out.

The following committee will be available for the tests: Dean Reudiger, representing George Washington University, to serve as chairman; Dr. Frank W. Ballou, Washington city schools; J. W. Crabtree, the National Education Association; President E. C. Broome, of Philadelphia; Dr. George Johnson, the National Catholic Welfare Conference; Dean Florence Bamberger, the Johns Hopkins University; Miss Bess Goodykoontz, Assistant Commissioner of Education.

Mr. Walter H. Newton, secretary to President Hoover, has written at his request a letter on June 22 to the governors of the states requesting them to participate in the organization of a test of the value of sound films in public-school education.

SURVEY OF THE SUPERVISED PLAYGROUNDS IN NEW YORK CITY

A SURVEY made last spring by the United Parents' Associations of New York City shows, according to the New York *Times*, an urgent need for providing a substantial increase in the 1932 budget of the Board of Education for after-school athletic centers.

The survey disclosed a wide-spread desire on the part of principals for an increase in the appropriation for these centers for supervised play in school playgrounds after school hours. More than half the centers were said to be open only two days a week. On the whole, there is better provision for boys than for girls.

The summary issued by the association points out that it is obviously difficult to build up a habit of attendance if the centers are open only twice a week. It is no wonder that the number of accidents to children under 16 years of age between 3 and 6 in the afternoon does not decrease when school playgrounds are locked after school hours and so many children are still deprived of the benefit of supervised play in a safe place.

Part of the $50,000 increase obtained for

after-school athletic centers in the 1931 school budget has been used to finance two experimental centers on Saturdays, one in the Bronx and one in Brooklyn. The larger appropriation also made it possible this year to provide more and better equipment for use in the centers, but there is still room for considerable improvement in equipment.

The complete report of the survey probably will be available in September.

The summary just issued says:

There is a difference of opinion as to the value of indoor playgrounds, especially in the warm weather of Fall and Spring. From 230 reports from schools having centers, 19 reported using indoor playgrounds only; 10 outdoor playgrounds only, and 183 schools said they used both indoor and outdoor playgrounds. Some principals failed to answer the questionnaire.

The general program of the centers does not provide activities for children of 4B grade or below. However, fourteen centers report caring for these smaller children. Sixty centers would admit these smaller children if they had more space and teachers. The fact that the centers do not generally care for the smaller children on their playgrounds has brought out the criticism that, as younger children are more liable to street accidents, they should be cared for on the playground as well as the older ones.

Sixty-eight centers report that they have children from other schools attending. This at least shows a desire for playground space by children outside of the schools in which the center is held.

Information given as to the number of children playing in the street near schools operating centers is not sufficiently detailed to permit of drawing any definite conclusions. For example, reports for schools having sessions on different days for boys and girls do not state whether the worker visited the school on a boys' or a girls' day. However, in general, the reports show that the number of children playing in the street near a school operating a center is, on the whole, noticeably smaller than near schools without centers; also that more girls play in the streets near schools which operate centers for boys only, and *vice versa;* also that more very young children play on the street near schools operating centers than children of the age admitted to centers. In the neighborhood of the schools without centers, the number of children playing on the streets at the time of the visit was generally much larger than near schools having centers.

GIFTS AND BEQUESTS TO UNIVERSITIES AND COLLEGES

THE New York *Telegram-World* reports that although official figures are not available, it appears that benefactions to higher institutions of learning have been larger during the depression than before. Counting only substantial contributions announced, the total donated to some of the more prominent eastern institutions approaches $75,000,000. Public gifts and bequests to the same colleges and universities in the year ended in June, 1930, totalled about $50,000,000.

The account in the *Telegram-World* continues:

About one third of the money given is to be used for building. Never before, it appears, have American colleges and universities been engaged in such an extensive program of physical expansion.

Among the heaviest contributors, as usual, have been Edward S. Harkness, John D. Rockefeller, Jr., the General Education Board and the Carnegie Corporation. There were two other outstanding bequests, one of from $10,000,000 to $25,000,000, by the Wendel estate to Drew University, and $3,159,766 left to Yale by the will of Mrs. Sarah Wey Thompkins.

Harvard, according to an unofficial estimate, tops all universities except Drew in gifts received. It has announced receipts of $14,571,697, compared with $11,265,775 last year. Included is the $4,410,239 gift of Mr. Harkness for the new house plan, an unrestricted gift of $2,261,800 by the estate of Stuart Wyeth, a scholarship fund of $1,280,193, established by the estate of Walter Hastings, the $1,025,155 Artemas Ward memorial fund and $1,001,973 from the International Education Board for a new biological laboratory.

Mrs. Thompkins's gift to Yale will be used for a surgical building, a new headquarters building for athletics and endowment. Total gifts to Yale were more than $12,000,000, compared with $22,050,074 in the previous year, when the university received large gifts for a new house plan and on its completed endowment drive.

During the last year $1,018,000 has been received on endowment pledges, $2,000,000 for maintenance of the Sterling Library, $1,500,000 from the John W. Sterling estate for five professorships, $1,154,961 for the Mary E. Hawley fund and $1,021,020 additional from the estate of Chauncey M. Depew.

Columbia received $2,500,000 in two large gifts,

one of $2,000,000 by the will of Edwin B. Parker to establish a school of international relations and another of $500,000 from Edward Harkness to be added to the $2,000,000 he had previously donated for residence buildings at the Medical Center.

Columbia also announced the gift of a huge library building by Mr. Harkness, the amount of the gift being kept secret. Gifts to Columbia in the previous year totalled about $1,400,000.

New York University received about $3,500,000, including $2,000,000 under the will of Dr. William H. Nichols and $1,000,000 from the late Mrs. Emma Baker Kennedy.

Princeton received $1,250,000, including $500,000 from Thomas D. Jones, lawyer and capitalist, for increasing faculty salaries.

Cyrus H. K. Curtis contributed $1,000,000 unrestricted to the total of about $2,000,000 the University of Pennsylvania received.

Of the University of Chicago's more than $3,000,000 in gifts, $2,215,000 was donated by John D. Rockefeller, Jr., for an international house.

Other large endowments were:

Amherst—$1,000,000 given by Dwight Morrow, Edward S. Harkness, the estate of Henry C. Folger and others, for six professional foundations.

Bennington—$1,261,969 collected toward the endowment for this new progressive women's college to be opened in the fall of 1932.

Boston College—$500,000 for a school of journalism given by the widow of William Taylor, formerly of the *Boston Post*.

Cornell—More than $400,000.

Lafayette—$1,250,000 toward a $3,500,000 fund to be raised by 1932.

Massachusetts Institute of Technology—$500,000 by the will of William E. Nickerson, Boston inventor.

Mount Holyoke—$640,000, including $375,000 from the General Education Board.

Syracuse—A $500,000 building for citizenship and public affairs study from George H. Maxwell.

Vassar—$399,290, including $125,580 for a gymnasium and sports building.

Carleton College—In Northfield, Minn., $1,500,000 from the General Education Board, with the promise of $4,000,000 if the college can raise an equal amount.

Carnegie Institute of Technology—Promised $8,000,000 by 1946 by the Carnegie Corporation if the institute can raise $4,000,000 within that time.

Wesleyan—$1,000,000 toward a $3,000,000 centennial fund sought.

ONE-ROOM SCHOOLS

AN Associated Press despatch from Washington says that rural schools of the country with their water buckets in the corner and their stoves in the middle soon may fall before the march of consolidation.

Some of the schools have only five to ten pupils. To unite these schools with others will be a project discussed at the National Education Association in Los Angeles, June 27 to July 4. A program looking to such legislation will be formulated. About 20,000 educators are to attend the convention.

The little one-room school, often snowbound in winter and sunbaked in summer, with its one lone teacher, is one of the principal educational problems of to-day in this country. There are 161,531 of these schools scattered over the country.

While the average number of pupils in each school is 29, many of them have a much lower attendance. One school in Missouri, which kept open two months, paying the teacher his $60 a month salary, did not have a single pupil. The teacher, hired for the season, unlocked the door each morning, read the paper until 10 and departed.

Ten thousand of the rural teachers have only eighth grade education. They do all kinds of work, including janitor service, for the $855 annual salary, yet even this amount is now hard to meet in many communities.

To relieve the situation the National Education Association proposes consolidation along with abolition of the country superintendency as a political office. The new program would have a man appointed by the Board of Education.

Rural schools in certain areas where there is a large foreign population are overcrowded, while many in New England and the middle West where there are few foreigners have not enough pupils.

THE PENNSYLVANIA SUPERINTENDENT OF PUBLIC INSTRUCTION

DR. JAMES N. RULE, recently appointed Pennsylvania's Superintendent of Public Instruction by Governor Pinchot, prepared for the teaching profession at Washington and Jefferson College where he was graduated with the bachelor of science degree in June, 1898. Immediately following graduation, he taught one year in the Washington, Pennsylvania, High School. He then accepted the position of teacher and assistant principal of the Washington and Jefferson Academy. While serving in this position, he took up and completed the work required for a higher degree and in 1901 received his Master's Degree in Science from Washington and Jefferson College. He served seven years as assistant principal of Washington and Jefferson Academy, and in 1907 was made principal of that institution.

In 1912, he was offered and accepted the principalship of the Central High School, Pittsburgh. He served in this position until 1916 when he became principal of the Schenley High School. In 1918 he was made associate national director of the Junior American Red Cross and in 1919 was advanced to the national directorship.

In 1921, upon the invitation of Dr. Thomas E. Finegan, Dr. Rule entered the Department of Public Instruction and became Pennsylvania's first director of science. In that position, he outlined the science course of study for the twelve years of the public-school system. In 1923, he was promoted to the second deputyship and was placed in charge of secondary education. Upon Dr. J. George Becht's advancement to the state superintendency, Dr. Rule was made first deputy superintendent and continued in charge of secondary education. In 1925, the State Council of Education made him its first executive secretary.

Not only did he continue to develop the state's secondary education program, but he identified himself with a wide range of educational activities. Some of these are the following: executive secretary, Commission to Study the Distribution of State Subsidies to School Districts; chairman of the Education Congress Program Committee; president, 1930, Association of Colleges and Secondary Schools of the Middle States and Maryland; executive secretary, Commission to Study the Present Plan for the Financing of Public Schools and Related Matters; representative of Department of Public Instruction on Joint Commission of College Presidents' Association and the Department of Public Instruction to Study the Relations of Secondary and Higher Education in Pennsylvania (this study is being conducted by the Carnegie Foundation for the Advancement of Teaching under the auspices of the above Commission); member, Commission on Higher Institutions, Association of Colleges and Secondary Schools of the Middle States and Maryland; chairman, Joint Commission of Commission on Secondary Schools and Commission on Higher Institutions, Association of Colleges and Secondary Schools of the Middle States and Maryland. Dr. Rule's other professional affiliations are: life member, National Education Association; member, Department of Superintendence, N.E.A.; member, Board of Directors, Educational Records Bureau, New York; member, Board of Governors, Educational Service Bureau, Pittsburgh.

Dr. Rule has been active in the progressive educational movements the state has undertaken in the past decade. As a tribute to his contribution to educational advancement, Washington and Jefferson College conferred upon him the degree of doctor of science in 1927. At various times during his service in the Department of Public Instruction, and particularly during Dr. Keith's illness, Dr. Rule directed the affairs of the Department of Public Instruction. On January 24, following the death of Dr. Keith, Governor Pinchot appointed him acting superintendent of public instruction, and on May 27, named him superintendent of public instruction for the constitutional term of four years. The State Senate unanimously confirmed Dr. Rule's appointment. On May 28, Secretary of the Commonwealth, Richard J. Beamish, administered to him the oath of office.

EDUCATIONAL NOTES AND NEWS

Amherst College at its commencement exercises conferred honorary degrees on Mr. G. A. Plimpton, of the firm of Ginn and Company, and on Dr. Henry Franklin Cutler, of the Mount Hermon School. President Arthur Stanley Pease, in conferring the degrees, read the following citations: George Arthur Plimpton, for fifty-five years an alumnus and for thirty-six years a trustee of Amherst College, in the development of which no living man has had a larger part; I confer upon you the degree of Doctor of Laws. Henry Franklin Cutler, of the class of '86, wise and experienced in teaching and in counsel, and for over thirty years principal of the Mount Hermon School, I confer upon you the degree of Doctor of Humane Letters.

THE doctorate of laws of the University of Michigan was conferred at commencement on Dr. Max Farrand, director of the Huntington Library and Art Gallery at San Gabriel, California; on Dr. Lotus D. Coffman, president of the University of Minnesota, and on Dr. Ernst Freund, professor of jurisprudence and public law at the University of Chicago. The degree of doctor of letters was conferred on Professor Edward Capps, of Princeton University, director of the American School of Classical Studies in Athens and former United States minister to Greece. Mr. Thomas B. Bronson, of the Lawrenceville (New Jersey) School, and Dr. George M. Kline, commissioner of the Massachusetts Department of Mental Diseases, received the master of arts degree.

FIVE honorary degrees were conferred at commencement by the University of Wisconsin on June 22. These were: Thomas J. Walsh, U. S. Senator from Montana, a graduate of the University of Wisconsin Law School, doctor of laws; Professor John R. Commons, of the University of Wisconsin department of economics, doctor of laws; Charles Edward Brown, director of the state historical museum, and curator of the State Historical Society, master of arts; Dr. Irving W. Bailey, professor of botany at Harvard University, doctor of science; Professor Harry F. Ward, of the Union Theological Seminary, New York City, and director of the Civil Liberties Union, doctor of laws.

THE University of Rochester on June 15 conferred the doctorate of literature on Dr. John H. Finley, of the editorial department of the New York *Times*. The doctorate of laws was conferred on Dr. Evarts Boutell Greene, DeWitt Clinton, professor of history at Columbia University, and on Dr. William Zebina Ripley, professor of political economy at Harvard University.

RHODE ISLAND COLLEGE OF EDUCATION at Providence conferred the degree of doctor of education on June 23 on Dr. Walter E. Russell, principal of the State Normal School at Gorham, Maine; on Mr. Frank H. Beede, superintendent of schools at New Haven, Connecticut, and on Superintendent Stanley H. Holmes, who holds a like position in New Britain, Connecticut. Professor W. Elmer Ekblaw, of Clark University, delivered the commencement address on "Russia To-day." Governor Norman S. Case and Dr. Walter E. Ranger, state commissioner of education, also spoke.

ARTHUR W. RICHARDS, retiring as head of the mechanic arts department of the Ethical Culture Schools, New York City, a position he has filled for thirty-two years, was guest of honor at a testimonial dinner recently given by the board of governors at the City Club. As a further token of the esteem of his associates Mr. Richards was presented with a purse by the board of governors, the Parents and Teachers' Association and the alumni of the Ethical Culture Schools.

A PUBLIC reception was tendered to Mr. Wells A. Hall, superintendent of schools at Concord, Massachusetts, on June 24, in recognition of his twenty-five years of service in the school department of the town. The school committee and the Parent-Teacher Associations of Concord and West Concord were in charge of the reception, to which all parents and friends of the public school children were invited.

DR. JOHN W. WITHERS, dean of the New York University School of Education, will direct the program of the Chautauqua Summer School of Education, which opens on July 6 for its fifty-eighth session.

THE REVEREND FREDERICK G. BRATTON, professor of religion in the University of Rochester, has been named to succeed Arnold E. Look as professor of biblical literature and character education and director of the graduate course in education in the Springfield "Y" College. Dr. Look will become president of Ellis College in Philadelphia.

MISS ANNA D. WOLF, associate professor of nursing and superintendent of nurses at the University of Chicago Clinics, has been appointed director of the School of Nursing and director of nursing service of the New York Hospital She will begin her new duties in the autumn.

MRS. MABEL BARBEE LEE, of Cambridge, Massachusetts, has been named director of admissions of the new Bennington College for Women. Mrs. Lee was formerly dean of Colorado College and adviser to women at the Harvard Summer School.

MR. ARTHUR L. PERRY has been elected superintendent of schools of Rahway, N. J., to succeed W. F. Little, who retired on July 1.

SUPERINTENDENT F. E. CONVERSE, of Beloit, Wisconsin, has been reelected for his thirty-fifth year as head of the school system.

SUPERINTENDENT C. A. KROUT, of Tiffin, Ohio, has retired after serving for forty-one years.

DR. EDWARD HAYWARD has resigned as superintendent of schools at Cohoes, New York, after a service of thirty years.

IT is reported in *The School Board Journal* that when William F. Geiger, who had served as superintendent of schools for twenty years, tendered his resignation, the board of education of Tacoma, Washington, adopted resolutions which stated that "As a teacher and a leader of teachers he has enjoyed the confidence and cooperation of the school corps to a remarkable degree. His spirit of kindliness and fair play has been a predominating characteristic."

MERVIN MONROE DEEMS, assistant professor of history in Carleton College, Northfield, Minnesota, has received the fellowship for 1931–1932 of the Albert Kahn Foundation for the Foreign Travel of American Teachers. The fellowship, which is valued at $5,000, was established in 1911 by Albert Kahn, of Paris, "to increase the number of men who have some personal and direct knowledge of other countries than their own—some understanding appreciation of other civilizations."

PROFESSOR E. M. GALE, lecturer in oriental languages and chairman of the oriental department of the University of California, sailed from New York on June 27, to visit the principal centers of Chinese studies in Europe. He will make an investigation of the methods of teaching far eastern languages on the continent and a survey of the libraries of Chinese works at Paris and at some of the German universities. Professor Gale plans to spend some time at the Institute of Sinology at the University of Leiden. While at Leiden he will attend the eighteenth International Congress of Orientalists, to be held in September.

DR. CLARENCE H. HARING, professor of Latin-American history and economics at Harvard University, recently sailed from New York for South America, where he will be engaged in study and observation for four months.

DR. DANIEL L. MARSH, president of Boston University, and Mrs. Marsh, will spend the summer in England and on the continent. They sailed from Boston on June 27.

PROFESSOR L. E. COLE, of the department of psychology of Oberlin College, will lecture at the summer session of the University of North Dakota.

MR. R. V. HUNKINS, superintendent of schools at Lead, South Dakota, will give courses in educational administration in the summer school of the State College at Brookings. Superintendent Hunkins was president of the South Dakota Education Association last year.

DR. J. E. WALLACE WALLIN, head of the department of psychology and director of the psycho-educational and mental hygiene clinic in Atlantic University, Virginia Beach, Virginia, will lecture on mentally handicapped children and conduct a seminar on physically handicapped children during the summer session of the State Teachers College at Buffalo, New York.

DR. M. LYLE SPENCER, president of the University of Washington, delivered the first commencement address to be given at Northern Montana College. His subject was "The Educational Purpose."

THE commencement address at Pennsylvania State College on June 8 was delivered by Dr. David Allan Robertson, president of Goucher College, on "The Communication of Ideas."

FRANCIS GREENLEAF ALLINSON, professor

emeritus of Greek literature and history at Brown University, where he taught for thirty-two years, died on June 23. Professor Allinson received the honorary degree of doctor of laws at the recent commencement exercises of Haverford College. He was seventy-four years old.

JUDGE FRANK IRVINE, formerly dean of the Cornell Law School and State Public Service Commissioner, died on June 23. He was seventy-two years old.

THE death is announced of Sir Harry Reichel, rector emeritus and vice-president of University College of North Wales, of which he had been principal from 1884 to 1927. He was editor of the Moseley report on American education, and also of a report on university education in New Zealand.

DR. S. W. BEYER, dean of the Division of Industrial Science at Iowa State College, died on June 2 at Iowa Falls as the result of an automobile accident. Mr. Beyer was born at Clearfield, Pennsylvania, on May 15, 1865, but lived nearly all of his life in Iowa. He received his first degree from Iowa State College in 1889, and the doctorate from Johns Hopkins University in 1895. Beginning in 1890, he held positions in the departments of zoology, mining engineering and geology. For thirty years he had been professor of geology, and in addition to his research and teaching had carried on work for the Iowa Geological Survey.

THE annual meeting of the Association of American Colleges will be held at Starrett's Netherland Plaza Hotel, Cincinnati, on January 21 and 22, 1932.

DEDICATION of the new $300,000 Harry Elkins Widener Memorial Science Building, the gift of Dr. and Mrs. Alexander Hamilton Rice, of New York, in memory of Mrs. Rice's son, Harry Elkins Widener, preceded the annual commencement exercises of the Hill School at Pottstown, Pennsylvania, on June 22. Mr. Widener was graduated from the institution in 1903 and died in the Titanic disaster in 1912. The keys to the building were presented to Mrs. Rice by Charles Z. Klauder, the architect. Mrs. Rice in turn gave the keys to Clarence A. Warden, president of the board of trustees of the school. Dr. Julian L. Coolidge, professor of mathematics at Harvard University, gave the dedicatory address, stressing the importance of a preparatory school having a building devoted entirely to the teaching of the sciences. Dr. John H. Finley, of New York, gave the address at the commencement exercises.

THE regents of the University of California have accepted an offer by the trustees of the Boys' and Girls' Aid Society to turn over the property of that organization in San Francisco for the support of child welfare work. This property is situated at Baker and Grove Streets, and is valued at $100,000. The Board of Trustees will maintain its legal existence for the purpose of acting in an advisory capacity should the need ever arise.

THE Spelman Fund, New York, has contributed $91,000 for research in adolescence by the Institute of Child Welfare of the University of California.

BY the will of the late Augustus Hemenway, of Boston, Harvard University receives $70,000 and the Boston Museum of Fine Arts $50,000.

THE American Academy of Arts and Sciences received $110,401 under the will of the late Mrs. Anno Bowman Blake Dodd, author and authority on French history.

COLGATE UNIVERSITY recently announced the establishment of eighteen new competitive entrance scholarships ranging from $1,500 to $1,000 for the four years of college. These scholarships were made possible by the will of the late Colonel Austen Colgate, who was a trustee of the institution and who made Colgate a beneficiary to the extent of over $1,500,000, the income from which is to be devoted to the promotion of student scholarship. In addition to the entrance scholarships, two $1,000 fellowships are provided for ranking seniors who are going on to graduate schools, and all undergraduates who maintain a superior standing will be eligible to receive scholarships graduated up to the full cost of tuition, $300.

BECAUSE of employment conditions, the Secretary of Labor, W. N. Doak, has suspended for the time being the practice of admitting foreign industrial students who come to the

United States and take temporary employment for the purpose of gaining experience in American industrial establishments. Such students are for the most part recent graduates of technical schools who are paid a nominal wage by employers here. In some years nearly 200 such students have been admitted under a reciprocal arrangement which assured that like numbers of American industrial students would be permitted to take employment in the foreign countries concerned. However, it is said that only five or six American young men have availed themselves of this privilege. Secretary Doak's order does not affect industrial students sent to the United States by foreign governments, or those who are brought here by employers desirous of training foreigners with a view to employing them as representatives in foreign countries.

A SPECIAL report to the New York *Times* dated from Chicago on June 26 states that the situation created among unpaid public servants in Chicago by the lack of available funds in governmental treasuries has reached the stage of rebellious mass meetings. While printing presses rolled off the scrip which the Board of Education hopes to hand its teachers and other employees in lieu of nearly $10,000,000 back pay, the teachers met throughout the city and in every case united in refusing the scrip. Superintendent Bogan joined in the movement. While protest meetings were held at schools throughout the city, Governor Emmerson received copies at Springfield of a petition bearing the signatures of 11,250 Chicago school teachers. It urged him to authorize the sale of tax-anticipation warrants against the 1931 state distributive fund. There is $3,200,000 available in that fund. The Cook County Board, whose employees have already had one payless payday, put vacations without pay into force as an economy measure, and was considering the adoption of the scrip method of meeting payrolls.

QUOTATIONS

FEDERAL LIBRARY GRANTS

IT is an inopportune moment to ask for a Federal grant of $100,000,000 for any new project, even if distributed over ten years. But such a request by the council of the American Library Association, in aid of rural libraries, will at least serve to call attention to the fact that there are forty million people without public library service in the United States, the estimate of three years ago being 45,069,890, of whom 93 per cent. live in the country or in places having less than 2,500 population.

It is a question whether the Federal Government should ever undertake to provide libraries. They are a phase of public education which lies within the unsurrendered functions of the states. There is, to be sure, the Library of Congress, which has become a national library, making its books extensively available as well as intensively useful under its own roof. The outside service may be still further extended, with the development of the agencies of distribution at the command of this great central library, in which all copyrighted books find shelter. The Congress that appropriated a million dollars and more for incunabula might easily find itself justified in spending as much for enlarging the circulation of recent books.

There is, of course, much to be said in justifying help in making a literate citizenry intelligent about its own affairs. But it would be logical first to aid the states to become literate. There are at least five million identified illiterates in America, and nobody knows how many there are who are to all intents and purposes illiterate, since they do not read what is within their reach.

The American Library Association should continue its splendid work in getting states and communities to make their own public library provision with such private assistance as is often available. Yesterday mention was made of what Mr. Owen Young had done for the public school in his native village. That sort of cooperation is even more readily practicable in providing libraries. The peril of Federal grants is that communities will come to look for them instead of making sacrifice to win what such grants would offer. A library with local support becomes a measure of the community's own aspiration and enterprise. Out of the forty millions there can not be even four millions that would not be able to make some provision for themselves if only they had the ambition to do so. The radio instead of being a competitor may even be an aid in stirring the desire which only the printed word can satisfy. —*The New York Times.*

PARENTS AND THE SCHOOLS

Representing 161 local parents' organizations of this city with a membership of 20,000, the United Parents' Associations, of which Mrs. Henry S. Pascal is president, has sent a letter to State Commissioner of Education Frank P. Graves urging that the proposed investigation of New York City's public school system be "thorough and comprehensive" and pledging aid to secure any special appropriation that may be needed from the next legislature.

Not only are these parents' associations convinced of the need of such an investigation, but they are already taking steps to "develop a body of citizens with larger vision, a better understanding of public education in its broader aspects and a more intelligent critical attitude toward the public school system."

This kind of citizen interest and initiative is the most heartening thing in civic life to-day. It is exactly what Lieutenant Governor Lehman means when he reminds the public: "Unless you take an interest in government, you will not get good government, and you are responsible for it, not necessarily the legislator or the government."

More power to this type of parent and voter. Its increase is the guarantee of New York's future.—*The New York Telegram and World.*

THE CHICAGO SCHOOLS

The 14,000 Chicago public-school teachers are again experiencing "payless pay days." They have received no salaries since April 2, and with no immediate prospect of cash in sight. The auditor of the board of education ventured the guess that cash might be available by the middle or the last of June.

There has been but one tax payment in about three years' time, and with constant agitation of real estate groups for a "taxpayers' strike," the banks are uneasy about loaning money on tax-anticipation warrants which bear no due date, even though they draw 6 per cent. interest.

The board of education has $55,000,000 worth of 1931 tax-anticipation warrants for sale, with no buyers. The banks have intimated that, if a certain financial reform legislation is passed by the General Assembly, they will at once buy the 1931 warrants.

Meanwhile, the teachers are much concerned. At a recent hearing before the board of education, they pleaded the seriousness of the situation to the trustees. The latter inquired whether the teachers would be willing to take tax-anticipation warrants in lieu of cash for payment of their salaries. The teachers decided against this. The teachers plan to begin a friendly suit in court and to try to secure a judgment against the board of education for their salaries. They believe the banks will loan money on a court judgment.—*The School Board Journal.*

BOOKS AND LITERATURE

A History of Women's Education in the United States. By Thomas Woody. New York, 2 vols. The Science Press, 1929.

Much has been written upon the transformation of the modern world through the application of science to industry and to all fields of human activity and thought, even more perhaps, upon the transformation of human society under the ever-extending sway of new social conceptions and their resultant practices. But those who have attempted to discover and interpret the basic forces explaining the passing of feudalism with all its oppressive restrictions and taboos have thus far largely overlooked the part which the gradual emancipation of women has played in the social and intellectual evolution of the last two centuries. It may well be doubted whether there is a single phenomenon more significant for the entire social order than the gradual rise of women from a position of dependence and oppression to that of freedom and leadership. In this great movement the United States has played a most important part. It is surprising, therefore, that the third decade of the twentieth century had nearly passed before any outstanding scholar attempted to give a worthy account of the history of the rise of the education of women in this robust new-world republic. This is the task which Thomas Woody set himself to some ten years ago, a task which has reached its conclusion in his two volume work recently published under the title of "A History of Women's Education in the United States."

Recognizing that the ideas controlling the practices of female education in the United States were in the beginning inheritances from European backgrounds, the author devotes the first two chapters of Volume I to a consideration of the conception of woman's position and education in Europe, first before, and then after the Renaissance. Chapter 3 carries the reader to the United States and permits him to behold the changes in the concept of woman's ability, position and education, characterizing the nineteenth and twentieth centuries. The three successive chapters describe the education of girls in New England, the Middle Atlantic States (New York, Delaware, Pennsylvania and New Jersey), and the South during the colonial period and the eighteenth century. The remainder of Volume I traces the rise of academies and seminaries for girls and young women, describes the entrance of women into the teaching profession, discloses the beginnings of women's teacher-training institutions, and closes with an account of the new educational opportunities for girls ushered in by the modern high school. Volume II, consisting of ten chapters, treats in succession the changing economic status of women, the rise of vocational education for women, physical education for women, women's colleges, coeducation and coordinate colleges for women, women's higher professional education, the relationship between women's emancipation and education, suffrage and the woman's club movement.

Much of the charm of these volumes is due to the author's style. He writes in a clear and entertaining manner, revealing a keen sensitivity to perspective and relative values. Institutions and individuals alike are properly subordinated to the great movements in which they have played a part. Although giving due attention to the rise of women as educational leaders, the author resists the temptation to attempt to give a complete biography of any leader, however stimulating such an account might be. Although many of the chapters can be read as accounts of what appear to be almost separate movements, nevertheless the unity of the work is preserved by definitely relating each to the great movement of which it was a constituent factor. The usability of these volumes might have been increased by the introduction of summaries at the close or the beginning of each chapter. In like manner the treatment might have been simplified at certain points by assembling in tables the data which appear in almost baffling numbers on many of the pages.

However, all such criticisms appear trivial when viewed in the light of the real achievement represented by this scholarly work. Indeed, no review can do justice to the wealth of concrete and illuminating material contained in each chapter. So numerous are the excerpts from original sources, and reproductions of early cuts, plates, announcements, advertisements and reports, that each volume constitutes a veritable storehouse of source material. Information of great value can be gleaned from the description in the appendices of the text-books and studies offered in educational institutions for girls and women from the middle of the eighteenth to the middle of the nineteenth century. The extensive bibliography, closely printed and covering 109 pages, is suggestive of the monumental task undertaken by the author and the zeal and care with which he has devoted himself to it. Not only students of the history of education, but those of all other social sciences will find in these two volumes a rare and valuable collection of material which up to the present time has been almost inaccessible. In gathering this material, in organizing it, in relating it and interpreting it, Dr. Woody has not only rendered a lasting service to all students of the history of education, but has placed upon future writers in this field the obligation of giving the movement which he has chronicled the place it has so long merited.

FLETCHER HARPER SWIFT
SCHOOL OF EDUCATION,
UNIVERSITY OF CALIFORNIA
AT BERKELEY

SOCIETIES AND MEETINGS

THE NATIONAL CATHOLIC EDUCATIONAL ASSOCIATION

The chief event of the year in Catholic education in this country took place from June 22 to 25 when more than three thousand delegates, representing Catholic schools, colleges, seminaries and universities of every state, assembled at Philadelphia for the twenty-eighth annual meeting of the National Catholic Educational Association and its departments. The meeting place was the newly completed municipal auditorium of Philadelphia, which has a main hall seating 12,000 and eight other rooms of varying size. In addition to the delegates, many others attended the sessions, particularly the opening meeting.

The four-day program included two general sessions on June 23 and 25; five meetings of the college department, with one meeting of the affiliated conference of colleges for women and three of the library section; four meetings of the secondary-school department; four meetings of the parish-school department, with one meeting of its superintendents section, one of the Catholic deaf-mute section and one of the Catholic blind-education section; one meeting of the vocational education and guidance group; four meetings of the seminary department; four meetings of the minor-seminary department; and also committee and commission meetings, religious services, music demonstrations, an orchestral concert, an exhibition of work in art education in Catholic schools, and a commercial display of books and school supplies.

At a reception on the evening of June 22, the visiting delegates were presented to His Eminence, D. Cardinal Dougherty, who, on the following morning, celebrated at a largely attended pontifical mass in the Cathedral of SS. Peter and Paul.

General Sessions of the Association

A short address by the president general of the association, the Right Reverend Francis W. Howard, bishop of Covington, opened the general session on the morning of June 23. "We may thank God," Bishop Howard said, "for the splendid courage with which Pope Pius XI maintains the position of the Holy See against the Italian Government. We sympathize from the depths of our hearts for the trials he is now facing."

As a formal message from the convention the following cablegram was addressed to the Pope at Vatican City:

> The National Catholic Educational Association, comprising Catholic educators from every part of the United States of America, assembled at Philadelphia at its twenty-eighth annual meeting, offers its expression of veneration, homage and affection to Your Holiness with a fervent prayer that God may help you to safeguard the rights of the Church to impart Christian education to youth. We implore your Apostolic benediction.

The leading address of the entire four-day meeting was delivered at this session. It was "The Philosophy of Catholic Education," by the Reverend Edward B. Jordan, D.D., department of education, the Catholic University of America. Dr. Jordan began by declaring that "Catholic doctrine does not change. Like its divine founder, it is 'the same yesterday and to-day and forever.' . . . And what is true of Catholic doctrine is true of Catholic education. We hear a great deal nowadays of education for the needs of life, education for a changing civilization, the education of to-morrow, progressive education, and education and the good life. Men are seeking for a system of training adapted to the social, political and industrial conditions of our era. They have proposed all sorts of modifications in educational theory and practice. They have demanded a reformulation of our educational philosophy in the light of what they have been pleased to call our changed conceptions of man and of his universe."

> It might be well if our educators were to center their attention more on the universal and permanent characteristics of human nature and less on the changing situations that confront men from one generation to another. As we shall point out later, it is precisely on these universally human attributes that the Catholic theory of education is based. For this very reason we maintain

that in the principles of Catholic education we have the groundwork for such reorganization of our schools and our teaching as may be necessary to meet the exigencies of our times. In other words, we hold that there is no need of a radical reform of education such as is proposed by Dewey and his followers. What education needs is ''a conservative revolution, a renaissance, that is to be attained only by a re-baptism in that eternal fountain of youth, the educational philosophy of the Catholic Church.''

Dr. Jordan went on to say that "Catholic education has met the needs of life for well-nigh two thousand years; it has taught its disciples to live the good life here that they might attain to the good life hereafter; it has kept step with, rather it has led, the march of all true progress; it has survived the vicissitudes of changing civilizations. In fact, it would be more correct to say that it has produced our civilization."

Pointing out that other theories of education "have had their day and ceased to be," Dr. Jordan said that "in the meantime Catholic education has maintained its hold and has never ceased to be a power in the world. . . . In spite of all concerted attempts to belittle, to hinder and to destroy the work of Catholic education, the Church has continued to be the teacher *par excellence* of the children of men."

The source of this abiding strength lies, the speaker said, "in the unchanging truth of the Catholic philosophy of life. Catholic philosophy has a very definite conception of man and of his place in the universe. It has arrived at a very positive understanding of the meaning of life. This conception and this interpretation are based not only on the data of science but on the teaching of Divine Revelation. Hence, they are essentially and universally true. Science may add to our knowledge of man and of his world and thus necessitate some modification of our concept; but so far as the essential nature of man, his origin and his destiny are concerned, our knowledge of these we have obtained from the Author of Truth and this is not subject to error. For Catholic philosophy, man, whether he be ancient or modern, primitive or civilized, Jew or Gentile, is a creature of God. He is composed of body and soul. He is endowed with free will and is responsible for his acts. He has been redeemed by the Blood of Christ. He is called to membership in the Church which Christ established for the salvation of men. He is destined for eternal life."

The main difference between the Catholic theory of education and modern systems, as set forth by Dr. Jordan, is that "the former lays greater stress on the unchanging, the latter on the changing aspects of human life." He expressed his opinion that the "domination of the specialists has been one of the greatest curses of modern education, particularly American. We have suffered more perhaps than any other nation from the propaganda carried on by these one-sided educationists. The psychologists have been among the worse offenders. . . . We have no science of psychology in the sense that we have a science of chemistry or of physics. What we have is an array of conflicting psychologies. Yet each claims to be exact and demands that the school be reorganized in accordance with its ideas. The result is what we might expect, *viz.*, chaos."

Dr. Jordan similarly criticized "the methodologists," the "curriculum constructors with their various plans for the reformation of the course of studies," and "the vocationalists" who demand "particular types of training."

Dr. Jordan, in closing, opposed "the impression that Catholic educators are thoroughly satisfied with themselves; that Catholic education is a perfect system which admits of no improvement; that modern reformers can hope to make no impression on this stronghold of conservatism. . . . This is far from being a correct statement of the facts. . . . Catholic educators are willing and anxious to learn from others. . . . They are not afraid to try the new, provided it is likewise true; nor are they afraid to lay the old aside when it is proved to be no longer serviceable. They are conservative; they are not carried about by every wind of doctrine."

Yet they are ever ready to ''walk in newness of life.''. They have a rich educational inheritance which they are unwilling to sacrifice for a mess of pedagogical pottage, but they are fully aware of the obligation that binds them of adding to the heritage they have received. They can not rest satisfied with the accomplishments of the past; they must be ever on the alert to meet the demands of the present and to anticipate the needs of the future. For the doctrine they teach is not of any particular day or age; it is of all time.

The one other address of broad interest was that of the Reverend Brother Thomas, of Manhattan College, New York, who led the superintendent's section, at a dinner and meeting on the evening of June 24, on the topic, "The Future Development of Catholic Education." According to an official abstract of his paper, Brother Thomas stated that the outlook in the United States is bright, as evidenced "by the splendid progress in all branches of educational endeavor from the kindergarten to the university in the last quarter of a century."

Brother Thomas said that the latest figures available showed 2,350,000 pupils in attendance in Catholic schools under the direction of 60,000 religious teachers. "This is a most encouraging growth," he commented, "but the ever-increasing demand for more Catholic schools is a source of real anxiety. The problem of the future is to provide additional school buildings of the most modern type and the teachers needed to staff these schools satisfactorily."

Brother Thomas praised "the nation-wide effort being made by Catholic teachers to secure advanced college and normal school instruction for the improvement of the quality of their classroom work." He urged "the desirability of employing every possible effort to encourage the number of young men and women to take up the work of a religious teacher." He pointed out the heavy financial burden placed upon religious communities and the Catholic laity in providing funds for the erection of schools and the preparation of teachers. He felt that "the time-proven generosity of the Catholics and their heroic sacrifices" would be continued.

Resolutions of the Convention

At the closing meeting of the association at noon of June 25, resolutions were unanimously passed which included the following:

Be It Resolved, That in view of the profound economic and social disturbance in which society is involved, the members of the National Catholic Educational Association join with all Catholic educators the world over in expressing our deepest gratitude to the Holy Father, Pope Pius XI, for his recent letters, ''Quadragesimo Anno'' and ''Casti Conubii.'' Embracing as these encyclicals do along with His Holiness's letter on the Christian Education of Youth, the teaching of the Catholic Church in the most important problems that confront the world to-day, we pledge our Holy Father that they will be our constant inspiration, and will furnish our schools material for courses of instruction, and will be the foundation stones of our teaching in wider spheres wheresoever our influence may reach.

The Association through its history has always advocated the recognition of the natural rights of the individual, of the family, and of the Church in the field of education. These rights are fundamental to liberty and opposed to the varied forms of absolutism and autocracy in education. The Association expresses its profound loyalty to the Holy Father who, by his unequivocal assertions of these rights, proves himself the guardian of human liberty and the defender of the freedom of education.

Officers were elected for 1931–32 as follows:

President General: Rt. Rev. Francis W. Howard, Covington, Ky.

Vice-Presidents General: Rt. Rev. John B. Peterson, Somerville, Mass.; Very Rev. James A. Burns, Notre Dame, Ind.; Rev. John B. Furay, Mundelein, Ill.; Rt. Rev. Msgr. William P. McNally, Philadelphia.

Secretary General: Rev. George Johnson, Washington, D. C.

Treasurer General: Rt. Rev. Msgr. John J. Bonner, Philadelphia.

College Department

A resolution calling upon the ninety-one colleges and universities having membership in the National Catholic Educational Association to establish "a six-semester course in social problems in the light of Christian principles" was adopted by the college department of the association at its closing meeting on June 25. This action was ascribed to "the Holy Father's recent recommendation that the Catholic faithful in general and Catholic students in particular acquaint themselves with the social problems of to-day." A committee was appointed to draw up a syllabus for the course.

The department also adopted a resolution favoring the "reservation to education of a reasonable share of radio channels."

At the morning session of June 24, Dean W. F. Cunningham, of the College of St. Thomas, read a paper on "The Purpose of the Comprehensive Examination on the College Level." Dr. William S. Learned, of the Carnegie Foundation for the Advancement of Teaching, reported on the comprehensive achievement examination given in Pennsylvania colleges. Dean Cunningham and Dr. Learned both criticized the credit system, the former saying that "the greatest single incubus resting on the college right now, from the standpoint of promoting scholarship, is the credit system." In the discussion Dean J. S. Reiner, of the College of Arts and Sciences, Loyola University, Chicago, took issue with the speakers, declaring that "the comprehensive examination plan becomes more of a menace to education than the credit system. The latter has served us very well."

The program of the conference of colleges for women, on June 22, included a paper by Sister Lioba, dean of Mount Mary College, Milwaukee, on "Some Distinctive Problems of Our Colleges for Women."

Library Section

Among the librarians who read papers at the three sessions of the library section were Sister M. Incarnata, Our Lady of the Lake College, San Antonio, Texas; Mrs. Grace E. Cartwell, Queens Borough Public Library, Jamaica, New York; Dr. Asa Don Dickinson, University of Pennsylvania; William T. O'Rourke, College of the Holy Cross; Miss M. Lillian Ryan, Loyola University, Chicago; Paul R. Byrne, University of Notre Dame; Irving T. McDonald, College of the Holy Cross; the Reverend C. J. Farrell, St. Benedict's College, and Dr. Francis E. Fitzgerald.

The library section voted to withdraw from the National Catholic Educational Association, and this action was announced by the secretary general, Dr. George Johnson, at the association meeting on June 25.

Secondary-School Department

Subjects of papers and discussions at the various meetings of the secondary-school department included "Catholic Action in High Schools," "Visual Education in High Schools," "The Prayerbook: a Factor in Teaching Religion," "Activity Periods and Club Organizations in High Schools," "Athletics in the High School," "The High-School Student and the Library," "The Fundamental Problem in Secondary Education," "Provision for the Poor in the Private High School" and "The Problem of First-Year Failures in High Schools." There were twenty-five scheduled speakers in this departmental program.

The Catholic Vocational Guidance Conference, which held its first meeting with the National Catholic Educational Association this year, voted unanimously, at its final session on June 24, "to submerge its identity for the time being with the secondary-school department." A resolution was introduced to study "what is now being done in Catholic schools in the way of education in vocational guidance and what are the needs in this field."

The Right Reverend Edwin V. O'Hara, bishop of Great Falls, Montana, read a paper on "The Catholic Philosophy of Vocational Guidance." Historical sketches were presented on the vocational-guidance movement in Europe and in America. Papers were read on a vocational-guidance curriculum in a Catholic high school and on a guidance program as exemplified in case studies.

Raymond Walters
Swarthmore College

EDUCATIONAL RESEARCH AND STATISTICS

A METHOD OF FORECASTING COLLEGE SUCCESS

The chief problem that faces any of those who exercise the functions of admissions officer is to determine to what degree an applicant will make a success of college work. If we can solve that problem we are not particularly concerned with the minutiae of his technical preparation. We have tried entrance examinations and have to acknowledge that they can be speedily and artificially prepared for. We have tried the entrance certificate and in spite of the excellence of the school have found it of varying value. We have insisted on the recommendations of principal, teacher, and alumnus, and have learned to be suspicious of individual judgments. We have tried various sorts of objective tests only not infrequently to be disillusioned.

All of these have been of value, but even combined have not been unfailingly accurate. It is, of course, too much to expect any certain method of forecasting success in college. Too many factors are involved, including the elusive moral factor which is so hard to measure, and which nevertheless is frequently a determining element.

By a kind of chance another method of making a prognosis of student success has emerged in compiling certain statistics in the registrar's office at Allegheny College. It is, of course, only "another method," but when used in conjunction with others has proved of value. In any case, the statistics show some striking results and can not be thoughtlessly dismissed.

The study began three years ago in an attempt to see if there was any relation between a freshman's foreign language preparation and his college record. It was begun as a result of a conversation with the president of the college. At Allegheny we still require four units of foreign language for entrance to all courses. The only modification is that in case a student presents thirteen other units, we accept him with but two language units, with the stipulation that he take two additional years of language in college above college requirements. The president raised the question of the wisdom of maintaining the four unit entrance requirement in the face of the fact that so large a proportion of colleges require but two. My reply was to support the present requirement, but with the explanation that it was not because my own university training had chanced to be in language, but because I believed it guaranteed us a better grade of matriculants. It was to verify this contention that the study was undertaken.

The result of the first year's study in 1929 was so surprising that I was not at all certain that it could be typical. I have therefore postponed drawing any inferences until the same study has been made for three successive classes. The three sets of results are so harmonious and the number of cases now so numerous that it seems safe to deduce some conclusions.

The method of the study was to divide all freshman matriculants into groups according as they presented for entrance two, three, four, five, six, or seven units of foreign language. No consideration was made of the grade received or of what language was offered. The study was wholly quantitative. At the end of the first semester, each student's average grade in all subjects was then secured, and an average numerical grade was calculated of the whole number of students in each group. The results for the three years were as follows:

Number of freshmen	Number of language units	Average grade in all subjects
103	2	68.91
63	3	73.19
249	4	76.85
64	5	78.24
90	6	83.04
21	7	84.40
590		

The number of cases, 590, is believed to be large enough to justify generalization, especially as the results in each of the three years are essentially identical.

The inevitable generalization is that college grades are likely to be very closely correlated to the amount of entrance language. The correlation is too close to be accidental.

But it is obviously possible to draw various conclusions from the exhibit. The enthusiastic teacher of language may reason that it is quite clearly indicated that foreign language is the most valuable vehicle for intellectual training and that college success is guaranteed by linguistic preparation. Let us, therefore, require more language for entrance. The writer believes that this is a *non sequitur*. The facts would rather indicate that language study in the secondary school is not the cause but the result. That is, students are not generally excellent because they take language, but they take language because they are excellent. They are not afraid to tackle a subject widely advertised as difficult, and consequently they have the courage and moral stamina to avoid the easy way and merely superficial interest.

If this reasoning is correct, it follows that we can get a fair prognosis of what a student will do in college by observing the amount of foreign language offered, a prognosis which will be strengthened if we find an excellent record in language as well. Is this not after all a kind of moral test we have felt the need of?

Then naturally, after this examination was completed, the question raised itself as to what relationship there is between college grades and other subjects presented for entrance. A similar investigation was then made for mathematics, natural science and social science. No study was made for English, as almost all students presented four units and there were not enough variants to make statistics valuable. The results were as follows:

MATHEMATICS

Number of freshmen	Number of units	Average grade in all subjects
64	2	72.09
151	2½	77.76
210	3	76.50
70	3½	79.08
95	4	76.98
590		
	SOCIAL SCIENCE	
22	1	79.70
119	2	78.61
237	3	76.41
212	4	75.62
590		
	NATURAL SCIENCES	
158	1	79.05
194	2	76.53
157	3	75.48
81	4	73.86
590		

It is clear from these tables that the amount of mathematics corresponds roughly with college attainments, but that the correlation is much less marked than in language. In the fields of social science and natural science the surprising result is shown that the relationship is the exact opposite of that of language.

This bears out the earlier interpretation. There is yet in the secondary schools a feeling, whether well or ill grounded, that the social and natural sciences are inherently less difficult than language and mathematics. The result is naturally that the less intelligent and particularly the less industrious students flock to these subjects. The subjects, when properly taught, are not to be burdened with the blame. That must be attached to the student.

In any case, to the officer charged with the duty of evaluating entrance credits, so often in the case of our small colleges the registrar, the study of the quantitative offerings in the various fields may be of value in helping to come to a correct foreknowledge of an applicant's success in college. And, at least, it is a method easy to apply.

I may add, in conclusion, that Dean Rivenburg, of Bucknell University, has seen some of the statistics given in this paper, and has conducted a similar investigation at Bucknell, with quite the same results.

C. F. ROSS

ALLEGHENY COLLEGE

NEW BOOKS IN EDUCATION

Elson Basic Readers. Pre-Primer: Pp. 40, $.12; Primer: by William H. Elson, Lura E. Runkel and William S. Gray. Pp. 144, $.56. Elson and Gray: Book I: Pp. 176, $.60; Book II: Pp. 240, $.68; Book III: Pp. 336, $.76; Book IV: Pp. 383, $.80. Illustrated. Scott, Foresman.

FIELD, W. S. and O. T. JOHNSTON. *Teachers' Salaries in the Los Angeles City Elementary and High School Districts.* Pp. xxx + 178. Los Angeles City Board of Education.

FRASIER, GEORGE W. and WINFIELD D. ARMENTROUT. *An Introduction to the Literature of Education.* Pp. xiv + 562. Scott, Foresman. $2.00.

GREENLAW, MILES. *Literature and Life Student's Guide.* Book IV. Pp. vi + 138. Scott, Foresman. $.40.

JESSOP, J. C. *Education in Angus.* Pp. vii + 328. University of London Press. 5 shillings.

STORY, E. M. *A Study of "The Ring and the Book."* Pp. 184. Basil Blackwell, Oxford, England. 7s/6.

TRESSLER, J. C. *Grammar in Action; with Answers.* Pp. xi + 404. Heath. $1.28.

WARD, C. H. and H. Y. MOFFETT. *The Junior Highway to English.* Book I, revised. Pp. xv + 317. Scott, Foresman. $.96.

EDUCATIONAL REVIEW

Edited by WILLIAM McANDREW

EDITORIAL COMMENT

A CONVERSATION IN A SUBURBAN TRAIN

"HELLO, Professor."

Without looking up, I knew this must be a man from the South or West. I hadn't been complimented or ridiculed with that title since the good old Illinois and Michigan days. Sure enough, there was Abraham Flexner, from whom twenty-five years and more of Baltimore, New York and other cities haven't removed the old Kentucky style of neighborly speech.

He lifted my package of new school books and holding them in his lap sat down beside me.

"You libeled me in SCHOOL AND SOCIETY," he said. "You wrote the article 'Flexner Reflexes.' "

I didn't need to make a shield of my arm against any Dreiser demonstration, for Arthur May, Riverda Harding Johnson, Sheldon Davis and Otis Caldwell were all sitting on Abraham's knees, and he was too well picketed to go on strike.

"On the whole," continued the Flexner, "you did pretty well. It was one of the most thoughtful and suggestive reviews that have come to my attention."

"I am the authors' pet."

"What do you mean by that?"

"So far as I know, the only readers I have are the authors whose books I review. They call me honey."

"Well, that gives you a dozen appreciations a month. You are lucky. Few critics get so many."

"You didn't read the review of any book beside your own," I said, half hoping.

"I turned two pages by mistake and read a line or two on another book. But never mind. I won't do it again. I have a bone or two to pick with you. I did not undertake, in my book, to say what other people's idea of a university should be. Looking at society as it now stands I said what I think a university should be. A university should be an adaptable institution, as should a religion and a school.

M. "Then, doctor, you wouldn't dynamite my university if I ran it on a principle contrary to yours."

F. "You'd possibly dynamite your own after you had run it awhile. You seem, in your review, to get excited over the 'ad hoc' idea. Of course everything a human being does is 'ad hoc' sooner or later; but the question is whether so costly an instrument as a university should divert its energies to manufacturing ice cream or training manicurists. Again, when I speak of an aristocracy of intellect you get needlessly disturbed about democracy. But my idea is the most democratic in the world. Search for brains in every boy, no matter who his father is. Let the university address itself to the development of such for the benefit of the world. Isn't that real democracy?"

M. "It has democracy in it."

F. "It is not a leveling democracy. That kind means ruin. You ought to know. Your Chicago board knocked your merit system galley west and wherever politics could do it wrecked the scheme of promotion of teachers according to civil service, didn't it?"

M. "Thou speakest true, O Socrates."

There were other matters of present-day moment discussed on this short ride, which ended with each passenger confirmed in his own beliefs and cheerfully according the other undisputed right to his own. Also each invited the other to luncheon.

ON REVIEWING BOOKS AND GETTING TEACHERS TO STUDY

CHESTER LANE, of Ypsilanti, afterward of Fort Wayne, was especially fond of a little piece of Edward Gibbon's autobiography:

"It was on that day, or rather night, of the twenty-seventh of June, 1787, between the hours of eleven and twelve, that I wrote the last line of the last page of the 'Decline and Fall of the Roman Empire.' It was in a summer house in my garden at Lausanne on the shore of Lake Geneva. After laying down my pen I took several turns in a covered walk of acacias which commands a prospect of the country, the lake and the mountains. The air was temperate, the sky was serene, the silver orb of the moon was reflected from the waters, and all nature was silent. I will not dissemble the first emotions of joy on recovery of my freedom and perhaps the establishment of my fame. But my pride was soon humbled and a sober melancholy was spread over my mind by the idea that I had taken an everlasting leave of an old and agreeable companion, and that whatsoever might be the future fate of my history the life of the historian must be short and precarious."

To-night, exactly 144 years later, in a little old house on the edge of Setauket Bay, I finish reading a 1,037th book on education. My night is also serene. Bright old friends spangle the sky. They are as brilliant as over Lake Geneva in 1787. The Long Island Lighting Company's brighter constellation twinkles through the branches of silent locust trees and makes visible the white houses of hospitable neighbors.

Gibbon was only fifty. I can see seventy without a telescope. He had finished the obituary of a dead giant. My 1,037 volumes portray the rise and progress of a universal force, changing, growing, perfecting itself. The education toward which the most of these books are moving is something to stir the blood and to make one wish to live longer and to help more.

A correspondent writes that our reviews praise too much. The publishers of his book never sent me a copy or he would be in the chorus of authors who affirm that the appraisals of School and Society are very proper stuff. When Walter Page was my boss he said a book review ought to be a refreshment counter. When a schoolmaster goes the round of classes he soon learns that he improves production if he gets the habit of looking for something to praise. I take my cue from the travel-club lecturers who waste no time running down poor places.

There is no decline or fall in the professional literature of teaching. All of us are decidedly better read than when the same Mr. Page, thirty years ago, advised us to emulate the average physician. We are handicapped by lack of the compelling competition which keeps other professions alert. We instinctively resent compulsion. But the reading-circle requirements here and there, the rewards provided in many a salary schedule, the persuasive recommendations of principals and superintendents are, according to our sharpest critics—Rugg, Snedden, Prosser—moving us ahead. Eliot, in 1900, considered us in practice fifty years behind uncontradicted theory. Charters, in 1930, thought this gap reduced to ten years.

In England, Sir Michael Sadler says the British school people's avoidance of professional study is appalling. With us the persuasive Withers continues to spread the conviction to school managers that no teacher shall be allowed to stop studying and growing. Progress means change. Resistance to it is still too common a feature of the public school.

Ella Young used to say to the Chicagoans: "It is not enough to have progressive teachers and principals scattered here and there in goodly numbers throughout the system. The poorest and laziest must equip himself with the best knowledge and skill."

Lotus Coffman suggests that if you do not encourage change, outside pressure will put some one in your place who will do it. Thomas Briggs startled the New Englanders by suggesting that the state's attorney might indict the schoolmaster for wasting public money by poor teaching. I heard a speaker at a Michigan Parent Teachers Association ask it to petition the school board to reexamine every five years the superintendent and all the teachers to see whether they are up to standard in the science of their profession.

Paying the Readers

This will come, no doubt. Locomotive engineers, army and navy persons, airmen get it. Some persuasive or indignant enthusiast will slip a law through the legislature requiring each of us to show satisfactory absorption of the contents of ten books a year. In 1930, I found 248 volumes no hardship. If I had been driven to study them by a law or a superintendent no doubt I would have found it a burden. But if on some salary schedule I could have been paid ten dollars for every written abstract you can not imagine the joy it would have given my Scottish heart. Necessity and gain do keep the physician at his reading. Money used for a similar purpose in school systems is well spent, isn't it?

James Greenwood, famed school superintendent of Kansas City, used to ask teachers, "What are you reading?" When I tried that form of questioning it used to seem to me that many teachers took it as a sort of rebuke. How can I get the teacher thus interrogated out of the inferior place of being quizzed to find out his sins of omission?

Try this in the course of your conversation: "By the way, you know I have to keep up to date in all your subjects. What do you think is the best book for me to study on the methods of modern arithmetic?"

Watch your questioned friend flounder. Keep still. Don't apologize. Mitigate, correct or express surprise. Use that gentle, humble request for help every time you talk with a teacher or a principal. In all well-regulated school systems the tip will fly by wireless to all concerned and pretty soon you'll get an answer:

"I think you'll find Rowantree and Taylor pretty good."

"I'm glad to know that. What do they say about forming the habit of reliability in the fundamentals?"

In deep water, again. But no one is criticized, reprimanded or hurt, except as he embarrasses himself.

The efficiency of this method of promoting professional reading is rated by a high-school friend of mine, principal of ninety-two teachers, so high that he promises strychnine in my coffee if I tell his name. The golden triumph of his scheme is that, coming into a school with a teaching corps mostly of unburied dead, he found himself invited at the beginning of his second semester to a weekly meeting of his teachers at which he heard the new professional books discussed.

The notion that pedagogy is pretty dry stuff fades out if you can start the neglectful person on the best book of a human and unirritating writer like Cubberley, Strayer, Bagley, Rugg, Judd, O'Shea, Sisson, Bode, Mossman, Morrison, Kilpatrick, Gates, Peters, Finney or Pulliam.

The July collation is now spread on the counter. Step up and taste.

REVIEWING NEW BOOKS

HAROLD RUGG—AGAIN

ANOTHER superb book in the Harold Rugg social science course is ready.[1] These volumes are for school children. They are the most generous assemblages of present-day ideas of vital importance ever attempted for common-school use. The text, the unusual pictures, the strong and simple narrative style everywhere show the work of a man who knows children throughly.

What are the problems the generation now in school will have to face? Unemployment, multiplication of desires, unequal distribution of wealth, plight of farmers, increased leisure, conflicting theories of government. What is an essential foundation for the thinker soon to be faced with these critical situations? The past experiences of our people in similar circumstances, the proposals public-minded men are making to meet the difficulties. The school texts of the previous generations treated our history as an account of glorious victories, or of troubles past and gone. In our debating clubs, extra-curricular, we learned some things about unjust practices by trusts, bribed juries and crooked politicians. But as far as direct teaching by the school people was concerned, America was a triumphant democracy—the admired of all the world.

Bunk, says Harold, but in more reserved and polite language. History is not merely an entertaining tale. Let us study it with reference to our present needs. Accordingly, history is of the struggle for democracy, the breaking of the monarchy, the crisis after the revolution, the union of 1787, the power of the politicians, spoils systems, government by big business, revolt of farmers and laborers, the wars, the schools, the Indians, the amusements, manners and morals, the present problems of democracy.

Noah Webster, than whom it would be hard

[1] Harold Rugg, "America's March Toward Democracy. A History of Her Government and Culture." Ginn & Co., New York. 635 pp. $1.96.

to find a more capable student of American needs, wrote, 144 years ago, that the schoolmaster thinks the Revolution is over, whereas it has only just begun and must continue until the ideals of an honest, generous, just democracy is obtained. If Noah should come back to earth, methinks he would clasp Harold to his bosom.

OUR NATIONAL LIFE AND THE SCHOOLS

YOU might well entitle the latest Harold Rugg book "A Mirror for Americans."[2] He calls it a preface to a theory of life and education with a tentative program to meet the staggering problems of social reconstruction." He portrays the potential American, the dream of the Founders. He proposes the school-centered community needed to produce such a man. Our present situation is a tragic absurdity. We have the requisites for an almost ideal civilization. Engineers and economists of prestige estimate we have concentrated capital enough, powerful machines enough, intelligence enough, sufficiently matured engineering plans to provide every man, woman and child in America with a comfortable standard of living. What use do we make of these? Leaders of government resort to one petty makeshift after another—unplanned building of public works, contributions of workers to relief of their fellows, governmental charity. As in every task, accomplishment depends on what we have to work with and what we intend to make out of it. Apprehend American civilization and culture; build individual and group life on a program of collective action—on a planned régime of economic, political and social life. Education is the means and process for it.

Here is no eccentric Fourrier, Noyes nor Alcott, planning to gather a group of enthusiasts into a community apart. The essay is a program for calling the public schools to their original purpose, identical with the principles of our political union, a direct and immediate turning of education to the general welfare.

In half of the book you find the characteristic forces of American life assembled and analyzed—our technology, our artistry, our pragmatism, our democracy, our philosophy, our national character. The second half covers the lag of the schools, the civic-social program that is needed, the school-centered community, the community-centered school, the teacher and educational reconstruction.

Not once in this century and a half has the cirruculum of the school caught up with the current of American life. The American school is essentially academic. What does that mean? When a court declines to give a verdict on a matter of no importance and calls it academic, he is paying no compliment to us schoolmasters.

THE PIFFLING HIGH SCHOOLS

Only to-day I was one of the throng at the graduation exercises of a big high school in a neighboring town. The youngsters, 120 of them, were dressed exactly alike: girls in white gowns, each skirt starting eighteen inches from the floor, lavender rayon stockings, white shoes; boys in black shoes, white-flannel trousers, navy blue jackets and identical neckties. They marched, counter-marched, formed bars, squares and x's; they sung a class song about dear old Maple High. A class history recounted only dances, picnics, suppers and athletic triumphs. Prizes were given to individuals who got the best ratings in Latin and English, in high-school mathematics and in games. The whole precious galaxy then came in again dolled up in academic robes, with the flat betasselled tomfooleries on their heads. As each took his silly roll of paper he moved the dangler from the right side of his vanity piece to the left, or maybe from the left to the right. What did it matter? What did the whole expensive mummery amount to? Or what use to the town, taxed to pay for it, did the whole four years signify, culminating in this meaningless festival? Was the whole thing a show?

America is playing a costly game with its schools.

Harold says public education is potentially a giant, actually a small and impotent weakling, bound by fear and mesmerized by the vaporous halo of a cultural glory that is of scant use to the school children and worth less to the toiling masses who pay the bills.

What are the schools doing to prevent the danger, depression and unhappiness of the mil-

[2] Harold Rugg, "Culture and Education in America." Harcourt, Brace and Company, New York. 628 pp. $2.75.

lions out of work? What discussions are sincerely concerned with providing continuous employment for the nation and a decent comfort-standard of living? How hard are the schools trying to get the coming citizen to consider the inequitable distribution of income, to be self-guarded against the propaganda with which he will be surrounded, to repair the current ignorance and indifference to our mutual responsibilities of government?

The business of the high school from the days of its birth and obligated by the nature of the sources of its cost is to visualize the community and direct its development. So promised Jefferson, Rush, Clinton, Mann and the campaigners for free school laws. Governor Sullivan, as early as 1787, told the Massachusetts lawmakers that the only justification for taxing all the people for the education of other men's children was to give the commonwealth the schools that would concentrate on doing what Rugg, five generations later, says they ought to be doing now.

Chief Justice Chipman, of New Hampshire, in Sullivan's time, warned the teachers to remember that we are a nation of growth and change. Our young, he said, must be trained to make our civilization different and better. Webster scathed the schoolmasters for a lazy and timid clinging to subjects that had nothing to do with improving democracy. Rugg keeps clear of bitterness and fault-finding but finds schoolmasters continuing to defend academic faith, protagonists of things as they are, reflecting the old opinion of the community.

Youth must be guided to a frank study of political problems. They must be shown the futility of current statesmanship, the lag of motive and of wise use of human resources behind technical invention and mass production. Our young people must be shown their responsibility to create a new public opinion and to build a new governmental order, that will give all creative persons rôles coordinate with those of promoters, financiers and politicians.

Again I am reminded of those earliest promoters of the American public-school idea who asserted that the instructors of youth should be expert economists, professors of civic affairs, masters of statecraft.

How expert are you in these things? How much of them was I qualified to teach in my high school?

In a book of French nursery tales my neighbor's little daughter reads to me is one of Bonhomme Pierre, who made a long journey to the fair. After many days he came to town and asked for the fair. "Why, that moved from here long ago. Why didn't you ask?"

"I did. I asked old Jean, who lives in the woods. He came to the fair, once."

"By the blue, man, the fair moves about from place to place. One doesn't go to the wood to learn of the town."

By the same token must we go to Latin, literature, algebra, geometry, general science, athletics, or to any of the vast majority of high-school subjects to find the way to democracy?

Pooh, pooh, come out of the wood.

SOCIAL LEADERSHIP

MR. HALL modestly says his big book[3] is not an encyclopedia. He could have claimed this for it and more. He calls it a record. It aims to tabulate organized efforts in the United States to deal with social conditions and problems. He says in his preface he wants suggestions and criticisms. Here's one for Mr. Hall himself. Set the book upright on a mantel and if ever you feel blue stand in front of it and realize that it is a monument of industry and success. Tell yourself that the idea of compiling a year book on a dictionary model is a stroke of genius that should be imitated by all compilers forevermore. Understand that your cross-references, inserted in their alphabetical places, your "consults," your "related articles," put where they belong, your list of topical references classified, your "History and Present Status," with which each topic begins, your "Development and Events," your "Legislation," given with each theme, make this the most serviceable handbook for school superintendents, charitable societies and social workers ever published.

This book reminds me of a guest room in Dr. Abram Elkus's house. The completeness of conveniences in it was secured first by a consultation between sir and madam. After the chambers were supplied with everything these

[3] Fred S. Hall, "Social Work Year Book." Russell Sage Foundation. 600 pp. $4.00.

two conceived might be needed, they packed their bags as if to travel; they put themselves up in one of their own guest rooms; they noted whatever needful thing had been omitted and supplied it.

The Social Work Year Book lists alphabetically, and thereafter according to field, 455 national social agencies. What do they include? Alumni, adult education, service for feeble-minded, for blind, for handicapped of all kinds, museums, psychiatry, school physicians and nurses, university women, child health, safety, library, nature study, mental hygiene, vocational, community chests, junior league, behavior, big brothers and sisters, boy scouts, boys' clubs, campfire girls, rural life, character education, child study, drama, motion pictures, pageants, playgrounds, home economics, education, progressive and ordinary—well, the mere list covers eighty-two large pages, and gives the purposes, officers and number of members of each society.

Do you care to know what the present conception of mental hygiene is? Turn to this dictionary and find among mental clinics, mental deficiency, mental diseases, a three-page account of how Clifford Beers organized his Connecticut society, how the national organization sprang up, what it has done and is doing, how it aids adjustments in school and college and what the best books on the subject are. Parent education has two enlightening pages. The objects, history and status of the parent-teacher movement is covered by Anna Beach Pratt, director of the White-Williams Foundation. Lois Hayden Meek furnishes the information on nursery schools. Every article is signed.

Milnor Dorey writes of progressive education. He is free of the wild and glad claims too often raising a smile when the completely emancipated addicts let themselves go or castigate the rest of us. What the movement is, according to the account here, is "a new attitude and a new technique—the child as a whole, freed from predetermined criteria." Its spirit, we are told, affects all schools in this country and abroad. John Dewey is claimed as its outstanding spokesman, Charles W. Eliot having been his predecessor. Decroly, Rotten, Ferriere, Hauser, Ensor, Harold Rugg, Shumaker, Naumberg, Washburne, Stearns, Cobb, Whitehead, Johnson and Mearns are listed as promoters. The enrolled supporters number 7,000.

Thus, from accident prevention through zoning, runs this first year book, 600 enheartening pages concerned with man's humanity to man.

SOFT PEDAGOGY AND DYNAMITE

I SEE public education to-day between two fires, says Dr. Bagley in his latest offering.[4] On one side it is tempted by soft sentimentalism of the extreme freedom theory; on the other side it is assailed by the hard materialism which calls educational funds "sanctified squander." Education is not only between the devil and the deep sea; it is between the upper and the nether millstones.

You have learned to accept from Bagley an adequate assembly of facts and a temperate interpretation of them before proposing any conclusions. He here cites enough reminders of the present situation to fix your mind on the enormous saving of human labor that now results from American industrial invention and management. What are you going to do with this appalling leisure and unemployment?

He reviews the increase of crime and political corruption. He considers the handicaps of character education. He objects to Professor Livingston Scholtz's views of the Bagley position, he calls on France and Germany to tell why their criminal record shows so much better civic conduct than ours, he pictures the peril of those so-called progressives who are playing with education; he sees the sorry results of a weakened discipline; he evokes an idealism and a fitness for the changing times.

Keynote: Educational doctrines that open paths of least resistance and follow them are, in a country like ours and under the conditions that now prevail, charged with dynamite.

COLLEGE FUTURE

DR. PAUL ARTHUR SCHILPP, associate editor of *Social Science,* California professor of philosophy, dedicates his symposium[5] to you: "To all who realize that the future of the

[4] William C. Bagley, ''Education, Crime, and Social Progress.'' The Macmillan Company, New York. 581 pp. $1.20.

[5] Paul Arthur Schilpp, editor. ''Higher Education Faces the Future.'' Horace Liveright, N. Y. 408 pp. $3.00.

United States depends largely upon the American College and University." A larger proportion of Americans go to college than is the case in any other country. With us, religion, crime, prohibition, machine-age problems, sex, college and sport get the most attention in print.

Caustic and savage criticism of college is abundant and increasing. Departures from academic tradition do result from these attacks. The only way to find out what fills our national need is to experiment. What shall we try? I have no axe to grind, says the editor, I sought answers from these nineteen contributors, specifically requesting them to speak untrammeled.

In the collection William Bagley treats the upward expansion of man's education. John Dewey covers philosophy and education. Alexander Meiklejohn is for progressiveness. President Lowell treats self-education in Harvard. Dorothy Canfield Fisher is for new leaders. Ray Wilbur holds that instead of maintaining a fixed procedure college must meet the changing civilization and adapt itself to the Americans of college age. The university should, however, be relieved of the immense amount of really high-school work it is now doing. Junior colleges are helping, President Leigh details the experiment in Bennington, Vermont. President Coleman outlines the eighteen years of freedom from tradition enjoyed by Read College, Oregon. President Holt describes the unconventional policies of Rollins College, Florida. Professor Elwood, Duke University, develops the theme of service to a democracy. William M. McDougall, also of Duke University, sees the function of the endowed college to be that of ministering to the intellectually superior. The Oxford and Cambridge type appeals to him. Max McConn is not here because he has written a whole book himself on the problem. Antioch is missing because King Arthur's Knights of the table round are said to be preparing a volume. But the straightforward discourses are full of meat, positive ideas, and generally indicative of an evolution going on.

THE CHEERY VIEW

WE have now reached a national maturity which requires that we remove teaching from the list of temporary employments. We are now in a position to require applicants to think of the ultimate possibilities of the profession, to be professionally minded in the sense that a medical or a dramatic student is. We are now able to exact from training schools the insistence that their students regard teaching as a great and honorable profession. Young people are ignorant of the broad and varied types of opportunity before educators to-day.

Many young men affected by a low traditional regard for this line of public service would be attracted to it if they realized the advance it has made in science and in respect. Professor Riverda Jordan, born Missourian, now Cornellian professor, furnishes an enheartening view[6] of where we are now and what we are coming to. Opportunities, duties, salaries, rewards in public and private schools, present aims, new stresses and a high-class survey of the field are ably presented.

WHY IS THE PRIVATE HIGH SCHOOL?

IN J. Dover Wilson's collection of essays entitled "The Schools of England," Head Master Alan Rannie, in good Scottish fashion, makes an unsubstantiated claim that private secondary schools, "justly rated by Anglo-Saxon judgment as superior to the free high schools," are fast growing up in the United States, in Scotland and in all parts of the Empire.

Few things are more irritating to a Scot than a positive declaration by a Caledonian. I could hug Leonard Koos[7] for starting his new book with a quotation from our national office of education showing that the percentage of private schools has shrunk since 1890 from its then 39.2 per cent. to its present 11.9 per cent. The percentage of students enrolled in private schools has fallen from 31.9 per cent. to 7.4 per cent. The reputation Dr. Koos has established for letting facts speak for themselves is sustained in the present study. "I have no interest in propaganda," he says, "but my work in Minnesota assembled a large amount of interesting information on high schools. As I study the situation in the entire country I have

[6] Riverda Harding Jordan. ''Education as a Life Work.'' The Century Company, New York. 303 pp. $2.00.

[7] Leonard V. Koos, ''Private and Public Secondary Education. A Comparative Study.'' University of Chicago Press. 228 pp. $2.50.

reason to believe the Minnesota facts may be taken as typical of the United States."

Dr. Koos summarizes the reasons for private high schools as formulated by Carson Ryan and again by George A. Boyce.

They are presumed to be better in fitting for college. The facts given as a result of the researches described at length fail to substantiate the claim.

They provide education in communities that can not afford the public school. This evaporates on examination.

They serve as centers of innovation and experiment. On the contrary the courses are more conservative. There is very little experiment attempted.

They are a substitute for unsatisfactory home life. Maybe. The claim is magnified. An occasional public school has made a meager beginning toward meeting such a need by establishing a dormitory. Maybe public schools will take over this peculiar service of the private school.

They can render better service to the religious denomination concerned. A genuine science of society is too remote to admit of satisfactory evaluation of this claim. It may not comport with the best good of an integrated democracy.

The book's chapter, "Who Attends and Why," is an account of the reasons given on the thousands of question sheets. For the religious schools the answers are what you would expect, but the boys and girls of the undenominational schools seem to me chary in saying what most of such children's mothers who have spoken to me allege: Better manners, more exclusive, higher toned, leads to higher social connections.

From John Adams and Noah Webster to Dallas Lore Sharp these are the reasons many Americans have urged for supplanting the old academies and seminaries by institutions for all the children of all the people.

Dr. Koos, with tables and charts, compares the two sorts of service as to achievements of students, success in the university, curriculums and teachers.

THE WHITE-HOUSE CONFERENCE

The Century Company is issuing some books of addresses and other matter appertaining to child health and protection as gathered at the 1930 White-House Conference on this theme. The first volume,[8] now available, has an introduction by Secretary Wilbur, President Hoover's address, Secretary Wilbur's speeches and papers on education of parents, medical service, school activities, vocational problems, the handicapped, and lists of the various committees of the conference. It is a comprehensive assembling of facts and services brought up to the modern moment. You have in your library many books on the teaching of subjects. You'll wish to add this on those you teach the subjects to.

CHILD INTEREST IN SCHOOL SUBJECTS

Silver, Burdett and Company's new psychology[9] is planned for the "usual" school-child and subject with a teacher as mediator. The school studies are products of social development. They sprang from human minds. They have within them accumulated human interests. What, then, to do? asks Professor Wheat, the author, whom, now, that I know his harvesting, I venture to call well named.

The task is to aid the teacher to get these interests uncovered and suited to attract the juvenile mind. Whereupon the professor marches into some terse paragraphs on the psychology of learning, considers the mentality of children in different school grades, treats the psychology of the school program and thereafter works out the introduction of the pupil to the school subjects and their adaptation to child mind, language, arithmetic, reading, handwriting, spelling, social science, history, geography, their psychologies, bring the book to the final chapter—the psychology of pupil behavior. Do habits of punctuality, orderliness and those concerned with "the school virtues" function anywhere other than in the school? We all used to claim they do. After you have followed Dr. Wheat through his notably modern assemblage of facts, tests, proofs and conclusions, you will have a clear idea as to what was the matter with the schools of yesterday. I can't after several profitable evenings with his book avoid quoting a motto I saw over the

8 "Addresses and Abstracts. White House Conference on Child Protection. 1930." The Century Company, New York. 363 pp. Boards, 50 cents; cloth, $2.00.

9 Harry Grove Wheat, "The Psychology of the Elementary School," Silver, Burdett and Company, New York. 440 pp. $2.00.

agricultural classroom door in a Michigan high school:

"Intelligence and care
And wheat without a tare."

MARRIED LIFE A FESTIVAL

IF you want a pocket companion for straight forward advice on the physical and mental health of children and parents, get Mrs. Selbert's attractive work.[10] You can get sustenance from it in odd moments. The author, who hails from the College of Medicine, Ohio State University, has developed an attractiveness and simplicity of speech in teaching classes and mothers' clubs. She gives plain talk on courtship and marriage. The happiest unions are those in which the man accepts leadership; the wife unifies her interests with his. Home-life is not a mere duty, it's a festival. Remember this, my son: Wife expects courtship after marriage, all her life long. There is matter in this book which you daren't tell teachers nor they communicate to high-school children. But it is here told so properly, it has so much to do with health and happiness that you can well take trouble to see that the information is transmitted. The book is suitable for the high-school library and for recommendation by teachers. It covers, marriage, birth, child care, high-school and college health, work and leisure.

ANGELO PAIDOSOPHOS

ANGELO PATRI explores the old familiar field of childhood and charts his route in a volume[11] of twenty-two short conversations on manners, truth, timidity, stealing, homework, college, punishment, fourth of July, fathers and all. He is talking to teachers of home and in school. The qualities that have made Angelo a favorite in America and abroad are losing none of their charm. For thirty-five years Angelo has taught, loving the job more and more. He and I have worked in the same district. I have seen him exposed to prejudices of clan and creed and race. He knows what it means to be weary and discouraged and misinterpreted to boot. With never a whine, with the soul of an artist, he has refused to lay aside his rose colored glasses. Read his chapter on "What's wrong with teaching?" It will surprise and comfort you.

RESTLESS YOUTH

I FIND Professor Frederick Bolton's Adolescent Education[12] a vigorous piece of writing skilfully working out from facts established by researchers, a guide for teachers, principals and parents concerned with the welfare of youth. Bolton, himself, has to his credit a good deal of objective and statistical study but it hasn't dried the sap out of him, nor carried him to extremes. For instance, he wants you to be careful about swallowing all that intelligence testers offer you. When they find 50.1 per cent. of 581 students rated, as to IQ, too low to do satisfactory college work but actually doing it creditably, these appraisers mustn't be too cocksure. Their examinations, valuable as they may be, says Dr. Bolton, are at best crude and limited. They in no way test emotions, will power, moral qualities, leadership, or mechanical abilities. These things are as important as academic knowledge. He reminds me of Frank Rexford at teachers' meetings discussing some new project. After all have said their say Frank sums up, "Now, my dears, you have clearly shown it can't be done, now go ahead and do it and show how able you are."

The Bolton book will not accept the conclusions from the studies of teachers marks that such ratings are utterly unreliable. Even when they are given by different teachers their predictive value of scholastic success is high, seventy to eighty.

He is an intellectual democrat. The warnings of Presidents Hopkins of Dartmouth and Faunce of Brown that too many men are going to college and that the aristocracy of brains is threatened, the seemingly similar fear of Glenn Frank, are answered by the fact that the people own the colleges, never intended them as creators of intellectual lords, and send their children not to fit the college but to be fitted by it.

Self government, he says in another place, may be harder to endure and to guide than the old regulation by rule and decree but the schools were established in America on the

[10] Norma Selbert, "Child Health." W. B. Saunders Company, Philadelphia. 261 pp. $1.60.

[11] Angelo Patri, "The Questioning Child." D. Appleton & Company, New York. 221 pp. $1.60.

[12] Frederick Elmer Bolton, "Adolescent Education." The Macmillan Company, New York. 506 pp. $3.00.

promise that they would make government by the people of more advantage than any monarchy had ever been. Actual participation in government is the most effective means of teaching the ideals of government. Without this phase of learning the real understanding of our republic can never be satisfactory. The important thing in school participation is not the machinery but the motive.

The book is new and fresh. It discusses adolescent growth, mentality, diseases and disturbances peculiar to the period, imitation, imagination, emotions, intelligence, ministration to individuals, paramount objectives, and devotes two strongly fortified chapters to youth, crime and character.

PROGRESSIVISM IN A PUBLIC SCHOOL

MARTHA PORTER is now directing elementary education in Roslyn, New York, where education in my younger days was kept to a high grade by Commissioner James Cooley. Every real estate dealer on the north shore will tell you that Roslyn schools are good schools. At any rate, a very good book[13] is this of the Roslyn director lady. She sees the gains and the drawbacks in letting children do only what they wish. She insists on arousing their curiosity in worth while things; she outlines the direction of interests into reading, writing, drawing and the things we all must do. Ingeniously and effectively Miss Porter adapts the usages of the rich and famous progressive schools and shows how these ways can be used in the traditional and poverty-stricken class rooms of hard-up country towns.

THE I STUDIES ME

PRESIDENT DAVIS, of the State Normal School of Dillon, Montana, had he gone into salesmanship, would have been one of those reliables who had rather lose a customer than persuade him to buy something not needed or wanted. You know that sort of agent, the one you come back to after chasing rainbow bargains, the solid salesman who won't stretch the truth to get an order. Dr. Davis knows that teaching is in the front rank of respectable services and not entirely respected. He begins his survey[14] of the teacher's place in society by an honest admission of the points in which education has failed. It hasn't taught every American to read. We don't lead the world in literacy. Even if we did, reading is not enough. Ten times as many know how to read as what to read or what to believe of what they have read. Schools were made a part of the American democratic scheme so as to get people to think and to improve our political affairs. The proponents of laws to require the whole people to pay for the education of the children of those who had any promised to save the cost of schools by reducing the expense of courts and jails. "More teachers, less policemen," said Horace Mann. Now we have a greater number of both. Education has not adequately developed an inner sense of duty. This generation rejoices in freedom from responsibility. Of all the influences able to save civilization from disaster, education is the force on which thinking men rely. Education is a living force. Our American theory expects it to function mostly through teachers. The most respectable thing about a teacher is that combination of motive, patriotism, intelligence, industry and skill which he nurtures and develops within his own breast. All of this clean, trenchant, sympathetic, patriotic book is a masterly persuasion to teachers to keep the faith, to continue the respectability of an indispensable, interesting and enjoyable profession.

A refreshing quality of the book is its freedom from cant, from coddling the hard-worked teacher, and from sympathy with protests against modern responsible supervision.

School boards thinking of the days of the five-cent cigar and the dollar-a-day wage for ten hours work may think present salaries too high. Teachers are as unreasonable in repeating that they are underpaid. Dr. Davis's chapter on salary and tenure will seem reasonable both to board members and teachers.

The chapters on relation to the school board, to administration, to supervision, to colleagues, to parents, to the community, to the profession, to self, are, it would seem, based upon a collection of all sorts of incidents sympathetically observed by a level-headed schoolmaster, dis-

[13] Martha Peck Porter, "The Teacher in the New School." World Book Company, Yonkers, N. Y. 312 pp. $2.00.

[14] Sheldon Emmor Davis, "The Teacher's Relationships." The Macmillan Company, New York. 415 pp. $1.80.

cussed, adjusted and stored away in memory until used in this novel and salutary book.

At times, as I read it, I imagine the author an earnest young chap of thirty, at times, a wise old grandfather. Albert Marquis, who knows, says Dr. Davis is fifty, came from Missouri, studied in Germany, and knows Montana from the Black Hills to the Kootenai. However that may be, he does know how to make educational discourse decidedly human.

THE MORRISON MONUMENT[15]

CHICAGO UNIVERSITY, according to my recollection, got Henry Morrison about a dozen years ago. I sat in a shady porch on the university campus with him there in 1920 and told him he was a western pioneer in spirit and outlook, breaking new paths and building an education for future time among people not content with the sleepy methods of the fathers. I had seen him in his native Maine and adopted New Hampshire telling lovable New England schoolmasters what delicious fooling was going on under the guise of teaching and how easy it is to solace our souls with theories that please us although real investigations disprove them every day. Morrison, as superintendent of schools in Portsmouth at his age of 28 and State Commissioner for New Hampshire at 34, had early fallen in love with the experimenters. Lured to the State Department of Connecticut, the commonwealth that turned Henry Barnard's hair prematurely white and lacked the foresight to keep him, Morrison couldn't have a happy time, for I have never been able to get him to speak of it. But have you ever noticed that you can't stop a man who knows where he's going? Morrison had a head full of beliefs that he was set upon trying out. Chicago University had laboratory schools. So,

"Strength and ease in graceful union meet
Though polished, subtile, and though poignant,
sweet."

After seven years as director of experimenting in the schools of the university, the Professor of Education published what is the recognized chief of high school guides.

Go to an examination for secondary-school teachers' certificates in any system. What is the source of most of the ideas in the answer papers? Morrison, "The Practice of Teaching in the Secondary School."

Now comes a revised edition. What need? Let the author tell. "A very considerable amount of new material has accumulated in the laboratory schools and elsewhere. It has been so substantial that I have had to rewrite many chapters." "Conduct is better understood than it was five years ago. Individual differences have become the basis of school and class management." "I find no reasons, however, for fundamental changes in the basic principles set out in the earlier volume."

What are those principles?

This is one, that our teaching does not give the thorough and genuine learning we are entitled to.

It must be founded on a coherent grasp of the whole field of teaching capable of being organized into a practical system.

No book of methods suffices. Teaching can not be perfected by such. The immense variety of schoolroom situations need solutions by the teacher on the spot. Morrison's analysis of the teaching process is a general guide from which you make the deductions proper in particular cases. But he does not fail to use, as illustrations of principles, method enough to satisfy a reasonable appetite for the concrete.

The plan of the revised version is that of its forerunner—What the secondary school is and what for, products of lesson-learning, appraisal of progress, control of the learning in classes and persons, organization, recitation, conduct, problem pupils, separate discussions of the teaching of different high school subjects.

The title of the book is not satisfactory to me. The volume has so much of what is needed in most of the primary and college classes I have seen that if I had the say I would add to the title the words, "and elsewhere."

PRINCIPLES OF LEARNING REACH HISTORY

MISS KELTY follows her "Beginnings of the American People and Nation" with a com-

[15] Henry Clinton Morrison, "The Practice of Teaching in the Secondary School." Revised Edition. University of Chicago Press. 688 pp. $4.00.

panion volume.[16] In this talented woman you have a reformer who has uncovered the purpose of national-history teaching and who has given to every one who undertakes to benefit a class by means of this subject, a guide for getting the purpose realized. The prime use of silent reading, as our eminent researchers have been for some time telling us, is apprehension of ideas directly from print. In intermediate grades the place for the present text, history study, should be silent reading. What Miss Kelty has done is the difficult task of building a history on a scientific basis of laws of learning and at the same time producing a text which will appeal to boys and girls. She has done it with admirable skill. The book talks to children in a way they like. Its historical content is from the union of 1787 to the unsolved problems of now. Its handling of our science, our social life, our inventions, our domestic intranquilities, our work and play, is with a fine sense of proportion. Patriotism as duty, not so much with a gun as with tongue, pen, and vote, is the aim of the book, even to the end, where runs the last line: "America is waiting to welcome you to her service."

SPIRITED LITERATURE

I find "The Spirit of America in Literature"[17] a real delight. Two professors of English in the Chicago Normal College, both experienced as magazine editors, have assembled 135 selections of prose and verse, specimens of Franklin, Tom Paine, Irving, the New England galaxy, and a preponderance of present-day favorites, forty of whom are contemporary with the present generation. The editors have made their knowledge of the preferences of American youth the basis of choice. We must take, they say, American boys and girls as we find them and allure to brighter fields and lead the way. It is not enough to fit literature comfortably to youth. We have chosen our matter on the basis of significant content and artistic quality. There is much vigorous writing in the book new to school use. The selections are grouped under adventure, out of doors, human nature, humor, fancy, old America, America to-day. Each section has copious lists of other readings of similar bent. There are many pictures, all new and done by Keith Ward. Each extract is followed by a short critical comment and by suggestions for discussion. The editors want their notes to help the enjoyment and profit of the reading. Therefore they put each one on the page where the need is.

DEBATING

James O'Neill, University of Michigan professor, wrote a manual of debate and oral discussion ten years ago. Rupert Cortright, Detroit, now joins with him in revising and expanding the work.[18] Besides furnishing a text for class instruction the authors have adapted the book for clubs and societies which have no instructor.

THE SUPERINTENDENT AND PUPILS' READING

"Learn to read slow, all other graces
Will follow in their proper places."

I am sorry I do not know who first said this. My old teacher John McGill—he would be more than 110 years old now if still on earth—had us write those lines on the fly leaf of our Hillard's School Reader. Arthur Gates keeps hammering away on the damage of crowding reading too fast. He is out with another book[19] this time, for the superintendent. Here is a nifty little work that you can slip into your pocket on the way to a school and use to freshen your mind for an intelligent conversation with the teacher of the beginning classes most of whom are more up to date in this "heart of the curriculum" than is the man higher up.

Dr. Gates has codified his own and others' investigations so as to offer a quickly bound summary of each essential fact appertaining to these standard school pursuits: Oral work, silent reading, vocabulary, instruction in different grades, diagnosis, measurement, correctives and standards.

[16] Mary C. Kelty, "The Growth of the American People and Nation." Ginn & Company, New York. 631 pp. $1.32.

[17] W. Wilbur Hatfield, H. D. Roberts, "The Spirit of America In Literature." The Century Company, New York. 650 pp. $2.00.

[18] James Milton O'Neill, Rupert L. Cortright, "Debate and Oral Discussion." The Century Company, New York. 274 pp. $1.25.

[19] Arthur L. Gates, "Reading for Public School Administrators." Teachers College Press, Columbia University, New York. 126 pp. $1.50.

ILLITERACY

What is the present illiteracy of the United States? How much education have we to boast of as compared with Denmark for instance? How does our illiteracy affect our social situation? Who and where are the illiterates? For answer see the very careful study by Professor Winston.[20]

STRONG STUFF ON STUDENT JOURNALISM

The president of the Pennsylvania School Press Association has in his considerable experience matured many ideas for the management of school publications. The gist of his conclusions is made available in twenty-one chapters,[21] covering the training of school journalists, the canvass for advertisements, style, make-up, faculty advising and related matters. Frederick Law, of the Stuyvesant High School, New York, who, long ago, wrote the best manuals on speech-making anybody ever read, introduces author Greenawalt as responsible for the best high-school paper in the U. S. A.

You are likely to be attracted to the book by its positive stand that getting out a school paper takes too much precious time and energy to be permitted to produce shallow stuff. On the first page is a declaration of stiff principles:

> A student publication should show the students and the general public that the school is the hope of America.
> The student periodical should not be extra-curricular but an allied curricular activity.
> It has academic and vocational values.
> If written by teachers it is a cheat.
> Many errors in a school paper are preferable to a student publication written by the faculty.

Mr. Greenawalt carries this healthy tone into his ideas of what the faculty adviser of a student paper should be and do. He ought to be as well trained for journalism as is the field-sports coach for athletics. He needs to know journalism, English, finance, advertising, printing. He needs a broad vision of the place and duty of a school in a democracy. The paper is the organ of American education. The community must be kept in favor of good schools. What good the schools are doing the town and district must be kept before the readers in a modest, unbragging but interesting manner. Doing something for the school is an exercise of general welfare spirit, a service promised when schools were made a tax upon all. But the community is bigger than the school and has almost the entire cost of educating the boys and girls. Doing something in return is obligatory on every sharer in this benefit. Town spirit is harder to maintain than school spirit, and worth more.

With a penetrating insight into a thousand and one bothersome preventives of getting the academic, vocational, civic training, out of conducting a school paper, cognizant of an immense binding and propulsive power the periodical can be brought to possess for almost all the worth while activities of a school and town, this experienced manager and sympathetic admirer of high school students has produced a manual of management as bright as it is extensive.

CLUBS ARE TRUMPS

Dr. Martin V. O'Shea's Experimental Education Series has reached its eighth volume.[22] The newest book is a striking surprise. Dr. Osburn, Ohio State University, professor and director of research, gave a talk in Milwaukee eleven years ago on the wasteful lockstep treatment of pupils. Ben Rohan, Superintendent in Appleton, Wisconsin, came to him and said, "Your suggestions sound sound to me."

"Then why don't you sound 'em by practice?"

With Osburn as coach Rohan furnished the players—pupils and teachers.

The book is a spirited account of the game, along with related information, philosophy, and incidental observations.

There are entertaining appraisals of the earlier adventures in fitting schools to varying capacities—Wm. T. Harris's rapid promotion plan, Shearer's Elizabeth effort, the Cambridge, Le Mars, Portland, Denver, New York, Santa Barbara, Batavia, Pueblo, Newton, Burke, Winnetka, Dalton, Ambridge and Car-

[20] Sanford Winston, "Illiteracy in the United States." University of North Carolina Press, Chapel Hill, N. C. 168 pp. $3.00.

[21] Lambert Greenawalt, "School-Press Management and Style." McGraw-Hill Book Company, 370 7th Ave., New York. 420 pp. $3.00.

[22] W. J. Osburn, Ben J. Rohan, "Enriching the Curriculum of Gifted Children." The Macmillan Company, New York. 408 pp. $2.00.

terville projects. The disadvantages of pushing bright pupils into grades composed of children decidedly older require, in the opinion of the authors, some scheme for keeping the abler boys and girls supplied with plenty of educative pursuits and for giving them associates of suitable age.

Happy thought—Clubs!

Here are these extra-curricular botherations harrassing schools all the time. They have the vitality of weeds. They have in many quarters been considered a pest in the school garden. How Osburn and Rohan made clubs an integral part of school procedure, made membership depend on standing in studies, guided the youngsters into club-work of high educative and service value, capitalized the interests of gifted children, developed a scheme for individual differences that can be worked in a city building of fifty classrooms or in a one-room country school are related with much sprightliness and verse.

Steam had been fussing around in kettles for thousands of years before Watt harnessed it to service. I believe your reading of this ingenious book will bring you to regard the authors as having made a famous discovery and utilized it in a notable invention.

BODY AND MIND

ALMOST at the close of their brilliant disquisition[23] the three wise men of Gotham—Caldwell, Skinner, and Tietz, remind us: "in the last analysis education must begin with and rest upon the physical child that human biology describes. The school's business is to develop normal inheritance and to guide it." To clarify an understanding of behavior as resulting from heredity and environment the authors contribute this text on the biology of man as a thinking and progressive entity. They desire to assist in an improvement of the philosophy of education and in a betterment of individual living. The body, the glands, the nervous system, the brains, mind, culture, inheritance, growth, work and fatigue are the main topics covered. It is an offering of men who have tried the topics on young people and whose work here set forth is worth infinitely more than most of the old stuff still doled in school.

[23] Otis W. Caldwell, Charles Edward Skinner, J. Winfred Tietz, "Biological Foundations of Education." Ginn & Company, New York. 534 pp. $2.72.

PLATOONERY

DR. CUBBERLEY, in his introduction to Professor Case's book,[24] reports over two hundred American cities conducting almost eleven hundred platoon schools enrolling more than twenty thousand teachers, 750,000 children. Burris, Bourne, Spain, and Sullivan have published books concerned severally with this type of school as found in Gary, Detroit, and Akron. Unnumbered magazine articles have discussed the plan; experts and laymen have fought over it. Dr. Case digests the arguments, the experiences, and the results. He comes through as Dr. Cubberley has often done before, with the conviction that William Wirt's scheme is based on sound thinking and fits the profound social and industrial changes taking place in American life. Wirt's original contribution in Bluffton and Gary were applications of Dewey principles. The modest and quiet Indiana schoolmaster has profoundly modified school organization and instruction in this country and abroad. Twenty years ago Wirt told me, with a twinkle in his eye, that a procession of school superintendents were passing through his schools every day taking copious notes to prove to their boards at home that the Gary system should not be adopted. Chicago agents of teachers' organizations were exhorting the Gary school workers to revolt. Subsidized agitators in New York organized parades of school children shouting "Down with the Gerry sisters," so intelligently did they know what they were howling down. Now comes this dignified volume from the press of a great university dedicating the book "To William A. Wirt, father of the platoon school in America."

It outlines briefly the history of the platoon system. It comprehensively shows how these schools are operating in the United States. It has half a hundred pictures, charts, and tables. It treats of underlying theories, experiences of cities with the plan. It elaborates cost problems, equipment programming, pays careful attention to the auditorium, to departmentali-

[24] Roscoe David Case, "The Platoon School in America." Stanford University Press, California. 366 pp. $3.00.

zation, to loss of "Mothering," and other serious or trivial prejudices. The comparisons of pupil standings, promotion success in high school and college, hard-worked teachers' attitude of parents, pupils, and teachers are illuminating.

It requires more brains, care, and skill, to run an effective platoon school than is employed in the ordinary one, says Dr. Case. A special training of workers is necessary. His book is primarily for the instruction of such. Accordingly each chapter is accompanied by questions and problems.

HOME ROOM

ON Professor Inglis's text, "The aim of the home room is the training of the citizen" two junior-high school researchers offer a manual[25] for fulfilling that purpose. It is concerned with counselling, helping to study, self-government, celebrations, and a lively lot of programs, ready to hand.

A REFRESHING VIEW OF SYSTEM

YOU who know Carlos Ellis as a schoolmaster could have told the Professional and Technical Press that when it got him as editor in chief of a series of books for educational executives the output would not be a rehashing of old meat.[26] The regimen of bewildering duties which now belong to school management has here been worked out by two men of Rooseveltian mold who consider that the way to dig a Panama canal is to dig it. The preponderating purpose in maintaining a principalship to-day is to provide for efficient teaching. All the tests of pupils show greater achievement of those of supervised teachers than of the children of teachers who are let alone. A reason why so many principals are afflicted by office blight is because they can not or will not supervise. No schoolmaster in his senses believes that he has to take school time for correspondence, telephoning, or receiving visitors. No thoroughly honest executive will go on spending his dollar time on ten-cent activity. A not unknown opposition of teachers to supervision is due to many causes. One is they don't have enough of it to get wonted. Another reason is that neither principal nor teachers fully realize that in supervision both of them are learning valuable and encouraging things. The old what's-he-up-to-now attitude evaporates under the principal's frequent appearance.

Messrs. Morgan and Cline base their system of administration on, as they say, organizing the how so as to realize the why. They are against the elaborate and spectacular. They are for the simple and unobtrusive. They are for thorough instruction of teachers by the principal and by staff discussions so that every one will grasp the purpose of the school and the reasons for different features of its organization. They have some solid arguments for employing young teachers. Teachers meetings can and must be cleared of the unpopularity clinging to them quite generally due to stupidity in the man higher up. Pupil participation in government is a laboratory practice in the main duty expected of pupils after they leave school. Teachers who want to see the principal "just a moment" are confirmed time-eaters. It is a poor principal who lets them form the habit. It is necessary to educate visitors, telephone callers, and school superintendents to realize that the value of the principal varies inversely as the ease with which he can be kept in his office. In rating teachers the middle rating is the average. Any rating above or below this requires unusual facts to justify it.

There can't be any doubt that this book is a masterpiece. It quietly brushes off the sentimentality, laziness, illogical hobbies, or other infelicities that have prevented school management from receiving from business executives the respect which is due. It treats organization of the staff, extra-curricular, office business and equipment, teachers' meetings, discipline, finnances, records, and reports, opening and closing of terms, with a completeness, richness and every-day reasonableness that is altogether refreshing.

YOU DAREN'T BOAST OF IGNORANCE[27]

THE first superintendent I worked under, a graduate from the university's department of

25 Iris Cleva Good, Jane M. Crow, "Home Room Activities." Professional and Technical Press, 420 Lexington Ave., New York. 325 pp. $3.25.

26 M. Evan Morgan, Erwin C. Cline, "Systematizing the Work of School Principals." Professional and Technical Press, 420 Lexington Ave., New York. 374 pp. $3.25.

27 Walton W. Blanche, Jay Speck, "A Gateway to Music." D. C. Heath & Company, Boston. 178 pp. $1.48.

liberal arts, used to say without a blush, "I know nothing at all about music." I didn't, either, but I was ashamed to say so. Victor Yarros, who, while carrying a heavy load of other studies has made himself a gentleman of refined musical taste, says a school manager, supervising instruction, who doesn't equip himself with knowledge of music and the plastic arts, is only part of a superintendent and less of an educated man.

Very well, what to do?

Dr. Blanche, who is a professor of language, Director Speck, who is a professor of music, present a music reference book which is for high-school students. But I find that its discourse upon the symphony instruments, its musical history, its brass-band chapter, its treatment of terminology, give me a handy book to make me less ignorant when milady takes me to the concert.

THE RIGHT TO VOCATIONAL TRAINING

I HOPE you are acquainted with Professor Arthur Mays of the University of Illinois. If so you admire his high-grade conception of the whole educational purpose. This is the third work[28] of his I have read on the subject of vocational instruction. I do not know of any more reasonable and persuasive demonstrator of the need of vocational information in school and college.

Nicholas Murray Butler's attack upon it is rebutted here with quiet indignation. Vocational education is necessary for everybody, and becoming increasingly difficult. The public increasingly demands it. Schools have to take care of 171,466 pupils who ask for agriculture. Thirty-four per cent. of high school children enroll in commercial courses. From the beginning American education has favored those intending to be preachers, doctors, and lawyers. Democracy demands vocational instruction for all workers. Professor Mays reviews the history of this kind of training. He covers vocation and culture, economic and social backgrounds, agriculture, business, homemaking, practical arts, all in the lower school, then discusses them as of college grades.

28 Arthur B. Mays, ''Introduction to Vocational Education.'' The Century Company, New York. 323 pp. $2.00.

UP IN THE AIR

THE boys in this house are fascinated by Hugh Allen's airship articles.[29] These are carried in nineteen profusely illustrated chapters with anecdotes of Franklin, the Montgolfiers, Blanchard, Gifford, Santos-Dumont, the Wright Brothers and the indomitable Zeppelin. Z. was observing balloons here during the Civil War. He was nursing the plan of a dirigible balloon until his retirement from the army at the age of fifty-six gave him leisure to study and design. By the time he was sixty-two he had convinced most of the world that he was a visionary Darius Green. Pluck, grit, indomitable industry brought him his great success at the age of sixty-eight, when the scientific and governmental highbrows flocked to his support.

Mr. Allen's accounts of foreign and domestic aeronautics of the docks or hangars, the improvements in design, safety, tactics of navigation, the gas, the motors, training, commercial airlines, notable flights, the Akron works, his chronological tables and bibliography, make an engaging story. I recommend several copies for the school library.

ALEXANDER'S PRESENT HELP

BANKRUPT school boards, cuts in teachers salaries, extravagant land and building payments, bank failures and other disasters to schools have, in these hard times, become common, indeed. You may not know when you will be the next to be hit. I recommend for your immediate perusal a short compilation by Carter Alexander.[30] It occurred to him to gather from eighteen recent studies on administration, those findings and provisions covering the loss and the protection of school funds. He desires to be of aid to school administrators especially in the present financial crisis. Alexander is the first person I would run to for advice in any matter of school monies. He was researching in this field more than twenty years ago. We used his advice in salary adjustment campaigns in New York and Chicago. He wrote the financial chapters in numerous school surveys. His present book is a service for which you may have cause to thank him from the bottom of your school bank account.

29 Hugh Allen, ''Story of the Airship.'' Publication Department, The Goodyear Company, Akron, Ohio. 71 pp. 50 cents.

30 Carter Alexander, ''Educational Finance Studies. Summaries for School Administrators.'' Teachers College Press, Columbia University. 92 pp. $1.50.

SCHOOL AND SOCIETY

EDITED BY J. McKEEN CATTELL

WITH WHICH IS COMBINED THE

EDUCATIONAL REVIEW

EDITED BY WILLIAM McANDREW

Volume 34 SATURDAY, JULY 11, 1931 Number 863

THE CONTRIBUTION OF RESEARCH TO THE MENTAL HYGIENE PROGRAM FOR SCHOOLS[1]

By Professor PERCIVAL M. SYMONDS

TEACHERS COLLEGE, COLUMBIA UNIVERSITY

IN discussions on education at the opening of this century adjustment was frequently referred to as the outstanding aim of education. As the term was used in these earlier discussions there was an attempt made to make education function as a tool in shaping the environment to suit men's needs. Learning was not for its own sake but was expected to aid man in adapting himself more adequately to his environment and to alter his environment to better fit his desires and wants. As Ruediger[2] expressed it "to educate a person means to adjust him to those elements of his environment that are of concern in modern life, and to develop, organize and train his powers so that he may make efficient and proper use of them."

Or O'Shea, writing on "Education as Adjustment" in 1903, said:

> Adjustment seeks ever to give the individual mastery over those phases of the environment that he must understand in order to realize most fully the possibilities of his being. And it aims to lead society as a whole to a mastery of the world in its totality so that in reality each member thus becomes adjusted to all features of his environments. One who is guided by this aim will plan his educational system in view of the environments that are to be adjusted to.

Adjustment, then, was the sanction for the present academic curriculum which aims to train a child in those knowledges and skills which would enable him to successfully cope with the environment which he would be expected to meet as an adult. Perhaps our increased industrial productivity to-day can be traced back in part to this emphasis on adjustment as mastery.

There is at the present time a renaissance of adjustment as an aim of education, but in quite a new sense. Instead of preparing a child to meet a static environment in a distant future, we are concerned that he make satisfactory school and home adjustments in the immediate present. Adjustment has become a matter of health, and the child who unsuccessfully reacts to the intricate and baffling problems of his own childhood and adolescent environment is lacking that vigor of adequate function-

[1] A paper presented at a meeting of the American Educational Research Association, Detroit, February 24, 1931.

[2] W. C. Ruediger, "Principles of Education," Houghton Mifflin Company, 1910.

ing that characterizes a desirable state of health. In short, mental hygiene has suddenly emerged as a primary concern of education, for somewhere in the educational process are to be found those conditions that contribute toward the sanity and poise of effective and happy living.

This new conception of adjustment shares with the earlier ideas the importance of shaping the individual to cope adequately with his environment. But whereas the older notions emphasized mastery of the environment, the newer point of view stresses the education of conduct. Our maladjustments to-day are due not so much to lack of control of our physical surroundings or to failure to provide the necessities and comforts of life, but to failure to manage the social order and to educate for social living. To be mentally healthy a man must be socially adequate and the newer education is coming more and more to believe that its big job is to provide children the opportunity to be socially adequate in order that they may be mentally healthy. Whenever one sees a criminal, a pauper, a prostitute, a neurotic, he sees a failure of our modern educational system.

To-day we are concerned not only with the academic child, the child who must acquire the skills of language and mathematics, the principles of science and the knowledge of history, but with the whole child, which will include his attitudes and ideals, his likes and dislikes, his fears and worries, his conflicts and inhibitions, his unified and integrated outlook on life and the many little habits and skills of social adaptation. Studies by Reavis,[3] Rosen,[4] Johnson,[5] Olson,[6] Flemming,[7] Turney,[8] and our[9] own studies indicate a substantial relationship between school achievement and desirable behavior which indicates either that satisfactory achievement has a salutary effect on personal adjustments as evidenced by behavior, or that poor adjustments become reflected in low achievement, and probably indicates both. A study of the factors related to these newly recognized outcomes of education gives research a new opportunity and a new responsibility.

The first major contribution of research to the mental hygiene program of schools has been the development of techniques for measuring the adjustment of individual pupils.[10] Three main lines of attack have been opened up. The first of these is the method of *rating,* immediately after the war somewhat discredited, but now staging a lusty comeback. The possibility of using ratings in the study of problem children was first proposed by Haggerty[11] in 1925

[3] W. C. Reavis, "Pupil Adjustment," D. C. Heath & Company, 1926.

[4] E. K. Rosen, "A Comparison of the Intellectual and Educational Status of Neurotic and Normal Children in Public Schools," Contributions to Education, No. 188, Teachers College, Columbia University, 1925.

[5] E. H. Johnson, "School Problems in Behavior," Hartford School of Religious Education, 1925.

[6] W. C. Olson, "Problem Tendencies in Children," University of Minnesota Press, 1930.

[7] C. W. Flemming, "A Detailed Analysis of Achievement on the High School," Contributions to Education, No. 196, Teachers College, Columbia University, 1925.

[8] A. H. Turney, "Factors Other Than Intelligence that Affect Success in High School," The University of Minnesota Press, 1930.

[9] P. M. Symonds and C. E. Jackson, "The Relation between School Marks, Achievement, Conduct and Intelligence." Paper read at the Americal Psychological Association, Iowa City, December, 1930.

See also R. H. Paynter and P. Blanchard, "A Study of Educational Achievement of Problem Children," The Commonwealth Fund, Division of Publications, 1929.

[10] P. M. Symonds, "Diagnosing Personality and Conduct," to be published in the Century Psychology Series.

[11] M. E. Haggerty, "The Incidence of Undesirable Behavior in Public School Children," *Jour. Educ. Res.* 12: 102–122, September, 1925.

and the method has more recently been validated by Olson.[12]

He followed up twenty-nine cases that had been referred to the Minneapolis Child Guidance Clinic and found that these cases tend to receive high percentile ranks on the rating scale. Studying the subsequent history of a group of rated pupils Olson found that 95 per cent. of the offences in a certain school and all of the serious offences were made by boys above the median of the general population on the rating scale.

The work of Hartshorne and May[13] provided us with variations of the traditional rating methods, and one known as the "Guess Who" method promises to be of considerable value in studying the adjustments of school pupils, particularly the extreme deviates, both those well adjusted and poorly adjusted. Our own[14] studies indicate that this device, which we have elaborated under the heading "Identification Sheet," has considerable promise as a method of locating early in the school year pupils with behavior difficulties.

The other technique is the *adjustment questionnaire* or psycho-neurotic inventory. Wickman has shown us that the obvious, extrovert, troublesome behavior of active wide-awake youngsters is not nearly so serious from a mental hygiene point of view as the unsolved conflicts of children which only get expressed in daydreaming, shyness, withdrawing, sensitiveness, and the like. The questionnaire is admirably adapted as an instrument for permitting children to reveal their inner tensions, worries, fears and unhappiness. This particular technique can be traced to the work of Woodworth, who first proposed the psycho-neurotic inventory. Since its original use in the war for determining the stability of men for active fighting service, it has had many adaptations for use with school children and college students by Mathews,[15] Johnson,[16] Cady,[17] Laird,[18] House,[19] Thurstone,[20] Rogers,[21] and others.

Rogers,[21] who devised such a questionnaire along with other similar devices for measuring personality in connection with his work with the Institute of Child Guidance of New York City, declares his "test of personality adjustment gives diagnostic scores which are as valid as a rating by a clinician who knows the case."

Our own use of this type of questionnaire[22] indicates that except for deep-seated mental conflicts with roots going back into early family experiences, most

12 W. C. Olson, "Problem Tendencies in Children," University of Minnesota Press, 1930.

This particular scale has recently been printed by the World Book Company under the title "Haggerty-Olson-Wickman Behavior Rating Schedules."

13 H. Hartshorne and M. A. May, "Studies in Service and Self-Control," The Macmillan Company, 1929.

14 P. M. Symonds and C. E. Jackson, "An Adjustment Survey," *Jour. Educ. Res.* 21: 321–330, May, 1930.

P. M. Symonds, "Group Methods for Conducting a Mental Hygiene Survey of High-School Pupils," SCHOOL AND SOCIETY 32: 501–506, October 11, 1930.

15 E. Mathews, "A Study of Emotional Stability in Children," *Jour. Delinquency* 8: 1–40, 1923.

16 B. Johnson, "Emotional Instability in Children," *Ungraded* 5: 73–79, 1920.

17 V. M. Cady, "The Estimation of Juvenile Incorrigibility," *Jour. Delinquency Monograph*, No. 2, 140 pp., 1923.

18 D. A. Laird, "Detecting Abnormal Behavior," *Jour. Abnormal and Social Psychol.* 20: 128–141, 1925.

19 S. D. House, "A Mental Hygiene Inventory," *Arch. Psychol.* No. 88, New York, May, 1927.

20 L. L. Thurstone and T. G. Thurstone, "A Neurotic Inventory," *Jour. Social Psychol.* 1: 3–30, February, 1930.

21 C. R. Rogers, "Measuring Personality Adjustment in Children Nine to Thirteen," Contributions to Education, Teachers College, Columbia University, 1930.

22 P. M. Symonds, unpublished data.

maladjustments are specific, depending on failure to adapt to some special situation.

Our own experience leads us to believe that instruments of this kind enable a principal or teacher to select early in the year pupils who have incipient behavior or personality difficulties. Of ten pupils who scored low on an adjustment questionnaire in a certain high-school class, seven were designated later in the year as "problems" by their teachers and one had left school because he was not able to get along satisfactorily. Likewise of ten pupils who showed the largest number of undesirable behavior characteristics by their fellow pupils, seven were declared to be "problems" by their teachers before the end of the term.

The third of these methods is *observation*. This method has had its greatest use and development with infants and small children primarily because research workers are forced to resort to observation when the child being studied can not express himself adequately in language. Valuable contributions have been made in this field by Dorothy Swaine Thomas[23] and Olson.[24] Probably the greatest single recent advance with this technique is the use of time intervals as a measuring unit. By breaking the period of observation up into short intervals and noting the occurrence or non-occurrence of the act or habit during each interval the observation may be increased in reliability. These intervals may be mere segments of a continuous period, or they may be intervals coming on separate days. Olson measured the incidence of nervous habits in school children by noting the number of occurrences of the habit in twenty-five minute periods. Miss Parten working under Miss Goodenough[25] extended Olson's technique by obtaining forty observations over *one minute* intervals. Except for the fact that certain acts such as cheating, borrowing, teasing, and the like require longer time intervals, there would seem to be no limit to the increase one could obtain in reliability by decreasing the size of the observation interval, increasing the number of observations properly spacing the observations.

To most persons mental hygiene means mental mechanisms, complexes, neuroses. But these are the unhealthy, pathological aspects of mental life. In a favorable environment these ugly mental deformities would have little chance of arising. Schools should be interested in so ordering their daily régime that so far as they are concerned mental health is established and maintained. Such a positive program of mental hygiene for schools goes to the very heart of education, for it concerns the curriculum, methods of instruction, the classification and grouping of pupils, the social program of the school and a régime which avoids fatigue and permits efficiency. The *second* major contribution of research provides facts concerning the relation of the school's organization and program to individual adjustment of the pupils. It must be admitted, however, that most investigations on the curriculum or methods of instruction have been more concerned with testing them against the criterion of achievement than against adjustment in the larger sense.

Research on the mental hygiene aspects of the curriculum has been scanty. Studies like that of Goodwin Watson on

23 D. S. Thomas and Others, "Some New Techniques for Studying Social Behavior," Child Development Monographs No. 1, Teachers College, Bureau of Publications, 1929.

24 W. C. Olson, "Measurement of Nervous Habits in Normal Children," Institute of Child Welfare, Monograph Series No. 3, University of Minnesota, 1929.

25 F. Goodenough, "Measuring Behavior Traits by Means of Repeated Short Samples," *Jour. Juvenile Research* 12: 230–235, 1928.

factors related to happiness,[26] however, point the way by indicating that a curriculum which concerns itself merely with the academic is not fulfilling its highest function in educating for a life of satisfactory adjustment. He says:

> There are those who pretend (whether at least they really believe it I never could quite decide) that life will be richer and happier for those who know better how to read efficiently, who know languages, philosophy, and mathematics. It is refreshing to note how little support, even in the academic group itself (of teachers), there is for such assumption.

Interest studies help us avoid the dangers of over-abstraction, classicism and pedantry and to select out of the abundance of available knowledge and skills those which fundamentally are adapted to the development of growing boys and girls. Significant studies have been made of interests in reading, writing, play, science and other school subjects.[27] In general these studies indicate that we have been shooting wide of the mark in our traditional curriculum. If it is true that pupils have shallow interests who like to read "Freckles," "Daddy Longlegs," "Pollyanna," and books of romance, adventure and mystery, certainly the schools are not helping greatly to raise the standard of enjoyment which continue to prescribe Emerson's Essays, Burke's Speech on Conciliation. And if pupils prefer to write on personal experiences, their summer vacations and travels, teachers are not helping pupils to write for enjoyment who ask for compositions on "The Deserted Farmhouse," "Silas Marner at Raveloe," or "Honesty is the Best Policy."

If interest studies tend to cause curriculum makers to lose perspective with regard to social demands of education, usage studies afford a helpful corrective, although usage studies tend to turn our attention backward to the age that is receding into the past instead of directing our attention forward to the needs of a rapidly changing civilization. Only too often usage studies have been concerned with the form of learning in connection with punctuation, capitalization, map location, words for spelling, arithmetic operations instead of searching out the habits and skills that really condition effective and happy living. Usage studies have been conditioned by the traditional curriculum rather than by the needs of life. The curriculum is a concern of mental hygiene because good mental health depends more than anything else on a daily routine of activities that keeps alive curiosity and enthusiasm.

The instructional process itself is intimately related to mental health, for out of the experiences of the classroom come those feelings of success and security, or failure and self-deprecation that condition the child's immediate sense of happiness

[26] G. B. Watson, "Happiness among Adult Students of Education," *Jour. Educ. Psychol.* 21: 79–109, 1930.

[27] A. M. Jordan, "Children's Interests in Reading," The University of North Carolina Press, 1921, 1926.

L. M. Terman and M. Lunia, "Children's Reading," D. Appleton & Company, 1925, 1926.

W. S. Gray and R. Monroe, "The Reading Interests and Habits of Adults," The Macmillan Company, 1929.

C. W. Washburne and M. Vogel, "Winnetka Graded Book List," American Library Association, 1926.

M. B. Huber, H. B. Bruner and C. M. Curry, "Children's Interests in Poetry," Rand, McNally and Company, 1927.

C. S. Crow, "Evaluation of English Literature in the High School," Contributions to Education, No. 141, Teachers College, Columbia University, 1924.

H. C. Lehman and P. A. Witty, "Psychology of Play Activities," A. S. Barnes and Company, 1927.

D. Oberteuffer, "Personal Hygiene for College Students," Contributions to Education, No. 407, Teachers College, Columbia University, 1930.

and well-being, and probably set habits of confidence or failure for the rest of life. Although it is customary to think of mental hygiene in connection with the intimate conduct of the classroom with all of its social give and take, it is probable that the larger problems of school organization have an even more important part to play in mental health. In attempting to adjust to individual differences schools are also helping to solve a knotty problem for mental hygiene. Perhaps no issue is more vitally important at the present time than the matter of the classification and grouping of pupils. Recent researches by MacGaughy,[28] Burr,[29] and Keliher,[30] and the practice in the Horace Mann School as described by Reynolds[31] have thrown wide open the question of grouping by ability. One outcome that these studies have demonstrated is that homogeneous grouping does not solve the whole problem of individual differences, and that further adjustments must be made by the teacher in the classroom. Although these studies have emphasized the specificity of abilities and make a plea for a consideration of the whole child in grouping, it is not at all clear that everything about a child should be considered in determining in what group he shall be placed. Particularly it does not seem that we have any basis for considering attitudes or ideals or appreciation in forming groups. I am certain that we do not want children brought together because they have certain racial prejudices or similar attitudes, to take one example. The policy of segregating those who have behavior problems seems unwise if we believe in the influence of social education. But to fail to consider abilities in forming groups is to very definitely limit children's capacity to profit by group activities. The child placed in a class that is studying long division who has never learned subtraction or multiplication is definitely handicapped in his learning. Abilities must be a prime consideration in forming groups. The evidence on the specificity of ability shows that in the elementary school homogeneous grouping contributes but little to the whole problem of individual differences, but in the secondary school where one may group by subjects the importance and value of grouping by ability increases.

An issue, long the subject of debate, for which practically no trustworthy evidence exists to-day, concerns the attitudes formed by various methods of grouping. On the one hand there are those who maintain that ability grouping results in the formation of deplorable attitudes of superiority and inferiority. On the other hand it is maintained that individual comparisons are most intense in a class of heterogeneous abilities, and that comparisons between groups are largely a result of administrative practices and policies. The answer to this issue awaits the results of research.

Even more pertinent to the problem of adjustment to individual differences are the proposals for individual instruction such as the Winnetka plan for the elementary school and the Dalton plan or its variations for the secondary school. From the standpoint of mental hygiene the advantage comes from permitting each indi-

28 J. MacGaughy, "Homogeneous Grouping," *Childhood Education* 6: 291–296, March, 1930.

29 M. Y. Burr, "A Study of Homogeneous Grouping in Terms of Individual Variations and the Teaching Problem," Contributions to Education No. 457, Teachers College, Columbia University, 1930.

30 A. V. Keliher, "A Critical Study of Homogeneous Grouping in Elementary Schools," Contributions to Education No. 452, Teachers College, Columbia University, 1931.

31 R. G. Reynolds, "Report of the Principal of the Horace Mann School to the Dean of Teachers College," contained in "Report of the Dean," *Teachers College Bull.*, 22nd Series, No. 1, November, 1930.

vidual to proceed at his own rate, giving him either the sense of mastery instead of the half-mastery or failure in group instruction, or gives him release from the necessity of loafing and bluffing with its accompanying boredom and dishonesty. But individual instruction has disadvantages from the hygiene point of view, inasmuch as it fails to provide social experiences, puts a premium on marks and other external expressions of achievement, and fails to stimulate an interest in the activities for their own sake.[32]

The problem of incentives in the classroom strikes at the heart of the problem of the hygiene of instruction. Research which has shown that competition is a successful drive,[33] that described situations have little motivating power,[34] that rewards and encouragements have more effect in some situations than punishments and nagging,[35] often have little bearing on the hygiene side of instruction. It is one thing to demonstrate that certain methods produce results in achievement, it is another to consider the *total* results of these methods. Although we can prove that competition produces higher achievement, we can not prove that it is a good thing that people be goaded on to achievement only under the spur of competition. At every turn the time has come to weigh methods of classroom instruction in the light of their influence on personality adjustments.

Considerable work has been done in studying marking systems and objective measures of achievement and in determining the conditions which make them more valid and reliable. Practically no investigations have been carried out to determine the effect of examinations and marks on the attitudes of pupils. Rumors abound as to the emotional shock accompanying examinations. We know rather definitely that such accompaniments have little influence on the results of examinations as measures of achievement, but there is no evidence as to the wider reverberations on attitudes, effort, encouragement and discouragement and the total adjustment to school life. If there is truth to these rumors it should be displayed with objective evidence so that educators can modify the use made of tests in the light of the facts.

Every boy and girl needs a certain amount of play, recreation and social activity. Experimental schools have shown how the whole school program in the lower grades can be reorganized on this basis, with the older academic subjects of reading, language and arithmetic contributing their share toward the common group activities. In the secondary school the recreational side of school is still considered extra-curricular, although we have now reached the point where the extra-curricular is deemed essential. More recent work has shown how the social program of the school forms a very wholesome balance in the interests of normal personality development to the older strictly academic type of school. The Germanes[36]

32 See W. H. Kilpatrick, "An Effort at Appraisal," in *Adapting the Schools to Individual Differences* in the Twenty-Fourth Yearbook of the Nature Society for the Study of Education, Part II, 1925.

33 J. B. Maller, "Cooperation and Competition," Contributions to Education, No. 384, Teachers College, Columbia University, 1929.

34 P. M. Symonds and D. H. Chase, "Practice vs. Motivation," *Jour. Educ. Psychol.* 20: 19–35, 1929.

35 E. P. Gilchrist, "The Extent to which Praise and Reproof Affect a Pupil's Work," SCHOOL AND SOCIETY 4: 872–874, 1916.

G. S. Gates and L. Q. Rissland, "The Effects of Encouragement and Discouragement upon Performance," *Jour. Educ. Psychol.* 14: 21–27, 1923.

E. B. Hurlock, "An Evaluation of Certain Incentives Used in School Work," *Jour. Educ. Psychol.* 16: 145–159, 1925.

36 C. E. Germane and E. G. Germane, "Character Education," Silver, Burdett and Company, 1929.

have shown how the home-room organization contributes definitely to group understanding and adjustments. Fretwell,[37] McKown,[38] Foster,[39] Cox,[40] Jordan[41] and others have discussed the possibilities of the extra-curricular program and have suggested helpful and stimulating activities and their organization. Studies have been made of the extent of participation, and the relation to achievement, but investigations directly evaluating the social and hygienic outcomes of the extra-curricular program have yet to be made.

As to the arrangement of the school's program to make working (and playing) conditions efficient and to prevent fatigue little direct evidence is available, although basic facts from physiology and from research in industry provide certain clues. It is quite certain, however, that education has failed to study adequately the possible injurious effects that may result from too-long continued and monotonous work.

These five aspects of school organization —the curriculum, pupil placement, instructional methods, the social program and the avoidance of fatigue—when wisely planned make the school a mentally healthy environment in which children may develop. Along with these should go a guidance program which would help children to make wise choices based on adequate information. As a child approaches a decision with respect to curriculum, vocation, work outside of school, cooperation at home, choice of companions, games and sports, management of leisure time, he needs a knowledge of the road ahead, a knowledge of his interests and abilities, and a synthesis of the two. The classroom teacher is in a position to contribute much to successful adjustment, and the homeroom plan of organization provides an opportunity for teachers to maintain intimate contacts and dispense helpful counsel with a limited group of students. But the increasing specialization in our schools has resulted in no one being responsible for the child as an individual. In older days the teacher could mother the child, but now she is only responsible for teaching him English or mathematics or science. To care for the whole child a program of guidance should be organized to be directed by a special counselor with psychological training whose duty it is to supplement the work of the teacher particularly with special or difficult cases, and to give leadership to the program and supervise teachers in their guidance activities. Only too often teachers have been assigned to guidance activities without training for the work. To understand adequately the individual through the use of tests, questionnaires, interviews, and other techniques, to know the educational and vocational possibilities in the local situation, to understand motives and behavior mechanisms is not something that is merely a matter of common sense which can be picked up casually on the side. Considerable technical knowledge and skill are necessary to do effective work as a guidance counselor. If the school is adequately to serve the whole child, some sort of organized system under the leadership of those trained for the work is indispensable.

The third major contribution of re-

[37] E. K. Fretwell, "The Place of Extra-Curricular Activities in Education," SCHOOL AND SOCIETY, 31: 633–639, May, 1925.

[38] H. C. McKown, "Extra-Curricular Activities," The Macmillan Company, 1928. "School Clubs," The Macmillan Company, 1929.

[39] C. R. Foster, "Extra-Curricular Activities in the High School," Johnson Publishing Company, 1925.

[40] P. W. L. Cox, "Creative School Control," J. B. Lippincott, 1927.

[41] R. H. Jordan, "Extra-Curricular Activities in the Elementary and Secondary Schools," Thos. Y. Crowell, 1928.

search to the mental hygiene program of schools has been the experimentation with forms of organized guidance in schools, the development and critical study of measures of capacity and interest of pupils, the study of occupations and analyses of the results of guidance.

Probably to most persons mental hygiene in schools refers to the study and treatment of problem children. Unfortunately because the school and home have not provided adequate training for the child's personality in a positive program of mental hygiene, problem pupils exist, and special study and treatment are necessary. The increase in juvenile delinquency in our larger cities has made the problem acute on the one hand, and on the other hand the increasing specialization in our schools has resulted in no one being responsible for the pupil as an individual.

The responsibility of the school is apparent when one considers that it has been estimated that one out of every twenty individuals becomes a patient in a hospital for mental diseases during the lifetime of a generation; that the chances of contracting a psychosis or severe incapacitating neurosis whether sent to a hospital or not, are somewhere near one in ten; and that the number of persons in prisons and reformatories at any one time is half as large as those in mental hospitals. A large number of those who in later life become criminal probably show delinquent tendencies as problem children while in school. Certainly the school is in part responsible for locating, diagnosing and doing what it can to ameliorate the conditions of those pupils who in all probability are destined in later life to become enemies of society. Society can afford to spend as much in attempting to eliminate delinquency in youth as it does in providing for the isolation of those who develop criminal tendencies in adult life.

A fourth contribution of research to the mental hygiene program of schools has been experimentation with clinical methods of studying and helping the problem child. A considerable body of experience has been accumulated in understanding the exceptional child, both the unfortunate deviates who are mentally deficient, as well as the gifted child, and there is increasing understanding of the value of the special class. The *clinical* study of problem children is a comparatively new development in the administration of schools, and there is meager experience to draw upon, but the need is pressing and educators everywhere are experiencing the necessity for establishing some sort of psychological service for the study of problem children. Such experience as is available has come on the whole from without the school where child guidance clinics, usually under the directorship of a psychiatrist, have rendered valuable service.[42]

Best practice to-day makes the study of problem children a part of the guidance program of the school, under the direction of a trained psychologist or psychological counselor. Most of the problems arising in schools are educational taken in the larger sense, and few are so distinctly pathological as to require the services of a psychiatrist. The clinical service in schools should be under the direction of a psychologist trained in a school of education with a broad background of understanding of the educational process, of the mechanics of behavior adjustment, and of the functions of the school. The work of the school should be in the hands of educators not physicians.

Usually psychological service where it has been available in schools has been in

[42] G. S. Stevenson, "The Child Guidance Clinic—its Aims, Growth and Methods," paper presented at the First Internat. Congress of Mental Hygiene, May 9, 1930.

connection with research bureaus, and it has been characterized by a narrow conception of the work of the psychologist.[43] Studying problem children involves more than giving a mental test and finding the I. Q. It requires an exhaustive study of the situation including observation of the pupil, interviews with the pupil, his teachers, his parents and others who know him, as well as the results of whatever tests, ratings and questionnaires are available. The diagnosis can not be made by merely dividing a mental age by a chronological age, but must be based on a careful study of the total situation, a keen interpretation of the findings, a knowledge of the possibilities for remedial treatment, and balanced judgment in making the recommendations. The training necessary for this type of work goes far beyond that usually received by psychologists in most universities or teachers colleges.

Finally, one discovers that most behavior problems are not the fault of the school's organization and régime, but go back eventually to the home. If schools are ever to complete their task of education to include the whole child, they must reach out to educate the parents. The nursery school movement and the adult education movement have made rapid strides in parental education. But the intimate cooperation between school and home is still embryonic. The visiting teacher is a necessity if there is to be adequate understanding and cooperation between the school and home. Existing organizations such as parent-teacher associations can do much. But if the interests of the whole child are to be conserved, schools must either take over more of the functions of the home, or, by the use of bulletins, the public press, conferences, adult classes, demonstrations, and the like, carry on a vigorous campaign of parental education.

This program of mental hygiene in the schools whose broad outlines have been merely sketched in this paper[44] offers an outstanding challenge to school administrators. Every so often there appears on the horizon a new point of view in education whose importance is so compelling as to make immediate changes in theory and practice. These new principles which are gathered around such catchwords as "personality adjustment," "mental hygiene," "education of the whole child" offer educators an opportunity to readjust the school program and practices to care more adequately for the integration of character and wholeness of development of the individual child.

To those interested in research this new point of view of education as personality adjustment offers a challenge unparalleled in a decade. The scientific movement in education originated with the development of instruments for measuring intelligence and achievement. There are many who believe that these instruments have reached a refinement and precision which is quite adequate for present needs in education. We have been told that our tests measure only a small fraction of the desirable educational outcomes. To measure attitudes, interests, adjustment, and personal integration, to determine the facts of individual differences for these newer educational objectives, to determine the relationships holding between these outcomes, and to establish the influence of various educational practices on these outcomes is the new task set for educational research. Teachers are somewhat in doubt as to the effects on personal adjustments of various devices and are looking to research for

[43] H. B. Chapman, "Psychological Services of Educational Research Bureaus," *Educ. Research Bull. of Ohio State University* 6: 92–98, March 2, 1927.

[44] See the report of the Committee on Mental Hygiene in Schools of the White House Conference on Child Health and Protection for a fuller statement of this program.

guidance. If educational research has reached a stalemate in its inquiries on the E. A. and A. Q. it may look forward to new fields of service in discovering the facts relating to the conditions underlying personality adjustment.

EDUCATIONAL EVENTS

ANTI-SEMITIC DISORDERS AT THE UNIVERSITY OF VIENNA

A WIRELESS despatch to the New York *Times* from Vienna on June 23 states, anti-Semitic disorders among students of the University of Vienna followed a decision on June 23 by the Austrian Constitutional Court that the famous "Students' Racial Regulation" was unconstitutional and must be set aside.

The regulation in question, decreed a year ago by Count Glaispach, late rector of the school, classified the students into racial associations and was hotly protested by Jewish groups.

When students from Nationalist groups heard of the court ruling, they rushed into the Aula with shouts of "Germans, awake! Jews, retreat!" and belabored Jewish students with cudgels. Jewish students soon were battered and bleeding, while one, who jumped from a window, lay motionless in the street until removed by a police ambulance.

Police charged the raised approach to the university and drove off the assailants, but were unable, under academic law, to enter the premises of the school. They withdrew at the order of the rector, Professor Uebersberger, but warned that they would charge again if new disorder broke out. The rector protested their action to the Minister of Education.

Nationalist students, meanwhile, decided to enforce a "Jewless week" at the school, planning to drive out every Jewish student who appeared. At the end of the week they intend to serenade the rector because of his sympathies with them.

Under the regulation set aside, Austrian students of "pure Teutonic blood" were classified as Germans and included in the German organization. Those with Jewish blood were classified as Jews and forced to enter a Jewish club, regardless of their personal feelings, whether they adhered to the Jewish faith, or how little Jewish blood might be theirs.

The court declared that Count Glaispach created a type of association not foreseen in the common law regarding associations and therefore it was not admissible, while the discrimination was contrary to public policy.

DECREASE IN ILLITERACY AS SHOWN BY THE CENSUS

CONTINUING a decline noted through six decades, the number of illiterates in the country last year comprised only 4.3 per cent. of the population as compared with 6 per cent. in 1920, according to figures released July 1 by the Bureau of the Census and summarized in the *U. S. Daily*. The data cover only persons 10 years old or over.

The decrease in illiteracy was termed "most gratifying" in oral statements at the Department of Commerce and the National Advisory Committee on Illiteracy. The census statistics show that the absolute number of illiterates has fallen 13 per cent. during a 10-year period in which the total population gain was 16.1 per cent.

The number of illiterates 10 years old or over was shown to be 4,283,749 in 1930, as against 4,931,905 in 1920.

Every state and the District of Columbia reported a drop in the percentage of illiterates. This recession is viewed by the committee as capable of giving a renewed impetus to its already extensive campaign in progress throughout the country to blot out illiteracy.

The percentage of illiteracy in the several states ranged from a minimum of .08 per cent. in Iowa to 14.9 per cent. in South Carolina. Not only did all states show a percentage decline, but most of them also experienced a decrease in the number of persons returned in the census as illiterate. The exceptions were found in those states which had considerable increases in their total population.

The drop in the illiteracy percentage has been steady since 1870, when it was 20. By

1880 it declined to 17 per cent., and it was 13.3 per cent. 10 years later, 10.7 per cent. in 1900, 7.7 per cent. in 1910, 6 per cent. at the end of the ensuing decade and 4.3 per cent. in 1930.

Only seven states had 10 per cent. or more illiterates among their inhabitants. These were all Southern States in which the Negro population is large, with the exception of New Mexico and Arizona, which have a rather large proportion of Mexicans.

Louisiana, although reporting 13.5 per cent. of its population as illiterate in 1930, has made remarkable strides in educating its people, for the 1920 census showed 21.9 per cent. to be illiterate.

The census, it should be pointed out, defines as illiterate any person 10 years of age or over who is unable to read or write. A person able to read and write in his native language was not counted as illiterate, even though he could not read or write English.

In addition to Louisiana, the states having 10 per cent. or more illiterates were North Carolina with 10 per cent. even, South Carolina with 14.9 per cent., Alabama with 12.6 per cent., Mississippi having 13.1 per cent., New Mexico with 13.3 per cent. and Arizona with 10.1 per cent.

Only Iowa had a percentage lower than 1, but 14 more states had a percentage lower than 2. The west north central division of states, comprising Minnesota, Iowa, Missouri, North Dakota, South Dakota, Nebraska and Kansas, outranked all other sections of the country. Its percentage of illiterates was only 1.4, the only state going over 2 per cent. being Missouri with 2.3.

The east south central region, including Kentucky, Tennessee, Alabama and Mississippi, had the most unsatisfactory proportion of illiterates. The division reported 9.6 per cent. of the population as unable to read or write.

New York, with 10,513,933 persons 10 years old or more, reported only 3.7 per cent. illiterate.

ENDOWMENT FUNDS OF THE AMERICAN LIBRARY ASSOCIATION

THE campaign for an endowment fund of $1,000,000 was completed at the third general session of the New Haven meeting, when subscriptions from the floor and telegrams from friends throughout the country carried the fund well over the goal. By completing the fund the association qualifies for another $1,000,000 offered by an unnamed foundation.

Subscriptions to the fund were mainly in the form of sustaining and contributing memberships at $100 and $25 a year, respectively, under a plan going into the future which capitalized the subscriptions at twenty to one.

In the face of adverse economic conditions and with library appropriations severely cut, the librarians have succeeded since January in raising nearly $500,000 by this plan. The remainder was assumed by individuals, library and college trustees and others who took sustaining memberships.

The Carnegie Corporation gave the association $1,000,000 in 1926. The 13,000 members have raised a second million and expect a third from a "friendly foundation." The endowment will be used for library extension and adult education.

Under a resolution passed by the council the congress will be asked to appropriate $100,000,000 as an equalizing and stimulating fund for rural public library service to be expended over a period of ten years.

The resolution carried with it memoranda defining several alternative methods for the administration of the fund. In any event it is desired that the money should be divided among the states, territories and possessions of the United States on the basis of their rural population as indicated in the latest national census.

AWARD OF THE GARVAN SCHOLARSHIPS

THE eighth and final series of Garvan scholarships, paying tuition and $500 annually at any college or university in the United States, was awarded on June 29 when Dr. Ray Lyman Wilbur, Secretary of the Interior and chairman of the American Chemical Society essay contest committee, announced the names of the six winners, all high-school students.

The winners are: Anne Stringer, the Roland Park Country School, Baltimore, subject, "The Purification of Municipal Water"; Elizabeth Day, Arkadelphia High School, Arkadelphia, Arkansas, "The Rôle of Chemistry in Music,

Painting, Chemistry, Radio and Motion Pictures"; Frances Gelabert, Tulsa Central High School, Tulsa, Oklahoma, "Fertilizers in Agriculture"; Geraldine E. Rhodes, Belleville High School, Belleville, New Jersey, "Is the Use of Gas in Warfare Justifiable?"; John Stewart Barney, Brattleboro High School, Brattleboro, Vermont, "How the Home Can be Made More Livable through Chemistry"; Marjorie Schumacher, Girls Preparatory School, Chattanooga, Tennessee, "Chemistry and the Utilization of Waste Materials."

Mr. and Mrs. Francis P. Garvan, of New York City, instituted the essay contest for high-school students in 1923 in memory of their daughter Patricia. Since that year forty-eight high-school students, including this year's winners, have received college or university tuition for four years and a substantial sum annually to help them win a college education. More than thirty states have produced winning contestants.

In addition to the college tuition and $500, more than $6,000 have been distributed every year for eight years to 306 winners in the preliminary and territorial contests leading up to the national championship contest. Altogether, Mr. and Mrs. Garvan have contributed more than $500,000 to this aid to the development of chemical research.

THE CHAUTAUQUA INSTITUTION

The formal opening of the fifty-eighth summer session of Chautauqua Institution under the auspices of New York University took place on July 2 with Dr. Arthur E. Bestor, president, presiding. Mrs. Grace Morrison Poole, first vice-president of the General Federation of Women's Clubs, was the chief speaker, taking as her subject "The World from Day to Day."

The program launched an eight-week season, which includes music, opera, lectures and collegiate courses covering many academic fields. Many new courses of study have been included and the most modern pedagogic systems will be followed with a complementary program of discussion in open forum by diplomatists, professional men and women and students of world affairs.

Among the speakers who will address the institute during the summer are Rear Admiral Richard E. Byrd, who will tell of his Antarctic experiences to the accompaniment of sound pictures made by him on the expedition; Governor Franklin D. Roosevelt, Mrs. Poole, Dr. G. Clyde Fisher, curator of visual instruction and astronomy at the American Museum of Natural History; Hanford MacNider, U. S. Minister to Canada; Major Thomas Coulson, of the British Military Intelligence Department, and Dr. Edgar J. Fisher, dean of Robert College, Istanbul.

Those attending the institute will have a choice of 225 courses, 100 of which carry credit in colleges in the United States. The school of education again will be under the direction of Dr. John W. Withers, dean of New York University, who has drawn up programs of wider range than before attempted by the institution, designed to meet not only the requirements of various state educational agencies, but to assist teachers, administrators, prospective teachers, graduate and high-school students and others desiring to add to their fund of general information.

The curricula will include courses in English, French, Spanish, German, Latin, mathematics, geography, general science, nature study, biology, chemistry, physics, music, physical education, art education, arts and crafts, librarianship, speech, business, self-expression, story-telling and history.

THE INTERNATIONAL HOUSE OF THE UNIVERSITY OF CHICAGO

The International House of the University of Chicago, which will be a center for foreign students, is, according to *The Christian Science Monitor,* approaching completion.

The "house," which rises nine stories in its principal wing and which occupies the width of a city block, is to provide living quarters and club facilities for students from more than fifty nations who are enrolled in thirty-six institutions of higher learning in Chicago.

Though Mr. John D. Rockefeller, Jr., presented the $3,000,000 fund for the center to the University of Chicago, it is known that the building is to serve students in the other institutions also. Members of the faculty of Northwestern University and the Y. M. C. A. College are on the committee for organization and program. The location was chosen with a view to accessibility for students of other schools. It is on the Midway front of the university near good transportation. Its site is that of the old Del Prado Hotel, which served the university's visitors until it was razed for the present construction.

Chicago's International House will be the third in the country, Mr. Rockefeller having already made possible erection of similar club homes in New York and in Berkeley, California.

Living quarters for 500 students are provided, as well as club conveniences for all of the 2,000 foreign students estimated to be in the city. To enable the American students to participate in the center, provision is made that from 25 to 30 per cent. of the residents may be from the United States. Two thirds of all the residents will be men, according to present plans.

The building is designed to harmonize with other buildings of the university. It is of Indiana limestone in an adaptation of the English Gothic style. In addition to living quarters, it will contain a great social hall, an assembly room, a refectory and rooms for the various national groups.

THE ALUMNI UNIVERSITY OF THE UNIVERSITY OF MICHIGAN

THE Alumni University at the University of Michigan, which was held over a period of five days from June 23 to June 27, enrolled 92 alumni students. This is an increase of 20 over the number returning for the first session held last year. The program this year included ten series of five lectures in philosophy, drama, child psychology, music, art, economics, heredity, geology, local government and social evolution. These were given by ten different members of the faculty, with the program so arranged that an opportunity was furnished for those enrolled to attend a maximum of five lectures daily. Many of those enrolled followed out the whole program from nine o'clock in the morning until three in the afternoon and the courses were all equally well attended.

A special reception was held on the opening night at the William L. Clements Library of American History, when Dr. Randolph G. Adams, director of the library, gave an illustrated talk on the Gage and Clinton papers.

The alumni attended performances of Noel Coward's "Private Lives," Ibsen's "Ghosts" and Shaw's "Arms and the Man," given in the Lydia Mendelssohn Theater. This program was given by a company which included Tom Powers, Violet Heming and Ernest Cossart of the Theater Guild.

Of those enrolled, 79 were alumni of the University of Michigan. Eight were husbands or wives of alumni in attendance, and five were graduates of other institutions. Four were graduates of the Engineering College, six of the Law School and four of the Medical School. Seven held degrees from the Graduate School. While a large proportion of those enrolled, 68, were registered from the State of Michigan, 6 came from New York State, 5 from Pennsylvania, 3 from California and 3 from Illinois.

MASTERS OF COLLEGES AT YALE UNIVERSITY

ANNOUNCEMENT of three masters of colleges was made by President Angell at the recent alumni luncheon at Yale University. Dr. Angell said: "We have been keenly aware of the need that science should be adequately recognized in our new Quadrangle Colleges, and I am happy to announce the appointment by the corporation of three new masters representing not only scientific interests in general, but in two instances representing directly the Sheffield Scientific School.

"I take great pleasure in announcing, first the appointment of Dean Charles Hyde Warren, of the class of 1896 Sheffield Scientific School, who has served with distinction for nine years as dean of the Scientific School and who had, prior to that time, achieved a notable reputation as a member of the geological faculty of the Massachusetts Institute of Technology. I need not enlarge upon his obvious fitness for one of these new and highly responsible posts. We regard ourselves as peculiarly fortunate in securing his services, not only because of his personal and professional qualities, but also because of the marked advantages during the period of adjustment to the new plan of having in the council of head masters the dean of Yale College and the dean of the Sheffield Scientific School, both of whom are now enlisted in this new and significant development.

"I announce next the acceptance of a mastership by one of the leading bacteriologists of the country, Dr. Stanhope Bayne-Jones, who comes to us from the University of Rochester in 1932 as master of college and professor of bacteriology. Graduate of Yale College in 1910, of Johns Hopkins Medical School in 1914, and professor and head of his department at Rochester since 1923, he has been widely recognized for his outstanding scholarship and administrative abilities. He saw continuous and active service during the war, first with the British Army and afterward with the American Expeditionary Force. He has both the British Military Cross and the Croix de Guerre, and was repeatedly cited in connection with the general orders of the 26th Division of the United States Army. This year he is vice-chairman of the Division of Medical Science of the National Research Council and next year will be its general chairman. We are securing in him a man of distinguished scientific attainments and with the personal qualities which are so indispensable for the successful execution of the duties of the college masterships.

"I have to mention third the appointment of Professor Elliott D. Smith, of the Sheffield Scientific School, a graduate of Harvard College in 1913 and of the Harvard Law School in 1916, where he took extremely high rank and was case editor of the *Harvard Law Review.* Subsequently he practiced law in Chicago, during the war became connected with the Council of National Defense, and was director of research for the Tariff Commission in 1919. He was connected with the Dennison Manufacturing Company from 1919 until he came to Yale in 1928, and while there was division manager in charge of an extremely important section of that large and flourishing company. Since coming to Yale he has made a position of marked distinction for himself, has published widely, particularly on the side of personnel management and is everywhere recognized as a man of forceful and imaginative intelligence and with the finest personal qualities.

"With these three new members of the council of head masters, we are willing to believe that there will no longer be any question of the conspicuous position which science is to occupy in the organization of the new colleges. We thoroughly disbelieve in the disposition to exclude science from the group of the true humanities. We believe that in the modern world science properly conceived is at the very heart of humanistic studies and our present action in bringing these three distinguished men into charge of new colleges is testimony to our faith."

EDUCATIONAL NOTES AND NEWS

School and Society expects to print next week an adequate account of the Los Angeles meeting of the National Education Association. Officers were elected as follows: *President,* Miss Florence M. Hale, state supervisor of rural education in Maine; *treasurer,* Henry Lester Smith, of Indiana University; *vice-presidents,* Sadie M. Alley, of Detroit; George C. Baker, of Moorestown, New Jersey; Ernest W. Butterfield, of Hartford, Connecticut; J. G. Collicott, of Columbus, Ohio; Edith Grosvenor, of Washington, D. C.; Oren E. Long, of Honolulu; W. T. Longshore, of Kansas City; Elizabeth McCormick, of Superior, Wisconsin; Charles Priest, of Carson City, Nevada; George W. Wannamaker, of Griffin, Georgia, and Carleton S. Woodruff, of Vermont.

Dr. Nicholas Murray Butler, president of Columbia University, received an honorary degree of doctor of philosophy at the University of Prague on June 25. Foreign Minister Eduard Benes attended on behalf of the government. Dr. Butler made an address on the importance of universities in the development of humanity.

At the recent commencement of the University of Michigan, Dr. Lotus D. Coffman, president of the University of Minnesota, delivered the principal address. This was printed in last week's issue of School and Society. The degree of doctor of laws was conferred on Dr. Coffman, the citation of President Ruthven being as follows:

Lotus Delta Coffman, president of the University of Minnesota since 1921. Called to direct the affairs of a great university after long and effective service in the study of educational problems and the practice of teaching, he has greatly increased the material and intellectual resources of the institution which he so ably represents. Skilled in expressing the purpose of education in its relation to state and society, and competent to give force and direction to his plans, he seeks by progressive administration to extend the horizons of research and to enrich the content of life through knowledge.

WESLEYAN UNIVERSITY has conferred the degree of doctor of laws on Dr. Henry M. Wriston, president of Lawrence College, Appleton, Wisconsin, and on Dr. Robert E. Blackwell, president of Randolph-Macon College, Ashland, Virginia. The doctorate of humane letters was given to Dr. Payson Jackson Treat, professor of history at Stanford University.

THE University of New Hampshire conferred at commencement its LL.D. on Dr. James N. Pringle, state commissioner of education. The L.H.D. was conferred on Dr. Henry C. Morrison, professor of education in the University of Chicago. Dr. William O. Thompson, president emeritus of the Ohio State University, delivered the address on "Our Changing Citizenship."

THE doctorate of laws has been conferred by Providence College on Dr. Charles Carroll, of the Rhode Island College of Education.

MISS MARY WILSON, president of the Headmistresses Association, and Mrs. Laura L. Scales, warden of Smith College, received the degree of L.H.D. at the Smith College commencement.

THE honorary degree of doctor of the humanities was conferred at the commencement exercises of the University of Cincinnati on Miss M. Edith Campbell, director of the Cincinnati Vocation Bureau, and a member of the Board of Education.

DEPAUW UNIVERSITY has conferred the degree of doctor of literature on Dr. Earl Marlatt, professor of religious education at Boston University.

PROFESSOR EMERITUS GEORGE LINCOLN BURR, of Cornell University, was presented with a volume of historical essays by his former students, during the fiftieth anniversary ceremonies of his class. The book is entitled "Persecution and Liberty"; most of the essays deal with some aspect of the history of heresy, witchcraft, persecution or toleration. The volume contains an introduction by Dr. Franklin Jameson. President Farrand formally presented the book to Professor Burr, mentioning the fitness of the tribute to one whose animating purpose for more than fifty years has been the fight against persecution.

AT the completion of twelve years of service, Mr. F. L. McNown, city superintendent of schools, at Basin, Wyoming, was presented with a document which set forth the appreciation of the community of his services and which bore the signatures of hundreds of persons.

As a tribute to the founder of the Knapp loan fund of $25,000, the University of Wisconsin has compiled and presented to Mr. Kemper K. Knapp, of Chicago, a book of letters from those having charge of the funds and those benefiting from it. The book was compiled by Professor Julius E. Olson, director of loans, and it contained, in addition to a letter from Professor Olson, letters from President Glenn Frank and Maurice E. McCaffrey, secretary of the board of regents.

DR. HENRY R. LINVILLE, of New York City, was elected president of the American Federation of Teachers at the Chicago meeting. He succeeds Miss Mary C. Barker, president since 1925. Dr. Linville had been vice-president.

DR. J. HAROLD WILLIAMS, associate professor of education at the University of California at Los Angeles, has been elected president of the California Educational Research Association.

DR. ROBERT J. ALEY, who recently resigned as president of Butler University, Indianapolis, has been made president emeritus. Dr. Aley went to Butler University in 1921, since which time it has moved to a new campus. In tendering his resignation, Dr. Aley presented to the university his home near the campus, valued at $26,000. Dr. Aley was formerly president for twelve years of the University of Maine.

DR. SAMUEL HOWARD ARCHER, dean of Morehouse College, Atlanta, since 1920, and acting president during the past year, has been elected president of the college to succeed Dr. John Hope, who resigned to devote his full time to the presidency of Atlanta University.

Dr. Fred Griffee, assistant director since May 1, 1930, of the Maine Agricultural Experiment Station, has been appointed director. He succeeds Dr. Warner J. Morse, who had been connected with the University of Maine from 1906 up to the time of his death on March 25.

Dr. Robert D. Baldwin, from 1926 to 1930 president of the Central State Teachers College at Stevens Point, Wisconsin, will take over the administration and reorganization of Haskell Institute, Lawrence, Kansas. He succeeds Mr. H. B. Peairs, formerly director of education in the Indian Service, who retired on June 30 after forty-four years of continuous service. The appointment is the first of a series of ten appointments covering five superintendents of Indian Schools and five superintendents of education on reservations.

Dr. Eugenie A. Leonard has become dean of women at Syracuse University. Since September, 1930, she has been acting dean. Dr. Leonard succeeds Dr. Iva Lowther Peters.

At the University of Michigan, Dr. William Clark Trow has been promoted to a professorship of educational psychology, Dr. Orlando Worth Stephenson to a professorship of the teaching of history and Dr. Margaret Elliott to a professorship of economics and personnel management.

Dr. A. N. Jorgenson, who has been associate professor of education at the Michigan State Normal College since 1927, will go to Buffalo, New York, next year where he will be a member of the faculty of the newly organized School of Education at the University of Buffalo.

Dr. Helen G. Saum, of the University of Cincinnati, has been promoted to a professorship of physical education.

The resignation is announced of Dr. John J. Richeson, superintendent of the Youngstown, Ohio, schools for the last five years.

Dr. Franklin B. Dyer, of Cincinnati, has resigned from the Board of Education. Dr. Dyer was formerly for five years superintendent of the Boston schools.

Professor Joseph Quincy Adams, professor of English at Cornell University since 1919, was appointed director of research of the Folger Shakespeare Memorial Library in Washington at a recent meeting of the Amherst College Board of Trustees. William A. Slade, chief biographer of the Library of Congress, has been appointed librarian.

Dr. Ivan R. Waterman, assistant director of the Department of Educational Research and Service in San Francisco, has been appointed chief of the Division of Text-books and Publications of the California State Department of Education. Dr. Waterman will direct all editorial and publication activities of the department. The development of materials to assist in evaluating text-books under consideration for state adoption will be one of the first responsibilities to be undertaken.

Mr. Joseph M. Murphy, assistant to the director of university extension in charge of extramural courses at Columbia University, has been appointed assistant to the president of the Catholic University of America in Washington, D. C.

Dr. Frank J. O'Brien, director of the Louisville Psychiatric Clinic, has been nominated by the New York City Board of Superintendents as assistant director of the new Bureau of Child Guidance, which will open next fall. The head of the bureau is Dr. Leon W. Goldrich.

Dr. Frank B. Bomberger has resigned as director of the extension service of the University of Maryland and as chief of the State Department of Markets.

Mr. Christopher Morley has been appointed to a Rosenbach fellowship in bibliography at the University of Pennsylvania and will deliver a series of addresses under the auspices of the university during the fall and winter.

Special lecturers in the Harvard Graduate School of Education, appointed for one year beginning on September 1, include: Dr. Edward Ellis Allen, education of the blind; Dr. Richard Day Allen, vocational guidance; Dr. Burdette Ross Buckingham, elementary education; Russell Ames Cook, teaching of music; Dr. Ransom Alphonso Greene, mental diagnosis of children; Arthur Orlo Norton, history of education; Dr. Zenos Edmund Scott, educational administration, and George Wallace Woodworth, the teaching of music.

Dr. Henry E. Schradieck, formerly president of Urbana College, Urbana, Ohio, was fatally injured on July 23 when his automobile overturned.

The death at the age of sixty years is announced of Dr. Kurt E. Richter, assistant professor of German at the College of the City of New York.

A conference on examinations was held at the Grand Hotel, Eastbourne, England, on May 23, 24 and 25, under the auspices of the Carnegie Corporation, the Carnegie Foundation and the International Institute of Teachers College, Columbia University. Twenty-seven members of the conference attended, representing England and Scotland, France, Germany, Switzerland and the United States. The members from the United States were Dr. C. H. Judd, dean of the School of Education, University of Chicago; Dr. Frederick P. Keppel, president of the Carnegie Corporation, New York City; Dr. Paul Monroe, director of the International Institute, Teachers College, Columbia University; Dr. Henry Suzzallo, president of the Carnegie Foundation; Dr. Edward L. Thorndike, professor of education, Teachers College, Columbia University.

Special conferences on "Unemployment and Adult Education" and "Radio Education" will be held in Vienna, Austria, during the week of August 17, in connection with the annual meeting of the council and executive committee of the World Association for Adult Education. The conference on unemployment will be addressed by Colonel Rees and Mr. Miller as the representatives, respectively, of employers and of employees in American industrial education. The conference on "Radio Broadcasting as a Means of Adult Education" will be under the chairmanship of Mr. Levering Tyson. Americans in attendance on the Vienna meeting will include: Morse A. Cartwright, director of the American Association for Adult Education, who is a member both of the Executive Committee and of the Council of the World Association; Spencer Miller, Jr., director of the Workers Education Bureau of America and member of the council; Colonel Robert I. Rees, of the American Telephone and Telegraph Company; Levering Tyson, of the National Advisory Council on Radio in Education, and Philip N. Youtz, of the Pennsylvania Museum of Fine Arts. Colonel Rees, Mr. Miller and Mr. Cartwright are members of the executive board of the American Association for Adult Education, while Mr. Tyson and Mr. Youtz are members of the council of that organization. The governing bodies of the World Association are scheduled to discuss the launching of a new periodical to be known as the *World Education Quarterly*. The American Association for Adult Education, according to Mr. Cartwright, will cooperate both in financing the new journal and in shaping its editorial policy.

An informal conference of university teachers of international relations will be held in Geneva during the forthcoming twelfth ordinary session of the League of Nations Assembly. In a growing number of universities, posts have in recent years been created for the teaching of "international relations" in general—as distinct from, and usually additional to, the teaching of international law. It has been suggested that an opportunity might usefully be made for persons engaged in the various countries in this relatively new department of teaching to become mutually acquainted and to compare points of view in matters of common concern. At the desire of the executive committee of the International Conference of Institutions for the Scientific Study of International Relations, Professor Zimmern, director of the Geneva School of International Studies, has offered a room in the Conservatoire de Musique, Place Neuve, where it is thought gatherings might be held during, at any rate, the opening week of the assembly, the first two to take place at 8:30 p. m. on Tuesday and Thursday, September 8 and 10. Teachers of international relations expecting to be present are requested to communicate, as soon as they conveniently can, with Professor Zimmern, suggesting at the same time any particular matters they would wish to have brought forward for discussion. This should enable them to be individually notified in advance of the order of the proceedings proposed to be followed at the meetings. Communications should be addressed to Professor Zimmern, at New College, Oxford, up to June 15, and thereafter at the Conservatoire de Musique, Place Neuve, Geneva.

NINE American economists from colleges throughout the country have sailed for Europe as guests of the Carnegie Endowment for International Peace. Arriving in Paris on July 6, the professors will be divided into three groups, visiting the British Isles, Central Europe and Southeastern Europe, remaining abroad for about three months. After completing their studies the three groups will meet in Geneva in September. Mr. Henry S. Haskell, assistant to the director of the Carnegie Endowment, will accompany the group visiting Southeastern Europe. Members of the party are: Arthur B. Adams, University of Oklahoma; Malcolm M. Willey, University of Minnesota; Edwin E. Witte, University of Wisconsin; Walter R. Sharp, University of Wisconsin; George W. Stockin, University of Texas; James F. Zimmerman, University of New Mexico; William M. Duffus, College of Commerce and Administration, the Ohio State University; Sidney L. Miller, University of Iowa, and W. N. Wanlass, dean of the College of Agriculture at Logan, Utah.

THIRTY-EIGHT girls between the ages of 20 and 35 have been admitted to the Barnard Summer School for Women Workers in Industry, which opens on June 27, according to an announcement made by Dr. Ernestine L. Friedman, supervisor of the summer courses. This year, although 100 applications from women workers had been received, only thirty-eight could be accepted, owing to the decrease of funds available. Last year fifty-one students received free training at Barnard in addition to the evening lectures, open to all members of the garment trade. Three instructors and volunteer assistants will be in charge of the teaching. Miss Ernestine L. Friedman, formerly head of the economics department at Wheaton College, will teach American economic history; Professor John Kennedy, of Brookwood College, will be in charge of a course called "Our Economic Organization," while Miss Esther Swenson, head of the Vail-Deane School, Elizabeth, New Jersey, will conduct the classes in literature and English. Special courses will be given in the evening and open to men as well as women workers who are not in attendance during the day. It had been the intention of the directors, according to Miss Friedman, to admit men this year to the Barnard Summer School, but owing to the reduced budget this plan had to be abolished. Forty applications from men had been received and invitations were sent to these applicants to attend the evening sessions, given twice a week.

AT the one hundred and ninety-first commencement of the University of Pennsylvania President Thomas S. Gates announced that Mr. Cyrus H. K. Curtis, Philadelphia publisher, had "made an unrestricted gift to the university of more than one million dollars," stating that the university "never had received so large a gift in a single sum from one individual." He said that in all likelihood the gift would be kept intact at the "Cyrus H. K. Curtis Foundation for the Permanent Endowment of Teaching and Research." President Gates also announced that the late Charles Day had left $100,000 as an unrestricted fund to the university.

IT has been decided to use the Cyrus H. K. Curtis gift to Bowdoin College of $50,000 made during the past college year for a $500 salary increase for all professors, assistant professors and associate professors on the faculty and a $350 increase for instructors.

HAMLINE UNIVERSITY has raised the $500,000 which was needed to claim a gift of $250,000 offered in 1923 by the Rockefeller Foundation. The gift raises the school's endowment fund to $1,865,000 and its total assets to $2,525,406, with no indebtedness except the current year's operating expenses.

A CONDITIONAL gift of $100,000 and bequests of more than $75,000 to Bates College have been announced. The $100,000 gift is from the Board of Education of the Northern Baptist Convention and is conditioned upon gifts of $900,000 from other sources by 1936.

DISCUSSION

INSTRUCTION IN OUR GRADUATE SCHOOLS—A PROTEST

"IN twenty-five years there won't be another intelligent teacher of literature in America," a friend of mine said rather recklessly the other day, and this started me thinking. Both of us were doing advanced study and both of us had suffered from the fact that the teaching of literature was among the living dead.

In reality such a study should be both intensely interesting and valuable, for in literature we have the inspiration of the noblest thought clothed in poetic beauty. All great literature has ennobled and enriched life; literature is thrilling, it throbs with life and has in it the breath of humanity; all life is its field, but graduate professors make it a boresome task to be memorized. They are primarily interested in arbitrary literary forms, and they do not attempt to impart to the students an appreciation of the great masterpieces. Minutiae and detail stifle the breath and life that the writing possesses, and the study too often concerns the influence of Ben Jonson on John Donne on John Fletcher on William Drummond on George Wither on Robert Herrick on Vaughan on Carew on Milton on Wordsworth and on and on, and what difference does it make? Two thirds of the literature that a graduate student is taught and must memorize in order to buy his degree could be advantageously discarded. Graduate courses in literature are pathetically dull and uninteresting; graduate study is a course in trivialities, not in great and profound thinking and appreciation.

The professors drone through the dull periods about dates, influences and details. What does that have to do with the novel or essay or poem that you are reading? Suppose Shelley did elope with a young girl who later committed suicide, how does that fact help you to enjoy or appreciate his "Ode to the West Wind"? Such details distract the attention from the poem to the anecdote. Will locating the lake region of England on a map help one to hear the water fall, the birds sing, or to see the trees sway in the wind? Dates, influences, map exercises and other such irrelevant details do not aid one's enjoyment or understanding; in fact, they disconcert, and divert the attention. Yet because a professor discusses a mass of details about something else, he thinks that he is a scholar, and a teacher of literature. In reality he is preventing the enjoyment of the study; he is dulling an appreciation of it. If he is doing anything, he is killing the life that was there.

Graduate study, with its mass of detail, places that which has nothing to say about life and that which possesses no significance on the same plane with that which has; consequently all appreciation and discrimination is lost, and all literature becomes one gray monotony and mediocrity. The study of literature should be a study of masterpieces, for only that which has something to say about life will be stimulating to thought, and only that which stimulates will be learned. But in our great schools of higher learning, the greater the scholarship, the greater is the mass of trivialities emphasized. As Max Eastman said, "The study of literature as it is taught in most of our graduate schools for three years isn't worth three weeks, and the best lovers of literature know this."

A professor of literature should be an actor; he ought to be able to so read a work that it becomes alive and lives again in his hands; he ought to dramatize the speeches so that the characters speak and move. Instead of that the professors tell you that Byron had a club foot and that he disliked his mother, or that Jane and Carlyle led a stormy married life together. To teach an appreciation of literature, an instructor ought to bring out what the essay, story or poem has to say about life. The great literature, written centuries ago, still has something to say about our own life, and to bring that out is to relate the literature of the past with our own times, to make an old story still have meaning for us.

But this takes intelligence. It is far easier for a teacher to parrot details than to attempt to develop in one's students an appreciation. To create and develop an understanding and appreciation takes great skill; it is a high art and requires genuine intelligence; to parrot details requires the mentality of a phonograph record, and after all, intelligent men can't very well be attracted to our graduate schools.

Pedantry has supplanted intelligence, and—

except for my friend and me—I can't see any hope for the intelligence of the profession. Only a grind, only one who is entirely devoid of imagination and a larger view of the values of life will submit to the present system of graduate study. Overhanging one's three or four years' preparation for the doctor's degree is always the dread and fear of the examination in the background, inhibiting and poisoning any genuinely true love for study. Take the examination at Columbia and Harvard: the candidate is brought before the faculty, and like the torturers of the Inquisition they question him for hours. Each of these teachers, specialists in his own field, questions the candidate on the most minute details of his own field. One after another, and hour after hour they grill away at him until the candidate becomes almost exhausted. To have one's professional ranking after years of study to be determined by this examination is a nerve-wracking ordeal that seems scarcely comprehensible. Even then, one might forgive this grilling if the questions were worth asking, but I shall never forget the glee with which our professor in the seventeenth century course told us that he had thought of a new question to ask in a doctor's examination. The question was concerning an obscure detail of an unimportant author, and the professor's eyes shone with pleasure: a candidate might not expect a question on such a topic. To study with one thought always in mind: I must know this because they may ask about it in the examination—to study this way is to kill any spontaneity, any liveliness or genuine interest that one could have. Only a pedant, one without the juices of life, will submit to such worthless pretense. Such a barrier that the universities put up to keep a man from getting an education either keeps the intelligent away or stamps out the intelligence once the study has started.

Personally I would like to have a doctor's degree in order to increase my salary a hundred per cent., but the study would be too deadly. No matter how difficult or great were the obstacles, though, I would work for this advanced degree if I could believe that the study was worth while or even interesting. But I have found it to be neither worth while nor interesting. And so far as I am concerned, as long as the formal study for the doctor's degree in literature is worthless, I am not willing to get one.

What is needed in graduate schools is research and experimentation in teaching as well as in subject-matter.

GEORGE MORLAN

INDIANAPOLIS, INDIANA

SPECIAL CORRESPONDENCE

EDUCATIONAL ORGANIZATION AND REORGANIZATION IN NEW MEXICO

EDUCATIONAL DEVELOPMENT IN NEW MEXICO

THE problem of providing an adequate educational system in New Mexico has always been a difficult one, chiefly because it is immensely complicated by questions of race and religion, and by the paucity of wealth and population. During the entire period of Spanish rule, which ended in 1821, there existed no public school or college in the territory of New Mexico.[1] Such educational work as was carried on owed its impetus entirely to the Catholic clergy, and the studies consisted primarily of the catechism, Christian prayers, and the Spanish language. Education was conceived as incidental to the more important object of colonization, the civilizing and Christianizing of the Indian population. The wealthy Spanish population, which was not large, depended upon private instruction or sent their children to Europe to be educated.[2]

Little improvement in the school situation can be found during the Mexican régime from 1821 to 1845. Evidence exists that there were a few primary schools in some of the principal towns between 1827 and 1832. But two years later there was no school at Santa Fé.[3] Attempts to reopen the schools by means of private subscription failed. In 1826, as a result of a show of interest by the clergy, a poor sort of college was set up at Santa Fé.[4] Finally, Colonel Al-

[1] R. E. Twitchell, "The Leading Facts of New Mexican History," Cedar Rapids, 1912, 1: 475.

[2] *Ibid.*, 2: 169.
[3] *Ibid.*, 2: 184.
[4] *Ibid.*

bino Perez, who became governor in 1835, issued a proclamation requiring the creation of a system of public schools. This gesture was, however, not followed up, and no schools were established.[5]

After New Mexico was annexed to the United States, although greater interest began to be shown in educational matters, the advance toward an adequate school system was lamentably slow. As always, progress was retarded by climatic and physical conditions. In 1850 the density of population was only .3 person per square mile, as against 7.9 for the United States at large; at present the density is only 3.5 per square mile.[6] Sparse settlement is, of course, due largely to the aridity and poverty of a considerable part of the state. New Mexico is still among the poorest of the states.[7]

Such advance as was made in the provision for schools during the Territorial period arose largely out of the efforts of the churches. The Right Reverend John B. Lamy, sent by the Catholic church in the United States into New Mexico, established day and boarding schools in Santa Fé, and was also instrumental in the founding of the Loretto Academy and St. Michael's Academy in that city. Between 1849 and 1878 schools or colleges were established by other sects, notably Baptists, Methodists and Episcopalians.[8] All efforts to secure public funds for school support failed prior to 1860, and the masses remained in poverty and ignorance. In 1860 there appear to have been 600 pupils in the various schools of the state, taught by 33 teachers. Out of a total population somewhat above 90,000, nearly sixty thousand were illiterate.[9] An act of the legislative assembly of 1859–60 finally provided for a school in each settlement to be supported by a tax of a half-dollar for each child. Attendance was required from November to April; the administration of the schools put into the hands of justices of the peace and probate judges.[10] In 1882 a tax of three mills on the dollar was provided for school purposes.[11] These acts were steps in the right direction but quite insufficient to the need.

Towards the end of the century the coming of the railroads and the influx of settlers from the United States gave a new impetus to the educational movement. In 1886 the New Mexico Educational Association was founded. Partly as a result of its activity the need for further legislation was brought before the legislature of 1890–91 as the most important matter demanding attention. The secure establishment of the public school system of New Mexico dates from a law of 1891 which became the basis of school legislation for the remainder of the Territorial period. Besides provision for free public schools supported by public money, a Territorial Board of Education and a superintendent of public instruction were created, the latter to be appointed by the governor. The board was entirely ex-officio, consisting of the governor, the state superintendent and the presidents of the University at Albuquerque, The Agricultural College at Mesilla Park and St. Michael's College of Santa Fé.[12] The existing state administrative organization, as provided by the Constitution of 1912 and by statute, still shows the influence of the laws of the Territorial period.

The Existing State Educational Administration

The present state organs for the administration of Education in New Mexico resemble closely in fundamental those of about two thirds of the other states. The existing organization is of the all too familiar dual-headed type, with a state board of education of seven members and a state superintendent elected by the people.[13]

The school code provides that of the five appointed members of the board one must be a county superintendent, one a head of some state educational institution, one an experienced educator. The remaining two members

[5] *Ibid.*, 2: 55.

[6] "World Almanac" (1931), p. 196.

[7] "World Almanac" (1931), p. 315.

[8] C. F. Coan, "A Shorter History of New Mexico," Ann Arbor, 1928, Part 2, 202–3.

[9] *Ibid.*, p. 202.

[10] Twitchell, v. 2, p. 322.

[11] Twitchell, v. 2, p. 491. (Note.)

[12] The size and make-up of the board were altered several times prior to statehood. See reports of superintendent of public instruction, Territory of New Mexico, June 15, 1908; June 15, 1910. Twitchell, v. 2, p. 507. Session Laws 1891, Chapter XXV, pp. 45–60.

[13] The following provisions are taken from the Constitution of New Mexico, Article XII, and the school code, published by the superintendent of public instruction.

may be laymen. The governor and the superintendent of public instruction are members ex-officio. The term of board members is four years, and the appointments are made at each regular biennial session of the legislature. The terms expire for only two or three members each biennium so that the board is a continuous body.

The state board is the supreme agency of the state in educational matters, possessing the power to determine educational policies of the state—"enact and publish by-laws for the administration of the public school system"—which—"shall have the force of law." More specifically it is empowered to perform the following functions:

(1) Adopt text-books for the first eight grades and provide for purchase and delivery thereof.

(2) Hold or direct the holding of examinations for teachers' certificates for elementary and high schools, and determine the qualifications requisite for certification, as well as revoke certificates for cause, after notice and opportunity for a hearing.

(3) Prescribe rules for its own government and for the government of the schools.

(4) Require reports from public schools, state educational institutions and private schools.

(5) Prescribe and enforce the course of study for elementary and secondary schools.

(6) Supervise the work of the state superintendent.

(7) Remove county superintendents after notice and hearing, for malfeasance, immorality, etc.

(8) Act as state agency for the administration of the federal vocational education and vocational rehabilitation acts.

(9) Prescribe rules governing teachers' institutes, adopt regulations on the establishment of part-time schools and classes and on industrial education.

The state superintendent is elected by popular vote for a term of two years, and is eligible for only two consecutive terms. The qualifications required are that he shall be thirty years of age, a resident of the state five years at the time of his election and an "experienced educator." Subject to the superior direction of the state board, the superintendent has "general supervision of public instruction." His powers are also set forth in greater detail as follows:

(1) Supervise all municipal and rural schools.

(2) Confer and visit with boards of education of counties and cities and the governing bodies of state educational institutions.

(3) Suspend county superintendents after notice and hearing, or begin proceedings for their removal.

(4) Render legal opinions with consent of the attorney-general.

(5) Visit schools of each county as often as practicable, hold teachers' meetings, awaken and guide public sentiment relating to education and diffuse information.

(6) Furnish necessary blanks, make an annual report, keep the record of the state board as its secretary, compile and publish the school laws.

(7) Employ an assistant superintendent who must know both Spanish and English, and prescribe his duties.

Thus it is seen that the state board and the superintendent acting together possess fairly wide powers over the state educational system.[14] With respect to local educational agencies, the power of the state organs is broad. The county superintendents are declared to be "subject to the superior and supervisory power" of the state board and the state superintendent, and commanded to obey the "legal instructions and decisions" of the state superintendent.

The chief financial officer for education is the educational budget auditor, appointed by the governor for an indefinite term. Together with the superintendent, he apportions the state school funds among the counties of the state. Other duties include the compiling and preserving of information on school finance and administration, reporting violations of the budget law to the governor, supervising the preparation of budgets and estimates of all public schools and state educational institutions, and in collaboration with the State Tax Commission, prescribing the forms to be used for reports and budgets. He is generally charged with the duty of consulting and advising with the state superintendent in regard to financial matters affecting all schools. The state treasurer and the state auditor possess merely formal powers relating to educational

[14] It is said, however, that the state board has insufficient power in certificating teachers. (*New Mexico School Review*, Feb., 1931, p. 5.)

administration. Aside from the above-mentioned officers the employees of the educational administration are very few and scarcely adequate to the legitimate needs of the department.[15]

NEEDED CHANGES IN STATE EDUCATIONAL ORGANIZATION

Educational leaders in New Mexico have been for some years sensible of certain defects in the present state agencies for educational administration. The suggestions which have been offered for reform center about the state superintendency and the state board. The dual control of education which becomes manifest when an appointed board must rely upon an elected superintendent for the execution of its policies may lead to discord and inertia. The proposal has often been made by educators in New Mexico that the superintendency be taken out of politics by changing it from an elective to an appointive post.[16] The best opinion in the state appears to favor giving the power to appoint the superintendent to the board of education and allowing it to determine his salary and the conditions of his employment.[17] The New Mexico Educational Association has sponsored a constitutional amendment providing for this reform, but thus far political opposition in the state legislature has prevented action.[18]

Closely connected with the above suggestion are some proposals for the reform of the state board. It is generally conceded that the board should be principally a legislative body to determine educational policies for the state, and that the superintendent should become the executive organ of the board. In order to secure a fairly representative board and a logical set of relations between these two agencies, opinion in this state favors the following plan:

(1) The state board shall be composed entirely of lay members, all appointed by the Governor. Seven members finds greatest favor, with terms overlapping so that the board shall be a continuous body. The Governor and the superintendent will then cease to be members.

(2) The members of the board shall be appointed without regard to race, religion, sex, occupation, residence, or party affiliation. They shall not be paid any salary, but shall receive only necessary expenses.

(3) The board shall have power to appoint the superintendent of public instruction. His qualifications, tenure, salary, etc., shall be determined by the board. The board thus becomes possessed of an executive officer responsible to it for the execution of its policies.[19]

(4) The powers of the board should be increased in some directions, and the permanent school funds and school lands removed from political control.[20]

It will, of course, be noted that the suggestions herein mentioned follow closely the principles of several state reorganizations and the recommendations of many state surveys.[21] It remains for the leaders of educational thought and opinion to bring their influence to bear upon people, press and legislature, so that the difficulties incident to putting needed changes into law, in the face of public indifference, the opposition of politicians, and the cumbrous procedure of constitutional amendment may be overcome.

EARL C. CAMPBELL
LEO P. KIBBY
NEW MEXICO STATE TEACHERS COLLEGE, SILVER CITY

QUOTATIONS

STATE APPROPRIATIONS FOR THE UNIVERSITY OF NORTH CAROLINA

As *The Review* goes to press it is difficult to determine just what the appropriation made the University by the long-sitting 1931 General Assembly totals. Included in the appropriations bill, passed on the last day of the 141-day session, is $721,000 for each year of the bien-

15 They include a chief clerk, certificate clerk, high-school inspector, rural school inspector, supervisors of agricultural education and home economics, clerks and stenographers.

16 *New Mexico School Review*, v. 7, Nov., 1927. (Nanninga, S. P., p. 17.)

17 *New Mexico School Review*, v. 7, Nov., 1927 (Nanninga, S. P.). See also *Ibid.*, v. 8, Feb., 1929, p. 26, Nov., 1930 (C. B. Redick).

18 *Ibid.*, v. 10, Sept., 1930.

19 *Ibid.*, v. 7, Nov., 1927, p. 18.

20 *Ibid.*, v. 10, Nov., 1930, p. 25. Also Feb., 1931.

21 E. P. Cubberley, State School Administration (1927), Chapter XI.

nium for the university's maintenance budget. The bill also provides for a ten per cent. cut in salaries of all state employees other than constitutional officers. Whether the ten per cent. salary cut means that the university will receive only ninety per cent. of the $721,000 or whether the ten per cent. salary cut is considered as taken from the university appropriation thereby reducing it to $721,000 is a point in doubt.

The $721,000 was arrived at by the joint committee of the Senate and House which undertook to reach a compromise figure which would be acceptable to both bodies. The House had passed the university's appropriation as $724,000, while the Senate appropriation bill had set the university appropriation at $759,000. The report of the conferees, which was accepted and passed by both houses on the final day of the session, fixed the university's appropriation at $721,000, providing a cut thereby even under the figure contained in the House bill.

For North Carolina College for Women the appropriation as finally passed amounted to $380,000, and that for North Carolina State was $357,800. Both these figures are considerably lower than the amounts appropriated for 1930–31.

In addition a flat refusal to protect the state educational institutions from further cuts during the next biennium than those already made by the Legislature was made when the Senate voted to table a bill introduced by Senator Francis O. Clarkson to prohibit the director of the budget from reducing the amounts voted by the Assembly.

The fixing of the university's appropriation for the next year at $721,000 marked the culmination of a long fight for the institutions of higher education in North Carolina. The university bore the brunt of the movement at all times, and even when its figures had been set proportionally higher than its sister institutions President Graham sought to secure increases for those institutions.

Early last January President Graham made public the university's request for an appropriation for maintenance for 1931–32 of $875,000, the same as the appropriation of 1929. This figure had run the gauntlet of strict and watchful economy both in faculty and trustee scrutiny. The report of the Budget Bureau, however, came forward with the proposition that the university be cut back to $573,000 or 34 per cent. less than the appropriation of 1929.

Appearing January 29 before the joint committee of the House and Senate on appropriations, President Graham made a masterful presentation of the devastation that such figures would bring about in the life of the university. Following his appearance the joint committee voted to appropriate to the university $875,000 for each year of the 1931–33 biennium. Soon thereafter, however, the committee reconsidered its action and voted to slash $75,000 from its first figure. The university, though vitally in need of the full amount, agreed through President Graham to cheerfully strain to make out on the $800,000.

The report of the joint committee on appropriations was then carried to the two houses. In the House, where the report came up first for consideration, a majority of the House members on the joint appropriations committee reported favorably to cutting the university appropriation to $724,000, even though the joint committee report had the figure placed at $800,000. The $724,000 figure passed the House. In the Senate the committee report carrying $800,000 for the university was accepted. Later, however, the Senate cut the figure to $759,000. The appropriation as finally passed therefore was $3,000 less than the House figure, and $38,000 less than the Senate figure.

Support for the appropriation request of the university came from all parts of the state. Newspapers of North Carolina continued to suggest that the university appropriation be not mercilessly cut back, and editors in big papers outside the state wrote feelingly on the subject.

But the appropriation was finally fixed at $721,000. The difficulty now is to know just what the $721,000 means. Perhaps a more complete statement can be made in the July issue of this magazine.—*The Alumni Review of the University of North Carolina.*

REPORTS

THE STATE UNIVERSITY AS THE DEVELOPMENTAL ARM OF THE STATE

THE phrase "developmental arm of the state," presumably coined by former President David Kinley, of the University of Illinois,[1] has been characterized as a "sagacious and appealing" designation of the state university by Chancellor Melvin A. Brannon, of the University of Montana.[2] Undoubtedly the locution is a happy one, pregnant with meaning which may clarify the somewhat cloudy prevailing concepts of the relation between the state and its institutions of higher education.

In a recent case[3] the supreme court of Montana has seized upon this phrase and exhibited it in support of a decision which compels the department of chemistry of the state college of agriculture and mechanic arts at Bozeman to analyze samples of gasoline and other petroleum products offered for sale in the state, wholly without compensation for personal services, either in the form of salaries or of fees. When this was resisted on the ground that a unit of the university (the University of Montana comprises five higher educational institutions at different locations, including the state university at Missoula and the state college at Bozeman) could not be required to perform duties unrelated to and antagonistic to its principal function of higher education, the court pointed to the fact that solicitude for the public welfare was the basis of the gasoline inspection law and asserted that the legislature may "broaden the functions of the university or any of its units . . . and for the public benefit may require the discharge of functions in new fields." "In other words," says the court, "the state may extend, and add power to, its developmental arm."

Of course the decision rests chiefly upon principles of constitutional law governing the interpretation of statutes, the discussion of the function of the university being incidental; and even if the educational theory of the court be wrong, the practical situation is one for which the court can not be held responsible, since it could be corrected only by means which are outside the province of the courts, namely, legislative or constitution-making action by the people or their representatives. With a view to this possibility, scrutiny of the facts of the case and of the educational philosophy involved seems worth while.

The statute[4] providing for the licensing of vendors of gasoline and kerosene charged the public-service commission with the duty of its enforcement, and required the commission to secure suitable samples of the vendors' wares for inspection from time to time. The act also designated the head of the department of chemistry at the state college of agriculture and mechanic arts as state chemist, and made it his duty to perform all analyses and tests required under its provisions, without compensation or fees. It permitted him to delegate the work to an assistant, employed by and subject to the rules of the state board of education (the governing board of the University of Montana). The work was performed until August, 1929, when the state chemist refused to make any further tests of samples transmitted to him, whereupon the public-service commission began an original proceeding in the supreme court for a writ of mandamus to compel him to proceed, naming the state board of education, Chancellor Brannon and the state chemist as defendants. Respondents answered that the state chemist was ready and willing to perform the work provided that funds for the payment of its actual cost, exclusive of compensation and fees to the state chemist, be furnished by the commission from a lawful source; that the commission had paid this cost out of the gasoline inspection fund from the passage of the act until the summer of 1929, when it refused to cause or permit its payment; that neither the state chemist nor any of the respondents had any funds from any lawful source for the payment of this cost, and that to compel the department of chemistry (at the college) to pay the expenses of the analyses would be violative of the constitution of the state.

It appeared that there was sufficient money in the gasoline inspection fund to defray the necessary laboratory expenses, and to that ex-

[1] National Association of State Universities, *Transactions and Proceedings*, xix, 108–109, 1921.

[2] *Ibid.*, xxvi, 30–31, 1928. Also published in SCHOOL AND SOCIETY, xxix, No. 753, June 1, 1929.

[3] State *ex rel.* Public Service Commission vs. Brannon *et al.*, (Mont.) 288, p. 202, 1919.

[4] Laws of Montana, 1927, Ch. 109.

tent the commission was willing to pay claims. But respondents refused to allow analyses to be made unless the commission should pay portions of the salary of an assistant to the state chemist. Prior to June, 1929, the commission had permitted an allocation of the assistant's salary, the commission paying for such portion of his time as was taken up in making analyses for it. The same policy had been followed by the commission under an earlier statute very similar to the one in question, which had been operative from 1919 to 1925. The real question at issue, therefore, was the payment for the time of an assistant required in making tests of gasoline and kerosene for the commission.

Applying principles of statutory interpretation, the court, speaking through Mr. Chief Justice Callaway, arrived at the conclusion that the construction given the law by the officers who allowed a portion of the salary of the assistant to be paid out of the gasoline inspection fund was palpably erroneous. The opinion then deals with respondents' contention that since the university is established by the constitution for educational purposes, and since the management thereof is vested in the state board of education, the legislature is without power to impose a non-educational and antagonistic function upon one of the university units. Of this the court said:

> While its functions are not specified in the Constitution, no one will dispute the assertion that the main function of the University is the education of youth. Yet its activities go farther than that. The University of Montana . . . while established and maintained primarily for educational purposes, has wider functions than mere scholastic instruction. The activities of modern universities embrace a wider scope than mere teaching. When sufficiently financed, research and experimental work of great value to the public is constantly being carried on by them. As a part of the work scientific treatises, of high practical worth, are put forth which contribute substantially to state and national progress along industrial, economic, and cultural lines. Indeed, the potentialities of service which may be rendered through these agencies can not be compassed by any small measure. The knowledge diffused by these institutions radiates far beyond the student body.

It seems that the court confuses education with mere instruction, treating the two terms as synonymous; and that the distinction between research and mere routine activity is not clear. Conceding that the university has functions other than teaching, it is a bit difficult to see how routine inspection of gasoline could be classified as research or experimentation. The educational function of a university is commonly regarded as including (1) resident instruction, (2) extension teaching, and (3) research, experimentation and publication; but this leaves no room for routine duties involved in the enforcement of the state's police regulations concerning the sale of petroleum products. If the university can be charged with such a duty, what is to prevent its being used as an agency for the enforcement of pure food and drug laws, laws regulating the sale of feeds and fertilizers, the transportation and disposition of diseased livestock, and so on through the whole gamut of state laws designed to promote the public health, safety, morals or convenience? In short, the situation in Montana would seem to open the gate to the use of the university as a mere agency for the enforcement of laws enacted under the state's police power, to the exclusion or subordination of its educational functions, if the legislature so chose. Nevertheless the court declared: "We fail to see how the work required is antagonistic to other functions of the college. . . . Nor do we see how the principle is destructive of the concept of the functions of the college."

On the question of the constitutionality of the act, the court quoted the pertinent clause of the constitution,[5] emphasizing the final phrase by placing it in italics:

> The general control and supervision of the state university and the various other state educational institutions shall be vested in a state board of education, *whose powers and duties shall be prescribed by law*. . . .

From this premise, the opinion proceeds as follows:

> The assertion that the legislature is without power to prescribe or regulate the functions of the University or one of its units can not be admitted. That the board of education is ''within the scope of its functions, co-ordinate and equal with the legislature'' must be denied. . . . The board of education is a part of the executive department, and is but an agency of the state government. The legislature may prescribe the extent of the

[5] Constitution of Montana, Art. 11, Sec. 11.

powers and duties to be exercised by the board in the general control and supervision of the University of Montana.

Accordingly, the peremptory writ of mandamus was granted. It is noteworthy that this decision definitely denies to the University of Montana the position of constitutional independence which is held by the state universities in Idaho,[6] California,[7] Minnesota,[8] and Michigan,[9] and the state agricultural colleges in Oklahoma[10] and Michigan.[11] The theory of constitutional independence for state institutions of higher education is expounded in the footnote references. At present we are concerned merely with the policy of imposing non-educational functions upon an educational institution without its consent and over its protest. It is submitted that, regardless of whether the legislature technically possesses such power, the policy can not be defended, because it points definitely toward cramping, subordinating, or even excluding important educational activities of the institution. The university should be the developmental arm of the state in the educational sense as undoubtedly meant by Messrs. Kinley and Brannon; not in the sense of an appendage for the enforcement of police regulations, as intimated by the Montana supreme court. A quotation from the paragraph in which President Kinley first used the phrase will emphasize the distinction:

> Such an agency is one whose work is to search out the paths the people must follow in order to progress; to discover how the culture of the people, using that phrase to include the totality of their life activities, may be improved; to find new truths and new ways which will make it possible for the people at large to attain a higher life, economically, socially, intellectually, culturally. The state university is, therefore, the fourth division or arm of the state, organized by the state although it is not categorically so recognized. It is fundamental to all the rest, so far as concerns the necessity of depending on positive legislation for the crystallization of progress. We must look to the state university as the agency which will open up new worlds of truth on which to base legislation.

Although this is a lofty, not to say grandiose, statement of the research function, it scarcely seems to have been meant to include the routine testing of samples of gasoline and kerosene from every commercial pump in the state. Such duty is not research, nor is it instruction, nor is it educational in any sense; and there is merit in the contention that it is non-educational and antagonistic to the principal function of a state university. Speaking not of law, but of policy, the imposition of such duties upon an educational institution is difficult to defend; and legislatures might do well to hesitate before following the example of Montana in this matter.

In view of the fact that funds for educational purposes are never too plentiful, and that the educational function is never too well performed, the wisdom of imposing extraneous duties upon educational institutions is open to question. Without disputing the state's power in the field of public health, safety, morals and convenience; and without attacking the judicial interpretation of existing statutes, one may see clearly the educational issue involved. Ought not education, in its broad and full sense, to be sure, to be the sole preoccupation of a state university? Of course it is impossible for any institution to abstain from subsidiary non-educational enterprises, in the maintenance of its own physical plant and in the disposition of the by-products of many kinds of experimentation; but should not the policy be to have the university engage in no non-educational tasks except such as are necessarily incidental to its educational functions? A state university is a quasi corporation created for a particular public purpose, without power to incur obligations not necessary to the execution of that purpose, unless such obligations be imposed upon it by statute. If it is allowed to remain restricted

[6] State *ex rel.* Black *vs.* State Board of Education *et al.*, (Idaho) 196 P. 201, 1921.

[7] People *vs.* Kewen, 69 Cal. 215, 10 P. 393, 1886; Williams *vs.* Wheeler, (Cal. App.) 138 P. 937, 1913; Wallace *vs.* Regents, (Cal. App.) 242 P. 892.

[8] State *vs.* Chase, (Minn.) 220 N.W. 951, 1928.

[9] People *ex rel.* Drake *vs.* Regents, 4 Mich. 98, 1856; Weinberg *vs.* Regents *et al.*, 97 Mich. 245, 56 N.W. 605, 1893; Sterling *vs.* Regents, 110 Mich. 369, 68 N.W. 253, 34 L.R.A, 150, 1896; Regents *vs.* Auditor General, 167 Mich. 144, 132 N.W. 1037, 1911.

[10] Trapp, State Auditor, *vs.* Cook Construction Co., 24 Okla. 805, 105 P. 667, 1909.

[11] Bauer *vs.* State Board of Agriculture, 164 Mich. 415, 129 N.W. 713, 1911; State Board of Agriculture *vs.* Fuller, Auditor General, 180 Mich. 349, 147 N.W. 529, 1914.

to resident teaching, research and extension activities, it will have an ample field in which to function as the state's "developmental arm," without becoming an agency for the exercise of the police power or undertaking any other routine non-educational functions.

M. M. Chambers
Ohio State University

SOCIETIES AND MEETINGS

CONFERENCE ON UNIVERSITY TRAINING FOR THE NATIONAL SERVICE

This conference, which will meet at the University of Minnesota, from July 14 to 17, and which will be sponsored jointly by the University of Minnesota, the U. S. Civil Service Commission, and other agencies and departments of the national government, will provide a means of contact between authorities of American universities and of the United States government to discuss common responsibilities with respect to the training and recruiting of university graduates for the national service.

Opportunity will be afforded to consider the following questions among others: (1) the career aspects of the national civil service for college and university graduates; (2) student and faculty attitudes towards the public service; (3) the functions of the universities as centers for training for the public service and resulting problems of curricula; (4) the courses now offered by colleges and universities as training preparatory to entrance into the national services; (5) existing methods of informing qualified students regarding vacancies in the national service; (6) the form and content of the specifications promulgated by the national government relative to the training required for various positions; (7) types of examinations now given by the United States government for entrance into the service; (8) salary ranges, opportunities for promotion and other conditions affecting the career aspects of the national service, and (9) possibilities for pursuit of graduate work within government departments.

While some attention will be given to the entire range of the employment in the national service, the conference will pay particular attention to the following fields of work: economics and statistics, law, agriculture and forestry, physics and chemistry, social welfare, engineering and the consular and diplomatic service.

The following officials, representing the national government, have accepted invitations to attend the conference: Governor Thomas E. Campbell, president, United States Civil Service Commission; Dr. A. F. Woods, director of scientific work, Department of Agriculture; Dr. W. W. Stockberger, director, Office of Personnel and Business Administration, Department of Agriculture, Dr. G. K. Burgess, director of the Bureau of Standards, Dr. L. B. Tuckerman, Bureau of Standards, Mr. H. A. Edson, chief examiner, Civil Service Commission, and Dr. L. J. O'Rourke, director of the Research Bureau of the U. S. Civil Service Commission.

Others from Washington, D. C., who have agreed to attend if it is at all possible include: Hon. Ray Lyman Wilbur, Secretary of the Interior; William H. McReynolds, United States Bureau of Efficiency and director of the Personnel Classification Board; G. Aaron Youngquist, assistant attorney-general, Department of Justice; Lewis Meriam, National Institute of Government Research.

The following representatives of universities, colleges, institutes or associations have already signified an intention to be present: Louis Brownlow, director, Public Administration Clearing House, Chicago; Dr. R. E. Buchanan, dean of the Graduate School, Iowa State College; Dr. W. L. Burlison, head of the department of agronomy of the University of Illinois; Dr. John M. Gaus, professor of political science, University of Wisconsin; Dr. J. A. James, associate dean, College of Agriculture, University of Wisconsin; Dr. Chester Lloyd Jones, professor in the school of commerce, University of Wisconsin; Dr. Isidor Loeb, dean of commerce and administration, Washington University; Dr. F. A. Middlebush, dean of commerce and administration, University of Missouri; Mr. Guy Moffett, Spelman Fund, New York; Dr. W. F. Ogburn, professor of economics and sociology, University of Chicago; Dr. B. F.

Shambaugh, chairman of the Department of Political Science, University of Iowa; Luther Steward, president of the National Federation of Federal Employees; Dr. Harvey Walker, professor, political science, the Ohio State University.

Others who have been invited and whose attendance is expected include members of the new Council on Personnel Administration of the U. S. government, of the Personnel Committee of the American Political Science Association, of the Committee on Training of the Assembly of Civil Service Commissioners, and of the Committee on Public Administration of the Social Science Research Council.

The committee on arrangements proposes to have a small number of meetings each devoted to a special field of work. These meetings will be opened by a representative of the national government who will discuss the problems of training and recruiting for a particular service. A representative of a university will then consider the problem of training for that branch of the service as viewed by the universities. General discussion will follow. In addition to these open meetings, there will be arrangements for small round table meetings for those having specialized interests. One session will be devoted to how best to carry out a nation-wide study of training for the public service.

EDUCATIONAL RESEARCH AND STATISTICS

ABSENCES, LATENESS AND DROP-OUTS IN THE NORTHEAST HIGH SCHOOL, PHILADELPHIA

ABSENCE from school and lateness of students at Northeast High School, Philadelphia, Pennsylvania, reached a peak in the school years 1924–25 and 1925–26. At that time a steady and concerted effort was begun to correct the tendency. There was a more careful check on the excuse notes, and each boy who was late more than twice was required to bring one of his parents to school that the school might enlist the cooperation of the home to secure more prompt, more regular, and more studious school attendance. The work has been done by a group of six men who have been given some roster concessions to allow for the time consumed. There has been a feeling on the part of some that so much insistence upon promptness might be leading to an increase in absences. The boy would rather take his chances with a forged note for absence than meet the certainty of reprimand and punishment for lateness. To afford an answer to this question a study was made of the records for the past ten years. Absence records, lateness records and drop-out records were secured from the monthly reports of the school to the superintendent of schools of the city. Much to our surprise we find that all three show a clear downward trend, and there is no evidence that pressure on the boys on account of lateness is increasing absence. (See Graphs I, II and VI.) The graphs show certain crests that defied explanation with the information at hand. In the absence graph (No. I) for example, why do we find crests in 1922, 1925–6 and 1928? In the drop-out graph why do we find similar crests at about the same times?

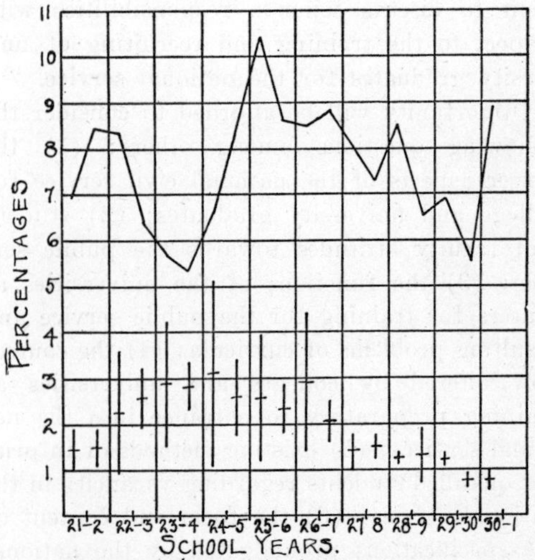

GRAPH I (UPPER) ABSENCES.
GRAPH II (LOWER) LATENESS—RANGES MEDIANS.

(The data, upon which the graphs and discussion in this paper are based, are so bulky that it does not seem worth while to reproduce them here. If desired, copies can be secured by addressing the writer.)

It was felt that general business conditions and general health conditions would probably affect these school statistics, and information on these factors was secured from the Philadelphia Chamber of Commerce and from the Philadelphia Board of Health. The Chamber of Commerce furnished a copy of Leonard P. Ayres' Graph of Business Conditions. This is here reproduced as Graph III, with acknowledgment to Dr. Ayres and to Mr. E. E. Bach, of the Philadelphia Chamber of Commerce. Graph V was derived from Graph III by plotting for average conditions of business during the school year. For this purpose the business index as of February was taken.

Data on health conditions were furnished by the Philadelphia Board of Health. From a table giving deaths in Philadelphia by weeks the deaths in each semester and in each school year were determined. Graph V, derived from these data, shows the death rate by school years only. The parallelism between the prosperity curve (Graph IV) and the death rate curve (Graph V) is difficult to explain and is quite

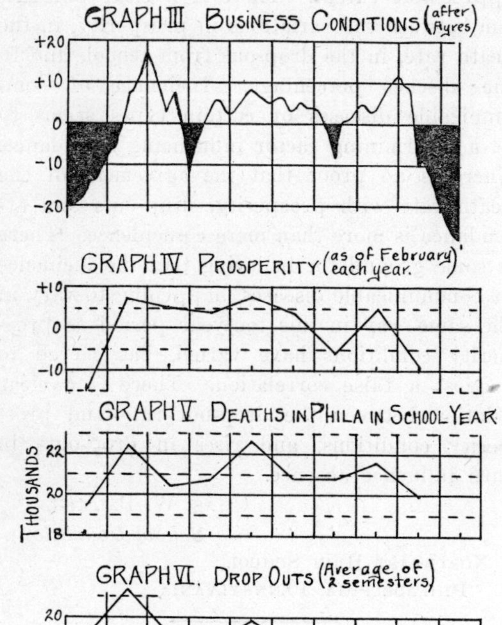

contrary to the general impression that the death rate is higher in periods of depression. For this ten year period we find that the reverse is the case. The question naturally arises, Is this a matter of cause and effect or is it merely a coincidence? To answer this question one should have data as to causes of deaths, incidence of epidemic conditions, and a careful correlation of all of the facts. It is hoped that a future paper will deal with this phase of the problem.

The Philadelphia Board of Health furnished further data on the incidence of communicable diseases. Some of these are not fatal to any great extent, and therefore have little bearing upon the death rate. They do have a marked effect upon school attendance, however, and these data will be discussed in that connection later in this paper.

Graph VI for drop-outs shows parallelisms with the peaks and depressions in the curves showing prosperity and deaths. It is believed that there is a definite cause and effect relationship between drop-outs and prosperity conditions. When boys under sixteen can not get work they must remain in school. Boys over sixteen are much less likely to withdraw from school and to interrupt their education if they can not get work. When periods of prosperity come there is a tendency to withdraw to help to make good the family losses incurred in the periods of depression. The clear downward trend of the drop-out curve shows the influence of two factors. The school has been making an effort to reduce the drop-outs, and to that end requires all boys who wish to withdraw to see the school counselor. If they are under sixteen they are required to bring a parent to the school before the preliminary blank is issued. If they are over sixteen they are usually asked to bring a note from a parent before they are allowed to turn in their books. The interviews with these boys are, of necessity, brief; but many boys are persuaded to continue in school to the end of the school year or longer. There are many cases where there is some small matter that needs adjusting to make the boy feel that he should remain. In some cases this is in a school relationship. In many cases it is a matter of finances, buying school supplies, gymnasium suits, or carfare and lunch. These cases are investigated and helped by the school scholarship fund when they seem worthy.

The other factor that is reducing drop-outs

from school is the increasing insistence of employers upon higher educational training. Many people express scepticism as to the values of modern education, but employers are insisting, with the present trends toward over-supply in the labor market, that educational training levels be raised. Even the telegraph companies in this city will no longer employ, as messengers, boys who have not completed eighth grade, and they prefer one year of high-school training.

Absence from school is reported monthly to the superintendent of schools. Calendar months contain varying numbers of school days. In a few cases the monthly averages were weighted and the semester averages were determined, but it was found that the results agreed with the raw figures. Graph I, derived from the semester averages of attendance, shows peaks that are roughly parallel with those of the graphs we have been considering. Both peaks and depressions are greater than we find in the other graphs, however, and these differences call for an explanation. The parallelism between the drop-outs and absences is to be accounted for in part by the fact that boys who are unsettled in school will frequently be truant for the purpose of looking for work. At times when they think work can easily be found they will be truant to look for it. When they know the finding of a job is hopeless, truancy is reduced. Health conditions will be found to answer for at least a part of the differences in the curves. The incidence of nine commonest communicable diseases, as the physicians of the city have reported them to the Board of Health, shows wide variations.

It is commonly recognized that chicken pox, German measles, mumps and whooping-cough have low mortality rates. I am informed that the mortality rate for scarlet fever has been much reduced in recent years, so that it can be added to the list of those diseases with high incidence and low mortality rates. These are all diseases that influence the attendance at school. And this is true, even where the child is not sick. Quarantine keeps all of the children of the family from school in many of the cases. It is worth while to point out that the highest peaks in absence occurred in 1922, 1925–26 and 1928. These are all years when measles had very high incidence, and when the total reported csaes of the nine diseases were above the average.

The remarkable rise in the absence rate during the first semester of 1930–31 calls for an explanation. This explanation is not furnished by the table. We remember that there were many cases of a mild form of influenza that affected both faculty and students, causing much absence, but not severe enough to merit report to the board of health. The latest data secured show that the death rate of the city for January, 1931, was well above the average, and that there were many reported cases of chicken pox, pneumonia and scarlet fever. The absence from school during January, 1931, was the highest for the month during the ten-year period.

Absence, lateness, and drop-out records at Northeast High School show an improvement in the ten-year period 1921 to 1930. There is no evidence to show that the drive to eliminate lateness has raised the absence rate to any appreciable extent. There is a clear parallelism between the variations in prosperity, in the death rate, in the drop-out from school, and in the absence percentage. Incidence of communicable diseases of certain types seems to be a determining factor influencing attendance. There is no proof that the agreement of the death rate with prosperity, drop-outs and attendance is more than mere coincidence. There is some ground for believing that the incidence of communicable diseases, happening to vary in the same way in this ten-year period as prosperity conditions have varied, has served to suggest a false correlation. There is a clear relation between the drop-out rate and prosperity conditions, and rises in drop-outs in turn influence absence.

CHAS. W. PALMER,
School Counselor

NORTHEAST HIGH SCHOOL,
PHILADELPHIA, PENNSYLVANIA

NEW BOOKS IN EDUCATION

HECK, ARCH O. *A Study of the Ohio Compulsory Education and Child Labor Law.* Pp. xii + 210. Ohio State University. $2.00.

HODNETT, EDWARD and MINNIE S. KEYES. *Plain English.* Pp. xiii + 209. Ronald Press. $2.00.

Report of Department of Research and Education, Federal Council of the Churches of Christ in America. The Public Relations of the Motion Picture Industry. Pp. 155. The Council, New York. $.50.

SCHOOL AND SOCIETY

EDITED BY J. McKEEN CATTELL

WITH WHICH IS COMBINED THE

EDUCATIONAL REVIEW

EDITED BY WILLIAM McANDREW

Volume 34 SATURDAY, JULY 18, 1931 Number 864

INTELLECTUAL FREEDOM AND INTEGRITY[1]

By ADAM STROHM

PRESIDENT OF THE AMERICAN LIBRARY ASSOCIATION

CONSCIOUS of the dignity and influence of this seat of learning whose guests we are privileged to be, we may well pause to inquire in how far we may follow its leadership and embrace its ideals.

Certainly in the case of a public institution, whereof I am but an imperfect deputy, its policy is not that of operating on the high levels of scholarship or being a claimant to such intellectual influence as is part of the traditions and accomplishment of Yale University. As an impetus in our own service we look to institutions of this kind for the creation of leaders—men whose careers are outstanding, not only if measured in terms of professional prestige but whose distinction and lasting impression on the popular mind rest on the clarity and courage of their minds and probity of ideals. It would be ungenerous if we did not honor institutions of higher learning by recognizing their chartered responsibility in the formation of national character, their mastery in assaying and purifying the human and intellectual ore brought to their laboratories. The greatness of any university finds its popular recognition through the service it renders the people in a national sense, through its share in developing and crystalizing a national genius which should be intelligible to and cherished by all.

Such institutions require a good many distributing points in order to realize their most cherished hope—that of far-flung service to mankind. Among such agencies for the distribution of knowledge the public library takes its humble but now definitely established position. The leaders of public libraries are not charged with the pursuit of scholarship, but as promoters of sound public thinking we may perhaps speak in the same faith as our academic colleagues, as we are both defenders of the bill of rights of a self-governing people to intellectual freedom; we can be faithful to such a trust only if we preserve the integrity of our declared purpose.

During the past decade the American Library Association achieved an unprecedented growth in membership and specialization in service activities. It was an era when the national energy was tuned up to a production and expansion that took on the dimensions of an economic world conquest. This prosperity wave carried everything before it—among other American institutions, the American library. Like all other corporations we de-

[1] Address given at the first general session of the annual conference of the American Library Association, Yale University, June 22, 1931.

cided to reorganize. The national headquarters was departmentalized; specialists and boards were set up, charged with the responsibility of advisory service and exploratory undertakings. They were called upon to outline service policies to meet the standards of the new social, industrial and educational life which the national spirit was endeavoring to interpret on the high wave of prosperity and power. Leadership at headquarters gave impetus to the new advance and met with generous support from all ranks; friends and powerful patrons registered their practical good will. We struck a fast pace, we gained territory, we achieved some objectives well worth while. Much remains to be done.

America is in a state of flux like the rest of the world. The industrial era has given us riches; it has also generated new conceptions of a life worthy of man, wherein sanitation, comfort, freedom and fellowship take their place in a new social order, where new capacities of living are revealed. A delicate interplay between rights and duties enters into a growing understanding of human relations. Modern transportation has brought restlessness about; we have no permanent anchor ground; the old farm, the village of our boyhood, our home town are but archaic terms, welcome to our sense of humor—occasionally even serving as a springboard for the sarcastic flights of our scribes. Our state of opulency, of sacred memory, supplied us with costly social upholstery and standards of simonized physical comfort. When the fountains of financial fuel ceased to spout we were brought up sharp in our plunge to make a short cut to success.

We have heard laments about the arid wildernesses in America where no library service is available. It is reported that approximately forty million people are without such contact. Accustomed as we are to associating popular educational service with print and other library accessories we are prone to forget that simplicity of surroundings, even hardships, have educational effects often enriched by the fact that these untaught people are masters of their own destiny, humble as it may be. With confusion and helplessness all about us we might be tempted to ask if standards of life—national or individual—and character-making are not realized in the quiet corners of our land where life is a little primitive quite as soundly as in the great centers of energy where life is a little hectic and under the whip of the sensational.

No doubt it has been within the experience of our field workers to meet and be honored with the confidence of the simple, kindly folk of rural habitation, where the friendly return of a greeting and many other expressions of good-will—with no thought of profit—are forthcoming quietly and in accordance with an ancient, unwritten code. These people know little of organized welfare work, but they have the ability to stand on their own feet—give a lift where it is needed, help their friends without imposing upon the self-respect of either.

Many of these folks of broken speech have their sanctuaries both within themselves and in the open where nature has revealed herself to their seeing eyes. Thither they wander in their hours of ease and commune with the mysterious truth of life, feeling its strength, as does the Arab kneeling on his prayer rug. Out of such golden threads are woven folk history, national culture and deep attachments—the soil out of which national literature blossoms and comes to harvest. We might find that more human virtues and a deeper unselfish affection are born and kept alive in the "wee hoose in the heather" than in the Alpine country of American skyscrapers.

The independent nature of these simple folks, their unwillingness to be imposed upon or to be patronized calls to mind the story told about a people whose lives also run in a minor key—the Shetlanders. As an example of the self-satisfied and withal independent nature of the average Shetlander, the following remark made by an old islesman to a storm-stayed visitor from the South may be cited:

"You must find it terribly dull living in this out-of-the-way place," said the stranger, "seeing you can not get your letters and papers when the weather is bad. Why, I don't suppose you know what we are doing in London from one week's end to the other."

"That's true," was the reply, "but yir just as badly aff in London, for ye dinna ken what we're doin' in Shetlan'."

Obviously we can not do our part in community service if we live marooned in an institution not in contact with the pulsing life of our day. We are citizens deputized by other citizens to administer a special service for public good. We must organize our full strength, keep our resources fluid and our libraries registered as intelligence bureaus to enterprises where creative work and practical skill construct some of the footings to which a civilization of human welfare must be anchored. The craftsman, the artist, the thinker are brothers, and the enrichment of life will be the more substantial if these minds are joined in a fraternity of civilization.

The industrial era of our age has widened the front of our advance. While harkening to the new calls we should not forsake old loyalties. The full chapter of the machine age is still to be written. Like all revolutions it filled a need, it corrected a wrong. The drudgery of toil, the drabness of primitive human shelters were cast off like unlovely garments. Work began to have a new meaning, a new recognition, a man's way of qualifying for social, economic and intellectual emancipation—the trademark of a wealthy nation.

We are emerging from a century in which science through the genius of many taciturn men all over the world placed at the service of mankind the latent forces of nature, and equally ingenious minds multiplied the talents placed in their keeping. The British Association for the Advancement of Science, meeting this year to celebrate its one hundredth anniversary, will also pay honor to the centenary of the great discovery by Michael Faraday, the obtaining of electricity from ordinary magnetism. Its bearing upon modern thought and modern life is well known to us all. We have received a rich inheritance from him and other masters of science. The technical details of their discoveries are beyond the understanding of most of us; their application for human comfort and power are within the experience of all. Indeed, the economic foundation on which the civilization of to-day rests is the gift of men of science who bequeath their findings to posterity.

Brilliant and amazing are the successes achieved at an accelerating speed within the wide domains of technique. Every difficulty is a challenge to new forces, new methods. Divers human needs have been met, a growing security against the daily struggle of old with unyielding nature has been achieved. Work has produced wealth, some of it flowing back into channels of industry, while large amounts have been dedicated to human needs other than material ones. American men of wealth tend to be a group of cheerful givers, unostentatiously practicing the theory of certain Roman philosophers which allowed "the wise man to possess, even to seek riches, but only as a means for exercising social virtues such as generosity, magnificence and the like."

Having submitted this imperfect brief for the modern industrial era, should not the honorable counsellor for the other side also be heard before a verdict is reached? To be sure, he will concede the value of concentrated energy and cooperative efforts, but as part of his exhibit he will also point to symptoms indicative of a life exhausted in centrifugal motions! Mental efforts are directed to outside life—technology, world events, national and international economic competition. Nobody has time to nourish his personal inner life. The rest period vibrates with nerves and overstimulation, a state of mental tension, demanding another spurt.

In this enervating craving for action and more action, the weary chase for "a good time," we repeatedly respond to the crack of the whip and surrender our heritage of manhood, our mental freedom, our right to a balanced individual life of thoughts and emotions, of memories and experiences, of yearnings and lofty ambition—the ingredients which are essential for poise and a personality. Our eyes are riveted on the untiring whirl of humans short-circuiting their power instead of preserving it.

The wonted dignity and calm of our libraries feel the reaction; we also are a part of an intricate machinery and have surrendered to a powerful collective will and demands, ever growing in numbers and insistence. We have joined forces with others in training intellect day after day to convey information and knowledge in order to keep the machines working and nature yielding its resources. Are we in danger of being industrialized? Certainly we occasionally stumble upon certain features that we have in common with industry. Laboratory devices are multiplied, daily working hours are reduced and yet there is a lamentable want of time, strength and seclusion to enrich our inner selves, to learn the art of husbanding our forces only to release them for the deeper satisfactions of life. Our social education has succeeded in collecting and uniting our moral and spiritual forces in a community structure of law and order where all people have a deepening sense of solidarity. Reaching for the perfection of organization, we are in danger of forgetting the individual, who, if he is to reach his full stature and adult growth, must be free to develop untrammeled by organization standards.

We librarians also are organized and classified; we have our departments, card catalogs and bureaus; our statistics are often our most solemn proclamations, though they express nothing but the mechanics of our service. Our chapter in the history of popular education can not be written merely in algebraic equations, our contributions to the spiritual emancipation of the individual call for careful auditing.

The danger of the machine age, the benumbing tempo of the lockstep are realized, and various devices and agencies are functioning for stimulating mental development and public intelligence. The library has many competitors, our superiors in aggressiveness and ingenuity. Certain organs of print ceaselessly furnish machine-made opinions which, mechanically conveyed, are accepted by many who without time and desire to do their own thinking submit to this polite forced feeding. In the name of culture, men's minds are being knocked about by plausible, sententious speculations and appeals gently sent out on the wave-length, the terminal letters of which may be identified with gullibility and conceit of individuals and groups.

If it be our part to assist in promoting sound public opinion based on orderly processes and tested truth, if we desire to be recognized for integrity of intellect and purpose, then it behooves us to protect and guard the birthright of others, their right to honest goods from whosoever sets himself up as their mentor and counsellor. Not for us to be field agents for the pretender, the hypocrite, peddling his shoddy wares in words of printed cant and platitudes. Be not impatient with the unlettered man, do not exalt the intellectual. Only those are servants of public good who through personal effort without thought of gain serve their fellows well and, if occasion arises, through a noble action. Those men are evil who distort truth, who perform sibilant lip service, who profiteer on simple minds, prejudice and false sentiment.

Those who intrude themselves upon the inner life of a man must come clean. Our high warrant for laboring in the vineyards of the so-called adult education must contain as a leading sentence the promotion of adult emancipation and intellectual freedom. Those attributes of manhood are the gangway to useful activity, to success and to rugged self-dependency.

He who takes flight or refuses to surrender his own judgment to conventional public opinion should, however, heed the truth that it is the analytical, investigating mind which triumphs against unbridled impulse and passion.

The main building of an old university in northern Europe bears this inscription, which greets the students as they enter:

> Great is the thought that is free,
> Greater the thought that is right.

In accommodating all those who come for printed sources of information of a theoretical and practical nature we are properly recognizing the life of to-day. If we are also spreading our wares to those who are interested in human emotions and the esthetics of life we are honoring those interpreters of events and peoples who with their artistry and fancy present a deeper and truer understanding of life than reality itself.

In making a plea for such library service we have no sympathy with the individual who substitutes reading for thinking or retires from his fellows in gloomy self-introspection. Too much reading, even educational, may be as stupefying and enslaving as the treadmill rounds of brute labor. One-sided intellectualism travels on the lonely trails of the arid, unfrequented regions. Books and reading should lead to the highway of freedom, alertness and usefulness.

National culture, the development of a race, will not attain its fulfilment if the recreational needs of the individual are neglected; if tactfulness, graciousness, fine taste and other manifestations of good breeding are absent. The colorful stratifications of adult education contain the elements of a spontaneous, sound joy of life, sensitiveness to beauty, good will and responsiveness to our fellows.

I like to deal with him who is not helpless and low-spirited when deprived of upholstered leather chairs and the beseeching appeals of the radio. I am for the man who has the courage to live his own life, whose wings are strong in mist and sunshine, whose zest of life has no hectic tempo—such a man makes a good companion and is a power in social education. Virility, steadiness in the hour of decision, sturdy humanity, the love of one's mother tongue enter into the structure of all national culture. The abundant life is achieved through the balanced intelligent enjoyment of one's physical and mental self and the sharing of the happy hours with others.

Books like "The Story of San Michele," "Giants in the Earth," "Death Comes for the Archbishop," "Lambs in March," the racy flavor of native humor as rendered by Mark Twain, the suppressed yet exquisitely fluent idealism of Galsworthy sound the depths of human sympathy and good will. They are a testament of noble sentiments from those who with deep affection have lived very close to the heart of nature and life. If education means understanding, then we serve faithfully in placing such printed messages in the hands of our fellows. There may still be voices from down in the pit speaking in praise of increased per capita book circulation—they are but droning words from the accounting department where the sun never shines.

A good book touching the mystery as whispered in the silent woods or giving us the jubilant notes heard under the open sky carries us toward the heights as do music and song. If it comes our way in our daily service to introduce to others such melodies of the delicately attuned and inspired human mind, then we experience a reward more precious than rubies—we have had a share in the making of a *life,* and not merely advised as to how to make a *living.*

ADVENTURES IN EVOLUTION

By Professor EDWIN LINTON

UNIVERSITY OF PENNSYLVANIA

A FEW weeks ago I found in my mail box at the laboratory the program of a debate to be held at the Metropolitan Opera House. The question proposed for debate was: *Resolved,* That the Facts of Biology Sustain the Theory of Evolution. The speakers were: Affirmative, Dr. Schmucker, formerly head of the department of science, West Chester State Normal School; negative, Harry Rimmer, president of the Research Science Bureau, curator of the Museum of Natural History, K. S. T. C. Auspices: The Prophetic Testimony, Philadelphia.

Impelled, it must be confessed, by a feeling of curiosity, I attended this debate, and, since my wife accompanied me, The Prophetic Testimony was richer by one dollar because of my desire to see how this word-tilt would be fought out.

Upon entering I found that the spacious orchestra was already well filled. By the time the speaking began the audience had increased in numbers until, upon a safely conservative estimate, it comprised at least 3,000 persons. First, a word concerning the speakers. I had known of Dr. Schmucker as an acceptable lecturer on biological subjects, but refreshed my memory by looking up his record in "American Men of Science." I considered him to be well qualified to handle any topic which could properly be introduced into the discussion of the question proposed for debate.

Of Mr. Harry Rimmer I had heard through a correspondent in Little Rock. Mr. Rimmer, who is a stirring evangelist, had taken a lively part in the anti-evolution referendum campaign in Arkansas. I learned from a leaflet which was handed to me as I was entering the hall that, in addition to the titles accredited to him on the program, he is also cleped archeologist; but in spite of this garland of decorations which he has gathered by the way, Dr. Cattell overlooked his name when compiling his "American Men of Science."

Dr. Schmucker presented arguments based on familiar objects in simple, untechnical language. Thus, instead of the rudimentary hallux of the *canidae,* he used the dog-fancier's name dew-claw. In like manner, instead of such oratorical flourishes as the vestigial metacarpals of the *equidae,* he talked to his audience in easy, everyday words about the splint bones of the horse. He also made some passing reference to an insect which has figured much in biological research of recent years, but gave it its common name of fruit-fly. His opponent, on the other hand, flourished scientific words and phrases of much oratorical moment, as a knight of old might brandish his tilting-lance. His repeated use of the generic name *Paramecium* made one think of that blessed word Mesopotamia; also, when he came to speak of the fruit-fly, he took care to use the generic name *Drosophila.* But his favorite word was *Euglena.* His use of scientific terms, and particularly his reiteration of the euphonious word *Euglena,* recalled Father Tom's praise of the figures of speech.

". . . For unless we thrate them Fathers liberally to a handsome allowance of thropes and figures they'd set up heresy at onc't, so they would."

"It's thru for you," says the Pope; "the figures of spache is the pillars of the Church."

"Bedad," says his Riv'rence, "I dunna what we'd do widout them at all."

"Which one do you prefir?" says the Pope; "that is," says he, "which figure of spache do you find most usefullest when you're hard set?"

"Metaphour's very good," says his Riv'rence, "and so's mettonymy,—and I've known prosodypeia stand me at a pinch mighty well,—but for a constancy superbaton's the figure for my money. Devil be in me," says he, "but I'd prove black white as fast as a horse 'ud throt wid only a good stick of superbaton."

Just how these interesting animals were to be regarded as facts antagonistic to the evolution theory did not appear, but they assuredly came trippingly off his tongue, and appeared to leave us under the impression that Calkins, Morgan and Woodruff, whose names were skilfully intermingled with his swarming words, were whole-heartedly on the side of the negative.

When the debate was ended the presiding officer stated that the audience would be called on to render a decision as to which of the speakers had won the debate, but before the vote was taken, he would ask—very happily, as it seemed to me—all those whose opinions before they had listened to the arguments had been favorable to the affirmative side of the question to rise. While I was on my feet I made an attempt to count the number of those who were on the side of the affirmative. I did not make a note of the number at the time, but my recollection is that there were exactly thirty-one of us in the orchestra on our feet; from where I stood I could not see the other parts of the house. Then a similar expression of opinion was asked of those whose sentiments before hearing the arguments were on the side of the negative. So far as I was able to judge all the remaining 2,969 of the estimated 3,000 rose to their feet. As might have been surmised the vote on the question as to which side had presented the better argument did not differ materially from the previous expression of opinion.

Although at first somewhat surprised at the great majority who, in the judgment of one familiar with the natural objects which had been made to figure in the discussion, would have to be rated as incapable of distinguishing between wheat and chaff, I reflected that if the human race at the present day, the world over, were to be asked to vote on the question as to whether the earth is round or flat, an overwhelming majority would be returned for a flat earth. In neither case, however, would the processes of nature be affected. While I was listening to this debate, and, I think, giving good attention, I yet found time to carry on a parallel line of thought. I was wondering if, with an hour at my disposal, a few lantern slides, a blackboard and a supply of colored crayons, I could win any of that majority for the time being away from their feelings, so that their common everyday reasoning faculties might have untrammelled play.

I should have had them consider a group of living things with which, as it happens, I have some first-hand knowledge, and that is the lowly, but interesting group of helminths to which the human tapeworms belong. The audience could be shown that there are free-living forms in fresh-water ponds whose anatomy is sufficiently like that of the tapeworms to indicate relationship, and thus point to a common ancestry. Further, they could be shown that there is a vast number of species of tapeworms, all of them parasitic, many of them peculiar to a single species, or to closely related species of mammals, birds, reptiles, amphibians and fishes. Again, that these species of tapeworms are of such diversity of form as to admit of arrangement into the various groupings of varieties, species, genera, families, etc., known to systematic zoologists.

These animals have, in the course of their parasitic existence, developed many kinds of hold-fast organs, hooks, suckers, and the like, structures which have no corresponding parts in their free-living relatives, but which have arisen, in some way, in response to their surroundings, just as, for example, such structures as the dorsal fin of the porpoises appeared after their ancestors left the land and adopted a purely aquatic life.

Now, how are such facts in nature as the hold-fast organs of the tapeworms to be accounted for? I see no escape for the teacher of biology from the conclusion that they are the results of what we term natural processes which have been in operation ever since the time when the free-living ancestors of cestode worms joined the ranks of the entozoan.

Even if there were but one species of tapeworm, instead of the three thousand or more already described, and that species one of those peculiar to man, still that would be a fact to be accounted for. When did it appear, before man, or subsequent to his advent?

Evidently Mr. Rimmer was looking for some argument based on such indisputable facts in nature as those which are furnished by parasitic forms, for, greatly to my surprise, he admitted that degenerate forms have descended from less degenerate ancestors.

But in making this admission he surrenders a very important position, as may be seen when it is noted that such degenerate forms as have been cited have themselves followed the same law of descent with modification which is seen when any one takes the trouble to study any considerable group of animals or plants.

Moreover, how are these believers in a changeless world to account for the diverse races of mankind except by employing much such lines of reasoning as naturalists employ when they attempt to account for different species of snails?

It should be noted that Mr. Rimmer's use of the word species is bewildering. Of course, I am well aware that the idea which is represented by the word species is not a sharply defined one, but no systematic zoologist would think of giving it the content which Mr. Rimmer gave it when speaking of such family groups as cats, dogs and horses.

A few days after I had sat at the feet of Harry Rimmer, "Archeologist," I had the good fortune to be present at a meeting at Thomson Hall, College of Physicians, of Philadelphia. The speaker of the evening was the archeologist, G. Elliot Smith, professor of anatomy in the University of London; the subject of his address: "The Peking Man."

It is altogether unlikely that any one of that great majority of Mr. Rimmer's audience was present to hear this report. I am pretty sure, however, if any of them had been present, that, given an opportunity, they would have cast their votes against the speaker's conclusion, that these bones, which were lately found near Peking, China, bridge over the gap between the generically different ape-man, *Pithecanthropus,* and the Piltdown man.

And here a few remarks, based on my experiences as a teacher of biological subjects covering the period 1882–1920, inclusive, and as an investigator during the past decade, may be indulged.

Occasionally, in the course of my teaching, when the various members of the class happened to be at work on the same type of material, and some interpretation was called for, differences of opinion arose. I might then suggest that we settle the question in dispute by a majority vote. This usually had the desired effect. The students changed about from disputants into investigators. I was not so much concerned as to what they believed as I was to see that they were trained into correct habits of arriving at reasoned conclusions.

I trust, and am inclined to believe, that no one of my former students, unless he is in the grip of the *idée fixe* that there is an infallible authority which has already pronounced in favor of the negative, would have been found, had he been present, among the 2,969 of that Metropolitan House majority.

I have the confession to make, however, and I think that my former students will bear me out in this, that I had in the course of my teaching little occasion to make use of the word evolution. This was not because of any prejudice against the word, and certainly not on account of any lack of appreciation of the orderly and dependable processes of nature which the word should connote. I am sure that the discussions of the part played by the environment in the origin of varieties, the meaning of vestigial structures, the significance of homologous parts, and the various attempts which have been made to explain how particular conditions have come about were given proper consideration. But in and through it all, as I look back along the lengthening vista of years, I do not recall that I made use of the word evolution. What we ordinarily mean by the word, I suppose, must have been taken for granted, much as we take for granted the action of gravitation.

Now that my memory is stirred by these recollections I do recall that once, near the end of an introductory course in geology, in the early years of my teaching, I had a request from the class to give them a lecture on evolution. My reply was that I did not have the time to prepare a formal lecture, but reminded them that if they had been giving reasonable attention to the subject-matter of the course, they had already had an introduction to the ideas which underlie all theories of evolution.

It was then that I bethought me of a friend,* at that time the pastor of one of the churches in our town. I invited him to give the class a talk on evolution. He consented and gave to the class a summary of the general theory, beginning with a consideration of the probable genesis of the solar system and coming down to the human era. His presentation of the subject was a model of lucidity and exhibited a sympathetic understanding of the interpretation of nature by scientific minds. I do not think that any group of astronomers, or biologists, or geologists, would have found any serious criticism to make of his exposition of the conclusions of science. This lecture was repeated before succeeding classes and was discontinued only when my friend left our town to take the chair of theology in a theological seminary.

So far as I can recall, my nearest approach to the expression of evolutionary opinions in any didactic way was to give it as my view of the course of events, that if we could have a moving picture of the successive incidents as they had taken place at the particular point of latitude and longitude on which my classroom was

* The Rev. Dr. James H. Snowden.

situated, and the picture so timed that it would show in one hour what had occurred in any 5,000-year period since living organisms had made their appearance, we would probably not be any more conscious of change than we are as we contemplate the record of the 5,000-year period which has just closed. Furthermore, as the picture was passing, we would find ourselves interpreting the streaming events as we do those which now fall under our observation, and saying with Huxley: That in all the vast progression there is no breach of continuity, no point at which we can say: "This is a natural process, and this is not a natural process."

Thus, it appears that, without fully realizing what I was doing, I was conveying ideas which to-day would contravene in spirit the laws of Tennessee, Mississippi and Arkansas, and, according to statistics given by Maynard Shipley (*Current History,* May, 1930) would be taboo in 70 per cent. of the secular schools of this republic.

In short, like the often quoted character in Molière's comedy, who to his astonishment and delight learned that he had been talking prose all his life, I discover that I have been teaching evolution through a long series of years although, probably, not having been quite alive to the fact. In this connection I recall a conversation with Professor W. K. Brooks in the summer of 1901, in which he said: "People ask me: 'Are you an evolutionist?' I tell them I don't know; I am a naturalist." As a profoundly philosophical student of the processes of nature Professor Brooks had peers, it may be, but no superiors.

Two other adventures in the anti-evolution jungles of America are deserving of brief notice, since they are typical of experiences which teachers of biological subjects may expect to undergo. Both of them were reactions to a paper entitled: "Scientific Method and Authority," which was read at Kansas City in December, 1925.[1]

The first hostile gesture that came to my attention was the demand for my immediate resignation from the University of Georgia, which was made by no less a personage than the Prime Minister of the Supreme Kingdom, Dr. William J. Mahony, in a public address delivered in Atlanta on Sunday, February 14, 1926. In answer to an inquiry over the long distance telephone from the city editor of the Atlanta *Georgian,* Mr. Lamar Q. Ball, I explained that, while it was true that my name did appear in the catalogue of the medical department of the University of Georgia, the position was purely an honorary one which imposed no duties and paid no salary, so that my withdrawal from the university would not be a matter of consequence either for good or ill to any one.

A very satisfactory account of the incident appeared in the *Georgian* of February 16, 1926, and there, so far as my information goes, the affair rests. It is a delight to me to be able to say that during my four years residence in the beautiful city of Augusta, Georgia, at which time I was afforded the privileges of the laboratories of the medical school, my relations with the university were in every way most pleasing. It may be added, by way of offset to the disapproval of the P. M. S. K., that, among the many letters which I received commending the Kansas City address, was one from a distinguished member of the board of trustees of the University of Georgia.

The other inimical gesture towards my views concerning the scientific method and authority, which I have chosen for comment, appeared in the *Bible Champion* for August–September, 1926, a marked copy of which publication was sent to me. In this magazine, one of the editors, Leander

[1] *Science,* 62: 171–178; 195–201.

S. Keyser, D.D., finds fault with my address thus: "It is not a calm and judicial article giving the reasons for evolution, but rather a hectic attack on Fundamentalists." Further, he complains: "But in this whole amplified article not one established fact is cited to prove evolution, not a word occurs to prove spontaneous generation, or transformism, or man's animal pedigree. It is all taken for granted and then the antis are unmercifully scored because they do not believe the theory."

In a note published in *Science* (Vol. 64, p. 526), referring to the criticism that no arguments for evolution had been presented, Dr. Keyser's attention was called to the fact that the address in question was made at a meeting of zoologists, and that, since the topic discussed did not deal with any phase of the evolution problem, the citation of proofs for or against any theory of evolution would have been inappropriate. Further, it may be remarked, that for an audience of zoologists, in the absence of any attempt to explain how some natural phenomenon was brought about, the word evolution is a convenient term for the processes of nature which we see going on about us, and of which we are a part, of which also, some record is preserved in the earth's crust, and elsewhere in the visible universe.

It is altogether improbable that an appeal to the common sense as against the feelings of that majority of 2,969 to 31 can have any immediate effect. But that majority should be shown that they are following unsafe leaders.

Any scientific theory that is worthy of consideration will be tested by specialists, who are the only ones that are qualified to judge of the validity of any proposed explanation of facts with which they have first-hand acquaintance. Therefore, if Mr. Rimmer has made discoveries in his investigations on the fruit-fly which nullify the conclusions of other investigators, as he allowed his audience to infer from his whirling words, he should make no delay in bringing them to the attention of Morgan and his coworkers. Also, instead of making misleading statements concerning the splint bones of the horse family, in his appeal to the feelings of a popular audience, he should show Professor Lull that the late Professor Marsh was mistaken and that the exhibit of fossils in the Yale Museum should be rearranged.

But these are matters of small concern. What is of serious moment is that the recognition of real values is put on the same footing, if it is not actually made to depend on a belief in traditions which are not in accord with demonstrable facts.

Consider, for example, the values which are enshrined in the Prophet Micha's words concerning what is required of man: To do justly, to love mercy and to walk humbly with thy God; and St. James's testimony as to the content of true religion: To visit the fatherless and widows in their affliction, and to keep himself unspotted from the world.

Latimer, with the hindrances to religion of his day in mind, wrote: "For religion, pure religion, I say, consisteth not in wearing a monk's cowl, but in righteousness, justice and well-doing." If he were speaking to-day he might well say, instead of "wearing a monk's cowl," the insistence on a belief in the literal truthfulness of every tradition recorded in the Hebrew canon.

The danger which lurks in the Fundamentalists' position arises from their weighting the recognition of the truth of such expressions of values as these with insistence upon belief in the literal truthfulness of traditions such as accounts of the creation of the first man and the first woman, a universal deluge and the confusion of languages at Babel, to go no farther.[2]

Doubtless Mr. Rimmer and the majority of those who choose him and his like for mentors are immune against the devastating effects of new ideas concerning the universe, but there are those to be considered for whose education they are responsible. Some of these young men and women will continue their studies beyond the grammar school. They will learn that reputable geologists decline to consider the Noachian spate as of world-wide extent. In like manner they will find that teachers of the philosophy of language hold quite different views concerning the origin of dialects and languages from those who explain these phenomena by the confusion of tongues on the plain of Shinar. They will note that astronomers fail to discover a solid firmament in the sky, and that those who strive to decipher the testimony of the rocks find a different story there recorded from that which is set down in Hebrew tradition.

It is far from my purpose to chide any one for ignorance, or even lack of information, for the wisest of mankind knows but little of the structure and processes of the material universe. When, however, one who would be a spiritual guide to his fellows engages, albeit, to affirm what he holds to be the truth, in disputations concerning material things of whose nature he is ill informed, a situation arises which demands that he be called to account, and that, too, for the sake of those spiritual values which, to use the recent words of an English biologist, count for everything in the real universe.

* * * * *

[2] The reaction to criticism of authority of Judge Raulston, of the inglorious Dayton, Tennessee, trial, is significant. Thus, he is reported as having given voice to the fear that if he lost faith in Genesis he might lose faith in that part of the Bible which says: Thou shalt not steal. (New York *Times*, November 9, 1925.)

In January, 1926, I agreed to talk to the Chautauqua Circle of the Woman's Club of Augusta, Georgia, and gave as the subject of my address, "The Scientific Method and Authority." The preliminary notices, which appeared in the papers, announced the title in the portentous words: "The Scientific Method and Authority of Evolution." Upon this I made the following comment, which was included in the published report of the address:

> It would appear that to many people in these days the word evolution behaves as King Charles's head did to Mr. Dick. No matter what they set out to say or write, sooner or later it obtrudes itself.
>
> If by the theory of evolution is meant attempts to explain how things come to be what they are, then, while we may find many reasons for differences of opinion and, consequently, grounds for discussion concerning natural processes, there should not be and, assuredly there is not, among people who are free from prejudice, any occasion for controversy.—*Augusta Chronicle,* Jan. 31, 1926.

The *Augusta Chronicle* for April 29, 1926, contained a report of an address made before the Exchange Club of that city, by the Reverend Father Foulkes, S. J. The subject of the address was "Evolution."

Two brief extracts from the somewhat extended report will be sufficient for the purpose of this paper.

> The theory of evolution does conflict with the Bible because it is not a truth, and very few real scientists accept it as a truth.
>
> It is the general opinion of Christian scholars that the theory of evolution as advanced by Darwin is untrue, and this theory has found many opponents among learned religionists, such as William Jennings Bryan.

It would be an unkindness to Father Foulkes to quote his arguments based on natural phenomena as they appear in this report.

As so much publicity had been given to the matter it seemed to me that Father Foulkes's attention might well be directed to an interesting book, a copy of which I had received from the author a few days before.

This was done in a letter to the *Augusta Chronicle,* published May 3, 1926. The letter, however, was buried in an extensive report of an interview with Father Foulkes under the heading: "Church's Stand on Evolution Explained by Father Foulkes; Says Research Should be Done."

This is my letter:

Concerning the statement which Father Foulkes is reported as having made regarding the theory of evolution, as published in Thursday's *Chronicle,* attention might well be called to a treatise by Father Ulrich A. Hauber, Ph.D., entitled: "A Catholic Opinion on the Evolution Controversy." Copyright, 1925, by St. Ambrose College, Davenport, Iowa.

This treatise carries on the second page the authorization of high dignitaries of the Catholic Church.

Thus: Nihil Obstat (nothing objectionable)
William P. Shannahan,
Censor Deputatus
Imprimatur (let it be printed)
Edward D. Howard,
Auxiliary Bishop of Davenport

The following wise words of Father Hauber should, if generally understood, go a long way towards allaying the fears of timorous souls, and quelling the belligerency of a tumultuous multitude:

> The theory that all things come to be what they are through an age-long process of evolution rests exclusively upon scientific evidence with which religion is not concerned (p. 12).

Whether due to the impressive official approval of Father Hauber's treatise or to a realization that he owed allegiance to an authority which can adjust itself to a changing world, or, however it is to be explained, there can be no doubt that Father Foulkes's views, as brought out in this interview, had undergone some change from those which dominated his address before the Exchange Club.

The inconspicuous place which had been given to my communication, which called attention to Father Hauber's book, seemed to call for one more letter to the *Chronicle,* which appeared in the issue of May 12, 1926, under the editorial caption of: "Theologian and Biologist." Following are extracts from this concluding communication:

The controversy . . . in which the words science and religion are used . . . would cease, or would be transformed into amicable discussion if agreement could be reached on the definition of terms. Thus, . . . I think that Father Foulkes, as a theologian, and I as a biologist, will agree with St. James in his definition of religion, and with Micah as to what is required of man.

Concerning evolution, considered simply as a theory to account for things as they are . . . I hope that we shall not find ourselves so very far apart. . . .

From the point of view of one who has given some attention to comparative anatomy, when I consider such facts in nature . . . as the small bones at the posterior end of the human skeleton, known . . . as the coccyx, I am forced to the conclusion that thereby there once hung a tail. I am quite ready to be shown my error, but until the comparative anatomists and embryologists of the world unite on a better explanation I must hold to what seems to me to be a reasoned conclusion.

Again, as I read Genesis 2: 4–25, I understand the narrative to be of the nature of ancient folklore. But here, as in the case of the human coccyx, I am without prejudice, and am ready to be set right by the proper specialists.

Now, Father Foulkes and I may hold very different views concerning the explanation of the human coccyx. We may differ widely as to whether the second of the two creation stories included in the book of Genesis is to be regarded as veritable history or not, but, be it noted, in these matters concerning which we may differ religion has nothing to do.

Our best chance of getting at the truth of the first is to listen to what the specialists in the sciences of comparative anatomy and embryology have to say; and of the second to learn what light the sciences of historic criticism and comparative theology have to shed upon it.

Concerning the truths of religion, however, as taught by St. James and the Hebrew prophet, Micah, and as testified to by the lives of the saints, Father Foulkes and I and every one may verify by putting it to the test in his own life among his fellows.

EDUCATIONAL EVENTS

REPORT OF THE INTERNATIONAL EDUCATIONAL CINEMATOGRAPHIC INSTITUTE

The results of an inquiry conducted by the International Educational Cinematographic Institute into the educational influence of the cinema with special regard to the use of the film in schools, have recently been made public and are summarized in the London *Times*. Towards the end of last year the institute supplemented the inquiry it was making among schools by a second questionnaire addressed exclusively to teachers. The purpose of the questionnaire was to facilitate a study of the cinema based on the opinion of the teacher rather than on the impressions of children and adolescents.

Italy alone furnished more than 3,000 individual or collective replies from teachers, male and female, of all classes and kinds of schools, rural and urban, elementary, vocational and secondary. The first question related to the real utility of the cinema as a means of entertainment pure and simple. On the whole the replies suggest that most teachers regard the cinema as a source of physical and mental rest and recreation, especially for those whose work is manual rather than intellectual.

The answers to the questionnaire indicate that in order to profit children, the commercial cinema must conform to the following requirements: (1) For reasons of health, cinema should not be visited too often and performances should not be too long; (2) serious steps should be taken to make cinema theaters safe and healthy; and (3) by a policy of cheap seats, facilities for visiting the cinemas should be given to the very poor as a means of escape from their surroundings.

The value of school films in teaching is almost universally admitted. Teachers state, according to the report, that wall diagrams and fixed projections are being supplanted by the more easily assimilated film, and that the screen's lesson is often more intelligible and profitable than the words of an intelligent and conscientious teacher. The report continues:

> The importance of such a statement is more than theoretical when it is borne in mind that these replies emanate from persons in daily contact with children who are in a position to appreciate the value of new methods. The spoken word, however eloquent and persuasive, is wearisome in the long run. It is also not strong on detail. Mural diagrams and fixed projections have the static value of lifeless matter. The cinema, it is considered, has all that they lack—movement, illusion of real life, with a wealth of technique beyond the reach of any other art; its mastery of detail makes it especially effective as a means of communicating knowledge. Moreover, the cinema, unlike these older instruments of teaching, amuses at the same time that it instructs. The mind of children and adolescents requires distraction, and the teacher's work is greatly facilitated by the mixing of the powder with the sugar. To judge from other correspondents, teachers who hold a contrary opinion are few. Even they are not diametrically opposed, but advance a psychological argument of some force. School films, they say, do not altogether fulfil their function, because by their instructional aim and purpose they arouse an instinctive opposition in the child and thus have less effect than they should.

The report also deals at length with the influence of the cinema on the formation of character. Although nearly all teachers acknowledge the cinema's strong powers of suggestion, they are far from unanimous in admitting that films exercise an influence on the formation of character. On this point opinion inclines towards the negative, or is, at the least, doubtful.

PHYSICALLY HANDICAPPED CHILDREN IN ILLINOIS

More than 10,000 physically handicapped children have been located in Illinois and it is estimated that there are fully 6,000 others who have not yet been found, according to a report recently issued by the State Commission on Physically Handicapped Children, which has been making a state-wide survey.

Infantile paralysis is the most frequent cause of physical handicap, the report points out. This disease was responsible for 2,308 or 23 per cent. of all the handicapped cases recorded. Next in importance as a single cause came tuberculosis of the spine, which accounted for

650 cases. There were 1,062 cases described as spastic paralysis and 907 as bone infections, but these conditions arise from various causes, the report states.

Accidents were charged with 555 of the crippled conditions, while congenital deformity of an unspecified nature accounted for 497, clubfoot 418 and bowlegs from rickets 386.

The commission recommended that facilities be provided immediately at the medical college of the University of Illinois in Chicago for the hospital care of the down-state cases which would profit by surgical treatment. It further recommended the creation of a permanent commission made up of the directors of public welfare and public health, the state superintendent of public instruction and five others named by the governor. The maintenance of a registry of the physically handicapped population of the state was recommended.

Particular emphasis was laid in the report upon the lack of medical and surgical treatment which would rehabilitate many of the cripples discovered. Clubfoot, for example, can be corrected in nearly all cases by appropriate surgical treatment during early childhood.

The very large part played by infectious diseases in the production of the physically handicapped gives to this problem an important public health feature. Control of infantile paralysis through the use of convalescent serum and the pasteurization of milk, and the complete eradication of bovine tuberculosis would, according to the report, cut down the production of physically handicapped population by fully one third.

NEW YORK CITY BUDGET FOR RECREATION

NEW YORK CITY spent $3,290,095.85 for recreation activities last year, the greatest amount spent by any of eighteen principal cities, but its *per capita* expenditure of 47 cents was fifteenth, according to the year book of the National Recreation Association, recently published. Chicago came next to New York in total expenditure, with $2,517,810.13, with a *per capita* rate of 74 cents.

Boston led the *per capita* expenditure rates with $2.02 and with a total of $1,580,465.46, was fifth. Cleveland was third in total expenditures, with $1,713,026.04, and second in *per capita* expenditure, with $1.90. New Orleans trailed the list in both total and *per capita* expenditures, having spent $63,341, with a *per capita* rate of 13 cents.

The Brooklyn Park Department spent $907,082.75 for land, buildings and permanent equipment, the largest single expenditure in the city. The total recreation expenditures of the department were $1,181,747.75, which also led the eight agencies. The second highest single expenditure was that of $892,811.25 for leadership by the Board of Education, whose total expenditures for recreation were $991,440.32.

The other totals were Manhattan Park Department, $641,070; Bronx Park Department, $272,660; Queens Park Department, $94,402; Children's Aid Society, $94,000; Recreation Center Committee, Community Councils, $7,785.78, and Brooklyn Parks and Playgrounds Committee, $6,980.

The expenditures of the eighteen major cities follow:

City	Total Expenditure
New York	$3,290,095.85
Chicago	2,517,810.13
Cleveland	1,713,026.04
Detroit	1,639,597.04
Boston	1,580,465.46
Los Angeles	1,229,167.31
Milwaukee	913,886.97
San Francisco	897,704.66
Philadelphia	820,967.92
Newark	530,338.35
Cincinnati	511,249.36
Baltimore	510,687.79
Pittsburgh	485,392.51
Minneapolis	390,579.40
Buffalo	368,806.00
Washington, D. C.	352,458.64
St. Louis	341,178.17
New Orleans	63,341.00

THE INCREASE OF HIGH-SCHOOL STUDENTS IN NEW YORK CITY

THE expected registration in the New York city high schools of 205,000 students in the fall of 1932, an increase of 25,000 over the last term, will make necessary the appointment of more than 1,000 additional teachers. According to Dr. Harold G. Campbell, deputy and associate superintendent of schools, in charge of high schools, this would be the largest increase in teaching positions ever allowed by the Board of Education at one time for day high schools. Of these positions, 400 would be needed for the fall of this year and the remaining 600 for the spring and fall terms of 1932. Their employment will raise the salary budget for high schools in 1932 to more than $30,000,000, an increase of nearly $3,000,000 over this year. An additional $100,000 also will be expended for supplies.

The registration in the high schools at the close of the 1930–31 school year was in the neighborhood of 180,000. It is expected that 189,000 will be registered in October; that 201,000 will be registered in the spring of 1932, and that by the fall of 1932 this registration will have increased 4,000 more to the unprecedented total of 205,000.

Despite the large increase in registration, Dr. Campbell explained that there had been a decrease in the *per capita* cost of instruction in the day high schools during 1930. He said the *per capita* cost in the high schools was $170.93 during last year, in comparison to $174.66 in 1929. The *per capita* cost per hour was $0.17576 in 1929, and $0.17126 last year. In 1928 the *per capita* cost per hour was $0.18081.

THE GROWTH OF COLLEGE AND UNIVERSITY EDUCATION IN THE UNITED STATES

College and university education has shown a remarkable growth in the United States in the past ten years, both as to enrolments, variety of courses offered, income and property, Walton C. John, associate specialist in graduate education, announced in a survey made public by the Federal Office of Education on July 6.

The annual income of the institutions now totals more than $500,000,000 while the total value of property approximates nearly $2,500,000,000. Twenty-two publicly controlled and 162 privately controlled institutions have endowments valued at $1,000,000 or more each. Nearly 870,000 students are reached now by 1,076 institutions of higher learning, which granted almost 97,000 degrees in 1928.

For the 25 years preceding the war the number of colleges and universities remained practically constant. In 1916–17 the number reporting was 662, including 82 junior colleges. In fact, during the 25-year period mentioned there had been a slight decline in the number of universities and colleges, and even by 1920 the total number had reached only 670. However, in 1926 the number had increased to 975, and in 1928 to 1,076, an increase of 107 institutions reporting for the biennium and 412 for the nine-year period.

The growth of the student body in the colleges and universities has been very great. In 1920, the enrolments, excluding preparatory students, reached a total of 462,445; in 1926 they reached 767,163; and in 1928 they were 868,793, an increase, respectively, of 65.9 per cent. and 88 per cent. over the enrolments for 1920. The enrolments in 1928 were 8.8 per cent. greater than those for 1926.

The colleges and universities in the United States in 1928 granted 83,065 baccalaureate degrees. In 1926 the figure was 71,529, and in 1920 it was 38,552. This represents an increase over the 1920 figure of 85 per cent. for 1926 and 115 per cent. for 1928.

The number of graduate degrees granted in 1928 was 13,834, of which 1,447 were the Ph.D. degree. In 1926, 11,451 graduate degrees were granted, which included 1,302 Ph.D. degrees. In 1920, 4,853 graduate degrees were granted, including 532 Ph.D. degrees.

The total income for the 1,076 institutions reporting in 1928 was $546,674,266. Excluding additions to endowment, the income was $496,529,309. The total income for 975 institutions in 1926 was $479,774,664, and excluding additions to endowment it was $47,400,056. In 1920 the total income for the 670 institutions was $240,141,994, and excluding additions to endowment it was $189,235,242.

In 1928 the publicly supported institutions received 41.1 per cent. of all higher educational income and the private institutions received 58.6 per cent. The increase in income is shown also. In 1928 the total income of all colleges and universities was 21.9 per cent. higher than that of 1926 and 162 per cent. higher than that of 1920. In 1928 the public institutions received an income 17.9 per cent. greater than that of 1926, and the 1928 income of private institutions was 24.8 per cent. greater than that of 1926.

The total value of property for the 1,076 institutions in 1928 was estimated at $2,413,748,-981; in 1926 it was $2,334,307,421, and in 1920 it was $1,257,614,739.

A comparison between the amounts and proportions of the value of property of publicly and privately controlled institutions is given. As the figures for 1919–20 can not be segregated, it is necessary to compare the figures of 1921–22 with those of 1927–28.

The value of all property, including productive endowment funds, in publicly controlled colleges and universities in 1921–22 was $360,-184,477; in 1927–28 it was $664,290,782. This indicates an increase in six years of 84 per cent.

"UNIVERSITY CITY" OF THE UNIVERSITY OF WISCONSIN

THE regents of the University of Wisconsin have announced plans for the creation of a "university city" on the ridge land overlooking Lake Mendota. The proposed university city would consist of dormitories, as well as sorority and fraternity houses. Each unit, according to an announcement made by the regents would be platted, landscaped and planted with trees and shrubs and would be an area "picturesquely unique" in the United States.

The regents' proposal follows an investigation of student housing facilities made by a committee of regents, faculty members and students. This investigation showed that the present dormitory system cares for only 500 men and 365 women, that fraternity and sorority houses care for only 1,500 men and 600 women, and that the remainder of 6,000 students stay in rooming houses.

On account of the financial limitations of the rooming-house owners, student rooms are badly ventilated, poorly heated and lighted, are without adequate toilet facilities.

To better the housing situation the committee has recommended that in the area west of the university two dormitory areas and the university city area be established. In all these groups, privately financed, will be permitted to build houses on the group or attached house plan. Each unit is to house thirty students.

In encouraging the construction of these group houses, the university will offer to furnish the land at a nominal rental, control the building plans, finance the construction of any dormitories, furnish heat at low cost, control the care of the grounds and maintenance of the buildings. When a fraternity or sorority wishes to build, the university believes the groups themselves should do the financing, the university retaining the title to the land.

Actual carrying out of the plan will be delayed until 1933, as permission must be obtained from the State Legislature before the land can be used for such purposes.

THE ATLANTA UNIVERSITY LIBRARY

GROUND has been broken for the Atlanta University library, which is designed to provide a cultural center for the university and the two affiliated schools, Morehouse College and Spelman College. Plans for the building, which will be of Georgian architecture, have been drawn by James Gamble Rogers, architect for Yale, Northwestern and other American universities.

The new library, which has been made possible by a grant from the General Education Board, will cost in the neighborhood of $300,000 to construct and equip. In accordance with the terms of the gift, it is the aim and purpose of Atlanta University to make the library serve not only Atlanta University and affiliated colleges, Spelman and Morehouse, but the other institutions of higher learning in Atlanta, namely, Morris Brown University, Clark University and Gammon Theological Seminary, which may enter into cooperative arrangements with Atlanta University for the use of the library.

In planning the library special provision has been made for adequate facilities for undergraduates to do required reading and for advanced students to conduct research. These objectives will be reached by the provision of a large reserve book room, with a delivery desk and seats for 104 students, a general reading room, seating 234, and by a series of seminar rooms for graduate groups. At the same time attention has been paid to the recreational reading facilities which will encourage students to read for their own cultural development. Reading habits will be encouraged by the presence of a spacious periodical room, seating 42, and a generously-proportioned browsing room where books on open shelves may be available to all. In the four tiers of book stacks will be space for 118,400 volumes, which it is believed will care for the needs of the university for many years to come.

The building, which will face north, thus affording a maximum of natural light, will consist of a full basement and three floors.

A reading room, two stories in height and extending the entire length of the building, will comprise the greater part of the second and third floors. On the second floor also will be the librarian's offices, a library work room, and the upper tiers of books stacks. On the third floor will be three class rooms and two offices.

In discussing the scope of the library's work, Dr. Hope, president of Atlanta University, has said: "It is my impression that Atlanta University will have an opportunity to render some service to Negroes in the field of adult education. For nearly ten years I have had this in mind and had hoped that we could do something in Georgia. It looks to me now as if with this library something like that may be begun. We may think also of an extension service that the library can render. This is practically a new field in the South for all people and so far as Negroes are concerned, it is virgin."

THE FIRST INTERNATIONAL RECREATION CONFERENCE

The Department of State, in compliance with the request of the National Recreation Association, has authorized American diplomatic officers to transmit to the governments to which they are accredited, and through certain of them to the governments of their dependencies oversea, for communication to those to whom it may be of especial interest, an invitation to the First International Recreation Conference. American diplomatic officers are to make clear that the congress will be held under private auspices and that the invitation is transmitted not on behalf of the Government of the United States but on that of the National Recreation Association.

The National Recreation Association, a body having an interstate directorate and headquarters in New York, has been accustomed to meet annually in furtherance of the purposes for which it was founded at the Playground and Recreation Association of America. The Association now proposes to hold at Los Angeles, Calif., from July 23 to 29, 1932, the First International Recreation Congress.

This congress will consider the problem of providing, for persons of all ages and tastes, opportunities for play, recreation and the recreational use of leisure. Such aspects of the problem will be discussed as programs, facilities and direction for public parks and playgrounds, for games and athletic sports, for camping, handicrafts, musical and dramatic entertainments and other recreational activities. Emphasis will be laid on the desirability of providing these facilities for the public at large and for amateur rather than for expert participants. The president of the United States has consented to act as honorary president of the congress. An international advisory committee is being formed; and it is hoped that many countries will be represented.

The authorities of the congress hope that among the representatives of each country will be individuals able to furnish accurate data as to recreational activities, public and private, in their own lands.

Further information and additional or later announcements may be obtained from the Secretary, Recreation Congress Committee, National Recreation Association, 315 Fourth Avenue, New York.

THE INSTITUTE OF POLITICS OF WILLIAMS COLLEGE

The Institute of Politics has completed its program for the eleventh annual session of the institute, which opens on July 30 and continues until August 27. Newton D. Baker, of Cleveland, former Secretary of War, will deliver the convocation address on July 30. Among the distinguished persons from abroad who will come to Williamstown are Professor Herbert von Beckerath, of Bonn University, an economist; M. Le Neveu, Director-General of L'Union Coloniale of Paris; Professor Luigi Villari, of the University of Rome; Dr. William E. Rappard, director of the School for Higher International Studies of Geneva, and Professor

Theodore E. Gregory, of the London School of Economics.

From Canada, Dean P. E. Corbett, of the Law Faculty of McGill University, and Professor Frank H. Underhill, of the University of Toronto, will be at Williamstown.

In the group of outstanding Americans who will take part are Malcolm C. Rorty, of New York; Dr. George S. Counts, Columbia University; Professor George M. Stratton, University of California; Professor Arthur N. Holcombe, Harvard University; Professor Jacob Viner, University of Chicago; James G. McDonald, New York, and Dr. George H. Blakeslee, Clark University.

The project adopted for discussion is the general subject of "World Economic Planning," a study of economic organization under the individualistic capitalist system, the Fascist system and the Communist system. Mr. Rorty and Professor Gregory will deliver two lectures on the capitalist system. The "Economics of Fascism" will be described by Dr. Villari; the "Economics of Communism" will be dealt with by Dr. Counts. Professor Viner and Professor T. E. Gregory are to conduct two round table conferences on the various aspects of the capitalist theory of national economy, Mr. Viner taking the subjects of trade, exchange and money, and Mr. Gregory those of production and distribution.

The lectures to be delivered by Dr. Beckerath are on the "Economic problems and policies of present-day Germany," and those by M. Le Neveu concern the situation in France. These lecturers, it is expected, will discuss the recent changes as affected by President Hoover's moratorium plan.

Other round tables will include one on "the social psychology of international conduct," under the leadership of Professor Stratton, in which an opportunity will be given for an appraisal of the importance of such questions as racial antipathies and the effect of commerce upon the attitude of nations towards one another. Also a conference has been organized for the discussion of "The Future of Democracy," under the direction of Professor Holcombe.

Two other conferences will be held, one on "The British Commonwealth of Nations," to be conducted by Dean Corbett; the other, on "The International Political Situation in Europe," will be under the direction of Dr. Rappard.

EDUCATIONAL NOTES AND NEWS

CARLTON W. STANLEY, professor of Greek at McGill University, has been appointed president of Dalhousie University, Halifax. He succeeds Dr. A. Stanley Mackenzie, who is retiring after twenty years as president of the institution.

DR. F. NAGAOKA has been appointed first president of the Osaka Imperial University of Japan, which has been recently transferred back from city to governmental control.

PROFESSOR JOHN STRONG has been appointed pro-vice-chancellor of the University of Leeds, in succession to Professor W. Garstang.

PROFESSOR ARTHUR D. WRIGHT has been chosen president of the John F. Slater Fund and the Jeanes Foundation, to succeed Dr. James H. Dillard, who has been head of these organizations for nearly twenty-five years. These foundations are organizations for the assistance of Negro education.

THE King of England has bestowed the honor of knighthood on Frank W. Goldstone, the retiring general secretary of the British National Union of Teachers.

DR. WILLIAM Z. RIPLEY, professor of political science at Harvard University, has received the honorary degree of doctor of laws from Bucknell University.

DR. RALPH L. WATTS, dean of agriculture at the Pennsylvania State College, received the degree of doctor of science at the recent commencement of Rhode Island State College.

MR. LESTER A. PROEBSTEL, superintendent and organizer of schools at Ipoh, Perah, Malay Straits Settlement, and Charles Rice, superintendent of schools at Portland, Oregon, have received the degree of doctor of laws from Willamette University.

OHIO NORTHERN UNIVERSITY has conferred the degree of doctor of pedagogy on Mr. J. T.

P. Calkins, superintendent of schools of Hempstead, Long Island, New York.

A complimentary dinner in honor of Dr. Frank H. Miller, of New York, retiring as trustee of Cornell University after twenty years of service, was held on June 5 at Willard Straight Hall. Professor Simon H. Gage, '77, presided. President Livingston Farrand gave the leading address.

Dr. Raymond Drewry, of Kingsville, Texas, has been appointed dean and professor of education at the College of Puget Sound to succeed Dr. Allan Clark Lemon, who has resigned that post to become professor of educational psychology at the University of Idaho.

The title of Dr. Francis D. Curtis, of the University of Michigan, has been changed to that of associate professor of secondary education and of the teaching of science and head of the department of science in the University High School.

Dr. J. C. Dewey, formerly superintendent of schools at Galesville, Wisconsin, has been appointed head of the department of education at Lindenwood College, St. Charles, Missouri.

Mr. V. Don Hudson, superintendent of the Novinger consolidated schools of Novinger, Missouri, for the past two years, has accepted a position on the faculty of the State Teachers College, at Kirksville.

The *School Board Journal* reports that Mr. F. E. Corbin, who has been a school official for forty-five years, the greater part as superintendent of schools at Southbridge, Massachusetts, has retired, having reached the compulsory retiring age. Mr. E. L. Brown, for seven years assistant superintendent of schools at Denver, Colorado, will retire on September 1, having reached the age limit.

Dean James Alton James, head of the history department at Northwestern University and dean of the Graduate School, has been appointed to serve as chairman of the historical committee of the Chicago World's Fair of the Century of Progress Exposition.

Dr. Walter M. W. Splawn, formerly president of the University of Texas, has been appointed to conduct a survey of power control, looking to the possibility of bringing the great electric holding and management corporations under governmental regulation. His appointment was initiated by the Power Commission.

José Padin, Porto Rico Commissioner of Education, has been in Washington in conference with government education officials relative to the educational situation in the territory. He has presented to the U. S. Commissioner of Education his annual report. It shows that there are in the public schools of the island 193,396 pupils, in contrast with an enrolment of 21,873 in 1899 when the island became a U. S. Territory. School expenditures for the past year were $5,386,923, of which 7 per cent. is supplied by the Porto Rico government and 30 per cent. from local taxes.

Dr. Archie M. Palmer, associate secretary of the Association of American Colleges, has been giving a weekly series of radio talks over WEAF on the general theme "In Search of an Education." Talks already delivered have been on the topics: "After the High School—What?" "Who Should Go to College," "Which College," "Financing a College Education" and "Gaining Admission to College."

Five college executives are explaining the theories and practices of their universities during the thirty-second summer session of Columbia University. Dean Herbert E. Hawkes, of Columbia College, opened the series with the "Columbia Plan" on Wednesday, July 8, followed by Dean Alfred C. Hanford, who spoke on "Harvard"; "Swarthmore" will be the subject of Dr. Frank Aydelotte, president of Swarthmore College, on July 22; "Wabash," of Dr. Louis B. Hopkins, president of Wabash College, on July 27, and "Chicago," of Professor Chauncey S. Boucher, dean of the College of Arts, Literature and Science, University of Chicago, on August 5.

The Reverend Dr. John A. Marquis, formerly general secretary of the Presbyterian Board of National Missions and president of Coe College, died on July 6, at the age of sixty-nine years.

Former Judge E. W. Biddle, president of the board of trustees of Dickinson College for the last nineteen years, died on July 4, at the age of seventy-nine years.

DR. A. L. WOLFE, head of the department of classical languages at Park College and a member of the teaching staff since 1889, died on July 2.

DR. FRIEDRICH GUNDOLF, professor of literary history at Heidelberg University, has died at the age of fifty-one years. He was widely known as a translator of Shakespeare.

THE Sixth World Conference of the New Education Fellowship will be held in France during the first two weeks of August, 1932. The theme of the meeting is to be "Education and Social Change." It will be a conference of teachers, parents and other students of education from all parts of the world to discuss their problems with educational leaders of many nations.

THE International Conference on the Child, organized by the *Association générale des Institutrices des Ecoles maternelles,* will be held in Paris from July 26 to August 1. The accompanying exhibition will remain open until August 8. There are five sections: General organization of the education of children between the ages of 2 and 7 years in France and foreign countries; premises, furniture and material; method and curricula, training of staff; education in art, games and celebrations; health and welfare work. The president of the Organizing Committee is Mme. Herbinière-Lebert, Directrice d'Ecole maternelle, 12 rue des Grands-Champs, Paris (20e).

A DELEGATION of twenty-seven students, selected from the leading universities of the British Isles to attend the British and American Students' Conference to be held in Ann Arbor, Michigan, under the auspices of the Carnegie Endowment for International Peace, has arrived in New York. Problems of international importance, including limitation of armaments, international regional organizations, and the issues that have arisen following the signing of the Treaty of Versailles, will be discussed at the conference by representatives from British, Canadian and American universities.

THE University of Pennsylvania Fund has received gifts and bequests amounting to $2,231,356 during the fiscal year of 1930–31, and, since its establishment in 1925, it has received a total of $17,543,343, according to an announcement made by Thomas S. Gates, president of the university. The largest single gift received by the university was the one from Mr. Cyrus H. K. Curtis for more than $1,000,000. This gift was announced at the recent commencement exercises, and unrestricted. It is now announced that this sum will be added to the endowment fund of the university and named for its donor. From the Rockefeller Foundation the university received $160,000, from the Julius Rosenwald Fund $75,000, while the Carnegie Corporation gave another $75,000.

GIFTS and bequests amounting to $258,793, received during the last academic year, have been announced by New York University, the largest item being $111,342 from the estate of the late James Arthur, who in 1926 gave to the university a collection of clocks which has become one of the most representative and complete in the world. The New York University gymnasium fund, for the erection of a five-story building on the campus at University Heights, the first unit of which is now under construction, was increased by $31,867, of which $30,000 was given by two anonymous donors.

BY the will of the late O. M. Eidlitz public institutions receive direct bequests and remainder interests amounting to more than $750,000. These include $229,576 to the Presbyterian Hospital; $153,050 to the Roosevelt Hospital, and $54,666 each to the Hospital for the Ruptured and Crippled, Fifth Avenue Hospital and the Manhattan Eye and Ear Hospital. Cornell University receives $25,000 for a scholarship in the engineering department.

YALE COLLEGE and various branches of Yale University have received $426,658 from the estate of Samuel Rossiter Betts, retired patent attorney, who died December 13, 1930.

A PROGRAM to raise $3,000,000 for the construction of a new plant for Colby College has been authorized by the board of trustees. This announcement was immediately followed by the receipt of an unconditional pledge of $100,-

000 from the Board of Education of the Northern Baptist Convention which is to be used in developing this program.

THE trustees of Columbia University have established two annual fellowships of $1,600 each for graduates of a college of high standing in Vermont. The awards were made possible by a bequest of $75,000 left to Columbia University by the late George W. Ellis, of Vermont.

AT the commencement of Goucher College, held on June 1, President David Allan Robertson announced the receipt of the gift of $50,000 for the establishment of the Agnes Latimer and Clara Latimer Bacon Fund, the income of which will ultimately be used for salaries for teachers and for free scholarships. During the lifetime of Professor Clara Latimer Bacon, of Goucher College, the income will be received by her.

THE Goldsmiths' Company has offered to the University of London a sum not exceeding £50,000 towards the cost of erecting and equipping the library building on the Bloomsbury site. The university library, at present housed in the Imperial Institute, South Kensington, contains a total of some 260,000 volumes and pamphlets.

WE learn from the *School Board Journal* that a million-dollar high school is in process of construction at Port Chester, New York. The board of education has issued a folder which gives all the cost figures as well as the data on capacity and the like. The site occupies 23 acres and cost $242,000. The furnishings, including athletic field and stadium construction, cost $350,000. The building will be ready for opening on January 1, 1932.

A DISPATCH to the New York *Times* states that the Board of Education of New York City has formally accepted a gift of a newspaper press, valued at $100,000, for use in the Central Printing Trades Continuation School. The press was offered by the New York Newspaper Printing Pressmen's Union, No. 2, through its president, Mr. Andrew R. Armstrong, and will be installed without cost to the Board of Education.

FROM a dispatch to the New York *Evening Post* we learn that plans for bringing together twelve Jewish schools under the direction of a single federation are being considered by rabbis and officials of Jewish schools. The schools are Yeshiva Chaimberlin, Rabbi Jacob Joseph School, Yeshiva of The Bronx, Yeshiva Eitvchaim of Brooklyn, Yeshiva Solomon Klugh, Yeshiva Torah Vodath, Yeshiva Tifereth Jerusalem, Yeshiva Torath Chaim, Yeshiva Torath Emeth, Yeshiva of Harlem, Yeshiva Moshea and Yeshiva of Flatbush.

DR. A. S. W. ROSENBACH, president of the American Friends of the Hebrew University, has announced that seventeen scholarships for students in the Hebrew University at Jerusalem have been established to help those who are having difficulty finding work to attend school.

THE Ministry of Education of the Chinese National Government has asked the League of Nations to establish a permanent system of exchange professorships between Chinese universities and European institutions. It is proposed that three professors, in geology, history and English, should be sent to the Central University at Nanking.

THE State Teachers College at Hays, Kansas, has obtained permission to be renamed the Fort Hays State College. Pre-professional school training will be emphasized, so that students can carry on there the early college work preparatory to entrance into schools of engineering, law, medicine, business, education and the like. The college can grant A.B. degrees. The Kansas State Agricultural College at Manhattan changed its name to the Kansas State College of Agriculture and Applied Science.

CORNELL UNIVERSITY has adopted a group insurance policy which protects the faculties and staffs of all its colleges and schools including the Agricultural Experiment Station at Geneva, New York (but not the medical center in New York City), and the employees of the administrative and operating departments. All full-time employees of the university are eligible to protection in amounts ranging from $1,000 to $10,000, according to salary received and the position occupied. Approximately 1,200 persons will receive protection under this plan. The total amount of insurance involved will approximate $4,500,000 and the premiums will be paid under the contributory plan, with the insured employees themselves paying part of the premiums and the university assuming the remainder of the expense. There is a provision in the plan whereby payments in sixty equal monthly instalments will be made in the event of total and permanent disability. Cornell is the fifteenth educational institution to acquire group insurance for its employees through the Prudential Insurance Company of America. Included in the list are the University of Chicago and Princeton University.

THE New York State Education Department announces the names of the winners of the special scholarships for soldiers, sailors, marines and nurses awarded as a result of the examination held on September 12 under the provisions of Chapter 690 of the Laws of 1930. This chapter provides for 450 state scholarships for the benefit of resident soldiers, sailors and marines who shall have served as such in the army, navy or marine corps of the United States in the world war and been honorably discharged from such service, and for the children of such soldiers, sailors and marines who died while serving in the armed forces of the United States or as a result thereof, and trained nurses with a similar record of service, and who shall have or acquire the necessary qualifications as to secondary or other preparatory education, to be required by the Commissioner of Education under rules and regulations to be established by him as hereinafter provided. Each of such scholarships shall entitle the holder thereof to his tuition, in a sum not exceeding one hundred dollars per year, in any college, university, normal, technical or trade school of his selection, within the state, such tuition to be paid by the state together with an additional sum of one hundred dollars per year for the maintenance of the holder of each such scholarship while in attendance upon instruction under such scholarship, provided however that no such annual payment shall be made to the same individual for a period longer than four years. Only 35 scholarships were awarded and there were only about 40 candidates for these scholarships.

DISCUSSION

THE DISCUSSION TECHNIQUE

IN your issue of May 23 you present an analysis of "The Discussion Technique" by Drs. L. R. Delong and H. B. Smith. They seek to answer the question, "What method or methods will produce the best results in insuring changes in behavior among mature students?" In analyzing this article certain subsidiary questions occurred to me to be basic to the original study but not referred to in it. For instance, what is the psychology of the learning process that underlies "insuring changes in behavior."

If students are encouraged in talking, there are various possible outcomes: first, more talking may result; second, if they proceed in a certain manner, less talking and more verification may be the outcome. If, however, there is any sound psychological basis for the doctrine that "we learn by doing," we must have in the learning process itself the kind of "doing," that is appropriate to the kind of "doing" that we wish to have as an outcome.

In what follows one thing should be kept clearly in mind: I believe very firmly that education must always be in relation to the learner rather than subject-matter, that the learner's question should be challenges for redirecting his inquiries and doings, and that the learner's problems should be opportunities for putting him in the way of working out his own solutions.

The writer discusses the value of "interludes" and sets up criteria such as that of the number participating during an interlude. If interest is focused upon changes within the individuals that compose the group, there may be some justification for this criterion. However, one interlude with only one participating may easily be more enlightening than forty with three hundred participating. Perhaps enlightenment may be a legitimate end in higher education.

Is talking itself a virtue—so said the defenders of the "socialized recitation." The outcome was often many discussions and less scholarly research, less studious learning. Certainly *some* of the "interludes" should be made to yield a very substantial return. We are apt to take it for granted that "egging on" discussion will take the place of substantial scholarship and absolve us as instructors from many rigorous labors. In some manner there should be adequate provision for following up nearly all, if not all, vital issues to some satisfying conclusion. It is here that true scholarship is necessary even though one may simply guide the learner to do his own researching.

This is not to be construed as a defense of either the "lecture" method or the "assignment and re-citation" method. It is but a conviction that we must guard against considering desirable education as issuing from a series of meaningless and unfruitful acts. Marshalling of evidence, clear elucidation of ambiguities, rigorous and well-disciplined economies in reaching solutions, the desire or "drive" for the most valid verification possible, such items as these are to be given due consideration if the right kind of education is to take place.

Thus we come to the place of wide experience and scholarly knowledge in the educative processes. There are some pertinent questions here. First, will throwing open a question to a group guarantee that all of the factors will be considered? Second, will any group be well disciplined enough to conduct in large part its own educational enterprise? And this raises a third question, as to what should be the function of a leader or instructor in the educative processes if we are considering "discussion" as a method. I have seen so much abuse of this procedure in high school and in college that it has made me feel that the criticism often made by students may have real foundation, and that is, "We can listen to each other talk on the street corner and we don't have to pay any tuition for that privilege. What we want here is that which can be contributed by scholarship."

Hence, while it may be desirable that as many as possible participate, while it may be only logical that education must take place largely through participation, a doing on the part of the learner, is it not also true that just participation itself is as apt to be vicious as helpful? Is it not also true that one contribution of no more than a question may be more richly educative than twenty or a hundred statements? Witness the interlocutor who smashes a three-hour debate by an incisive query that dispels all of the smoke screens that have been created—such are the real "salt" of democracy.

In regard to criterion eleven, "the amount of discussion continued informally by the members of the group after the adjournment of the recitation,"—who has not witnessed with real satisfaction, educationally, a vast silence follow a discussion? Perhaps if it were added that, "if the continuing of the discussion were fruitful," then the above criterion would be an excellent one. Who has not grown weary of discussions that should have ended immediately by some simple experiment or investigation? It reminds one of the student in the Middle Ages who brought to a close, or who by bringing in a horse threatened to bring to a close, a very persistent argument as to whether or not horses had teeth in both the upper and lower jaws. It is said that he was expelled immediately. I fear that we have been often too well pleased with our discussions to proceed to a settlement of them by some simple experiment or investigation. Are not most quarrels of this character! What can last longer, grow more intense, involve more people, and create more human comedy! So, in regard to this criterion, is there not a danger to be guarded against in our criteria-loving age? What can be so sweeping as a criterion, so devastating! However, the authors may turn upon me and say, "Are you not now exemplifying education by discussions?"

It may be that each criterion should be accompanied by a number of sub-criteria. I hope, for instance, that there may be some value in this analysis, as I feel convinced there is real value in the analysis made by the authors. I feel convinced that such criticism leads to desirable clarification and elaboration of issues. We need, perhaps, this enrichment of concept, this clarification of validity and process, if we are to arrive at some more fruitful educational procedures.

One issue that should be kept clearly in mind and which does not seem to be so clearly distinguished in the article by Doctors DeLong and Smith, is that when we are thinking of educational ends rather than of production as an end, very different criteria apply to the procedure. When changes within the individuals who are participating in the discussion, is the end in view, very different criteria must be applied than if we have efficient production as an end. Anything that does not lead to greater productive efficiency is out of place in the latter case, while anything that produces desirable changes in the individual and the group may be very appropriate in the former, even though the end-point of the discussion may be but indirectly approached.

The tendency seems to have been largely to espouse one particular method and to throw mud at all the rest. Different procedures are appropriate for different ends. One end may be that of an adequate solution of a problem. If that is the sole end, then the particular interests and educational status of the individuals present can not be considered. If, on the other hand, the end is that of desirable educational changes in all present, then even the original end itself might conceivably be sacrificed. We need to consider the value of different procedures as different ends are in view. The lecture method probably should have a substantial place in education. There would seem to be a point at which scholarly reorganizations and presentation of appropriate materials would be desirable, and since we do not publish and probably should not publish all such reorganizations and interpretations, there would seem to be a very legitimate place for the lecture method in higher education.

In regard to the discussion method, again it may be reiterated that participation and discussion may simply end in more discussion, and will so end unless by chance or purpose such discussion is connected with developing more effective thinking, speaking, doing, etc. If it is a sincere process of discovering new means for the clarification of problems, or, setting up experimental, dialectical, or informational procedures, such as will lead on to a more adequate solution of problems, then discussion may be valuable. But may it not be that under certain circumstances the lecture method will accomplish these and other results also more efficiently? In some cases the real point of the occasion is that of bringing to the group a certain amount of recently developed facts or newly discovered facts, and these are most adequately presented usually by the scholar himself. What degree of desirable education takes place through the participation of the members of any group must of necessity depend upon the appropriate qualifications of that group. The scholar must in some form or other provide new materials, either through directing the learner how to get them for himself or by presenting them directly. We can not afford to sacrifice the functions of scholarship to general participation.

Allen O. Hansen
University of Illinois

THE CONTRACT PLAN IN RETROSPECT

What is the ogre in our high schools that frightens the students, keeps their heads bent, sucks their enthusiasm, and kills their energy? It's the contract system. It's like a poison unwittingly administered by the teachers.

Miss Smith, teacher of civics, smiles at her students, and, since it is a rather pleasant morning, the students smile back. Miss Smith rises, a pile of mimeographed sheets in her hand. The eyes of her audience take on a variety of expressions—bewilderment, perplexity, disdain, contempt, resignation, hatred. The sheets distributed, Miss Smith holds one up for view.

> As you will see, this is contract number seven, due next Monday. Now, at the bottom of the second page are the requirements. For D grade, you must read the text, pages 50 to 61. For C grade, you must write out answers to these questions. For B grade, you must read at least ten pages in one of the references, and for A, you must either read 15 more pages or do an original project, preferably a notebook.

The ogre begins his cruel work. Industrious Helen rushes home to get it all done in one night. There are always Helens in every class. Unfortunately, I was one. I spent my afternoon in outlining the text. The sun might shine; the neighborhood might play baseball; the family might sit on the back porch contemplating the garden; but I sat in the living room where I put down facts in neat rows. In an hour, I was well started in the process of writing out the questions. While dinner was cooking and my sister and brother read the "funnies" in the evening paper, I laboriously wrote question five in the margin, ran my finger down a page of the lesson, and, finding the answer, copied it word for word, one eye on my paper and the other on the books. Grudgingly I put down the book and set the table, contriving to think of notebook material while hacking at bread and dumping milk into the pitcher. Dinner over, I carried the dishes into the pantry and went through the customary task of washing them, at the same time continuing to hunt mentally for something original in the way of a project. Then, back I rushed, hunted up one of the reference books which I had checked out, skipped through it and began to look for pictures of anything pertaining to government. Magazines were hauled in from the garage and flipped through, scissors whacking out stray pictures of capital buildings, election campaigns and other inspiring things. By eleven I was half done, and by twelve the notebook lay on the table, pasted, bound, and covered, while I was a bundle of nerves. When I finally got into bed without taking down my hair or brushing my teeth, I set myself to the task of going to sleep. I forced myself to relax; I counted sheep; I looked at the moon; I even swore, but all I could think of was civics. The next day I had such a case of nervous indigestion that I wished I were dead.

Now, Jimmy next door was different. The ogre at school had no terror for Jimmy. He always rushed home from school and out into the street to join in baseball. He could go out and see if the radishes were really being demolished by worms. He could absorb "funnies." He whistled as he brought in his wood and he spent his evening in reading pirate yarns. His father would ask, "Haven't you got any school work to do?" "Oh, no, civics isn't due until Monday; I got a week yet." Then, on Monday morning, Jimmy sighed and spent his study-hall hour in dashing off answers to questions. Perhaps he poked his nose into a reference book, stared at the pictures and went to class. He was a failing student, according to the teacher, because he lacked initiative. But he had no idea how a sick stomach felt.

Between these two extremes hovered the average students. If they felt like studying, they studied. But usually they didn't. They were uncertain as to what grades they were aiming for, but who cared? Civics was dry old stuff anyway. If they had originality, they hid the gift for experience had taught them that the teacher would suggest some tiresome project to do. If they lacked such imagination, they might skip through the additional fifteen pages, all depending on how they felt.

It may be true that the teacher finds out the caliber of her class by the grade each student strives for, but that alone does not justify the system. When the contract system was first introduced in our school, it was vaguely explained as a preparation for college. "You must learn to distribute your time." All very well, but what an unendurable apprenticeship! One contract is finished; another appears. The discussions increase the dislike because the class period could otherwise be spent in preparation of the contract. Discussions don't amount to much anyway, for having outlined the lesson and written out answers the students have rushed off to the extra work, leaving not a remnant of the text in their minds.

Quantity replaces quality. The formula is: Get it done; hand it in; forget it. The exact position of examinations is unknown. In some classes there is an examination for every grade; if a student wants a C he takes the D and the C examinations. If he wants an A he takes the B and A examinations, too. But the teacher is buried in papers. For protection she sometimes resorts to one examination and somehow averages it in. The purpose of the teachers has degenerated to that of a clerk who looks over written papers, creates contracts, creates examinations, and files away or destroys the mass of class work that comes in. She is no longer there to create an interest in the subject. The student must dig things out. Exponents of the plan claim that high-school students must develop initiative, but I'd much rather have a little interest for flavoring.

After three years of contract system, during which I learned to substitute quantity for quality and failed to learn to distribute my time, I graduated and prepared to enter college. Theoretically, my three years of apprenticeship should have accustomed me to the new atmosphere. Imagine my disgust upon finding that there are daily assignments in college! After the teachers had told us that daily assignments were grade-school stuff, the college even dares to have them. Something must be wrong! Another sad revelation was that in college quality strangely displaces quantity. After outlining the text, it pays to learn what one has written so that the knowledge can be reproduced in blue books. The habits of three years must be unlearned.

And as I try to fit into the new environment, I can't help wondering what an advantage it would have been to my health, happiness and grades if the daily assignment plan had been followed in high school.

I get all stirred up inside as I watch the ogre swing his whip over my sister and other high-school students as he smiles, "Due next Monday!"

ALISON COMISH

OREGON STATE COLLEGE,
CORVALLIS, OREGON

QUOTATIONS

REQUESTS FOR FREE COPIES OF TEXT-BOOKS[1]

UNREASONABLE demands upon publishers for free books on the part of teachers, administrative officers, school boards, and text-book commissions are characterized by some of the bookmen interviewed as a serious problem in carrying on their business. In general it is contended that no other business enterprise is expected to distribute free samples of its wares in any such wholesale fashion as book companies are compelled to do, and that members of the teaching profession itself do not make such demands in purchasing other necessary school supplies and equipment. The net result of the practice is higher prices for the books which are sold to the school public, since all the expense of marketing, as well as the cost of production, must be liquidated in the revenues from sales.

The most emphatic objections relate to demands for free sample copies of books "for examination." Arguing that "the system is wrong in principle," one manager says the "self-respecting superintendent should demand of his board that all samples needed should be bought and paid for." The value of gift copies of school books sent out by publishers is estimated by one representative at from 3 to 10 per cent. of the value of the books sold. Another states that for every 15 college texts sold, one is given away. The number of samples sent out by one company last year is given as 192,850 copies, and the writer adds that "we are considered by some teachers as stingy." The protest against this practice is fairly summarized in the following quotation:

> It takes a sale of at least twenty books to pay for one free sample, and the demand on the publisher for free samples has steadily increased in recent years. This is to no small extent due to the lavish and foolish waste of sample copies on the part of representatives of some publishers, but it is also due to the increasing demand for copies on the part of educational authorities. This organization of committees within committees, followed by a demand for a separate sample copy for each member of each committee, results in such a demand for sample copies in the minor cities that the eventual sale hardly pays for it, especially as there is more than a suspicion that these sample copies are eventually used for study, to take the place of books that would otherwise be bought.
>
> Moreover, there is a strong suspicion that these sample copies are sometimes sold by thoughtless educational persons, which results in their going into the second-hand trade and materially reducing the legitimate sales. If a teacher does not want the books given him, is it too much to ask him to return them to the giver?
>
> It can fairly be expected that any city ought to be able to select its books without expecting the publisher to give away twenty to thirty copies. This is the only business which I know of where a merchant is expected to give away unlimited quantities of his product in order to secure a sale. Admitting that it is impossible to select a book wisely without examining it, it still is reasonable to ask that the educational authorities have copies submitted for examination used by more than one person, and not expect every person who has the slightest claim to a chance to examine the book

[1] Extract from "The Text-book in American Education," prepared by the Committee on the Text-book, National Society for the Study of Education: W. C. Bagley, B. R. Buckingham, G. T. Buswell, W. L. Coffey, N. B. Henry, F. A. Jensen, C. R. Maxwell, Raleigh Schorling and J. B. Edmonson (*chairman*). Assisted by the following members of the society: Ellwood P. Cubberley and Herman G. Richey. Issued: Spring, 1931.

to be provided with a separate copy. As I have said before, this evil is partly due to the publishers themselves.

A further demand objected to by some of the publishers is that they furnish free "desk copies." Continuing the statement just quoted:

An evil which, however, is not due to the publishers to any extent, is the demand that, after a book has been adopted, the teachers shall be supplied with free desk copies. Educational authorities do not demand that their teachers be supplied with free chalk, free erasers, free stationery, free desks, or any other part of their school equipment, but they unhesitatingly demand that they be supplied with free books in many parts of the country. The schools do not gain anything by this, for if the custom grows instead of decreases, the price of twelve books will have to be raised to cover the cost of thirteen, assuming that the thirteenth must be given away as a desk copy.

Objection is made also to the not infrequent practice of requesting free sets of books ''for trial with classes'' with a view to adoption. This practice is an imposition upon the text-book companies, but competition does not permit the companies to refuse such requests.

It is suggested also that the growing practice of requesting publishers to donate books for a library for a school or a college should be discouraged. Some publishers feel that they must comply with such requests; and of course all such demands upon the companies must indirectly affect the price of books which are sold. Also the complaint is made that these libraries of text-books are not always so administered as to make the books which are provided by the publishing companies conveniently serviceable to the people they are expected to serve.

An instance is cited by a representative of one publishing company, of a request he received from the head of a department in a state university where such an exhibit of books is maintained, asking for the publications of this company in his particular field as a contribution to the text-book library for his department. When reminded that such publications had already been furnished the library maintained at his institution, he replied that there were too many books in the library and that it was impossible for anybody to find what he wanted.

REPORTS

EDUCATIONAL PROBLEMS OF PENNSYLVANIA[1]

FOLLOWING my memorandum of several days ago indicating that a committee was to be appointed to study certain fundamental problems in education, a committee of twenty-six school men and women met in Harrisburg on Tuesday, June 11, 1931. The personnel of the committee, which is to be known as the "Commission for the Study of Educational Problems of Pennsylvania," is given on the attached sheets.

Dr. William John Cooper, U. S. Commissioner of Education, was present at this meeting. The commissioner has assigned Mr. W. S. Deffenbaugh, chief of the Division of American School Systems, U. S. Office of Education, as his representative in connection with our study to develop a ten-year program of public education in Pennsylvania.

At the present time the Office of Education has three major surveys under way. These are a survey of secondary education, a survey of teacher preparation and a survey of school finance. A fourth survey on special education will be started on July 1, 1931. It is evident, therefore, that the commission may draw heavily on the results of these various studies in connection with the formulation of a program for Pennsylvania.

The commission approved a general plan of organization which provides for the following:

1. Director, James N. Rule
   Superintendent of Public Instruction
   Associate Director, W. S. Deffenbaugh
   Chief, Division of American School Systems
   U. S. Office of Education
   Washington, D. C.
2. Four committees are to be appointed immediately:
   1. Committee on Guiding Principles
   2. Committee on School Organization and Administration
   3. Committee on School Finance
   4. Committee on Recodification of School Laws

[1] Memorandum sent by Dr. James N. Rule, superintendent of public instruction, to county and district superintendents and presidents of State Teachers Colleges.

3. A small executive committee to be appointed to organize the various study committees and to coordinate the work of the Commission. The following executive committee was appointed:

Dr. Francis B. Haas, president, State Teachers College, Bloomsburg.

Dr. Albert Lindsay Rowland, superintendent, Cheltenham Township Schools, Elkins Park.

Dr. W. Grant Chambers, dean, School of Education, The Pennsylvania State College.

Dr. Ben Graham, superintendent of schools, Pittsburgh.

This group, of which the superintendent of public instruction is also a member, will constitute the executive committee.

The executive committee, which met the following day, authorized the appointment of the following chairmen of study committees. These groups are to begin work at once:

1. Committee on Guiding Principles
   Chairman: Dr. John Minnick
   Dean, School of Education
   University of Pennsylvania
2. Committee on Unit of School Organization and Administration
   Chairman: Dr. J. Linwood Eisenberg
   President, State Teachers College
   Slippery Rock, Pennsylvania
3. Committee on School Finance
   Chairman: Dr. LeRoy King
   School of Education
   University of Pennsylvania
4. Committee on Recodification of School Laws
   Chairman: Dr. Francis B. Haas
   President, State Teachers College
   Bloomsburg, Pennsylvania

For each study committee there will be a small executive group responsible for coordinating and organizing the work of the committee as a whole. It was suggested that this group be appointed at once so that the members might begin the collection of needed materials. Meetings of these small committees will be held within the next few weeks.

A preliminary report of the work of the Committee on Guiding Principles will be presented at the Superintendents' Conference at State College. This conference will be held during the latter part of July.

The commission adjourned to meet in the Department of Public Instruction on September 21, 1931.

I am making this report at this time to advise you relative to the work of the commission and also to enlist your support in connection with the various study committees. We want this to be a cooperative enterprise which will involve the entire teaching personnel of the state. While the committees must necessarily be small, we do hope to secure the advice and cooperation of all school men and women of the state.

I shall attempt to keep you advised from time to time relative to the progress of each of these committees and shall appreciate it if you will take time to make a critical analysis of the preliminary outlines as they come to your desk. Any pertinent comments relating to the problems which are under observation will be appreciated and will be placed before the appropriate committees.

I shall also appreciate it if you will give the widest publicity possible to the work of the commission.

Sincerely yours,

JAMES N. RULE,
Superintendent of Public Instruction

SOCIETIES AND MEETINGS

DETROIT MEETING OF THE AMERICAN HOME ECONOMICS ASSOCIATION

SEVENTEEN hundred persons were registered at the twenty-fourth annual meeting of the American Home Economics Association held in Detroit, from June 22 to 27.

The central theme of the meeting, "The Rôle of the Home in Individual and Family Development" was discussed from the standpoint of the factors contributing to individual and family growth. Speakers at the general sessions included Honorable Wilbur M. Brucker, governor of the State of Michigan; Mr. Frank W. Cody, superintendent of city schools, Detroit; Mr. F. J. Kelly, chairman of the education section of the White House Conference on Child Health and Protection; Mr. William Lyon Phelps, Lampson professor of English language and literature, Yale University, and Mr. Royal B. Farnum, education director, Rhode Island School of Design. Each speaker presented the thesis of the home as the vital social unit in community or national life.

The divisions and the departments of the association each held two meetings. The speakers at the meetings of the divisions, which comprise the phases of family life included in family relationships, family economics, the house, food and nutrition, and textiles and clothing, were: Dr. John Sundwall, of the University of Michigan; Miss Frances O. Davis, of the Merrill-Palmer School; Mrs. Edith Hale Swift, of the American Social Hygiene Association; Mr. Wells A. Sherman, of the U. S. Bureau of Agricultural Economics; Miss Florence Davies, of the *Detroit News;* Miss Gertrude Zurrer, research fellow of the National Safety Council, and Miss Flora M. Thurston, of the National Council of Parent Education. Prominent speakers at the meetings of the departments of the association were Dean Abby L. Marlatt, of the University of Wisconsin; Mrs. J. K. Pettengill, formerly president of the Michigan Congress of Parents and Teachers; Miss Lita Bane, of the staff of the *Ladies' Home Journal;* Miss Flora Rose, of the New York State College of Home Economics; Dr. Chi Che Wang, of the University of Cincinnati; Professor E. L. Austin, of the Michigan State College, and Miss Mary I. Barber, of the Kellogg Company of Battle Creek, Michigan. The departments of the association represent home economics in business, in colleges and universities, in elementary and secondary schools, in extension service, for the homemakers, in institutions, in the fields of research and social service, in student clubs and for workers in child development and parental education agencies.

At the association business meeting an informal presentation of home economics interests in national conferences was made by Dr. A. J. Carlson, of the medical section of the White House Conference on Child Health and Protection, and Mr. James Ford, acting executive secretary of the President's Conference on Home Building and Home Ownership.

Newly elected officers are: *President,* Miss Frances Swain, supervisor of home economics in the Chicago Public Schools, reelected; *Vice-president,* Miss Margaret Edwards, director of school of home economics, Alabama College; *Secretary,* Dr. Marie Dye, dean of home economics, Michigan State Agricultural College; *Councilor at large,* Dr. Henrietta Calvin, supervisor of home economics, Philadelphia Public Schools; *Controller,* Miss S. Agnes Donham, specialist in income management, Boston, Massachusetts; *Treasurer,* Mr. H. Gale Turpin, Baltimore Trust Company.

The 1932 meeting will be held in Atlanta, Georgia, during the week of June 20.

EDUCATIONAL RESEARCH AND STATISTICS

THE INFLUENCE OF PRACTICE ON INDIVIDUAL DIFFERENCES[1]

DOES equal training make a group of individuals more alike or more different in their achievement? The solution to this problem is tied up not only with the old question of the relative importance of heredity and environment in the achievement of individuals, but also with questions of public policy in education. If individuals under the same training become more alike in their achievements it is said that this result is due to environment. On the other hand, if they become more different, it is said that this result is due to heredity. If our great system of public education will have the result of increasing the social, political and economic inequalities between individuals, then it fails in one of its major purposes, and many of our present educational practices accomplish just the opposite for which they are intended; but if it decreases the inequalities between individuals, then our present gospel of equality of opportunity is well grounded, for the theory underlying the latter doctrine is that inequalities between individuals will not be great if all individuals have an equal chance.

The conclusions of experiments upon this

[1] Paper read before the Kansas Psychological Association at Wichita, December 13, 1930.

problem before 1923 may be summed up in the conclusion drawn by Thorndike from his experiment published in 1916, namely: "The effect of equalizing opportunity is thus to increase individual differences. This result now found with many different functions furnishes perhaps the strongest argument that differences in achievement are largely due to differences in original capacity."

In 1924, I published a paper in which I called these conclusions in question, and pointed out that if gains are measured in terms of time per unit of work instead of work per unit of time, the facts justify an exactly opposite conclusion. The data of my experiments at that time justified the opposite conclusion when the results were measured by the ratio of highest to lowest before and after practice, ratio of Q_3 to Q_1, and correlation between initial performance and per cent. of gain.

In 1925, Kincaid applied many measures to the data of twenty-four experiments. Of these measures, the standard deviation and gross gain show that practice increases individual differences while the coefficient of variability, per cent. of gain, and correlation between initial ability and per cent. of gain show the opposite effect just as clearly. On the other hand, the ratio of worst to best, ratio of next worst to next best, and correlation between initial ability and gross gain show about the same amount of evidence on each side of the question. Such results demonstrate the necessity of finding valid measures before our problem can be solved.

I made a critical analysis of all these measures and finally selected the three following measures as valid for the purposes of our problem: the ratio of the average of the three highest individuals to the average of the three lowest individuals at the beginning of practice compared with the ratio of these same individuals at the end of practice, the coefficient of variability (standard deviation divided by the average), and the correlation between initial performance and per cent. of gain.

I was interested in finding out what conclusions could be drawn from previous experiments on this problem when these three measures were applied to the results. I, therefore, went over every experiment on which I could lay my hands, and calculated the above three measures so far as the data permitted. Whenever possible, I used the calculations already made by Kincaid, Peterson and Barlow. Out of fifty-nine experiments from which I was able to calculate the ratios of the highest to the lowest at the beginning and end of practice, I found that in 95 per cent. of the cases they decrease as a result of practice. This shows the effect of practice on the differences between the extremes of a distribution. Out of the seventy experiments from which I was able to secure the coefficients of variability, I found that in 77 per cent. of the cases they decrease as a result of practice. This shows the effect of practice on the middle two thirds of a distribution. Out of fifty-eight experiments for which I was able to get the correlation between initial performance and per cent. of improvement, I found that in 93 per cent. of the cases they are negative. This shows the effect of practice on the group as a whole. In other words, practice nearly always decreases the variability in the achievement of a group of individuals. This seems to be true for all kinds of tests, mental or motor, simple or complex. The amount of the decrease seems to vary directly with the amount of the initial difference between individuals and the length of practice and inversely with the initial level of achievement. All this suggests that the limits of improvement that are set by uncontrollable factors are much closer together than those due to training, and that as individuals approach these limits because of equal opportunity and training, their relative differences in achievement are decreased.

In order to discover if these conclusions needed modification, we made two new experiments—one a motor test, and the other a series of tests of achievement in elementary school subjects. The motor test was done by a group of thirty-seven college students and consisted of one hundred eighty minutes practice in throwing the yo-yo top. The task was to throw the top down and allow it to roll back on the string into the hand. If it did, such a catch was considered one success. The number of catches in ten minutes was the score. During 18 practice periods, the average number of catches increased from 82.51 to 445.63, the coefficient of variability decreased from 1.02 to 0.25, the ratio of the average of the three highest to the average of the three lowest decreased from 49.42 to 1.31, and the correlation between initial performance and per cent. of gain was –0.43. All these measures are consistent in showing that practice decreases individual differences. If we apply Thorndike's technique, divide the individuals into seven groups from highest to lowest, and calculate the average gross gain of each group, I find that the gain increases from 368 in the lowest to 418 in the middle group, but from this point on, the gain decreases to 189 in the highest group. If by good fortune I could have excluded the upper half of my group, I could have verified Thorndike's contention that gross gains are proportional to initial achievement, but when I include them, this theory is spoiled. It is interesting to notice, however, that the relative gains increase consistently from 63 in the highest group to 12,267 in the lowest group. If the gains are calculated on the basis of time per 10,000 catches, I find that the gross gains increase consistently from 130 in the highest group to 33,064 in the lowest group; and that the relative gains increase from 38.8 per cent. in the highest group to 99.1 per cent. in the lowest group. Here we notice that the relative gains, whether calculated on the basis of amount of work per unit of time or amount of time per unit of work, consistently show that they are inversely proportional to the initial achievement. But the gross or absolute gains calculated from these two measures are inconsistent. This is one more evidence that judgments of the effect of practice on individual differences can not be based on gross or absolute scores. Ignoring this measure, the results from this experiment consistently show that practice decreases individual differences.

In the investigation with the tests of achievement in elementary school subjects, the Stanford Achievement and the Compass Survey Arithmetic tests were given in October, February and May to 137 school children for Grades II to VIII inclusive. The following measures were applied to the results of each period of testing: (1) The ratio of the average of three highest to the average of the three lowest in the October tests, and the ratio of these same individuals in February and in May; (2) the standard deviation divided by the average; (3) the ratio of the 75 to the 25 percentile in October, and the ratio of the same individuals on these points in February and in May; (4) the ratio of the 60 to the 40 percentile in October, and the ratio of the same individuals on these points in February and in May; (5) the correlation between the October scores and the per cent. of gain from October to May. The first four measures were calculated for the children of each grade. The first, second and fifth measures were calculated for all the children treated as one group. For most of these calculations I am indebted to Mr. C. J. Edwards, superintendent of schools, Elizabeth, Colorado, who worked up the results for a master's thesis. The tabulation of the results by grades cover a number of pages. However, we may summarize them. The chances are 96 in 100 that equal practice will reduce the differences between the extremes of a group, 85 in 100 that it will reduce the variability of the central two thirds, 76 in 100 that it will reduce the variability of the middle half, and 67 in 100 that it will reduce the variability of the middle 40 per cent. of the group. If we calculate the results by tests for the entire group of 137 pupils regardless of grade, we find that the ratio of the average of the three highest to the average of the three lowest shows a marked decrease from October to May for each one of the ten tests. The same is true for each of the coefficients of variability for each test. All the coefficients of correlation between initial performance and per cent. of gain from October to May are negative. They vary from –.42 to –.75. All these facts together point to the conclusion that the training ordinarily given in the public schools reduces the variability in the achievement of the individuals that make up their populations. Our results, therefore, justify the policy of equal opportunity as a means of reducing the inequalities in achievement among individuals.

For a much fuller discussion of this problem as well as a presentation of the data, the reader is referred to my monograph entitled: "The Influence of Training on Changes in Variability in Achievement," Psychol. Rev. Co. Princeton, New Jersey.

H. B. REED

FORT HAYS STATE COLLEGE

SCHOOL AND SOCIETY

EDITED BY J. McKEEN CATTELL

WITH WHICH IS COMBINED THE

EDUCATIONAL REVIEW

EDITED BY WILLIAM McANDREW

Volume 34 SATURDAY, JULY 25, 1931 NUMBER 865

SOME PROBLEMS IN EDUCATION[1]

By Dr. WILLIS A. SUTTON

PRESIDENT OF THE NATIONAL EDUCATION ASSOCIATION, SUPERINTENDENT OF SCHOOLS, ATLANTA, GA.

NEVER before have responsibilities so heavily pressed upon the educational world as in the last eighteen months. H. G. Wells has said that civilization is a race between education and disaster, but the very existence of our globe is dependent upon knowledge, training and education. The very existence of education has been threatened during the period of depression through which we are now passing. The duties and responsibilities of a great organization in such an age have been almost unbearable. Thousands of our teachers can find no place to work and yet the need for teachers was never greater. This is a strange age, and a strange time. Never was there so much bread on the face of the earth, and never such a crowd of hungry people; never so much cotton in the fields and wool on the sheep's back; never so many shivering human beings; never so many teachers in all the world, and never so many people who needed teaching and yet a half million teachers in America are without work. In every city, in every hamlet, in every school district in America, the cry has gone up for retrenchment and it has been a popular thing to claim that schools have overtaxed the people and that education is bringing bankruptcy. The problem that confronts the teachers of America is the solution of the unemployment problem.

It is strange that we have not found the cause of our depression in the 15 million men who were killed in the World War. It is strange that we have blamed none of our difficulties upon the $250,000,000 destroyed in that great war. We have reached a period of readjustments and of paying for such a conflict. It is strange that we have found no reason for this depression except that the people were overtaxed for education. It is the business of the teacher and the business of the educator to see that the public is better informed. We have reached a readjustment period. The world must pay for its loss of life and destruction of property, for its speculation and wild orgy of extravagant living, but we, in the educational work, must see that this responsibility is not laid at the door of the one agency that will enable us to weather this storm and to come out victorious on the other side. The greatest problem confronting the educators of to-day is to see that the childhood of this generation is not robbed of its right by lowering educational standards, reducing salary schedules and lessening the educational offering.

[1] Address before National Education Association, Shrine Civic Auditorium, Los Angeles, California, June 29.

To meet this problem we must have courage, courage to tell the truth, courage to speak with absolute sincerity, courage to meet this impending disaster. It is not education, it is not culture, it is not the taxes that come as a result of this education and culture that is crushing America, it is the burden of taxation caused by wars past, present and to come. It is the burden of mortgaged property brought on by the personal extravagance of our people. It is the burden of taxation as the result of a wonderful and marvelous road system for the country, itself a great necessity and a great pleasure and a great maker of values, but we must be willing to pay the price. Education now requires less than 20 per cent. of the money expended for crime in America.

It may be true that the expenses of education have increased. It may be true that such an increase has not been absolutely essential. It may be true that extravagances have been committed by individuals, but it is not true that money has been wasted in education. The very evidences of prosperity that are about us are the results of our best educational efforts, and continued expenditures for better schools and better teaching will enable us to stem this temporary stream of depression and land us in the harbor of prosperity.

In this work of teaching the public, each individual teacher must assume his or her own responsibility. The humblest teacher in this land must see to it that the parents of those children whom he or she teaches understand that the basis of business is education—that the barometer of business is culture—that the background of business is knowledge. This, I think, is our first great duty. The second great problem of education is integration of all educational forces. "United we stand—divided we fall" was never truer than in the educational field, and in America to-day the great educational forces are dividing. Too often the college is railing at the high school; too often the high school, forgetting the arduous duties of the elementary schools, are complaining that children are not sent up to us properly prepared. There is lack of coordinating force to educate a child. Too few college men recognize what the high schools are doing, too few high-school teachers understand the aims and objectives of college life. The church and the community, the extra-curricular activities engaged in through Y. M. C. A., Y. W. C. A., Boy Scouts, Girl Scouts and other activities need to understand the program of education, and education needs to understand the character building powers of these agencies. Our great business concerns maintain educational departments, but oftentimes they are not correlated with the educational systems of the state or city. When will America learn that the making of a life is much more important than the learning of a subject? How many teachers are dealing with your boy and mine—how many are putting a "patch," so to speak, on his educational garment instead of working and weaving a robe of purple to bedeck an integrated soul. Just as a child is required to stand an examination of proficiency in any subject, so each teacher that takes over a child should be given an examination in what he knows about the background of a child's life, including his individual life, his heredity and the life of the race. Just so we need the integration of all educators of all types of education in order that we may present a united front for the great cause of knowledge and culture.

The third problem in education, and possibly the greatest of all, is that the teachers themselves and the public in general shall realize that every child in every state should have something like an equal opportunity to develop his God-given powers. The problem of equalization of educational opportunities for the city child and the country child, is possibly the greatest problem before the American education administrators. When I recall the fact that one third of our children are still in a one-teacher school, under the direction of a teacher whose training scarcely extends through the high school, and whose experience is practically nil; when I tell you that in the states of this union there are discrepancies in the amounts spent upon children running from two to one, and from seven to one, a child, I am asking you, as educators, to see that justice is done to the children of this nation; whether you live in the city or in the country, whether you are county superintendent or city administrator, whether you teach in a marble palace or a one-room school house. If you are a real teacher, and you have the spirit of school education, you must be interested in seeing that justice is done to every child. I therefore appeal to you that you interest yourselves in this conference on rural life; you will see to it that the teachers of the rural sections of this country have pay equal to that given in the city districts, and that the children of the farmers have an equal chance with the boys and girls who live on the boulevard.

THE PROFESSION OF TEACHING[1]

By Dr. WILLIAM C. BAGLEY
PROFESSOR OF EDUCATION, TEACHERS COLLEGE, COLUMBIA UNIVERSITY

THE first part of this paper will record the work of a committee appointed by President Sutton late last fall and known as the temporary committee on the appointment of teachers. Reports had come to the headquarters of the association that the unemployment situation, already serious among those who had been trained for teaching but were unable to secure first appointments, was likely to extend to experienced teachers, especially those who had resigned their positions to take further training and who now found themselves, with their savings exhausted, looking for new posts in an over-crowded market.

The profession quite obviously could not hold itself responsible for the inexperienced teachers, but some members of the profession—among them the present speaker—who believed that the profession should concern itself with the welfare of those experienced and successful teachers who, through no fault of their own, and often from a most commendable desire for professional improvement, found themselves temporarily caught in the tangled skein of the wide-spread economic depression.

Against the advice of many of my friends and colleagues who did not share this view of professional responsibility, I accepted the request of President Sutton and Secretary Crabtree to head a temporary committee to study the situation, determine how serious it was, and devise plans to provide relief if such relief were found advisable. The present paper is not an official report of this committee, but merely a statement of the chairman regarding its work together with some personal comments and suggestions for which he is alone responsible and which do not constitute in any sense a statement of official recommendations by the committee as such.

Fortunately, the situation during the year just ended was not so serious as might have been reasonably anticipated. While many public-school teachers have received few salary payments in actual cash on ac-

[1] Address before the General Session, National Education Association, Los Angeles, California, June 30, 1931.

count of the difficulty of raising taxes in several sections of the country, the schools have been kept open and the teachers have been able to meet living expenses through local credits.

In order to have a fund with which to meet such emergencies as might arise, especially in the several cases of teachers who had completed advanced training and were unable to secure employment, the committee sent a request for contributions to a limited group with which the chairman has been associated for many years—namely, the heads of education departments in colleges and universities and the faculties of normal schools and teachers' colleges. Contributions were also asked from publishers of school text-books—a business which at that time had not been seriously affected by the depression. Later college teachers in departments other than education were asked to contribute. Funds were not solicited from public-school workers because very generally these—whether teachers, supervisors, or executives—were not only contributing to local unemployment funds but also drawing generously upon their salaries to provide food and clothing and especially shoes for children in their classes whose families were destitute. In my judgment, the efforts and sacrifices of the public-school personnel in this connection deserve the highest praise and commendation from their fellow-workers in other branches of the educational service.

The temporary fund raised from the sources that I have indicated was not large, but it sufficed to care for nearly all the *bona-fide* cases reported to the committee that could not be provided for in other ways. A brief notice of the establishment of the fund and its purpose was carried by the Associated Press. The first letter received in reply to this notice was fairly typical of the cases for which, in the present writer's judgment, the profession as a whole should share some measure of responsibility. A man had resigned his position as a high-school teacher to accept a new position just created in another community. With the opening of the school year, however, the latter community found itself unable to provide a salary for the new position and the engagement was necessarily canceled. The man made a diligent search for other employment, but aside from a few weeks of unprofitable house-to-house canvassing nothing appeared. His family was in desperate straits, having had but one meal in three days, when the wife, reading our press notice, wrote me.

I got in touch at once with the superintendent of schools in the small city where the teacher and his family were then living, asked him to investigate the case, and if he found it as represented, to provide if possible work which would be of value to education for which payment could be made from our fund. The superintendent acted upon this request, stated that the situation was indeed desperate, and offered to furnish temporary employment in his office. Later substitute teaching was found, and at the end of the month the man was placed on the regular payroll as a teacher.

In another case, a teacher in a denominational college was thrown out of employment because the depleted college treasury necessitated a combination of departments and reduction of offerings. This teacher was living at the time close to one of the state universities. The dean of the school of education was asked to investigate the case. He reported that the teacher was in financial straits, that she seemed to be highly competent, and that he could put her at work in completing a rural school survey for which also the funds had been exhausted. He wrote later that the work had been completed, the teacher's financial distress at least temporarily relieved, and a real contribution made to the cause of education.

In many of the cases reported to the committee employment was found with drawing upon the temporary employment fund. The local communities took care of them once the need was brought to their attention. Several cases, too, proved on investigation to be of the "unemployable" type. Some of these were pitiable in the extreme, but the policy of the committee has been to use its funds only to provide work for the trained and efficient who were unemployed because of the depression, and especially to protect these teachers from the sting of asking for or accepting charity by actually employing them in work that will be of unquestioned value to education.

In every case except one, the employment for which payments were made from the fund covered a period of from four to eight weeks. In other words, practically all those aided from the fund soon found regular employment — which indicates fairly clearly that we were not providing doles for inefficient members of our guild. At the same time we were making it possible for these fellow-workers to maintain their self-respect and their professional pride during a critical period when their self-respect might easily have been sacrificed and their professional pride shattered.

In the one case in which a longer period of employment was paid for from our fund, a highly trained teacher, incapacitated for physical work, and the sole support of aged parents, was employed during the entire latter half of the year. He lived in one of the sections devastated by the drought. It was found that not far from his home, but in another state, was a junior high school literally crowded with pupils and very seriously understaffed on account of lack of funds. The principal was only too glad to have this teacher attached to his school, and the teacher rendered on the testimony of the principal most excellent service. The county board of education has requested me to convey to the association the deep and sincere gratitude of the community for helping them in a time of real need.

With the exception of a small amount paid to an unemployed teacher for addressing envelopes, the cost of administering the work of the committee has not been a charge upon the fund itself; nor has it been a charge upon other funds of the association nor upon the time of headquarters staff except that all contributions were received by and all payments made from Dr. Crabtree's office—the latter upon the recommendation of the chairman of the committee, who has assumed sole responsibility for the justification of all expenditures.

As has been suggested, the economic depression did not during the year just ended affect our profession in a profound way in so far as unemployment among experienced and successful teachers is concerned. It did hit us hard enough to inaugurate the little experiment in professional cooperation that I have just described and thus to suggest a possible way of meeting the problem if it should appear in the future in a more acute form and on a more extended scale.

What, then, are the prospects for the coming year? A few weeks ago I addressed an inquiry to the state superintendents and commissioners of education asking whether the number of teachers in the public schools would be likely to be decreased or increased during the coming year; and, if reductions were in prospect, how many teachers were likely to be thrown out of employment by combinations of classes, curtailment of programs and other "economy" measures.

I have received answers to this inquiry from forty-two states. In seventeen states a reduction of the total number of teachers employed is predicted. In most of these states, doubtless, this will be the first significant reduction in the number of teachers employed since the public schools got their first real start.

I asked for estimates of the number of teachers likely to be displaced in terms of ranges: fewer than 50, 50 to 100; 100 to 150, etc. Taking the aggregate of the lower ranges checked, it seems that in these seventeen states the total number of teachers whose contracts will not be renewed will be in the neighborhood of 4,000. I have reason to believe that these estimates are very conservative and may be safely taken as a reliable basis for any policies that the representative assembly may wish to consider regarding its possible responsibilities during the coming year. I should add that a very few states anticipate small increases in the teaching-personnel, but these may be disregarded, since few openings in these states are likely to be filled by displaced teachers from the states in which substantial decreases are predicted.

One can only guess at the proportion of these 4,000 displaced teachers who will need such assistance as an employment fund can provide, but it is clear enough that the number will be much larger than during the year just ended. A few of the state education associations have permanent welfare funds which might possibly be drawn upon to provide temporary employment for displaced teachers, but those fortunate associations are in states where serious unemployment is not predicted. Nor is transfer to other occupations likely to solve the problem, for the states in which unemployment among teachers is predicted are also the states in which the general problem of unemployment is likely to be the most serious.

If the representative assembly decides that the profession has a responsibility to discharge in connection with the situation that seems bound to arise during the coming year, I suggest that it consider the advisability of establishing what I may call an experimental welfare fund to be available during the coming year for meeting the needs which were met during the past year by the temporary employment fund and possibly for other welfare purposes. I suggest the designation, "experimental welfare fund," because it would be possible to determine through a year's experience whether it would be advisable for the association to have a permanent welfare fund. Such an experimental fund could be initiated without imposing a serious burden upon any member of the association. When the bills for annual dues are sent out in the fall, a request could be made that each member, if he is willing to do so, add to his remittance any sum from ten cents to one dollar as a contribution to this fund. An average contribution of five cents from each member would mean a fund of $10,000.

I am making this proposal merely as a personal suggestion and not as anything that represents a recommendation of the committee. I included in my letter to the state educational officials a question asking them whether they were or were not in favor of a permanent welfare fund for the National Education Association. Of the forty-two replying, sixteen were in favor of this policy, twenty-one were opposed and five were undecided.

The objections, in so far as reasons were given, were based in part upon the assumption that the just and honest administration of such a fund on a nation-wide basis would be impracticable, and in part upon the conviction that the problem is a state and local problem and not a national problem.

The first objection seems to be fairly met by the experience of the past year. It is not impossible to administer a national welfare fund for teachers both equitably and honestly, because in every case action can be guided by the investigations and advice of local educational officials of known responsibility. Payments were made from our temporary fund upon certification by responsible officials (1) that the application represented a real need for remunerative employment, (2) that neither state nor local educational unemployment or welfare funds were available for meeting the need, and (3) that employment of value to education could and would be found without displacing other workers. I believe that a larger fund could be administered in much the same way for unemployment and for other welfare purposes with a minimum of waste and injustice.

As to the contention that the problem is exclusively a state and local problem, it would appear that the experience of the past year in the general field of unemployment-relief supplies a convincing answer. President Hoover, who last year opposed national relief for unemployment, has recently approved a plan of cooperation between the Red Cross and local community chests which would involve the collection of a national fund and its distribution to the communities where relief is most needed. The fundamental principle back of a national welfare fund is, of course, one which the association has repeatedly indorsed with regard to the support of education.

One would not deny, of course, that the primary responsibility for unemployment relief and for other forms of welfare-service in our profession should rest with the state and local education associations. We have already seen, however, that few state associations have welfare funds, and, in addition to this, cases have been reported to our committee that such funds could not relieve. For example, a teacher living in a state in which she had never taught was seriously ill, penniless and with elderly parents dependent upon her for support. Her earlier teaching experience had been in four different states, and the most recent experience had been for a very short period. Which of these states should assume responsibility for her relief? This is a purely academic question, for in no one of the states did the state education association have the machinery to provide relief, but it illustrates clearly enough the function that a national welfare fund might justly and legitimately discharge.

The Pennsylvania State Education Association has a welfare fund by means of which it supports a teachers' home and provides annuities to the extent of $12,000 each year for retired teachers who, for one reason or another, do not come under the provisions of the state pension system. In so far as I know the Pennsylvania association is the only one that makes provisions of this sort. Such provisions are needed if a certain proportion of our fellow workers are to spend their declining years with a reasonable measure of comfort.

THE SIXTY-NINTH ANNUAL MEETING OF THE NATIONAL EDUCATION ASSOCIATION

By WILLIAM DOW BOUTWELL

EDITOR, OFFICE OF EDUCATION, DEPARTMENT OF THE INTERIOR

Father Junipero, founder of California missions, spent much of his life walking up and down the coast, and Californians have been going to conventions ever since.

So when it was announced that the sixty-ninth annual meeting of the National Education Association would be held in Los Angeles from June 27 to July 3, thousands prepared for a journey. They thronged the southern metropolis of Southern California. They clustered like bees around the National Education Association registration desk, using up all the ample supply of cards. They rolled up the largest attendance ever—16,500 registrants. Of these, 1,422 were delegates, some from California, the rest from all the states in the Union and many territories.

Rural education, the relation of business to education, and integration of all education were the three outstanding problems discussed at the meeting.

Out of the full day conference on rural education called jointly by the National Education Association, United States Commissioner of Education, William John Cooper, and the National Congress of Parents and Teachers, came a resolution asking the President to call a conference on rural problems comparable to the White House Conference on Child Health and Protection.

Speaker after speaker fastened attention on the educational handicaps suffered by the country boy or girl, although most of them recognized that the disabilities arise largely from the economic ills of agriculture. "The cards are stacked against the boys and girls of the countryside," declared President C. C. Swain, State Teachers College, Mayville, N. Dak., and, he added, "A sound educational policy can only rest upon a sound fiscal policy." To present aspects of this overshadowing conditioning factor of education in rural schools, the National Education Association enlisted for the program representatives from agencies outside the profession—Governor George H. Dern, of Utah, Mrs. Charles W. Sewell, American Farm Bureau Federation, M. C. Gay, representing the Federal Farm Board, and Clarence Poe, farm magazine editor—but these speakers did not successfully illuminate the dominant problems of rural education which, concededly, lie beyond schoolroom walls.

Mrs. Sewell urged the Brand Bill by which $100,000,000 in federal money for rural education would be matched by the states. She advocated this on the ground that "the Nation has long accepted the principle of Federal aid for highways as valid. In the same way Federal aid for our rural schools is valid." Educators on the program, hewing strictly to their own line, secondary though it was, brought more light to the problems of the conference. Agnes Samuelson, state superintendent of public instruction, Iowa, presented the surprising fact that because of the economic situation only one consolidated school has been organized in Iowa since 1923, although consolidation is strongly recommended as a solution of rural education deficiencies. Miss Florence Hale, state director of rural education in Maine, and new president of the National Education Association, asked for "adjustment of taxation and administrative units in such a way as to lead to the reorganization and enlargement of units so that . . . rural communities may provide both primary and secondary education for their children." Other speakers echoed the demand for larger rural school districts, although the practical political problems that such a course waits upon were not explored by the conference. Miss Samuelson set up a program for inquiry with five questions for research: (1) What should be the minimum educational program for every child in the state? (2) What will it cost? (3) What part of the burden should be borne by the local school district? (4) What should the state contribute? (5) Should the federal government contribute? If so, how much and on what basis?

One of the best received addresses of the conference, which was given by President Earl E. Harper, of Evansville College, Evansville, Indiana, was not limited to education in rural schools. Throwing off the robes of a prophet in which many National Education Association speakers array themselves, Dr. Harper contented himself with the task of reporting what young people think about. From records of hundreds of personal conferences he finds that "the overwhelming field of interest and question among high-school students is one which I call by a hyphenated name, 'vocational-educational.' I have found it utterly impossible to practically separate the educational interests of high-school youth from their vocational interests. Culture for culture's sake is not aspired to by many of our youth." Following in order of importance came, second, "socio-moral" questions "in ethics of social fellowship and in fundamental moral principles"; third, religious questions; fourth, athletics; fifth, personal deficiencies, complexes and emotional disturbances; sixth, general information, and seventh, art and music.

"Any one who fears that our youth are overwhelmingly obsessed by sordid considerations of sex may be relieved," the speaker declared. "There is a freedom, too often a license in thinking, talking and in acting in terms of sex interest which would be startling if we had not positively refused to be startled or shocked by anything. But on the whole this field of interest falls into a fairly normal place, altogether subordinate to others. . . . Abnormal influences and surroundings, abnormal stimuli and abnormal hours all have their tragic influence. But God help us to refuse to lose faith in our youth, individually or collectively, because when victimized by abnormal conditions they react exactly as any student of human nature should expect normal youths to react."

Depression and wide-spread retrenchments in teachers' salaries naturally brought education's relation to business to the fore. Yet here again the convention did not seem to come to grips with fundamental facts. Most speakers for education demanded that investments for education be maintained in face of financial difficulties, resting their case on emotional appeals. Speakers for business made the usual request that what they want is schools that will turn out boys and girls with common sense, whatever that is. United States Commissioner of Education William John Cooper summoned pertinent facts to show the close relation of the growth of the American market and the elimination of illiteracy. One of his observations deserves especially wide attention. "School people," the commissioner declared, "have been self-critical because some business men succeeded despite little schooling. Perhaps business would not be in such a bad state at the present moment if its leaders had had a little more education."

Superintendent A. L. Threlkeld, of Denver, renewed the demand for a more equitable system of taxation geared to modern conditions.

Since the convention met in Los Angeles it was natural that a representative of the motion picture industry appear before the National Education Association. Carl E. Milliken, associate of Mr. Will Hays, spoke on Monday night when various stars were introduced to a capacity audience. He invited the National Education Association to establish a previewing committee to consider educational aspects of pictures, a committee comparable to the one established by the American Library Association and other national organizations. "We will provide the projection room, show you the pictures," said Mr. Milliken, "and let you decide for yourselves which pictures fit normally into your program." Recent controversy between certain national organizations and Mr. Hays' organization lent added interest to Mr. Milliken's exposition of the motion picture industry's methods of "cooperating with national agencies."

President Sutton's interest in integrating all education prompted him to include many unusual features in the convention program. At the first session representatives of various fields of education described the contributions of particular institutions. Dr. George D. Strayer, of Columbia University, spoke for the public schools; Colonel Thomas A. Davis, president of the San Diego Army and Navy Academy, for the private schools; Sister M. Raphael, of the Catholic University of America, Washington, D. C., for the parochial schools; William J. Hutchins, president of Berea College, Berea, Ky., on the college, and Mary Yost, of Stanford University, on the university. Speaking on the subject of integration in his major address, President Sutton said: "Too often the college is railing at the high school; too often the high schools, forgetting the arduous duties of the elementary schools, are complaining that children are not sent up properly prepared. There is a lack of coordinating force to educate a child. The church and the community, the extra-curricular activities engaged in through the Y. M. C. A., Y. W. C. A., Boy Scouts, Girl Scouts, and other activities, need to understand the character-building power of these agencies. . . . When will America learn that the making of a life is much more important than the learning of a subject? How many teachers dealing with your boy and mine are putting a patch, so to speak, on his educational garment. Just as a child is required to stand an examination of proficiency in any subject, so each teacher that takes over a child should be given an examination in what he knows about the background of a child's life including his individual life, his heredity, and the life of the race."

Dr. Sutton is also interested in the establishment of a department of student activities in the National Education Association, "where boys and girls and college men and women coming together under the guidance and direction of educators, administrators and teachers may really integrate education in such a way that the mother and father in the home, the club and scout leader in the community, the teacher in the school, and the student from kindergarten to college, all working together shall really make an integrated program of education."

As an opening gun in the movement to establish this department one morning program was given over to young men and women students, a refreshing innovation. Herschel Langdon, a student from the University of Iowa, was frequently applauded when he spoke on "What I Would Do If I Were a College President."

Many others speakers of note addressed the convention. Dr. William C. Bagley, of Columbia University, departing from his listed topic, gave the report of the committee on unemployment which, during the past year, has aided many qualified and able teachers until they were able to get permanently reestablished. William McAndrew, associate editor, SCHOOL AND SOCIETY, urged teachers to be more outspoken in the cause of good government. "When I ask intending teachers what they do if crooks are nominated for office in their home town," he said, "I am told that they do nothing. Why not? With all the ridicule heaped on teachers for talkativeness, foolish investments, and other things, let us not, in God's name, have the added slur that we are cowards."

The campaign to save part of the air rights for schools, which is led by Joy Elmer Morgan, editor of the *Journal of the National Education Association*, is receiving increased attention. His constant and impetuous attack on the almost exclusive use of radio for advertising purposes, which he renewed at Los Angeles, seems to be arousing educators to the crisis in this field, and it is commanding much space in newspapers.

Miss Florence Hale was unanimously elected president of the National Education Association, a selection which assures that the interest which President Sutton generated in problems of the rural schools will be continued. Walter R. Siders, for years chairman of the board of trustees, was replaced by E. G. Doudan, secretary, State Board of Normal School Regents, Wisconsin. Joseph Rosier, president of the Fairmont State Normal School, Fairmont, W. Va., was reelected to the executive committee. It was decided tentatively that the next meeting would be held in Atlantic City.

Afternoons were given over as usual to meetings of the various departments, allied organizations and conferences, numbering 39 in all. Relatively small attendance at some of these sessions can be accounted for by the enthusiasm of Los Angeles hospitality and Los Angeles sunshine. Sixteen departments held meetings; Adult Education, Business Education, Classroom Teachers, Deans of Women, Elementary School Principals, Kindergarten-Primary Education, Lip Reading, Rural Education, School Health and Physical Education, Secondary School Principals, Science Instruction, Social Studies, Supervisors and Directors of Instruction, Supervisors and Teachers of Home Economics, Visual Instruction and Vocational Education. A conference on special education was called with the object of forming a new department of the National Education Association.

Six conferences were held. Some of the following represent interests that are strong in West Coast education circles: Art education, citizenship, thrift and conservation, American Library Association and the National Education Association, student participation in school government, and a Pan American Conference which concerned itself especially with Mexico.

The National Council of Education met on the two days prior to the convention. Other allied organizations which held sessions were: The American Classical League, Counselors Association of Southern California, National Association of Journalism Advisers, National Commission on the Enrichment of Adult Life, National Congress of Parents and Teachers, National Council of Administrative Women in Education, National Council of Geography Teachers, National Council of Teachers of English, National Federation of Modern Language Teachers, the National Geographic Society (an illustrated lecture, "The Geography of the Stars"), National League of Teachers Associations, National Secondary Education Association, National Vocational Guidance Association and the School Garden Association of America.

The airy hall housing exhibits was thronged at all times. On the main floor were exhibits of commercial companies and national agencies; on the balcony elaborate and impressive exhibits of the activities of Los Angeles schools. Cost of express and freight to the West Coast, limitations on book sales arising from California's state text-book laws and other factors brought some gaps in the regular roster of firms exhibiting. Their places were taken by Los Angeles business houses. The presses of Stanford and Chicago universities combined to present an unusually impressive display. Oxford University Press was there, too. University publishing is a trend of higher education growing yearly in importance. A novel globe introduced at the convention has the world's cities in fine print on a roll of paper within the shell. A fixed magnifying glass permits the user to read the city's longitude and latitude, turn the globe and find the location.

The report adopted by the committee

appointed for the National Conference on Rural Education was as follows:

The First National Conference on Rural Education, called jointly by the National Education Association, the United States Office of Education and the National Congress of Parents and Teachers, meeting in Los Angeles, California, on July 2, 1931, believes:

That a wholesome and happy rural life is fundamentally essential to the highest social, economic and political achievement of America. It believes that the foundation for such a life can be found only in adequate education and cultural opportunities for both children and adults in farm communities.

This conference believes that the problems of rural education are so far-reaching and difficult as to require for their solution the combined efforts of many lay and professional agencies.

This conference recommends that there be held in the nation's capital a national conference on rural education and culture, following the general plan of the White House Conference on Child Health and Protection; that this national conference be followed by similar state conferences to be arranged by the governors in cooperation with the educational agencies and organizations of the various states.

This First National Conference on Rural Education recommends that the president of the National Education Association, in cooperation with other agencies, appoint a committee to take up this project with the President of the United States, to the end that there may be a vigorous nation-wide campaign for equal opportunity for rural children and the development of an adequate rural culture in America.

JOSEPH ROSIER, *chairman*
AGNES SAMUELSON
CLARENCE POE
GEORGE H. DERN
KATE WOFFORD

Resolutions adopted by the convention are as follows:

The National Education Association, in its sixty-ninth annual convention in the City of Los Angeles, California, July 3, 1931, reaffirms its belief that the foundation of the nation is the education of its youth and that a democracy can attain its full fruition only when each of its members is trained to the highest level of his intelligence. To this end the National Education Association commends to the nation thoughtful consideration of the following statements of policy:

I. FINANCING AND SCHOOLS

In the United States the continuous maintenance of an efficient public school system is fundamental. To cripple the schools financially, even for a year or two, means a serious loss in school morale, in educational leadership, in qualified teachers, and in the quality of our future citizenship. The present economic depression should strengthen our determination to fit the new generation to solve future economic problems.

1. *State and Education:* The state should provide from public funds a system of free schools extending from the kindergarten through the university and open to every child.

2. *Taxes and School Support:* Financing the public schools requires a system of taxation which is equitable, wide in its application, and which establishes a fair balance between direct and indirect taxes. Better support of progressive education is largely dependent upon the study and revision of our present tax systems. Continued research should be made to find the best sources of support for schools. The National Education Association commends the study of school finance now being undertaken by the Office of Education under the authorization of Congress. Legislation initiating and revising systems of taxation which will provide adequate support for public schools should follow such findings.

3. *Federal Aid for Education:* Funds should be provided by the Federal Government to assist the states in making available to every child a basic education, in equalizing educational opportunities, in meeting the many acute problems of rural education, and in preventing the interruption of education during floods, droughts and other widespread emergencies.

4. *Budgets and Salaries:* The National Education Association condemns ill-considered cuts in school budgets, reductions in teachers' salaries or other shortsighted policies advocated because of the present economic depression, realizing that education is the basis of our national wealth and of our economic and social stability.

II. CURRICULA

The curricula should take into account the aptitudes, attitudes and abilities of individuals on the different levels of attainment and should provide opportunities for training and growth in vocational and cultural subjects.

1. *Health Education:* Adequate provision should be made for physical and mental health in accordance with the conclusions of the White House Conference on Child Health and Protection—to the end that habits of clean and wholesome living

may be developed in childhood and youth. Schools should continue to emphasize the evil effects on the human organism of alcohol and of tobacco and other narcotics.

2. *Character Education:* Character education should be a major objective in education. The activities of the school should be fully utilized for character training and in securing law observance and intelligent participation in public affairs.

3. *Law Observance:* The National Education Association reaffirms its stand in favor of the eighteenth amendment and of the laws enacted thereunder. It argues their vigorous and impartial enforcement and pledges its support to an active educational campaign in the schools in behalf of habits of living for which the eighteenth amendment stands.

4. *Special Education:* The National Education Association believes that exceptional and handicapped children should receive the special care that their condition requires. A survey by the Office of Education as to the needs of these handicapped children would provide the basis for an adequate educational program.

5. *Rural Education:* The National Education Association recognizes the necessity of providing educational opportunities for children in urban centers and the pressing need for a revision of the rural school curriculum to meet the needs of rural life to-day. The association urges the government to make, through the Office of Education, a thorough study of rural education throughout the nation.

6. *Vocational Education and Guidance:* As a measure for the conservation of human energy, the National Education Association recommends that school programs provide for vocational education and guidance, the study of occupations, and a placement service for those who leave school to become wage earners.

7. *Adult Education:* Ample opportunities should be provided for adults to remedy deficiencies in their education, to develop personal talents, to improve their vocational efficiency, and to enrich the cultural aspects of life.

8. *Education by Radio:* The National Education Association believes that legislation should be enacted which will safeguard, for the uses of education and government, a reasonable share of the radio broadcasting channels of the United States.

III. Teachers

The primary purpose of all education is to provide for the children of America the best possible training for good citizenship and for happy and successful living. Since this training depends almost entirely on the teachers, the fundamental thing in providing adequate education is to set up conditions which will secure and train most effectively the best teachers.

1. *Standards:* The National Education Association recommends that requirements for beginning teachers be immediately increased in all states. Trained teachers are now available in sufficient numbers to offer an unusual opportunity to reach the goal of four years training beyond the four years high school—the minimum standard recommended by this association for all teachers.

2. *Teachers and the Profession:* All teachers, regardless of position or title, are workers in a common cause. The public as well as the teachers should be interested in improving the status of the profession through appropriate legislation and higher professional standards. The growing tendency to permit initiative and independent action by teachers is commendable.

3. *Teacher Training and Certification:* Upon the preparation of each teacher depends the ultimate success of education. It is important that teacher training opportunities be adequate, rich in content and practical in application.

4. *Retirement Systems:* Legislative provisions for sound teacher retirement systems are essential to efficiency in public school systems.

5. *Salaries of Teachers:* The compensation of teaching should be adequate in order to attract and hold in the service men and women of marked ability and thorough training.

6. *Tenure of Service:* The National Education Association believes teachers should hold their positions during competence and good behavior. The association favors the enactment of tenure laws which will protect teachers from discharge for political, personal, religious, or any unjust reasons, but which will not prevent the dismissal of teachers for incompetency, immorality or unprofessional conduct.

IV. Federal Relations

Education is a state and local function. The product of education is good citizenship, but citizenship is national, not local. The Federal Government is, therefore, vitally concerned in the product of education.

1. *Qualifications for Citizenship:* The ability to read and write English understandingly and a general knowledge of the history and principles of the United States Government should be made qualifications for citizenship.

2. *Department of Education:* The Federal Government should aid the states and localities to

equalize educational opportunities through the dissemination of authentic information scientifically evaluated by experts. This service can best be rendered by a department of education with a place in the Cabinet of the President. Until such a department is established, the National Education Association recommends that the funds and authority of the Office of Education be materially augmented to the end that its efforts may be increasingly effective.

V. EDUCATION AND INTERNATIONAL RELATIONSHIPS

Realizing that science and invention are every day bringing each nation closer and closer to its neighbors, we recognize the imperative need of a clear understanding of the problems of each nation by the people of every other nation, for the problems of one nation may vitally affect all nations.

1. *Relations in Education:* We favor the exchange of students and professors, the formation of international education associations, and the holding of international education conferences, for all these promote world understanding, friendship, cooperation and peace.

2. *World Federation of Education Associations:* The National Education Association commends the activities of the World Federation of Education Associations and heartily indorses its program for world understanding as outlined in the Biennial Conference at Geneva in 1929.

3. *Pact of Paris and the World Court:* The National Education Association recommends that the Pact of Paris be taught in the schools and favors the accession of the United States to the Permanent Court of International Justice under the terms of the protocols now awaiting approval by the Senate of the United States.

VI. OBSERVANCES

The National Education Association urges the continued observance of American Education Week, and of International Good Will Day, May 18. The association recommends that the schools participate in the nation-wide observance of the 200th anniversary of the birth of George Washington, and the 150th anniversary of the surrender at Yorktown.

TO LOS ANGELES

The National Education Association acknowledges the many courtesies and the hospitality of the citizens of Los Angeles and sunny California. We extend our special thanks to Superintendent Bouelle, the educational staff, of the city, the teachers and pupils, the Boy Scouts of America, the press, the broadcasting studio, KFI, and others who have cooperated in making successful the 69th annual convention of the National Education Association.

JOSEPH H. SAUNDERS, *Chairman*
EDITH LOUISE GROSVENOR, *Secretary*

EDUCATIONAL EVENTS

PHYSICAL AND PSYCHOLOGICAL EXAMINATION OF SCHOOL CHILDREN

THE Belgian correspondent of the *Journal* of the American Medical Association reports that at the recent meeting of the Congress of the International Association for the Protection of Children a resolution was adopted to the effect that in all institutions of learning a physiological and mental examination of all pupils or students be made and that record cards be employed for the classification of the pupils. As regards the physical examination, in the large cities and the important communes it is desirable that school inspection be entrusted to physicians who devote themselves exclusively to the work. Where the number of schools and of school children justify the outlay, a woman physician should be designated for the kindergartens and the girls' schools. Visiting school nurses, with the aid of the instructional corps and, if need be, of a teacher, male or female, especially delegated, will give emergency aid in small matters, including the application of certain treatments prescribed by the school physician, or the specialists will take the children to the offices of whatever children's society is indicated. The nurses will discover the existence of contagious disorders, will make social inquiries and will keep in touch with the parents. It is desirable that the record books shall be of adequate size so that they can be utilized from the day the child enters the day nursery up to the time he finishes his studies, and, if possible, up to the time of entering the military service, so far as the boys are concerned. The health record book should furnish at least the following information and should call attention to everything that is abnormal: administrative information, date of birth, occupation of the parents, schools attended; also information on the pupil's antecedents: composition of the family, stages of physiologic and mental development, vaccinations, diseases and accidents; results of physiologic examinations pertaining to weight, the sitting height, the chest girth, the mouth, the teeth, the nose, the throat; the respiratory, digestive, urinary and genital apparatus (puberty), the skeletal system, the spinal column, the nervous system, hernia, skin, scalp, endocrine disorders, and general condition of the blood.

As concerns the mental and pedagogic examination: I. Mental examination: It is desirable that all pupils entering the school and also any pupils who have any trouble with their studies should be examined from the standpoint of their mental aptitudes. II. Pedagogic examination: It is desirable that the pedagogic examination shall consist of standardized tests adapted to each country and taking account of the pupil's previous program of studies so that exact comparisons may be made with respect to the grade of scholarship attained by the pupils. The record card on which the results of the mental and the pedagogic tests are recorded should be of such a nature that the information thereon can be utilized not only with regard to the pedagogic measures to be adopted but also with reference to decisions in connection with vocational guidance.

EDUCATIONAL BROADCASTING

MORE than 10 per cent. of the "time on the air" of American broadcasting stations is devoted to programs which they construe to be educational in character, according to a survey made by Federal Radio Commissioner Harold A. Lafount, on the basis of questionnaires sent to the entire roster of stations.

Based on returns from 522 stations of the 605 licensed as of February 1, 1931, the tabulation shows that 3,457 hours and 50 minutes were devoted to educational programs during the week from January 11 to 17, inclusive, selected by the commissioner for the survey. The stations were on the air for 33,785 hours and 45 minutes during that week.

Of the 51 licensed educational stations, the survey shows that 42 replied to the questionnaire. These stations broadcast an aggregate of 286 hours and 9 minutes of programs considered entirely educational, out of 1,027 hours on the air, according to the survey.

Nine questions were asked, the totals representing an average of the answers of the 522 stations to each question. The first question was as to the number of hours used in broadcasting educational data from studios. The educational stations responded that a total of 128 hours and 18 minutes was used for this purpose, while all the stations reporting showed a total of 1,007 hours and two minutes.

The number of hours used in broadcasting programs originating in educational institutions aggregated 431 hours and 33 minutes during the week for the entire group of 522 stations. Stations operated by educational institutions reported 70 hours and 1 minute.

A total of 2,021 hours and 32 minutes was utilized during the week in broadcasting other data considered educational, but not necessarily broadcast by professional educators. Of this total, educational stations broadcast 89 hours and 50 minutes.

The total of these three items showed the figure of 3,457 hours and 50 minutes for the broadcasting of educational data. Of this total the educational stations contributed 286 hours and nine minutes.

For the broadcasting of data prepared or supplied by the Federal Government, 741 hours and 15 minutes were devoted. Educational stations broadcast 50 hours and 30 minutes of this total. The time used in broadcasting data provided by city, county and state agencies was 390 hours and 6 minutes, of which 23 hours and 16 minutes were broadcast by the educational stations.

A total of 792 hours and 23 minutes was devoted to the broadcasting of speeches of general character. Educational stations contributed 46 hours and 17 minutes to this total.

The largest single total was that of hours used in broadcasting classical music, which totaled 5,782 hours and 40 minutes. The 42 educational stations broadcast 200 hours and nine minutes of such programs.

Time devoted during the week to broadcasting for the Red Cross, Community Chest and similar organizations was 469 hours and 56 minutes. The educational stations devoted 14 hours and 45 minutes for such programs.

PUBLIC EDUCATION IN ARKANSAS

A RECENT dispatch to the *New York Times* states that education in Arkansas has greatly improved during the past year. About $4,000,000 has been spent on public-school buildings alone; the organization of the system has been improved; school revenues have been increased, and a survey of all Arkansas public schools has been made for the purpose of working out a plan providing standard elementary and high school advantages for every child in the state. So marked has been the improvement in Arkansas that Dr. William John Cooper, U. S. Commissioner of Education, recently characterized the report of the State Department of Education as "the most promising item of school news which I have encountered during the course of the depression."

Since almost 80 per cent. of its school population is rural, Arkansas is now waging an active campaign against the one-room schoolhouse. Rural school facilities have been consolidated and modernized, and numerous additions made. During the past year 110 consolidated country schools have been built in sixty of the state's seventy-five counties. The value of public school property in 1930 reached a total of $35,000,000 as compared with $17,400,000 in 1920.

How seriously the state has entered on its campaign is seen in the levies made to supply the additional funds. All proceeds from the sale of state lands, income taxes, tobacco dealer licenses, cigarette and cigar taxes, slot machines and professional licenses have been appropriated for an auxiliary fund, which represents an annual increase of about $1,000,000 to the regular fund of about $9,500,000, and $2,000,000 has been raised to pay delinquent salaries.

Arkansas school laws have been revised and simplified. Special school elections are now held entirely apart from political elections. Types of school districts have been reduced from seven to one and every rural school district is now included in a high school territory.

Hand in hand with the effort at improvement, also, has been an effort to help more children take advantage of the facilities. Since 1925 the number of buses operated in transporting rural children to school has increased from 108 to 1,508, and the number of school children receiving free transportation has risen from 3,000 to approximately 50,000.

The length of school terms for both white and Negro children in Arkansas has been increased, until about three fourths of the public schools now have a nine-month term. The public high-school enrolment has grown more than 60 per cent. during the past five years. In 1930 it reached a total of 40,535 as compared with 5,684 in 1910. The number of students graduated from the high schools last spring was greater than the total high-school enrolment twenty years ago.

COURSES IN MENTAL HEALTH AT TEACHER TRAINING INSTITUTIONS

A MARKED increase in mental hygiene activity in teacher training institutions throughout the United States is reported by Dr. Charles E. Benson, of the School of Education, New York University, who has completed a nation-wide survey of the subject for the National Committee for Mental Hygiene.

Questionnaires were sent to 205 teachers' colleges, state normal schools, city normal schools and private teacher-training institutions, and the large majority of the 239 who replied reported instruction in some phase of mental hygiene in the curriculum.

A very large percentage (80.7 per cent.) report that the subject is presented in some form in connection with various courses. Fifty-two (21.7 per cent.) of the 239 institutions offer a regular course in mental hygiene. Fifty-six (23.4 per cent.) have special lectures in mental hygiene. One hundred and eighty-eight (78.6 per cent.) offer regular courses in mental testing. Sixty-three (23.3 per cent.) offer courses on mentally defective, backward or problem children. The survey indicates that in the large majority of teacher-training institutions the work in mental hygiene is under the direction of the department of psychology or in connection with work in psychology. In a number it is a part of the general health program.

Thirteen (5.4 per cent.) report that they have

a psychiatrist in connection with their institutions or available for their students. Thirty-two (13.4 per cent.) state that they have a mental-hygiene clinic in connection with their institution or available for their students.

Comparison with a previous survey shows that there has been marked progress in the work in mental hygiene in teacher-training institutions during the past ten years and a rapid growth of interest in the subject and its possibilities. While very few institutions reported regular work in mental hygiene in 1920, 92 institutions now report regular courses or special lectures relating to this subject.

The states that have the greatest number of teacher-training institutions emphasizing mental hygiene by course or lecture are New York, with 16; Massachusetts, with 8; Pennsylvania, with 5; California, Connecticut and Illinois, with 4 each, and Minnesota, New Jersey, Ohio, Oklahoma, Tennessee and Virginia, with 3 each.

The states that have a low percentage of teacher-training institutions emphasizing mental hygiene in proportion to the number reporting are Alabama, Maine, Missouri, Nebraska, North Dakota, Washington and Wisconsin.

The survey also finds that in previous years emphasis in the work in mental hygiene in the field of education was upon the abnormal child and his difficulties. Since then the point of view has considerably broadened, and the major aim to-day is to keep the normal child normal.

INVESTIGATION OF SITES AND SUPPLIES OF THE NEW YORK CITY SCHOOLS

THE New York City Board of Education, at a special meeting called by its president, Dr. George J. Ryan, on July 20, received information from its special committee recently appointed to investigate the letting of repair contracts, and ordered the immediate suspension of seven inspectors who had been questioned by the committee. The inspectors will be tried on departmental charges to be prepared at once by the corporation counsel.

According to the report in the *New York Times,* Mr. Leonard M. Wallstein, special corporation counsel investigating impropriety in the city's acquisitions of school sites, questioned Joseph Horowitz on his ability to foretell where schools were to be built. His explanation was that he merely guessed and bought parcels suitable for school sites. Real estate men who have testified as experts for the city in condemnation matters have been examined.

The special committee's exposure last month of "irregularities" carried on in the board's Bronx Bureau of Construction and Maintenance already had resulted in the indictment and surrender of six contractors and a Board of Education clerk, who was alleged to have admitted receiving at least $20,000 in "gratuities."

The report which the board has now received and approved said that "the evidence indicates that the practice confessed by Grossman was not confined to the clerical staff of the Bronx, nor to clerks alone." It went on to say: "It shows that, excepting the Borough of Richmond, where work of this character is comparatively negligible, and where the investigation has not yet been concluded, payments were regularly made by contractors of furniture repair to certain of the clerical staff in practically every other borough, these payments varying from 5 per cent. upward on the contract price."

The report, together with almost 1,000 pages of testimony taken in the five-borough inquiry, was presented to the board by Louis S. Posner, head of the investigating committee. Commissioners Arthur S. Somers and C. C. Mollenhauer are the other members of the committee. Five of the seven members who were present immediately voted the adoption of a resolution approving it and requesting the corporation counsel to draw up charges against the seven inspectors.

Most of the payments to clerks and inspectors, it was explained by Mr. Posner, were made by contractors in consideration of their confining invitations to bids on "tissue specifications" to the contractors' ring and in consideration of a speedy and not too exacting inspection of the repair work when completed. "Tissue specifications" are for contracts involving less than $1,000, for which public letting is not necessary under the law. While most of the "gratuities" in those cases were so-called "small graft," which, however, might have great cumulative value, the report showed that there were several instances of contracts let by advertised competitive bidding, in which "testimony shows that 5 per cent. was paid to the inspector in charge of the work covered by such competitive contracts." This type of contract sometimes runs into tens of thousands of dollars.

The ring of contractors are said to have carried on their part of the system in a business-like manner, with private meetings and a treasurer who acted as the go-between to pay the city employees in cash for their favors.

CHICAGO'S NEW EXPERIMENTAL SCHOOL

TAKING advantage of the greater freedom from traditional routine which is practicable in vacation schools, Superintendent William J. Bogan arranged that the new Lewis-Champlin Experimental School should open on July 1 as one of the city's vacation schools, and hold its first sessions during the summer. A special committee of the Superintendent's Advisory Council has aided in planning the scope and program for the new school.

Through contributions from interested citizens and the cooperation of civic organizations an excellent beginning has been made toward furnishing special equipment and services beyond those available to the regular city schools. Besides the six classroom teachers and three special teachers of the vacation school, there will be a year-around home and community worker, a psychometrist, and a recreation worker. The summer session will also have a nurse, doctor, trained librarian, accompanist, clerical assistant and other special services.

Excursions will be an important feature of the school program. During the first week various grades visited the Field Museum, the Chicago Historical Society, the Old Fort Dearborn Replica, built for the Century of Progress Exhibition, and the Municipal Airport, where in their study of transportation they witnessed the landing and unloading of mail planes.

The Lewis-Champlin School has been placed under the supervision of Assistant Superintendent James E. McDade. Before organizing the school Mrs. Edna R. Meyers, the principal, spent a month visiting progressive schools throughout the country. The school has been equipped for a modern activity program, and will carry on its work throughout the year, with the purpose of developing curricula and procedures which will be applicable to the regular work of the city school system.

THE TENT COLONY OF THE UNIVERSITY OF WISCONSIN

REPRESENTING states from New York to Oregon and from South Dakota to Kentucky, 64 families, consisting of approximately 200 persons, including about 60 children, have established their summer homes at the University of Wisconsin summer-school tent colony.

Seventeen states are represented in the 1931 tent colony, which is located on the shore of Lake Mendota, about three miles west of the university. With 19 families present, Wisconsin leads all other states in residents at the colony.

Other states represented and the number of families from them are: Ohio, eight; Illinois, five; Indiana, four; Iowa, Kansas, Nebraska, Michigan, Minnesota and Pennsylvania, each three; Kentucky, Missouri and New York, each two; and Idaho, Oregon, South Dakota and Wyoming, each one.

Combining their pursuit of higher education at the university with the pleasures that are afforded them as residents of the colony, the colonists have completed the organization of their little lake-shore village, and have settled down for the summer.

Fathers and in many cases mothers are not the only ones who attend classes while residents. From the ages of three and up, the children residents of the camp learn to swim under the instruction of a life-guard, provided by the university. Classes in nature lore, woodcraft and scout-craft are also conducted by various members of the camp.

Founded in 1912 by Dean Scott H. Goodnight, director of the summer session, the colony during its early years consisted only of four tents and but few male inhabitants. At that time, gasoline launches took the campers across the lake to their classes.

During the next nine years the colony slowly expanded, with Madison students largely occupying the living quarters. Then the colony suddenly gained popularity. In 1921 only three women were included among the residents. One year later the female population had increased to five, and since 1923 the population has been made up almost entirely of families.

With the growing demand for reservations in recent years, registration in the colony has been limited to out-of-town school men of small incomes, and their families. Organized under a pseudo city government with the offices of mayor, alderman, city clerk, sheriff and treasurer delegated to various members annually, the camp is designed as an individualistic enterprise in which the campers furnish their own transportation facilities and equipment, and do their own housekeeping.

LIBRARY OF THE UNIVERSITY OF KENTUCKY

The University of Kentucky has completed its new library at a cost of over $400,000. The building is fireproof, of Georgian architecture, and consists of four floors and basement. The stack section is in a separate portion of the building and has eight levels. In the various reading, browsing and seminar rooms, seats are provided for more than 500 persons. A total of 200,000 books can be contained within the present structure with ease. A staff of 15 full time and 20 student employees is necessary to properly man the building.

The basement of the structure consists of various service rooms including work rooms, rooms for preparing books for the bindery, janitors' rooms, and a fireproof vault for rare and autographed publications as well as first editions.

The first floor contains a large main lobby which will be used as a museum for rare books, coins, etc. Glass wall cases will house poster displays and announcements of new books. A check room off of this lobby will be maintained for the convenience of visitors. To the west of the main lobby is the reserve reading room and to the east is the periodical reading room. At the present time about 750 periodicals are regularly received by the University of Kentucky Library.

On the second floor is another fair sized lobby containing the loan desk and the general card index files. Back of the loan desk is the main entrance of the stacks. To the north of this lobby, a long room illuminated with soft indirect lights, and upholstered in restful overstuffed furniture is set aside as a browsing room, a location where students and faculty can relax, help themselves to the books on the shelves at will, and read for the sheer pleasure of it. This browsing room gives a fine view of an expanse of campus in front of the building. The east wing on this floor contains the offices of the employees of the library, bibliography room, cataloging department, as well as another storage vault. The office of Mrs. W. T. Lafferty, in charge of women's club work throughout the state, is also in this section. The west wing on this floor is used as the main reading room.

On the third floor, a balcony partially encircles the main reading room, the desk lobby, and the browsing room extend up two stories. This floor, however, has a classroom and a study room with individual desks for those studying library science.

The fourth floor will be used as a graduate floor. One entire room will house the Carnegie Art Library and another room will be given over to a medical collection. Numerous seminar rooms will be available.

Ninety individual study booths or carrels have been constructed in the stacks for members of the faculty and advanced students who must do research with a large number of books at hand. Permits will be issued to those allowed to use these carrels. An automatic elevator and booklift gives service to all floors of this building. Cork floors are used throughout. A special system of stairways behind the stacks are available for employees, and rest rooms are conveniently located throughout the building. It is planned to place in the building portraits of past presidents and faculty members of the university.

EDUCATIONAL NOTES AND NEWS

Josephine A. Rathbone, vice-director of the Pratt Institute School of Library Science, Brooklyn, has been elected president of the American Library Association for 1931–32. Other new officers are: Charles E. Rush, Yale University Library, New Haven, Connecticut, *first vice-president;* Beatrice Winser, Public Library, Newark, New Jersey, *second vice-*

president; Matthew S. Dudgeon, Public Library, Milwaukee, Wisconsin, *treasurer,* and George Woodruff, Chicago, *trustee of endowment funds.*

PHILLIP COATES KING has been named president of Washburn College, Topeka, Kansas, where for the past year he has been associate president.

DR. CHARLES L. WALLACE, for twenty-five years an active leader in the North Dakota Conference of the Methodist Episcopal Church, has been elected to succeed Dr. Edward P. Robertson as president of Wesley College at Grand Forks, North Dakota.

PROFESSOR EMERY FILBEY, assistant to President Robert M. Hutchins, of the University of Chicago, will become acting vice-president and dean of the faculties in the absence of Vice-president Frederic Woodward, who will be abroad as a member of a mission inquiry commission during the coming academic year.

DR. THOMAS S. GATES, president of the University of Pennsylvania, has been given the degree of doctor of laws by Dickinson College.

W. LELAND THOMPSON, member of the board of regents of the University of the State of New York, has received the honorary degree of LL.D. from the Rensselaer Polytechnic Institute, Troy, New York.

AT the commencement exercises of the College of Wooster the honorary degree of doctor of science was conferred on Professor C. G. Williams, director of the Ohio Agricultural Experiment Station.

THE Roumanian Government has honored President Robert Johns Trevorrow, of the Centenary Collegiate Institute, with the Order of the Crown of Roumania in the degree of commander. This was conferred in recognition of services rendered in connection with the relations existing between Roumania and the United States.

DR. HOMER A. WATT, chairman of the English department of the Washington Square College, New York University, has been honored with the diploma and decoration, Order of St. Sava IV, by King Alexander I, of Jugoslavia, for his work as a member of the Serbian Educational Commission.

DR. SAMUEL W. STRATTON, chairman of the corporation of the Massachusetts Institute of Technology, formerly director of the Bureau of Standards, celebrated his seventieth birthday on July 18.

DR. PIERCE BUTLER, associated with the Newberry Library in Chicago for the past fifteen years, will become professor of library science in the Graduate Library School of the University of Chicago. He will teach courses in the history of printing, the problems of librarianship and the history of scholarship.

DR. PAUL H. VIETH has resigned from the International Council of Religious Education, which he has served as superintendent of educational administration and director of research for the past six years, to become associate professor of religious education in the Divinity School of Yale University.

PROFESSOR EARL E. CUMMINS is leaving Wooster College to accept the position of professor of economics at Union College, Schenectady, New York.

DR. RAYMOND MYLAR MOSHER has resigned from the University of Idaho to accept the position of professor of psychology at the State College at San Jose, California.

DR. FRANCIS DUMONT has been appointed professor of French and head of the Romance language department at the Pennsylvania State College.

DR. HAROLD H. SPROUT, who has been acting assistant professor of political science at Stanford University for the past two years, has accepted a position in the department of politics at Princeton University.

MISS MILDRED LEWIS, formerly Kentucky state supervisor of music, has been appointed instructor of music at the University of Kentucky.

AT a recent meeting of the State Board of Education of Arkansas, Mr. C. M. Hirst, state superintendent of public instruction, resigned and was unanimously elected commissioner of education by the state board. The recodification law enacted at the last session of the legislature abolished the office of state superintendent and created that of commissioner. The *Journal of Arkansas Education,* in announcing this change, says: "For the first time in history, Arkansas has a commissioner of education selected by the state board on the basis of fitness for the position rather than a superintendent who was elected as other political offices are filled."

DR. GEORGE J. MOHR has been appointed director of the new Child Guidance Clinic of Pittsburgh.

MRS. GLADYS SPEARIN, of Fort Fairfield, Missouri, has been appointed field representative for rural schools for the State of Maine.

CARL H. MILAM, secretary of the American Library Association, has been reelected to membership on the executive board of the National Advisory Council on Radio in Education, for a term expiring on June 30, 1934.

DR. CHARLES H. GRANDGENT, professor of Romance Languages at Harvard University, and exchange professor to France for the second half of the academic year 1930–31, gave an address at the Hôtel de Ville, Paris, on June 18, as representative of the American universities at the celebration of the four hundredth anniversary of the Collège de France. He completed in May a course of public lectures at the Sorbonne on "Le Théâtre Américain contemporain."

DR. HARRY ALLEN OVERSTREET, head of the department of philosophy of the College of the City of New York, will give a series of three public lectures this summer at the University of California. The lectures and dates are announced as follows: Monday, August 24, "Building a Modern Mind"; Wednesday, August 26, "The Foundations of a Sound Philosophy," and Friday, August 28, "A New Philosophy of Life."

DR. PEDRO J. LEMOS, director of the Stanford Museum and the Art Gallery, and editor of the *School Arts Magazine,* will be in Mexico during the next two months, having been asked to make a survey of its arts and crafts. During this trip Mr. and Mrs. Lemos will also visit and study the public art schools of Mexico as guests of Señor Juan F. Olaguibel, Minister of Education.

AT the meeting of the International Union for Scientific Investigation of Population Problems held in London on June 15, Colonel Sir Charles Close, formerly director general of the British Ordnance Survey, was elected president to succeed Professor Raymond Pearl, of the Johns Hopkins University. The third general assembly of the union will be held in Germany in 1934.

JOHN T. NICHOLSON, a district superintendent in the New York City schools for the past sixteen years, died on July 17, at the age of sixty-six years.

FERNANDO A. CARTER, for twenty years director of the Syracuse Museum of Fine Arts, died on July 18, at the age of seventy-five years.

SAMUEL A. B. ABBOTT, formerly president of the board of trustees and acting librarian of the Boston Public Library, died on June 19. From 1897 to 1903 he was director of the American Academy at Rome.

MRS. HARRIET D. PARSONS, music supervisor and instructor at the Cleveland Board of Education for twenty-two years until her retirement two years ago, died on July 15.

DR. ESTHER S. DAVIES, assistant professor of home economics at the Massachusetts State College, died on July 14, at the age of forty-six years.

THE REV. ALBERT OVERTON HAMMOND died on July 20, at the age of ninety years. Dr. Hammond went to Centenary Collegiate Institute, Hackettstown, New Jersey, to teach Greek and Latin in 1878. Although he had not been actively teaching for the last five years, he was continued as a member of the faculty. In 1928 the trustees of the school presented to him a loving cup in honor of fifty years of service.

AN exhibit of portraits of fifteen university presidents and faculty members belonging to the University of Wisconsin was displayed at the Memorial Union, during the university's commencement week. The portraits include Dean W. A. Henry, Professor S. M. Babcock and Dean H. L. Russell, by A. Nyholm, artist;

Dean John Butler Johnson, by Frederick W. Freer; Dean Frederick E. Turneaure, by Carl Marr; Professor Benjamin W. Snow, by Merton Grenhagen; Professor Richard T. Ely, by Johnson C. Johansen; President John W. Sterling; Professor David B. Frankenburger, by J. R. Stuart; President Charles Kendall Adams, by S. S. Nicolinis; Dean H. S. Richards, by R. S. Stebbins; President E. A. Birge, by Christian Abrahamsen; President Charles R. Van Hise, by C. S. Pietro; President Thomas Crowder Chamberlain, by Lorado Taft; and Edwin E. Bryant, by J. R. Stuart.

MR. MALCOLM G. WYER, city librarian of Denver, is dean of the new school of librarianship of the University of Denver, which will open in September. Municipal library facilities will be largely employed in practice training. Miss Harriet E. Howe, of the University of Chicago, will be Mr. Wyer's principal assistant.

UNIVERSITY OF WASHINGTON executive officers recently discussed their work to a high school radio audience. Through special arrangements a Seattle station and a Spokane station cooperated in presenting the program, a third of a series during last spring. At the first program university requirements were stressed by a group of speakers, under the direction of Registrar E. B. Stevens; on each of the two successive programs four university deans spoke briefly on opportunities for advancement in their fields. Special arrangements were made with high school principals throughout the state whereby schools listened to the programs.

THE National Advisory Council on Radio in Education has designated the University of Chicago Press as its official publishers. The proceedings of the first annual assembly of the council will be issued under aegis of the University of Chicago Press, and a list of publications on radio and education comprising six or seven titles has already been arranged for.

COMMENCEMENT exercises for the 1,000 or more convict students, who have been studying with the University of California extension division and in the prison school, were held at Berkeley on July 6. At exercises presided over by Warden James J. Holohan, the "graduates" received certificates which may be used for credits in the possible continuation of further studies after dismissal. The occasion marked the dedication of a new $50,000 school building, the first of its kind to be built within the prison walls. Addresses were delivered by Dr. Vierling Kersey, state director of public instruction; Dr. R. L. Alderman, federal government educational director, and H. A. Shuder, head of the San Quentin educational system.

WESLEYAN UNIVERSITY announces the award of Olin Scholarships amounting to $2,000 each for the college course to six of the candidates from various parts of the United States who recently took special examinations. The scholarships are a memorial to Stephen Henry Olin, '66, and are awarded to candidates who have first been selected by alumni as giving the best indication of possessing Mr. Olin's traits of scholarship, character, manhood and interest in the various extra-curricular activities. The committee on award consists of President J. L. McConaughy; Vice-president L. A. Howland; Professor J. W. Hewitt, dean of freshmen; Olin F. McCormick, '07, of Philadelphia, and Francis B. Upham, Jr., '15, of Mamaroneck, N. Y.

Two junior colleges, William Woods, of Fulton, Missouri, and Crescent, of Eureka Springs, Arkansas, have organized chapters Alpha and Beta, respectively, of Pi Alpha Gamma, an honor education sorority for students in junior colleges and normal schools. The purpose of Pi Alpha Gamma is to promote a professional spirit in the teaching service and to give recognition and encouragement to education students who show high attainments in health, character and scholarship.

A BILL to amalgamate all educational administrative bodies in Wisconsin into a centralized board of education has been killed by the Assembly, 62 to 29. The bill would have abolished existing boards of vocational education, trustees of institutes, normal school regents, university regents, directors of schools for the blind and deaf, and the office of the State Superintendent of Public Instruction. The measure proposed to replace these with a department of education composed of fifteen members appointed by the Governor subject to confirmation of the Senate.

Contributions by teachers within the last school year, approximating $500,000, will make it possible for the New York City Department of Education to continue its relief activities through the vacation months. Up to and including last month the sum of $441,000 was contributed by teachers to the school relief fund. The final contributions for the year now being collected in the schools from the May pay checks, will reach about another $50,000. On June 30, it is estimated, a balance of $100,000 will remain in the fund. This will be used chiefly to supply milk and crackers in summer schools and playgrounds through the Bureau of Extension Activities, headed by Mr. Eugene C. Gibney. Home relief work will be continued through the summer by the Bureau of Attendance.

The local education authorities of England and Wales, according to an announcement in *The Christian Science Monitor,* have given notice of their determination to revise the scales of salaries for teachers in the public elementary and secondary schools. The number of teachers affected is 200,000, and the amount of money spent on their salaries every year is more than £40,000,000. Teachers' salaries are settled by a standing joint committee called the "Burnham Committee," after its chairman, Lord Burnham. This committee consists of representatives of local authorities and teachers. The present salary scales were agreed to in 1925, and they will remain unaltered until March 31, 1932. The present year will be spent by the committee in negotiating a new set of scales to supersede them on April 1 of next year. The local authorities have two objects in view in giving notice to terminate the agreement. They wish to effect a reduction in the amount spent on teachers' salaries, and they wish to redress certain anomalies. The chief anomaly is the existence of four scales, differentiated according to locality. The London scale is the highest, the large provincial towns are next, small towns come next, and the lowest scale is paid in the rural areas. The difference between the salary of an assistant master in London and that of one in a rural area is £96 per annum.

It is understood that the French Government has introduced a measure into the Chamber of Deputies to provide funds for new premises to house the Institut Français du Royaume Uni, now situated in Cromwell-gardens, South Kensington. The Office of Works is stated to be desirous of obtaining possession of the premises for the use of the Royal College of Art. The Institut Français is affiliated to the Universities of Paris and Lille, and its educational work is carried out in three departments: (1) Educational classes for French children and English children in London; (2) lectures, chiefly to English people, on French subjects; (3) the university section for preparing students, generally English young men and women, for French degrees.

DISCUSSION

VOCATIONAL GUIDANCE AND MENTAL HYGIENE

Most phases of vocational guidance have been subjected to thorough scrutiny and evaluation in recent years. The emotional, the mental hygiene side of guidance, however, has been given only scant attention by most counselors, perhaps because it does not lend itself readily to standardization.

Yet a vocational analysis of an individual, which does not take into consideration his emotional make-up, his mental conflicts and the compensations he is seeking in his chosen vocation will remain inadequate. Ability alone is not a criterion of success. If the work is constantly creating an emotional disturbance it will fail to stimulate the efforts of the worker. Shyness will make the most intelligent person with the best commercial education a failure as a salesman. Similarly a salesman can not be convincing if in his youth he has acquired fear, dislike or mistrust of the article he is to sell or of anything related to it.

On the other hand a person with serious

handicaps may be very successful in an occupation which satisfies some emotional urge or creates an outlet necessary to his happiness.

In studying the personality tendencies of eighth-grade students before advising them in their choice of high-school course we have used the regular questionnaire, consisting of a list of occupations. The children were asked to mark the occupations which they would like to follow, those they would not mind pursuing and finally those which they would dislike. In this manner we discovered not only the general occupational tendencies of each child but also the general emotional response by the number of definite likes and dislikes as against the neutral reactions and the emotional coloring of each occupation. Besides, the pupils were asked to give reasons for their likes as well as dislikes. These answers led us on the trail of those children who needed help in their adjustment to life and society before vocational advice could be considered. More generally we learned from these answers a good deal about the personality of each child. We found out whether a boy was an independent thinker or a follower from his tendency to choose independently or to follow the occupation or advice of relatives. We learned how seriously each student thought of his career by the seriousness or superficiality of his reasons. We found the children who lacked fundamental information about their chosen occupations—the girls who wished to be nurses, because of the pretty uniforms they should wear, but were shocked when some phases of the work involved were revealed to them.

From this information, combined with a short family history and school history, we tried to construe the personality of each child for present and future vocational guidance purposes. Wherever we found discrepancies or signs of mental conflict, compensation or other emotional difficulties, we made a more thorough investigation. For example, Joseph registered a violent dislike for most occupations usually cherished by boys. He hated elevator operating, aviation, electricity and engines. He disliked the idea of being a policeman, chauffeur or chemist. And the reasons he gave for all these dislikes implied fear. He might get caught in the straps of the engine. The elevator might drop down the shaft. He feared the contact with a charged wire in electrical engineering. As for airplanes—he preferred to die in his bed. So all other occupations called out in his mind first their perils. Teaching, bookkeeping and gardening were about the only occupations which he considered safe. Joseph was a strong, husky boy with mediocre abilities for whom any one of the occupations which he scorned would have suggested itself. He was, however, an only child, and the cause of his attitude was an over-anxious mother. In spite of an improvement under mental hygiene treatment such an attitude is too deep-rooted to be safely ignored by the vocational counselor.

Elizabeth F. wanted to be a stenographer or librarian. Reason in both cases: "Because you have a nice, clean, quiet place all to yourself."

Her father was a shoe repairer, who had his shop in the family living room. In the three-room flat that was Elizabeth's home, there lived father, mother, five children and two boarders. The important consideration in a case of this kind is to determine whether the child's abilities and general interests coincide with her emotional urges and which are the more important in determining her future success and happiness.

Anna M., a bright but rather self-centered child, planned to be a surgeon, because "it was thrilling to think of cutting people up, putting them together again and seeing them walk then." All very well, but on second thought: "I should love to strap my enemies to the operating table and cut them to pieces."

When Anna was five years old, her father was brought home from mines with an injured skull and severe internal injuries. The child witnessed this scene, which of course involved considerable emotional strain. The doctors decreed that only a famous surgeon from a distant city could save the man. The surgeon arrived and saved the father by his skill. Later the family went through many hardships and disappointments. Both parents were inclined to blame their "enemies" for their misfortunes. Although they are at present in comfortable circumstances they remained skeptical and distrustful.

Here the parents' cooperation was enlisted

and Anna was helped to acquire a more wholesome attitude toward the world and her fellow human beings. With a better sense of proportion she might make a very good surgeon indeed.

George was a very pleasant, friendly boy with a great ability for friendship and for inspiring confidence. But he was not very bright. He barely passed his subjects in high school, his showing on intelligence tests was mediocre and all his teachers, though very fond of George, admitted that he was slow, but a steady, hard worker. And George wanted to be a physician. His reasons showed a thorough understanding of the education and the duties required from a physician. George's enthusiasm for the profession was great. His uncle was a physician and the boy's ambition to be one dated way back in his childhood.

George's intelligence and school record did not justify encouragement of his ambitions. But as the emotional urge was great and the boy's personality was admirably suited for his chosen profession, he was advised to plan to go to a college with not too high standards, the graduation from which would, however, enable him to enter a medical school.

In this way the general tendencies of a personality find their expression in vocational choices. If the abilities of the individual are such as to enable him to follow the chosen occupation, the emotional compensations and urges are of course an added guarantee of success. The difficulty arises when the physical and mental make-up of a person is at variance or even contradictory to the person's emotional needs. To the counselor then falls the difficult task to advise wisely with a happy well-balanced human being in view. It remains to him to study each case thoroughly in order to determine whether the vocational choice indicates a wise and necessary compensation or emotional outlet, or if it merely points to a hopeless self-deception.

It would have been an exceptional vocational counselor who would have advised Demosthenes to carry out his ambition to become an orator. And very few would have encouraged the delicate Roosevelt to join the Rough Riders. And yet they as well as many others succeeded in the face of apparently impossible odds. And their success has meant to them the winning of self-confidence, mental health and happiness.

On the other hand failure in the chosen occupation as well as an occupation that is unsatisfactory from the emotional point of view may mean complete loss of mental balance.

It is to be hoped that with the rising interest in mental hygiene in the schools, vocational guidance will develop along these lines as it has along others. More thorough methods even than have been outlined above will be developed to insure vocational adjustment, which would serve the greatest happiness of every individual.

JOSEPH MILLER,
Director of Guidance, City Schools
WILKES-BARRE, PENNSYLVANIA

A NEW MODE OF ATTACK ON THE COLLEGES

SYMPTOMS of a curious change in the attitude of high-school educationists towards the colleges reveal a new attack of some ingenuity upon our college system—provisionally upon the first two years of the standard college course.

Twenty years ago the high schools were busy declaring their independence of college domination. They were diluting the classical high-school courses to the extent of from twenty-five to fifty per cent. with industrial, economic, artistic and other branches belonging to the new "culture." They were experimenting with various forms of student-government among their pupils. They were organizing high-school students into classes and cliques for social, athletic, and other "cultural" purposes. They cut out of the standard five-class-per-week program two or three of these weekly exercises and introduced "supervised study-hours" so that the students, freed from the necessity of home-work, would be able to attend games and dances and crash the gates of moving-picture theaters. It was believed—or at least suggested—that the improved technique of the new education would enable the high-school student to learn, in the reduced time, as much English, mathematics, science, etc., as he had heretofore acquired—or at least as much as he would ever need.

The results have not quite come up to expectations. High-school students, it must be admitted, accepted the new order of things with pronounced enthusiasm. They govern themselves with a fine, artistic abandon of traditional prejudices. They have developed high proficiency as movie, radio, and baseball fans. They have learned to dance, play football and hockey, drink, and, on occasion, commit adultery. Their "culture," in the Freudian sense, has notably increased.

These unexpected results have pained both parents and educationists, although the latter, manifesting an automatic defense mechanism, try to make light of it. Parents have begun to note that the industrial subjects taught in high school are of even less actual, monetary value to the high-school graduate than the much maligned Latin and Greek of the classical curriculum. Notwithstanding high sounding courses in civics, economics and sociology, high-school graduates romp joyously into the modern vortex of political and social pollution without showing any sign that the philosophical and moral presentations of the high-school curriculum have made the slightest dent in their adolescent obtuseness.

What the educationists did not anticipate was the effect of their curricular dispositions upon student attitudes. From their cutting down of the time formerly devoted to English, arithmetic, and language the students naturally assumed that these things were no longer a vitally important part of education. The new branches introduced were obviously the real essentials. Consequently students came to consider the drudgery of learning to spell, "figger," and parse as something to be avoided as far as possible, something to "get by" with minimum effort, so that they would have more time to devote to the new "cultural activities."

But what pains the educationists most is the stubbornness of the colleges against lining up with the new order of things. Endowed universities are using methods of constantly increasing rigor in selecting their freshmen. State schools, unable to reject unsuitable high-school graduates at the outset, flunk them out as soon as possible, with results to the individual rejectees more disastrous than original elimination would have been. Parents resent this, and educationists resent parental criticisms of the high schools.

It was not to be expected that the educationists would meet this situation by any reform of secondary curricula or instruction. Such an attempt, in the face of the intellectually demoralized youth of the nation, would be a labor of Hercules. Rather, they have launched a flank attack upon the college system itself—an attack against which the new junior colleges, in particular, will have little effective means of defense.

It is almost amusing to note how, of late, they have piped down on their erstwhile resonant declarations of educational independence. They are playing up again the old moan of college domination. They have enlisted the services of such eminent educational administrators as President Glenn Frank to point out the lamentably rigid interdependence of the various stages of our educational system upon each other. They have applied to education Lincoln's dictum that the "nation can not continue half slave and half free"—without stating whether the high school is slave and the college free, or the high school itself half slave and half free. More recently they have organized a formidable "Committee on the Relation of School and College" which, while heavily weighted with high-school men, includes a few outstanding college educators. They ask for an extension of "progressive" high-school experimentation into the first two years of college work, knowing full well that if they can get by with this, the whole college system, including the graduate school, will soon be at their mercy.

It is to be hoped that the colleges will do a little research of their own before turning the high-school experimenters loose in their freshman and sophomore departments. They have at their disposal, in the form of high-school graduates, abundant material upon which to base judgments of the educational effectiveness of recently developed educationist techniques. If they find that the new education has brought forth fruits at all commensurate with its vast claims, it will be time to consider possible applications of the new techniques to college teaching.

It can be taken for granted, at the outset, that all the "adjustments" and "cooperation" will be on the part of the colleges. The high-school system, impregnably secure behind its political defenses, will never concede a single point to help the colleges realize thir own ideals. It will be a matter of give and take—give on the part of the colleges and take on the part of the high schools. Let the colleges therefore, beware of giving up anything they do not want to lose, for they will certainly never get it back again.

G. WAKEHAM
UNIVERSITY OF COLORADO

QUOTATIONS

CHILD LABOR IN INDIA

THE Report of the Royal Commission on Labor in India, published on Thursday, is a document of great social and educational, as well as industrial, importance. Mr. Whitley and his colleagues found that many troubles in the factories arise from lack of education. In India nearly the whole mass of industrial labor is illiterate—a state of affairs not to be found in any of the other seven countries which rank with India as of the greatest industrial importance. The commissioners find it almost impossible to overestimate the consequences of this disability, which are obvious in wages, in health, in productivity, in organization, and in several other directions.

Many employers have endeavored to do something toward making good the deficiency by means of factory schools. The commissioners saw some schools which are admirable examples of their kind, and represent a big outlay in cost and thought. There is a fairly general tendency to concentrate in such schools on the education of half-timers. Useful work is done in some cases, but the truth is that too often the results are incommensurate with the effort. The report lays down the incontestable fact that a child is seldom capable of putting in five or six hours' work in a factory and learning properly in a school after that work ends or before it begins. This is especially true of children whose heredity and environment do not predispose them for mental work. Mr. Whitley's experiences in Yorkshire as a social and educational worker in earlier years are probably reflected in the observation that the half-timer, from his own point of view, is merely undertaking an extra task until the law permits him to earn a higher wage, by which time he is too often ready to forget what he has learned. It is added that a further factor which diminishes the value of concentrating on half-timers is that in some instances they are few or unknown, and in others their numbers are diminishing.

The conclusion is reached that the child who is not working is likely to get much more advantage from factory schools than the half-timer. The difficulty is the economic pressure which tends to drive the child to work at an early age. Elsewhere in the report it is recommended that the present legal maximum of six hours' work a day for persons between the ages of 12 and 15 should be reduced to five hours.

The commission was well advised to point out that the main responsibility for education in industrial areas must fall elsewhere than on the employers. The task is primarily one for the community, acting through local bodies and government. It is argued that the industrial areas have a special claim to attention. Most industrial workers spend their childhood in villages and not in cities; but there are many children in industrial areas who will subsequently enter industry. Mr. Whitley and his colleagues hold that these areas should receive preferential treatment, in view of the economic results to be obtained. Since universal primary education is still a somewhat distant ideal, on account of financial and general difficulties, claims for preference are made on all hands; and the trend to-day is to ask for women's education to take precedence, because of the leeway to be made up.

Most educationists acquainted with Indian conditions will share the view of the commission that for rapid progress the application of compulsion is desirable. In some parts of India it was found that there was a tendency for municipalities applying compulsory methods to exclude wards peopled by factory labor on the ground of the backwardness of the population. The Bombay Municipality, on the other hand, has recently applied compulsion to two wards chiefly inhabited by millworkers—a step commended by the commission. Attention is called to the desirability of bringing the upper age limit for compulsory education at least up to 12 years, the minimum age for factory employment. The present system in Bombay, under which compulsory education stops at 11, involves the loss of a valuable year and jeopardizes the results already achieved. It is suggested that employers might assist by lending buildings in the workers' lines or the factory compounds, or by equipping schools. The combination of the educational experience of the authorities and the practical wisdom of employers might lead to valuable improvement in the ordinary curricula.

The commission pays tribute to the educational side of welfare schemes of a number of industrial concerns. The Buckingham and Carnatic Mills in Madras have given a lead in such matters, as is well known, to the rest of industrial India. Mr. Whitley and his colleagues were particularly impressed with the educational facilities provided by this company. These included a sound elementary course, some technical classes, and training in hygiene. The British India Corporation in Cawnpore and the Empress Mills (Tata's) in Nagpur also come in for honorable distinction. One of the handicaps in the way of welfare work has been the tendency of the worker to be suspicious of anything new, even when it is to his advantage. —*Educational Supplement of the London Times.*

REPORTS

MASSACHUSETTS STATE COLLEGE

ON April 15 the Massachusetts Agricultural College changed its sixty-eight year old name to Massachusetts State College by act of the Legislature and the approval of the Governor. The question has been asked frequently why the name of the college was changed and what its policy and program are to be under the new name.

The reason why the name was changed is briefly answered by saying that the old name implied an institution of more restricted scope than actually existed and was, therefore, misleading. It has long been thought by many persons that a change in the name of the college was desirable, and as early as 1896 there was student agitation for such a change. It was felt by students that the college name and the agricultural terms applied to many courses such as agricultural education, rural sociology and the like, have constituted a sop to agriculture. This has been resented by the faculty in charge of the agricultural work of the institution who have felt that agriculture needed no subsidy of any sort and they now feel that the teaching program in agriculture will rest on a higher plane with the new name.

There is little doubt that the nature of the college and the service which it renders have been misunderstood by large numbers of citizens principally because of its name. Frequently, parents of prospective college students have been much surprised to learn that the facilities for a sound college education are available at this state institution and many have failed completely to realize what opportunities for higher education exist here, largely because the name has implied a restricted scope. The new name will doubtless help many citizens of the state to better appreciate the extent of the educational service provided by this college.

The passing of the old name brings pangs of keen regret to many alumni who have cherished "Aggie" through the years. The reputation made for the college throughout the world by her distinguished graduates is something in which all friends of the college take great pride and it is the hope of the faculty and trustees that the glory of the old name will be inherited by the new and that under the new name the institution will develop soundly and her achievements expand.

It should be emphasized that this change of name is not the result of a recent change in the scope of the college for that is no different now than it was sixty-seven years ago. To be sure, changing times have developed changing demands for service with the result that different phases of the work of the college have had to be emphasized to meet these demands. However, the basic laws governing the scope of the college remain unchanged and it is in accordance with these that the college has functioned and will continue to function as the Massachusetts State College.

There are four distinct types of service which the college renders to the commonwealth. First, there is the Experiment Station which is the research unit of the institution, studying the problems of agriculture in an effort to improve production and marketing practices. Then, there is the Control Service which regulates the sale of certain agricultural products for the purpose of protecting purchases.

The Extension Service undertakes the large responsibility of teaching adults and boys and girls throughout the state, who can not come to the college for instruction, better methods in agriculture and homemaking. Approximately 285,000 people in the commonwealth received help last year through this Extension Service.

The fourth phase of the service of the college is that of instruction to students on the campus. Approximately 1,000 young men and women are in attendance in the various courses offered and they are securing a sound training for useful lives and good citizenship. Several types of courses are offered. Besides such short courses as the winter school, summer school, the two-year course in practical agriculture known as the Stockbridge School, there are the four-year course leading to the bachelor of science degree, and the Graduate School which offers opportunity for study for advanced degrees.

The vocations in which the majority of the graduates of the college are engaged probably gives the clearest idea of the sort of training which is provided. The largest number are serving as teachers in schools and colleges or as specialists in extension education. The various phases of agriculture attract the next largest number and others listed in order are industrial workers; landscape architects and engineers; research experts and technologists in such scientific fields as chemistry, botany, entomology, bacteriology, etc., professional practitioners, such as physicians, lawyers, ministers, etc., and a wide variety of miscellaneous callings.

On the campus, teacher training is, at present, one of the popular courses and those who are going out as teachers in high schools are frequently combining this work with athletic coaching. The college has trained many very successful athletic coaches and more than fifty graduates of the college are now engaged in this work. The college has just completed a splendid new physical education building which provides practically every modern facility for this type of training in addition to the splendid recreational program which it makes possible. The college continues to offer a splendid training in the fields of agriculture and horticulture. Closely related to these is the course in landscape architecture. This college was the first in the country to organize such a department and it has long been prominent for its work in this field. Among its graduates are some of the leading landscape architects of the country.

The courses in the physical and biological sciences are popular with present-day students. They include such subjects as bacteriology, physiology, botany, chemistry, entomology, zoology, geology, physics, mathematics and veterinary science. Many prominent scientists are numbered among the graduates from these courses and many valuable contributions to present-day life have been made by them. The work in entomology has attracted particular attention to the state college. Members of the staff or graduates of the college were the first to discover the presence in this country of many foreign insect pests including browntail moth, oriental moth, gypsy moth and European corn borer. Steps for the control of these pests were recommended and usually carried out by the college and much destruction to plant and animal life has been avoided by this service.

In recent years enrolment of women students at the college has increased largely so that there are now 175 women students enrolled. They find an interest in the home economics courses, in teacher-training and also in some of the scientific and horticultural subjects. One of the attractive features of the campus, and a very useful addition to the facilities for home economics teaching, is the home management house known as the Homestead. This home was recently restored and furnished and is typical of the Connecticut Valley architecture of one hundred and fifty years ago.

In addition to these special fields of teacher-training, physical and biological sciences, agriculture and home economics, the curriculum includes strong supporting courses in the humanities, such as the languages and literatures, economics, history and sociology. The aim is to give to each student as high a degree of efficiency in some particular branch of learning as is possible without sacrificing the breadth of knowledge and training which should characterize the well-rounded college course.

The cost of an education at Massachusetts State College is comparatively low. Opportunities for self-support, loan funds and scholarships make it possible for most any earnest student who really wants a college education to get it here even though he may lack parental financial support. A nominal tuition fee of $60 per year is charged to residents of the state and the fee to non-residents is $180 per year. The necessary expenses of the college course need not exceed $550 per year. Eighty per cent. of the students enrolled are partially dependent financially upon their own efforts for an education.

The foregoing is a brief description of the newly named Massachusetts State College. Further information concerning any of its activities may be secured from the secretary of the Massachusetts State College at Amherst. It is generally recognized as a progressive institution offering a high grade of educational service to the commonwealth of Massachusetts.

A CORRESPONDENT

EDUCATIONAL RESEARCH AND STATISTICS

PRELIMINARY REPORT ON MEDICAL APTITUDE TESTS FOR 1931–32

AT the Denver meeting of the Association of American Medical Colleges last October a report[1] was given of the experimental work over a period of two years, on the use of Medical Aptitude Tests in predicting success in medical school and in selecting students for admission to medical schools. Following the report, these resolutions were adopted by the association:

(1) That the association record its sense of the importance of the study and of the value of aptitude tests in relation to the selection of students for medical schools.

(2) That the association recommend the use of aptitude tests as one additional criterion for selecting medical students.

(3) That the next year the tests be given the same day in all the premedical schools in the United States and a distribution showing the standing of all the applicants together with the names and scores of the individuals applying to each school be sent to the dean of the medical school concerned.

(4) That $1.00 be charged each applicant to cover the expenses of this service of the committee.

The committee appointed to conduct this work includes: Torald Sollmann, Western Reserve University, *chairman;* H. G. Weiskotten, Syracuse University; Edward Koch, University of Buffalo; Beverly Douglas, Vanderbilt University, and F. A. Moss, George Washington University, *secretary* and *director of study.* Steps were immediately taken to organize the work for giving the aptitude test to all students applying for entrance to medical schools this year.

CONSTRUCTION OF NEW TEST

Two forms of the aptitude test had previously been developed for use in the experimental work. In order that no applicant should have an unfair advantage over others because of having seen one of the previous forms, it was necessary first to construct an entirely new form of the test for use in this year's testing. Immediately following the Denver meeting, work was begun on the construction and standardization of the new test. The various items of the two previous forms of the test were studied in detail with a view to determining which items gave the best indication of success in the medical school. New items were constructed along these same lines and were tried out with a group of known ability. The most of this preliminary work was done by Thelma Hunt, Donald Stubbs and Leon Gordon under the direct supervision of the secretary of the committee. On the basis of the preliminary work a draft of the new test was made and sent to the various members of the committee for criticism and suggestions. In the light of their suggestions, the final draft of the test was made. The test consists of six parts: (1) Scientific Vocabulary, (2) Visual Memory for Anatomical Drawings, (3) Memory for Descriptive Material, (4) Premedical Information, (5) Learning and Retention of Material and (6) Understanding of Difficult Printed Material. The total working time required for taking the test is one and a half hours.

[1] *Journal* of the Association of American Medical Colleges, January, 1931.

Cooperation

Excellent cooperation in carrying out the testing has been given by medical schools and premedical schools. All the medical schools cooperated in the preparation of a list of schools and colleges training premedical students; and many of the medical schools aided directly in securing cooperation in the premedical schools from which their applicants come.

The premedical schools cooperated in the administration of the test to their applicants, and in forwarding the papers to our committee for scoring. The total number of premedical schools in which tests were given in February is 547. This number includes premedical schools in every state of the United States, three in Canada, one in the Philippine Islands, one in Porto Rico and one in Hawaii. In addition, correspondence with a number of premedical schools that had no students applying for admission this year, indicated their willingness to cooperate in years when they have applicants to the medical schools. In the schools the tests were given by a designated member of the staff, usually a member of the teaching staff of a department in close touch with the premedical work of the college.

Many helpful suggestions for carrying on and improving the work have been received from both the medical schools and the premedical schools.

Giving and Scoring of Tests

The tests were given on February 13 at the same hour in all the schools throughout the country. After being given, all the tests were forwarded to the office of the committee for scoring and tabulation. As soon as the tests arrived a corps of examiners and statisticians began scoring of tests and tabulation of results. The first report was sent to the deans or admissions officers of the medical schools March fifteenth.

Making the Results Available

Results on the tests were supplied to the medical schools in two ways.

First, a list of all the students taking the test was sent to each medical school. This list gave for each student his total score on the test, and his percentile rating, or relative standing in the whole group tested. This list was arranged by states and by premedical schools within the state.

Second, a more detailed record was sent to each medical school for those students who had indicated that they are applying or would apply for admission to a particular medical school. This record gave for each student a detailed analysis of his test, giving separate scores on the six parts of the test.

All the premedical schools cooperating have received a report on their own students, giving each student's total score and percentile rating. No results have been returned to the applicants themselves, and the premedical schools have been asked to regard the reports as strictly confidential information.

Summary of Results

A total of 9,220 students applying for admission to the medical schools took the test. Table I shows the distribution of this number

TABLE I

Distribution of Number Taking Test by States

State	Number	State	Number
Alabama	168	Nebraska	184
Arizona	8	Nevada	10
Arkansas	63	New Hampshire	100
California	390	New Jersey	58
Colorado	61	New Mexico	17
Connecticut	105	New York	1,450
Delaware	5	North Carolina	225
District of Col.	245	North Dakota	33
Florida	48	Ohio	658
Georgia	133	Oklahoma	111
Idaho	11	Oregon	100
Illinois	400	Pennsylvania	1,097
Indiana	265	Rhode Island	47
Iowa	219	South Carolina	73
Kansas	135	South Dakota	42
Kentucky	143	Tennessee	118
Louisiana	150	Texas	339
Maine	26	Utah	65
Maryland	125	Vermont	43
Massachusetts	301	Virginia	225
Michigan	308	Washington	90
Minnesota	185	West Virginia	154
Mississippi	52	Wisconsin	132
Missouri	247	Wyoming	6
Montana	27	Foreign	23

TABLE II

Percentile Ratings on Aptitude Test

Scores	Percentile rating	Scores	Percentile rating
240	100	133	49
215–239	99	132	48
210–214	98	131	47
205–209	97	130	46
200–204	96	129	45
198–199	95	127–128	44
196–197	94	126	43
193–195	93	125	42
191–192	92	124	41
187–190	91	123	40
185–186	90	121–122	39
183–184	89	120	38
181–182	88	119	37
179–180	87	118	36
178	86	117	35
176–177	85	115–116	34
175	84	114	33
173–174	83	113	32
172	82	112	31
170–171	81	111	30
169	80	109–110	29
168	79	108	28
167	78	107	27
166	77	106	26
165	76	105	25
164	75	103–104	24
162–163	74	102	23
161	73	101	22
160	72	99–100	21
159	71	98	20
158	70	96–97	19
156–157	69	94–95	18
155	68	92–93	17
154	67	90–91	16
153	66	88–89	15
152	65	86–87	14
150–151	64	84–85	13
149	63	82–83	12
148	62	80–81	11
147	61	78–79	10
146	60	76–77	9
144–145	59	74–75	8
143	58	72–73	7
142	57	69–71	6
141	56	67–68	5
140	55	65–66	4
138–139	54	55–64	3
137	53	45–54	2
136	52	35–44	1
135	51	Below 35	0
134	50		

by states. The test scores for these students ranged from 15 to 240. The total distribution is shown in Figure 1. The median score of

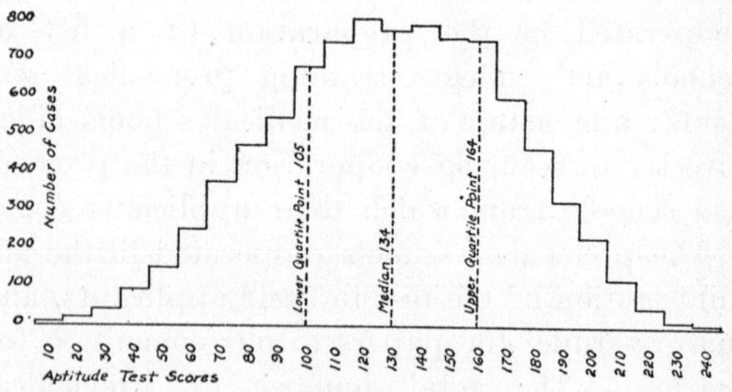

Fig. 1

the group is 134, the upper half making scores of 134 or above, the lower half below 134. The Upper Quartile Point is 164, the highest fourth making 164 or above. The Lower Quartile Point is 105, the lowest fourth falling below this score.

Table II gives the percentile ratings based upon the total distribution. The percentile rating indicates where the student falls in relation to the whole group taking the test. For example, if a student's score is 104, his percentile rating is 24. This means that he falls 24 per cent. of the way to the top of the group; he makes as high or higher than 24 per cent. of those taking the test, and 76 per cent. are above him. Or, if a student has a score of 204, his percentile rating is 96. He makes a rating as high as or higher than 96 per cent. of those taking the test, only 4 per cent. are above him. These percentile ratings have been used in reporting the scores in order to give an indication of the relative ability of the applicants.

The exact use that will be made of the test results and the exact standards to be required on the test will vary according to the local conditions in the medical schools. Most of the medical schools will give equal weight to three criteria in admitting students, as follows: (1) Aptitude Test rating, (2) scholarship as indicated by grades in premedical work, and (3) personal interview ratings, letters of recommendation and other indications of personal fitness.

F. A. Moss

George Washington University

SCHOOL AND SOCIETY

EDITED BY J. McKEEN CATTELL
WITH WHICH IS COMBINED THE

EDUCATIONAL REVIEW

EDITED BY WILLIAM McANDREW

Volume 34 | Saturday, August 1, 1931 | Number 866

THE SUPERINTENDENT AS THE CHIEF INSPIRATION AND EXECUTIVE IN MAKING THE WHITE HOUSE CONFERENCE EFFECTIVE[1]

By Dr. EDWIN C. BROOME
SUPERINTENDENT OF SCHOOLS, PHILADELPHIA, PENNSYLVANIA

The White House Conference, called by President Hoover in Washington on November 19 and 20, 1930, brought together over three thousand leaders in education, health and social service, to discuss ways and means of advancing the interests of childhood. The purpose of the conference was clearly stated in the President's call: "To study the present status of the health and well-being of the children of the United States and its possessions; to report what is being done; to recommend what ought to be done and how to do it."

The number attending, the importance of the membership, the object of the conference, the completeness of its findings and the significance of its recommendations ought to make the work of this conference of inestimable value to the forty-five millions of growing children of our country. Its value to these children will depend upon three things: The seriousness with which we regard the recommendations of the conference, the effort we make to study and comprehend them, and the thoroughness and effectiveness of their application in the communities of the United States.

The responsibility for securing the maximum advantages of the White House Conference rests mainly upon boards of education and school executives. The superintendent of schools is the key to the situation. To him boards of education look for advice, and through him their policies are made operative. The superintendent of schools, therefore, whether state, county, or district, becomes, as the title of this paper suggests, the "chief inspiration and executive in making the White House Conference effective."

The clearest and most complete statement of the ultimate purpose of all agencies for the advancement of the nurture, health and training of childhood is found in the opening paragraph of the report of the Committee on the School Child:

> The first cardinal principle in education and training for a democratic society is that each individual child should develop to his highest possible level of attainment. This calls for the opposite of the lock-step in education. It demands full recognition of the individual differences among children. Each child must be considered as a unit—mind, soul, body. The child must be

[1] Address before the National Education Association, Los Angeles, California, July 1, 1931.

seen as a whole, sent to school as a whole, trained in school as a whole, and sent out from school as a whole with the best that education can give him, that he may be more adequately equipped to live abundantly in service and satisfaction.

How is this ideal to be realized?

Ten definite lines of action must be followed:

1. More complete cooperation between the school and the home.
2. More effective cooperation between the school and other community agencies which are organized for service to children.
3. School buildings, grounds, and equipment designed to promote the maximum of safety, health and happiness of the children.
4. Teachers trained and guided to appreciate the cardinal principle of education and training, as stated above, and only teachers whose characters and reputations command respect.
5. The introduction of child-centered, rather than subject-centered curricula.
6. An adequate program and proper physical facilities for promoting the health, recreation, and physical education of all children.
7. The guarantee of opportunities for rural and village children equivalent to those enjoyed by the children of better circumstanced municipalities.
8. Adequate provisions for the nurture and training of under-privileged and handicapped children, as well as for the children of socially handicapped races.
9. Entrusting the vital function of the education of children to people professionally trained for that purpose, with equal confidence with which we entrust the care of the sick to trained physicians.
10. Effective methods of intelligently interpreting the aims and practices of the schools to the people of the community, to the end that they will understand and appreciate the work of the schools, and will give to the enterprise of public education the cooperation which is necessary to make it successful.

It is along these lines that progress must be made if we are to make it possible for all America's children to live successfully and happily in a democratic society. This is a mighty challenge to the superintendents of the country.

Considerable progress has been made, especially in the more progressive city school systems, towards realizing proper standards of child health and training. The findings of the White House Conference are in no sense a reflection on communities which are providing for the education and welfare of children to the extent of their capacity. Nor was any question raised as to the adequacy of the general education which children in the public schools are receiving throughout the land. The reports of the several committees, however, did show that very generally our provisions for health, physical education, and recreation; provisions for the physically, mentally, and emotionally abnormal children; and provisions for the healthful, and profitable use of leisure time *are* inadequate. It is along these lines that our shortcomings are most evident.

Physical, Health Education and Recreation

Even in the most progressive cities the program of physical, health education and recreation is inadequate. One large city whose school system holds high repute is spending $25 a pupil in its academic high school for Latin and $3 for all forms of physical and health education. There is hardly a community which can not afford to double its support of physical and health work, even, if need be, at the expense of corresponding retrenchment in other forms of service.

Colleges, also, are not without blame. Many colleges willingly spend large sums on stadiums and training tables for "varsity" teams, but are niggardly in furnishing adequate facilities for the health and all 'round physical development of the great body of students who bring no glory or advertising to the institution.

We should not wait for legislation to

force upon us ill-thought-out programs, promoted by propagandists, but should meet the challenge now.

Much can be accomplished by cooperation with various organizations already existing—*e.g.,* Boy Scouts, Girl Scouts, Campfire Girls, Catholic Boys Brigades, the Y. M. C. A., the Y. W. C. A., the Y. M. and Y. W. Hebrew Associations—organizations which already provide health-training and recreation for over 10,000,000 children a year. Much progress has been made since the World War in provisions for health education and recreation; but how many communities can show that they have attained the standards of the White House Conference? To wit, one acre of play space for every 100 inhabitants, all school playgrounds in use by the children after school hours, and at least a half hour of physical education daily.

Provisions for Handicapped Children

The committee on special classes found the following:

Four hundred and fifty thousand pupils in elementary schools are so mentally retarded as to require special classes, but only 60,000 are as yet provided for;

Six hundred and seventy-five thousand present serious behavior problems; and only 10,000 are now in parental or special schools. Most of these are undoubtedly mental hygiene cases; but as yet we have made only a feeble effort to understand and treat cases of mental disorders;

Six million are under-nourished, but only 40,000 are in open air classes;

One million children have weak or damaged hearts; but very few communities are giving special attention to such cases;

There are at least 50,000 partly-seeing children, but only 5,000 are in special classes;

Three million are hard of hearing, but only 18,000 are in schools or classes for the deaf;

There are 300,000 crippled children, but only 11,500 are receiving special attention in classes organized for them;

One million have serious defects in speech, but only 60,000 are receiving corrective training.

In brief, according to reliable estimates, we have over ten million children under eighteen years of age who are abnormal or subnormal, physically, mentally, or emotionally, and less than two per cent. of these are receiving the special educational, physical, or mental treatment which their cases demand. One large city, which has done comparatively well for various types of handicapped children for over a decade, expends only 5.3 per cent. of its budget for the handicapped of all types. Communities will willingly spend large sums for the education of the so-called average, or normal children, or normal children in traditional courses of study, but they can not see the advantage in spending a proportionate amount for the treatment of the handicapped children. There is no average child. There are the average in weight, and the average in height, because those factors can be mathematically determined. But when we consider physical health, mental health, and emotional health, there are no averages. In these respects every child is an individual, and must be dealt with as such. What comfort is it to a parent to be assured that his child is having superior instruction in the three R's, when his boy has failing eyesight, or defective hearing, or is likely to succumb to tuberculosis if he does not receive special treatment?

For years we have been constructing buildings, furnishing them, preparing courses of study, and training teachers for the *average* child. We have assumed that the large majority of children are *normal.*

But those who have carefully taken an account of stock know that that assumption is incorrect. They tell us that between 30 and 40 per cent. of the children entrusted to our care are not normal, that they have abnormalities ranging all the way from those whose teeth are so defective as to impair digestion to those whose mentalities are so low that they should be in institutions.

We have been altogether too willing to leave the treatment of handicapped children to outside, privately supported institutions and organizations, unmindful of the fact that every handicapped child will become a social and economic liability upon the entire community, unless he receives the special treatment which his condition deserves. The proper nurture and training of all children, the handicapped as well as the normal, is a total community responsibility which must be squarely and intelligently met.

"I believe," said Horace Mann, over eighty years ago, "in the existence of a great natural law, antecedent to human institutions, a principle of divine origin which proves the absolute right to an education of every human being that comes into the world."

The superintendent of schools is the leader to whom the community should properly look to bring this to pass. Before sufficient funds can be secured to provide proper treatment for handicapped children, well-directed publicity is needed so that the community will appreciate the seriousness and the extent of the problem, and will become persuaded to make reasonably adequate appropriations. Also it is necessary to have properly qualified teachers, who not only understand the technique of teaching various classes of handicapped children, but who are in sympathy with them, and can see hope where others have seen only failure. It is also important to enlist the effective cooperation of hospitals, clinics, and other organizations in the community which are dealing with different phases of the problem of the underprivileged child.

We must not overlook the specially gifted children. We can not safely assume that they will take care of themselves. They can, and many do, become community liabilities, not because they lack capacity, but because, unless wisely guided, they may develop bad habits and unsocial attitudes, dissatisfaction with commonly accepted educational standards, and, instead of becoming tolerant and socially cooperative, they may acquire a superiority complex which makes them contemptuous of those of lesser endowments, and of little value in a world where intelligent cooperation is the chief guarantee of useful service.

Careful findings reveal the fact that there are at least a million and a half especially gifted children in our public and private schools, but that in only about forty cities are special classes or groups provided for them. To-day we are reaching approximately three tenths of one per cent. of the gifted children in the country. More and more do the industrial and social problems of our country need the influence of gifted minds. The gifted pupils in our schools represent an invaluable asset to society, one which we can least afford to squander.

The Extra-School Life of the Child

Probably what children have in the way of amusement and recreation out of school hours has as profound an influence upon their health and general welfare as what they do during school hours. It is especially important that care should be given to the extra-school life of children, because, first, the out-of-school influences are to a large extent irresponsible, and, secondly, because children are under the control of out-of-school influences for more than twice as long a period, every day, as they are under the influence of school. Allowing five hours a day for school and nine for sleep, there are ten waking hours every day, with all of Saturdays, Sundays, and at least eighty-five other days during the year when the child is under influences and controls other than those of the school. In fact, of the 5,475 waking hours of the child during the year, 1,000 hours, at the most, are spent in school. Measured by time alone, the outside influences have a leverage of nearly four and a half to one over the school influences upon the life of the child. Or, to put it another way, the school, in its effort to develop good habits in the children and to bring them under good influences, is under a handicap of four and a half to one in the case of children who are under unfortunate or disintegrating influences on the street, the back lot, or in a bad home environment. The wonder is not that so many turn out badly, but that the majority of children become creditable and useful citizens.

Much can be done, and every year more is being done, within the school to cultivate in boys and girls a taste for healthful and mentally and morally wholesome forms of amusement and recreation. We already recognize our responsibility for preparing the rising generation for the proper use of leisure. The White House Conference emphasized that as a proper and important function of the school.

In many school systems this is being done consciously through the development of appreciation of good literature, art and music, and through supervised play and games. Much is being done through what are commonly called extra-curricular activities. Unfortunately extra-curricular activities have not entirely emerged from the fad stage; and in some schools silly and meaningless projects have been undertaken so that all groups in the school may have some assignment for the extra-curricular hour. Extra-curricular activities are valuable only to the extent that they are organically associated with some regular branch of study. Such extra activities as foreign language clubs, which meet for practice in conversation and correspondence, home-economics clubs, which make a study of practical problems in home-making, also debating clubs, public-speaking clubs, crafts clubs, press or publishing clubs, good government clubs, nature study and hiking clubs, which make practical applications of the principles learned in the regular studies of the curriculum, are examples of legitimate and useful extra-curricular activities. As such, they form valuable training for the proper use of leisure time.

The most serious danger which confronts the school is the type of commercialized amusement and entertainment to which children are often exposed out of school hours. Commercialized amusements have grown to tremendous proportions since the World War. It is estimated that the American people expend over $500,000,000 annually on various types. Unfortunately, the promoters of commercial entertainment expect to make money, and are influenced by the profit motive rather than motives of public service or human welfare. The test, therefore, of the success of a feature is not its uplifting influence on the public mind but the success with which it "goes over." The result is that certain forms of entertainment, which otherwise might be elevating and beneficial, become at the best mediocre, and, at the worst, demoralizing, especially for younger people.

We need not have much concern over the effect of the legitimate theater upon the ideals of children. The report of the

White House Conference is authority for the estimate that not one child in twenty thousand patronizes the theater. But, according to the same report, motion pictures, prepared for adults, are seen by nearly 40,000,000 young people each week. Herein reside great possibilities for either good or evil.

No intelligent citizen will condemn motion pictures, or the radio, or dancing in a wholesale way as demoralizing as such. Many motion picture reels are artistic, educative and morally above reproach, and possess extraordinary power of interesting people of all ages. But cheap, vulgar, violent and risqué features are bad for all ages, and especially harmful to children. The influence of the superintendent of schools is impotent with the motion picture producers, except in individual instances where local theater managers will seek his counsel. But he can do much in a field where he is not impotent. Through meetings of parents and bulletins sent to the homes he can appeal, with considerable success, to the parents of school children to see that their children see only suitable picture shows, in so far as possible to determine. He can, through the proper use of a picture machine in the school, develop a taste for good pictures, and to some extent, lessen the desire for unsuitable commercial reels.

Vulgar and indecent books and periodicals, which are readily available in many public book-stalls, and are passed from pupil to pupil, are more dangerous than the lowest order of motion pictures, because they are more difficult to control, are inexpensive, and are more subtle and pernicious in their influence. No measures, except the elimination of the traffic in indecent publications, will avail. They are published and sold with vicious and contaminating intent. The control of this traffic, like the control of dope peddling, is a responsibility upon police and courts, and should be courageously met. In our own school system principals are instructed to confiscate any pieces of indecent publications that they discover in school, get all possible particulars as to source or place of purchase, and send the publications, with the facts obtained, to the chief of police. We have had uniformly fine cooperation from police and courts in the arrest, conviction and sentence of offenders.

The radio has tremendous educative possibilities, as everybody concedes, but we shall not begin to realize those possibilities until, perhaps as a condition of receiving a license, every broadcasting station will be required to devote a definite proportion of its schedule to educative programs, free from advertising. The broadcasts of Walter Damrosch are of the type we have in mind. It is doubtful that the radio as an instrument of regular class-room instruction, or as a substitute therefor, offers much promise. As a method of instruction, it has all the shortcomings of the lecture method which we have been condemning for years; it is practically impossible to plan a radio feature which will appeal with equal profit to an audience of children differing widely in age, maturity and interests; and it is impossible to imagine an educational radio program, made up for broadcast over a wide area by a committee of educators, perhaps sitting in Washington, which can approach in educational value, and in adaptation to varying ages of pupils, a well-planned course of study. But as an extra-curricular feature, the radio has great possibilities as a means of presenting to an entire school if a secondary school, or a department if an elementary school, examples of literature finely read, or of music beautifully rendered, or as a means of broadcasting a speech of the President or some other distinguished person whom the pupils may never hear in any other way, the radio offers valuable possibilities for supplementing the regular instruction of the school and, at the same time, if rightly used by school authorities, of developing in pupils a wholesome radio-receiving judgment and taste, analogous to a taste for good reading which all schools regard it a duty to cultivate.

Dancing is a healthful exercise, and, when done gracefully, has high esthetic value. But the average public dance hall is not a suitable place for boys and girls to frequent. Again we have a case of a useful art which the school must recognize as a desirable element in education, if done under proper auspices. It is possible by having dancing as a school exercise and done at school under school supervision, to eliminate, through the cooperation of parents, much dancing by school children in unsuitable places, and in improper company.

The school can not be expected to counteract entirely the harmful influences of improper motion pictures, radio features or dancing in harmful surroundings, any more than the school can be expected to prevent the use of all slang in conversation. But the schools, and the superintendent who directs the schools, must recognize the fact that these forms of entertainment make a strong appeal to young people, and that they do now, and will continue increasingly to claim a large share of the outside time of pupils. In any plan, therefore, for the preparation of children for the proper use of leisure it becomes the duty of the school to cultivate in children a refined movie, radio and dancing taste to the same degree that the school already has accepted the duty of developing a refined taste for literature, art and music.

To sum up, while the White House Conference dealt with many phases of child health and welfare, it laid especial emphasis upon the need of better and more extensive programs for health and recreation, more effective provisions for the proper treatment of handicapped children, and the development of a program for preparing children to make wholesale and intelligent employment of leisure time. Every school superintendent should have an adequate program to meet in his own school system the responsibilities which the White House Conference has so clearly defined. We can expect that the same outside agencies which are now cooperating will continue to do so, but they need guidance and they will accept it, if it is tactfully offered. The conclusion is that American communities are taking a much broader view of education than they did twenty-five years ago. They expect the school to promote the health and general welfare of their children, as well as their strictly educational interests, and the superintendent of schools rightly becomes the chief inspiration and executive to whom the people look for results.

EDUCATIONAL EVENTS

ENGLISH TEACHING IN JAPAN

A Tokyo correspondent to *The London Times,* writing on teaching of English in Japan, gives information concerning the founding and work of the Institute of Research in English Teaching. Approximately ten years ago the former vice-minister of education, Dr. Sawayanagi, suggested to Mr. Harold Palmer, who was then lecturing on methods of language study at University College, London, that he should come out to Japan as a linguistic technician with the mission of examining the situation at first hand, to discover what were the causes for the comparative failure of English teaching in Japan and to suggest remedies. This plan was subsequently carried into effect through the generous financial support of several wealthy Japanese, and the Institute of Research in English Teaching, the first of its kind in the world, was founded in Tokyo. The institute has on its board a number of eminent Japanese scholars, and is under the chairmanship of the head of the Imperial Academy of Japan. Notwithstanding lack of funds (apart from the small initial grant it has been self-supporting), it has not only justified its existence by the efforts it has successfully made to bring about a reform of English teaching in Japan, but has made a scientific approach to many problems arising out of the teaching of foreign languages, and has incidentally thrown much valuable light upon the linguistic study of English.

The institute, according to this correspondent, has played and is playing an increasingly important rôle in the training of teachers and is gradually organizing special courses in language teaching methods in accordance with the principles elaborated by the director and his associates. Its research work has not been limited to the investigation of the teaching situation in Japan. In the course of the last few years it has been specially concerned with researches on speech psychology, making use of and carrying further work done by individuals in various parts of the world, based upon the fundamental principle that language in its essence is "not a codification of concepts, nor a means of communication, but the instrument of thought itself, the thing that we think with, in short, 'speech.'" The results of these inquiries have been embodied in a series of pamphlets, text-books and in a fundamental study of the romanization of Japanese, which is the first serious and systematic study of a vital question affecting linguistics in the Far East. The director's inquiries into lexicology have led to the establishment of a new lexicological technique, differing from that adopted by Dewey, Thorndike and the American and Canadian Committees on Modern Languages. The results obtained so far, it is understood, are encouraging and seem destined to have far-reaching results. The same may be said of the work done in connection with the making of educational gramophone records, which mark a considerable advance on those produced so far in other countries.

THE DECLINE IN APPROPRIATIONS FOR OHIO STATE COLLEGES AND UNIVERSITIES

The Ohio State University Magazine gives information concerning the General Assembly's adherence to its announced policy of cutting approximately ten per cent. of the appropriations for wages and salaries in the five state-supported colleges and universities. An appropriation bill passed on June 25 virtually puts the Ohio State University back where it was four years ago. The university is granted $7,939,826 for the biennium 1931–32 as against $9,879,206 on which it operated during 1929–30.

The university is confronted with a marked reduction in outlay for capital equipment and maintenance. More serious, however, is the decreased appropriations involving salaries and wages. For the two years this bill carries $6,131,530, while the present payroll of the university, according to President Rightmire, stands at approximately $6,500,000. The university was granted $6,020,000 the previous biennium for salaries. In the meantime the enrolment had increased by 2,000 students, requiring additional faculty members to take care of them.

How the shortage will be absorbed is at present undecided. It is said, however, that there must be marked increases in the size of classes, which will hamper President Rightmire's program of reducing the size of sections and thus reaching more effectively the individual student. A general salary decrease, however, seems improbable, as other means of trimming the payroll will probably be tried first. It is hoped that the suggestion of Senator Earl Lewis that the universities reduce the amount paid to the high-salaried men can be avoided, as such action might cause the better men to accept positions in other institutions. It is also hoped that internal adjustments can prevent a general reduction for the lower salaried teachers.

The extent that the institution's income has been reduced is shown by the comparison with some other Western Conference universities for the same biennium: Wisconsin, $8,376,336; Michigan (for the first year) $4,920,000; Minnesota, $9,008,000; Illinois, $11,345,000.

The magazine comments: "Failure to increase the utilities excise tax, a move which was blocked time after time during the session by one of the most powerful lobbies known, prevented the state from foreseeing sufficient revenues to carry on a progressive régime, and witnessed the passage of an appropriation bill which not only has set back education, but which sees all state agencies marking time, and no progress made. It seems significant that other legislatures were able, in the face of the depression, to carry along their educational programs."

THE LINGUISTIC ATLAS OF THE UNITED STATES

Preliminary work on the Linguistic Atlas of the United States, sponsored by the American Council of Learned Societies, will be started in New England next month. Professor Hans Kurath, an authority on American dialects, will direct the compilation of the atlas.

In announcing its plans the society states that social prejudice in word pronunciation is very strong. Each locality believes its particular method is correct and that any deviation is wrong. One of the results it is hoped to achieve through the publication of the Linguistic Atlas is a more charitable point of view towards local dialects. It will be able to show, for example, that a million people in a given locality are in the habit of pronouncing a certain word in a particular way. The fact is that, for the given locality, that pronunciation is correct. In some other place, because of habits and customs of speech, some other pronunciation might be quite as acceptable.

A standard of pronunciation is not desirable except for the stage and that represents such a small portion of our national life. For the sake of art, it might be well to have such a standard but its use would be limited. It should not serve as a measuring stick or basis for criticism of some locally accepted dialect. According to the ideas expressed by those conducting the investigation, the United States is the only important country which has made no intensive study of its dialects. All the western European countries have made one or more such researches. Professor Jakob Jud, of the University of Zurich, co-author with Professor Carl Jaberg, of a Linguistic Atlas of Italy, Sicily, Sardinia and southeastern Switzerland, is a consultant in preparing the atlas in this country.

Professor Hans Kurath and Professor Miles L. Hanley, of the University of Wisconsin, will begin the research in New England in August, collecting data in Connecticut. Dr. Guy Lowman, recently returned from the University of London, where he has studied for the past two years in preparation for the atlas, will conduct the work in Vermont. Cassil Reynard, formerly of the Case School of Applied Science at Cleveland, will gather material in the Plymouth area of Massachusetts, and Martin Joos, graduate student from the University of Wisconsin, will handle the detail in western Massachusetts.

Additional workers who will gather data in New England this fall are being trained by Professor Jud in the Linguistic Institute at the College of the City of New York. Other workers are taking preparatory courses in the summer session in Columbia University.

Some idea of the resultant maps which will comprise the Linguistic Atlas of the United States can be gained by glancing through a volume of Professor Jud's study in Italy. The word "ant," for instance, has 1,200 different pronunciations, spellings and substitute words. These variations are all charted on a map showing phonetically exactly how the word sounds as used in each locality. The tracing of race histories is assisted by such comparative researches.

In the United States, it is quite common for the same object to have different names in different localities. The greatest variety is shown in the names of kitchen utensils and the parts of houses. A skillet is the same as a frying pan and a spider, while a tin cup may be called a dipper, cup, gourd or tin, and a porch is a stoop, veranda, portico, gallery or piazza.

Dr. Kurath writes that:

> While the atlas can not be completed for perhaps ten years, the field work in New England will take only about fifteen months. When compiled, edited and published, it will present a well-organized collection of the facts of our speech,

which is extremely diversified, for local and class variations are striking in this country. If the study begun here in the East is carried into other sections of the country, we shall learn why the Southerner drawls as he does, why the Easterner is as definitely marked by his speech as a Middle-westerner or one from the far West. These dialects can then be compared with foreign ones in sections of England, Ireland, France, etc., until we obtain a real view of the genesis of our speech.

The success of the "Dictionary of American Biography," which reflects the thought, culture and activities of contemporary American life through the biographies of representative men and women, has encouraged the American Council of Learned Societies to undertake the first comprehensive study of native dialects ever made in this country, which will be called the "Linguistic Atlas of the United States."

THE INFLUENCE OF THE ECONOMIC DEPRESSION ON VOCATIONAL EDUCATION

EVIDENCE of a realization on the part of state governments of the necessity for continuing their support of vocational education programs, even in the face of the economic depression, is found in a statement made public by Dr. J. C. Wright, director of the Federal Board for Vocational Education.

A summary of the situation discloses that the vocational education program in this country has stood the test of the world's economic depression, a depression which has resulted in the curtailment of public expenditures in many fields. The depression has served to emphasize the fact that the necessity for vocational education in giving training to those persons who desire preparation for work as well as for helping those out of a job to adjust themselves to new occupations is even greater in times of depression than in normal times.

Nineteen states report an increase in state appropriations for the current fiscal year, amounting to $800,000. Only seven states report decreases in their vocational training appropriations. These decreases total $70,000, which leaves a total increase in the appropriations for the 46 states reporting of nearly $750,000 available for additional schools and classes in vocational education.

Four states have increased their appropriations for vocational rehabilitation work, amounting in all to $18,503, while only one state reports a decrease.

The encouraging feature of the reports made by the 46 states is the upward trend in the financial support for vocational education and vocational rehabilitation by local communities throughout the country. Only two states report less support from local communities during the current year. On the other hand, one state reports a material increase, 20 states a general increase, and 11 states a slight increase; while 3 states indicate that the local support will be the same as last year.

Every indication points to an increase in enrolment in vocational classes in agriculture, trade and industry, and home economics, the three fields with which vocational education has to do, in 31 out of the 46 states reporting. Four states report that the enrolment will probably be about the same as for the previous year.

New York is planning the greatest program of expansion of any of the states from which we have reports. The state legislature has increased its appropriations for vocational education $300,000 over last year. It is expected, according to authoritative reports, that fifteen new departments of vocational agriculture and fifty departments of home economics will be added within the year, and an increased enrolment is anticipated in the day schools in trade and industrial instruction. A feature of the past year's program in this state has been the enrolment of several thousand persons in special classes organized for the unemployed.

Thirty states report no changes in the size of their staffs for the current year, and eleven states have increased their personnel by the addition of 16 supervisors. A decrease reported by four states gives four supervisors. Only one or two states indicate any tendency to reduce salaries.

PRISON EDUCATION IN NEW YORK CITY

EDUCATION will be brought within prison walls for the first time in a New York City penal institution in the near future, according to the announcement of Deputy Commissioner Joseph F. Fishman, of the Department of Correction, printed in the *New York Tribune*.

Establishment of the first prison school, a joint project of school and prison officials, proposed by Commissioner of Correction Richard Patterson, Jr., is virtually assured at the New York City Reformatory for Male Misdemeanants at New Hampton, Orange County, N. Y. This institution has been selected tentatively for the first school by a committee of public school officials called in by Commissioner Patterson early this summer. If present plans materialize the school will be housed in an educational building of special design suited to its unusual purposes.

The Board of Education will be asked to assign a member of the school department to New Hampton to undertake a survey to determine the education, mental capacity, aptitudes and physical condition of each inmate. On the basis of his findings, expected to take six or eight weeks, the organization of the school and its needs for apparatus and equipment will be determined.

The committee reporting on its intensive study of prisons recommended informally the establishment of the proposed new school. On the committee are: George H. Chatfield, director of attendance; Dr. John S. Roberts, district superintendent representing Superintendent of Schools William J. O'Shea, I. David Cohen, principal of the Brooklyn Boys' Continuation School, District Superintendent Oswald Schlockow, in charge of continuation schools; Edward Zabriskie, principal of Washington Irving High School, and Dr. Charles Harper, principal of the Murray Hill Industrial High School for Boys.

The New Hampton Prison was selected as having the most hopeful class. The committee states that many of its inmates have been chronic truants, have served time in protectories, are hardened criminals or just "tough city kids." It is a model farm prison for those between the ages of sixteen and thirty sentenced from Manhattan, Queens and Richmond. With a maximum sentence of three years it offers a comparatively stable group with which to start.

The survey to be conducted there will determine whether academic, vocational, trade or guidance work should be given and in what proportions.

THE FINANCIAL SITUATION OF THE SCHOOLS OF CHICAGO

A SPECIAL dispatch to *The New York Times* states that the Chicago School Board's floating debts have reached a total amount of $101,462,730 and the board is in the market to borrow $34,000,000 more.

A large part of the debts are secured by tax anticipation warrants, another part by participation certificates in a trust composed of tax warrants, and the remainder is composed of unpaid bills and overdue salaries, some of which are delinquent four months.

Paying of the warrants depends on the collection of taxes. Not enough taxes have been gathered to pay off all the 1928 warrants, less than 65 per cent. of the 1929 taxes have been collected, and the 1930 taxes have not been levied.

Paying of back salaries to teachers and janitors and the bills of supply men and contractors hinges on the board's ability to sell more tax anticipation warrants, which buyers so far have refused until the board pays some of the old debts.

Under these conditions the board must decide whether it will trim expenses, other than the elimination of one Lincoln, four Packards and four Buicks, which have been purchased, operated and maintained for trustees.

The board voted at its last meeting to abolish the automobiles and thus save $30,500. Taxpayers have been paying chauffeurs $200 a month each to drive the trustees.

President Myers has recommended that $3,620,065 additional be saved and last week it was reported the trustees had agreed to eliminate about $2,400,000. Since then, however, five unions of teachers and the janitors' and engineers' unions have threatened to persuade the trustees to oppose this retrenchment.

At the pace the school board is going its debts will mount to $107,207,000 before it is time to open its schools in September.

To pay these debts the board has whatever taxes which may be paid in the meantime, which has been estimated at less than $6,000,000. This money, according to the requirements of the statutes, must be used to pay off tax anticipation warrants first, so that taxes can not possibly be relied upon to pay the past due salaries and bills.

THE WORLD FEDERATION OF EDUCATION ASSOCIATIONS

THE World Federation of Education Associations opened its meeting on July 26, at Denver, Colorado. The federation was welcomed by Governor Adams and officers of the state board of education. Miss Florence M. Hale, newly elected president of the National Education Association, extended greetings on behalf of the American teachers and school authorities.

The effect on international friendship of military training in schools and colleges; further extension of the practice of exchange of students and teachers, and the establishment of a world university, are included among the topics to be discussed in the sectional conferences scheduled for each morning of the week's program.

Dr. Augustus O. Thomas, of Augusta, Maine, is the president of the world federation. The vice-presidents are: Sir Frank Goldstone, of London; Hirotaro Hayashi, of Tokyo, and D. D. MacDonald, of Toronto.

According to a statement issued by these officers of the federation, it will be the purpose of the Denver congress, and the world organization of teachers, to promote friendship, justice and good will among the nations of the world; to bring about a world-wide tolerance of the rights and privileges of all nations, regardless of race or creed; to develop an appreciation of the value of inherited gifts of race and nations.

It will seek to secure more satisfying information and more adequate statement of facts for text-books used in the schools of the different nations; to omit from teaching materials statements which tend to misunderstandings and false impressions; to foster a national comradeship which will produce a more sympathetic appreciation among nations; to bring together the experiences of the races and the achievements of the various peoples as a basis for teaching international understanding and good will; to foster the dissemination of information concerning the progress of education in all its forms among nations and peoples.

Finally, it will endeavor to teach the interdependence of nations, that each nation is possessed of certain inalienable rights, among which are the rights to develop its natural resources, to carry on trade and commerce, to cultivate the gifts peculiar to itself and to provide for the welfare, progress and happiness of its people.

EDUCATIONAL NOTES AND NEWS

THE trustees of Allegheny College have announced that Dr. William Pearson Tolley will be inaugurated as the thirteenth president of the college on Friday, October 9. The committee in charge of the inauguration consists of The Honorable Frank P. Miller, Dr. Clarence F. Ross, and Dean J. R. Schultz, all of Meadville, and Dr. William P. Beazell, of New York City.

DR. HOWARD R. OMWAKE, dean of Franklin and Marshall College, has accepted the position of president of Catawba College.

DR. CORNELIUS BETTEN has been named acting dean and director of the State Colleges of Agriculture and Home Economics at Cornell University to fill the vacancy created by the promotion of Dean Mann to the office of provost of the university.

DR. HEINRICH LUEDERS, professor of Indo-Aryan Philology at the University of Berlin, has been elected rector of the university to succeed Professor Diessmann.

MR. ARTHUR L. F. SMITH has been appointed rector of the Edinburgh Academy. He succeeds Mr. P. H. B. Lyons, who has been appointed head master at Rugby School.

DR. RUDOLPH D. LINDQUIST has resigned as assistant superintendent of schools at Oakland, California, to accept the position of director of university schools and professor of education at the Ohio State University.

DR. ALBERT B. WRIGHT has been appointed head of the school of business administration at Duquesne University, Pittsburgh.

DR. WALTER J. SAUPE and Dr. Ralph K.

Watkins have been promoted to full professorships of education at the University of Missouri.

Appointments to the faculty of the summer session of the University of Cincinnati include: Dr. Harvey L. Eby, associate professor of rural education of the University of California at Los Angeles, and Dr. Gladstone H. Yeuell, professor of secondary education and head of the department of the University of Alabama.

Raymond Leslie Buell, research director of the Foreign Policy Association, has been appointed lecturer in the School of Public and International Affairs at Princeton University.

Mr. Arthur M. Seybold, for five years principal of the Thomas Jefferson Junior High School, Brooklyn, N. Y., has resigned to become head master of Oak Lane School of Temple University, Philadelphia.

The Reverend Joseph H. Dulles, librarian of Princeton Theological Library for the last forty-five years, retired on July 31, and will be succeeded by the Reverend William B. Sheddan.

Miss Charlotte Templeton has been appointed librarian of the new Atlanta University library. She is second vice-president of the American Library Association and president of the Southeastern Library Association.

Mr. Andrew J. Kolar has been elected president of the board of directors of the Chicago Public Library.

Dr. Albert B. Meredith, dean of school administration at New York University, has accepted the chairmanship of the American Council on Education.

Dr. D. C. Cabeen, professor of Romance languages at Vanderbilt University, has been elected president of the Vanderbilt Chapter of the American Association of University Professors. Other officers are: Dr. W. E. Garrey, *vice-president,* and Dr. C. B. Brown, *secretary.*

Mr. Patrick Henry Callahan has been appointed on the board of trustees of the National Child Labor Committee.

Brother Paul, formerly superintendent of St. Mark's Industrial School at Baltimore, has been elected superior of the Xaverian Order throughout the world for six years.

Dr. James T. Quarles, formerly university organist, and now dean of the College of Fine Arts of the University of Missouri, was honored at the commencement exercises of Denver College of Music with the degree of doctor of music.

Miss Flora Rose, professor of home economics at the Ohio State University, was awarded an honorary degree in pedagogy by the New York State College for Teachers on June 14.

Miss Grace Owen, honorary general secretary of the British Nursery School Association, was awarded the Order of the British Empire in the King's Birthday honor list. After holding lectureships in education in the Universities of Manchester and Reading, and at Leeds City Training College, she was from 1917 to 1924 principal of the Mather Training College for teachers of junior schools and nursery schools, and on the amalgamation of the Mather and Manchester Training Colleges, she was appointed the first principal of the combined foundation. Miss Owen, who is a sister of Mrs. J. McKeen Cattell, received the bachelor's degree from Teachers College, Columbia University, in 1905.

The Oberly Memorial prize this year has been awarded to Everett E. Edwards, U. S. Department of Agriculture economist, for his publication, "A Bibliography of the History of Agriculture in the United States," by the Eunice Rockwood Oberly Memorial Fund committee of the American Library Association. Eight bibliographies were submitted for the prize, which is awarded triennially in honor of Eunice Rockwood Oberly, Federal Bureau of Plant Industry librarian, who died on November 21, 1921. Miss Oberly was widely known in scientific circles for her preparation of bibliographies of scientific literature.

Three American professors of economics and commerce—Dean Adams (from Oklahoma), Professor Willey (from Minnesota), and Professor Witte (from Wisconsin)—arrived in London on July 11 as the guests of the Carnegie Endowment for International Peace for the purpose of making an extensive tour of Great Britain and Ireland and studying the general economic conditions. They remained in London until the end of the month, and during August will visit Liverpool, Manchester, Newcastle, Edinburgh, Glasgow, Belfast, Dublin, Swansea, Cardiff, Bristol and Oxford. On August 31 they will proceed to Geneva.

DR. NICHOLAS MURRAY BUTLER, president of Columbia University, who had just returned from a European trip, addressed the students of the summer session of the university on "This Changing World" on July 29.

Dr. L. P. JACKS, principal of Manchester College, Oxford, will lecture in various cities throughout the United States during the next academic year.

DR. STEPHEN P. DUGGAN delivered the first of a series of lectures at the University of San Marco, Lima, Peru, on July 18. He spoke on "The Character of the North American Civilization." Dr. Duggan was made an honorary fellow of the university.

MEMORIAL services for Dr. Frederick Gordon Bonser, formerly professor of education at Teachers College, Columbia University, were held on July 20 in the Milbank Chapel of Teachers College. Dr. Bonser died on June 8 after an illness of several months. Dean William F. Russell presided and Dean Emeritus James E. Russell was the speaker.

MISS HENRIETTA SCHMERLER, a candidate for the Ph.D. degree in the department of anthropology of Columbia University, aged twenty-three years, has been murdered on the Fort Apache Reservation, Arizona, where she was engaged in a study of the ceremonial and tribal home life of the Apache Indians.

A CONFERENCE of representatives of eastern states to consider the general situation in connection with an outbreak of infantile paralysis in New York was held in New York City on July 27, according to information received by the Public Health Service. The states participating, according to this information, under a call from the Health Officer of the State of New York, included all of New England, New York, New Jersey, Pennsylvania and possibly Maryland.

A PINT of milk every day in the week will be delivered during the summer vacation to ten thousand needy school children in New York City, who have been under the care of the school authorities, according to announcement of the Board of Education. The cost of the summer milk, which will be approximately $50,000, will be defrayed by the School Relief Fund, maintained by the voluntary contributions of teachers, principals and supervisors. The milk will be delivered in accordance with lists made out by the teachers, naming children whose families are not able to buy the milk. The list will be rechecked from time to time during the summer by attendance officers.

CLASSES in the continuation schools of New York City for retraining unemployed adults will be continued this fall and for such time next year as they are considered necessary, according to a statement made by Mr. Arthur S. Somers, chairman of the budget committee of the board. Funds have been tentatively set aside for the employment of thirty-nine teachers in addition to the regular staff of the continuation schools. Their salaries will amount approximately to $117,000. They will be able to teach about 2,000 part-time students. Two continuation schools are maintaining retraining classes this summer, but this feature of the work is not expected to be continued next year. The board, however, will decide next year whether summer classes are necessary in 1932. If employment conditions are better the classes will not be organized. Introduction of "retraining classes" last winter benefited approximately 3,700 jobless adults, many of whom have since been able to obtain work.

YOUNG Jewish scholars from America will be beneficiaries of seventeen new scholarships founded at the Hebrew University in Jerusalem, given by benefactors in the United States. The awards will be made on the basis of competitive examinations, which will be held at the beginning of the fall semester.

THE home economics curricula of some of the leading women's colleges of Japan and China will be studied during the coming year with the view of making them serve adequately the home life of the native people. Dean Ava B. Milam, of the school of home economics at

Oregon State College, under a year's leave of absence, has departed for the Orient to make the study. Dean Milam spent a year and a half in China in 1922–23, where she made a study of Chinese home life and on her findings based the first collegiate Chinese course in home economics, which was established under her direction at Yenching College.

SAN MARCOS UNIVERSITY, the oldest university on the American continent, recently celebrated its 380th anniversary. San Marcos was founded May 12, 1551, by the Spanish Emperor, Charles V, "with the same privileges, franchises and freedom as Salamanca University."

The Christian Science Monitor reports that the Greek government has increased fivefold its annual assistance to the University of Athens, to enlarge its activities, complete its buildings and acquire long-needed apparatus and furniture. The university will now be able to execute its plans at an estimated cost of 100,000,000 drachmas ($1,300,000). These funds will cover a period of four years. After the construction plan has been carried out, the annual subsidy to the university will be raised to 25,000,000 drachmas.

DESPATCHES to the daily press state that entrance to the two universities in Bulgaria is to be limited under plans of the educational authorities. The census showed that whereas the population had increased by 13 per cent. and the enrolment in primary schools by 11 per cent. in the six years between 1924 and 1930, the university enrolment had grown by 80 per cent. The authorities have advised parents to teach their sons and daughters trades, warning them that hundreds of young people who graduate from the universities are unable to find "white collar" jobs and have to undertake labor for which they are not fitted.

THE Budapest University recently celebrated the two hundred and ninety-sixth anniversary of its foundation and the one hundred and fifty-first anniversary of its restoration, according to the *Journal* of the American Medical Association. In his opening speech the rector of the university, Professor Louis Nékám, outlined the progress of the past seventy years. He made known the great sacrifices made by the neighboring countries. It is desirable, continued the rector, that a strong university and a strong ministry should cooperate. Also the community has to move in the interest of the university. He complained that the university met with little understanding in its present adverse position. In 250 years the Hungarian gentry (which spend millions and millions on race horses) altogether have made only four foundations, while the business men and the city of Budapest, so to say, did not support the institution with anything at all. He expressed his hope that henceforth rich merchants, manufacturers and noblemen will bear in mind the difficult financial position of the university and will lend helping hands as is done in the cultured Western states.

AN Associated Press dispatch reports that nearly 300 schools at Jerusalem with more than 22,000 children have been closed as a consequence of refusal of the Hebrew Teachers Union to accept a reduction in pay prescribed by the Jewish agency executive. Teachers have not received their salaries since December and some of them are said to be starving.

BELGIUM will set up a national bureau for the care of minor children who have lost the support of the family bread-winner through industrial accident, it has been announced at the Children's Bureau of the Department of Labor. The bureau, which is authorized in a law recently enacted, is directed to supervise in behalf of this class of children and enforce the child-welfare laws. It will administer the pensions awarded under the workmen's compensation law, handle matters affecting the minor's property, and give pecuniary aid when needed. In addition to these functions, the bureau will supervise their general education and vocational training. It will be represented by local committees in the provinces and cities. Through these committees, welfare "visitors" will be appointed to advise the mother or guardian. They must have certain prerequisites in education, experience and character. In administering to the children's well-being, the visitors will serve without compensation. Women are preferred for the work where young children are involved.

DISCUSSION

WHY THE WISCONSIN EXPERIMENT WAS BOUND TO FAIL

THE Wisconsin experiment has frequently been obscured from view by the clouds of incense and vituperation which hover about the heads of Messrs. Frank and Meiklejohn, on the one hand, and their opponents on the other. Mr. Showerman's able article has drawn floods of condemnation upon his person, while the principles for which he contends have been contemptuously thrust aside with a mere gesture. I wish to steer clear of all personalities for once and direct the public eye to facts and considerations which to my knowledge have not yet appeared in print and yet touch the very core of the actual situation in Wisconsin.

In brief, my thesis is that the Wisconsin experiment bore the germs of its failure in its very constitution, and it ultimately came to an end because its own faculty sabotaged the scheme and its students deserted it. Confirmation of these assertions should dispose of the notion that the university faculty was too reactionary to let the experiment succeed, as well as the notion that the Experimental College was to demonstrate some principle or other once for all. Arguments pro and con have completely lost sight of the truism that the failure of an experiment may prove only that it was badly devised.

It is probably true, as Mr. Showerman asserts, that a majority of our faculty was opposed to the Experimental College from the start, and has remained unconvinced down to the present date. It is also wholly irrelevant. For in point of fact the experiment went its way without obstruction either on or off the campus; and whatever discouragement may have resulted from informal expression of adverse opinion on the part of faculty members was more than offset by the very vocal approval which has resounded from platform and press ever since the venture was first announced.

More serious difficulties resulted from certain other factors which were stressed in campus discussion but have not been widely understood elsewhere. The predominantly vocational education which our state universities impart, especially in the case of men students, was a poor soil in which to plant an experiment which certainly did not primarily aim at preparation for a gainful career. The indefinite character of the actual training afforded by the Experimental College rendered very difficult the evaluation of that training in terms of "credits," *i.e.*, those measuring units for academic work which, for better or for worse, are the accepted currency on the academic market. Finally, there was something anomalous in a scheme which set the student free during his first two years and then sent him back into the more rigid harness of upperclass study. However, it may confidently be asserted that these problems did not contribute essentially to what I term the inevitable failure of the experiment, although to be sure they may well have accelerated its downward course.

At this point the question is in order as to why the defective character of the experiment was not recognized at the outset, if, as I claim, it was doomed to failure before it ever began. The answer is very simple: nobody knew how the experiment was actually to be conducted, and the vast majority even of well-informed persons do not know to this day what went on in the Experimental College. Mr. Meiklejohn's addresses and publications are disappointingly vague with respect to all the technical details of the experiment, and even the L. S. faculty did not obtain much insight into these matters until a committee appointed by the dean, in accordance with the terms of the original legislation establishing the experiment, undertook a careful investigation of the work of the Experimental College and the progress it had made. The committee was ably manned and went about its work with intelligence and energy; and it published a report which was a masterpiece in the art of saying nothing in as many (truthful) words as possible. This was an act of magnanimous restraint which has so far gone unheralded. For if the committee had published its actual findings, the effect upon the prestige of the Experimental College would have been little short of devastating. The failure of the experiment, in short, would have been patent to all seeing eyes, and Mr. Meiklejohn's work might have been seriously hampered. It seems to me, however, that the public should no longer be denied such information as is by now in the possession of every well-posted person on the Wisconsin campus.

Into Mr. Meiklejohn's original scheme were written the following specifications, among others which do not concern us here: (1) Each faculty member was to teach everything; (2) instruction by lecture was not favored; (3) faculty and students were to live together in a cloistered community; (4) formal instruction was to consist of one group conference per week and one individual 50-minute conference per student per week. Let us see some of the implications and results of this technique.

1. The requirement of universal instruction reads very beautifully in Mr. Meiklejohn's able and eloquent presentation of it. Faculty and students marching together along the same road, emulating each other in their efforts to reach the same or a similar goal, making simultaneous discoveries in a new and exciting world—such is about the tenor of the proponent's words. In actual practice, however, it was as unfortunate a plan as could well be imagined. I can only touch upon the disadvantages which it would seem that any expert pedagogical eye would have discerned in it. To begin with, it meant an overworked faculty, since the staff had to inform themselves along all sorts of lines which had hitherto been outside their regular fields of thought. But with all their effort, their students were bound to be or to become discontented, for a teacher in the guise of a fellow-student can hardly achieve that leadership that the teacher-student relation normally requires. Certain restrictions of the curriculum followed inevitably, for neither foreign language, nor exact science, nor mathematics, nor for that matter English, could be taught by an all-knowing faculty on the basis of one hour per week. Yet these are subjects which surely deserve some place in a program of liberal education, and the lack of suitable training in them must seriously affect a young man's preparation for his future work in life. Finally, a loyal acceptance of this program, which precluded the pursuit of a special field of study on the part of most members of the faculty, practically cut them off from advancement except within the framework of the college, since promotion seldom comes to a man who does not distinguish himself along some particular line of thought or work. In my judgment, the Experimental College would have eventually been destroyed by this specification alone.

2. Very severe and disconcerting things have been said about instruction by lecture, and there is no doubt that the average academic lecture is a variable whose pedagogic value approaches zero as a limit. I am in no mood to defend it, having touched zero in my own experience as a student. But for certain purposes we have nothing better, indeed nothing else: the best proof of which is that the faculty of the Experimental College, swearing it would never consent, consented (ultimately) to give its students about as many lectures as the average L. S. freshman has always had.

3. The cloistered college community was another beautiful dream—on paper. Or rather, to be perfectly fair, it was really marvelous for the students. But it drove the faculty to despair. The students of the Experimental College, who were not overburdened with those assignments that keep the ordinary freshman's nose to the grindstone, liked nothing better than to drop in at 8 in the evening and stay through till midnight. And that is precisely what they did, while the opportunity lasted.

4. I have already hinted at the reasons why neither the group conference nor the individual conference really amounted to very much from a pedagogical point of view. The group conference, as will be clear upon a little reflection, was only too often bound to degenerate into a sort of free-for-all in which certain voluble students easily got the lead and kept it. What could any but a very superior instructor do to prevent this? Had he been conducting a quiz-section in a field which he commanded, he could have held the discussion within bounds and led it back and back to the basic essentials that his knowledge and experience indicated as either fundamental, and hence requiring infinite repetition, or else difficult of mastery, and therefore calling for particular emphasis. While the same considerations apply in a somewhat lesser degree to the individual conference, a new factor of much importance enters at this point. I refer to the very great technical difficulty of this mode of instruction. In this connection, craving my readers' pardon for rubbing in the fact, I wish to call attention emphatically to the

circumstance that the only fixed appointment the Experimental College student had was this weekly conference with his instructor. I have taught for many years, and regard myself (of course) as a good teacher; but I should hesitate to take the responsibility for guiding the education of a young person on the basis of one hour per week. And I know that able members of the Experimental College faculty were discouraged by their relative failure to handle their conferences effectively.

I said above that the faculty of the Experimental College sabotaged the scheme. It is now possible for me to elucidate that statement, at the same time disclaiming any idea of reflecting upon their loyalty, which in fact was uniformly intense and highly inspiring. I mean by sabotage something much more subtle and more vital, a tacit admission that the original scheme could not be made to work, and consequent modifications of it which in some instances approached repudiation. A case in point is the treatment of lectures in the Experimental College curriculum, already referred to above. Let me mention a few other significant examples.

Certain members of the staff conducted voluntary conferences in their several fields of interest (cultivated prior to their appointments to the Experimental College staff). These were attended by students really interested and conducted in each case by a master of the subject. The value and interest of these conferences, as compared to those of the Experimental College curriculum, was an eye-opener to both staff and students, and their success demonstrated the inadequacy of the latter type.

A very considerable percentage of the students sought instruction "on the hill," as we say at Wisconsin, in subjects outside the Experimental College curriculum, notably in foreign language. This work had to be done in addition to their studies in the college. Obviously, for these students the Experimental College course did not completely satisfy the requirements of a liberal education. What would these students have done had the L. S. college not been close by with its wealth of organized classes?

The cloistered community idea was an early victim of faculty rebellion. After the staff had given it a good trial, they found that their intellectual existence was endangered, and they very properly pulled up stakes and left the young monks to roam the cloisters alone. In other words, the Experimental College teachers did just as the rest of us do: they posted office hours, which they probably kept as well as we do, and for the remainder of the time they retired behind the bastions of their homes.

Most serious of all, the faculty struck entirely, so to speak. That is, they came to feel, most of them, that a continuous post on the Experimental College staff would be a professional and personal impossibility. Some abandoned the ship altogether and left in disillusionment and dismay; others toyed with the idea of a sort of alternation, serving two years (say) in the Experimental College and returning for the third to what a great former president has taught us to call normalcy. Just what an independent college would do with the 33 per cent. of its staff that wanted to be off duty each year is not clear to me. But it is perfectly clear that the Experimental College at the University of Wisconsin could safely be called a failure from the moment when its staff—all handpicked and able men—ceased to regard it as offering a desirable life berth for any man.

Finally, I must explain the assertion that the students deserted the Experimental College, again with a disclaimer as conciliant. The loyalty of the students on campus to the experiment, their faculty, and their director, was perhaps the most gratifying feature of the entire venture and was at the same time a tribute to the magnetic and inspiring personality of Mr. Meiklejohn. And yet we must face the inescapable fact that in spite of this campus solidarity, in spite of a publicity campaign in Wisconsin which exceeded any effort the university had ever made, and in spite of nation-wide commendation of the Experimental College, the student enrolment, which only barely reached the desired figure in its first year, has dropped from year to year and is now only about one half of the anticipated norm of 125 per class. What does this mean? For me the conclusion is plain that in the eyes of the home-going student the experiment was a failure. He may even have been satisfied for himself; but either he could not conscientiously urge his younger brother, or his high-school friends, to follow his example, or what he had to tell about his year in the Experimental College held out no lure for them.

Let me drop our imaginary probe a little farther into the soul of the Experimental College student as he goes home. How has his year differed from that of his college mates and friends? He has had the same sports and amusements, has participated in that "college life" that the young man is supposed to regard as the chief object in signing up for a higher education. He has very likely had more time, in fact, to enjoy that life than his classmates, with their 16-hour schedule and steady grind of themes, quizzes, reports on outside reading, and the like. What is the matter, then, that he is not uttering paeans of joy and begging all his friends, "come on in, the water's fine!"? The only answer I can find is one which throws a better light on his character than our professional crape-hangers are wont to shed; it is my firm conviction that he feels he has somehow been cheated, that he hasn't got his (or his parents') money's worth, that the education imparted to him in the Experimental College is not the equal of what his friends on the hill received in the same time.

And now you know why (at least in the writer's opinion) the Wisconsin experiment was bound to fail: because it offered an inadequate form of collegiate education in competition with one which, with all its admitted faults, is more substantial and better suited to its day and its geographical location, and the students, doubtless inspired by the tenets of a merchandising age, are determined to "accept no substitutes!"

Ole Man Ribber

QUOTATIONS

CHILE'S STUDENTS

Until very recently Chile had succeeded in resisting the wave of political unrest engendered by the economic depression which has been sweeping over all of South America. Now her dikes have been broken. Just as in Argentina, Brazil, Peru and Bolivia, a long smoldering resentment has broken out against officials so unfortunate as to be in power at a time when economic conditions are beyond their control. President Carlos Ibanyez finds himself assailed from all sides with demands for his resignation.

The spearhead of this unrest is the student body of the University of Chile. A rapid series of Cabinet changes failed to moderate their attacks upon the Government, and, having barricaded themselves in the university buildings, they have been defying the troops and calling upon Ibanyez to surrender his power. It is futile to speculate on how much support their movement has in the country as a whole, but whatever the outcome of present disturbances they afford a striking demonstration of the political influence which students in Latin-American countries so often exert.

According to reports, these patriotic young men threatened to burn down the buildings, regardless of their own lives, should the troops attack them, while on the other hand they promised to get out peacefully if President Ibanyez "restored full freedom to Chile." Just how these threats and promises could really help their country is something which perhaps only the student agitators could adequately explain. Economic depression is the real problem with which Chile is faced, and under present circumstances political questions are necessarily subordinate to the measures undertaken to alleviate economic distress. And obviously on such matters the student body of the University of Chile is hardly qualified to know what should be done or even to criticize the Government's program.

In a stable country it is a great thing to have student interest in politics. It is often regretted in this country that the students of our universities and colleges are often so apathetic in regard to public questions. But between a student body which takes advantage of an economic crisis to defy the Government and provoke unrest and disorder and one which is content to restrain its political impulses until they can be expressed through the ballot box, the choice would fairly seem to lie with the latter.—*The New York Evening Post.*

THE HIGH-SCHOOL CURRICULUM

The high-school teachers of the land at last demand that their institutions shall serve the students and the public rather than college entrance committees. This proposal of the National Secondary School Association at the National Educational Association meetings in Los Angeles received relatively little publicity. Yet it dwarfs into insignificance such heralded educational items of the last year as the proposed reform of collegiate athletics or the dropping of Latin at Yale. Indeed, if the plan is put through in thorough fashion it may well be regarded as the outstanding educational reform of our generation.

The most tragic travesty in our educational system has been the conventional high-school curriculum. The greatest waste of conscientious pedagogical effort has been the work of our high-school teachers. About one high-school student out of ten goes to college. Yet our high schools have been prostituted to the service of college entrance committees rather than being devoted to training young men and women to live more adequately in human society.

The high-school curriculum has been determined by the demands placed upon students for college entrance. The subjects thus required have had singularly little relation to fitting anybody to live more satisfactorily in twentieth century civilization. The successful high-school teacher has been judged according to the number of boys and girls he can get by the college board examinations, not in relation to his shrewd and understanding guidance in the problems of human living. Progressive educators have observed this tragic waste and misdirection of teaching effort and have long murmured "O Lord, how long?"

Now it appears that the long-suffering secondary schools have burst into open rebellion against being regarded as lackeys of the colleges. It is proposed that the old curriculum be scrapped and that subjects be introduced which will prepare students to meet the responsibilities of life in more intelligent fashion. It is recommended that more attention be given to the natural and social sciences, to psychology, "because it is essential that young people know something about the laws that govern mental health," to subjects that develop motor skill, to health education, and to an appreciation of the fine arts.

The green mould of the past lingers on in the proposal that two units of Latin or higher mathematics still be required, and rather too much time is to be given to the formal teaching of English. Yet the proposed reconstruction as a whole is sane and far-reaching. The results hoped for are well stated by the committee:—

"This program, if conscientiously carried out, we confidently believe will solve most of our secondary school problems. It will produce symmetrically developed citizens interested in the varied activities of the social organization equipped for complete living. This means social-minded, service-rendering men and women. It means also a far larger proportion of creative mentalities than this country or any other country has ever possessed. More than that, it means a happy, prosperous and ever-developing type that will rule the world, not by its dollars or its governmental authority but by its creative spirit, its ideals and its universal service."

I agree heartily and hope that the proposal will pass beyond the rhetoric of reform. The high school is the one opportunity which we have to train the majority of the mentally capable to be intelligent and honest citizens.

It is time that we realized the opportunity and responsibility involved. The high school must no longer be a despised and incidental adjunct to higher education.—*Dr. Harry Elmer Barnes in The New York World-Telegram.*

REPORTS

THE NATIONAL COUNCIL OF EDUCATION

AN outstanding feature of the program of the National Council of Education, held in connection with the National Education Association at Los Angeles on June 26 and 27, was the presentation and discussion of "The Philosophy at the Basis of Understanding and Good

Will," based upon a source book entitled "Human Relationships—Individual and Collective," prepared by the Bureau of Cooperative Research of Indiana University, Bloomington, Indiana, under the direction of Henry Lester Smith and Harold Littell, of that institution. The discussion was led by Mrs. Susan M. Dorsey, superintendent emeritus of schools, Los Angeles, California.

Some conclusions growing out of these materials and their interpretations pointed to the fact that in practically all periods of history from the beginning of time there have existed thinkers and writers who perceived and pointed out the necessity for abolishing wars and even recommended the establishment of leagues of then existing nations which, in some instances, were carried out. The problems to be solved in developing and maintaining satisfactory human relationships were held to be difficult but probably not insurmountable, and education was accepted as an indispensable factor in attaining the goal. Instances of the influence of the prejudices of adults, especially parents, on the human relations of youth were cited, and a plan suggested for the education of parents as a means of correcting such situations.

Henry Lester Smith, joint author of the source book and president of the National Council of Education, brought before the council "Some Suggested Theses Together with Related Questions bearing upon the Subject of the Philosophy of Education." These nine theses and the twenty-seven questions relating thereto were in printed form and distributed to the council for consideration.

Other interesting portions of the program included:

(1) "A Review of Educational Progress during the Year," based on the biennial survey of the United States Office of Education and read by Mrs. Katherine M. Cook, chief of the division of special problems, United States Office of Education. In this résumé were emphasized the expansion of educational service through the public schools to new groups and to increasing numbers of all groups; equalization of funds for school purposes; enlarged powers of state boards of education, and important curriculum revisions. Attention was drawn to the fact that while we have approximately four and one half million youths in the public schools—fifteen to eighteen years of age—there are still approximately four million out of school that need educational aid.

(2) "A Look into the Educational Future," presented by Dr. Willis A. Sutton, superintendent of schools, Atlanta, Georgia, and president of the National Education Association. Dr. Sutton declared that we do not give youth the challenge of "hard work and the making of new discoveries." We dwell entirely too much in our education on what has been accomplished and too little on the still unknown, undiscovered and uninvented. We also think and act in terms of things rather than of people, and the higher values of life are overlooked. Dr. Sutton cited an investigation which disclosed that when one thousand of our best citizens were speaking, seventy-eight words out of every hundred were spoken of real estate, stocks, bonds, houses and material possessions; six words out of every hundred were purely in fun or gossip; while only sixteen words out of every hundred concerned the development of the social, intellectual and moral life of the people.

(3) "Some Problems Reviewed by the California Commission for the Study of Educational Problems," by Mrs. Susan M. Dorsey, superintendent emeritus of schools, Los Angeles, California, and chairman of the commission. This report outlined a careful study of educational problems by a commission of nine members, appointed by the governor of California, for this purpose, for a period of one year. Thirty major educational problems were studied, and both sides of the question set up in each case, followed by a summing up of evidence and such recommendations as the case seemed to warrant. The report consisted of five major divisions: (a) "Student Problems"; (b) "Teacher Problems"; (c) "School Organization Problems"; (d) "School Costs and Revenues," and (e) "Miscellaneous Problems." A remarkable feat of the commission was the expenditure of only $30,000 out of the $50,000 appropriated for the work, thereby reserving $20,000 for some future investigation.

(4) "Report of the Committee on the Reorganization of Membership of the National Council of Education," by Joseph H. Saunders, superintendent of schools, Newport News, Virginia, and chairman of the committee. This report was based on recommendations made some months earlier by Dr. Henry Suzzallo for a reorganization of the council, and offered definite recommendations for the same to be acted upon one year hence—after the members had time to study the report and evaluate the recommendations.

New officers were elected as follows:

President: Dr. William C. Bagley, professor of education, Teachers College, Columbia University, New York City.

Member Executive Committee: Miss Minnie J. Nielsen, Valley City, North Dakota.

Members of Membership Committee: Joseph H. Saunders, Newport News, Virginia, and Mary McSkimmon, principal, Pierce School, Brookline, Massachusetts.

ADELAIDE S. BAYLOR

EDUCATIONAL RESEARCH AND STATISTICS

AN EXPERIMENT IN REMEDIAL READING

THE purpose of this experiment was to ascertain the effect of some remedial instruction in reading on students of the freshman class, Teachers College, University of Nebraska, first semester, 1930, who scored definitely below the reading norm for the tenth grade.

On October 23, 1930, form *A* of Whipple's High School and College Reading Test was given to 273 freshmen in the Teachers College. This test is a short test requiring only ten minutes for its administration and is one of the few tests published for use in the high-school and college levels. Remedial classes were instituted during the last week in October for those who were below the tenth-grade norm in reading score. Thirty-eight students took the work. These classes met once a week for eight weeks. Each student was tested individually for speed and comprehension. A study of each subject's eye movements was made in an attempt to determine the specific difficulty of each student. Each one was advised as to his or her particular difficulty and was given definite remedial treatments. Each student was given a "Manual of Reading Exercises for Freshmen," by Dr. L. C. Pressey. This book is one of daily exercises which require a minimum of six weeks.

Each student represented a case study on the part of the instructor and of the one in charge of the experiment. Remedial treatment was recommended on the basis of individual diagnosis. As soon as those in charge felt it would be profitable for the student, different types of reading were taken up. On January 13, 1931, or near the end of the first semester, form *B* of Whipple's Reading Test was given. Because the results appear to show that there is no true difference between the performances of the whole group, forms *A* and *B* were subjected to statistical treatment in order to ascertain the reliability and validity of these instruments. The reliability was found to be .51 and the validity was found to be .71 upon the assumption of a perfect criterion. The chances are much in favor of the validity being much lower than this figure.

The data were subjected to group comparisons and paired comparisons. The paired comparisons were made by selecting one student from the practice or remedial reading group and pairing him with one student from the control or unselected group. The pairing was made on the basis of percentile rank on the Ohio State University intelligence examination and the reading score. No pair was selected which varied more than 2 percentiles in the intelligence test or 2 scores on the reading test. This method yields individuals paired on the basis of 3 variables: Intelligence, reading score, and class-standing in the university. It was possible to obtain only 26 pairs by this rigorous method of selection.

A. Group Comparisons: The distribution of the freshman class closely approximated a normal curve on the basis of the initial test in reading. The median of the distribution was 10, showing that this teachers college freshman group scored slightly superior to the norm for normal schools and teachers colleges and slightly inferior to the norm for arts colleges undergraduates as given by Whipple. The range was from a score of 3 to a score of 19 upon a scale of 20.

TABLE I

Total Group Comparisons (N = 273) Reading (Whipple)

	Mean	S. D.
Initial test (form *A*)	10.28	2.93
End test (form *B*)	10.13	2.51
Difference	.15	.42
Critical ratio	.94	3.80

The above Table I shows that the mean on form *A* of the distribution is found to 10.28 with a standard deviation of 2.93. The mean in form *B* given for the group was found to be 10.13 with a standard deviation of 2.51. The obtained difference of .15 is statistically unreliable, being much less than 4 times the probable error of the difference, which is .2135. The critical ratio of .94 indicates that there is slight chance that a real difference was obtained in view of the low reliability and validity coefficients of the test.

The following table indicates the number of students in the various categories of delinquency employed by the University of Nebraska.

TABLE II

Delinquent Students with Reading Score Below Tenth-Grade Norm (Whipple)

	No. cases	Failure	Incomplete	Condition	Total
Remedial group	20	3	0	6	9
Non-remedial group	32	12	4	6	22
Total group	52	15	4	12	31

Table II shows the number of the fifty-two, or 18.8 per cent., of the freshmen who scored 7 or below which is below the norm for the tenth grade who were reported as being delinquent. Of these fifty-two students, thirty, or 57.6 per cent., were reported down in from 1 to 4 courses at the first quarter. Thirty-one, or 59.6 per cent., of these fifty-two individuals were reported delinquent or failed in one or more subjects at the end of the semester. It is to be noted that proportionally fewer of the reading group were delinquent than the non-remedial group.

These results seem to show that this test indicates little difference in the ability to read after a semester's work in the university. Furthermore, there is indicated the fact that students of low initial reading score who took the remedial reading work were more successful in avoiding failure than individuals who did not receive this instruction.

In another attempt to make a comparison the scores of the students in the remedial reading class were extracted from the groups. These students (38 in number) made up the experimental group. The remaining members of the class (235 in number) formed the control group.

TABLE III

Group Comparisons Reading (Whipple)

	Mean	S. D.
Remedial group N = 38		
Initial test	6.81	1.65
End test	9.55	1.46
Difference	2.74	−.19
Critical ratio	11.42	1.12
Non-Remedial group N = 235		
Initial test	11.27	2.77
End test	10.78	2.73
Difference	.49	.04
Critical ratio	2.88	.33

The above Table III shows the mean of the experimental group on the initial test was 6.81 with a standard deviation of 1.65. The mean of the end test was 9.55 with a standard deviation of 1.46. This represents a gain of 2.74 or a gain of more than 4 times the probable error of the difference. The chances that this is a true difference are better than 99 in 100. It must be stated that this difference is found on the basis of only 38 cases and that there is, therefore, some skepticism as to the absolute legitimacy of these results. The mean for the control group in the initial test was 11.27 with a standard deviation of 2.77. The mean for the end test was 10.78 with a standard deviation of 2.73. The probable error of the difference indicates that there is slight chance that a real difference was obtained in this group. On the basis of these data it appears that the remedial reading group probably made a definite gain in ability to read as measured by the reading test used.

B. Paired Comparisons: The following Table IV gives a statement of differences found among the groups selected by pairing individuals upon the basis indicated above.

TABLE IV
PAIRED COMPARISONS

	Mean	S. D.
Remedial group		
Initial test	7.38	1.12
End test	9.50	1.54
Difference	2.12	.42
Critical ratio	8.48	2.33
Non-Remedial group		
Initial test	8.81	1.633
End test	8.42	1.817
Difference	.39	.184
Critical ratio	1.22	.80

The above Table IV shows the mean for the reading group in the first test was 7.38 while the mean for the second test was 9.5 or a gain of 2.12. The mean for the control group for the initial test was 8.81 while the mean for the end test was 8.42 or a loss of .39. The errors of measurement would nullify this loss. The critical ratio for the control group shows that there is no gain indicated while the critical ratio for the reading group indicates that there is little doubt but what an actual gain of substantial size was made by the reading group.

The significance of the difference between the means of the experimental group and the control group was computed. The critical ratios were 5.50 for the means and 2.70 for the standard deviations. This indicates a reliable difference in favor of the control group obtained at the initial testing. Critical ratios of 3.37 for the means and 1.26 for the standard deviations indicate that in all probability a real difference in favor of the experimental group is shown by the end test. On the basis of these findings the remedial reading groups were definitely inferior to the control group at the initial testing and distinctly superior to the control group in the end test.

The total aspect of this experiment seems to show that definite improvement in reading was possible for college freshmen in a relatively short period of time. It also seems evident that, as a whole, freshmen do not improve in reading during the first semester of college work. While the suggestions for the improvement of reading were treated in regular class work in an orientation course given all freshmen there is seen to be no effect. However, when remedial treatment is given on the basis of individual diagnosis there is positive improvement obtained. In spite of the fact that the reading classes met only once a week for eight weeks and that the work was entirely optional with the student, the results show that definite gains were achieved. It is to be pointed out that the reading test used in this experiment, although highly recommended, is of relatively low reliability and validity. The evidence in this experiment seems to suggest that poor readers constitute potential failures in college work.

SUMMARY

1. 18 per cent. of the Teachers College freshman class had less reading ability than the average child in the tenth grade.

2. 59 per cent. of poor readers of the Teachers College freshman class constituted delinquents for the first semester.

3. College freshmen as a group do not improve in reading ability after a semester of college work.

4. Remedial reading classes improved the students' ability to read in a short time.

5. The evidence yielded by this investigation suggests that poor reading is a potential factor in the failure of freshmen to succeed in the first year of college work.

WILLIAM H. THOMPSON
TEACHERS COLLEGE,
UNIVERSITY OF NEBRASKA

EDUCATIONAL REVIEW

Edited by WILLIAM McANDREW

EDITORIAL COMMENT

MEMORIES OF THE MEETING: LOS ANGELES

What Mr. Boutwell printed here a week ago, on the great meeting of the National Education Association, does it and him credit, but if, each week for the rest of the year, an article upon that convention were run there would be material enough left for other pages. In all the sixty-nine years' life of the association no meeting has reached this one in crowds, cordiality, color and compliments.

Everybody assumed that the hard times would reduce attendance. But on Monday the usual number of registration cards was exhausted and a rush order given a printer for a thousand more. These were filled by Tuesday noon. Five thousand more were sent for. When I visited Secretary Crabtree's headquarters, Saturday morning, members were still registering. A gentlewoman of the staff estimated that over 16,000 persons had enrolled. To this might be added participants who never register; wives, relatives and visitors, bringing the attendance up to staggering figures.

The habit of many school superintendents to have presented to meetings of their staffs ideas gathered by attendants on the convention will spread this meeting over a still larger multitude. The various state educational publications will distribute impressions still further. The pressroom in Convention Hall had representatives from many cities. The *New York Times* sent its educational editor. The Associated Press had a direct wire from the meeting place. The reporter told me the papers of the country were eating up all he could send and asking for more. These things justify calling it a great convention.

Dr. Crabtree's dozen years as master of ceremonies, the experience of his associates, Allan, Martin, Chase, and Shankland, the executive and hospitable genius of Willis Sutton I think could carry on a brilliant program anywhere. The addition of Los Angeles talent results in a triumph unique in school annals. For visitors arriving by train across the sizzling plains and stepping out on the Los Angeles station platform the first sight is that of pretty girls proffering iced orange juice. These are Ione Kirk and her committee. Flags, banners, and welcomes flutter over the streets; Schoolmen Chandler's and Wilson's staff saw to this. Morley Sellery, E. B. Lefferts and associates provided for first aid. Marie Larkey, C. F. Palmer and a large company of teachers had inspired school children to cultivate flowers for convention guests. Result: a profusion of blossoming glory across the stage at every meeting, on the tables at every breakfast and banquet. Lester Rogers, Wm. Bryan, Gordon Watkins, F. L. Thurston and helpers got us lodgings at whatever prices our necessities determined. We were all advised back home where we were to sleep. There were twenty-six of these local committees under the general charge of Mr. Bouelle, the superintendent of schools. They were tireless, smooth-running, and Californianly cordial. They distributed a handbook of information so full of entertainment and hospitality as to make you feel like the Sultan Shah-Zaman come to the city of Ispahan.

A Topsy Town

Los Angeles is a combination of Cannes, Paris, Detroit, Oil City, and Gopher Prairie. It has acres of smart shops where France, Tokio and Persia meet. Its hundreds of acres of square-fronted, one-story marts are sandwiched between magnificent boulevards embowered and perfumed with tropic blooms. Its used-car repositories outnumber those of any city in the world. Whole trains of electric coaches run on the main streets along with motorbuses of the brightest colors. A traffic policeman held his protecting arm around me in the middle of the street while he told me how to reach the First Congregational Church. Fire engines and ambulances have sirens of a thousand-shriek power. They are in charge of grown-up boys whose main delight is to race up and down the town with the noise valve locked open. The self-serving dining halls surpass all the Eatitoriums on earth for variety and savor. They insist on keeping your check far below the dollar mark. With all its sunny climate the city seems not to have discovered the continental charm of outdoor eating. Theaters are as thick as churches and almost as modest in admission price. There were no beggars in the streets. The men and women are the cleanest, brightest, most attractively dressed to be found anywhere out of Ypsilanti, Michigan. I met neither flies nor mosquitoes nor nights uncomfortably warm. To the north and south are shadowy mountains, red in the morning, pink in the afternoon, blue or melting lavender in the evening. East are miles of orange groves, walnut trees and lines of red-barked eucalyptus. West is the best-behaved of oceans. All around are more than sixteen thousand of the hope of the nation listening to 1,137 speeches, discussions and resolutions. Two propositions never fail to get applause: that our country ought to have a National Minister of Education and that the people howling for repeal of the Eighteenth Amendment are short of general welfare sentiment.

Educational vespers are a habit with us by this time. Eleven years ago when we met in Salt Lake City, Hugh Magill preached us a Sunday sermon in the Mormon Temple. Two years later the program of the Oakland meeting called the Sunday afternoon program a vesper service. Since then the pleasant project of an out-of-door meeting on the Lord's day has come to be a regular feature of the summer session. Los Angeles gave it a beautiful setting. We sat in front of a park temple of music. Across its stage were the lilies, dahlias and roses grown by the school children for us. On each side, tall columns are surmounted by lovely ladies blowing golden trumpets. Vines have climbed up to and over them. Our Lady Sinestra is prettily veiled with the green. Madam Dextra is quite hidden by verdure and flowers and toots her horn from behind its thick screen. Leroy Allen's All-City High School Band and the handsome Rufus von KleinSmid delight us, the first with the music of much brass, the second with the melody of his velvety speech. I enjoyed most the singing of young high-school boys in charge of Louis Curtis. The fourth lad from the right edge of the front row gave us a thrill. He was all words and music. The afternoon sun picked him out for attention. He was illumined without and within. The cynicism of disappointment, the monotony of repetition haven't dulled him against the ring of a paean. "I am the master of my fate; I am the captain of my soul," he sang, meaning all of it.

So am I, Buddy, let's not allow the scorners to laugh us out of it.

Marvelous Musicians

It seems to me I have never attended a meeting comparable to the one in the civic auditorium Monday night. The amazing curtain went up and disclosed an orchestra of more than two hundred boys and girls. Many of the little adorables had trombones or cellos or drums bigger than themselves. Jennie Jones, who is the head supervisor of Los Angeles Elementary orchestras, led these youngsters through a snappy number. Six women in succession, each a handsome full-size specimen such as you would nominate for a committee of appeal to a legislature, conducted this same musical multitude through colorful selections. The harmony was marvelous—not a sour note in the whole long program. Phrasing, shading, climaxes were done with the assurance of veterans. None of the large women conducting indulged in any flummery copied from any eccentric stager. They indulged in no rapping, impressive waits or attention antics. They stood up, made a sweep of the baton and off we floated upon waves of sweet sound. Who can forget the straight-standing violinists hardly out of the cradle, the chubby little trumpeters, the crowd of trombone players who swung up the long bright tubes with an irresistible gesture? In the front row of these was a masterpiece in yellow curls. She was small enough to pack in a suitcase. I claim a good conduct card for that I didn't steal her and take her home with me. Wonder stroke of all —these miniature virtuosos played their last number without a leader and in perfect time and tune.

Nearly Naked

Another wonder of this Monday meeting was the nearly naked commercial propaganda of the Motion Picture Producers and Distributors of America, Inc. After the Bishop of Los Angeles had prayed, accompanied by the click of a stenotype operated between him and God in order that the archives of heaven may be kept in a businesslike manner, Carl Milliken, vice-president of the Federal Council of Churches of Christ, member of the Clergy Club, and secretary of the motion picture syndicate, told us of our duty to see that the coming generations solve the problems of our country. We must train the children to see that their parents take them to the movies. A wise teacher can make a movie audience squeeze the last drop of juice from a film. Teachers should pay attention to the offerings of the local picture houses.

The people near me were thinking of the New York despatches of the morning, recording the protest of a council of churches against block and blind booking which prevent local theaters from eliminating objectionable pictures. We were wondering why Carl suggests that we butt against the stone wall. We were recalling the film shows at this moment advertised in Los Angeles: "The Man in Possession," "with risqué moments and even more risqué innuendoes," "Born to Love," "The Girl Habit," "Tabu," "Uncivilized Love," "Strangers May Kiss," "Behind Office Doors," "Kiss Me Again," "The Sin Ship," "A Night in Reno," "Confessions of a Co-Ed" and "The Tarnished Lady." We were recalling various National Education Association resolutions against encouragement to speakers who have propaganda to spread and to various agencies which seek to serve private ends through school publicity. Mr. Milliken invited us all to confer with him in his temporary office maintained during the convention. He introduced us to a number of bored men, women and children, film stars "in person." Then they and most of the audience left, the president's annual address being scheduled to close the meeting. Dr. Sutton gave it superbly, without petulance at the amazing demonstration of relative interests shown by educators. Mary McSkimmon whispered to me, "We still have many who choose the Colosseum rather than the forum," and then she added proudly, "We have no movies in our town." Farther along in the general program is printed, "Hollywood motion picture stars will be introduced at several of the general sessions." What's the great idea? Is this a contribution of the association's division on "the enrichment of life"? or the department of visual instruction, or a committee on character education or maybe of a section for the use of schools for the promotion of business. Really, where is the hook-up in purpose between the schools and the Motion-Picture Producers, Inc.? Do we get quit of Mother's Day propaganda of dealers in flower baskets; do we slough off apple week, tooth-brush makers, dairymen and power trusts only to be easy marks for the Picture Producers, Inc.? One of us is born every minute.

A Banquet of Builders

The "lifers'" dinner, planned and executed by Harriett Chase, was in celebration of the enrolment of over 4,500 continuous members in the association. We who have been let in are the starred and the undecorated. If we pay our own fifty dollars for membership our virtue is its own reward. If a faculty, a club or a philanthropist buys the commission for us our names are preceded by the asterisk which usually means "deceased." We are assured that we are upper-class, for every life member must be recommended by an organization, or a superintendent or a college president or a life member. We are all listed as "Builders of the Profession." When you come to analyze us we are not without our laugh-provoking side. Here we are, the agencies proposed by the makers of the nation to carry out the American doctrine of equality, abolition of caste, disuse of artificial distinctions. And here we are, telling ourselves that life-membership is a distinction. One must be recommended to it by a distinguished person or organization and pay fifty dollars for the honor.

Piffle!

Why don't we print the honest truth that any

educator who has the brains and patriotism to hope that a great benefit will come to our country by a well-equipped and well-financed union of school people should do his duty by paying the cost, not for his personal prominence, starred or unstarred, but for the general welfare? We are not beyond the need of purging ourselves of pride. A well-known school official, by some reason omitted from head-table listing, went this evening into a sulk and out of the room. Why have head tables? The early Christians and the later Washington Irving High School faculty had none at their communions. Education is for democracy, isn't it?

For all that, Miss Harriett is responsible for a brilliant affair, so big it crowded the huge Biltmore dining hall and drove participants into the galleries. Everybody compliments her in the Washington headquarters; at conventions she scores A plus.

A Cubberley Club

At our table someone started to talk about the brilliant record of California in the educational world. We were all from east of the Mississippi, but amongst us we named Royce, Howison, Lange, Lang, Almack, Snedden, Suzzallo, Rowell, Dorsey, Swett, Wood, Cooper, Jordan, Terman, Francis, Wilbur, Hunter, Wilson, Cook, Schallenberger, Griggs, and Cubberley as our candidates for tablets in a hall of fame. Somebody said that Stanford University wants to commemorate Dean Cubberley. So do we. Here is a teacher, school superintendent, and professor who has preached a gospel of progress in Indiana, Harvard, Columbia, Chicago, and on the Pacific Coast for forty fruitful years. He has excavated the strata of educational history down to the azoic layers, cleaned, polished and mounted his discoveries, to the end that we can traverse the whole collection without a yawn. The risk of the historian is to be pulled into the past by his researches. Cubberley yanked them into the present. Surveyor indefatigable of schools in Maryland, Montana, Oregon, Utah, California, Washington, New Mexico, and for National Commissions, he has fused his observations of past and present into educational practice treatises which have given American school theory and performance a notable Cubberley turn.

Gilbert Wrenn told me the tireless dean is going to retire from professional life in two years.

Absurd!

Think of Socrates or Franklin or Gladstone retiring at sixty-five! Cubberley may change his work but he won't retreat from it. He's too young to quit and too old to get the loafing habit.

Nevertheless three different groups, east and west, are planning a memorial. They are combining into a national body with Henry Suzzallo as chairman. An Ellwood Cubberley Institute of Educational Research, a Cubberley Hall to house the Stanford School of Education, a Cubberley celebration in 1933, a Cubberley volume of letters by those who realize their debt to him, a Cubberley endowment for lectures, a Cubberley portrait, a biography, are projects already under way. My guess is that as soon as the intent of the initiators is known a multitude of good people will want to be let into the commemoration. It affords a focus for a constantly brightening professional pride. Satisfaction at being in a high-grade public service was never so keen among teachers as now. Never were there so many and well-reasoned declarations by public-minded Americans upon the reliance that must be placed upon our schools. The memorials in foreign lands, marking the service of other than military leaders, invariably impress the thoughtful travelers as a contrast to our custom at home. The time is ripe for reminding ourselves of what education means to America and for putting personality into our commemoration of the nation's pattern set for educating the people. The starters of this move could not have chosen a better leader of progress than this scholar, planner, and executive. It is in order, now, to write G. Gilbert Wrenn, at Stanford University, your request to be enrolled in the Cubberley Club.

Everywhither

The Los Angeles Herald attempted a high-grade project; a symposium on educational trends. Reporters tackled people pointed out as leading educators and asked them whither schools are going. The result was not Paul Hanus's famous "All sails set and going nowhere." It was rather "Headed where my hobby leads." As you read *The Herald's* collection you will find that education is to be more vocational, more for leisure, more for health, more individual, less individual, more adoptive of radio, more insistent on letting the teacher exercise her personality, more or less almost everything and sometimes W and Y. Much less bewildering was Sutton's brilliant feature, a symposium of youth. He presented a galaxy of boys and girls from east, west, north and south who told us schools are democracy's means for keeping itself pure. We must dedicate our brains to the perfection of our political system. We must give our youth practice in government, using the school as if it were the wider community and state.

On every hand I heard that this event was Sutton's greatest contribution to a phenomenal program. It is a feature that ought to be as usual as is the present use of children as entertainers by means of their concerts, their calisthenics, their dramatics, their pageantry and their dancing shows. Get them out of the side-shows into the main tent! Let up on the supplementary and stress the fundamental!

Pursuing a Principle

I followed hot-foot every cue I could find to the big American idea: the establishment of schools by community funds not for individual advantage so much as for community benefit. George Strayer opened the first meeting by hammering home the old truth that America made schools a public charge for public, not personal, benefit. Willis Sutton's presidential address nailed the flag to the mast reiterating that the schoolroom must solve the problems that vex the body politic. For this the framers of free-school legislation justified making everybody pay for schools. Brother Bogan told us that by the teaching of democratic ideals the schools have made democracy, with all its weaknesses, indestructible. Ann Brewington, from that same Chicago, pointed out the failure of education to address itself to real social problems. The average American has more property and money than any one in the world and commits more crimes. The native-born among us rates at the worst, the Negro, next; the foreign-born citizen has the cleanest record in court.

Newsman Bradfield, of the *Evening Herald,* asked me why is it that the greatest school system in the world, asking for support because it is the bulwark of democracy, hasn't produced a generation able to keep the most richly endowed country on earth from going to the dogs criminally and economically.

For answer I showed him a paragraph in his own journal: "Following the youth symposium, a teacher was heard to remark to a neighbor: 'Those youngsters don't really think the things they say, they just think they should think them.' Replied the other: 'You're all like that. Your ideals are the things you think you ought to think.' "

"You mean," asked Bradfield, "that educational aim is mostly talk?"

"It has often been so charged. Everybody knows that public schools are part of our self-governing system as much as are legislatures and courts. The statesmen who set schools up proposed that the classes would be manned by teachers especially prepared in politics, government, economics and general welfare. The creators of the public school said it should make training in these its main duty. For every school you name so organized and functioning I'll give you a dollar."

Bradfield. "I lose. My school never referred to politics."

Myself. "Noah Webster said the Revolution never reached the schoolmasters."

Bradfield. "What is to be done about it?"

Myself. "Keep pushing the idea under their noses."

Here's a citation for Bradfield; he microscoped every day's proceedings for signs of public education's birth certificate and when he found some speakers exhorting to get public service into public schools he featured it in his newspaper. So there's another happy warrior added to our squad along with Richard Welling, John Chewning, Harold Rugg, David Snedden, John Greenan, Thomas Finegan, William Bagley, John Tildsley, Chester Rowell, Bessie Pierce, Edna Stone, Director Kelso, Alsworth Ross, Ira Brinser, Helen Marquand, Claire Epler, Professor Maverick and some others.

A CHALLENGE FOR FLORENCE HALE

Are we downhearted?

Not a bit.

It took the Roman republic 480 years to fizzle out. We have, at that rate, 338 more years in which to get public education onto the track it was built for. The National Education Association will be brought around. The women presidents, for some unexplained reason, swing the programs into the larger patriotism. Mary Bradford at Pittsburgh, Charl Williams at Boston, Olive Jones at Washington, Mary McSkimmon at Philadelphia, Cornelia Adair at Minneapolis, Ruth Pyrtle at Columbus, kept the civic fundamental to the fore. With enthusiastic acclaim we, at Los Angeles, elected the radiant Florence, Hale and Hearty, for president and patternmaker of the next meeting. No one has any doubt of the outcome. The Lady of the Aroostook will put on a program up to any high mark yet made. Atlantic City schools can not be counted on to do much entertaining. We have, with various supplementary conventions, been a heavy load on nearby teachers and children. But a series of rousing addresses, on the big theme, by Borahs and Bakers, Morrows, Fosdicks, and such speakers as Harry Garfield can recommend, will do much to keep us out of the educational eddy—in which the youngest university president, even Rob. Hutchins of Chicago, says we are—floundering around failing to substitute civic intelligence for stupidity, prejudice and fear.

TASTES OF BOOKS

We now open the doors of our booketeria. Help yourselves to pads and pencils. Select your viands. Proceed to the easy chairs. May good digestion wait on appetite. The offerings to-day are history, civics, economics, imported pedagogics, administration, psychology, methods, mathematics, business, science, logic, philosophy, reading, linguistics and literature.

BOOK REVIEWS

BECKER AT HIS BEST

To Carl Becker, Professor of History, Cornell University: It is nine years since I told you that your "Declaration of Independence," which Harcourt, Brace and Company has just published, is so written as to give the reader a feeling of personal intimacy with the words and thoughts of the inspired men who framed it and adopted it. Yours is the rare talent of bringing the dead past to life. No one surpasses your power to free the sublime visions of early Americans from the crust of cynicism laid on by some who would ascribe our failures to overstatements of ideals when the land was young. In your books, "Beginnings of the American People," your "Eve of the Revolution," your "Experiment in Democracy," your "Spirit of Seventy-Six," you revive the American fundamentals with such calm and logical presentation and such force withal as to shame our laziness and indifference. When I open a handsome new volume[1] on recent history, "Becker" on the title page means, "Here will be facts so linked together as to facilitate learning. Here will be found men and deeds so set on the stage that the dramatic quality of past events will make them intimate." I am right. I find your new history so engaging as to interfere with work, play, correspondence and other duties until I have read it through. It has a continuity as if you had written it at one sitting. Your review of the world's approach to modern times, all in thirty-five pages, is a feat of condemnation without squeezing out the sap. Your comforting suggestions to me and other readers in the matter of dates and memorization, hints introduced so as to forestall our inclination to skip them, are decidedly agreeable. Your chapter-

[1] Carl Lotus Becker, ''Modern History, the Rise of a Democratic, Scientific, and Industrial Civilization.'' Silver, Burdett and Company, N. Y. 850 pp. $2.24.

and paragraph-headings are the brightest things I ever saw in any history. They mind me of the most engaging novels I used to read as a boy. Your hook-up of American events with European doings freshens my home history and puts it in a broader light. Your approach to great events—what we older schoolmasters call "preparing the mind" for the lesson—has the quality of expectation in it skilfully used, your diagrams depicting the gist of the chapters are original and impressive. Your pictures are delicious, nothing less. You will be thinking my enthusiasm is running away with me. Why not? Every day I've been getting Becker and Becker. I have profited so highly by this week's daily perusal of the doings of mankind from the beginning of civilization to the last naval conference, I see such enjoyment and benefit coming to teachers and to boys and girls from following your lead, that I have to pay tribute to your labor, your skill, and your knowledge of the way of holding attention and of inclining the mind to wisdom. You may tell yourself that you have produced a masterpiece that will charm, edify and benefit the world. Add my satisfaction to yours.

FOR THE COMING CITIZEN

Here's another admirable Munro text.[2] It includes not only the survey of the machinery of government, but is concerned with those questions of economics, sociology and international relations that the citizen to-day, if he is worth his salt, is obligated to consider. The author is working to imbue the young student with American principles. The rights and duties of the citizen, the blemishes on municipal and higher government, the unsettled problems loom large in the Munro treatment.

EVERYBODY'S LIVING

Professor Eliot, chair of sociology, Northwestern University, has made a reading book for college and high school students, for teachers, and for householders.[3] He has made it as pertinent to these hard times as if he were publishing a news magazine. His introduction might be summarized in this: the standard of living is set by what you want; the plane is what you get. Here is a timely shot: "the consuming public needs courses in salesmanship resistance." With an expert's sense of what is sound, with a newsman's scent for what is interesting, with a doctor's intuition of what is needed, Professor Eliot has gathered short essays by Edward Devine, Grace Abbott, Mary Simkhovitch, Simon Patten, Trufant Foster, Wadell Catchings, Richard Ely, Edward Filene, Ellen Richards, Edward Ross, Stuart Chase, and others: nearly two hundred crisp discussions of earning, saving, spending, enjoying, and enduring, city life, farm life, laborers, professors, misers, spendthrifts, luxury, comfort, births and funerals, and the costs thereof are treated by people who do know how to write.

When I was a boy our town hall used occasionally to harbor performances advertised to give "entertainment and edification combined." Professor Eliot has presented a great collection of topics that are of immediate use. They are as full of vital interest as a best-selling novel.

For classroom use, and for the solitary reader who is up to the Abbe Dimnet's grade, there are questions with each selection. They come before, not after, the reading. This authenticated method of getting more meat more speedily has been in use a few years in silent reading classes. By introducing it into a book for the high school and college Professor Eliot should have the ribbon of the A. G. T. (Adopters of Good Things.)

BRITISH DISCUSSIONS OF SCHOOL TOPICS

Very early in an illuminating series of talks on modern education[4] by masters, professors, physicians and clergymen, Dr. Cyril Norwood, head master of Harrow, notes the English people passing through a period of disintegration when all values are brought into question and

[2] William Bennett Munro, "Our Democracy and its Problems. Social Civics." The Macmillan Company, N. Y. 693 pp. $1.72.

[3] Thomas D. Eliot, "American Planes and Standards of Living." Ginn and Company, N. Y. 931 pp. $5.00.

[4] Harrow Lectures on Education, series of addresses by Twenty-One Masters. Cambridge University Press, Macmillan and Company, N. Y. 227 pp. $3.50.

old loyalties brought under review. Assistant master Coade finds uncertainty of aim to be "a very devil, a disease undermining the work of the cleverest of men. Much energy and initiative are at present wasted, especially among the conscientious younger teachers, because of vagueness of vision and uncertainty of aim." There is, through the book, much sober reflection upon the low tone of the press, the stage, and politics. Dr. Norwood argues that the future of Britain is not only to be saved by the schools but created there. "The Roman Empire was built by character as all enduring political systems must be. The achievement of our race is also due to character but to maintain it in the twentieth century more attention must be paid to brains."

As you read the offerings of the prominent English educators represented here you note indications that the neglect of science, the preponderance of games, the absence of measured proofs of old English educational claims are considered by many British masters as things to be corrected. "We might win all the international sports trophies and not advance one step in solving the problems which press upon our country. Our schools have opprobrious terms for the hard-working student but none for the complete ignoramus who is good at games. In science we are falling behind the French and the Dutch. We are weak in economics, politics and social service. Our people are making the country uglier every year."

The discussions include understanding the adolescent, sex problems, the classics, art, hygiene, other subjects of high-school grade, a jolly good talk on discipline by Head Master Vaughan of Rugby, and six discussions on character and religion.

PROFESSIONALLY MINDED

It is exactly fifty years since William H. Payne, professor of education in the University of Michigan, repeatedly told us that teaching is a profession because it is based on science, requires practitioners of high character, skill and devotion to service, and insures an honorable career. If any of his students intended to remain long enough at the service to make a career of it they concealed the idea under their hats. In Chicago our superintendent, George Howland, used frequently to admonish us to tend to our knitting and not to waste time arguing that teaching is a profession. There was more ridicule than approval, from inside and out of the calling, for the attempt to professionalize teaching.

Having read the new Carpenter and Rufi book[5] I am persuaded that it can be shown that teachers are, at least, professionally minded. These two members of the faculty of the University of Missouri base their treatise on the thesis that a thorough understanding of an extensive list of relationships of teachers to the profession, to one another, to the principal, the supervisors, the superintendent, the school board, the community, the state, and the nation is as necessary to a teacher as knowing the special subject he has prepared to teach. Positive and reasonable demands for this knowledge mark the several chapters devoted to it. Besides there are discussed school law, opening of the term, discipline, records and reports, extracurricula, parents, buildings and equipment, measurements, health, safety, economy, closing the term. The book is a mine from which a high-school principal can easily get solid material for staff meetings. It will save much time and searching in preparation to pass examination for a high-school teaching certificate. It is a clear-cut text for classes of intending teachers. The prevailing postulate is cooperative management of high schools with every member sharing responsibility for policies and management.

WRONG GUESSES IN PICKING A TEACHER

How can you tell among the increasing applicants, those would-be teachers, who will render the best service? Professor Roy Ullman submits a dissertation[6] on this highly important problem. In the manner now demanded, in order that the doubting Thomases may review every tabulation of facts and measurements,

[5] W. W. Carpenter and John Rufi, ''The Teacher and Secondary School Administration.'' Ginn and Company, N. Y. 460 pp. $2.00.

[6] Roy Roland Ullman, ''The Prognostic Value of Certain Factors Related to Teaching Success.'' A. L. Garber Company, Ashland, Ohio. 133 pp. $1.50.

Professor Ullman brings you to a disconcerting scepticism as to the value of the elaborate examinations now used to decide upon teaching certificates. How he reaches the assertion that in the cases worked out by him psychology, history of education, methods, and other favorite standbys of teacher-preparatory courses all tallied below successful practice teaching, you will find distinctly set forth in his snug little book.

LOWTH AGAIN

A SECOND enlivening piece of work comes from Frank Lowth.[7] He writes for the hundred and fifty thousand one-room rural teachers. He loves 'em all. Many he has taught in his normal school at Janesville, Wisconsin, a college devoted to the preparation of teachers for the country schools.

His book, without waste, goes at once into the ways of getting education to live up to its promise of making this an honest, law-abiding, generous, everybody's government. Citizenship, character, lessons, practices, all the work and problems of the country school are treated here in practical fashion, not without enthusiasm and faith.

MAKING A MAN OF HIM

BOTH Engelhardts, Nickolaus in Columbia University, Fred in the University of Minnesota, have built their reputations on the inductive method: facts first, survey, comparison, conclusion, teaching. Both have pioneered in building a comprehensive program for school management involving definite standards of pupil progress, specific planning, economical material equipment, exact financial accounting. In my reviews, printed here in March, I noted Fred Engelhardt's smaller book: the "Syllabus of School Organization and Management." Now I have the big work.[8] It is a delight. The dedication is a choice family jewel: "To my brother Nickolaus whose life, to me, has been the challenge."

What the researchers, experimenters and testers have been piling up in the past thirty years is the framework of the book, the conclusions being arranged in appropriate chapters, reasoned out to principles, recapitulated, then documented by surveys and a bibliography. When there is yet no objective data for confirming a principle, Fred says so and hopes you'll do your share in collating definite facts and comparisons to establish an authentic procedure.

The whole book is, because of its abundance of measured facts, a campaign volume for real management of education.

What is the difference between any successful productive organization and a failing one? Management. In business you hear it often said success is nine parts management, one part luck and other things. This is true of schools. For the first seventy years of school superintendency, little effort was made to train educational managers until 1900. Universities and teachers' colleges to-day consider the training of a superintendent a necessary service.

Most superintendents are high-school principals elevated. Minnesota requires courses in school administration before a superintendent's certificate is awarded. When traits requisite for a good superintendent are considered the judges rate them in this order of importance: leadership, good judgment, breadth of interest, resourcefulness, poise, intelligence, force, adaptability. At the tail of the list of twenty-six virtues come punctuality, magnetism and industry.

Objective studies of the superintendency are few. There is a huge and important field for investigation here. What are the chief causes for which school systems lose good superintendents? What are the best school systems in the United States? What are the circumstances that make them such? Select two cities of about the same size and sort of population in the same state. Get a school board quietly to agree to support the kind of supervision recommended by an expert in this art and science. Leave the superintendent of the other city to the mercies of the board, ignorant that their school system has been selected as the control. At the end of three years survey both systems with a thoroughness such as never was.

[7] Frank J. Lowth, "The Country Teacher at Work." The Macmillan Company, N. Y. 541 pp. $2.00.

[8] Fred Engelhardt, "Public-School Organization and Administration." Ginn and Company, N. Y. 593 pp. $3.60.

As you study Engelhardt's book you will observe that the extensive advances made in education in our day is only a beginning. There are enough problems to keep would-be doctors of educational philosophy supplied with thesis subjects for years to come.

As an experienced surveyor this author is not deluding himself nor you with the gay thought that all's well with the world in education. Although experience in other fields and tests of school systems never fail to show that the supervised worker produces better results, yet the researchers do not find teachers, nor mankind as a whole, glowing at a white heat of enthusiasm to be supervised. High-school teachers, says our author, are less keen for supervision than those in the elementary schools. Against this might be set a quotation from "Undergraduates," the study made at the suggestion of the Association of American Colleges: "The best teaching is in the elementary schools, poorer in the high schools, worst in the colleges."

Says author Engelhardt, any one who has had to do with the administration of any enterprise knows from experience that in practice individuals must be protected from their own notions. The mutual interests and benefit of community and teachers can not be maintained without inspection, oversight and supervision. The work of the most superior teacher is improved by supervision. It does not curtail any initiative or freedom that is essential to development and improvement.

Engelhardt's tables tell much in a short space. In the absence of objective measurements in any case he gives judgments of groups of persons. At present writing 14 per cent. of his respondents are for announced visits of a supervisor to a class so that the teacher may be seen at his best. Thirty-eight per cent. favor unannounced appearances. The preference for a long inspection is 36 per cent., for a short one 46 per cent., for none at all 2 per cent., indifferent 16 per cent. Sixty per cent. of the voters prefer informal tests prepared by teachers as superior to standard examinations.

Vigorous without overstatement, extended without dullness, based upon individual studies to be found only in scattered volumes, this work is a thesaurus of resources in the circumstances surrounding a school superintendent. School law, boards of education, personnel, high schools, health libraries, business, finance, the public, the state, measurement, research, modern proposals, and many other pertinent matters are given separate and adequate presentation. This book will give the superintendency another push toward the respectability fitting the importance of the service.

THE SATISFIERS AND OTHERS

Dr. Edward Thorndike delivered a series of lectures on the Messenger Foundation at Cornell University. Possibly you did not hear him. You may now do so at your leisure. The Century Company is bringing out fourteen books in its Psychology Series. The fourth to appear is made up of these Messenger Lectures.[9]

The nature and evolution of learning is the theme. The Thorndike doctrine of bonds, satisfiers, the Gestalt theory, conditioned reflexes, and the future changes in teaching as influenced by experiment and discovery make a progressive dissertation on what science and scholarship have done with man's inheritance of truth and error. We are learning more things and truer ones, and learning difficult things more quickly and pleasantly. As far as you are concerned the preponderating necessity is that you don't stop.

GOOD AND EASY

Ralston and Gage say they want to make a psychology[10] for students, parents and friends who are not familiar with the subject and who ought not to be frightened away from the science by dismal language. They wish to keep the teacher of elementary school and the parent of children. The work assumes no knowledge of psychology by the reader. It takes nothing for granted beyond everyday intelligence and common sense.

How human beings live and behave is the theme. Back of the how is the psychologist's endeavor to find out the why. The student is

[9] Edward L. Thorndike, "Human Learning." The Century Company, N. Y. 202 pp. $2.25.

[10] Alene Ralston, Catherine T. Gage, "Present Day Psychology, an Objective Study." J. B. Lippincott Co., Philadelphia, 404 pp. $2.40.

living his psychology while he is studying it. The teacher is a psychologist, whether realizing it or not. His success depends on his use of interests, strivings, urgings, joys, struggles, pleasures, loves, hates, purposes, annoyances, experiences, problems, aches, pains, fears, habits, drives, satisfactions, feelings, actions, wishes, wants, desires,—all those kinds of behavior that differentiate man from the inanimate world.

For thousands of years psychologists have reached conclusions by thought and observation. They have, if eminent enough, attained the name of sage or philosopher. Too much of their teaching is based on a personal whim picturesquely worded, as, "truth is beauty; beauty truth." In our day the method of scientific experiment, measurement, observation of thousands of cases compared with controlled situations, has offered more reliable principles than the Orphic sayings of the village cobbler. These two authors have gathered from James, Thorndike, McDougall, Watson, Pintner, Terman, Bertrand Russell, Colvin, Gates, Cattell, Gesell, Pyle, Dewey, Judd, and others so much as well to justify their title "Modern."

The relation of mind and body is treated with full references to the glands. The adrenals are the standbys of the fighter and the coward. "The behavior of these glands is rather well established. The medical men in the World War discovered that the soldiers who couldn't go over the top had not enough adrenalin and therefore lacked in force, energy, pep." Maybe all your hopes, fears, loves and hates affect and are affected by your thyroids, pineals, pituitaries, ovaries, testes and adrenals. Who knows but we shall have an endocrine psychology, next?

I find the treatment of instincts, heredity, means of modifying behavior, habits, emotions, learnings, fatigue, testing and measuring, admirably complete and conveniently grouped under living, learning and measuring. I find controversial topics pretty fairly treated and the whole work so concrete and well-illustrated and documented as to make it what the authors intended: easy and good.

A SPECIAL PSYCHOLOGY

For seven years, Fred Moss, M.D., has given lectures on psychology in the Central Training School for Nurses, Washington, D. C. You can have all the discourses and more, bound in a readable and valuable volume.[11] As you have to be your own nurse oftentimes you should not be without the information given here about the traits you have in common with the rest of us, factors involving behavior, effect of bodily conditions on conduct, how drugs affect you, the influence of your surroundings, mental disorders, causes of delinquency, individual differences and emotional outlets. These topics are the contents of this well-indexed, utility volume for teachers, school-masters, parents, and intelligent citizens.

P. S. The title might shoo you off. If so, you would lose a decidedly entertaining experience, for Dr. Moss knows how to tell good stories, true ones.

ELEMENTARY SCHOOL WAYS NOW

How reading used to be taught, how spelling, how grammar, arithmetic, music and many other things were imparted, and how they are handled now, make a unique and highly interesting feature of Professor Claude Phillips' exposition of methods in elementary education.[12] His treatment of objectives fails to give training for political participation the prominence it deserves, but when he comes to his chapter, "Character Education," he gives the citizenship duty decided stress and definiteness. The persistence with which Dr. Phillips makes objectives of every study and exercise prominent indicates that his experience in directing teachers is fresh in his Missouri mind and full of punch.

SCHOOL DELIGHT

If left to themselves, asks Marian Stevens,[13] of the Ethical Culture School, New York, what do children do? She lists 45 natural performances. Why do they do such things? Because they want to. A natural need is satisfied. If these tendencies are guided into valuable and

11 Fred A. Moss, "Psychology for Nurses." Houghton Mifflin Company, Boston. 289 pp. $2.50.

12 Claude A. Phillips, "Modern Methods and the Elementary Curriculum." The Century Company, N. Y. 521 pp. $2.50.

13 Marian Paine Stevens, "The Activities Curriculum in the Primary Grades." D. C. Heath and Company, Boston. 440 pp. $2.00.

educative channels your school will go farther in developing valuable members of society than will a course of teaching based upon merely an adult's estimate of the value of school subjects. On this line the author fills 425 bright pages of projects, constructions, games, holidays, festivals, work and play, bringing in reading, spelling, arithmetic and other old standbys, more concerned with making themselves agreeable and welcome than they used to be when they had the rod, the slap and the backing of the school-ma'am police behind them.

THE LIFE OF MATHEMATICS

Payson Smith would like some would-be doctor of philosophy to work out the marvelous increments of value by which a group of persons whose educational value is represented by X get together, read original papers, discuss topics and go home with an average worth of X^n. The National Council of Teachers of Mathematics might do this. Their year books waste few words on annals of work done. They are full of plans for better doings to-morrow. "A new era in the teaching of mathematics is dawning," says David Eugene Smith in the sixth year book.[14] "Tradition is giving way to a nobler conception of what all sciences mean in relation to one another and to the higher ideals of humanity."

The papers in this year's book are on the applications of mathematics to the social sciences, to biology, the humanities, religion, investments, agriculture, pharmacy, physics, and statistics. The contributors are Fisher, Harris, Keyser, Smith, Hart, Roe, Spease, Walker, Brown and Birkhoff.

A TEACHER'S JUNIOR HIGH SCHOOL MATHEMATICS

Thomas Alexander and Rosamond Root, editing the Johnson Education series, announce the first definite attempt to offer professionalized materials in junior high-school mathematics.[15] Dr. Schaaf, the author, works in the field covered by his work. He has in mind a large proportion of junior high-school teachers promoted hurriedly from the seventh grade and conscious of the need of different objectives and methods in their new field. The author supplies these needs in their mutual relations. The historical and social aspects of measurement, geometry, graphs, arithmetic of home, of community and business, money, banking, investments, insurance, algebra, functions, roots, powers and problem-solving throw an unusual interest into what for too many children is a dull and boresome branch of knowledge.

EDUCATION FOR OFFICE WORK

Function before form, the why before the how, presumption of brains, belief that the schools are teaching the children to think, are the foundation on which three high-school teachers of New York City build a guide[16] for young office workers. It is a text for junior and senior high schools. It covers the bank from the depositor's view-point, the technique and etiquette of telephoning, mail, correspondence, filing, office machines, express and telegraph, reference books, and so on. It is generously illustrated. There is a bright chapter on the first year's experience of a young office worker during which some of the real refinements of business work are admirably brought out.

SCIENCE OF TO-DAY AND TO-MORROW

The dying sun, the new world of physics, matter and radiation, relativity and the ether, fill the first four chapters of a review[17] by Sir James Jeans. In the final chapter, "Deep Waters," you are advised of the fatuity of the scientific concept of thirty years ago, holding the universe to be a mere machine. To-day there is a wide measure of agreement that the universe is rather a great thought.

The decorations of this book are also mysterious and, in places, sublime.

[14] National Council of Teachers of Mathematics, "Mathematics in Modern Life." Teachers College Press, Columbia University, N. Y. 195 pp. $1.75.

[15] William L. Schaaf, "Mathematics for Junior High-school Teachers." Johnson Publishing Company, Richmond, Va. 439 pp. $2.00.

[16] Abbie A. Morrill, Mabel A. Bessey, John V. Walsh, "Applied Office Practice." D. C. Heath and Company, Boston. 376 pp. $1.96.

[17] Sir James Jeans, "The Mysterious Universe," The Macmillan Company, N. Y. 163 pp. $2.25.

LOGIC IS NEW

A LOGIC text-book ten years old will not suffice. Highly significant contributions have been made to this science. Bosanquet and Muirhead believe the late discussions of the nature of inference revolutionize the entire science. To equip yourself with the result of recent discussions, to clarify your views of naming, of categories, predicables, intention, extension, definition, division, judgment, propositions, premises, syllogisms, inferences, fallacies, etc., I commend to you Robinson's "Principles of Reasoning."[18]

A son of Indiana, Bowdoin-prize-winner, world-war veteran, professor of philosophy, Miami University, has a way of presenting what is commonly regarded as an abstruse subject so as to keep you at it long after bed time.

LOGIC IN SHORT

FATHER COTTER has taught logic in Jesuit houses of studies for ten years. His experience in direct and clarified presentation he puts at your disposal in a terse contribution.[19]

NO TESTERS BOTHERED THEM

WHEN Thomas Aquinas, Duns Scotus and Roger Bacon discoursed upon their various quiddities no tables of medians, modes and averages had to be appended to their tractates to let the reader see for himself whether the conclusions were sound or no. Apt marshalling of sayings of Aristotle, Seneca and St. Augustine, nimble juggling of enthymeme, dilemma and epagogue, prodigious accumulations of authority established eminence for those wordy old boys. Their method held in educational discussion up to the time of many living schoolmasters. The fat volumes of the National Education Association abound with the phrases, "As William T. Harris has pointed out," "As Charles W. Eliot observes." Where are they now, those amiable and positive reasoners on what the policies should be? Smothered by the researcher's statistics. Unless we are knowing what, where, how often and how much, we can't be listened to. A quaint taste of the stately reasoners of old time is the set of two trim volumes[20] from Scribner's.

Sample: "As regards authority I proceed thus. Boethius saith in the second prologue to the Arithmetick that if the inquirer lacks the four parts of mathematicks he can in no wise discover truth. Whosoever hath neglected these hath lost the doctrine of all wisdom." Thus may we see, dear children, how Roger Bacon in the Opus Majus, A. D. 1264, did prophesy the reign of Edward, the Thorndike, and his court.

CLEVERNESS LESS THAN CHARACTER

AN observing and delightfully human professor in the University of Virginia is at the same time supervisor of rural schools. The combined experiences of these two positions illumine a book on character.[21]

You can imagine the spirit of the book from the author's opening: "We are spending thousands of dollars in our search for the best ways of teaching the three R's. But we must spend still more to discover the most effective process of training in honor, truth and righteousness in daily living."

Old assertions as to how good boys are made have lost their universal support. The teacher of to-day is puzzled. One of the best principals of one of the best Chicago schools says we want to teach these things but we don't know how. Commissioner Ernest Butterfield tells his Connecticut school superintendents that the daily question from service clubs, civic organizations, everybody, is "What are the schools doing to make America more decent?"

Professor McLester discusses the present situation, various attempts, practical suggestions, and then describes her own experiments and outcomes. It involves truthfulness, clean speech, friendliness, courtesy, honor, orderli-

18 Daniel Sommer Robinson, "The Principles of Reasoning: An Introduction to Logic and Scientific Method." D. Appleton and Company, N. Y. 393 pp. $2.50.

19 A. C. Cotter, S. J., "Logic and Epistemology." The Stratford Company, Boston. 234 pp. $2.00.

20 Richard McKeon, "Selections from Medieval Philosophers, from Augustine to William of Ockham." Charles Scribner's Sons, N. Y. 1030 pp. $2.50.

21 Amelia McLester, "Development of Character Traits in Young Children." Charles Scribner's Sons, N. Y. 123 pp. $1.25.

ness, good habits in general. It does this with a directness and clarity so pleasing as to persuade you that patience and intelligence will greatly ameliorate the poor quality of the present unspanked generation."

GATES TO READING

Arthur Gates' last contribution[22] to the teaching of reading is based on findings by the Institute of Educational Research of Teachers' College, New York. What is it that produces an enthusiasm for reading? How do you increase the reader's power of comprehension? The conclusions derived from more than twenty extensive experiments are here presented. Among them is the question of how many different words may be effectively used in the reading books of children of different grades: enough words to maintain curiosity, sufficiently few words to prevent what many teachers have found a mysterious loss of interest. Now, these are the flavors which make school reading palatable: surprise, liveliness, doings of animals, conversation and plot.

It is a new and vital thing for a superintendent, a principal, a teacher, or a reading book maker to conceive at the start what outcomes should be secured by the teaching of reading at any grade. The books of thirty years ago were like a miscellaneous magazine. Dr. Gates' treatise discusses linguistic abilities, dramatic, artistic and exploratory traits. His experiments develop a more effective method than the present excessive use of flash cards gets. He notes specific improvements in diagnostic tests of various reading abilities.

In the various reading manuals that different experts are furnishing, it is notable how little they suggest to make reading contribute to the type of honest, cooperative, courageous citizens the country needs. Did the old primers, saturated with moral lessons, overdo it? Among my cronies, white-haired old boys who never carry a gun and who respect the Volstead Law, the matter of the morals of the present generation comes up a good deal. This leads into the question: "What are the influences which have tended to keep you straight?" All these patriarchs include the school books in their list. None of the witnesses feel that adequate civic duty for times of peace got into their cosmos from their school. This is only their guess. They are not a controlled experiment. All the same, Ernest Butterfield says that the questions following his addresses to service clubs and laymen's societies show a large amount of desire for more successful inculcation of civic virtue. Come on, then, Institute of Educational Research! You are, sure enough, improving the teaching of what we have. Give us more help in methods for what we ought to teach!

DRAMA AT REDUCED COST

Clever, competent, complete is Professor Wayne Campbell's treatise on the school and college theater.[23] Often called upon to advise instructors who have no money nor place for dramatic presentation, a resourceful artist, Wayne Campbell, has developed a canny talent for making high-class bricks where there seems to be no straw. The class-room theaters he has equipped, almost at no cost, are a triumph of Scottish economy. The high tone of his dramatic concept is evident throughout, even extending to the beauty of print, pictures and binding of the book itself. He has one of the richest discussions of stage fright and its cure you will meet in many a day. Choosing a play, casting it, rehearsing, staging, make-up, scenery, lighting and ingenious ways of making inconvenient halls suffice are treated in a businesslike and thorough manner. The amount of royalties demanded by authors of clean and wholesome plays are given. Five non-royalty, one-act plays are printed entire.

SILVERN SPEECH

A lot of very practical suggestions, based upon an affectionate regard for the often cruelly tortured audience, are given by Mr. A. C. Edgerton in a manual for speechmakers.[24] Be prepared. Extemporaneous remarks that

[22] Arthur I. Gates, "Interest and Ability in Reading." The Macmillan Company, N. Y. 264 pp. $1.50.

[23] Wayne Campbell, "Amateur Acting and Play-Production." The Macmillan Company, N. Y. 374 pp. $3.50.

[24] A. C. Edgerton, "A Speech for Every Occasion." Noble and Noble, 76 5th Ave., N. Y. 427 pp. $2.00.

hit the mark come only from superior geniuses. After they grow old enough to write their memoirs you find their extemporaneity was faked. They laboriously gathered ideas, rehearsed them, and were always loaded. Mr. Edgerton's more than 200 short speeches are grouped together according to occasion—social, commemorative, political or what not.

PERSUASION TO POETRY

OF all the literary influences, poetry sinks deepest and lasts longest. So begins a delightful educational essay[25] by Professor Seely. He groups his thoughts under "Poetry and the Teacher," "Poetry and Appreciation," "Poetry in the Classroom," "Poetry as a Stimulus to Composition." Professor Seely has seen teachers who seem to prefer the photograph of a pansy to the perfume and color of the flower itself. This type will analyze the form and structure of a lyric, load its allusions with facts and dates, dissect the living body and leave a corpse. Dr. Seely wastes little time correcting such as these but talks inspiringly on what he heard and saw and did in the high schools in which he has taught.

LITERARY WORK FOR FRESHMEN

How shall you avoid the platitudinous and, on the other hand, keep almond frosting off what you say and write? Anatole France asked this. He revised everything over and over to get rid of exaggerations and strains. It is hard to be both vivid and true. Three wise men of the West tell how they work along this line in Ohio University and in the University of Illinois.[26] I would like to see the freshman clever enough to bluff through an English course using this book. These authors during the past three years have been trying the lessons of this volume on all sorts of conditioned and unconditioned first-year college students. There is offered, now, what may be considered an almost hundred per cent. penetration of the freshman skull. They begin with a fundamental essential: you must conceive and work for a reader. Get the thought of yourself and your writing out of your head, first, and think well of the persons, real or imaginary, for whom you are writing. For the sake of mercy, have some one in mind other than your professor. Amazing it is that college freshmen, after all their composition in the public school, don't know what to write about. This book gives sixty themes from which to choose at the start. That gives the instructor a basis for moving from the known to the unknown in grammer, spelling, form of manuscript, and the mechanics of discourse. Preliminaries and review occupy the first third of the book after which, with an abundance of examples from masterly writers, paralleled by exercises in the same field, the whole gamut of effective discourse is run. If you wish a spirited manual for putting a student into workmanlike habits, here it is.

WHAT IS THE WORD WORTH?

STANDARD third readers contain over nine thousand words. Many, no doubt, need not be taught. Others need only to be explained far enough to serve the purpose of the paragraph and then be left to their fate. Others should be thoroughly taught and reviewed. "Which ones?" asks Edward Thorndike, and proceeds to the answer.[27]

From various counts of the words in children's books, the Bible, English classics, newspapers, letters, etc., involving more than five million words, Dr. Thorndike gives in alphabetical order the twenty thousand words occurring most frequently in all the places examined. With each word is given a number showing the relative importance of this word as to frequency. In preparing your reading lesson, if you are in doubt as to how thorough teaching should be given to "true," turn to the wordbook. You find "1-a." This means "true" comes in the first five hundred most frequently used words. "False" comes in the first two thousand important words. What conclusions, not mentioned by our author,

[25] Howard Francis Seely, ''Enjoying Poetry in School.'' Johnson Publishing Company, Richmond, Va. 267 pp. $2.00.

[26] Bernard L. Jefferson, Harry Houston Peckham, Hiram Roy Wilson, ''Freshman Rhetoric and Practice Book.'' Doubleday, Doran and Co., Garden City, N. Y. 674 pp. $2.00.

[27] Edward L. Thorndike, ''A Teachers' Word Book.'' Teachers College Press, Columbia University, N. Y. 182 pp. $1.50.

might a moralist get out of these graded lists when he finds "love" in the first class of freqence; "hate" in the second; "honest" second class; "cheat" fourth order; "virtuous" fourth; "unchaste" twentieth? Pretty good, isn't it, if man is what his words are? Digging a little deeper, however, you will be shocked by the greater number of negative, unlovely shameful words in the American and English vocabulary than there are positive and pleasing ones. The synonyms to "clean" are as four to the five equivalents of "dirty." The same sorry proportion shows with "wise" and "foolish," "good taste" and "vulgarity," "hope" and "despair," through a long list of virtues and vices. There is still work for you character-moulders to do. "Politics" is in the sixth class of frequent use, "sports" in the second, "business" in the first.

Although the always sober author of this monumental list doesn't suggest it, I can see how it can be used in many an edifying game. I'll give you some names to rank in the order of frequent mention in the vast body of reading examined for the Thorndike list. When you check your list by the book you find this unlooked for order: Washington 2nd, Lincoln 3rd, Jackson 5th, Wilson 7th, Jefferson 8th, Napoleon 8th, Roosevelt 9th, Edison 14th, Nelson 14th, Dewey 17th, Harding 19th, Coolidge and Hoover, not yet.

Have you time for another? Here are the frequencies of use of a different group of words: American 1st, German 2nd, Englishman 4th, Scot 5th, Frenchman 6th, Irishman 10th. Yes, I know what you are thinking of. I saw that myself. It seems to me you have here a strikingly useful book. You may well say of Thorndike:

'Twas he that ranged the word at random flung,
Pierced the fair pearls and them together strung.

STANFORD'S RARE BOOK

STANFORD UNIVERSITY comes into the group of makers of rare and beautiful books with a handsome edition of Robert Burton's "Philophaster."[28] The famous author of "The Anatomy of Melancholy" wrote the drama, "Philophaster," in 1606. It was produced in 1617 and remained unprinted over two hundred years. It is a satire on Oxford, requiring, says Dr. Jordan-Smith, but few penstrokes to make it fit abuses of this present.

SPEEDING UP FRENCH

BY teaching French in different high schools ending with service under the guidance of Teachers College, Columbia University, by guiding her teaching in accordance with the newer educational psychology, by collating the essentials of an extensive professional literature on language teaching, Florence Baker made preparation for producing a usable book[29] for the improvement of high-school practice in teaching this language. Miss Baker finds teachers eager to reject the traditional inheritances which hamper linguistic success. Among the newer practices elaborated in this treatise is silent reading. Put speaking and writing into the background. Get the same kind of reading, *viz.*, unspoken, as a good reader employs when getting printed English to impart its ideas. Break the literal-translation habit. Don't interrupt with questions. Ask them before the passage is read so as to furnish a definite motive. Unless and until a habit of silent reading has been formed don't assign home work.

Miss Baker treats aims of the study, the pupils' objectives, the cultural aims, the teacher's attitude, when to use English, skills, tests, methods, younger children, bringing the study up to general educational progress. This is an unusual book, stimulating, reasonable, and constructive.

EASE AND COMFORT

THERE are now ten titles in the Chicago French Series. The last is Hector Malot's "Sans Famille."[30] It is an ingenious rendition of a connected story so easy as to come into use after lesson X in beginning French. The "comprehension exercises" for each chapter are in French and almost automatic.

[28] Paul Jordan Smith, Translator and Editor, "The Philophaster of Robert Burton, with other minor writings of Burton in Prose and Verse." University Press, Stanford University, California. 283 pp. $5.00.

[29] Florence M. Baker, "The Teaching of French." Houghton Mifflin Company, Boston. 286 pp. $2.00.

[30] Ruth Elizabeth Meade, Grace Cochrane, Helen M. Eddy. Malot's "Sans Famille." University of Chicago Press. 134 pp. $1.10.

SCHOOL AND SOCIETY

EDITED BY J. McKEEN CATTELL

WITH WHICH IS COMBINED THE

EDUCATIONAL REVIEW

EDITED BY WILLIAM McANDREW

Volume 34 | Saturday, August 8, 1931 | Number 867

OXFORD

By H. P. PERKINS

NEW YORK CITY

Oxford does a great deal to make sure that most of the business of education has been completed before university life is begun. That is the real secret of her success. It is not merely a question of relying upon strong currents of English culture to lay hold upon a youth and sweep him into the way that he should go. Important steps are taken by the university to encourage these tendencies in the schools.

Each college has a large number of scholarships, and there are twenty-one colleges. The scholarships are given in every conceivable subject. There is always a financial reward attached, ranging from $1,000 to $50 a year. Some of the scholarships are restricted to particular schools or to particular districts.

Speaking generally they serve as a reward for good work in the school and an incentive to good work at the university (since they will be taken away if the student rests on his laurels). Naturally many boys could not go to the university if they did not exist. When they are won by a well-to-do boy the stipend is commonly resigned to the next man on the list until a needy man is found, but the title with its honors is held by the winner. The main reason for having them is that the work is better done than it would otherwise be.

The effectiveness of this scholarship system depends on the nature of the examinations on the basis of which scholarships are given. If the examinations are so framed that everything the student has to offer is called forth, competition will make the school training more and more thorough. If the examination is put together stupidly one kind of preparation will serve about as well as another. Or, what is worse, the mechanical and short-sighted kind will be most effective, and there will be no tendency for the school training to become more educative. Now with so many scholarships and so many examinations there is bound to be a good deal of variety. It would take a more intimate knowledge than I possess to make a precise estimate of the system. But it is clear that an attempt is made to test the candidate's thinking power, his command of English, and his mastery of English history and literature, as well as his knowledge of the subject in which the scholarship is given.

This helps to explain the comparative maturity of the English freshman, his tendency to know what he wants to study at the university. He has a good basis for making a choice between different disciplines.

Say it is a classical scholarship which he

has been pointed at since he was fourteen or fifteen. He has been brought to the point at which he could read the most difficult Latin and Greek literature at sight in large quantities. He is a thorough master of two grammars and to a surprising degree this knowledge has been reduced to illuminating principles of language structure which make the later attack on German, French and Italian much easier for him. And naturally French and Italian are easy when approached with a first class Latin vocabulary, while many of the compounds in German are made in the same way as in Latin.

This has been done largely by work in small groups or alone with a master. He knows what concentrated independent work is long before he comes to the university. This has a direct effect on his capacity for choice of university work. He has had a good deal of provocation to think, and naturally he thinks about himself. This would be true of any material which was taught concentratedly and thoroughly in small groups, but Greek and Latin literature have a peculiar tendency to stimulate self knowledge. And of course he thinks about other things, the impulse having been aroused. His home has usually supplied him with plenty of excellent modern material for thought.

But his classical scholarship is not given merely for mastery of Greek and Latin. The examination will demand an essay, calculated to test his powers of original thought and expression, and a general paper which demands a fairly thorough saturation in English history and literature. Here again the school has gone out of its way to "polish him up" and the result is that he has had plenty of experience in concentrated reading in fields other than the classics. These fields also have a peculiar suitability for provoking thought about himself.

Thus his elections are likely to be rational, and a change in the university is likely to represent an organic development of his personality.

These changes are frequent. The best classical scholar of my year had specialized in mathematics at school until he was thirteen or fourteen. Of the four men in my class at Queen's who distinguished themselves in classics at the end of their second year, two went over to European history. Professor A. N. Whitehead, now of Harvard, did classics at school, and has since distinguished himself principally in mathematics and philosophy. It is erroneous to think of this scholarship system as fixing the boy's line of development. In a way it makes change more likely by insisting that the boy get a thorough taste of what he first elects to do at school. And it is sufficiently well rounded so that there are several disciplines he will be able to pursue with success.

In many American colleges you will find a majority of the best students working at English literature. You will find a great many more good men working at European history and at the social sciences. This seems to be a logical way of trying to comprehend one's environment. At Oxford nearly all the best men are studying Greece and Rome instead of a modern civilization, and they are concentrating on Greek philosophy. Oxford looks hidebound. It is difficult to see how any one who emerges from a prolonged bout with Plato and Thucydides can be ready for "Sex" and "Labor."

At Oxford very few of the good men bother with a training in English literature or European history. They have already been pretty well saturated in these things at home, and the scholarship system encourages it in the school. The interest has been built up so well that it can be trusted to nourish itself. The English undergraduate is infinitely better prepared for labor problems by drinking in politics at every pore than is his American equivalent by a course in American National Problems. English families sometimes eat and sleep politics, American families tend to be bored by them. I do not mean to say that the English undergraduate is really well prepared for labor problems, I only say that he is better prepared than the American freshman. He has read much more about his own country's history, and in better books. It is hardly our place to sneer if the Englishman feels at eighteen that he will now learn more about his country by going a long distance away to look at it. He already knows it directly better than we know ours, and he can afford to try another angle. He goes to Greece and Rome.

First in Honor Mods a year and two-thirds, or five terms, of epic, drama, and oratory. Aristophanes, Euripides, Sophocles, Aeschylus, Homer, Lucretius, Demosthenes and Cicero. Remember that he is quite capable of getting through the thousand odd lines of the "Bacchae" in one long night when he first appears in Oxford. Then on this foundation Greats—two years and a third, or seven terms of history and philosophy. Thucydides, Herodotus, Livy, and Tacitus, and most of all Plato's "Republic" and Aristotle's "Nichomachean Ethics." This is supplemented by Bury and Meyer in Greek history and by Descartes, Hume, Kant and Croce.

Readers who are acquainted with the "Republic" will remember how it begins with an appeal to traditional wisdom and proceeds to discuss a minor Greek poet. Homer is cited again and again, Aeschylus appears here and there. The English student of Greek philosophy is able to begin the "Republic" with a background as much like that of Plato as any modern youth can attain. In Honor Mods and at school he has been saturated in the same poets. He can supply an apt quotation where Plato has not bothered to do so. He becomes intimately acquainted with Greek history and Greek institutions. He is able to deal with Plato as the quintessence of the Greek mind. After he has worked out Socrates' refutations of sophists who are as Greek as himself, the student passes on to criticisms of the Socratic position in the notes of Aristotle. He has thus explored a grand civilization in a number of its aspects.

When he uses a Greek idea as a clue to his own environment, his suggestions are not the abstractions of a doctrinaire philosophy out of touch with its fellow men. They represent in the students' own mind the reflections of philosophic genius on a society which was itself a work of genius, a society whose depths had been lit to their furthest reaches by flashes of poetic fire. All this background of the philosophy has been made accessible to the student.

For this the command of the language is an absolute *sine qua non*. *Inexperto crede.* I have attempted at various times to become familiar with Greek, but have not had much success because of my late start. The more I try to understand the major monuments of the Greek world, the more I am baffled by my inability to be sure exactly what significance is to be attached to the expressions on which arguments and descriptions turn. A smattering is better than nothing, and so is a dictionary, but there is no substitute for intimacy.

The student returns from his long tour with the scaffolding of a civilization laid bare, the structure and interconnection of its parts outlined in bold relief. He looks for such connections in his own environment with a boldness which often astonishes. He says, for instance, that experts ought to rule, that there is a connection between wisdom and good government.

This positive approach to modern problems is fostered at Oxford by dogged insistence on a method.

Thought requires the preliminary selection of an opinion which serves as an hypothesis for discussion pro and con. In the course of the student's work on a number of different fields within his chosen Honor School he considers several such hypotheses. But if the work is to be done with care the number of them must be small. And they must be related, so that the discussion of different suggestions begins to interact and provoke thought.

Greek philosophy offers very attractive hypotheses. This is not the same as saying that Plato is nice to read. Most of the dominant currents of western life were concentrated at Athens, and wherever the same interests come together again the Greek way of finding a place for all of them is bound to exercise a powerful fascination. Moreover a method had been evolved by abstract philosophizing for dealing with these various interests. An intensity of social life had been achieved which fused them together in the common consciousness and demanded the highest type of poetic expression for the new unity. Plato formulates the conclusions of a very complete civilization, and only a very incomplete one could fail to find them worth discussing.

''The Greeks,'' says Nietzsche, ''are simple. That is why they make the best teachers.'' For a brief moment in the world's history the complexity of human life seemed to melt away before the eye which had been sharpened by centuries of careful looking, and certain clear principles were laid down which have served ever since as threads in the labyrinth.

Not, mind you, as final answers, but as something which defines the issue. They are far from being final, rather they provoke discussion by their very simplicity. Plato is often definite to the point of being doctrinaire. I have in mind things like his banishing of the poets, and his treatment of the family. He is so extreme and so definite that he provokes explicit testing. And the material itself is just such a testing by discussion—it takes the form of dialogues. Nothing could illustrate more strikingly the completeness of Plato's unification of the major forces in our western world. It is as though these forces had become self-conscious and started to talk.

It is discussion of hypotheses drawn from the ''Republic'' which we find in the Oxford tutorial. Talk was also the method of Socrates.

It is hardly possible for any one who knows the dialogues to describe the method of Socrates except by quoting.

Socrates: I can not help feeling, Phaedrus, that writing is unfortunately like painting; for the creations of the painter have the attitude of life, and yet you ask them a question they preserve a solemn silence. And the same may be said of speeches. Is there not another kind of word or speech far better than this . . . an intelligible word graven in the soul of the learner . . . the living word of knowledge which has a soul, and of which the written word is properly no more than an image? . . . Then he (the wise man) will not seriously incline to write his thoughts in water with pen and ink, sowing words which can neither speak for themselves nor teach the truth adequately to others . . . in the garden of letters he will sow and plant, but only for the sake of recreation and amusement. . . . But nobler far is the serious pursuit of the dialectician, who, finding a congenial soul, by the help of science sows and plants therein words which are able to help themselves. . . .

Socrates: . . . the midwives know better than others who is pregnant and who is not? . . . And by the use of potions and incantations they are able to arouse the pangs and soothe them at will; they can make those bear who have a difficulty in bearing, and if they think fit they can smother the embryo in the womb. . . . Did you ever remark that they are also the most cunning matchmakers, and have a thorough knowledge of what unions are likely to produce a brave brood? . . . Well, my art of midwifery is in most respects like theirs, but differs, in that I attend men and not women, and I look after their soul when they are in labor, and not after their bodies: and the triumph of my art is in thoroughly examining whether the thought which the young man brings forth is a false idol or a true and noble birth.

Those who want to get to the bottom of individual instruction should read the "Apology" and the "Meno" with care.

But does it not strike the reader as curious that I should be urging the advantages of the dialogues as material for a conversation when they are exactly the written work which Socrates deplored? If the process of discussing hypotheses is to be a real discussion, is it not necessary to follow Socrates' precept and example in throwing over books?

There was no carping about mistakes in reporting other men's opinions, no minutiae of scholarship. Socrates knew no language besides his own, and he would never have bothered to choose any particular set of books as the center and starting-point of education.

Is not the Oxford tutor guilty of the usual mistake of apotheosis? Has he not insisted too vigorously on the importance of the dialogues, and thereby missed precisely what is most important in them, Socrates' refusal to start from any one point of view?

Socrates did not teach philosophy by turning to the history of philosophy. He dealt with the issues of the day. He went straight for the young man's own belief.

These objections to the Oxford method, as is natural in arguments which express scorn for use of the past, are rather inaccurate in their statement of fact.

If we know anything at all about it, Socrates was one of the most scholarly historians of philosophy the world has seen. So strong was his interest in the past that it remained the one characteristic common to all the opposing schools which looked to him as their founder and ideal. Even the Cynics with their exaggerated individualism were unable to fight the tendency down, and we find their successors, the Stoics, struggling to find their own views in Heraclitus, who died several centuries before they appeared upon the stage. Plato scarcely knows how to philosophize except by opposing the views of his predecessors one to another. Aristotle is the great historian of philosophy.

Socrates, it is true, did not always talk in terms of past philosophy. Instead he often appealed to past poets. But there was nearly always some traditional point of view about which he was questioning the youth he taught. If he himself did not suggest such a view, it was certain to be brought forward by the youth himself. Socrates always accepted it as a valuable starting-point for discussion. "Shall we say that this is right?"

The objections to the Oxford method (which I have just attempted to answer) provide an interesting illustration of what I am driving at. They do not attack the use of Greek philosophy directly. They take a past example of successful teaching, an example which is all the more forcible because it happens to be Greek, so that those on the other side ought to respect it. They attempt to show from this example that there *can* be successful teaching without a reference to the past. It seems a little strange to use history to show that history is not very useful. But it is very difficult for two people to argue without making references of this sort. The chief difference in method is not between citing an opinion and not citing it, but between misstating it and using it accurately. Every one has to have a springboard to give him a running start at the problem, and history provides the springboard.

Of course there is an important truth in the statement that Socrates usually began by asking about his neighbor's opinions, not by asking him what Simonides said. No one wants to discuss the view of some one else unless it is closely related to something he himself believes.

Now it happens that in the Greece of the fifth century B. C. the number of points of view which one would encounter if one went about interrogating one's neighbors was relatively small. One scarcely needed the common center or common starting-point for discussion which is supplied by an older statement of an idea. It was so usual to agree with Homer that one cited him because one could (having memorized him at school), and because it was after all a pleasant thing to do, rather than because one felt bewildered by the various possible opinions.

Nothing is more astonishing to the modern mind than the ease with which Socrates refutes the sophists. The sophist gives in when the modern reader thinks that he has been merely tricked by a play on words, and that if he had been more than a fool he would have had a retort ready. A great many arguments used by Socrates have been called sophistical which are really perfectly valid when one attaches the meaning to them which was attached by both parties to the dispute. It was rather difficult for a sophist to disagree with Socrates, since both were starting from the intellectualist presuppositions of Greek morality. Socrates was only a little clearer in his deductions from these principles.

Greek life was very concentrated, and it had a surprising degree of unity. No great effort was needed to find hypotheses for discussion. Any traditional opinion would serve, so long as it was trenchant enough. And it was these traditional opinions, often in the form of quotations, which Socrates extracted from the youth of Athens.

This is a good deal truer of the modern world than would appear at first sight. A point of departure for a good discussion can still be found if you can get a young man to say what he thinks, and if he will find a line of Shakespeare or Milton to represent his thought. We always have a good deal in common with it. The largest difference between the ancient and the modern world is that it had memorized its classics, and we have not. The very form of a modern classic like Ulysses makes apt quotation practically impossible. We have a goodly store of traditional wisdom, but we have lost the habit of repeating it in a form which strips away non-essentials. Our talk is too much cluttered up to serve as a definite beginning.

The form of our answers to Socratic questioning is complex, and this is more than an accident. It indicates that our life has become more complex than that of the Greek world. (The reader may think that this statement might have gone without proof. But I insist that our life is not nearly so complex as it has been made to look. The disagreement between Socrates and the sophists is still the only issue in philosophy. I think that it is impossible to find any other description of conduct than the intellectualist ones on which Socrates and the sophists were agreed.) No one can question that a good many new ways of stating the fundamental issue have been discovered, and these are confusing. Hence the pressing need for clearly formulated problems, and the greatly increased importance of the older thought with its precise statements of various hypotheses. It is just because the world is so modern that it must go to school with the ancients.

I do not feel that this necessarily involves going to school with Plato, and I should be willing in many cases to put something else from the more recent past in place of the Greeks.

I apologize for stating this theory in terms of the teaching of philosophy. I feel that it has universal applicability, and I hope that my views will find sympathy among teachers of other subjects who will take the trouble to convert them into their own language.

It is pretty generally recognized that one

can not cut oneself off from the past. But many people fail to take the idea at its source, where it is likely to have been expressed with the greatest simplicity, and to carry all the force of the conviction which compelled its discovery. With ideas of a relatively subordinate class these conditions may be repeated, and the second or third statement may be more effective than the first. Major ideas represent a very complex combination of influences, and if any one experiences all of them again in their unity it will be the student of history for whom these influences are already dead. Even if he is himself a genius his impulse will be to express something quite different from the original discovery, while the ordinary student of history will merely expound and analyze. If you want the idea alive you must go to the original.

From the point of view of the hostess as well as from that of the philosopher books make admirable beginnings in a conversation. Yet I do not seem to meet many people who can give much of an idea of a book they have read to any one who has not read it. I do not mean "give a good analysis," I mean an adequate picture such as would stimulate the imagination of the hearer, something in the same category with the things a poet will pour out on one when he is bursting with an unwritten *chef d'oevre*. The comparison may seem exaggerated. Yet with such an enormous amount of reading and such an enormous amount of talk as one finds in modern society it does seem as though our imaginations might be a little stimulated.

It is true—to some extent—that we are not all poets. But the one thing in which we can all imitate the poet is in frequent repetition of the same picture. Goethe carried Faust in his head for forty years before the publication of the First Part. Of course if we are poets we can afford to concentrate on chapbooks now and then—though even Goethe found it necessary to come back to Homer again and again. Not being poets, we are faced with the not altogether dismal necessity of concentrating on works of genius. The thing which now chiefly distinguishes us ordinary fellows from poets is our failure to devote our time to a few pictures. It ought to be an axiom that any book which is worth reading at all is worth reading a number of times.

The Oxford way of allowing long vacations establishes a very nice balance between the processes of saturation and gestation on one hand and of definition and formulation on the other. The work which is to be gone over in the eight weeks of the Oxford term has been assigned at the beginning of the previous vacation, which varies from six weeks (Christmas and Easter) to four months (summer). It is an unwritten law that you must not attempt to take as the basis for a formal essay anything which you are reading for the first time.

The success of these reading vacations depends first of all on the school which has built up a habit of independent work, and on the home which has also contributed to this, and provides peace and quiet, and an atmosphere in which serious reading is taken for granted. It is I think noteworthy that when the Oxonian goes home for his six weeks' Christmas vacation he attends five or six dances in the course of this period. Sometimes he goes abroad, or to some part of England other than his home, with a group of kindred spirits. The possibility of making steady progress without help from his usual instructor naturally grows with his experience of university life. And the concentration of his program makes much of his vacation reading repetition—a new attack on an old favorite, with many suggestions and problems of formal study to mull over and clarify in a fresh stream of impressions. The principal works are usually begun in the vac, then given considerable attention in a series of essays, then browsed over at odd times. Some months later they will again form the staple of vacation review preliminary to the final grind.

Within the last few years an attempt has been made at Oxford to encourage a study of modern civilization taken in the same unified way. Naturally it is very difficult to achieve the same coherence in dealing with a material so much more varied than classical literature. A good many of the books which might have been studied have had to be left out. The background in French and German literature is ignored or left to the student's casual reading. The curriculum includes English political, economic and constitutional history from 1760, the history of European philosophy from Descartes, some modern economic theory, political theory, and then for concentrated study a choice of two out of the three following groups: Kant, "Critique of Pure Reason" and "Foundation of the Metaphysic of Morals"; Adam Smith, "Wealth of Nations," and Ricardo, "Political Economy"; and some books on political theory and descriptions of modern governmental procedure. This is philosophy, politics and economics, or Modern Greats.

This program does not hang together very well. There is a sharp division between the philosophy, which belongs to the seventeenth and the eighteenth centuries, and the history and economics and government, which is pretty largely nineteenth century and English. Nor is it easy to see how this wound could be healed with good results for the student, since English philosophy from 1739 to 1876 does not often repay intensive study.

On the other hand, this material is quite useful as an addition to the classical curriculum described above (Honor Mods and Greats totaling four years). Able Oxonians are tending more and more to devote five years to university life before entering a profession. After the excursion into Greece and Rome they take a year to do some economics and brush up on English history and have one good bout with Kant.

The man who does this survey of modern civilization without the full classics program as a prelude will usually take two years to it. He is either a foreigner with a degree from some other institution, or else he is a classical scholar who has had his year and two thirds of Greek literature (Honor Mods) and has decided to give up the Greek and Roman history and Greek philosophy. Then there will be a few men who start off in Modern Greats after two terms or two thirds of a year of some preliminary study like history or the *pass* school in classics (Pass Mods). Of these only the renegade classicist spends four years in completing his work for a B.A. The foreigner usually has no preliminaries and gets his degree in two years, the rest with their preliminaries take three years to it.

All these people have a rather fragmentary program, judged by the standard of the classics curriculum. There is no such command of French and German to start with as we find in the case of Greek and Latin. In fact the standard set for modern languages at Oxford, if we except the very small number of people who do one of the modern language Honor Schools, is below that of the American college. This means that it is very low indeed. Nothing has been done to connect this survey of modern civilization with the small number of scholarships which encourage study of the modern languages. These ought to be more numerous. Nor has the ordinary beginner in Modern Greats the same familiarity with philosophy or economics or constitutional theory as the Greats man has at the start with philosophy and Greek and Roman history. The latter has always read some Plato at school, while for most men in Modern Greats the field (if we except the strictly historical portions of it) is new.

It follows of course that the undergraduates who do have a good background in modern European literatures, and who are really masters of French and German, are for the most part failing to work at modern philosophy, history and economics. To the American this may not seem surprising. But Oxford has set so high a standard of unity, has done so much to insist on the inevitable connection between command of language, appreciation of literature, and understanding of abstract ideas, that it seems too bad it can not do more to link these things together in its treatment of the modern world. Perhaps we on our side of the Atlantic can do it more effectively. We have only to learn from Oxford the paramount importance of controlling the schools by a scholarship system, and work out a college program with French and German classics, science, philosophy and social organization. "Only!" exclaims the reader. It could be done. A successful college depends on somehow having brought it about that most of the work has been done before freshman year. The program which I have just hinted at leaves out all language training and all assigning of history and English literature for explicit study. It would be absolutely necessary to bring it about that these had been so well cultivated at home and in the school that their further development could be left to the student. If that were done—and schools can do it if we demand it—four years would not be too little for a thorough training in the ideas which lie at the base of modern civilization.

Something would have to be done to weave in the ideas which come to us from mechanical and biological science. Here again Oxford has fallen far short of her own standard of unity. The scholarships which are given for work in the sciences do little to encourage the sort of work which could find a place in a reflective study of modern civilization. The holders of the scholarships are usually absorbed in strictly scientific inquiry. Obviously that is an excellent thing, but there ought to be some way of providing another sort of work at science which could be made to fit more readily into a literary and philosophic program. This is the most pressing problem which confronts the modern educator.

Both the classical and the modern program have been put together on the assumption that the abler men must deal with a civilization as a unity, and that this involves a good deal of work with abstract concepts. Philosophy forms the heart of the most important Oxford programs. But for those who do not feel attracted to the more abstruse disciplines there are the schools of modern history and English, and the lately developed schools in the various European literatures.

Then for the pass man there are all sorts of piddling little curricula. Neither the principle that most of the work must be done at school, nor that the university work must be concentrated and unified, have been applied to the pass man. There has been very little effort to find material which is adapted to his development.

The subjects for discussion normally fall into a fixed series, determined by the tutor. It is nearly always possible for the student to suggest an alternative subject in any one week provided that it is not outside the general field which has been selected by the tutor for the work of the term. The student could alter this field only by changing over to another Honors School. The order of the fields within the School, as well as the order of the weekly subjects within the field, will vary from tutor to tutor, though he is influenced to some extent by the tradition of the college, and of course he has to cooperate with others. Here is a sample sequence for Greats, the last half of the classics program: first two terms the "Republic'' and general Greek history, third term, "Nichomachean Ethics'' and Herodotus, fourth term, moral philosophy and Thucydides, fifth term, logic and Roman history, sixth term, history of modern philosophy and more Roman history, seventh term, review. The lectures are suggested by the tutor to parallel the term assignments.

Where one finds a subject like logic in place of a book in this program, three or four standard works are usually suggested, and from these the student selects one or two. His choice may be more or less directed by his tutor, as the latter will often tell him for instance to write an essay on Judgment after reading Bradley's second chapter.

The student does all his work for his tutors. Usually he has several of them, in different subjects. After he has begun Greats or another Honor School he may write an essay a week for each of them. Since this is the only task which is assigned for performance in term, they are expected to absorb a good deal of his time. I think it would be usual to assign a minimum of four hours and a maximum of fifteen hours to the reading of material for and the actual writing of one essay. Multiply the average by two or three and you have the work which is officially demanded in each week of term. Much of the preliminary reading has been done during the vacation. The writing of essays does not usually absorb all of the working time in term, so that one has a chance to do reading which is related in some general way to the comprehensive examination, and one can also browse.

The fact that most of the rereading is done for essays makes it practically a fresh reading. You have a problem set you. It is not likely that you thought of that particular problem very definitely when you were reading the book before. You now scrutinize it carefully with just that question in mind. A little later you may read exactly the same pages again, but with quite a different interest.

Any other way of reading simply heaps up tangled facts, but preparation for the writing of essays will build up a notebook that is organized. For instance: "Athenian Democracy:'' Herodotus offers us this, Thucydides has another point of view; Grote brings this material to bear on the problem; Bury suggests this analysis; here are a couple of points picked up in hastily glancing at Wilamowitz-Moellendorf, and a couple of quotations from Aristophanes which do not seem to have had much attention in handling this problem.

Obviously not all of Thucydides can be brought under this heading of Athenian democracy, and we have to read him again when we come to the Peloponnesian War in its military aspects. The result of this organization is that the book is remembered.

Tutors usually listen to the essays, sometimes they also read them over beforehand. Interruptions are likely to be frequent while the essays are being read, and this may lead quite far afield if the student is ready to talk. Some tutors attempt to pull the threads of the discussion together at the end of the period. There is a good deal of criticism of the style and form of the essay, and this becomes intensive in the last term, which is devoted to trial examinations. In the papers of the actual degree examination persuasiveness, clarity and coherence will play as large a part in determining the ranking as the substance of the thoughts expressed. The attacks of the tutorial on bad diction and incoherence come as a reenforcement of much practice writing at school, which helps to make them successful. And the student is usually well acquainted with fine writing, both ancient and modern.

In the first two years the classics student (Honors Mods) does a large part of his work for small recitation classes or groups meeting with a tutor. He does not often write essays. He will also have conferences alone or with a tutor for the correction of assignments in Greek prose composition and the like. In other preliminaries and in the Pass Schools there is likely to be some writing of essays, just as in the scientific schools there will be some writing out of solutions to problems for discussion with the tutor alone or in pairs.

In the other Honor Schools groups of two men are often taken together in a tutorial for an hour. Sometimes a group of from three to six will meet together for two hours. In Greats one man is frequently tutored alone for one hour. The success of these conferences is closely connected with the smallness of the groups. The conversation hews to the line with no interruption by others who see the issue differently. It is largely the smallness of the group which prevents the tutorial from becoming a bull session. This is also thwarted by the thoroughness of the student's training at school and in the university, and by his familiarity with the subject to be discussed. He does not always present a brilliant analysis. To the Oxford tutor he often seems slack and indifferent. But it is rather rare that he has not made an effort to digest the material and present a coherent view of it. He is in a fairly good position to comprehend the tutor's attacks, and he repels them with the same bluntness with which they are presented. The tradition of English school and college life heightens this bluntness by encouraging a brutal disregard for other people's feelings, even when it insists on the forms of polite intercourse.

It has been noticed in debates between English and American teams that the Englishman is usually ready to discourse on any point whether he has investigated it carefully or not, and that he usually scorns elaborate analysis of fact. This is what strikes one at the Union, and in the college debating societies. Obviously it has its defects as an intellectual attitude, especially when it is carried over into the tutorial. On the other hand it does encourage the pupil to cast around for something with which to meet the tutor's argument, and prevents him from regarding him as some one whose statements of fact sweep away all possibility of opposition.

There has been a good deal of talk about the informality of the tutorial, talk which gives an impression that the tutor's wisdom somehow oozes in. It does—when there has been a rigorous training at school, and when one goes through this mill faithfully, so that one is prepared to understand his criticisms. The tutorial is informal in the same way that any meeting of two men is informal when they have work to do and are anxious to get to the point. To cut a tutorial is a serious sin. There is nothing optional about it. Of course the tutor is quite friendly, and takes a personal interest—though this is usually manifested on the fringes of the interview, and soon gives place to the grindstone of discussion. English tutors who visit this country and begin asking questions in Honors groups often strike American students as brutal. They are scornful of academic pretense, and when they see an opening they try to swing from the canvas.

If it were merely a matter of smoking a pipe and being friendly there would be a great deal of tutoring in our Pullmans.

Many Americans seem to believe that Oxonians are not made to go to lectures. This is quite erroneous. The undergraduate at Oxford attends about as many lectures as his American equivalent. In his first two years he will be carefully checked up for attendance, and even in the last two the roll is sometimes taken at the lecture. The more diligent pupils are naturally not watched with as much strictness as their fellows. Supervision is in the hands of the tutor and the college authorities, not of the lecturer. There are no preparations to be made for lectures. No assignments or examinations are given by the lecturer.

It should be remembered that these lectures are given to men who are well prepared for hard work, and on subjects with which they are quite familiar. They rarely go to lectures except on books they have read a number of times, and are now explicitly digging out for essays and discussion with the tutor. The lecture supplies a fresh analysis of material which they wish to consider from a good many different sides. They already have some analysis of their own, with problems confronting them on this point and that. The lecture is not aimed at a vacuum, nor does it pretend to supply them with more than a tithe of the relevant considerations. This may have an important bearing on the number of the lectures they are able to attend with profit.

When I wrote the last paragraph I was thinking of those who read Greats. This is a picked group within the Oxford undergraduate body. A very large part of it holds scholarships. Hence what I have said would be less true of men reading History or English. These men listen to the same number of lectures, though I am inclined to believe they ought to have fewer. However it must be kept in mind that the whole of the group which gets into Oxford is carefully selected. These students have more highly cultivated families and better schools behind them than the majority of American undergraduates. I am speaking now not only of those who have been polished up for scholarships—which is naturally larger than the group which actually wins them—but of the whole undergraduate body at Oxford. This has a very decided bearing on the amount of lecturing they are able to digest.

There are also written examinations perhaps once a term. The marks have no bearing whatever on his degree, but the writing gives the student practice, and forces him to get his work into coherent form. The tutor uses these examinations as a guide to further assignments, besides subjecting them to the same sort of criticism which would be given to an essay.

The comprehensive examination on which the granting of degrees is based consists of ten or a dozen three hour papers to be done within a week, and summing up the work of two years. Most of the things which one has studied or taken notes on or written essays about are relevant—if one sees the connection. In the grading of the papers a premium is put on ability to bring out the connection in colorful and accurate English, with a persuasive movement of thought. Clarity must be combined with the appearance of having just evolved this particular answer, so that it has all the flavor of a new discovery. Naturally this ideal is not often achieved.

This is the intellectual test of a prospective tutor. He gets a job if he takes his B.A. with distinction and lives up to the other requirements of the college which seeks a tutor. There is no graduate work for him to do, except to the extent that many potential tutors are now adding Modern Greats and making a five year job of it. In some cases a would-be tutor in English or History will take that Honor School (for another B.A.) after Greats. More usually he works into English or History in the course of his teaching. Nearly all the tutors have gone through the classics mill, whatever their present subject may be.

That it is this sort of test which picks the teacher makes for vigor and absence of pedantry. A very large proportion of those who distinguish themselves in this examination remain to teach. The fact that there is usually no formal graduate work to be done is very helpful when one has been through a school and university routine of this sort, and knows how to study. For the years after the first appointment it will be largely a matter of keeping ahead of the cleverer pupils—who have the most unbounded contempt for a young tutor—keeping fresh on the material to be gone over with them, discovering new points of application for it, new connections with it, and branching out gradually into remoter fields. This has the advantage of demanding constant application and use of new studies right through the period which would in this country be devoted to graduate work. It also tends to keep new additions to the store hinged pretty tightly upon the old. The new tutor will usually work up a set of lectures, but these must be fitted into the program for undergraduates.

THE RELATIONSHIP OF TRAINING AND ADVANCEMENT OF TEACHERS IN ELEMENTARY SCHOOLS[1]

By FRANK W. BALLOU
SUPERINTENDENT OF SCHOOLS, WASHINGTON, D. C.

Every important condition attending the preparation, appointment and salaries of teachers contemplates improvement after appointment. The limited amount of practice teaching provided in our best normal schools and teachers colleges; the appointment for a probationary period of time, the salary schedule providing for increased pay from year to year, all indicate that the teacher is not fully equipped for the profession when appointed; that she is expected further to prepare herself for the teaching profession after appointment, and that the increased financial reward usually provided each year in the regular salary schedule is intended for increased professional service on the part of the teacher for a number of years after appointment.

It is a generally accepted principle in school administration that advancement both in salary and rank or official position should be on the basis of merit.

Two different procedures are to be found to-day relating to the advancement of teachers in service. One is the single salary schedule, and the other is a higher salary schedule for superior teachers.

The single salary schedule provides for the increased compensation of teachers primarily or largely in accordance with the professional growth of teachers as represented by the systematic courses of instruction that they pursue from year to year.

The higher salary schedule for superior teachers involves determining who are superior teachers and advancing such teachers to the higher salary schedule.

The salary schedule enacted by Congress in a law approved June 4, 1924, provides a salary schedule for superior teachers $400 higher than the maximum salary of the great body of teachers. The law further provides that teachers shall be promoted to the higher salary schedule "on the basis of such evidence of superior teaching and increased professional attainments as the Board of Education may prescribe."

The essential difference between the

[1] Address before the Municipal Normal School and Teachers College Section, Ballroom, Detroit-Leland Hotel, Detroit, Michigan.

above procedure lies in the fact that in the case of the single salary schedule, advancement is contingent on academic and professional courses pursued in accredited institutions, whereas the fundamental basis for the promotion of teachers to a superior salary class is the character and quality of classroom and related service that such teachers have rendered and are likely to continue to render in the school system.

The single salary schedule tends to promote the pursuit of courses, sometimes to the extent of substantial deterioration in the classroom work of teachers who are devoting too much time to their own individual study and too little time to their classroom work. The fundamental difficulty in operating a salary schedule for superior teachers grows out of the problem of determining who are superior teachers.

Through the cooperation of officers, teachers and the Teachers' Council in Washington, the following definition of a superior teacher was formulated:

> A superior teacher is one who renders superior service to the children whom she teaches, to the school in which she teaches, to the local community which she serves, and to the District of Columbia as a whole. A superior teacher is one who possesses broad scholarship, who is thoroughly familiar with the present-day educational theory and practice in the line of work which she teaches, who is doing constructive educational work of the highest order in carrying out the established educational program in the school where she teaches, who is actively and constructively promoting the educational welfare of the community in the vicinity of her school, and who participates in the improvement of education in the District of Columbia as a whole.

The plan for determining who are superior teachers may be indicated in general by the following outline showing the distribution of 1,000 points in an examination that consists largely of the submission of credentials or the assembling of official information.

SCOPE OF EXAMINATION AND APPORTIONMENT OF CREDITS

	Maximum number of credits Dist.	Total
A. *Recorded Success in Teaching*		325
Determined by the five official discriminating ratings, in the office of the superintendent, immediately preceding September 1 next after the date of examination, considering only the marks ES, E, VG (ES–65; E–50; VG–35).		
B. *Educational Preparation*		140
Courses successfully pursued in accredited institutions of learning within the fifteen years immediately preceding the announced date of the examination, over and above those required for eligibility.		
(Ph.D.—10 credits; A.M.—4 credits)	10	
(a) Courses in education	80	
Graduate courses, maximum 8 credits each.		
Other courses, maximum 6 credits each.		
Courses are classified into the four groups given below. The maximum value of a course will be given if in the first group; one less if in the second group; two less if in the third group; three less if in the fourth group:		
Group 1. Courses in the teacher's line of work (maximum number of courses, 6);		
Group 2. General course in educational psychology and the profession of teaching (maximum number of courses, 6);		
Group 3. Courses in subjects allied to the teacher's line of work (maximum number of courses, 6);		

	Maximum number of credits Dist.	Total
Group 4. Other courses in education (maximum number of courses, 4);		
(b) Courses in subject-matter (*i.e.*, Content) (maximum 5 credits each)	50	
Courses are classified into the three groups given below. The maximum value of a course will be given if in the first group; one less if in the second group; two less if in the third group:		
Group 1. Courses in the teacher's line of work (maximum number of courses, 7);		
Group 2. Courses in subjects allied to the teacher's line of work (maximum number of courses, 5);		
Group 3. Other subject-matter courses (maximum number of courses, 4);		
C. *Approved Constructive Educational Work*		100
Constructive, well-organized written educational investigations and plans made to official superiors and by them deemed worthy of adoption to carry out or improve the established educational program of the local schools or of the system as a whole, including distinct contributions made to the work of important educational committees and individual investigations.		
1. *Investigations*	50	
Covering any or all of the following: methods of teaching; organization and management of school, and line of work; educational welfare of local school community.		
2. *Plans*	50	
Covering any or all of the following: methods of teaching; organization and management of school, and line of work; educational welfare of local school community.		
D. *Professional Interest and Growth (other than under B and C)*		35
1. Publications or manuscripts on educational subjects	20	
2. Affiliations with educational associations	6	
3. Travels	9	
E. *Civic Interest—distinct from special educational work*		50
1. Civic associations and similar associations	30	
(a) Membership—maximum 6.		
(b) Participation—maximum 24.		
2. Lectures, articles, etc., prepared, of a non-professional nature—maximum number five, 2 credits each	10	
3. Other outside contacts	10	
F. *Assigned Work other than Teaching*		50
G. *Familiarity with Present-Day Educational Theory and Practice*		200
Related to the candidate's line of work. Determined by a written examination one hour in length.		
H. *Personal Equipment*		100
Determined by questions on any of the foregoing parts of the examination and matters pertinent thereto.		
Total		1,000

While it is generally recognized that the administration of a salary schedule for superior teachers is a very difficult problem, it is gratifying to record the fact that almost complete unanimity was reached with regard to every detail of the procedure set up for determining superior teachers. It is to be noted also that among the teachers and the school officers concerned there is very general satisfaction with the manner in which the boards of examiners organized and conducted the examinations.

EDUCATIONAL EVENTS

FREE MEALS FOR THE SCHOOL CHILDREN OF THE IRISH FREE STATE

SOCIAL reformers, who have long advocated a comprehensive scheme for the provision of free meals for necessitous children attending national schools in the Irish Free State, express great satisfaction that the movement is now receiving a large measure of governmental time and attention, according to *The Christian Science Monitor*.

Last year an act was passed for the preservation of the Irish-speaking districts of the Gaelthacht, and among its most important provisions was one to provide free meals for the indigent children of the area. The scheme is now in full swing and is working admirably.

A new bill, which has for its purpose the extension of the movement to small towns throughout the country, is passing through Parliament and has the support of all political parties. Though introduced by a private member, the measure has been adopted by the Minister for Local Government and is expected to become law this year.

Under legislation passed some years ago, local authorities in cities and large towns were empowered to provide school children's meals at public expense in their own districts.

Unfortunately, however, there are many instances in which the act has not been put into operation, and efforts are being made by the National Council of Women and the Irish Women Citizens' Association to stimulate local bodies into taking full benefit of the act. If this can be achieved, fully 75 per cent. of the urban national school population of the Free State will be brought within the scope of the scheme.

The Minister for Education is being urged to rearrange school hours in urban areas to allow time for a substantial midday meal. This is a reform which is widely demanded by parents and teachers; it is necessary in all schools, national or otherwise, as under the existing régime the children are only allowed time to eat a few sandwiches.

It is maintained that it is highly detrimental to a child's welfare to be compelled to work for a stretch of six to eight hours without a warm and substantial meal. The minister is being approached with a view to the introduction of a system on continental lines, which will enable the children to return to their homes for a midday dinner and resume their school work after.

THE LIBRARY OF CONGRESS

THE Library of Congress, after 130 years of growth, has now become the National Library of the United States and one of the ranking libraries of the world.

With a collection of 4,103,000 books and pamphlets, 1,160,000 maps, 1,060,000 pieces of music, nearly 500,000 prints, it is now surpassed in the number of books and pamphlets by only one library in the world, the Bibliothèque Nationale, in Paris. The Library of Congress acquires annually 190,000 books and pamphlets.

Founded in 1800, the library was housed in the Capitol until 1897, when the present building was completed. The collection was destroyed in 1814, when the Capitol was burned by the British. Through a purchase of the library of Thomas Jefferson, a new collection began, and has been increased year by year until it has attained international importance. It suffered a setback in 1851, when a second fire almost wiped away all the acquisitions since 1814.

The present building, the largest library building in the world, represents a cost to date of $7,868,951. It will accommodate 900 readers, including 49 separate rooms and over 125 study tables for research workers. In addition to stacks, study rooms, and the general reading room, the building contains an auditorium which will seat 510 persons. Much space is given over for exhibition halls in which various collections are displayed for the interest and enlightenment of the public.

In addition to its numerous books and

pamphlets, the library contains more than 1,000,000 pieces of manuscript.

Scholars seeking information on American history and politics will find in the National Library the most complete collection of material. It is also possessor of the most complete collection of bibliography and library science material. Its file of federal documents is equaled only by that of the Office of the Superintendent of Documents.

One interested in foreign studies will find a wealth of information. Probably the largest collection of Russian books anywhere in the world outside of Russia reposes in the Library of Congress. The same is true with reference to books on China and Japan. The Vollbehr Collection of Incunabula is the most recent fifteenth century acquisition.

Collections of works on economics, law, science and technology which have been added to the library are unsurpassed in the United States. It has an unequaled collection of publications of learned societies, and within its manuscript group are papers of nearly every President of the United States and many statesmen. Through the Rockefeller grant, the collection is being enriched by transcripts of manuscripts in European libraries.

There are about 50,000 rare books and manuscripts housed within the edifice. These include many first editions, books of rare bindings, about 25,000 early American pamphlets, and 3,357 incunabula.

Its stock of 1,135,000 printed cards contain about 80,000,000 names in all. Over 5,000 libraries, firms and individuals purchase cards to the amount of over $250,000 annually. The depository sets of the Library of Congress cards are now housed in 63 libraries, including those of 8 foreign countries.

A staff of 962 workers handles the increasing labors of the growing institution. Appropriations for the current fiscal year amount to $3,698,522, and income from gifts and endowments administered by the Trust Fund Board amounts to approximately $290,000.

STATE APPROPRIATIONS FOR NORTH CAROLINA SCHOOLS

The *Christian Science Monitor,* in reporting on the financial status of the North Carolina schools, writes that salaries of state officials, state employees and school teachers were cut, and the act providing for the operation of public schools gives further evidence of the pruning hook to be applied during the next biennium.

The entire scheme of financing public education was changed in its tax reduction program, and the experiment of full state support for six months out of each year will be put into operation when the schools open next fall.

From a state that spent only $1,000,000 on public education in 1900 to one that now spends more than $30,000,000, North Carolina has assuredly advanced rapidly. In the early 1900's the value of its public school property was negligible. The present total is more than $100,000,000, and along with the increase in the amount invested in school houses, enrolment, attendance, scholarship and teaching efficiency have advanced.

The revenue bill adopted by the 1931 Legislature takes a load of $16,500,000 off the counties, and, consequently, off farms and homes for the six months' term, and about $1,500,000 for extended terms. It also reduces the *ad valorem* tax rate for school support from 52 cents on the $100 valuation to 15 cents.

Taking over the county highways by the state will relieve the counties of $8,000,000 a year for maintenance. This, also, will be reflected in local taxation, as will the saving to be effected through the operation of the county finance control act, whereby the state will scrutinize and pass upon all county transactions.

The total amount in property tax reduction reflected back to the counties will be about 57 cents on the $100 valuation.

As soon as the Legislature was under way, it was seen that the schools of the state were at the cross-roads. Early in the session, Angus Dhu McLean, Representative from Beaufort County, introduced a bill providing for state support of the six months' school term. This is the minimum term allowed by the constitution. Many of the county schools run for eight months and most of the city schools for nine months.

The question then was how to finance the load the state had taken over. Two groups contended and went into a deadlock that extended over a period of more than two months and caused the session to last until spring was well advanced. One group advocated a sales tax, the other opposed such a move. The latter finally won. The McLean law remained in force, and the state, with the revenue bill adopted by both houses, will take over the public schools.

Summed up, the various measures passed by the 1931 Assembly will take a total tax load of nearly $25,000,000 from the counties. While the state will support the schools for only six months each year, the local communities will be responsible for all the time their schools are operated beyond the constitutional limit. However, even in this, state aid will be available.

PART-TIME IN NEW YORK CITY SCHOOLS

FALLING registration in the elementary schools is helping the New York City authorities to make progress against the part-time problem. According to a report in the New York *Sun* at the close of the semester last June there were 20,535 elementary school children on part time, and none in the junior high schools. The aggregate was not only the smallest on record ever since part time became a problem, but it represented an insignificant proportion of the enrolment—2.6 per cent. At one time, in 1913, 12.9 per cent. of the elementary junior high-school population was on part time, or, as it is now officially termed, short time.

The fact that the elementary school enrolment fell by more than 3,000 between June 30, 1930, and June 30, 1931, was an important factor in the war on part time, since the new buildings opened were available entirely for the relief of overcrowding. In the high schools, for example, the enrolment is still increasing so rapidly that the best the school authorities can do is to keep part time in check. Last year, despite an increase of 18,000 in register, the high school reported no increase in part time; in fact, they showed a decrease of 296, bringing the total to 28,620. The junior high schools wiped out the 1,081 short-time figure they had a year ago.

The 20,535 short-time pupils in the elementary junior high school division last month compare with 33,027 on June 30, 1930, and with close to 90,000 in 1923.

The figures for part time and the percentage they constituted of the total elementary junior high school enrolment since 1911 follow:

1911	65,387	10.71
1912	72,633	11.67
1913	81,495	12.90
1914	35,652	5.44
1915	33,866	4.81
1916	30,778	4.29
1917	34,431	4.78
1918	30,519	4.19
1919	40,976	5.56
1920	58,524	7.86
1921	82,569	10.57
1922	85,545	10.71
1923	89,223	11.02
1924	71,661	8.66
1925	56,117	6.74
1926	39,994	4.79
1927	46,345	5.48
1928	41,127	4.82
1929	43,188	5.03
1930	33,207	3.84
1931	20,535	2.6

The greatest amount of part time was found in the schools of Queens, where 10,536 elementary school pupils and 6,019 high school students, a total of 16,555, were so designated. Manhattan reported 10,033 on short time, all in the high schools.

At the close of the school term a total of 1,053,534 were enrolled in all day schools, a net increase of 21,979 for the year. The high schools accommodated 178,222, the junior high schools 101,092, the training schools 1,935 and the elementary schools 765,220.

Thirty-three classes with registers of over fifty pupils were reported, a decrease from the sixty-two such classes in existence in June, 1930. A total of 945,609 attended school on regular sessions, 58,770 on special schedules.

THE AMERICAN COUNTRY LIFE CONFERENCE

THE Fourteenth Annual American Country Life Conference meets at Cornell University, Ithaca, New York, August 17–20, 1931, under the presidency of Dr. Liberty Hyde Bailey. The topic of the conference is "Rural Government." Its discussions will be carried on in six forums, one of which is devoted to public education, and will consider local units of school government. Dr. Francis B. Haas, president of the State Teachers College, Bloomsburg, Pennsylvania, is chairman of this forum and Julian E. Butterworth, of Cornell University, is secretary. The topics of the four sessions of the forum are "Some Types of Local School Units," "Criteria for the Establishment of Local Units of School Government," "Problems in the Development of the Central Rural School District in New York," and a joint session with the forum on Public Health and Welfare on "Problems of Coordinating School with Health and Welfare Services." Many of the leaders in the study and administration of rural schools as related to local government are on the program, which may be obtained from Professor Dwight Sanderson, Ithaca, New York. The program follows:

GENERAL TOPIC:
Local Units of School Government.

Tuesday afternoon, August 18

Some Types of Local School Units.

The California High School District. Dr. W. M. Proctor, Stanford University.

A Plan for Cooperative Reorganization in Vermont. Mr. A. J. Holden, Vermont Commission on Country Life, Burlington, Vermont.

The County School District. Dr. R. E. Jaggers, Director of Rural Education, Kentucky State Department of Education.

The City-County School District. Mr. John M. Foote, Director Research, Louisiana State Department of Education.

General discussion.

Wednesday morning, August 19

Problems in the Development of the Central Rural School District in New York.

Criteria for Laying Out the Central District. Mr. Ray P. Snyder, Director of the Bureau of Rural Education, New York State Department of Education.

Types of Problems in Providing Educational Facilities for those Areas Lying Near Cities. Dr. J. Cayce Morrison, Assistant Commissioner for Elementary Education, New York State Department of Education.

The Function of an Intermediate Unit in Making Available More Adequate Educational Facilities. Dr. Francis B. Haas, Bloomsburg State Teachers College.

Guiding Principles in Dealing with the Foregoing Problems. Dr. Harlan Updegraff, Educational Adviser for Griffenhagen and Associates, Trenton, New Jersey.

General discussion.

Wednesday afternoon, August 19

Joint session with the Public Health and Welfare Forum.

Thursday morning, August 20

Criteria for the Establishment of Local Units of School Government.

As Revealed through a State Survey of School Districts in Ohio. Dr. C. C. McCracken, President of the Connecticut Agricultural College, Storrs, Connecticut.

Curricular Demands on the High Schools of the Future Affecting the Size of the Local School District. Dr. E. N. Ferriss, Professor of Rural Education, Cornell University.

Educational and Social Factors. Dr. M. G. Nelson, New York State College for Teachers, Albany, New York.

General discussion.

THE NATIONAL SURVEY OF SCHOOL FINANCE

DR. WM. JOHN COOPER, U. S. Commissioner of Education, has announced the appointment by the Secretary of the Interior of 17 finance specialists from various sections of the United States to act as consultants in the Federal Office of Education's four-year National Survey of School Finance, which was officially launched July 1.

These specialists, who will serve in an advisory capacity to those conducting the survey, are: Wm. G. Carr, director of research, National Education Association, Washington, D. C.; Lotus D. Coffman, president, University of Minnesota, Minneapolis; Albert S. Cook, state superintendent of schools, Baltimore; N. R. Crozier, superintendent of schools, Dallas, Texas; Fred R. Fairchild, professor of political economy, Yale University; Mark Graves, state tax commissioner, Albany, N. Y.; Robert M. Haig, professor of business administration, Columbia University; Arthur N. Holcombe, professor of government, Harvard University; L. F. Loree, president, Delaware and Hudson Railroad, N. Y.; Harley L. Lutz, professor of public finance, Princeton University; Felix M. McWhirter, president, Peoples State Bank, Indianapolis, Ind.; Fred W. Morrison, state tax commissioner, Raleigh, N. C.; Henry C. Morrison, professor of education, University of Chicago; Orville C. Pratt, superintendent of schools, Spokane, Washington; George D. Strayer, director of educational research, Teachers College, Columbia University, New York, N. Y.; Fletcher Harper Swift, professor of education, University of California, and Rolland A. Vandegrift, director of finance, State Department of Finance, Sacramento, California.

Timon Covert, Federal Office of Education specialist in school finance, and Eugene S. Lawler, senior specialist in the finance survey, are now conducting preliminary survey investigations. Dr. Carter Alexander, Teachers College, Columbia University, and Dr. Mabel Newcomer, professor of economics, Vassar College, are cooperating in the preliminary investigations.

The school finance survey, authorized by the Congress at a cost not to exceed $350,000, is the third national educational study now being directed by the Federal Office of Education, and the finance survey administrative organization will be similar to that of the other two studies, the Survey of Secondary Education, and the Survey of Education of Teachers. Commissioner Cooper is director, and Professor Paul R. Mort, director of the School of Education, Teachers College, Columbia University, is associate director in active charge of the survey.

An appropriation of $50,000 for the current fiscal year has been made for the school finance study.

EDUCATIONAL NOTES AND NEWS

PROFESSOR GILBERT MURRAY has been reelected president of the International Commission for Intellectual Cooperation of the League of Nations. Mme. Curie and M. Destrée have been reelected vice-presidents.

PROFESSOR JAMES HENRY BREASTED, director of the Oriental Institute of the University of Chicago, has been appointed chairman of the American delegation to the Eighteenth International Congress of Orientalists, which will meet in Leyden, Holland, from September 7 to 12. Dr. Breasted was appointed to head the group of ten American orientalists by Secretary of State Henry L. Stimson.

DR. THOMAS JEFFERSON WERTENBAKER, professor of history at Princeton University, has been honored by being made a freeman of the University of Göttingen, where he has been lecturing as exchange professor.

AT the recent annual commencement of Ohio Wesleyan University, President George F. Zook, of the University of Akron, was awarded the honorary degree of LL.D.

DR. JOHN G. BARRY, mining geologist and engineer, has been elected president of the Texas College of Mines and Metallurgy.

DR. LOUIS J. RETTGER, for forty years a member of the faculty of the Indiana State Teachers College, has been elected vice-president of the institution.

THE REVEREND GEORGE R. KISTER, director of education at the St. Xavier College, will become president of the University School of Divinity when it moves from St. Louis to St. Mary's College, St. Mary's, Kansas.

MR. JOHN ELLERTON LODGE, for twenty years associated with the Museum of Fine Arts at Boston, has resigned his position as curator of the Department of Asiatic Art, which he has held since 1915, in order that he may give full time to the directorship of the Frear Gallery, at Washington, D. C.

THE REVEREND C. F. ATKINS, pastor of the Church of Christ, Congregational, Milford, Connecticut, for the past ten years, has resigned and will become a member of the faculty of Columbia University.

PROFESSOR JOHN HARROWER has resigned from the position of Regius professor of Greek at the University of Aberdeen, Scotland. No appointment has yet been made to fill the position.

Miss Edith P. Stickney has been appointed professor of history at the Constantinople Woman's College.

Those promoted to the rank of professor at the University of Missouri include Harry H. Charlton, professor of anatomy; Ella V. Dobbs, professor of applied arts; Arthur S. Emig, professor of sociology, and Eva Johnston, professor of Latin.

Mr. Lon Luvois Fuller, who is now professor of law at the University of Illinois, has accepted an offer from Duke University. He is teaching this summer at the University of Washington.

The summer session faculty of the University of California includes the following foreign members: Dr. Raoul Blanchard, director of the Institute of Alpine Geography at the University of Grenoble, in the department of geography; Diego Rivera, artist, of Mexico City, in the department of art; Professor Daniel Mornet, of the Sorbonne, in the department of French; Professor R. Courant, of the University of Göttingen, in the department of mathematics, and Professor J. W. Bridges, of McGill University, in the department of psychology.

Dr. Charles B. Fowler, associate professor of economics at New York University, will run on the Democratic ticket for mayor of White Plains, New York.

Alta B. Claflin, librarian of the Federal Reserve Bank of Cleveland, has been elected president of the Special Libraries Association for the year 1931–1932.

Dr. D. M. Douglas, president of the University of South Carolina, died on July 31. Dr. Douglas became president of the university in 1927. Prior to that he was president of Presbyterian College of South Carolina at Clinton for sixteen years.

Dr. Hugo K. Schelling, emeritus professor of German at the University of California, died on July 24, at the age of seventy years.

Miss Sarah G. Foote Sheldon, for over twenty-five years a volunteer full-time assistant to the late J. H. Paarmann, curator of the Davenport Academy of Sciences, now the Davenport Public Museum, died on July 2 at the age of about seventy-five years.

George D. Dietrich, for nineteen years superintendent of schools of Carrollton, Kansas, has died at the age of sixty-eight years.

A library of over 700 volumes, dedicated to the memory of Dr. Bird T. Baldwin, pioneer in the field of child study in the University of Iowa, has been opened in Iowa City for the use of university staff members and graduate students in child welfare. The library contains 3,000 pamphlets on child welfare and includes the late Dr. Baldwin's personal library, bequeathed to the university. Dr. Baldwin, who died in 1928, directed the first child welfare research station in the United States at the university.

Mr. Julius Rosenwald, of Chicago, has made a gift of $1,000,000 to the city of Berlin for the establishment of a children's dental clinic.

Drew University has opened a program of expansion, planned since its inheritance in March of more than $15,000,000 from the estate of Miss Ella Wendel, of New York, with the purchase of twenty-seven acres of land.

Because of the success of the first conference of school superintendents held last month on the University of California campus as a part of the summer session program, Professor F. W. Hart, director of the conference, has announced that efforts will be made to hold similar conferences annually. Sixty-five school leaders registered for the conference, which lasted approximately two weeks during the middle of July. The subjects considered were: Administration of the teaching personnel, making and administration of the school budget, organization and administration of curriculum revision, organization and administration of the business department, educational guidance, administrative use of tests and measurements, sources of revenue—taxation, enlarged responsibilities in the field of administration, organization and administration of research departments, multiple *versus* unified administrative control.

The executive board of the Special Libraries Association voted to transfer the general office of the association from Providence, Rhode

Island, to New York City, where headquarters are now established at 345 Hudson Street.

AT a recent meeting of the trustees of Vermont Academy, which has hitherto been a coeducational institution, it was decided to confine registration to boys only.

THIRTEEN new public schools will be opened in Baltimore during the next scholastic year, according to Dr. David E. Weglein, superintendent of public instruction. When schools open in September, it is estimated there will be an increase of 3,400 in the student population.

A PROJECT to house 9,000 University of Wisconsin students is planned by the board of regents of the University of Wisconsin. Because university fraternities are operating under $3,000,000 in mortgaged debts, and 6,000 students are inadequately housed, the regents hope to set aside a district near the university for construction of enough dormitories and state-owned buildings to house all students. Buildings would be erected on private funds, but titles would accrue to the university in thirty years. It is hoped to furnish and heat the buildings at nominal cost.

A COMMISSION of sixteen members to study the problems of child health and protection in Iowa was appointed, June 9, by Governor Dan W. Turner. Seven of the sixteen members are physicians: Drs. Channing G. Smith, Granger, president of the State Medical Society; Daniel C. Steelsmith, State Health Commissioner; Mae H. Habenicht, of the State Children's Bureau; John H. Peck, president of the Iowa Tuberculosis Association; J. F. Edwards, of the health and hygiene department, Iowa State College; Milford E. Barnes, professor of hygiene, State University of Iowa College of Medicine, Iowa City, and Fred Moore, Des Moines, who was a member of the White House Conference. The state medical society adopted a resolution at its recent annual session that the governor be requested to promote through existing agencies a Conference on Child Health and Protection in Iowa. Two conferences have already been held, section and subcommittee chairmen appointed and plans made to study the entire field of child welfare work in the state and to work out plans for coordination and more efficient operation of the various projects and activities.

ACCORDING to the *Journal* of the American Medical Association, the St. Louis Tuberculosis and Health Society in cooperation with a committee of sixteen physicians sponsored a posture contest in St. Louis, from July 8 to 10. One hundred and seventy-five children between the ages of 6 and 12 were entered. They were given preliminary examinations, and silhouettographic pictures were made of their posture and from these the posture was classed as excellent, good, poor or bad. Those in the excellent class were called for reexamination and two winners were selected. All children entering the contest were given photographs with printed instructions on how to correct such defects. The society plans to have the children return within a year to determine whether any improvements have resulted. The Shriners' Hospital for Crippled Children was in charge of making the pictures.

THE celebration of the fourth centenary of the Collège de France began on June 18, when Professor H. Vincent, member of the Institut de France and of the Académie de Médecine, delivered an address on Claude Bernard and the Collège de France.

THE city of Madrid, Spain, has decided to create 200 schools in the city and suburbs since, although education is legally compulsory, there are many thousands of children unable to obtain admittance for lack of space. In three months Don Marcelino Domingo, the Minister of Education, has taken measures for the creation of nearly 5,000 new schools.

THE growth of elementary education in Mexico during the past half decade is shown by figures compiled by the Mexican Bureau of National Statistics. These data show that the republic had only 29,015 school teachers in 1925, but that in 1929 there were 42,310. Of this latter number 21,182 taught in schools maintained by state and municipal governments, 14,792 in Federal Government schools, and 6,336 in private institutions. In that year the pupils numbered 1,662,371—slightly more than 10 per cent. of Mexico's population—and schools 18,412, of which states and municipalities conducted 9,338, the Federal Government 5,925, and private interests 3,149. Radio has become a prominent factor in Mexico's rural school system. Practically every country school house has a receiving set. Even primary seats of learning in villages eight days' horseback ride from the nearest railroad station have this equipment. Wireless has dramatized education for the rural population. The Minister of Public Education gives daily broadcasts from its stations in Mexico City. Radio has tended to make each town schoolhouse a social center for formal instruction. The Minister's broadcasts include musical programs, lectures on domestic science, dressmaking, etc., and folk tales for young and old. The enthusiasm for education has embraced the study of English, which is being taught and studied throughout the country. Most Mexicans of culture know English well. Many natives of the republic who have never been out of the country speak and know the language.

THE first step to fulfil China's request to the League of Nations to aid the country to reorganize its educational system was taken by the Intellectual Cooperation Committee to-day. It appointed a committee of experts composed of Professors Becker, of Berlin; Falski, of Warsaw; Langevin, of Paris, and Tawney, of London, who will leave within a fortnight for a five months' tour of China to survey the situation. Frank Walters, secretary to Sir Eric Drummond, the League Secretary General, will accompany the party as a special adviser. Henry Bonnet, director of the Institute of Intellectual Cooperation, will join them later. China has offered to send some of her leading scientists, writers, philosophers, historians and archeologists to lecture in European universities if the league will arrange for the dispatch to China of specialists in medicine, natural science, law and particular science, drawn from Germany, Austria, Scandinavia or Switzerland and capable of lecturing in English as well as one professor representing the Anglo-Saxon educational systems. The committee appointed Professor Parjes, of Geneva, to lecture on geology at Nanking University and Professor Credner, of Germany, to lecture on geography at Canton University. Part of their salaries is to be paid by the League. League work for the reconstruction of China, which includes economic, financial, transportation and health, as well as educational problems, is being financed out of back dues to the League, which China is now beginning to pay.

WE learn from *Nature* that at a meeting of the Court of the University of London held on May 13, the principal, Dr. Edwin Deller, read his annual report of the work of the university for the year 1930–31. The statistics for that year have brought out some facts concerning the number of students. For example, the number of matriculations has almost quadrupled since just before the war. A great increase has taken place in all branches of study. For the year 1913, the numbers of matriculations, first degrees, and higher degrees were 6,638, 1,636 and 171, respectively. The corresponding numbers for 1929 were 23,832, 3,436 and 510, and for 1930, 25,544, 3,543 and 548. The total number of degrees, diplomas and certificates awarded for those three years were 11,937, 36,633 and 39,323. During the last decade, the inspection and examination of secondary schools have received much attention and the growth of the school examinations has been specially noteworthy.

THE municipal education authorities of Manchester, England, are planning to spend £1,260,682 during the next five years in erecting new schools and extending and reconditioning existing ones. The projects include two new secondary schools, a big extension to the College of Technology, six new senior public elementary schools, two new junior and infant schools, and the development of special services.

DISCUSSION

THE TRIANGLE OF LIFE

IN the presentation of the "Triangle of Life" the physical development is taken as a constant, as it is the basis of all success. Without a well-developed body, character development and educational development are practically impossible or limited. Man at birth is handicapped as he can not talk, can not walk, is without teeth and generally without hair. The mind is a blank negative ready for impressions good or bad that are presented. We gradually overcome these handicaps by proper nourishment, care, fresh air and environment. The first information a college or industry desires in examining an applicant for admission is to know of any physical defect so they can be corrected by proper supervision in physical educational work. Some industries have recreation facilities for the development or correction of the physical defects of the men they employ. In colleges they have a department of physical education for the training of young men, with special classes for the correction of physical defects. In business life the executive of the industry recommends that the employees have some avocation in order to rest their minds and perhaps develop a better physical condition, as in the playing of golf, swimming, gymnasium work, boating and other forms of recreation. Intramural sports are as necessary in college work as interdepartment contests are in industry. The first question a personnel man of the industry asks a college graduate when his application is being considered for a place is, "What do you do when you are not studying?" or "What is your avocation?" Some form of exercise is necessary for the business man as well as the college student if he expects to stay fit for life and build a successful triangle.

The second most essential development is character. By character development is meant the development of personality, the light shining through the windows of your soul produced by proper contact in the world of business and education. This character development is produced by contacts with your fellow men in a business and social way, in service clubs, chambers of commerce, religious organizations, college publications, and other activities beneficial to your community. By your contact, in business and in pleasure, with your fellow men, you are taught to play the game of life fair and square, to give and to take with a smile and emphasize the fact that it is not so important as to whether you have won or lost but how you played the game. A large number of people think that athletic events, in our high schools and colleges, are only for the display of athletic prowess, but it is very essential for character development. The man who has never had the opportunity to mingle with his fellow men in school, on the street and in business can never appreciate life to its fullest extent. The character development line when perfect, the same as the line for educational development, is taken as a line perpendicular to the line of physical development. The space between these three lines, physical development, character development and educational development, is known as the field of infinite success. Jesus of Nazareth was the only one who has ever had perfect qualifications, so our lines must be intersecting lines producing a triangle having as the base the perfect physical development and designated as the "Triangle of Life." The field

THE TRIANGLE OF LIFE

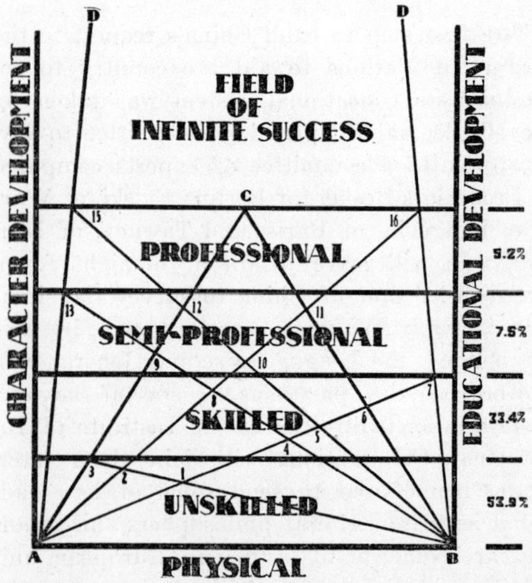

of infinite success is divided into four divisions —unskilled workmen, skilled workmen, semi-professional and professional. You will note the numbers occupying the different divisions become less and less, the larger being those in the unskilled class. As a man develops he passes upward through each division until his perfection may place his intersecting lines in the field of infinite success.

In a tabulation made by the Welfare Council of New York City of the migrating Bowery population or the army of drifters who occupy the Bowery hang-outs, the following was found:

Total homeless	14,198 men
Unskilled workmen	73 per cent.
Skilled workmen	22.6 " "
Semi-professional (clerk)	3.5 " "
Professional	0.3 " "

The ages of the men were as follows:

15 to 20 years	1.3 per cent.
20 to 29 years	14.0 " "
30 to 39 years	26.0 " "
40 to 49 years	30.7 " "
50 to 59 years	18.0 " "
Over 60 years	10.0 " "

The record also shows that

9.5 per cent. of the men are married,
56.0 " " are native born Americans,
20.0 " " come from Northern and Eastern Europe,
15.0 " " come from British Isles, and
9.0 " " come from the rest of the world.

These statistics emphasize the fact that the typical Bowery bum is a native American, more than forty, unskilled workman, unmarried and unemployed. The best way to keep men from becoming bums is to educate them in some trade or occupation when they are young. The youthful loafers of to-day are the bums of to-morrow. Employers of unskilled labor hire only husky young men, under thirty years of age. Keep the young men in school; teach them a trade—if they refuse to accept an education.

Educational development or training needs no argument, as every one recognizes how essential it is to know your own business. It matters not whether a man receives his training in college or in the "school of hard knocks." It is absolutely essential in this day of competition for success. A business man can not afford to stop studying unless he expects to retire. Business competition is based on knowledge and knowledge is power. The intersection of the line representing character development and educational development forms the "Triangle of Life." A man may be well developed in character but his educational training may produce a triangle in the unskilled field, and also a man may be restricted to a certain field due to lack of character development. The ideal triangle would be where the lines intersect at a place equal distance from each side and in the field of infinite success. The triangle is not complete until the end of life, and every one should strive to improve from day to day his undeveloped characteristic in order to improve his triangle. I would not want to be a business man if I was not considered by my business associates honest. I would not want to be a teacher if I was not regarded by my students as fair and square. I would not want to be an executive if I did not have the confidence of my associates, as their friend. Humanity stressed in industry and education is the key word to success. To-day and not to-morrow is the time to improve ourselves as to-morrow may never come, and to-day is not to-day for we keep step with the revolving world so closely that the twilight of to-day becomes the dawning of to-morrow.

C. C. Hedges

Department of Chemistry
and Chemical Engineering,
Agricultural and Mechanical
College of Texas

SPECIAL CORRESPONDENCE

"THE PEOPLE'S UNIVERSITY"—PROFESSOR IORGA'S EXPERIMENT AT VĂLENII-DE-MUNTE, ROUMANIA

The low standard of education of pre-war Roumania had its reflection in the post-war conditions of Greater Roumania. However, the whole Roumanian nation is showing a tremendous interest in education which, in general, may be said to be of two types: official education, and education supported and directed, though under official supervision, by private individuals and private foundations.

One of the most beloved and best-known educational centers of Roumania is the "People's University" of Professor Nicolae Iorga, present Premier of Roumania, in a little town, north of Bucharest, under the Carpathian Mountains, where for over twenty years the leaders of national cultural life have found their inspiration. The Roumanians, living outside the boundaries of their country, had no cultural support for their educational efforts until Iorga established in 1908 his "summer courses." Their reputation spread very quickly and many an enthusiastic nationalist secretly crossed the Roumanian boundaries to reach Vălenii-de-Munte. Here they were taught the rudiments of Roumanian civilization, the historical background and the contemporary conditions of Roumania. Thus the courses had two aims in view: cultural and culturally irredentist, the latter favoring the ultimate union of all Roumanians in a national state. But the state, strangely enough, was suspicious, and it was only in 1912 that a small subvention was granted to Iorga. The World War interrupted these efforts.

The post-war years saw the steady development of Iorga's attempt to encourage popular education. The irredentist tendencies were now useless; the aim now is to elevate the cultural level of the nation and to create one Roumanian national soul. Of great importance is the insistance of Iorga that all minorities in Roumania be included in these summer courses and treated in the spirit of understanding and cooperation. Numerous foreign lecturers attend here annually and deliver lectures on problems of a cultural nature.

The university differs somewhat from the schedules of our American extension courses. In general, no serious attempts are made to popularize culture and science for the masses, but to add to the general education of the graduates of high schools and universities. Iorga is convinced that his students lack general educational foundations, being specialized in one narrow line. This results in a spiritual vacuum, so well known to our American civilization.

The writer participated in this "summer university" and could not but admire the enthusiasm with which the youth and aged flocked to this admirable institution. The intimate relations between the students and lecturers is most commendable and something very seldom existing in European university and college circles. Mutual discussions of problems add to the atmosphere of the place. The session is limited to one month during the summer and is open to everybody. As a number of girls attend the picture of the sessions with the national costumes is very picturesque. The presence of all Roumanian intelligentsia makes Vălenii-de-Munte the spiritual and cultural center of present-day Roumania.

Connected with the summer university is Iorga's press, "Datina Romanescă," which was used originally by the founder, Dr. Iorga, to reprint old and forgotten works of Roumanian literature. The press is now serving the needs of Roumanian scholars. Literary and historical-literary works of outstanding Roumanian personalities here find a publisher. Recently a cultural foundation, "Cuvântul," was established in connection with the press, and edits, under the leadership of Iorga, historical and literary works for the general public.

There are several other institutions located in Vălenii-de-Munte which are of greatest importance to the educational aims of Iorga. A special "School for National and Cultural Women-Missionaries" is here housed. A cultural center of Roumanian minorities also grew up here after 1925. Another cultural institute of Iorga cares for the national artist-painters.

The importance of the efforts of Iorga is evident from the fact that King Carol of Roumania is planning to build a palace here for his son and heir, Michael, who spends a part of each year here, growing under the tutelage of Iorga in the atmosphere of cultural and educational aims of the nation, which he will some day rule.

JOSEPH S. ROUCEK

CENTENARY JUNIOR COLLEGE,
HACKETTSTOWN, N. J.

QUOTATIONS

THE WEEK-END SCHOOL

WITH the shortened week and the consequent periods of week-end leisure every year, it is now proposed that recreation should let education have a portion of it. In California there has recently been developed, according to a report made by Dr. James A. Moyer, of Boston, the president of the National Commission on the Enrichment of Adult Life, to the National Education Association at Los Angeles, the week-end community school, "reminiscent of the folk-schools in Denmark and the week-end colleges in England."

There are school buildings and equipment idle at week-ends that might be available for such uses. Particularly the consolidated school of the rural community is suggested as a center in which enriching experiments of this nature might be carried on. But whatever the subject of the study, it should not be restricted to the merely formal. Even hobbies might have free course, to be glorified as educational endeavors. When the avocational zest of spirit permeates a course of study it becomes both educational and recreational. The commission goes even further and urges that for the conditions of modern living "an avocation developed as a real hobby is essential to good mental health," and becomes an "equivalent to mental life insurance."

One can imagine a whole community transformed by week-end activities which look toward the enrichment of life, stimulating the creative powers for whose development the vocation does not provide the opportunity. It is coming to be recognized that education must be thinking not only of the work-time but of the leisure-time as well; and not for the few only, as in ancient Greece, but for the many—in fact, for all, since leisure has now come to all.

The week-end school for adults suggests also that education does not end with high school or college, or even the university. And it may illustrate the fact that an educated man may, after all, have little formal education. One of the phrases in Ramsay MacDonald's definition of an educated man was "happy when alone." This sort of continuing education should perhaps, above all else, contribute that particular happiness to life.—*The New York Times.*

THE TEACHERS' TURN TO BE HELPED

Chicago's school-teachers and other educational employees, by their loyal work during the last two payless months of school, have given a magnificent demonstration of their professional ethics. That "the schools must go on" is a rule among teachers everywhere. The Chicago members of the profession have lived up to this standard.

Fortunately some teachers have reserve funds, saved perhaps for a vacation trip or summer school, which will see them through the present crisis in school board finance. But others will face an increasingly serious problem as the vacation months wear on and the pay they should have received in May and June is not forthcoming. Some neighborhood banks have closed and teacher depositors can not draw upon the money they saved for just such emergencies.

What can they do? A teacher will think a long time before applying for financial aid from the county or from the United Charities. And should he conquer his pride and seek public help, he probably will not get it. The hard-pressed social agencies feel that their limited funds must go to aid the families of the unemployed. School employees, they say, should be able to get credit. But this is not always easy to do.

There is one way people of means in the community could show their gratitude for the service of city teachers. While the board of education finds itself unable to get a loan from the banks, individuals with money to lend for philanthropic purposes could make an excellent investment in good will which would return their capital as surely as the city collects its taxes.

The Chicago school board owes about $9,000,000 in salaries. Individuals with money might set up a fund to cash the teachers' pay checks, holding them until the school board can deposit the funds which will make them good. It would not be a big risk, but it would be a big service.

During the trying economic conditions of the last year teachers contributed freely from their own salaries to feeding hungry school children and they gave hours of unpaid service to finding them clothes. What they have taught their pupils by their example of working without pay can not be evaluated in dollars. Surely some immediate financial assistance is only their due. —*The Christian Science Monitor.*

SOCIETIES AND MEETINGS

THE NEW HAVEN MEETING OF THE AMERICAN LIBRARY ASSOCIATION

COMPLETION of the million dollar endowment fund of the American Library Association was achieved at the fifty-third annual conference of the association, held from June 22 to 27 at Yale University, New Haven, Connecticut. The conference, the largest in the history of the association, was attended by more than 3,200 librarians and friends of libraries from the forty-eight states, Canada and Mexico.

The final sum was raised in half an hour at the third general session of the conference, when subscriptions from the floor and telegrams from all over the country carried the fund well over the goal. The association now qualifies for another million dollars which is believed to be in sight from a friendly foundation.

With the endowment fund completed, the association is able to carry on important projects in library extension, education for librarianship and personnel service and adult education. As previously stated by officers of the association, the increased income from new memberships and from the anticipated new endowment is not for expansion. It is to take the place of funds formerly received from other sources which are not to be received from those sources in the future.

"Intellectual Freedom and Integrity" was the subject of President Adam Strohm's address at the opening general session of the conference, in which he deplored the fact that industrialism is invading even the atmosphere of the public library.

Frederic Allen Whiting, president of the American Federation of Arts, speaking at the second general session, emphasized the need of "Coordinating Community Programs for Art Appreciation." Pointing out that there are probably few public libraries which are not doing something constructive towards developing an appreciation of art in their communities, Mr. Whiting stated that the American Federation of Arts is especially interested in the problem of coordinating community programs in arts, and that its facilities are at the disposal of any one who cares to make use of them. The federation headquarters are at Washington, D. C., with a staff of about twenty people, which will be increased as the demands for service and the income permit. A department of education is under the direction of Erwin O. Christensen, who has charge of the traveling exhibitions, illustrated lectures, etc. The department of advisory service under Miss Mechlin is in constant touch with communities all over the country which need help in planning programs or which come to her for advice because of her experience of twenty-two years in this field.

There is now a national realization in England that the librarian, like the schoolmaster, occupies a position of authority, E. Cockburn Kyte, of the Douglas Library, Queen's University, Kingston, Ontario, declared in an address on "Recent Developments in British Librarianship." The British librarian is recognized as a part of the machinery of government, Mr. Kyte pointed out, and as such promises to become one of the best investments of the taxpayer.

Discussing "Leisure in a Machine Age," Stuart Chase, New York author and economist, said that no group of workers in the whole community life of America to-day is more strategically located or can do more valiant service in promoting constructive leisure than librarians. The battle is joined, Mr. Chase declared, between genuine and rewarding uses of leisure, and "pulling the levers of jumping-jacks"; between people who have some conception of life's real values, and the high pressure salesman who wants to sell the nation more leisure-time goods and services.

Other general sessions' speakers were Andrew Keogh, librarian of Yale University, who spoke on the Sterling Memorial Library; William Lyon Phelps, author and lecturer, of Yale University, who discussed "The Librarian's Opportunity," and Elizabeth Pomeroy, supervisor of Hospital Libraries, U. S. Veterans Bureau, who talked on "Hospital Libraries."

Reading services to college alumni were described at a program of the college and reference section during the conference. President Henry M. Wriston, of Lawrence College, in an address on "The College Library and Alumni Reading," stated that there was some fear that the establishment of the Lawrence alumni reading service would have all the virtues of novelty, and that after the first rush of enthusiasm had died away the usefulness of the project would begin to decline. Such fear has been allayed, however, by the fact that the service has grown (at the same time that costs have been cut in half) until to-day 43.5 per cent. of all those receiving the lists of books have asked for volumes.

Two noted authors and editors, Henry Seidel Canby, editor of the *Saturday Review of Literature,* and May Lamberton Becker, reader's guide for the *Saturday Review,* editor of *St. Nicholas Magazine* and book editor of the *Scholastic,* were speakers at conference section meetings.

In his discussion of "Reading Habits of the Intelligent Reader," Dr. Canby pointed out that in our determination to keep free speech "we have lost sight of a very important distinction between freedom to express opinion and freedom to use any method of selling printed matter which will bring profit." Of all reading in newspapers, magazines and books, not more than one third is positively valuable for the intellect.

Romance and adventure form the mental meat of boys and girls between the ages of twelve and sixteen, Mrs. Becker told members of the Young People's Reading Round Table. But reading habits may change radically in the 'teens, she pointed out. "You may go into them hand in hand with Louisa Alcott and come out arm in arm with Bernard Shaw."

A resolution advocating a federal appropriation of $100,000,000 to develop rural library service over a ten-year period was passed by the council of the American Library Association. The fund would be "divided among the states, territories, and possessions on the basis of rural population according to the latest census." Three alternative methods of administration were suggested, all under the direction of a federal library commission.

A new association by-law, raising two dollar membership dues in the A. L. A. to three dollars and abolishing the initiation fee, was passed at the third general session of the conference. This change, which will go into effect next January, is intended primarily to finance *Bulletin* improvements. Plans for the improved bulletin will be outlined in that periodical later.

Annual rather than biennial conferences were overwhelmingly favored by A. L. A. members, 2,651 of whom voted for the former as against 1,580 for the latter.

The need for adequate library service during the period of economic depression was stressed in the following resolution passed at the close of the A. L. A. conference:

The present economic depression with its accompanying unemployment has stimulated the demand for library service, increased the circulation of books and enlarged the contribution which libraries make in the preparation for new types of employment, in the profitable use of leisure time and in the maintenance of public morale. We call these facts to the attention of the governors and legislatures of the various states and to all public officials of counties, cities and towns, and urge them to allow no reduction of appropriation for books and service, but to maintain the libraries of the county in their full efficiency in this period of special need.

The Newbery medal, given annually to the author of the most distinguished contribution to children's literature, was awarded this year to Elizabeth Coatsworth for her book, "The Cat Who Went to Heaven." Mary Gould Davis, chairman of the A. L. A. Section for Library Work with Children, presented the medal at an afternoon program of the section.

Twelve winners in the poster contest, conducted by the association among junior and senior high school students of thirteen Southern states, were announced at a dinner for members of the A. L. A. School Libraries Section. The first prize of $100, won by Elizabeth Hoover, of Birmingham, Ala., enables Miss Louise Roberts, the school librarian, to select forty-three books from the new A. L. A. list of "Books for Recreational Reading." Each book will be marked with a book plate bearing the winning student's name. Two $50 prizes, four $25 and five $20, of the same character as the first, were also awarded. Prizes were given by the National Association of Book Publishers.

Josephine Adams Rathbone, vice-director of the Pratt Institute School of Library Science, Brooklyn, was elected president of the American Library Association for 1931–32. Other new officers are: Charles E. Rush, Yale University Library, *first vice-president;* Beatrice Winser, Public Library, Newark, New Jersey, *sec-*

ond vice-president; Matthew S. Dudgeon, Public Library, Milwaukee, Wis., *treasurer,* and George Woodruff, Chicago, trustee of Endowment Funds.

Members elected to the Executive Board are Gratia A. Countryman, Public Library, Minneapolis, and Sydney B. Mitchell, School of Librarianship, University of California, Berkeley. New council members are: Henry B. Van Hoesen, Brown University Library, Providence, R. I.; Anne Morse Boyd, University of Illinois Library School; L. L. Dickerson, Public Library, Indianapolis, Ind.; Adah Frances Whitcomb, Public Library, Chicago, and J. T. Gerould, Princeton University Library.

E. H. D.

EDUCATIONAL RESEARCH AND STATISTICS

GROUP DIFFERENCES IN ART JUDGMENT

MARKED progress has been made in the measurement of complex mental traits since Binet constructed and published his first intelligence test in 1905. Psychologically this movement would be inconsequential if the sole outcome had been the measuring instruments themselves. It gains in importance, however, when these instruments are used to analyze various mental functions and when individual and group comparisons are made. To illustrate, the knowledge of an individual's I.Q. is meaningless unless it is possible to interpret his degree of brightness in terms of more meaningful concepts. When, therefore, the relation was sought between intelligence as measured by stock examinations and school progress or possible occupational destination, the significance of those examinations was magnified. The usefulness of these tests was further accentuated when comparisons were made between the sexes, various races and nationalities, and certain artificial and academic classification of pupils.

Now that the movement to measure psychological traits has reached the point where attempts to measure art judgment have definitely taken form in the Meier-Seashore and McAdory Art Judgment Tests, attention is naturally directed towards differences between groups. The two instruments that are available for this purpose have sufficient reliability to warrant group comparisons and, even though one may be dubious in regard to the validity of these tests, he can not deny that they show marked differences between a group of artists whom one could suspect of possessing at least a slight degree of critical judgment in the field of their speciality and a group of novices.

With the Meier-Seashore and McAdory tests as a basis, it becomes the purpose of this paper to present certain group differences derived chiefly from the application of these tests to college students. The questions for which data were sought may be stated briefly as follows:

1. To what extent do the sexes differ in art judgment?
2. What differences in art judgment exist between various subject-matter major groups at the college level?

Traditionally the assumption has been made that women as a group are endowed with aesthetic judgment to a greater degree than are men. Since this supposition has been based upon casual observations, more precise methods of comparisons are desired. When such assumptions have been checked with scientific measurements, they have frequently been found to be misinterpretations of comparisons on related traits. That is not the case, however, when men and women are compared on the Meier-Seashore and the McAdory Art Judgment Tests.

The Meier-Seashore test was given to all the students entering the College of Education at the University of Minnesota during the fall quarter, 1929. The mean score for 655 women in the group was found to be 75.15 (Table I). For 164 men, the mean was 70.00. The difference of $5.15 \pm .43$ is unquestionably significant for it is almost twelve times greater than its probable error. It appears that an assumption based upon casual inspection is substantiated in this instance by scientific fact, for, when measured objectively, women show a higher degree of art judgment than do men.

In order to eliminate the effect that art majors may have upon the comparisons of sex differences, the means of the men and women

TABLE I

SEX DIFFERENCES AMONG COLLEGE STUDENTS ON THE MEIER-SEASHORE ART-JUDGMENT TEST

	N	Mean	PE_M	S. D.
Total Group				
Women	655	75.15	.19	7.21
Men	164	70.00	.39	7.31
Difference		5.15		
PE_D		.43		
D/PE_D		11.98		
Total	819	74.12		7.50
Art Majors Eliminated				
Women	556	74.10	.20	6.89
Men	161	69.85	.39	7.26
Difference		4.25		
PE_D		.44		
D/PE_D		9.66		

were calculated with such majors eliminated (Table I). In this instance the mean for the women was 74.10 ± .20 and for the men, 69.85 ± .39. The difference of 4.25 ± .44 remains significant for it yields a ratio of 9.66.

A similar observation was made with the McAdory Art Judgment Test (Table II).

TABLE II

SEX DIFFERENCES AMONG COLLEGE STUDENTS ON THE MCADORY ART-JUDGMENT TEST

	N	Mean	S. D.	P. E.
Women	210	184.86	24.53	1.14
Men	28	163.93	15.43	1.97
Difference		20.93		
$P.E._D$		2.28		
D/PE		9.20		
Total group	238	182.40	24.61	1.08

Although the number of men in the comparison is relatively small, the difference is in the same direction and of approximately the same degree of significance. The women earned a mean score of 184.86 while the mean for the men (163.93) was 20.93 points lower. This difference is greater than nine times its P.E.

The McAdory test was also given to groups of borderline and superior children. Considering the groups as a whole, the scores for the borderline children are distinctly below those for the superior group although partial overlapping is readily apparent. The comparison of the sexes within these groups reveals a similar tendency to that observed for the college students. The average scores for the borderline boys was found to be 102.37 (Table III) and

TABLE III

SEX DIFFERENCES AMONG BORDERLINE CHILDREN AND SUPERIOR CHILDREN ON THE MCADORY ART JUDGMENT TEST

	N	Average age	M	PE_M	S. D.
Borderline Children*					
Girls	24	14.98	130.42	4.01	29.15
Boys	19	15.62	102.37	2.92	18.87
Difference			28.05		
PE_D			4.96		
D/PE_D			5.66		
Total group	43	15.26	101.28	2.59	25.15
Superior Children†					
Girls	24	15.75	168.75	1.90	13.79
Boys	19	13.20	145.53	3.46	22.36
Difference			23.22		
PE_D			3.95		
D/PE_D			5.88		
Total group	43	13.37	158.49	2.20	21.44

* The average I.Q. for the borderline group is 71. The range is from 61–80.

† The average I.Q. for the superior group is 132. The range is from 119–154.

for the borderline girls, 130.42. While the difference of 28.05 ± 4.96 is larger than that observed for the college groups it does not appear to be as reliable. In spite of this fact, which is undoubtedly attributable to the smaller number of cases, the girls have a significantly higher score than the boys. The sex difference in the group of superior children is even more marked. A concluding statement is evident. In all of the groups, girls and women possess keener art judgment as measured by the Meier-Seashore and the McAdory tests than do men.

Meier[1] has shown that the median score of a group of art students who took the art judgment test was six points higher than the median score of a group of high-school seniors. He does not present data to show the extent to which the art students differ from those who are majoring in other subjects Such compari-

[1] "Art Judgment Test," Examiner's Manual, p. 15.

TABLE IV

Differences in the Mean Scores Between the Art Majors and Eleven Other Major Groups on the Meier-Seashore Art Judgment Test

Major	N	M	S. D.	PE_M	$D_{M_1-M_2}$	PE_D	D/PE_D
Art	95	81.74	5.02	0.35			
Biological science	13	72.54	5.03	0.94	9.20	1.00	9.20
Commercial education	30	73.33	5.84	0.72	8.41	.80	10.51
English	60	74.93	6.93	0.60	6.81	0.70	9.73
Foreign language	26	73.00	6.35	0.84	8.74	0.91	9.60
History and social science	60	72.13	6.96	0.61	9.61	0.70	13.73
Mathematics	23	75.35	7.21	1.01	6.39	1.07	5.97
Physical education	162	71.25	7.89	0.42	10.49	0.54	19.43
Physical science	13	72.69	5.91	1.11	9.05	1.16	7.80
Professional education	27	75.96	7.33	0.95	5.78	1.01	5.72
Public school music	90	74.04	6.77	0.48	7.70	0.59	13.05
Special curriculum	69	74.36	6.24	0.51	7.38	0.61	12.10

sons were available within the group of entrants to the College of Education. Table IV contains the average scores for the various major groups. The column labeled $D_{M_1-M_2}$ designates the differences between the average score of the art majors (M_1) and the other major groups (M_2). For example, the average score of the art majors is 81.74. For the group of 13 individuals majoring in biological sciences the average is 72.54. The difference of 9.20 ± 1.00 is decidedly significant. When divided by its probable error the ratio obtained is 9.20. A glance at the column of ratios reveals that each designates a significant difference if interpreted in terms of the generally accepted criterion. The greatest difference obtains between the art students and the physical education majors. In all the comparisons the average score for the group of art majors is higher. It is clear, therefore, that the test does differentiate between the students who are pursuing special work in art and those who are following sundry curricula. Whether this difference is one of innate capacity or one resulting from training rests purely upon speculative inferences. The data at hand do not warrant a dogmatic generalization.

When differences between all possible combinations of major groups are obtained, only 4 of the 55 differences are greater than four times their probable errors. These are found in the comparisons of the physical education group with the majors in English, professional education, public school music, and special curriculum. None of these differences is as great as the least significant of those found between the art majors and the other major groups. It is obvious that the test measures a unique trait or quality possessed to a greater degree by art majors than by other major groups.

The answers to the questions raised in regard to group differences in art judgment may be recapitulated in the following terms: (1) Women and girls attain significantly higher scores on the Meier-Seashore and the McAdory Tests of art judgment than do men and boys. (2) College students majoring in art exhibit decidedly keener critical ability in the field of their speciality than do students majoring in any other subject.

Alvin C. Eurich
Herbert A. Carroll
University of Minnesota

NEW BOOKS IN EDUCATION

Case, Clarence M. *Social Process and Human Progress.* Pp. 336. Harcourt, Brace. $2.50.

Dolch, Edward W. *The Psychology and Teaching of Reading.* Pp. 261. Ginn. $1.80.

Goodsell, Willystine, editor. *Pioneers of Women's Education in the United States.* Pp. viii + 311. Illustrated. McGraw-Hill. $2.25.

Hill, Clyde M. and Raymond D. Mosher. *Making the Most of High School.* Pp. 288. Illustrated. Laidlaw. $.96.

Swift, Fletcher H. *Federal and State Policies in Public School Finance in the United States.* Pp. 472. Illustrated. Ginn. $3.80.

Woodhouse, W. J. *The Fight for an Empire: A Translation of the Third Book of the Histories of Tacitus.* Pp. xx + 173. Angus and Robertson, Sydney, Australia.

SCHOOL AND SOCIETY

EDITED BY J. McKEEN CATTELL

WITH WHICH IS COMBINED THE

EDUCATIONAL REVIEW

EDITED BY WILLIAM McANDREW

Volume 34 SATURDAY, AUGUST 15, 1931 Number 868

SURVEY COURSES AND THE JUNIOR COLLEGE

By Professor WALDO SHUMWAY

UNIVERSITY OF ILLINOIS

THE liberal arts college has traditionally required four years of residence for its degree, although unusually gifted or studious scholars have been able to graduate in three and a half or even three years. Fifty years ago the course of studies was entirely prescribed and was based on a foundation of Latin and Greek, mathematics and logic, history and philosophy, with some options in French and German and the natural sciences.

Under the pressure of applicants with less training in Latin and Greek and an increasing interest in modern languages, the sciences, and, more recently, the social sciences, new courses of studies were introduced with distinctive degrees such as Bachelor of Literature, Bachelor of Sciences, Bachelor of Philosophy, etc. Harvard under the leadership of President Eliot effected a major revolution by adopting the elective system, so-called because the student might select his courses from year to year subject to certain prerequisites designed to secure a reasonable sequence within each department.

Somewhat in the nature of a revulsion against this bold stroke, the colleges began to experiment with restricted electives, imposing such restraints as the requirement that a certain amount of work be taken in specified fields such as foreign languages, the natural sciences, etc., during the first two or three years, the so-called system of "group requirements." This system is admittedly a compromise between the hard and fast requirements of the old college with its small number of departments, and the cafeteria system of the university college with its many newly created departments, each clamoring for recognition. The result is that instead of every student taking a course in natural history, for example, he is offered a choice among botany, geology and zoology, with perhaps bacteriology, physiology, entomology or geography thrown in for good measure. With increasing specialization and the growth of college constituencies, an increase in the number of departments could scarcely have been avoided. But even now it is difficult for an undergraduate, although aided by a host of advisers and deans, to secure a modicum of information from each of say twenty departments, and absolutely impossible to correlate the information so obtained in two or three years preparatory to later specialization.

Accordingly there has come a demand for broad introductory surveys of the larger fields of human knowledge cutting across the lines of departmental specialization. Variously denominated, as survey courses, orientation courses, or cultural courses, they have already been introduced in several of the more liberal universities and colleges. Chicago has given for several years a survey of natural science under the title "The Nature of the World and of Man"; Columbia has a notable course on Contemporary Civilization; while Dartmouth is experimenting with courses on Evolution and on the Social Order, and still others are being offered or are in state of preparation.

The boldest synthesis yet attempted is that of the Experimental College at the University of Wisconsin where Professor Meiklejohn directs a project in which the students spend the first year in the study of Athenian civilization during the time of Pericles, and the second year is devoted to a study of modern American civilization. It has been announced that this experiment will be discontinued and it is indeed a question whether the majority of high-school graduates or of college teachers are prepared for so abrupt a transition from departmentalized thought.

These tendencies indicate a general agreement among educators that the work of the earlier years should be devoted to a broad general foundation upon which to rear the more intensive cultivation of special studies in the later years. Corroborative of this conclusion is the rapid increase in the number of junior colleges during the years since the World War. These institutions offer two years only of college work, yet more than four hundred are now in existence, of which over half have come into being during the last fifteen years. They have a total registration of over 60,000 students, the great majority of whom will not secure any further college training.

The existence of these colleges as well as the implicit division of the four-year college into a junior and a senior division suggests that this affords a basis for separating the work of the liberal arts college into two divisions according to the separate purpose which each must serve. *In brief it is my proposal that the work of the first two years be re-designed to give a survey of the principal factors of modern civilization which shall be sufficiently sweeping in its scope to satisfy a primary objective of orienting the high-school graduate to the world in which we live.* Following this should come comprehensive as well as aptitude examinations designed to select the superior students adapted to the *departmental system of education already in existence. No others should be admitted to the work of the last two years.*

Such a junior-division or pass-division college is not, however, to be considered as a machine for selecting superior students. Its prime purpose is to offer a kind of education, complete in itself, which will supplement the work of the high school on the one hand, and preface the advancement of selected graduates in the senior-division or honors-division college on the other.

In such a program it seems unavoidable that the college discard completely all formal admission requirements save graduation from an accredited high school, and all the present machinery of credits, semester hours, grades, and departmental machinery incident to the existing bachelor's degree, and evaluate anew the content and methods appropriate to the aims of its respective divisions.

First let us consider the articulation of the junior-division with the high school. Here we must bear in mind that this unit no longer acts as a college-preparatory school, but is attempting to work out a program of studies which will form a complete whole, superimposed on the work of the elementary school system. Parenthetically, it may be remarked that the high school now is experimenting with a junior and senior division which stand in closer correlation with the work of the elementary school and the college respectively. As a result of these changes in the educational policies of the high school, college teachers have long been aware of the inadequacy of high-school preparation for the present type of college organization.

Let me illustrate by two examples. In the study of foreign language it is customary to evaluate a year of high-school credit as equivalent to a half-year of college credit, although the classes in high school meet as many times a week as those in the college. Even so, the student who has suspended the study of Latin or French for one or two years frequently finds himself incapable of continuing the subject in college. Teachers of science, chemistry, physics, and biology in particular, are all but unanimous in stating that a year of high-school science is not even the equivalent of a half-year of the same subject in college. In the University of Illinois there are two introductory courses in chemistry, one designed for students who have had no previous training in the subject, the other for those who have had a year of chemistry in high school. It has been the experience of that department that students who took chemistry in high school at least two years previous to entering college are unable to carry the work of the second introductory course and must be transferred to the first.

There have been many explanations offered of such discrepancies as stated above, ranging from criticism of high-school teaching methods or of the ability of the students concerned, to criticism of the educational practices of the college. It has occurred to me, and doubtless to many others, that the trouble lies in the fallacious assumption that French is French and chemistry is chemistry no matter at what age in years or mental development the subject is studied. We must face the fact that although teaching is an individual matter and teachers vary as much as students, nevertheless comparative studies indicate that individuals tend to pass through successive levels of "teachability" corresponding to their attainment of more or less definite mental ages. According to this principle, high-school physics and high-school history differ from college physics and college history far more widely than we have assumed in the past, and the existence of high-school credits in these subjects should not be considered a valid reason for excusing college students from elementary entering courses at the college level. So far as organization is concerned the junior-division college should take the position that its matriculants have graduated from high school; they are to start out on new adventures in learning, regardless of the particular pieces of information they have acquired in the past; they are to consider that they have attained not learning itself but a method of learning suitable to the intellectual age they are quitting, and which is to be supplemented by new methods appropriate to their advancement.

So, in general, the course of studies will be similar for all new students regardless of the particular subjects for which they have received credit. Later I shall call attention to a method of sectioning for ability which has been employed to advantage in segregating students of superior and inferior ability from those in the average group.

It has become conventional that the student carry some fifteen credit-hours per semester, with the assumption that each hour represents a clock-hour in lecture or recitation or some fraction of a clock-hour in laboratory or field work. Under our departmental organization different courses carry credit varying from one to five or more such semester-hours, so that the number of courses carried per semester may vary considerably. Assuming that our conventional system has some basis in reality, and recognizing that there are great advantages to the student in daily preparation, I should propose further that the junior-division be organized with three courses meeting daily for five or possibly six days per week.

We may assume that in the junior-division curriculum the student will be required to carry three such subjects for four semesters, a total of twelve units of instruction. Each of these is to be a survey course, cutting across present departmental lines, and therefore the product of interdepartmental groups, something after the order of the new divisions proposed by the University of Chicago. Such courses, to be sure, will vary from institution to institution according to the personnel of the groups charged with administering the instructional work. They might be complete in themselves or form parts of sequences. Personally, I lean towards the idea of sequence in three great groups, literature, science, and the social sciences.

One course each semester, for example, should be devoted to the study of literature, either English, or, in translation, foreign masterpieces, with due attention paid to ideas and their influence in the development of human thought as well as the literary form. Such a course should not only teach the student to read, at first under close instruction, later independently, but it should acquaint him with the use of library facilities, and by means of oral and written reports lay stress upon the correct use of the mother-tongue.

Another course each semester should be devoted to the survey of some field of science, such as biology, viewed as the study of life in its varied aspects, geology and astronomy with particular reference to the earth as a developing unit in a larger cosmic system, chemistry and physics from the descriptive view-point. The organization of such courses should represent problems in omission and condensation and can be developed only through the greatest cooperation and mutual forbearance of the groups concerned. They must eschew all aims of teaching techniques or imparting the swollen vocabularies of their sciences, and attempt to formulate principles and indicate how these are applied in modern life. Here is a challenge to the professional scientist which he will do well to heed unless he wishes to see the college teaching of science follow the classics into that limbo of lost hopes, the history of education.

The course in social science awakens the greatest curiosity in my mind because I have even less personal knowledge in that field than in any other. So my sole contribution can be to suggest what sort of course I should myself enjoy and profit by. This would be a course which sought to interpret the succession of the most important events of history in terms of economics, political science, and sociology.

The formulation of such courses presents problems in organization of subject-matter, in methods of instructions, and in utilization of physical facilities which may appear almost insuperable. But the success attending such preliminary experiments as have been made at institutions such as Chicago, Columbia, and Dartmouth gives ground for hope that, granted a broad-minded and liberal administration, we may put our faith in the hands of the teachers, secure in the belief that when the storm of battle abates, something worth while will supervene.

Certain difficulties with the proposal

here outlined are immediately apparent. For example, what will become of the course in Freshman Rhetoric almost universally required, but slowly disappearing in those universities, like Columbia and Harvard, which are admitting only carefully selected students? It has been proposed that a certain amount of instruction in the use of the mother-tongue be given in connection with the courses in literature already described. In addition it may appear necessary to offer a two-hour course in the essentials of English composition to students whose preparation is evidently deficient.

Another problem is that of the foreign languages. Here is a question rendered increasingly complex by a situation peculiar to American education. It has been pointed out in an earlier section that the classics were at one time fundamental in the college curriculum, and that they were gradually supplanted by modern foreign languages. Now it appears that even these have only a traditional value in education at the college level, granting that there is no longer any basis for the theory of formal discipline. Studies reported a few years ago indicate that less than one half of all college graduates ever have occasion to read a word of a foreign language and fewer still will ever speak or much less write a word. There seems to be no basis for the cherished belief that a liberal education demands at least a reading knowledge of some language other than the mother-tongue. On the other hand students who will continue into the senior-division may desire to specialize in foreign language studies and certainly those who expect to do research must be prepared to read at least French and German with sufficient facility to understand technical articles in these languages. While it is still entirely possible to obtain a reading knowledge of a language in the last two years of college, and some graduate students have picked up enough French or German to worry their way through technical zoological papers in less than that time, there should be provided facilities for ambitious students with high standing in aptitude tests and high-school records to continue or initiate their work in these "tool" subjects by means of three-hour courses in addition to the required curriculum.

This is true also of mathematics; courses in solid geometry, algebra, trigonometry and analytic geometry, meeting approximately three hours a week, should be open only to high grade students intending to prepare for the senior-division.

Instruction in music and fine arts has been excluded from the curriculum, with the understanding that courses in appreciation of art will be offered to students in the senior-division and that public lectures without university credit will be available.

Military science, physical education, and hygiene have also been omitted from this curriculum and with deliberation. Military science certainly should not be given credit for an academic degree but treated like an extra-curricular activity under especial supervision. Similarly, while all possible facilities, including organized supervision, should be afforded for athletic activities, it is manifestly absurd to consider such training as an integral part of higher education. Hygiene is also an anomaly in the college. Practically all students have had some work in high-school physiology; under the scheme proposed above, the required course in the principles of biology will pay some attention to the mechanism of the human body.

The next question relates to the method of instruction. This is of particular significance in the junior-division college because here we have a transitional method between the high school with its text-book, recitation, examination-in-fact method, and the university lecture, independent-reading, conference, report, examination-in-rationalization method. The college must introduce the student gradually to the lecture method and teach him to take notes; introduce him to the library and teach him to take more notes; teach him to rationalize about these facts in conference with his teacher and classmates, in written reports, and on searching final examinations. Since it is generally admitted that the best way to learn a new technique is to keep practicing it by increasing application, it appears logical that the survey courses should commence at once with lectures and library assignments in the minor fraction of the assigned hours, with conferences and reports in the major fraction until the student commences to find himself. In the second year, lectures and library assignments should occupy the major portion of the student's time, while conferences and reports consume a smaller portion.

This assumes a division of the instructor's time between lecturing and conferences, with of course a large amount of assistance in conferences and the reading of reports and examinations. It also assumes that there are capable instructors willing to do such work.

Our standardizing agencies of one kind and another have much to answer for. In their bland assurance that the Ph.D. represents the minimum requirement for successful college teaching, they have overlooked the fact that this degree stands for investigational rather than interpretational scholarship. Trained in the mechanics of research and imbued with the idea that the only way to promotion and increased pay lies in the production of more and more pages of facts gleaned from a smaller and smaller field of specialized learning, the teacher comes to feel that the university would be a fine place in which to work, "if it were not for the students."

It is squarely up to the officers of administration to seek out efficient teachers and see that these are encouraged to develop their especial gifts. While not abandoning in the least the high ideals of true scholarship, and carrying even further the present tendency to reward those who are carrying the torch of learning into new territories by rapid promotion, increased salaries, more complete exemption from administrative assignments and gradual relief from all but the most specialized and advanced teaching, it is the plain duty of the college to reward in commensurate fashion the great teachers of each generation by corresponding advancements in rank and salary without inquiring too closely into their formal contributions. To paraphrase an ancient motto, if learning maketh man, then let us honor that "productive" scholar whose labors result not in papers but in men.

The organization and administration of the junior-division college should be taken immediately from the control of departments. So it seems advisable to place each of the half-year survey courses in the hands of an interdepartmental committee with explicit instructions that they are to serve as individuals rather than as members or representatives of their departments. These committees might elect representatives to an executive committee in each of the three groups mentioned above, literature, science, and social science, with the function of correlating the four survey courses in each group. The group committees in turn might elect representatives to an executive faculty which, with a dean as executive officer, should direct the appointment and assignment of teachers, the registration and progress of students, and all the other details which can profitably be decentralized from the general administration of the institution. The dean and chosen representatives should, of course, be members of the council, senate, or whatever the central governing body of the institution be called.

To the office of the dean, there should be attached a personnel force comprising officers to scrutinize the high-school record and to administer aptitude tests on the basis of which to divide the registrants into conference groups of superior, average, and inferior standing. These ratings should not be considered permanent but sufficiently flexible to admit of readjustment in the middle of each half-year course. These same officers would be charged with a scrutiny of the progress of students as represented by grades of superior, average, and inferior, turned in at the middle and end of each course. Inferior students might at the option of the instructor and dean be required to repeat any course. A well-trained physician and psychiatrist should form part of the staff in order to aid in the cases of students deficient in physical or mental health.

A vocational counsellor also should have charge of a student employment and a placement bureau for graduates. Faculty committees with executive secretaries from the administrative corps should be charged with college discipline and the control of extra-curricular activities. There should by close liaison between all these agencies and those of other colleges in institutions of university rank, and very likely budgetary requirements might result in the centralization of several of the offices contemplated above.

Finally we turn to the graduation of these students and their admission into the senior-division college. Our scheme of organization requires that comprehensive examinations in the three groups here described be administered by the executive committees on these groups and that only students doing, let us say, superior work in the field of specialization chosen and average work in the other two be so admitted. All others meeting the average requirements as determined by the executive faculty should be graduated with a degree, *e.g.*, Associate in Arts, as now awarded by some junior colleges.

In the senior-division college is the place for our system of departments made up of instructors who divide their efforts between research and teaching. Freed from the requirement of administering large elementary courses, these instructors will find themselves confronted by a highly selected and well-read group of students ready for intensive work and rapid specialization.

Lectures and seminaries, laboratory and field projects, and the preparation of semi-original reports will occupy the time of the student. He should be freed from all administrative restraints except that of carrying successfully fifteen hours of class-work per semester, under the advice of a departmental adviser. The instructor will turn in grades at the end of each course according to whether the work of the student has been superior, average, or inferior in quality. No regulations as to attendance or extra-curricular activities should be in force. At the end of two years, or whenever he has earned sixty hours of credit with a certain proportion of superior grades, the senior-division student should receive the degree of Bachelor of Arts. Such a student, provided he has taken the courses in education required by state boards, is prepared to do high-school teaching. He should be prepared to enter graduate professional schools or to enter upon graduate courses in a field of academic specialization.

Such a two-year program as that suggested above might easily be tested in an experimental college attached to the college of arts and sciences in one of our great universities or in an independent junior college. It may not prove to be a practicable method of imparting a general education, but at least it aims at the goal of interpreting modern life and that is more than can be said of most college curricula.

READING FOR HONORS WORK AT THE UNIVERSITY OF OREGON

By Professor C. V. BOYER

UNIVERSITY OF OREGON

In School and Society for February 14, 1931, there appeared an article entitled "Honors Work in Institutions Accredited by the Association of American Universities," the occasion for which was the same as that which has led to the writing of this paper, namely, the desire of persons interested in higher education for further details of a plan which is spreading more and more widely throughout the colleges and universities of the United States. It was found that 81 institutions, or about 35.7 per cent., of the 227 on the accredited list were offering honors work. "Of these, 11 had enrolments of less than 500, 36 had enrolments of from 500 to 1,500, and 34 enrolments of more than 1,500." No significant difference was found between the practice of the smaller and the larger institutions. Differences there are, to be sure, but they have nothing to do with size. Swarthmore with its 500 students has as complete and successful a system as Harvard with its thousands. Since the word "honors" was used with various meanings in the catalogs, however, signifying at times simply high grades, the compilers of the statistics in School and Society adopted a definition of "honors work" which I have accepted for the purposes of this paper, *viz.*, "a program of independent study, under the direction of a faculty adviser, superseding either in part or as a whole regular classroom work."

Certain significant conclusions may be rather briefly stated without burdening your minds with the statistical tables printed in the magazine. It was found that 16 institutions permit as a maximum only one sixth of the upper-division work to be carried for honors; 21 institutions allow from a sixth to a third. "On the other hand, 19 universities and colleges offer a complete honors program in the upper division." Harvard, Dartmouth and Swarthmore are examples of institutions of this sort. Where complete programs are not offered, the number of honors students is not large, only nine institutions having more than 60, and 13 having only from one to six. Nevertheless, all evidence points to the success of the honors plan: favorable reports were received from the deans of 52 institutions; there has been a steady increase in the number of institutions adopting it; and no college is known to have discarded the plan after having once put it in operation.

As regards the selection of honors students, nearly all of the institutions require a high grade in lower division work for eligibility to honors. Dean James H. Gilbert, of the University of Oregon, who made a first-hand study of honors systems in eastern institutions in the fall of 1929, states in his report that "In all the institutions visited, honors work does not begin until the junior year." The reason for this, as pointed out by Abraham Flexner in "Reading for Honors at Swarthmore," (Introduction) is that our educational organization in the schools is on such a low level as to render selection of competent workers unreliable. "The elementary schools level down; the high schools level down. The schools therefore do not locate exceptional ability and do not train it." Nevertheless, the actual selective process does begin much earlier at Swarthmore and other institutions of limited enrolment where entrance examinations are given and the number of applicants is far in excess of those accepted. Where students are admitted on certificate, as in state universities, the student's record after he has entered college is the only reliable test of his mental capacity for such work as the reading for honors imposes. Dean Gilbert states that "the common practice is to pick the upper twenty-five per cent., although in some cases an absolute standard is set (all A and B record or 2.6 average) and all students who attain this standard are eligible irrespective of the number or percentage of the student body. At the beginning of the Swarthmore experiment about ten per cent. were picked for honors privileges but steady improvement in the quality of the student body . . has raised the percentage to about 35."

The practice at Oregon has been to admit to honors work the upper one third of the men and the upper one third of the women at the end of their sophomore year. Over a period of three years the average grade for women who were within this third was 2.5 and for men 2.9. As a result, these figures have been definitely adopted, but as students who have been here two years have not always cleared the lower-division requirements and are consequently not in position to carry the extra burden of honors work, eligibility has now been fixed at 2.5 and 2.9 respectively for women and men at the time of granting the junior certificate. The grade average is not, however, the exclusive determinant of eligibility. Experience has shown that, for one reason or another, the ablest students are not always among the upper third of the class at the end of their sophomore year. On this account, students who are highly recommended for mental strength and initiative by instructors who know them personally may be made eligible by action of the honors council. The placement is in no case final. Any student who has registered for honors may at any time be asked to withdraw if his capacity or interest appears inadequate to the work required.

The proper conduct of the honors system has everywhere been found to be expensive. At the outset the direction of honors students, which is in the nature of tutorial work, is an extra burden voluntarily assumed by instructors for the good of the cause. In the survey printed in School and Society little evidence is to be found that colleges make special provision for honors work by additions to the faculty, except in those institutions just noted which have been able to offer a complete program in the upper division. The extra work which one man can carry in addition to his regular schedule is by the nature of the case limited; at least one hour a week is required for conference, whether the conference be attended by one student or ten, and the amount of preparation on the part of the instructor is often greater for an honors conference than for a classroom lecture. As honors groups must be small, and as a teacher carrying a regular load can meet but few of these groups, the number of students who can be cared for is limited and the growth of the system impeded if extra funds are not forthcoming. In the 81 institutions surveyed, the student-instructor ratio ranged from 4 to 16. Where special provision is made for honors work by engaging instructors, a class is opened for two students and an enrolment of seven is regarded as the maximum for efficiency. How great the expense of such a system is obvious. The work at Dartmouth was confined to English until an endowment of $1,500,000 made it possible to extend the system throughout the college (James H. Gilbert, "A Brief Survey of Certain Educational Programs and Policies in American Universities and Colleges"). Swarthmore was able to offer a complete program only because the General Education Board made a grant of $240,000 for this purpose, a grant supplemented by a $50,000 gift from the Carnegie Foundation for library purposes and numerous gifts and scholarships from private individuals. (Robert C. Brooks, "Reading for Honors at Swarthmore.") Only a vast endowment makes Harvard's tutorial system possible.

Since the object of honors work is to promote independent study and research it is the custom in most institutions, though not in all, to excuse honors candidates from regular classroom attendance. Sometimes, as at Dartmouth, they attend on recommendation of the instructor such lectures as will presumably help them in their independent studies; sometimes, as at Yale, the dean of the college determines how many hours may be carried for honors in addition to the schedule which is required. At Oregon, honors courses themselves carry credit and the number of hours taken is limited only by the offerings and university requirements. The student is allowed much freedom in his choice of courses, the final comprehensive examination being regarded as a sufficient guide to his choice. Because his knowledge is to be finally determined by this examination, he is also privileged to attend or not, as he chooses, the course examinations during the last two quarters of his senior year.

The content of the program in different institutions varies in many minor details but in only one significant detail. We might divide the honors systems into two types, the one comprehending those colleges which provide a complete program for the work of the upper division, the other taking in the remainder of the institutions where honors work is incidental. The method at Dartmouth and Swarthmore impresses me as ideal, assuming that the purpose of the system is to cultivate alertness of mind, original thinking, and a critical spirit. The method, indeed, is not unlike that of a graduate seminar.

In addition to attending such regular lectures as may interest him, the honors candidate meets with his group once or twice a week, in the afternoon or evening, in sessions officially of two hours each but often lasting twice that long owing to interest aroused in the discussion. Each student prepares a paper once a week or once in three weeks, according to the size of the class and the nature of the paper. An incomplete bibliography, usually of classical works on the subject, is supplied but the student is supposed to supplement this with later books and articles. Where two or three weeks are allowed to the preparation of a paper, copies of the papers are supplied to other members of the group before the meeting of the class in order to improve the quality of the criticism when the paper is read.

The group meeting to discuss papers consists of one or two teachers, five or six student members, and visitors, who may be undergraduates not enrolled for honors or campus visitors of distinction in the very subject under discussion. Any one may take part in the debate. Because those present have had every opportunity to inform themselves on the subject-matter of the meeting, the writers of papers are stimulated to do their best and to leave no source of information unexamined. In the discussion itself the paper is criticized for its diction, its syntax, and its organization, as well as for its accuracy and the cogency of its reasoning. The presence of two instructors who take part in the debate and often uphold conflicting opinions adds no small zest to the conference. From an educational point of view nothing could be sounder than a method which demonstrates that difference of opinion on social and scientific matters may exist in spite of the most honest intellectual efforts to arrive at the truth. Submission to *ex cathedra* utterances or to the mere name of authority is not likely to survive as a mental attitude after such training. Prejudice breaks down and with it the tendency to condemn departure from herd-mindedness. On the other hand, the assumption of the ignorant but conceited undergraduate that a shrug of the shoulders and a contemptuous epithet suffice to destroy an argument fares just as badly. Such training as that offered by these discussion groups could hardly be improved upon for cultivating a considerate and rational attitude of mind.

Where the full program is not in force, the conduct of honors assumes various forms. At Brown, for example, the supervised reading plan is used in the departments of English, foreign languages, and philosophy. In other departments the so-called "course plan" is followed, including "double courses" giving extra credit for collateral reading, and seminar courses. At Oregon we have worked out two plans: one is called "Honors with Thesis," the other "General Honors."

In the former, the student attempts to cover one subject thoroughly. The English department has published a list of books and authors ranging from Greek tragedy to American comedy, a critical knowledge of which will be expected of the candidate when he comes up for examination. In addition, he is required to write a thesis on some phase of one subject. The object is to cover a wide field intelligently and to cultivate a small field intensively. A course called "Honors Reading," carrying an elastic number of hours of credit, is offered for juniors and another for seniors. Students register in these courses singly or in groups. If several students register with one instructor and if they are all equally well prepared by way of background, he directs their joint reading, asks for papers, and discusses them with the group. If their needs are different he meets them separately one hour a week. The mental attitude of the student affects the nature of the assignments. He may be a person who asks for definite assignments, or he may be one who wants liberty to read in his own way. The former type we regard as not, properly speaking, of honors caliber; we hope to develop in him intellectual curiosity and capacity to direct his own work. Such students are usually attracted to honors work by the lure of the distinction of having their names on the Commencement program rather than by any native desire for independent research.

In addition to courses called "Honors Courses," any upper division course may, with the consent of the honors council, be taken for honors. Before granting its consent, the council demands a description of the course showing how its program is to be differentiated from the same course as given for regular students. The usual procedure is to demand broader reading than is asked of the ordinary student and to require a term paper calling for independent work in investigating and organizing material. The rules of the council would permit of a special section being made up of honors students to be conducted with greater rapidity or greater intensity according to need, but so far there has been insufficient demand to justify the establishment of such a section.

The scheme called "General Honors" is an attempt to avoid specialization and to relate the knowledge of several fields. The catalog announcement states that the student shall study in three related fields, such as English, philosophy, and history, or education, psychology, and sociology, over a period of two years. Owing to the difficulty of getting teachers of different subjects to relate their courses for the benefit of the honors student, the current practice has been to allow students to take a course in philosophy, one in English, and another in education, say, without actually binding them together, but requiring of the student extra work in each course. The results have not been nearly so satisfactory as in the scheme of honors with thesis. The students have not been as carefully coached; they have not read as widely; nor have they an equivalent fund of knowledge or the same critical attitude towards it.

The scheme of general honors, nevertheless, is an experiment in the right direction. It is a failure, but a failure on account of lack of teachers and funds to do what is being successfully done in private institutions with ample funds at their disposal. Honors work in English at Swarthmore, for example, was conceived "as a study of the development of English thought and culture as embodied in literature, history and philosophy, rather than the history and appreciation of literature alone." (Philip M. Hicks, "Honors Courses in English." *English Jour.* 18: 230–7, March, 1929.) One half of the student's time is allotted to English, one quarter to history and one quarter to philosophy. To prevent the work from becoming a glorified survey course, a survey of the whole field is demanded as a prerequisite. The program is then divided into six parts:

I. English literature of the periods of Chaucer, Shakespeare, and Milton.

II. The social and political history of England from the Black Death to restoration of Charles II.

III. The transition in England from Mediaeval to Modern thought during the Renaissance and the Reformation.

IV. English literature from the French revolution to the end of the nineteenth century.

V. History of England from the French revolution to the end of the nineteenth century.

VI. Philosophy and science in the eighteenth and nineteenth centuries.

To carry out this scheme Swarthmore has bent every effort. The candidates are organized into small groups of five or six students and two instructors, who meet every week for papers and discussions as above described, each instructor being required to direct and pass on the work in all three subjects. Each instructor will probably conduct three groups. That such a system has led to "renewed vigor in the classroom teaching of the instructors engaged in it" and to the breaking down of inter-departmental barriers is not to be doubted, but without question it calls also for a highly paid staff with plenty of leisure, a demand that the state universities are unable to meet, the taxpayers of the state having not as yet been converted from the so-called democratic notion of quantity education to that of quality. That is why our system of general honors breaks down.

In nearly all institutions offering honors programs the custom prevails of final comprehensive examinations. The practice is variable in respect to written or oral examinations and as regards the requirement of a thesis. Swarthmore relies almost entirely upon written examinations which are read by outside professors. The examination period covers a period of five or six days during which period the student writes from eight to twelve three-hour papers which are mailed to the examiners as fast as written. After the completion of this test the examiners come to the campus to conduct the final orals in order to satisfy themselves concerning any doubtful candidates. During the first few years greater stress was laid on the orals, but as the written examinations were found to be adequate and as the number of candidates increased to such an extent as to render oral examining physically difficult, reliance was placed more and more on the written test.

At Oregon we have in the past depended on the oral examination supplemented by the thesis. This test is given a week or so before the regular examinations and the thesis must be ready in time to allow of its being read before the examination. The examination lasts for two hours and is attended by a committee of the department and one member of the honors council who is not a member of the department. These examinations have been a rigorous and satisfactory test, and although something of a strain on the candidates have not proved injurious. There is a good deal to be said in favor of the oral test as a means of determining the candidate's ability to respond readily under trying circumstances and as a type of test much more frequent in actual life than the written examination. Nevertheless, as the number of candidates increases, the difficulty imposed by time approaches the insuperable. The instruction of regular classes continues during the week that honors students are being examined, and as the end of the academic year draws near faculty duties increase; the number of extra two-hour periods that a busy man can find at this time is limited. On this account we shall, if there is any perceptible increase in honors students, be compelled in another year to resort to written examinations.

I have enumerated in passing some of the obstacles that stand in the way of the operation and expansion of the honors plan. The difficulties noted in the survey that I have several times referred to are lack of student interest, indifference or hostility of faculty members, and the need of extra help and funds. The hostility of faculty members usually springs from this lack of help and funds, on account of which they are compelled to sacrifice independent research activities of their own and assume tasks that are too burdensome for them. The lack of interest among students is connected closely with the other difficulties.

There is the initial difficulty of overcoming the inertia of students, their habitual reliance upon daily assignments and frequent examinations to keep them up to the mark, the tendency to loaf, the excitement and prestige of outside activities, the lack of prestige of intellectual excellence, and the absence of any real intellectual curiosity. James Bryce, in "The American Commonwealth," long ago noted the absence of the spirit of study in our institutions of learning. "Accordingly," he wrote, "those who in American Universities regret what they think the deficient interest taken by undergraduates in their studies and the preponderating attraction of inter-university contests in such games as football, have begun to canvass the question whether the introduction of honour courses and of competitions for literary and scientific distinctions may not be needed. Observers from other countries have long expected that such a debate would some day arise, and await with curiosity its issue." The implication is plain that the observers from other countries believe that the rousing of interest in study depends upon an appeal to the instinct of competition. Abraham Flexner's statement that an adequate contribution by the United States to civilization—"to the art of government, the art of living, to science, literature, and art"—depends upon a substitution of excellence for mediocre ability and mediocre training (Introduction to "Reading for Honors at Swarthmore,") justifies, if we accept the statement, the introduction of an honors plan, yet still leaves us groping for an incentive to the successful operation of such a plan. The mere opportunity to study independently is perhaps inducement enough to the few students in every college in whom intellectual curiosity is already stirring; appeals by professors to the ambitions of the exceptionally gifted may arouse others; and course-work itself may so expand the minds of still others as to swell the number of applicants for admission to candidacy. All these incentives do, as a matter of fact, operate, and the students moved by them constitute now our honor roll. But the numbers are not sufficient; too many men of latent intellectual power are unmoved; other activities in which their pre-eminence is recognized by the mass of students draw them away from honors courses. This state of affairs can be best remedied by competition, by the meeting in groups, as is done at Dartmouth and Swarthmore, where mind is brought sharply in conflict with mind and every incentive to excellence that operates on the athletic field, in class politics, in social organization, is called forth in the contest for intellectual supremacy. Lack of men and money prevents us from demonstrating as we should like what might be done. Nevertheless, every forward step that we make in enlisting the interest of the stronger student intellects brings us nearer our goal by producing the very type of leadership that we need to assist us.

EDUCATIONAL EVENTS

SITE OF THE AMERICAN UNIVERSITY CENTER IN PARIS

ACCORDING to a special cable to *The New York Times* the Commission on Sites and Monuments of the Department of the Seine has approved the American students' center projected by the philanthropist Mr. Edward Tuck. When an option was taken on the property where Mr. Tuck proposes to construct this modern university center, supplying for American students in Paris the facilities and recreational advantages available on American campuses, there was some protest. This property is part of the land belonging to the Marie Thérèse Infirmary and its gardens had been the home of Chateaubriand for several years.

The idea of building an American students' center on this ground was repugnant to lovers of literature and of old Paris, and the government was asked to list the site as a historical one so that no changes could be made and its appearance would be preserved as in the time of Chateaubriand.

The Commission on Sites and Monuments was instructed to conduct an investigation and has now made its report, which favors authorizing the American project. The commission first examined the property to ascertain its exact connection with Chateaubriand, and it was found that he actually inhabited it from 1826 to 1838. The buildings in which he lived, however, had been completely altered and his memory seemed principally associated with the gardens.

Chateaubriand in his writing recounts that he planted three cedars of Solomon, two druidical oaks and a double alley of chestnuts. After examining the plans for the American center the commission discovered that the chestnuts had disappeared and in the garden only two cedars remained and the oak trees had vanished.

Thus the student center as arranged in the plans would change nothing of Chateaubriand's day. The garden he lingered in will be preserved as well as the two trees he planted. The only change asked of the American architects is that they construct a grille fence instead of a solid wall so that Chateaubriand's garden will be visible to the public from the Boulevard Raspail. As the new American buildings will be screened by foliage, they can be built without detriment to the site.

EMPIRE TRAVEL FOR BRITISH STUDENTS

AN article in *Nature* states that for the past eight years parties of Canadian undergraduates, numbering from 50 to 150, and representing most of the universities of Canada, have made a summer tour in Europe under the auspices of the Overseas Education League. The party usually leaves Montreal for Glasgow towards the end of June, and spends about a month in Great Britain, visiting such centers as St. Andrews, Edinburgh, Grasmere, Bangor, Stratford-on-Avon, Oxford, Cambridge, London and the south coast of England. A further fortnight is then spent in Switzerland, Germany and France, before the party embarks for Quebec. Last year the continental section of the tour included visits to Geneva, Innsbruck, Oberammergau, Munich, Stuttgart and Paris.

These tours represent one activity only of the Overseas Education League. Organized in 1910, on a definitely non-commercial basis, by Major Ney, of Winnipeg, the league was originally designed to foster understanding between Canada and Great Britain. Its scope has gradually widened, and now it "seeks to emphasize the significance attaching to citizenship in the British Commonwealth of Nations, to interpret Britain and France to the two great branches of the Canadian people through a closer educational and cultural association, and to develop a consciousness of the rôle of education as a means to international understanding and amity." It organizes summer schools of English, French, music, drama, etc., at Oxford, Paris, and other centers; and, in all, some six thousand teachers and undergraduates have taken advantage of its arrangements. The governor-general of Canada is honorary president of the league, and among other patrons and supporters are the governor-general of the Union of South Africa; Lord Plumer, the Right Honorable L. C. Amery, honorary vice-presidents; the primate of all Canada, president, and Major F. J. Ney, vice-president and honorary organizer.

This summer, for the first time, a return visit to Canada of a party of university students from Great Britain has been arranged under the auspices of the league. A group of about twenty men and women students of the University of St. Andrews, representative of the various years and faculties, have sailed for Canada in the company of the home-going Canadian undergraduates and various other Canadian parties. Professor John Read, professor of chemistry in the United College, St. Andrews, is leading the party, and the tour will occupy a period of about five weeks. The visit will be restricted to the eastern provinces, and the party will visit such centers as Quebec, Montreal, Ottawa, Toronto and Kingston. The return journey from Toronto to Quebec will be made by water via the Thousand Islands. Throughout the tour opportunities will be afforded the members of gaining a first-hand knowledge of the educational institutions, culture, home-life and resources of the Dominion. The undertaking is said to provide the first instance of an organized visit to a British Dominion by a body of university students from Great Britain.

PLANS FOR A SURVEY ON EYE STRAIN

A comprehensive study of the strain on eyesight in school activities is being undertaken as a joint project of various departments of Columbia University and the National Society for the Prevention of Blindness, it is announced by Lewis H. Carris, managing director of the Society for the Prevention of Blindness.

Plans have been completed for this research, after a year of planning by Teachers College, staff members of the department of ophthalmology in the medical school, authorities in related fields within the university, and staff members of the National Society for the Prevention of Blindness.

Serious concern is felt over the fact that children spend a large proportion of their school time in work demanding close, careful eye work, as in reading and writing. Yet, there has been no investigation made heretofore on the possibilities of reducing this so-called "eye-load."

In most schools there is no standardization of lighting and seating arrangements; the printed materials with which the children work may vary from very large print to very small print; and in many instances the vision of the pupils frequently does not receive even a cursory examination.

Among the problems to be studied are: How much time ought a child with normal vision to spend in reading? Which materials would cause him least fatigue? Which materials are best suited to children with eye defects? Ought children of five and six years of age to engage in close eye-work? What kind of lighting is best suited to the varying age levels of readers? What degree and intensity of lighting is best?

The proposed plan of research recognizes the complexity of the problem. Extensive research extending over a period of several years and engaging educators, ophthalmologists, illuminating engineers and others will be necessary.

It is expected that the results obtained from this investigation will justify a readjustment of school procedures related to the use of vision. For instance, one size of type may be advantageous under a certain kind of lighting, but another type may be better under different lighting conditions.

Four factors seem predominant in the problems: (1) the vision of the child; (2) the lighting conditions under which he works; (3) the materials he uses; and (4) the length of time he uses them. A program of research which takes into consideration among other factors these four predominant factors should eventually produce practical results that will lead to sound educational practice.

A general plan has been formulated for this program of research under the general direction of Professor M. B. Hillegas, of Teachers College. Members of the faculties of Columbia University will advise upon those aspects of the problem within their fields. Graduate students in different departments will work on parts of the program under the advisement of the professors concerned. The National Society for the Prevention of Blindness will assist in the work.

Miss Roma Gans, research associate at Teachers College, will be in direct charge of the investigation. Her association with the research work in the college will make it possible to enlist the assistance of graduate students within the college and also the help of those who occupy positions in the schools in various parts of the country.

No time limit is set for the completion of the work, neither is the scope of the problem being limited to fit a given group of workers. The plan is to carry the investigations over as long a period of time and into as many fields as is necessary.

Steps have already been taken toward a definite starting-point in the work. A comprehensive survey of the eye-load of the school children from the ages of five to ten years is in process. This survey is taking into consideration the four important phases previously mentioned. Separate studies in the fields of physics and sight-saving classes have been started.

EXPERIMENTAL ENTRANCE PROGRAM AT THE UNIVERSITY OF SOUTHERN CALIFORNIA

THE University of Southern California has announced that it will inaugurate in September a three-year experiment with a group of 70 selected entrants to measure validity of tests of scholastic aptitude and of high-school grades as entrance criteria for admission to college. The experiment will be carried on in the College of Letters, Arts and Sciences. Admission and instruction of the experimental entrance group go forward according to the following plan:

A group will be selected who are secondary-school graduates, of age not to exceed twenty-one years, who do not meet the set entrance requirements in certain particulars as announced for the University of Southern California. Individuals will be selected by the use of entrance-test criteria which measure scholastic aptitude and two personal judgments as to scholastic promise, one of which should be from a high-school principal. Students in the experimental entrance group will not be permitted at any time in their college careers to compete in intercollegiate athletics, and during the time that they are members of this group may not hold membership in campus clubs or societies or other campus groups, and may not be pledged to a fraternity or sorority, or live in a fraternity or sorority house. They will be required to live in the university dormitories or in the homes of their parents.

The earning of a scholastic average of 1.5 or higher (a grade between a B and a C) for the work of the year in a special study program will be accepted as sufficient evidence to justify full admission to the university with advanced standing in the subjects for which a passing grade has been made. Each case of scholarship average between 1.5 and 1.0 will be considered on its merits. Members of the experimental entrance group who do not earn a 1.0 scholastic average will be denied further enrolment in the University of Southern California until the usual entrance criteria have been met.

The group will be closely observed and given guidance based on scientific studies with the view of developing, if possible, methods of study and work which will increase the probability of collegiate success. The group will be divided into two groups of 35 each for instructional purposes, so that significant contrasts will be made possible. Examinations on which selections for the year 1931–1932 will be based are scheduled for August 28 and 29.

ENROLMENT AT THE SUMMER SESSION OF COLUMBIA UNIVERSITY

COLUMBIA UNIVERSITY's thirty-second summer session has an enrolment of 14,016, the largest in the history of the college, according to official figures issued by the university. The highest previous registration was 14,007 in 1928.

Business and professional men and women, undergraduates and students from Algeria to Newfoundland and from every state in the union, are entered in one or more of the 1,086 courses offered. Of those registered 68.5 per cent. are women.

The largest single group enrolled is studying for an A.M. degree in philosophy. The second largest group is taking regular work in Columbia College, while those seeking a master's degree in political science form a close third.

Registrations in courses in pure science, education, law, architecture, engineering and business are likewise "impressive."

Geographically, the greatest number of students come from the north Atlantic states, including New York, Connecticut, Maine, Massachusetts, New Hampshire, New Jersey, Pennsylvania, Rhode Island and Vermont. Second is the north central group. The south provides the third largest, while the far west ranks fourth. Thirty-seven foreign countries and all the island possessions of the United States are represented.

A vocational analysis of the figures indicates that of those engaged in the teaching profession, the greatest number were from secondary schools. In this division, 4,095 were enrolled, while elementary-school teachers numbered 1,258.

Other registrations include 967 teachers in higher educational institutions, 439 school principals, 266 supervisors, 255 private school teachers, 221 teachers in normal schools, 169 school superintendents, 121 teachers in hospitals and 33 school librarians.

Students journeyed from thirty-seven foreign countries and all the island possessions of the United States to attend the summer school, which is entering its final week. Countries represented this year which sent no students in 1930 included Abyssinia, Algeria, Australia, the Bahama Islands, East Africa, Czechoslovakia, Newfoundland, Poland, Russia, Scotland and Switzerland.

BENNINGTON COLLEGE

GROUND was broken on August 7 for the five projected buildings which will constitute the founding of Bennington College. Over one thousand people were present at the ceremonies.

Mr. Robert Frost, a trustee of the institution, read a poem, and Mrs. Dorothy Canfield Fisher, also a trustee, spoke on the new education. Dr. William E. Rappard, formerly an official of the League of Nations, discussed education and international relations, and Dr. William Allan Neilson, president of Smith College, welcomed Bennington to the ranks of New England institutions for women.

Other speakers on the program were Governor Stanley C. Wilson, of Vermont; the Reverend Vincent Ravi Booth, who turned the first shovelful of earth, and Dr. Robert O. Leigh, president of the college. The Rev. Dr. Anson Phelps Stokes, canon of the Washington Cathedral, pronounced the benediction.

Among the guests were Dr. Harry A. Garfield, president of Williams College and chairman of the Institute of Politics, as well as a large number of others from Williamstown, which is only eighteen miles from Bennington. Construction on the new college buildings—four dwelling halls and a commons—began on the morning after the exercises. A large red barn forming three sides of a square will be remodeled to house temporary recitation rooms, laboratories, a library and administrative offices. The college will open in September, 1932, with a freshman class of eighty.

UNEMPLOYMENT AND THE PROLONGATION OF SCHOOLING

AT a conference of the President's Emergency Committee for Unemployment on August 5 a plan was worked out to encourage students to remain in educational institutions instead of seeking employment.

Objectives outlined during the conference are:

1. To take advantage of the present period of unemployment and part-time employment by encouraging the greatest possible utilization of opportunities for preparation for future positions and for the enrichment of American life.
2. To keep all children under 16 years of age in school in this time of surplus labor and increasing demands of industry for skill and judgment.
3. To encourage undergraduates and members of 1931 high-school and college graduating classes to remain in school.
4. To urge that increasing effort be made by institutions of learning for guidance programs that will direct young people not only into fields of usefulness but into fields where their services will be in demand.

The plan, as explained by Miss Olga Jones, who is directly in charge of the work, is to obtain the cooperation of local school officials and civic and business organizations in urging those to continue in some sort of educational training who have not yet graduated or otherwise discontinued their schooling.

The plan proposes to provide employment for those most needing it and to make possible greater opportunities for young persons through preparation for future positions.

Included among those attending the conference were W. W. Husband, assistant secretary of labor; James E. Cummings, National Catholic Welfare Conference; W. Ellwood Baker, general secretary, National Congress of Parents and Teachers; Miss Edith Rockwood, National League of Women Voters; Louis A. Kahlbach and Maris M. Proffitt, U. S. Office of Education; Joy E. Morgan and L. W. Ashby, National Education Association; Miss Katherine F. Lenroot, Children's Bureau; John Cummings and Frank Cushman, Federal Board for Vocational Education. Other organizations have indicated that they will cooperate.

THE OHIO STATE UNIVERSITY AND PROFESSOR MILLER

EXONERATING Dr. Herbert A. Miller, professor of sociology at Ohio State University, from all charges preferred against him by the trustees of the Ohio State University, and from all the alleged grounds of his summary dismissal on May 21 of this year, the investigating committee of the American Association of University Professors, in a preliminary report, released on August 10 from the association's office in Washington, points out that the action of the trustees was a grave violation of "every essential safeguard" in preserving freedom of speech and the security of the professor's tenure of position. The attitude of the Board of Trustees, according to the committee, is in this case "directly opposed to sound public policy, to good educational practice and to long established university ideals."

Examining the "Bombay incident," in which Professor Miller was alleged in a public statement of the trustees to have "incited the Hindus to civil disobedience," the report finds that his brief remarks were "a proper expression of opinion from an authority in Dr. Miller's field, and that it (the speech) aroused no objection with respect to its propriety in any responsible quarter other than the Board of Trustees of Ohio State University." As to the complaints which the board declares it has received for several years against Dr. Miller's alleged radicalism on social and racial questions, the investigators were unable to discover any evidence of such dissatisfaction. On the contrary, Dr. Miller is found to have been moderate and well-balanced in his expression of views on such problems.

The report claims evidence of bad faith in the handling of Professor Miller's case by the trustees and the university administration. President George W. Rightmire, of the university, it is shown, gave the reassuring impression last October to the dean of the college, to the head of the department of sociology and to Dr. Miller himself that the charges would be fairly investigated and full justice done. Yet between that time and the date of his dismissal, on May 21, Professor Miller was not informed of any charges or given further intimation that he might be discharged. As a result of the evidence, the committee records its conviction that personal animus against the professor, on the part of one or two members of the Board of Trustees, was solely responsible for the arbitrary action.

A protest against Dr. Miller's dismissal, signed by 153 members of the Ohio State faculty, was presented some time ago. This protest the investigating committee regards as fully justified, because the confidence of many faculty members in the official protection of freedom and tenure "has been destroyed by the temper and actions of the present board and the president." According to the report, "The board has insisted throughout on its position of legal authority and has failed to recognize its position of public trust. Until the board is ready to concede that there are no university acts, procedures or policies, whether relating to academic freedom, to security of tenure, to 'fundamental purposes of the university' or to 'clear responsibility to the people of Ohio,' including decisions by the board itself on these matters, which are not proper topics for discussion within the faculty, between faculty and the board and by the public, it can not assert that freedom of speech prevails at the Ohio State University."

Finally, the report asserts that acceptance of the views of academic freedom, tenure and of the reinstatement of Dr. Miller as contained in the recent faculty statement "is necessary if the university is to regain in any reasonable time the esteem of intelligent opinion throughout the country."

The complete report of the committee will be published in the next issue of the *Bulletin* of the American Association of University Professors. The investigating committee consisted of Professors Arthur B. Coble, University of Illinois, *chairman;* A. O. Craven, University of Chicago; J. W. Martin, University of Kentucky, and A. J. Todd, Northwestern University.

EDUCATIONAL NOTES AND NEWS

Mr. Charles B. Boyer, superintendent of schools of Atlantic City, N. J., for the past twenty-seven years, retired on August 1, after completing forty-one years in the service of the Atlantic City schools. The school board of Atlantic City, in accepting Mr. Boyer's resignation, adopted resolutions of appreciation and respect, and appointed him superintendent emeritus.

Dr. J. Freeman Guy has been appointed first associate superintendent of schools of Pittsburgh, in the immediate capacity of representative of the superintendent of schools.

Dr. Carl G. Wallenius has been elected president emeritus of Wesley Academy and Theological Seminary, Chicago.

The *Columbia Record* reports that Bernard M. Baruch, New York financier and a native of South Carolina, has been suggested to succeed the late Dr. D. M. Douglas as president of the state university.

Mr. Harry V. Meissner, non-partisan member of the school board of Milwaukee, Wisconsin, was elected president of the board on July 7. Mr. Meissner succeeds Mrs. Elizabeth M. Meehan. Mr. W. F. Buech, a Socialist, was elected to fill a vacancy on the board.

For the first time since the Alvan T. Simonds annual economic contests were established in 1921, both the prizes of $1,000 and $500 for 1930 have been awarded outside of the United States. Mr. C. E. R. Sherrington, who won the first prize of $1,000, was for a time instructor in economics at Cornell University. He is now lecturer in transport at the London School of Economics and Political Science. Mr. Frederick Geidt, who won the second prize of $500, is connected with Morton Brothers, stock and share brokers, 97 Gresham Street, London. The subject of the 1930 contest was "Government Interference with the Free Play of Economic Forces."

The degree of doctor of philosophy of the Charles University of Prague has been conferred on Madilene Veverka, supervisor of the kindergarten and primary grades of the Los Angeles public schools.

Prime Minister Pandeli Evangeli, of Albania, has bestowed the Order of Scanderbeg on Mr. C. Telford Erickson, founder of the Albanian-American Institute at Kavaja, Albania, the first college to be established in that country. Dr. Erickson is field representative of the foundation and is the first American to be made a member of the order.

Four new professors have been appointed in the Cornell Medical College, New York City. They are Dr. Eugene L. Opie, now of the University of Pennsylvania, as professor of pathology; Dr. Herbert S. Gasser, now of the Medical School of Washington University, as professor of physiology; Dr. George S. Amsden, now of the New York Post-graduate Medical School, as professor of psychiatry, and Dr. James M. Neill, now of the school of medicine of Vanderbilt University, as professor of bacteriology and immunology. It is understood that these professors will not take up active teaching until the completion a year hence of the new center of the New York Hospital and Cornell Medical College.

Dr. J. J. Janney, of the Rockefeller Foundation, will be in charge of a model health department established by the Rockefeller Foundation and the Johns Hopkins School of Hygiene and Public Health in Anne Arundel County, Maryland, to work out problems of preventive medicine.

Gretta M. Smith, librarian of the fine arts department of the Carnegie Institute in Pittsburgh, has been awarded a fellowship for the study of display methods in commercial and industrial expositions and museums in America and Europe, with a view to determining how they are applicable to libraries. Her work will be done under the direction of Dr. E. S. Robinson, head of the department of psychology at Yale University.

Miss Margaret Brewer has been appointed dean of women at Washington College, Chestertown, Maryland.

Mr. Allan D. Mainds has been appointed professor of fine art and director of the King Edward VII School of Art at the University of Durham, England. He has since 1909 been on the staff of the Glasgow School of Art.

Mr. W. S. Angus, at present deputy academic registrar of the University of London and warden of the Connaught Hall of Residence, has been appointed registrar of Armstrong College, Durham.

Ward H. Biddle, of Indiana University, has been elected president of the National Association of College Bookstores. William E. Pearce, of Rochester University, was chosen first vice-president.

Dr. George E. Vincent, formerly president of the Rockefeller Foundation and honorary president of the Chautauqua Institution, gave the dedicatory address at the opening of the Smith Memorial Library, erected through a bequest of $60,000 in the will of Mrs. A. M. Smith Wilkes, of Washington and Chautauqua.

Dr. Charles E. Spearman, professor of psychology in the University of London, arrived recently in this country to lecture at the Ohio State University. Following his present visit he will return to England to stay until September when he will give a lecture course at Teachers College, Columbia University.

Ashley Dukes, author and dramatist, of London, has accepted an invitation to teach in the University of California summer session of 1932, from June 20 to July 30.

Dr. John Franklin Crowell, at one time president of Trinity College, now Duke University, died on August 6, at the age of seventy-three years.

Dr. Walter Platt Cooke, formerly chancellor of the University of Buffalo, a trustee of Cornell University, died on August 3, at the age of sixty-two years.

Dr. Thomas F. Hamblin, for thirty-six years professor of Greek at Bucknell University, died on August 7, at the age of seventy-six years.

Mr. M. P. Stone, formerly state superintendent of public instruction for California, died on July 8.

Mr. G. Lloyd Palmer, superintendent of Frederick County schools, Maryland, for eighteen years, died on August 7, at the age of sixty-two years.

Specific bequests of more than $175,000 were made in the will of Dr. Richard Alexander Fullerton Penrose, Jr. The residue of his estate, which may amount to $1,000,000, is bequeathed to the American Philosophical Society and the Geological Society of America. The bequests are made in the form of endowment funds and only the income is to be used by the societies. The University of Chicago receives $50,000 to be used for the benefit of *The Journal of Geology,* of which Dr. Penrose was one of the editors for many years. The Economic Geology Publishing Company is given $25,000 to be used for the benefit of its journal.

The will of Worcester R. Warner, formerly president of the Warner and Swasey Company, gives $100,000 to the Western Reserve University and $50,000 to the Syrian Protestant College at Beirut.

The General Education Board has given $300,000 to Grinnell College. The sum will be added to the present endowment fund.

The Lenox Library Association, Massachusetts, has received the sum of $40,000 through the will of Mrs. Hannah M. Lydig.

The Pennsylvania State College reports the largest summer session enrolment in its history during the term just closed. The gross registration was 3,924, of which approximately 16 per cent. was in the graduate school. At the commencement exercises on August 6 a class of 183 was graduated including 120 baccalaureate, 61 master's and 2 doctor's degrees.

The Barreiros Agricultural School at Pernambuco, one of the largest in northern Brazil, has been closed by the state government in order to reduce expenses.

The *Journal of Western Education* states that foreign educational institutions in China have been given until the end of August to register with the National Government and to comply with the regulations drawn up last year. Despite protests from some missionary organizations, the government adheres firmly to its original contention that the regulations must be observed, and it is believed that the date now set will be made final, as the time limit already has been delayed from the end of 1930. Missionary institutions which register pledge themselves not to make religious instruction compulsory. The regulations do not object to voluntary courses in Christianity or any other religion. They provide that Chinese educators must be the heads of registered schools, although foreign educators may occupy important positions.

A London dispatch to the New York *Sun* announces the appointment of Mr. Charles Holden as the architect for the rebuilding of the University of London. The task of constructing the new buildings on the Bloomsbury site to the north of the British Museum is expected to extend over thirty years. The cost is estimated at from £2,000,000 to £3,000,000. The first buildings to be erected will include the administrative offices, the university hall and library, premises for the Officers' Training Corps, and buildings for the Institute of Historical Research and the Courtauld Institute of Art.

The corner-stone for the new students' home in Sofia, Bulgaria, was laid recently. It will form a unit in the cultural quarter of the city near the university, the museums, the National Assembly, the Cathedral and the Holy Synod. The first collection for this purpose, according to *The Christian Science Monitor,* was made before the Balkan wars. By the time the world war had been concluded the collection had lost 29-30ths of its value, dwindling to only $2,000. The campaign was started over again, this time among a people no longer able to give liberally. But thanks to contributions from students in Europe and America, the erection of the building is now assured. The home will provide living quarters for 500 students and dining facilities for 2,000. It will also contain lecture halls, a library and a study room. There are nearly 4,000 students in the Sofia State University, of which somewhat more than a fourth are women. A third of them are from the villages and most of the rest from small towns. Two thirds of them are very poor, living on no more than $10 a month for board and room.

The French Association for the Development of Technical Education, under the patronage of the Under-Secretary of State for Technical Education, the Municipal Council of Paris, etc., is organizing in Paris, from September 24 to 27, in connection with the Colonial Exhibition, an International Congress on Technical Education. The following subjects among others will be dealt with: (1) Vocational guidance. (2) Cooperation between government departments and industrial associations of employers and employees in the organization of vocational education. (3) Recruitment and training of teachers in trade schools, including that of workshop instructors. (4) Recruitment and vocational training of salesmen. (5) The place of general education in the technical training of the engineer. (6) The use of the cinematograph in vocational guidance; its use in vocational training, whether in the workshop or the school. Persons desiring further information with regard to the congress should address themselves to the Secretary of the Organizing Committee, Avenue Alexandre III, Grand Palais (Poste Côte Champs-Elysées), Paris, VIIIe.

The University of Denver School of Commerce has completed the first year of a survey of infant mortality in Denver. Registration of all infant deaths for another year will complete the survey and following this definite conclusions and recommendations will be announced. Professor A. D. H. Kaplan is in charge of the work and is assisted by the city government and various public and private agencies.

According to the survey made by the School of Education of the University of Maine in conjunction with the Maine Development Commission, as reported in the daily press, evidence has not been found to support the development of additional institutions for women, nor for the development of additional professional schools at the present time. Abundant evidence is available to demonstrate the need for the improvement of existing enterprises and for the enlargement of facilities already established. With the provision of considerable increase in support, the report states that the four institutions, Maine, Bates, Bowdoin and Colby, which are now functioning, can care for any number of students which may reasonably be expected to desire higher education, and their progress may be studied, modified and improved to provide ample and adequate higher educational facilities for the state during the next few years. In a digest of the survey, a paragraph on the need for higher education in Maine, it is stated that a study of student migration in the United States by President Zook for one year, 1922–23, indicated that while Maine produces as many students in proportion to her population as the average state, yet 40 per cent. of them seek their higher education in other states. The survey also showed that enough residents of other states attended Maine colleges to reduce the net loss to 19.9 per cent. for 1922–23.

The Massachusetts Institute of Technology has adopted a plan according to which before accepting appointment to the faculty, professors must agree to pay over to the institute fifty per cent. of fees received for services rendered during the term to parties other than the institute, such payments to constitute a professors' fund to be employed for providing further salary increases, leaves of absence, etc.

Approximately $275,000 of group life insurance has been provided for the employees and members of the faculty at DePauw University through a contract with the Equitable Life Assurance Society. The cost of the insurance will be shared by the university and those protected by it.

A general system of retirement allowances has been established at Johns Hopkins University, so that each member of the faculty, on retirement at the age of seventy years, will receive an annuity for life. The pension system provides retirement allowances for teachers of the ranks of professor and associate professor, under which a minimum annuity of $3,000 will be available for those who come within the scope of pension expectations from the Carnegie Foundation. For all other professors and associate professors the plan provides a retirement allowance at the age of seventy equal to half of salary up to a maximum of $4,000. The plan also provides for certain exceptional cases of high-salaried teachers whose present age is such that the regular provisions are inadequate. Since 1927, it is reported, there has been in effect a contributing pension plan for the school of hygiene and public health and a similar plan in the institute of law since 1929.

The dedication of the Children's Hospital Pediatric Research Foundation in Cincinnati, on May 20, is reported in the *Journal* of the American Medical Association. The foundation, which is housed in the Research and Clinic Building of the Children's Hospital, was established in January, 1928. The cost of that building with equipment is $800,000 and it has an endowment of $3,000,000. Mr. William Cooper Procter donated the entire amount. The new structure contains laboratories for chemistry, bacteriology and metabolism, animal quarters, set of shops, medical illustration and photography unit, library, auditorium, store rooms and offices. It also houses the main pharmacy of the hospital, recreation facilities and a complete out-patient department, which units are not directly connected with research. The out-patient department is so arranged that from the time a patient enters until he leaves, he has no contact with any other patient. He waits in a cubicle, is weighed and measured in another set of cubicles, and passes on to individual examining rooms. There is also an isolation unit for children suspected of having contagious disease. The Children's Hospital is linked to the University of Cincinnati College of Medicine in care of patients, teaching and research. There is an affiliation whereby the professor of pediatrics in the college of medicine is the medical director, chief of staff and director in the Children's Hospital; this position is held by Dr. A. Graeme Mitchell. The staffs of the two institutions are largely the same. Dr. Leonard G. Parsons, professor of pediatrics, University of Birmingham, England, spoke at the dedication, among others, on "Pediatrics: a Backward and Forward Glance."

SPECIAL CORRESPONDENCE

SCHOLARSHIPS OF THE CULVER MILITARY ACADEMY

Scientific methods of selection are being employed by a committee of educators in the bestowal of twelve newly created scholarships in Culver Military Academy, probably to a greater degree than has ever before been applied in the making of scholarship awards. By such methods the academy expects to discover twelve superior youths, each of exceptional promise not alone in scholarship but also in civic mindedness and public service.

The successful candidates must achieve, in competitive tests devised by leading educators and psychologists, above-average ratings in mental ability, emotional control, life purpose and faculty for social adjustment. Possession of these qualities will entitle them in effect, to a rating of extraordinarily high "citizenship expectancy."

With a valuation of $6,000 each the scholarships rank among the most generous offered in the United States. They cover all school expenses for three years, at the end of which the holders will have earned their diplomas. The scholarships were established by the trustees of the academy in the name of the wife of the founder, Emily Jane Culver, who was his steadfast support in the academy's early struggles. They will be awarded by states to the winners of state-wide competitions; four each year for three years, beginning with the opening of school next September.

Although the donors are not expecting to find child prodigies such as Mr. Edison sought by his competitive questionnaire, they do want the Culver awards to go to boys of outstanding qualities who are making the maximum use of their talents and opportunities. In other words, the scholarships are intended as a stimulus to the boys of greatest capacity for useful citizenship; for youths such as President Hoover had in mind when he referred (in discussing the White House conference on child health and protection) to the "specially gifted children who have 'gifts' that must be nurtured. . . ."

Culver, with a curriculum in which the emphasis is on guidance of the individual and flexibility of courses that permits ready adaptation to the particular needs of each, and with its program of military and physical training for the cultivation of leadership and physical stamina, is in a position to nurture the "gifts" to which the president alluded and the scholarship offer is one way of searching for the boys who have them. The academy contemplates giving the boys of greatest capacity the opportunity to exercise those capacities to the limit.

The testing which the scholarship committee is conducting represents progress toward the goal foreseen by Dr. Lewis M. Terman, of Stanford University, one of the chief authorities in the science of mental measurements, when he said:

> Neither science nor common sense has yet solved the riddle of genius but psychology has made a beginning. Sometime budding geniuses will be discovered early, tended and looked after as the most prized asset of the nation. Even now the search need not be a blind one. It is possible to identify with considerable certainty the youth who is endowed with talent.

Tests developed by Dr. Terman and his associates and by Dr. Arthur B. Otis, another noted authority, were adopted for use in the Culver competitions which have been described as the "most interesting scientifically yet applied to scholarship competitions," by Dr. M. V. O'Shea, of the University of Wisconsin, psychologist and editor of the *Nation's Schools.*

Having offered tempting prizes to "gifted" boys, the donors were confronted by the problems of definition and measurement. It was realized that the terms honored by long usage—"brightest boys," "most promising," "most intelligent," or "best scholars," were all too vague and meaningless for the purpose. Some dependable yardstick of science had to be applied.

But investigation revealed that there were not established tests or other systems of measurement comprehensive enough to fit the unusual and exacting pattern that had been agreed upon. Interest in the problem was aroused among educators and the aid of a small group, representing the universities and public schools of the states to which the first four scholarships were allotted, was enlisted. A committee was formed to draft the plans and write the specifications on qualification.

Places on this committee were accepted by such distinguished educators as Dr. Henry W. Holmes, of the Graduate School of Education of Harvard University; Dr. George F. Arps, psychologist and dean of the College of Education of Ohio State University; Dr. Clarence S. Yoakum, vice-president of the University of Michigan and a specialist in educational research; Dr. James B. Edmonson, president of the North Central Association of Colleges and Secondary Schools and dean of the School of Education of the University of Michigan; Dr. Walter S. Monroe, dean of the College of Education of University of Illinois; Dr. Charles Scott Berry, psychologist of Ohio State University and an authority on special education; Dr. Bancroft Beatley, professor of education of Harvard University; Professor Arthur W. Clevenger, of the University of Illinois, secretary of the North Central Association of Colleges and Secondary Schools, and Dr. Jesse B. Davis, professor of education in Boston University.

The experience and view-point of public-school administrators are represented in the committee by Dr. M. R. Keyworth, of Hamtramck, Mich.; Dr. Frank A. Jensen, of Rockford, Ill.; Irving O. Palmer, of Newton, Mass.; and Dr. Robinson G. Jones, of Cleveland, Ohio.

The general requirements adopted are that applicants must be recommended by the principals of their schools as outstanding students worthy of the committee's consideration; that their parents be unable to pay their tuition in Culver; that they be between 14 and 16 years of age, and graduates of the ninth grade.

Further, eligibles must be in the upper third of their class; must stand well with their associates and be disposed to group cooperation; be participants in general school activities; have emotional stability, good health and physique, be ambitious and have a settled purpose in life.

With these qualities required for a start and the tests applied in the course of the preliminary and final competitions, it may be said without dispute that the survivors are made of stern and durable stuff, with scientifically tested capacities for achievement far above the average.

One of the particularly interesting features of the scholarship enterprise is the possibilities it allows for "testing the tests." As members of the Culver corps of cadets all the winners will live to an exceptional degree in what educators call a "controlled situation," because of their being under constant supervision and military regulation. This provides an ideal condition for studying the twelve survivors of the examinations and observing to what degree the tests applied in measuring their aptitudes and abilities are valid and dependable by their progress and conduct.

The 1931 scholarships were allotted to the

states of Illinois, Massachusetts, Michigan and Ohio. Over 900 boys applied for consideration. In each state ten candidates were selected for final examination and the winners, one from each group of finalists, are to be selected early in June by committees in which the sciences of education, psychology and medicine will be represented.

Earle Hitch

Culver, Indiana

OUR CHRYSALIS CLUB

We are a commercial school, striving to give as much cultural work as we can to our pupils while throwing the emphasis on their commercial studies. As there are three other high schools in the city specially training for college, we enrol a very small percentage of pupils with a cultural or social background. Our upper 10 per cent. scholastically are frequently timid pupils socially undeveloped. Very few of this upper 10 per cent. were ever elected to school offices—these offices going to their more aggressive, less mentally well-equipped comrades. Hoping to remedy this state of affairs and wishing to awaken any dormant social abilities these pupils might have, with the consent of the principal, I, five years ago, organized our Chrysalis Club, and drafted into the club the upper 10 per cent. of the first-year pupils at the end of the first semester. I drafted them into the club; otherwise I should have defeated my purpose, as the very ones I wanted would have been too timid or socially backward to join, if I had made joining optional.

"Chrysalis" seemed to be a good name for a club such as I wanted, for these first-year pupils are in a chrysalis stage of development. The members are always quite pleased with their name after they grasp its meaning and what they are expected to do for themselves. The motto of the club is—See big, think straight, act square; the purpose—to make the mentally brightest pupils in the school the most attractive, the most popular and the most useful.

At our first meeting each one tells who he or she is, what junior high he came from and any outstanding things he did there. We do not elect officers until we have had time to get acquainted. At each meeting I give them something specifically to do for themselves and for their classes, to carry out their motto and their purpose. We talk about how to become attractive, how to make the most of our personal appearance, bringing out our strong points and minimizing our defects. One of the requirements is to dress up for each meeting so that we can all look our best, being sure that we join the bath-tub brigade. We practice standing and walking correctly; making our voices pleasing and cultured, our eyes shining with interest in our fellow man. At each meeting we decide on something to be done to beautify the classrooms, some way members can help their classmates, and make their mental ability count for something in the groups with which they are thrown; suggest ways of making the advisory period in the morning more interesting and profitable. After the first two meetings and after the officers have been elected, different groups take over the program for the meetings, the program to illustrate some one idea of the motto or the purpose of the club. One of the most important things the club does is to emphasize the value of making acquaintances and friends. I always set the members the task—it is a task for some of them—of getting acquainted with as many of the teachers as possible. We have over fifty. It takes several meetings and much encouraging persuasion to get some of the members to go up to teachers who do not teach them and introduce themselves. The teachers, of course, are all primed ahead of time to meet them more than half way.

We always wind up the year with a party, managed entirely by the members, to which they have invited the entire faculty. Those in charge of the invitations are usually members of the art class and the invitations they send out are beautifully decorated and printed. At our annual spring festival, a festival for all the activities of the school, the officers of the Chrysalis Club present flowers to the distinguished guests of the occasion.

If in their second and third years in school the Chrysalis Club members could be drafted into a public speaking club much more could be done for them, but I have to leave them to their own initiative after the first year. Most of the boys do go in for public speaking, but there is no such club for the girls during the school session, and I do not feel justified in drafting pupils for an after-school session, however much I may believe in public speaking as a developer of personality and usefulness.

What results have I obtained in five years? More and more are these pupils being elected to the school offices of proctors, bank directors, etc. Some of the most worth-while but timid pupils have learned to inhibit, to a certain extent, their timidity and to get recognition from their classmates. Some of the aggressive, conceited ones have learned that aggressive conceit is not "comme il faut." All the upper 10 per cent. know each other, and I have a group in each year's class that I can count on to cooperate intelligently in setting and maintaining the standards for the school. Discipline takes care, for the most part, of itself.

LILLIAN PIERCE

ATLANTA, GEORGIA

QUOTATIONS

SEVEN HUNDRED MILES OF BOOKSHELVES

FACTS from the new 1929 library census of national public, society and school libraries, recently analyzed by the United States Office of Education, are impressive. It shows that libraries have lengthened their shelves seven hundred miles since 1923. This has been done to accommodate the 33,500,000 books which have been added since 1923 to libraries having 3,000 books or more. There are now approximately 162,000,000 books in American libraries —public, society and school—which is, we are told, equivalent to about 40 libraries the size of the Library of Congress. Interpreted from another angle, this total means that the average number of books per person in American libraries is now one and one third. The nation-wide average of 29 library books to every 25 persons revealed by the 1923 book census has risen to 33 books to every 25 persons.

Radio notwithstanding, the use of libraries seems to increase along with the increase in the number of books. Libraries of 3,000 books or more have 6,000,000 more borrowers' cards in use than they had in 1923. Also, 130,000,000 more books were circulated in 1929 than in 1923. "Americans," say the libraries, "are reading more books."

Californians use their libraries more extensively than do the citizens of any other state, boasting an average of 6.2 books circulated per capita by libraries of 1,000 volumes or more. The average for New York is 4.1, although this state leads in the number of libraries with 3,000 volumes or more.

Citizens of the District of Columbia have access to the largest number of books, the average here being 17.54 library books to each person. The next best book-shelved state is New Hampshire.—*The Publishers Weekly.*

SOME PRACTICES IN TEACHER SELECTION

THE experiences of the year in the appointment of teachers lead to the conclusion that the economic pressure which is upon the country is asserting itself in some phases of the school-administrative service. While the tendency toward retrenchment has been manifested in a general way, there has also been a more discriminating attitude on the part of the school authorities in the selection of teachers.

Home talent has been favored more than ever before. The rules against the married women teachers have been tightened to a considerable degree. The community spirit has leaned toward provincialism. Nepotism has asserted itself with greater frequency. The law of self-preservation has asserted itself with exceptional vigor. The rule which places the selection of the teaching personnel in the hands of the superintendent has come into conflict with the board member who proposes his own candidate.

"The four most particularly objectionable practices in respect to the selection of teachers," says Professor J. B. Shouse, of Marshall College, "are the following: nepotism, patronage, partisanship, provincialism." He then explains that: "While nepotism, strictly speaking, refers to the employment of relatives, it can be made to include the employment of close personal friends. Patronage takes up the case where nepotism leaves off (wherever that is), and refers to the exercise of employing authority for the discharge of obligations or the building up of an obligated clientèle. Partisanship is likely to be operative in patronage, but may operate independently; it simply means favoritism founded upon common membership in a group or party; it is the place where political connection determines the fitness of candidates. Provincialism marks the preferring of local candidates for teaching positions; in more extreme form it may go so far as to include refusal to employ other than local candidates."

The question which arises here is whether the evil complained of exists in the degree that some educators would have us believe. The board-of-education member who is conscious of the duties of his office does not countenance the irrelevant, the unwise, the harmful in the selection of teacher talent. He knows that such selection does not lie within his province, and rather feels relieved in the thought that the burden rests upon other shoulders.

It is our firm conviction, that while the practices complained of must be condemned, they are highly exceptional and do not stand as a charge against the modern board of education. It may be well to point out the lapses and shortcomings into which the appointing authorities may fall, and in a few cases have fallen, but it is also well to distinguish between the general and the occasional.—*The School Board Journal.*

REPORTS

NATION-WIDE SURVEYS IN READING, ENGLISH USAGE AND VOCABULARY

The Psychological Corporation in October, 1930, launched a five-year study, nation-wide in scope, to provide essential data for the improvement of instruction in English usage, reading and vocabulary, and for more effective allocation of subject-matter within curricula. The study is undertaken in cooperation with the English Council, and is directed by Dr. L. J. O'Rourke. To date, the program has been confined to a study of English usage, approximately 825,000 pupils throughout the United States and its territories having participated in survey and achievement tests of English usage during the past school year. The program has been conducted in forty-eight states, Hawaii, Porto Rico, and the Philippine Islands.

Estimate blanks received by the Psychological Corporation from schools throughout the country indicate that approximately a million pupils will participate (in 1931–32) in the October–November nation-wide surveys in reading, English usage and vocabulary. The survey will be conducted with the grades grouped in two sections, the first including grades three to six, the second, grades seven to thirteen.

The English Usage Survey

Some of the aims of the English usage survey are (1) to bring a closer agreement as to which phases of English usage are essential and which may well be eliminated from the elementary and secondary school curricula; (2) to determine the level at which each specific phase of usage should be given major emphasis, and the points at which and the extent to which the teaching of that phase should be reinforced by review; (3) to evolve a general English usage curriculum which may serve as a guide for the schools of this country, even though they do not adhere strictly to it.

The Reading Survey

The purpose of the reading survey is to determine, through controlled research programs, (1) the degree of interpretation which is achieved at different age and grade levels; (2) the different types of interpretation attainable at these levels; (3) the appropriate instructional responsibilities at various grade levels.

The reading survey will also be divided into two parts on the basis of school grades, the first part including grades three to six, the second, grades seven to thirteen. Attention will also be given to reading courses such as those conducted for freshmen by the University of Chicago. The purpose in studying such courses will be to determine the extent to which mastery of different types of interpretation is related to mastery of subject-matter in various courses, as well as the extent to which progress in the mastery of types of interpretations is indicative of improvement in various courses.

The data secured by means of the survey conducted during October and November will indicate the extent to which certain types of interpretation differ from each other, and the extent to which these types are related or interdependent. Such data will also be a valuable guide in determining at what grade or age level different types of interpretation can most profitably be introduced, and at what level given major emphasis.

The Vocabulary Survey

The objectives of the vocabulary survey are closely allied with those of the reading study, and the results of this survey will supplement those of the reading study. In the vocabulary survey one test will cover grades three to thirteen.

Results

National norms are being completed and will be sent to all schools that cooperated in the English usage study last year, in order that they may compare the achievement of their pupils with national standards. The analysis of records which have so far been tabulated shows that the items involving problems of sentence structure presented the greatest difficulty to pupils of grades seven to thirteen. In order of difficulty, the remaining classes of items ranked as follows: adjective, adverb, preposition, conjunction, verb, capitalization, punctuation. Items dealing with the case of pronouns were found to be least difficult. These differences in difficulty held practically constant for grades seven to thirteen in both the October and April surveys. Items involving the correct use of pronouns, aside from case, and other miscellaneous items are not included in making this comparison, because of the limited number of such items and the diversity of their content. The final report will show, for each grade from three to thirteen, the degree to which pupils have mastered each phase of usage included in the test.

The relative progress in the mastery of phases of English usage which is made by pupils during the seventh to the twelfth grade is indicated to some extent by the degree of overlap shown in the following figures. On the entire tests twenty per cent. of the seventh grade pupils made better scores than ten per cent. of the twelfth grade; ten per cent. of the seventh grade made better scores than twenty per cent. of the twelfth grade. Twenty per cent. of the eighth grade made better scores than twenty-eight per cent. of the twelfth grade; ten per cent. of the eighth grade made better scores than forty-two per cent. of the twelfth grade.

Unquestionably, the low degree of mastery of English usage found to exist generally throughout grades three to thirteen shows the need for more exact determination of essentials and greater concentration on these essentials.

The extent to which pupils' responses to items are affected by the form in which items are presented is indicated by the following items:

"I didn't expect it to be he when I answered the telephone," was correctly changed by 71 per cent. in the seventh grade, 71 per cent. in the eighth, 75 per cent. in the ninth, 76 per cent. in the tenth, 73 per cent. in the eleventh, and 72 per cent. in the twelfth.

When an item involving the same phase of usage was presented in April in the correct form—"I did not expect the man with the mask to be him"—it was answered correctly by only 53 per cent. in the seventh grade, 50 per cent. in the eighth grade, 51 per cent. in the ninth, 48 per cent. in the tenth, 49 per cent. in the eleventh, and 53 per cent. in the twelfth grade. When these percentages are corrected for chance, the results even more strikingly show the low degree of mastery.

This is but one example to show that, even with large numbers of cases, the mere giving of items and totaling of results may result in data that give an extremely misleading idea of the degree to which phases of usage have been mastered and thus misdirect our efforts with regard to revising curricula and teaching methods. The problem, then, involves setting up controlled projects not merely to secure comparable data but to make possible statistical analysis that will insure valid and reliable conclusions.

All schools are invited to take part in the study. For the English usage survey a fifty-item test is provided for use in grades three to six, and a 75-item test for use in grades seven to thirteen, inclusive. Each of these tests is printed on a single sheet of paper and requires but 40 minutes of testing time.

Convenient tabulation and remedial sheets have been developed by Dr. O'Rourke for use with the tests, and these sheets will be furnished to all schools taking part in the program. Teachers will not be expected to compile data unless they wish it for their own use, since a number of schools sufficient to determine national norms will prepare records for the achievement tests. Teachers who do prepare these blanks, however, are requested to send copies of their data to The Psychological Corporation.

The excellent reports submitted by superintendents, English teachers and directors of research who cooperate in the study indicate that the schools recognize the importance of the study and are doing everything possible to make the program of the greatest possible value.

Owing to limited grants, the corporation is conducting the surveys on a partially self-financing basis and consequently there will be a nominal charge for the tests to cover research programs and trials incidental to development of materials, analysis of data, writing reports, and printing and mailing of several thousand free samples of tests, and teachers' materials. Answers to thousands of specific inquiries in regard to objectives, methods and analysis are among the items that grants are not sufficient to cover.

For samples of the tests and further information in regard to participating in the October–November Achievement Test Program address The Director of English Program, The Psychological Corporation, Washington Office, 3506 Patterson Street, N. W., Washington, D. C. Samples will be sent gratis to school officials who forward their school address. In accordance with the request of school officials, tests will not be sent to any one at a private address.

Paul S. Achilles,
Secretary.

SOCIETIES AND MEETINGS

CONVENTION OF AMERICAN INSTRUCTORS OF THE DEAF

The twenty-seventh biennial convention of American Instructors of the Deaf met in the school of the Province of Manitoba, near Winnipeg, from Monday to Friday, June 22 to 26, under the presidency of Dr. E. A. Gruver, of the Pennsylvania School for the Deaf. Characteristic of changing conditions in the education of the deaf was the almost universal presentation of the papers read and the discussions before the convention by two simultaneous speakers, one serving as the interpreter, one of the two using the "word of mouth" and the other the "manual signing." At least one third of the 230 registered in attendance would have little profited from the proceedings without the manual presentation, since they were not only teachers of the deaf, but also deaf teachers. But they were people considerably advanced in age, for the days of the deaf teacher of the deaf are counted.

There is no demand any more for young deaf teachers of the deaf except in very, very rare instances for teaching trades in a few institutions which still have a number of pupils too old to master the oral method which is inevitably superseding the method of systematic signing. This ought to be made clear, especially for the benefit of young deaf people in our colleges, who are likely to conceive the idea that the most natural profession to which a college education might lead them would be to become a teacher of those likewise afflicted. As a matter of fact, that is the very profession from which the deaf college graduate is nowadays and will be forever rigorously excluded. The teacher of the deaf must hear normally in order that she may aid the deaf children in learning not only to speak, but to speak normally.

The modern education wants to make the deaf an integral part of human society, not the kind of social outcast, or intellectual leper, that he used to be. And to reach this aim, the deaf child must learn to speak well enough to be understood by his future employers and hearing associates. Since hearing people will never universally learn to "sign," the deaf must learn to "speak" in the true sense. The minority must adapt itself to the majority.

Estimating the relative importance of the various discussions on the program, one may say that about 22 per cent. of the total time of the convention was devoted to primary language instruction, about 12 per cent. to arithmetic teaching, and 8 per cent. to methods in more advanced instruction in using the English language. About 18 per cent. of the time was devoted to all the other elementary school subjects. Industrial training of older children and the general problem, tremendously important, of finding employment for the deaf people, to make them self-supporting, received about 16 per cent. of the time of the convention. The remaining fourth of the proceedings was given to a variety of subjects, such as methods of ear training, the use of educational tests, the preparation of deaf high-school students for college entrance, the best utilization of the summer by the teachers of the deaf, etc. A discussion of the place and methods of religious instruction in a school for the deaf, intended to last only a few minutes, aroused so much interest that it lasted an hour, revealing a great diversity of opinion as to the methods to be used, which in this case are unusually controversial.

What organized body should establish and enforce standards for the certification of properly trained teachers of the deaf is an important problem in the education of the deaf. It was apparently solved by referring a tentative outline of such standards to the conference of executives of the American schools for the deaf, which already has a permanent and efficiently working organization and is undoubtedly the only body that can fix such standards because it consists of those whose duty it is to employ the teachers.

The convention of 1933 will take place in the school of New Jersey under the presidency of Dr. T. S. McAloney, of Colorado.

The fact that this convention took place on Canadian soil made possible a sincere expression by those in attendance of the advantage of international amity in this branch of education as in the general problems of education.

MAX F. MEYER

UNIVERSITY OF MISSOURI

EDUCATIONAL RESEARCH AND STATISTICS

STANDARDS OF MEASUREMENT OF TEACHING ABILITY

THERE is great need in institutions of higher learning of objective means of measuring the teaching ability of members of instructional staffs.

Until measurement becomes possible, it will likewise be impossible to distinguish good from poor teachers upon any other basis than that of more or less ill-informed and purely subjective opinion. In this circumstance it is difficult indeed to see how improvement in teaching can actually be brought about, since it will be impossible to determine with any assurance either the best teachers or the most effective teaching methods.

In this connection, the present tendency to employ objective tests of acquisition as a means of measuring or judging teaching ability is apparently to be deplored. It is true that they have the character of objectivity. Yet at most they measure only temporary possession of knowledge. This should probably be regarded as a false standard of measurement as applied to quality of instruction. Too great a discrepancy is apparent between the mere acquisition of knowledge on the one hand and its retention on the other; and this discrepancy is apparently greater still between acquisition and use in later life. Any plan that seeks to measure the quality of a teacher's work by the test of mere acquisition seems therefore ill-advised; and this is true regardless of whether the test is objective or subjective in character. Moreover it is apparently as serious an offense against truth and justice to evaluate methods of instruction as to measure teachers by this standard. Unfortunately, it is about the only one that has so far been applied to the measurement of either.

In view of the foregoing, it is clearly necessary to find other standards or criteria, if we desire to measure true teaching ability. What shall be their nature is not quite clear. It is entirely possible that the standard to be used in any given case will depend upon the nature of the instruction. Furthermore, we may find that not one criterion but several should normally be applied in judging the effectiveness of a given instructor's work.

A number of criteria have been suggested as more or less satisfactory substitutes for acquisition tests in the measurement of teaching ability. Several of these are stated and briefly considered below:

(1) The percentage of failing grades given: Some have felt that this criterion would have considerable significance in that it would reveal alike the identity of those who offer "snap" courses and those who are unreasonable in their demands upon students. While it may do this, it seems to put in the latter category certain teachers who apparently do not deserve to be branded as poor teachers for the reason that by giving failing grades, they are simply stopping incapable students early rather than "prolonging the agony" for other teachers by allowing such students to continue in work in which they must eventually fail. It is therefore not to be regarded as a satisfactory criterion.

(2) Correlations of grades given with mental test scores of students: This criterion, if used, must rest upon the assumption that it indicates the degree in which the teacher secures from his students achievement according to their respective abilities. Obviously, it is not a practicable standard since teachers would have only to observe the mental test scores of their students in determining the marks to be given and assign grades accordingly.

(3) Results of ratings given to instructors by their respective classes: It has been demonstrated that there is a notably high degree of agreement on the part of students when they are asked to rate their instructors in this manner. However, it has not been shown that the scores are given in recognition of teaching ability rather than some other quality or qualities. Until this is done, the results should, it seems, be regarded with some degree of suspicion.

(4) Degree of retention by the students of the knowledge taught, as shown by deferred, unannounced tests: This is obviously a far more valid measure of teaching ability than acquisition tests of any kind. In view of the fact that there appears to be a high correlation between retention and use of knowledge, it may apparently be regarded as a relatively sound criterion of teaching ability, provided sufficient time has been allowed to elapse before the deferred tests are given. Its limitation seems to lie in the difficulty of applying it under ordinary college conditions.

(5) Quality of work done by students of the teacher under consideration when enrolled later in related courses: This measure of teaching ability appears valid if we accept the conventional belief that good teachers should make their students "stronger" for the work that they are to do in related courses later. Since teachers seem actually to differ considerably in this important respect and since such difference is capable of objective determination through examination of grades received by students in later related courses, it may apparently be regarded as a fairly satisfactory criterion.

(6) Percentage of an instructor's students who complete satisfactorily the sequence of related courses of which his subject forms a part: This criterion rests upon the two-fold assumption that a good teacher should strengthen the purpose and determination of his students to "carry on" to the end of their undertaking, and that the effects of such inspiration may be expected to show in an increased percentage reaching the end of the related sequence in which the instructor is working. The standard seems essentially sound but in common with the one just preceding, is subject to such limitations as are imposed by the fact that not every subject really belongs to or functions as a component part of a related sequence.

(7) The percentage of an instructor's students who return voluntarily for later elective courses in the same subject-matter field: This represents, as did the last above, a measure of inspiration. While perhaps somewhat less significant than that one, it has the advantage of being applicable to the work of teachers whose subjects do not happen to be included in related sequences.

Included in the program of research in higher education at Iowa State College within the past 18 months have been three studies whose purpose was to determine the practicability of the sixth and seventh criteria above as measures of teaching ability when applied under ordinary college conditions. A fair measure of validity was assumed for the two standards referred to.

The studies were made in three different departments, each of which teaches a sequence of related subjects required of large numbers of college students. All teachers in the respective departments who had taught these subjects to any considerable number of students within the periods under consideration were included in the investigations. The first included 13 teachers, the second 9, and the third 14.

It was deemed necessary in connection with each of the studies to equate the student groups from the standpoint of ability. This was somewhat roughly done by means of the prediction scores determined for the students at the times of their entrance as freshmen. The accuracy of these scores was such that when rated on a five-step scale approximately 93 per cent. received a rating that was shown by their later college achievement to have been either correct or not more than one step removed from the correct rating. For the purposes of these studies, the students were classified upon the basis of the above ratings in three groups, the first of which consisted of the highest 25 per cent., the second of the middle 50 per cent., and the third of the lowest 25 per cent.

It was then determined for each teacher of any given subject (1) how many students of each grade of ability had been enrolled in his classes in the subject in question during the period embraced by the study; (2) the average grades of these students in later related courses; and (3) the percentage of each group who had eventually completed the sequence satisfactorily.

Results of the studies can not be given in detail. Among them, however, were several that were wholly unexpected and quite surprising. It was found in every case, for example, that teachers of any given subject to students of the same ability really differ widely when measured by the standards named. Thus a group of 45 average students, who had taken a given subject from a certain instructor received an average grade in all subsequent related courses of 78.9 per cent.; and 62 per cent. of the entire group finished the sequence. At the same time, another group of 40 average students who took the same subject from another instructor received an average grade of 67.4 per cent. in later related courses, and only 45 per cent. of the group completed the sequence. Differences nearly as great as these were so numerous throughout the three studies as to leave little doubt that they actually exist.

Another disclosure no less surprising from the studies was that teaching skill, if these measures are valid, is not general in character but tends to be specific with respect to particular subjects and particular grades of student ability. Hardly a person was found who was not notably successful in teaching at least one subject to students of some specific grade of ability. Yet no matter what might be the teacher's special adaptation as to subject or type of students, it was found that in nearly every case he was notably unsuccessful either in teaching other subjects or in teaching the same subject to students of other orders of ability.

Another rather startling indication was that the instructors, who appear by these tests to be doing the most effective work at any given point, are in many cases not the ones who have been generally regarded as the best teachers of the department. Indeed, each of the studies referred to seemed when finished to demand a more or less violent change in the ranking of instructors as to their relative values to the respective departments.

The results seem to mean that the distinction commonly drawn between good and poor teachers is largely imaginary, or at least that we should be less concerned with making it than with the discovery of the subjects and types of students which each instructor is best adapted to teach.

W. H. LANCELOT
DEPARTMENT OF VOCATIONAL EDUCATION,
IOWA STATE COLLEGE

NEW BOOKS IN EDUCATION

ATKINS, RUTH E. *The Measurement of Intelligence of Young Children by an Object-Fitting Test.* Pp. xii + 89. University of Minnesota Press. $1.50.

BOHAN, JOHN E. *Students' Marks in College Courses.* Pp. 133. University of Minnesota Press. $1.50.

HANEY, JOHN L., Editor. *The Barnwell Addresses.* Volume I, 1922–30. Pp. xvi + 436. The Mary Gaston Barnwell Foundation, Central High School, Philadelphia.

HILLEGAS, MILO B. *The Elements of Classroom Supervision.* Pp. 224. Laidlaw Brothers. $1.76.

PITKIN, WALTER B. *How We Learn.* Pp. 263. McGraw-Hill. $1.60.

RUGG, HAROLD. *Introduction to Problems of American Culture.* Pp. 616. Illustrated. Ginn. $1.96.

VAN BUSKIRK, EDGAR F. and EDITH L. SMITH. *Workbook for Use with "The Science of Everyday Life."* Pp. 216. Illustrated. Houghton Mifflin. $.72.

WEBB, WALTER P. *The Great Plains.* Pp. 525. Illustrated. Ginn. $4.00.

SCHOOL AND SOCIETY

EDITED BY J. McKEEN CATTELL

WITH WHICH IS COMBINED THE

EDUCATIONAL REVIEW

EDITED BY WILLIAM McANDREW

Volume 34 SATURDAY, AUGUST 22, 1931 Number 869

EDUCATION FOR THE PROFESSIONS[1]

By Dr. MALCOLM W. WALLACE

PRINCIPAL, UNIVERSITY COLLEGE, UNIVERSITY OF TORONTO

Mr. President, and Members of the Baltimore University Club:

IT is my first duty to thank you for the very great honor you have done me in inviting me to address you to-night. I am always conscious of a peculiar pleasure when I receive an invitation to address an American audience, but an invitation from Baltimore is in a class by itself. For no university man is likely to forget that it was in this city that the modern conception of a university had its birth, that from this city went forth those influences which have wholly transformed our idea of a university. Those influences have been hardly less potent for good in Canada than in the United States. My predecessor in the Chair of English in University College, Toronto, was one of Gildersleeve's students, and from Professor Alexander I learned to think of Baltimore not only as the most distinguished university center in America, but as a city in which the indigenous culture of the South, its care for letters and good manners and hospitality still shed a romantic light in a world obsessed by business and busy-ness. Many others of my colleagues and friends have graduated here, and have been glad to confess the great debt which they owe you. Accordingly it is not easy for me to feel quite like a stranger in your midst, much less a foreigner.

Hitherto I have had in mind the debt which Canadian universities, and Toronto in particular, owe to Johns Hopkins on the side of the humanities. Our Medical Faculty is perhaps in even greater debt to you. Here, however, we may claim that in some measure we have attempted to repay what we owe. At any rate I am sure that some of the men whose names you delight to honor laid the foundations of their mature achievements in our Canadian schools. Of these Sir William Osler is only the most illustrious in a goodly company, a man whose unique achievements in medicine only deepened and widened his sympathies in the fields of education and literature. And you will pardon my recalling at this time with peculiar satisfaction that I have the great honor of being a member of the Tudor and Stuart Club of this city of which Sir William was the distinguished founder.

I have been much troubled as to the choice of a subject on which I might venture to offer you some considerations. It is often said that no subject lends itself as does the subject of education to commonplace and platitudinous treatment. That reflection should give a wise man pause.

[1] An address delivered before the Baltimore University Club on Friday, April 17, 1931.

And indeed I have hesitated seriously before deciding to address you on a subject on which many of you have thought much more profoundly than I am able to do. Nevertheless, as university men we have a peculiar responsibility both for the theory and the practice of education in our own day, and both theory and practice are in constant need of reexamination, of restatement in order that the necessary readjustments may be made to the changing needs of the world. The name of Baltimore is forever associated with the boldest, the most fruitful of modern departures from contemporary practice in university education, and I shall let this consideration encourage me in asking your attention to a brief survey of what seem to me some educational problems of our day that call most loudly for examination.

My first commonplace will be to remind you that we are living in a day when there is hardly an established practice in any great field of human endeavor that has not been called in question. There is a wide-spread conviction among thoughtful men that we are near the end of an era, that great changes will be wrought in the affairs of men, that the times are big with events the character of which we can only vaguely forecast. The prevailing confusion of thought is nowhere more evident than in the matter of education. Perhaps men have never been able to make up their minds as to just what good results they should aim at in the educational process. It is strange to recall Aristotle's complaint regarding the muddled thinking of his own contemporaries. "What education is," he says, "and how children ought to be instructed, is what should be well known; for there are doubts concerning the business of it, as all people do not agree in those things they would have a child taught, both with respect to their improvement in virtue and a happy life: nor is it clear whether the object of it should be to improve the reason or rectify the morals. From the present mode of education we can not determine with certainty, to which men incline, whether to instruct a child in what will be useful to him in life; or what tends to virtue, and what is excellent: for all these things have their separate defenders." Aristotle's own opinion was that the principal aim of education should be to produce good citizens and to teach men to enjoy leisure honorably. Plato thought that "an intelligent man will prize those studies which result in his soul getting soberness, righteousness and wisdom, and will less value the others." In the nineteenth century Herbert Spencer thought that education should be mainly occupied with the care of the body and the perpetuation of the physical life of the race. Matthew Arnold regarded the intellectual and moral life of the race as of far greater importance.

However various the theories as to the object, and however disappointing the results of education may have been in any given period, wise men have never doubted that true education, if it could be discovered and practiced, was an instrument of unique potency in shaping human affairs. I think it may be said also that wise men have always agreed that all education is one—that without good secondary schools good universities can hardly flourish, and that a solid cultural basis should first be laid by those who aim at scholarly attainments in the professions or in any field of specialized study. In his inaugural address President Gilman laid down certain principles from which I believe few of you will wish to dissent. "At the moment," he declared, "there is nothing which seems to me so important, in this region, and indeed in the entire land, as the promotion of good secondary schools preparatory to the universities." And again,

"The object of the university is to develop character—to make men. It misses its aim if it produces learned pedants, or simple artisans, or cunning sophists, or pretentious practitioners." "The best scholars will almost invariably be those who make special attainments on the foundation of a broad and liberal culture."

If we may proceed on the assumption that these are essentially sound ideas it may be worth our while to examine the situation which confronts us to-day, to inquire whether in the half century which has passed since the foundation of Johns Hopkins we have succeeded in furnishing to the universities a student body more satisfactorily equipped for the pursuit of the higher learning. We may inquire incidentally whether the great multitude of those who leave our secondary schools with no thought of carrying their formal studies further are being more satisfactorily equipped to take their places as members of an intelligent democracy. "These are such," in the words of Ecclesiasticus, "as are not found in the high places, neither shall they sit in the seat of the judge, nor understand sentence, yet these maintain the state of the world." Does the state of the world promise to be better maintained in our day than formerly?

To-day our educational practice is being shaped very largely by two phenomena—the vast increase in the sum total of human knowledge, and the vast increase in the number of students who are seeking secondary and higher education.

Since the war, the increase in the numbers enrolled in high schools and colleges is something that could not have been dreamed of a few years ago. Even in the poverty-stricken countries of Europe the number of students has increased surprisingly, though not nearly to the same extent as on this side of the Atlantic. In the United States there are twenty-odd thousand high schools and over four million students attending them: some universities boast of fifty thousand students. No doubt the democratic idealism that grew out of the war was to a large extent responsible for this development. Empires and kingdoms had been overthrown, the heroic qualities of the common man had been proved, and henceforth democracy was to give us good government and to make war impossible. But the common man must be educated for his high task, and secondary education for every child of the nation seemed a reasonable and attainable ideal. It was a noble ambition, and if we are to judge by statistical evidence it has been realized to an astonishing degree. Incredible sums of money have been spent during the past decade on new buildings, expensive equipment and the salaries of teachers and administrators. School and university budgets have grown to proportions which a few years ago would have seemed utterly impossible, and there is an insatiable demand for the executive type of ability which can organize these huge plants and make their facilities available to the huge numbers who crowd their classrooms.

And yet if we are skeptical of statistics, if we refuse to be impressed by mere numbers and the complexity of the educational machine, and insist on examining its product, our enthusiasm for the whole new system is given pause. It was perhaps inevitable that the increase in numbers should involve some deterioration in the product of the educational process. But the volume of criticism that is being expressed to-day by competent educationists reveals a degree of dissatisfaction which must come as a shock to any one not familiar with the subject. The graduate of the American or Canadian high school, it is generally agreed, can not be compared to the graduate of a European secondary school. "It will be almost universally admitted," says Dr. Pritchett, "that the secondary school (in England, France and Germany) succeeds in imparting to its pupils a quality that our schools do not, and that along with the intellectual quality which is developed by hard and constant work, the student acquires also a pleasure and a satisfaction in the intellectual life. . . . The (American) boy or girl who has finished the secondary school and entered college, in many cases is unable to write or speak good idiomatic English. He has not learned to enjoy good books. On the other hand the graduate of the German *Gymnasium* or of the French *lycée* or of the English *public school* can speak and write his mother tongue with clearness and discrimination, and he reads." "The cult of the average," says Dr. Learned, "determines not only the spread, but also the quality of our education." "The breakdown of the high school in its attempt to educate the whole people has been due to failure to keep clearly in mind wherein genuine education consists." "Efficiency methods in the mass production of cheap articles seems to have been carried over instinctively from commerce to education." Dr. Flexner recognizes the fact that there are many good schools which he regards as exceptions to the rule. Moreover he recognizes the great and unheard-of achievement of keeping the door open for all classes of the population for four years, as the high school does. "But," he concludes, "the high school is too elementary, too broken-up, and too miscellaneous to constitute for most students anything more than an elementary education. As to the quality of the achievement, no nation has ever so completely deceived itself." "Our secondary schools," declares Professor Briggs, of Teachers College, Columbia University, "have failed, more lamentably than is commonly realized, in their attempt to administer the traditional curriculum . . . to so large a proportion of the adolescent population as has been permitted and encouraged to attempt it. And in this failure they have squandered the public investment and weakened the State." And again, "The lowering of standards that a respectable percentage may pass is fair to students at neither extreme. Those with exceptional academic abilities are not challenged as they should be to the high accomplishments of which they are capable; those with abilities of other kinds are wasting their time in attempting a program for which nature did not equip them, and in which they are doomed to insignificant achievements or to failure." Foreign students of the American system agree with these judgments. For instance, André Maurois, writing in the *Gazette de Lausanne* of February 12, 1931, says: "The American High School which corresponds to our *lycées* gives a much less thorough course than does the *lycée*. The two first years of the American university correspond very closely to the last two years of our *lycées*." Dr. Savage, the well-known English Inspector of Schools, declares that "the Canadian, like the American boy, starts his secondary school career at least two years later than does the English boy—and never catches up, at least at school."

If there is practical unanimity among American critics as to the facts, there is also a surprising degree of agreement as to the causes. It is generally recognized that the high ideal of extending opportunities for secondary schooling to as large a proportion of the population as possible has made the maintenance of real educational standards very difficult. The merely physical problem of handling multitudes of students, of assigning them to classes and teachers, and of testing the quality of their achievement would be a staggering task under any circumstances. Schools become elaborate organizations in which the emphasis almost inevitably is laid on administration, statistics, equipment and budgets. Under such circumstances there must be a strong tendency to make instruction mechanical, to herd together in large classes students of varying grades of ability and of preparation, and to retard educational progress to a pace not faster than that which can be attained by the average student. Nevertheless, these critics do not write merely to give counsels of despair. They have very definite convictions as to where the root of the trouble is to be found. We may conveniently group these criticisms under three different headings.

First, the curriculum, with the system of "electives" and "credits." Only a small proportion of students graduate from high school, it is maintained, after having pursued a coherent, organized course calculated from the beginning to modify the student's outlook on the world. "American high schools," says Dr. Learned, "give access to a nondescript, unorganized mass of courses at a single level and that a low one: Europe prefers to offer carefully organized groups of curricula suited expressly to at least three varying types of ability." "The high school," says Dr. Flexner, "used to be a sieve of a certain kind. But American democracy objects to sieves. . . . It is (now) a kind of bargain counter on which a generous public and an overworked and underpaid teaching staff display every kind of merchandise—Latin, Greek, science, agriculture, business, stenography, domestic arts—leaving the student, with such advice and direction as he may get from teachers, parents, and college matriculation requirements, free to piece together under restrictions which sometimes amount to much and sometimes to little, a course of study that by the end of four years will yield 'counts' or 'units of credit' enough to win a diploma or to enable him to satisfy the entrance requirements of the college of his choice." It is the lack of continuity of interest, of coherence in the effort which is put forth that negatives every reasonable ideal of true education. At best the graduate of such a system can be possessed of a certain amount of disconnected elementary information, for there is no final test of his total performance. Professor Briggs declares that 42.5 per cent. of the students who elect French in American high schools drop the study at the end of one year, and 79.5 per cent. at the end of two years. Dr. Learned quotes by way of contrast the instructions issued to examiners in German schools. They are "to note particularly the student's intellectual grasp, his judgment, his comprehension of the whole field with which he deals, and his power of presentation." "An arbitrary succession of questions having no internal coherence or connection should in any case be avoided." "Is it possible," exclaims Dr. Learned, "that these examiners do not understand that every well-bred examination should consist of ten distinct questions, each of two or five separate parts, and each question having a value of ten credits?"

Closely related to this criticism of the unorganized programme of studies is the fact that a large proportion of high-school students leave school after one or two years. The wastage represented by this fact both of the student's and teacher's effort can hardly be exaggerated. Dr. Learned points out that "English school authorities require an assurance from the parents, often under penalty of money forfeit, that the pupil will finish the curriculum; we, on the contrary, urge that any fragment of a curriculum is proportionately desirable.''

A second defect of the American high school that is being widely criticized to-day is the practice of giving instruction in the same class to bright and dull pupils, to the industrious and the lazy, to those of scholarly tastes and capacities and those whose abilities are mediocre or worse. From an administrative point of view it is of course much more convenient to do this. The American high school knows almost nothing of testing and segregating of true capacity, and as a result there is no standard of high excellence at the top. There is an urgent demand among American critics that the best fourth or fifth of the pupils be drawn off and given a genuinely coordinated programme taught by scholarly teachers. Such a class would provide for high intellectual performance, would be an immense stimulus to the morale of the whole school, and would free able pupils from the deadly effects of the lock-step method. But such a plan, it is argued, would be undemocratic. If democracy is to be defined in these terms it carries in itself the seeds of its own dissolution, for it is hardly conceivable that a society can be healthy which is indifferent to the highest possible development of its ablest minds.

The third major weakness of American secondary education, on which our critics concentrate, is the character of the teaching body. Partly because of the recent demand for a greatly increased staff, partly because the teachers are themselves the product of a system of uncoordinated courses and of ''credits,'' genuine scholarship, which is the fundamental qualification demanded of English, French and German teachers, has become rare in American high schools. On this point there is substantial unanimity among competent observers. ''The plain fact,'' says Professor Briggs, ''is that there are not enough good teachers, even reasonably good teachers, to staff the secondary schools.'' . . . ''We have complacently, or even with pride entrusted our children to teachers whom we have no evidence for believing (to be) more than nurses, policemen, and amateur practitioners in the art of instruction.'' Dr. Gordon Laing, Dean of the Graduate School in the University of Chicago, writes: ''I do not think that I am exaggerating when I say that scores of masters are graduating each year without having attained even the slightest appreciation of the higher culture. Nor do they acquire it later. Large numbers of them regard the degree as a gilt-edged teacher's certificate, and having obtained it they do not pursue their studies further. They are through. If you doubt my statement, study the published output of the secondary school teachers of this country (and it is in the secondary schools that the masters are for the most part to be found) and compare it with the publications of secondary school teachers in England, Germany or France. You will find that our secondary teachers make but a pitiful showing beside the others.'' Dr. Flexner writes: ''There are, I have gladly admitted, here and there men and women on the superintending and teaching staffs who are cultivated and well educated. In strange ways, industry, ability, a fine spirit and scholarship occasionally appear in a sea of mediocrity and incompetence; but it is unpardonable misrepresentation to attribute these characteristics to even a considerable portion of the rapidly changing teaching staff.'' ''The high school,'' he continues, ''is such a welter of subjects and activities, the high school teaching staff is so largely occupied in teaching subjects that the teachers themselves do not know, that grading and certificates are well nigh meaningless." "The teaching staff," writes Dr. Learned, "while usually composed of admirable men and women, is not a staff of scholars. . . . Excepting many scholarly and fully competent teachers, usually to be found working under impossible conditions in our larger cities, the staffs of our public high schools are amateurish and superficial in their knowledge. Mediocrity reigns. . . . They have been given no responsible, independent experience in educating themselves, nor have they been selected on a basis of well-tested intellectual capacity and achievement."

This is certainly a dark picture and forms a strange contrast with European conditions. In France the teachers in the *lycées* have been subjected to the most highly competitive examination that is known, and the ranks of teachers in French universities are recruited almost exclusively from the teachers in the *lycées.* It is assumed that scholarship is as fundamental in secondary schools as in universities. In Germany the selection of secondary school teachers is hardly less rigorous; for instance, in certain teacher-training courses in recent years one half to one third of the candidates have been rejected. Now it may be true that a first-rate scholar may be a poor teacher, but it is incredible that a poor scholar can be a good teacher. It may be true, moreover, that it is easier in the Old World to persuade men of first rate ability to enter the teaching profession than it is here, and assuredly the smaller number of posts simplifies the European problem. But when all allowances have been made the contrast is painful and humiliating.

Of the substantial truth of this picture my own experience of Canadian schools leaves me in no serious doubt. In other words I believe that our average high-school teacher is far inferior in scholarship to his predecessor of twenty-five or fifty years ago, that no serious provision is made for segregating the youths of unusual ability in order to test them by real intellectual standards, that the average high-school graduate has only the slightest tincture of either cultivated tastes or scholarly capacities. Recently a friend of mine had to undergo an operation on his eyes in one of our large hospitals. He was shocked to discover that neither of his nurses (they were both high-school graduates) could read aloud to him intelligently. Many of our Toronto graduates continue their studies in English or Continental universities, and in general they feel immature in comparison with the best European students. In our graduate classes in English in the University of Toronto during the present session we have one student from Germany and one from Switzerland. Both are definitely superior to our own graduates of the same age in their capacity to organize their thought, in initiative, in power of presentation. We welcome them to our classes, but their presence is a silent rebuke.

One practical problem suggested by these observations seems to me most urgent if we are to preserve a sense of values in our society. It is more urgent than in former times because the high-school graduate of our day who enters any field of higher learning finds his whole time claimed by the highly specialized studies of his profession. In other words the high-school holds the key to the problem of how we are to have lawyers, doctors and engineers who are broadly educated, cultivated gentlemen as well as highly trained specialists. If they have not laid the foundations of a liberal education in the secondary school it is hardly conceivable that they will have an opportunity of doing so at a later stage. To-day we have all become specialists, and must depend for even our social intercourse on the narrow circle of our fellow-specialists.

It would seem as if organized society

were bent on widening the gulf which separates men from one another, on confining its members within more and more restricted fields. In the desire to secure the highest efficiency of service, society delights to honor the great scientist, the great engineer, the great surgeon, the great captain of industry, who has become most expert in the technique of his craft, irrespective of his development as a man. If he insists on devoting a portion of his energy and time to becoming acquainted with the story of the human race and their achievements in art, literature and science, he does so at his own peril, for all his time and all his energy are inadequate for the business of perfecting himself in his craft. I shall not labor the point at greater length, for all men are familiar with the fact and a multitude are in dumb, if futile rebellion against it.

It is true that much of our present practice is unavoidable. It is true that each of us must be content to share in only a fraction of legitimate human interest and experience. But this is true only within reasonable limits. We are all so dazzled by the marvelous achievements of modern science and their application to our comforts and conveniences that we seldom stop to consider the price of the achievement. That price is nothing else than the divorce of most men from the deepest sources of abiding human happiness. Even those who are most successful in meeting the insatiate demands made upon them are often the most dissatisfied with the results. If I know much of physiology, is that a recompense for my knowing nothing of Homer and Dante and the great men of my own race? If I am minutely acquainted with the philology of the Teutonic group of languages am I rewarded for my ignorance of modern physical science or for an intelligent acquaintance with the causes of the nations' difficulties in finding the basis of enduring peace among themselves? Society seems to demand of most of its members a service that negatives many of their aspirations as human beings.

Matthew Arnold has pointed out that human progress has ordinarily been achieved by the method of giving full swing now to one set of instincts—intellectual, moral, imaginative—now to another, and that when one set is uppermost it is necessary to insist on the value of those which are being temporarily ignored. In other words, men are incurably addicted to the doctrine that there is one thing necessary, that if we pursue it strenuously we may safely disregard other things. To-day the one necessary thing in the minds of most men is efficiency in our calling, and a capacity for hard work directed toward that end is the chief virtue. Science has achieved such an incredible series of triumphs during the last half century, it has added so enormously to our physical comforts and conveniences, it has put such powerful instruments into our control, that men's imaginations have been fired with the ambition to push on to new conquests and to achieve more and more of knowledge and of control over nature. Now I do not propose to make myself ridiculous in your eyes by denying for a moment the magnificence of these feats. They have added enormously to men's well-being and even more wonderfully to the potential well-being of the future. But they carry with them the fallacy of there being only one thing necessary, and many men are vaguely conscious that science has not contributed to happiness, nor taught us how to live satisfying lives to as great an extent as we might reasonably have expected. We are not much nearer a solution of the problem of living peaceably one with another, nor of providing adequate food and clothing and shelter for mankind. We can produce goods on an almost unlimited scale but we do not know how to distribute them. We do not even know how to set men at work doing anything, and unemployment has become a chronic malady of most states. Moreover, our current literature portrays an unhappy world, pessimistic, cynical regarding most of our established institutions, inclined to denounce the existing, and skeptical regarding men's capacity to organize their lives satisfyingly.

Now I have no panacea to offer for these evils. I do not believe that there is one thing needful and that that one thing will work our salvation. Rather I wish to urge that it is our exclusive devotion to practical aims that is at the root of our present *malaise*. There is a duality in human nature which we can never safely ignore either in our education or in formulating our ideals. It is well to be efficient members of society but not at the cost of sacrificing our own individualities. It is well to develop the rational side of our nature and to pursue knowledge, but we are imaginative creatures, also, and our emotions demand satisfaction. It is well to work hard to achieve ends, but it is also well to dream and speculate and take counsel together as to *what* ends we shall pursue.

There is only one great problem of education: how shall a man learn to spend his life satisfyingly? And a tentative answer is that he must make provision for satisfying different sets of his human instincts. He will want to render service to his community, and to secure that most real of earthly honors, the "Well done" of his fellows who know. But he will also want to be conscious that the process of growth goes on in himself apace, and that he is in more and more intimate communion with the best minds of his race. And in our day it seems to me that we need especially to be reminded of the importance of finding time for the development of our imaginative life and for our becoming more and more familiar with the general ideas that are, or should be, of common interest to all intelligent men. There are two very obvious reasons why we should take time from our professional labors to cultivate our love of beautiful things, to improve our personal acquaintance with the great poets and the great thinkers of the world. And the first of these reasons is that in this way we shall contribute largely to our personal happiness. The man who loves music or pictures or poetry has within himself an inalienable source of delight. The man who has cultivated an interest in general ideas as illustrated in the biographies of great men or in the most significant events in the history of government or science has a precious capacity for occupying himself happily.

A very busy medical friend of mine told me recently that he was getting tremendous enjoyment from reading the Odyssey after he went to bed at night. An old friend of mine, eighty-four years of age, and confined to bed, was utterly absorbed when I last visited him, with the situation which confronted Murray in Quebec immediately following Wolfe's death. As we talked, my old friend's infirmities were forgotten, and he was living imaginatively through a great historical event where vital issues were at stake. As long as a love of beautiful things and of general ideas can accomplish these results men will not willingly forego their advantages.

But there is another advantage that comes to the professional man who refuses to be utterly absorbed in technique, who cultivates his imaginative life. He is thereby increasing his general capacity, his mental caliber. A capacity for happiness, a habit of serenity, are powerful aids to efficient thinking: largeness of view and sanity of judgment will hardly be present in the thoughts of the unhappy, irritable, exclusively practical man. Unless our imaginative life is fed and nourished and exercised constantly, our generous impulses will degenerate into sentimentalities; our critical sense of values will degenerate into acceptance and parrot-like repetition of current conventions. Familiar daily acquaintance with literature and history—

that more intense, more significant world than this in which we dwell—can alone furnish us with a criterion for the constant re-interpretation of life which is the program of every man who is fully alive. To accept our world, and the dominant conventions of our day, is to have anticipated the period when we shall cease to live. To meditate on the ideas that informed past civilizations, to unsphere the spirit of Plato, and to commune with the most vital human beings who have preceded us in the world, is to drink at the most life-giving source, is to regulate our own speculations on right and wrong, on beauty, on justice, on human values. It is puerile to assume that it is easy to know what is right, or just, or worth while in our own day. It is supremely difficult, and we can say nothing about it so surely true as this, that the standards of yesterday will not serve us without modification. Even the sages can do nothing but assist us: the truths to which they attained have become half-truths, and even these may have become invalid for us. To believe otherwise is to be guilty of the fundamentalist heresy—that truth, and standards of conduct or of value, are static, that they have been revealed to the Saints once for all, and that our duty is merely that of passive acquiescence.

The truth is that every generation has to meet the challenge of new and difficult problems, and no society is healthy unless it can count upon the eager and intelligent cooperation of a large number of its members in arriving at decisions. "The future of mankind," said John Stuart Mill, "will be gravely imperiled if great questions are left to be fought out between ignorant change and ignorant opposition to change." All the great sources of human suffering and unhappiness, he believed, were conquerable more or less by human effort, but it must be by intelligent and informed effort. And where are we to find this intelligence and this information if not among the men who make up the great professional classes? Consider the problems that are clamoring for solution to-day. What about the relation of the great mass of men to religion and the Church? Are we providing the most intelligent education—primary, secondary and advanced—to the multitudes who are demanding it? Our international problems depend for their solution on a large body of informed opinion in each nation. Our economic and social problems—problems of unemployment, of distribution and marketing, for instance, are very acute. Or consider, again, the fact that everyday society is becoming more and more organized into huge corporations. Does this tendency not involve of necessity a modification of the highly individualistic and competitive ideals of our Western civilization? These things should not be fought out between "change and ignorant opposition to change." Nor can they be decided by highly trained specialists whose vision has been confined to a narrow field, whose imagination has atrophied because it has not been nourished at the perennial sources from which only it can derive its sustenance.

In a word, gentlemen, I wish to plead for an ideal of the professional man as something other than a great technician. It is true that society legitimately demands efficient service from us, but she should also demand that we develop our faculties in as rounded a fashion as possible, in order that we thereby become able to take counsel together as to how the world is to be made better, more satisfying for each individual, as to how the inevitable changes are to be made. A democracy needs a body of educated men in this sense of the word. Too often our great specialists to-day—in business or the professions—make themselves absurd by public pronouncements on subjects with which they have only the most superficial acquaintance. In our contemporary society we have lost much of the delight of being associated with our fellows in an intelligent, unselfish effort toward a common end conceived as good. Many a soldier found it in the war—a strangely grim satisfaction which had been denied to him in civil life. The professions should seek to foster this satisfaction in public service, but in order to do so they must cultivate among their members a love of its history and literature and general ideas, a consciousness of our common life, the effort of the race, its achievements and aspirations, its enduring possessions—Shakespeare, Homer, Burke, Darwin.

To foster this sense of community must surely be one of the chief aims of education unless our sense of values is hopelessly awry. And it is surely not too much to expect of a secondary school that it should lay a solid foundation for these things in the heads and hearts of at least the more gifted youth of our country. In a carefully planned and coordinated high-school course extending over eight years—the only kind known in Europe—it would be reasonable to hope that an able boy might achieve among other things some real acquaintance with the story of man's development as recorded in the history of the most significant nations of the past, and especially in the people of his own blood. He might also know in outline the story of man's increasing understanding of the nature of his physical environment. At the same time he could learn to take delight in beautiful things, in music, painting and particularly in the poetry and general literature of his own tongue. He should have developed some capacity to deal with general ideas especially as they bear on the well-being of the community—ideas relating to education, religion, politics, economics. He should have acquired a consciousness of membership in the society of those who feel responsibility for clear thinking on all problems of *general* human welfare. These, or some of these things, he must have achieved if he is to be a citizen of the world, an intelligent member of a democracy, if his education can deserve the epithet "liberal." How sadly many of our university graduates fall short of such an ideal to-day I need not insist. That this should be necessary I do not believe. An enduring basis of liberal culture can be laid in our secondary schools, provided we are genuinely interested in securing such a result, and provided that we abjure the heresy that school-mastering is the task of second and third-rate persons. You will remember Hippocrates' ideal of medicine as "a profession of a cultivated gentleman." Should the day come when that ideal is regarded as obsolete, not only in medicine but in all the learned professions, it is my own conviction that magnificent additions to the sum of human knowledge may have been purchased at too great a price.

WHAT I WOULD DO IF I WERE A COLLEGE PRESIDENT[1]

By HERSCHEL G. LANGDON

SENIOR CLASS, STATE UNIVERSITY OF IOWA

"To qualify as an educational expert," according to Professor Munro, "one needs only to be a glib fellow away from home." I am now 2,000 miles from Iowa. Unless I come within that definition I am not an authority on education. I sought assistance in the preparation of this address. When I put to college presidents the ques-

[1] Address from the point of view of the college student before a General Session, National Education Association, Los Angeles, California, June 29, 1931.

tion, "What would you advise me to do if I were a college president?" the answer invariably came, "Resign!"

What is the purpose of a college? To answer this question would be my first problem. Is it the sole purpose of a college to impart factual information? Is it to train adolescents in vocations that they may be better able to obtain a livelihood upon reaching maturity? Is it to teach a trade or trades? Is it to develop a class of intellectuals, who, because of intensive training, will be better fitted to take advantage of their fellow men? Is it to train men to be physically superior in order that they may break records on the athletic field? "No! Emphatically no!" would be my answer to such questions. A college may do all of these things, but if it stops there, it has, in my opinion, failed to accomplish what should be its main purpose, which is to turn out men and women who, in the best sense of the word, have an education.

I hear your protests. "Education" is a loose word. It is difficult to define. But that difficulty should not deter its use; rather it should emphasize that perhaps an education is something more than a curriculum.

It has been said that the business of colleges and universities is the "conservation of knowledge and ideas." It is more than that. Not only should a college conserve knowledge; it must stimulate new ideas. It should turn out men and women who are individuals, not just members of the crowd; individuals who can, and do, think for themselves—creative personalities. Too many colleges grind students through a process that does exactly the opposite; a process which tends toward the suppression, rather than the expression of original thought. It should be the function of a college or university to encourage both the development and the expression of new ideas.

But the college must go further. Ideas are of little value unless they are brought to humanity in an acceptable manner. Professor Sumner has enunciated a fundamental truth that colleges sometimes ignore: "Book learning is addressed to the intellect, not to the feelings—but the feelings are the springs of action." One is reminded of the old gentleman who, when told that his son was studying Latin and Greek, remarked, "What is he studying them damn things fer? Nobody speaks 'em." I do not mean to suggest that Latin and Greek are anything but excellent subjects; I do want to say that more college students should obey the scriptural injunction, "Get wisdom; and with all thy getting, get understanding."

The development of men and women, who are above all things human, who have active minds and pleasing personalities, who have knowledge, judgment and wisdom, ideas and the courage to express them—this, to my mind, is the function of the college. To accomplish this, if I were a college executive, I should consider the selection of a faculty my most important duty. I confess it would be a gigantic task. And I am frank to say that I might not have the ability to select a good faculty. Besides sheer ability it would require great courage; for the selection would necessarily involve both acquisition and elimination. But this address is, after all, hypothetical. I shall assume that I am a keen judge of men and of human nature, that I am possessed of indomitable courage, and that I would be able to select the kind of faculty that I have in mind.

Faculties are made up of many types. Two are chiefly necessary—those who are interested in and capable of research, and those who are interested in and capable of teaching. My emphasis in selection would be on the teachers. It does not follow that persons who are able to do research are capable as teachers. The spirit of research a good teacher must have, for it is true that, though one speak with the language of science and philosophy, and have not the spirit of research, he has become as sounding brass, or a tinkling cymbal. But I would not select my teachers on the basis of research; I would select them as individuals, for their ability to teach, to inspire, to lead. It is not necessary that one should excel in research in order to be a great teacher; witness Jesus and Socrates, the greatest teachers of all time, yet so far as the records show, neither ever wrote a single line. Nor would my faculty be selected on the basis of degrees alone, for a degree, in many cases, represents nothing more than the completion of so much routine work, together with a thesis that is gratuitously assumed to contain a bit of new information.

Once having selected a faculty, I should consider it my duty to let the professors alone. These teachers would be free men and women. I should regret exceedingly the existence of even unconscious suppression of any kind. Teachers free to live and teach as they might see fit would be my ideal. "Ideas about teaching, like those concerning government, are all created free and equal." My teachers would be permitted to carry out their own ideas. Their results, and not their technique, would measure their success.

There should, I believe, be less emphasis on administration, and more on teaching; less concern about the "how," and more about the "what." Not a few of the weak points in higher education are the result of applying administrative methods of secondary schools to colleges and universities. Too many professors are concerned not with what should be done, but with what, under the circumstances, may be done. It is not that they feel the hand of control; it is rather that they unconsciously fear to step beyond a certain line, lest they meet the censure of high authority.

I emphasize the faculty and its intellectual environment because I feel that it is upon these things that the real success of a college depends. I would not emphasize buildings. I would not emphasize equipment. For no matter how magnificent the buildings, how beautiful the campus, or elaborate the equipment may be, they are indeed hollow and meaningless without an inspired faculty. Whereas, an inspired faculty, even though the buildings be shacks, and the equipment meager, will make a great college or a great university.

In my college I should expect to have professors who would be more than scholars—to their students they would be intimate friends rather than cold intellectual gods; they would be teachers with imagination who would inspire and stimulate as well as inform and translate; living personalities who would be, not just tolerated, but respected; teachers whose courses would appeal, not as a means for gaining credits, but as opportunities for rich intellectual experience.

At the same time, I am convinced that a college or university can not succeed unless the faculty has intelligent students with which to work. By intelligent students, I do not mean those who are naturally adept at gathering information from books and hence likely to be awarded high grades. The intelligence of which I speak is that intelligence which is best described as common sense. So far as I know no tests have been devised which will accurately, or even approximately, measure this uncommon gift. But it is apparent that some selection must and should be made. "We should have, not students who will give expected answers, but students who will ask unexpected questions." Between the high school and the college I should place the hurdles high.

If there is a distinction between the college of which I am speaking and the better colleges in America, it is to be found, not in the basic structure, but in emphasis. In my college I should expect the emphasis to be placed on culture rather than upon skill and vocations. I am convinced that specialization in undergraduate work misses the very target at which it aims. For the most part, it is a waste of time that might be better spent in getting an education that is, if not technical, at least broad. To permit undergraduates to specialize in vocational subjects is to give them training that has but one dimension—length. It has neither breadth nor depth.

An excerpt from an address on "The More Than University," by Professor Shambaugh, of my own University of Iowa, describes what I should like to find in my college: 'Less of organization, less of regimentation, less of supervision, less of timing; less of testing, less of grading, less of classification, and less of standardization; more of synthesis and less of analysis; more of creation and less of manufacturing; more of the individual and less of the crowd; less of methods and more of morals; less of efficiency and more of living; less of the letter and more of the spirit.''

Perhaps my college would not be popular. It might not even be large enough to have a football team; but I believe it would turn out graduates who would be, first of all, cultured and human; graduates who would, in all walks of life, by virtue of their understanding, by the very freshness of their ideas, coupled with their knowledge and wisdom, be able to lead their fellow men into the good life, to better thoughts, and to greater love for the good, the true, and the beautiful.

EDUCATIONAL EVENTS

THE CARNEGIE UNITED KINGDOM TRUST

THE seventeenth annual report of the Carnegie United Kingdom Trust gives, as reported by *Nature,* by way of introduction to its record of the events of 1930, a short general survey of the five years 1926–1930 and a statement of the main heads of policy which the trustees have decided to pursue during their fourth quinquennium, 1931–1935. Their operations range over a wide field, shared now with the Pilgrim Trust, of charitable enterprise in Great Britain and Ireland.

The trust's income of roughly £120,000 a year has been distributed since 1925 mainly in grants under the headings: libraries (47 per cent.), playing fields and play-centers (21 per cent.), rural development, adult education, and music and drama. In their library development work the trustees have exploited the possibilities of coordination and cooperation, and this policy led to the establishment in December and January last of two regional schemes of the greatest experimental importance, one in the north of England, based on the library of the Newcastle Literary and Philosophical Society and embracing libraries in the four northern English counties; the other serving Warwickshire, Staffordshire, Worcestershire, Shropshire and Herefordshire, and based on Birmingham City Library. In each area the trustees are meeting the initial cost of creating the necessary union catalogue. If these schemes, after a short trial period, turn out to be on sound economic and administrative lines, the trustees hope to invite the libraries of two or three other areas to adopt the same policy.

To "special" libraries, including those of many industrial research and other scientific associations, grants amounting to more than ten thousand pounds were paid last year. These, in turn, have made their collections available to the general public on application from the National Central Library. The Association of Special Libraries and Information Bureau, which has enjoyed the financial support of the trust during the six years of its existence, has recently decided against a projected amalgamation with the Library Association—a decision involving, the trustees observe, competition and possible overlapping with the university and research section of the Library Association.

The trust's playing-fields policy, inaugurated in 1927 with an allocation of £200,000 spread over four years, has been carried into effect in collaboration with the National Playing-Fields Association. It has aimed at stimulating and encouraging local effort, and its success may be gauged by the fact that already 356 grants, varying in many cases from only one tenth to one sixth of the total cost, have sufficed to enable some 5,000 acres to be preserved permanently for the playing of organized games. Apart from this playing-fields program, the trustees have not during the past year been pursuing any concerted policy for ameliorating the physical welfare of the masses, but they have offered a grant of £30,000 for the erection of a Physical Training College for Men Teachers at Leeds and have helped the National Council of Girls' Clubs to employ two physical training instructresses. The main feature of the college will be a one-year course based on the principle that physical instruction is better given by teachers who also take part in the ordinary work of the school than by specialists with no other qualification and with little, if any, hope of being usefully employed after they reach 40 to 45 years of age. The Girls' Clubs instructresses conduct short intensive courses in large towns, giving special attention to instruction in the organization of team games for clubs with limited playing spaces. The experiment is an entirely new one and the results so far are reported to be most encouraging.

THE COMPARISON OF SALARIES AMONG URBAN AND RURAL TEACHERS

SALARIES of public-school teachers continue to advance for the country as a whole, according to a statement made by W. H. Gaumnitz, senior specialist at the Federal Office of Education, to a representative of the *U. S. Daily,* in announcing a forthcoming study in salary trends now in process of compilation.

The increase in salary appears in practically every class of school. The findings, however, refer to the median salaries. They admit that in some individual instances there has occurred a drop.

A sharp contrast is apparent between the wages of urban and rural teachers. Between 1921 and 1930, inclusive, rural median incomes advanced 7.5 per cent. while urban ones mounted 16.2 per cent. for the country as a whole.

In actual dollars, the median salary of the rural teacher stood at $926 in 1930 compared with $1,771 for the city teacher.

The lowest salary paid to any class of teachers is received by the one-room teacher group. The elementary teacher in the larger cities receives two and two-thirds more income than the one-room teacher. It appears equally true that salary seems to be progressive in proportion to the type of school in which the teacher instructs.

The median income for the one-room teacher is $788, for the two-room teacher is $829, for the three-room and over type, it is $980 in the rural areas. The rural consolidated school teacher enjoys a median of $1,037, while in the village schools it is $1,157.

Another aspect of incomes of teachers is that the larger the city the higher the salary. School revenues, obviously, are higher in the larger cities. The median salary for the teacher in a city with population from 2,500 to 5,000 is $1,162; in a city from 5,000 to 10,000, it is $1,303; in a city from 10,000 to 30,000, it is $1,428, while in a city between 30,000 and 100,000 population, it reaches $1,609. Teachers in cities in excess of 100,000 population have a median salary of $2,118.

The teacher in the public schools of a city with a population above 100,000 then receives 161.7 per cent. higher income than the one teaching in a rural one-room school.

In 1921, the rural teacher received a median salary of $861 compared with $926 in 1930; the city teacher received $1,524 in 1921 compared with $1,771 in 1930.

Although the median salary trends are upward for the nation as a whole, New Mexico, North Dakota and South Dakota show a downward trend.

Salaries of Negro teachers, in those states which segregate the Negro children from the whites, continue very low. The median for the rural white teachers in the 17 states is $945 while that of the Negroes is $388.

The forthcoming survey is based on statistics submitted by a majority of the county superintendents and gives in more detail the rural salary situation. It will contain 25 tables devoted to salary distribution, median salaries, and salary trends state by state.

THE SCHOOL BUDGET FOR NEW YORK CITY SCHOOLS

WITH the approval of a school budget of $146,338,848.48 for 1932, the Board of Education sets a new record for the amount of money New York City will be asked to contribute to the maintenance of the public school system. In asking for an increase of $5,953,963 over the record budget for last year, the board is preparing to cope with a phenomenal increase in high-school registration which it believes is due to the business depression and the desire of unemployed young men and women to continue their schooling.

In addition to the amount asked by the Board of Education for elementary and secondary education for 1932, there will be other expenses incurred by other city departments. An estimate of $30,000,000 is made for the acquisition of school sites and enlargement and construction of new schools, and about $35,000,000 will be required for interest on and amortization of bonds.

The total amount, therefore, which it is estimated will be devoted to public school purposes in this city in 1932 reaches approximately $212,000,000. This record sum, which averages about $1,000,000 a day for every day of the school year, is estimated as $9,600,000 more than was spent for public-school purposes in 1931.

The committee on finance and budget, which prepared the estimates, made the following report in regard to the situation in the day high schools:

> The largest single item of increase in the budget estimate for 1932 is due to the phenomenal growth in the day high school register. This increase in the register is due largely to the economic depression, which has caused young people to remain in school because of the fact that there are no openings for them at the present time in the business world. There is also a constantly increasing demand on the part of parents for high school education for their children.
>
> The raising of the compulsory education age in recent years has also had the effect of increasing the day high school register. Not many years ago it was the exceptional boy or girl who went to high school; now it is the exceptional boy or girl who does not go to high school.

Anticipating that the day high-school register will increase by about 20,000 pupils by the fall of 1932, the board has provided for more than 1,000 additional teacher positions. There will be 350 new teachers for the fall of 1931, about 500 for the spring of 1932 and approximately 135 for the fall of 1932. The number of teacher-in-training positions also has been increased from 350 for 1931 to 400 for 1932.

THE EXTENSION DIVISION OF THE UNIVERSITY OF MISSOURI

THAT an ever increasing number of people in the state are becoming identified with the University of Missouri is indicated in a report of the Extension Division of the University of Missouri which shows that 2,810 individuals took extension courses during the year ending last month. Three thousand five hundred and twelve courses were given in correspondence, extension class, extension center and Smith-Hughes work.

By means of the Extension Division, established in January, 1910, the university is bringing a complete practical education within the reach of every citizen of the state, according to Professor C. H. Williams, director of extension work. The report of the extension department shows that 2,307 students enrolled during the year in correspondence courses, 211 for extension center courses, twenty-six for Smith-Hughes work, 377 for extension class courses.

More correspondence students enrolled for undergraduate credit than graduate credit, the totals being 1,706 and 142. Three hundred and thirty-five enrolled for high school work, two for non-credit courses. There were thirty Negro students. In extension classes were 377 enrolled for undergraduate credit.

The largest enrolment was in the departments of education, English, agriculture and history. Other departments in which courses were offered are: Accounting and statistics, Bible, classical languages and archeology, economics and finance, French, geography, German, home economics, journalism, Latin, mathematics, physical education, physics, physiology, political science, preventive medicine, psychology, rural sociology, Spanish and zoology.

The Extension Division has expanded rapidly since its beginning twenty-one years ago. Its original purpose, that of offering a thorough course of training at the lowest possible cost to all who have been unable to attend established institutions, has brought the division into seven lines of service: Correspondence courses, extension class courses, department of public information, visual education service, debating service, municipal reference bureau and department of alumni service.

Through these various services the Extension Division enrols students from all parts of the world, but by far the greater number are natives of the State of Missouri who are engaged in some occupation that prevents them from attending the university in person, but who are interested in some special training.

BOOKS FOR CHILDREN

President Hoover's Rapidan River School in Virginia has been presented with a collection of children's books, the gift of the American Library Association.

Fifty-eight book titles most often asked for by rural and mountain children were selected by a committee of the school librarians section of the association. Members of the committee were: Euphemia K. Corwin, librarian of Berea College, Kentucky; Edith Johnson, librarian of the Berry Schools, Mt. Berry, Georgia; Virginia Harnsberger, late librarian of State Teachers College, Harrisonburg, Virginia, and Mildred P. Harrington, of the Graduate Library School, University of Chicago.

The list includes such well-known titles as "Alice in Wonderland," "Hans Brinker and the Silver Skates," "Just So Stories," "Little Black Sambo," "Pinocchio," "Robinson Crusoe," "Story of Dr. Doolittle," "Treasure Island," "Wild Animals I Have Known" and editions of the "Arabian Nights" and "Mother Goose."

Other titles which complete the collection are: "All About Pets," by Margery Bianco; "Around the World with the Children," by F. G. Carpenter; "Book of Legends," by Horace Scudder; "Boy Collector's Handbook," by A. H. Verrill; "Boy's Life of Roosevelt," by Hermann Hagedorn; "Burgess Animal Book," and "Burgess Flower Book," by T. W. Burgess; "Careless Jane," by Katherine Pyle; "Child's Garden of Verses," by R. L. Stevenson; "Children's History of the World," by V. M. Hiller; "Daniel Boone, Wilderness Scout," by S. E. White; "Dutch Twins," by L. F. Perkins; "Eskimo Stories," by M. E. S. Smith; "Everyday Manners for Boys and Girls," South Philadelphia High School; "Fables," by Aesop; "Fairy Ring," by K. D. Wiggin and N. A. Smith; "Fairy Tales," by H. C. Andersen; "Fifty Famous Stories Retold," by James Baldwin; "Golden Numbers," by K. D. Wiggin and N. A. Smith; "Heidi," by Johanna Spyri; "Hoosier Schoolmaster," by Edward Eggleston; "Household Stories," by Grimm Brothers; "Housekeeping for Little Girls," by O. H. Foster; "Japanese Twins," by L. F. Perkins; "Lisbeth Longfrock," by Hans Aanrud; "Little Folks' Handy Book," by Lina Beard; "Little Lame Prince," by D. M. M. Craik; "Little Men" and "Little Women," by L. M. Alcott; "Lonesomest Doll," by A. F. Brown; "Magic Forest," by S. E. White; "Nursery Tales from Many Lands," by E. L. and A. M. Skinner; "Older Children's Bible," by A. Quiller-Couch; "Overall Boys," by E. O. Grover; "Page, Esquire and Knight," by Marion Lansing; "Peggy in Her Blue Frock," by E. O. White; "Rebecca of Sunnybrook Farm," by K. D. Wiggin; "Secret Garden," by F. H. Burnett; "Seven Little Sisters," by Jane Andrews; "Story of My Life," by Helen Keller; "Sunbonnet Babies' Primer," by E. O. Grover; "Suppose We Do Something Else," by Imogen Clark; "Toby Tyler," by J. O. Kaler; "Two Little Confederates," by T. N. Page; "Viking Tales," by Jennie Hall; "What Happened to Inger Johanne," by Dikken Zwilgmeyer; "When Mother Lets Us Garden," by Frances Duncan.

THE YALE SUMMER EDUCATIONAL CONFERENCE

Yale University's first Summer Conference for Advanced Students of Education, which brought together a small group of graduate students and men and women of wide educational experience for the study of important problems in the field of education, came to a close on August 8. Pointing out that the conference has been undertaken as a three-year experiment, Professor Clyde M. Hill, chairman of the department of education and director of the conference, said that "if the next two sessions of the conference are as enthusiastically received as the session this summer has been, there is no doubt in my mind that it will become a permanent feature of the work in education at Yale University."

Twenty-six states were represented among the students, who lived in Yale dormitories. The faculty, made up of leaders in important educational fields, included Professor Boyd H. Bode, of the Ohio State University; President Walter A. Jessup, of the University of Iowa; Professor Truman L. Kelley, of Harvard University; John W. Studebaker, superintendent of city schools, Des Moines, Iowa; Professor Edward L. Thorndike, of Columbia University, and Professor Hill. Special lectures were given by Professors Hughes Mearns and A. F. Myers, of New York University, and by Professor M. B. Hillegas, of Columbia University.

The work was characterized by much freedom, there were no courses in the ordinary sense of the term, and each student was expected to contribute to the success of the conference by making available to the group the results of his reading, thinking and general experience. Small group discussions and opportunities for individual conferences with members of the faculty were important features of the work. No classes were scheduled during the afternoon and evening, this time being reserved for reading, for group discussions and for personal conferences with members of the faculty.

The student body included principals of high schools, elementary schools, and junior high schools; city school superintendents; supervisors in normal schools, teachers colleges, and elementary schools; college, teachers college, and normal school teachers and graduate students. Approximately fifteen per cent. of the group had received the Ph.D. degree, and eighty-six per cent. the M.A. degree. Sixty-eight colleges and universities were represented.

In planning the conference for next summer the department of education expects to make generous use of suggestions which have come from members of the 1931 group. Frequent personal interviews have been held with students and faculty members. These interviews have been supplemented by a questionnaire designed primarily to find out the least satisfactory features of the conference. The replies showed enthusiastic approval of the work. More than 80 per cent. of those who replied to the questionnaire have applied for admission to the conference next year.

TEACHERS OF CHEMISTRY AT BUFFALO

Teachers of chemistry from schools and colleges in all parts of the United States will gather at Buffalo on August 31 to celebrate the tenth anniversary of the founding by the late Dr. Edgar Fahs Smith of the Division of Chemical Education of the American Chemical Society.

The meeting of teachers, to be held in connection with the eighty-second convention of the society, will pay tribute to the contributions made by Dr. Smith, for seventeen years provost of the University of Pennsylvania, to American scientific education. Reforms long advocated by him will be discussed throughout the week in papers and addresses. A feature will be a joint session of the Divisions of Chemical Education and of the History of Chemistry. Dr. Smith was the first chairman of both sections.

"Progress in the teaching of chemistry in this country owes a vast debt to the inspiration and zeal of Dr. Smith," said Professor R. A. Baker, of the College of the City of New York, secretary of the division of Chemical Education. "Ten years ago Dr. Smith created a new section of the American Chemical Society by gathering together a group of teachers of chemistry. That new section now known as the Division of Chemical Education has grown to be one of the largest of the society, having about 1,200 associates and active members. Its aim is to offer a common meeting ground to those interested in chemical education, to aid the training of future chemists and to develop a wide-spread appreciation of chemistry."

Dr. Smith was born in York, Pennsylvania, on May 23, 1856. He was graduated from Pennsylvania College in 1874, receiving his Ph.D. two years later from the University of Göttingen. Later in life he received many honorary degrees. He became provost of the University of Pennsylvania in 1911 and held the post until his death in 1928.

EDUCATIONAL SCIENCE AT THE CENTENARY MEETINGS OF THE BRITISH ASSOCIATION

Sir Charles Grant Robertson has chosen for his presidential address to the Section of Educational Science a subject in full accord with the special nature of the centenary meetings of the British Association, namely, "Educational Development: 1831 and 1931: A Centenary Retrospect and a Forecast." The address is to be delivered in the Great Hall of the university on the morning of September 24. Dr. E. Deller will follow with a paper on "London as a Pioneer in University Education," and in the discussion afterwards Sir Frank Heath, Sir Robert Blair, Sir Philip Hartog, Sir William Beveridge, Sir John Gilbert, and the Reverend Scott Lidgett will take part.

On the second morning two subjects, Imperial in nature, will be considered: "The Establishment of a Central Institute for Imperial Education," and "The Education of Backward Peoples." Lord Eustace Percy, Professor F. Clarke and Mr. F. H. C. Butler will give papers on the former, and Sir Michael Sadler, Dr. Maxwell Garnet, Sir Percy Nunn, and Major A. G. Church will speak in the discussion. Papers on the latter subject will be read by Mr. S. Rivers Smith, Major H. A. Harman, and Dr. A. R. Paterson, and in the discussion the Honorable Hugh A. Wyndham, Lord Raglan, Mr. A. Victor Murray, Mr. C. W. Hobley, and Miss M. F. Perham will speak.

The next session is to be devoted largely to problems connected with school clinics and child guidance. Three papers are to be given: Dr. G. A. Auden will deal with "The Maladjusted Child," Dr. W. Moodie will follow with "Environmental Factors in Maladjustment," and Dr. A. Macrae will give the third paper on "Psychological Examination as an Aid to Vocational Adjustment." Dr. C. W. Kimmins, Dr. Emanuel Miller, Dr. J. R. Rees, Dr. C. L. C. Burns, Dr. R. G. Gordon and Mr. D. T. John will also state their views. The session will close with a paper and discussion on "Eugenics in Education." Professor R. Ruggles Gates is reading the paper, and Professor Julian S. Huxley, Professor E. W. MacBride, and Sir Arthur Thomson will take part in the discussion.

At the final session "School Broadcasting" will be dealt with by Mr. Frank Roscoe and Lord Eustace Percy. There will be an appropriate demonstration, and Sir Walford Davies will open the discussion and Miss Mary Somerville will answer questions. A paper on "Adult Education Broadcasting," by Professor Winifred Cullis, will follow, and Mr. C. A. Siepman will take part in the discussion and questioning.

The reports of three special committees will be presented during the meeting. Sir Percy Nunn and Mr. G. W. Olive will report on "General Science in Schools with Special Reference to Biology"; Sir John Russell and Mr. C. E. Browne will present a report on "Education for Life Overseas," and Sir Richard Gregory and Mr. J. L. Holland will deal with the report of the Committee on Educational and Documentary Films.

EDUCATIONAL NOTES AND NEWS

The Rev. W. C. Martin has been elected by the board of trustees of Murphy Collegiate Institute, Tennessee, to succeed the Rev. B. Lloyd Black as president of the school.

The Rev. Joseph S. Dinneen, S.J., formerly vice-president of the Jesuit novitiate of St. Andrew-on-Hudson, has assumed the presidency of St. Peter's College, Jersey City. He was appointed some time ago to the post by General Wlodimirus Ledochowski, head of the Jesuits in Rome. He succeeds the Rev. Joseph J. O'Reilly.

In view of the approaching retirement of the chief librarian of the National Library of Scotland, Dr. William Kirk Dickson, the trustees of the National Library announce the appointment as his successor of Dr. Henry William Meikle, at present keeper of manuscripts in the National Library. Dr. Meikle will be succeeded as keeper of manuscripts by Mr. Marryat Scott

Dobie, an assistant in the library. Both appointments have been approved by the treasury and will come into effect when Dr. Dickson retires on November 24.

IN the School of Education of the Pennsylvania State College the following appointments are announced: As professor of educational administration and assistant director of correspondence instruction, Dr. Frank H. Koos, for nine years assistant superintendent of schools in Winston-Salem, North Carolina; as assistant professor of psychology, Dr. Robert G. Bernreuter, of Stanford University; as assistant professor of music education, Miss Willa C. Williammee, recently of New York University and for several years an instructor in the Penn State summer session; the following promotions have also been approved: Dr. F. A. Butler, from assistant professor to associate professor of education; Dr. George W. Hartmann, from assistant professor to associate professor of educational psychology; George J. Free, from instructor to assistant professor of nature education; Miss Edith V. Harding, from instructor to assistant professor of home economics; Hummel Fishburn, from instructor to assistant professor of music education; William M. Lepley, from assistant to instructor in psychology.

PROFESSOR ALEXANDER STEWART FERGUSON, Regius professor of logic and philosophy at Aberdeen University, Scotland, and Dr. Brand Blanshard, of Swarthmore College, will be visiting professors in the department of philosophy at Columbia University during the next academic year. Dr. L. Susan Stebbing, reader in philosophy at Bedford College for Women at the University of London, will be visiting professor at Barnard College.

DR. B. M. BOWEN, of Scarritt College, Nashville, has been elected to the faculty of Candler School of Theology, Emory University, to succeed Dr. W. A. Shelton as professor of Hebrew and Old Testament literature.

NEW appointments to the faculty of Colby College include for next year: Hans Christian Thory, associate professor of Latin; Charles Manning, instructor in English; Frederick Martin Phelps, instructor in business administration; Joseph Selwyn Ibbotson, librarian; and John White Thomas, director of music.

DR. M. M. CHAMBERS, formerly assistant professor of political science in the Oregon State College at Corvallis and recently assistant in school administration at the Ohio State University, has accepted appointment for 1931–1932 as chairman of the department of social sciences in the Teachers' College of Kansas City, Missouri.

DR. RAYMOND E. MURPHY, recently head of geography and geology at Concord Teachers College, West Virginia, has been appointed assistant professor of economic geography at the Pennsylvania State College.

DR. CHARLES MCNEIL, senior physician in the Royal Edinburgh Hospital for Sick Children, has been appointed to the newly founded Edward Clark chair of child life and health at the University of Edinburgh.

PROFESSOR MAURICE A. BLAKE, chairman of the council of athletics of Rutgers University, will be the head of a newly combined department of student health, physical instruction and intercollegiate athletics.

MR. L. N. HELSBY has been appointed lecturer in economics at Durham Colleges. During the last year he has been assistant lecturer in economics at Exeter University College.

THE REV. NORMAN WALKER PORTEOUS has been appointed to the chair of Hebrew and Oriental languages in the University of St. Andrews in place of the late Professor Alexander Reid Gordon.

PROFESSOR BERNADOTTE E. SCHMITT, of the department of history of the University of Chicago, is to serve during 1931–32 as professor of the Graduate Institute of International Studies, the seat of which is at Geneva, Switzerland. The institute was founded in 1927 to promote advanced study of present-day international questions.

MR. HARRY C. HAWKINS, for the past year professor of foreign trade at the University of Oregon, has resigned to accept a position as economic adviser in the Department of State.

MAYOR CERMAK has appointed Dr. Leonard D. White, professor of public administration in the University of Chicago, a member of the Civil Service Commission of the City of Chicago. He is a trustee of the National Institute of Public Administration and of the Bureau of Public Personnel Administration.

MR. FREDERICK DIELMAN has resigned as art director of Cooper Union after being associated with that organization for thirty-six years. Mr. Austin Purves, who has been instructor at the National Academy of Design for the past two years, will succeed Mr. Dielman.

MRS. GEORGE C. MANGOLD, of Los Angeles, California, has been appointed chairman of the Child Welfare Committee of the National League of Women Voters. Mrs. Mangold will be in charge of the league's child welfare program in the state and local branches and will advise on the legislative program. Maternity and child care, one of the major legislative interests of the league, fall within the scope of this committee.

PLANNING to utilize his annual vacation trip for gathering of information on foreign trade, David E. Faville, dean of the School of Business Administration of the University of Oregon, sailed on August 1 from Vancouver, B. C., to Kobe, Yokohama, Nagasaki and Shanghai. Each year Dean Faville takes a similar trip.

THE death is announced of Professor Horace A. Hollister, for twenty-six years until his retirement in 1928 professor of education at the University of Illinois.

W. F. TREUB, formerly professor of economics in the University of Amsterdam, and Netherlands Minister of Finance from 1912 to 1918, died on July 24 at the age of seventy-two years.

ARTHUR GEORGE PESKETT, a life fellow and former tutor of Magdalene College, Cambridge, died on July 26.

SHERMAN DAY THACHER, founder of the Thacher School in Ojai Valley, California, one of the West's leading preparatory schools for boys, died on August 6.

THE American Country Life Association opened its fourteenth annual conference at Cornell University on August 17. Dr. Albert R. Mann, provost of the university and former dean of the College of Agriculture, welcomed more than 200 delegates from all parts of the country. Dr. Bailey, chairman of President Theodore Roosevelt's original Country Life Commission, held to his thesis that development of the individual is the goal of country life. Governor Roosevelt spoke on Wednesday night and Frank O. Lowden, former Governor of Illinois, spoke on Thursday. Forums are being conducted on county organization and management, under the chairmanship of Robert H. Tucker, dean of Washington and Lee University: Village and township government, E. C. Branson, professor of rural social economics, University of North Carolina; taxation, C. R. White, president of the New York State Farm Bureau Federation; public education, Francis B. Haas, president of State Teachers College, Bloomsburg, Pa.; public health and welfare, David H. Holbrook, secretary of the National Social Work Council, New York, and rural planning, C. E. Ladd, deputy commissioner of the Department of Conservation, Albany.

THE Institute of International Relations for Educators was held at Haverford College, June 22 to July 3, under the auspices of the American Friends Service Committee. There was an attendance of a hundred and forty, although this was the first such conference held by the committee. Full-time courses were given by Dr. Herbert Fraser, Swarthmore College; Edward W. Evans, the University of Pennsylvania; Henry Cadbury, Bryn Mawr, and Dr. Leyton Richards, of Carrs Lane Church, Birmingham, England. Other lecturers included Professor William H. Kilpatrick, Columbia University; Sidney Fay, Harvard University; Augustus O. Thomas, president of the World Federation of Education Associations, and Agnes McPhail, only woman member of the Canadian Parliament.

COLGATE UNIVERSITY, of Hamilton, New York, will receive $50,000 under the will of the late Henry Thompson, attorney. The bequest was made for the creation of an endowment fund. Five years ago Mr. Thompson made a similar bequest to establish scholarships under his name.

A GIFT of $20,000 to the University of Cincinnati to establish four scholarship funds is made by the will of the late Mrs. Blanche

Cleneay Webb, widow of William A. Webb, president of the Hunnewell Soap Company.

Colby College has been left a bequest of $10,000 under the will of the late Waldo E. Pratt, of Wellesley, Massachusetts. Other educational institutions mentioned in his will include Northfield Schools, Northfield, Massachusetts; Good Will Home, Hinckley, Maine; Berry School, Inc., Mt. Berry, Georgia.

The will of the late Edward W. Howe, Dorchester, Massachusetts, leaves $5,000 to the president and fellows of Middlebury College, for its general purposes. It also leaves $1,000 each to the Appalachian Club and to the Society of Civil Engineers.

Construction is about to be started on a new dormitory, to cost approximately $92,000, for the Evanston campus of Northwestern University. The building when completed will accommodate forty-five persons and will be used exclusively by the Austin scholars and their proctors and faculty advisers.

The new Library Commission of South Carolina, established by the Legislature, providing for the ways and means of maintaining its public libraries and for the undertaking to stimulate and develop public libraries, especially in rural districts, has been organized. The state formerly was under public school library supervision both for workers and for support. By this new plan the Board of Education is separated from such jurisdiction.

Operation of the act passed by the last California Legislature, providing a fund through which dependents of veterans who were killed in action or died in service during the war can continue their education, will begin on August 16, according to George M. Stout, secretary of the Veterans' Welfare Board. The board is in charge of the administration of the act, which provides that applicants for educational aid must be over sixteen and not more than twenty-one years of age, must be children of deceased veterans and must have resided in the state for five years previous to filing application.

The Senate of Texas has passed, and the House has favorably reported, an appropriation of $16,000 to provide for the operation of the new Child Welfare Division of the State Board of Control effective on September 1.

The establishment of a national minimum standard for child labor is treated in a special bulletin of the Children's Bureau, publishing findings of the White House conference committee on vocational guidance and child labor. Night work would be barred for boys and girls of 16 or 17 with entrance prohibited into occupations known to be physically or morally hazardous. A maximum work week of 44 hours in eight-hour days was recommended. No child under 16 should be permitted to leave school to go to work. Regulation of child labor by the states was described as "slow and uneven and the cause of grave injustice."

At the Los Angeles meeting of the Department of Visual Instruction of the National Education Association the following resolution was passed: "That the Department of Visual Instruction of the National Education Association earnestly recommends that a course in visual and other sensory aids in teaching be required of all persons preparing for the profession of teaching, and that Teacher Training Institutions in every state be requested to organize and offer such courses, beginning with the scholastic year of 1931–1932."

The London Teachers Association has issued its annual "Register of Recommended Hotels, Boarding Houses, and Apartments for 1931." The addresses in it have all been recommended by members of that association. The booklet can be obtained from the offices of the London Teachers Association, 11, Pilgrim Street, E.C.4.

A number of students from St. Andrews University, representative of the various years and faculties, left home on August 20 for a tour of the eastern states of the Dominion of Canada, under arrangements made by the Canadian Overseas Education League and the University Court. The party will sail in the *Empress of Australia,* and at Cherbourg they will be joined by the Canadian students who recently visited St. Andrews and by various other Canadian parties. Quebec will be reached by August 27, and the party will go by special train direct to Montreal, where the program is in the hands of Lieutenant-Colonel Wilfrid Bovey, of McGill University. From Ottawa the party will go to Toronto, where the arrangements are being made by Miss Rhoda Howe, of the Overseas Education League. By a happy coincidence the Canadian National Exhibition

takes place at Toronto during the visit of the St. Andrews students. From Toronto a visit will be paid to Niagara Falls. Leaving Toronto on September 12, the lake steamer will take the party to Kingston, where Queen's University will be visited, after which the lake journey will be continued by way of the Thousand Islands to Montreal. The party will sail in the *Duchess of Bedford* down the St. Lawrence River to Quebec, where two days are to be spent. Mr. E. W. Beatty, the president of the Canadian Pacific Railway and Chancellor of McGill University, has arranged to entertain the party at dinner in the Château Frontenac on the last night of the tour. They will sail for Glasgow by the *Melita* on September 19. The party numbers about 20 (including supervisors), and is in charge of Professor John Read, professor of chemistry in the United College, St. Andrews. The organization of the tour is in charge of Mr. David J. B. Ritchie, assistant registrar.

A report issued by the British Commission on Educational and Cultural Films points out, according to the London *Times,* that though the commission has not yet completed its labors it has arrived at the conclusion that the following provisions will be indispensable if the scheme which it is preparing for submission to the government is to work satisfactorily: (*a*) That it must be adequately financed, either by the government, by a university, or by a substantial endowment from trust funds; (*b*) that it must be in close touch with film-producing firms, with whom it will collaborate, without being in their hands; (*c*) that it must be able to undertake for the government any certification of films as educational, which the government may sponsor, whether national or international, and its imprimateur must be based on an expert review of the films presented to it; and (*d*) the provision of adequate premises, including a demonstration theater. The commission was established in November, 1929, by the unanimous vote of more than a hundred educational and scientific bodies, which felt that the film was a powerful instrument in national life which should be used constructively in the interest of education in the widest sense. The commission began its work without funds but with the cordial support of the government departments concerned with the subject, most of whom are represented by a responsible officer on the commission, and also of the Federation of British Industries.

The *Journal* of the American Medical Association reports that following an investigation in Lanarkshire schools by the Department of Health for Scotland on milk consumption and the growth of school children, it was decided that the influence of the addition of milk to the diet of school children is reflected in a definite increase in the rate of growth both in height and weight; that there is no obvious or constant difference in this respect between boys and girls, and that there is little evidence of definite relation between the age of the children and amount of improvement. The investigation is said to be the first in which a government department made itself responsible for a daily milk supply to 10,000 children. The number of children under observation was 20,000, of whom 5,000 received raw milk, 5,000 pasteurized, and the remaining 10,000 were used as controls. The milk supplied was grade A, each child receiving three fourths of a pint daily. Sixty-seven schools were included in the investigation, the selection of representative children being left to the teachers, the age group including those of from 5 to 12 years. Cards were printed in distinctive colors for the children receiving raw milk, for those receiving pasteurized milk and for those used as controls. As each child was weighed and measured at the beginning of the investigation, the results were added to the cards, which, at the conclusion of the investigation, were sent to the department of health for statistical analysis. The measuring and weighing required the full time of five physicians and seventeen nurses.

According to *Nature,* the report of a British consultative committee, under the chairmanship of Sir W. H. Hadow, which was appointed by the Board of Education to inquire into the courses of study suitable for children (other than children in infants' departments) up to the age of eleven years, with special reference to the needs of children in rural areas, has just been published under the title of "The Primary School." The report may be regarded as the logical complement to the consultative committee's report on the "Education of the Adoles-

cent" (1926) (Hadow Report), dealing as it does with the upper stage of primary education. This important period in the development of children has, up to the present, been comparatively neglected by physiologists and psychologists. Recognizing this fact, the Consultative Committee obtained memoranda on the physical growth and mental development of children up to the age of eleven years from Professor H. A. Harris and Professor Cyril Burt. The data contained in these memoranda in addition to administrative problems included questions of the internal organization of primary schools on the problem of retarded children at the primary stage of education, dealing especially with the chief causes of retardation, are discussed. The views of the committee on the general problem of the curriculum for children up to the age of eleven are given. The sections on the "Study of Nature," and the memorandum on the anatomical and physiological characteristics and development of children between the ages of seven and eleven, by Professor H. A. Harris, and that on the mental characteristics of such children, by Professor Cyril Burt, are of special interest.

DISCUSSION

JOLTING THE COLLEGES

Mr. William McAndrew is to be sincerely thanked for stating, with all the authority of his brilliant reputation, the educationist attitude towards colleges and universities. Progressive college teachers will heartily agree with many of his dicta. All children and youth should have equal educational opportunities. The true democracy should give every potential citizen a chance to attain the highest degree of mental, moral and physical development of which he is capable. It should furnish facilities for ascertaining both the aptitudes and the inherent limitations of individual cases and guiding their efforts into the channels which promise the greatest individual fruitfulness. The school system, taken as a whole, should offer to every student the type of instruction most suitable to his individual needs.

It is almost incredible that the educationists, after analyzing the need so clearly, should nevertheless still confuse the idea of equal educational opportunity with that of equal educational capacity. It is now widely recognized that the attempt of the American school system to create all children equal was a blunder of cosmic magnitude. It bullied, brutalized and all but wrecked millions of subnormal children and quenched the brighter lights of the gifted few by its uniform mediocrity. Yet Mr. McAndrew quotes, with apparent approval, Professor Henry Morrison's statement that "any one can be taught any thing"—one of the many *reductiones ad absurdum* of behaviorism which are fast driving that curious cult of pseudo-psychology from the realm of serious thought.

Democracy has elsewhere been defined as "that form of government which most promptly proves that all men are *not* created equal."[1] The most rapid developments and crystallizations of class distinction—rich and poor, landlord and serf, intellectual and ignorant—take place under the freest forms of government. Democracy, therefore, should recognize not only the wide variations in the types of intellectual endowment but also the immense individual differences in total intellectual and physical capacity, and try to meet the needs of all classes. The desperate and utterly illogical attempt of American education to compel a thousand varieties of seed to bring forth the same kind of fruit has caused its most lamentable failures.

One hardly expects so large a mind as Mr. McAndrew's to be bothered by the bane of consistency, but lesser intelligences can not forbear noting certain discrepancies. He freely admits, for example, that professional schools must "pick and choose their boys and rigorously weed them out when deemed unable to reach a professional standard (after telling us that 'anybody can learn anything!'). . . . The public must be protected from unsafe railroads and falling bridges." But he denies the special functions for which colleges of liberal arts were originally founded. They, it seems, must be the dumping ground for those who can not get by anywhere else. If they can not learn what the college offers, it is the fault of the professors—or they should be given something which they

[1] *The Independent*, July 11, 1925, p. 39.

can learn and passed on with a degree, as per usual. Ideally, all of our young people should have degrees. The next step is to give them all Ph.D.'s. Even this may not be the ultimate *reductio ad absurdum* of modern educational logic.

How often must college authorities point out that the "goodness" of the rejected applicant for admission is not in question? How about the "goodness" of would-be engineers who have no aptitude for mechanics? It seems pitiable that Mr. McAndrew should raise again this oft refuted and utterly absurd misconception. Is he not content that Wisconsin has hardly yet recovered from the effects of flunking young Lindbergh?

Liberal arts colleges were founded to train certain types of leaders. The theory of educational equality denies not only their function but the very need of leadership. Mr. McAndrew's illustration that many small lights are more useful than a few great ones is patently specious. A uniformly diffused luminosity, without point or shadow, would be more devastating to human progress than total darkness. Let there be, by all means, as much light as possible, and as widely diffused. But there is constant need for greater lights—the sun and the moon, with stars of many magnitudes—to serve as standards and incentives.

The fight to maintain reasonable standards for college degrees is daily becoming more critical. A college degree should mean something. The educationists would reduce it to a mere mental and moral birth-certificate. Alumni should not—and generally do not—claim any inherent mental or moral superiority, but they should—and often do—command knowledge which may prove useful to their communities—knowledge which the average man has not had the inclination or capacity to attain. Alumni do not pretend to know everything, but they should—and often do—know where to find what they don't know. The colleges may be mistaken in their choice of subject-matter and faulty in their teaching methods, but they do honestly try to maintain standards which shall secure some approximation of the end to which they were established. And they do not try to keep out a single boy or girl who is inherently capable of even half way realizing their ideals.

Mr. McAndrew's inference that college professors are lazy and vicious, and chiefly interested in preserving a layer of superior persons calling themselves alumni, can not be too vigorously denied. Recent events have shown that large majorities of supposedly conservative faculties are capable of expressing liberal and even radical opinions, even to the point of risking their jobs. They never question the antecedents of their students. They pass every student who even approaches their standards. They work very hard to fill up the woeful gaps left by secondary education. And they are always fighting alumni who want them to pass unintellectual athletes.

Over and over again Mr. McAndrew refers scathingly to Princeton's "62.5 per cent." of rejectees. In the first place, Princeton passes no mental or moral judgment upon those who do not meet its own highly specialized requirements. In the second place, the application of this figure to the general college situation is a gross misrepresentation of the facts. Hardly ten per cent. of college students, on the whole, "flunk out" of school. They leave for a hundred other reasons. State universities do their darnedest to keep as many students as possible. Subfreshman classes, vocational advisers, readmission boards and a dozen other devices work overtime to coax, cajole, entice, beg and all but force weak students to remain.

It is complained that the colleges act as a sieve. All life is a sieve. Business, salesmanship, factories, trades and even vagabondage are sieves. In the very nature of things some go to the top and others to the bottom. The mesh of the college sieve has been made so fine that almost nothing but the most impalpable dust of sub-intelligence gets through.

College teachers would rejoice to see some indications, in their freshman classes, that secondary education is "not trifling at sloppy scholarship." But the fond hope that improved teaching technique would make possible the present over-loading of high-school curricula without any sacrifice of scholarship has not been realized. Many a college teacher who has followed the progress of his own children through high school knows that it is now possible for children to take long courses with passing grades and at graduation not remember

a single fact that was taught in some given course—not even that they had ever taken the course. This could not be done in the old high school.

The chief difference between bad high-school teaching and bad college teaching seems to be that the college teacher knows his stuff but not how to put it over while the high-school teacher has a technique of presentation with very little knowledge of the subject-matter. Colleges teach subject-matter but not the art of presentation. Normal schools train prospective teachers in the art of presenting what they don't know. You may take your choice.

As a matter of fact, the state universities are now doing pretty much what Mr. McAndrew demands of the liberal arts colleges. They take almost everything that comes. They offer a multiplicity of courses calculated to meet the needs of almost every type of endowment, save only the complete lack thereof. They maintain a complicated machinery of intelligence and aptitude tests, vocational advisers, etc., and try to consider individually the thousands who apply, shunting them to departments in which they will get the most good and do the least mischief. No professor who has labored and sweated through hundreds of hours of gratuitous committee work, at grievous sacrifice of his own teaching and research, can accept the implications of Mr. McAndrew's attack. And however diligently professors may work to find a place for every student in the university, they will never assent to Mr. McAndrew's denial of the specific function of the liberal arts college and open it up to general dumping.

We can not admit that every one should go to college, even in the ideal state. We can not all be kings and priests. Some of us must earn our daily bread by the sweat of our bodies as well as by the sweat of our brows—and this without the slightest inference of "superiority" or greater "goodness" on the part of those whose particular brain-kinks make them capable of specialized knowledge. Education, while realizing that some of us have ten talents, some five, and some one, should help every mother's son of us not to bury a single talent, whether we have many or few, but to cultivate them all to the general good. And not the least duty of education is to show the one-talent student how to put just as much goodness into life, and get just as much happiness out of it, as the proud possessor of a dozen degrees.

G. WAKEHAM

UNIVERSITY OF COLORADO

SPECIAL CORRESPONDENCE

EMPLOYMENT OF CORNELL GRADUATES

AN employment survey at Cornell University reveals that a majority of the members of the recent graduating class already have jobs and that the prospects for the others securing employment have improved during the past few weeks.

The large number of requests for engineering graduates from small concerns represented a marked change from the experience of previous years, when employment directors of large corporations absorbed practically the entire output of the engineering colleges at Cornell. For the first time in the experience of the placement bureau here, small concerns were able to compete for the services of the exceptional men, normally attracted to the larger corporations.

Of eighty-four seniors in the College of Mechanical Engineering at Cornell University, seventy-five, or 89.29 per cent., were able to find employment upon graduation. Two of these seventy-five will continue their studies at the Harvard Business School, but since it was necessary for them to be interviewed before being admitted to this graduate school, they were regarded as having accepted positions.

Of the entire class of eighty-four, that left only eight without work. Two of these men are foreign, and one other of the eight is a woman. The foreigners will in all probability return to their homes. The six remaining seem quite likely to find places before very much time has elapsed. One has stated that he is not seeking employment.

Salaries for beginners have not dropped, according to Professor J. R. Bangs, Jr., director of personnel, who has for the past several years

undertaken to establish an employment bureau for Cornell men in mechanical engineering. The average salary for a trained mechanical engineer is about $150 per month at the start.

Fifty per cent. of the graduates of the civil and electrical engineering colleges at Cornell are reported as already employed. This number is slightly less than last year, the decrease being largely among the electrical engineers. The reason ascribed for this condition is that a large number of electrical engineering students have specialized in communication, and that at present this field is somewhat inactive. However, recent inquiries point to a number of new jobs being available in this field. Extensive road-building operations and public works programs all over the country are absorbing graduates of the college of civil engineering.

Graduates in architecture had more trouble in finding jobs this year than ever before. In previous years entire classes have been placed several months before the completion of their work. This year most of the placements will occur during the summer and fall.

Candidates for teaching positions have been faced with more competition than ever before. The number placed was, however, much better than expected from indications of conditions at the beginning of the college year.

Graduates in the agricultural college applying for positions found not much change in conditions. Approximately three fourths of the seniors in that college have been placed. A small number of these will return to their own farms. Some will enter the teaching field, and others the dairy and fruit businesses. Many will enter the numerous scientific fields of activity. A large group this year is entering soil survey work, and others are going into extension.

In forestry and floriculture, fewer found employment than before, although the number of foresters who have jobs will be increased with civil service appointments which have not yet been made definite. Forestry graduates are usually slower than others in finding positions, because they must take civil service examinations and then await appointment.

Even in the law school, whose graduates do not have to find positions for more than a short period before entering business for themselves, more than two thirds have found employment that may, if they wish, be permanent.

On the whole, except in the teaching field, the outlook on employment for college men, according to men at Cornell who have familiarized themselves with the situation, is a favorable one, and much better than was expected at the beginning of the college year.

L. C. B.

QUOTATIONS

THE SCHOOL BUDGET

The budget prepared by the Board of Education for 1932 is more than one-fourth of the city's annual outlay for all purposes. The estimated increase over 1931 is nearly six millions ($5,953,963.14), the city contributing $4,200,000 more and the State and Federal Governments approximately $1,700,000 more. If the estimated expenditures for school sites and buildings, interest on bonds, instalments paid as the city's share of the teachers' retirement fund, with money spent by other departments for the benefit of the pupils—as the Health Department and the Department of Water Supply and Electricity—are added, the total is pushed up to $212,000,000. This sum is one-third of the city's total budget and $9,600,000 larger than the total estimated expenditure of 1931 for school purposes.

Increases in the school budget proper are accounted for almost entirely by the additional teaching positions required by reason of increased attendance, especially in the high schools. Fifty years ago the legality of the high school was still being discussed—and New York had none except the preparatory departments of the City College and Normal College. It was the exceptional boy or girl, even a few years ago, who went beyond the elementary school. Now "it is the exceptional boy or girl who does not go to high school." Moreover, the depression has caused larger numbers to continue in school, since fewer opportunities are open to them in industry and business. It is figured that the increased requirement for the day high schools alone will be more than $3,-000,000. This does not include the junior high schools, which are classed with the elementary schools in the budget.

In the elementary schools, while no more enter than in earlier years, more remain, with a resultant growth in the upper grades. The increase in the number of elementary teaching positions is due in part to the commendable reduction of oversize classes. The compulsory continuation schools, it is anticipated, will show a falling off in registration, because fewer young people will be finding employment and so will appear as full-time pupils, whether in the upper grades or in high school. This is one of the few decreases. Another, the only one to prompt question, is the reduction of the amount proposed for the evening elementary schools. It would seem that there should be special support for these schools in times of increased idleness.

It is to be said that the budget as presented is a clear and succinct document. Salary increases are for the most part mandatory, and the increase in the number of teachers is made necessary by the larger number of pupils and classes. There is every indication of a purpose to keep the schools up to their normal standard.—*The New York Times.*

EDUCATIONAL RESEARCH AND STATISTICS

CORRELATES OF INTELLIGENCE IN COLLEGE STUDENTS

INTELLIGENCE has been correlated so many times and with so many things that it may seem that there is nothing new under the sun to be said about it. But since the college at which this study was made has not contributed much of the material used in previous investigations, and since the experimental method requires the collection and consideration of a large amount of evidence, it may be of interest to review the data collected here.

One part of this study was suggested by the numerous investigations conducted by Terman and others, of children's intelligence as related to the occupational grouping of their parents. It was decided to study the intelligence of Barnard College students as measured by the Thorndike intelligence examination, in relation to the occupations in which the fathers of the students were engaged. The problem was to discover if the general impression, backed up by the results of investigations in secondary schools, that children of fathers engaged in professional pursuits tended to be superior intellectually, held good at the college level and in a college such as Barnard, in which approximately two thirds of the students come from public high schools.

Another part of the study was to discover whether there was a tendency for bright students to select particular subjects, such as the sciences, for majors, and for mediocre students to select certain other subjects. A third problem was to find the correlation between intelligence score at entrance to college and earnings after graduation.

The data for the study were furnished by the members of the seven classes at Barnard College who were given the Thorndike intelligence examination at the beginning of their freshman year. These were the classes graduating in 1926, 1927, 1928, 1929, 1930, 1931, and the present seniors. The classes were not studied separately but as a whole. Transfer students from other colleges are not required to take the entrance intelligence examination, so this excludes about twenty per cent. of the graduates in the seven classes. Also, information in regard to the father's occupation was not obtained in some cases. Leaving out those who had to be omitted because information was lacking on one or the other of the points studied, there are 855 cases in the study of fathers' occupations and intelligence test scores, and 1,118 cases in the study of majors and intelligence test scores.

Reports of earnings were available for three of the classes, those of 1926, 1927, and 1928—231 graduates in all. Many students from these classes were going on with graduate or professional study, and so could not be included in the earnings report.

Intelligence Score and Father's Occupation

The Thorndike intelligence examination is in three parts and requires two hours and fifty minutes of actual working time. It includes several hundred questions and has a maximum score of 120. Table I gives a summary of the results found in the study of intelligence scores in the seven Barnard classes, correlated with the occupations of the fathers.

TABLE I

Father's Occupation

	Number of cases	Median	Q	Range
Professional	240	81.82	7.27	48–113
Business and technical	533	81.55	7.05	45–112
Skilled mechanical	38	81.67	7.47	47–96
Semi-skilled	41	79.64	7.29	59–106
Unskilled	3	75.33		61–85
Total	855			

The median psychological scores for the first three groups are very nearly identical, varying by only a fraction of a point. The professional group, as we have been led to expect, heads the list, but by only .15 of a point. At the University of Buffalo it was found that the tendency was for the children of skilled mechanics to excel the children of business men in scholarship, and at Barnard we find that the tendency is for these children to excel those from the business group in psychological score. However, the very great difference in numbers in the two groups is much more significant than the slight difference in score, a difference of .12. At Buffalo, the numbers in the two groups, business and skilled or semi-skilled, are very nearly the same, while at Barnard there are 533 in the business group as against 79 in the skilled and semi-skilled group. This would seem to signify that only those of outstanding ability in the latter group, as compared with others of their economic class, come to Barnard College. It is probably true that others of this skilled and semi-skilled group, who have the ability to do the quality of college work demanded at Barnard, are prevented by financial considerations from coming, and it is probably also true, as suggested with reference to Buffalo, that the larger amount of money available for education in the business group is responsible for the fact that some students from that group are in college despite a lack of interest in scholarship.

The number coming from the unskilled group is negligible. There is in addition the chance that the fathers of these three students, by reason of language difficulty or other circumstance, may not be in the economic class to which their intelligence would entitle them.

TABLE II

Professional

Father's occupation	Number of cases	Median	Q	Range
Teacher	39	85.75	7.22	53–102
Engineer	42	84.29	5.59	67–113
Architect	10	83.33	4.69	65–85
Writer	13	82.50	9.15	60–102
Lawyer	49	81.39	6.17	60–102
Dentist	15	79.50	8.69	58–104
Scientist	4	78.50		75–82
Physician	49	78.41	10.61	50–104
Clergyman	19	76.88	9.17	48–104
Total	240	81.82	7.27	48–113

Reference to Table II shows that the children of fathers in four professions, teaching, engineering, architecture, and writing or editorial work, are above the median for the group (81.82), while the children of the other six professional groups are below the median. The table as a whole bears some resemblance to the Army Alpha hierarchy of occupations.

Intelligence Score and College Major

Miss Rogers in a study of four classes at Goucher College found a marked tendency to select the humanistic studies. She says, "It is especially noteworthy that relatively few women are concentrating in the natural sciences and that almost half are majoring in the social sciences." The classes studied at Goucher were those graduating in 1922, 1923, 1924 and 1925, so that the study at Barnard begins where the Goucher study leaves off. In the last class studied at Goucher, 16 per cent. were majoring in foreign languages, 19.8 per cent. in English,

TABLE III

FREQUENCIES OF SCORES FOR STUDENTS SPECIALIZING IN FOUR FIELDS

Barnard College
Classes of 1926–1932

Thorndike scores	Foreign languages	English	Social sciences	Natural sciences
	Per cent.	Per cent.	Per cent.	Per cent.
30– 39	0	0	0	0
40– 49	1	0	0	1
50– 59	3	2	3	2
60– 69	20	10	14	11.5
70– 79	30	30	28.5	32
80– 89	34	36	37.5	33
90– 99	10	15	15	16.5
100–109	2	6	2	4
110–120	0	1	0	0
Cases	241	269	318	266

45.2 per cent. in social sciences, and 18.8 per cent. in natural sciences. At Barnard the students are divided much more evenly in the four fields, the percentages being: foreign languages, 21.5 per cent.; English, 24 per cent.; social sciences, 28.4 per cent.; natural sciences, 23.8 per cent. Education is included in the social sciences at Goucher, and that fact may account for the large proportion of students listed as majoring in social sciences. At Barnard, students do not major in education, since they may take courses in that subject at Teachers College during their junior and senior years, and since many students, who intend to teach, now plan for a master's degree in education after the completion of their undergraduate course.

Miss Rogers thought her data suggested that, while there was much overlapping between the four groups studied, the natural sciences tended to select a superior set of students. The median score attained by the four groups at Barnard varies by only a little over three points. The median for the majors in English is 82.22 (Q 6.81), for natural sciences 81.25 (Q 6.79), for social sciences 81.17 (Q 7.21), and for foreign languages 79.13 (Q 7.87). The fact that the students majoring in foreign languages are often the children of foreign parentage, and that they may make a lower psychological score while keeping up a scholarship average in the subject in which they have a special advantage, perhaps accounts for the somewhat lower score for foreign language majors. At Buffalo it was found that the students of foreign parentage were likely to be low in vocabulary and in speed of work, both of which are important factors of intelligence examinations.

Listing the majors according to a somewhat

TABLE IV

MAJORS

	Number of cases	Median	Q	Range
English	269	82.22	6.81	49–113
Natural science	266	81.25	6.79	43–112
Social science	318	81.17	7.21	53–108
Foreign language	241	79.13	7.87	45–108
Total	1094	80.96	6.64	43–113

Omitting religion, art and music (24 cases).

TABLE V

HUMANITIES

	Number of cases	Median	Q	Range
Philosophy	14	81.66	9.17	50–97
Art	17	77.50	9.31	71–99
Religion	1	85.00		
Greek and Latin	53	77.75	7.70	53–102
Romance	164	79.22	7.83	45–108
German	24	82.00	11.07	51–92
English	269	82.22	6.81	49–113
Music	6	75.00		61–89
Total	548	80.69	7.47	45–108

TABLE VI

SOCIAL SCIENCES

	Number of cases	Median	Q	Range
Psychology	37	83.25	6.62	61–100
Economics and sociology	77	80.91	6.59	53–103
Government	35	79.58	8.66	60–103
History	152	80.74	7.32	55–108
Anthropology	3	92.66		79–104
Total	304	81.15	7.21	53–108

TABLE VII

Physical Sciences

	Number of cases	Median	Q	Range
Mathematics	128	82.75	6.70	63–112
Physics	4	95.25		87–104
Chemistry	73	78.55	7.48	43–105
Geology	9	79.37	6.09	74–99
Total	214	80.89	6.85	43–112

TABLE VIII

Biological Sciences

	Number of cases	Median	Q	Range
Botany	22	78.75	7.88	59–92
Zoology	30	83.57	6.55	48–105
Total	52	81.67	7.9	48–105

different classification—humanities, social sciences, physical sciences and biological sciences—we find still less variation between the groups but interesting differences within the groups. The highest median score for the four groups is 81.67 for biological sciences (52 cases, Q 7.9), the lowest, 80.69 for humanities (548 cases, Q 7.47). Considering the individual subjects within the groups, the four physics majors have a median score of 95.25 (the highest median score made in any subject), and the three anthropology majors a median score of 92.66. The 30 zoology majors maintain a median score of 83.57 (Q 6.55), the 37 psychology majors a score of 83.25 (Q 6.62), and the 128 mathematics majors a score of 82.75 (Q 6.7); all these are higher than the median for their particular group whether physical, biological or social science, and all are higher than for any subject listed among the humanities (excepting one student who majored in religion, with a score of 85).

In the social science group the students majoring in the closely related fields of history, government, and economics and sociology make median scores centering around 80, while the psychology and anthropology majors are noticeably higher. In the physical science group the mathematics and physics majors are considerably higher than the majors in chemistry and geology, and in the biological sciences the majors in zoology are nearly four points ahead of the botany majors. This division within the groups themselves suggests that certain sciences attract superior students.

The lowest scores were made by students majoring in Greek and Latin (53 cases, median 77.75, Q 7.7), art (17 cases, median 77.5, Q 9.31), and music (6 cases, median 75). It is quite probable that a student might be able to excel in such studies as music and art without being able to make a high score in this examination. Probably, too, interest and excellence in music, art and the classics depend more upon the emotions than upon the intelligence.

Intelligence Score and Earnings

All the correlations of intelligence score and earnings are too low to be statistically important, but are included in this report, since we were trying to see whether or not there was any correlation at all between these two factors.

Fifty-nine members of the class of 1928 reported, for 1928–29, earnings ranging from $825 to $2,100, with the median at $1,419.64. The correlation of intelligence score and salary is $-.324 \pm .063$. The graduates who were making the most money in their first year out of college were not, in general, the students who had made high psychological scores. The fact that those who were going on with graduate study were not included in the report probably eliminates many of the higher intelligence scores. A recent study at Yale has indicated that men going into business receive in their first years out of college a much greater financial return than do the men going into the professions. The results of this study would imply that the same thing is true of Barnard graduates.

Ninety-one members of the class of 1927 reported earnings ranging from $900 to $2,800, with the median at $1,758.93. With this class which had been out of college two years the correlation of intelligence score and earnings is $+.016 \pm .071$. This means that there is practically no relation at all between intelligence and earnings for this group.

Eighty-one members of the class of 1926 reported earnings of from $837 to $4,200, with the median at $1,831.25. Here the correlation of intelligence score and earnings is $+.126 \pm .070$. So with this class out of college three years there begins to be a slight positive correlation between intelligence score in college and earnings after graduation. We may assume that the correlation will increase, but we have no way of telling what the limit will be or when it will be reached.

In a study of the earnings of Barnard alumnae as reported in 1929 it was found that the median earnings for those with the A.B. degree were $2,377, for those with the A.M. or M.S., $2,968, and for those with the Ph.D. degree, $3,590. An investigation conducted by Miss Elliott and Miss Manson, of the earnings of college women in the United States, showed the median for those with the A.B. degree to be $1,750, while for those with the Ph.D. the median was $3,150. In both of these studies the possible intelligence score can only be inferred. If graduate study requires a higher type of mind than undergraduate study, these figures indicate a positive relation between intelligence and earnings.

SUMMARY

The results of this study of Barnard graduates and students in seven classes may be stated as follows:

(1) No startling differences in intelligence test scores are found in the students from the five occupational groups, professional, business, skilled, semi-skilled and unskilled.

(2) The differences in numbers from each group are more significant than differences in intelligence scores. Ninety per cent. of Barnard students come from the professional and business classes.

(3) The students whose fathers are engaged in the professions of teaching, architecture, engineering and writing or editorial work rank highest in the Thorndike intelligence examination.

(4) The few students whose fathers are in the skilled occupations rank higher than those from the business group and higher than many in the professional group. The probable explanation of this is that only outstanding students come to Barnard from the skilled mechanical group.

(5) The students from the semi-skilled and unskilled groups rank somewhat lower than others in the intelligence examination.

(6) No large differences in median intelligence scores are found among the four groups of subjects in which students may major—humanities, social sciences, physical sciences and biological sciences.

(7) Certain subjects, as physics, anthropology, mathematics, zoology, psychology and English seem to select students of superior ability.

(8) Students majoring in art, music and the classics make median scores which are appreciably lower than the median for their group. This may be explainable by the fact that interest and excellence in these subjects may depend more upon the emotional make-up than upon the intellectual quality of the individual.

(9) For the first two years after graduation the correlation between earnings and intelligence is zero or less than zero. With the third year after graduation there begins to be a slight positive correlation between earnings and intelligence score, which we may assume will increase.

(10) It is probable that the professions attract graduates of the highest intelligence and that the financial rewards of such professional women are in the long run greater than for those in any other line of work.

FRANCES M. GILLIS

NEW EDUCATIONAL BOOKS

BENNETT, WENDELL CLARK. *Archaeology of Kauai.* Pp. iii + 156. 15 plates. 56 figures. Bernice P. Bishop Museum, Honolulu. Bulletin 80.

BIGELOW, HENRY B. *Oceanography.* Pp. vii + 263. Houghton Mifflin. $2.50.

CHRISTOPHERSON, ERLING, and EDWARD L. CAUM. *Vascular Plants of the Leeward Islands, Hawaii.* Pp. 41. 16 plates. 3 figures. Bernice P. Bishop Museum, Honolulu. Bulletin 81.

FITZPATRICK, F. BURKE. *Supervision of Elementary Schools.* Pp. 128. F. A. Owen Publishing Company.

GREGORY, HERBERT E. *Report of the Director for 1930.* Pp. 36. Bernice P. Bishop Museum, Honolulu. Bulletin 82.

HANDY, E. S. CRAIGHILL. *History and Culture in the Society Islands.* Pp. 110. 6 plates. 13 figures. Bernice P. Bishop Museum, Honolulu. Bulletin 79.

MEAD, MARGARET. *Social Organization of Manua.* Pp. 218. Bernice P. Bishop Museum, Honolulu. Bulletin 76.

National Committee on Standard Reports for Institutions of Higher Education. Suggested Forms for Financial Reports of Colleges and Universities. Pp. 87. Lloyd Morey, Chairman of Committee.

SCHOOL AND SOCIETY

EDITED BY J. McKEEN CATTELL

WITH WHICH IS COMBINED THE

EDUCATIONAL REVIEW

EDITED BY WILLIAM McANDREW

Volume 34 SATURDAY, AUGUST 29, 1931 Number 870

EDUCATION AND THE ECONOMIC DEPRESSION[1]

By Professor JOHN K. NORTON

TEACHERS COLLEGE, COLUMBIA UNIVERSITY

A RECENT newspaper report ascribes to Henry Ford the statement that business depressions are good for the country in that they constitute the only periods in which we do any thinking. It is my purpose this afternoon briefly to review certain sectors of the current American scene and to think through with you their meaning for education.

The school is a social institution. It does not work in a vacuum. It can be intelligently planned and properly administered only when considered in relation to the society which it serves.

The industrial revolution which began about a century ago and is still going on all about us is setting loose a train of forces which affect every phase of modern life. As a result of the application of scientific methods and the machine to production, the whole center of gravity of economics has been changed.

Let us recall that through the ages of man's upward struggle his principal aim has been to produce enough. The crying need of the eighteenth century in England was how to increase productive efficiency to a degree that a sufficient supply of the bare necessities of life might be produced. A principal purpose of Adam Smith's fundamental inquiry into the nature and causes of the wealth of nations was to point the way to increased production so that a considerable proportion of the British population might be lifted from a condition of serious deprivation.

And now with the twentieth century less than a third gone, the age-long quest of the race has been rewarded. Man in the United States can not only produce enough to meet his basic material needs, but is able to do it in a fraction of the time which he is able to work each day.

I recognize that there are many in the country to-day who are not getting all they need in the way of food, clothing, shelter and other basic commodities. But this is the result of a wasteful and unplanned economic system rather than basic inability to produce. The fact is that the farmers of the nation, even with their present inefficient methods, can grow and harvest more agricultural commodities than the nation can consume. Equally striking is the situation as it concerns manufacturing. One reliable economist has estimated that the manufacturing establishments of the nation even in the most prosperous years produce at but 72

[1] Address delivered at Seventeenth Annual Conference of Superintendents of Schools of Massachusetts, Bridgewater, Mass.

per cent of capacity, and that in periods such as the one we are now in, the ratio of actual to possible production is little over 50 per cent. Even more significant is the fact that most signs indicate that the reign of the machine has only just begun.

Let me invite your attention to a few facts given in a recent publication, "Insecurity in Industry," *The Annals of the American Academy of Political and Social Science, March, 1931, page 20.* A tractor now plows eight acres of soil in the time required for a man with a horse to plow one acre. Since 1910 agricultural output has increased 28 per cent with a labor force reduced 6 per cent. In the building industry, a power shovel will dig and load as much soil as four hundred men used to do. One man used to turn out 450 bricks in a day. Now a brick machine turns out 40,000 bricks in a day. In the boot and shoe industry, one shoe-making machine replaces from six to ten artisans. One cigar-making machine now turns out a quantity of cigars equivalent to the former production of fifteen men. Prior to 1910 all glass tubes were made by skilled glass blowers. To-day a machine does the work of 600 such artisans. One man used to saw a hundred feet of lumber a day. Now, with the aid of machines, he can saw ten thousand feet of lumber in a single day. Steel companies can now produce three times as much pig iron as in 1904, with the same force of men. These are but a few of many examples which might be cited. In the twenty years from 1899 to 1919 the production per wage earner increased 11 per cent. In the ten years 1919 to 1929, production per worker increased 53 per cent.

These things have all happened since the men in this room reached adulthood. Within three decades we have had changes which formerly were the work of centuries.

Thus far we have allowed the forces set into play by the machine to run riot. There has been but little effort to control these forces and to mitigate the severity with which they fall on the individual. If "canned" music throws thousands of musicians out of work, if the type-setter is first displaced by the linotype operator, who is in turn thrown out of employment by the invention of a still more advanced machine, we are perhaps sorry, but we leave it to the individual to take care of himself.

The present economic depression is the normal outgrowth of such an unplanned economic system. Can one imagine a more irrational situation than the one in which we now find ourselves? Here is a nation abundantly supplied with the natural resources and raw materials necessary to production—land, coal, oil, water-power, iron, and all the rest. We are in an extremely favorable position as to the implements of production. No nation has gone so far in applying the machine to industry and agriculture. We possess an abundant supply of labor, anxious to work, and more intelligent than any other large body of workers in the world. Our 125,000,000 people enjoy an annual income which in 1929 approximated ninety billions of dollars, which is roughly equivalent to that of all the other inhabitants of the globe. Their tremendous purchasing power and general desire to maintain a high standard of living make the American people the customer market *par excellence* of the world. But what are we doing with this unparalleled situation? Hundreds of factories are completely closed down, and thousands more running at a mere fraction of capacity. Thousands of farmers are unable to sell their products at a price sufficient to pay for their production. From five to six million workers are out of work, which means, if we consider their dependents, that some twenty million persons in the United States are a prey to all the demoralizing influences which trail in the wake of unemployment.

Abundantly supplied with the raw materials and implements of production, amply provided with competent labor, inhabited by a population constituting the world's greatest market, yet the nation continues in an economic impasse in which factory wheels do not turn, farms lie fallow, the unemployed continue idle and want even for food, and the legitimate wants of many millions are but partly satisfied.

Somebody has said that if the other planets are inhabited, there seems justification for believing that the earth is their lunatic asylum. The present situation in the United States flavors the remark with something more than humor.

But here is where we get back to Henry Ford. Undoubtedly, the economic dilemma in which the United States now finds itself is inspiring much hard thinking. Leaders in all walks of life are predicting dire consequences to our civilization if the forces turned loose by the industrial revolution continue to run riot. Dean Donham, of the Graduate School of Business Administration of Harvard University, opens his recent book, "Business Adrift," with this statement: "The recurrence of depressions and unemployment emergencies of anything like the serious nature of our current problem must be prevented if capitalistic civilization is to endure."

Although the remedies which are suggested for the future vary widely, all those which make a serious effort to go to the bottom of the difficulty agree that some form of social planning is essential if civilization is to escape the fate of Frankenstein. Otherwise, the tremendous size, the great complexity and the increasingly rapid pace of civilization will outrun our power to control the forces which have it within their power to destroy the very foundations of society.

What does all this mean for the school and for those who are in positions of educational leadership? One can not study the literature dealing with our great society without concluding that any effort toward social planning and economic regulation, adequate to control the forces which the machine age has turned loose, must lean heavily upon education, and upon a system of education which is far more extensive and dynamic than that now in operation.

Some one has said that the population of a nation may be divided into three groups, first a small class which makes things happen, second a larger class which watches things happen, and third a much larger class which has no idea as to what is happening. The remainder of this address will urge that we as educational leaders should equip ourselves to take our places in the ranks of those who *make things happen*.

If we, through education, are to play a major rôle in bringing about the economic adjustment and social planning which are essential if civilization is to avoid a collapse, we must become students of the society which the school seeks to serve. If the school is to play a major rôle in the coming decades it must take its cue from contemporary civilization and build its program with the demands of practical life clearly in mind. What are some of the facts of contemporary life which call for educational responses?

The first fact of contemporary life to which your attention is invited is that the environment of children in their out-of-school hours is becoming progressively less educative. President Hoover recognized the problem clearly in his introductory speech before the White House Conference when he said:

> In the last half a century we have herded 50,000,000 human beings into towns and cities where the whole setting is new to the race. We have created highly congested areas with a thousand changes resulting in the swift transition from a rural and agrarian people to an urban, industrial nation. Perhaps the widest range of difficulties with which we are dealing in the betterment of children grows out of this crowding into cities. Problems of sanitation and public health loom in every direction. Delinquency increases with congestion. Overcrowding produces disease and contagion. The child's natural play place is taken from him. His mind is stunted by the lack of imaginative surroundings and lack of contact with the fields, streams, trees and birds.

Let us consider some values which the typical farm child of a generation or two ago gained from his out-of-school environment. He gained a concrete, first-hand knowledge of work. He performed the chores with which the farm abounds. As soon as he was old enough, he aided in such fundamental farm operations as sowing, hoeing and harvesting. When the horses needed shoeing he drove with his father to the blacksmith shop and saw the glowing iron fashioned at the forge and fitted to the horse's foot. The milk bottle did not mark the limit of his knowledge as to the source of milk. He did not have to go to a zoo to see a cow. He knew all about their habits, and the chores connected with them from first-hand experience. Nearly every hour of the day brought him increased understanding of, and training for, life. He knew how real work was done, and learned how to do it.

Compare this situation with that of the child living in the congested city. There is much less in the typical urban community that children can do. The grocer brings the eggs, machines milk the cow, and the baker bakes and delivers the bread. Actual participation in the work of the city is prohibited by child labor laws; and it is difficult to observe what goes on even at second hand, for "keep out" is posted in large letters at the entrance to the factory and shop. Often turned loose with nothing to do, children have to choose between play upon the crowded city street, association with the back alley hoodlum, or attendance at the cheap movie show.

Here is a condition which offers a double opportunity to education, first for supplying the child with the raw material out of which to build an understanding of life, and second for protecting the child in his out-of-school hours from the negative educational influences with which the city abounds. The modern school at its best has already made substantial progress in meeting the first need through its expanded and enriched curriculum. The second responsibility has not been faced as yet. We school people have been content to wash our hands of responsibility for what happens to the child, after three-fifteen on school days, on Saturdays and during the summer vacation. We have hoped that the home would meet the problem, or that the Boy Scouts or some other agency might step into the breach. But existing social agencies are falling far short of offering the child the protection he needs in his non-school hours.

Here is an example to illustrate our point. First comes the machine, then the congested city with its many pitfalls for children. Society, and particularly the school, fails to respond to the new factors which have come into child life. It is satisfied to continue to function essentially as it did in an agrarian civilization. Juvenile delinquency, gangdom and crime are the result. And so we have one of the strongest influences for social deterioration in modern day life, millions of children unprotected from the negative forces which play upon them in our cities during much of their out-of-school time.

Here is a problem which should have vigorous presentation during the coming decades as the nation seeks for a more intelligent use of its tremendous economic power. Is it too much to hope that it will increasingly become the practice for superintendents of schools to take the lead in calling conferences of civic leaders to devise community plans for guarding the out-of-school time of children. Around the table will sit representatives of the home, of the public playgrounds, of the church, of the Boy Scouts, and of every community agency capable of making a contribution to the protection and education of children.

Out of these conferences will come a community plan, the aim of which will be to protect every child from negative, and to place him under positive, educational influences, throughout the 365 days of the year.

The creation of conditions in our cities in which all children may properly develop to normal adulthood is a social need of prime importance. If it is properly presented by the nation's educational leadership it can not fail to receive recognition in the programs of social planning which must be evolved during the decades of the future.

A second major feature of contemporary life calling for an educational response is the growing realization of the tremendous significance to later life of the early years of childhood. The White House Conference has the following to say on this matter:

> The outstanding problem of this period (of life) is the establishing of basic habits of physical care and of attitudes and adjustments toward objects and persons. Since the mental health of later years is built on the foundations of the early years, the widest possible recognition should be accorded to this important period.

In 1930 there were sixteen million children under six years of age in the United States. It is not necessary to swallow behavioristic psychology whole, or to exaggerate the importance of the research which has been carried on in nursery schools in order to justify the statement that long before they enter school many of these children have proceeded a considerable distance in developing personality traits of a highly unsocial nature. The employment of mothers, apartment house living, small families with the resulting relative isolation of many children, are destined to increase the significance of the problem.

The schools have only begun to face this issue. A considerable proportion of communities have established kindergartens, which enrol children of four and five years of age. But we have hardly begun the more basic approach to the problem through a broadly conceived program of parental education which will not only seek to instruct mothers in the education of younger children, but offer them some relief each day from the incessant demands which the care of young children involves.

The future program to meet the educational problems of children under six can not be predicted in all its details. Perhaps it will require the extension of the school at the pre-school level to include nursery classes. Perhaps it will involve the training of teachers of the early grades or the employment of visiting teachers, so that they may effectively counsel mothers of young children. But when it is worked out it will offer a plan whereby the school and the home may get together on the care of children from their earliest years to the end that they may develop healthy bodies as well as integrated personalities.

Here is a problem which calls for educational leadership of a high order. The facilities for further research on the development of young children must be provided, as well as the means whereby the findings of such study may be translated into appropriate educational facilities. This problem deserves important recognition in any program of social planning looking to a better use of our tremendous resources in economic energy. Such recognition will be received only as we who are in school-work equip ourselves to interpret its significance to the public in general, and to those who are in positions of leadership in particular.

As a third plank in the platform which educational leaders should propose in the coming era, I suggest a dynamic attack upon the problem of adult education. By adult education is not meant merely devices for patching up the educational deficiencies of mature illiterates, nor the coaching of immigrants for naturalization examinations, nor a few elementary academic or vocational courses offered in an evening high school. These may be essential features of a modern educational program, but they do not go to the heart of the adult education program of the future.

One of the writers in the recent *Annals of the American Academy of Political and Social Science* (March, 1931, p. 34), dealing with "Insecurity in Industry," makes this statement:

> The day will come when the training of youth will be recognized as the lesser half of the educational obligation, and its processes the lesser demand upon the educator. In a civilization as instinct with change as is ours, no processes centered upon the young can be esteemed to be educationally sufficient.

This conclusion is supported by a whole series of considerations. First, let me refer to Thorndike's researches indicating that the typical person does not reach the point of greatest efficiency as it concerns ability to learn, until several years after he ordinarily leaves school, and that his ability to learn continues at a relatively high level for thirty years and more after this time. The old aphorism—an old dog can not learn new tricks—has little applicability so far as man is concerned. This, combined with the additional fact that the mature person brings a background of experience to the learning situation, places him well above the child as to ability to profit from study.

Even more impelling is the fact that growing numbers of our people have got to keep on learning if they are to survive. So long as the supply of knowledge was limited, and relatively static in character, we could afford to treat Dorothy Canfield Fisher's question, "Why Stop Learning?" with indifference.

Rapid extension of knowledge is taking place in every field of life as a result of scientific inquiry. The knowledge which is applicable to everyday life is not only increasing in extent, but is also continually changing. Witness, in the field of diet, the rise of the lowly calves' liver from the status of dog meat to that of a delicacy in the menu of men, selling at ninety cents a pound. And when we come to the occupational field, adult learning is increasingly a condition for survival. Imagine the physician who leaves the medical school at thirty and continues to practice, but not to learn, until he is sixty. Consider the wagon maker and the cobbler. They have had to "learn or perish." The whole tempo of life has been tremendously stepped up. But even more significant is the fact, as one writer has recently phrased it, that "the changes of the past twenty-five years will look like stagnation in the perspective of twenty-five years hence."

Means of communication once changed only in centuries; now they are remade in lifetimes. Grandfather, father and son once worked at occupations which changed little if at all during many generations. Now an occupation may be obliterated or totally remade in half a lifetime. No man can be sure that he will not wake in the morning to read of some epoch-making invention, or combination of inventions, which will make it necessary eventually to start all over again so far as his means of livelihood are concerned, whether he be accountant, musician, linotype operator or teacher.

A whole series of signs points in the same direction and agrees in indicating that increasingly in the future education throughout life will be necessary if men are to adjust successfully to the rapid changes of the modern world.

We live in an age when no mere extension or refinement of educational facilities for youth can be adequate for a lifetime. Schools for the young should be made as effective as possible, to be sure, but the great need is for a vertical, rather than merely a horizontal, extension of the provisions for education.

Is society going to recognize these conditions and set up means whereby the evils resulting from technological unemployment, and other phenomena of the machine age, may be mitigated? To what extent will the social planning of the future include adequate provision for the continued education and reeducation of practically all adults? The answers to these questions will depend principally upon the leadership exercised by those of us who occupy positions of responsibility in the field of education. To the extent that we increasingly become students of the complicated scene in which modern life is carried on, to the extent that we take our places beside leaders in other walks of life in developing economic controls and social plans adequate to the solution of the problems which the machine age has created, the school may be expected to play a major and an increasingly important social rôle in the future. When H. G. Wells stated that the present age is a "race between education and catastrophe" he had in mind the problems with which we have been dealing this afternoon. Any social program seeking to meet the problems of the machine age which does not include education as its keystone is destined to eventual failure. It may be true that education alone can not solve the problems of modern life, but it is equally true that it is one of the essential ingredients which must enter into their solution.

Before closing, it is appropriate to indicate some recognition of the immediate and practical problems with which the typical superintendent of schools must struggle whether times be good or bad. Every suggestion that the school shall do more carries with it the accompanying expectation that more money is to be expended for education. Under present conditions, with the bulk of school support coming from a property tax, levied in the locality, it will be extremely difficult to secure the money necessary for an expanded educational program. Yet basically we have resources sufficient to finance a far more extensive educational system than that now in operation. By increasing the size of the political units responsible for the financing of education, and by broadening the base upon which school taxation rests, it should be possible eventually to secure sufficient support so that the types of educational service demanded by the modern era may be supplied.

Equal in significance to these considerations is the fact that in the long run it is in the communities which are spending the most money for education that it is easiest to get still more financial support. When we offer a modern school program, one which the people of a community feel is accomplishing something vital for their children and for the community as a whole, they are far more likely to approve an increased educational bill than when a different feeling exists.

From this fact we may draw a lesson as we think through the current period of business depression. To the extent that we are able to offer an educational program in the coming decades, which seems to promise a substantial contribution to the solution of the problems created by the machine age, we may expect education to receive adequate support. If we fail in this duty, many of these problems will go unsolved, or at best, will be but imperfectly solved. In this respect, we, as educators, bear a heavy responsibility. If we are content merely to confine ourselves to the relatively routine tasks of running schools as they are, important though this may be, catastrophe rather than education may win the race. If, on the other hand, we become students of this complicated age, and dare to develop the new types of educational service which practical life is already insistently demanding, we can expect to play a major rôle in the economic and social planning which is essential if we are to make the machine the slave rather than the master of man.

ATHLETICS AND ALUMNI EDUCATION[1]

By WILFRED B. SHAW

DIRECTOR OF ALUMNI RELATIONS, UNIVERSITY OF MICHIGAN

"WHAT do college students think about and talk about?" This query was addressed recently to an undergraduate in one of our large universities. A further question pointed the matter more precisely, "Do they spend much time over athletics—talking about the football team, for instance?"

Rather startling to one of an older college generation, was the reply, "No, you don't hear so much about athletics now-a-days; students have too many other interesting things to talk about."

Behind that reply, which the writer is convinced might be duplicated in any number of colleges and universities, lies more than may first appear. If its implications are at all representative, and there is reason to believe that they are, we find ourselves almost unaware in the midst of a revolution in college thought. New interests are emerging—new patterns in the tapestry of college life, and in this present-day scheme athletics represent only one motive in the design. More and more, thoughtful athletes are acknowledging that glory yields a doubtful recompense for hard work and loss of time. Students who sacrifice a place on the team for a Phi Beta Kappa record or for an honors course are no longer rare; neither are they misunderstood and scorned by their fellows as would once have been the case.

Such an attitude and such motives would have been unthinkable a few years ago. Sentiment and pressure, to say nothing of alumni enthusiasm, all ran the other way. The problems of intercollegiate athletics, the merits of the team, or of some player, were the topics which absorbed undergraduate life and thought and colored every discussion wherever a group of undergraduates assembled.

To-day we are facing a significant lessening in undergraduate support of intercollegiate athletics, even though, as far as it concerns football, this decline may be thought of as a definite cooling of white hot interest rather than any actual de-

[1] This article was written and submitted for publication prior to the appearance of the supplementary report on athletics of the Carnegie Foundation.

crease in attendance during the football season. While the realization of this change in temper has come suddenly, the forces behind it have been developing for some time. It is all a part of the more realistic questioning attitude of the modern student who refuses to be carried away by a victory or unduly oppressed by a lost championship. Philosophical and somewhat detached, the modern college man becomes an enigma to the bewildered "old grad." He goes to the games, it is true; he sits in the cheering section and responds perfunctorily to the antics of the cheer leader, or else he grouches over the seats assigned him and in that respect anticipates his future status as an alumnus. But, after all, the game for him is only a spectacle; his withers are unwrung. It has been as interesting, perhaps, as a good movie. But whatever the outcome he returns in an equable spirit to a leisurely dinner, winding up a pleasant day, perhaps, with a Saturday night dance or a week-end trip.

Needless to say, this attitude is not always and everywhere the rule. Sporadic bursts of the old Adam still arise occasionally, even in those institutions most infected with this newer sophistication; moreover, the virus has not spread equally over the country, for the old spirit still seems to flourish undiminished in the South and the West, with the Mississippi and the Ohio rivers serving as frontiers. But that there has been a geographical shift in the centers of football enthusiasm will be acknowledged by any newspaper reader who even glances at the sporting page. The old "headliners" in football are passing; a new and farther flung series of leaders in the world of college sports is emerging, while the forces in the eastern colleges that set the waves of enthusiasm in motion some forty years ago are dying down.

College athletics, however, even with all the overemphasis they have received, have had a beneficial as well as a detrimental aspect. The tally is not all on the debit side. Not only have intercollegiate sports brought the students of different institutions into healthy fellowship, but they have provided outlets for undergraduate energies which might have been dissipated in less harmless channels; they have forged a bond between the youth and the man, and have served to carry the play spirit over into adult life. The cult of athletics, too, has stressed the importance of physical fitness, an emphasis we are beginning to incorporate in our educational programs. In a recent discussion of "The Education of the Whole Man," Principal L. P. Jacks, of Manchester College, Oxford, emphasizes the "coeducation of mind and body," suggesting that a truth known by the Greeks was lost sight of when their culture died out.

Finally, a very tangible benefit has come to our educational institutions through the impressive additions to physical plants which this athletic cult has brought—the playing fields, the gymnasiums and stadiums which rise in the academic landscape. Their development on so grandiose a scale would have been inconceivable save as a consequence of the rise of intercollegiate sports, particularly football. Whether the impulse continues to grow, or a period of decreasing interest on the part of the public supervenes, this equipment survives, to be used in the development of the new and different programs stressing physical health and intramural sports, which are claiming more and more the real energies of the student.

While the present commercialization of intercollegiate athletics, and the nation-wide emphasis accompanying it, was inconceivable in 1890 when football was first becoming popular, the seeds of the expansion to come even then were sending forth their shoots. This was revealed in a growing concern in college athletics on the part of the alumni. Later came a growth of newspaper publicity which in turn led to an intense interest on the part of the general public, with the enormous attendance we have been witnessing at the more critical games as an inevitable result.

Meanwhile, great business and coaching staffs were called into existence, and in this expansion the fact that football and other forms of college sports were after all primarily a student activity came to be almost completely overlooked. Million-dollar structures to accommodate the throngs, composed not alone of students and alumni but also the general public, marked a later stage. And now, we have as a final step, a growing indifference on the part of the student. Perhaps this critical attitude may be in part a case of *autre temps, autres moêurs,* but even more, it may well be the logical result of the elimination of the student from any share, even remote, in the control and direction of these games. Ultimately a similar falling off in alumni enthusiasm is almost inevitable, save possibly for those reared in the tradition of twenty years ago.

Thus a progressive evolution over what we may assume to be a half century of athletic big-business is bringing us to a place where the public, stimulated by the sporting pages, will prove at the end to be the only factor retaining the primitive absorption in the spectacular elements of college sport. Football will become just one of the manifestations of a many sided program in intercollegiate sport, which in time will relate itself more definitely to a well-rounded academic development.

Are we not already witnessing a shift from college to public in the proprietary attitude expressed by the press in their growing insistence that a share of football receipts be devoted to charity? To ask our institutions of higher education, *as a matter of right,* to provide a Roman holiday in the guise of charity, as has been demanded of some state institutions at least, is a commentary on the distance we have traveled from the normal and legitimate in college athletics. This attitude on the part of the public is a real evidence that we are reaching, or have already reached, a final phase. The time is coming when our colleges and universities, in self defense, must refuse to encourage and maintain college sport for the benefit of the world at large, particularly if the sharp edge of college enthusiasm be dulled. When that time comes we shall return to a period of simpler things, of intercollegiate athletics that express honestly the play spirit which represents one side of American college life.

Hardly evident as yet, a lessened graduate enthusiasm must be the eventual consequence of this present student attitude. The time may well come when we shall look back upon the present intense intercollegiate rivalries in football with much the same sentimental tenderness we cherish for those picturesque extravagances of the gay 90's and the years immediately succeeding. Intercollegiate football will continue, most of us would hate to think of its abandonment, but its present all-absorbing manifestations will become history. An extravagant picture? Perhaps. But there are signs which seem to justify its projection.

Right here some cynic may ask, "If the college student no longer centers his life and thought in the team, what is there for him in college life?" In theory the answer is easy to those of us familiar with the main springs of student thought; others may find the answer not so simple. Nevertheless a growing conviction seems to emerge that a greater respect on the part of the student for his college work, his studies and his teachers is developing.

College spirit is indestructible; it will survive despite the saddened convictions of some alumni, though it may be that it is to be interpreted in new terms, which will express, in part at least, the present efforts of our colleges and universities to bring about a more reasonable correlation of curricula, a more careful selection of students. Admittedly our educational institutions are beginning to ask more of their students and this attitude is already reflected outside the classroom as well as in it. The average college man may not be acquiring better grades or lead a more industrious life. Such diversions as "dates," dances and movies, to say nothing of automobiles and week-end trips, may seem to negative any serious conception of a college career; but the student of student life recognizes that these are only obvious manifestations of youthful spirits. They rise like white patterns on the wave that runs strong with the impulse of an underlying current.

Just now, it must be acknowledged, the average alumnus, which by interpretation means the one most vocal in the stadium and at alumni gatherings, is still apt to reveal the over-athletic emphasis of his own undergraduate days. But the alumnus of to-morrow will almost certainly turn from his present preoccupation in college sports to affairs which relate themselves more properly to a better rounded out academic program. Interests and fashions of thought change in the college world as in society at large, and in this respect, at least, we seem to glimpse the portents of a new period, in which a different group of motives and ways of thinking will inform both undergraduate and graduate attitudes and relations.

While this conception of a certain periodicity has reference here only to one phase of the relations between the institution and the alumni, careful study will reveal other and broader tendencies in university development which parallel this movement. Certainly there has been a reorientation in undergraduate programs, marked particularly by the emphasis on scientific studies, which roughly falls within the same limits. Moreover, a recent discussion of the relationship of the American college president to the alumni[1] divides the development of American universities into three periods—an unorganized alumni period, before 1821; a period of early organization, from 1821 to 1893; and a late organized alumni period, in which most of the alumni activities with which we are familiar developed, extending from 1893 to 1928. It is significant that this writer suggests for the future a program of instruction of undergraduates in the rights and duties of alumni. He feels that the college president's rôle as far as the alumni are concerned, is "less financial prodding and more educational stimulation." One thing is sure, in more academic fields than that of alumni relations, our whole university life seems to be entering upon a new phase.

Within the last few years an expanding vision of educational possibilities, lying in a greater college and university body composed of the students, faculty and the alumni, has been developing. In these latest years alumni organizations, originally developed on a basis of traditional loyalties and social interests, are almost without exception seeking a more fundamental and reasoned justification for their existence. Opportunities are being sought for constructive and thoughtful support through alumni cooperation wherever and whenever it can be provided. We now see the alumni, not only as an educational

[1] W. S. Stover, "Alumni Stimulation by the American College President," Columbia University, 1930.

end-product, with the degree of their success a check-up of the effectiveness of the process, but also we discern great reserves of moral, spiritual and financial support within the body of graduates, forces which may mean everything, not only to the individual institution, but to the progress of higher education.

It is not then entirely surprising that a more constructive conception of the alumni relationship should be emerging. If college students are coming to assume a more critical and questioning spirit in the various phases of undergraduate life and studies, possibly viewing more wholeheartedly the educational function of college and teacher, there are indications that the alumni, too, are endeavoring to march with the educational advances in their institutions. Moreover, the colleges themselves are beginning to feel more free to ask for alumni support.

An analysis of the activities of almost any alumni organization, the trend of the leading articles in almost any alumni publication, will show this is true. One result has been an expansion of the conception of adult education. Originally conceived in terms of the educationally underprivileged, the idea of education for adults is found to be valid in the college world as well. Here, however, it has become "alumni education" or "continuing education," a force designed to carry the educational effort of undergraduate years over into the post-college period. The vision underlying the familiar commencement platitude, that graduation is not the end but only the beginning of a lifetime of education, is thus becoming interpreted in practical and constructive terms.

It is only very recently, however, that a number of American colleges and universities have begun to work out on a small scale, by what might be called a trial and error process, practical methods for maintaining an intellectual contact with those who were once their students. It must be acknowledged that the going is sometimes difficult, since educational theory as well as practice, up to the last few years, has failed to recognize any opportunity or obligation in this direction; the students, undergraduate and graduate, have filled the whole academic horizon. Nevertheless a recent investigation has shown that of one hundred and forty-one institutions that answered a request for information on this point, seventy-six have undertaken efforts designed to keep the graduates in intellectual contact with the institution, while eighteen others reported definite plans under consideration by faculty and alumni committees.

We are thus beginning to look at the various phenomena of contemporary life through wider lenses, and we seem to find indications that measures looking toward continuing education will not be without positive result. The widening circulation of newspapers and journals dealing with accurate, even though popular, information in fields of literature, science and public affairs, may be taken as one indication of a developing cultural maturity. Where a few years ago no self-respecting newspaper would have opened its columns to a scientific discussion, save when presented in the most sensational guise, we now find everywhere scientific and educational information accurately presented with several national agencies developed for the dissemination of just this type of news, material that is eagerly awaited by the newspaper editor. Publishers' catalogues can also be taken as an index; for books on history, biology, popular science and *belles-lettres* are more conspicuous in book lists and windows than are contemporary novels—even the ubiquitous detective story, for which most of us, including various presidents of the United States, acknowledge an unashamed fondness. The lists of "best sellers" bear further witness. The part the colleges have played in this changing emphasis toward the more substantial can not be, of course, precisely defined, but their influence has undoubtedly been considerable.

Every sign, therefore, seems to point to a new and stimulating era in which our colleges and universities may achieve a more effective participation in contemporary life and affairs through improved personal relationships and educational contacts with the students actually in residence, as well as through the widening impact of an intellectual fellowship beyond the college years. That loyalty to one's own institution, so characteristic of college life in America, is not a thing of the past. But the channels through which it flows seem to be shifting.

May it not be that the impulse toward a distinctly educational alumni interest will come to play a more conspicuous rôle in the future? One hesitates to become either dogmatic or too optimistic, but the indisputable evidence of graduate sympathy for projects which look in this direction affords some justification for the idea.

It may also be suggested that if there is a certain periodicity revealed in the rise and threatening decline of athletics as the focus of student and alumni attention, the same wave motion will be evident in the future. The era from which we seem to be emerging has been marked by what may be considered as, in fact, an immense publicity program for college sports which has spread from students to alumni and thence to the newspaper-reading legions. Although this propaganda can not be said to have been subsidized, or even to have had behind it a marked directive agency, the results have been the same as if some such force were in existence. A flood of popular interest has carried us along, and up to very recent years such efforts as have been made to stem the tide have been ineffective.

But the effects of this nation-wide emphasis give rise to a fair question: Were one tenth of the effort which has done so much to build up our present athletic system directed toward continuing, into the lives of college graduates, the educational, spiritual and cultural contacts and inspirations of college days, might we not at least determine the fundamental character of the new era we are anticipating? The more thoughtful attitude of the present-day student, the effort on the part of alumni organizations to find a basis of real cooperation in educational programs, and a growing sensitiveness on the part of the American public, whether college bred or not, to literature, science and art, in forms which go a little deeper than the ephemeral, all seem to suggest the possibility of a broader and truer basis for the coming relationship between college and graduate.

EDUCATIONAL EVENTS

THE BRITISH MUSEUM LIBRARY

The London Times, in reporting on the progress and the plans for rebuilding the British Museum Library, states that the first structural stage has now been completed, the two supplementary rooms to the west of the new North Library having been converted into four-story galleries ready for the reception of bookstacks. The plans for the complete reconstruction of the old Iron Library of the museum involve the treatment of each quadrant separately, but it has been necessary to find accommodation for the books from the first quadrant to be attacked.

The supplementary rooms, saloons 32 feet high built a century ago, offered a site ready for conversion, since they were until last year merely lined with stationary bookcases. The books from these shelves were removed last year to temporary wooden cases in passageways, and the structure of the supplementary rooms strengthened and fireproofed to allow of the insertion of three new floors of steel filler-joists and concrete at intervals of eight feet. These floors have now been completed, and the seven windows lengthened from 15 to 31 feet so as to light each story satisfactorily.

Beneath each of the new floors, and beneath the newly reconstructed floor of the second and third Egyptian rooms ("Mummy Rooms") above, rails running the length of the galleries have been placed, which will in the next few months be fitted with hanging steel book-stacks upon runners. Each book-stack will be equipped with six to eight adjustable steel shelves, and since no shelf will be higher than about seven feet from the floor immediately beneath, every book will be accessible to an attendant of average height without the necessity of a ladder. Movable steel book-stacks have been installed for some years in the old Iron Library, but these have been moved forward transversely, while in the new rooms the book-stacks are designed, on a system more economical of space, to slide lengthwise along their rails. The supplementary rooms are 36 feet wide, and their length is, respectively, 62 feet and 55 feet. The four floors will allow of the reception of 1,100 book-stacks, and a beginning will be made in the installation of these and the removal of books from the northwest quadrant of the Iron Library in September. The floors have been connected by a steel and concrete staircase, and an electric lift will carry books and attendants from floor to floor, while upon the ground level room has been found to provide a new study for a deputy-keeper. Panel radiators have been placed in the reveals of the windows, and the windows themselves have been glazed with plate-glass divided by small squares of wire, so as to avoid the risk of large fragments falling inwards in case of fire.

It is hoped that the book-stacks will all be installed and the northwest quadrant of the Iron Library emptied of its books by the end of January. The area of the Iron Library is to be extended by the absorption of the carriage-way on the western side, and new walls built, which will contain four stories instead of the present three, and will be strong enough to carry two more stories in the future. All the work so far completed has been done without removing books even temporarily beyond the call of the reading room, or of the staff engaged on the compilation of the new British Museum catalogue, and it is intended that the shifting of books from the old buildings to those reconstructed shall continue without interrupting the service of the museum.

TEACHERS OF PORTO RICO ATTENDING SUMMER SCHOOLS

FORTY per cent. of the 4,500 active school teachers of Porto Rico are attending school this summer, according to Dean J. J. Osuna, of the College of Education of the University of Porto Rico. As reported in the New York *Times*, these teachers and others are to be found in the summer schools of the university, the Central High School, San Juan, and at similar schools at Caguas, Ponce and Mayaguez.

Latest reports on enrolments at these various schools show more than 2,600 in attendance. At the university at Rio Piedras there are more than 1,200 students—fully 1,000 of them teachers in the island public schools—while at the Central High School there are 900. The Caguas Summer School has 200, and Ponce and Mayaguez each have 150. At Rio Piedras the school is under the direction of the university. Elsewhere the courses are being directed by the extension service of the Department of Education.

Both at the university and at the Central High School enrolments were greater than expected and at the last moment additional teachers were employed for the summer term.

In part, at least, the record attendance at the summer sessions this year is attributed to the fact that teaching requirements are more exacting than formerly and there is a desire on the part of teachers now employed in the public schools to come up to the newly-established professional requirements, while those who have not yet qualified for teaching certificates must meet the new standards before they may seek appointment.

Not all the summer students at the university are school teachers. There are a good many who are either trying to get ahead with their college work or else are trying to make up past deficiencies. All those in attendance, however, are students of college grade.

English and Spanish classes have the largest enrolments. What might be called professional subjects for the teacher-student group also are in great demand, including introductory educational and vocational education courses.

THE POST-GRADUATE MEDICAL SCHOOL AND HOSPITAL AND COLUMBIA UNIVERSITY

IN accordance with the agreement between the New York Post-Graduate Medical School and Hospital and Columbia University, effective on July 1, by which the former became the Post-Graduate School of Medicine of Columbia, an administrative board of post-graduate studies in medicine has been established on which will be represented members of the governing body of the university, the undergraduate medical school and the post-graduate school of medicine.

Under the terms of the affiliation, this board will have general oversight and control of all post-graduate instruction in medicine offered by the university, whether at the Medical Center, the Post-Graduate Medical School or elsewhere in the city, and is constituted as follows: Dean Willard C. Rappleye, *chairman,* Dr. Linsly R. Williams, Dean Howard Lee McBain, Director James C. Egbert, Dr. Walter W. Palmer, Dr. James W. Jobling, Dr. Frederick Tilney, Dr. Arthur F. Chace, Dr. Herman O. Mosenthal, Dr. Howard F. Shattuck, Dr. Edward H. Hume, Dr. Harry S. Dunning, Dr. Lewis F. Frissell and Mr. Frank D. Fackenthal.

Dr. Edward H. Hume has been appointed director and Dr. Alan R. Anderson associate director of the New York Post-Graduate Medical School.

This incorporation of the New York Post-Graduate Medical School into the teaching system of Columbia University as its post-graduate school of medicine, distinct from the undergraduate school, carries into fruition, after some forty-nine years, the ambition of the seven founders of the Post-Graduate who resigned from the faculty of the New York University upon the refusal of the trustees to grant them a separate building for post-graduate instruction and, early in the year 1882, organized the present New York Post-Graduate Medical School and Hospital.

Dr. D. B. St. John Roosa, first president of the institution he helped to found, in his inaugural address in November, 1882, pointed out that while temporarily undertaken in an independent institution, this type of medical education rightly belonged with other forms of professional instruction within a university, and closed with the forecast, "the time will come when this institution will be included within a great university."

SURVEY OF TEACHER-TRAINING INSTITUTIONS

THE Office of Education in its biennial survey of teacher-training institutions shows that the total receipts of all the teacher-preparing institutions in the United States more than doubled during the decade. The income from states, cities and counties advanced from $19,670,253 in 1919–20 to $43,240,309 in 1927–28, a gain of $23,570,056, while the receipts from all sources increased from $31,395,389 to $70,016,988, the gain being $38,621,599, or 120 per cent. The average receipts per individual institution were $91,532 for 1919–20, as compared with $229,564 for 1927–28.

The difference in amount of receipts in the case of single institutions is very great, ranging in 1930–31 from surprisingly low sums to as high as $904,000, the total operation and maintenance income of the school at Cedar Falls, Iowa. The next largest incomes for operation and maintenance are reported by Western State Teachers College, Kalamazoo, Michigan, with $901,400, and State Normal College, Ypsilanti, Michigan, with $874,155.

Expenditures for construction of new buildings and other capital outlay have increased steadily during the decade. The largest amount expended by any individual school for capital outlay was $176,675 in 1919–20. More than a score of teachers colleges expended amounts in excess of this sum in 1930–31 when there were at least three institutions that reported expenditures of more than $40,000 for permanent improvements.

The chief source of income of state teacher-preparing institutions is from public taxation. More than three fourths of the income of typical state teachers colleges is provided by the state. About one fifth of the income is from student fees and similar institutional collections. The remainder, a comparatively small percentage, is secured from permanent endowments, local taxation and federal funds.

While no significant changes are noted in the relative proportions of income derived from different sources during recent years, the amount of state support given to-day is in distinct contrast to that afforded early in the history of teacher preparation when this function was regarded largely as a private enterprise.

The assumption by the state of the responsibility and function of teacher preparation, involving also its support, constitutes one of the most significant chapters in the history of this basic educational activity.

According to the survey the full effects of the economic depression existing at the close of the decade have not yet been felt by teacher-preparing institutions. Reduced receipts from taxation, however, are general and a growing number of institutions may be forced temporarily to curtail their programs. It is anticipated that such curtailment will not be permanent except where local conditions already render some fundamental readjustments advisable.

SCHOOL FINANCE AND THE STATE

THE failure of states to make adequate provision to meet mounting costs of an educational program due to high standards set up by the states is throwing a heavier burden on the local school taxing units, according to a survey of the Federal Office for Education.

States actually show a tendency to bear less of the cost than formerly, the report brings out. New standards for which the states are responsible, such as introducing longer school terms, extending the compulsory school attendance age, and raising the teacher qualifications, have resulted in increased expenditures locally.

Failure on the part of law makers to make adequate provision to meet the mounting costs of the educational program results in throwing a constantly heavier burden on local school taxing units. Public schools of 7 states received 40 per cent. or more of their revenue in 1917–18 from state sources, whereas this was true in only 2 states in 1927–28; those of 11 states received 30 per cent. or more in 1917–18, but the schools in only 9 states received as much in 1927–28; those of 23 states received 20 per cent. or more in 1917–18 and of 21 states in 1927–28; those of 34 states received 10 per cent. or more in 1917–18 and of 35 states in 1927–28. Some state funds were provided for the public schools in all states both years. The median per cent. in 1917–18 fell between 19.1 and 17.7, while in 1927–28 it fell between 16.9 and 16.2.

The general trend downward in percentage of total public-school expenditure derived from state sources continued during the biennium 1928–1930 in most states, but in a few the percentage increased.

That the general property tax has been overworked as a source of revenue is an accepted truism to-day. Since localities depend chiefly on this type of tax for their revenue and since, as has been pointed out, localities have borne the brunt of the burden of increased school costs, there is an imperative need for states in their process of raising revenue to tax other forms of wealth if localities are to be relieved.

Accordingly, much study concerning new sources of wealth and new types of taxes is in evidence. Financial surveys and investigations by legislative and other important committees have been made during the decade in practically all states with the view of bringing about improvement in taxing systems.

Such investigations were under way in more than one half the states during the biennium 1928–1930. Reports and recommendations of most of these were placed in the hands of the 1931 legislatures.

THE TEACHER RETIREMENT FUND IN MINNESOTA

MINNESOTA has secured a new retirement fund law which is a revision of the first and present act passed in 1915. This subject has been brought before each legislative session for ten years but has never reached a vote until 1931. Had there not been the present law on which to base a revision, any attempt at an original statute in these days of stress and unrest would have been futile. The new law, passed at the legislative session that closed on April 22 and signed by the governor on April 25, repeals the present inadequate law and becomes effective on August 1 of this year. Briefly, its main provisions are:

(1) Payment by member-teachers of 5 per cent. of the annual salary, no part of a salary above $2,000 being counted.

(2) Teachers under 25 years are exempt until reaching that age, but *may* join under the age of 25.

(3) All teachers employed this year in the schools of the state, to which the act applies, *may* join but are not required. The law is applicable to public schools, except for three main cities which have their own local funds; it covers the six state teachers colleges, county superintendents and the State Department of Education.

(4) "Arrears" may be paid, in part or whole, basis being 5 per cent. of average salary for the latest five years. The state assists on arrear payments for years in excess of fifteen on a graduated plan.

(5) To retire, the member must teach 30 years or have attained age 55. Option is then given between a life annuity or one for term of 15, 20, or 25 years. The annuity is such sum as the member's "savings," principal and accumulated interest, will purchase. The state matches this annuity. Disability retirement is granted after 15 years.

(6) On ceasing to teach prior to retiring, the member may withdraw all payments with interest. Similar option is offered on retiring.

(7) Present annuitants, those retired under the 1915 act, will be continued for life and receive the sums now being paid to them.

This is the only general educational act passed in Minnesota this year. The Minnesota Education Association and trustees of the present fund, with the State Commissioner of Education were the sponsors of securing enactment.

THE CHILD EDUCATION SECTION OF THE NATIONAL SAFETY COUNCIL

The National Safety Council has organized a child education section corresponding to the other sections of the council dealing with industrial and public safety problems.

There are already seven hundred school members affiliated with the council, and these will form the nucleus of the newly organized section. It is hoped that at least one executive from each school system will eventually become affiliated. Dr. Randall J. Condon will serve as chairman of the child education section and Dr. Thomas W. Gosling, of Akron, as vice-chairman. There will be committees on elementary education, secondary education, vocational schools, program and membership. The activities of the section group themselves under two heads, exchange of experience and supervisory service and publication service. As these various committees carry on their work they will issue reports and studies from time to time which will be available to school members.

The first meeting of the child education section will be held in connection with the twentieth annual Safety Congress, to be held in Chicago from October 12 to 16. The topics for discussion at the education sessions at the Hotel Stevens follow:

Wednesday morning, October 14, at 9:30 a.m.

General Meeting: *Chairman,* Dr. Thomas W. Gosling, superintendent of schools, Akron, Ohio.

The Problem of Safety Brought up to Date.

Round Table:

How can we Apply the Safety Recommendations of the White House Conference on Child Health and Protection to the Schools?

Safety Education Luncheon.

Wednesday afternoon, October 14, at 2:00 p.m.

Group conferences have been arranged in order to provide opportunities for informal discussion.

Group I: Successful Experiments in Teaching Safety to High School Students.

Group II: Constructing a Course of Study for the Elementary School.

General Meeting: *Chairman,* William J. Bogan, Chicago Public Schools.

The Challenge of Safety Education:

What Can Safety Contribute to Education?

What Can Education Contribute to Safety?

The Place of Safety in the Progressive School.

Thursday morning, October 15, at 9:00 a.m.

Round Table:

Organized Safety Activities for Boys and Girls.

Ten-minute Discussion.

Source Material for Teachers:

Traffic Safety.

Safety and the Steam Railways.

Fire Prevention.

During the eight-year period from 1922 to 1929, accidental fatalities to persons of all ages mounted from 76,420 to 98,258—an increase of almost 29 per cent. In the same period deaths of children under 15 decreased 2.3 per cent. Since about 1924, when child safety work began to receive special emphasis, actual decreases in child fatalities have occurred, in spite of the increasing number of children exposed. Entire credit, of course, can not be given to the work in the schools. Cities have been attacking other angles of the problem by providing playgrounds and recreation centers, and more adequate traffic safeguards. The natural ability of children to adjust themselves quickly to dangerous situations is another factor to be considered.

The student accident reports submitted by schools to the National Safety Council yield some interesting figures. At present schools and school systems with a total enrolment of more than 400,000 students are keeping records and reporting their accident experience. During one four-months period a total of 2,973 accidents was recorded with an average time lost from school of 2.8 days per accident. Eighteen of these resulted in death. More accidents happen to children in their homes than at or going to and from school, indicating how important it may be, from the school's point of view, to carry over safety lessons from the classroom to the home.

EDUCATIONAL NOTES AND NEWS

DR. EARL B. MCKINLEY, director of the School of Tropical Medicine of the University of Porto Rico, who was recently appointed dean of the School of Medicine at the George Washington University, will take up his work on September 1.

MRS. EDITH FOSTER FLINT, professor in the department of English of the University of Chicago, has resigned as chairman of the Women's University Council to become director of the organization and administration of work in English composition in the college under the reorganization plan. Mrs. Flint has been succeeded, temporarily, as chairman of the council by Mrs. Adeline deS. Link, assistant professor of chemistry. She has served as dean in the Colleges of Arts, Literature and Science since 1925.

PROFESSOR GEORGE H. SABINE, of the Ohio State University, has accepted a call to Cornell University as professor of philosophy.

DR. A. B. WOLFE, formerly of the Ohio State University, has accepted a position as professor of economics at the University of California.

PROFESSOR U. G. MITCHELL, of the University of Kansas, has been appointed head of the department of mathematics, succeeding Professor C. H. Ashton.

MR. JEAN HEBRARD has been appointed professor of architectural design at the College of Architecture of the University of Michigan for the next academic year.

MR. THOMAS ARKLE CLARK, for thirty years dean of men at the University of Illinois, has retired.

DR. HARVEY A. WOOSTER, head of the department of economics at Oberlin College, has been named director of studies to be made by a special Ohio State Commission on the Stabilization of Unemployment.

DR. P. E. MCNALL, of the department of economics of the Wisconsin College of Agriculture, has been chosen by the Wisconsin Railway Commission to represent the state's agricultural interests at the hearing on the railroads' proposed rate increase, to be held early in September.

DR. W. S. TAYLOR, dean of the College of Education at the University of Kentucky and a member of the Kentucky State Crippled Children's Board, has been appointed a member of the education committee, International Society for Crippled Children.

PROFESSOR J. H. HERRIOTT, of the Spanish department of the University of Wisconsin, who recently obtained a fellowship from the American Council of Learned Societies, will spend next year in Spain studying an Aragonese text of Marco Polo.

DR. C. E. GEHLKE, professor of sociology at Western Reserve University, will be absent on leave during the first half of the academic year to permit him to give his time to preparation of a report for President Herbert Hoover's Commission on Social Trends. Professor E. H. Sutherland, of the University of Chicago, will collaborate with Dr. Gehlke in the work.

The American Council of Learned Societies will be represented at the Second International Congress of Linguists at Geneva, which will be held from August 25 to 30, by Professor George M. Bolling, of the Ohio State University; Carl D. Buck, of the University of Chicago, and Franklin Edgerton, of Yale University. The council will be represented at the Eighteenth Congress of Orientalists meeting at Leyden from September 5 to 12, by Mr. Mortimer Graves, assistant secretary of the council; Mr. Arthur W. Hummel, Library of Congress, and Professor William F. Albright, the Johns Hopkins University.

Dr. L. J. Richardson, director of the University of California Extension Division, has returned to the university after a year spent in Europe studying adult education methods and conditions.

Dr. Jesse H. White, president of James Millikin University, gave the commencement address at the close of the summer session in the University of Kentucky, on August 21.

Dr. John William Dickman, president of Upper Iowa University, died on August 22. He had been connected with the university for forty years, becoming its president in 1928.

Dr. L. Pearl Boggs, professor of education at Athens College, died at Pasadena, California, on August 15, at the age of fifty-seven years.

Miss Mary Etta de Vanna, principal of the Centre School in New Canaan, Connecticut, since 1926, died on August 21, at the age of fifty-six years.

The first National Congress for Social Service for children in Argentina will be held in Buenos Aires from September 20 to 26, 1931. The president of the congress will be Dr. G. Araoz Alfaro, president of the National Department of Hygiene.

The American Vocational Association will hold its annual convention at the Hotel Pennsylvania from December 9 to 12. President George J. Ryan, of the New York City Board of Education, is chairman of the general committee in charge.

School attendance and pupil adjustment officers of New York State held a five-day conference under the auspices of the Graduate School of Education from July 13 to 17. Problems of school attendance were discussed in informal talks and meetings. Professors Riverda H. Jordan, Rolland M. Stewart and Julian E. Butterworth were on the committee in charge of arrangements. Professor Butterworth welcomed the delegates. Professor Jordan spoke on "The Home and School Relations of the Attendance Department." Officials of the State Department of Education were also present.

The sixth annual Industrial Training Conference at Rutgers University, attended by New Jersey plant executives, will be held on September 10 and 11. The two-day program has been prepared to accord with a recent analysis by the Rutgers extension director indicating that educational budgets for the coming year in large corporations will suffer no curtailment.

Middlebury College has inaugurated the new degree of doctor of modern languages, according to the Boston *Evening Transcript*. The requirements for the new D.M.L. are rigid. They include a year's work in a foreign country, residence at Middlebury College equivalent to five-year courses, teaching one year under supervision, final oral examination conducted in the major language by native faculty members covering phonetics, pedagogy, literature, philology and stylistics, a minor language tested by an oral and written examination and a speaking knowledge of German.

Three recent school elections in a single county of South Carolina are regarded as significant. The constitutional six months' school term, heretofore supported by the counties with state aid, has now been taken away by the state, with the counties bearing one fourth instead of three fourths of the cost. Extended terms are maintained by districts through taxes voted by the electorate. The last legislature reduced the number of petitioners necessary to call an election to remove such a tax from 50 to 25 per cent. of the electorate. In Wake County, which contains the state capital, three such elections have been held and in each of them the tax was retained by a large majority.

The Board of Education of Detroit has called upon 100 married teachers to take a year's leave of absence without pay. The move is part of a $1,300,000 economy program. All those requested to take a leave are wives of men employed in the school system.

WHILE the regular summer session at Columbia University has closed after a record enrolment of 14,016 students, a few are remaining to follow special inter-session courses. Included are 200 teachers, principals and superintendents taking advanced courses in education under the direction of Dr. Lester M. Wilson, professor of education at Teachers College and an associate in the International Institute. One group of students, preparing to teach in the Philippines, Germany, the Orient and other foreign countries, is making an intensive study of the organization and administration of state and local schools in America. Students in the course on "Research in European Education" are carrying on special investigations in this field, in addition to attending four lectures a week on significant contributions being made by European schools to the field of education.

ACCORDING to the *Journal* of the American Medical Association the department of public health of Toronto offered immunization against diphtheria by the use of "toxoid" to the school children of the city from December, 1926, to June, 1929. A systematized record was kept of all notifications of diphtheria cases together with tallies when the immunization was given. Among 36,189 school children passing through the hands of the toxoid team, 8,980 received no toxoid, 1,386 one dose, 8,994 received two doces and 16,829 received three doses. The diphtheria rate, during the observation period of two and a half years during the campaign and fourteen months following completion of the campaign, was about 25 per cent. of the rate in children who did not pass through the records of the team. Among the 120 cases that did occur subsequent to coming under observation of the toxoid team, twenty-two were in the group of children who were given no toxoid and twelve occurred within one month of receiving the first dose of toxoid, four within one month of the second dose. In the 120 cases the case fatality was definitely less than in the cases occurring in the balance of the school population. This 75 per cent. reduction in cases and 80 per cent. reduction in deaths in the whole group (with about 90 per cent. reduction in cases with no deaths in those given three doses of toxoid) is said to have been obtained without producing one severe reaction.

ACCORDING to the New York *Times,* following a study tour of the United States undertaken by M. André Honnorat and M. Jean Branet, and after examining a general report that they presented to him, John D. Rockefeller, Jr., presented to the University City of Paris, under date of July 17, 1928, a gift of $2,000,000 for the construction of the building destined to offer to the students of its various foundations a common dormitory, with restaurants, library, rooms for physical culture, lecture halls, banquet halls and conference halls. A detailed study of the plans of the building brought out, however, that to carry out the program drawn up by M. Honnorat and M. Branet, the gift, large as it was, would be insufficient. Mr. Rockefeller therefore invited M. André Honnorat to come to New York in company with M. Lucien Bechmann, the architect of the Cité Universitaire. As a result of his conversations with them and with his counselors, Mr. Rockefeller decided to increase his gift, donating three and a half million dollars in place of two million.

THE London *Times* announces that in May of this year the French Embassy intimated to the British Government that the Government of France had decided to allot annually as from November, 1931, the sum of 40,000 francs for five studentships with free tuition for British graduate students desirous of spending an academic year at a French university. As a result of correspondence between the Foreign Office and the committee of vice-chancellors and principals, the Universities Bureau of the British Empire was charged with the duty of setting up a selection committee to choose the five students from among those nominated by the vice-chancellors of the Universities of Great Britain and Ireland. The committee consists of Sir H. Frank Heath, *chairman,* Professor Ernest Barker, Sir Henry A. Miers, Sir Theodore Morison, Professor E. S. Prior, and Miss M. J. Tuke. M. L. E. Genissieux, director of the Office National des Universités et Ecoles Françaises, has consented to act as an assessor to advise the committee on university conditions in France.

DISCUSSION

THE PLACE OF ADULT VOCATIONAL EDUCATION IN OUR PUBLIC SCHOOLS

We are accustomed to regard organized education as a service for youth only, but the adult also has needs and rights which have been greatly neglected or ignored. The American public has centered its attention upon the education of youth largely on the theory that young people constitute our future citizenship. It has been the theory that if the youth is properly trained, things will be improved in the next generation. Meanwhile, we have rather unconsciously assumed that it is too late or unnecessary to do anything for the present generation of adults.

There is another reason why an interest in adult education has been delayed. It is perhaps best expressed in the common saying, "He is too old to learn," or perhaps worse still, that "I am too old to learn." It is true that children learn easily, especially when the teaching process is correct. However, the adult has certain advantages which he did not possess as a child. In the school of life, the adult has been "through the mill" and he has a background of facts and ideas which enables him to make a greater use of any new information obtained. Recent studies by eminent psychologists prove that we can all learn long after we have left the halls of the public schools and colleges. It has been stated that "adults come to their full capacity to learn after life has given them the experience with which to learn."

As a result of these exploded educational theories and the trends in our social and economic order, there is developing in this country a genuine interest in all phases of adult education. The "machine age" has given the American people time and additional facilities for learning. In addition, it has created many new problems of complex nature. That an adequate program of adult education will do much to help solve these problems is the growing belief of an increasing number of economical, industrial, social and educational leaders.

One may rightfully ask, what need is there for a systematic program of adult education? Why should such a program include occupational training? Why should the public school assume any responsibility of providing for the educational needs of the adult citizenry? These are pertinent questions.

There are at least two fundamental reasons why we need a systematic program of adult vocational education. The first is quite apparent when we but suggest the complexities of our modern civilization.

Due to the development of science, invention, and the effect of the machine upon agriculture, commerce, industry and the home, our civilization is passing through a series of changes, the complexity of which is unparalleled in the history of the world. Occupations are constantly changing in their demands and opportunities. Likewise, new occupations are arising making new demands. As we view the modern processes of production, the methods of transportation, the means of communication and the way we amuse ourselves, it appears as if there is no limit. We frequently wonder what is "just around the corner."

The unemployment condition in this country points to a specific need for adult education. A large number of America's idle workers are innocent victims of a "technological unemployment" situation. By "technological unemployment" we mean the displacement of men by machines, and mergers. Without an opportunity to adjust themselves to new conditions and to the new demands of industry, many of these individuals will fall by the wayside and become idle parasites living off the work of others; or dependents, criminals and unnecessary victims of the iron man. Society faces a new responsibility. We must provide a program of re-education which will assist these people to adjust themselves to new conditions, to acquire new skills and to return to useful employment.

Such a re-educational program must be a continuous one. Charles Austin Beard, in speaking of these "dislocated soldiers of industry," states that "adult education can not solve the problem of unemployment, technological or otherwise; but it has a function to discharge in our progressive society where new knowledge pours from laboratories, studies and workshops with bewildering rapidity, offering new powers and opportunities while altering historic occupations. That function is to make continuously available to all inquisitive adults a realistic knowledge that furnishes a shield and a sword in the struggle for existence." Vocational education will not solve unemployment, but unemployment can not be solved without vocational education.

Adult education is the only kind of training which a large part of our people can receive if they are to be adequately prepared for the tasks of life. The United States Office of Education is responsible for the statement that of all of the boys and girls who enter the fifth-grade in our public schools, two thirds never enter high school, and only 14 per cent. finish high school. It is evident that this large group of people who do not go on to school are inadequately prepared to meet the economic and social problems of the present day. A program of part-time or evening school education would enable these people to increase their social and vocational efficiency.

A review of the facilities which provide for our after-school training reveals that there are many valuable agencies which contribute to the educational needs of the adult portion of our population. It would be extremely difficult to name all of them. A partial list includes evening schools, college extension courses of varied nature, literary clubs, reading circles, libraries, churches, theaters, movies, art galleries, museums, magazines, newspapers, and the radio.

A further study of these numerous agencies shows that a number are organized primarily for educational purposes; such as the evening school, the extension service and the public library. On the other hand, there are many agencies which are organized primarily for commercial or entertainment purposes but disseminate news and ideas to a large group of adults. The press, the movies and the radio are examples of this class.

It is impossible to estimate to what degree each of these many agencies contributes to the welfare of our individual lives. However, it is evident that the great bulk of our adult population receives after-school education in an unorganized and unsystematic manner. Where, then, may the adult turn in order that he may receive guidance and instruction which will enable him to bring order to his learning process? It is the growing belief of many that the answer will be found when the public schools provide a well-organized program of adult education. Such a program must provide for the training of social as well as vocational efficiency.

We have in this country an organized educational machinery called the public school. It is to this typically American institution that we have been accustomed to look for systematic educational service. It has been built to serve the youth. At the present time it is probable that the majority of the teaching personnel is not equipped in the technique of adult education. Only in a limited way has the machinery been organized to train the adult. We hear much about the equalization of educational opportunity. Many accomplishments have been made which have expanded the educational program horizontally in order that all youth may be served more efficiently. Is it not also logical that we may equalize educational opportunity by extending the public school program vertically? Apparently the public school could be organized so that the adult might have a place where he could receive systematic instruction. At least much could be done to help him organize his learning process.

Such a program has many proponents. As an example, Roger W. Babson, the statistician, addressed a group of industrial and educational leaders who were assembled in Boston only a few weeks ago. This meeting was held for the purpose of finding possible solutions to the present unemployment situation. Mr. Babson proposed that each community should establish a public employment clinic where the men out of work could register. Then during the period that the adult is out of work the public school plants could be used for night classes where he could improve himself in a trade or learn a new one.

Someone stated that "to the sober eye of wisdom the vocations of men are like the walls of a building. Poorly built foundations will presently cause the distortion and crumbling of the upper walls and rooms, no matter how solidly and decoratively these may be constructed. The man or woman who is not well grounded and secure in a good vocation can have at best only insecure and disordered foundations for his culture, his religion, his political cooperation, his good fellowship or his family life."

It is evident, therefore, that the successful solution of our problems and the future of our nation demands a well trained citizenry. Dorothy Canfield Fisher suggests the answer in her little book "Live or Perish" when she states, "All thoughtful people have been reached in the last decade if not sooner, by a conviction of the folly of imagining that enough education can be crammed into the years when youth sits in the classroom. . . . Everyone who observes at all has realized that the necessary intricacies of a great modern country can not be maintained unless that country can depend upon a population which does a powerful amount of learning after school days are over."

There is an abundance of evidence which shows that adults will attend vocational classes when such educational opportunities are provided. During the fiscal year ended June 30, 1929, more than one third of a million of people were enrolled in vocational evening school classes in the United States. This entire program was conducted by the public schools of the country under the provisions of the Smith-Hughes Act.

That the adult citizens of Iowa are interested in a program of adult vocational education is indicated by the fact that during the fiscal year ended June 30, 1930, over 6,000 men and women were enrolled in vocational evening school classes. It is also significant that this enrolment was double that of the previous year. Preliminary reports just received by the state board for vocational education indicate that the adult program for the present year will greatly exceed that of a year ago.

In conclusion may I state that there are trends which indicate that our public schools will become, in not a far distant future, centers of adult education. These centers should provide evening school classes where a banker, a day laborer, a clerk, a doctor, a merchant, a machinist or a truck driver might have an opportunity to better equip himself for the necessities and the finer things of life. The greatest immediate return to a country comes through the efficiency of its adults. Therefore, an adequate program of adult education should pay big dividends.

F. E. Moore

State Board for Vocational
Education, Des Moines, Iowa

SPECIAL CORRESPONDENCE

THE EVOLUTION OF HEBREW ELEMENTARY EDUCATION IN PALESTINE

Palestine, although small in area and in population, is a country on which the interest of many cultured peoples is focused. The old national dream, cherished by generations of Hebrews and now growing gradually into a reality, of coming back to the beloved fatherland and rejuvenating both it and themselves, has made that country the center experimental station in the world.

By many people Zionism as a whole is looked upon as an experiment which can not yet be fully judged. This is not my own point of view for I am convinced of its ultimate success; however, this is not the place for discussing that problem. Whatever may be one's opinion in the matter, one aspect of that movement, namely, the cultural, or, more precisely speaking, the educational one, is admittedly a striking achievement which deserves the admiration of all.

Hebrew education in Palestine has proved to be very influential upon the cultural state of Jewry all over the world. What does its power consist of? Of two important achievements:

(1) Hebrew has become the sole language of instruction there, and from the school it has passed to the street and home, until it has reached its culmination in being recognized by the government as an official language of the country.

(2) The secular subjects have become in Palestine an integral part of the curriculum.

The first is one of the most wonderful results the Jewish national movement has already attained. Some think of it as almost a miracle. Hebrew had been a semi-dead language during many centuries. It was the language of prayer, but not of conversation. It has never ceased to live in literature, to be sure, and so has kept in touch with human thoughts and feelings; furthermore, it has always served among Jewish people as the language of correspondence, even in business matters. Yet it has not been spoken, and has also kept a certain isolation from many developments of modern life, particularly the technical. Thus, about forty years ago, nobody could believe that some day this semi-dead language would be a modern living tongue, the sole vehicle of expression for many thousand children in Palestine and in other countries. This "miracle" has been performed chiefly through the endless endeavors of the first Hebrew schools in Palestine.

It would take too long to tell in detail how this important achievement has been attained, but since it has played such a significant rôle in the history of the schools in Palestine a few words about it should be said.

It was natural for the Zionistic movement to include in its sublime aspirations the revival of Hebrew, the symbol of that ancient glory and national creative power, which the Jewish people is attempting to regain. But even so, such a prompt happy solution of the problem as has been achieved was not expected. When first trials along this line had been made, they were a target for derision. Ahad-Haam, the greatest Hebrew thinker of our day, has strongly criticized the idea, considering it harmful to the intellectual growth of the children. He particularly assailed the teaching of science in Hebrew, for the language then lacked many needed words and expressions. (He later changed his view.)

To a person interested in linguistic developments there is nothing more fascinating than this heroic chapter in the history of education in Palestine. Dr. Isaac Epstein, one of the greatest Hebrew educators, and so-called "father" of the modern Hebrew school in Palestine, tells us in a most charming way about his first steps in creating the Hebrew elementary school with Hebrew as the sole language of instruction. He finishes his narrative as follows: "About thirty-seven years have elapsed since those days, and comparing the smallest school now with the institution I presided over in those days, I admire the great distance we have passed."

This successful outcome of the endeavors was due to the zeal of the first educators and new settlers in Palestine, who came from Europe with the firm decision to build a new life, based upon the old Hebrew culture. "Many a social group adopted the rule of imposing a fine upon its members when in the heat of discussion they slipped from Hebrew into German, Yiddish, French or Russian." ("Recent Jewish Progress in Palestine" by Henrietta Szold, Philadelphia, The Jewish Publishing Society of America, 1915. p. 128).

Success, however, was also the result of a social factor. The Jewish people, owing to its dispersion, has been disunited into many "races," the two most important being "Ashkenasim" and "Sefardim." The former are those Jews who live mainly in eastern and central Europe and in the New World, and have adopted the Yiddish, an offspring of German, as their spoken language; while the latter remained in the Orient and in some parts of Europe, and their spoken language, called "Ladino," is of Spanish origin. There are many differences in the ideals and manner of life which mark the two parts of Jewry. The way of pronouncing the Hebrew letters is also different, and there are two pronunciations; an Ashkenasian and a Sefardian. For example: "Hebrew" is expressed by the five-letter word עברית. The word is pronounced "Ivrit" by the Sefardim, while the Ashkenasim call it "Ivris." Due to many causes which can not be dealt with here, when the new Jewish settlement in Palestine was started about forty years ago, there were many Sefardim to be found in Jerusalem and other Palestinian cities. When the two Jewish races came in contact, they had no common language which both knew, except Hebrew, although their pronunciations differed. Thus the Hebrew language in the Sefardian pronunciation which prevailed and became the dominating one in the country, served as a bridge to unify remote brothers and to create a mutual understanding between them.

The second important feature which gave Hebrew education in Palestine its vigor and vitality was concerned, as it was pointed out above, with the curriculum of the elementary school. From the pedagogical standpoint there was no innovation in introducing the secular subjects into the curriculum, and the emphasis upon that fact would seem strange to an American or to people of other countries. Yet in Jewish life it was a real revolution. This is another result of the Jewish national movement. What were, and still are, the educational conditions for a Jewish boy or girl in Europe and America? They always wear, as it were, two garments, the one of a Jew and the other of a citizen. The Jewish child was, and is, a sacrifice to this painstaking duality. He gets his "human" education in the morning, while toward the evening he becomes Jewish and attends the Hebrew school where he is taught the language alone. This situation is an inexhaustible source of spiritual conflict, and may be considered, in its deeper meaning, the chief cause for the national movement. It makes impossible the shaping of an integrated Jewish personality. The Hebrew school in Palestine removed this situation completely. It functions in the same way as schools in other countries do. The child there is not placed between two worlds, but lives a sound natural life in his own small milieu in which the entire world is reflected.

These two features in Palestinian schools have brought about a marvelous growth of the Hebrew School in Palestine and have given birth to further developments of particular viewpoints, according to the different types of the Jewish population.

Three main streams of development are now becoming evident in the Hebrew educational system in Palestine.[1] They are:

(1) General
(2) Mizrahi (representing the religious element)
(3) Labor.

Each of the above has its own schools, the budgets for which are covered by the Zionist organization. "The following table shows the comparative distribution of the three types of schools for the current year 1928–1929." (Educational Year-book of the International Institute of Teachers College, Columbia University, 1928, published 1929, p. 185.)

	No. of schools	No. of full-time teaching posts	No. of pupils	Per cent. pupils of Total
General ...	123	413	12,000	63
Mizrahi ...	58	185	5,977	31
Labor	46	64	1,272	6
Total ...	227	662	19,249	100

I should give some information about the curricula of these schools and the philosophy underlying them, but for the sake of greater clearness I think it worth while and necessary first to trace briefly the evolution of elementary education in Palestine from its very beginning.

It has already been stressed above that the language problem was an overwhelming one in the first period. The school then presented a sharp contrast to real life, but not to the aspirations of the best element of the population. Hebrew was not spoken by the parents; and the school, which tried to teach the subjects in Hebrew, was thus circumscribing the pupils' thought and therefore was unsatisfactory to them. The necessity of opening a "preparatory" class for children 4 to 5 years old, with the sole purpose of preparing them in Hebrew speech, has thus arisen on the *ordre du jour*. "The pedagogical value of those 'preparatories' was negative. The whole work consisted in 'What is this?—This is a chicken,' etc.; the older children were taught to write and to read, the teachers being young girls who had an 'education' of four elementary grades and not any training in teaching" (from a Hebrew source). The purpose was nevertheless attained, and when those children afterwards entered the school, the teacher could speak to them about things and not only words. Thus, indirectly, those preparatory classes had a pedagogical value too. A few years later those classes expanded and took the form of a regular kindergarten, which since then has become a very important cultural factor in the life of the Jewish settlement in Palestine.

[1] Many agencies are developing educational activities in Palestine, but the most important are these two: The Government and the Zionist organization, the former being concerned mainly with the education of the Arabs, and the latter of the Jews. As the name of this paper implies I am not dealing with the schools designated for the non-Jewish population; furthermore, the discussion is confined to the educational system of the Zionist organization alone, since other schools, both public and private, have been much influenced by it.

The schools, too, were on a very low pedagogical level. Grading was done not according to the age and mentality but according to the knowledge of Hebrew. The teaching of arithmetic and science was very poor. Nobody thought of drawing, singing, physical education and manual work. Yet there was a continuous growth, and in the course of time much was improved.

A turning point in the whole situation of elementary education was the foundation of the Association of Teachers in Palestine (1903). At first, this association was not largely concerned with the economic interest of the teachers, but it took the greatest interest in the pedagogical and administrative aspects of the schools. It elaborated a program to be followed by all the schools and they obeyed; it provided for better teachers (through an examination by the Central Committee of the Association). Since the teaching of science in Hebrew was an innovation, and the lack of a standard terminology resulted in great disorder, every one using his own terms, the Association established in Jerusalem an "Academy of the Hebrew Language" to decide about all the words and expressions in use and to create new ones.

A further step in the way of perfecting the pedagogical aspects of the school was the establishment, by the Association, of "Kohelet"—a book-publishing concern with the purpose of providing text-books for the schools, and this was followed by many other important achievements, such as summer courses for teachers, a pedagogical library, and finally a pedagogical magazine, which marked a new era in the history of education in Palestine. The old epoch, characterized by emphasis on mere language, gave place to a new one distinguished by a policy of strengthening the education itself, a policy of making the school pedagogically sound. This movement had its influence upon the kindergarten too.

Educational methods and procedure now became the chief concern of the teachers, and no longer was the fostering of the language their sole interest. And here we come to the split of the educational system. As long as the work was concentrated on the language there was more or less unison in the ranks of the teachers and the population. It was something like a *union sacrée* in war time, when all the political factors are throttling their voices to share in the common cause. After this language fortress was conquered, and new educational theories sprang up, the divergence of opinions among different classes became conspicuous, and new ways of education were sought to fit their respective demands. The religious element was looking for a synthesis between tradition and modern education, and to this end established a new type of school which laid special emphasis upon religious matters, although they did not neglect the requirements of modern education. The labor class, on the other hand, which in Palestine represents the most intellectual and idealistic part of the population, had its social claims and tried to establish another extreme type of school. Thus the three types, given in the table above, came into existence. This differentiation became possible especially after the war, when the new political situation of the Jews and Palestine led to the formation, under the auspices of the Zionist organization, of a Department of Education for the Jewish population in Palestine which supplies the budgets of all those schools and provides for adequate supervision.

The first task of the Department of Education (called in Hebrew: "Mahlekat Hahinukh") was to formulate, after many consultations with the teachers, a definite program for the various types of schools. Here are two tables, taken

TABLE I

OFFICIAL TIME SCHEDULE FOR GENERAL SCHOOLS

Subjects	Classes or grades 1	2	3	4	5	6	7	8
Bible	periods not assigned	periods not assigned	6	5	6	5	5	4
Hebrew			7	7	6	5	5	5
Mishna			...	...	...	...	2	2
Moledeth (Heimatkunde)			7	...	...	...	...	...
Geography			...	4 (Geography and Nature Study)	2	2	2	3
Nature Study			...		3	3	3	3
History			...	...	...	2	2	3
Arithmetic			4	4	5	5	5	5
Drawing			...	2	2	2	2	2
Singing			2	2	2	2	1	1
Gardening			...	2	2	2	2	1
Calisthenics			2	2	2	2	1	1
English			...	...	4	4	4	4
	23	23	28	28	34	34	34	34

from the "International Year-book," showing the respective schedules of the general type and of the Mizrahi type. The labor type has no special curriculum, its schedule being roughly related to that of the general, although there is a difference in *methods.*

TABLE II

TYPICAL TIME SCHEDULE FOR MIZRAHI SCHOOLS

Subjects	Classes or grades							
	1	2	3	4	5	6	7	8
Prayers	periods not assigned	6	6	...	...	...	...	...
Bible		7	9	9	8	7	7	5
Ceremonies		...	...	2	2	...	...	...
Mishna		...	...	5	...	...	...	...
Talmud		...	...	...	8	10	10	12
Hebrew		8	5	4	4	4	4	4
Moledeth		...	4	...	...	...	...	...
Geography		...	...	2	2	2	2	2
Nature Study		...	...	2	2	2	2	3
History		...	...	...	2	2	2	3
Arithmetic		4	4	4	4	3	4	4
Calisthenics		...	...	1	1	1	1	...
Singing		...	...	1	2	1	1	1
Drawing		...	...	1	1	1	...	...
English		...	...	...	...	5	5	5
	25	25	28	31	36	38	38	39

These tables show us that:

(1) The Hebrew elementary school in Palestine is an 8 year course.

(2) The Mizrahi school differs from the general type both in the number of hours per week and in the subject-matter taught. The emphasis is laid upon religion. More Bible is taught; Talmud and religious customs are added at the expense of some other secular material.

(3) There are no assigned periods in the two lower grades (in the Mizrahi school this is true only in regard to the first grade), as those grades are the transition from the kindergarten, where the child enjoys complete freedom, to the definite curriculum of the upper school. In these first two years, reading and writing and some arithmetic are freely correlated with *Anschauungsunterricht,* which is the chief concern in the third and fourth grades. Frequent trips usually serve as the point of departure for that instruction, as they do for *Heimatkunde* and nature study in other grades as well. The theories of Pestalozzi and his followers have had much influence on the teachers' work in the lower grades.

(4) The Bible receives much emphasis in the schools. This is not for the sake of religion, but is due to three main factors:

A. National, the Bible being the precious monument of Jewish past glory.

B. Linguistic, the Bible still remaining the most invaluable model of pure literary Hebrew in both form and style.

C. Educational, the Bible being in Palestine a realistic book which is readily grasped and felt, in spite of the distance of thousands of years separating us from the times of its creation.

The labor schools differ from the general type in their method of instruction and somewhat in their educational aims as well. While the general school is more or less the traditional school of Europe with its constant endeavor to improve methods of instruction, the labor school represents the movement of revolutionizing the very heart of education. Teachers here try to run the schools according to modern theories of education. You find here some resemblance to the *Arbeitschule,* the children being engaged in supplying their own needs to a great extent. The schools being chiefly designated for the children of the working class, their tendency is to adapt their atmosphere accordingly.

It would, however, be difficult to draw a line of demarcation between the two types of school, labor and general. There are indeed fundamental differences in procedure and in tendency, but personal ability and preference still play a great rôle. As a rule, all the schools reveal a high level of ability and devotion, and after visiting them one can not help exclaiming: "It is not a school but a great family!"

L. I. RIKLIS

QUOTATIONS

A NEW WOMEN'S COLLEGE

A MORE beautiful site for a school for women than that chosen for Bennington College, ground for which was broken last Sunday, would be hard to find—or a more appropriate. The round, green Vermont hills over which it will look; the near-by village, with its fine old white houses and sturdy Colonial memories; the whole tradition of Yankee simplicity and individualism which permeates the neighborhood, all fit in with the independent and adventurous spirit back of this experiment.

The ground-breaking ceremonies took place in a barnyard, the big barn itself being an integral part of the future college campus. Dr. William Rappard, who had come over from the Williamstown Institute of Politics to speak, said that he was reminded of some of the cantonal meetings in his own Swiss mountains. The speakers—Governor Stanley G. Wilson, of Vermont; the new college's president, Dr. Robert Devore Leigh; Dorothy Canfield Fisher and others—talked from the base of an abandoned silo. The buildings, which are to be opened a year from now, will be dwelling houses in the New England tradition rather than cloisters or monuments borrowed from an older world and another age.

Briefly, Bennington College is the outgrowth of the "progressive" schools—those, that is to say, which have discarded the more or less medieval intellectualist tradition for emphasis on the child's whole personality, on direct experience and integrating formal education with contemporary life. In admission requirements, in accent on the student's enthusiasm for and grasp of his work rather than on written examinations, even in such matters as the spacing between term times and vacations, Bennington will venture on various experiments and what some of the orthodox may even regard as heresies—a vague program, necessarily and unfortunately, but an interesting one.

To build a new college from the ground up is no simple task at any time, even with plenty of initial funds. President William Allan Neilson, of Smith College, spoke humorously at the Bennington ceremonies of the difficulties all women's colleges face in wangling their share of available funds from the hard-boiled and ravenous men's universities, and he mentioned one great university which, during last year alone, had received in gifts a sum equal to all that Smith College had accumulated in its fifty-five years of life! One to fifty-five, Dr. Neilson said, just about measured the American man's comparative indifference to the education of his daughters. The special difficulties which any new educational institution faces in such a year as this need not be pointed out.

However that may be, the Bennington trustees did not start digging on their Vermont hillside until they saw their way clear to at least the start of the new school's life. And their future work will not be cramped by the dogmatism and personal crankiness of the fairy godfather who occasionally blesses such enterprises. The new college has enthusiasm on the part of its faculty and the more or less concrete backing of an unusually well informed and alert portion of the public, and its progress will be watched with lively interest.—*The New York Herald-Tribune.*

TESTING THE EXAMINERS

THAT an examination may test those who draw up the questions rather than those who answer them is a fact illustrated in a ruling made this week by Dr. Charles H. Elliott, State Commissioner of Education of New Jersey. He has decided that a series of tests given last June by the Irvington school authorities to 116 aspirants for teaching certificates did not constitute "an adequate instrument of the work of the normal schools and can not be regarded as valid tests for the selection of teachers."

The Board of Education at Irvington estimated that it would need about twenty more teachers for the fall semester. In view of the large number of unemployed normal-school graduates the superintendent made the examinations unusually severe, a practice adopted by most examining boards when the number of applicants for appointment as teachers is markedly in excess of the number of vacancies. In Irvington the plan worked too well; not one of the 116 aspirants managed to achieve a passing mark.

If it had been only the disappointed candidates who protested the incident might have ended there, but since most of the candidates were graduates of the state normal schools taxpayers, too, were aroused. Had they been paying for the support of colleges and normal schools whose graduates could not qualify for certificates, or were the tests unfair yardsticks for measuring the output of the training courses? A committee appealed to Dr. Elliott, whose decision must be gratifying to all parties except those who prepared the examinations.

It is the same sort of controversy which the New York City Board of Education has submitted to Dr. Frank P. Graves, the Commissioner of Education. Last May a committee of the National Republican Club charged that graduates of the city's elementary schools had made a lamentable showing in examinations which graduates of up-state schools were required to pass; the inference it drew was that the city's schools were inefficient. Officials of the school system denied the allegation; branded the tests as unfair, in view of the city's curriculum, and asserted that the method of scoring was faulty and inconsistent. The Board of Education requested Dr. Graves to investigate the "pedagogical efficiency" of the system.

New York, however, moves more slowly than New Jersey in such matters. Dr. Graves plans to begin his inquiry next fall.—*The New York Sun.*

REPORTS

AMERICAN EDUCATION WEEK[1]

NOVEMBER 9–15, 1931

AMERICAN EDUCATION WEEK is a concerted effort on the part of teachers everywhere to increase the appreciation of the public for its schools. Because of its extensive observance, and the cooperation of many nationwide organizations, the interest of the press, the radio and the pulpit, it offers an effective means of beginning or strengthening a continuing program of interpreting the needs, aims and achievements of the schools. For ten years the interest in the observance of American Education Week has steadily increased. It promises to become a great national festival during which the American people redevote themselves to the ideal of popular government based upon an enlightened citizenry.

In the present trying economic conditions the schools need more than ever before the sympathetic cooperation and support of the people. Only a recognition of the significance of the schools will cause citizens to sacrifice last the education of their children, in communities where it is found necessary to reduce support for public enterprises. The sponsors of American Education Week have endeavored to make the 1931 program point to the significant accomplishments of the schools. It is intended to help teachers in their efforts to maintain the present high standards of educational service at a time when every public service must be highly valued by the people if it is to receive continued effective support.

[1] Prepared by the Division of Publications of the National Education Association.

The general theme of American Education Week is "What the Schools are Helping America to Achieve." Nationwide cooperation in inspiring the public with a renewed sense of the value of the schools through programs built around this theme will be of incalculable aid in maintaining the gains made in recent years toward providing every child with a fair start in life.

The Day by Day Topics

Monday, November 9—Theme: *What the Schools are Helping America to Achieve in Economic Progress.* Show how education increases and refines human wants, making larger demands upon the products of industry and business. Show how schools help students select occupations for which they are best fitted because of their interests and abilities, and give training in vocations, helping industry and business effectively to staff and man large-scale operations. Point out the work of the schools in promoting ideals of honesty and ethics without which modern business could not be transacted. Show how the schools contribute to the stability of government without the protection of which business and industry could not operate.

Tuesday, November 10—Theme: *What the Schools Are Helping America to Achieve in Child Health and Protection.* The work of the White House Conference on Child Health and Protection, carried on under the direction of President Hoover and Secretary of the Interior Wilbur, has recently been completed. Many of its findings are now available for use in school and community. They constitute a great charter of the rights of American childhood to a fair start in life. They should be in every city and school library. This topic offers an opportunity to familiarize the community with the epochmaking recommendations of the White House Conference. (Have citizens inventory the child welfare provisions of the entire community in light of these recommendations.) Show what the schools do to protect children from poor health, exploitation and moral delinquency.

Wednesday, November 11—Theme: *What the Schools are Helping America to Achieve in Citizenship and Loyalty to Law.* Visualize the schools as the great unifying force in American life. It is universal education which makes our widely separated people one in loyalty and devotion to the flag and the constitution. Show how our schools encourage youth to emulate the lives of our country's noblest characters; how they create a respect for our national aims, and inspire a sense of responsibility for personal right, conduct and observance of law. Point out the dependence of a democratic form of government upon enlightened citizens. Explain the work of the schools in teaching the privileges and duties of citizenship.

Thursday, November 12—Theme: *What the Schools are Helping America to Achieve in the Improvement of Rural Living.* Farm life faces a reconstruction that is as fundamental as the industrial revolution. These far-reaching readjustments call for the most capable leadership the nation can produce. Many of these leaders must come directly from the farm. Point out this challenge to the rural school to train farm youth for new needs and new conditions. Show what has already been done in spite of meager support. Agriculture is firmly based on the solid rock of human necessity. From the farm have come many of our great leaders in politics, business and the professions. Upon agriculture the whole world depends for food. Show why a fair start in life for the rural child should be of concern to every citizen.

Friday, November 13—Theme: *What the Schools are Helping America to Achieve through a Higher Level of Intellectual Life.* Point out the contribution the schools have made to the welfare of the nation in even the simplest and most common skills they teach—the ability to read and write. Education for all extends far beyond these fundamentals. American citizens have attained the highest average intellectual life ever enjoyed by any nation. Show what this means in increased enrichment of living and the general advance of civilization.

Saturday, November 14—Theme: *What the Schools are Helping America to Achieve through the Enrichment of Adult Life.* Since psychologists have shown that youth is not the only learning age, adults have applied themselves in increasing numbers to study and the development of new skills. Increased opportunities for adults in night schools, in colleges and libraries have been the result. Show the growing significance to individual happiness and national welfare of facilities which enable adults to spend their constantly expanding leisure time in these worthwhile ways. Survey the adult education opportunities of your community, and point out ways in which they may be improved and extended.

Sunday, November 15—Theme: *What the Schools are Helping America to Achieve through High Ideals of Character and Home Life.* Plan the cooperation of home and school and church in inspiring noble character based upon high ideals and wholesome habits. Ideals and habits grow largely out of the environment in which people live. It is the privilege of home and school and church to promote the clean and elevating activities of community life. The churches will usually take the lead in carrying out this program, which may well be the theme for an entire Sunday service.

The Division of Publications of the National Education Association, 1201 Sixteenth Street, Northwest, Washington, D. C., will send free to any teacher or school officer an outline of the program for American Education Week, with suggestions for carrying it out. The Division of Publications has prepared attractive bulletins and posters to use locally during and previous to American Education Week. These may be obtained ready to use at the cost of publication and distribution, or they may be reproduced in school print shops or in other economical ways, and used in whatever way local committees find most effective.

EDUCATIONAL RESEARCH AND STATISTICS

EDUCATIONAL APPOINTMENTS AND POLITICAL APPLICATIONS

The extent to which partisan politics affects the selection of presidents of state institutions of higher education has been observed in varying degrees by most of us, perhaps, but few of us have tried to extend our observation beyond the cases that incidentally come to our attention. A recent selection of a college official on what seemed to be purely political grounds prompted the writer to extend his observations. Although he suspected that political affiliation was a primary requisite for such positions in many states, he wanted to see exactly to what extent such was true. He wanted to know definitely what he already knew indefinitely.

His procedure was simple. He went to the Office of Education *Bulletin,* 1931, Number 1, for the names of the heads of the state universities and colleges, of the state junior colleges, and of the state teachers' colleges and normal schools. He limited himself to the forty-eight states of continental United States. Only the names of present heads were noted; acting presidents and presidents emeritus were not considered. Then the writer consulted "Who's Who in America" for the political affiliation of each president or principal and also for the date when each entered upon his present position. With these data in hand, the writer went to "The World Almanac" for each year that a college head took his position and found the politics of the governor of the state at that time. No effort was made to learn the politics of any other officer or of the members of the boards of trustees of the various state institutions of higher education, or of the manner in which the trustees were selected. No effort was made either to see whether there was a change in the personnel of a board of trustees after the inauguration of a governor and before the selection of a college head. This study, then, instead of showing the extent of political influence in the selection of presidents for state institutions of higher education, shows the extent of coincidence of political affiliation by the college heads and the governors of the states at the times of their selection.

The results of the investigation in the first two references examined are shown in Table I. This table shows for the heads of the various types of institutions the number listed in "Who's Who in America" and the number so listed who gave the data necessary for this study.

TABLE I

Data on College Heads

	Listed in Educational Directory	Listed in "Who's Who in America"	Necessary data in "Who's Who in America"
Universities and colleges	93	80	37
Junior colleges	20	2	2
Teachers' colleges and nor. schools	198	130	89
Total	311	212	128

Since only two heads of junior colleges were listed in "Who's Who in America," junior colleges were dropped from further consideration. Only the 37 presidents of universities and colleges and the 89 presidents or principals of teachers' colleges and normal schools for whom the necessary data were available are considered hereafter in this report.

The more significant data of this study in coincidence are shown in Table II. In Table II are shown the extent to which the political

TABLE II

Incidence of Political Affiliation of College Heads and of State Governors

	Same party			Not same party		
	Democrat	Republican	Total	Democratic Governor and Republican College head	Republican Governor and Democratic College head	Total
Universities and colleges	16	13	29	3	5	8
Teachers' colleges and normal schools	29	43	72	12	5	17
Total	45	56	101	15	10	25

affiliations of the college heads and of the governors of their states at the times of their selection coincide, the extent to which they differ, and the political parties involved. All governors concerned were either Republicans or Democrats except one, who was a Progressive. But since this governor was a Republican before and after the short life of the Progressive party, he is considered here as a Republican. No college head was bold enough to classify himself as other than Republican or Democrat.

With four fifths of the presidents or principals of the state institutions of higher education being of the same political faith as the governors of their states at the times of their selection, one might be curious about individual states in the matter. A detailed report would probably be tedious, but there are some states especially which deserve consideration. There were a number of states in which all the college heads included in this study were of the same political complexion as the governors considered. These should be announced. Their attainment should not go unpublished. The states listed below are those that had two or more college heads of the same politics as the governors and none of different politics. These might be called the "hundred percenters." After each state named appears the number of state college heads included in the study, all of whom claimed the same politics as the governor.

Democrat "Hundred Percenters"		Republican "Hundred Percenters"	
Alabama	5	California	4
Arkansas	2	Illinois	3
Georgia	6	Indiana	2
North Carolina	3	Maine	4
Oklahoma	6	Michigan	3
South Carolina	2	Minnesota	3
Tennessee	3	Pennsylvania	6
Texas	9	Wisconsin	4
Virginia	2	Total	29
Total	38		

"Hundred Percenters" under alternating parties

Arizona	1 and 1
New Mexico	2 and 2
Total	3 and 3

The following conclusions concerning the incidence of political affiliation of the heads of state institutions of higher education and the governors of the states at the times of the selection of the college heads can be deduced from the above data:

(1) There is a coincidence of political affiliation of the governors and the college heads to the extent of four fifths of all cases for whom data were available, and there is practically no difference between the presidents of the state universities and colleges and the presidents or principals of the state teachers' colleges and normal schools in this ratio.

(2) The Republican party seems to enjoy more of this coincidence than the Democratic party.

(3) Certain states, all located in the South, are responsible for most of the coincidence of Democrats. These states are "hundred percenters" in this regard. Certain other states, mostly in the Great Lakes region, are "hundred percenters" for the Republicans and are responsible for most of the coincidence for that party. Two states, the newest ones of the Union, are also "hundred percenters," but the two major political parties share equally in the honors there.

J. R. SHANNON
INDIANA STATE TEACHERS COLLEGE,
TERRE HAUTE, INDIANA

NEW BOOKS IN EDUCATION

CARNEGIE FOUNDATION FOR THE ADVANCEMENT OF TEACHING. *Twenty-fifth Annual Report of the President and of the Treasurer.* Pp. vii + 206. The Foundation. Gratuitous.

CARR, WILLIAM G. and JOHN WAAGE. *The Lesson Assignment.* Pp. ix + 98. Stanford University Press. $1.50.

FITZGERALD, IRENE H. and ROBERT H. MAHONEY, editors. *Prose and Poetry for Précis Writing.* Pp. xiii + 184. Catholic Education Press. $1.25.

INTERNATIONAL INSTITUTE OF INTELLECTUAL CO-OPERATION. *Centres of Reference for International Affairs.* Pp. 163. The Institute, Paris. $1.00.

KITSON, HARRY D. *I Find My Vocation.* Pp. xvi + 216. Illustrated. McGraw-Hill. $1.40.

LYON, LEVERETT S. *Education for Business.* Third edition. Pp. xvi + 586. 16 figures. University of Chicago Press. $3.50.

PIPKIN, CHARLES W. *Social Politics and Modern Democracies.* Volume I. Pp. xxxiv + 377. Volume II. Pp. vii + 417. Macmillan. $7.50 the set.

REED, P. I. *Writing Journalistic Features.* Pp. xiii + 373. McGraw-Hill. $3.00.

SCHOOL AND SOCIETY

EDITED BY J. McKEEN CATTELL

WITH WHICH IS COMBINED THE

EDUCATIONAL REVIEW

EDITED BY WILLIAM McANDREW

Volume 34 | Saturday, September 5, 1931 | Number 871

TEACHERS BY THE GRACE OF GOD

By Sir JOHN ADAMS

UNIVERSITY OF CALIFORNIA AT LOS ANGELES

Mr. Floyd Dell is probably right when he tells us in his "Were You Ever a Child?" that we are all potential teachers, that we all want to teach. The ordinary human being when asked the way by a passing stranger *likes* to tell—if he *knows*. Irritation at such a question usually arises only if we are unable to supply the information desired. We enjoy the superior position of being the one who knows. It pleases us to talk with authority. A phrase has been coined to express this satisfaction. When we talk of "speaking *ex cathedra*," we really betray our schoolmaster attitude. For the two Latin words mean merely "from the chair," the reference being to the professor's chair, and the professor is after all only an elevated schoolmaster.

Even children pose as little schoolmasters and take pride in communicating a bit of knowledge of which they have the monopoly. The newspaper reporter's "scoop" is accompanied by a state of mind that is quite at home in the nursery, for there one of the most characteristic declarations is "*I* knew it *first*."

Passing from the numberless swarm of potential teachers, we find that in the United States there are round about eight hundred thousand professionals, of whom the vast majority have gone through a regular training for their work. Normal schools and university education departments seem to Americans part of the nature of things. It does not occur to them to ask whether a teacher should be trained to do her work. That is taken for granted. It is assumed that her occupation is a profession, and therefore demands a serious preparation. Accordingly, there is not the same need here as in England for the initials I like to use as a parallel to the popular T. B. M. which everybody knows stand for the Tired Business Man. My letters are T. G. G. standing for Teachers by the Grace of God.

The T. G. G. are those who believe that teaching comes by nature, so they have no need for any special training in the art. Most of the civilized world agree with Americans in demanding from their teachers the same sort of training as is exacted from the members of other crafts that claim to be professions. But in England there is a small group of secondary men-teachers—it used to be a very large one—who resent the suggestion that they should be called upon to undergo a training like their medical, legal and ecclesiastical friends. They regard it as an insult to be asked to show that they are qualified to do their work. A young man went through Oxford or Cambridge, took a good degree, and then proceeded straight to a school, and began to teach. In the few cases of "the born teacher" all went well, but in the case of the T. G. G. things did not usually go quite so satisfactorily. The plan strangely enough did not seem to work badly, so far as the careless observer could see. The agony of the T. G. G. during their first year or two was hidden from the general public. If the Grace of God scheme were challenged its supporter would ask: Do you deny that the teaching in our public schools is good? The critic, being a fair-minded man, had to admit that the work in these schools was in most ways admirable, and as a result of this admission he was occasionally at a loss to justify his demands for training.

But when we look a little closer we find the weak spot. While the secondary schools of England in those pre-training days were well taught at most stages in the school, there were almost always certain classes (under men fresh from the university) that suffered rather badly while their teachers learned their business. For these young men had to learn their craft somewhere, and if not in a training institution then it had to be in the actual school classroom. It is true that no training college or school of education can produce perfectly trained teachers, but they can turn out young people who have at least acquired skill in learning how to teach. Such beginners have been saved from making hundreds of blunders that the untrained make and repair at the expense of the pupils. After spoiling two or three classes, these untrained raw teachers did acquire the necessary skill. In point of fact they reached a stage at which they could legitimately claim to be trained teachers who could do their work as well as those who had taken a professional course, the difference being that the expense of their training was borne not by themselves but by their pupils. The process of their training is graphically described in a set of verses in *Punch* some years ago, in which a brilliant young schoolmaster describes what the untrained beginner went through in his first year or two of teaching. The story ends happily, as in real life it usually did. I quote the last verse from memory:

> But now the scene has somewhat changed,
> His past is growing dim.
> He's making men of boys because
> They've made a man of him.

It will be noted that I have used the masculine all through this account, the justification being that the English women secondary teachers from the beginning adopted a favorable attitude towards training. They recognized that if they wanted their craft to rank as a profession they must fulfil professional requirements. How could they expect the public to treat them as professionals if they themselves proclaimed that there was nothing to be learned about their profession—that it could be picked up in passing?

Once the government began to pay grants for education, the elementary teachers in England did not have the choice of training or not training. The educational authorities saw at once that if teachers had to be responsible for the huge classes that economy imposed upon them, they must be properly trained for their work, and a rather crude but very effective training was at once set up.

In America education has always been taken very seriously, so the need for training was readily recognized and there was at the beginning none of that contempt for normal schools that arose in England because only elementary teachers went to them. It took a while for the resentment against training to get a footing, and it never gained a very firm hold. There were two forces working for the establishment of a superiority complex against the normal schools, and later against the education departments of universities. There was first the very natural pride of the high-school teachers in the advanced nature of their curriculum as compared with the simpler subjects of the grades. This feeling of superiority is to be found among secondary teachers all over the world—though less in the United States than elsewhere. But the second cause of cleavage was found in the universities themselves. With the rise of the education departments there developed a split in the whole faculty. It fell into the two parts that for convenience may be called the "pedagogics" on the one hand and all the rest of the instructors on the other, who may for our purposes be labeled "academics." Gradually a slight superiority complex developed among the academics, though it is noteworthy that this was not balanced by a corresponding inferiority complex among the pedagogics.

The academics did not realize that in essence the university was originally a great training college. When a man got through his university course successfully, and in the idiom of that time "went home a wise man," he carried with him a document that conveyed to him the *jus ubique docendi,* the right to teach in any of the universities of Christendom—really a teacher's certificate. It has to be admitted that the curriculum leading up to this certificate included no deliberate training in teaching, though the constant discussions and debates must have provided an excellent preparation for the lecturing which was at that time the recognized method of teaching. The present detailed form of training is the outcome of the great development of different ways in which teaching may be carried on. A recognition of this necessary complexity is one of the factors that have produced a certain favorable reaction of the academics towards the pedagogics.

What has hitherto strengthened the superior attitude of the academics is the enormous importance they attach to the subject-matter they teach. The thing to be taught bulked much more largely in the mind of the professor than did the person he taught. The faculty were much more impressed by their knowledge of the subjects than by their knowledge of their students. The old-fashioned schoolmaster was much prouder of his knowledge of Latin than he was of his knowledge of John to whom he taught it, and truth to tell his knowledge of John was hardly massive enough to warrant much pride. In the past the teacher drove subject and pupil tandem, subject being in front and pupil in the rear. But while John had to take place behind Latin, and therefore incidentally nearer the whip, a reversal would not have mended matters. Neither must be in front: they must be driven side by side.

For the four words "subject to be taught" let us adopt one word. Though it is a Latin one it involves the saving of three words every time we use it. So the reader will perhaps excuse *docendum.* It has at least the authority of a brilliant writer—no less than De Quincey—behind it.

All the academics have in the past taken refuge behind the *docendum,* and have rather neglected John. But now the multiple-John of the university classroom has wakened up to his own importance, and the professors are beginning to realize that he must be taken into account. Since the same awakening is observable among the senior pupils at the high schools, academics on the university faculty are beginning to adopt a somewhat more friendly attitude towards their pedagogic colleagues, and seem to be even wondering among themselves whether there may not be something after all in this "training" that might possibly be of use even to full rank professors.

Listening to the complaints of outside lay critics, and even to the criticisms of their own students as expressed in such printed productions as "The Students Speak Out," the academics are beginning to ask themselves whether after all it is enough to be masters of their *docendum,* or whether there may be something to learn about how to "put it over" to their students. These conscience-stricken academics may still say to themselves that of course these pedagogics have certainly erred in not paying sufficient attention to the *docendum* and that the academics have been justified in describing the education men as professors who are experts in teaching but have nothing to teach. Still the generous minded academics may reflect that this reproach may apply to all experts —that they know everything about their own subject and precious little about anything else. In any case the time has come when the academics seem to think they had better give the pedagogic a chance to show what he has in him.

In view of this approach to a friendly tone of repentance it may be permitted to mention without offence one of the possible reasons why in the past the academics regarded with disfavor the schools of education that began to invade Academia. It must be admitted that it was unpleasant to realize that into one's own institution came fellows who taught the students the principles of teaching. For when all is said professors are teachers, and these upstarts were laying down the law about how the thing was to be done. To be sure the instruction given in the schools of education was specially addressed to students whose life-work was to be in the ordinary schools of the nation. But in the last resort teaching is teaching the world over, and at all stages of advancement, and the students who attended lectures on teaching could not help applying what they learned to criticize how they were themselves taught by the academics. Whether they would or no the students of education could not help noticing how frequently pedagogical principles were disregarded by the academics. It is not in human nature to hold one's peace about such matters: they crave for discussion, so a wave of criticism began to sweep over the campuses of the country, and uneasiness reigned in the ranks of the academics. Among the nobler of them there was a quickening of conscience, and a personal examination to see whether there was any ground for the criticism in their case. It is probable that the total result of the disturbance was all to the good. It is true that those of the baser sort experienced nothing but an increased irritation with those troublesome pedagogics. But the net result of the whole was the present slightly favorable change of attitude towards the pedagogics.

Fortunately there has been a corresponding change of heart among the pedagogics. They are beginning to realize that perhaps they have taken up a too exclusively expert attitude, and have been working in a too abstract atmosphere, maybe following the airy nothings of their craft to unreasonable distances from the actual school and college. It is not impossible that the student criticism that aroused the consciences of the academics has had a good deal to do with the pedagogic change of heart. It is bad enough to be criticized by students because we do not teach them Latin and physics as expertly as we ought: but it is harrowing, and gall and wormwood, and boiling oil, and the rack and all the other standard horrors to have students finding fault with us because we do not teach them as we ask them to teach others. The better sort of the pedagogics live in an unhappy state of self-criticism. They realize all too clearly how difficult it is to live up to the high level they set before their students. Accordingly, they are only too willing to sympathize with the academics who resent, but do not care to speak about, this undercurrent of criticism that has its source in the classroom of the school of education.

So keenly do many of the pedagogics feel the sting of this suppressed criticism that they themselves bring into being, that they are inclined to adopt the counsel of despair that underlies the recommendation to their pupils: "Don't do as I do: do as I tell you." Cynical as it sounds, it embodies a quite sound philosophy that deserves elaboration. In the meantime an excellent application of this apparently depressing doctrine may be made by using it as a means of drawing together the two hitherto opposing groups in the university faculties. If educational progress and the development of means of intercommunication among the universities of the world have roused a cosmic critical attitude of students towards their instructors, it is highly desirable that the academics and the pedagogics should join ranks and make common cause against the weaknesses pointed out by their critics. A beginning of this cooperation has already been forced on the training colleges where a certain amount of academic work has to be carried on simultaneously with professional training. The lecturers in these subjects are specialists, but they are not called lecturers in this or that, but lecturers in the teaching of this or that. The lecturer in the teaching of physics is really an academic and a pedagogic rolled into one. What is to hinder the two sides of the faculty working together by the academic side appointing specialists to represent the various elements of the *docendum* on the education faculty? They need not be full-time members in the pedagogic school: it will be enough if they are specially good teachers of their branch of the *docendum,* and expert enough in the subject itself to command the respect of their fellow academics. They would serve as *liaison* officers to keep the two sides in friendly touch, and would do invaluable service in lubricating the wheels of the university machine.

THE CONTRIBUTION OF PUBLIC EDUCATION TO THE WELFARE OF THE NATION[1]

By Dr. GEORGE D. STRAYER

PROFESSOR OF EDUCATION, TEACHERS COLLEGE, COLUMBIA UNIVERSITY, NEW YORK CITY

Education is a function of the state. Public education is the foundation upon which the democratic state is built. The perpetuity of our form of government and the improvement of our society rest alike upon the work which is done in the public school system.

Students of government have from time immemorial emphasized the importance of education in the development of the democratic state, no one more adequately than the late president of the United States, Woodrow Wilson. In his noteworthy treatise entitled, "The State," he says:

> . . . Education is the proper office of the state for two reasons. . . . Popular education is neces-

[1] Statement before general sessions, National Education Association, Los Angeles, California, June 27, 1931.

sary for the preservation of those conditions of freedom, political and social, which are indispensable to free individual development. And, in the second place, no instrumentality less universal in its power and authority than government can secure popular education. In brief, in order to secure popular education the action of society as a whole is necessary; and popular education is indispensable to that equalization of the conditions of personal development which we have taken to be the proper object of society. Without popular education, moreover, no government which rests upon popular action can long endure; the people must be schooled in the knowledge, and if possible in the virtues, upon which the maintenance and success of free institutions depend. No free government can last in health if it lose hold of the traditions of its history, and in the public schools these traditions may be and should be sedulously preserved, carefully replanted in the thought and consciousness of each successive generation.

It may be well to emphasize the fact that through the development of public education in our nation has come the largest degree of realization of that promise of democracy which proposes that men shall enjoy equality of opportunity. The pronouncement of the Fathers that in this nation men should have guaranteed to them life, liberty and the pursuit of happiness has been in some degree realized through the opportunities for achievement presented by the public-school system. In increasing degree in the United States all boys and girls are finding it possible to achieve up to the limits of their intellectual capacity, their ambition and their character.

Certain it is that the schools are open to the more ambitious and that no obstacle of class or other social distinction prevents the progress of boys and girls through the school system from its beginning in the kindergarten through the professional or graduate school of the university. In increasing measure the several states of the Union are enacting legislation and providing support which tend to equalize opportunities throughout their borders.

In one state the smallest rural school is guaranteed by the state a support of not less than $1,500 per year. In many of the states special provision is made for the transportation of children to larger centers in order that those living in the rural areas may enjoy opportunities comparable to those provided in the cities. In ever increasing measure children of high intellectual capacity are finding the road to higher education more certainly open to them than was true a generation ago.

The ideal acknowledged by our forefathers has been in process of development, particularly during the past sixty years. To state that we have not yet fully realized the ideal is not to deny its validity nor to question its importance as a most significant contribution in the development of the democratic ideal.

That equality of opportunity is not merely a catch-word of the demagogue or the hope of the idealist, is indicated by the great advancement that has been made in recent years in the adaptation of our public school system to the needs of the whole population. We no longer believe that a single-track school system provides equality of educational opportunity. In our more progressive school systems, the traditional elementary school and senior high school have been replaced by schools which seek to provide unique opportunities for boys and girls who vary greatly in their ability to acquire skill or knowledge, in their power to undertake precise thinking, in their capacity for growth in power of appreciation, and in their ability to do creative work. Instead of the old-fashioned elementary school with a single course of study, we have provided schools in which individual instruction is given, others in which groups are organized with respect to their general intelligence or special abilities, classes for those who are backward, delinquent, physically handicapped, and the like. For that part of the school system which was once merely a repetition of the work done in the first six grades, we have established the junior high school with its broadening and finding courses, with its earlier beginnings of mathematics beyond arithmetic, foreign language, science, and a variety of opportunities in industrial and household arts. For the high school, which was available for only the top ten per cent. in intelligence, we have provided the comprehensive high school with multiple curricula. We have added to the lower end of the school system the nursery school and kindergarten. At the upper end we have extended the program to include the college and the university. We have paralleled the work of the high school with the continuation and vocational schools. We are beginning to develop a program of adult education which may prove to be the most significant of all changes in our school organization.

The recognition of individual differences has been the key to progress. We have sought diligently to adjust our schools to the needs and capacities of those who are registered in them. City school systems, large and small, have developed organizations for the study of the problems of curricula. Teachers, supervisors and superintendents, under the direction of well-equipped specialists, have moved our schools beyond the stage that they occupied when the text-book was the only guide provided for the teacher. More and more certainly courses of study are offering suggestions to teachers which will enable them to make significant adjustments to individual needs. Our curricula are less traditional and more certainly related to the social demands which the schools are organized to meet. The interests, enthusiasms, and creative abilities of children are given a larger place in our modern courses of study.

That our public-school system has made a real contribution to the welfare of the nation is measured objectively by the fact that a larger percentage of boys and girls of secondary school age are to be found enrolled in these institutions than is the case in any other country in the world. It may be proposed that we have come to accept secondary education as the common heritage of all our people as we had sixty years ago come to believe in the necessity of free elementary schools for all children. Fifty-five per cent. of all boys and girls between fourteen and eighteen years of age are to be found enrolled in American high schools. It seems entirely possible, with the development of this part of our school system and its adaptation to the needs and capacities of the individuals composing the whole group, that we may look forward to a time when an even greater proportion of the total population may be enrolled in secondary schools.

But public education has not stopped with the secondary school period. One of the most notable contributions to the welfare of our people has been found in higher education supported by taxation in the several states of the Union. In the state colleges and universities so maintained we have provided for the liberal education of an increasing percentage of the total population and for the special technical and professional education of those who are to serve in these most important fields. Even more significantly our state institutions of higher learning have contributed in the field of scientific inquiry. There is no process or undertaking in everyday life that has not been modified by contributions made at institutions of higher learning, supported by public taxation.

Whether we inquire concerning the increased productivity of the soil, the improvement in machinery or management in industry, the marketing of goods, the dissemination of information or the expansion of human knowledge, in every case we can trace much of the development of the past fifty years to the contribution made by public education as represented by the institutions of higher learning.

It is possible to point out, not merely in general terms, the contribution which has been made by public education, but also to indicate in detail the effectiveness of this social institution. We enjoy a common culture in the United States to-day, primarily by virtue of the work done by the public schools. In no other way could the diverse elements which make up our total population have been moulded into a unified people. We have one language. When one stops to consider the millions of those who have come to live with us, speaking foreign tongues, he can not but marvel at this achievement of the public-school system. We have, with the exception of a small and constantly decreasing minority, a people who are literate. We have achieved, by virtue of public education, a social solidarity which has enabled us to act as a unit in times of crisis. We enjoy a "likemindedness," the fundamental basis upon which a working society must be constituted, due to the possession of common ideals, beliefs and loyalties.

Our schools have encouraged boys and girls to believe in the virtue of individual initiative, while at the same time they have taught them to acknowledge their responsibility to the whole group. The philosophy of education which guides the work of the teacher in our public schools places highest sympathy and cooperation with one's fellows in working for the common good.

We are a more healthful people than were our grandfathers. Knowledge of the laws of personal and community hygiene and right habits of living have been taught in the public schools. In increasing measure the literacy of the population, together with the instruction given in public education, is freeing us from the influence of the "quack." The nostrums that were commonly sold and the "cures" for which people once gave their substance are less commonly accepted by our people than they were a generation or two ago.

Mention has already been made of the application of science to agriculture, industry and commerce. It is no idle claim to propose that the economic strength of our people is attributable in large degree to our program of public education. It is inconceivable that one should be successful in the modern economic world except upon the basis of a system of education offered free to all.

Among the countries of the world those that show the greatest economic strength are those in which education has most certainly been made available for the whole population. Careful students of the economic experiment now being carried on in Russia have proposed that it may fail because of the lack of education provided both in the past and for the present generation of young people.

The standards of appreciation in the fine arts have been raised during our lifetime. Tens of thousands of children in the public schools in the United States are learning to enjoy better music. Other thousands are participating in a significant manner in work carried on in the graphic and plastic arts. Almost universally the boys and girls and young men and women in our public-school system are becoming acquainted with the literature of our language and are receiving significant training in expressing their thought and feeling in their mother-tongue.

The public schools of the United States have always recognized character building as a primary objective of education. It is worthy of note that the Ordinance of 1787, for the government of the Northwest Territory, proposed the following mandate with respect to the schools:

Religion, morality and knowledge being necessary to good government and the happiness of mankind, schools and the means of education shall be forever encouraged.

The contribution of public education to the welfare of the nation can not be considered as having been made. Public education has to contribute to each generation all that has been claimed for it in the generations which are past. Even more certainly public education in the years that lie ahead must contribute to the solution of our modern economic and social problems. We must hope to develop, through education, a generation of men and women whose sympathies are as broad as their common humanity; a group of individuals who, while seeking to achieve up to the limits of their capacities, acknowledge their responsibility for the welfare of the whole group; men and women tolerant of the beliefs of others and yet guided in their thinking by science rather than by superstition or tradition; a nation of individuals whose scale of values places highest the good, the true and the beautiful.

Our public schools, from the kindergarten through the university, must continue to be the instrument used by the nation for perpetuating and for improving our society. Our faith in public education has been justified. Still greater tasks lie ahead. The forces of ignorance, superstition and social injustices always remain to be conquered. Enjoying the confidence and good-will of our people, the public schools may be counted upon to make an ever increasing contribution to the welfare of the nation.

EDUCATIONAL EVENTS

COMPULSORY EDUCATION IN SOVIET RUSSIA

MR. WALTER DURANTY, in a wireless dispatch to *The New York Times,* comments on the fact that August 14 was the anniversary of the publication of the Soviet decree ordering four years of compulsory education throughout the Union of Socialist Soviet Republics for children from 8 to 11 years old, inclusive, and a further three-year period for children from 11 to 14 in so far as possible.

The dispatch says that a summary of the results to date show that 15,500,000 children are taking the four-year course, which is 97.1 per cent. of the children between the ages mentioned, in the Russian Socialist Federated Soviet Republic (the largest unit in the Soviet Union), 98.2 per cent. of the children in the Ukrainian Socialist Soviet Republic, and 97 per cent. of the children in the White Russia Republic.

Other republics in the union show lower percentages, but the grand total amounts to 10 per cent. above the program originally planned. In addition, more than 2,000,000 children from 8 to 11 are getting the extra three years' training, making the total 17,600,000, as compared with the peak figure under czarism of 7,200,000. Education is conducted in 70 different languages.

Mr. Duranty states that President Kalinin, of the Soviet Union, expresses great satisfaction in the leading editorial in the newspaper *Izvestia* as to the number of children attending school, but mentions several shortcomings, such as inadequate buildings, poor equipment, the shortage of teachers and their lack of qualifications, and the unwieldy classes, as a result of which, he said, even children finishing the seven-year course "still do not properly know their own language and grammar."

He adds that improvements also are necessary in developing "social" education—that is, from a proletarian, Socialist standpoint—but he stresses particularly the need for teaching children from an early stage to understand and respect the dignity of labor, especially physical labor. For this purpose he advocates such "practical" studies as helping with the harvest on fruit and truck farms and mechanical instruction for future workers in the towns.

Andrey Rubnoff, commissar of education of

the Russian Republic, asserts that generalized Socialist education got a real start only this year. The chief task now, he says, is to direct it towards higher polytechnic training, and on this basis the educational system and the teaching staff require further organization, which, when accomplished, will permit the participation of adult workers and members of farm collectives in the educational movement.

M. Rubnoff says that he is confident that it will not be long before polytechnic training for all children up to 17 years of age will be successfully organized. He stresses the need for righting "Right" and "Left" tendencies in political or "social" training, and he said that the aim is "to lay a sound educational foundation for the whole country, which has now entered the period of socialism."

ADULT EDUCATION

Millions of adults throughout the United States are now pursuing systematically some form of instruction, according to a report issued by the Federal Office of Education.

Approximately 4,000,000 persons are thus reached by adult education which the specialist asserts "is having a powerful influence in bringing to the fore the importance of public libraries and museums."

Only 17 per cent. of the rural population, Mr. Alderman adds, has access to public libraries compared with 90 per cent. of the city dwellers. Additional information from the study follows:

Alabama, California, Connecticut, Delaware, the District of Columbia, New York, Louisiana, Pennsylvania and South Carolina have made progress in promoting the instruction of grown-ups.

In a number of states school officials have endeavored to find, at the time of taking the regular school census, the names and addresses of those who are in reality functionally illiterate. It has been found that this information is of much greater value than that procured by the federal census. It also has been found that the expense of procuring these names and addresses is relatively small.

The states of Nebraska and Delaware, in connection with their school census, have gathered valuable information as to the educational needs of their adult population. The city of Tacoma, Washington, for a number of years has gathered such information at the time of the regular school census. It is evident that school administrators should have full information as to the educational needs of the community.

School officials are becoming more aware of the importance of the influence of parents upon the education of children. Wherever studies have been made it has been found that children of illiterate or poorly educated parents are greatly handicapped in their quest for an education. Growth in the parent-teacher work in this country shows most clearly that parents are vitally interested in bringing about better conditions for the rearing of children. Leaders of this movement claim that the most effective means of bringing about more wholesome conditions for children is to be found through the education of parents.

The education of adults is going on in all kinds of ways, and it is estimated that there probably are 4,000,000 grown-ups who are pursuing some kind of instruction which is so continuous and of such a nature that it may be classified as adult education. The number probably will increase manyfold as it becomes generally known that adults can learn and as courses that fit their needs become more numerous.

Adult education is having a powerful influence in bringing to the fore the importance, as educational agencies, of such organizations as public libraries and public museums.

It is regrettable that only 17 per cent. of our rural population have access to a public library, while over 90 per cent. of our city dwellers have such privilege.

Public museums are taking a larger place in public education, and it is very likely that such museums will be organized more as educational exhibits and will be even much more popular than they have been in the past.

THE CARNEGIE FOUNDATION FOR THE ADVANCEMENT OF TEACHING

According to an official summary of the twenty-fifth annual report of the president and of the treasurer for the year ending June 30,

1930, Dr. Henry Suzzallo assumed, on August 1, 1930, the presidency of the foundation. Dr. Henry Smith Pritchett, president of the foundation since its beginning in 1906, became on that date president emeritus.

Dr. Suzzallo served from 1915 to 1926 as president of the University of Washington. During 1927–28 he was visiting Carnegie professor of international relations in Europe with the Carnegie Endowment for International Peace. He served also as director of President Hoover's National Advisory Committee on Education to study and to offer recommendations concerning the federal government's relations to education.

Dr. Pritchett was associated with Andrew Carnegie in organizing the foundation. From 1897 to 1900 Dr. Pritchett was superintendent of the United States Coast and Geodetic Survey, and from 1900 to 1906 president of the Massachusetts Institute of Technology. He continues his association with the foundation in an advisory capacity.

For the year 1930–31, the officers of the foundation's board of trustees are President John Grier Hibben, of Princeton University, *chairman;* President William Allan Nielson, of Smith College, *vice-chairman,* and Provost Josiah Harmar Penniman, of the University of Pennsylvania, *secretary.*

The report reviews the financial history of the foundation and lists in detail the studies and publications with which the foundation has concerned itself. The resources of the foundation are held in five separate funds.

The general endowment of $10,000,000, since its transfer to the trustees on April 16, 1905, has been increased by $6,801,000. Of this addition, Mr. Carnegie provided two millions in 1911 and one million in 1912, and the Carnegie Corporation provided two millions in 1920, a total of five million dollars. The rest of the increase of $1,801,000 was produced by reinvestment. The remaining $14,000,000 and more of the foundation's resources constitute three special reserve funds and the endowment of the Division of Educational Enquiry.

During the twenty-five years of its history the foundation has issued twenty-five reports, twenty-five bulletins, and about two score of smaller publications. These publications, amounting in all to some ten thousand pages, have been distributed without charge to interested persons in editions usually of 7,500 copies, frequently of 10,000, and sometimes of 20,000 copies.

The Carnegie Foundation's Division of Educational Enquiry in the eighteen years of its existence has expended more than $1,039,000 in studies relating to universities and colleges. Among these studies the inquiry concerning legal education has received more than $222,000 up to June 30, 1930; the study of secondary and higher education in Pennsylvania about $164,000; the foundation's study of dental education more than $64,500; and its enquiry into college athletics upwards of $96,300. These studies have been financed out of income from the permanent fund of the Division of Educational Enquiry, which totals $1,270,000.

ANALYSIS OF COSTS PER CHILD IN THE SCHOOLS OF NEW YORK CITY

APPROXIMATELY $86 out of every $100 of the taxpayers' money spent by the New York City Board of Education is applied directly to the instruction of the city's 1,200,000 public school pupils, and about $3 out of every $100 is spent for administration according to figures recently made public by Dr. George J. Ryan, president of the board.

The compilation contained an analysis of how $100 is spent in the school system. The figures were for the fiscal and calendar year 1930 and did not include the cost of erecting new school buildings and additions, as these expenditures are from a separate budget administered jointly by the board of education and the board of estimates.

The total annual and recurring expenses of the board of education were slightly more than $135,000,000 as of 1930. Besides approximately $42,000,000 was spent to carry forward last year's school-building program.

According to the board of education's analysis, each $100 spent in the school system may be itemized as follows:

For the salaries of teachers and principals......	$83.06
For supplies, text-books, library books, etc.	2.88
For playgrounds, after-school athletics, community and recreation centers, baths, school lunches, &c.; salaries and supplies...	1.01

For rentals and leases of school buildings, the transportation of pupils and teachers and fees for instruction of children in outside institutions	.77
For general repairs to school buildings, repairs and replacements of furniture and pianos, the salaries of draftsmen, inspectors, mechanics and others	3.89
To pay custodians, elevator operators, firemen, stokers and cleaners and for the supplies used by custodians for the care of buildings and property; for coal, wood, water and the salaries of fuel inspectors	5.29
For educational administration, including the salary of the Superintendent of Schools, the salaries of the Associate Superintendents, the Board of Examiners, the directors of various activities and others and the supplies for these officials	2.03
For business administration, including the salaries of the Auditor and his staff, the Superintendent of Supplies, the Superintendent of Construction and Maintenance and the Superintendent of Plant Operation	.79
For general administration expenses, including the salary of the secretary of the board, the salaries of the secretaries of the board members, printing in the secretary's office, &c.	.25
For other incidental expenses, payments under the Workmen's Compensation law and damage judgments	.03

In explaining how the sum of $86 was arrived at as the amount that went directly to the instruction of children, the statement showed that this was the sum spent to pay the teachers and to buy the school books and the copy paper. The remaining $14 out of every $100 was used to keep school buildings in good condition, to supply them with coal in the winter and a playground in the summer, and also to provide for the staff of workers which administers the affairs of the school system.

THE FINE MEMORIAL HALL AT PRINCETON UNIVERSITY

MATHEMATICAL equations and geometrical figures appear in the stained glass windows designed for Princeton University's latest building which has been erected in memory of Dean Henry Burchard Fine, professor of mathematics and until his death dean of the department of science at Princeton University. This structure will be dedicated in the autumn. Miss Gwethalyn Jones, of Chicago, who with her uncle, the late Thomas D. Jones, prominent Chicago lawyer and Princeton trustee, presented to the university $500,000 for the building and its endowment, will attend the dedication.

In keeping with the study and research which will be carried on within the walls of the building, in one window is a curve of the fourth order expressed in polar coordinates and in another is a hyperbola with the axes as asymptotes. Even the gargoyles have a mathematical meaning, one of them, on the fireplace of the common room, illustrating the merbius strip or one-sided surface.

Constructed of red brick in the collegiate Gothic style, Fine Hall, joining Palmer Physical Laboratory at the lower end of the campus, is elaborate and modern to the last detail. It provides studies for members of the teaching staff, similar facilities for graduate students, large lecture rooms and seminar rooms and a spacious library occupying the entire third floor. On the second floor are two small kitchens equipped with every device to minimize labor, including dishwashing machines. There are several conference rooms and the common room, in which will hang a portrait of Dean Fine. The class rooms are equipped with sliding blackboards and all rooms have indirect lighting.

Dean Fine died in 1928 as a result of injuries he received when struck by an automobile.

A DISTINGUISHED CITIZEN OF GEORGIA

THE State Legislature of Georgia, according to the *Christian Science Monitor* has recognized the accomplishments of two well-known women of the state by declaring them "distinguished citizens."

To be declared a "distinguished citizen of Georgia" one must have accomplished some service for the state or have done something of outstanding interest.

The only two women in the recent history of Georgia to win this distinction are Miss Martha Berry, of Rome, and Mrs. Richard P. Brooks, of Forsyth. Recognition came to Miss Berry at a former session of the General Assembly. That to Mrs. Brooks has been but recently bestowed.

Miss Berry is more than a Georgian figure.

Her reputation is nation-wide and probably extends beyond the borders of the United States. She has for a number of years been engaged in a great educational work in Georgia. She is the active and successful head of the Martha Berry School for Mountain Children in Rome. She has a campus of 20,000 acres, largely of tilled and productive land and buildings valued at $5,000,000.

The *Monitor* writes:

This development has come about within the last twenty years or so. It began when Miss Berry, as a young woman, entertained three mountain children at her home in the country near Rome, on a Sunday afternoon. She played the old-fashioned melodeon for them, recited a Sunday school lesson and invited them with true Georgia hospitality to "come again." They did so, and brought others with them. So the flock increased, until Miss Berry, seeing the need of education for such youngsters, was inspired to start a school. Thus was formed the nucleus for the great institution she has to-day.

Mr. and Mrs. Henry Ford have helped her in her work. Former President Coolidge has commended her efforts, and Colonel Theodore Roosevelt, when President, was enthusiastic over what she was doing. A monthly magazine conducted recently a national contest to select America's 12 most useful women, and Martha Berry's name is high up on the list. The New York Town Hall Club gave her a medal for achievement of lasting merit.

THE FINANCIAL STATUS OF THE SMALL COLLEGE

According to a report published in the *New York Herald Tribune*, Senator Simeon D. Fess, of Ohio, former president of Antioch College and long connected with educational affairs, has arranged the conference at the instance of a number of college heads. The purpose is to get the President interested in what is known as the liberal arts college movement and to ask him to give it his indorsement and to speak to the country in its behalf in an address which will be broadcast throughout the United States.

Fear of the small colleges that they will be more and more overshadowed and eventually swallowed by the great colleges and universities with huge endowments or resources furnished by the states is back of the liberal arts college movement.

Senator Fess, in a statement explaining the forthcoming conference with President Hoover, said:

"The liberal arts college movement originated in a conference in which 280 colleges were represented, meeting in Chicago March 18 to 20, 1930. Direction of the movement was intrusted to a committee of fifteen under the chairmanship of A. N. Ward, president of Western Maryland College. This committee includes representatives from all sections of the country and from all religious groups, both Protestant and Catholic, which have large interests in higher education. The second conference of the movement was held in Indianapolis January 21, 1931. An executive secretary has been appointed and offices opened in Chicago. Some 230 colleges have joined the movement since its beginning.

"Catholic as well as Protestant colleges are associated in the movement and the one Jewish college in the country also is a member.

"Liberal arts colleges, most of which represent from 300 to 1,000 students each, have made outstanding contributions to the production of leadership in this country and are continuing to render that service with increasingly modern plants, equipment and better trained personnel. In respect to their relation to the country, however, they recognize a growing disadvantage which this movement is intended to offset.

"Many colleges, such as Davidson, Randolph-Macon, Carleton, Center and Pomona, are located in comparatively small communities. They are unable, acting individually, to secure the public attention and interest which comes unsolicited to immense universities, located in urban centers and reinforced with the attention secured through professional schools, scientific achievements in the graduate departments, and receipt of large gifts; yet within their more limited field the independent standard colleges are doing a work of education grade equal to that of the universities."

Arrangements are being made for a broadcast on a national hook-up some time this fall. Dr. John H. Finley, of New York, will preside and announce the speakers. President Hoover will be asked to give an address at this time and a number of prominent speakers will be on the program. The tentative date is Saturday, November 14.

EDUCATIONAL NOTES AND NEWS

SIR DONALD MACLEAN has been appointed president of the board of education of England in the new national government.

DR. JOHN D. BLACK, of Harvard University, has been appointed chief economist of the Federal Farm Board, to succeed Dr. Joseph S. Davis.

DR. GEORGE B. CUTTEN, president of Colgate University, has been elected to the presidency of the National Council of Education of the Young Men's Christian Association.

FREDERIC L. BALLARD has been appointed to succeed the late Charles Day as vice-chairman of the executive board of the trustees of the University of Pennsylvania.

THE REV. THOMAS F. RYAN, dean of arts and sciences at St. John's College, Brooklyn, since 1923, has been named president of the institution.

DR. JOSEPH S. ILLICK, former state forester of Pennsylvania, was appointed head of the department of forest management of the New York State College of Forestry at Syracuse University by recent action of the board of trustees of the college.

DR. CHARLES E. SPEARMAN, professor of psychology at the University of London, will retire at the end of the coming academic year. He will be succeeded by Dr. Cyril L. Burt, professor of psychology at the London Training College.

THE following appointments have been made at the school of education of New York University: Peter L. Agnew, Jr., Louis Berg, Francis J. Brown, Helen Cox, John C. Duff and Ray E. Haines as instructors in education; J. Warren Erb, Frank Luker and Dorothy Mulgrave as assistant professors of education, and George C. Minard as associate professor of education.

JAMES E. MORLOCK has been named to succeed Professor Paul G. Cressey as head of the department of sociology at Evansville College. Dr. Morlock is president of the Southwestern Indiana Teachers Association.

DR. HARRIET E. O'SHEA, of Madison, Wisconsin, who has been director of personnel, director of the pre-school laboratory and professor of educational psychology at Mills College, California, has resigned her position there to accept a similar position in Purdue University.

MR. CHARLES CALVIN MADEIRA has been elected superintendent of the schools of Gloucester, New Jersey. He succeeds John C. Groome, who will continue with the school system as principal of the high school.

DR. VICTOR C. MILLER, professor of English at the Indiana State Teachers College, Terre Haute, is spending two years in advanced study in Germany and England.

ACCEPTANCE of the position of permanent secretary to the Social Science Research Council, with headquarters in New York, by Professor Robert T. Crane, of the political science department of the University of Michigan, will not definitely terminate his connection with the university, since he is not resigning but will be granted an indefinite leave of absence. He has been on Michigan's faculty for eighteen years and has been connected with the governing body of the Social Science Research Council for ten years. Professor Crane succeeds Dr. Robert S. Lynch, who has become professor of sociology at Columbia University. Dr. R. S. Woodworth, professor of psychology at Columbia University, is president of the council, having succeeded Dr. E. B. Wilson, professor of vital statistics in the School of Public Health of Harvard University.

DR. GEORGE H. BRIDGMAN, president emeritus of Hamline University and for twenty-nine years president of the institution, celebrated his ninetieth birthday on August 2.

RAYMOND MACFARLAND, formerly professor of secondary education, Middlebury College, has opened the Aurora School of Personality at East Aurora, New York, on the site formerly occupied by the Meade School.

DR. JULIAN D. TAYLOR, who resigned from Colby College two months ago, after teaching Latin in that institution for sixty-three years, has been nominated by Governor William T.

Gardiner, of Maine, as the "Grand Old Man" of Maine. In his message to President Franklin W. Johnson, the governor said: "I have noticed recently by the public prints the honors and attentions which have been bestowed upon Dr. Julian D. Taylor, of the Colby faculty. It was a pleasure to note, likewise, that the Italian ambassador was moved to recognition of Dr. Taylor's service as a teacher of Latin in Colby for a period of over sixty-three years. With your permission and that of Dr. Taylor, I want to nominate him the 'Grand Old Man of Maine,' confident that neither the field of letters nor yet business or public service can produce a man in our state who has done more, over a longer period, for the people of Maine, than has this Nestor of professors." Simultaneously with this honor Dr. Taylor was elected an alumni trustee of the college by the largest vote ever recorded.

DR. J. MCKEEN CATTELL, editor of SCHOOL AND SOCIETY, sailed for England on August 26 in order to attend as the delegate of the American Association for the Advancement of Science the centenary meeting of the British Association.

PROFESSOR JAMES T. SHOTWELL, of Columbia University and the Carnegie Endowment for International Peace, is in Poland in connection with the completion of the Polish volumes of the economic and social histories of the world war.

DEAN THOMAS U. TAYLOR, of the University of Texas, has been given a silver medal by the society of the Red Cross of Jugo-Slavia, in recognition of his kindness to students from that country since the world war.

DR. MILTON S. J. WRIGHT, who has been studying at the University of Heidelberg during the past year, will resume his duties as dean of Sam Huston College at the beginning of the academic year.

PROFESSOR GEORGE ELLSWORTH JOHNSON, associate professor of education at the Graduate School of Education of Harvard University, died on August 26 at the age of sixty-nine years.

DR. RICHARD PAUL KOEPKE, professor of modern languages at the University of Detroit, died on August 30.

THE death is announced of Mrs. George Wood Bacon, one of the founders of the New School for Social Research and a member of its board of directors.

THE school of education of the University of Chicago has dedicated a bronze drinking fountain as a memorial to Katharine Martin, for nearly twenty-five years and until her death a teacher in kindergarten-primary education. Miss Martin held the positions of critic teacher, instructor and assistant professor, respectively. The fountain, modeled by Mrs. Mabel L. Torrey, of the Midway Studios, Chicago, was presented to the university by students and alumnae of the department.

A TWO-DAY conference is to be held under the auspices of the Child Study Association of America, at the Pennsylvania Hotel, in New York City, on October 19 and 20. The speakers will include Mr. Eduard C. Lindeman, *chairman.* Dr. Nicholas Murray Butler, Dr. Rachel Stutsman, Dr. Caroline B. Zachry, Mr. Harry M. Schulman, Dr. Ruth Brickner, Mr. Robert Lynd, Mrs. Sidonie Matsner Gruenberg and Dr. William A. Neilson.

THE Pennsylvania State College is sponsoring, through its school of education, a conference on guidance and personnel to be held on October 30 and 31, 1931. At that time, Mr. F. O. Holt, of the University of Wisconsin, will discuss the conference theme, "School and College Relations." Speakers from Pennsylvania will also address the meeting.

A GIFT of $25,000 to Northwestern University has been made by Mrs. Minnie G. Newman, the income to be used for scholarships in the law school. The fund was established by Mrs. Newman in memory of her husband. In accepting the gift President Walter Dill Scott said that the school stood in urgent need of scholarships at this time, when more than an average number of students need financial help and jobs are unusually scarce.

THE will of the late Ira B. Blackstock, of Springfield, Illinois, graduate of DePauw University and member of its board of trustees since 1911, grants that institution a section of land in Barber County, Kansas, reputed to be worth approximately $50,000. Mr. Blackstock also left a large piece of land in the same county to the DePauw chapter of Delta Tau Delta, of which he was a member.

UNDER the provisions of the will of David J. Gibson, who died on August 1, $20,000 was left to the board of trustees of Wesleyan College at Buckhannon, West Virginia.

THE opening of the public schools of New York City has been ordered postponed from Monday, September 14, to Tuesday, September 22, because of the continued prevalence of infantile paralysis.

TWENTY-FOUR grants have been made to Harvard University professors from the appropriations of the General Education Board for studies in the humanities. Most of the funds will be used to continue studies already going on. Others will be used to preserve photostatic or published copies of rare manuscripts.

MORE than 1,500,000 are dependent on school buses for transportation in the rural sections of the forty-eight states each day during the school year, and approximately $35,000,000 is expended annually for this service, according to the National Association of Motor Bus Operators. In 1930, 16,547 schools were served by motor buses covering 451,013 miles of route. The southeast, with its sparsely settled areas, leads in the number of children using school buses daily, a total of 410,771, the association pointed out, with North Carolina having the largest number of schools served.

THE opening of classes on October 1 at Meharry Medical College, the largest professional school for the training of Negroes in the world, will see that institution established in its new $2,000,000 set of buildings. Meharry Medical College needs its new facilities on account of its steadily accelerated growth from an institution of two teachers, five students, and one department at its founding in 1876 to one of eighty teachers, four hundred students, and five departments at the close of the academic year 1930–31. Meharry's undergraduates may study in the fields of medicine, dentistry, nurses' training, pharmacy and dental hygiene. Three thousand students have been graduated from Meharry Medical College since its founding, and its alumni, who are recognized by all examining boards as graduates of a Class A medical college, practice in almost every state of the Union and in foreign countries. According to a report from the college recently Meharry was recognized and its graduates allowed to sit before the Royal College of Surgeons in London and the Royal College of Physicians. Meharry's new buildings house modern equipment for the teaching of medicine and its allied sciences. Under their roofs, for the first time, doctors, dentists, nurses, pharmacists and dental hygienists will be trained in the same building, the same laboratories and by the same teachers. The main building is to be divided roughly into two parts, the southern half containing 150 hospital and out-patient beds, the northern half the laboratories, classrooms and amphitheaters for the teaching of medicine.

A CENSUS recently taken in connection with the London County Council Education Library, as reported in *The Times Educational Supplement*, showed that 14,579 volumes, or a third of the library, were out on loan in one day. Of books in circulation during the year, literature was first with 27,801, history second with 18,290, and geography third with 17,044. Then came art, music, hand work, and science, followed by psychology, religion and philosophy. Methods of education came next, but the theory and history of education were only sixteenth and seventeenth on the list. The last two of the thirty-four classes were education and the state and school architecture. About a quarter of the members of the council made use of the library—2,466 of the officers, and 16,447 of the teachers—the net increase in membership for the year being over 1,000. Over 4,000 books were added, of which about three fifths were duplicates. The circulation scheme embraces three training colleges and 67 secondary schools. This section comprises some 7,450 volumes, and the number of books issued amounted to 5,921. The section dealing with literary institutes and those institutes having cycle courses included 18 institutes. The number of books issued was 3,606 and the stock amounted to 6,745. In addition 1,003 volumes were lent to central schools. Progress with the three years' program, as regards books and apparatus, is marked by an increased capitation allowance for books, while the sum of £5,000 has been expended on replenishing school libraries in a third of the schools and building up "permanent cores" of English literature. The remainder of the schools will be dealt with in the next two years.

EDUCATION in India in 1928–29 is reviewed briefly by the educational commissioner with the Government of India in a pamphlet recently issued by the Government Publications Branch, Calcutta. According to an abstract in *Nature,* the number of scholars in institutions of all types in 1929, namely, 12,165,839, shows an increase of 3 per cent. in twelve months. During the same period, expenditure on education increased by 5 per cent., to Rs. 27,07,32,253. Expenditure on universities and colleges, providing instruction for 94,257 students, amounted to 13.5 per cent. of the total expenditure and showed an increase of 13 per cent. over the expenditure of the preceding year. The report suggests doubts as to whether this rapidly increasing expenditure is justifying itself by results. Of the University of Bombay, it is recorded that "the average student does not bother to read his texts, but is content to learn by heart second-hand opinions on them, gleaned from cheap bazaar cram-books." The University of the Punjab "is burdening itself, and is encouraging the colleges to burden themselves, with a very large number of students who have little or no chance of completing the course successfully and on whom the expenditure of money intended for higher education is very largely wasted." There is similar wastage also in the University of Rangoon. The number of Indian students in Great Britain is now well over two thousand. Including students at universities on the Continent and in the United States of America, the total number who are abroad in one year is not far short of 2,500.

THE *Journal* of the American Medical Association reports that the Educational Ministry of Japan has received the results of the physical examination reported by the local health officers of all the prefectures in Japan. Ten million children were examined in the primary schools. The proportion of children with carious teeth is 95 per cent. in cities and 70 per cent. in the country; that of children suffering from trachoma is 20 per cent. in cities and 80 per cent. in the country; the number of feeble-minded children is 2,200,000 (20 per cent. of all those examined). The ministry, therefore, held a meeting of school health experts for three days, in the department, in order to eliminate the causes of apprehension for the younger generation. Besides several plans, which are to be laid for the improvement of their health, such as the establishing of the school-health committee, the ministry intends to establish highland sanatoriums as well as health centers in large cities for weak children. In Tokyo, 203,000 children from about 200 primary schools have been examined, and the results show that the children of from 7 to 12 years of age in Tokyo are taller by 3 cm. than the average children of this country. In the children examined, the average height of the boy of 7 is 110.1 cm and of the girl of the same age, 108.7 cm. The average weight of the boy of 7 is 18.5 kg. and of the girl of the same age, 17.4 kg. These weights are greater than the average of the children in this country. Ninety-five per cent. of the boys of 7 years and 93 per cent. of the girls have carious teeth; 11,200 of the children are near-sighted in both eyes, and 8,176 of the children are suffering from trachoma, although the number of cases is fewer than in preceding years.

PROPERTY of a private school operated for profit is exempt from taxation, the Oklahoma Supreme Court has held in a case entitled Board of County Commissioners of Tulsa County *v.* Tulsa Business College. Referring to the Oklahoma statutes on the subject, the Court said: "These provisions specifically exempt from taxation all property used exclusively for schools or colleges. They make no mention as to whether they are private schools or public schools. Neither is there any mention made as to whether or not they shall be run for a profit. The requirement is that they shall be used exclusively for schools or colleges. Under these provisions, as we view it, it is immaterial as to whether or not the institution produces a profit or a loss. If it had not been the intention of the framers of the Constitution to exempt a private school then there would have been no necessity for including the word 'schools' in the constitutional provision because all property of the public schools is public property and exempt from taxation. "It is the use to which the property is devoted and not the presence or absence of pecuniary profit to the owners which determines whether or not the property is exempt from taxation," the opinion continued. "In the present case it is admitted that the property is used 'exclusively' for school purposes. Since it is used exclusively for school purposes we think it clearly comes within the exemption."

GRADUAL displacement of the small rural school by the "consolidated" school has brought to school boards throughout the United States another problem—that of providing and paying for child transportation. Data which are expected to be of aid in solving this problem are given in a bulletin issued by the Office of Education on "Factors Affecting the Cost of School Transportation in California," prepared by Frank O. Evans, director of administrative research, Los Angeles Public Schools. By comparison with other states, California transports its school children longer distances. Approximately 26 per cent. of the high-school pupils there live more than 10 miles from their school. The average student pays $41.35 per year bus fare to and from school, while the cost for the same privilege to the average elementary school pupil is $28.86 per year. A school bus on the Pacific Coast makes a daily trip of 37.7 miles on the average, and carries an average load of 30.6 pupils. The expenditure for "school transportation" has come to occupy third place in the budget of union schools in the state, and amounts to 11.5 per cent. of the total current expense. The present large expenditures seem to be justified both as an economy and as a means of enlarging the educational opportunities of more than 30,000 children in the state.

DISCUSSION

OBJECTIVE EXAMINATIONS AND HABITS OF HONESTY

THE problem of honesty both within and without the schoolroom has been examined experimentally by many students of character education. It seems established by May and Hartshorne's studies of "Deceit" that there is a relatively low relationship between the behavior of children in the classroom and in the life situation where honesty is concerned. Further, children's attitudes about honesty in the two situations are different. Whether pupils are inhibited by fear of authority (law) when tempted to take a purse and yet do not feel that it is wrong to cheat in the schoolroom situation is a point yet to be determined. What seems to be brought out by these studies, as well as others, is that habits of honesty are rather specific habits. To remove cheating, then, in the classroom would necessitate building up desirable habits in that situation. With this in view the present discussion deals with controlled examinations as a factor in developing habits of honesty.

It is the writer's observation, after teaching introductory classes in general psychology for a period of time in three different universities, that a careful inspection of the eye-movements and postural changes of students when given their first quiz in the course will reveal that some students have habitual tendencies of looking on their neighbor's examination paper. They are probably motivated to do this only when they confront a question for which they have no information ready at hand with which to answer it. It is the writer's opinion that these students, who have a tendency to cheat, have probably formed this habit earlier in their life experience in the schoolroom situation. That is, that some time in their school experience they met their first task to solve, under examination conditions, for which they had no adequate repertoire of responses ready as answers. Now under these conditions the pupil probably showed a bit of frustrated behavior, restlessness, moving and squirming in his seat; these postural changes, too, were accompanied by eye-excursions, yet with probably no intention of cheating. But suddenly his eyes fell upon the intent performance of his fellow student next to him. He was attracted to this. He read. What he read gave him a clue to the answer of his question and thus began the habit of depending not upon himself for information, when thinking was required, but upon the geographic position of a friend whom he knew always to be prepared and who always made a good mark on examinations. This habit, of course, was made easier for the potential cheater by the old essay examination which furnished the same questions in the same order for all students. Now these same students, when they get to college, are the ones who can not control their eye-movements—and thus signs of exploring other peoples' papers are manifested. Somewhere, then, between the early grades (at the very early grade level the little fellow is rather individualistic in attitude and wants to do his own task) and later secondary school period, when the awareness comes of what grades mean, does he learn to borrow from his fellow student. Herein lies the problem then of controlling the examination situation so that the pupil may not establish habits toward which society registers disapproval. This leads us to a point or two about the type of examination used as a means of building desirable character habits. Since it has already been hinted that the old type of essay examination may facilitate habits of dishonesty, it is now claimed that alternate forms of the new type objective examination may remove that condition.

It seems agreed by most authorities that examinations of any kind should not only motivate students to cover thoroughly and adequately the material presented but also habits of wholesome competition should develop during the process of training. And as a further by-product of the processes of competing on a uniform basis it is the writer's opinion that the character trait of honesty may be developed by using objective examinations.

If two forms of the objective examination are always administered, while progress is being measured, and the student is aware of the fact that this is the type of examination he may expect, will he not learn, first, to depend upon himself while preparing for the examination? Secondly, will not the situation be such that as he grows from day to day and from year to year in his school work that there will be no examination-situation which favors cheating? Consequently when frustrated by encountering questions which he does not know he will face his problem and will not build up the habit of seeking information from the neighbor's paper. The very situation then will prohibit modes of adjustment—cheating—which society calls dishonest. Then when he gets to college there will be no behavior patterns indicating his previous experiences of cheating in school examinations. Of course, the real test would be to tempt him to see if he could withstand temptation. But here again we must take a chance on his previous habits of honesty functioning rather than new habits of dishonesty being started. After all it is on the basis of one's past ways of reacting toward his life situations that we are able to predict his future conduct. The kind of examination, then, it seems, can incidentally be a factor in building up honesty in children. Not only may we expect the accruing of habits of honesty but also self-reliance and wholesome competitive attitudes may be acquired. In this way, then, the kind of examination given may influence the building of character in either a positive or a negative way. A neat little problem it is and one which can be solved experimentally by some researcher in the field of testing. Scientific information along this line might throw new light on the so-called honor systems in vogue in some schools.

JAMES R. PATRICK
OHIO UNIVERSITY

HE GAVE DE MAUPASSANT A GRADE OF B

THE student was doing about *B* work. The young instructor thought the compositions were good, but not exceptional. One of the themes, however, was strikingly like something the instructor had read in de Maupassant. Upon looking up the French writer's story, the teacher found that the composition and the story were the same. He checked over the other themes that the student had written and found them all to be stories of de Maupassant that the student had copied and had handed in for his own, and for which he had received a grade of *B*. The teacher had given the great de Maupassant a grade of *B*. Sometimes teaching develops little minds; minds that look for commas and semicolons, and miss entirely the swiftness or beauty of the whole, having become slaves to rules and details.

To show his own cleverness the teacher had told this story of finding the student's plagiarism, but in reality, though he was successful in detecting the boy's dishonesty, the teacher was revealing his own failure as an instructor. The student and teacher had both failed. The student had failed in his personal adjustment to the course, had failed to really develop himself in his attempt to appear successful. But the dishonesty of the students is a test also of the teacher or of the school. In the degree that the students are dishonest, to that extent the schools have failed. To that extent they have failed to really interest, to genuinely stimulate the students, who have sought grades instead of knowledge. If, however, the students see the usefulness and purpose of their study, if the teaching has been really successful, the students will be interested in really mastering the subject instead of obtaining a dishonest grade. Dishonesty in school is an indication of failure in education, and the proportion of student dishonesty is the proportion of failure or success of education.

The instructor deserves credit for detecting this bit of plagiarism, but his success revealed his own failure as well. He had given de Maupassant a *B*—this because he had failed to really stimulate and command the real interest of the student.

George Morlan
Columbia University

THE PERILS OF COEDUCATION AND CIGARETTES

A recent newspaper item stated that 44 out of 46 "co-eds" in a certain college said they did not expect to be kissed the first time they were out with their boy friends, and that two said it didn't make any difference. Presumably the 44 thought it made no difference the second time they were out with their boy friends.

The coeducational system is another of those "noble experiments" that have been weighed in the balances, and found wanting. It is high time to return to the old, tried, true system of segregating young men and young women in high schools and colleges. It is high time to consign drinking and petting parties to the limbo from which they came. It is high time to call a halt to a system of education that opens private smoking rooms for young women where the bloom of maiden innocence and modesty is besmirched in an atmosphere of vile cigarette smoke. If the American people had but a slight realization of the ruinous effects of drinking and smoking upon the morals of young women, they would rise up as one American giant, and bury coeducation deep in the sulphurous pit from which it came.

The passionate period of youth is a perilous time even when the surest safeguards are thrown about our sons and daughters. We who have passed through that veritable Valley of Peril know its temptations and pitfalls. Coeducation adds fire to fire by throwing young men and young women together at the most impressionable sex period of life. The fire cools when they are separated. Out of sight, out of mind.

Under the system of coeducation, the chief purpose of education is defeated; for how can young people study when allurements of sex are all about them? How they stand it, I do not know. But I know this: well-educated men and women, strong men and women, are not produced by coeducation. Sex ran truer to form under the old system.

Charles Hooper
Coeur d'Alene, Idaho

SPECIAL CORRESPONDENCE

GRADUATE WORK FOR HIGH-SCHOOL TEACHERS OF THE SOCIAL STUDIES

Graduate work for high-school teachers has become a common requirement in large school systems, and many teachers with no purpose other than improving their qualifications for high-school teaching are becoming candidates for the degree of master of arts. In subject-matter fields, where the high-school and university organization is similar, relatively little difficulty is found in arranging satisfactory graduate curricula, with a major in subject-matter and a minor in professional training or with credit allowed for the latter on the major. The field of social studies presents a more serious problem. In all but some of the largest high schools it constitutes a teaching unit, but in universities and colleges it is broken up among four or five departments, each with its own major and minor requirements. On the undergraduate level this has been met in many colleges of education by a combination social studies major that includes work from the various fields. On the graduate level the problem is still to be solved, and a new program at the University of Missouri is one attempt to meet it.

This new curriculum is not thought of as merely a fifth year of college education; rather it is visualized as a definite stage in the training of the teacher. It was built directly upon two programs—the state high-school course of study and the requirements for a B.S. in education with a social studies major. This last program includes a forty semester hour minimum in social studies content, thirty-five hours of which are specified courses covering on the college level the same ground as the high-school courses—or as near that as could be found among the standard departmental courses in the university. The new graduate program requires this forty hours of undergraduate work—and twenty hours of professional work in education—as an absolute prerequisite. The majority of the students registering for the graduate program thus far have been forced to carry some undergraduate work without credit in order to come up to this standard.

The graduate program is based upon the same principles as the undergraduate—a specified minimum of professional courses and broad training in the subject-matter of the social studies that prepare for high-school teaching. It is visualized best in terms of total training, graduate and undergraduate. At the granting of the M.A. degree the student will have had at least the following training: Twenty-six hours of required professional work in the field of education specifically selected for training high-school teachers of the social studies. Thirty-three hours of history, eight of which are elective among a group of specified courses, and which include a thesis. Eighteen hours of required social studies other than history and education. Fifteen hours of social studies, elective among specified courses in various fields. (Those interested may obtain a detailed statement of these requirements by applying to the Graduate School, or to Professor Jonas Viles, University of Missouri, Columbia, Missouri.) It may be noted that the above program is stated in terms of minimum requirements, and although they are maximum for most students who have had their undergraduate work some years ago, many of the more recent graduates will exceed this minimum considerably.

The question of including a thesis was the subject of the most discussion during the organization of the program. There was general agreement upon the aim of specialized training for high-school teaching, rather than specialized training for research. It was generally felt, however, that an understanding of research and at least a brief experience with it is highly valuable for a high-school teacher. For that reason a thesis is included, with the specific understanding that it will represent about half of the quantity of work that in the past has been the unusually large requirement for the M.A. thesis at the University of Missouri. This practically requires a thesis in history. The social studies course of study for the state of Missouri is made up of approximately two thirds history and one third in the other social studies fields. Consequently the content side of the teacher training program is weighted heavily on the side of history, so that under normal conditions this is the only content field in which the student has had sufficient training to do research. In a few cases where a student has pyramided his graduate and undergraduate electives in one of the other social studies, the thesis might be written in that field.

These, in substance, are the regulations that went into operation with the summer session of 1931. Although the high prerequisites make it a more difficult program to complete than older major and minor combinations, its essential soundness appeals so strongly to the high-school teachers that the registration in it is surprisingly heavy. It is not thought by any one to be a final solution of the problem, but rather a fundamental readjustment in the right direction.

ELMER ELLIS

UNIVERSITY OF MISSOURI

QUOTATIONS

BRITISH IMPERIAL EDUCATION

EDUCATION is the greatest link of Empire, and the fact is slowly being realized in England and in the Dominions oversea. English humanism or culture, or whatever term may be used for the spiritual and intellectual forces that make a nation, has been very fortunate in the soils to which the wings of fortune have brought it. Emmanuel College, Cambridge, gave to New England Harvard College in the seventeenth century, and that great university now dominates, as one of its many activities, the growth of culture in the West and Middle West of the United States of America. England came to South Africa in the first decade of the nineteenth century and she found that great Dutch scholar and educational administrator, de Mist, already at work and willing to communicate his gifts to the English colony. De Mist was one of the world's great educationists, and his works follow him. In Canada England had the great French tradition to follow; while in Australia Englishmen built on the old English model, and soon, in very early days, not only had an educational system, but a school of literature all her own. In New Zealand and, indeed, in all the farthest outposts of Empire and in the nearer islands, and to-day in West and East Africa, education proceeds apace and the benefits of education are freely given to peoples that once were slave races.

The interest of English educationists in Imperial education was not obvious fifty or sixty years ago. They had their own problems and little energy for work oversea. We must not forget the efforts made by the great School Societies and by the Church of England itself, and the fact that one of the earliest efforts for elementary schools in England was made, more than a hundred and thirty years ago, by Dr. Bell, from Madras. Nor must the work of the University of London be forgotten. The external students are an important part of the university. But the educational services of England to the Empire were in a sense sporadic. Now there is full recognition of the fact that Imperial education is an entity and that all the parts, like all the parts of the Empire itself, contribute to that entity. The Educational Adviser to the Colonial Office is playing a great part in the education of native races, and, as was mentioned last week in the *Supplement's* weekly article on India, that Adviser, Mr. Arthur Mayhew, contributes to a Hindu educational journal "a weekly article on movements and tendencies in the field of education in every part of the world." The Church of England is keenly awake to the needs of oversea education, and supplies through St. Christopher's College, Blackheath, trained women educationists to many parts of the empire, and specially to Canada for work in regions far distant from towns. There is, moreover, exchange of teachers between England and the Dominions, though on a comparatively small scale. This method of exchange of teachers needs encouragement on a great scale, since if English teachers, highly trained and enthusiastic, go oversea for a year, the best methods of the best training colleges in the world will be given to the Dominion schools. On the other hand, Dominion teachers have much to teach, not only in our schools but to our education authorities. Many of their difficulties are our difficulties, and new solutions are very welcome. There should be frequent exchange of professors of education between the universities of the empire and exchanges of many other chairs. In such practical ways the links of imperial education can be brought together by the aid of various boards of education and of the various universities. Voluntary work can do much, as the development of the school journey shows. Another and very practical way is the rapid extension throughout the empire of the scout and guide system. Lord Baden-Powell has told us recently what great advances have been made in New Zealand, Australia and South Africa. The scout system in South Africa is being extended to the native races. The cause of imperial education seems in safe hands to-day, but there is much linking up to be done and there are many problems to be solved. Only knowledge and enthusiasm can solve them.—*The London Times Literary Supplement.*

REPORTS

EDUCATION UNDER THE NATIONAL GOVERNMENT

By J. McKeen Cattell

ON July 4, 1930, a patriotic date,[1] Dr. C. R. Mann, chairman of the National Advisory Committee on Education, and Dr. J. W. Crabtree, secretary of the committee, signed the following "Foreword" to a report entitled: "Federal Relations to Education: A Memorandum of Progress by the National Advisory Committee on Education":

> The National Advisory Committee on Education desires counsel from every interested source before crystallizing recommendations for action consistent with the principles which it agrees are basic to sound relations between the Federal Government and education.
>
> Wide-spread understanding of the problem, full discussion and constructive suggestions are wanted. To that end, this memorandum of progress has been prepared. It includes an analysis of the present situation, a series of proposals tentatively approved by the committee, and several alternative propositions submitted to date. Nothing has been finally accepted.
>
> The recipient, be he layman or educator, is invited to forward comments to the committee at 26 Jackson Place, Washington, D. C., before September 14, when the Steering Committee meets.

As the report tells us, President Hoover, in his annual message to the Congress on December 3, 1929, said: "In view of the considerable difference of opinion as to policies which should be pursued by the Federal Government with respect to education, I have appointed a committee representative of the important educational associations and others to investigate and present recommendations."

The committee was organized by Secretary Ray Lyman Wilbur, of the Department of the Interior, in May, 1929, and consists of fifty-two members. Its purpose, as then defined by Dr. Wilbur, is "to give us the proper chart by which to steer our educational course."

The report continues:

> The committee had not proceeded far before it became apparent that detailed study was required to assemble the evidence necessary for making a reliable chart. Under the direction of Dr. Henry Suzzallo, this study has been under way since November. Significant records and testimony from government departments, private organizations and individuals were obtained in numerous conferences, both in Washington and in the field.
>
> While all committee members were kept continuously informed of the progress through communications, a steering committee of twelve met from time to time to discuss the evidence. Members of this committee were: S. P. Capen, Frank Cody, L. D. Coffman, J. W. Crabtree, W. M. Davidson, C. H. Judd, U. W. Lamkin, C. R. Mann, J. E. Russell, W. F. Russell, Henry Suzzallo, George F. Zook.

The distinguished members of the "steering" committee represent the composition of the committee as a whole, although some leaders, as Professor Dewey, are missing, and some members were appointed to represent politically influential organizations, as Messrs. William Green and Matthew Woll, president and vice-president, respectively, of the American Federation of Labor. It might be expected that a committee of this size and character would present a safe, sane and colorless report. It may be, however, that the numerous presidential commissions are not intended so much for information and guidance as to supply reports that will give support to policies that the government wants to see adopted.

This appears to be the case with the National Advisory Committee on Education. Mr. Hoover and Dr. Wilbur did not wait for the report of the committee, but, in accord with the general policies of the present administration, proceeded to minimize the part to be

[1] In answer to an inquiry sent just a year later as to "what has happened to the National Advisory Committee on Education," Dr. Mann replied on July 8: "I am *glad* [italics not in the letter] to report that the National Advisory Committee on Education has not met as a whole during the past year." He says that it will meet early in the autumn and that "whatever is approved by the committee at its fall meeting will be transmitted to the President as soon as practicable after the meeting."

taken by the Federal Government in education. A committee appears then to have been arranged that might be expected to make recommendations supporting this policy.

Secretary Wilbur let the committee know what he expected it to report. In 1929 he changed the name of the Bureau of Education to Office of Education in order, as he tells us, to mark "its present dissociation from administrative burdens," and in his annual report for that year he emphasized his opposition to a Department of Education. The report reads:

> The plan of reorganization of the Office of Education has been completed and is in process of execution. Its principle is the establishment of the Office of Education as a research organization rather than an administrative agency. It will transfer to other agencies its present administrative activities so far as possible and concentrate on fact-finding and research in the many fields of education. Known in the past as a bureau, its present dissociation from administrative burdens will be marked by a change of name. Hereafter it will be known as the Office of Education.
>
> Local government in education is, in the Secretary's opinion, the keystone of proper training for citizenship by universal public education. There is a distinct menace in the centralization in the National Government of any large educational scheme. Abnormal power to standardize and crystallize education which would accompany that financial power would be more damaging to local aspiration and local self-respect and to state government and state self-respect than any assistance that might come from the funds.
>
> A Department of Education similar to the other departments of the government is not required. An adequate position for education within a department and with sufficient financial support for its research, survey and other work is all that is needed. That is the aim of the newly reorganized Office of Education and that will be its position in this Department.

The demotion of the Bureau of Education[2] and the proposal to take from it all administrative functions apparently were intended to block any movement for the establishment of a Department of Education.[3] To take this action without awaiting the report of the National Advisory Committee on Education may have been the best way to accomplish the objects in view, but it is not clear that it is good politics to ignore the Congress. An appropriation had been made for the Bureau of Education, not for an Office of Education deprived of administrative work. It appears that legal advice was secured; but this does not mean that members of the Senate and House would approve the action if it could be brought to their attention. Dr. Wilbur, Secretary of the Interior, sees "a distinct menace in the centralization in the National Government of any large educational scheme." As a trustee of the Rockefeller Foundation he seems to approve the control of higher education from 61 Broadway.

The circumstance that Dr. Wilbur is president of Stanford University and a trustee of the Rockefeller Foundation indicates that his sympathies are with private educational institutions and with the control of education by the private philanthropic trusts. This does not necessarily disqualify him from being head of the educational work of the Federal Government, but it should lead him to be particularly careful to act in his official capacity as attorney for the people rather than for the special interests. It is natural that Mr. Mellon should not like a surtax on incomes or an inheritance tax; but as Secretary of the Treasury he should try to dissociate his public actions from his personal affairs. These remarks are in no sense a reflection on the intelligence or the integrity of distinguished cabinet members. John Bright, one of the noblest of men, an advanced liberal for his day, defended the em-

2 The title of the United States Commissioner of Education has not as yet been changed to chief clerk of the Office of Education.

3 In an article written to accomplish a definite purpose, it is not feasible to discuss problems from all sides and from a completely objective point of view. The present writer fully realizes the difficulties and dangers of centralized control under the National Government. For twenty years he has maintained that the present Department of the Interior should be transformed gradually into a Department of Education, Science and Public Welfare, perhaps without any change in name. None the less he would like to see a Department of Education established now, if only as a symbol of national ideals. In so far as it can be obtained, we want local initiative and local responsibility. But we should advance education and public welfare when, where and how we can.

ployment of small children in the cotton mills of Lancashire.[4] Bright was a cotton spinner.

The present writer happens to have been the first professor of psychology in any university in any country; while his work has in the main been the exact measurement of individual differences rather than wide generalizations on behavior, he can perhaps make statements concerning the effects of personal interests on conduct with about as much authority as any one else. He believes that Mr. Mellon is not competent to decide on income and inheritance taxes, that Dr. Wilbur is not in a position to dictate the relations of the Federal Government to public education.

It probably did not even occur to Dr. Wilbur that in appointing Dr. C. R. Mann as chairman of the committee and Dr. Henry Suzzallo as its "director," he was not making the best possible selections. These are men who, like himself, have been taken over by the private foundations and are supported by them owing to their ability and experience in educational affairs. Their opinions and policies would naturally agree with those of Dr. Wilbur, and what better evidence of their competence could be asked? For the same reason Dr. Charles H. Judd, director of the school of education of the University of Chicago, and Dr. James E. Russell, dean emeritus of Teachers College, Columbia University, and his son, Dr. William F. Russell, dean of the college, would obviously be suitable members of the "steering" committee. These men of outstanding ability have been most wisely selected by our patrons of education and their foundations to conduct schools of education which far surpass in their magnitude and standing any that the politicians are willing to support.

As Voltaire said, "It is a pity that good people are so stupid." It may also be regarded as unfortunate that when one sups with the devil it is likely to be in good company. But those familiar with the economic control of history will understand that where the gold is there are the souls. They are not bought in any sinister way but are just naturally there. This is what makes it so difficult to dispossess a plutocratic society or a kleptocratic government. Most of the nicest and cleverest people are part of the system.

Dr. Wilbur apparently does not see any impropriety in a government committee appointed by the President of the United States to make recommendations for the Congress on the relations of the Federal Government to education having its salaries and other expenses paid by a private foundation. The committee doubtless would not bite the hand that feeds it; in any case Dr. Wilbur would take it for granted that none but a mad dog would bite such kind hands.

The Memorandum of Progress, prepared under the auspices described, is a queer document. The larger part of it (29 pages) is a kind of N. E. A. convention address, in which, however, the rhetorical platitudes are directed against the government taking any part in education. Thus a section entitled "A Confused Policy and Public Fears" reads:

> Federal participation in the management of our education has become a public issue. All attempts to extend federal financial aid to general elementary or secondary education, and to important associated aspects, such as decreasing illiteracy, have failed, though fundamental education on the common school level is basic to the national interest. Further financial aid to equalize educational opportunity among the states has been feared because every recent federal subsidization has enlarged the actual power of the Federal Government over local education. Proposals to coordinate educational activities under a single department of education in the National Government, wholly devoted to intellectual assistance and coordinated cooperation, is [*sic*] feared for the same reasons.

And again it is remarked:

> A decentralized system of management and control of schools is the one absolutely reliable antidote to the easy capture of schools by the propagandists of an economic, social, or political cult.
>
> A class or party may capture a central government by revolution or by some exigency of politics; it cannot as readily capture forty-eight states, or the 120,000 local school communities which really determine American educational policy and procedure.

[4] Here and now the Federal Administration and the Office of Education do not concern themselves with the child labor atrocities. "Suffer the little children to come unto me, and forbid them not"; for of such is the profit of Wall Street. This doubtless sounds demagogic, but the words anathema on western farms give the correct rhythm.

It is not made clear who is responsible for the two essays, one entitled "American Education," the other "Principles and Policies," which contain these and similar observations; but it is said that they were presented to the committee on June 20 and 21, 1930 (the former by the "director"), and it is implied that they were approved by it. There are, however, seven proposals for action drafted by the "steering" committee, and it is said that the committee of fifty-two "unanimously voted tentative approval." Three objections, however, are recorded and those who raised them were added to the "steering" committee on the principle that if a member complains of the food served at a club he is put on the house committee. The objections were on the one hand to the abolition of the federal appropriations for the state agricultural colleges and for vocational education. On the other hand the Rev. George Johnson, secretary of the Catholic Educational Association, objected to any federal headquarters for educational research and information.

The recommendations "unanimously voted tentative approval" by President Hoover's National Advisory Committee on Education of fifty-two are:

1. Increase the federal appropriations for educational research and information service by the Office of Education, by the Federal Board for Vocational Education, and by the Extension Service and the Office of Experiment Stations in the Department of Agriculture, and provide ample means to these offices for supplying to all concerned the results of research and statistical studies through publications and conferences.

2. Create an adequate Federal Headquarters for educational research and information, so organized as to serve both as a cooperating center for all federal agencies with respect to the educational aspects of their work, and as a reliable source of comprehensive, correlated and accurate data on education for all concerned.

3. Provide one unallotted annual grant to the States of $2.50 per child under 21 years of age, with the sole restriction that these federal funds be used for support of educational operations, making each State responsible for budgeting the grant within the State school budget in such manner as, in the judgment of the State itself, will best develop all the talents of all the people.

4. Repeal all laws that give annual federal grants in any form to the States for special phases of education of interest to particular groups of the people, or that authorize federal officers to supervise state educational or research activities, approve state plans, or withhold funds in order to compel state compliance with federal requirements.

5. Provide that for the next five years each State must allot to each specific purpose for which it now receives federal funds as much of the new federal grant as is now received from the Federal Government for that purpose; and that after five years the State may allocate all federal monies received for support of educational operations as it decides will best promote its own educational program.

6. Require that each State submit each year to the appropriate federal office a financial audit and that it publish a report describing specifically how the federal monies have been used; and that the Federal Government publish all forty-eight reports in one volume for comparative study by all interested.

7. Readjust the amount of the flat *per capita* federal grant to the States for support of education at the end of each ten-year period as the new census figures, the past experience and the then existing situation may indicate to be appropriate.

These recommendations allow federal appropriations for educational research and information and a federal grant of $2.50 to the States for each child to be used for "educational operations"—and there an end of the nation's concern for education and public welfare. It seems that a whole range of fifty-two mountains was in labor to give birth to these two little mice, the one represented by the present Office of Education, the other surely still-born.

It may be futile to kick a dead mouse. But there is no more important problem than the part that the National Government should take in education and the welfare of the people. The present writer consequently drew up a statement for the committee on some of the things that the Federal Government might do for education and prepared a questionnaire intended to ascertain the attitude of others toward the auspices under which the report was prepared and its recommendations. The proposals and the questionnaire were submitted to Secretary Wilbur; Dr. Mann, chairman of the committee; Dr. Suzzallo, "director" of the committee, and Dr. Cooper, U. S. Commissioner of Education, for their information and advice. The proposals are printed as an appendix to this article. The correspondence with Secretary Wilbur is given in a footnote.[5]

The questionnaire was then sent in August last to 600 of those holding leading positions in educational work, a random selection of 100 from each of the six following groups: Presidents of publicly controlled universities and colleges; presidents of private universities and colleges; presidents of publicly controlled teacher-training colleges; heads of departments of education in publicly controlled institutions; heads of departments of education in private institutions; school superintendents in cities of over 50,000 population. They were the first two named in each state, according to the alphabetical arrangement in the "Educational Directory" of the Office of Education, the 100 being completed by the third named in larger states.

With the questionnaire was sent the following memorandum:

On the enclosed galley slip are printed extracts from the annual report of the Secretary of the Interior, the proposals of the National Advisory Committee on Education, and some suggestions that I plan to present to the committee. In order to learn the attitude of leaders in education toward the report of the committee and the auspices under which it was prepared, I venture to ask those to whom this communication is addressed to be so kind as to check and return the enclosure.

Only 159 replies definitely checked were received, so in January a second request (again with stamped envelope for return) was sent with the following memorandum:

[5] *To the Secretary of the Interior, July 30, 1930*

In response to the request of the chairman and secretary of the National Advisory Committee on Education for comments on its tentative report, I plan to ask a number of workers in education for answers to the questions given on the enclosure. Will you be so kind as to inform me in case you regard it as undesirable to ask these questions at the present time or find any of the questions inadvisable.

I can scarcely hope that you will like the questions which are intended to ascertain whether there are others who share my point of view as to the provisional report of the committee and its implications. I am sure, however, that you will approve of an open discussion.

From the Secretary of the Interior, August 11.

Your letter of July 30th has just reached me here. Naturally it is disappointing to find in a subject of such vast importance as the relationship of the national government to education that even in higher educational circles personalities are brought into decisions. I suppose that this is because of the emotionalized state in which a good many people are in connection with the question. Insofar as your questionnaire is concerned I can say frankly that parts of it seem to me to bring up questions of little concern as to the fundamental issues. With your particular leadership in the field of education I would venture to hope that you would focus the question upon fundamentals rather than upon some incidental questions in regard to persons. Anything that you can do to facilitate the most clear-cut and open discussion of the whole question will be of real service. It has been presented with that point of view.

To the Secretary of the Interior, August 27.

I beg to thank you for the courtesy of your letter which I especially appreciate in view of the character of the questions that I propose. I do not, however, admit that these bring in personalities. It is not a question of the character or ability of the men named, but of the foundations with which they are connected. There is no one for whom I have had a higher regard than for President Eliot. When he opposed the extension of educational work under the government, it might be taken as a token of his superior wisdom. But when in his book on ''University Administration'' he says ''the best number of members for a university's principal governing board is seven,'' and somewhat later remarks that it is a curious and interesting fact that the president and fellows of Harvard College number seven, one smiles. Perhaps if I had had as bad a time in a state university as I had elsewhere, I should be suspicious of the public control of higher education.

It is also the case that we are here concerned with political issues, where the emotional appeal, even in reference to personalities, is legitimate. The people elected a President of intellectual distinction, he selected a Secretary of the Interior with the same high qualities, together they appointed an admirable Commissioner of Education. Now why do these three of the ablest representatives of our most progressive state favor a limitation of government work for education, instead of planning to advance it, as did, for example, President Harding? Why do the schools and scientific institutions get on better in New York City under a Tammany mayor than under a reform administration?

My own proposals regarding the relations of the federal government to education are given on the enclosure. If I should print these in SCHOOL AND SOCIETY they would receive but little attention. I regard the report of the National Advisory Committee as very bad, and believe that it can best be discredited by the method that I am using.

After the National Advisory Committee on Education had printed its Memorandum of Progress, stating that "the committee unanimously voted tentative approval both of the foregoing principles and of the seven proposals presented by the steering committee," and in view of its invitation for comments by "layman or educator," the undersigned sent the enclosed series of questions to some leaders in education. These included a random selection of 100 from each of the six following groups: Presidents of Publicly Controlled Universities and Colleges; Presidents of Private Universities and Colleges; Presidents of Publicly Controlled Teacher Training Colleges; Heads of Departments of Education in Publicly Controlled Institutions; Heads of Departments of Education in Private Institutions; City School Superintendents.

This second request is now sent to those who did not reply to the first, for it is hoped that the returns will be complete. Doubtless some have not replied because the questions appeared to have an aspect of propaganda rather than to be simply a request for information. This is in part the case, as is explained in the correspondence with the Secretary of the Interior and the Chairman of the National Committee, which is enclosed herewith. It seems reasonable, however, to ask for a reply as the blank permits the check to be "no answer." The undersigned certainly hopes to use the replies to obtain a reconsideration of the proposals of the committee, but the results will be reported with scientific precision.

Again the replies were unexpectedly few, 87, making the total number 246, only 41 per cent. of the 600 addressed. Replies were received from about one half the heads of departments of education and from about one third the presidents and superintendents. In addition some 47 letters were received, discussing the situation one way or another.

Questionnaires are notoriously a nuisance, but that does not account for the failure to reply by such a large proportion of those addressed. The questions asked were of public interest and were sent to those officially concerned. The answers required only a check after "yes," "no" or "no reply." While some failures to answer were due to the usual causes, which account for the 10 per cent. of failures in a previous questionnaire, that still leaves 50 per cent. unaccounted for. There is apparently only one reasonable explanation. Presumably these people[6] in the main agreed with those who replied, but did not regard it as desirable to say so, especially to one who had criticized the controls of wealth and had been dismissed from a professorship in our biggest university. "Safety first" is on the ikon carried by presidents, professors and superintendents. At Columbus and at Los Angeles a resolution in favor of a Federal Department of Education was unanimously adopted. At Washington some of the same people unanimously supported recommendations burking such a department. The existing organization and management of our schools and universities, the legislatures and boards of trustees, the benevolent millionaires and philanthropic trusts, with their doles and controls, make "cowards of us all."

The present writer is the author of books entitled "University Control" (1913) and "Carnegie Pensions" (1919). The first of these reviews the situation in our universities controlled by absentee trustees and autocratic presidents; the second relates and criticizes the misuse of money and power by one of the foundations.[7] Dr. Mann, chairman of the

[6] The word originally used was "men," for they are nearly all males. It might be better if we had in our schools more men teachers and more women administrators.

[7] The endowed foundations have performed services of great value to education, public welfare and scientific research. They have in most cases been administrated by men of ability and good will. Whether what they have accomplished is more than counterbalanced by the harm done through the retardation of the same work under public auspices, the controls of wealth, the great influence of a small group subservient to wealth, and the intimidation of workers in education and science, may be an open question. Thirty years ago the present writer remarked ("Concerning the American University": Phi Beta Kappa address at the Johns Hopkins University, *Popular Science Monthly*, June, 1902): "We know that the lack of money is the root of all evil. Our private educational corporations, dependent on the generosity of millionaires, are in a remarkable and almost anomalous position. Yet it is evident that this unique phase of development has not only kept the university in advance of popular appreciation, but has also tended to maintain the stability of society. At a time when large fortunes and monopolistic corporations are needed for the material development of the country, the generous gifts of a few men of great wealth have done much to allay popular clamor. It seems likely, however, that in the end the people will control monopolies and the universities supported by the profits of monopolies.

Hoover-Wilbur committee, now director of the American Council on Education, supported mainly by foundations and private institutions, was formerly an agent of the Carnegie Foundation. Dr. Suzzallo, "director" of the committee, and presumably the author of its reports and recommendations, has now succeeded Dr. Pritchett as president of the Carnegie Foundation. These two men are primarily responsible for the report of the committee giving *ex post facto* support to the policies of Dr. Wilbur, representative of the private universities and foundations. Most educators might hesitate to oppose a scheme sponsored not only by the present federal administration, but also by the Rockefeller and Carnegie corporations, with their hundreds of millions of dollars and the vast influence which these dollars purchase.

But even the most timid of us must take up arms when the corporations, representing vested wealth and interests, endeavor to control the relation of the nation to the public schools. It is ominous for a state university to accept subsidies from these foundations; it is a disgrace for a public school system to solicit a survey by one of them; it is a scandal to let them dictate the part to be taken by the National Government in education and public welfare. Most workers in education would not express themselves so emphatically;[8] but the answers to the questions sent them leave no doubt concerning their attitude. A copy of the

There is no more reason for depending on the generosity or caprice of millionaires for our universities than for our ships of war.''

The danger from self-perpetuating trusts controlling education and science may be illustrated by what has happened in the case of one of them. When in 1919 the present writer asked university professors whether the plans of the Carnegie Foundation for the Advancement of Teaching were satisfactory, of 753 who replied only 13 (an unlucky number) said that they were. The some 200 letters written in returning the questionnaire were nearly all condemnatory of the activities of the foundation. It may be worth while to quote from some of them:

''The great calamity befalling professors in recent years was the giving of the Carnegie millions. Would that he had kept them.''

''Any scheme which tends to give the Carnegie Foundation, directly or indirectly, control of, or influence over, our educational institutions, methods and aims is *in* and *per se* evil and not to be tolerated.''

''It has always been a mystery to me that every single teacher in private conversation sympathizes with your point of view while very few of them dare openly react against the continued humiliation inflicted upon our profession. . . Carnegie plus our academic system of administration has broken our back-bones.''

''I have no sympathy with the methods of 'The Carnegie Foundation for the Control of Teaching' (and teachers) because it has been so repeatedly shown that they were based on incomplete data, bad logic, and inexpert specialists, even if they were not tricky or worse.''

''Pritchett and Butler are so completely discredited in the eyes of the teaching profession, so far as my information goes, that no one can now put the slightest faith in any of their propositions. We all owe you a great debt of gratitude for your vigorous leadership in exposing the true nature of the Carnegie Foundation's management. Success to your arm!''

''In my opinion the Foundation has failed utterly to do that for which it was founded. I don't care to express any opinion as to the incompetence or dishonesty of those who have been managing it, but I can't see how they can escape one charge or the other.''

''I entirely agree with you that the Carnegie system was one which was fraught with the greatest danger to freedom of thought and the development of the social sciences. I am glad that it was so poorly planned that its failure is assured.''

''Words can scarcely be framed to express the criminal and selfish culpability of the trustees of the Foundation. This, however, is only one of the many symptoms of the disease affecting our colleges, 'presidentitis.' ''

''The conduct of the Carnegie Foundation has been an insult to the intelligence and an affront to the integrity of the teaching profession.''

''All these private 'foundations' and 'endowments' are abhorrent to me in any form. Whether intentionally or not, their effect is to shackle the freedom of speech and action of those who should be most free—the teachers of the nation.''

''I regret and deplore the existence of any institution having the objects, apparent or concealed, and the consequences, whether intended or merely inevitable, of the Carnegie Foundation.''

''It is going to be hard enough to teach in an American university and retain one's self-respect apart from the activities of this Foundation. What I think we ought to do is to utterly ignore the Carnegie Foundation and all its works. Moreover we should make it clear that we do so because it has brazenly disregarded all its promises and because its only apparent *raison d'être* is to exercise an external, non-academic control over the souls of American university teachers.''

[8] Ruskin somewhere made a remark to the effect that as he grew older he realized as fully as ever the evils of society, but no longer had the ability to express his censure in adequate words. The present writer wishes that he had the powers of invective of a David or a Jeremiah; with the actor in the company on the road, he can only say: ''Please do not throw anything at Hamlet; he is doing the best he can.''

form used is here reproduced and within the parentheses left blank for the checks is given the number who checked "yes," "no" and "no answer."

Of 197 who expressed an opinion, 186 held that it is not "desirable for a Secretary of the Interior who undertakes to determine the relations of the Government to public education to be president of a private university and a trustee of the Rockefeller Foundation." Of 202 no fewer than 184 believe that the expenses of the committee should not be defrayed by a private foundation. Of 206 there are 162 who disapprove of the change in name of the Bureau of Education. By a vote of 184 to 26 it is held that it "would be desirable for the activities of

REPLIES TO QUESTIONS CONCERNING THE COMPOSITION AND POLICIES OF THE NATIONAL ADVISORY COMMITTEE ON EDUCATION

Is it desirable for a Secretary of the Interior who undertakes to determine the relations of the Government to public education to be president of a private university and a trustee of the Rockefeller Foundation?

Yes (11); No (186); No answer (29).

Does the National Advisory Committee on Education organized by the Secretary of the Interior adequately represent public education in the United States?

Yes (37); No (131); No answer (48).

Should the salaries and other expenses of the committee be defrayed by a private foundation?

Yes (18); No (184); No answer (27).

Is it desirable for the chairman of the committee (with his office as headquarters of the committee) to be a former agent of the Carnegie Foundation for the Advancement of Teaching, now director of the Council on Education supported mainly by private institutions and foundations, for the "director" of the committee and the author of its report to be a trustee of the Carnegie Foundation, now its president, previously dismissed (however unjustly) from the presidency of a state university, and for two members of the "steering committee" to be the past and present deans of Teachers College, Columbia University?

Yes (20); No (138); No answer (49).

Do you approve the change in name of the Bureau of Education to Office of Education by the Secretary of the Interior (without congressional action) in order, as he states, to anticipate a limitation in the scope of its work and presumably to prevent its development into a Department of Education?

Yes (44); No (162); No answer (21).

Should the Office of Education have administrative functions?

Yes (110); No (82); No answer (26).

Would it be desirable for the activities of the Government concerned with education, science, health and public welfare to be in part at least brought together in a group of related bureaus?

Yes (184); No (26); No answer (22).

Do you approve the resolution passed by the National Education Association at its 1930 meeting, namely, "The National Education Association reaffirms its belief that the control and direction of education must be maintained as an independent function of each state. It further believes that public education is a matter of such vital national importance that it is entitled to the scientific leadership and fact-finding which have been provided by the Government in the fields of agriculture, commerce and labor. The association therefore urges the establishment of a Department of Education with a Secretary in the President's cabinet and the efficient integration of the educational activities of the Federal Government in this department."

Yes (163); No (51); No answer (11).

Is it desirable, as recommended by the committee, for the Congress to distribute to the States $2.50 (in place of any other grant) for each minor in the States to be used for "educational operations" in any way that the State decides?

Yes (46); No (123); No answer (50).

the Government concerned with education, science, health and public welfare to be in part at least brought together in a group of related bureaus." By a large majority a Department of Education with a Secretary in the President's cabinet is approved. The proposal of the committee to "distribute to the States $2.50 (in place of any other grant) for each minor in the States to be used for 'educational operations' in any way that the State decides," is decidedly opposed, though many would favor such a grant if it did not interfere with other forms of cooperation.

There are no considerable differences in the returns from the several groups, but the heads of departments of education in publicly controlled institutions are somewhat more decided in their opposition to the constitution of the committee and its performance than the heads of departments in private institutions. The superintendents were more adverse than the presidents of the universities and colleges, but there was no significant difference in the replies from state and endowed institutions. The first question is typical of the others. The vote to the effect that it is undesirable "for a Secretary of the Interior who undertakes to determine the relations of the Government to public education to be president of a private university and a trustee of the Rockefeller Foundation" was as follows: Presidents of publicly controlled universities and colleges, 17 to 1; Presidents of private universities and colleges, 24 to 0; Presidents of publicly controlled teacher training colleges, 35 to 3; Heads of departments of education in publicly controlled institutions, 43 to 1; Heads of departments of education in private institutions, 39 to 6; City school superintendents, 28 to 0.

The damning judgment of these answers is obvious. All those addressed occupy high executive positions in education. Most of them, in order to secure these positions, must to a certain extent conform to the standards set by authority. It is truly encouraging for the future of our schools and of our country that they hold the opinions here recorded. It may be taken for granted that teachers in schools and colleges, representatives of the people in congress and legislatures, those of the people who are informed, would in even larger measure condemn the Hoover-Wilbur committee and its proposals. A vote of censure has been passed. What next? Will Secretary Wilbur and his committee submit to the judgment that has been meted to them? This is the only proper course under a constitutional and democratic government.

APPENDIX

PROPOSALS SUBMITTED BY J. McKEEN CATTELL FOR THE CONSIDERATION OF THE NATIONAL ADVISORY COMMITTEE ON EDUCATION

(1) The Department of Education established by act of the Congress in 1867 should be re-established. It might be a Department of Education, Science and Public Welfare and might develop by gradual transformation of the present Department of the Interior. It is unbecoming for the United States to be the only nation having departments of agriculture, labor and commerce, but none of education and public welfare. As stated in the resolution of the National Education Association adopted at Columbus in July, 1930: "The National Education Association reaffirms its belief that the control and direction of education must be maintained as an independent function of each State. It further believes that public education is a matter of such vital national importance that it is entitled to the scientific leadership and fact-finding which have been provided by the Government in the fields of agriculture, commerce and labor. The association therefore urges the establishment of a Department of Education with a Secretary in the President's cabinet and the efficient integration of the educational activities of the Federal Government in this department." All activities of the Government concerned with education, science, health and public welfare should not, however, be placed under one Department of Education, for they are the concern of all the departments.

(2) There should be a Department of National Defense, including the present War and Navy Departments, with military aviation. To this department military pensions should be transferred. Legislation should be enacted providing that all appropriations for national defense shall automatically carry an equal appropriation for the budget of education and public welfare. Money spent for military defense may be desirable insurance. Money expended on education, science, health and public welfare contributes more to national defense than armaments and is an investment yielding on the average economic profits far

greater than 100 per cent. The investment would consequently finance the expenditures of the Department of National Defense.

(3) The Department of Education, in cooperation with the Department of State, should have charge of the return of all interest on the foreign war debts to be used by the nations concerned for education, as was wisely done in the case of China and the Boxer indemnity. We should ourselves profit beyond the amount of money returned by the better education of people in foreign nations and their greater good-will to us, and to an equal extent by the lesser need of military expenditures, if we abandon policies likely in the future to cause friction. We should not dictate to other nations, yet the money should be spent in ways leading to international cooperation in education and the promotion of the welfare of all nations, so a Department of Education would have here a difficult and important function.

(4) The Department of Education should cooperate with other nations in the establishment and control of an International University to be established in Switzerland or Holland, or on an island or territory internationalized for the purpose. Such a university would be a center for international congresses, conferences and commissions, and a place for the determination of standards, the collection of statistics, the preservation of archives, etc. There would be resident professors and directors of departments from the several nations and also visiting professors, fellows and students. Such a university would not only contribute to the advancement of science and productive scholarship for the benefit of the world, but would also give useful practice in methods of international cooperation.

(5) Under the Department of Education there should be a National University in Washington which would utilize existing federal laboratories, collections, libraries and archives. The professors, say a hundred at first, should be the ablest obtainable, being given the salaries of Justices of the Supreme Court and the same permanence of tenure. About half of them should be temporarily absent in exchange with foreign universities, as visiting professors at State Universities, and on foreign and domestic missions. Professors at State Universities should have temporary appointments in Washington, the salaries of those especially invited, say at first fifty each year, being paid by the National University. The students and fellows would in large measure be instructors in State Universities and others engaged in public education.

(6) The Department of Education would have charge of the formal education and cultural activities of the Military and Naval Academies, for the District of Columbia, Alaska and our political dependencies, for native peoples treated as wards of the nation. This involves a population twice as large as that of New York City, and unless the National Government is less liberal than that city would require 50,000 teachers and an annual expenditure of $300,000,000. This is work for which the National Government must be responsible, however it may be delegated. When the Secretary of the Interior says that the Office of Education is to be relieved of all administrative "burdens" it is not clear to what bureau or department he wants them to be transferred.

(7) There should be under the Department of Education, as recommended by the National Advisory Committee on Education and as a development of the present Office of Education, a bureau to collect and disseminate statistics and other information and a bureau for educational research. Statistics and research should be published, and releases should be sent, as is now done, to the daily press and other publications. The office should not, however, publish, as it does at present, a monthly journal, given away or sold at a nominal sum, in direct competition with the *Journal* of the National Education Association and the state educational journals. [Since these proposals were submitted to the U. S. Commissioner of Education the character of *School Life* has been somewhat changed. It now contains more reports from the office.]

(8) In addition to a bureau of educational research in Washington, appropriations should be made for Educational Experiment Stations in each State of at least the amount that is now appropriated for the Agricultural Experiment Stations. The research of the agricultural stations has repaid their cost many fold to the farmer and to the nation. It is almost incredible that the National Advisory Committee on Education should propose to abolish the grants for agricultural experiment stations, for in the first place this would be most unwise and in the second place there would be no chance of favorable congressional action. The method should be extended, in the first instance to educational research to improve methods of selecting and training teachers for the schools, and methods of selecting and training children in the schools. This work should be taken up in Washington as agriculture is by the Department of Agriculture, but there should also be stations in each State as in agriculture. They could effect improvements and economies that would pay their cost ten times over. Each of the larger States should have a school of education not inferior

to the privately owned and admirably conducted Teachers College of Columbia University. It is a national scandal that most of the leaders in the administration of public education should do their advanced work and obtain their point of view from private universities supported and controlled by the owning classes and their foundations.

(9) In addition to research stations and colleges of education, and of agriculture and the mechanic arts, the extension of the method of national and state cooperation to other subjects should be considered. The so-called mechanic arts should not be subordinated, as is now the case, to agriculture, but should be extended in independent institutions to cover industry and engineering in all their aspects. A similar development should be favored for forestry, mining, transportation and commerce. The present economic depression is due to lack of knowledge and the deficiencies of our schools. There is need of research stations and colleges in the fine arts, including the drama and music.

(10) Radio is an interstate problem that must be taken over by the National Government. It is a federally controlled monopoly, it disregards state limits, payment for the service can be obtained only by taxation. Radio broadcasting is now mainly supported by advertising. The Federal Government should have a chain of stations within hearing of every citizen and should send out continuously the best possible educational and social programs. Every school and every individual can be reached with lessons, addresses and music. The difficult questions involved are being taken up under the auspices of the Carnegie Corporation with a former Columbia University publicity man in charge, but should not be left to them. The Secretary of the Interior has indeed appointed an Advisory Committee on Education by Radio which recommends a section devoted to education by radio in the Office of Education, while the other Advisory Committee ignores the subject and the Secretary of the Interior would relieve the office of all administrative ''burdens.'' This radio committee curiously recommends that $200,000 be obtained from ''*interested* [italics not in original] persons or foundations'' for a ''high-grade program.'' Large appropriations by the National Government, perhaps ten million dollars a year, should be made to support the best possible broadcasting service. The money can be obtained by a small progressive tax on radio sets when sold.

(11) The distribution of publications by the post office, the interstate shipment of films, the provisions of the Mann act, and similar problems are of considerable educational and social interest. It may be that illiterate, feeble-minded, diseased or delinquent children and adults should not be permitted to move freely from State to State. But presumably the Federal Government should not so much concern itself with censorship and prohibition as with supplying the best there is to all the people. It does send out books from the National Library, and several of the bureaus distribute educational films. It might well arrange traveling libraries of books, as also collections of natural history and of art, for exhibition throughout the country. It might provide lectures, plays and concerts. Other nations have national museums and libraries (as we have) and also national operas and theaters (as we have not). We have accomplished more than any other nation in establishing national parks, reservations and monuments. A Department of Education and Public Welfare should determine the best methods of extending culture and recreation.

(12) The Federal Government should cooperate with the States in all educational efforts in which expert knowledge is in advance of common practice or one part of the country in advance of other parts. This is the case with vocational education and home economics. The Government has done well to take up these problems and the National Advisory Committee on Education is unwise in proposing to abolish them instead of making recommendations for their improvement. In the case of the Negroes and the immigrant classes there is an interstate problem of vast consequence. If their education and social welfare are not properly cared for in certain States, and they are allowed to move to other States, we have a national problem that must be solved. It is a challenge to a Department of Education, not a matter for private charity.

(13) Problems of health in our schools are of measureless importance. Thanks to the development of a Department of Agriculture, we limit and control the diseases of plants and animals, not only in interstate commerce, but also within the States. As we have no Department of Education, the more fundamental work of suppressing contagious diseases and alleviating constitutional and other illnesses, defects and deficiencies is neglected. Most of all we need prolonged and intensive research that can only be undertaken on a sufficiently large scale by the Federal Government. Any one familiar with what the Rockefeller Foundation has accomplished with limited means will realize the possibilities of the situation. We can reduce the death rate of children and the incidence of incapacitating illness and defects to

one half. Apart from the contribution to human welfare, the economic saving would finance not only the health work, but the whole program here proposed for a Department of Education.

(14) There might be appropriated say $10 for each illiterate according to the census of 1930 to those States that will use it to reduce illiteracy. When people move freely from State to State illiteracy concerns the nation as a whole. *The New York Times*, not a publication favoring centralized control, advocates editorially federal efforts to reduce illiteracy. There might also be a *per capita* appropriation of one dollar for adult education in those States that would undertake to use it for this purpose. The National Advisory Committee on Education recommends an appropriation of $2.50 to the States for each child under twenty-one years of age, in lieu of all other grants to States, to be used for "educational operations" in such a way as the State may decide. This is too crude a method of redistributing wealth. It would not be approved by the wealthy States, nor would the poorer States like to be treated as charity patients. None the less it is true, as the Advisory Committee points out, that taxation is becoming increasingly national. Added to the tariff and internal revenue taxes, we now have the corporation and personal income taxes. The inheritance taxes will soon be increased as in other countries. By the nature of things these should all be national taxes, and the large sums required for education, scientific research, health and public welfare, even if these are promoted only to the extent that they are profitable investments, can be obtained only by national taxation.

(15) A Department of Education and its Secretary, who next to the President would hold the most responsible office under the Government, must take up the problems of the economic support and social welfare of the dependent classes. The ill, the disabled, the feeble-minded, the lawless, may perhaps be left to the States, though this is doubtful. In the case of children and the aged the National Government must ultimately intervene, as it only can obtain by taxation the immense sums required. The family can no longer be expected to bear costs that are primarily the concern of the nation. Child labor should of course be prohibited; this is a national issue. But when we require school attendance to the age of sixteen, ways must be found to relieve the economic burdens of the parents. The family is now easing its problem by having so few children that schools will soon be depopulated, the nation regressive. Thanks to scientific research and its applications there is ample wealth; the most difficult of all political questions is how it shall be properly distributed. Most individuals earn during their lifetime more than they cost and add to the national wealth. But we have now advanced the time of self-support to sixteen or eighteen years, to twenty-five years for the professional classes. There is said to be greater difficulty than formerly for older people to obtain employment. The problems are too complicated for discussion in detail here, so only two definite plans are proposed for a beginning—first, allow pensions to teachers in public schools on the same basis as now applies to military service; second, grant $100 a year for each child who stands in respect to ability, character and health among the upper tenth of the children in the public school that he attends. If any one says that such measures are socialistic the reply is that all public and compulsory education is socialistic. It is only a question of how little or how much we shall do for education and welfare.

(16) Education we are told means to lead out the abilities of the child, but etymologically it may equally well mean to select the "dukes," the leaders for a democracy. This selection is the most important and the most neglected function of our lower and higher schools. We try to teach children what they need not learn at ages at which they are especially unfit to learn it. We could do far more for them by determining what they can do and giving them a chance to do it. Among the twenty million children in our schools are large numbers who are as able as those who have done the most for the nation and the world. By giving each of these children opportunity to do the work he can do best, and by training him to do it in the best way, the average economic production of each individual from the moron to the man of genius can probably be more than doubled, and happiness would be increased in equal measure. We can thus finance any expenditure for education, even though it may be counted by billions of dollars. Lastly, we not only can select individuals for their work, but also the individuals themselves. Eugenics is the great problem of the future.

(17) A Department of Education, with a Secretary in the President's cabinet, can and should be established at once. The problems here enumerated will require a generation for their solution, and the more we accomplish the more numerous will be the new problems brought into view. Any political party in an intelligent democracy that makes education and public welfare its platform will prevail. If the old-line parties do not realize the situation, a new party will arise.

EDUCATIONAL REVIEW

Edited by WILLIAM McANDREW

EDITORIAL COMMENT

A BOUQUET FOR VALPARAISO

A FRIEND of Valparaiso University writes to my easy overlord, "In the June 6 issue of SCHOOL AND SOCIETY, McAndrew, in a review of Flexner's 'Universities,' makes the statement: 'The Indiana Ku Kluxers, if they become a corporation and undertake teaching stenography, using the name Valparaiso University, might be ridiculed by an Oxford don.'"

I was showing that the original meaning of the word "universitas," as well as later usual usage, justifies its employment as "university" in any case even though an Oxford don might ridicule.

"I trust," continues the letter, "that correction will be given due prominence. I do not know whether McAndrew tried to be funny in his statement. I can not rid myself of the feeling that it was a nasty statement. In 1923, a newspaper story stated that the Indiana Ku Klux Klan was thinking of taking over Valparaiso University. It has never been possible to find where this story originated. Certainly there was never any intention on the part of the university trustees at that time to make such a deal. In 1925, the Lutheran University Association bought the property for the purpose of establishing a first-class educational institution. Steps were taken to reorganize the school on a sound educational basis. The college of Liberal Arts was accepted by the North Central Association of Colleges. Other boards and associations have given it recognition. The same is true of the Law School, the College of Pharmacy and the College of Engineering.

"McAndrew is repeating a fable which he should know never had any existence in fact."

Is this a chip on the Valparaiso shoulder? I like chips and scrappy educators. We are short of both. Ask Professor Thurstone. Let's see what my Valparaisic friend is hot about. "The Indiana Ku Kluxers, if they become a corporation using the name Valparaiso University might be ridiculed by an Oxford don." When I shall put the Flexner review into my complete works, I'll say, "The Indiana Ku Kluxers, if they should become a corporation and should take over Valparaiso University as a newspaper story in 1923 said they were thinking of doing, might be ridiculed by an Oxford don."

Oh, come, take off the chip, here's rather a bouquet:—All the people of my acquaintance who took work at Valparaiso University said it was time well spent. Its plan was to concentrate on the business of education without waste or distraction. Will Hayward, alongside of whom I taught for years, who is in the front rank as teacher, author, New York high-school principal and quiet efficiency expert, long ago taught me that Valparaiso, his Alma Mater, was nearer the type of educational institution suitable for a democracy than are most of the higher institutions in America.

Come, my corrective friend, put that in your buttonhole.

I'll do more, I'll say that I have studied the sixty-ninth year-book of Valparaiso and noted its array of courses such as self-respecting universities give, including public health and sanitation, nursing, medicine, teaching (with an option for the teaching of citizenship and plenty of instruction in games and sports), Latin, Greek and languages galore, religion and ethics, politics, sociology, summer sessions and all.

Vive Valparaiso!

SOME HOT SUMMER SHOTS

FOR four years, ending in 1928, the EDUCATIONAL REVIEW used to distribute, each month, return sheets on which the readers were asked to note what features of the magazine most suited and displeased them. The publisher was disconcerted to find that the feature "What the Layman Thinks," a collection of newspaper editorials, received more commendation than any other particular. It was prepared by aid of shears and paste-pot and with less use of brains than was employed in preparing and choosing the more solid articles of masters of pedagogy. Either the school people are not so indifferent to the opinion of mankind as they are often said to be or else they feel the danger of isolation.

My notebook and I have been attending public meetings devoted to consideration of educational service. There is a what's-wrong-with-the-schools wave in our neighborhood. We older men can remember many. Richard Grant White stirred up one; Rebecca Harding Davis, another. There were successive surges caused by James Rice, Charles W. Eliot, Colonel Larned, Michael Friedsam, and Edward Bok. Charges were made, defenses published and more or less benefit gained.

A researcher with time and skill could measure the amount of discontent printed in samplings of newspapers at stated periods and plot the curve of criticism. It happens that the entire number of addresses I heard this month were devoid of praise, compliment, satisfaction and complacency.

Dr. James Sheerin, standing on the Washingtonian maxim that only an enlightened public opinion can make popular government honest, pointed out the amazing ignorance of all of us when we go to the polls. We don't know what the candidates stand for. We don't know whether they are honest men or crooks. What is the remedy? A Citizens Union publishes the record of those running for reelection but the majority of voters are not sufficiently warm with the love of honest men to go to the polls and to urge others to do the same. Civic duty we continue to believe would be strengthened if the public schools would address themselves to what they were founded for: the purification of politics. So says the Reverend Sheerin.

Stupidity and Prejudice Rife

I found the youthful president of the University of Chicago mincing nothing in his survey. Education has singularly failed so far, is his opinion, in training intelligence and substituting it for stupidity and prejudice. What have schools and universities been doing all these years if they have been unable to prevent our present parlous state? What must education do? Switch to the study of human problems, train thinking independence, direct consideration of civic ills near at hand, eliminate the time-wasting subjects that inadequately contribute to civic training; substitute such as aim directly at a higher social, political morality and intelligence. So urges President Hutchins.

Goodwin Watson, on the day I heard him, ranked as high as Dr. Hutchins in vigorous demand to discard the traditional non-essentials of the school course. Every investigation of government, he said, shows the failure of what the schools thought they were teaching as citizenship. Hundreds of thoughtful teachers are frittering away their lives because they are in a treadmill divised for an old and outworn educational philosophy. The new plan of the University of Chicago is better than most others but it doesn't go far enough; its graduates still may be a moral menace and political grafters.

Jesse Newlon's discourse, shortly after, said education is too busy remembering to have time or energy for thinking. It is a buttress to an established order. That order contributes no solution to present ills. It makes teachers automatons, little better than employes in a factory.

My cherished William of the clan Kilpatric held that American children are vaccinated against thinking on economic and political problems. Our school system is sold out to the past. Schools are timorous and cowardly, teaching only generally accepted creeds, steering clear of controversial issues.

The hottest shots of the summer were fired by Norman Thomas, guest speaker of Columbia University at its luncheon in its Faculty Club. The high schools, he said, have sterilized thinking about things that matter. The educators keep the children away from controversial matters. Thought is sterilized. Political morons are graduated by the millions. We face the most bitter peace-time winter ever known, and the citizens turned out by our public-school system are going, as usual, to let things drift because they have not been habituated to think out problems of the general welfare.

Not Teaching What Needs to Be Known

Lotus Coffman's jeremiad stirred his hearers as no school talk I ever heard has done. Poverty, misery and unemployment, said he, stalk in the midst of plenty. Captains of industry, with their feet mired in the clay of their own making, tell bedtime stories to send mankind chasing rainbows. Government by expedient rather than on principle is upon us. Communism will not yield to negation. The only solution Americans seem able to use is to wait for time. Schools have not taught their graduates what now they need to know of economics, civic intelligence and world relations. The times need that the promises put forward as to the results of education be realized in the kind of work it does. So much from Coffman.

I heard Lewis Maverick declare that school citizenship's greatest weakness is in the eternal drawing of parallels that get nowhere. Citizenship must participate in civic life. The school graduate doesn't participate. A man is not a good citizen unless he pulls his weight in the boat. The frequent salute to the flag and repeating an oath of allegiance is soporific. It degenerates into formalism and even antipathy. Commanders have learned that. Not form, not ceremony, not memorized passages, but real issues discussed, thinking and personal conclusion based on principles of fairness and general welfare must be had in school.

The admirable Reisner, christened Edward, who uses the calmest manner in delivering the hardest blows, said what you need is punch and power. You educators are now and have been all along supine before the organized forces of corruption and personal advantage. The human output of your schools are like you. The original purpose and continuing obligation of your position, management and teaching is the development of persons who can and will be effective in civic warfare for improvement.

Playing School

Well, brothers, what does it mean to you?

There is nothing new in it. Presidents Washington, Adams, Jefferson, Madison, Monroe, Lincoln, Roosevelt, Coolidge and Hoover have said it. Dr. Franklin, Dr. Rush, Noah Webster, Governor Sullivan, Justice Chipman said it more than a hundred years ago.

In prosperous times you can play with this American idea. You can go on teaching the machinery of government, while those who know all the anatomy of it that your text-books teach are manipulating politics for their own advantage. Then come hard times like these and with all our wealth, resources and school graduates we haven't a public opinion enlightened enough to select a remedy.

The men who coaxed the legislatures to take over education and charge the cost to the whole community, parents and childless, promised that the expense would be more than saved from the cost of crime, corruption, police-courts and jails. We spend more per capita on education than any other nation. We have more crime and corruption in proportion to population than any other country. There isn't a single public school based on the American idea. The course of study, according to the men responsible for making education a public charge, was to be: more perfect union, justice, domestic tranquility, common defense, general welfare, blessings of liberty now and in the future. To train in these desirabilities, the proponents of public education said, the teachers should be experts in economics, politics, justice, defense, general welfare government, civil affairs. Where is there a public school so manned?

Simpler Than Your Present Scheme

Often in the nearly 150 years since the group of statesmen outlined their ideas for American public education have the DeWitt Clintons, the Horace Manns, and lesser lights exhorted that education turn away from its prerevolutionary idols and tackle its promises. Harold Rugg's, Martin O'Shea's definite proposals that the elementary schools be organized on such civic-social aims as are suitable to young children are not so elaborate as the complex objective of the schools we have.

Edward Reisner's urge that high-school and college study those programs of social and political improvement which are discoverable and make them the direction-posts of education is the same sound advice that the prize-winners of Franklin's invited writers upon the proper educational system for the United States advocated generations ago.

What's hindering you?

Teachers who have spent time and money preparing to teach Latin, Algebra, French, German and standard school subjects are a hindrance. Gentlemen who have money invested in text-books are an obstacle.

School boards who know no other conception of education than the old standard are in the way.

Parents whom we have taught that our brand

of education will advance their children are clogs upon you.

Politicians who fatten on public ignorance of what they do have you by the neck.

Everybody's indifference and laziness discourage you.

You are behind a stone wall.

Butt your head against it!

On the other side of it, I just heard Lotus Coffman say, are insurrection and misunderstanding, human slavery. The time has arrived when your buildings, your athletics, your dramatics, your 1,001 secondary things, must be pushed aside and the original responsibility of public education be assumed by you.

It will be the riskiest adventure you ever tackled.

It will give you the opportunity to sympathize with your brothers in unemployment.

It will correct a not uncommon fling at schoolmasters that their motto is "safety first."

It will give you something of the inner glow that Montressor noted in that early American schoolmaster, Nathan Hale, who, when he mounted the scaffold, Montressor wrote, had an expression on his face as if he had attained a great satisfaction.

PROFESSIONAL PROVENDER

Out of a hundred and six good-looking volumes sent by their excellencies, the publishers, this month, I have ventured to prescribe the following for your professional sustenance. As advertisement to the nutritive value of this table service I publish without permission the following testimonials.

"I use your book reviews as basis for expenditure of our library fund." Charles M. Herlihy, principal, State Normal School, Fitchburg.

"I read what you say about all the books and some of them I buy." Thomas H. Briggs, professor of education, Teachers College, Columbia University.

Proceed, therefore, upon the following path of duty.

BOOK REVIEWS

FRANKLIN WAS HOT

Versatile and lovable old Ben, so Dr. Woody[1] reminds us, held a life-long contempt for the system of higher education which wastes upon Latin and unapplied mathematics the time that could have been devoted to preparing youth to serve the public. Among the Franklin experiences, assembled in this volume of the McGraw-Hill education classics, the academy adventure reads like educational fiascos of here and now. Franklin was the father of the project. He drew the prospectus and gathered the money. Here was to be an institution released from tradition and conditioned by public need. Life was too short and obligations too pressing to permit youth to devote precious time to dead languages and unapplied science. However, trustees of wealth and position must be got on the board. They are for the good old curriculum suitable for a gentleman and a scholar. Franklin, according to his life-long principle, takes half a loaf as better than no bread. He compromises on a school with two courses—a classical, an English. Then follows the oft-played educational game of putting the prospectus in the cupboard and throwing away the key. Like Ezra Cornell's or Jacob Tome's educational purpose, Franklin's, in the hands of educators, gets more and more moulded into the traditional pattern until it is hardly recognizable.

Absent in Europe and busied with the affairs of the Revolution, Poor Richard scarcely knows what the old-liners are doing to his project. But old, sick and within a year of his death, the philosopher wrote one of the most scathing reports ever submitted to a school board. It consists of a series of minutes from the board records, exposing a startling contrast of resolutions with performances. "From the beginning, the contempt of your employes for the new, the English, course has been allowed to damage it. They got you to give the Latin master a title. You gave none to the English principal. To the Latin head you gave £200; to the English, one half as much money and twice as many boys. You voted £100 to buy

[1] Thomas Woody, "Educational Views of Benjamin Franklin." McGraw-Hill Book Company, New York. 270 pp. $2.00.

Greek and Latin books, nothing for English. I flatter myself, gentlemen, that from the board minutes it appears that the original plan has been departed from; that the subscribers have been deceived and disappointed, that good masters have been driven out of the school and that the trustees have not kept faith."

Woody reprints the entire report. It is enriched by quotations from Locke, Trumbull and ancient authors. It is vigorous writing.

It must strike you that Franklin's disappointment with the course of his academy, left to the management of traditional educators, would be paralleled and intensified if he were to compare our tremendous public school and college performance with the plans of the men who persuaded the legislatures to tax the people for the schools. The promise was that the schools would be run for public benefit. The fact is that the schoolmaster continues to conduct them for Latin, for geometry, for individual benefit or ornament, as if education were still paid for by parents for their children rather than by the community for community benefit. Educators have done to that new objective what the masters did to Franklin's modern system—starved it.

Professor Woody gathers Franklin's educational activities and presents them as an engaging story. Education of youth, of adults, of self, each is elaborated in interesting detail. It is, when you come to see it in this light, an added respectability that Woody is giving us. Asked to name America's great educators, the average man doesn't get beyond Charles Eliot and Horace Mann. These Woody and Hansen, and similar books that are coming out, give us claims to Benjamin Franklin, Thomas Jefferson, Noah Webster, DeWitt Clinton and a galaxy of statesmen whose brilliant success in other fields should not fade their educational service but give it and all teachers an added glow.

MASTER EDUCATOR

WHEN I was in the dear old Ypsilanti Normal School, fifty-one years ago, we recited the names of Comenius, Basedow, Luther, Sturm, Ascham, Locke, and other distant worthies as the eminences of our profession. I can not recall anything there learned of Horace Mann nor any American except Oswego Sheldon, who, alas, doesn't appear in Dr. Thomas's big dictionary of biography, nor in Cubberley's index nor in Dr. Dexter's "Education in the United States."

Professor Woody, if you read his "Franklin," makes the addition of that name inevitable among great educators, Roy Honeywell[2] establishes Jefferson there with no fear of dislodgment. In theory, in research, in planning, in devotion of time, strength and money, in sacrifice, in ultimate success, the educational service of the great Virginian as portrayed in the superb volume published by the Harvard Graduate School of Education puts Jefferson at the head of the founders of the public school system.

In selecting Professor Honeywell to write the book, the Graduate School avoided risk of a narrow view, for he is a trainer in history and government in Boston University. His father was, in New York, a life-long promoter of education for community benefit.

The Harvard book begins with a sketch of Jefferson as an educated man and of the means that made him such. Digging into personal correspondence from 1750 to 1826, the author presents, in their inception, growth and change, the educational ideas of the constructive statesman. Mr. Jefferson, accepting doctorate degrees from various colleges, learned to look upon them as aristocratic vanities out of place in a democracy. He feared domination of the faculty by the president of his university. While Jefferson lived he secured that the professors would elect one of their own number as head to hold office only a year. He favored the self-government of students, as observed in Edinburgh, with sufficient appeal to their honor and self respect, but was too practical to commit the whole affair of discipline to a mob of young cubs uncontrolled at home. He played upon their loyalty to the institution and urged them to make a reputation for the University of Virginia.

Dean Page, in Charlottesville, eight years ago, when I quizzed him on discipline, outlined existing policies. Honeywell, now, in quoting Jefferson, is describing the usage observed by

[2] Roy J. Honeywell, "The Educational Work of Thomas Jefferson." *Harvard Studies in Education*, Harvard University Press, Cambridge. 295 pp. $3.00.

Page. I imagine, Mr. Principal, that if you returned to your present school in 2037 A.D. and found an intelligent and successful executive announcing as the policy of government the one you worked up and used in 1931, you would have a pleasant thrill of your own. My writers on school administration find half of us prone to throw out all the policies of our predecessors after an examination both cursory and cursery.

Jefferson, like Franklin, modified theory by experience. He found there was a limit beyond which reliance on the manliness of boys wouldn't work. In his latter days he was convinced that the element of fear was needful. Professor Honeywell's narration of the ups and downs of Jefferson's public-school and university projects, of the growth and change of his ideals, catches its romance and adventure, rising to epic levels. Honeywell does justice to the splendor of Jeffersonian ideals. They were a majestic dream of political, social and moral progress through universal education. Their realization, still short of the vision and behind what could at this moment be achieved by concentration in line with his purpose, is, in material equipment and cost, beyond the record of any other people.

The appendices to this book, the thirty large pages of authorities and sources, are a generous piece of work. As we recall Jefferson's methodical habits and his constant urge that the full utility of every project be realized, we are sure the thing he would desire which would give this splendid book a value after it is read is an alphabetical index. One could be made, dear Graduate School, in a week, by one of your students. Why don't you give it out as a research assignment and bind it into the later issues?

AN ALLURING HISTORY

MABEL CASNER, teaching in New Haven, wondered why American history had to be so complex as to bewilder her children. She made her own selection of fundamental necessities. She had her pupils use what books were available in school and in the public library. The waste of time in getting and copying material made the work irksome. Often the matter was above the brain-power of the seventh graders. She consulted Yale Professor Ralph Gabriel, editor of "The Pageant of America," issued by the University Press. For several years these two made the history lessons from month to month and put them out in mimeographed form. They tried these on the pupils, they modified the scheme from time to time. Harcourt, Brace and Company came into the project. They enlisted J. Russell Smith, the geographer; William Kimmel, social-studies expert, and Robert Harmon, professor of education, as advisers. Result: a new history.[3] To know a people we must sing their songs, think their thoughts and look at the world through their eyes. The book abounds in lovely music, descriptions of sports, pictures in profusion, diagrams of famous structures, marvelous maps and novelties once found only in children's books and magazines unrelated to education. What fascinated there is employed here when it is valuable in connection with our history. The authors divide the book into units and problems. They are generous with outlines for class discussion, pupils' thinking exercises and activities, words to understand. Sprinkled here and there are stories of the time. What Miss Casner and her youngsters spent so many hours looking for in libraries is all here and more, between the two red covers beginning with the world before 1492 and closing with the London Conference on disarmament.

A CLEVER CHRONICLE

WHAT president was born on July 4? What three died on Independence day? Who kept his cabinet intact during his full term? Why is Hoover called the 31st president when we have had but 30? Who was the youngest president? The oldest? Who received all but one of the votes of the electoral college?

Dr. Johnson used to carry in his pocket a book of problems to take out now and then to give his mind exercise. Auburn S. Cunningham's little volume[4] is replete with entertainment and fact skillfully arranged. The qualifications, duties, oath, powers, salary and expenses, flag, salute and residence of the chief executive are described. A brief biography of

[3] Mabel G. Casner, Ralph Henry Gabriel, "Exploring American Hitory." Harcourt, Brace and Company, New York. 812 pp. $1.96.

[4] Auburn S. Cunningham, "Everything You Want to Know about the Presidents. A. C. McClurg and Company, Chicago. 135 pp. $1.00.

each president, giving parentage, birth-place, education, business, marriage, party, terms, death and burial; a similar tabulation of vice-presidents; lists of all the cabinets; accounts of 33 parties from Federal to Ku Klux; outlines of conventions and elections; tables of victories by states; and two hundred remarkably engaging questions—answers a little further on, the whole closed with a handy index, make this one of the particularly valuable books of the year. No school library should be without it. The history teacher needs one under his thumb.

WHAT INTERESTS AMERICANS?

As if written to fit into Dr. Cunningham's book comes a joint product of the American Library Association and Chicago University.[5] It is a report of the first two years of a study fostered by the Carnegie Corporation and the American Library Association. It summarizes previous investigations, determines the interests of typical adult groups, centers on non-fiction, indicates subjects needing new books, finds "the next war" getting its chief attention from Iowa medical students and from other groups in this order: Minnesota students of education and home economics, housewives, high-school teachers, women factory workers, telephone operators, and elementary teachers. Chicago men in high schools prefer to read of statesmen and politicians, criticisms of political policies, international attitudes, prevention of specific ills, self-improvement, birth-control, etc. They avoid business, biography and management, personal beauty, changing status of women, styles, art, movies, theaters, sports and the home garden.

The book is full of meat, interest, surprises, encouragements and of hints of practical value to educators, librarians, authors, politicians and preachers.

THE BEST OF LANGUAGE FACTS IN ONE BOOK

MAY I call the attention of junior and senior high-school workers to a new treatise on foreign languages?[6] Dr. Cole, who was head of the department of French and Spanish in the Lawrenceville School and is now professor of secondary education, calls attention to the wreckage of good old opinions. This havoc the researchers have done. Teaching a subject is not enough. You must know the changes you are aiming to secure in John and Mary. The book is founded on the thesis that the language teacher must set up his objectives and must use the material and methods, which experimentation has shown to be those best known, to realize the objectives.

You have here the presentation of these aims and means as developed in the past fifteen years.

Better English does not come from studying other languages. It is usually hurt by such study. You must make it an aim and see that better English comes. The days of fights for language when hot air was the only weapon are gone. The experimenters have given you solid shot in the form of results piled up by standardized tests. Dr. Cole collects and arranges a wealth of philosophy, psychology, argument, method and result with lesson types, pictorial and dramatic aids, supervision, technique, questions, and bibliography that make a manual indispensable for every school and college attempting modern-language teaching.

EASY SPANISH

ANOTHER urge upon teachers of foreign language to drop the wasteful usage of oral reading comes in Silver, Burdett and Company's neat book[7] of anecdotes, biographies, descriptions and conversations in Spanish.

In celebration of its fifteenth birthday the work has been given a new dress and valuable jewels in the form of pictures. It is an example of text-book engineering in which the builders tried various alluring extracts upon pupils in the early stages of study. The most successful selections were gathered, graded and made into this volume of entertainment and instruction usable from the fifth to the tenth month of Spanish classes. By questions according to modern text usage the reader is led into getting the gist of interesting stories of *el canal de*

[5] Douglas Waples, Ralph W. Tyler, "What People Want to Read About." University of Chicago Press. 312 pp. $3.25.

[6] Robert D. Cole, "Modern Foreign Languages and Their Teaching." Appleton and Company, New York. 598 pp. $3.00.

[7] Lawrence A. Wilkins, Max A. Luria, "Lecturas Faciles." Silver, Burdett and Company, New York. 266 pp. $1.44.

Panama, la ciudad meridional del Ecuador, la Republica Argentina, and of much of Latin America and of Spain.

PARLOUS STATE OF LANGUAGE TEACHING

MILLIONS are studying foreign languages. Theories and methods in endless variety come and go thick as the litter of picnickers in Vallombrosa. In spite of honest efforts to find universal validity, teachers are divided into many camps. Consideration of this leads Dr. H. R. Huse of the University of North Carolina to investigate principles of the studial learning of foreign languages.[8]

Those loyal souls who are disposed to resent the oft-repeated fling that the poorest teaching is above the elementary school will get little comfort here.

Foreign language teaching is an anarchy both in theories and works. No one knows how vocabulary should be presented, how words should be defined, what kind of exercise should be effective for what purposes. There is no experimental investigation leading to conclusions on these points. There is no agreement among language instructors as to what to teach. There is no consensus and little scientific information as how best to teach even common details. Determination is infinitely complicated by dozens of different aims: as reading knowledge, speaking ability, appreciation of the life of a foreign country, development of mental power, ability to write, better comprehension of English grammar and English words, ideals, etc.

Dr. Huse does a direct service in taking up, one by one, a large number of researches—he exhibits a bibliography of 13 pages of these—and by contrasting them with one another and by giving each a Missouri scrutiny, he leaves you convinced that the mind of enquiring teachers must be in a state of bewilderment.

For instance, there is the problem of giving a speaking ability in the foreign language. Charlie Vopicka, Chicago board member, proposes reform in the local high schools because the children graduate without being able to converse in their French, German or Spanish. Dr. Huse assembles the findings of investigators showing that at best only a classroom dialect is attainable, useless in business or society. It's a matter of mathematics. A pupil can get practice in speaking about three minutes a week, two hours a year, a quarter of a day for his whole course; on the other hand, to acquire one's own language the learner talks all day and would drive a school teacher to exasperation by repeating over and over original productions and what is heard. Worse yet, studies of bilingual children show that one language interferes with the other; neither are mastered so well as the child of one speech uses it. To command two languages is to lessen ability in other fields.

What language teaching needs is simplification. Get rid of the multiplicity of aims and it becomes essentially a memory problem; it is the learning, for recognition and recall, a fixed list of units of expression.

After clearing away much rubbish H. R. H. blocks out specifications for procedure. Simplify your objectives. Get measurements before the teaching begins, enlist sufficient numbers to bring conclusions as near universality as possible; get scores at the end of definite periods, compare results, find the weak spots and go at it again.

It must appear to you from the study of the Huse proposals and from the facility of enlisting language teachers into a working organization that the need of ending the present confusion can be satisfied in large measure. It would not only be a service of civic virtue in improving the public investment in language teaching, but it would enhance the self-respect of this large multitude of teachers whose reason for being is so widely doubted. H. R. H.'s book shows him so hard-boiled when confronted with mere rationalizing and opinion that no one really digesting it would be willing to repeat the fatuity of the famous Classical Investigation with its armchair working of beliefs into masquerading guesses put forth as facts. We have been fed on this sort since education organized itself, B. C. What brought alchemy into the respectability of chemistry ought to put high-school teaching on a firmer foundation. Experiment, with testing, free from the will to believe, is due in language study; *n'est ce pas?*

[8] H. R. Huse, "The Psychology of Foreign Language Study." University of North Carolina Press, Chapel Hill, N. C. 231 pp. $3.00.

HUMAN GRAMMARIAN

"THE trouble with grammar," says our Setauket Squire, who was prize man in English, class orator and editor of the college paper forty years ago, "is that there ain't no consistency in it. The master tells us the verb must agree with its subject and then he reads from the platform 'now abideth faith, hope, and charity, these three.'"

"If you said 'ain't no consistencies,' Squire, instead of 'no consistency,'" said the schoolmaster, "you would be grammatically correct though colloquial, for 'ain't' is short for 'am not' or 'are not'; but to use it for 'is not' is, my dictionary says, illiterate. As for 'now abideth,' your contention is that the verb doesn't agree, because there are three subjects; and so, the passage, being accepted as good English, never having been corrected all during these 300 years, is right and shows inconsistency. Wait a minute. 'Now abideth faith' is correct, isn't it?"

"Of course! It's in the Bible."

"Then 'now abideth faith' is right, and, by itself, consistent?"

"Certainly."

"The whole verse is right. 'Now abideth faith, now abideth hope, now abideth charity, these three,' is what is meant, as plainly as 'you shut the door' is the proper expansion of your speech when you use only the last three words."

I had stopped in at this rendezvous of village sages on the way home from the post office. I was carrying a package which, when opened, enriched me with the trim "Syntax"[9] just off the Heath press. I turn to the table of contents. There is a chapter on agreement between subject and predicate. In a minute, I find, on page 54, "When the verb precedes a number of subjects it is often in the singular: 'There is little illustration and no side lights' (G. W. Lewes's "Aristotle") 'And now abideth faith, hope and charity.'"

One of the strongest recommendations for a book is its readiness to tell you what you want to know. Can I find anything on the Squire's "ain't"? I do. I also find "aren't" and "amn't," and quotations showing their varied use. Simplicity and economy have made "ain't" serve for "am not, are not" and "is not."

Still further, why did the schoolmaster pass over the Squire's "ain't no"? I search Curme again. "Double negation. In better literary English and in current popular speech, two or three negatives are felt as stronger than one on the same principle by which we drive in two or three nails. 'I can't see no wit in her': (Lamb: letter to Coleridge.)"

Dr. Curme's "Syntax" is a teeming thesaurus. Not only are the older English classics sifted for examples, but mountains of current literature and floods of living speech have been panned for treasure. The arrangement, the table of contents, the chapter headings, the index, are masterly. The classification numbers and the page captions are ingenious and effective. This is a piece of work that awakens your admiration and enthusiasm. I like this combination of exact scholarship with everyday human interest. "Good English," this author says, "is not a starched shirt for all occasions. Evening dress is out of place at a football game. Loose, colloquial English, as often described in these chapters, is frequently as appropriate as a loose-fitting garment in moments of relaxation. The lesser grammarians in their insistence on strait-jackets not only show bad taste but they do a good deal of harm in that they impart erroneous ideas of language."

I had a teacher, once, who corrected me, "not 'garden,' Willie, say 'garding.'" Curme, bless his heart, sees such clearness, force and charm in some of the expressions attacked by little grammarians that he discards the technical term "vulgar" as having acquired a disparaging meaning and classifies his many racy expressions under the head of "popular speech." For the honest user of the speech of his fathers who is bewildered by fear of violating the rules of a school book now abideth charity.

[9] George O. Curme, "Syntax" (vol. III of the Kurme-Kurath English Grammar). D. C. Heath and Company. 616 pp. $5.00.

STRESSES IN MATHEMATICS

THE teacher sends the pupils to the blackboard and assigns to each a theorem. The demonstrations are written out in full. Each boy sits down when he is through. This wasteful performance, the most common class exercise that Professor Ernst Breslich meets on his tour of schools, is one of the many traditional performances his "Problems in Secondary Mathematics"[10] will ameliorate. "Come, let us reason together," says the author. "It is of no value to listen to a recitation of a proof the boy already knows. Such pupils as do not understand get no thought-training in listening to such things. They agree and accept. They contribute very little." The whole book is a criticism and correction of mathematics teaching of the traditional type. The coming of testing and research has determined the most efficient of various methods found in use. The Breslich book is based on the findings of such appraisals. It espouses the theory that distinct units of a subject should be mastered. It illustrates in detail the best ways of getting them mastered. It stresses the necessity of effective assignment of lessons, the indispensable habits of study to be taught, the most profitable ways of directing class work, motivating mathematics study, ministering to each person according to his abilities and needs. It effectively demonstrates the need of arithmetic on the part of all high-school students. It is a fresh and inspiring guide for making arithmetic, algebra, geometry and their varied extensions the valuable contribution to one's mental equipment by virtue of which mathematics holds place in public education.

THE LONG HUNT FOR TRANSFER

After fifty years and more of attacks upon the theory of mental discipline, the question of transfer of power from one study to a general ability will interest almost any company of schoolmasters. James Robert Overman in a late work[11] confines himself to a limited field as affording opportunities for more exact results than the earlier appraisals obtained. He gives, however, a valuable condensation of the work of various investigators: Jastrow, Thorndike, Starch, Poffenberger and others in their search for the ever evasive transfer. Author Overman is impelled by a commendable hope. By means of a complete description of the tests he made, Mr. Overman shows you that his children gained in useful amounts a transfer from one type of example to another. He devises complete plans for the continuance and expansion of his experiments by such other teachers as are willing to do the careful work necessary to determine how the hard task done in one part of the arithmetic may be utilized with less work and more success in other parts.

No old schoolmaster has any doubt that the thrashing he gave one boy, for raising Cain in the class of a substitute teacher, effectively, though mysteriously, transferred an observance of good order to many other little devils and kept them quiet, though unlicked, all day long. But why the neat papers, gentle voices and charming manners practiced by all high-school boys and girls in the presence of Miss Fanny Gray didn't affect the boisterous rough-house nor mussy papers of these same youngsters in the classes of Mr. Hubert Brown was the unsolved wonder of my old schoolmaster. He said so. He also preached and no doubt believed that the hard study of Latin syntax was making us men of high character. Mr. Overman is searching for the teaching methods that will make the transfer greater and finds some. He considers important the suggestions of Bagley and of Judd that by exhorting to a general habit of neatness in all situations where it is worth while, by generalizing experience, by inculcating ideals, a teacher may train us all to sweep a room as by God's laws and make all actions fine.

MISMANAGED AND MUDDLED

In cozy little hamlets, in bewilderingly large cities, the selection of incompetent nobodies as school trustees has so often put the greatest of the public expenditures into the hands of blunderers as to warrant Fletcher Harper Swift[12] to say that at no time in our history have revenues for schools been disbursed in a manner likely to realize sufficient returns. At no time has it been adequate to needs. Select from fiscal policies anywhere the ones that are the most unsound, disastrous, and indefensible; these are the ones that will be found most widely used in the support of schools.

[10] Ernest R. Breslich, "Problems in Teaching Secondary School Mathematics." The University of Chicago Press. 348 pp. $3.00.

[11] James Robert Overman, "An Experimental Study of Certain Factors affecting Transfer of Training in Arithmetic." Warwick and York. Baltimore. 609 pp. $3.12.

[12] Fletcher Harper Swift, "Federal and State Policies in Public School Finance." Ginn and Company, New York. 470 pp. $3.80.

Formerly it was general practice, in many places it is still the rule, to exclude the superintendent of schools from participation in the financial policies of the system. Assuming that a schoolmaster knows nothing of business, board members have often managed to keep him in that condition. Teachers colleges and departments of education in universities have been for a few years training school men toward ability to break through the barrier. Professor Swift, early specializing in administration, soon saw the futility of training superintendents in educational practices far beyond realization with the funds available. His studies made him sought by state authorities as financial adviser. His surveys gave him acquaintance with diverse situations at home and abroad. Twenty-five years ago he published "Common School Funds." From 1922 to 1925 he issued four volumes of studies in public school finance, East, West, North, South. He is now professor of education in the University of California.

In this present volume he gives to statistics, with which the book is richly documented, an interest for the general reader by animated stories of the struggle of progressive citizens to secure national and state endowment for the public education service. He narrates the creation, increase and squandering of the federal heritage, the mismanagement and loss of school funds. He describes and explains the increase of school costs, the declining importance of State aid; and the evils of decentralized support. The quest for new sources of revenue, the problems of apportionment, remedies required, typical systems, tables and comparisons of methods, all made usable by a full index, make this an invaluable book for rural, village or city dweller concerned with putting the schools on an efficient basis.

FOR ORDER IN KNOWLEDGE

LOVERS of order will thank Librarian Bliss[13] for his productive study. He realizes that the problem of the organization of libraries involves the systemizing of knowledge and affects civilization's tasks. John Dewey praises the wide and solid scholarship of the book. Its dominant concern is educational. Social knowledge and cooperation are the only means that will bring us out of our desperate straits. If leaders and teachers had addressed themselves to social and economic studies we wouldn't be in this mess. The world has resources and science enough to give a decent living to everybody. A completer, more effective organization of science, technology education, government and social team work must be applied to life. The classification of Plato, Aristotle, Leibnitz, Compte, Spencer, modern systems, their failures and approaches to adequacy are presented. Organization is defined and elaborated. The improvements desired so that a system may be competent to cover the enormously expanded and specialized fields of knowledge are proposed and defended with notable clarity and in a broad and liberal spirit.

13 Henry Evelyn Bliss, "The Organization of Knowledge and the System of the Sciences." Henry Holt and Company, New York. 433 pp. $5.00.

LINGUISTIC INTERLUDE

To rest your mind for the other reviews necessary for your month's supply of bookish information, try this:

The English language needs many more words. With the millions of literal combinations not yet used, the absurdity of making one word serve for decidedly different concepts ought to be remedied.

A school principal of Newark—there are at least nine Newarks in the United States; take your choice—was called to the aid of a young girl teacher, whom he found standing in a corner threatened by a boy pupil, the other children paralyzed with terror. Mr. Principal felled the youth, lifted him and booted him out of the door. An excited boy shouted. "Bully!" and was immediately thrashed for calling the principal names.

TRAITS OF PRE-SCHOOLERS

BESIDES the qualities usually measured by the now common tests there is much else that is valuable in one's make-up. Dr. Nelson goes after these things as observed in pre-school children.[14]

She describes her study and conclusions as to resistance, persistence, talkativeness and spontaneity of little children.

14 Janet Fowler Nelson, "Personality and Intelligence." Teachers College Press, Columbia University, New York. 62 pp. $1.50.

A MYSTERY SOLVED

ALL the lovely music-teachers and supervisors it has been my fortune to work with are a mystifying puzzle in one respect. Why did none of them get their children to engage in vocal and written composition? The English teachers, drawing teachers, manual trainers, domestic art and science ladies were all giving their children the joy of creation, but I never found a music instructor in the public schools who had the children make up tunes or who could tell me why not. In a few minutes I could get any class I ever visited to set "Jack and Jill" or any Mother Goose stanza to an original melody. I must ask Hughes Mearns why the tuneful members of our service are so lacking in this line. Silver, Burdett and Company have sent me a new book[15] which I, not being a musician, find decidedly unique in that it is so written that an ordinary school superintendent can understand it. I am convinced that a study of it will enable a common man to ask questions that will help break the tradition that the music of his schools is a holy-of-holies wafer that he is to swallow with his eyes shut.

I search this book for solution of the mystery of absence of composition from school music exercises. Apparently it is not absent from Kansas City where Miss Glenn, one of the authors, is supervisor, nor from Lawrence College where the other author, Professor Mursell, teaches education. In many places throughout the book such matter-of-fact reference is made to "creative projects" as to imply that what I couldn't find a few years ago is tripping gaily through the schools from kindergarten to junior college. In the little town in France which harbored milady and me for some years, the boys and girls wrote their melodies as commonly as ours do their English compositions.

In the third grade, remarks my Glenn-Mursell advisers, the child should be able to develop significant music of his own. It is developed by feeling for phrases, not for separate notes. An attempt to have the child build his tune by deciding what the next note ought to be will inevitably fail.

This book is not written for music supervisors, the authors declare, but for the working teacher. Accordingly, technical aspects are avoided. Relevant studies are translated into teaching situations.

When we first saw drawing introduced into school we heard a protest that the training of draughtsmen or artists was no proper aim for public education. All of us have been pretty well supplied with the answer. English composition is not taught with the aim of making authors. We don't have school plays so that we may train for the stage. The Glenn-Mursell doctrine is that appreciation is the central aim of music education and, as amateur painting is a prime aid to the enjoyment of art and nature, so are school singing, playing and composing direct aids to the refining and perfecting influence of music upon the soul.

The psychology herein presented is elevating and dignified but it doesn't get out of sight in the high empyrean where some of the dear school musicians are wont to soar.

It tackles the monotones, real and make-believe, voice-building and control, toy orchestras, rhythm training, tests—practically everything you are likely to meet in school and especially the nature of the youngsters whom you teach, what music should do for them, and how it should be directed in order that it will do this.

[15] James L. Mursell, Mabel Glenn, "The Psychology of School Music Teaching." Silver, Burdett and Company, New York. 378 pp. $2.40.

AS GREEK MOTHERS TOLD 'EM

IN the midst of the tests, researches, yearbooks and other solidly nutritious plants of the Browns' garden of publications springs an exquisite little flower "Greek Tales for Tiny Tots."[16] From the cover in black and gold to the last baby design on the back, the book is a delight. The Crawfords say it was fun making it for their children. It shows it. Even the publisher dances with the joy of it through a preface not at all dignified. Because it is absurd to believe that little Pericles or baby Alcibiades first got their myths direct from Homer, Papa and Mama Crawford, one with words and one with pictures, put the grand old tales charmingly into the form that Bill and Jack and the other kiddies adore. Pictures? They're an enchantment! I have to take my hands from writing this so as to clap them. Christmas is coming. Better list this for the kindergarten class.

[16] John and Pauline Crawford, "Greek Tales for Tiny Tots." Public-School Publishing Company, Bloomington, Illinois. 83 pp. $1.25.

SCHOOL AND SOCIETY

EDITED BY J. McKEEN CATTELL

WITH WHICH IS COMBINED THE

EDUCATIONAL REVIEW

EDITED BY WILLIAM McANDREW

Volume 34 | Saturday, September 12, 1931 | Number 872

ARE STATE UNIVERSITIES DIFFERENT?[1]

By Professor GEORGE H. SABINE

OHIO STATE UNIVERSITY

THE subject about which I am to speak to-day is perhaps a little off the usual path of commencement addresses. Possibly I may be allowed to plead as an excuse that this occasion is, in a sense, a graduation for me as well as for you, marking as it does almost the close of my membership in the faculty of this university. For the Ohio State University, if not my alma mater, has been and will be in a very intimate sense my university, because of the happy years of work done here, because of the uniform kindness which I have received at the hands of the students, because of the friendships which it has been my good fortune to form among its distinguished body of teachers, and because of the consideration given me by its governing officers. For all these I give grateful thanks to you, ladies and gentlemen, and to you, Mr. President, as the official head of the university. Perhaps, then, it is not inappropriate that I should talk to you for a few moments, as a friend to friends, about a question of policy which is of deep concern to state universities, and which is, therefore, of interest to all of us as members of one of the greatest of them. It is a question about which your experience as students has given you an excellent opportunity to form an opinion and about which your judgment ought to be of peculiar value. Besides, your opinion is not only valuable; it may also be influential. As alumni you will have no inconsiderable power to make this university what you believe that it ought to be, since you will help to form the really enlightened public opinion of the state about its work. For this reason I intend to anticipate the outcome of to-day's ceremony and to speak to you as alumni who both know what the university is doing and also have some vision of what it can and ought to do.

It needs no argument to show that any important policy pursued by the state universities is a matter of major concern to the whole community, both state and nation. For the state universities and institutions like them have come to play an astonishing part in the whole educational work of the country. Of all the students enrolled in schools of collegiate rank more than half are in those which are supported by the states, and even if the teacher-training colleges be omitted, something like 38 per cent. are in schools that receive public support. Of all those who, like yourselves, will be graduated this year by the colleges and universities of the United

[1] A commencement address delivered at the March Convocation, 1931, Ohio State University.

States a very large proportion will receive their degrees either from state universities or from colleges which, like the state universities, are supported chiefly by money raised through taxation and which form a part of the public school system. As a result, the type and the quality of the work done by the state universities will go far to determine what shall count in America as the marks of an educated man or woman. It may well be doubted whether any of the agencies supported by the states are doing a work which has, actually and potentially, any more significance for the life of the country than that done by the state universities, and indeed, these institutions absorb no small proportion of the revenue which the states collect as taxes and expend upon public services.

The question which you are asked to consider, then, is whether these state universities are different—different, that is, from other universities which are supported by private endowments and controlled by boards which may expend their incomes as they see fit, instead of being supported by money which the state takes from the taxpayers and controlled by boards responsible to the people. Have they a different purpose? Do they furnish higher education to a different class of students? Ought they to offer a different type of work? More especially, ought they to require a different standard of excellence for the degrees by which they mark the successful completion of their courses? And finally, to be explicit, are the state universities justified in setting a really high standard of scholarship, a standard equal to that set by the best privately endowed universities, where such standards have been accompanied by a process of selecting among applicants for admission and of excluding those who are little likely to complete the course with success?

Unless I am mistaken, many persons take for granted that the answer to these questions is a foregone conclusion. They would assume that the state universities are and must be different; that private universities may rightly select their students but that state universities can not and ought not. The reasons for this view, whether it is sound or not, are perfectly easy to understand. The state universities are a part of the whole public school system, the apex no doubt, but still a part, and a normal continuation of the high schools. Now the American public school system has of necessity assumed the truly colossal task of providing education for the whole population. We have indeed long since ceased to look upon education as a private right. Up to the age of fifteen or thereabouts we have made it compulsory by law. But legal compulsion tells only a small part of the story. We have not unnaturally thought it a distinct gain when a larger and larger proportion of children could be kept in the schools as much beyond the legal age limit as possible. And in fact, the public desire for education has proved to be more extraordinary than any optimist would have foretold. Never before have so many students carried their education through the high school. Never before have so many graduates of the high schools entered the colleges. The change is undoubtedly a major social phenomenon of the last twenty-five years. It is not strange that the value of the public school system has been measured largely in terms of the number of students it reached.

It is a very easy and simple matter to look at the state universities also from the point of view just sketched. These universities are the next step in the school system beyond the high schools. Hence it is felt to be right and inevitable that the universities should take in a large proportion of those who finish the high school, or indeed, that they should take in all who choose to come. Admission to the state universities, it has been felt, must depend solely upon the volition of high-school graduates, and any process of grading or selecting students according to their probable success in doing university work is felt to be out of place. But this argument gets a still further application. As it is felt that the state universities must make admission easy, so it is sometimes felt that they must make remaining in the university easy. If admission is easy, it necessarily follows that many who enter are not really very much interested in the work to be done there; a thousand and one attractions bring students to college besides the desire for further study. It follows also that many will not have the capacities needed to do a very high grade of intellectual work and that their attainments in science or literature or the arts will always be mediocre. Obviously, then, the state universities will have to set their standards accordingly. Probably no one has ever gone to the length of believing that literally every student who wishes to stay in a state university ought to be permitted to do so, and still less that all who stay ought finally to be given degrees, but there has been at least an inclination to believe that state universities justify themselves to their constituencies by the numbers they teach as much as by the excellence of their courses. In a considerable degree their success tends to be measured by their size.

If this argument is stated baldly, as usually it is not, it amounts to the truly horrible doctrine that democracy means mediocrity. And this is a truly horrible doctrine because, if democracy is condemned not only to be mediocre but to try to be mediocre, then it stands before the world self-condemned. If the friends of democracy put themselves in this position, there is nothing worse that its enemies can do. In education it amounts to saying that state supported schools must teach large numbers, without inquiring whether most of those taught have any real interest in learning, or the ability to learn enough of the subjects taught to make any effective use of them afterward. It means that the most a state university can aim at is a good average standard of educational mass-production, leaving to the privately endowed universities the greater part of those kinds of education which aim at a really high level of scientific or scholarly or artistic accomplishment. It means also that, if we are frank, we should advise the most gifted and ambitious students to seek universities that offer such students the chance to go as fast and as far as possible in developing their unusual talents. If this conclusion is sound, state universities are indeed different, different in the profoundest of all possible ways. For while the private university is free to seek the highest qualitative standard of education, the state university is condemned not only to reach but actually to seek mediocrity.

Now the conclusion is not sound but fallacious, just as the doctrine which equates democracy with mediocrity is a counsel of despair. In fact, the state universities, and the men who have made them what they are, have never, as a class, accepted the philosophy of mediocrity in all its implications. They have sometimes been forced by circumstances to act upon it, but they have never been guilty of believing it. In spite of difficulties caused by often overwhelming numbers, the history of the state universities over a period of years has been a history of improving quality. Especially in the last two years of their undergraduate courses, and in their professional and graduate schools, the best state universities have offered at least the possibility of a high type of education to a high type of student. Those who have thought clearly about state supported education have never really believed that the universities could justify themselves to the people they serve by offering mediocre education in the mass instead of the best education to those that can profit most from it.

Undoubtedly this problem needs thinking through, especially if we are to see just why the argument that would fix educational mass-production on the state universities is a fallacy. Like most fallacies the argument is not all wrong, for if it were, it would deceive no one. It gets a certain plausibility because it includes some elements of fact that are not only true but important, and these facts must be taken into account by any one who wishes to form an intelligent opinion about what state universities ought to be. Let us try, first, to concede all that truth requires; in this way the final untruth of the philosophy of mediocrity will be all the more evident. The argument includes two important facts which it would be folly to deny. In the first place, it is a fact that the state universities must keep in touch with the high schools and that the whole school system must offer continuous and developing lines of study which can be followed straight through from the elementary schools to the top. But this is really no truer of the state universities than of the others, which also must draw the vast majority of their students from the public schools. No privately endowed university which receives undergraduates at all has ever even contemplated closing its doors to properly qualified students who have come up to them through the high schools. In the second place, it is a fact that there now exists a public demand for state supported education which will take a considerable number of students some way beyond the last year of the high school. Such a demand is warranted by the fact that young people need not be forced into gainful occupations at an early age and also by the fact that a complex industrial civilization needs a relatively long period of schooling. At all events the demand is real and a government which is highly responsive to public opinion must grant it.

Let us agree, then, that our state system of education must include continuous lines of study which may be followed from the top to the bottom and that the top, for large and increasing numbers of students, must extend beyond our present high schools. Does it then follow that all education beyond the high school must try to be university education, designed to lead through a four year course to one of the recognized degrees? By no means. There are many lines of education—almost any form of purely vocational education will serve as an illustration—which may well be worth a year's time for those who want it and which may properly be given at the state's expense, but which is not and never can be university education. From no point of view is it justifiable to erect such courses into an imitation of university education. It is not justifiable from the student's point of view because such courses do not lead to a profession or to any form of calling which warrants four years of scholastic preparation. And for the same reason it is not justifiable from the state's point of view. From the point of view of the university it can not be too strongly insisted that the university has its own work to do, and this work is too important to be endangered by the distraction of trying to do three or four other things at the same time. The university is devoted uniquely to giving advanced instruction in the sciences and the arts and in those professions which need an advanced and an exact knowledge of the sciences and the arts. This work only the university can do and this it must be free to do well.

When we say, then, that more students are to go beyond the high school, we do not say that they must be gathered helter skelter into the university. What seems rather to be indicated is more differentiation of state supported education at the top, much of it organized in schools other than the university, opening more lines of education beyond the high school and offering more choice according to the interests and the capacities of the students. Just what these lines of education should include is not a question to be settled offhand, but what is needed is certainly not past finding out. Nor is it beyond our power to give boys and girls more help in finding themselves and placing themselves more quickly in a sort of education suitable to their needs. For the university this means a selective standard of admission planned to take in students who are able to do from the start a good grade of university work.

As things stand, nearly all the students who continue in school after finishing the high school flock into the colleges, and especially into the state university, since the better privately endowed schools have long since adopted selective standards of admission. Any one who watches the working of this system year in and year out in the state universities must be profoundly disturbed by what he sees. It is perfectly apparent that very large numbers of entering students are misfits in the university. Many of them are manifestly not much interested in the work which the university offers. Even with the most careful attention to teaching many of them are able to do only very poor work, according to the standard which the university must set for those who go on to a degree. An appalling proportion of those who start follow their course for only a year, or perhaps two years, and never come within sight of a degree. In the majority of cases this is not because the university dismisses them but because they become discouraged, for nothing is more discouraging than to be always trying to do something you can not do well. Their work fails to satisfy them and they drop out voluntarily.

Thus out of every thousand students who enter this university from high school, approximately two hundred and fifty, or one fourth, have failed to return by the fourth quarter following, or the beginning of their sophomore year. Similarly, in the course of another three terms another one fourth has disappeared, so that the thousand has shrunk to something like five hundred in the junior year. In the end only about one in four or five receives a degree. There are about a hundred and fifty of you who are to receive your first degrees to-day, but you are the selected remainder from six or seven hundred who started. Make no mistake about it: education in the state universities is already highly selective if judged by those who succeed in taking a degree. It is selective with something that suggests the ferocity of selection in the biological world.

It would certainly be false to say that this failure of entering students to take degrees represents nothing but wasted effort. Many who finish only a year or two doubtless profit by their studies. But as one watches the process one can not seriously doubt that there is a great amount of waste in it. One can not avoid the conclusion that entirely too many of these students get no return that is commensurate with the time and money they have spent, or with the effort and the money that the state has expended upon them. There is certainly some loss of money, though that is the least important factor in the situation. The serious losses fall upon the human values concerned. No one can imagine that it is good for a young person to spend a year or two trying to do something for which he is ill fitted, following studies in which he is not really interested, and gaining a slipshod acquaintance with subjects he will never know enough about to appreciate or use effectively. No sympathetic person can believe, surely, that a boy of eighteen is inspired to make the most of whatever abilities he has by doing a year or two of unsatisfactory work, pending the time when he shall become sufficiently discouraged to drop out. A sense of failure is not as a rule the soil in which future successes grow. Finally, there is serious loss in this state of affairs even for those students who succeed in their university work. For the university can not possibly do its best work when its classes, especially in the first two years, are filled in a large measure by students who ought not to be there. In the last resort the standards of a university are set as much by the students as by the teachers. The loss to the university lies in its inability to do from the start the very best that it might do for those students who really want and need a university education.

Now there is, of course, an easy way out, but like most easy ways, it is the wrong way. Just here the philosophy of mediocrity crops up with the inspiration that the right thing to do is to coddle the poor student. If he is discouraged by failing in his work, pass him. Encourage everybody. Be democratic. Pretend that all students are equally promising. Set a pace that every one can keep. In short, bore the good students to death while you wait for the slow ones to catch up. But this is not an argument; it is arrant sentimentality. There is no kindness in teaching a person what he really does not need to know, or in encouraging a person to go on with what he is really unfitted to do. There is no democracy in fostering the illusion that excellence does not matter and that anybody can succeed at whatever he turns his hand to. This sort of sentimentality would turn the university into a fool's paradise. Students are going to succeed or fail in a world that needs trained faculties and judges a man mostly by what he can do. There is going to be very little sentiment wasted on students after they are out of school, and the sooner they realize it the better. In the long run nothing is more unkind than sentimental kindness. True humanity and true democracy in education consists in helping people to find out what they can do well and in giving them the training needed to do it. University education is not a panacea; it is a rather special kind of training for a fairly unusual sort of person.

I said a moment ago that it was fallacious to argue that state universities must open their doors to all comers. The truth is that no university which is supported with money taken from all the people of the state can justify itself merely by the number of its students. The disproportion is too great in any case between the number who benefit directly and those who can not avail themselves of the university's services. There must be at the present time in the state of Ohio somewhere near four hundred and fifty thousand boys and girls between the ages of eighteen and twenty-two, that is, of about the age to go to the university. Suppose then that we have on this campus some ten thousand students, while in all the state-supported colleges of the state we have somewhere near twice that number. It will still be true that only one or two in forty-five of those who are of the right age actually profit in their own persons by what the state provides. Suppose that those who go to the university be increased in any fantastic way you choose to imagine, that for example the number be doubled. Would the argument be much better if the ratio were three to forty-five? In any case the argument from numbers alone is bound to be fatally weak. For on the score of numbers alone, how can you justify taking money from all the people of a state in order to give an expensive education to one boy or girl, while more than forty are unable to avail themselves of the same privilege?

In any case the state universities must be justified not by the number of students they teach but by the intrinsic importance of university education and by the quality of the work they do. The benefit which states derive from their universities can not be measured by the proportion of the population that passes in and out at the university's doors. In every civilized community those callings which require especially a well-trained mind and a high degree of artistic or scientific skill have an importance out of all proportion to the number of persons who practice them. The physicians upon whom your health and happiness largely depend, the lawyers to whom you turn for counsel and who largely protect your rights, the teachers who educate your children, the journalists who bring you the news of the day together with their comments on it, the business men who manage your significant enterprises, the engineers who direct your more technical industries, the men and women who, outside their particular callings, set the higher standards of taste and civic virtue, are not important because they are numerous. In any society we can imagine they will still be a small part of the whole. They are important in so far as they do their work well, and the contribution which they make to civilization is a contribution of excellence.

And where shall a state look for men and women of this kind if not to their state university? For what does a university exist except to train men and women of this kind—men and women freed from the bonds of superstition and convention, imbued with the best that has been thought and written in the past, clear-sighted to grasp the problems of the present, endowed with the creative imagination to see new possibilities, open-minded to follow an argument even to an unwelcome conclusion, patient and judicial to weigh evidence and to test their ideas relentlessly before the bar of fact, courageous to follow their conviction once it has been formed, humanly sympathetic to rise above the interests of their class and place. Here or nowhere is your university justified. In so far as it can train and elicit qualities like these, no price is too great to pay for it. The argument for excellence is amply strong to carry all the load that can be put upon it.

Those who profess to be learned in reading the popular mind will perhaps tell us that such an ideal for the state universities is not sanctioned by public opinion, that whatever university men may think, the people at large, who pay the bills, want a university in which the standards will not be too severe and in which the average rather than the gifted student will be at home. Perhaps it is true that such a public opinion now exists, but if it does, the simple answer is that it must be changed. Moreover, it can be changed. What we call vaguely public opinion on any subject gets its tone mostly from the persons who are really interested. In the case of a state university this is mostly the alumni, who have had a chance to test what the university's degree is really worth, the school superintendents and high-school principals, who are closely in touch with the training of students to enter the university, and the trustees, who are responsible to the state for a far-sighted direction of the university's policies. These persons are the interested and the instructed nucleus by which the larger and vaguer public opinion ought to be formed. These are the natural leaders; if they want quality, the public opinion of the state will follow them.

In this matter of public opinion and its effect upon universities, we shall do well not to imagine a vain thing. An unenlightened public opinion can no doubt starve and ruin a state university, but it has very little power to make good university education anything but what it is. In science, in art and in scholarship there is a standard of excellence which neither a state, nor all the people in a state, can change, whatever they may think about it. A scientific investigation will still add, or not add, to our knowledge and use of nature, whether people like it or not. The worth of a poem, or a novel, or a picture is not fixed by counting heads. For this reason the kind of education that universities give is not needed merely because people think so. The need exists deep in the structure of society; public opinion does well to understand the need but it does not create the need. Even the reputation of a university does not depend upon public opinion in the usual sense of the word. The public that finally judges a university and the value of its teaching is the world of scholars within and without the state. It is *this* public which finally awards or withholds the repute of work well done.

The propriety of high standards and the selection of suitable students is in fact just as clear in the state universities as in those that are privately endowed. The public pays the interest on the endowments of private institutions of higher learning as surely as it pays taxes. In both cases the public must look for its return to a high standard of proficiency on the part of graduates in those callings, professions and walks of life for which a university education is the best preparation. Let it be repeated that the proper work of the university, the work which it alone can do, is indispensable. But that work, to be worth anything at all, calls for special abilities and special interests. All universities, no matter how supported, must be justified, if at all, by the excellence of the work they do. And selection is inseparable from excellence. Selection of a kind you already have in the process that reduces five entrants to one graduate. The question is not whether you will select, but when and how. For wise selection is not the simple reduction of numbers; in itself a small number is no better than a large one. The purpose is to help boys and girls to find the places where they can do their best work, and it is the part of wisdom to do this as quickly as possible, as accurately as possible, and with the smallest possible loss to the human values at stake. So far as the university is concerned this means picking out at the beginning the students who are destined for a degree and avoiding the heavy toll of failures which is incident to our present system of selection.

How then shall we answer the question, Are state universities different? If we pass over details and go at once to the heart of the matter, the answer is emphatically, No. In its underlying purpose a state university is exactly like a privately endowed university. Both exist to preserve and extend those higher reaches of science and art and technology without which a civilized community can neither hold its own nor progress. Both impart a specialized training to students who must always be a small proportion of the total population and who possess interests and capacities somewhat unusual as compared with the total range of human interests and capacities. In both, the success of the training depends upon finding as soon as possible the group of somewhat unusual students who are qualified to take it. In both the success of the training will be limited if effort is distracted in the direction of teaching a considerable proportion of unsuitable students. In both the excellence of the work done is the condition of its being really useful. In the end the state universities must follow the policy already adopted by the best private universities of selecting their students from among those applicants for admission who have the interest and the capacity for a relatively high type of intellectual effort. For in this way only can they conform to the ideal of a university education and justify the confidence which a really enlightened public opinion reposes in them.

OBJECTIVES IN RELIGIOUS EDUCATION

By PAUL H. VIETH, Ph.D.
INTERNATIONAL COUNCIL OF RELIGIOUS EDUCATION OF CHICAGO

THROUGHOUT this discussion, the term "religious education" will be used to mean education in the Christian religion.

During the past quarter century religious education has risen to a place of major importance in the life of the Christian church. When the church was taking but scant notice of the Sunday school held beneath its roof, there was little call for religious education to define its objectives. Since, however, religious education has been accorded a recognition to the extent of ranking as a major activity in many progressive churches, there is urgent need that it state clearly its purpose and function.

In the traditional type of religious education which prevails in most of our churches, it is easy to define the objective. It is the teaching of the Bible. The advance of education generally, however, from emphasis on subject-matter to emphasis on experience, has not left religious education untouched. A period of transition is upon us, bringing hesitation and confusion in its train. Small wonder that there are those who have felt that religious educators themselves do not know where they are going.

The demand that religious education define its objectives in clear and simple terms is heard from both its friends and its foes. Its friends want to understand it better in order that they may use this new instrument more effectively. Its foes want it to become more articulate in order that they may refute its claims the more easily.

For its own development, religious education needs to define its objectives. Only in the light of clear objectives can it give meaning to its processes and test its results. Only as a clearly defined purpose is wrought out may teachers of religion be expected to develop whole-hearted enthusiasm and fruitful method.

Moreover, religious education needs to define its objectives in order that its distinctive field may the more clearly be marked out. On the one hand, the church, with its many and varied activities, is seeking to know what religious education is proposing to do in order that it may be given its rightful place among these activities. On the other hand, the movement for character education, which is gaining ground steadily in our schools and relieving the church of much which was once assumed as its task, though inadequately performed, is demanding that the contribution which religious education can make be indicated. Religious education can not longer postpone defining its distinctive field of work.

What, then, are the objectives of religious education?

George Albert Coe finds the objective of religious education at the point where the essential nature of education and the primary emphasis of the Christian religion meet.

(1) Education to-day expresses its aims in terms of growth. Growth of the young, and happy self-realization in and through the social group is its objective. Social participation in the life of a group is indicated as the way to growth. Education then becomes a matter, not of transmitting a way of life, but of introducing growing persons to the problems and responsibilities of living in a social group and giving them a creative share in learning to live in a social group. Thus may the seeds of self-criticism and social reconstruction be sown which alone will fit each new generation for its life in a changing civilization.

(2) Jesus laid primary emphasis on the worth of human personality. Education will be Christian only to the extent that it enhances the development of personality. "To be a person is to have satisfactions and dissatisfactions that are one's own and that are discriminated, compared and weighed by the one whose own they are, and to act in view of this discriminating, comparison and weighing."[1] Thus, religion and education would both find their highest fulfillment in creative personality.

It is here that education and religion meet. Both are concerned with persons. Both want to bring to pass the largest possible growth on the part of the persons. Both see the possibility of growth taking place through creative self-activity in response to the varied situations of life.

This view sets education as the transmission of a culture in sharp contrast with education as creative experience in which the pupil shares. True, in any process of education there are bound to be both transmission from the past and response to the present. But the problem of religious education becomes one of whether it shall have as its primary purpose the handing on of traditional beliefs or the creation of a new world. Religious education in the past has conceived its task as being primarily that of transmitting a faith to the growing generation, as found in the Bible and the dogmas of the church. That it has never succeeded very well in doing this is a failure which grows out of the nature of education. As Coe points out, religion changes in the act of teaching it. It is never just the truth which is transmitted, but the truth as interpreted by the teacher and as understood against the background of experience of a particular pupil. One needs only to ask whether under even the same teacher, the words "love your enemies" would have the same meaning in 1912 as in 1918 or again in 1931, to show how even the teaching of the meaning of identical words is dependent upon surrounding circumstances. Granting then that religion is going to change in the teaching thereof, would we not be wiser if we were definitely to plan to give both teacher and pupil a creative share in the development of our faith as a part of our educational endeavor? Is not education better concerned with helping the pupil to learn *how* to think than *what* to think? Is not the teacher better employed when he is a guide to unborn to-morrows than when he is a merchant of dead yesterdays?

When religious education conceives its objectives in terms of creative self-realiza-

[1] Geo. A. Coe, "What is Christian Education," page 69.

tion of persons, it has resolved a conflict which has harrassed it for years, namely the conflict between technic and content.

There are some who feel that religious education is given too much to technic of teaching, and too little to the content of religion. A dean of a theological seminary declares that the trouble with religious education is that religious educators do not know theology. Some one else has voiced the same sentiment in the statement, "Religious Educators can teach anything, but they have nothing to teach." This conflict can not exist when the development of creative Christian personality is the major objective, for the test of success lies not in the content which has been transmitted, nor in the skill with which this has been done, but in the amount of growth which has taken place. Both technic and content must minister to this essential process of self-realization.

Let us now turn to the question,—Does religious education possess something distinctive in its objectives which sets it off from general education, and from moral education, both of which might readily subscribe to the personality principle? The International Council of Religious Education representing over forty Protestant denominations, after extensive investigation, has stated a series of seven distinctives for the guidance of its work in curriculum construction. The leaders in this organization would, I think, readily subscribe to the principles discussed above. But they would yet feel that there is needed more specific guidance concerning what constitutes the Kingdom or Democracy of God, and self-realization therein. These objectives, shorn for the sake of brevity of all their specific interpretations, are as follows:

I. To foster in growing persons a consciousness of God as a reality in human experience, and a sense of personal relationship to him.

II. To lead growing persons into an understanding and appreciation of the personality, life, and teaching of Jesus Christ.

III. To foster in growing persons a progressive and continuous development of Christ-like character.

IV. To develop in growing persons the ability and disposition to participate in and contribute constructively to the building of a social order embodying the ideal of the fatherhood of God and the brotherhood of man.

V. To lead growing persons to build a life philosophy on the basis of a Christian interpretation of life and the universe.

VI. To develop in growing persons the ability and disposition to participate in the organized society of Christians—the church.

VII. To effect in growing persons the assimilation of the best religious experience of the race, as effective guidance to present experience.

From these general objectives, certain conclusions follow:

(1) Religious education seeks to touch life at all points where the most vital experience is taking place, and to guide the growing person in understanding and interpreting that experience in terms of a religious conception of life.

(2) Growth may be continuous, throughout the years of life, from earliest infancy to oldest adult-hood. The church's responsibility is equally imperative at every point along this road, and everything the church does to bring about genuine growth in Christian living may be regarded as a part of its work in Christian education.

(3) Fellowship between the more mature and the less mature in meeting common problems and pursuing common purposes is one of the most important educative factors. Teaching is not so much bringing the new generation to the level of the more mature, as of each assuming its share in a common, worth-while enterprise.

(4) Many of the most vital experiences which enter into the growth of Christ-like character take place in the home. There-

fore, Christian education must seek to Christianize home contacts and seek to train parents to be first of all teachers of Christian living.

(5) The religious culture of the race is important as the material of religious education, but it is always important as a means to the achievement of creative living, and not as end in itself.

Granted the validity of creative education, and of comprehensive objectives such as these, let us conclude this discussion with asking and answering four questions, which normally follow:

1. *What place has religious education like this in the modern church?* The objectives just stated would probably be accepted as representing fairly well the objectives of the work of the church as a whole. This identity of objectives is inevitable if religious education is to find its purpose in the message and program of Christianity, and not in some separate sphere of its own. Moreover, the development of creative persons who are willing and able to share in the building of the Kingdom of God is an ideal accepted by an increasing number of pastors for their entire congregations. If then religious education presents a new method whereby the purposes of the church may be realized, does not the answer to the question concerning its place in the church depend on the extent to which the educational method is adapted to the accomplishment of these purposes? Even now churches are experimenting with the idea of the whole church as an educational enterprise. This does not mean that the Sunday-school is "swallowing up" the church. It means that the Sunday-school is losing itself in a larger whole which is the church.

2. *What responsibility does this lay on the pastor?* If religious education presents a valid and effective method, it lays upon him the responsibility of using the educational method as a basic approach to his work. This is but another way of saying that he must use those methods which will most effectively produce the results which he is seeking. Having set his purpose in the development of creative Christian personality, his concern must be to discover the ways in which that kind of personality is most readily developed. Which means further that the training of the minister must include not simply courses which will assist him in defining high objectives, but courses also which will help him to understand the conditions under which character grows, and how they may be utilized.

3. *What then will become of the teaching of the Bible?* We assign worth to the Bible because of its value in personal and social living. Unless we are afraid to put this basis of valuation to the test, we have nothing to fear from an education which puts at the forefront of its objectives personal values and the problems of the Kingdom. One would suppose that education such as this would lead to better understanding and higher appreciation of those portions of the Bible which are of genuine human value.

4. *Does this allow adequately for evangelism?* No religious education which understands itself will seek to accomplish its work without direct appeal to individual persons, without leading them into the experience of being saved from sin, without bringing them into clear expressions of loyalty to Christ and his ideals of life. Such personal decision for Christ is a necessary part of Christian living, and must therefore have a place in Christian teaching.

If by evangelism we mean the regenerating work of God's spirit in the soul of man, religious education has this as its highest aim. If, however, we identify evangelism with a sudden, momentary conversion experience, then religious education has a different method of work. Its very foundation is laid on Bushnell's proposition that the child is a child of God and should never know himself to be otherwise. Growth there must be, and decisions—not one, but many decisions for Christ as the countless situations of life unfold before the growing child. It is true that these decisions are of differing intensity, and one may even overtop all others as *the* decision. But no completed Christ-like character can be had in the twinkling of an eye. Religious educators do not deny the possibility of a momentary conversion experience. They maintain only that Christian nurture as a constant approach toward God, making unnecessary a turning-about experience, is a better and surer way. Even when birth into the Kingdom is by some sudden experience of conversion which completely reverses the former trends of life, it has usually been preceded by unnoted or forgotten educative influences, and must in any case be followed by a long process of education before Christ-like character is established.

No greater task rests on the church than that of helping young and old to be aware of the meaning of the Kingdom of God and to find happy self-realization therein. Religious education offers itself to the church as a means of realizing this objective.

EDUCATIONAL EVENTS

BRITISH EDUCATIONAL BROADCASTING

THE British Broadcasting Corporation, according to the London *Times,* has issued a program containing particulars of broadcasts to schools arranged by the Central Council for School Broadcasting, comprising the program from September, 1931, to June, 1932, and the syllabus for the autumn term, 1931.

A preface, signed on behalf of the Central Council by Mr. H. A. L. Fisher, the chairman, says that the council have now entered on their third year of office. A technical subcommittee appointed by the council is engaged in the effort to devise proper standards of reception. The council take the view that broadcast lessons in the school should be regarded as supplementary to and not in any degree supplanting the efforts of the class teacher. Certain general principles are, they say, already coming into view. It is hoped that during the coming year much assistance will be received from teachers in schools and from training centers in which experimental work is being done. In this way a body of tested experience will be gradually built up which will serve as a guide to teachers in the use of this new medium.

The program for the period from September to next June includes history, English literature, French and German, nature study, music, biology and hygiene, rural science, geography, speech training, stories and talks and concerts and dramatic readings. From the syllabus for the autumn term this year it appears that among those who will give talks will be: Mr. Norman H. Baynes, on history; Sir Walford Davies, on music; Professor Winifred Cullis, on biology and hygiene; Mr. C. E. Hudson and Sir John Russell, on rural science; Mr. E. Parker, on nature study; Mr. G. Heard, on science; Mr. S. P. B. Mais, on English literature; Mr. B. Tunstall, on history; M. Stéphan, on French, and Dr. E. Deissmann, on German. Mr. Baynes' historical talks will be illustrated in alternate weeks with dramatizations by Miss Rhoda Power, who, with Mrs. Williams-Ellis, will also be responsible for stories to be told to young children. Mr. A. Lloyd James, university reader in phonetics at the London School of Oriental Studies, will give speech-training lessons on new lines. Travel talks will be broadcast by various speakers, and Friday afternoon stories and talks will be given by Mr. Frank Roscoe and others. There will be six concerts and six dramatic readings.

SCHOOL REGISTRATIONS

THE Federal Office of Education in estimating school attendance states that elementary and public high schools of the United States will enroll upwards of 25,000,000 boys and girls; college and university registration will boost the enrolment to nearly 26,500,000. All other school enrolments, both public and private, will raise the total American school population to approximately 31,000,000, more than one fourth of the nation's population. Estimates furnished by the Federal Office of Education are based on the average yearly increase in past school enrolments.

The first day of school is, for the average American child, the first of 172 days of school work. The school year constantly lengthens. It now averages 10 days more than in 1920.

A boy or girl living in a rural community and attending a small rural school, for instance, may not start to school on the first day after Labor Day. Office of Education statistics show that the typical rural school year is 21 days shorter than the city average of 184 days. The shortness of the rural school term generally is evident in the later date of fall opening and earlier spring closing.

Many children of school age will not, however, be included in the long September school lines. Geographical location, climate, size of school, wealth of school and numerous other circumstances all play a part in determining the date of fall school opening and the length of the school year.

Upwards of 3,500 Negro schools in the United States have terms of only five months or less, according to information collected by the special problems division of the Federal Office of Education. These do not, in most cases, open their doors in September. Neither do about 1,200 white schools which report school terms of five months or less. A September opening for these short-term schools would mean a closing in midwinter. Children attending some rural schools of short-term duration, however, will go to class within the next three weeks, but their school term will be interrupted time and again both in the fall and in the spring so that they may assist in the fields. Suspension of school activity for extended periods is not uncommon in potato-raising areas, fruit sections, beet- and cotton-growing localities and other rural regions where farming is the leading industry.

All-year schools have been attempted in Nashville, Tennessee; Newark, New Jersey; Omaha, Nebraska; Columbus, Georgia; Aliquippa, Pennsylvania; Gary, Indiana; Lakewood, Ohio, and several other cities. They have been well patronized by pupils anxious to complete a four-year high-school course in three years, by those eager to "make up" courses failed previously and by those who wish to take part in the summer leisure or educational opportunities schools offer.

In Europe, according to the foreign schools section of the Federal Office of Education, September is the month of vacations, so that schools generally do not open until the latter part of the month or in October. Boys and girls in Norway and Belgium go to school ten months a year and enjoy six- to eight-week vacations, generally fixed by decree of the Ministry of Education. While American children generally have a five-day, twenty to twenty-five-hour week, Belgian school children attend six days and spend thirty-four hours a week in school. Belgium is typical of most European countries in this respect.

COLLEGE CREDIT FOR VOCATIONAL EDUCATION

A BULLETIN recently issued by the Federal Board for Vocational Education discusses the present practices of vocational teacher-training institutions in granting college credit for trade experience, vocational teaching experience and for supervisory and administrative experience in vocational education.

Eighteen out of thirty-eight colleges and universities offering courses for prospective vocational education teachers allow college credits for one or all types of practical experience. The number of credits varies from five in one university to eighty in another, and the minimum number of years of experience on which these credits are granted ranges from one to six.

By thus providing an incentive to individuals with a background of practical experience such institutions are securing a selected group of students who are not only more mature than high-school graduates but who have already demonstrated successful leadership ability. Professional training given to such individuals can not but reflect ultimate credit to the institutions granting degrees under these conditions, since the individuals are already successful teachers, supervisors and administrators in educational work.

Particular attention is called to the fact that thirty-one out of thirty-eight colleges offering credit for practical experience gained either in wage-earning employment or in the vocational education field announce summer courses for teachers or prospective teachers or leaders in vocational trade and industrial schools. Of these twenty-nine provide for vocational industrial teachers in service, twenty-two for supervisors and administrators of vocational education, and twenty-six for prospective vocational industrial teachers.

Conspicuous among the announcements of summer school courses is that of the Colorado Agricultural College, perhaps the leading advocate of the idea that college credits should be granted the vocational trade school teacher for practical experience in the occupation which he is teaching. For the past six or seven years this institution has been developing training courses intended to assist an individual who is already engaged in the field of vocational education as a teacher, supervisor or administrator. Under its plan the Colorado institution is allowing a maximum number of credits to such individuals. In addition, an attendance of eighteen weeks in residence is required of those who would qualify for a degree, a requirement which can be met by attendance at three summer sessions of the college.

The practical character of the courses offered for vocational teachers at Colorado Agricultural College is attested by the personnel of the summer vocational course faculty. It consists of experts who are actually engaged in the field with which their courses deal. For the summer of 1931 the vocational course faculty consisted, among others, of the personnel and employment manager in charge of occupational training for a large corporation, a state director of vocational education, the principal of a vocational continuation school, a state supervisor of vocational education, the principal of a trade school, the director of one of the most prominent privately endowed trade institutions in the country, and the educational consultant of the Federal Board for Vocational Education.

Only individuals who are employed in trade and industrial vocational education work and who have shown distinct ability on their jobs are encouraged to attend the summer course. Those desiring professional training for vocational education are advised to attend other institutions.

The putting in operation by the Colorado college and other institutions of plans whereby credit toward a college degree in vocational trade and industrial training courses is granted for practical experience is the outgrowth of the requirement of local school boards that industrial vocational teachers shall have a college degree or of the policy frequently followed by such boards of making a degree a condition of promotion or salary increase. It is obvious, of course, that few industrial vocational teachers can give four years to acquiring a college degree. The summer school courses offered by the vocational teacher-training institutions provide opportunity for this group to fulfil the residence requirements for such a degree.

PER CAPITA COST OF EDUCATION IN OREGON

GOVERNOR JULIUS L. MEIER, of Oregon, in a communication sent recently to the state board of higher education, discusses a report made by a survey commission for the board. His statement is in part as follows:

The survey shows that both the per capita expenditures for operation and maintenance and the outlay for fixed capital in Oregon are very high as compared with other states. For the former we pay $3.12 per capita as compared with an average of $1.68 for all the states. In capital outlay we invest $13.24 per capita as compared with an average of $6.31 for the country as a whole.

If these figures are correct, it is apparent that substantial savings can be effected without reducing our publicly supported educational institutions to a level of which we need be ashamed. A reduction of $1 per capita for operation and maintenance would still leave us well above the average for the Nation and would, at the same time, help materially in reducing the deficit in sight.

Along the line of economy the survey reveals two important facts about our student enrolment. First, we have a rate of attendance for each 10,000 of population of 112 students as compared with 49 for the country as a whole. After making due allowance for the greater percentage of all students who are educated in public institutions in Oregon, we still find that our institutions contain over 50 per cent. more students in relation to population than the average for the country as a whole.

In the second place, the proportion of Oregon students who fail to graduate is almost double that found on the average in the public institutions of the United States. This indicates that our large attendance is abnormal and wasteful, and that high pressure methods of student recruiting are inducing many young men and women to enroll in institutions of higher learning who are not able, financially or scholastically, to complete the curriculum.

Each student costs the State of Oregon $276.99 a year, which in itself is $62.07 per student in excess of the rate for the country at large. Included in our enrolment are 1,613 students from outside the State of Oregon. The survey suggests that many of these may have come on account of the lower standards maintained in Oregon institutions.

The tuition fees charged do not begin to cover the cost of educating this large number of out-of-state students. In fact, at the rate of $150 per year charged by the college for nonresident tuition, the state loses $126.99 per year on each out-of-state student, or a total of $204,834.87 per year. Here is a clue to a means of saving money for Oregon without in any way impairing the efficiency or lowering the standards of our educational institutions.

THE EDUCATION OF TEACHERS IN NEW YORK STATE

Approximately 75 per cent. of all high-school teachers in New York State are college graduates, according to a study made by the educational research division of the state education department and summarized in *The New York Times*. The study shows that 91.2 per cent. of all high-school teachers in the state were graduated from high school; 18.8 per cent. are normal school or city training school graduates; 55.6 per cent. have taken summer and extension courses, and 15.7 per cent. have graduate degrees.

Under the item of general training of teachers in each subject group the study shows that for all teachers 10 per cent. more majored in college in the same subject that they now teach than did not. Under the item of professional training the report declares "that there is considerable evidence to support the contention that professional training among high-school teachers of each subject is of a meager and irregular character." On the whole less than 3 per cent. of the teachers of the different subjects have a college major in education.

The teaching experience of teachers was considered from two aspects: (1) Teaching experience in present positions; (2) total teaching experience. The median number of years in present position of all teachers who reported in this aspect of the study is 3.84. The middle 50 per cent. of teachers have served between 1.96 and 7.55 years. The median number of years of total teaching experience of teachers in cities is 10.19 years; villages, 5.94 years; supervisory districts, 4.05 years. The middle 50 per cent. of the high-school teachers in cities have taught between three and seventeen years; in villages, between three and eleven years; in supervisory districts, between two and nine years.

The data for the number of subjects taught show that in New York City 90 per cent. of the teachers teach only one subject. In other cities of the state more than 80 per cent. teach one subject, 14.1 per cent. two subjects, 1.8 per cent. three subjects and .2 per cent. four subjects. In villages 75 per cent. teach one subject, 19 per cent. two subjects, and 5 per cent. three subjects. In supervisory districts 38.8 per cent. teach one subject, 37.2 per cent. two subjects, 17.2 per cent. three subjects, 5.1 per cent. four subjects, and a few more than four subjects.

The study also gives data regarding subject combinations of teachers who teach three or more subjects, the extent to which each subject is taught as a first or only subject, the extent of first-subject combinations, the variety of teaching certificates held, the nationality of high-school teachers, the occupations of fathers. Under the heading of salaries the report indicates that the average salary for high-school teachers varies as to size of community. Villages have a median salary approximately $300 higher than supervisory districts, while cities have a median salary that is much higher than villages.

SCHOOL ATTENDANCE AND UNEMPLOYMENT

A COMPILATION by the Children's Bureau of the Department of Labor states that, despite a decided decrease in employment opportunities for young people, more than 103,000 children fourteen and fifteen years old received first regular employment certificates permitting them to leave school for work during the calendar year 1930, according to reports from twenty-three states, the District of Columbia, and forty cities of 50,000 population and over in eleven other states.

These 103,000 children entered jobs which might have been available for older persons without employment had the children remained in school. Although the depression caused a decrease of one third in the number of fourteen and fifteen year old children leaving school for work in 1930 as compared with 1929, yet in a few localities there was actually a slight increase in the number of children receiving first regular employment certificates in 1930, as compared with the previous year.

The report states that, while millions of adults were idle, the 103,000 child workers under sixteen were leaving desks and playgrounds to assume part of the burden of family support. In one large city in which about 1,000 children fourteen and fifteen years old received their first regular employment certificates in 1930, the reporting official gave unemployment of adult members of the family as the "main reason for those who have quit."

The seriousness of this termination of schooling is indicated by the fact that in five states and thirty cities in other states among those reporting on the educational attainment of the children, less than 60 per cent. had completed the eighth grade and in four states and eleven cities from 30 to 71 per cent. had completed no grade higher than the sixth.

The kind of work which the children found to do is not limited to messenger and delivery service, errand work and jobs of like character. Practically as large a percentage as in previous years—42 per cent. of 30,154 children fourteen and fifteen years old for whom the type of work was reported—entered manufacturing and mechanical industries and 24 per cent. mercantile occupations.

For those states and cities for which comparable information was reported to the bureau for the two years 1929 and 1930, the number of fourteen and fifteen year old children receiving first regular employment certificates in 1930 represented a decrease of 34 per cent. as compared with the previous year.

In those places able to furnish monthly records this decrease ranged from 28 per cent. in January and March to 56 and 64 per cent. in July and August, respectively. In the states reporting on this subject the decrease ranged from 23 per cent. in New York to 55 per cent. in Vermont and Wisconsin, and in the cities from 10 per cent. in Lansing, Michigan, to 82 per cent. in Rockford, Illinois.

Though nearly all states require fourteen and fifteen year old children leaving school for industrial and commercial employment to obtain certificates, a much smaller number require sixteen and seventeen year old minors to do so. In six states, the District of Columbia and 31 cities in other states having this standard and reporting to the bureau, 66,837 boys and girls in this age group received first regular employment certificates in 1930. Where comparative figures are available for the two years this represents a decrease of 27 per cent. over 1929.

THE ALLEGANY SCHOOL OF NATURAL HISTORY

The Allegany School of Natural History, located on Quaker Run in the Allegany State Park, has ended its fifth successful session. The school, which is sponsored by the New York State Museum, the Buffalo Museum of Science and the University of Buffalo, has a curriculum containing the following five subjects with advanced courses in each: Zoology, geology, botany, bird study and nature study.

Believing that there should be a close relation between the educational system of the state and the huge state parks system, and that without detracting in the least from the recreational value of the parks, they may also be made to contribute much to education under proper guidance, Dr. Charles C. Adams, director of the New York State Museum, has supervised the educational work of the school. There is no similar school elsewhere in state parks where work of college grade trains outdoor leaders in such a fascinating atmosphere. Registration at the school this year was unusually high, and most of the students were of more mature years than usual, several of them having advanced degrees. Any one who has completed high-school work or its equivalent, however, may enter the school.

The students of the school this summer represented the following educational institutions: the Maxwell Training School for Teachers, Brooklyn, N. Y., Columbia University, the College of the City of New York, the University of Chicago, the University of Illinois, Fordham College, Bryn Mawr College, the Illinois State College, Hunter College, Pennsylvania State Teachers College at Mansfield, Mount Holyoke College, Susquehanna University, Wellesley College, the State Normal School at Bridgewater, Massachusetts, Syracuse University, the University of Rochester, the State Normal School at Geneseo, New York, Miami University, the University of Wisconsin, Lake Erie College, Antioch College, the North Carolina State College for Women, the University of North Carolina and the North Central College of Illinois.

This year an open-air museum was opened at the school, where all sorts of plants, birds' nests, rocks, insects and even some mammals were displayed. The annual series of free, illustrated, popular science talks which were given on Wednesday evenings was especially well attended.

Dr. R. E. Coker, of the University of North Carolina, is director of the school and also instructor in zoology. Many students of former years have either returned for additional courses themselves, or have sent new students. Each year distinguished visitors stop to observe the school program and the methods employed to present the subjects ecologically.

EDUCATIONAL NOTES AND NEWS

NEW appointments at the University of Buffalo include: Mr. Kenneth A. Agee, head of the department of education at Mount Holyoke College, professor of education; Dr. Albert N. Jorgensen, professor of school administration at Michigan State Normal College, Ypsilanti, professor of education; Mr. Basil S. W. Buffam, of the Canadian Geological Survey, assistant professor of economic geology; Dr. Eleanor L. Lattimore, acting professor of sociology at Bryn Mawr College, assistant professor of sociology; Mr. Henry C. Mills, associate professor of education at Acadia University, assistant professor of education.

PROFESSOR T. ELIOT BENNER, formerly with Columbia University, has assumed the duties of dean of the college of education at the University of Illinois, succeeding the late Dr. Charles E. Chadsey.

DR. MITCHELL DREESE, of Grinnell College, has been appointed assistant professor of education in the school of education of George Washington University.

DR. CLIFFORD L. BARRETT, assistant professor at the University of California at Los Angeles, will go to Princeton University next year as assistant professor of philosophy. Professor Donald A. Piatt, of the University of Texas, will go to the University of California at Los Angeles for the year 1931–1932 as visiting professor of philosophy.

DR. MAX FARRAND, director of research at the Huntington Library, San Marino, California, and Dr. William Linn Vesterman, professor of history at Columbia University, have been appointed to membership on the advisory committee of the John Simon Guggenheim Memorial Foundation.

MR. RICHARD BOMBERGER, formerly head master in the Donaldson School at Ilchester, Maryland, has been elected dean of Franklin and Marshall College.

JAMES R. MCDONALD, secretary of Little, Brown and Company, publishers, of Boston, has been elected president of the trustees of Lawrence Academy, Groton, Massachusetts, to succeed the late Honorable Albert E. Pillsbury.

SIXTEEN new county superintendents in North Carolina have assumed office for the years 1931–1933. The new superintendents are: J. B. Hash, Ashe County; George M. Bowman, Avery County; D. B. Burgess, Camden County; J. Gary Allen, Carteret County; J. A. Abernethy, Edgecombe County; H. C. Sawyer, Gates

County; J. H. Moody, Graham County; A. B. Alderman, Greene County; J. H. Gentry, Iredell County; J. B. Madison, Jackson County; Joe R. Nixon, Lincoln County; J. C. Manning, Martin County; N. H. Yelton, Mitchell County; B. B. Kesler, Onslow County; H. G. Robertson, Tyrrell County; J. T. Reece, Yadkin County.

MR. OSCAR C. HANSON has been chosen dean of men for the coming term at Waldorf Junior College, Forest City, Iowa.

MISS JULIA HAHN has resigned as supervisor of the kindergarten and primary grades of the San Francisco Schools to accept a position as supervisor of kindergarten grades in the public schools of Washington, D. C.

PROFESSOR W. F. SHAFFER, of Princeton University, has accepted the position of head of the Greek department at Gettysburg College.

DR. ELEANOR TUPPER has been appointed head of the department of history at Lindenwood College. She succeeds Dr. Berntha Reuter, who has accepted a position at Baylor University.

DR. DANIEL HOUSTON BUCHANAN, formerly of Harvard University, has accepted a position as associate professor of economics in the George Washington University.

PAUL PHILIPPE CRET, professor of design at the University of Pennsylvania, has been appointed architect of the Institute of Fine Arts of the University of Chicago, founded by Max and Leola Epstein, as the new building devoted to study and research in the field of art is formally to be known. It is expected that the structure will be completed by January, 1933. Mr. Cret, who was born in Lyons, France, in 1876, was a student at the art school of Lyons and at the Ecole des Beaux Arts of Paris.

MEMBERS of the several departments of the school of education of the University of Chicago, together with alumni and friends, have obtained funds to secure a portrait of Dr. Charles H. Judd, who has been director of the school since 1909, although his title was recently changed to dean of the school of education. The portrait was painted by Louis Betts, from whose brush have come several of the portraits in the university's collection.

DURING the summer months, in addition to the details of the conduct of the Office of Education at Washington, Dr. William John Cooper took the opportunity of meeting a large number of teachers attending summer schools in various parts of the United States and others attending educational conferences. He gave addresses at five Illinois state teachers colleges, at the Colorado State Teachers College at Greeley, and at three other institutions of higher education in Colorado, at the New Mexico Normal University at Las Vegas, the Kansas City Teachers College, Marshall College, Huntington, West Virginia, and the University of New Hampshire.

DR. CLYDE AUGUSTUS DUNIWAY, chairman of the department of history at Carleton College, has just returned to the United States from a year's leave of absence spent as visiting professor in Australia and Japan for the Carnegie Foundation for International Peace. Dr. Duniway gave a series of lectures on historical subjects in Australian and Japanese universities.

DR. JOHN PATERSON, professor of Hebrew and Old Testament exegesis, formerly of Dunbarton, Scotland, will deliver the matriculation address at the opening of the sixty-fifth year of Drew University on Thursday afternoon, September 17.

PROFESSOR ANDREW SETH, from 1891 to 1919 professor of logic and metaphysics at the University of Edinburgh, and fellow of the Royal Academy, died on September 1 at the age of seventy-five years.

PROFESSOR CLIFFORD H. MOORE, Pope professor of Latin and dean of the faculty of arts and sciences for the past six years at Harvard University, died on August 31 at the age of sixty-five years.

DR. LLOYD JONES, professor of education at the University of Wisconsin, died on September 3. He was sixty years old.

THE death is announced of the Reverend Dr. George Bryce, who had charge of the first Presbyterian church at Winnipeg and was a cofounder of the University of Manitoba, where for many years he was a lecturer. He was in his eighty-eighth year.

DR. HENRY T. MCKINNEY, professor of education at Bethany College since 1925, died on August 30.

ADDED facilities and innovations announced by the University of Southern California include more than fifty new staff appointments, the change from a school to a college of architecture with entrance direct from high school, the location of the State Bureau of Juvenile Research on the Southern California campus, the inclusion of a number of new courses, and a new "experimental entrance program" to "measure the validity of scholastic aptitude and of high-school grades as entrance criteria for admission to college," with a selected group.

PRESIDENT HOOVER will be one of several speakers who will participate in a radio program on November 14 in the interest of the continuation of the liberal arts college as an important unit in the American higher educational system. The broadcast is announced as a concerted effort to interpret the needs, the aims and the achievements of the American liberal arts college, to strengthen the appreciation of the public for the contribution the college has made and is making to American civilization and to enlist the sympathetic cooperation and support of the people in the enhancement of the services the colleges are rendering. Other speakers include: Mrs. Thomas J. Preston, widow of President Cleveland; Dr. John H. Finley, of *The New York Times;* Robert L. Kelly, executive secretary of the Council of Church Boards of Education of the Association of American Colleges, and Dr. A. N. Ward, president of Western Maryland College and chairman of the liberal arts college movement.

FOR lack of funds the People's Institute, which is about to enter on its thirty-fourth season, may have to close its school at the Muhlenburg Branch Library, in New York City. In order to avoid this a committee of students of the institute has been working to raise the $2,500 required, appealing to all students for contributions.

THE trustees of Martha Washington College at Abingdon, Virginia, have announced that the college will not open for the regular session this fall, on account of economic conditions. The school is owned by the Holston Conference, Methodist Episcopal Church South, and was opened seventy-five years ago.

UNDER the presidency of Lieutenant-Colonel J. M. Mitchell, secretary of the Carnegie United Kingdom Trust, the British Library Association held its fifty-fourth annual conference at Cheltenham from August 31 to September 5, preceded by meetings of the International Federation of Library Associations.

THE seventeenth national council of the Phi Beta Kappa Society met at Providence, Rhode Island, from September 9 to 11. The society was the guest of Brown University during the convention.

THE international conference of the World Association for Adult Education was held on August 20 and 21 at Vienna. The conference was opened by Dr. Czermak, minister of education. Mr. Levering Tyson, director of the American National Advisory Council of Radio in Adult Education, was in the chair. British organizations were represented by Sir John Reith, of the British Broadcasting Corporation; Mr. J. W. Brown, of the World Association for Adult Education, and Mr. G. H. Baker, of the London County Council.

A CONFERENCE of economists was held at the Stevens Engineering Camp, Johnsonburg, New Jersey, during the week of August 28 under the auspices of Columbia University and the Stevens Institute of Technology.

PENNSYLVANIA'S ten-year program of educational development will be the central theme of the 1931 Education Congress, which will be held in the New Education Building, Harrisburg, on November 4 and 5. A feature of the opening session will be the dedication of the new Education Building. The dedicatory address will be delivered by an outstanding leader of education of national prominence whose name has not yet been announced. Governor Pinchot and Mr. James N. Rule, state superintendent of public instruction, will also deliver addresses at the opening session. Following these addresses, there will be presented the report of the committee on guiding principles for the ten-year program by John H. Minnick, dean of the School of Education of the University of Pennsylvania. Opportunity to ask questions and discuss this report will be given the delegates in attendance. At the evening session, U. S. Commissioner of Education W. J. Cooper will speak on "Federal Cooperation with the Pennsylvania Self-Study."

THE state government of Vera Cruz, Mexico, has demanded the resignation of all Catholic teachers of the Vera Cruz Preparatory College, which has been closed by the faculty in protest against a raid by police who searched the students for arms. The government has promised that the school will not be subjected to police action again so long as there are no Catholic teachers on the staff.

WORK of construction on both the men's gymnasium and the women's gymnasium at the University of California at Los Angeles is expected to start about October 1. The two buildings will cost about $900,000. Both of the buildings will have swimming pools, and both will be modern in every appointment. The men's gymnasium will also provide space for an armory in compliance with the military training policy of the university. George W. Kelham, of San Francisco, supervisory architect for the university, has designed the men's gymnasium. The firm of Allison and Allison, Los Angeles architects, has designed the women's gymnasium.

DISCUSSION

THE COLLEGE AND THE CURRENT BUSINESS CRISIS

IN spite of economic depression, American colleges and universities witnessed a remarkable increase in enrolment in 1930–31 as compared with 1929–30. Dean Raymond Walters, of Swarthmore College, after a careful study of college enrolments last fall,[1] made the following significant statement: Attendance this year at American colleges and universities shows an upward trend exceeding that of the past several years and approaching the percentage increase of the post-war period." Out of 421 colleges and universities, 254, or 60 per cent., showed increases in 1930 over 1929. There was an increase in the small as well as the large colleges. The registration of 426 institutions combined exhibited an increase of 3½ per cent. over the totals of 1929. The increases were mainly increases in the number of men students, since a number of colleges for women reported decreases in enrolment and since even many coeducational institutions reported decreases in the number of women students.

The causes for these increases in enrolment are of two main types: First, the faith of American parents in higher education; and, second, the present scarcity of jobs.

American parents have abounding faith in the efficacy of a college education both for their sons and their daughters. They express this faith in periods of economic stress as well as periods of economic stability. The past academic year is no exception to the rule. They have sent their offspring—particularly their sons—to the universities even at the expense of digging into their savings. Hard times, instead of halting, merely heightened their faith in higher education.

More students than usual turned toward the educational centers during the past year because they could not find employment. Fathers, due to the necessity for retrenchments, did not need their sons in their own businesses. Positions elsewhere were also scarce. Since young men could not find anything at all to do, or since at most they could obtain only certain types of jobs to which slight opportunities for advancement were attached, they presented themselves in large numbers to the professors for further training. Even many who had already stepped from high school, or who had resigned from college to enter into the business world, found themselves let out by lay-offs; these likewise turned to the professors. Consequently, the colleges and universities found themselves with larger student bodies than usual and were confronted at the same time with decreasing incomes with which to provide facilities to handle these student bodies.

While economic depression has increased the supply of college students it has had the opposite effect on the demand for college teachers. Educational institutions have not expanded their faculties during the past year, nor will

[1] SCHOOL AND SOCIETY, December 13, 1930.

they during the coming year, as they did during the post-war period. The supply of teachers, however, has not diminished. On the contrary, the growth of graduate schools has tended to increase the supply. The result is that increasing numbers of graduate students, prepared for college teaching, are seeking employment in vain. University presidents and deans during the past few months have had their offices literally deluged with inquiries for teaching positions. Almost every day brings from one to five inquiries to each department of instruction. The answer given in each case is usually the same: "No openings are anticipated for another year."

The current business collapse has greatly decreased the income of colleges and universities. Many state institutions are facing budgetary crises. While enrolments are increasing, appropriations are standing still or are decreasing. In almost every state in the Union, legislatures have either reduced appropriations or have held them the same. In some cases these reductions have taken the form of decreases in salaries as well as decreases in expenditures for operation, for maintenance and for construction of new buildings. The immediate future of state colleges and universities is uncertain. Unless enrolments are "pegged" or unless they are actually reduced, most state institutions will be greatly handicapped and their work seriously impaired during the next biennium.

The situation is not altogether dissimilar in many privately endowed institutions. The flow of income from endowments has tended to decrease. The stock market crash of 1929, together with the decreased earnings of corporations, has greatly reduced the income of a large number of privately endowed institutions from their investments as well as the market value of the investments themselves. Since the churches have also been hard hit and donations for religious education have been greatly reduced, some small colleges dependent almost wholly on denominational support are almost threatened with extinction.

While the flow of endowments may not yet have been affected by the economic depression, this flow will undoubtedly be affected sooner or later. When business enterprises are operating at a loss or when they are at most standing still, dividends are not forthcoming and stockholders and business managers are not adding to their store of wealth. This naturally results in less wealth available for endowments. Gifts that have been made to colleges and universities during the past eighteen months have originated from past accumulations of wealth. Since these accumulations have been checked by changes in the business cycle, gifts in the immediate future are not likely to be so great as they have been in the past. This means that privately endowed institutions will probably face more serious difficulties during the next few years than they face at present.

But the influences of economic stagnation have not been limited to the administrative activities of the colleges. They have also extended to the students. Students have assumed a more serious attitude during the past year than they have in previous years. They have recognized as never before the sacrifices which parents have usually endured to make college training possible for their offspring. They have paid less attention to social activities, to athletics and to extra-curricular activities and more attention to things intellectual. They have resorted less to self-indulgence and more to serious self-improvement.

Moreover, parents themselves have been more seriously concerned with education during the past year than they have in former years. They have constantly prodded the students to keep up their scholastic achievements. When they have received reports of bad grades from the university, they have immediately gotten in touch with their sons and daughters and issued an edict to them either to improve their intellectual standing or else return home. Parents refuse to provide funds for educational purposes in eras of depression unless the recipients thereof show an appreciation of the use of funds by achieving high scholastic results.

College students are more economical in their personal expenditures during a period of business depression than they are during a period of prosperity. Their monthly allowances are usually smaller and they feel that what funds they secure must be made to go as far as possible. Expenditures for dances, for clothes and for other articles of personal use are reduced to a minimum. In some institutions during the past year student groups have agreed to combine their social activities into a few all-university functions rather than to carry on a multitude of separate functions, thereby effecting greater economies in the giving of fraternity dances, and in the handling of other similar social activities.

More students during hard times than at other times naturally earn their way through the university. In many institutions during the past year there were scores of students struggling to hold on. With curtailed allowances they still attempted to get an education. Many students whose families could not give them any financial assistance at all, still felt the urge to educate themselves.

The present economic crisis has aroused uncertainties in the minds of young people of college age. It has exhibited to them as never before the increasing complexities of modern civilization. They, looking toward the future, feel the necessity of higher education if they are to adjust themselves successfully to the changing economic and social order. Under such circumstances they are willing to make any kind of sacrifice to attend college and to acquire the means with which to meet the dangers which they think they see ahead. Consequently, they have come to the colleges and universities, whether they have money or not. This action on their part has thrown a tremendous strain on these institutions—in particular on the offices of the deans of student affairs and in general on the communities in which the institutions were located.

The current business crisis has caught the colleges, at least temporarily, between the familiar upper and nether millstones. The pressure from above is increased enrolment. The pressure from below is decreased income. Are the colleges likely to be crushed? The result will hardly be as disastrous as that, but they will be at least tightly squeezed during the next two or three years, unless some action is taken or some event occurs to remove either one or both millstones.

W. J. Matherly

University of Florida

REDUCING WASTE IN THE WORK OF STUDENTS

Seven years ago, when I started to build up our course in "Methods of Study," I made what use I could of the text-books then available, but found none that came close enough to actual assignment preparing to furnish the help we sought.

In assembling and shaping material for the course I had experiences like these:

The chief essential, as well as difficulty, was to make the study skills carry over from the methods course to the work on the several subjects. Most members of the class admitted, for example, that they lacked the power to concentrate. When I tried to remedy this defect by explanations and exercises calculated to show how attention could best be focussed and how attention led to interest and interest to concentration—it all tended to remain just psychology with only slight transfer.

And yet guidance must come from applied psychology and educational experimentation. I believe if deductions from these sources were culled out, shaped and adapted to class work by some one with a clear perception of the needs of students invaluable aid would thereby be rendered. But their incidental or unskilful use is not likely to meet the study situation: Experiments in memory seem to prove that the number of readings required to memorize a series of units increases, not in arithmetical, but in geometrical proportion to the length of the series. Here is a valuable hint on memory work under the aspect of the whole and part method. But it needs to be shaped so as to reach direct touch with assignments, as these come before the freshmen.

To treat major areas independently of each other under the plan of orientation, present status, direction of development and class room work entails an unwarranted repetition of essentials common to them all, such as problem-solving, memory work, etc. Selected projects from the major areas give scope for planning and manipulation with less waste.

Practical disciplines like note-taking should be adapted to the plans which the several instructors follow in conducting their courses.

No handy expedient or intellectual leverage can be shaped and handed over to the freshmen. The most useful procedures can generally be reduced to simple lines: The freshman finds the work of composition writing onerous because he attempts to do at least four difficult things at the same time. The technique here would be: "Concentrate on one thing at a time. (1) As a first step select a subject to which you are related or one to which you can readily become related (Explanation). (2) Assemble your material as a second step and see to it that you assemble it in convenient form for organization (Illustrated by examples). (3) Concentrate on its organization as a third step (Illustrated). Finally, (4) proceed leisurely to give it literary form with your powers centered on this one procedure (Explanation).

Our course "Methods of Learning"[1] has finally become shaped so that it falls into two main divisions. The first includes considerations that help the freshman to pursue his work with a full asemblage of his powers. Some matters taken up in this connection reach far beyond formal study. They are seen to be inseparably bound up with the efficacy of study skills. A few of the topics treated in the course are:

A preliminary lecture and discussion in which it is made clear that the purpose of the course is to reduce the student's expenditure of his time and energy. Facts are given to show how such waste comes about.

Study perspectives: It is believed that if the entering student can from the outset be caused to view his entire program in relation to its end aims, he will be steadied as he goes on and at the same time gain a mind-set towards unity in his pursuits and also a desirable discrimination among study values.

The dynamics of attitudes: What is here meant is such directing as will quicken the student's inborn driving forces into action—conscious purpose and intent, the satisfaction of making progress, keeping the power of initiative alive, attitude towards the instruction and the instructors, discovering one's self, what constitutes a good recitation.

Some elements in the second main division, which is concerned with study skills and techniques, may advantageously be brought in earlier than is here indicated that use may be made of them at once.

The student's workshop technique: The workshop, the tools of study, continuity in the work instalments, the technique of reading as study, mechanistic aspects of study, presence and close-up, wholeness, unity.

Special procedures and working arrangements: Length of drill and study periods, how improvement in skill takes place, the impulsion of ideas, planning, study schedules, time and place adjustments.

Getting ideas from print: How rapid readers read, preparing a reading assignment, unequal value of the subject-matter, how to bring main values into relief, marginal outlines, marginal commentaries, graphic representations.

Note-taking and constructive work: Notes from spoken and dictated matter, from reading and study, research papers and note-taking.

Work on specific assignments: Here most subjects of the freshman and sophomore years are taken up. Several typical assignments from each course in history, economics, literature, composition, physics, geometry, sociology, are worked out as exhaustive preparations. Others are briefly outlined.

Adapting the working plan to the subject: How an assignment in a subject best opens up; the nature of the subject as determining what is most profitable to do in a specific piece of work.

The study of foreign languages: Why the undirected student has to look up a Latin word some twenty times before it is a part of his Latin vocabulary, making the context disclose meanings, exercises in directed study of foreign texts.

Other topics included in the course are "Principles of Memorizing," "Problem-Solving," "Improving the Power to Concentrate," "Taking Examinations."

The discussions and exercises connected with the topics here given converge on a series of major projects. These are carefully prepared, usually by the instructors whose domains they invade. Material is provided for a prompt start. The class is resolved into working groups, following the principles of division of duties when this seems expedient. If the project has to be left incomplete at the end of the session care is taken that everything is left in shape for a prompt "pick-up" when the class reconvenes.

In these projects the instructor has his best opportunity to guide his class towards direct and time-saving procedures. The writer has

[1] Now being prepared for publication.

with the assistance of his colleagues prepared twenty-four such major projects from which selections will be made for the work of the coming year.

The teacher of "Methods of Learning," like the teacher of composition, would like to expedite the transfer of his disciplines into the activities where they are expected to function. To this end the most promising ways are: (1) Directed work on units of the other subjects; (2) a working alliance with the other instructors.

In these efforts to minimize waste in student work much help would be rendered by a study calculated to state the usual amount of wasted energy in terms of greater exactness than we have at present. Whether the results of such a study would show the ordinary loss to be about 75 per cent., as some have conjectured, or 90 per cent., as one psychologist points out in a particular discipline, it is not likely that educators would continue to view such appalling loss with indifference.

P. H. PEARSON

UPSALA COLLEGE,
EAST ORANGE, N. J.

SPECIAL CORRESPONDENCE

RECENT TENDENCIES OF THE ROUMANIAN EDUCATIONAL SYSTEM

THE educational system of Roumania is now rapidly undergoing changes which are planned to make up for the deficiencies of the past, due to the lack of thorough historical roots and to the disunity springing from the additions of territory to the kingdom of Roumania after the war. It was not until 1838 that the first Wallachian official decrees were promulgated in which directions were given for the organization and the upbuilding of schools, to be attended not for the whole year, but during the winter season only. The result was 29 grammar schools, and between 1838–1864 259 additional schools came into being. The creation of schools in the other provinces of pre-war Roumania was imposed by the state as early as 1832, but up to 1850 only 25 grammar schools were established in villages and 30 in the cities.

The educational acts of 1864 created the principle of free and compulsory education "where schools were available" under state supervision. But because of financial and organization deficiencies the laws could not be applied very effectively. The foundations of the present Roumanian system were laid by the decrees of 1896, supplemented in 1901, 1903 and 1908. The four years' attendance was introduced, and the state imposed on itself the duty of supporting and extending education and providing for the training of teachers. Though the development of education was rapid after 1896, the number of illiterates remained rather large. In 1909, for example, 73.2 per cent. of the men and 53.9 per cent. of the women of the cities could read and write, but in the villages only 51 per cent. of the men and 17.4 per cent. of the women were literate.

In Transylvania, formerly a part of Hungary and now the most important provinces of Roumania, each commune having more than 30 children had to establish and support a school. The Magyar government granted the schools, which were not supported by it, certain financial support if the Magyar language and traditions were taught there. In 1911 there were 2,655 schools with 2,767 teachers, mostly the product of, and under the control of, the church. In Bukovina the Austro-Hungarian government was rapidly denationalizing the Roumanian children and in 1914 there were 179 Roumanian schools with 35,131 pupils out of the total of 541 schools. In Bessarabia the conditions were much worse.

After the war there is noticeable a remarkable growth in the number of schools, pupils and teachers. In 1920–21, the estimated number of primary schools was, according to the Near East Year-Book (1927), 13,398 primary schools, 25,745 teachers and 1,516,198 pupils. According to the official figures, the number increased as follows: 16,824 schools, 52,995 teachers and 2,216,206 pupils. We should also notice that while the Magyar government did not support one school teaching the Roumanian language, the Roumanian government was subsidizing, in 1922, 600 Magyar schools, 89 German and 73 other language schools.

The educational policy of the Roumanian

government has been based on the desire to make up for the lost time of the past and to retain Roumanian control of every school. Dr. Angelescu and the Liberal government reorganized the whole system by the decree of July 24, 1924. The four years' course of the primary school was lengthened by three years for additional education in civics and practical subjects. However, the pupils desiring to attend the higher schools need only four years of the primary schools. For the children from four to seven years of age, the kindergartens were introduced. Adult courses were organized, and the length of training of teachers in normal schools was lengthened.

The present educational system of Roumania is divided into four categories: elementary, secondary, graduate and superior. Compulsory education is applied only to the elementary schools.

The new law of May 15, 1928, made some changes in higher education. In addition to the seven years of secondary work one year of preparatory work for the entrance to a university was provided. After four years of university studies, the students get the degree of master of arts; but in order to teach, the students must include in their studies special pedagogical courses and pass a special examination which entitles them to teach in the secondary schools. There are no residence requirements for a doctorate, as in the United States.

Professor Iorga, who besides being prime minister of Roumania is also minister of education, plans a rather thorough reorganization relating to the years of studies, subjects and the granting of diplomas and degrees. The first steps in this direction were taken this year. The "maturity" examination, which allows the student to enter a university, on the basis of the recent change, now favors the minorities of Roumania. The examining commission is composed of the professors speaking the minority language of the candidates. Furthermore, only professors with higher classifications are selected for these commissions. The candidates can select either German or French as the modern language requirement. A written examination in the Roumanian language is compulsory for all the candidates, and the other examinations can be written either in Roumanian or in the language of the respective minority.

The last National-Peasant government especially favored agricultural development. This tendency is evident from the requirements raised for the teachers of agricultural subjects in teachers' schools and colleges. Special examinations are now required. Only those holding the degree of agronomical engineer and doctor of agronomical science, and graduates of other higher institutions, are allowed to take the examination, consisting of two written and additional examinations. The former consists of the examination in the higher agricultural studies and the pedagogical studies. Other requirements are two practical demagogical examinations in the class and in the field or a garden with the pupils and a practical examination in the laboratory. All candidates must have two years of agricultural practice and the certificate of attendance and "graduation" from a university seminar. Only in case that there are not enough candidates with agricultural practice, these with the practice in pedagogy, in natural sciences and geography are admitted to compete. Three days before the examination, all candidates must pass a rigid physical examination before a commission of three physicians.

In America much attention has been paid to physical education in recent years. Roumania, as all other European countries, pays by no means so much attention to the physical development of the students. Before the war, physical training was intimately connected with the military requirements. There existed only military physical-training schools for the under-officers, and teachers of fencing and physical training. During the war this activity ceased entirely, and in 1919 the ministry of war opened the Military Physical Training School, the pupils of which were recruited from the civilian classes and after their graduation drafted into the army, where they have ranks from the sub-lieutenants to the captains.

In 1922 the Institute for the Physical Training of the Nation (O. N. E. F.) was established. Its task is to popularize physical training among the masses of population, to take care of the premilitary training of the youth and the preparation of instructors in the army and the schools. Another duty of the institute is to see that each Roumanian community be given lots for playgrounds by the state. Professional publications for other sporting and training institutions are systematically published and special attention is paid to tendencies abroad to improve this endeavor. The institute itself is a state institution, and its committee is composed of the representatives of the ministry of education, war, health and work. Prince Nicolae is its honorary president.

The studies of teachers in this institute take three years, and from 1925 to 1927 diplomas were granted to 50 graduates, who have the right to teach in secondary schools. With the reorganization of the school system, the grammar schools have now four hours and secondary schools two hours of physical training. Every year special summer courses are given for the teachers, who did not graduate from the institute, in Techirghiol on the Black Sea or in Predeal and Calimanesti resorts in the Carpathian Mountains. It is planned to establish chairs of physical training in every Roumanian university.

In addition, the institute has a special one-year course for the officers and sub-officers of the army. Between 1925 and 1927 about 220 of them graduated. A number of students were sent abroad to become acquainted with foreign systems.

Altogether, 11,419 hectares of playgrounds, divided into 4,406 communities, are supervised. Heretofore the institute succeeded in organizing two main centers of physical education in Roumania. The first is located in Bucharest. It is a modern building for 100 women-students, 80 male-students, 30 officers and 30 sub-officers; it has also six lecture rooms, two gymnasiums, two halls for the practice of Swedish gymnastics, in addition to laboratories, playgrounds, stadium, swimming-pool. However, tennis courts, grandstands and a well-furnished gymnasium are lacking. The other center is the school Techirghiol on the Black Sea, where eight-months' courses are given for the village teachers and leaders of labor physical-training organizations. The attendance here is rather high, ranging from 300 to 40,000 in the whole of Roumania, and from 300 to 400 attending the monthly courses. Additional schools will be soon established in Predeal and Calimanesti in the Carpathian Mountains.

The students and graduates of the institute have founded a club, which with its public performances in Bucharest, Campina, Giurgiu and Constanza, is spreading the appreciation of its aims among the general public. The same aims are followed by the society of non-professionals, "The Friends of the Institute for Physical Education," which has branches all over the country and cooperates closely with the institute.

Besides this official activity, private initiative is represented by the Roumanian athletic federation of Bucharest, in which there are centered numerous Roumanian sporting clubs. It sent its representatives to the Olympiads of 1924 and 1928. It also cooperates fully with the institute, its motto being the same—"For the Health of the Roumanian youth."

J. S. ROUCEK

CENTENARY JUNIOR COLLEGE,
HACKETTSTOWN, N. J.

QUOTATIONS

EDUCATIONAL JOURNALS IN INDIA

THE names of new members of the Indian Round-Table Conference recently published as having been added to the Federal Structure Committee include that of Mr. A. Rangaswami Iyengar, the editor of the *Hindu,* one of the most widely read and ably conducted daily newspapers under Indian control. Mr. Iyengar has made a useful contribution to the inadequate educational journalism of the country by the issue, since the beginning of 1927, of a weekly supplement under the name of *The Hindu Educational and Literary Supplement.* Mr. Arthur Mayhew, who had long and practical experience in the Indian Educational Service and at Eton, and who is now Educational Adviser to the Colonial Office, writes a weekly article on movements and tendencies in the field of education in every part of the world. Mr. T. Earle Welby, the well-known literary critic, contributes a regular article on new books. The Supplement serves, besides, as a forum for the discussion of educational aims and methods which are being advocated or tried in India generally, and in South India in particular. Articles by specialists on music and the other fine arts are also published at regular intervals.

Another development in the interchange of educational thought in India is the issue since the autumn of 1928 of *Teaching*, a quarterly technical journal for teachers, published by the Oxford University Press. It was founded under the editorship of Dr. H. R. Hamley, then principal of the Secondary Training College, Bombay, now Reader in Education at the University of London. The quarterly aims to provide an inter-provincial platform for the discussion of Indian educational problems from a practical point of view, problems which are often to a great extent common to all parts of India. The need for such a platform was emphasized by the Hartog Auxiliary Committee of the Indian Statutory Commission, and the view was endorsed by the Commission. Each article is intended to be a practical contribution to the science of teaching, and no encouragement is given to merely "hot-air disquisitions on general or semi-political topics loosely akin to the subject of education. The paper has no official subsidy, though one province at least ensures (by paying their subscriptions) that all its high-school head masters, inspectors, and deputy inspectors regularly receive copies.

A journal known as *Indian Education* was issued monthly by Messrs. Longmans, Green and Co., for 15 years to 1921. Publication ceased when the Department of Education stopped its subsidy of Rs. 1,000 a year. The gap was partly filled on the Bombay side by the establishment in July, 1924, of the *Progress of Education* (at first published in alternate months), which has been issued monthly for the past two years. It is devoted to the discussion of problems relating to the theory, practice, and administration of education, particularly in the Bombay Presidency. It is edited jointly by three college professors and two schoolmasters in Poona, and is published by Mr. A. V. Patwardham, a well-known public worker and a member of the Servants of India Society. The monthly discusses all sorts of educational problems, but has so far concentrated on those of secondary schools. The editors have shown a commendable desire to open their pages to contributions by schoolmasters, men who are tackling the numerous details of educational efficiency in their own way. Not only has the *Progress of Education* helped to remove the shyness of schoolmasters; it has also tended to develop a preference for the views of the men who work in place of those of the men who talk and criticize.

This outline of some recent developments in educational journalism in India shows that real progress is being made. Under Indian conditions, however, subscription prices have to be kept very low if the journals are to reach the rank and file of a very ill-paid profession. Such journals can seldom, if ever, be remunerative to the proprietors, and a measure of government support in the form of paying the subscriptions of some members of the teaching staff or of advertising official notifications would seem to be a necessity.—*The London Times Educational Supplement*.

SOCIETIES AND MEETINGS

THE NATIONAL ASSOCIATION OF COMMERCIAL TEACHER-TRAINING INSTITUTIONS

THE National Association of Commercial Teacher Training Institutions comes before the commercial teaching world with a new program worthy of the support of all commercial teacher-training institutions and all commercial teachers. The fourfold objective of the association is stated as follows: Improvement of programs for training teachers of commercial subjects; elevation of standards for the certification of teachers of commercial subjects; promotion of research in commercial education; development of proper recognition amongst schoolmen of the significance of commercial education.

In working toward this objective, the association has in the past followed a fact-finding program and attention has been given to determining (1) what are the practices in the teacher-training field with regard to curricula, and (2) what should be the practice with regard to teacher training curricula. A study was undertaken and the principles of curriculum building for commercial teacher-training were formulated by Dr. Paul S. Lomax and Dr. Herbert A. Tonne, both of New York University.

In the year 1930–1931, the work of the association, under the leadership of the president, Miss Ann Brewington, of the University of Chicago, undertook the formulation of a definition of commercial education and a statement of the obligation and position of business education in our social and economic order. This attempt to define the scope, the obligations and the position of business education, it will be noted, is basic to the realization of all four parts of the objective of the association. It will be noted further that such a definition should serve particularly to assist in achieving parts 3 and 4 of the objective as stated above.

Only a beginning was made in this work during the past year. Members of the association, realizing the importance of the work, decided at the Detroit meeting on February 27, 1931, to continue the study to secure a better formulation of the definition, representing the best and most careful thought of business educators throughout the country. This important work was turned over to a committee with Mr. Frederick G. Nichols, of Harvard University, as chairman. The association expects to publish the results of this study when the work is completed, which study will be sent to members.

The officers for the year 1931–1932 are as follows:

President: C. M. Yoder, president, Whitewater State Teachers College, Whitewater, Wisconsin.
Vice-President: Alfred Sorenson, University of California, Berkeley, California.
Treasurer: Paul A. Carlson, Whitewater State Teachers College.
Secretary: Helen Reynolds, Ohio University, Athens, Ohio.

The directors who are serving now are: Ann Brewington, University of Chicago; A. A. Miller, North Texas State Teachers College; F. G. Nichols, Harvard University; Paul S. Lomax, New York University; E. G. Blackstone, University of Iowa.

Membership in the association is of two kinds, institutional and associate. Institutional membership is open to recognized universities, teachers colleges and normal schools, doing commercial teacher training. This membership entitles the holder to a voting representative at all meetings of the association; the fee is $10 a year. Associate membership is open to instructors in institutions eligible for institutional membership, to graduate and to fourth-year students specializing in commercial education in the schools eligible for membership, and to public-school administrators and supervisors in charge of commercial education. The associate membership fee is $2.00.

Under the leadership of Mr. Yoder, the new president, the association will make an important contribution to the professional life of its members. Institutions doing commercial teacher training are urged to ally themselves with the other leading universities and teachers colleges in the country in contributing to and profiting by the work of the association. Individual teachers will find it worth their while to join with the other representative business educators of the country. Send your application for membership to the secretary, Helen Reynolds, School of Commerce, Ohio University, Athens, Ohio, in time to make your contribution to the 1932 meeting.

EDUCATIONAL RESEARCH AND STATISTICS

A COMPARISON OF THE FIRST AND THE SECOND SEMESTER PROGRESS OF PRIMARY PUPILS

IN a recent experiment in class size in the primary school,[1] assumed differences in first and second semester achievement were held constant by arranging primacy of experimental groups so that one half of the 24 rooms used were in small class situations the first semester and one half in large classes. After the report was written, it seemed worth while to investigate

[1] Whitney, F. L., "The Trinidad-Pueblo Experiment in Class Size in the Primary School." *Colorado Teachers College Education Series No. 12.* Colorado State Teachers College, Greeley, 1931.

the relative truth of the assumption usually held that pupil groups do much better in their work during the first half of the school year.

The achievement records of 529 of the subjects of the experiment were used, constituting 24 classrooms—127 in grade one, 133 in grade two, 112 in grade three and 157 in grade four. These groups had been tested three times during the experiment, in September, in January and in May.

Grade one
- January, 1930, and May, 1930
  - Los Angeles Primary Word Recognition Test, Form 1
  - Los Angeles Primary Reading Test, Form 3

Grades two and three
- September, 1929
  - New Stanford Achievement Test, Primary Form V
- January, 1930
  - New Stanford Achievement Test, Primary Form W
- May, 1930
  - New Stanford Achievement Test, Primary Form V

Grade four
- September, 1929
  - New Stanford Achievement Test, Advanced Form V
- January, 1930
  - New Stanford Achievement Test, Advanced Form W
- May, 1930
  - New Stanford Achievement Test, Advanced Form V

To get the facts of differences in achievement, the January score of each individual pupil was subtracted from the September score, and the May score from his January score. Then, the second semester gains were subtracted from the first semester gains. This was done for each subject in each grade, and distributions of individual gains tabulated. Table I illustrates the results for the six first grade classes in English.

It will be seen that the summation figures at the bottom of the tables make possible a comparison of first and second semester gain in school achievement in terms of average differences, the probable error of averages, and the relation of these two units for each distribution. The interpretation was that an average difference was *significant*, if it was at least twice its PE, and statistically *reliable*, if at least four times its PE.

TABLE I

THE DISTRIBUTION OF DIFFERENCES IN GAINS IN ENGLISH FOR THE FIRST OVER THE SECOND SEMESTER MADE BY SIX FIRST GRADE CLASSES (127 PUPILS) IN THE TRINIDAD, COLORADO, PUBLIC SCHOOLS, 1929–1930[a]

Difference	Frequency
1	2
40 – 44.9	2
35 – 39.9	1
30 – 34.9	1
25 – 29.9	2
20 – 24.9	8
15 – 19.9	8
10 – 14.9	9
5 – 9.9	12
0 – 4.9	21
– 5 – – 0.9	20
–10 – – 4.9	12
–15 – – 9.9	17
–20 – –14.9	9
–25 – –19.9	5
N	127
Average	1.28
Sigma	13.98
$PE_{av.}$	.837
$\frac{Av.}{PE_{av.}}$	1.53

[a] The Los Angeles Primary Word Recognition Test, Form 1, and the Los Angeles Primary Reading Test, Form 3.

The results of this calculation are reported in Table II. It is seen that (column 4) only in one case was there a greater average gain during the second semester. This was in fourth-grade social science; but this is a measure of mediocrity, as both semester gains were negative. Two of the eight first semester gains are not significant, according to the criterion of the paragraph above; and three are not reliable. This leaves a preponderance of group gains

TABLE II

THE DIFFERENCE IN GAINS OF THE FIRST SEMESTER OVER THE SECOND SEMESTER FOR 529 PUPILS IN GRADES ONE TO FOUR INCLUSIVE IN THE TRINIDAD, COLORADO, SCHOOLS IN 1929–1930, AND THE RELIABILITY OF THESE GAINS IN TERMS OF PROBABLE ERROR OF THE AVERAGE

Grade and subject	Average of differences	Probable error of the average	Semester showing greater gain	Was the gain significant?	Was the gain reliable?
1	2	3	4	5	6
Grade One					
English	1.28	.84	First	No	No
Grade Two					
English	13.10	1.39	First	Yes	Yes
Arithmetic	4.78	1.69	First	Yes	No
Grade Three					
English	15.89	1.40	First	Yes	Yes
Arithmetic	9.64	1.99	First	Yes	Yes
Grade Four					
English	17.33	2.93	First	Yes	Yes
Arithmetic	2.77	1.81	First	No	No
Social science	12.17	2.79	Second	Yes	Yes
Physiology	7.04	1.37	First	Yes	Yes

both significant and statistically reliable. However, there seems to be no consistency in subject gains. English shows a reliable first semester gain in only three out of four cases. Arithmetic reveals a similar mixture of results. Perhaps the first semester gains were weighted slightly because of the fact that the September tests were not given until near the close of the month. This undoubtedly gave opportunity for reviews, and rapid relearning may have obviated in part vacation forgetting.

On the whole, the data seem to point to rather consistent differences in achievement gains in favor of the work of the first semester, so far as these 24 classrooms in grades one to four inclusive are concerned. It might be worth while to extend the investigation to other situations and to public school work beyond the primary school.

FREDERICK L. WHITNEY
CHARLES G. SWANSON
COLORADO STATE TEACHERS
GOLLEGE, GREELEY

THE ART ABILITY OF MEXICAN CHILDREN

IT is commonly supposed that Mexican children are gifted in art. References to this alleged talent are frequently found in discussions of the Mexican people,[1] and many teachers of Mexican children in American schools think that they are more artistic than children of ordinary English-speaking stock.

The recent development of instruments of measurement makes it possible to begin at least to submit this hypothesis to actual test. The study made by the authors was based upon the use of the Meier-Seashore Art Judgment Test and the McAdory Art Test. These tests, it will be remembered, require the pupil to choose between two or more art products. In the first, one attempts to choose the better of two renditions of a painting or other work of art. In the second, a series of plates is presented, each of which has four representations of clothing, furniture and other objects, and the four are to be ranked in order. Theoretically, then, these tests give a measure of aesthetic judgment and to that extent of art ability. Meier and Seashore, indeed, think that standing on their test is an especially valuable symptom of art ability in general. Presumably, the one thing which an artist needs above all else is the ability to know when a thing is beautiful and when it is not.

In our study these two tests of art judgment were given to eighty-two Mexican children and one hundred three non-Mexican white children in the Washington Irving Junior High School of San Antonio.[2] The Mexican and other children were enrolled in the same classes. The Mexican children were on the average a half-year older and, according to the records of a

[1] See, for example, Carleton Beals' ''Mexico'' and Manuel Gamio's ''Mexican Immigration to the United States.''

[2] Grateful acknowledgment is made to Principal C. A. Arnold. The tests were administered by Miss Stolz.

National Intelligence Test given just before entering the junior high school, had intelligence quotients about ten points lower.

A brief comparison of the two groups as a whole is shown in the following table:

TABLE I

AGES, INTELLIGENCE QUOTIENTS, AND SCORES ON THE MEIER-SEASHORE AND MCADORY TESTS

	Mean		Difference of means	Critical ratio[3]
	Mexican	Other white		
Age	13.9	13.4	0.5	3.0
N. I. T. IQ	94.1	104.8	−10.7	3.5
McAdory	104.6	107.6	− 3.0	0.8
Meier-Seashore	77.1	73.5	3.6	2.9

Neither group compares favorably with the authors' norms. On the McAdory test both are below the mean score (115) reported for one hundred sixth-grade children. On the Meier-Seashore test the Mexican children are at the 27th percentile and the other children at the 18th percentile of junior high school pupils.

The Mexican children made poorer scores on the McAdory test and better scores on the Meier-Seashore test. Of the two differences only the latter is statistically reliable.

The Mexican children were slightly less variable.

Correlation of the two tests of art judgment and of each of these with intelligence quotients were made for age groups 13 and 14, in which the number of cases seemed sufficient to make a useful comparison. The correlations are reported in Table II.

TABLE II

	Age 13		Age 14	
	Mexican	Non-Mexican	Mexican	Non-Mexican
McAdory and Meier-Seashore	.07 ± .12	.58 ± .08	.31 ± .13	.37 ± .13
McAdory and IQ	.00 ± .11	.20 ± .11	.00 ± .15	.29 ± .14
Meier-Seashore and IQ	.42 ± .09	.26 ± .11	−.08 ± .15	.55 ± .10

[3] Difference of means divided by sigma of difference.

The correlations in general are relatively low and less for the Mexican children than for the other children. It seems probable that the two art judgment tests measure somewhat different functions and that this difference is greater in the case of the Mexican children. Intelligence seems to be at least a small factor in the art judgment tests of the non-Mexican children.

When the various parts of the McAdory test are considered separately, the Mexican children are generally inferior to the others. They make their best relative showing on "colors" and "textiles and clothing" and their poorest on "furniture and utensils."

As a final summary, it may be said that although the alleged superiority of the Spanish-speaking children in art ability finds a little support in our results with the Meier-Seashore test, the results of the McAdory test do not support this hypothesis, and the average of both groups is far below the authors' norms. The number of cases is too small, however, to permit the drawing of general conclusions from these data.

ALBERTA STOLZ
H. T. MANUEL

UNIVERSITY OF TEXAS

NEW BOOKS IN EDUCATION

ANDERSON, LEWIS F. *Pestalozzi.* Pp. ix + 283. McGraw-Hill. $2.00.

HOLLIDAY, CARL. *The Dawn of Literature.* Pp. x + 367. Illustrated. Thomas Y. Crowell. $3.50.

LAIDLER, HARRY W. *Concentration in American Industry.* Pp. xv + 501. Thomas Y. Crowell. $3.75.

LUMLEY, FREDERICK E. and BOYD H. BODE. *Ourselves and the World.* Pp. viii + 591. Illustrated by Guy B. Wiser. McGraw-Hill. $2.00.

MITCHELL, W. N. *Production Management.* Pp. xi + 422. University of Chicago Press. $4.00.

REMMERS, H. H. and J. M. STALNAKER. *Studies in Higher Education.* No. 17. Pp. 31. *Division of Educational Reference,* Purdue University. $.50.

SANCHEZ, NELLIE V. *Stories of the States.* Pp. x + 380. Illustrated. Thomas Y. Crowell. $2.50.

STETSON, F. L. *Studies in Secondary Education in Oregon.* No. 1: *The Organization and Administration of Standard High Schools.* Pp. 205–296. University of Oregon Press. $.75.

SYMONS, FARRELL. *Courses on International Affairs in American Colleges.* 1930–1931. Pp. xviii + 353. World Peace Foundation. $5.00.

SCHOOL AND SOCIETY

EDITED BY J. McKEEN CATTELL

WITH WHICH IS COMBINED THE

EDUCATIONAL REVIEW

EDITED BY WILLIAM McANDREW

Volume 34 SATURDAY, SEPTEMBER 19, 1931 Number 873

TEACHER TRAINING FOR LARGE CITIES

By Dr. GEORGE F. ZOOK

PRESIDENT OF THE UNIVERSITY OF AKRON

FOR many years there has been, quite properly, deep concern relative to all forms of rural life in America. To those who have devoted themselves to this problem, the rural and village school has seemed to be one of the most obvious ways out. Hence a great deal of time and attention has been given to the development of rural education. In these discussions the teacher is always the center and hope. How to secure and to keep capable and adequately trained teachers in the rural and village schools has been the subject of countless educational meetings and volumes of printed proceedings.

I do not wish to suggest one whit less emphasis on this problem. We need all the guidance in its solution that we can possibly get. But I do wish to raise another problem relative to teacher training for large cities which so far as I know is seldom, if ever, discussed. It, too, has serious aspects. If we could solve it we should not only do greater justice to the cities than is now usually the case, but, as is so often true, perhaps we should also render a great service indirectly to the smaller communities.

Teacher training has presumably been more definitely accepted as a state function than any other form of higher education, except agriculture. So thoroughly is this true that the efforts of other types of higher institutions, privately endowed and municipally supported, are often not regarded as being very serious factors in the total teacher-training program. Under these circumstances it would seem that the states should make ample provision for the training of teachers in all types of communities, including the large cities. That they do not do so, but should do so, is the subject of this paper.

The state teacher-training institutions are seldom located in the large cities. The following examples are cited as evidence of this situation. The examples are selected from those states which have one or more large cities.

Massachusetts: There are 10 state teacher-training institutions in Massachusetts, but none of them are located in Boston, the largest city of the state.

New York: In New York there are 11 state teacher-training institutions, but only two of the seven cities above 100,000 in population, including New York City, have state teacher-training institutions located in them. Yet the seven cities above 100,000 contain 67 per cent. of the population in New York state.

Pennsylvania: Pennsylvania has 14 state

teacher-training institutions, but none of them are located in Philadelphia or Pittsburgh, which contain 27 per cent. of the population of the state. Other large cities, such as Erie, Wilkes-Barre, Scranton, Reading and Johnstown, have also been consistently avoided by the state.

Ohio: Ohio has eight cities, Cleveland, Cincinnati, Toledo, Columbus, Akron, Dayton, Youngstown and Canton, each with population over 100,000 and containing 40 per cent. of the state's population, but all the state's teacher-training institutions, with the exception of the state university, have been located in small towns.

Indiana: Indiana has one large city, the capital, located in the center of the state; but the state institutions of all kinds, including teacher training, are located elsewhere in the state. The other large cities, Gary, South Bend, Evansville and Fort Wayne, have also been missed by the state when locating its educational institutions.

Illinois: Chicago contains 44 per cent. of the population of Illinois, yet all the state teacher-training institutions find it desirable to be located in towns not exceeding 15,000 in population. The resolution which a representative from Chicago recently introduced in the state legislature to petition Congress for the formation of a new state comprising the present city of Chicago was perhaps not so foolish!

Michigan: Detroit contains 33 per cent. of the population of Michigan, but the nearest of the five state teacher-training institutions is 28 miles from Detroit. Other large cities, like Flint and Grand Rapids, have not been chosen by the state for the training of teachers, yet they pay a large percentage of the state's bills in higher education, including teacher training.

Wisconsin: Wisconsin has but one large city, Milwaukee. Fortunately, it induced the state to locate one of the state teacher-training institutions within its borders.

Minnesota: There are two large cities in Minnesota, Minneapolis and St. Paul, containing 29 per cent. of the population of the state. In one of them the state university is located. Like other state universities, it leaves the training of elementary school teachers to the teachers colleges and normal schools. There are six of these, all except Duluth located in small towns of the state.

Missouri: Missouri has seven state teacher-training institutions besides the university, but none of them are located in St. Louis or Kansas City, which contain 34 per cent. of the state's population.

Maryland, Kentucky, Tennessee, Alabama, Oregon, Maine, Colorado and Nebraska have each one city of considerable size; but their respective state legislatures decided years ago that for some reason it would be unwise to locate state teacher-training institutions in Baltimore, Louisville, Memphis, Birmingham, Portland (Oregon), Portland (Maine), Denver and Omaha, respectively. They have not thus far repented.

These examples are certainly sufficient to show that the large cities have received quite inadequate consideration when the respective states were engaged in the establishment of teacher-training facilities. Indeed, of the 100 largest cities in the United States containing 30 per cent. of the total population, only 16 have been fortunate enough to secure state teacher-training institutions. In seven other cities there are state universities or land-grant colleges which confine their teacher-training programs almost entirely to secondary schools.

There are certain important implications which seem to result largely from this almost consistent but very unwise policy.

The graduates of high schools in large urban centers do not have as easy access to state teacher-training facilities as to other forms of higher education, and as their residence in large centers of population justifies. The result is that when the residents of New York City, Syracuse, Rochester, Philadelphia, Pittsburgh, Baltimore, Passaic, Detroit, Cleveland, Cincinnati, Toledo, Akron, Louisville, Birmingham, St. Louis, Kansas City, Chicago, St. Paul, Indianapolis, Los Angeles, San Francisco, Portland (Maine), Portland (Oregon), New Orleans, Atlanta, Dallas, Ft. Worth, Houston, Oklahoma City, Tulsa, Omaha, Denver and Spokane wish to attend a state teacher-training institution they must be at the expense of leaving home, often a modest one, to do so. This is a serious inconvenience which many students can not afford. Consequently a large proportion of them forego the desire for entrance into the teaching profession and enrol in other types of institutions located in their respective cities. Some of these institutions may possess some facilities for training high-school teachers. Few of them are prepared or inclined to train teachers for the elementary schools. Under the circumstances just cited, the state teacher-training institutions are naturally attended primarily by students who live in rural areas, villages and small towns. Numerous studies testify to this statement. In other words, the state is not giving itself the benefit of attracting students from the urban centers into its teacher-training institutions. Had the states pursued the the urban centers into its teacher-training institutions in part in the large cities, it is easy to believe that the number of students enrolled in teacher training would have been much larger. We should not then have had so difficult a time to supply the schools with adequately trained teachers as has been uniformly true throughout the country.

Many studies in recent years seem to show clearly that state teachers colleges and normal schools, usually located in rural areas, villages or small towns, and drawing a large proportion of their enrolment from these same districts, are not only not securing a representative cross-section of our American population as prospective teachers, but they often do not obtain students whose native ability averages as high as those enrolled in other types of institutions.

To whatever extent these statements are true is extremely unfortunate. In our schoolrooms we need a fair proportion of teachers with the background of industrial and commercial life as well as those who come from the farm. Such a variety of experience and background should add strength and virility to the educational program.

That we often secure our teachers from groups of students who average lower in native ability than those enrolled in other courses of study should also be cause for grave concern. Whether better provision for state teacher-training facilities in the urban centers would improve this situation can not be proved readily, but there is considerable reason to think so. In the recent Missouri survey, the local teacher-training facilities in St. Louis and Kansas City certainly stood up well in a comparison of students with those of the state institutions. The municipal teacher-training institutions in Detroit, Chicago, Cincinnati, Akron, Cleveland and New York City can and do exercise considerable selection of students as against the practices of the state teachers colleges and normal schools in their respective states. The students attending municipal junior colleges have almost uniformly equalled or exceeded in native ability the students attending the state teacher-training institutions. I am convinced, therefore, that the states could generally raise the level of the student body attending teacher-training institutions if they would make a conscientious effort to provide teacher-training facilities for the students living in urban centers.

The absence of state provision for teacher training in the cities affects the elementary schools particularly. The endowed colleges as well as the state universities often train a large proportion of their graduates for teaching in the secondary schools. They seldom enter effectively, however, the very much larger field of preparing teachers for the elementary schools. This task is left almost exclusively to the state teachers colleges and normal schools. For their elementary teachers, therefore, far more than for their high-school teachers, the cities must look to the state teacher-training institutions.

In general, state teacher-training institutions which are located in villages or small towns can not train teachers well for schools located in the large cities. The students themselves for the most part are not from the cities. The practice-teaching facilities seldom approximate the school conditions of the large cities. The cities want elementary teachers with more special training and a longer preparation than the usual two-year course of the state teachers college. The entire atmosphere, indeed, is usually primarily rural, village or small town—not city.

As has been said, the location of state teacher-training institutions in villages and small towns places these institutions at a distinct disadvantage relative to practice teaching facilities. Often there are actually such a small number of children in the community as to make it difficult for the institution to arrange for their students to secure adequate observation and practice teaching assignments. Almost invariably there are disagreements with the local school superintendent, and the state is called upon to build separate practice schools for both elementary and high-school grades in order that they may have these schools completely under their control. This disposition of affairs is expensive to the state. It is likely to result in a selection of children in these schools. In fact, it is not a normal situation. I do not say that the location of state teacher-training facilities in cities would entirely eliminate the necessity for these expensive observation and practice schools, but it would certainly greatly reduce the need for them. Teacher-training institutions, both state and municipal, which are located in the large cities, usually find it more economical and desirable to use the local public schools for observation and practice-teaching purposes. In them prospective teachers usually get a longer practice-teaching experience under perfectly normal school conditions. There is much to be said for this method as against short assignments in abnormal state-conducted practice schools.

There is another advantage which the state is losing by its almost consistent disregard of the cities in teacher training, namely, the in-service work. A state teachers college or normal school located in the country is in a very awkward position when it attempts to carry on extension work in a neighboring large city. As a result, there is at present no field of in-service training which is so poorly organized as that for elementary school teachers particularly. Yet in all centers of population there are large groups of these people who are waiting for real opportunities to improve themselves. Unfortunately, these large groups are cared for only by the uncorrelated efforts of state teacher-training institutions, usually located miles away, or by privately endowed institutions which either neglect the problem entirely or attack it in an unconvincing manner. Otherwise, these teachers go to summer school. It would be entirely feasible for teachers to secure a large proportion of what they desire at home if only the several states would adopt a policy of taking into serious consideration the teacher-training needs of the cities as well as the needs of the small towns and rural areas.

The state teacher-training institutions are nearly always closely identified with the state department of education. Indeed, the state department or state board of education is often the governing board of the state teacher-training institutions. The state department is usually concerned more definitely with county, rural and village school systems than it is with the school systems of large cities. There is indeed often very little contact and sometimes only mild mutual respect between a city school system and the state school administration. The location of the state teacher-training institutions away from these centers of population and the placing of them under an administration which is not on a high professional level has a still further tendency to emphasize the gap between the two. We can not possibly place the state department of education on a proper professional plane until the city school systems cease their localism and get interested in matters of state educational policy. But, on the other hand, it will be difficult to make an effective appeal to the city school administrators to do this kind of thing until the states are willing to pay greater attention to the needs of the cities, including a more comprehensive policy relative to the training of teachers.

Failing the location of state teacher-training institutions within their borders, a large number of cities have felt compelled to supply their own facilities along this line for their citizens. Some of them have done this through the establishment of municipal universities; others through city normal schools. Among these cities are New York City, Cleveland, Cincinnati, Akron, Toledo, Louisville, St. Louis, Boston, Kansas City, Chicago, Detroit, Omaha, Rochester and Syracuse.

In all these instances, the city teacher-training institutions not only take care of a very large proportion of their residents who desire this form of higher education, but they supply a large proportion of the teachers who are appointed in the public schools of their respective cities. Yet, instead of showing any gratitude for the way in which the city teacher-training institutions relieve the state in this important work, with minor exceptions in Missouri and New York State, the states make it necessary for these cities to tax themselves doubly, first for a full share of support of the state institutions which relatively they do not attend and secondly for their own teacher-training facilities which their citizens are anxious to use.

In support of this statement the situation in the three cities of Akron, Toledo and Cincinnati, Ohio, may be cited. State teacher-training institutions have been located from 11 to 25 miles from each of these three cities. At the present time there are about 200 residents of these three cities enrolled in all the Ohio state teacher-training institutions combined. On the other hand, there are approximately 1,000 residents of the same three cities enrolled in the teacher-training divisions of the three municipal universities located in these cities. This situation shows clearly that the residents of large cities will enrol for teacher training if they are only given a reasonable chance to do so. The state teacher-training institutions which somehow got located in Buffalo, Salt Lake City and Milwaukee show the same thing.

The intense desire of the urban population for all types of higher education, including teacher training, has enabled most of the teacher-training institutions located in large cities, whether municipal or state, to increase the minimum preparation required for graduation considerably above that which is possible for a state institution located in a rural area. The minimum course of study for elementary teachers in Cleveland is three years, in Akron four years, in Cincinnati five years. In New York City the courses of study for elementary teachers in the three municipal teacher-training institutions have recently been increased from three to four years.

As long as the states persist in confining their teacher-training facilities to institutions located in villages and small towns they will tend to perpetuate a low level of teacher preparation. If they would take advantage of the desires of the city population for teacher training they could easily raise the present level considerably.

Those cities which do not choose to support teacher-training facilities of their own do not ordinarily employ inexperienced graduates of the state normal schools. Much to the disgust of the villages and small towns they continually raid these places for graduates of normal schools who have had several years of experience and who show signs of unusual teaching capacity. No one can blame them for this so long as the states locate their teacher-training institutions in the country, where it is difficult to train for conditions in city schools. With proper state teacher-training facilities located in large cities there is every reason to suppose that the continual drain on the small communities for experienced teachers would be greatly reduced. Such a situation should be a welcome relief to these communities.

The summary of this situation is, therefore, that the states have presumably very definitely assumed the function of training teachers for the public schools. Yet they have almost uniformly located the teacher-training institutions in the small towns and villages where they are not as easily accessible to the great masses of people living in large centers of population as they should be and where it is more difficult to train teachers for service in city schools. Consequently, our teacher supply is drawn largely from rural districts, villages and small towns, and to a less extent from the cities. Under these circumstances, prospective teachers do not have so great a variety of background nor so high a level of native ability as they should have. If the cities insist on having teacher-training facilities, they themselves must establish them and pay for them in addition to the financial support which they in common with the rest of the state provide for the state teacher-training institutions. If they do not establish their own teacher-training facilities, they are engaged in a continual raid for experienced and capable teachers in the small towns and villages. Finally, if the state teachers college or normal school is located in a small town or village, the state usually finds it necessary and expensive to erect its own elementary and high-school buildings for practice teaching purposes. Even here, however, the atmosphere and the facilities for training teachers for city school conditions are not entirely satisfactory.

What is to be done about these conditions? The states refuse to locate teacher-training institutions in the cities. Yet it is in the cities that a large proportion of the state's population, which wishes to attend them, live. It is the cities which pay for a large part of the support of these state institutions. It is the cities which ultimately absorb a large proportion of their product.

It seems clear that the states should more definitely recognize their responsibility relative to teacher training to the large populations living in urban centers. Many of them are greater in size than several of our smaller states. Either the states should locate state teacher-training institutions in them as is the case in Buffalo, Salt Lake City and Milwaukee or, under proper safeguards, they should assist local educational authorities financially to set up adequate teacher-training facilities for themselves as is the case in St. Louis and Kansas City, Missouri, and as has been suggested in Ohio for several years. The latter is doubtless far more economical for the state, because the local authorities are usually glad to supply adequate buildings and equipment and to bear all overhead expenses. The per capita expense to the state may therefore be reduced from one third to one half of what is necessary in state institutions.

Such a disposition of the teacher-training problem is in line with developments in other forms of higher education. Higher institutions, whether public or private, which are located in the cities usually find themselves full to overflowing with students, while those which are located in villages or small towns often struggle for existence. As each recurring census shows, there is a distinct trend of population toward the cities. People buy their clothes and amusements in the cities. The great mass of people want to secure their higher education there also. Municipal universities and junior colleges are becoming increasingly popular because they are accessible and inexpensive for the average student coming from a modest home in the cities. If other forms of higher education are desirable and economical in centers of population, so too is teacher training. It is time that our states adopted some consistent, fair and economical policy for serving the greatest possible number of citizens, including those living in cities, who wish to enter the teaching profession, and for supplying all the schools, both rural and city, with trained teachers.

COMMUNITY PLANNING AND THE PROBLEM CHILD

By Dr. NORMAN FENTON

CALIFORNIA BUREAU OF JUVENILE RESEARCH, WHITTIER, CALIFORNIA

In the attempt to explain social or psychological problems, one error of approach is the search for some simple formula. For example, it is the easiest thing in the world to attribute either to hereditary or to environmental factors the causation of juvenile delinquency and maladjustment. This is done as though heredity and environment were mutually exclusive, instead of being mutually interactive and dependent. As a matter of fact, we can not know the relative importance of heredity and environment in the causation of the symptoms shown, for example, by problem children. A minority of emotionally unstable problem children may be so as the result of constitutional factors. This is a conservative enough opinion. On the other side of the dilemma, to state that the problem child is entirely a reflection of social background or milieu is an overstatement. It seems thus to be more accurate to define the relationship between heredity and environment as mutually dependent, both presenting very serious considerations for any final solution of the riddles of personality presented by maladjusted children, and neither factor being capable of isolation. An example of the harmful effects of misinterpretation of the concept of heredity is to be found in the case of gifted children. Of serious social consequence has been the dictum, "genius will out," implying that the gifted child will rise to his level no matter what the difficulties in his environment. It is true that some men of genius have fought through seemingly insuperable difficulties, finally achieving what they were eager to reach. But in large part hereditary genius or superior mentality is dependent to a great degree for its social or intellectual achievement or realization upon purely environmental factors.

A number of important investigations in the United States recently have been very interesting and stimulating in presenting data indicating strikingly the influence of social background on the behavior of the child. For example, an important scientific contribution by Clifford W. Shaw, entitled "Delinquency Areas,"[1] points out that in Chicago the rate of delinquency *for a given neighborhood* year by year is fairly constant, though the human raw material of the neighborhood may vary with the changing nature of the immigrant stream. For example, the young Negroes of a certain district in Chicago now appear in the juvenile court in the same proportion as did the Swedes, Poles, Russian Jews, Irish, Italians and Germans who inhabited the same neighborhood before them. Crowd a neighborhood with the sordid trappings of factory industries, cram the people into close-packed tenements, force the play of the children into narrow alleys and crowded sidewalks, and the inevitable result is the development among a high proportion of the children living there of undesirable and anti-social types of behavior. Add to the squalor, noise and filth a traditional neighborhood tolerance of petty thievery from freight cars, stores or warehouses, and of other types of minor offenses, and the child's behavior leads to encounters with the police and the courts, and becomes definitely delinquent. The proportion of juvenile court admissions for those "delinquent areas" continues to remain fairly constant, though the people change in their national and racial origins. Furthermore, as various successive national groups move out of these areas into the suburbs, they leave behind them with the neighborhood itself their delinquent tendencies, and in the new environment their proportion of delinquency decreases.

What implications may we find in these arresting facts? Is it not the obvious conclusion that the well-planned community may hope eventually to reduce very significantly the socially aberrant behavior of its children? This conclusion would be justifiable only if we include in our concept of the "well-planned" city planning for adequate expression of normal childish interests and impulses, for excellence in human stimulation and guidance, as well as planning for sanitary and architectural excellence. A new technique and a new spirit in social organization are needed. The cities of America are confronted by the challenging ideal that the well-planned city of the future may be orderly and interesting, not merely in its geographic plan, but in the organization and structure of its human agencies and the resources provided for all types of athletic, cultural and social enjoyment.

This paper is concerned very definitely with the problem of what might be called environmental control. In other words, we are seeking to define techniques of community organization and integration which will lead to less stimulation of what may possibly be inherent anti-social traits in

[1] University of Chicago Press, Chicago, Illinois, 1929.

children, especially among those who might be designated prospective problem children. With fewer environmental factors calling into activity the socially undesirable traits of these children and thus contributing to the formation of anti-social habits, it is believed that the proportion of delinquent and maladjusted children in the community will decrease. Certainly the studies of Shaw and his colleagues offer significant evidence in both a positive sense as well as a negative sense to bear out these optimistic aspirations: negative in that a poorly planned and organized neighborhood produces a large proportion of delinquent children; positive in that in a well-integrated neighborhood there are few children who arrive at the juvenile court.

In our theories as to the individualized treatment of problem children we have passed beyond the stage of faith in the single expert, be he physician, pastor, sociologist, psychologist or psychiatrist. One person, no matter how wise or well trained, can not handle the problem of a seriously maladjusted child. Progressive communities are now looking with faith and hope to the newly developed clinical procedure. The problem child is put trustfully into the hands of a *group* of experts, consisting of a psychiatrist, a psychologist and psychiatric social workers. Individually these experts study the child in his relation to his home, his school and his neighborhood, as well as in the mysterious recesses of his own heart. Carefully they ponder their findings, and then in conference pool their information and arrive at a group opinion and a jointly planned program of treatment. With high hopes the community hails the child guidance clinic as the new panacea, the new guide to set within the narrow ways of righteousness the wandering footsteps of rebellious childhood.

And now we find that the clinic, too, is but a partial device. It is superior—greatly superior—to the isolated workers, but it is not enough. Some of the children who have been submitted to its careful and scientific analysis and ministration have kept on, none the less, in the way which leads to the juvenile court and to the state correctional school.

And so we must look to the next step. This seems to be the community *as a whole,* so organized in its program of child guidance that it can *supplement* the clinic and insure the carrying out of the clinical program and recommendations.

The experiences of the visiting child guidance clinic of the California Bureau of Juvenile Research during the past year have been very suggestive of the significance of community organization. This clinic, organized for the observation and treatment of problem children, was invited to communities under two types of auspices—one was that of a single agency, such as the county health department, the city school department or a service club; the other was that of a citizens' committee representing a combination of all social agencies active within the community, such as the school, the court, the probation department, the parent-teacher association, service clubs, etc. The committee plan proved, on the whole, to be by far the more desirable, for it had the effect of interesting the united community in the problems of each child. When remedial work for a child is undertaken by a single agency, conflict of interests among various groups all too often interferes with the smooth outworking of the planned program; the behavior difficulties of the social agencies begin to outweigh those of the child! When the coordinated backing of all agencies is utilized, all the social resources of the community are brought into agreement upon a program and every one is on his mettle, eager to do his part in the reconstructive work for the child. Many typical cases could be cited to illustrate the significance of community integration in connection with the adjustment of problem children. These cases, showing vividly the effects of good team-work among welfare and educational agencies in the community, bespeak more eloquently than any theoretical statement the value of cooperation among the child welfare agencies of the community. In these cases a number of social agencies worked together. The consequence was that by this coordinated effort the community, instead of throwing up its hands and sending a child away to a state institution, was able to keep the child at home and to make an adjustment there. Of about two hundred pre-institutional cases studied by the clinic only two were actually sent away from their own communities.

A town or city can accomplish much through the pooling of its resources and interests. Various attempts have been made to achieve a community consciousness of the social problems of children. In California there has been developed in certain communities the coordinating council or the child welfare council, fine examples of organized social efforts of this type. According to the plan in one community, representatives of the important civic departments—health, schools, charities, police, recreation, etc.—meet weekly for the discussion of individual cases of problem children and the formulation of a program of treatment. When the welfare of individual problem children is considered by such a representative group of community workers in collaboration with a child guidance clinic, the result is a fine technique for the control of juvenile maladjustment.

The above statement gives a suggestion regarding the coordination of all the social agencies in the community dealing with children and their integration in the most efficient way. However, we have still to consider perhaps the most important factor in the adjustment of children, namely, the attitude and interest of the rank and file of citizens toward child welfare activities. One unfortunate tendency regarding our treatment of the problems of juvenile delinquency is the assumption that all we citizens have to do is to establish courts of justice, build institutions, employ expert personnel, and we have done all that we can. Usually, if these social problems continue to be serious, we tend to concentrate our energies on finding fault with these courts, institutions and public officials. From a fundamental standpoint, the major error of democratic peoples in regard to the handling of many social problems, especially crime, is that they are slow to realize that democracy, to succeed, entails a number of community responsibilities on the part of the rank and file of citizens which can not be met by the delegation of authority to the most conscientious paid public officials. If there is any basis at all for pessimism regarding the effectiveness of democratic principles of government in everyday life, we may attribute it to the fact that the ordinary citizen has been expecting too much of democracy and giving too little. We shall never arrive at a better control of vice and crime until it becomes the accepted duty of every citizen to cooperate with these chosen public officials in a scientific program of crime prevention.

In this connection, one might draw an interesting parallel from another aspect of public service, namely poor relief. Many communities assign the problem of poor relief to paid public officials. In practically all of them the cost of this aspect of government is increasing. In the city of Elberfeld in Germany, another method of poor relief was tried out many years ago.

It has as its fundamental fact the personal service of responsible citizens, in addition to the assignment of the work of caring for the needy and unemployed to conscientious public officials. What was the result of this cooperation of citizens and paid public officials? The city of Elberfeld was able to maintain the cost of poor relief over a long period of time at a relatively constant expense to the community, while the city itself increased in population several times. Instead of merely doling out money, an effort was made to get to the root of the individual's problems and to make an adjustment. Charity in this community did not consist merely in giving money and then forgetting the individual until the next time help was sought. Rather, it was the ideal to help the individual overcome his difficulties through interested and sympathetic personal service. Through this understanding of his problems, the person in need might eventually become self-supporting instead of remaining a perpetual charge on the community. A thorough job was done the first time instead of some temporary makeshift.

There seems to be a parallel situation in the problem of crime. We are probably never going to succeed in our efforts to reduce the economic and human costs of criminal behavior until the concern about juvenile delinquency, especially, becomes the personal affair of conscientious citizens as well as the routine duty of paid public officials.

The child who gets into difficulty with society should, of course, be handled, where necessary, by public officials, especially experts in the social, psychiatric and psychological phases of child guidance, and by competent probation officers, judges and other public officials. But the final solution of the problems of many children is beyond the scope of these individuals, for the adjustment of these younger offenders depends so often upon the attitude of the home and neighborhood toward them. This is where the suggestion follows that, in addition to child guidance clinics and a cooperative organization of the public agencies dealing with children and their problems, *there should also be enlisted the services of citizens of the community, whose only compensation will be the satisfaction of public service.* The duty of these public-spirited citizens will be to learn at first hand about the sources of delinquency in a community or neighborhood, then to proceed, under the guidance of experts, to treat the causes of the difficulties of children and adolescents in the community. This rational procedure is far superior to throwing up our hands, growing rhetorical about a juvenile crime wave, and building more and more and bigger and bigger institutions. It should be clearly recognized by citizens in general, as well as by public officials, that each time a community builds an institution (except perhaps for special cases, such as the mental defective, the blind or the deaf), it is building a monument to its own indifference and selfishness. When the state builds institutions for children who, but for the influence of an evil environment, would be wholesome in their social outlook, it is a public announcement of the poverty of the social resources of the local communities from which these unfortunate children are sent.

Thus, fundamentally, what is needed in meeting the problems of juvenile delinquency and other maladjustment of childhood is more democracy—more personal concern and service on the part of the rank and file of citizens. When we develop better methods of social organization and integration for the treatment of erring and wayward children, then and only then shall we begin to cut into the crime problem in any fundamental sense. We can never accomplish anything fundamental in the way of overcoming juvenile delinquency and maladjustment until the rank and file of citizens realize that it is their duty and opportunity to take an active personal part in making communities more wholesome places for children and adults. Through conscientious citizens acting in collaboration with educational and welfare workers of the community, the causes of juvenile delinquency and maladjustment may be attacked at their source in the home and in the neighborhood. Few, if any, children who are behavior problems to their teachers and principals in school have not been previously in difficulty at home and in the neighborhood. No child is ever sent away to a state institution who has not previously been a problem child in the school and neighborhood. In other words, the boy or girl who becomes seriously delinquent usually has had a long biography of gradually increasing seriousness of offenses against society. A properly integrated community should study and treat the child's problems in the earlier stages when the chances of speedy adjustment are much greater. The alert community would have many resources to discover and to study children when first they show symptoms of asocial attitudes. Once known, there would be many methods used, many paid experts and volunteer workers ready to proceed with a scientifically adequate plan of treatment. For, only as we organize and integrate our community resources for child welfare and improve their general atmosphere and wholesomeness are we ever going to solve in a fundamental and efficient manner the numerous social problems that face our people, so many of which have their roots in childhood maladjustment.

EDUCATIONAL EVENTS

HEALTH CONDITIONS OF ENGLISH CHILDREN LIVING IN BASEMENTS

AN investigation into the condition of children living in basements has recently been carried out by the London County Council. This showed that the different types of basements in different parts of London are reflected in the health of the children. The inquiry affected families occupying basements in the boroughs of Kensington, Paddington, Westminster, Islington, Finsbury, Poplar, Stepney and Southwark. The school medical officer of the council, in a report published in the London *Times,* thus describes the inquiry and its results:

The basement children were examined in their schools, in company with a double set of controls—that is, two children not living in basements were compared with each basement dweller. These control children were selected by the head teacher for similarity in age and social circumstances, and they were of the same sex as the basement child. The identity of the basement dweller was not known to the examining doctor until the examination in the department was completed—254 basement children and 508 controls were examined.

The inquiry was divided into three parts—medical history, physical examination and school history. The latter included an assessment of the child's progress at school and the regularity of its attendance. The medical examination showed that basement dwellers were not far behind non-basement dwellers in cleanliness, but that they were not so well nourished, 35.7 per cent. of the basement children being definitely under-nourished, compared with 19.1 per cent. of the controls. Pallor of the skin or mucous membranes, indicative of anemia, was present in 44.1 per cent. of the children living in basements and in 38.8 per cent. of the controls. Defective vision was practically the same for the two classes of children. Throat and nose affections were found in 7.4 per cent. of the basement dwellers and in 3.3 per cent. of the controls. Symptoms of rheumatism were found in 2.2 per cent. of the children living in basements and in 0.8 per cent. of the non-basement children.

The educational inquiry brought out the fact that there were fewer children living in basements who were making normal progress at school than among the children selected as their controls. The head teachers returned 43.6 per cent. of basement children and 24.8 per cent. of the controls as definitely backward; 11.8 per cent. of the basement dwellers and 5.9 per cent. of the controls were irregular in their attendance at school. Although the numbers are not very large, the children were examined with great care and the investigation shows that the basement child appears to be deficient in vitality. This is demonstrated in its physical measurements, its physical condition and in its progress at school.

LIBRARIES OF THE WORLD

A SPECIAL correspondent to the London *Times* reports that the annual meeting of the Library Association was held at Cheltenham during the week of August 30. It was preceded over the week-end by sessions of the International Library Committee, which forms a link between the Library Associations of some 20 countries. The formation of such a committee to administer the affairs of the International Federation of Library Associations was proposed in 1927, when librarians from all parts of the world attended the fiftieth conference of our own Library Association at Edinburgh; the committee was formed in 1928, and has since held sessions in Rome, Venice and Stockholm.

While the principal European countries, together with the United States, Mexico, China and Japan, are represented on the committee, the financial crisis has made it difficult for delegates from all countries to attend at Cheltenham. The sessions which have been held here under the chairmanship of Dr. Isak Collijn, librarian of the Royal Library, Stockholm, have none the less brought together representatives from the United States, France, Germany, the Netherlands, Belgium, Czechoslovakia, Finland, Italy, Poland, Sweden and Switzerland. Great Britain has been represented by Mr. Arundell Esdaile, secretary of the British Museum, and Mr. John D. Cowley, county librarian of Lancashire. The secretary of the conference and permanent secretary-general of the federation is Dr. T. P. Sevensma, librarian of the League of Nations, who also represents the Commission of Intellectual Cooperation of the League, while M. Marcel Godet, Director of the Bibliothèque Nationale Suisse at Berne, represents the International Institute for Intellectual Cooperation in Paris, with which the International Library Committee closely cooperates.

Dr. Collijn, in his presidential address, referred to the important bibliographical works which have recently been initiated in several countries, and in particular to the compilation of the new British Museum Catalogue of Printed Books, and the parallel work of the Collected Catalogue of Prussian Libraries, now incorporating the libraries of Munich and Vienna.

Dr. Sevensma referred in his report to the discussions held in Paris during June by a League of Nations Committee on the use of popular libraries by workers in their leisure time, especially the leisure created by unemployment; and a report of the office of the International Federation formed a principal subject of discussion at yesterday's session.

Among other matters which occupied the first day's session was the question of a new edition of the "Bibliotheca bibliographica internationalis"—a complete list of bibliographical works. A Danish scholar, M. Grundtvig, has laid before the committee proposals for such an addition and these were provisionally approved. Members were asked for help in furnishing a list of organizations concerned with international bibliography. It was announced that an international code of bibliographical abbreviations had been compiled after one year's work by the International Institute for Intellectual Cooperation. It was recommended that all members should press for the adoption of these abbreviations.

THE NATIONAL ADVISORY COMMITTEE ON EDUCATION

RECOMMENDATIONS outlining the future relationship of the Federal Government toward education will be determined in the final sessions of the National Advisory Committee on Education opening on October 5 after two years of searching study, Chairman Charles R. Mann has stated orally to a representative of the *U. S. Daily.*

Though no conclusions have been reached, members of the committee have been studying tentative proposals during the summer, and they will act on them conclusively in the final sessions, he said.

Additional information was supplied as follows to the *U. S. Daily* from the U. S. Office of Education.

The purpose of the committee as defined by Secretary Wilbur was "to give us the proper chart by which to steer our educational course." Since its organization the entire scope of American education has been minutely examined. Nearly 300 field agents, regional consultants, members of cooperating committees, and research collaborators have participated in the investigation. Numerous conferences have been held with leading educators, representing various levels of American education, and out of the mass of information gathered some very significant proposals have been drawn up.

Among some of the outstanding problems the committee has studied at length are those involving federal financial aid to the states and the extent of its control over education, once aid has been given. The steering committee agreed that the Federal Government has an obligation to aid public education in the states, and the committee members endorse this principle.

Tentative proposals for action submitted by the steering committee in 1930 called for revolutionary changes in the present policy of the Federal Government. Since then, however, changes and modifications have resulted. One of the earlier tentative suggestions was to repeal all laws that give annual federal grants in any form to the states for special phases of education of interest to particular groups of people, and provide one unallotted annual grant to the states of $2.50 per child under 21 years of age. States were to be individually responsible for making up their educational budgets.

Also it was earlier proposed that there be created an adequate federal headquarters for educational research to correlate all data on education and coordinate the research of various agencies already existing.

These suggestions and others, however, have undergone considerable scrutiny since they were proffered. They served to stimulate interest and brought forth important discussion and additional suggestions. Those will be determined with finality when the committee holds its final sessions in October.

THE DECREASE OF ILLITERACY

THE portion of the nation's population which was not able to read or write, either in English or any other language, was reduced from 6 per cent. to 4.3 per cent. in the decade from 1920 to 1930, census figures disclose.

On April 1, 1930, there were 4,283,753 illiterate persons out of a total of 98,723,047 persons 10 years of age or over. Illiteracy among youths from 10 to 20 years dropped from 2.7 per cent. to 1.6 per cent. and among persons 21 and over 7.1 to 5.3 per cent. in the last decade, census figures showed. The percentage of illiteracy for males was 4.4 per cent. and for females 4.3 per cent., it was disclosed.

Of the illiterates in the United States in 1930, 2,407,218 were white, 1,513,892 were Negroes, and 362,643 were of other races. For native whites, the percentage of illiteracy was 1.5; for foreign-born whites 9.9; for Negroes 16, and for other races 25.

The highest percentage of illiteracy was found in the south where 8.2 per cent. of the population could not read or write. In both the north and the west, the percentage was 2.7 per cent. More than 19 per cent. of the Negroes in the south were returned as illiterates.

Iowa holds the state record for literacy. Only 0.8 per cent. of the persons in that state over 10 years of age were not able to read or write in 1930. In 1920, when Iowa also took first place, 1.1 per cent. of its population were illiterate. In 1930 Iowa was the only state with less than 1 per cent. of its residents illiterate. Other states with low illiteracy totals were Washington and Oregon, 1 per cent.; Idaho, 1.1 per cent.; South Dakota, Nebraska, Kansas and Utah, 1.2 per cent.; Minnesota, 1.3 per cent., and North Dakota, 1.5 per cent.

The greatest proportion of illiteracy was found in South Carolina, where 14.9 per cent. of the population could not read or write. This figure was a reduction from 18.1 per cent. registered 10 years ago. Louisiana in 1920 was the most illiterate state, with 21.9 per cent. unable to read or write, but it so improved its record during the ensuing 10 years that last year only 13.5 per cent. of its population were recorded as illiterate. Other states showing a high percentage of illiteracy in 1930 were New Mexico, 13.3 per cent.; Mississippi, 13.1 per cent.; Alabama, 12.6 per cent.; Arizona 10.1 per cent., and North Carolina, 10 per cent.

CONFERENCE OF THE INTERNATIONAL STUDENT SERVICE

EIGHTY American and overseas students and leaders in university circles attended the tenth annual conference of the International Student Service held at Mount Holyoke College from August 31 to September 9. There were also about 200 delegates at the conference, 125 representing 34 foreign nations and the remainder from the United States.

An official welcome to the United States on behalf of President Hoover was delivered to the delegates by Dr. Stanley K. Hornbeck, head of the Division of Far Eastern Affairs of the State Department. Dr. Mary E. Woolley, president of Mount Holyoke College, welcomed the delegation to the campus. The conference was opened by A. Buel Trowbridge, chairman of the American committee of the International Student Service.

Speakers at the conference, at which interest centered on the problems of "The University in a Changing World," included Dr. Henry Noble MacCracken, president of Vassar College; Dr. William Allan Neilson, president of Smith College; Dr. Arnold Wolfers, director of the Institute of Politics, Berlin; Dr. S. K. Datta, member of the Indian Round Table Conference; Dr. C. W. Guilleband, of the University of Cambridge, and Dr. Walter M. Kotschnig, of Geneva, general secretary of the International Student Service. Dr. Wolfers acted as chairman, with Dr. Woolley and Dr. Datta serving as vice-chairmen.

The delegates considered the universities' problems under present-day conditions, inquiring into overcrowding, unemployment in the professions, inadequate facilities for the study of international problems and the loss of contact between the universities and the outside world.

They also considered ways and means of furthering the organization's program. The International Student Service, which grew out of relief work for impoverished European students after the war, fills the need for a non-partisan world-wide university association to assist students in self-help and cooperative enterprises, in health problems, in the construction and maintenance of student houses, and in the ironing out of social and international difficulties.

Foreign delegates to this year's conference were entertained by Lucius N. Littauer at his estate in New Rochelle, N. Y., previous to the opening of the conference. Dr. and Mrs. Harry Starr, of the Lucius Littauer Foundation, and Dr. and Mrs. Solomon Liptzin were also guests.

NATIONAL FUNDS FOR STUDENTS

MR. FRED C. CROXTON, assistant director of the President's Organization on Unemployment Relief, reports that the following funds are available for qualified students in the different branches of learning:

American Association of University Women, national headquarters, 1634 I Street, N.W., Washington, D. C. Many local branches maintain funds to be loaned to worthy local girls.

Barrett—F. J. Barrett Foundation, 1600 Davison Avenue, East Detroit, Michigan, established a student loan fund of $100,000 in 1926. Juniors and seniors in accepted colleges are eligible for loans when they pass as to character and probability of paying as agreed; examinations, interviews and recommendations are required.

Business and Professional Women's Clubs, National Federation, 1819 Broadway, New York City. Many local clubs maintain loan funds for women. Information as to local addresses may be obtained from the National Federation.

Crawford Student Loan Fund, care of United States National Bank, Portland, Oregon, was established in 1924 with $250,000. Any student properly recommended is eligible, except those preparing for a professional career such as theology, medicine, law or music.

Harmon Foundation (Inc.), division of student loans, 140 Nassau Street, New York City. In 1922 a fund of $150,000 was established to be loaned to students in affiliated colleges. To be eligible a student must be of junior standing or above, working toward a bachelor or higher degree with satisfactory character references and approved budget. A Harmon-College cooperation loan fund is also established to aid students of sophomore grade and above. A special student loan fund aids juniors and seniors in unaffiliated colleges.

Hebrew Free Loan Society, 108 Second Avenue, New York City, lends to students, irrespective of nationality, religion, or race without interest if credentials are satisfactory.

Kiwanis International, 520 North Michigan Avenue, Chicago, Illinois, represents 1,750 Kiwanis Clubs in the United States. Many local clubs lend money to local students who are worthy.

Knights Templar Educational Foundation established an educational loan fund of $1,560,000 in 1922 to aid juniors and seniors of good character and application upon recommendation of the college and home community. The fund receives an annual addition of about $500,000. Applications for loans should be made to the grand recorder of the Grand Commandary, Knights Templar Educational Foundation, in the respective states.

Lions International, 332 South Michigan Avenue, Chicago, Illinois, represents local Lions clubs throughout the United States. Many of these clubs lend money to local men and women for the purpose of a college education.

National Congress of Parents and Teachers. Application should be made to state or local organization. Information may be obtained from national offices at 1201 Sixteenth Street, N.W., Washington, D. C.

Panhellenic—National Panhellenic Congress, care of Miss Louise Leonard, 150 Claremont Avenue, New York City, administers certain sorority funds for college women.

Rotary International, 211 West Wacker Drive, Chicago, Illinois. Many local clubs in cities of the United States have student loan funds. A booklet on Student Loan Funds is published.

State Federations of Women's Clubs or local federations, in most states provide student loan funds. Loans are made preferably to junior and senior college girls who are residents of the state in which the loans are available, and sometimes to girls who are freshmen or sophomores in college. Application for loans should be addressed to the loan scholarship fund committee in each state, or information will be given by the General Federation of Women's Clubs, 1734 N Street, Washington, D. C.

Young Men's Christian Association. Many local branches of the Young Men's Christian Association lend money to local young men. Inquire of the president or secretary of the local Young Men's Christian Association or 347 Madison Avenue, New York City.

MENTAL HYGIENE AND PSYCHOLOGY AT THE NEW SCHOOL FOR SOCIAL RESEARCH

THE New School for Social Research, New York City, one of the first institutions to inaugurate courses in mental hygiene, has announced its program for the fall term opening on September 28.

The most important advances in psychology in recent years will be reviewed by Dr. Joseph Jastrow. In each lecture he will discuss one of the important books of the year. Dr. Jastrow, as chairman, has also organized a course on the American contribution to psychology in which the foremost American psychologists will expound their view-points. The series is listed as follows:

October 1: "The American Contribution," Joseph Jastrow.
October 8: "The Philosopher's Version," John Dewey.
October 15: "The Behaviorist's Position," John B. Watson.
October 22: "The Psychology of Growth," Arnold Gesell.
October 29: "Psychology and History," Harry Elmer Barnes.
November 5: "Psychology at Work," W. V. Bingham.
November 12: "Reconstructing Humanity," William Healy.
November 19: "Experimental Psychology in Music," Carl E. Seashore.
December 3: "The Days of William James," James R. Angell.
December 10: "Freud in America," Joseph Jastrow.
December 17: "The Animal Mind," Carl J. Warden.
January 7: "The Biologist's Approach," E. M. East.
January 14: "The Psychiatrist," Abraham Myerson.
January 21: "The Psychologist and the Child," Ira S. Wile.
January 28: "The Program of Research," Robert S. Woodworth.
February 4: "The Social Empire," Everett Dean Martin.
February 11: To be announced.
February 18: "Intelligence and Achievement," Walter B. Pitkin.

Dr. George K. Pratt, medical director of the mental hygiene committee of the New York State Charities Association, gives a comprehensive survey of the field in "The Mental Hygiene of Everyday Life." It comprises lectures, case histories, conference and group discussions, with special emphasis on behavior and personality difficulties in otherwise normal children—maladjustments at home, at school, in industry, the mental hygiene point of view in the philosophy and technique of child training.

An advanced course is offered by Dr. Frankwood E. Williams and Dr. Caroline B. Zachry, who collaborate, in the order named, on "The Philosophic Aspects of Mental Hygiene: Their Applications to Education." Dr. Williams, editor of *Mental Hygiene* and formerly director of the National Committee of Mental Hygiene, gives the theory and traces its implications for thought and for practice. Dr. Zachry, director of the Mental Hygiene Institute of the Montclair State Teachers' College, supplements theory with concrete cases in personality adjustment, its effect on professional adequacy, *e.g.*, in adjustment of the student teacher to instructor and college life, to home and community. The importance of the practical application of mental hygiene to teaching techniques is consistently borne in mind.

In the "Study of Behavior Problems in Children," Dr. David M. Levy, chief of staff of the Institute for Child Guidance, continues his admirable, synthetic presentation of relevant psychological, sociological and medical view-points, using the clinical method of approach and illustrating with case material.

Courses in related fields include "Human Nature and Educational Ideals," in which Dr. Horace M. Kallen discusses the adequacy of the educational response to contemporary strains. "Problems of Social Ethics" is an analysis by Sidney Hook, of New York University, of the leading ethical philosophies of life and their impact upon contemporary social problems.

EDUCATIONAL NOTES AND NEWS

PROFESSOR GEOFFROY ATKINSON has resigned as dean of Amherst College. He will resume the full-time teaching in the French department which he has had to curtail while dean. Professor Charles S. Porter has been named acting dean of the college.

PROFESSOR WILLIAM CULLEN FRENCH will serve as acting dean of the school of education of the George Washington University during the absence of Dean William Carl Ruediger, who will be on sabbatical leave during the coming academic year.

WILLIAM A. SLADE, of the Library of Congress, has been appointed librarian of the Folger Shakespeare Memorial Library, in Washington. Professor Joseph Quincy Adams, who has been professor of English at Cornell University since 1919, will be director of research. The collection of the late Henry Clay Folger, which constitutes this special library, comprises the most extensive collection in the world of the first and rare editions of Shakespeare and books relating to him. There are about 25,000 volumes in all. It has an endowment of $10,000,000 for its maintenance.

INCLUDED among the thirty-one new appointments to the faculty of the George Washington University are: Dr. Alexander H. Krappe, assistant professor in the department of Romance languages; Dr. Charles Martel, professor in library science; Mr. Ernest Kletsch, lecturer in library science; Mr. Belknap Severance, associate in library science; and Dr. Daniel H. Buchanan, associate professor of economics.

DR. A. R. MEAD, head of the department of education at Ohio Wesleyan University, Delaware, Ohio, has been granted a leave of absence for the coming college year in order that he may join the staff of the University of Florida, for the purpose of organizing a laboratory school for the college of education there. The work will include the planning of a $350,000 building to house the school.

GENERAL CHARLES P. SUMMERALL, retired chief of staff of the U. S. Army, formally assumed his duties as president of The Citadel, the Military College of South Carolina, at Charleston, when it opened its fall term on September 13.

MISS NORAH E. EVANS, for three years director of physical education for girls at Hamilton, Montana, has assumed the duties of dean of women at Gooding College, Idaho, filling the vacancy caused by the death of Dean Edith F. Barrett.

Dr. Joseph C. Dewey has been appointed head of the department of education of Lindenwood College.

Dr. Benjamin A. G. Fuller, of the University of Cincinnati, formerly on the faculty of philosophy of Harvard University, has been appointed to the position of professor of philosophy at the University of Southern California.

Mr. Janusz Jendrzejewicz has been appointed Minister of Education of Poland to succeed the late Sladomir Czerwinski.

Dr. William J. Campbell, formerly of the Texas College of Arts and Industries, has accepted the position of assistant professor of education at the University of Southern California.

Professor John Burns Martin, of Harvard University, has been appointed to the department of English at King's College, Halifax, N. S., to succeed the late Professor Walter Douglas MacFarlane.

The faculty at the Junior College of Connecticut, Bridgeport, has been augmented by the addition of Mr. John Harold Hutchins, of the Alabama Polytechnic Institute, as assistant professor of English, Mr. William W. Everett, of Mercer University, as assistant professor in charge of biology, and Mr. Henry F. White, formerly of Amherst College, as associate professor in charge of all the college activities in the field of athletics, health and physical education.

Arthur M. Seybold, for six years head of the Thomas Jefferson Junior High School of Cleveland, has been chosen head master of the Oak Lane Country Day School, Philadelphia.

Mrs. Jessie E. Crownhart has been appointed by Governor La Follette as regent of the state teachers colleges of Wisconsin for a term of five years. She succeeds Mrs. John A. Aylward.

The Reverend Harry F. King has resigned as pastor of the Rivesville Methodist Episcopal Church South to accept an invitation to join the faculty of Morris Harvey College, Barboursville, West Virginia.

Willard P. Lewis, librarian of Wesleyan University, has accepted the position of librarian of the Pennsylvania State College. He replaces Sabra W. Vought, who left the college to become librarian and director of library service for the Federal Office of Education.

Milton F. Husted, for more than thirty-five years associated with the public schools of North Bergen, New Jersey, has resigned his office as superintendent. Mr. Husted, who is seventy years old, was for more than a quarter of a century head of the school system of North Bergen.

Dr. Charles F. Thwing, of Cleveland, president emeritus of Western Reserve University, has been elected a life senator at the national council of the United Chapter of Phi Beta Kappa.

Professor Bruno Roselli, professor of Italian at Vassar College, has received a gold medal from the Italian Ministry of Education for "spreading knowledge of the Italian language, literature and ideals in the United States." It is the first time such a medal has been given to an American.

Dr. Sidney Edward Mezes, president emeritus of the University of Texas and president of the College of the City of New York, from 1914 to 1927, died on September 10 at the age of sixty-eight years.

The Reverend W. W. Jackson, formerly rector of Exeter College, Oxford, died at Oxford on August 30 at the age of ninety-three years.

Dr. Edwin Greenlaw, head of the English department in Johns Hopkins University and formerly dean of the graduate school in the University of North Carolina, died on September 10 at the age of fifty-seven years.

Dr. John Alfred Faulkner, professor of church history at Drew Theological Seminary since 1897, died on September 8. He was seventy-four years old.

Mr. C. Stanton Belfour, assistant director of the university extension division of the University of Pittsburgh, reports that the university has recently completed its largest and most successful summer session. The total net enrolment for the 1931 session was 4,007, the largest summer session in Pennsylvania. There were 4,706 gross registrations. Graduate enrolments totalled 1,270 students. Branch sessions were conducted at the off-campus centers in Johnstown, Erie and Uniontown, Pennsylvania, as well as an evening session in downtown Pittsburgh. There were summer courses at the biological station at Presque Isle (Erie), and at the nature study and surveying camps in the Allegheny Mountains.

AN announcement in the *Baltimore Sun* states that methods are being sought by an influential group of educators to relieve Mississippi's four state institutions of higher learning of suspensions by the Southern Association of Colleges and Secondary Schools and to restore their credits. The suspensions, effective with September, were decreed because of Governor T. G. Bilbo's reputed political shakeup of faculty and domination of the schools.

BEGINNING this fall the Lincoln School of Liberal Arts at Northeastern University will offer a four-year program leading to the degree of associate in arts. The school will be coeducational and facilities for taking individual courses will be available for those who do not wish to pursue the program for a degree. It will be under the supervision of Dean James W. Lees.

FIVE prominent professors of history and economics will publish a weekly news magazine to supplement their text-books and correlate for the student the records of the past and the current events. They are Charles A. Beard, Harold G. Moulton, David Saville Muzzey, Walter E. Myer and Edward Alsworth Ross. Their magazine, *The American Observer,* will be published in Washington, D. C.

THE fourteenth annual conference of the Massachusetts state normal schools opened at the State Normal School at Bridgewater on September 9. A general business session and registration of delegates and addresses by Payson Smith, state commissioner of education, and Dr. Rollo W. Brown, of Cambridge, were on the first day's program. Miss Florence M. Hale, president of the National Education Association, and Dr. William C. Bagley, of Teachers College, Columbia University, gave addresses.

AN international congress on education for commerce will be held in London in 1932. The last triennial congress was held at Amsterdam in 1929. The forthcoming congress is being organized by the British Association for Commerce and Education, of which Sir Francis Goodenough is chairman.

THE award of the first Fidac Medal for this year, given to Princeton University for distinguished service "in promoting world peace and understanding," has been announced. Other medals have been awarded to Vassar College and Clark University. This is the second year that Fidac has awarded medals of honor to colleges and universities in each of the ten countries represented in its membership of almost 9,500,000 World War veterans of the allied forces. The American Legion is the member society of Fidac in the United States. Last year Columbia University, the University of Chicago and the University of California were chosen to receive the awards. The members of this year's board of award, on whose recommendation the Fidac International Congress made the choice of three American institutions of higher education, were Dr. Stephen P. Duggan, director of the Institute of International Education; Dr. Paul Monroe, director of the International Institute of Columbia University; Dr. David P. Barrows, of the University of California; President Robert Maynard Hutchins, of the University of Chicago, and General L. R. Gignilliat, of Culver Military Academy.

PREPARATIONS for the opening of eight cultural centers for Jewish students at colleges and universities have been completed by the executive committee of the Third District of B'Nai B'Rith, Jewish fraternal order. The student centers, where emphasis is given to Hebrew history and accomplishments, will be established at the University of Pennsylvania, West Virginia University, the University of Michigan, Ohio State University, Cornell University, the University of Wisconsin, the University of Texas and the University of California.

THE opening of Amherst College has been postponed until the end of September, owing to the prevalence of infantile paralysis. Similar action has been taken by Mount Holyoke College.

THE freshman class of the New York State College for Teachers will be limited this year to 300 students because of the overcrowded condition of the teaching profession. The college has been obliged to turn away more than 300 fully qualified students who wish to become teachers.

THE Education Building in Harrisburg, Pennsylvania, which was to have been completed last year, but which was damaged to the extent of nearly $1,000,000 by a fire last October, will be ready for occupancy the latter part of this month. It will be occupied by the Department of Public Instruction, which is now in temporary quarters, the Department of Welfare and the State Library.

THE first instruction unit of the Hunter College $10,000,000 group of buildings was opened to freshmen on September 18. About 750 students can be accommodated. The new cafeteria and social hall also are expected to be ready for use during the coming term.

APPROXIMATELY 3,500 properly certified teachers in California are unemployed, according to an announcement by the state department of education. In order to provide immediate relief in the present situation and to attempt to secure some permanent remedy, the state superintendent of public instruction has appointed a committee on teachers' unemployment. The committee consists of two sections, one for northern California and the other for the southern part of the state.

THE Union Society of King's College, London, will celebrate the centenary of the opening of the college on October 8. On that day there will be a service at St. Clement Danes, at which the Bishop of London will preach. In the afternoon a commemorative tablet will be unveiled in the New Pavilion (War Memorial) at Mitcham. There will be a centenary dance in the evening. Commemoration Week will be observed in various ways from December 10 to 21. On December 21 the Bishop of Winchester will preach at a service, and on December 22 Sir John Simon will deliver the commemoration oration.

THE Ministry of Education at Nanking, China, has ruled that Chinese students must hereafter refrain from attacks upon unpopular teachers and principals, devoting more attention to study and less to agitation. Students in several government schools this year have compelled unpopular presidents to resign and made their own nominations of successors. The Ministry says this procedure will not be countenanced hereafter, as it is not the business of the students to select their own teachers.

DURING the present academic year 81 Russian student engineers will enroll in 26 American colleges, of whom 18 will specialize in electrical engineering, 13 in mechanical and the others in chemical, aeronautical, civil and mining engineering.

THE University of Mexico has decided to establish correspondence courses in Mexican history and Spanish language, primarily to spread native culture. University credit will not be given for the courses. The course in Mexican history is divided into two parts, the first dealing with the pre-Cortesian epoch and early colonial and republican times up to 1900, and the second covering the modern period from 1900 to the present.

THE experiment, started by the London County Council five years ago, of allowing children at a number of elementary schools to spend some days in the hopfields as part of their summer holiday period, is not being repeated this year. In 1927, 28 schools took part in the experiment, and the total rose to 43 in 1928, but fell to 25 in 1929, and to 17 last year. Reports received by the education committee of the Council indicated that the children enjoyed the novel experience, but there was a division of opinion among teachers as to whether there was loss or gain in the results. There was an improvement in school attendance, but against this had to be set the loss of three days' teaching due to the fact that the special hop-picking holidays were three days longer than the ordinary school holidays. After careful consideration of the position, the education committee recommended a reversion to the ordinary holidays in all schools, but close observation will be kept on the effects of the change on school attendance.

THE number of students in the various Italian universities for the academic year 1929–30 was 29,630, as against 26,932 in the preceding year. The greatest number of students, 9,990, followed the careers of medicine and surgery. Law was next, with 9,864. There were 2,500 students in the faculty of letters and philosophy.

DEFECTS in the educational system of Mexico, it was pointed out in a statement issued by the National League of Teachers and reported in the *New York Herald Tribune,* are responsible for Mexican parents sending their children to schools and colleges in the United States. It is estimated that at least 5,000 Mexican boys and girls are students in these institutions. According to members of the league, parents have no confidence in Mexican schools because of their belief that they are impotent to provide their children with the scholastic preparation which will assure them success and which can be translated into well-being and happiness in their future lives; hence they make sacrifices to send their sons and daughters to foreign schools, where may be obtained what is not to be found here.

DISCUSSION

ACID IN THE LITERATURE OF EDUCATION

EDUCATORS do not frequently match wits against each other in the presence of trained umpires. Competition among educational administrators is for the favor of the lay populace, and competition among teachers is largely conditioned by the same desideratum. Perhaps here is a clue which may help to indicate why educational writing, by and large, exhibits a singular atrophy of the critical faculty.

Generations of experience in commercial advertising, from the days of Phineas Taylor Barnum and Lydia Pinkham down to the present, have proved that an immediately successful appeal to the public need not be entirely free from exaggeration, bombast and downright untruth. Can it be that the same technique must be pressed into service in order to "sell" education to the public, and that the literature of education must carry a heavy burden of this sort of ballast, along with the innocuous reports of pseudoscientific "experiments," to the exclusion of any soul-stirring clash of thoughtful opinions?

A heavy proportion of the writing in higher education, for instance, is done by university and college presidents. Much of this stuff is so obviously vitiated by several pervasive factors that an enumeration of them seems superfluous. The executive head of an institution, when he writes for publication, is likely to have trouble in subordinating:

(1) An inordinate desire to make his institution appear as a paragon of efficiency and progressiveness; (2) an exaggerated paternal solicitude for the supposed feelings of his faculty, such that the salving of their precious morale is a consideration which tinges every expression; (3) a discreet regard for the known pet prejudices of certain members of his governing board, or of certain elements in the institution's constituency; (4) a strange intuitive feeling that a lofty and grandiose style, little short of polysyllabic grandiloquence, is the only mode of expression in keeping with the dignity and importance of higher education. The list is by no means inclusive, and might be lengthened indefinitely.

It might be remarked that college presidents write most frequently about their own institutions, often to describe in favorable terms some promising innovation in administration which is to be a panacea for all educational ills. Who has not read scores of articles about "The Honor System at Siwash," "The Reorganization at Jerkwater," and "The Point System at Podunk"? New schemes of administrative organization, new methods of instruction, new intra-curricular or extra-curricular activities, since they do not lend themselves to immediate and exact measurement, may be seized upon as ready-to-hand vehicles of favorable publicity for the institution.

Let it be broadcast that Siwash is initiating a "significant experiment in higher education," and avid readers become thirsty for information on the details of the new cure-all. Eagerly they read anything which purports to describe the epoch-making novelty, but somehow precise information is painfully meager. Promising titles lead only to articles which grandiosely evaluate the results of the "experiment" ere it is scarcely begun, and "place Siwash in the forefront of progressive higher educational institutions," without descending to the point of demonstrating just how and why. Conscientious students of education peruse everything that relates to the allegedly new venture, and finish with a guilty feeling that somehow they must have overlooked something, because the central idea is still rather inchoate. The truth often is that the innovators themselves are equally hazy about details; that the "experiment" is all variables and no constants, and that the whole hullabaloo is a furious tilting at the windmill to persuade the public that the institution is not completely hidebound in its conservatism.

This is not to deprecate the progressive spirit in educational administration; it is only to deplore the tendency to publicize uncritically. Where is the literature that points out possible sources of weakness in the score of innovations that are now largely monopolizing the pages of educational periodicals with their ballyhoo? The profession seems blandly to choose the dictum that anything is worth trying, and anything worth trying is worth praising to the skies. Could anything be more abject?

Another type of production of college presidents, which gluts the periodicals, consists of their lofty effusions on occasions of academic ceremony, such as inaugurations, dedications and commencements. Almost any one knows the rest of this story. The glorious history of the grand old institution will come in for many fervid allusions; its still more glorious future will be the subject of an interminable and perfervid peroration. Particularly amusing are the presidents of state institutions when they launch into their favorite topic—the relation of the university to the state. Untrained in the law of the subject and often ignorant of the most elementary principles of public finance, they perspire to make their hearers wonder that the commonwealth did not founder before the institution came into existence, and persuade them that more money for the university takes precedence over shoes for the baby. Not desiring to disparage the claims of state universities for public support, one could sometimes wish that their case might be presented with a little less emotion and a little more evidence of professional competency.

At the risk of overdoing the job of properly forewarning the readers of presidential documents, attention must be called to their ubiquitous and uncritical devotion to various overstrained conceptions of democratic theory. A few allusions to some nebulous scheme of "faculty representation" or of "professorial participation" in policy-making will always serve as a bid for the good graces of the American Association of University Professors, and help to inflate the rapidly descending and poverty-stricken but genteel dignity of the local faculty. Actually, nine out of ten of such schemes serve only to waste the time of the faculty in futile committee meetings and debates which eventually so obscure the issues that the coast is absolutely clear for the exercise of presidential autocracy. Your true scholar in a professorial chair as a rule does not care to be bothered by administrative labors, and does not want even to hear the administrative cogs turn, so long as his living and working conditions are such that a scholar can be reasonably happy in them.

Under the same head come the innumerable monstrosities known as "student governments," designed to convey somehow the subtle but entirely false impression that the students are to be permitted to have charge of their own discipline. These elaborate organizations provide numerous high-sounding titles for the activity-hounds who came to college for the "contacts," enabling them to be everything from presidents to chief judges of the honor court, and any aspiring young-man-on-the-make who does not become at least a member of the senate is a failure indeed. These august official positions require the incumbents to dash hither and yon from meeting to meeting to pass upon grave issues when they should be studying, and it is an obtuse professor who can not see that a meeting of the student court transcends the importance of a lesson in the subject he is teaching.

The saddest feature of all this is the fact that

the student himself, if he is more than a moron, soon perceives the futility of such flapdoodle; and if he then persists in it, he does so at the sacrifice of his intellectual honesty, which is about the most priceless possession a student can lose. Like his professor, the real student prefers not to be annoyed with the endless petty details of administration, and not even to hear of them unless the breakdown of administration interrupts his opportunity for scholarly work, which is an occurrence not likely to happen.

The temptation is strong to turn to the increasing volume of educational literature purporting to be the result of rigidly scientific investigation, presented with mathematical accuracy and embellished with a redundancy of statistical refinements. But the curious absence of thought in much of this stuff has been often the subject of comment. One could not hope to duplicate the fine irony of Quintus H. Flaccus, the esteemed contributor to SCHOOL AND SOCIETY; and it would be a bold critic who would dip his pen in vitriol and attempt to imitate the sulphurous strictures of Dr. Abraham Flexner in his "Universities: American, English, German."

These, by the way, are hopeful dribblings of the much-needed *aqua regia* of which the literature of education stands in sore need. But their reception has been discouraging. Most of the reviewers of Dr. Flexner's book, instead of attempting to refute his penetrating thrusts, have striven to impeach the scholarly competency of the author. This is reminiscent of the over-strenuous efforts to "laugh off" the exceedingly pertinent observations in the famous *Bulletin No. 23* of the Carnegie Foundation, on American college athletics. Much the same treatment was accorded Max McConn's "College or Kindergarten?"

The fact that most of the current criticism of higher education appears in the "lay magazines" is not the result of accident. Whether from timidity or from preoccupation with pseudo-science, the bulk of the educational periodicals are inhospitable to critical contributions. Let us have more critics, lest we forget how to treat them honestly and capitalize their services. To be sure, the man who applies the acid sometimes burns his own fingers; but the corrosive agent is necessary for the reduction of dross. No professional literature can progress without liberal and continuous infusions of cauterizing criticism.

ROCOCO FAÇADE

DOING WITH A PURPOSE IN GRAMMAR

IF a teacher does not see a reason why pupils should study a certain lesson, if she does not see how it leads toward something important, she had better find out what the purpose is or not assign it. Certainly she can not make it valuable until she knows what value there is in it. Teachers, it seems to me, take too many lessons on faith. If they pause to justify them, they say, "These things have been taught for years. Anyway they will not do the children any harm." That is false. It is wrong, even for one day, to ask thirty children to study and recite about something which at the best will not harm them because there are so many things which they could be learning to equip themselves for present and future important occupations. Preparation time for this complicated life of ours is so short, and the children are so eager to learn. Surely they should move forward in every lesson toward intelligent living.

There is no reason why we should not take out of the grammar lessons those parts which have no immediate or ultimate needs or adapt them to the present day because there is nothing sacred about the grammar forms concocted by teachers who studied in the past and taught children to live in a past age. Though there may have been a reason for talking about dative indirect objects and nouns in the predicate nominative when English and Latin grammar were taught together in schools, there is no value now. To be able to recognize them does neither keep any one from making mistakes nor help him to write better sentences. The time so spent could well be employed in fixing the right habits in using the nominative and accusative cases of pronouns, in learning when to use "I" and "me," "he" and "him."

Work in grammar classes should be devoted to saying and writing the things that people need to say and write in order to get on in the world. The theory of grammar is not important to most people, but the practice is important to every one. Then why should thirteen year old children be asked on a test to give the possessive plural of *editor-in-chief* or *father-in-law?* Who would ever need to use the plural, much less the possessive of either? Editors-in-chief and fathers-in-law do not gather in groups, and if they did, they would not be apt to have anything in common. Such situations certainly need not worry children. There are enough possessive plurals that they might use every day if they only knew how. They might use them in telling about their camera club members or the business men's activities.

The children demand that the theory be in actual practice. I learned this lesson from Charles and Bill who helped me with lessons I was arranging. Charles insisted that all the *blah* be left out, and Bill in his polite way read a paragraph and then said, "But what are the kids to do about it?" I was disappointed that he had not been impressed by my neat explanation. He said, "Yes, that is all right, but the kids will just read it and turn the page." Bill was right—children do not want to read and then just turn the page. They want to do something. I am constantly overwhelmed by the eagerness for activity of ninth grade boys and girls. Hardly does the bell ring before the hands go up. "Please let me read my paper first." One boy does not finish answering a question before the hands are in the air. "I wanted you to ask me the next question." Such energetic exuberance wasted on nouns as predicate nominatives! No, there are things more immediately and more ultimately practical.

Grammar need not be theory for theory's sake. It is theory for the sake of practice and practice for the sake of getting on with people in this present day world. Theory only so far as it explains the correct practice in grammar and a knowledge of sentence structure in order to develop the ability to speak and write sentences are what we need. For example, it is necessary to know about adjectives and adverbs to be able to recognize them and to use them, not for any virtue in them of themselves but in order to be able to know when to use them. Many people now grown would have profited by more exercises than they had in using good and well in every day conversational sentences. It is necessary to know about adjective and adverbial phrases and clauses, that is, to be able to recognize them and write them with as much variety as possible because the ability to use them is equipment for enjoyment and for business.

HELEN RAND
EVANSTON TOWNSHIP HIGH SCHOOL,
EVANSTON, ILLINOIS

SPECIAL CORRESPONDENCE

CONSOLIDATING THE COLLEGES

I

So much ink has sluiced through the presses in the last few years regarding "house plans" and "inner colleges" and "quadrangles" that the small college has virtually become, in the popular mind, the educational Moses that is to lead us out of intellectual bondage in our land of Egypt. I should like to rise to a point of objection. I should like to submit that all this depends upon the quality of the small colleges.

It must be granted at once that a small college can stand in a closer relation to the individual student's inner life than the average large university can quite hope to do. It must be granted as well that this relation is greatly to be desired, as tending to evoke the higher and finer understanding. I contend, none the less, that a large university, humanly organized, can minister equally well to this personal development. Such a university can do what almost no small college can do: it can minister to the development of the faculties and abilities of able students toward this finer understanding, but it can also throw open the wider doors of the university mind. In a word, there is no magic in mere smallness.

This contention, it may be added, is not a solo of dissent, for Dr. Bernard Iddings Bell, of St. Stephen's College, one of the keenest of to-day's small-college leaders, argues "the need for the small college of a university integration," stating: "We believe the day of the small college, independent of the university, definitely to be over. Some of the well-endowed and fashionable ones may go on living for years, decades, but they will be fewer and fewer, and eventually even the wealthiest of them is likely to disappear."

Fewer and fewer they are already becoming.

We need not view this fact with alarm. We can conceive even that it may be for the best interest of our educational future. We have now, to banish darkness out from among us, no less than 1,000 institutions of collegiate grade within our national boundaries. Might it not have been better had many of these children of our pioneer days not been born at all, rather than born into the bleak and hard existence that has been their lot? Is it uncharitable to rejoice that in the last few years at least two dozen such institutions have been consolidated into half as many colleges, but stronger?

This urge to merge has been a noticeable trend, at any rate; hopeful, too. Consider the facts: There is so much duplication among our 1,000 colleges and universities, geographically and academically, that the independent existence of some has become wasteful and precarious, or even impossible. This condition has been merely inevitable in the light of the zeal with which colleges were founded as the country expanded.

In this movement the church was the crusader of light, as it had been in Europe before the universities came into being. It was therefore a blessing to the country, but not an unmixed one. It over-reached itself.

All the New England colleges were born of the Evangelical impulse. Nearly all, too, of the rest of the nine colonial colleges of the country were established primarily for religious purposes. Almost the only college in the present United States before 1800 that was not the child of the church was the University of Pennsylvania. Moreover, of the 119 colleges first founded east of the Mississippi, 104 were Christian colleges.

Especially was the Middle West virgin soil for the planting of church colleges, and it is in this region that their over-production has been most pronounced. It is here and in the South, too, that most of the college consolidations in recent years have been effected. Mergers were both needed and inevitable.

II

The great number of Western colleges formed a rude bridge that arched the flood of darkness in our untutored pioneering days. But after the first intellectual fever of the newer geographical regions had somewhat subsided, numerous colleges found no real field of educational usefulness left open to them. The various religious denominations, into the bargain, found them financially burdensome. And as the functions of education were taken over more and more by the state, the sectarian spirit in private colleges declined rapidly. This fact stripped them of their identity and usefulness as such. Indeed, even before this trend set in, the older colonial colleges had withdrawn from church control. Harvard, for example, early threw off its Unitarian character, Yale its Congregational affiliations. Subsequently higher education in the United States has become predominantly non-sectarian, and in general the highest standards are now considered to exist in colleges and universities that are not under church control.

Look, for a moment, at the other side of the picture. Many of the colleges still supported by religious denominations have never succeeded in escaping the austere poverty of their early years, nor in attaining and keeping high standards. Not even the modern treasure hunt of the colleges, as a result of which handsome benefactions have come to many of them, has frightened off the wolf of poverty that snaps inexorably at their heels. To-day we are wont to regard the average of such colleges as we regard the little old grandmother, with a certain affection, to be sure, but with a conviction that her useful days are over.

If you would see the excess of small, independent and struggling colleges, look, for example, at the state of Ohio. With an area of 41,040 square miles and a (1930) population of 6,689,837, it had in 1928 a total of fifty-two institutions of collegiate grade.[1] Six of this number receive public support, and the remaining forty-six are, in the main, privately controlled.

Only seven of these forty-six privately controlled colleges had total operating receipts for 1927–28 of more than $500,000 each. Only seven of the forty-six received more than $100,000 each from productive funds. Sixteen of the forty-six received less than $100,000 each from all sources; and of these sixteen seven

[1] U. S. Department of the Interior: Office of Education Bulletin (1929), No. 38.

received less than $50,000 each! Eighteen of the forty-six received less than $25,000 each from productive funds.

These figures mean merely that the colleges are so numerous that most are badly supported and that they can not, on that account, provide the equipment or the personnel needed to carry on their work at the proper college level.

As one aspect of their equipment, consider the libraries of the various Ohio colleges. "The true university in these days," declared Carlyle, "is a collection of books." Yet one university in the state, reporting a total enrolment of 1,797 for 1927–28, also reports that it has only 13,000 bound volumes in its library. Fourteen of forty-nine institutions have less than 10,000 volumes each in their libraries, and only four have more than 100,000 each!

An even drearier aspect of the colleges is their endowment per student. Out of a total of thirty-six Ohio private colleges listing their 1927–28 productive endowments, twelve had less than $1,000 per student each, and only seven had more than $5,000 per student each. Some institutions claimed no productive endowment at all, and one institution with 1,595 students had only $8.00 in endowment for each student enrolled! These thirty-six colleges so reporting had a total of 29,138 students and a total of $53,495,758 in endowments. The average for all is therefore $1,836 per student.

It is useless to invoke more statistics. Viewed under any aspect the picture is an unlovely one; and please bear in mind that Ohio is one of our wealthiest states and really believes in education.

As in Ohio, so elsewhere these limited collegiate resources mean inevitably limited work. And yet the struggle to enrol students goes on. Yearly hundreds of unknowing high-school students are induced to register at poor institutions by the blandishments of field agents, whose cry is that the small college is the only intellectual salvation of maturing minds.

Many of these recruited students are, unfortunately, only fuel for the educational machine, and their careers amid the green pastures of Academe average quite short. They emerge "finished and finite clods, untroubled by a spark." They give point to a remark by a Pacific Coast university dean: "As long as universities and colleges take the 'mill run' of students, many will be called and few chosen for academic degrees later on." As a fact, according to Dean Gauss, of Princeton, only 37½ per cent. of the men who enter college leave with diplomas.

None would be so foolish as to say that able men and women may not find in any college the kindling of the intellectual soul or the will to achieve. But no more can one ignore the logic of William Howard Taft, who believed that such people would emerge still better trained from schools where competition was stiffer and standards were higher.

III

College endowments in the United States amount roughly to $1,000,000,000. Outside of what is spent for room and board, the annual cost of conducting these 1,000 institutions is approximately $300,000,000. Neither of these sums is too large, or even large enough. My point is merely that the first sum is not so wisely invested, nor the second so wisely spent, as it might be.

What is likely to be done? In the first place, a smaller percentage of the youth of the land is likely henceforth to storm the colleges than we have seen enrol since the war. As a fact, the percentage of our population to which we are attempting to give higher education is immensely larger than that in the most highly civilized and educationally best-organized European countries. Sir Michael Sadler, of Oxford, pointed out not long ago that in Great Britain one out of every 1,000 in the population attended a university; in France, one out of 700; in Germany, one out of 650; and in the United States, one out of every 120. Is it cause for wonder that the spreading feeling in this country now amounts to a conviction that our universities are too thickly populated, and that the hordes who enrol get too little out of their experience?

In the second place, many informed persons here are convinced that we have altogether too many independent colleges. Because modern transportation facilities enable students easily to reach distant but better colleges, the usefulness of many a "local" college is now greatly diminished. Like "sweet Auburn," it has found that its population has fled to the centers of light.

Oddly, one encouraging ray of light amid our dark mediocrity is the contemporary scramble after "the best teachers of the time." But they are not such a numerous band, and they can not be sprinkled thinly over the soil of 1,000 colleges. They are, on the contrary, a gifted few. Men like Royce and James, Sumner and Lounsbury, Gummere and Lowes, are a heaven-sent few in each generation, and it is well for society that they should perform their kind labors in centers of the greatest influence, so long as their rare afflatus is not diluted by excessive numbers of students.

Of all these factors there is tacit recognition in the merging of more than two dozen colleges or universities since 1928 into these institutions:

Albright College Schuylkill College	Albright College, Reading, Pa.
Atlanta University Morehouse College Spelman College	Atlanta University, Atlanta, Ga.
Austin College Texas Presbyterian College	Austin College, Sherman, Texas
Centre College Kentucky College for Women	Centre College of Kentucky, Danville, Ky.
Chicora College for Women Queens College	Queens-Chicora College, Charlotte, N. C.
Columbia University New York Post-Graduate Medical School and Hospital	Columbia University, New York City
Hannibal College LaGrange College	Hannibal-LaGrange College, Hannibal, Mo.
Knox College Lombard College	Knox College, Galesburg, Ill.
Lane Theological Seminary Presbyterian Theological Seminary	In process of amalgamation
Miami University Oxford College for Women	Miami University, Oxford, Ohio
New Orleans University Straight University	Dillard University, New Orleans, La.
Pittsburgh Theological Seminary Xenia United Presbyterian Theological Seminary	Pittsburgh-Xenia Theological Seminary, Pittsburgh, Pa.
Rochester College of Optometry University of Rochester	University of Rochester, Rochester, N. Y.

Fundamentally, the purpose of these mergers is to make the best teachers and the best educational resources available to the best students.

IV

I am far from advocating that we should have fewer teachers, for I do not believe in making the country safe for unemployment. Signs point to the prevalent belief that we should have fewer students and fewer but more compact colleges, but, if anything, more teachers and better. Extremely few colleges are able to maintain the recommended ratio of one teacher to each ten students. Extremely few, for that matter, have learned what Henry Adams concluded: "No man can instruct more than half-a-dozen students at once. The whole problem of education is one of its cost in money."

This is precisely true. We must recognize the fact that a real college is not like a wild flower: it can not grow in poor soil. It requires careful planting and even more careful cultivation. It requires to be fertilized with money enough to equip it to do well the proper work of a college. It requires to be fertilized with highly sophisticated intellects ripened by stimulating contacts among their colleagues and humanized by ministering to the growing minds of eager students. It requires, in a word, to have for its goal the propagation of sound learning and pure manners. There is no other way to do this than to be excellent; there is no success in mediocrity.

A start toward this end has been made with the recognition by some boards of control that consolidations will concentrate the brains and the money to grow one better college where two or more poor ones grew before. These trustees recognize that our higher educational system is discrete and a shambles. They recognize the competition of the now myriad junior colleges. They recognize that the business of the real college lies in higher regions than that of the junior college, and they are accordingly seeking to raise their standards. They recognize, as President Emeritus Durham, of Transylvania University, has stated candidly, that the small sectarian and secluded college, uninfluenced by the fertilizing cross currents of modern financial and intellectual life, is in serious danger of extinction.

We shall need an even wider recognition of

this fact and of the way to meet it. We shall need a growth in vision to see that education is dynamic, not static; that any college or university that is continually to justify its existence must grow to meet the current demands of society upon it. We shall need more of the vision of men like Arthur E. Morgan at Antioch College and Hamilton Holt at Rollins College, who broke new furrows in ground, once fertile, that had latterly lain fallow.

We shall need, in brief, a clear recognition of the truth of Henry Adams's judgment that the whole problem of education is one of its cost in money. Colleges that deserve support will receive it. But they will have to make fresh adjustments to function vitally in a world greatly different from that which bred the small college of colonial pattern. That is the way to improve our national brood of small colleges. That way lies salvation for our system of higher education.

John A. Pollard

QUOTATIONS

SIDNEY E. MEZES

Though years of ill health have intervened since Dr. Mezes resigned the presidency of the College of the City of New York, the results of his administration still testify to the soundness of his constructive work. It is not too much to say that he gave the college its present form of organization. The preceding decade had been one of transition, physical and scholastic. The new college buildings on St. Nicholas Heights had been built and equipped; the requirements for admission had been heightened and the curriculum had been extended and enriched. But it was Dr. Mezes who consolidated what had been achieved in the several advances and brought the whole institution into an administrative unity.

The number of students, which had grown to 20,000 during his administration, has increased, according to yesterday's report, to 30,000, but the lines of expansion had been determined under his leadership. Special schools began to take shape. The College of Liberal Arts and Science was maintained in its integrity, but with it were developed schools of technology, business and education. Summer courses were inaugurated and the evening session, which has now 15,000 enrolled students—twice as many as in the regular courses by day—was strengthened and made of special use to those in the employ of the city. So does his educational statesmanship, which earlier showed itself in the University of Texas, where he was lately made president emeritus in recognition of his service there, show its fruits.

He was in his own person and accomplishments an ideal type of citizen to be set before college students. A scholar, a philosopher, a teacher who knew the heights of human culture, an intellectual aristocrat, he had profound democratic sympathies. He seldom spoke outside the college walls. He made his impression within, where it will be lasting.

Dr. Mezes rendered an international service during and following the war as chairman of the group of American experts (about 150 in number) who gathered information for use at the Peace Conference. His intimate relation on the one hand with those representing America in the conduct of the negotiations and on the other with the most highly qualified authorities made his position one of great responsibility and influence. But he came back to the college as soon as he could have honorable release, for there he felt he could do even more for the peace which he helped in this way to prepare.

Franklin K. Lane in one of his last letters, written only a few days before his death to one of his dearest friends, when he himself was still seeing things that he longed to live to do, said that he would like to gather around a fire a few men whom he loved—a dozen men they were whom he named—adding, after he had named them, "The real world is very small, isn't it?" Near the head of that list was "Sid," with whom he had been a student in the University of California and who had helped him materially as well as in other ways to make his own start—and the "Sid" of that small "real world" was Sidney E. Mezes. In such company he belonged.—*The New York Times.*

EDUCATIONAL RESEARCH AND STATISTICS

ADAPTATION OF TESTS IN SCIENCE TO DIFFERING ABILITIES

FOR a number of years the public high schools have been receiving in the ninth grade many children of chronological age fourteen or more and mental age thirteen or less, *i.e.*, one or more years retarded. The range of the intelligence quotient of girls in the first term of Grade IX in the South Philadelphia High School in February, 1931, was from 75 to 121. Many of them came from families in which either a foreign language or imperfect English was spoken.

If the function of the school is to develop the latent powers of the pupils and to supply them with a fund of useful information it is obvious that, with a wide range in intelligence and in cultural opportunities, differentiation of instruction is needed. With differentiation in instruction is necessarily correlated differentiation in tests for determining the effects of instruction. Limited memory span, limited power of association and inability to deal with abstract ideas are major defects of the less intelligent as compared to the more intelligent groups. It follows that the material of instruction for them should be concrete and composed of few units. It is also very important for the teacher in presenting the material to use language of concrete character and great simplicity. In spite of the very elementary character of their text-book it has seemed best to allow girls of I.Q. below 90 to do their reading at school where dictionary and teacher are available rather than at home, so limited and inaccurate is their English vocabulary. It was discovered by a teacher of the dullest girls that common English nouns of concrete significance, such as shavings, kindlings, kerosene, were unfamiliar to them.

Word Column Test on Conduction

After each of the words in column I place one of the two letters, A and B, according to whether the substance is a good or a poor conductor of heat.

I	II
1. Iron	A. Poor conductor
2. Water	B. Good conductor
3. Mercury	
4. Copper	
5. Asbestos	
6. Glass	
7. Air	
8. Silver	
9. Clay	
10. Wool	

Result of Test on Conduction

Group	Number of girls	Per cent. getting 7 out of 10 right
Lower I.Q.	26	70
Higher I.Q.	29	83

A matching type of test is suitable for determining degrees of accuracy in the association of ideas and in the use of terms. The results of a test of this character given to two groups, one of lower I.Q. (90 or below) and the other of higher I.Q. (above 90) are shown above. Both classes had performed experiments in the laboratory and had completed the reading in the text-book.

Another test given to similar groups required ability to distinguish between conduction and convection and properly to apply the terms.

Word Column Test on Conduction and Convection

After each of the words or expressions in column I place one or more of the letters in column II that stand for related ideas.

I	II
1. Wind	A. Heat moves from particle to particle
2. Conduction	B. Warm air escapes through an opening
3. Draft	C. Heated matter moves to cooler region
4. Ventilation	D. Cold air enters through an opening
5. Ocean current	

Results of Test on Conduction and Convection

Group	Number of girls	Per cent. getting 6–8 right
Lower I.Q.	27	22
Higher I.Q.	29	70

It is immediately evident that the second test is beyond the ability of most of the less intelligent girls, only six of the twenty-seven making the required score (6 points out of 9). The first test, however, is entirely suitable; eighteen out of twenty-six are able to pass it. One reason for this is the greater simplicity of the first test. The choice is limited to two possible associations instead of four. In addition each idea to be associated is expressed in two words which readily recall a simple experiment recently performed in the laboratory while in the second test a choice must be made between ideas less simply expressed and involving a choice from knowledge gained not merely from experience in the laboratory but also from reading and discussion.

Somewhat analogous results were obtained with tests designed to furnish information concerning ability to apply principles to situations varying slightly from those met in the laboratory. For this purpose a diagram, illustrating a coffee pot in section with two different levels indicated, was presented to members of segregated classes. The question was worded thus: "A shows the original level of the water. What did we do to make the level go to B? (Water was not added.)" In the group of higher I.Q. 90 per cent. were able to give the correct answer and in the group of lower I.Q. 80 per cent.

Another test involved a comparison of two balloons, one of slightly larger size than the other. The question was "We can make the small balloon as large as the larger balloon. How?" Only 20 per cent. of those of lower I.Q. gave the correct answer whereas 50 per cent. of the abler girls solved the problem.

The second of these tests is presumably more difficult because it requires visualization of the interior of the balloon and the presence of a gas whereas the interior of the coffee pot and the presence of the liquid is shown in the diagram. Coffee pots are also to them somewhat more familiar objects than balloons.

Fifty-six girls with I.Q.s from 89 to 121 and segregated according to intelligence into two classes (I.Q. 89–104 and I.Q. 104–121) were shown diagrams representing a silver spoon and a glass dish into which hot apple sauce was about to be poured. They were asked to explain why the spoon was placed in the dish. 40 per cent. of the more intelligent and 25 per cent of the less intelligent were able to apply to this problem what they had learned about conduction.

With a task of simple comparison they were more successful. In this diagram two pans, one of copper the other of iron, each containing a liquid, were shown over a flame. The task was to compare what would happen in the two cases. 90 per cent of the more intelligent and 79 per cent. of the less intelligent were able to give correctly more than two comparisons.

The difficulty which girls of I.Q. in the neighborhood of 75 to 80 have with a task of this kind is shown by the following samples of their answers.

Comparison of Pans of Copper and Iron

Iron and copper are good conductors of heat. So the water in the pans of copper and iron does not get hot so quick and does not boil quicker.

There is no differences and no likeness.

The iron pot of water and the copper pot of water are both good conductors of heat and therefore both of them come to a boiling point at the same time.

The only difference in between them are, that one is copper and the other is iron.

How alike: Iron and copper are both poor conductors of heat when the water gets warm, In the iron pan it also gets warm in the copper pan. the water will also expand in both pans although they are both poor conductors of heat. Iron and copper are both metals or solids.

How they differ: Iron and copper are poor conductors of heat but in time If the flame is left under both to the same length of time the Iron will get hotter than the copper because it is a better conductor of heat than copper.

A similar lack of ability to perceive simple relations is evident in their attempts to write directions for the performance of an experiment. To seventy-eight girls of a wide range of intelligence was shown the apparatus for determining the relative conductivity for heat of different substances. Without preliminary discussion or reading they were asked to tell what they would do with the apparatus to solve the problem.

Experiment on Heat Conduction

We took a piece of copper, iron, aluminum, glass, asbestos clay and took each and holded it over a Bunsen Burner. Then we took a test tube holder and put a piece of parrafin in it an lighted it.

We took a bunsen burner, copper, iron, aluminum, glass, clay, asbestos, test tube, paraffin. We then lit them to see if they were good conductors of heat. We watched them closely.

We took a little pot and put into it a strip of brass, copper, iron, aluminum, asbestor, clay, Glass and we used a test tube holder to put them in.

Contrast with these the following by a pupil of higher I.Q.

We took three metals and three non-metals. The metals were copper, iron and aluminum, the non-metals were glass, asbestos and clay. We also needed a bunsen burner, a test tube holder and a piece of pareffin. We heated each metal and non-metal supported by a test tube holder over a bunsen burner. After two minutes of heating we allowed it to cool for one minute and then put it against a piece of paraffin.

Characteristic of pupils of low intelligence is utter inability to generalize. They are, therefore, quite incapable of framing definitions. For example, after experimenting with a number of different substances such as chalk, starch, sugar, salt, etc., in order to determine their solubility in water and using in connection with each experiment such terms as solvent, solute, solution, suspension, a certain proportion will be unable to give a satisfactory definition of any of the terms. It is somewhat easier for them to detect the wrong use of the term when confronted with an incorrect statement. The difference between groups of higher and lower intelligence in this respect is shown by the results of a test given to two hundred and eighty-six girls of IX A grade segregated according to intelligence into four pairs of classes meeting at four different periods of the school day.

Definitions and Detection of Absurdities

Group	Definitions correct	Incorrect statement detected
Lower I.Q.	47 per cent.	61 per cent.
Higher I.Q.	74 per cent.	84 per cent.

In our work at the South Philadelphia High School with pupils of varying intelligence we have become convinced of the value of diagrams as testing devices. For those of lower intelligence they are a necessity because a majority of the unintelligent are deficient in power of vizualization. They can not readily construct a situation described in words. For those of high intelligence the diagram saves time and often avoids misunderstanding or misinterpretation.

During the past term the experiment was tried of presenting to classes of IXB grade, at the close of their laboratory work and reading on the subject of sound, a set of diagrams. One showed three stringed instruments; A, a lyre, B, a mandolin and C, a violin. Another diagram represented A, a simple xylophone with bars of metal on a wooden frame and a single stick for playing; B, an African marimba in which hollow gourds are placed below the metal bars and three sticks are used for playing. A third diagram showed A, human lips from which lines represented the direction of sound waves and B, a megaphone with lines showing the alteration in the direction of the sound waves from the lips. In each case the task was one of comparison and statement of the nature of the improvement in the production of transmission of sound.

The results of the three tests are as follows:

1. *Stringed Instruments*

0	1	2	3	4	5	6	7	Points
2	3	1	7	5	1	0	0	Number of girls (Lower I.Q.)
0	3	1	7	2	2	3	1	Number of girls (Higher I.Q.)

2. *Xylophone and Marimba*

0	1	2	3	4	5	6	7	8	Points
	3	13	1	2	0	0	0	0	Number of girls (Lower I.Q.)
	0	3	8	5	1	1	0	1	Number of girls (Higher I.Q.)

3. *Megaphone*

0	1	2	3	4	5	Points
1	7	7	4	0	0	Number of girls (Lower I.Q.)
0	1	7	3	6	2	Number of girls (Higher I.Q.)

From the results it appears that, for the majority, the test on stringed instruments is easier than the other two. The median score for both groups is three points. Over 30 per cent. of the less intelligent make more than three points and over 40 per cent. of the more intelligent. With the other two tests the median for those of lower I.Q. drops to two while for those of higher I.Q. it remains at three. Over 40 per cent. of the latter get more than three points on both tests. On the second test only 10 per cent. of the duller pupils make more than three points and none at all make more than three on the third.

The reasons for the differences in the results for the two groups are not far to seek. The scores more nearly coincide in the first test because the diagrams represent concrete objects with which all have some degree of familiarity and therefore less imagination is required to comprehend the problem. The diagrams used for the second tests represent a familiar object, the xylophone, and a less familiar one, the marimba. With a simple xylophone the children had had some experience in the laboratory. Many of them had attempted to play a tune with its single stick. While the design of the African marimba is in the main similar to the simple xylophone, the presence of the hollow gourds below the metal strips is new. It is also played with three sticks instead of with one. These features introduce a complexity into the comparison with which the majority of the duller children are unable to cope. A number of the more intelligent transfer and apply to this new situation what they have learned, in the laboratory and from outside experience, about resonance and harmony.

A child of low I.Q. is unable to visualize sound waves and therefore can not satisfactorily interpret the diagram used in the third test. Some of the children are able from personal experience to describe the difference in the sound of the voice as it comes from the megaphone and from the bare lips. The cause of this, however, since it requires manipulation of visual imagery, is beyond their powers. Those possessing superior intelligence have this control of visual imagery and therefore make higher scores.

In considering the application of the information gained from such tests to differentiation of instruction it must be remembered that children with similar I.Q.s are not identical in mentality. Intelligence tests do not divide the pupils so that all those in the superior class have superior reasoning ability, discrimination, power of observation, ability to follow directions, etc. There is no inevitable correlation between these various abilities. It may happen that a pupil of superior reasoning power is deficient in ability to observe accurately and to follow directions. Industry, power of application, is often greater in those of rather low I.Q. Children differ widely, too, in temperament and in the nature of their previous experience. These factors account, in large part, for the overlapping in the scores obtained with the tests. Then, again, there is little difference in the general intelligence of the lower end of the superior group and the higher end of the inferior group. If the dividing line is an I.Q. of 100 a pupil of I.Q. 100 in the upper group is unlikely to be noticeably superior to one of I.Q. 98 or 99 in the lower group.

When there is such overlapping of intelligence at the lower and higher ends of the two groups it is advisable to use with the less able group tests varying from the simplest to those of medium difficulty. The ablest of the superior group need the stimulus of exercises more complex and abstract, yet there must be included some of moderate difficulty if those of average intelligence are not to be discouraged. When segregation according to intelligence is not possible and within the class there is a wide range of ability a similar wide range of tests should be used so that all but the dullest or the laziest may make a passing score. The tests for those of lower I.Q. must present only a few items and those few must be of concrete nature. Complexity must be avoided. Application of principles to new situations can be expected only when the new situation differs but slightly from what is already familiar.

In order to discriminate ability to think from mere memorization there ought to be available to each teacher a well graded series of tests pertaining to the laboratory work and its application to real life.

In the administration and grading of the tests described in this article I have had the valuable assistance of other members of the department, namely, Miss Liebermann, Miss Snyder, Miss Dumm, Mrs. Pike and Mrs. McClellan.

M. Louise Nichols

South Philadelphia
High School for Girls

SCHOOL AND SOCIETY

EDITED BY J. McKEEN CATTELL

WITH WHICH IS COMBINED THE

EDUCATIONAL REVIEW

EDITED BY WILLIAM McANDREW

Volume 34 SATURDAY, SEPTEMBER 26, 1931 Number 874

THE ESSAY EXAMINATION AND THE NEW TYPE TEST

By Professor HULSEY CASON

UNIVERSITY OF WISCONSIN

THE epidemic of new type tests in the elementary school and high school has been accompanied and followed by a surprising number of true-false, multiple-choice, completion, simple recall and matching examinations in the colleges and universities; and for several years the essay examination has been referred to as the "traditional" essay examination. For a while I preferred the new-type tests for courses in psychology, and have used all the more familiar forms; but I have now become convinced that the essay examination is the most satisfactory kind of written examination for college and university students. The purpose of the present paper is to compare the two types of examinations and to present a number of semi-experimental observations which have been made during the past nine years.

Qualities of Research Professors: The most important general assumption underlying the new type test is that a person's knowledge and ability can be adequately measured and judged by counting some of the disconnected and disjointed details that he knows. Thorndike has defended this doctrine on numerous occasions, but it seems obvious that Thorndike's own knowledge and ability in psychology could not be adequately measured by a long new type test. It is possible that a younger psychologist might make a higher score, although Thorndike may have ten times as much psychological ability. If a university is selecting a research professor of psychology, it would be unwise to make this selection, for example, on the basis of a true-false or multiple-choice test, regardless of its range and length. A psychologist's monographs and articles give some indication of his ability and originality, but these publications bear a much closer resemblance to the kind of mental activity involved in the essay examination than to that which is involved in the new type test. There are probably few who would deny that there are some important activities and capacities that can not be adequately measured by the new type test.

The Work of Graduate Students: The essay examination is an aid in forming an opinion of graduate students' qualifications for the doctor's and master's degrees, and it is also of some assistance in judging one's ability to teach psychology. Graduate theses are supposed to show a certain grasp of psychology, some organization of the material, at least a few faint suggestions of originality and initiative, and they frequently involve a considerable amount of perseverance. These qualities and abilities, however, can not be measured by the new type test. Knowledge of some facts is of much greater value than knowledge of others, and some attitudes and general habits of thinking will carry a student much farther than others. A large number of educators and psychologists will probably agree that it is practical and desirable to judge a graduate student's ability by his performance on written examinations in regular courses, by writing special papers, making reports, his participation in class discussions, a comprehensive examination at the end of his whole graduate course, and also by some personal contact with him. Such a judgment can be and has often been made in a fairly satisfactory manner by experienced and competent instructors. One could make out a fairly strong case in favor of the proposition that several of the methods used in teaching and examining graduate students should also be employed if possible with undergraduate students.

The Undergraduate Major in Psychology: Instead of giving the undergraduate major in psychology a barrage of true-false, multiple-choice and other new type tests during his sophomore, junior and senior years, and then "counting" the score, there is much to be said in favor of requiring him to take regular essay examinations in all his courses, and of having him take a comprehensive essay examination on his major subject at the end of his senior year. The undergraduate student should be tested for his knowledge of psychology and also for his ability to use the information gained in thinking about psychological and other related problems. The process of putting one's ideas in writing is a distinctly beneficial exercise, and this benefit is probably as real for the student as it is for the professor. It has frequently been pointed out that students can not think effectively if they do not know certain facts, and that they may know a large number of disjointed facts without being able to think effectively. Thinking is in some ways an art, and it is difficult to measure artistic ability quantitatively. However, a general opinion of the requirements and desiderata for the undergraduate major in psychology can be formed in much the same way that one forms a general opinion of the requirements for the A.M. degree. It is also not particularly difficult to agree upon a general standard of proficiency for students who are taking their first course in psychology, and at all these levels of psychological ability there is more need now than ever before for relatively long, comprehensive, essay examinations.

Recall Examinations and Recognition Tests: Most of the paper and pencil studies that are ordinarily cited in support of the new type tests have been carried out on children in the elementary school and high school, but equally happy results have seldom been obtained with university men and women. One of the reasons why this is so is that the essay examination is concerned with recall memory and the ability to organize and think about the material learned, while some of the new type tests deal largely with the recognition memory of details that are often insignificant. The relation between recall memory and recognition memory does not require further investigation, as is sometimes claimed, because it is now well known that the correlation between recall and recognition is quite low. A person can generally recognize a large number of details that he can not recall, but when he can recall a fact he can practically always recognize it. A test for recall is a more complete and satisfactory measure of retention. The process of recall is more closely related to the higher mental activities of thinking, reasoning and imagination. It would appear therefore that some of the new type tests which are largely concerned with recognition can not be a valid or especially significant type of examination because they do not measure just the kind of ability that a university teacher is most concerned about.

Reliability of the Essay Examination: The essay examination has been used as the criterion in a number of comparative studies of the essay and the new type, and several of the reports on the unreliability of grading essay examination papers are grossly exaggerated. It is not a question of whether ten teachers give an English composition paper the same grade, but a question of the general value of an individual teacher's grades, when he grades the students in a class that he himself has taught, and when he uses an examination of his own making. At the beginning of their experience, most teachers learn that the rationalizations of their poorest students can not be accepted at their face value; but some instructors underestimate their efficiency in grading essay examinations when only their worst mistakes are repeatedly called to their attention.

Validity and Reliability of the New Type Test: It may seem that the essay examination does not cover as wide a range of specific topics as the new type test, but the range covered by the essay examination can be made wide enough; and the studies of the validity and reliability of the new type test show that it is quite unsatisfactory. One reason for the low reliability of most of the new type tests is the fact that students will guess at some of the questions they do not know regardless of the kind of instructions they may have received. In a test composed, for example, of 100 true-false statements, a student may know 50 items and guess at the remaining 50. Although the advantages and disadvantages of the true-false test do not depend upon statistical considerations alone, it is well to remember that there is a large and important difference in the results that are obtained when one penny is thrown 50,000 times and when 50 pennies are thrown all at once a number of times. The factor of chance is much more important in the latter case. One writer in his enthusiasm for the new type test suggested that the skeptical reader throw 10,000,000 coins!

The problem involved here is similar to the question of whether to take a chance in common stocks. For a long period of time the probability may be slightly in favor of the stocks going up, but it may still be better not to take a chance. There are additional reasons why certain individuals should not buy on margin. If a correlation of .70 is obtained between an essay examination and, let us say, a true-false test, it would probably be better simply to use the essay examination and avoid some of the risk. An individual diagnosis of the student is necessary, and one does not have to think of his grade merely as a most probable score. I have known good students who made ridiculously low scores on the new type tests, and I have also known poor students who made moderately high scores on the same tests. I am also inclined to believe that these observations are not as exceptional as has sometimes been claimed. The statistical questions of correlation and probability are for the most part beside the point. Teachers do not like to see a student's credit frozen on any occasion merely because his stocks happen to go down, and university officials certainly do not regard with great satisfaction the kind of examination and procedure in which a student's account is carried or closed out partly on account of the factor of chance.

Factors Which Should Be Considered in Grading: Before giving a student a grade in any course it is desirable to consider how long he has known the material, how long he will probably remember it in the future, and the extent to which he has crammed for the examination. It is easier to float to an A grade by cramming for the new type test than by cramming for an examination in which recall memory, organization and thinking are involved. It is also desirable to find out something about the student's general habits of thinking, his attitude towards the course he is taking, and what he has actually gotten out of the total experience of the course from his point of view. The effect of psychology courses on the undergraduate student is often a highly personal matter, and the nature and extent of this effect can be best appreciated by some kind of personal contact with him. The essay examination furnishes more information about the *quality* of the student's performance than the new type test. The essay examination is also of some help in judging the personal influence of a course, but from this point of view the new type test is of practically no assistance at all.

The Introductory Course in Psychology: The introductory course in psychology presents a large number of problems, and some of these are concerned with the type of the examinations. In the Psychology I. course at Wisconsin we have been giving five one-hour essay examinations at intervals of three weeks, and the final two-hour examination is also of the essay type. We try to avoid vague, indefinite and ambiguous questions, we attempt to select questions that can be graded intelligently, and we do not ask catch questions. The students are examined on important matters so that if they know the answer to a question they will know something important, and if they do not know it they will be obviously deficient. In this course, excellent students practically always get high grades, and poor students practically always get low grades. The course is not conducted as if the students were expected merely to acquire a number of specific bonds such as those involved in spelling and in the multiplication table. A considerable amount of the material included is general and "subjective," and we fail to appreciate just why we should lean over backwards in trying to make the examinations entirely specific and "objective."

The Objective-Essay Examination: The kind of essay question that we have frequently preferred may be called the objective-essay type, and it can be illustrated by the following examples: "State, and discuss briefly, James' four rules to be used in forming a new habit and in leaving off an old one," and "Describe in detail the Ladd-Franklin theory of color vision." If the students in Introductory Psychology are asked to "define, and distinguish between (A) Inherited, (B) Acquired, (C) Congenital and (D) Learned," there is certainly no acute problem connected with grading their answers. If the same students are requested to "describe the procedure used and the results obtained in Hunter's delayed reaction experiment," there is no chronic difficulty in determining which students are prepared and which are not. In order to grade the answers to these questions it is of course necessary to read the papers, and to read them carefully. It frequently happens that a professor does not have an assistant who is competent to grade his essay examinations, but any assistant can score a new type test if he is supplied with a key to the supposedly correct answers. This has been a good selling point for the new type test with professors and assistants alike.

Influence of the Examination on the Students: The essay examination can be made to have almost any kind of influence on the students that is desired; but the influence of the new type test is practically always undesirable. For several years I made an unsuccessful attempt to convince students that, when due account was taken of the factor of chance, the new type test was a fairly accurate measure of their knowledge and ability. They preferred it to the essay examination because it was easy to take, they did not have to think, they could guess at the questions they did not know, and they did not have to strain themselves in studying for the next examination. The conditions were almost ideal and the grades were noticeably higher when the students corrected their own papers at the end of the test! It is easier for students to take the new type than to take the essay in the same way that it is easier for a professor in the classroom to answer in a summary fashion, "Yes, I know this" or "No, I don't know that," than it is for him to write an article for publication. In the new type test, the students hurriedly read the statement, experience a brief pain, make a response partly by means of a "hunch," and then put the disagreeable subject completely out of mind. It is not surprising that they like it when it is so easy to take! The class as a whole also did not particularly mind when some good students got low grades and when some poor students were lucky; the good students were "grinds" anyway and it served them right, and as for the slow fellows why not "give them a break"? The principal purpose in giving the examination was to stimulate the students, and the resulting attitudes were not just the kind I had hoped to produce. The conditions of acquiring an education are more satisfactory if the students feel reasonably certain that when they are well prepared they will receive good grades and that when they are not prepared they will receive low grades. Cheating is easier and much harder to detect on the new type test; and in the case of those students who are not at all enthusiastic about the course anyway, a little guessing and a small factor of chance may have a disastrous effect.

Difficulty in Making up New Type Tests: Another serious disadvantage in such a test as the true-false is that it is extremely difficult to make up satisfactory questions. In this test one should formulate a large number of statements on important subjects, the statements should be absolutely true or false, and the factor of suggestion should not be present. Many of the most important subjects in psychology and the social sciences do not readily lend themselves to the true-false test, and the more widely read and intelligent a student is the more he is at a disadvantage. The percentage of students answering a question correctly should not be too close to 100 or too close to 50. The statements should be of such a nature that they will be marked correctly by about 75 per cent. of the class. This, however, is a practical impossibility. Courses in psychology generally change considerably from year to year, and if they happen to be taught in approximately the same fashion for any length of time, the method of using a standardized set of new type questions is highly impracticable because the student organizations generally maintain a more complete file of previous examinations than the professor giving the course. The instructor must actually try out a true-false question before he can know the number of students in the class who will mark it correctly, and when this has been done the question can not be used again! Those who have had experience with essay examinations can judge the approximate number of students who will answer each question satisfactorily. Those who have not had experience do not realize how accurately this judgment can be made. It is less trouble to write out a new set of essay questions for each examination than to prepare one or more forms of a new type test. The new type is also practically impossible for the make-up examinations which almost always seem necessary.

Absolute and Relative Systems of Grading: In most universities the grades have to be handed in as either A, B, C, D, E or F at the end of the term; and it is desirable for the instructor to have in mind the kind of performance or ability that corresponds to each of these grades. In forming such general estimates, one can consider the interest and intelligence of the students, the amount and difficulty of the material learned, the skill and ability acquired, and the total amount of time spent on the course. These factors should be considered especially in connection and in comparison with other courses being given in the same school. It is just as reasonable to form an opinion of the kind of performance that corresponds to an A, C or F grade as it is to decide whether to accept or reject a graduate thesis. In the last analysis a university teacher must have an absolute scale of grading.

One of the weaknesses in the relative system of grading according to the normal curve or the "normal law fetish" is the fact that different classes differ markedly from each other, and the same class also varies from time to time. Arriving at a general concept of the kind of ability that should be graded A, C or F is not particularly difficult with the essay examination; but with the new type test and with no result besides the resulting order of rank of the students there is no sensible means at all of estimating the kind of performance that should correspond to the different letter grades. It has been claimed that some instructors who use the new type almost exclusively do not know the color of their students' minds, and they do not appreciate how little work their students do and what an unfavorable attitude they have towards the course. It seems also that some instructors who are most extravagant in their praise of the new type test have not taught long enough to realize how accurate the standards of grading the essay examination may become in the hands of experienced and competent teachers.

Conclusions: The principal conclusions which seem justified are as follows:

(1) The agitation for the new type test has run quite a distance away from the cultural and personal needs of psychology students and the practical requirements of the teaching situation.

(2) The new type test is not a valid or reliable measure of a student's knowledge and ability in psychology.

(3) The influence of the new type test on psychology students is undesirable.

(4) Some form of the essay examination is the most valuable and practical type of written examination to use with both undergraduate and graduate students of psychology.

FEDERAL-STATE COOPERATION IN INDIAN EDUCATION[1]

By W. CARSON RYAN, JR.

OFFICE OF INDIAN AFFAIRS, WASHINGTON, D. C.

IN this whole Indian business we are having to do with individual Indians, with individual human beings. We tend constantly to talk about "the Indian," as if all Indians were the same. Actually there are, of course, at least fifty separate linguistic stocks represented among the American Indian population; our present-day Indians include everything from full bloods to almost pure white; and in the same small tribal remnant one may find some Indians living in tepees in a cold northern climate while other members of the identical group are among the success-

[1] Paper presented at the National Conference for Social Work, Minneapolis, June, 1931.

ful Indian students at the University of Oklahoma.

When we undertake, therefore, to discuss Federal-State cooperation in Indian education, we must understand at the outset that no uniform rule will work for every state or every Indian in the state. Certain principles we do assume, however:

(1) That the Indians can not and should not forever remain the concern of the National Government. Sooner or later all Indians, even in the Southwest, will become participating citizens of the state and local community as well as of the United States.[2]

(2) That whatever program we in the Federal Government undertake, this ultimate interest of the state in Indians as part of their population must be kept in mind.

The state of Minnesota offers an excellent illustration. The one fact that differentiates Minnesota's attitude toward the education of Indians from that of nearly all other states is that Minnesota assumes that Indians are citizens and are to be included in any and all plans the state has for its citizenry. This may seem like a little thing; actually it is all-important.

INDIAN CHILDREN AND PUBLIC SCHOOLS

The most obvious and most frequently cited development in Federal-State cooperation on Indians is the attendance of Indian children in public schools. It comes as a surprise to some people to learn that approximately half of the Indian children attending any school—38,000 out of 75,000—are in regular public schools, usually with whites. During the last school year we had contracts for tuition of Indian children with nearly 900 boards of education, aside from many communities where some Indian children attend without tuition payment. At first sight this looks like a great advance, and in a sense it is—especially as most of it has come within the past six or eight years, and much of it has been successful beyond anybody's dreams. Certain real reservations one must have with regard to it, however.

In the first place, this is not really Federal-State cooperation at all. The arrangements are between the Federal Government and the *local* communities, with the state as such seldom having anything to do with it. This is a violation of every right principle of Federal-State relationship in education, besides being administratively absurd. The National Government should not be dealing directly with local communities in this fashion—it should be dealing directly with the states. Contracts with local boards tend to perpetuate the conception of the Indian as somebody the Federal Government is always there to pay money for. The situation has become such that the wealthiest city in one state was not above putting in its plea for a few cents a day for its handful of part-Indian children, even though the usual justification on which Indian tuition is based—that the community is poorer by reason of untaxed Indian lands —would have been grotesque in this instance. Indeed, in more than one state having Indian population the real problem is going to be to help the state maintain its self-respect as far as possible in the apparently inevitable demand for Federal money for Indians supposed to be long since free of Federal control.

In the second place, there are some indications that in the past the change from government school to public-school attendance for Indians has sometimes been made too suddenly, with scanty consideration for the real needs of Indians. We are moving rather slowly on public school

[2] All Indians were made "citizens of the United States" by Act of Congress in 1924.

attendance at the present time, taking particular care not to turn Indian children over to the public schools until the community is reasonably ready for it. Hostility towards Indian attendance on the part of any considerable portion of the community, even though a minority, makes it exceedingly difficult for Indians to make the adjustments they should. When Indian schools were notoriously poor, it would have been difficult to prove that any change could be worse, but with the raised standards of Indian schools—teachers now going into the service with pay and qualifications above the average for the states in which the Indians are located and considerably above the standards for the districts in which the Indians live—the situation is altered. We hesitate to make the change unless we are sure the Indian child will get at least as good schooling as he is getting in the Indian school. Our education staff at Washington have seriously considered whether, if we are to insist on three and four years of training for our elementary teachers and pay them a minimum entrance salary of $1,680, we should not make rather definite conditions as a prerequisite for public school attendance. Some of our staff are inclined to think the Indian children ought to take "pot luck" with the rest of the population of the backward parts of rural America. Most of us are convinced, however, that we might rather lay down certain conditions for the sake of the whites as well as the Indians. We have usually insisted, for example, upon a hot midday lunch, rather hoping the white children would have a look in on it too. We usually furnish a so-called day school representative to follow up attendance—though I should dislike to have to confess to the attendance we accept as normal. We would like to make sure that school nursing, visiting teacher work and other services badly needed by Indians and white alike in these regions will have a fair chance to develop.

Some Recent Steps

While we hesitate somewhat to go much further into these Federal-local relations without setting up what we consider more adequate safeguards, we have taken certain steps that are definitely in the direction of Federal-State cooperation in education:

(1) First of all, we have asked and obtained the adherence of state educational authorities to a Federal-State program in education. At Milwaukee last December, the heads of state school systems accepted Federal-State cooperation as fundamental. The state departments have been particularly cooperative since that time in helping us in our effort to make the Indian schools come more closely to the better state courses of study that are being worked out.

(2) At the present time we are trying to revise our educational administration and supervision to accord with the conception of the state as a unit. Until recently we had nine general or district school supervisors each of whom roamed over a considerable territory. We are abolishing these positions, assigning in their stead supervisors of the special type for industrial training, home economics and the like, or supervisors of Indian education with the state or local Indian jurisdictions as the unit. If we put in highly qualified local Indian school superintendents, as we are about to do, for example, at Turtle Mountain, North Dakota; Pine Ridge, South Dakota; and the Pima-Papago reservations in Arizona; we shall expect them to work as closely as possible with state and local educational administration and with all existing non-school agencies for health and family welfare. In one state with a large Indian population we are

designating a state supervisor of Indian education. We have taken him from a Federal Civil Service list of eligibles furnished as the result of a recent non-assembled examination, but he is a school man from the state and came recommended to us by the state school authorities. He will have his offices in the State Capitol, with the state superintendent of public instruction. Those who watched the work of the General Education Board in the South in other days will recognize the plan at once. While Indian education may not be as much in need of the aura of respectability as Negro education was at the period when the General Education Board was beginning this type of work, Indian education needs very greatly to be looked upon as part of the state's educational program.

In another state, we stand ready to enter into a contract with the state department of public instruction, any time the state says the word, for the schooling of all the Indian children of that state, thereby abolishing our present—to my mind—indefensible method of dealing with local school boards. We are prepared to include in the contract funds to cover the salary of a state supervisor of Indian education under the state commissioner of education.

Both of these plans have been set up, it will be noticed, without waiting for the passage of the Swing-Johnson bill, which, as most of you know, would regularize this type of procedure for education, health and social welfare.[3] We can unquestionably carry on abundant cooperation without this legislation. It would not, as often erroneously assumed, "turn the Indians over to the States," but it would put the stamp of legislative sanction upon state-wide and partial plans for Federal-State work in all three fields.

(3) Still another direction in which we have made some tentative steps in that of encouraging signs of initiative on the part of Indians to work themselves free from dependence and take an interest in their own educational affairs. In the case of one tribe, the Choctaws, we recently arranged that we in the Indian Office would take no action regarding the education of their children without first consulting them. Under the law we spend for them some $55,000 annually of tribal funds for schooling. The principal chief of the tribe—who happens, by the way, to be a university graduate—has drawn up a plan whereby, in order to secure the education of Choctaw children, particularly orphans, in public schools rather than in institutions, children are to be placed in the families of other Indians and attend the public schools. Chief Dwight's plan contains some things that may be embarrassing to the Choctaws and the Government, particularly as it would, if fully carried out at once, probably put out of business several Catholic and Protestant Mission schools that are dependent upon Indian tuition for their existence. I feel sure, furthermore, that Mr. Dwight has not fully realized the difficulties in the placement of seventy-five children, and we shall try to get him to visit child-placing agencies to learn something about it. The point is, however, that the Choctaws, through him (for Mr. Dwight is acting as the result of a decision formally reached at a meeting of the tribe) are not only determined to have their people part of the main current instead of being isolated from it, but are plunging in to do their own experimenting as good citizens should, rather than waiting for the Federal or the state government to do something. Part

[3] This bill passed one house of Congress at the last session.

of the Federal Government's end of Federal-State cooperation would seem to be to turn over to the state as many *active* Indian citizens as possible.

School Superintendents and Visiting Teachers

In the meantime, we are strengthening our Indian educational program. If it is to be real cooperation, we must have something to cooperate with. Congress has given us the money for significant changes in the personnel of the Indian Service, and we are making them. Mention has been made of the new positions as superintendents of schools on the reservations. On at least a dozen reservations or groups of reservations this coming year we shall have unusually well-qualified educational men in charge of the educational program. This is in addition to new heads for some of our most important schools, and represents the first attempt—at least in recent years—at real educational leadership out among the Indians, away from the non-reservation boarding schools. These men are all graduates of leading universities, with considerable advanced work in the field of modern education. They know state educational conditions and should be able to adjust their programs to both Indians and the state plans, working quite as much, furthermore, with local health and welfare agencies as with organized school forces.

We are banking even more heavily on visiting teachers for a number of our Indian jurisdictions. In some cases, we shall put such visiting teacher at a boarding school, to see to what extent the Indian children in that school can be taken care of where they belong—back in their own communities. We make no secret of the fact that we hope to eliminate gradually practically all the Government Indian boarding schools in this part of the country, but we do not intend to do this until a real study is made of each school and the necessary guarantee of follow-up of the children is obtained. In other cases we shall assign the visiting teacher to what is already a public-school situation and have her provide the kind of service rural visiting teachers under the national committee have rendered so successfully in recent years. We hope to put such a worker also with the new consolidated school at Turtle Mountain, North Dakota, where a sort of inverted Federal-State cooperation is under way, where there is an unusual opportunity to build up a community around the school, and where whites and Indians both should be gainers by an experiment in providing superior educational facilities in rural regions.

The Public's Attitude

It has been suggested that any real cooperation between Federal Government and the states depends upon the public's attitude—in attendance of Indian children at public schools, for example. It is only fair to say that most of the opposition that usually develops is not racial, but is based on actual or assumed health conditions. This particular opposition is rather easily allayed where community nursing and similar services are provided. The argument of mental inferiority soon falls—all the evidence we have indicates the capacity of Indians to get along with other children, once reasonably good environmental factors are made possible. That there is a real cultural loss in this merging of the groups is certain—one might wish it could be avoided, or at least that some of the survivals might be rescued and developed as a contribution of this group to the life of all of us.

There is one form of obstruction to Federal-State cooperation, however, that we meet at every turn, and only an enlightened attitude on the part of the general public can do anything about it. Wherever a Government Indian boarding school exists, it is likely to be regarded as an entrenched interest, and the question tends to become, not one of the needs of Indian children and youth, but of the business demands of the community. When the new head of Bismarck School entered upon his duties last year, the local paper served notice in an editorial that the community must watch out lest somebody take this business asset from them. When the commissioner of Indian Affairs closed a small California boarding school last year because it had obviously outlived its usefulness, a howl went up that is still being heard. And when Mekusukey School, Oklahoma, was abandoned a year ago because of its dilapidated condition, lack of tribal support and general uselessness, a local official wired us two pages in which we were told that "every brick in this noble edifice is sacred" (the precarious condition of these bricks was one of the reasons for closing) and ended with the statement that it looked to him as if this administration was determined to "put responsibility back upon the people!" On the other side of the picture, we have the people in one Western state taking counsel among themselves as to how they may secure from the Federal Government the largest Indian school plant in their state—one of the best of the service—for a junior college.

It has been suggested that people in the states who know the state's institutional needs look over the existing Indian school plants to see whether any of them could be spared by the Federal Government for necessary state institutions. This would in many instances be helpful in a program of Federal-State cooperation. In any case, the least one should expect is that the people of a community will be willing to look beyond immediate selfish interests and determine whether some other kind of a program might be better for Indians and for the rest of the community than the segregated boarding school.

EDUCATIONAL EVENTS

HOMELESS CHILDREN IN PORTUGAL

A REDUCTION in the number of homeless children to one third of the total in 1927 is an achievement Portugal will submit to the International Congress for the Protection of Children when it meets at Lisbon in October, according to a special dispatch to the *Christian Science Monitor*.

After consideration of the three branches of its work, judicial, hygienic and pedagogic, the delegates to the congress will make a round of visits to institutions of public assistance and education and to orphanages and reformatories in Portugal.

They will find, according to Dr. Machado Pinto, director of public assistance, that after failing to give much attention to the general welfare of children until a few years ago, Portugal has now taken the destitute children under supervision so well that whereas in 1927 there were 6,000 homeless in the state, to-day over 4,000 of these are happily sheltered and cared for.

Judicial action for minors has been greatly modified since 1925, and the old repressive penal system has been completely put aside. Dr. Alfonso Costa, one of the leaders of the republic when it was first proclaimed in Portugal, was the founder of the "tutorias" or homes for minors who are destitute or have committed slight delinquencies. These homes, which have been greatly improved, are considered to be models of this system.

The state allows an annual sum of 6,000 contos (about $290,000) for the tutelar and juridical services for children, part of which is supplied by the sale of products from the minors' agricultural colonies, and the workshops of various charitable institutions.

The state insures obligatory and gratuitous

instruction all over Portugal, and under its protection have been established the municipal schools, "tortorias," correctional colonies, orphanages, reformatories, homes, puericultural and educational institutions which exist all over the country.

An agricultural school was recently established, where destitute minors are not only taught to work the land, but also learn various crafts. Primary instruction is given them and those showing greater ability are afforded facilities to attend colleges and universities.

In the summer, children's colonies are organized in the country and at the seaside, chiefly by private enterprise, which also supports over 5,000 charitable schools and institutions, besides those under state protection.

EDUCATION IN INDIA

SOME general conclusions on the educational position in India are given in the annual volume on British India presented to Parliament recently. The *London Times Educational Supplement* states that the writer, Mr. I. M. Stephens, is of the opinion that as time has gone on, since the introduction of the last reforms eleven years ago, education ministers in the provinces have shown increasing courage, enthusiasm and initiative. He points to the gradual elimination of the old, one-teacher type of village school and the increasing attention paid to the grant-in-aid system. The "considerable decentralization of control" of which he writes is known to have some serious drawbacks, but he is able to state that many of the municipalities and local boards are exercising their increased responsibility wisely.

Mr. Stephens notes with special satisfaction the increasing attention devoted to the education of children belonging to the depressed classes or untouchables. Exclusive of Burma and Assam, the number of depressed class pupils reading in all kinds of institutions in British India is well over 1,000,000. The figure represents 3.5 per cent. of the total number of persons of the depressed classes in the seven provinces concerned, as against an all-India figure for all communities of 4.9. A satisfactory feature is the increase in the number of depressed class pupils reading in the ordinary school and in that of caste pupils reading in the special schools intended for the depressed classes. As was pointed out some time ago by a committee appointed by the Government of Bombay, it is most desirable that such intermingling should develop.

In secondary and collegiate education, the analyst notes an increasing amount of attention being given to the admitted defects of the system. It is well known that secondary education in India is at once excessive in quantity and defective in quality. While the number of pupils under instruction is greater than that of the posts which at present are available for them, the standard of instruction is poor, on account of faulty methods of tuition, lack of interest and of adequate qualifications on the part of the staff, absence of organized corporate life and physical training, the predominantly literary bias of the curricula and the usually mercenary ambitions of the pupils. Even at the best, only a small portion of India's population can hope to pass beyond the stage of secondary education, and it is therefore essential that this education should be sound and complete in itself. Hence a growing desire is manifesting itself to separate secondary and university education more effectively, confining each to its proper sphere and making the former self-contained. Vocational training is also becoming steadily more popular, under the pressure of the very serious and widespread unemployment among the literate middle classes.

The defects of university education, writes Mr. Stephens, are, within their own sphere, not dissimilar in nature and origin to those from which secondary education has been suffering. Originally the Indian universities were examining bodies, established primarily for testing the attainments of students in groups of colleges which individually were often widely separated both culturally and geographically from each other. They lacked adequate organization, staff and equipment. The post-war period has seen considerable improvements. The old universities, with one or two important exceptions, have been remodelled so as to be both teaching and examining bodies, and new ones are being established. Colleges are being reorganized, new methods of administration adopted and new courses of instruction introduced. A drawback has been undesirable competition by new colleges for students; but the growing tendency toward specialization in the teaching of particular subjects should prove an antidote. A useful function is served by the Inter-University Board, which was set up in 1926, to coordinate the work of the large number of universities scattered throughout India. This has already done much to collect information and stimulate thought regarding current university problems.

THE LIBERAL ARTS COLLEGE MOVEMENT

THE recently organized Liberal Arts College Movement is making steady progress. It has been under way only a year and a half, but it is gaining in power and influence all the time. About 250 institutions are already enrolled. It may be predicted that practically all liberal arts colleges will be in this movement before long. Headquarters have been established in Chicago at 3016 Pure Oil Building, with Dr. B. Warren Brown in charge. Dr. Brown is editing the *Liberal Arts College Bulletin* and is preparing literature for the colleges which may be used by them in their appeals to their constituencies. The office of the chairman of the committee, President A. N. Ward, of Western Maryland College, is now located at Westminster, Maryland. The committee of fifteen having charge of the movement is composed of the following:

A. N. Ward, *chairman,* Western Maryland College; W. G. Clippinger, *vice-chairman,* Otterbein College; George L. Omwake, *secretary,* Ursinus College; Guy E. Snavely, Birmingham-Southern College; J. W. R. Maguire, St. Viator College; Albert C. Fox, John Carroll University; Rees E. Tulloss, Wittenberg College; H. J. Burgstahler, Cornell College; Homer P. Rainey, Franklin College; H. H. Sweets, Board of Education, Presbyterian Church in the United States; John E. Bradford, Board of Education of the United Presbyterian Church; H. O. Pritchard, Board of Education of Disciples of Christ Church; Irving Maurer, Beloit College; Harry M. Gage, Coe College; W. J. McGlothlin, Furman University; Joseph H. Apple, Hood College, *treasurer;* B. Warren Brown, *executive secretary.*

A committee of one hundred, composed of prominent citizens of the country, is being organized. This committee will sponsor the movement, and President Hoover has consented to serve as chairman. The full committee will be announced later in the fall.

The second annual meeting of the Liberal Arts College Movement will be held at Cincinnati during the sessions of the annual meeting of the Association of American Colleges. A strong program is being arranged. Through the cooperation of the National Broadcasting Company and a group of educators interested in the future of the liberal arts college as a vital unit in our American educational system, a national radio program on the general theme of "The Liberal Arts College" has been arranged for Saturday, November 14, 1931. This national broadcast is a concerted effort to interpret the needs, the aims and the achievements of the American liberal arts college, to strengthen the appreciation of the public for the contributions the liberal arts college has made and is making to American civilization, and to enlist the sympathetic cooperation and support of the people in the enhancement of the services that colleges are rendering.

The national directors who have general charge of the program are:

Mrs. Cleveland E. Dodge, trustee of Wells College; Albert C. Fox, dean, John Carroll University; Robert L. Kelly, executive secretary of the Association of American Colleges and of the Council of Church Boards of Education; Charles R. Mann, director of the American Council on Education; Albert N. Ward, president of Western Maryland College and chairman of the Liberal Arts College Movement; Albert St. Peter, 393 Seventh Avenue, New York, *executive secretary.*

Nine regional directors have been appointed to develop and intensify interest in the various sections of the country and to decentralize the administration of the program and aid in making arrangements for enlisting the cooperation of local agencies.

The sponsors of the broadcast have arranged the program in two parts in order that the full benefit may be enjoyed in different sections of the country. One part will consist of a half hour given over to talks by President Hoover, Dr. Robert L. Kelly, Mrs. Thomas J. Preston, Jr., Dr. John H. Finley and Dr. A. N. Ward, broadcast from the National Broadcasting Company studios. This part of the program will be given over the N. B. C. system and associated stations. The other part of the program is being left to the initiative of the college presidents in each community under the leadership of the regional directors. A local program for a half hour or longer immediately following or immediately preceding the national broadcast will be a very effective way of focusing attention and thought locally.

All colleges are invited to cooperate with the national broadcast, whether members of the Liberal Arts College Movement or not. All colleges cooperating are asked to plan alumni gatherings at convenient points on the evening of November 14, 1931, with place to be left in the program for listening-in during the national broadcast. Mr. Albert St. Peter, executive secretary of the national broadcast, has his office at 393 Seventh Avenue, New York City. Colleges interested in the broadcast should communicate with him.

LECTURES AT THE METROPOLITAN MUSEUM OF ART

The courses of lectures to be offered at the Metropolitan Museum of Art during the coming season cover a wide range of subject-matter. A pamphlet, containing a schedule and descriptions of the courses, designed for persons of various interests in the field of art has been issued by the museum.

Announcement is made of a series of Saturday afternoon conferences for workers, led by Roberta M. Fansler, museum instructor, to be held in the main hall of the museum, beginning on October 10 and continuing through May 29, with the omission of December 26 and January 2.

The course is intended particularly to meet the needs of men and women who are unable to come to the museum on week-days and who wish to make a serious study of museum material for the light it can throw on the culture and history of the human race. The material under discussion will be European art from the break-up of the Roman Empire to the year 1600.

The story hours for boys and girls and interested adults, illustrated by lantern slides and objects from the galleries, will begin on October 3. This series, continuing through May 29 next, will be given by Anna Curtis Chandler, museum instructor, in the lecture hall, on Saturdays at 1:45 P.M., and on Sundays, at 1:45 and 2:45 P.M. Miss Chandler will be assisted by Teresa Marie Bergamo, Susan Scott Davis, Agnes K. Inglis and Alice H. Nichols. The first talk will be in honor of Sir Walter Scott's centenary, and will be a story of jousting at a tournament with the Knight of Ivanhoe.

All Saturday afternoon and Sunday afternoon lectures, gallery talks, study hours and story hours are free to the public. Radio talks will be given during the season, to extend the museum's educational work. Public showings of the motion pictures, produced or distributed by the museum, are given on Thursday afternoons.

The courses for museum members, including lectures, gallery talks and study hours, beginning in October, will lead off with seventeenth-century French painters. The series offers gallery talks at The Cloisters and Saturday morning gallery talks at the museum for older children of members and story hours for younger children of members.

The Saturday and Sunday illustrated free lectures offer a wide range of subjects, dealing with the appreciation of the principles of art, the first opening on November 7 at 4 P.M., and the Sunday lectures on November 1, at the same hour. This series includes lectures and study hours for practical workers under the provisions of the Arthur Gillender Fund.

The courses of lectures offered free to teachers of the public schools of New York and to teachers and students of the training schools for teachers, the College of the City of New York and Hunter College will begin this month, and there will also be twenty-five courses under the auspices of New York University.

Courses for which fees are charged include the series listed for public school teachers, which are open to the public on payment of a tuition fee; study hours for employes of stores and of manufacturers, and special study hours for buyers and salespeople. These two are to be conducted by Grace Cornell, associate instructor at the museum.

SILVER ANNIVERSARY MEETING OF THE VINELAND LABORATORY

Meetings in celebration of the twenty-fifth anniversary of its research department were held at the Training School at Vineland, New Jersey, from September 3 to 5, with Henry H. Goddard, first director of the laboratory, as guest of honor. Some fifty leaders in the fields of education, psychology, sociology and medicine attended, and participated in the discussion of the various papers and addresses presented.

Edgar A. Doll, the present director of the research department, spoke on "The Trend of Future Research"; Arnold Gesell, director of the Yale Psycho-Clinic, on "The Study of Genetic Psychology"; Earl Barnes, prominent lecturer on education, on "Child Research and Social Progress"; William J. Ellis, state commissioner of institutions and agencies, New Jersey, on "Research in Public Welfare"; and E. R. Johnstone, director of the Training School, on "The Institution as a Laboratory." Dr. Goddard, following a banquet on the final evening of the meetings, also addressed the group, telling of his past association with the work, and commenting on research, present and future.

There was a general tendency to review the research activities of this laboratory since its inception. The Americanization of the Binet-Simon Scale, the initiation of the word "moron" to designate the highest level of mental deficiency, and the publication of "The Kallikak Family" and other important works are all traceable to this source.

With regard to the important findings of this and other child study centers, Mr. Johnstone, in his address, questioned whether the findings of the clinics are reaching their goals.

"Are there not teachers," he asked, "who do not know any more of the child who enters their rooms at the opening of school than that he has passed to their grades and must, in some way, be carried on to the next?

"Do the findings of the clinics reach the teachers, or are they too frequently considered too sacred for human hands or too technical for ordinary intelligent minds, and so find repose in the files of the clinic or of the principal? The testers and examiners are of the utmost importance. They must furnish the teacher with much more information than she ordinarily gets, if she is really to prepare the child for the future.

"To-day the physician, the psychiatrist, the psychologist and the school man all unite to tell us where we may aim to take the delinquents or those who are mentally deficient. Shall we not give the normal child the same advantages?"

Still questioning, Mr. Johnstone continued, "How far ahead shall the teacher look? Does that mean how far to-day? Or this year? Or shall she be given all the scientific information possible, so that she may envision him five or ten or even twenty years hence? May we not look forward to a much better understanding of a child's aptitudes and his possibilities? Every child who misses making a grade is a challenge to us. Every square peg in a round hole is an example of our ignorance.

"Shall we not see to it that the teacher shall know of the child's home life, the environment in which he lives outside of school hours, the educational and social standards of the home? I believe we must answer 'yes' to all these questions. There may have been plenty of reason for the teacher's lack of knowledge of those things in 1900, but we who believe in child research have no mean task before us, even in the enlightened year of 1931."

HEATHER G. COLLIER

RECENT APPOINTMENTS AT YALE UNIVERSITY

NEW members on the faculty of Yale University when it opens its 231st academic year on October 1 will include Charles Templeman Loram, chairman of the Native Affairs Commission and Director of Education at Natal, South Africa, an authority upon African native affairs, who joins the graduate faculty at Yale as Sterling professor of education, with especial interest in social science. Professor Loram, who is a member of the Mandates Commission, is a graduate of the University of Cambridge, and took his doctor's degree at Columbia University, which recently awarded him the medal reserved for distinguished foreign graduates.

Professor Edward Sapir, of the University of Chicago, noted anthropologist and linguist, joins the faculty as Sterling professor of anthropology and linguistics. Dr. Sapir will act as chairman of a new section of the department of the social sciences devoted to the development of study and research in the field of cultural anthropology. Through arrangements with the Peabody Museum and the Bishop Museum in Honolulu, this section will engage in field work, both in the United States and abroad. Professor Sapir will also be a member of the new department established in the graduate school to promote study and research in linguistics. In addition to his assignment to the graduate school, Dr. Sapir will be a member of the staff of the university's Institute of Human Relations.

Wilbur Marshall Urban, of Dartmouth College, comes to Yale as professor of philosophy. He is a graduate of Princeton University, and received his doctor's degree from the University of Leipzig. He has been successively reader in philosophy at Princeton University and professor of philosophy at Ursinus College, Trinity College and at Dartmouth College.

Thurman Wesley Arnold, dean and professor of law at West Virginia University, who has been visiting professor of law at Yale, becomes professor of law in the Yale Law School. Dr. Christian Richard Thurnwald, of the University of Berlin, has been appointed Bishop Museum visiting professor of anthropology. Dr. Thurnwald comes to Yale to give instruction and direct research in the problems of the Pacific area under the terms of the agreement by which Yale and the Bishop Museum at Honolulu are affiliated. Dr. Walter Richard Miles, who has been professor of experimental psychology at Stanford University since 1922, joins the Yale faculty as professor of psychology. Professor Eduard Prokosch becomes Sterling professor of Germanic languages, succeeding to the Sterling chair formerly held by Dean Emeritus Wilbur L. Cross, professor of English. In addition to Professors Loram and Sapir, Sterling professorships have been assigned to James Harvey Rogers, professor of political economy at Yale, and formerly professor of economics at Cornell University and the University of Missouri; and to Oystein Ore, now professor of mathematics at Yale University and formerly of the University of Oslo, Norway. These appointments have been made possible by the gift of $1,500,000 from the trustees of the estate of John W. Sterling, '64, for the endowment of five additional Sterling professorships. Another appointment under this gift is still to be made.

EDUCATIONAL NOTES AND NEWS

DR. ROBERT LEE STUART has assumed the presidency of Taylor University, succeeding President John H. Paul, who resigned last April.

DR. WALTER SCOTT ATHEARN, recently dean of the school of religious education and social service of Boston University, has been appointed to the presidency of Butler University.

THE overseers of Harvard University will act on September 29 on the selection of Kenneth B. Murdock as dean of the faculty of arts and sciences. He will be regarded as chief assistant to President Lowell.

THE sixty-fourth year of Cornell University will mark the beginning of the newly created office of provost of the university, with Dr. A. R. Mann, former dean of the state colleges of agriculture and home economics, the first incumbent. Dr. Cornelius Betten will serve as acting dean. Dr. Julian E. Butterworth, professor of rural education, will be director of the newly created graduate school of education. Professor C. A. Martin will serve as acting dean of the college of architecture during the absence of Dean George Young, Jr. Conant Van Blarcom, prominent builder of Cleveland, is the new superintendent of buildings and grounds, succeeding Charles E. Curtis, who retired last June.

RECENT additions to the faculty of the University of Michigan include: Professor M. S. Handman, formerly of the University of Texas, professor of economics; K. T. Rowe, assistant professor of English; C. C. Craig, assistant professor of mathematics; J. R. Abernethy, C. D. Jones and H. C. Van Engen, instructors in mathematics; C. J. D. Brown, E. P. Cheatum and K. A. Stiles, instructors in zoology; A. Benson and John Manley, instructors in physics; Lawrence Preuss, instructor in political science;

E. B. Greene and Norman Maier, instructors in psychology; S. H. Davies, instructor in philosophy; A. L. Hawkins, Robert Wetzel and M. L. Williams, instructors in English; B. O. Hughes, instructor in anthropology; S. A. Queen, lecturer in sociology; W. C. Steere, instructor in botany; V. A. Scanio, instructor in Romance languages; R. A. Winnacker, instructor in history.

THE following promotions at the University of Pittsburgh have been announced: in the department of chemistry, E. V. Hjort, from assistant professor to associate professor; in the department of psychology, Florence M. Teagarden, from associate professor to professor, and O. C. Held, from instructor to assistant professor; and in the department of zoology, G. M. McKinley, from assistant to instructor, and E. A Wolf, from assistant professor to associate professor.

DR. B. LAMAR JOHNSON has been appointed librarian and dean of instruction at Stephens College.

DR. BELISARIO PENNA, director of public health in Brazil, has been appointed minister of public instruction and health *ad interim*, in succession to Dr. Francisco da Silva.

PROFESSOR ERWIN PANOFSKY, of the University of Hamburg, and Professor Arthur Haseloff, of the University of Kiel, have been appointed to the faculty of New York University. They will offer new courses in the history of art.

MR. DAVID KIRBY, former president of Morris Harvey College, Barboursville, West Virginia, has been appointed professor of education at Davis and Elkins College to succeed Dr. C. W. Gwinn, who resigned to accept a similar position with the Pennsylvania State Teachers College, at Mansfield.

BY his own request Herbert W. Lull, after fifty-seven years of educational work, the last thirty-one as superintendent of schools at Newport, Rhode Island, was relieved from his duties on September 1, when he was made superintendent emeritus. Mr. Harold T. Lowe has been appointed to succeed Mr. Lull.

PROFESSOR O. V. JACKSON, for three years head of the department of Bible and religion at Cornell College, has resigned. He has accepted a position as chaplain of a church at Rolla, Missouri, and will conduct religious education work under the University of Missouri.

DR. C. RUFUS ROREM, formerly assistant dean of the school of commerce and administration at the University of Chicago, and since 1929 economist for the Committee on the Cost of Medical Care, at Washington, D. C., has been appointed by the Rosenwald Foundation to investigate medical care of persons of moderate means.

VAUGHN S. BLANCHARD, director of the health education department of the Detroit public schools, has been elected president of the Michigan Physical Education Association.

W. S. DEFFENBAUGH, chief of the division of American school systems of the U. S. Office of Education, has been assigned by William John Cooper, U. S. commissioner of education, to represent the Office of Education in connection with the study to develop a ten-year program of public education in Pennsylvania.

DR. FRANK AYDELOTTE, president of Swarthmore College, has been elected to membership in the Senate of Phi Beta Kappa.

MISS MARIE L. HINES, instructor in household administration at Western Reserve University, has been named director of dietetics for the university hospital group.

DR. DAVID STARR JORDAN, chancellor emeritus of Stanford University, died on September 19 at the age of eighty years.

JUDSON SUDBOROUGH HILL, president of the Morristown Normal and Industrial College, at Morristown, Tennessee, since 1881, died on September 14 at the age of seventy-seven years. His fifty years as president of the normal college, a pioneer Negro school, made him the oldest college president in point of service in the United States.

PROFESSOR FLETCHER HARPER SWIFT, of the school of education of the University of California at Berkeley, will present the final report of the committee of which he is chairman on a plan for an equalization fund for the state of California, at the annual meeting of the California Public School Superintendents' Association to be held at Riverside, October 5. The committee is composed of the following members: C. R. Holbrook, superintendent of schools, Santa Cruz, California; Walter E. Morgan, chief of the division of research and statistics of the California State Department of Education; Dr. Elmer H. Staffelbach, director of research of the California State Teachers Association, and Dr. Ivan R. Waterman, of the department of educational research and service of the San Francisco public schools.

A TWO-DAY conference on creative writing is to be held under the auspices of the school of letters of the State University of Iowa on October 30 and 31. There will be round tables on "Creative Writing and the Universities," "Creative Writing and Journalism" and "The Midwest in Letters." Among the speakers who will lead discussion are Addison Hibbard, Harry Hansen, Zona Gale, Floyd Dell and Ruth Suckow.

THE sixty-seventh convocation of the University of the State of New York will open on Thursday afternoon, October 15, with a reception in the rotunda of the State Education Building, and in the evening the first formal session of the convocation will be held in Chancellor's Hall, Chancellor Chester S. Lord, of Brooklyn, presiding. Sessions will be continued on the following day. "Health Education" will be the general theme of the convocation. With "Health Education and the Public Welfare" as the theme of the opening session, addresses will be given by Dr. Frederick G. Banting, of the University of Toronto, whose subject will be "Medical Research," and Dr. Ray Lyman Wilbur, U. S. Secretary of the Interior. Honorary degrees will be conferred after the addresses.

NEW courses to be given at the College of the City of New York include one on the history of education and one in educational sociology. Other courses are: Contemporary movements in education, problems of child behavior, educational measurements, intelligence tests, teaching in progressive and experimental schools, the management of a New York City school, visual instruction, health teaching, vocational information, play activities, current international relations, contemporary American problems and contemporary Russia.

AT the request of social agencies in the Rocky Mountain region and of Denver citizens interested in welfare work, the University of Denver has just opened a school in graduate professional training in applied social science, with Miss G. Eleanor Kimble as director. An administrative board, consisting of Chancellor F. M. Hunter, of the University of Denver, faculty heads of the university and officers and leaders of the principal social organizations of Denver, will supervise the work and give counsel.

A NUMBER of changes in the curriculum of the undergraduates of Yale University and in the requirements for the degree, as well as in the methods of instruction, are to be put into effect this year. The purpose of these changes is to emphasize the mastery of subject and method as the aim of the course of study rather than the acquisition of a given number of credits, according to the university announcement. Under the revised course of study midyear examinations and half-year courses are to be abandoned. There will be three reading periods during the year—a one-week period immediately preceding the examinations at the end of the year for all courses; two periods of two weeks each coming in each course at times designated by the instructor. The final examination in each course will be from three to four hours in length and will embrace the subject-matter of each course in a more comprehensive manner than at present, covering the field as outlined in advance by the instructor and not being confined to matter actually covered in lectures and recitations.

THE department of engineering extension of the Pennsylvania State College conducted its sixteenth annual industrial conference at State College during the week of September 7. Executives in many branches of Pennsylvania's diversified industries, business analysts, efficiency experts, plant foremen and economists of the college staff took part in the program. In conjunction with this meeting the department arranged a conference for retail merchants on Tuesday, September 8, the first of its kind on the campus. Many of the men attending this meeting, including department store executives, store managers and advertising experts, remained for the industrial conference.

A PLAN for merging the three theological seminaries of the American Lutheran Church—Capital University, Columbus, Ohio; Luther Seminary, St. Paul, Minnesota, and Wartburg Seminary, Dubuque, Iowa—was announced at the annual convention of the eastern district of that church. The announcement was made by Dr. Carl C. Hein, of Columbus, president of the American Lutheran Church, in response to a recommendation of a committee that activities in the educational field be curtailed. Dr. Hein said the effect of the merger, if carried through, would be to consolidate forces and eliminate duplication.

THE bulk of the $500,000 estate of Dr. Charles William MacFarlane, economist and engineer, who died on May 15, was left to Lehigh University because he believed "it would do more good if left to a smaller and less prosperous university." His will, as written in October, 1918, left most of the estate to Yale University, but in a codicil, dated February 24, 1927, Dr. MacFarlane revoked the bequest to Yale and named Lehigh as the beneficiary.

KAPPA DELTA PI, honorary society in education, announces an award of one thousand dollars for the best report of research dealing with the measurement of efficiency in teaching. The award is to be made in 1932.

THE Hershey Industrial School at Hershey, Pennsylvania, founded by M. S. Hershey, chocolate manufacturer, to educate orphaned boys, will be enlarged at a cost of $1,500,000 to accommodate 1,000 boys. The present school has an enrolment of 350 boys, who reside on the premises. Elementary and junior high-school academic and agricultural education work will be taught in the structures now standing, while the new buildings will provide quarters for orphaned boys of high-school age.

THE Daughters of the American Revolution will spend more than $150,000 in 1932 for child education, principally in the Southern mountains. Attention is being focused on the South because there the purest Anglo-Saxon stock in America has lived for generations with little contact with the outside world and practically no education.

THE Yonkers, New York, Museum of Science and Arts has, as reported in *Museum News,* made the first step toward carrying out its plan of extra-mural exhibits. With the cooperation of the director of art in the public schools and the principal of the Gorton High School a branch museum has been installed at the high school. In addition, arrangements have been made for the installation of exhibits in centrally located stores in the city, the display material provided by the museum being related to the goods sold in the stores. The exhibit material in the stores and in the school is changed from time to time. The teacher loan service of the museum has received recently twelve loan-carriage cases, made by the Saunders Trades School and given to the museum by the auxiliary. An enlarged board of museum commissioners is provided for by a city ordinance passed by the common council in December, making possible the appointment of commissioners representing a greater variety of community interests.

As the result of recent surveys of health activities, the Delaware State Board of Health has inaugurated a five-year plan of sanitation which will include improvement in milk pasteurization, eradication of typhoid, sanitation of canneries, food control work, sanitation of state institutions and oyster control work. According to *Delaware Health News,* it is hoped that this program will realize three objectives: the actual application of known sanitary laws to the sanitation of the community's water, milk, food, sewage, garbage and communicable disease; the actual provision of each citizen with the knowledge, means and incentive for promoting health and preventing disease, and the coercion of dissenters from accepted health and sanitary practices by legislation, wherever the action of such a dissenter might harmfully influence the health of others. Two inspectors were recently added to the state department of health, one of whom is to devote his entire time to collecting milk samples from all over the state, and the other practically all his time to the inspection of dairies. At present, it was pointed out, about 45 per cent. of the milk in the state is pasteurized, and the cows are 100 per cent. tuberculin-tested.

THE cooperation of American republics in

educational matters is on the way to realization, as the result of rapid progress in organizing the Inter-American Federation of Education, according to *The New York Herald Tribune*. Sixteen countries have appointed national cooperating committees, and five others—Colombia, Nicaragua, Paraguay, Peru and El Salvador—have promised their cooperation, although the personnel of committees is not yet known. The ministers of education of all constituent countries will constitute an advisory council. Plans call for an inter-American educational conference next year, probably at Mexico City, where it is expected that a long-range program will be adopted. The International Committee on Organization, besides the chairman, Dr. Glen Levin Swiggett, includes Dr. Helio Lobo, of Brazil, formerly consul general at New York, writer and diplomatist; Pericles Franco, of the Dominican Republic; Natalia G. V. de Morales, of Guatemala; Adolfo Berro Garcia, of Venezuela; Rafael Gonzales Rincones, of Venezuela, and a representative of Mexico, to be appointed.

DISCUSSION

A LIBERAL EDUCATION—PAST AND PRESENT

OLD as man is this question of what constitutes a liberal education, yet ever new. It probably puzzled the Neanderthals and helped to set those protruding brow ridges and primitive jaws that still intrigue the anthropologist. The Greeks, lovers of beauty, simple in their taste, thoroughly understood the theory of it and reached nigh unto perfection in all the arts. The Romans adapted it to practical life, contenting themselves with the reflection that "nothing is perfect in every part." The Middle Ages carried it to a fine art. Moderns proceeded to interpret, to analyze, to statisticize—and much was lost!

Seventy-five years ago our grandsires still clung to it in remnants, "it" being the classics, mathematics, history, and philosophy. Then, as some opine, came the dark. About twenty-five years ago vocationalists and "educationists" began to clamor: Why all this impractical twaddle? We must keep abreast of the times. Try this method; try that. Learn to do by doing.

Abreast of the times? Which times? Tomorrow is quickly a part of yesterday's sev'n thousand years.—Modernity? What is modern? Criticism of education? Hardly, that is hoary with the dust of ages. Hear the inspired invective of an educational iconoclast of the days when Nero fiddled: "I believe," he declared, upbraiding Professor Agamemnon—we have the words of Petronius for it—"I believe that our young men become absolute dolts in our colleges, because they see and hear nothing of real life there. . . . And if you will pardon me, it is you teachers above all others who have destroyed expression. . . . When originality flourished in art and literature, no 'doctor' from academic cloisters had ruined the intellect."

Liberal studies were all bosh to the *parvenus* of Professor Agamemnon's day. A prosperous canvas manufacturer, member of the local fire department—in Cumae, was it?—though he had mighty aspirations for his son, considered that he had become steeped quite enough in literature, and determined to have him "learn the trade of barber, auctioneer, or advocate, at least something that he could carry to the grave with him."

And the lazy-minded, epigrammatic Martial who called Domitian lord and king bitterly wailed: "Ah, what idiots my parents were to give me a liberal education! What good are literary critics and professors of eloquence to me? Break my trifling pens and tear up my poems, my frivolous muse, if a boot can give all this (elegance) to a cobbler." Elsewhere he admonishes: "Don't send your son to teachers and professors of liberal studies to have him waste his time over Cicero and Virgil. . . . If he shows an inclination to write verses, disinherit him. If he wishes to learn lucrative arts, have him learn to play the zither or flute for the dances" (guitar and saxophone would interpret it); "but if he is dull, make him an auctioneer—or a construction engineer!"

The younger Pliny was shocked at the spirit of the times, which was further registered by poor attendance or attention in the lecture halls, as he complained in a letter to Sosius Senecio (to whom Plutarch dedicated his Parallel Lives). The letter has such a deliciously familiar twang that the temptation is not to be resisted to translate it here *in toto:*

Gaius Pliny to his friend Sosius Senecio, Greeting.

This season has produced a great crop of poetasters. There's scarcely been a day in the whole month of April that someone hasn't given a lecture. I am delighted that literary pursuits are flourishing, and that the talents of men display and assert themselves; but people are slow to come to hear them. Most of the audience stand in the lobby and waste in gossip the time that they should be listening, and then they have some one report to them whether the lecturer has arrived or has finished his introduction, or has nearly completed his manuscript. At last they come in, but even then slowly and haltingly, and they don't stay through the lecture, but they leave before the end, some slyly, and stealthfully, others without embarrassment or any attempt at disguise. Heavens! Quite the contrary it was in my parents' day. They say that when the Emperor Claudius Caesar asked the reason for some applause that he heard while walking on the Palatine and was told that Nonianus was lecturing, he hurried to the lecture, appearing suddenly and unexpectedly. But nowadays even those with the most leisure, though invited far in advance and reminded again and again, either do not come at all, or if they do come, complain that they have wasted the day—just because they have not wasted it. But those enthusiasts are all the more laudable and praiseworthy who are not deterred from writing and public speaking by this laziness and indifference on the part of the audience. Now I for my part have hardly ever failed anyone. And certainly I have a great many friends, for there is scarcely anyone who loves literature who doesn't love me too at the same time. That's the reason why I have spent more time in the city than I intended. But now I am going to hunt up a quiet spot and write something myself—not to read in public, of course, for I don't wish those whose lectures I have attended to think that I have been not an auditor but a creditor. For as with everything else, so with the service of lecturing, the favor disappears, if a return is demanded. Fare you well!

Since the ancients are so modern in their practical bits of educational psychology, suppose we pry into the theory of their more thoughtful moments—not the theory of those who strove only for perfection, but of those who granted: *nihil est ab omni parte beatum.*

Cicero, the foremost orator and lawyer of his time, mayhap without a peer in any time, considered eloquence the chief qualification for a man in public life—the ability to sway an individual or a collection of individuals to a desired point of view, not only by conviction, but by wit and pathos and every charm of style or manner. Though recognizing natural endowment as a *sine qua non* of success, he laid extreme emphasis upon training—training that was partly technical, but strongly entrenched by liberal studies without which an orator becomes as sounding brass and tinkling cymbals. Law, political science, history, literature, including foreign language, and philosophy are among the subjects which he held to be essential for a successful lawyer or man of affairs. Add to these experience, observation, common sense, enthusiasm for the task, willingness to work, and one inevitably comes to his highest development, bringing his natural talents to their fullest powers.

Cicero is privileged to speak *ex cathedra* on the side of the professions, but for technical training, let us turn to a master builder, Vitruvius Pollio, who published a treatise on "Architecture" (covering building construction in general) in that great era of construction, the Augustan Age of the Roman Empire. His first chapter, interestingly enough, is on the education of an *Architectus,* that is, what we should call to-day a "construction engineer."

Vitruvius, like Cicero, starts with the assumption that every art involves theory and practice; that with practice alone an engineer will never reach a position of authority, while with theory alone he will find shadow, not substance. The two combined will bring achievement and authority. The formidable list of subjects which Vitruvius considered absolutely essential for the training of a construction engineer includes language and literature, drawing, geometry, astronomy, much history, philosophy, and—it may be noted with some wonderment—law, medicine and music.

It is diverting to mark the reasons, some of them naïve, which this master builder assigned for his choice of subjects. The study of language and literature, of course, is primary, as enabling one to convey his ideas to others, "to effect sounder records for posterity." Fortunate, indeed, would it be for posterity, had Vitruvius himself been a greater master of language. Although he has been "the object of continuous professional study from the Renaissance down to the present day," many an envied secret still lies concealed in his pages, so obscure and unintelligible, at times, is his meaning. In comparatively recent years, the late Professor Sabine, of Harvard, by reinterpreting certain passages, solved a number of important problems concerning acoustics.

The need of drawing, geometry and physics for engineers is obvious. Astronomy Vitruvius included for matters of location, climate, and the theory of sun dials. A wide knowledge of history he considered necessary in order to comprehend and explain ideas underlying the employment of ornamental parts. Philosophy is very important because no work can be rightly done without honesty and incorruptibility, and philosophy stresses not the profession but the individual, turning the attention to requisites not perquisites, rendering one courteous, just and honest. Law is highly desirable, at least enough to enable one to know about party walls, dripping eaves and drains, and to keep householders and contractors out of litigation. A knowledge of medicine is of advantage for questions of climate, air, healthiness of sites, and the use of different waters.

But the most interesting requirement urged by Vitruvius is the principles of music, recommended in order to give knowledge of canonical and mathematical theory and to tune projectiles to the proper key so that the strings will work in unison. All who are interested in amplifiers and in sound transmission will find entertaining reading in Vitruvius' section on the bronze contrivances in theaters which were "placed in niches under the seats in accordance with the musical intervals on mathematical principles. These vessels were arranged with a view to musical concords or harmony, and apportioned in the compass of the fourth, the fifth, and the octave, and so on up to the double octave, in such a way that when the voice of an actor fell in unison with any of them, its power was increased, and it reached the ears of the audience with greater clearness and sweetness." (The translation is Morris Hicky Morgan's with tense changes).

No one has a right, Vitruvius thought, to claim to be a professional engineer until he has climbed step by step to what he called the holy heights of construction. He saw a common bond of union and intercourse between all studies; that is what makes it possible to select and grasp such a wide range. One does not have to excel in each branch, but he should not be deficient in any. A liberal education forms a single body made up of many members.

And what did Professor Agamemnon retort (for Petronius) to his Neronian detractor? "Indeed," he said, "teachers are not responsible for the practices of the schools. If they don't lecture as the young people like, 'they will be left alone in the colleges,' as Cicero says. Like those who fawn upon the well-to-do to get invited out, they plan primarily for what they think will best satisfy their audience. . . . A professor is like a fisherman, if he does not put on his hook the bait which he knows will attract the little fish, he will have a long wait on his rock without any hope of a catch. . . . It is parents who deserve rebuke, for not wishing their children to become proficient through stern discipline. In their over-ambition and hurry to realize their hopes, they thrust their charges into a profession, while they are still babes and ill-trained." Professor Agamemnon's advice was that it should be of first importance to perfect the character of youth by the rigid law of simplicity and temperance, and to realize that a thing is not of the highest value simply because boys like it: those who show an eagerness for knowledge should be allowed to proceed step by step, reading much, training their minds by the precepts of philosophy, and acquainting themselves with high standards for imitation.

Where have we been—in the present or the past? Simply in the great world of ideas where we have discovered that the eternal verities are changeless; that truth is truth, and man is man, and ever the twain shall meet only through constant seeking and much disagreement between man and man. Can it be that a liberal education is a state of mind, a method of approach? Enthusiasm for the task, a willingness to work, a realization of the common bond of union and intercourse between all studies, an eagerness to know, proceeding step by step at one's best pace, a happy running to the source of knowledge—these have been characteristic marks of the cultivated man from the Neanderthals to the latest thinker, and this is the educational philosophy which the colleges to-day are endeavoring to inculcate through various experiments. Especially interesting among these experiments is the method of "reading for honors" which does away with "courses," breaks down departmental barriers, and opens the way to enchanting exploration; the system particularly attracts serious students, for it aims to prevent the waste of brains which one critic deplores in American education, and offsets the tenacity of methods of savagery which another detects. Clearly, culture, the illusive, is obtainable only by him who cultivates, rigorously and dauntlessly, through his own efforts. The professional man has it, the engineer has it, the scientist has it, the craftsman has it, the layman has it, if, eager and determined to know his domain in its entirety, he has been led into the liberalizing fields that underlie or bound or penetrate his own confines. A liberal education, indeed, appears to be something akin to what his faith is to a Quaker; an individual "experience" establishing closer communion with truth.

E. H. Brewster

Swarthmore College

FREE EDUCATION IN COLLEGE

The article on "College Tuition Trends" in the issue of School and Society for May 30, 1931, closes with the observation that public colleges and universities can not be considered in any plan of having institutions of higher learning charge their students with the cost of their education. "Their policy is to offer higher education at the expense of the state, thereby making it virtually free to students."

Is it not time that educators were beginning to face the question whether this should be the policy of public colleges and universities? It would perhaps mean political suicide for any head of a public institution to suggest that students ought to pay a fair charge for their education beyond high school. But there are many others whose experience has doubtless convinced them that not everybody should go to college and that those who are allowed to go at the expense of the state should be required to demonstrate their fitness for college by something more convincing than the fact of high-school graduation. Those who know should speak. It is not fair to the essential work of the state, in providing primary and secondary education for all, that increasing sums of tax-money should be poured into institutions of higher learning to give special advantages to some young people without cost to themselves.

It is possible that the best educational opinion will finally settle on the proposition that all young persons should go to college, because even though many of them are not well prepared and are not interested and are not intellectual, they get more out of college than they would get from four years spent anywhere else. But that proposition is not accepted yet, and there is considerable evidence that it is not true. College days for those who are not interested in college work encourage the formation of bad habits rather than of good ones. If we finally conclude that everybody ought to go to college, then we ought to prepare to place colleges within easy reach of youth everywhere, as we have placed our high schools.

The urge to go to college to-day does not come from a reasoned conviction that it is good for everybody to go to college. It comes from the political necessity of getting more students to get more appropriations from the state legislature in order to build more buildings to get more students to get more appropriations, and so on around the endless circle. In the case of private colleges, the political reason is lacking but the financial reason remains, for these colleges are more dependent on tuition receipts than are state-maintained institutions. Neither public nor private colleges, with a few glorious exceptions, have made any concerted efforts to test the fitness of applicants for college education. To give such education to the unfit is a waste of private funds or of state taxes. In either case it should be stopped.

This letter will be misunderstood. I believe that every boy and girl who graduates from high school and is qualified to do college work ought to have that opportunity, but not at the expense of the state. If the student's family can not pay a reasonable tuition charge, liberal scholarship arrangements should care for him. But after having made adequate provision for those who otherwise would be barred by poverty from a college education, the state has no obligation to educate in college or professional school the sons and daughters of the middle and upper classes at the expense of the taxpayers. Nor should the state receive into its colleges any person, rich or poor, who is not qualified by interest, ability and training to do college work.

Unless the policy of state-maintained institutions of higher learning to offer their courses practically without cost to the students but at the expense of the taxpayers is radically changed in the next few years, we shall be training a generation of parasites. If the state owes to every young person free of charge the superior advantages for profitable employment that come with a college education, every young person will begin to feel that the state owes more than the training. Why should it not also owe the job? If the state gives the college training free, why should it not also guarantee the job and the living? But the state owes no man a living. And the state owes to none except those relatively few who are otherwise barred by poverty the opportunities of college education without cost. Let young people get their college education as they must later get their livelihood, by paying as they go.

CHAS. J. TURCK

CENTRE COLLEGE,
DANVILLE, KENTUCKY

SPECIAL CORRESPONDENCE

STATE REGULATION OF PRIVATE SCHOOLS

ALTHOUGH every state in the Union has an excellent public-school system, there are many parents who prefer to have their children attend a private school, principally denominational, where they have to pay tuition and where, in many instances, the institution is not nearly as well equipped as are the public schools. During 1928, more than 280,000 pupils were enrolled in private high schools and academies.[1] In addition, there was a much greater enrolment in the private elementary schools and denominational colleges.[2]

"Practice in the United States, as well as constitutional or statutory provisions, charges the several state legislatures with the responsibility of providing a system of schools for all the children of the state adequate to their needs and efficient in fulfilling the educational ideals of the people of the state. Education is a state responsibility."[3] While citizens are compelled by law, through taxation, to support public schools, they may send their children to private educational institutions.[4] However, non-public schools receive no subsidy from the government.[5] They are supported by private funds. Strict justice would exempt the parents of the pupils who attend these private schools from taxation for the public schools.[4] Such a model of tolerance is the system of the Province of Quebec where the subsidies voted by the legislature for schools, Catholic or non-Catholic, are apportioned by the Superintendent of Public

[1] "Statistics of Private High Schools and Academies," Bureau of Education, Dept. of Interior, Washington, D. C., 1929.

Denomination	Schools	Students
Baptist	68	7,145
Congregational	15	1,265
Episcopal	82	7,310
Friends	23	2,571
Latter Day Saints	2	1,337
Lutheran	26	3,016
Methodist	71	8,411
Methodist Episcopal South	10	933
Presbyterian	60	5,405
Roman Catholic	1,345	158,612
Seventh Day Adventist	35	3,159
Other denominations	52	5,623
Nonsectarian	659	75,662

[2] No figures available.

[3] "A Manual of Educational Legislation," Bureau of Education, Dept. of the Interior Bulletin, 1926, No. 22, Washington, D. C., p. 2, 1927.

[4] Philip Schaff, "Church and State in the United States," Charles Scribner's Sons, N. Y., p. 74, 1888.

[5] Thirty-two states exempt school property from taxation.

Instruction, proportionately to the number of pupils enrolled during the previous year.[6]

The various states have passed laws regulating the private schools. "The nature of state regulation of a private school generally depends upon the class of such school and the scope of its work. If it is a degree-conferring institution, it must get from the state the power to confer degrees, and incorporation usually accompanies this grant of power. Methods of forming corporations, for educational purposes in general, vary in the different states. The methods, however, seem to fall into three divisions:

(1) Incorporation is effected by special act of the Legislature in

Connecticut	Maryland	New Jersey
Maine	Massachusetts	North Carolina
Delaware	New Hampshire	Vermont

(2) Incorporation may be effected either under general laws or by special act of the Legislature in

Dist. of Columbia	Indiana	South Dakota
	Louisiana	Tennessee
Florida	Ohio	Utah
Illinois	Rhode Island	Virginia

(3) In all the other states educational corporations are formed under general laws; which usually provide that a certain number of persons, varying as to number in different states, may be incorporated for educational purposes by filing in a specified office or offices, usually with the Secretary of State, and in some cases also with the County Recorder of Deeds, a certificate setting forth the name of the institution, the number of trustees, the object for which they wish to be incorporated, the location of the institution and sometimes other pertinent facts such as the amount of property to be held. Generally, the filing of this certificate is all that is required and thereupon the proper officer, usually the Secretary of State, issues the certificate of incorporation. There is, however, an important restriction in some states which requires that persons desiring to be incorporated must be citizens or residents of the United States and, in some cases, of the state where incorporation is sought. Educational institutions may be incorporated under general laws in about two-thirds of the states.

"There is a very large number of private schools and institutions in this country which are unincorporated. The regulation of schools of this type may be considered in two parts, (1) general regulation, and (2) specific regulation. Unincorporated private schools receiving only pupils not subject to compulsory education laws are usually subject only to general regulation such as required conformance to accepted moral standards, etc. Private schools, either incorporated or unincorporated, receiving children subject to compulsory school attendance laws, are subject to greater regulation, which is referred to above as specific."[7]

These specific regulations will be discussed now in detail. For the purpose of enforcing compulsory education of required standards, private schools in the following states must have the approval of public school authorities:

Alabama	Michigan	Pennsylvania
Indiana	Missouri	Rhode Island
Iowa	Nebraska	South Carolina
Kansas	New Hampshire	South Dakota
Kentucky	New Mexico	Virginia
Maine	New York	Washington
Maryland	North Dakota	West Virginia
Massachusetts	Ohio	

In some cases such approval is granted on the basis of submitted data and without visitation.

The laws of the following states provide for the inspection and supervision of private schools by public agencies:[8]

Alabama: Inspection of convents, reformatories, etc., as to sanitary conditions, manner of conduct and treatment of inmates.

Connecticut: State Board of Education may inspect registers.

Florida: Inspection of convents, reformatories, etc., as to general condition and treatment of inmates.

Illinois: Such charitable institutions as are educational in character may be visited.

Indiana: Schools attended by children of compulsory education age are to be "open to the inspection of local and state attendance and school officers."

[6] England and Belgium subsidize private schools; Holland and Hungary support them. *Statistical Year-book of Quebec*, p. 75, 1922.

[7] "State Regulation of Private Schools," Bureau of Education, Dept. of Interior, Washington, D. C., p. 2, 1928.

[8] "Oregon School Cases," Belvedere Press, Baltimore, Md., p. 925, 1925.

Kansas: The state board of education has the power of visitation, to see that the laws regarding the use of the English language and the teaching of civil government are enforced.

Michigan: The superintendent of public instruction and his agents may "investigate and examine" private schools as to "sanitary conditions, courses of study and qualification of teachers."

Nebraska: County and city superintendents must inspect private schools at least twice a year, regarding Americanism, course of study and qualification of teachers.

New York: The commissioner of education "shall cause to be inspected and supervise the instruction" in patriotism and citizenship.

Pennsylvania: Inspection of all children's institutions as to instruction, discipline, care, etc.

South Carolina: Private schools "must be supervised by the county superintendent of education or by the supervisor of public schools."

South Dakota: Private schools must be approved. The county superintendent "shall exercise the right of visitation and inspection" of private schools and private instruction.

Washington: Private schools should be examined and approved by the county superintendent. All institutions caring for children are to be visited twice a year.

West Virginia: Private schools must be approved for purposes of compulsory education. The state board of education is to supervise all teacher-training departments.

Wisconsin: Attendance records are to be open to the inspection of proper authorities.

Compulsory school attendance laws in each of the forty-eight states apply to all schools,[9] public or private. Furthermore all states have some regulations governing schoolhouse construction, and at least three fourths of the states have laws on the sanitary features of the building.[10]

States which require stated reports are:[11, 12]

Alabama—Statistical
Connecticut—Statistical
Delaware—Statistical
Illinois—Statistical
Indiana—Enrolment and attendance
Iowa—Statistical
Kentucky—Attendance
Maine—Enrolment
Maryland—Enrolment and attendance
Massachusetts—Statistical
Michigan—All reports required of public schools
Minnesota—All reports required of public schools
Mississippi—All reports required of public schools
Nebraska—Enrolment and attendance
New Hampshire—Statistical
New Jersey—Statistical
New Mexico—Attendance
New York—All lawfully required reports
Ohio—Enrolment and attendance
Pennsylvania—Enrolment and attendance
Rhode Island—All reports required of public schools regarding enrolment, attendance and instruction
South Carolina—Statistical
South Dakota—Attendance
Texas—Enrolment
Washington—Attendance
West Virginia—Attendance and instruction
Wisconsin—Attendance

Private school teachers must obtain certificates or licenses to teach from the public-school authorities in Alabama, Michigan, Nebraska, South Dakota.[13]

"In some states the power of the public school authorities to approve or disapprove the school has been construed to include the approval or disapproval of the teacher."[12]

The laws of the following states specify that the instructor must be competent: Arizona, California, Kansas, Minnesota, Mississippi, New Jersey and New York.

The curriculum requirements of twenty-nine states are:[14]

Alabama: Enumerated branches are to be taught in every elementary school.

California: The several branches taught in the public schools.

Colorado: Enumerated branches.

Connecticut: Enumerated branches.

Delaware: The subjects prescribed for elementary schools.

[9] Society of the Sisters *v.* Pierce, 296 Fed., 928.

[10] "A Manual of Educational Legislation," *Dept. of the Interior Bulletin,* 1926, No. 22, Washington, D. C., p. 67, 1927.

[11] "Oregon School Cases," Belvedere Press, Baltimore, Md., p. 930, 1925.

[12] "State Regulation of Private Schools," Bureau of Education, Dept. of Interior, Washington, D. C., p. 3, 1928.

[13] School laws for various States.

[14] "Oregon School Cases," Belvedere Press, Baltimore, Md., pp. 926–928, 1925.

Georgia: "The ordinary branches of an English education."
Idaho: Enumerated branches.
Illinois: Such branches as are taught in public schools.
Indiana: Enumerated branches.
Iowa: Enumerated branches.
Maine: "Minimum subjects prescribed for approved schools."
Maryland: Subjects usually taught in public schools.
Massachusetts: All studies required by law.
Michigan: Same as public schools.
Montana: Enumerated subjects.
Nebraska: Substantially the same instruction as in public schools.
Nevada: Equivalent instruction.
New Hampshire: Substantially the same subjects as in public schools.
New Jersey: Enumerated branches.
New Mexico: Courses of instruction approved by the state board of education.
New York: Enumerated branches.
North Dakota: Branches usually taught in public schools.
Ohio: Enumerated branches.
Oregon: Branches usually taught in public schools.
Pennsylvania: Enumerated branches.
Rhode Island: "Substantially equivalent" instruction.
South Carolina: Such subjects as are required in public schools.
South Dakota: Enumerated branches.
Vermont: "The same education" as in public schools.

The teaching of special subjects: the constitution, civics, and patriotism:

Alabama: Community civics.
California: The duties of citizenship and local self-government. The Constitution of the United States, in the 8th grade and throughout high school.
Connecticut: Citizenship.
Delaware: The Constitution of the United States and Delaware, in the 8th grades, throughout high school and in colleges and universities.
Idaho: The Court of the United States, in the 6th and 8th grades, throughout high school and colleges and universities.
Iowa: Civics in elementary and secondary schools.
Kansas: Civil government, patriotism and the duties of citizenship.
Kentucky: Constitution of the United States in 8th grade, and throughout high school.
Louisiana: Instruction in the constitutional system of the state and national government and the duties of citizenship.
Maine: Civil government, in all elementary and high schools.
Michigan: Constitutions of the United States and Michigan, in the 8th grade and throughout high school.
Minnesota: The Declaration of Independence and the Constitution of the United States, in the 8th grade and throughout high school.
Nebraska: Civil government, state and national.
New Hampshire: Constitutions of the United States and New Hampshire, in the 8th grade and throughout high school.
New Jersey: Constitution of the United States, beginning with the 7th grade, lasting through high school.
New York: Patriotism and citizenship.
Ohio: American government and citizenship.
Oregon: Constitution of the United States.
Pennsylvania: Civics in elementary school. The Constitution of the United States in the 8th grade and throughout high school.
Rhode Island: Government of Rhode Island, in the 7th and 8th grades; the Constitution and government of the United States and Rhode Island, in high school.
South Dakota: Patriotism throughout the elementary course. Constitutions of the United States and South Dakota, in 8th grade and throughout the high school.
Texas: Good citizenship.
Utah: Constitution of the United States.
West Virginia: Civics and the Constitutions of the United States and West Virginia.

In addition, twenty-eight states have passed laws concerning teaching in the English language.[15]

Recently the Supreme Court of the United States ruled that a state has the power, under the Federal Constitution, to provide free textbooks for children in private schools.

A few states require medical inspection:[16]

Florida: All school children shall be examined once each school year.
Indiana: There shall be medical inspection of all persons attending or employed in all schools.
New Hampshire: A medical inspector shall be assigned to each school.
Rhode Island: Medical inspection of all schools shall take place at least once each year.

[15] "Oregon School Cases," Belvedere Press, Baltimore, Md., pp. 928–930, 1925.

[16] "Oregon School Cases," Belvedere Press, Baltimore, Md., p. 931, 1925.

Vermont: Medical inspection of private schools shall take place when requested.

All teachers in Colorado, Ohio, Oklahoma, Oregon, Pennsylvania and South Dakota are required to take an oath of allegiance.

The only states that have attempted seriously to restrict the liberties of private schools were Michigan, Washington and Oregon. These states had the proposition placed on referendum, but Oregon was the only state that succeeded in passing the law on the referendum in 1922. This law required all children between 8 and 16 to attend a public school. "However, while not expressly prohibiting private schools, this act, which was to become effective September 1, 1926, was in effect a prohibition of patronage to such schools. On March 31, 1924, the Federal district court issued an injunction restraining the state of Oregon from enforcing the act upon the ground that it was unconstitutional. The issuance of this injunction was affirmed by the United States Supreme Court on June 1, 1925. Hence the Oregon law was never put into operation as it was declared unconstitutional before the date it was to become effective."

No supporter of the private schools can justly maintain that the regulation of such institutions in the United States is rigid.[17] His only concern might be that besides voluntarily supporting his denominational school because of conscientious scruples, he is taxed to support an institution from which he derives no direct benefits.

W. E. BELLEAU

QUOTATIONS

BRITISH CHILDREN AT THE SEASIDE

IT may well be the instinct of the islander, penned in cities, that impels him to take advantage of the new facilities of transport to the seaside. In any case, a centrifugal movement of population to the coast during the summer months is an outstanding fact in these days, an exodus which on a single bank holiday, by railway alone, is reckoned in millions. The same tale is told by the recent multiplication and growth of seaside resorts. Figures supplied from many of these places show that the extent of popular bathing, especially by children, is unprecedented. The question is a pertinent one: how are these children from the cities affected by the sea climate and by daily immersion in the sea?

In countries with a considerable seaboard, medical men are taking an increasing interest in marine health resorts. Witness the formation in 1914 of the International Congress of Thalassotherapy and its recent well-attended meetings in Italy, Roumania and France. In Germany there are associations of medical practitioners on the Baltic and the North Sea, and in Belgium a new international journal, *La Cure Marine,* has appeared in the present year. All these organizations have for their object the precise study of the effect of marine climates and bathing on health at all periods of life. Like some branches of physical medicine, it needs to be reclaimed from irrational empiricism. Dr. Ceresole in Italy, among others, has pointed the way to a much-needed physiopathological study of thalassotherapy.

It is often difficult, at home, to draw a clear line between normal and defective health, but a holiday at the seaside, with its abrupt change of climate and exposure to cold in bathing, often furnishes the test by which abnormal conditions of health may be detected. It is, to some extent, a therapeutic classification for delicate children. Normal school children and jaded but healthy adults can always, and immediately, find at the sea the complete change of scene, with the tonic influences of light, air and water, which are all that they need for a summer health holiday. But this is not at all the case with perhaps the equal number of persons in subnormal health who are to be found at the seaside; such are the catarrhal, nervous and chilly children, who perhaps are never ill and never well, but in whom a low and sensitive condition is a standing menace, and invites

[17] The strictest laws are probably found in Alabama, Michigan, Nebraska and South Dakota, where inspection, required reports, licensing of teachers and approval of the school are provided for in the laws.

a variety of infections. For them the strong prescription of the sea must obviously be applied with care. The use of sea climates and bathing for delicate children presupposes in the first place a selection and differentiation of cases referred to the coast, whether it be to the marine hospital, the convalescent home or the holiday center. It also presupposes observation after arrival, and especially the regulation of exercise, rest, degree of exposure to sun, air or sea, according to the reactions produced; and, lastly, proper measurements and records. Children tolerate so much that it may not be recognized that they react in the most varied ways to physical influences. The marine climate, and especially bathing in the open sea, with its low temperature and risk of shock, enormously increase the cooling of the body and make a heavy demand upon heat production, metabolism and nervous energy, and where these powers are defective may evoke unfavorable reactions, which time, patience and a course of reeducation could easily have averted.

It is on account of the frequent and gratuitous ill-effects—chills, catarrhs, gastro-intestinal disturbances, rheumatism, heart symptoms, nervous disturbances, febrile "sur-saturation"—that some seaside practitioners in different countries have expressed grave doubts whether, on the whole, sea-bathing for children is not more injurious than beneficial. They have been painfully impressed by its too prevalent abuses: the unwilling with the willing prematurely hurried into the water, without acclimatization, and perhaps immediately after a meal; the bathing in all weathers, too frequently repeated, and much too prolonged; the endless wading on the shore; and the spectacle of children blue with cold and shivering in the wind from excessive and uncompensated exposure. These questions have been under discussion by the new section of hydrology and climatology at the British Medical Association's annual meeting at Eastbourne. It is evident from reports from the British coasts that medical officers of health and practitioners, as well as local authorities, are not unaware of the dangers to which delicate children are exposed. At the more progressive seaside resorts efforts have been recently made to guard against them. Some, like Hastings, have published rules and hints for bathers. Others, like Margate, have set up excellent shelters on the beach and provide hot drinks and hot foot-baths after the bath, which are a great assistance to favorable reaction. In many places hot sea-baths, as at Eastbourne, have been installed for the use of those for whom cold open-air bathing is injurious; and these, as well as the marine climate, have been reported upon as beneficial for convalescents and others, including rheumatic subjects, who are, temporarily perhaps, in a low and exhausted condition of health. Another provision of special value for delicate children is the sheltered, comparatively shallow swimming pool of fresh sea water, as at Lowestoft, Hunstanton and Southport. In sunny weather the warmth and shelter of these pools make the water possible and pleasant for chilly subjects, and an effective means for the gradual reeducation to cold.

Tuberculous children are now treated in many countries with striking success on the coast, and the needs of non-tuberculous children are too little considered. In addition to the catarrhal, the nervous and the rheumatic, very many children are subnormal in nutrition and development, in peripheral circulation and in resistance to cold. These common conditions, equally with non-pulmonary tuberculosis, are amenable to physical treatment at the seaside. Dr. Carl Häberlin, whose opening paper we publish this week, gives a summary of his work for non-tuberculous children at Wyk, on the further side of the North Sea, where he directs a hospital of 300 beds, with various convalescent homes. He describes the methods and technique which belong to the marine hospital, especially the tests by which the reactions of children under treatment can be measured, and the results of treatment graphically recorded. In another place he has set forth the organization by which children from Berlin and Hamburg are selected by medical officers of friendly societies, schools and hospitals, and the ministry of health, and distributed to appropriate town clinics, marine hospitals or homes and holiday colonies, and has also described the system of subsequent after-care.

We are glad to hear that there is some prospect of an effective organization of medical men interested in the problems of thalassotherapy in this country. The 6,000 miles of seashore of the British Islands, with their temperate and invigorating climates, have a great variety of air and shelter, at different seasons, on the North Sea, and on the Atlantic, and on the long range of the South Coast. Such a provision of nature is unrivalled in Europe, and suggests large possibilities for the health of a crowded industrial population. It is possible that, especially for the children from towns and cities, something like a national preventive and curative régime might be made available at the seaside, under medical men of special experience and training.—*The British Medical Journal.*

EDUCATIONAL RESEARCH AND STATISTICS

COMPARATIVE DATA FROM A SAMPLING OF LIBERAL ARTS STUDENTS IN NEW HAMPSHIRE, TENNESSEE AND ALABAMA

THE following tables summarize information collected by the writer from his classes in education in liberal arts colleges in New Hampshire in 1927, Tennessee in 1929, and Alabama in 1930. The content of the responses, as well as the general spirit of readiness exhibited in writing them, indicated a sincere effort to be accurate.

(1) Alabama women are accelerated approximately a year in comparison with those of New Hampshire and Tennessee, due probably to summer school attendance both secondary and collegiate. The comparative retardation of the men at all three colleges presents a problem.

(2) The proportion having graduated from private secondary schools was largest in New Hampshire and smallest in Alabama. There are historical reasons why the reverse might be expected.

(3) When asked to state in a sentence or two their notion of true success in life, the two first-named groups were given the leading suggestion "wealth, fame, service to others, and so on." This lead was omitted with the Alabama group. Exclusively altruistic ideals are found more prominently among those to whom "service to society" had been suggested. If the third sample exhibits more faithfully the actual day-by-day point of view of students, an important problem of college teaching would seem to be indicated.

(4) Plans for a career in teaching show a reduced percentage in 1930 on the part of these education classes.

(5) The Southern groups report a larger number of hobbies.

(6) The students listed their three best liked college subjects in order of preference. A ranking of all the subjects named gives the first four places to English, mathematics, French and history in order as listed.

(7) Because of the fact that about two months had elapsed following the close of the preceding summer vacation, the students requested that their reports of vacation activities

CLASSIFICATION

		Freshman	Sophomore	Junior	Senior	Graduate	Total	Aggregate
New Hampshire	Men		30	14	4	1	49	
	Women		48	5	1		54	
	Both		78	19	5	1	103	103
Tennessee	Men	1	18	2	10		31	
	Women	7	22	12	8		49	
	Both	8	40	14	18		80	80
Alabama	Men			1	8	1	10	
	Women		3	14	31		48	
	Both		3	15	39	1	58	58
(Aggregate)		8	121	48	62	2	241	241

be accepted as approximations. A summer of thirteen weeks was taken as a basis for making estimates.

(8) New England women students worked for pay much more generally than did those of the South.

(9) Alabama students attended summer school to a much greater extent than did the others.

(10) No significant regional differences appear in amount of attention to popular music. The men in all three groups fell considerably below the women in control of song titles.

(11) As to books read, title and name of author were called for and as to magazines and newspapers, the names of those read somewhat regularly. In numerous cases the student could remember the book title but not the name of the author. Only stated titles were counted and indefinite replies such as "many" or "about a hundred" were omitted. No attempt is made here at qualitative evaluation. Even a quantitative appraisal is difficult because of a lack of objective norms. Amount of unconstrained study is surely one of the important and at

AGE: TYPE OF SECONDARY SCHOOL

		Median age	Age-range	Per cent. public high-school graduates	Per cent. private high school
New Hampshire	Men	21.2	18 to 40	75	25
	Women	19.3	16 " 26	74	26
Tennessee	Men	21.3	17 " 27	84	16
	Women	19.9	17 " 22	86	14
Alabama	Men	23.3	19 " 27	90	10
	Women	20.5	17 " 22	94	6

NOTION OF SUCCESS: CAREER PLANNED

		Ego (per cent.)	Alter (per cent.)	Both (per cent.)	No data (per cent.)	Per cent. choosing teaching	Other work (per cent.)	No data (per cent.)
New Hampshire	Men	49	29	18	4	78	18	
	Women	48	33	19		91	9	
Tennessee	Men	45	16	39		45	42	13
	Women	57	12	31		72	21	7
Alabama	Men	60	10	20	10	50	50	
	Women	88	6	6		88	12	

HOBBIES: PREFERRED COLLEGE SUBJECTS

		Median no. hobbies	Range	Four most popular college subjects	No. other subjects mentioned
New Hampshire	Men	1.8	0 to 5	Eng.; Hist.; Sociol.; Math.	20
	Women	2.3	0 " 4	Sociol.; Eng.; French; Math.	20
Tennessee	Men	2.9	0 " 5	Econ.; Hist.; Math.; Eng.	16
	Women	2.8	1 " 6	Eng.; Music.; French; Math.	16
Alabama	Men	3.6	2 " 5	Hist.; Ed'n.; Psychol.; Biol.	11
	Women	4.6	1 " 9	Eng; French; Ed'n.; Spanish	25

SUMMER VACATION EXPERIENCES

		Per cent. worked for pay	Per cent. attended summer school	Med. no. popular songs	Range	"None" or no data
New Hampshire	Men	88	.04	2.6	0 to 5	17
	Women	65	.019	4.2	0 " 11	3
Tennessee	Men	81	0.00	3.5	0 " "many"	2
	Women	27	.06	4.8	0 " 14	1
Alabama	Men	70	10.	2.5	0 " 8	3
	Women	30	42.	4.75	0 " 10	2

		Med. no. books read	Range	Med. no. magazines	Range	Med. no. newspapers	Range
New Hampshire	Men	2.3	0 to 9	3.0	0 to 6	2.2	0 to 7
	Women	3.3	0 " 9	3.6	0 " 7	2.6	0 " 4
Tennessee	Men	1.75	0 " 8	3.8	1 " 9	3	1 " 6
	Women	1.8	0 " 6	3.1	1 " 6	2.8	0 " 4
Alabama	Men	2.5	0 " 7	1.5	0 " 6	3.4	0 " 5
	Women	3.9	0 " 10	4.6	0 " 7	3.2	0 " 5

		Med. no. movies	Range	Med. no. other	Range	Med. no. dances	Range	Med. no. church	Range
New Hampshire	Men	5.8	0 to 78	1.8	0 to 12	4.7	0 to 52	6.6	0 to 20
	Women	9.5	0 " 35	.5	0 " 8	3	0 " 26	4	0 " 20
Tennessee	Men	15.3	0 " 40	3.7	0 " 10	3	0 " 30	10.9	0 " 35
	Women	12.6	1 " 65	2.6	0 " 14	1.75	0 " 25	10.9	1 " 30
Alabama	Men	1.5	0 " 52	.8	0 " 5	1	0 " 52	14.5	5 " 74
	Women	14	3 " 62	1.4	0 " 5	5	0 " 40	13.9	0 " 86

present unused measures of the quality of school education.

(12) Movie attendance increased from the 1927 to the 1930 group.

(13) There was a greater patronage of theatricals other than movies than the present writer had expected.

(14) The only college of the three permitting dancing on its campus is New Hampshire. The highest median is found at one of the colleges not sponsoring this type of diversion.

(15) Summer religious camps in Alabama continuing through several weeks tended to raise the medians for church attendance for that group. Three services daily were reported for some of these summer conferences. The students were directed to include this type of religious service in reporting such attendance.

The foregoing is a highly condensed and prosaic summary of a wealth of colorful detail, revealing of course only glimpses of the contents of the students' minds. It is just a fragment of what will probably be done in increasingly more complete form. The seven-year program of the Carnegie Foundation now under way in Pennsylvania is a significant illustration of personnel study on a comprehensive scale.

VERNON L. MANGUN

HOWARD COLLEGE

SCHOOL AND SOCIETY

EDITED BY J. McKEEN CATTELL

WITH WHICH IS COMBINED THE

EDUCATIONAL REVIEW

EDITED BY WILLIAM McANDREW

Volume 34 SATURDAY, OCTOBER 3, 1931 Number 875

EDUCATIONAL DEVELOPMENT, 1831-1931: A CENTENARY SURVEY AND A FORECAST[1]

By Sir CHARLES GRANT ROBERTSON

PRINCIPAL, BIRMINGHAM UNIVERSITY

THE honor of presiding over the education section at this centenary meeting of the British Association is no mean one, and I gladly acknowledge the pleasure that the invitation to be your president has given me, even though it inevitably carries with it the duty of inflicting on my audience a presidential address. My life as far back as I can remember has been concerned with one form of education or another, although I have successfully avoided on the whole the dubious duty of adding to the burden of printed books on the theory or practice of a subject which has been more than once described as more dismal and arid than even the dismal science of political economy, and more vulnerable even than theology to the charge that, in all such contributions to theory or practice from Zoroaster to, shall we say, Mr. Bertrand Russell, whatever is true is not new and whatever is new is flagitiously and demonstrably untrue. The world, as far as I can make out, has always teemed with educational reformers. The continuous puzzle for the historian has been to find out where the reforms of the reformers have gone to, or in what the reforms actually achieved have precisely consisted. At this moment in particular, standing alone in the tumbril which we politely call the presidential chair, I am acutely conscious that as a small boy I was part of a historic experiment in educational reform when I was sent to the school of R. H. Quick in Orme Square, Bayswater. Quick deservedly has, by a notable book on "Educational Reformers," a secure niche in the history and practice of education; but neither at the time nor since have I ever been conscious that under Quick I was learning new things in a new way. And the only convincing reason that I can give for this deplorable failure on my part is that if, in that misty past, I had been subjected to a Binet test I should have been at once shown up as, for my age-level, much below the normal metrical scale of intelligence.

In selecting the subject of my presidential address, I was confronted with one obvious difficulty. Presidents of this and other sections, I understand, usually can press into their addresses the fruits of their own independent and original research. But though for more than thirty-five years I have been an investigator, a

[1] Address of the president of Section L—Educational Science—British Association for the Advancement of Science, London, September, 1931.

teacher and an administrator, I have no fruits of research to offer you, unless a prolonged experience and still more prolonged reflection could be dressed up to look like the majestic divinity of research. I propose, therefore, to offer you some of these considered reflections in the form of a centenary survey which on this occasion is, I hope, both pardonable and appropriate.

My title, I agree, may mean little or nothing or much. Permit me, therefore, to explain briefly that I am not going to waste your time with a synthetic, unpalatable but probably familiar summary of the evolution of educational theory, practice, development and administration between 1830 and 1931; I am not going to drench you with dates, names and statistics, scientifically labeled and sorted with platitudinous or provocative adjectives dogmatically attached; least of all have I any desire to gut the large historical textbooks and the still larger squadrons of blue books and compress the vivisection into a miniature panorama of an astonishing century of effort and achievement. For astonishing it surely is. The more you study the situation round about 1830, the more you know from first-hand study of the sources of all that has happened after 1830 and the more that you know of the situation and tendencies of to-day, the more you will be impressed with the quality, quantity and scope of the work done and the results achieved. It is a commonplace to emphasize in the last hundred years the progress of physical and natural science. That progress has been equaled and in some respects surpassed by what has been done in education—and, to anticipate one of my conclusions, with the same broad general effect. Just as in physical and natural science, so in education the most striking result of a century of unflagging and remarkable progress has been the revelation of the extent of our own ignorance and of the difficulties of the fundamental and as yet unsolved problems.

My modest task, therefore, in the limited time at my disposal, is to invite you to accompany me on what the higher command of the army calls a staff ride. Our ground is a century; our object is to make both a strategical and tactical map—with future operations in our mind.

First, we must drive 1931 out of our consciousness, to be suppressed in a subliminal limbo until we are ready by and by to invoke it back for sublimated treatment; we must see the England of 1820 to 1830 as that generation saw it.

With Castlereagh's death in 1822 began the reform movement in every branch of the nation's life which culminated in the great Reform Act of 1832. The waters which for thirty years had been dammed up in England since the French Revolution began slowly to pour through the dykes, until finally the whole structure of our institutions and habits seems to be submerged. I emphasize in this intellectual and political ferment three general points, the significance of which will be, I hope, more apparent later on; first, the power of influence of the utilitarian group, the Benthamites, because they provide one more striking example of what can be accomplished by a small body of able men with a definite creed, a definite objective and the high and passionate seriousness that high and passionate purposes alone can inspire; secondly, the forces and personalities which made the Oxford Movement; Keble's sermon on "National Apostasy" in 1833 which, in Newman's judgment, started the Oxford Movement proper, only gave expression to a new interpretation of national life that had been fermenting for years, above all, in Oriel College, and Oriel College is for the Oxford Movement what Assisi is for the Franciscan revolution: in a word, the Oxford Movement brought into the arena a new conception of the spiritual as a formative force in life, and we shall fail to understand the nineteenth century problem of religion in education if we do not remember this: thirdly, I put the organized and wide-spread campaign against "ignorance" as an evil and a national vice, which led to the foundation in 1827 of the Society for the Diffusion of Useful Knowledge. There is no more entertaining guide to this period in our history than Peacock's novels, every one of which is a *roman à clef*. You will recall particularly in "Crotchet Castle," the delicious play that Peacock makes with "The March of Mind," that slogan, as we should say to-day, which captured the intelligentsia of England and was the direct creation of the Society for the Diffusion of Useful Knowledge and many other similar organizations. In the irresistible "March of Mind," England was to become united, happy, prosperous and free. Is it not the characteristic of all revolutionary movements that they start from an infallible faith in the perfectibility in a short period of the human species and end with a remorseless tyranny over a human species that refuses to perfect itself?

Study the correspondence of the leading figures in the decade from 1822 to 1832, and you invariably find either an extravagant fear that England is stumbling to her doom or a no less extravagant expectation that in a few more years of drastic reform England will have entered the Promised Land. To the one type of mind the question is: What can be saved from the coming cataclysm? To the other type the question is: What is the next Jericho whose walls will fall by the sword of the Lord and of Bentham?

Let us focus our attention on the strictly educational field. The primary sources are particularly rich, for apart from numerous pamphlets we have the *Parliamentary Debates*, the *Quarterly* and *Edinburgh Reviews* and (after 1824) the *Westminster Review*, the organ of the Benthamites, and for 1831–1835 the six volumes (and no more) of the *Quarterly Journal of Education*, supplemented by the letters in many biographies and many volumes of sermons and pamphlets. Remember, please, that Raikes had started his Sunday schools as far back as 1780, that Bell's "Madras System," Lancaster and Owen's epoch-making school experiments had long been topics for admiration, imitation and ferocious controversy; that Froebel at Keilhau, Pestalozzi at Yverdun had accomplished their work, and that before 1830 Herbart had thought out and published in German the substance of his system. But neither in the educational literature nor in the furious controversies of the time will you find that Froebel, Pestalozzi or Herbart were known or that any one supposed that in fifty or sixty years these would be spell-binding names in every text-book. The explanation may be, as Pusey maintained of the theology of this period, that only about three persons, of whom he was one, could read German with ease. At any rate, Froebel, Pestalozzi and Herbart, like the early plays of Bernard Shaw and like Mendel in biology, were to smite England after traveling from Germany to the United States and thence, somewhat battered rather than bettered in the process, back to our own country. In psychology, at any rate, if any book or system held the field, it was the elder James Mill's "Analysis of the Phenomena of the Human Mind" first published in 1829—and condemned to-day as a decayed fortress of the superstitions of faculty psychology and a discredited associationism.

That everything educational was in a profoundly unsatisfactory state every one at pains to investigate took for granted. So gloomy is the picture drawn that one is driven to wonder how there were any educated persons at all and particularly so many able to write such good English or construct such closely thought out and impressive arguments. The two universities and the only two, Oxford and Cambridge, were targets for savage criticism; the endowed public schools such as Eton, Winchester, Harrow, etc., were held to be expensive nurseries of vice, incompetence and pedantry; the old grammar schools were dilapidated, starved and useless; elementary education simply did not exist. Every established institution was threatened; we were recklessly flinging our doors open to an ignorant, irreligious and irresponsible democracy, without any adequate institutions or administrative machinery to cope with the dangers and needs of a new political nation.

The England that created the British Association concentrated, you will find, its attention on four main educational problems—what was to be done with the universities? How were the public schools to be reformed? How can this illiterate democracy be cured of its intolerable and dangerous ignorance? Where and how was the money to be found? And immediately, by this concentration, leaped straight into the educational vortex. Of the university aspect of the problem I will say practically nothing now or hereafter, because meeting as we do to-day in London, the foundation of the University of London and its significance naturally deserves separate treatment on this centenary occasion, and I leave it to the competent hands of Dr. Deller. But nothing illustrates better than the creation of University College and King's College the power of the utilitarian group and the reaction of the established Church of England to the challenge that University College implied.

But go back to that contemporary literature, even if your mind is full of 1931 and its controversies and at once, if the vocabulary and the environment be very different, you are on familiar—painfully familiar—ground. Here, for example, are three questions always coming up in the literature of the day and on which tons of ink were spent: What is the object of education? If it is not mere knowledge, what is it? The formation of character or the formation of a Christian character and a Christian citizen, and if not, what then? To whom is this duty to be left—the individual conscience of the parent, the church as the depository of Christian truth, or the state, with a compulsory power and the right to represent the civil mind?

Let me quote here a couple of sentences from the *Quarterly Review* of July, 1829: "Does any man believe that to furnish the future weaver or carpenter with the education of a scholar or a man of science will make him more contented in the sphere in which he is thrown? The more fitted he is for a higher station in society, the greater the effort of mind to keep him happy in that which fortune has fixed him." And observe the implications in the quotation. Or, take again, these sentences from Dr. Arnold, written in 1837: "The whole good that the University (*i.e.* of London) can do towards the cause of general education depends on its holding manifestly a Christian character; if it does not hold this, it seems to me to be at once so mischievous, from giving its sanction to a most mischievous principle, that its evil will far outweigh its good. . . . I have not the slightest doubt that it is better to go on with our present system, with all its narrowness and deficiency, than to begin a pretended system of national education on any other than a Christian basis." For in those sentences you have the essential core not only of Arnold's work at Rugby, but of his most passionate convictions on every form of education from the nursery to the universities and the life of the nation as a whole.

The years from 1825 to 1840 were a period of bitter but stimulating controversy; of positive achievement to be registered they may seem to be scanty, if not sterile; but three points of immense importance stand out from the dust that has been laid and the ashes, still treacherously hot. First, as regards religion and its part in the general conception of education as a whole, we note the transformation of an educational problem into a savage political warfare. The privileges and legal status of the established Church of England were challenged by the political and religious disabilities of nonconformist dissent. And the political battle was embittered by the controversies within the Church of England itself, which cut deep and wide into the fundamentals of the relations of church and state. It is profoundly significant that Scotland was at the same time rent by the issues which culminated in the epoch-making disruption of 1843, and that in Ireland the whole cause of education was thrown back for at least one generation, if not two, by the storm that centered in what may be conveniently called the "Maynooth Grant." In the political welter in all three countries the real educational issue was either submerged or driven on to the surf-smitten rocks.

Secondly, with the first parliamentary grant from national funds in 1833, the state stepped into the arena, with the reluctance of a man unable to swim and pushed into cold water out of his depth.

Abstract political theory—and I mean by that the definition of the functions and powers of the state in the sphere of intellect and of morals—at once became linked with the issues of controversial party politics. As early as 1840 it was grasped by all clear thinkers, irrespective of the school of thought to which they belonged, that henceforward the control of Parliament and of the power of the purse could be made, indeed must become, not the sole but the most powerful force in deciding educational issues.

Thirdly, all the issues contained in the term "curriculum," were in full and fierce debate from 1825 onwards, the real significance of which has often, I think, been missed, and largely because both attackers and attacked in a singularly copious literature failed to distinguish the real educational issue that had been raised. The champions of what to-day we should call modern studies—history (other than ancient history), modern languages, science and even of mathematics—as indispensable elements of any sound curriculum—only too frequently urged their case on the intrinsic merit of the subject as a branch of knowledge and without any reference to the result in the type of mind or character that a reformed system was to produce. And a dreary study of much dead controversy has left on my mind a depressing impression that conservatives and reformers alike completely forgot that the method and the amount of any subject in a curriculum may be even more important than the subject itself, intrinsically considered. Be that as it may, this period from 1825 to 1840 brought the whole question of curriculum into the disconcerting light of day; and if it is the duty of every generation when it can not solve a problem to make it impossible for its successors to evade it, the generation of the Reform Act at least did that part of its duty very faithfully.

The next thirty years, ending roughly in Forster's Education Act, were to be not less abundant in controversy but more fruitful in positive and lasting achievement. Superficially regarded, they might be called the age of royal and governmental commissions. The state was, therefore, proclaiming its right, bitterly contested and resented, to inquire into the working of educational institutions—universities, endowed public schools, secondary grammar schools—over which it had neither administrative nor educational nor financial control. The transition from education was an optional function, to education as a national duty of, the state was being rapidly effected in these thirty years.

But apart from this really momentous evolution of applied political theory, what else are we bound to note, in our staff ride, as peaks? Three points in particular. First, then, the slow revolution effected in the endowed public schools. We owe this to four pioneer head masters who, in an age of remarkable personalities, stand out preeminent. For the acid test and infallible criterion of the pioneer in all spheres of human activity is that after his work has been done, the sphere in which he has done it is qualitatively different. Only too often so decisively does the result pass into the texture of every-day thought and action that we can only judge its originality by a study of the conditions prior to the pioneer. It is thus that we judge the work of a Newton, an Adam Smith, a Niebuhr, a Darwin or a Pasteur. And it is thus that we can safely regard Arnold at Rugby from 1828 to 1842, Benjamin Hall Kennedy at Shrewsbury from 1836 to 1866, Edward Thring at Uppingham from 1853 to 1887, Haig-Brown, the second founder of Charterhouse, from 1863 to 1897; and if I extend my period considerably, I add a fifth, in Sanderson of Oundle, from 1892 to 1922. These were all men of very different fiber outlook on life, intellectual power and quality of scholarship. But they had one uniting link and characteristic, they were great teachers because they were great personalities; they were great organizers because they had the gift of leadership: and they left on their generation, on their staffs who knew them, on their boys, on all indeed with whom they came into contact an ineffaceable stamp of power and inspiration, the combination of individuality and experience, and they created an inexhaustible tradition for the institutions that they remoulded. In the firmament of education there have been, there are and there will be many lamps shining with different rays and varying intensity when focused in the spectrum of spirit and mind, but these five great names—Arnold, Kennedy, Haig-Brown, Thring and Sanderson—will always swing in our English firmament with a rare and undimmed splendor.

The second point is the advent of science. The nineteenth-century renascence of science may correctly date from 1831 and Faraday's discoveries, the centenary celebration of which has just preceded our centenary meeting, but the period from 1840 to 1880 is studded with great names and memorable discoveries. As far back as 1830 even the *Quarterly Review* was indicting the British neglect of science as compared with the state of things on the Continent; and I would remind you that as late as 1864 at Rugby alone of the older public schools and at the newly founded Cheltenham, was any science taught, and that it was unknown for example, at Eton, Harrow, St. Paul's, Shrewsbury, Charterhouse, Merchant Taylors and so forth. It was in the late sixties that the great educational struggle began seriously, which I term the advent of science, and I mean by that the battle for the principle that an adequate knowledge of physical and natural science is advocated not merely for its importance as knowledge or for its vocational or utilitarian value, but for its cultural indispensability. In other words, an adequate knowledge of, and training in, physical and natural science was proclaimed as an essential element in any education claiming to be liberal. If Huxley unquestionably is the Achilles and protagonist of this twenty years' battle for the capture of the classical Troy, do not let us forget that one of the first trumpets sounded in the fray was in the famous "Essays on a Liberal Education," published in 1867, in which J. M. Wilson, then a master at Rugby, afterwards head master of Clifton (1879–1890) urged the claims of science. Wilson died this year, aged ninety-six, fighting to the very end for high and noble truths. *Clarum et venerabile nomen,* indeed, whom in a meeting such as this we can salute with affectionate and grateful homage.

Thirdly, to the renascence of the public school, the renascence and advent of science, we can add neither a renascence, nor an advent, but the creation of a new element in the educational problem—the education of girls and women. The present generation can only reconstruct with difficulty and astonishment the conditions of girls' education in the first half of the nineteenth century. What a German educator said as early as 1786 was not wholly untrue sixty years later: "As to the feminine sex, especially that of the better classes, it seems as if the state cared little whether they grew up into human beings or into monkeys." "Madam," wrote a business man in 1858 to the head teacher of one of the better girls' schools, "as my daughter is not going to be a banker, I see no purpose in her being taught arithmetic." "Everything," said Miss Cobbe of her school in 1836, "was taught in the inverse ratio of its true importance. At the bottom of the scale were morals and religion, and at the top were music and dancing." To-day, if we choose, in page after page of the report of the Taunton Commission of 1864, which but for the pressure of five or six devoted and gifted women would never have illegitimately extended its reference from boys' to girls' schools—we can read the devastating facts and no less devastating comments of the commissioners. The dawn of the new era coincided with the year of political revolution, 1848, when Queen's College, in direct imitation of King's College, was started in Harley Street to "hold classes in all branches of female learning." Two of the first students in Queen's College were Frances Mary Buss and Dorothea Beale. To-day, when we visit the Frances Mary Buss Schools in North London, and the Ladies' College in Cheltenham, do we realize that we are seeing as great a revolution in education as when we visit Wykeham's foundations at Winchester and Oxford, or stand in the early quadrangle of Merton College at Oxford or of Peterhouse at Cambridge. In Miss Buss, whose creation of the North London Collegiate School came first and who was also the creator of the Head Mistresses' Association, and in Miss Beale, we have two pioneers who stand and always will stand, in a class by themselves. They are as great and creative revolutionaries as were St. Francis and St. Dominic in the thirteenth century. And yet Frances Mary Buss is omitted from the "Dictionary of National Biography"—perhaps because omission is a more eloquent testimony to distinction than four columns of obituary epitaph.

To these two I would add one other name, Sarah Emily Davies, who, if any one person founded Girton College, was that one person; and with the foundation of Girton College began the second part of the revolution—the admission of women to a university education.

I mentioned the Forster Education Act of 1870 casually because I have never been able to regard that act as a revolutionary or a creative measure in the true sense of the term. It was essentially a compromise; it gathered together into a single statute forces, movements and principles which had been operating for at least twenty years previously, but it expressed no new principle and enshrined neither really new methods nor new and constructive ideals. And its most conspicuous defect was that it made no attempt to correlate the elementary education that it reorganized with the existing system of secondary education, so as to bring the inevitable development of both into an organic and fruitful union. This is only another way of saying that Forster was not a great education minister; he was a high-minded statesman of remarkable ability, courage and independence, who showed greater imagination and vision in imperial policy than in education. And it is remarkable that from 1815 to 1916 we have no education minister or statesman of the first rank, no political mind of the first order devoting supreme powers of brain and imagination to education and leaving it permanently in his debt.

What would have been revolutionary in 1870 would have been the translation into legislation and administration of the principles of the Birmingham group who fought to make primary education "secular, compulsory and free," and who really compelled the liberal government of 1870 to legislate and were given the Act of 1870, which they denounced as a betrayal by the government and a treacherous surrender by the minister. If England does not love coalitions she loves revolutions still less, and, least of all, revolutions in education inaugurated by governments. In 1871 England was as unready for primary education, "secular, compulsory and free," as were the United States for prohibition in 1917.

I am getting near the end of my staff ride. After 1870 the two most conspicuous new elements (apart from the Act of 1902, of which my old chief, Sir William Anson, was one of the main authors) surely are first, the adult education movement, and the advent of psychology.

The first great chapter of the recognition and development of extramural teaching as a function of the university is contained in the history of university extension which started in Cambridge in 1872, spread to London in 1876 and to Oxford in 1878. The roots of this new growth go back to the movement for mechanics' institutes, which began in 1799 and took a fresh shape in the ideals of Frederick Denison Maurice and the foundation of the Working Men's College. The second great chapter dates from the foundation of Ruskin College at Oxford and the creation of the Workers' Educational Association, with which the name of Albert Mansbridge will always be associated. Well can I remember both those events, and, to use the familiar formula of our Oxford University Bidding Prayer, more especially am I bound to mention here that my College of All Souls—that reputed home of reaction and lost causes—was the first in any university to provide not only from its corporate revenues the first extramural university tutor, Mr. Tawney, but to allocate its hall in the summer term for his extramural classes. What the fusion of the older university extension movement with the principles, organization and ideals of the Workers' Educational Association has become and wrought is known to-day—even in Fleet Street.

The statesman who said thirty years ago that we were all socialists now would assert with more truth that to-day we are all psychologists. We do not indeed talk psychology (as Bourgeois did his prose) without knowing it. On the contrary, we do not know psychology and therefore we all talk it; in fact, it is better for a modern citizen to be guilty of kleptomania, which I understand is really only a functional parapraxis due to imperfect motivation or an intermittent disassociation affecting a polylocationary consciousness, than to deny a universal addiction in our friends, but, of course, not ourselves, to complexes and neuroses. The advent of psychology was ushered in by the re-discovery, in the eighties of last century, of Herbart and the application or misapplication of his principles to educational theory and still more to educational practice, to which the foundation of training colleges for teachers and the mania of publishers for small text-books gave an unlimited scope. It was fertilized by the astonishing advance in physiology in which British physiologists have played so memorable a part and by the tremendous impetus given by Wundt, James and Ward, to name only three of those no longer living, who with their successors and disciples have literally created a new and definable branch of science, requiring a specialized technique.

What material, I must now ask, has our rapid staff ride provided for a summing-up in the shape of a forecast? Let me summon to my aid my aged friend, Rip Van Winkle, versed in the educational problems that vexed the England of 1830, put to sleep when the British Association came into its cradle, waking up in this year of grace and taking stock of this world so new to him after a century of blissful oblivion.

I see, [he tells me] a vast and complicated administrative machine, spread like the electric grid over the whole country and coordinated, if at all, by a State Department of Education, as remarkable for its executive comprehensiveness as for its intellectual timidity, which, after all, is the characteristic of all bureaucratic organizations; this new president of the Board of Education, so strange to me, is a member of a party cabinet, with the inevitable political bias that his membership in his party involves, and dependent for the tenure of his office on the fate of his party on purely political issues: the century proves that education bills do not destroy ministries, but neither, however excellent, can they save them; hence, most party education ministers with political ambitions have to make their reputations elsewhere than at the Board of Education, because whether they are good or bad ministers of education, they will only stay in their office if their party stays in power. In 1931, as in 1831, education can only be kept out of politics by the determination of every party in turn not to allow an educational issue to jeopardize its general political fortunes. One issue, the so-called religious issue, alone threatens this. In 1931, as in 1831, I observe that no government will tackle it fairly and squarely, because a courageous solution of it would be unlike successful operations in surgery; the operation would succeed, the nation would recover and the operating surgeon, the minister, would die.

In 1831 we talked and dreamed of a national system of education. You are still talking and dreaming of it, but I begin to suspect that you (as we) were deluded by a catchword, cribbed by misunderstanding France and Germany. For national can have two very distinct interpretations which we jumble up—it is either a comprehensive unitary system, embracing every branch of educational effort controlled by a single national authority, however differentiated and delegated the powers of the sub-authorities and local organizations may be, or a system expressing the national character of the political community in accordance with its traditional principles and attitude to all national problems.

One feature in this hundred years is amazingly significant—the reform of the old and the development of the new universities, almost wholly endowed by private and voluntary benefactions. They are all literally co-educational. Mrs. Rip Van Winkle is even more astonished than I am, for she was with Miss Becky Sharp at Miss Pinkerton's Academy. But what puzzles and grieves her is not that girls should have their Etons and Winchesters or go to a university and become a Mistress of Arts or a Bachelor of Commerce, but that in a century which has labored so incessantly to secure rights for married women and which rightly regards motherhood as one of the fundamental bases of what you call sane and sound citizenship, you have, also, labored so hard to secure that girls and young women should almost universally be taught and controlled by spinsters. You seem to regard marriage in a man as enriching, but in a woman as impoverishing, the experience of life and capacity for service. You put married men at the head of your universities, colleges and schools, because you like the best of them, in the interests of the race, to marry; but you do not put married women in the same position, because apparently you wish to encourage the fools and the fribbles to marry, while the ablest women are subsidized to remain single—of course in the interests of the race.

To proceed; why when we are still a commercial and industrial nation have you done little or nothing scientifically to educate boys, girls, young men and young women for commerce and industry, particularly when you have done marvels for scientific research and all the professions, law, medicine, engineering, teaching, the religious ministry and so forth? As my friend, Adam Smith, once said in another connection, that omission is "altogether unfit for a nation of shopkeepers, but extremely fit for a nation whose education is influenced by shopkeepers."

Since I woke up I have been studying hard the best books from a vast collection of what I find is called psychology, and I have run through dozens of smaller books for teachers which profess to boil down—as you call it—scientific research into a practical compendium for the course called pedagogy or how to teach every subject to every kind of person, and this pedagogy based on psychological commandments seems to be compulsory in the training of all teachers in state schools, though why it is not compulsory for other teachers I do not know. The pupils learn the whole of psychology in a year, which shows how clever are your professors of education and the would-be teachers, compared with the professors and would-be teachers of my generation a century ago. This psychology delights me extremely. For it teaches me precisely how I get all my thoughts and feelings and what I do with them when I get them. It is explained with lovely diagrams that I can not do with the external stimuli anything but what I actually do; and if I seem to do something different from what I ought to do, it is either a conditioned reflex in which I have forgotten to obey the conditions or it is an unconditioned reflex which means that the conditions were there all the time or ought to have been there, but that I forgot to give the right or was rattled into giving the wrong, response—and nature very properly spanked my ego. I have, in fact, at last discovered, what used to puzzle me a hundred years ago, that I am what I am because I am not someone else. I learn, too, that I am the sum of all my responses and reflexes, together with those that I repress and tuck away in my subconsciousness, because I do not like them or they do not like me and which therefore wait either to pounce out on me unawares or pop up just to show me they are there; and then I sublimate them into something which I ought to like much better and if I do not sublimate them, they sulk and fester into a complex. But while I am simply the sum total, I am also the unifying something that collects and labels and separates, so that I am at one and the same time the man who gives you the ticket, the passenger who uses it on the train by which he must travel and the collector who takes it from the passenger when the journey is done, to prove that the passenger has come by that train and not by an illegitimate motor-nerve bus. But as I am only a beginner at this modern psychology, I have not yet found out whether my mind—if it is my mind and not merely a function of the physical stimuli—was there before I had any stimuli and responses, or whether the stimuli came first from somewhere and created my mind in order that I might recognize that it was a stimulus and give it the right label. What comforts me, however, is to be assured that I have an ego which is always different from, and yet the same, as all my reflexes and reactions—both those which I have had in the past, am having to-day, and those I am going to have presently.

Finally, [he concludes] I observe with immense interest that after a hundred years you are still arguing precisely all the fundamental questions that perplexed us. A friend sent me a book called "Education at the Cross-Roads," by a gentleman who had been a Minister of Education, and I thought I had by mistake been sent one of the many books of my own time, because we all declared then that education was at the cross-roads, and now a century after, I find education is still at the same cross-roads. We did not know what was the purpose of education—whether it was purely utilitarian to enable the educated to earn a better living than the uneducated or to make them better craftsmen or to train them for a profession or merely to become as virtuous and happy as they could make themselves or others would allow them to be. And I find you are arguing just as passionately as we did all these things to-day. In my time someone solved all our difficulties by saying that education was not for any of these things but for life. No one could say, unfortunately, what life was for which we were to be educated, and if he defined it, every one else said life was something quite different. Everything was altering so rapidly, and there were so many different lives and no one could say which of them was going to be the life of each different boy and girl, that we got very angry with each other and before anything could be decided, I fell asleep. And now that I am awake again, I am terrified at the world round me, not because it is so wonderful and strange with its motor cars, and aeroplanes and wireless and electric light and cooking and gas and fountains pens and typewriters and telephones and telegraphs and your wonderful newspapers which come out every hour, but because it is changing so rapidly every month and every day. People to-day are such a perplexing compound of primitive—for you thieve and murder and tell lies and get drunk and run away with each other's wives, just as we did—mixed up with the purely artificial which is the result of all your inventions—which are like a very tight corset all over a savage's body, that I do not know how you can educate for life to-day, because by the time that you have educated the boy and the girl the life will be absolutely altered. And so I end with a concrete question. For what kind of life do you educate a girl, just to be a voter, which she certainly will be if she lives till twenty-one, whether she wants a vote or not, or to be a film actress or a cook or a mother or an old maid, none of which she may ever be?

Thus far Rip Van Winkle. Hard questions, if I may venture to say so of my venerable friend and going to the root of many problems.

Let me conclude by inviting you to concentrate on four points which are bound to find a place in any forecast of the future.

First, the science of psychology is obviously only in its infancy—the stage which chemistry had reached when Dalton formulated his celebrated law which modern chemistry no longer accepts. What can we expect from psychology judging from what it has already done? I am not concerned here with the inexhaustible possibilities opening up in the medical, and particularly the pathological, sphere and the field of therapeutic action. No sound educational results, as far as I can see, are going to come from applications from the abnormal to the normal, unless we accept an assumption that it is the abnormal that is really normal, which is like assuming in medicine that disease is the rule and health the exception. I look to much real help coming from intelligence tests, however unsatisfactory they may be at present, and in two supremely important directions.

For, if we can once really establish what every one from Aristotle to the present board of education has assumed that children and adolescents and adults in varying categories and at different age-levels have definite limits of educability and that it is waste of time, effort and money to treat one category as if it were another, the doctrine of equality of opportunity will come to be regarded as a devastating superstition, and the grading of the categories on the educational ladder will be the beginning of an unparalleled social revolution.

Secondly, human activities, professional or otherwise, will have to be regarded socially and economically in proportion to the degree of trained intelligence and revealed aptitude that they require for their discharge. It is here that social and industrial psychology will find their true field. The difficulty will be the correlation of the industrial or occupational categories with the purely professional in the social organization, which means that the education, with the aid of psychology, will necessitate a revaluation of social values. Such a revaluation will at once raise the issue of the purely ethical values in the scale qualitatively considered. Through education, we shall decide potential function and then train, in Aristotelian language, potentiality into actuality.

And that raises my second issue—the functional differentia between the sexes. The nineteenth century revolution in the position of women went through two main stages. The first was purely educational. If girls had brains, they justified as good training as the brains of boys—hence, the revolution in secondary, which reacted on the primary, education of girls, and in its turn led up to the demand for admission to the universities. Simultaneously, the demand for careers for the educated girl was a logical consequence. The legal or social obstacles to opening the professions had to be removed: this, in turn, involved political rights: and the intellectual demand for equality in careers was merged with the demand for equality in citizenship and political rights. The movement was consummated with the grant of the vote in 1918 and with the grant of the degree at Oxford and the quasi-degree at Cambridge —the two last university strongholds of male monopoly to surrender. Women now have a virtual equality both in civic and educational status. Until 1921, it was inevitable that in the struggle for this dual equality, differentiation of function should be ignored or rejected. If women were to be able to do exactly what men did, their training must obviously be a copy of that which men had deemed necessary. But since 1921, when equality of opportunity for all careers had been conceded, a slow reaction began. Differentiation and specialization of function, based on differential sex qualities, reasserted their directive force—and will reassert it with increasing momentum.

Girls no longer feel it their duty to choose a particular career in order to emphasize a claim to equality of rights or to extirpate traditional social taboos. It must be the privilege of education to stimulate this marked tendency, and thereby to reduce a stupid competition of the sexes and cut down a costly social waste. For the social revolution, through which we are now passing, is slowly learning from the preceding political struggle for the so-called emancipation of women, that in a well-ordered society there are no monopolies of civic function or of intellectual or imaginative activity based on sex, but that there are limitations imposed on all in the form of physical, intellectual and moral qualities and aptitudes, inherent in the individual as such. Whether it be surgery or poetry, acting or nursing, teaching in a kindergarten or research, domestic administration or scavenging, aviation or dressmaking, a trained woman may be the equal of a trained man or she may be a great deal worse than an untrained man. But it is, also, becoming clearer every day that for certain activities the average woman, if trained, is better than the average trained man, and *vice versa,* and the difference in each case rests on a functional sex differentiation, of the criteria of which we are as yet amazingly ignorant. But until this obscure and baffling field of vast inquiry has been cleared up, social and, therefore, educational reconstruction continues to be like the game of billiards on an Atlantic liner in a storm—the truly hit ball may go into the pocket at which it is aimed or into the eye of the rival competitor, with a ripped tablecloth into the bargain.

Mark, I beg you, the educational consequences. Already many wise teachers are questioning seriously whether the education of girls from eleven plus ought not to be freed from the barnacles that have accumulated, since the ship of female education was brought to a static anchorage in the centuries-old harbor of male education. One of our greatest needs, therefore, to-day, is another Miss Buss or another Miss Beale, as free as were those great women from the inherited superstitions of their own sex and from the cramping complexes that obsess the male mind, with a new mission to start a second and even more revolutionary chapter in the emancipation of women and the reorganization of society.

This does not mean, of course, that any sane man or woman desires to wrench the clock back to tick out demoralizing hours in the dreary wastes of "accomplishments" or to substitute an amateurish sloppiness for a bracing intellectual discipline: still less does it imply that there can be feminine, as distinct from male, mathematics, Greek or logic. But when that woman reformer comes—or perhaps it will be a man—we shall, as usual with all reforms, not be surprised at the results but only wonder that the reform had not been made fifty years earlier.

I repeat that psychology, like physiology, is only in its infancy. Fifty years hence, neither the behaviorists nor the subjectivists nor any other of the present camps which end in an "ist" will demand unfaltering subscription to provisional and half-worked-out hypotheses dressed up as infallible decrees of a nature which may prove to be neither a radioactive force definable in mathematical symbols, only intelligible to a Newton or an Einstein, nor an accidental entity leaping into a void, after a fortuitous collision of electromagnetic units in an imaginary etheric universe.

Thirdly and lastly, as the preachers are supposed to say, the end and purpose of education has not yet been settled and, in the nature of things, can never be settled once and for all. We may, if we choose, hold differing views as to what mind is or how it originated or how, in the terms of a really scientific psychology, it works and can be distinguished from its manifestations. We may refuse to believe that mind can operate apart from the material medium analyzed by the pathologist, and the neurologist, or we may be convinced that the material medium is simply an imperfect instrument through which a spiritual reason alone can work for a structure of human society composed of imperfect physical units, which we call men and women, and that mind, apart from matter, is both prior to, and part of, a rational universe. But the one clear conclusion that no one can evade is that every society everywhere and, therefore, all such societies together on this tiny physical globe are and will continue to be the result of purposive human action, which by an increasing control of *all* the elements at its disposal has made things to be what they are, and is daily altering the process of adaptation, to fit the purposes, wise or illusionary that it selects as ends worth pursuing. My friend, Rip Van Winkle, had obviously taken from Huxley the conventional distinction between the process of natural selection and the arbitrary interference with that process by man the ethical artificer—*homo artifex*—for his non-natural but rational purposes—the relentless antagonism between a nature with one purpose and a human reason with a contrary purpose—between evolution and ethics. Rip Van Winkle could not be expected to know that that conventional distinction has long been shattered and that it only survives to-day, like the human appendix, because the majority of us are not affected by its vestigial existence, but when it tries to exercise an atrophied function, we have it cut out as an intolerable nuisance.

It is like the old metaphysics or the old psychology, when mind was regarded as working inside a self-sealed box and outside was the whole objective and material world, which surged upon the box, while the something inside the box exercised cognitive and apperceptive powers on the surge—a phenomenal world playing hide-and-seek with mind, which took off its blinkers, from time to time, just to see who was playing the fool with it. Except in Fleet Street, and some old-fashioned laboratories of science and some dusty classrooms of, shall we say, German philosophy, we educationalists (a horrible word) have long recognized that mind is as integral a part of nature and the processes of nature as the so-called natural forces. And that if, for example, nature has a pruning hook which we call war, it was forged by mind, put into nature's hand, *i.e.*, the hand of purposive men by mind, and that, as with other pruning hooks or scythes, when human minds are, as they can be, bad craftsmen or lose control, what was intended to cut down weeds gashes the user to death. You can make a razor and use it either to cut a human throat, or remove a carbuncle with an aseptic technique, or, like Peter the Great, shave your nobles as the first stage towards reconstructing your systems of government and in so doing you are natural and ethical at one and the same time and are taking the most appropriate step, as you conceive it, to achieve another stage in your interpretation of life, which is an inextricable mixture of the spiritual, the intellectual, the moral and the physical—a jumble which neither Piltdown man nor Mr. Bertrand Russell nor any one in the centuries between them has ever been able to disentangle into separate packets, much less prove that some of the packets are precedent in order of time and are, therefore, "natural," while others followed later and must, therefore, be termed "artificial"—or "anti-natural."

Beethoven and Dante are useless to the Patagonian because he can not fit them into his conception of social life, which really means his scale of social values. In the twentieth century, Fra Angelico may be for us only an item in a museum of dead junk, much as a modern housewife hangs a Tudor warming pan above her electric refrigerator—unless the vision of life that inspired Fra Angelico continues to have a value which can supplement or intensify the values determining the pattern of the life that we are making with the help of wireless telephony, the songs of Shakespeare or any other material or instrument that seems appropriate. The thin, starved, anemic and retarding life, whether of today or of the age of Tut-an-Khamen or of Siegfried and Brunhilde, is the life where purposive man let the scale of values shrivel and, in consequence, the aptitudes that might have flowered withered up and human appetites were degraded to a limited and purely carnal satisfaction; the fat, well-nourished, rich and expanding life of any epoch has always been when purposive man let the scale of values soar and measured an illimitable horizon, not by what mind cooperating with body had done or were doing, but what they could do if each of the two could be trained by an appropriate technique completely to work together for a unified end—above all, when he became intoxicated by the profoundest of all truths that the spiritual and the material are not in the nature of things antagonists, but allies.

To-day, a social revolution, largely due to the educational progress of the last hundred years, is steadily regrading and reshaping the whole commonwealth that we call the British Empire. Education has extended the scale of social values and increasingly intensified in millions of new recruits the power to devise and the desire to will the means to action. But the aid that our educational system can increasingly give to this complicated social and economic transformation is being limited because we have refused to solve the fundamental problem of religious instruction and to allocate to institutional religion its harmonious place in the task of training for life. Until we have done that, no matter how scientifically planned may be our educational machinery, or how loyally it may be worked, there will be a steady flow of grit clogging the gears and causing all the bearings to run red-hot. This is not the place, nor am I the person, to indicate how and where the true solution can be found; but if it be the supreme function of education to see life as a whole and to train every boy and girl, according to their powers and aptitudes, to a maximum of vision and of a willing reason, so that they can ultimately achieve their truest happiness and their highest efficiency in the new social order, based on the correct allocation of differentiated function, it is my unshakeable conviction that the fundamental place of religion in life must be regarded as an essential preliminary to any further educational advance.

A hundred years hence, Section L may be meeting in London to celebrate a second centenary of the British Association. Whatever else the president may have to say on that occasion, I trust that he will be able to record this as a mortgage inherited from 1931 and paid off to make a triumphant overture to another century of success.

EDUCATIONAL EVENTS

EDUCATION IN THE IRISH FREE STATE

Statistics of promotion from standard to standard give some measure of the efficiency of elementary schools, and those now available go to show that a slow but steady improvement is going on in the Free State mainly as a result of the school attendance act which came into force in 1926, according to a report published in the London *Times Educational Supplement*. On June 30 of that year there were 522,000 children on the elementary school rolls; of these 171,000 were in the infants standard, 75,000 in the first standard, 67,000 in the third, 45,000 in the fifth and 25,000 in the sixth. On June 30, 1930, there were 512,000 children on the rolls; 151,000 of these were in the infants standard, 71,000 in the first standard, 68,000 in the third standard, 49,000 in the fifth and 30,000 in the sixth. The tendency to lag behind, it will be seen, is still strong, but not nearly so strong as it was four years ago, when children were sent to school or kept at home as their parents judged most convenient.

The vocational education committees have now been brought into being, and are beginning to make preparations for the new system of education which should become operative next year. A very special interest attaches to their proceedings, for one of the most important features of the new vocational education act is the creation of local committees charged with the duty of administering a system of continuation education. As the new schools will be financed in part from the rates, the committees are elected by the local rate-levying authorities, but the electors are free to go outside their own numbers to secure the inclusion in the committees of men who have special knowledge of the problems involved in setting up a system of continuation education with a practical bias. The idea of financing education from the rates and giving a measure of control to the local ratepayers is of course not new, even to Ireland, but neither the teachers nor the clerical managers of the schools have ever been anxious to see it realized in the spheres of primary or secondary education. The teachers fear that a local committee may prove a more meddlesome master than the parish priest, and the church has of course always insisted that it must retain effective control over the teacher and the things taught in the school. Only in the sphere of technical education was control by local committees tolerated. This exception was made apparently because the church believed that technical teaching would not influence the pupil's character and outlook on life as a cultural education does. Of late years the hierarchy has been reconsidering its decision with a view to seeing how far it can fall in with democratic ideas, and it has let it be known that it will raise no objection to the creation of local committees empowered to finance and control school buildings, school sanitation, lighting, heating and such matters so long as the church retains its authority in regard to the teacher and the matter taught. But a more remarkable expression of the church's confidence in the affection and loyalty of the Irish people is found in its decision not to oppose the control of vocational education by local committees.

The first reports of the proceedings of the new committees suggest that the church's confidence in their loyalty will be amply justified. Recently a meeting of the County Cork vocational education committee was attended by 17 members, of whom one was a deputy with a seat in the Dail. Twelve others had seats on the local county or borough authorities; four were Roman Catholic priests, and one of these was in the chair. The most important business before the committee was to hear the Bishop of Cloyne, who had certain representations to make about the site of the new technical school which the committee proposed to erect at Cobh. The bishop's wishes were acceded to with the utmost courtesy and good will.

SECONDARY SCHOOL BUILDING IN NEW YORK CITY

The New York *Sun* reports that to relieve overcrowding in the secondary schools of New York City the Board of Education is considering more than a score of new buildings, with 70,000 sittings. The cost of these projects will aggregate $34,000,000, it is officially estimated, and they will increase the present capacity of the high school by nearly 50 per cent.

According to an official statement of the board, 19 buildings are now being "projected," including those under construction, those for which plans are being drawn and those for which sites are being authorized. The seating capacity in these aggregates 45,900. By the end of 1932, it is said by school board officials, five more schools with 24,700 seats will have to be authorized at a cost of $7,000,000.

Such liberal provision for new buildings is needed because of the short-time problem in the secondary schools. Out of a total register of 203,000 students, 33,197, or nearly 20 per cent., are on short time this fall.

The high-school construction program contemplates an addition to the Washington Irving High School, which should entirely eliminate short time in that school, and a new school for girls in upper Manhattan.

In the Bronx plans have been sketched for an addition to the Morris High School. A new school to relieve the Monroe School awaits the selection of a site. A third Bronx school, the Samuel Gompers, is already under construction. This will be a trade school. Two additional Bronx schools, one in the northeastern section of the borough and one in the western section, will probably be projected in 1932.

In Brooklyn the proposed Lafayette High School awaits the selection of a site. The Franklin K. Lane is already being planned. Sketch plans have been prepared for the Manual Training High School addition. A new school to relieve New Utrecht awaits selection of a site. Plans are being made also for an addition to Erasmus Hall and for an addition to the Girls High. In 1932, it is expected, a new building to relieve Tilden and Madison Schools, in Flatbush, and a new building in Borough Park will be authorized. The Boys Industrial High School in Brooklyn awaits the selection of a site.

In Queens the board is selecting sites for the Bayside and Woodrow Wilson high schools. Plans are now being drawn for the Andrew Jackson High School at Cross Island Boulevard and 208th Street. The Boys Industrial High School in Queens awaits the selection of a site.

In Richmond plans have been drawn for a vocational school, and plans are nearly ready for the Curtis addition. The new Tottenville High School awaits the selection of a site.

THE PICTURE RENTAL SERVICE AT LAWRENCE COLLEGE

The picture rental service at Lawrence College, as described in the *Liberal Arts College Bulletin,* is based upon the assumption that the way to learn to appreciate pictures is to live with them as part of one's normal personal surroundings, and upon the further assumption that if they are given a choice, students will normally choose the better things rather than the poorer.

The initiation of the enterprise was due to two phenomena which did not seem to fit very well together. On the one hand, the students showed a lively interest in the art exhibits which were hung outside the administrative offices and often purchased the less expensive pictures. On the other hand, their dormitory rooms were usually decorated with posters and advertisements. It seemed altogether likely that if better pictures were available at a cost within their means, students would choose the better rather than the poorer.

Through gifts, from a foundation, trustees, artists and friends, a collection of pictures has been built up. They have been chosen not only with care, but with the active advice and cooperation of the students, who were asked both as individuals and through representative groups what they desired from among the collections exhibited from time to time. The pictures when purchased were framed with extreme care. This proved more expensive than had been anticipated, but the educational results amply justified the cost.

During the college year, from time to time, beginning in November, 190 pictures were made available for rental at the flat rate of fifty cents a semester. Of this number 135 were rented. There are now 240 pictures ready for next year, and others are being added.

On the back of each picture is its title, the name of the artist, a brief biographical sketch and a description of the process by which the picture was made. It is now proposed to add a short bibliographical reference listing the books in the library which tell something of the artist, the picture or the process. Each picture is catalogued in precisely the same way as a library book, and the pictures are taken from the charging desk in the library precisely as books are taken. The reserve stock of pictures is kept in accessible cases, and representative samples are continuously displayed in one of the library's reading rooms.

The project requires a large part of the time of an enthusiastic promoter who knows how to deal with students. It can not be done casually and without the expenditure of a large amount of energy. But given those elements the basic assumptions seem to be more than justified.

UNEMPLOYMENT AND AMERICAN INDIAN EDUCATION

THE unemployment situation has compelled the Indian bureau to liberalize its eligibility requirements for Indian boarding schools, according to a letter addressed to all superintendents of Indian schools. Dr. W. Carson Ryan, Jr., director of education for the bureau, has issued instructions stating that practically all eligibles who apply shall be admitted to schools, even though it means overcrowding. He especially stressed the desirability of admitting youths who might compete in the labor market rather than large numbers of young children. The letter states that:

> Heretofore we have rightly been discriminating in our attitude toward the application of youth to our boarding schools, especially in those of our schools where conditions are crowded. I believe we shall have to reverse our policy and admit practically all eligibles who apply and be more liberal in our interpretation of eligibles, even though it means overcrowding, in order that we may hold these youths out of the competition with labor in the present emergency.
>
> This is believed to be much better than taking in large numbers of young children, a policy that has been urged upon us recently because of unemployment and bad financial conditions generally. To take older boys and girls, who would otherwise be competing in the labor market, does not have the same disastrous social effects that taking children does. In some instances we may even be able to help fathers of children by removing younger men and women who would otherwise be competing with them for employment.

The letter cautioned superintendents not to overlook the following obligations:

(1) To make surer than ever that young Indian men and women are given training that will really fit them for their future needs as workers.

(2) To accomplish this, regardless of any "preconceived notions about the sacredness of the old school program and organization."

(3) To connect up the idea of labor and education, trying by every means possible to have students work for their education.

He adds that "heads of our schools who have been interested in a 'pay for work' scheme as opposed to the present program should find the situation to-day a particularly good one in which to try out their ideas. The risk of inculcating dependence, always a serious one in the Indian work, is especially bad under the present conditions, and every experiment in developing responsibility for earning and spending wisely will be vigorously encouraged."

BROADCAST PROGRAM OF THE NATIONAL ADVISORY COUNCIL ON RADIO IN EDUCATION

THE National Advisory Council on Radio in Education announces that it will sponsor a program of radio addresses, consisting of two series of lectures—one on economics, the other on psychology—to be broadcast weekly on Saturday evenings, beginning on October 17, through the courtesy of the National Broadcasting Company. The programs will be on the air from 8:30 to 9:00, Eastern Standard Time. The half-hour broadcast will be divided into two fifteen-minute periods so that a lecture in each series may be presented every week. There will be thirty lectures in each series. President Nicholas Murray Butler, of Columbia University, will give a fifteen-minute introductory address preceding the first lectures.

The psychology lectures have been planned by a committee, consisting of Walter V. Bingham, *chairman,* Paul S. Achilles and Arthur I. Gates. The introductory unit of five lectures includes:

> "Psychology To-day: Its Relation to Other Sciences and to Social Problems," by James R. Angell, president of Yale University.
>
> "Psychology, a Modern Science of Human Management," by Professor Walter R. Miles, of Yale University, president of the American Psychological Association.
>
> "Learning and Forgetting: Some Recent Discoveries," by Dr. Edward S. Robinson, professor of psychology, Yale University.
>
> "Our Social Attitudes: Convictions and Prejudices, Their Origin and Control," by Professor

Gardner Murphy, professor of psychology, Columbia University.

"Current Trends in Psychology: The Middle Road between Behaviorism, Psychoanalysis and Other Schools," by Professor Robert S. Woodworth, president of the Social Science Research Council.

The second unit in the series on "Psychology To-day" will deal with "Child Development: Growth and Behavior from Birth to Adolescence." This unit has been arranged by a subcommittee of specialists, under the chairmanship of John E. Anderson. The speakers and their topics are:

"The Development of the Infant Mind," by Dr. Arnold Gesell, director of the Clinic on Child Development, Yale University.

"Children's Fears," by Professor Harold E. Jones, Institute of Child Welfare, University of California.

"Anger: Its Causes and Control," by Professor Florence L. Goodenough, Institute of Child Welfare, University of Minnesota.

"Social Behavior in Infancy and Childhood," by Dr. John E. Anderson, director, Institute of Child Welfare, University of Minnesota.

"Adolescence: The Difficult Age," by Professor Leta S. Hollingworth, Teachers College, Columbia University.

Later units will treat of educational psychology, changes in personality, animal behavior and industrial applications. A profusely illustrated pamphlet is being prepared to accompany each of the six units. Each pamphlet will not only summarize the separate addresses, but will also contain questions for discussion, hints for study and reference readings.

Since this is the first time that a series of educational programs of this type has been arranged for a nation-wide audience, those responsible for the series, while not yielding authenticity of subject-matter to popularity of presentation, are planning programs that will be interesting and important enough to encourage a considerable audience to tune in on the series regularly. The committees hope that some college and university professors will find the series of such value that they will advise their students to listen either individually or as a class.

EDUCATIONAL NOTES AND NEWS

Dr. Homer P. Rainey, formerly president of Franklin College, will be inaugurated as president of Bucknell University on November 13. Dr. Rainey succeeds Dr. Emory W. Hunt, who retired in June after serving for twelve years as president of the institution.

Dr. Isaac Butler Schreckengast, chancellor of Nebraska Wesleyan University since 1917, has presented his resignation, effective in the fall of 1932, to the board of trustees of the university. Dr. Schreckengast gives as reasons for his resignation ill health and the increasing burdens laid upon him by the financial difficulties to which the university has been subjected by the current depression. The trustees accepted his resignation and immediately elected him chancellor emeritus and professor of Biblical literature.

Dr. Kotaro Honda has been elected president of the Tohoku Imperial University at Sendai, Japan.

Professor Clemente Pereda, dean of the Middlebury College Summer School of Spanish, has resigned. Dr. Juan A. Centeno, assistant professor of Spanish at the University of Syracuse, has been appointed to fill the vacancy.

Mr. Frank Conner, of the University of Akron, has been appointed head of the McKinley Trade School, Wheeling, West Virginia, to succeed Mr. J. H. Lambert.

Changes in the faculty at Tufts College include the appointment as head of the department of economics of Assistant Professor Earle M. Winslow, who has been on leave of absence in Europe doing research work as a Guggenheim fellow. Mr. James R. Harrison has been appointed assistant professor of physics, and Mr. Walter Miller has been added to the department of mathematics as assistant professor. Professor Alanson T. Warren, formerly at William and Mary College, is to be professor of biology, taking the place of the late Dr. Fred D. Lambert. The Reverend Alfred S. Cole has been appointed assistant professor of homiletics, taking the place of Dr. Frank O. Hall, who has become professor emeritus.

PROFESSOR FLORIAN ZNANIECKI, of the University of Poznan in Poland, will be visiting lecturer on sociology at Teachers College, Columbia University, during the present academic year.

DR. RANDALL J. CONDON, formerly superintendent of schools at Cincinnati, and Dr. Charles G. Maphis, director of the Institute of Public Affairs of the University of Virginia, have been appointed to the National Advisory Committee on Illiteracy.

PROFESSOR ERNEST P. HORRWITZ, formerly professor of Sanskrit at the University of Dublin, and of Indo-European philology at the University of Bombay, will give two courses of lectures at Hunter College this winter on world literature and on French, German and Russian literature.

DR. PAUL W. PENNINGROTH, whose work has been in educational psychology and the social sciences, has been appointed head of the department of education in the junior college and school of art which was opened by Southern College, Lakeland, Florida, at Sarasota, Florida, on October 1.

MR. WILLIAM A. EVANS, for the past four years instructor in journalism at West Virginia University, has resigned to become director of public relations for the schools of Indianapolis, Indiana.

MISS ALICE H. HALEY, formerly state supervisor of home economics for Minnesota, has joined the faculty of the School of Education of Boston University.

DR. ROBERT D. BALDWIN, who has been director of graduate courses in educational administration at West Virginia University, has been appointed superintendent of Haskell Institute, government Indian school at Lawrence, Kansas.

DR. CHARLES SINGER, lecturer in the history of science at University College, London, who made an extensive lecture trip in the United States in 1929, expects to spend the winter of 1931–32 at the University of California at Berkeley. Between April 20 and May 20, 1932, Dr. and Mrs. Singer expect to lecture at a number of American colleges and universities. Inquiries as to their schedule may be made of Dr. George W. Corner, School of Medicine and Dentistry, University of Rochester, Rochester, New York.

MR. E. MARION JOHNSON, of Chicago, editor of the *Scholastic Editor,* will be the principal speaker at the thirteenth annual conference of the high-school editors of Kansas, at the University of Kansas, on October 9 and 10. Plans for the annual conference have been announced by Professor L. N. Flint, chairman of the department of journalism, under whose auspices the conference is held each fall. Seventy-eight high schools from all parts of Kansas were represented at the conference last year. The delegates registered included 55 teachers and supervisors, 109 boys and 165 girls. Delegates at the annual university dinner numbered 309.

DR. AUSTIN TAPPAN WRIGHT, professor of law at the University of Pennsylvania since 1924, died on September 19 at Las Vegas, New Mexico, from injuries suffered in an automobile accident.

DR. LUJO BRENTANO, professor of political economy at the University of Munich from 1891 to 1920, died in Munich on September 24, at the age of eighty-seven years. He was the author of "A History of the Economic Development of England."

MR. FRANK L. TOLMAN, director of the library extension division of the state of New York, has been elected president of the State Library Association. He succeeds Wharton Miller, head of the school of library science at Syracuse University. Ernestine Rose, librarian of the 35th Street branch of the New York City Public Library, was named as vice-president, and Milton J. Ferguson, of the Brooklyn Public Library, was elected to the council for 1931–1932.

DR. MAX C. STARKLOFF, city health commissioner in St. Louis, Missouri, for thirty years, was made president of the International Society of Medical Health Officers during the recent meeting at Montreal.

PRESIDENT ADA L. COMSTOCK, of Radcliffe College, one of the vice-chairmen of the American Council of the Institute of Pacific Relations, has sailed from Vancouver, B. C., to attend the fourth conference of the institute, which will be held in Hangchow, China, from October 21 to November 4.

MR. JAMES C. KIMBERLEY has made a gift of $100,000 to Lawrence College to be used for construction of a memorial to his father, which is to be an addition to the Institute of Paper Chemistry, affiliated with the graduate school of the college.

THE Buhl Foundation has made a grant of $30,700 to the University of Pittsburgh to establish a course in field training for graduate students in social work.

BOWDOIN COLLEGE has received a bequest of $50,000 under the will of the late Edwin Bradbury Smith.

THROUGH a special gift from an anonymous donor, the University of Chicago has been enabled to begin the development of a new department of music, with the appointment of Carl Bricken, Pulitzer prize winner in 1929, as assistant professor of music. Mr. Bricken will give his first classes during the autumn quarter, which opened on October 1.

THE Society for Ethical Culture of New York City has received permission from the Supreme Court to mortgage its property at the southwest corner of Central Park West and Sixty-fourth Street for $200,000, besides a present one of $445,000, to aid in the erection and equipment of an elementary school building on its property at Fieldston in Bronx County. The proposed structure will rise in the block adjoining the society's upper school building, which includes a junior high, high school and prevocational school. The cost will exceed $250,000, but the society expects to obtain the remainder of the money from other funds.

AT the dedication of a new building of the North Yarmouth Academy, Maine, on September 18, Mr. Cyrus H. K. Curtis responded briefly to expressions of appreciation. Mr. Curtis has made financial gifts to the academy, totaling $251,000, through which it is hoped it will regain the prominence it held in past years.

AN announcement in the New York *Times* states that salary decreases averaging 10 per cent. have been accepted by the faculty of Ohio Wesleyan University.

THE school of education of Boston University has announced the organization of an elementary education department. The staff consists of Professor Guy M. Wilson, *chairman*, Miss Mabel C. Bragg, Professor W. Linwood Chase and Mr. Donald D. Durrell. Dr. Wilson has just returned from a year's leave of absence for study abroad.

BUCKNELL UNIVERSITY will hold its sixth annual conference on education at Lewisburg on October 23 and 24. Speakers for the general sessions will be: Dr. Homer P. Rainey, who has been recently elected president of the university; Dr. Harold O. Rugg, of Teachers College, Columbia University, and Dr. Anna Y. Reed, of the school of education of New York University. There will be six sectional and subject meetings in addition to the three general sessions. The Susquehanna Valley Secondary Principals' Association collaborates with the university in its secondary education program.

THE twenty-eighth annual convention of the National Conference of Juvenile Agencies will be held in Baltimore from October 15 to 17, at the Lord Baltimore Hotel. Among the speakers will be Dr. Miriam Van Waters, former judge of the Children's Court, Los Angeles; Dr. Helen MacMurchy, chief, Division of Child Welfare, Ottawa; Dr. Charles H. Johnson, state commissioner of social welfare, New York; Dr. W. L. Nofcier, sociologist, Asbury College; O. H. Close, superintendent of the Preston School of Industry at Ione, California; Dr. C. E. Partch, dean of the school of education of Rutgers University; Leonard Mayo, of the New York School of Social Work, and others.

A PROPOSAL to found scholarships by state appropriation for the University of Maryland is being given consideration by the board of regents of the institution. State Senator E. Milton Altfeld, who asserts that scholarships now are being given students "talented in the muscle direction," although not provided by law, has proposed that sixty scholarships be created and granted for distribution by the state senators of the twenty-three counties and the City of Baltimore. At present there is no legal provision for scholarships at the university, in spite of the fact that the institution is maintained by state legislative appropriations.

THE Junior College of Connecticut, located in Bridgeport, Connecticut, has been registered with the New York state department of education.

THE strike of students of the University of Guayaquil in Ecuador was settled by a government commission on September 12, the students gaining their demands for certain replacements among their teachers. The strike started six weeks ago and was responsible in part for the resignation in August of President Isidro Ayora and his cabinet.

DISCUSSION

THE PROJECT PRE-EMINENT

IT is now nearly forty years since McMurry stated in his "General Method" that his purpose was "to apply the lever and to lift into prominence the moral-character-building aim as the central aim in education." At that time it had "no recognition in our school course." Theoretically it is now the goal of all education.

The National Education Association put down ethical character as one of the seven cardinal objectives, emphasizing at the same time its importance as follows: To consider moral values in education is to fix attention upon what should be the paramount aim. A schooling that imparts knowledge or develops skill or cultivates tastes or intellectual aptitudes, fails of its supreme purpose if it leaves its beneficiaries no better morally. . . . The greatest need of our boys and girls is character.

Harold Saxe Tuttle, in *Education* (November, 1930) says, "The general educational journals are devoting increased space to problems of character, while popular magazines are invading the field of education in a growing demand that the schools live up to their opportunities." The same writer states truly that all the leading educators of to-day place character first among educational aims. On the theory side of education then moral character comes into its own.

In achievement, however, not so. The moral status is anything but satisfactory. The product is admittedly disappointing. Mrs. Florence E. Allen, judge of Ohio State Supreme Court, in *The New Century S. S. Teachers' Magazine*, says, "When we look out into the nation around us, when we see the Supreme Court of one great state wiping out an entire city election because the whole proceeding was permeated with bribery and fraud; when we see the Supreme Court of another state holding its governor guilty of a felony; when we see in a metropolitan city armored cars manned by bandits patrolling the streets, large groups of lawless people putting themselves above the law, can we say that we have worked out our spiritual enterprise as efficiently as we have built the framework of our government?" S. O. Courtis, in SCHOOL AND SOCIETY (Vol. 26, p. 322) says: "Society is ill, very ill. Crime, ugly and menacing, persistently growing, is gnawing like a cancer at the very vitals of civilization." J. V. Collins, in *Education* (April, 1931), says, "We teach morals and our product is satisfied if it can evade punishment for wrongdoing." Again, "A large part of our population lives on a low level." William McAndrew is quoted in *Journal of Education* (July 20, 1931), as saying before the National Education Association at Los Angeles, "We seem to be all for learning—for grades. But the fact is that the crookedest crooks in our government have been well educated, and despite the early concept of our educational system there are more crooked officials, more corrupt judges, more crime and rotten politics in this country than in any other country in the world." Dr. J. E. Adams, in *Kentucky School Journal* (October, 1929), proves by statistics that "America is the most lawless civilized nation on the earth to-day."

A situation and a challenge! The daily detail of debauchery and the inordinate craving for such carrion, a time of moral degeneracy with its crime wave whose peak is formed by eighteen-year olds!—this moral breakdown, all too general, and this juvenile delinquency in particular, brings the matter of character forcibly forward as education's biggest problem and one which is becoming more and more formidable. Education can change the situation, but this it will not succeed in doing satisfactorily until moral character is not only theoretically the goal, but becomes, by whatever desperate effort required to put it there, the center upon which all activities are focused. Blind optimism and "the world's getting better" doctrine will hold many awhile longer in a fool's paradise, but unless there is a turn in the present trend a certain disillusionment is impending. Everything may depend upon an immediate awakening.

The project of all projects! Consciously or not we are ever on this project. Let it become the project preeminent, the great composite that it is, and worked at with deserving earnestness and enthusiasm, and a change will inevitably come. But for near-sightedness, every project decided upon, planned and worked would be consciously and purposefully related to this one major and made to contribute its full share toward the paramount objective, at the same time none-the-less serving its subordinate purpose. With the situation and the need impelling toward it, have we not here a logical basis for the integrating of all educational work? If not, why not? And when all educational forces of all levels are found really working on this project of projects; when all curricula are formed accordingly, materials selected, courses laid out, standards adjusted, measurements characterized, methods adapted, activities pursued, atmosphere created, cooperation won, and help from on high appropriated—then shall education "more than scratch the surface of moral training." With an efficient, adequate, unified force putting forth concerted effort utilizing all powers at its command, persistently, patiently, perseveringly working to the one great end, we shall presently experience a relief from "an intolerable situation," our civilization will be delivered from its threatening ruin, and education will be able rightly to rejoice as never before in the product of its labors and in the fulfilment of that prophetic supplication, "Yea, the works of our hands, establish thou it."

STANFORD CHAMBERS
PORTLAND CHRISTIAN SCHOOL,
LOUISVILLE, KENTUCKY

QUOTATIONS

LIBERAL EDUCATION IN JAPAN

We have received a visit from a well-known Japanese educator, Mr. Kuniyoshi Obara, who left us two illustrated pamphlets of great interest. One, entitled "Education of the Seijo-Gakuen, 1930," is the program of the school of that name, situated at Kinuta-Mura, near Tokyo. Founded in 1917, the Seijo-Gakuen was originally an elementary school. In 1922 the middle school was added, in 1926 the boys' high school, and the following year the girls' high school and kindergarten. Three famous educators, well known outside Japan, Messrs. Sawayanagi, S. Konishi and Kuniyoshi Obara, have presided over its destinies. The conditions for admission are severe, one of them demanding that the parents or guardians should be fully in sympathy with the school and its educational philosophy. The school bases its education on scientific principles, emphasizing the development of character, the formation of good habits of individual work, the love of nature and the education of the whole man.

The second pamphlet, "Education of the Tamagawa-Juku," describes a very important experiment carried out by Mr. Kuniyoshi Obara in the school founded by him, Tamagawa-Gakuen, at Machida-Machi, near Tokyo. This is a mixed school, ranging from kindergarten to college, and completed by a research institute for teachers. It was created so that children of parents who could ill afford to pay heavy fees might have the benefit of his educational ideas. The Juku educational system is specifically Japanese and already traditional. The Juku is a school where the masters and pupils alike share a life of hard work, each master being the head of a little family, all the little families forming one big family. Instruction is not gratuitous, parents are asked to give what they can towards the education of their children, the idea being one of self-sacrifice for the enlightenment of the race. In addition, the children earn a good deal towards living expenses at the school itself, for not only do they participate with the masters in the domestic work, but they are trained to cultivate the land, care for animals, make their own dwellings and furniture, print their own books and run cooperative stores, etc. In this way the school is entirely self-supporting. Mr. Obara believes that this system of educating men and women to be independent will make them honest, upright and capable of managing their affairs in whatever branch of life they may find themselves. Furthermore, he is convinced that the combination of manual productive work and intellectual work, a combination which relates the school to real life, will give to the child that complete education which will enable him to understand real beauty and true religion. Although founded for poor children, the school does not close its doors to the children of the wealthy whose parents believe in character training through work. Mr. Obara brought us a fine series of Pestalozzi's works in Japanese, printed by his pupils with type made by themselves and delightfully illustrated with Swiss engravings from the original edition. These volumes would do credit to any big publishing firm.—*Bulletin of the International Bureau of Education.*

EDUCATIONAL RESEARCH AND STATISTICS

DOES REMEDIAL INSTRUCTION PAY?

THIS question might as well have been, "Does it pay to give additional time for instruction on a teaching unit in physics?" The answer may seem rather obviously yes, but one might cite cases in which the answer would be no. For example, if measured achievement showed that the objectives of the unit had been met by every pupil, added time for instruction would be unnecessary. All the objective data available, however, show no known case of perfect achievement by all pupils in any teaching unit. As a matter of fact, poor achievement is the general rule. If, then, poor achievement be recognized by the instructor and the points of poor achievement discovered, remedial instruction should undoubtedly raise subsequent scores in a ratio which bears a close relation to the efficiency of the instruction.

One of several experiments[1] on a teaching unit in high-school physics carried on under the direction of the institute during 1930–31 sought to discover if an added six days of instruction would significantly raise achievement, measured by objective test scores. For the experiment a preliminary test preceded fourteen days of instruction, after which, Final Test Form A was given. Six days of remedial instruction were then followed by Final Test Form B, which test covered the same instructional objectives. Both forms had possible scores of 79. Table I presents the evidence in raw scores for 602 pupils in 21 schools.

[1] For descriptions of these experiments, see *North Central Association Quarterly,* 5: 485–489, March, 1931.

TABLE I

SCORE DIFFERENCES FORM B—FORM A WITH SIX DAYS OF INTERVENING INSTRUCTION

Mean score Form A	49.85 ± .54*
Mean score Form B (after six days)	62.24 ± .38*
Difference (B–A)	12.39 ± .34*

* Standard error.

Apparently there is a substantial gain, but this may show up because Form B is an easier test, or because of the practice effect on B of having had Form A previously. It happens that experimental data are available from other similar experiments conducted under the same time conditions, except that the additional six days were omitted, Form B following Form A a day later, there being no remedial instruction. Table II gives the data for these experiments for 1,423 pupils in 34 schools.

TABLE II

SCORE DIFFERENCES FORM B—FORM A WITHOUT INTERVENING REMEDIAL INSTRUCTION

Mean score Form A	52.38 ± .32*
Mean score Form B (one day later)	57.77 ± .27*
Difference (B–A)	5.39 ± .20*

* Standard error.

These data show higher mean scores on Form B. The question still to be answered is, "Is the difference (B–A) in Table I (with remedial instruction) significantly greater than in Table II (without remedial instruction)?" Table III makes the statistical comparison.

TABLE III

COMPARISON OF SCORE DIFFERENCES FORM B—FORM A WITH AND WITHOUT INTERVENING REMEDIAL INSTRUCTION

Difference between B–A (Table I) and B–A (Table II)	7.00 ± .39*
Difference divided by its standard error	18.0†

* Standard error. † Critical ratio.

NOTE: Standard errors were computed for correlated and uncorrelated measures, respectively, in the proper cases.

The critical ratio is highly significant, showing that the added six days of remedial instruction resulted in significantly higher achievement, on the average, for the whole group of pupils. In other words, objective test data give distinct evidence that remedial instruction pays in experiments similar to those conducted.

Another method of making comparisons is by considerations of single classes, transmuting scores in B to comparable A scores. Such transmutation may be done from superimposed (1) standard deviation, or (2) percentile graphs. For example, if the mean score of a class is 48.9 in Form A and 66.6 in Form B, the latter may be transmuted to a comparable A score of 60.8 by the standard deviation graph, or 62.9 by the percentile graph. The gain due to the six days of remedial instruction is then 11.9 score points (standard deviation graph), or 14.0 (percentile graph).

This procedure was followed for 33 classes in 22 schools enrolling 688 pupils. Graphs were constructed on the basis of 1,423 pupils in 34 schools, in which Form B followed Form A without remedial instruction, and all mean B scores transmuted to comparable A scores. Of the 33 classes, 28 made gains by the first criterion (standard deviation graph) and 30 by the second criterion (percentile graph). It is clear that a very few classes failed to make any gains. On the other hand, some classes made very great gains. The mean gain by the first criterion was 5.6 score points, and by the second criterion, 7.1 score points. It may be stated that for the classes making no gains, instruction was not definitely directed toward the objectives measured by the tests. In classes making great gains, on the other hand, instruction profited from the disclosures of Form A which stimulated efficient remedial instruction. It is to be understood that the method of preparing the graphs eliminated the practice effect of Form A on Form B so that the stated gains were due only to the added remedial instruction.

Remedial instruction does pay, then, in terms of measured achievement. This statement is premised by the supposition that instruction is directed toward the objectives which the tests are designed to measure.

A. W. HURD

INSTITUTE OF SCHOOL EXPERIMENTATION,
TEACHERS COLLEGE,
COLUMBIA UNIVERSITY

NEW BOOKS IN EDUCATION

CAPEN, LOUISE I. *A Workbook in Local, State and National Government.* Pp. 256. Illustrated. American Book Company. $.60.

CHAYER, MARY E. *School Nursing.* Pp. xvii + 292. Putnam. $2.50.

CORMACK, MARIBELLE and WILLIAM P. ALEXANDER. *The Museum Comes to Life.* Pp. 207. Illustrated. American Book Company. $.76.

FORESMAN, ROBERT. *The High Road of Song.* Pp. 208. American Book Company. $.68.

HALE, CHARLES B. and JAMES E. TOBIN, editors. *Contrast and Comparison.* Pp. xi + 476. Prentice-Hall. $2.00.

HOLY, T. C. *Survey of the Schools of Springfield, Ohio.* Pp. ix + 84. 22 figures. Ohio State University. $1.00.

JONES, EDWARD S., editor. *Improvement of Study Habits.* Pp. 118. Author. $.50.

KRINER, HARRY L. *Pre-Training Factors Predictive of Teacher Success.* Pp. 91. School of Education, Pennsylvania State College.

MCELROY, MARGARET J. and JESSICA O. YOUNGE. *Toby Chipmunk.* Pp. 80. Illustrated. American Book Company. $.52.

MILES, DUDLEY and others. *Literature and Life Student's Guide.* Book I. Pp. vi + 82. Scott, Foresman. $.28.

NYBERG, JOSEPH A. *Tests and Drills in First Year Algebra.* Pp. 176. American Book Company. $.52.

PETERS, CHARLES C. and F. THEODORE STRUCK, editors. *Abstracts of Studies in Education at the Pennsylvania State College.* Pp. 96. The College.

SMITH, E. T., editor. *A New Approach to American History,* by D. C. Bailey. Pp. xiv + 124. University of Chicago Press.

WARD, C. H. and H. Y. MOFFETT. *The Junior Highway to English.* Revised edition. Book II. Pp. xv + 334. Illustrated. Scott, Foresman. $1.00.

WHITFORD, WILLIAM, editor. *Theatre Art,* by Victor D'Amico. Pp. 217. 59 figures. 30 plates. Manual Arts Press. $3.25.

EDUCATIONAL REVIEW

Edited by WILLIAM McANDREW

EDITORIAL COMMENT

FRONT SEAT CLUB

When we stepped upon the stage to preach the educational gospel to the charming heathen of Pennsylvania in the old city of York, once the seat of the Continental Congress, a thrill of gratitude tingled through our old bones. All the empty seats were behind the audience. Quamobrem? Arthur Ferguson, superintendent of schools and director of the institute—he did it. As each teacher registered, a slip assigning a designated seat for the whole week was handed out. On it was the simple statement: "Our speakers are your guests. Your courtesy will not let you chill them by the sight of empty seats among us. Bare benches are the bane of public speaking."

Ferguson gave to each teacher the satisfaction that one gets from owning a box at the opera. He adds himself to the list of knowsome hosts who recognize their responsibility for seeing that the speakers are at their best. Ferguson thinks it incumbent on him to help the audience get the most out of the program.

Thus, he belongs to a courteous group in which I know, first hand, are Joseph Richey, of McKeesport, Albert Leonard, of New Rochelle, Edward Fuller, of Darien, Carroll Reed, of Minneapolis, Alice Leatherland, of New Canaan, John Scully, of Brockton, Payson Smith, of Massachusetts, Armond Strong, of Savannah, L. P. Hollis, of Greenville, and William John Cooper, always a Californian. These people make it their business to see that no educational meeting of theirs is chilled by the dismal beginning, "Will those in the rear please come forward." If you know of any Abou Ben Adhems that should be added, do send me their names that I may engrave them on the tablets as those who love their fellow men.

For it is a disgrace that education, which all our eminent statesmen have called the indispensable means of progress, should be given a smear of backwardness by its own people.

In most of the educational meetings I have attended this lack of respect, not intended, not conscious, is evident. Engineers when listening to a speaker don't chill him with empty front benches. Doctors don't, nor attendants at a prize fight.

A back-seat meeting indicates that the head officer doesn't know his business, or is short of courtesy to his speakers, or doesn't care. It is one of the situations in which leadership is needed. Come on in. Let's form the Front-Seat Club; seal—an empty bench with the motto, *Nullum in fronte.* Dues—nothing a year. President—Albert Edward Winship. Recorder—Thomas Briggs.

SHOTS FROM COLORADO

Of the return volleys batted toward me by Professor Wakeham, of the University of Colorado, one I claim as foul. This is it:

"Mr. McAndrew quotes with apparent approval Professor Henry Morrison's statement that any one can be taught anything—one of the many *reductiones ad absurdum* of behaviorism."

This careless shot might annoy the innocent bystander, Henry, himself. What the optimistic Morrison did say in addressing teachers in St. Cloud and what I did quote him as saying was, "Any one can be taught anything *if the right kind of teaching is applied to him long enough.*" Which it does seem to me is no more of a *reductio ad absurdum* than each and all of my beloved Professor Wakeham's arguments for permitting the liberal arts colleges, supported by taxation, to assume the function of a sieve and of training a certain type of leaders. Professor Wakeham declares liberal arts colleges were founded for this purpose.

In appeals for legislative support every plea of a liberal arts college I ever read sedulously avoided mention of the sieve and leadership, while stressing the democratic purpose of affording opportunity to all the children of all the people.

The sieve and leadership idea is the rock on which the current of educational proposals splits. On one side, there are I know not how many college professors and masters of preparatory schools; on the other, as set out in their department resolutions, are most of the superintendents and principals of public schools. We believe that our scholarly friends are assuming a principle which those who pay the bills are unwilling to endorse. We of the common schools want all American youth educated to the capacity of each. Law and demand have put the bright and dull into our hands. Demand is putting them, professor, into yours. One court has ruled you can not dismiss a student for failure to meet your requirements. The *obiter dicta* involve the suggestion that you try various exercises until you get something profitable the students can do.

Even if training leaders and casting out the unleading were a legitimate occupation for a state department of liberal arts, where is there such a state college that has on its faculty experts in training for leadership? Or courses in it? Or a record showing that the leaders of its commonwealth were trained by that college in such leadership?

That large assemblages of youth do give opportunity and practice in leadership every observer will note. That any adequate professorial provision for study and development of leadership exists is widely doubted. Anyhow, I'd like my boys, whom it might take much longer than four years to train as leaders, not rejected from college on the old irrelevant ground of poor scholarly ability. I'd be willing to have them taught intelligent and discriminating followship. I speak the mind of the ordinary taxpayer.

To differ with a gentleman and scholar on so vital a point runs the risk of offending him. Public-school men, some professors and presidents, many legislators, numerous citizens differ with Professor Wakeham fundamentally. In fact, as Dr. Wallace quotes Abraham Flexner, "American democracy objects to sieves." For Professor Wakeham I here record respect; for his educational doctrine, abhorrence.

THE BOY WHO BROUGHT THE VEGETABLES UP

WHEN, fifty years ago, I used to hear the speakers tell us young men that work, pluck and sticking to it would bring success as surely as in the days of our fathers, I had my doubts. When I hear the same sort of optimistic exhorters speak to this generation of school boys and girls, repeating the same old slogans, I think of the scarcity of jobs. Yet, here, right under my nose, this is happening. A rowboat rich with the red and green and yellow of carrots, beets and squashes touches the beach. A high-school boy taking a basket, runs up the slope to our camp and cheerily tells milady that he has the potatoes, spinach, peaches, melons, corn and tomatoes she ought to have. His white shirt and trousers, even his ten-cent white-cotton gloves that keep his vegetables from being touched by human hands, are part of an intelligent scheme. Whoever selected his boatload of provender and arranged the display of it and the white canvas to prevent wilting in the sun, had the mind-stuff that writers on business personnel keep complaining is hard to find in high-school graduates. The samples in his basket are winsome. His customers do leave the camps and go down to look at his stock. They do buy to-day and give orders for tomorrow. Two men with trucks and one with a motor-boat, earlier in the season, used to call at the resort to sell vegetables and fruits. They come no more. Harry has captured the whole trade. Tibbetts used to shuffle up to the cabin and drawl, "I don't suppose you want no termatters to-day." Negative stuff. Harry puts his tempting samples before your eyes and says he thought of you the minute he saw these.

Superintendents like John Beveridge, Frank Cody, Paul Stetson, Milton Potter, Des Moines Studebaker and Birmingham Glenn have been playing this perfectly reputable game on their constituencies for years. It is getting to be the style among teachers not to beg, with a whine, for better salaries, but to play up the positive. "We like this town. We like your children. We like to deliver the goods. We'd sooner stay here than move to where teachers are paid more money." Education, itself, has been displayed in its attractiveness. Children do beg to be allowed to go to school.

You wouldn't want me to get out of this sketch without a bit of preaching. Here it is. It isn't Harry's white clothes and gloves and cheery manner that hold his trade. It is his stock. He knows his stuff. The flair some superintendents have for business, for buildings and equipment won't last them long. That's only the boat. What's inside is what counts. With all the published standings of different school systems in the matter of what the children know and can do, the superintendent in demand is the one who knows what the educational product ought to be and how to get it. Isn't that true? It is.

AUTHENTIC COMPANY

After all, the best educational comment is what you make on reading the pronouncements of men whose ideas have been found good enough to make into permanent books. Enter in, therefore, to the company of searchers, scholars, recorders, critics, builders and promoters of educational thought.

COMMENTS ON NEW BOOKS

THE WEST IN HIS BLOOD

FOR an educator to have a work[1] selected by the Book-of-the-Month Club gives us a fraternal thrill, a delight which extends far into the night as we follow his enthralling story of what the great plains have done to our history and national character. They prevented the spreading of slavery; they led Daniel Webster into the course that smirched his reputation in the North; they modified the type of American manhood and womanhood; they made the revolver and Samuel Colt and Chicago. How they were formed, why they have tall grass, short grass or tufts, and no trees, what happened to the Indians and why, what the Spaniards did, and the cowboy and barbed wire, windmills, and irrigation, what their literature is, their romance, their spirit, and their meaning in American life, is told with the verve of an outdoor artist, a born Westerner, a present Texan, a professor of history, a full-blooded American.

UNBABYFIED NEWS

YESTERDAY, while I was caressing volumes which I do not own in the Macmillan Company's visitors' parlor and wondering why I, with my dreams of avarice, had not been born to buy all the books I want, Editor Knowlton, of that company, called my attention to their bound volumes of their "News Review."[2] "I have heard," said the complimentary Knowlton, "that you were the first to introduce newspaper study into the public schools."

Modest blushes suffusing me, then this question:

"Who said that?"

Knowlton: "You did."

Myself: "Wrong, my son, what I said was that I began it in the Hyde Park High School, Chicago, in 1887. But a Scot told me that he had seen it in Dunfermline before that."

The Macmillan venture among its excellences has these superiorities. It is not written down to children. They don't like their news babyfied. The Macmillans have free access to the print and pictures of the *New York Times,* on the presses of which the paper is printed. Here you have an international journal, offering, each week, the most significant news occurrences of the seven days and comment enough to bring, as John Finley says, the past and present into relation with the ideas fostered by the schools. The weekly editorials by Dr. Finley, William Allen White, Thomas M. Marshall, Hamlin Garland, Walter Lippmann, Hamilton Holt, Charles H. Judd, Stuart Chase, William C. Bagley, Arthur Gates, Owen Wister, Richard T. Ely, Frank Hackett, Vachel Lindsay, Norman Thomas, William Green, Martin V. O'Shea and Florence Hale, added to the selected unsigned ones by the *Times* staff, ought to please the English teachers as means of showing the pupils that the masters of discourse are not all dead. Editor Knowlton says that the first year's experiment has decided the Macmillans to continue the prospect. That is good news for you.

It's all meat. There are no advertising bones.

HOW READING-BOOKS ARE BUILT

As I study the new Lewis-Gehres-Rowland-Stephenson-Price-Hoopes reading books[3] I real-

[1] Walter Prescott Webb, "The Great Plains." Ginn and Company, Boston, 523 pp. $4.00.

[2] "The News Review," The Macmillan Company, New York. 8 folio pp. 36 issues yearly. 1 to 9 subscriptions, 60 cents each; over 10 subscriptions, 50 cents each, postpaid.

[3] William Dodge Lewis, Ethel Maltby Gehres, Albert Lindsay Rowland, editors; Eunice Stephenson, Hattie Longstreet Price, Florence and Mar-

ize what an easy life McGuffy, Swinton, Hillard, Cathcart and the other reader makers of my boyhood had. Copy short best extracts from well-known literary works, prose and poetry, guess which ones will do for different grades, fill up the gaps with articles of your own—the trick is done! Each reading book was little more than a fattened magazine, usually sufficiently beyond the capacity of the young scholar to give the teacher opportunity to shine as an oracle.

I happened to intrude upon Lewis during the long building of this series and lost any idea I might have had of such book-making as a pleasant pastime for winter evenings. He showed me elaborate summaries of studies of what the common difficulties of reading are and in what grades they occur. Many college students are shown to lack ability to read usual eighth-grade books. He showed me charts of specific reading skills, of words needed in a good vocabulary and where they are first to be tackled, and where, afterward, to be stressed again. It reminded me of my old days in the railroad office, building up freight-and-passenger timetables, getting to competitive points as quickly as rival lines, allowing for sidings to meet and pass other trains, slowing down where track is poor and catching up over the good stretches. Either Admiral Sims or native gumption has driven Lewis into the conviction, whither all good workers come sooner or later, that objectives must be set up first, scaled according to importance, and kept in the mind's eye all the time. These authors have on the walls of their workrooms "translation of print into ideas," "thinking about the subject," "thinking about other subjects in the course of study," "habits of thinking about worthwhile things out of school," "cultivation of a love of the stiffer kinds of reading, which is study," "growth of a loyalty for the beautiful, the true and the good," "cultivation of healthy humor," "development of kindness for people and dumb animals," "information of men and events," "othermindedness," "patriotism" and "a broad recognition of the brotherhood of nations." "I observe," I said to Lewis, "that you harp much on the 'basal idea.' You are carrying 'skill exercises' far beyond the grades we usually stop at."

"There you show," he answered, "how much of a back number you are. If the researchers have discovered anything, it is that the disabilities of reading in high school and college come from lack of remedial and strengthening exercises for the older children. Supervisors are clamoring for follow-up work in the higher grades. Don't you know that?"

"I do, now. Anyhow, you have done a first-class thing in providing that the children, themselves, learn that there are many kinds of reading they will have to do: Solving a problem for oneself, getting a fact for some one else, making an abstract, self-testing, and so on. The outlines of objectives you set up are certainly remarkable blazes into the woods and up the hills."

These particulars, Lewis reminded me, are merely bones. A reading book must be like a beautiful living creature, dynamic, inspiring, a beloved companion.

I confess to a prejudice for Lewis. I noted him in the Syracuse High School twenty-five years ago, a smiling assassin of traditional absurdities which a too efficient state organization was feeding. I remember him putting self-government and presumption of pupil ability into the William Penn High School, Philadelphia. When he wrote the book, "Democracy's High School," Theodore Roosevelt hugged him to his bosom. I recall him in the state department of Pennsylvania's schools calling the pedagogues together and reminding them that in their commonwealth the first fundamental school law was passed in 1787, declaring good government the purpose of American education. He thrust in their faces the record of political corruption in which the Keystoners stood in the first line. He shot a volley of Sims, Taylor, Ayers and Gulick at them: "Conditions, desirabilities, plans, trial, correction, and plan again." There issued one of the best public-school courses in democracy that I have seen. Citizenship and language have been his hobbies. As an educator he hit the mark. He returns to simple and effective teaching in his books, "Practical English," "Knowing and Using Words," "The Simplified Dictionary," "English for Use," and this splendid series.

garet Campbell Hoopes, illustrators. "The New Silent Readers," Pre-primer, primer and eight books. John C. Winston Company, Philadelphia.

From Lewis I should expect a brilliant work. No doubt had I known the other authors I would not appear to be slighting their credit. By their works, here, ye shall know them as educators extraordinary. Eunice Stephenson's colored pictures of children's doings and adventures give me so much delight I am glad to boast of my second childhood. Red, blue, yellow, green, brown, flesh color, black and white, dolls, houses, animals, airplanes, games, seasons, works, end-papers and blank spaces for the owner to make his own pictures are here. Hattie Price comes into book three, with animal and story pictures of particular charm. For the five upper grades Mesdames Hoopes brighten the pages with colored composition rich in imagination, historic detail and varied artistry.

On Miss Gehres and Superintendent Rowland devolved the task of trying the manuscript on living classes, excising parts that didn't take well enough to suit, and stiffening the practice exercises where it was thought necessary. So here comes a series of basal readers founded on purposeful activities, informational units, graded building of vocabulary, exercise in drawing conclusions, finding the gist of paragraphs, learning how to study, using books of reference, making summaries, correlating school subjects, recall, speed, self-testing, understanding, maps, tables and graphs, conversational ability, civics and character.

To secure these ends and at the same time get the allurement which signally marks these books the authors have gathered a remarkably fresh collection of pieces by writers of distinctive ability. It is a great work worthy of the advancement of teaching, for which this decade is distinguished.

TIGERT'S TESTAMENT

The revered William H. Payne, first to occupy a collegiate chair of education, University of Michigan professor of the science and art of teaching, once said, before the standard testers had shown us how logarithms, square roots and algebraic formulas can be used to establish our P.Q., that we could estimate our professionalism by the amount of effort necessary to get ourselves interested in an educational report. John Eaton was at that time United States commissioner of education, prefacing the name of every school superintendent with the political "Hon," so were they all, Dutton, Marble, Harris, Peaslee, Seaver, Sill, *et al.,* honorable men. The spotty nature of the annual volumes, the short quotations from local system reports, pushed in between statistical tables, was hard reading. If you could find yourself interested you could honestly claim a high professional quotient.

The blue and gold volume[4] received this week by School and Society from Washington is the work of the Bureau of Education, for a year and eight months of the time when Dr. John Tigert was commissioner to a date when there wasn't any. The first eighteen chapters are separate monographs by specialists on higher education, medical, legal, movements in city school systems, rural, secondary, health, industrial, home economics, commercial, adult, nursery-kindergarten-primary teacher-training, parent education, educational boards and foundations, Alaska, school buildings, educational foundations. The familiar tables of statistics occupy ten fat pages. Chief statistician Frank Phillips does the beneficent work of summarizing these in a chapter by itself. Interesting are his figures for popularity of high-school subjects. He shows the percentage of students in various classes at eight periods since 1890. Some of these choices for 1890 and 1928 (percentage of pupils enrolled) are as follows for public and private schools.

	1890	1928
Latin	34 per cent.	25 per cent.
French	9 " "	15 " "
German	11 " "	2 " "
Spanish	0 " "	9 " "
Greek	4 " "	0.3 " "
Algebra	43 " "	36 " "
Geometry	20 " "	20 " "
Physics	21 " "	7 " "
Biology	0 " "	13 " "
Hygiene	0 " "	8 " "
General science	0 " "	17 " "
Community civics	0 " "	13 " "
Sociology	0 " "	3 " "
Economics	0 " "	5 " "
Problems of democracy	0 " "	1 " "

4 U. S. Office of Education, "Biennial Survey of Education, 1926–28," Superintendent of Documents, Washington. 1,229 pp. $2.20.

If this were not a bad year in which to mention things that cost more money there would be a wail that the good old Harris days, when the commissioner's report made two buxom volumes, are succeeded by this present one when two years are put into one book. We miss the special studies of separate educational movements, Moseley commissions, the educational system of France. We long for those literary excursions on which Anna Tolman Smith embarked each year, going through the school policies of Europe. Never mind, prosperity is just around the corner, all the great men say. In time the governmental publications of the nation most famous for education will have all the pages they want. Meantime, what we do get is well conceived and handled. It is easy to show a high P.Q. with this volume in your hand.

Commissioner Cooper's survey is on the way. Timely parts of it are now attainable by sending ten cents for each pamphlet to the Superintendent of Documents: "School Administrations and Finance," "Exceptional Children," "Speech Defects," "School Health," "College and University Education," "Engineering Education." From the contents it looks as though we shall have two notable volumes.

DIRECT HIGH-SCHOOL SERVICE

SIX handy volumes of school-betterment studies have come from the Henry C. Frick Educational Commission of Pittsburgh. Mr. Frick set up a fund for giving to public education benefits that are not usually regarded as having a claim on the school tax. Over two thousand teachers were given financial aid for summer studies. For more direct appeal to the school children an allotment of the fund was used to secure assembly addresses in the high schools. The present books are the outcome of this program.[5] I don't find the modest Gerwig's name in five of the books, but his geniality sparkles in the narrative and comment. I remember him as secretary of the Pittsburgh Board of Education, writing books on the perfect-score school, the Declaration of Independence, Shakespeare's ideals, and so on. Now, as trustee of this commission and secretary of it, he marches through these tasty volumes, summarizing the youngsters' criticisms and comments on Lorado Taft, Henry Turner Bailey, Edward Howard Griggs, S. H. Clark and Bertha Kūnz Baker, who gave the talks on beauty. He does the same with the character addresses of Albert E. Winship, Mrs. Percy Pennybacker and Earl Barnes. There were others speaking on music, literature, sport, science and personality. One book is a reprint of the address of Nebraska University's dean, Lucius Sherman, who gave the boys and girls a straight talk on education and must have made some teachers lift their eyebrows when he told how the pupil has been left to grow to maturity and learn despairingly from others the meaning of moss and pine.

The reading investigation occupies a volume by itself, the work of Anne Campbell Rinehart. It is an illuminating study of what high-school seniors, after eleven years of school, seventeen of home, church, newsstands, movies, street and alley teaching, are reading.

The gentle Gerwig himself writes a character study. At no time in the world has character been so much in the mind of the country, he says. The national association puts character at the last end of its seven objectives. It should be first of all. In the courses of study there is no connection between the subject of character and rearing of approved citizens which is the character-training goal. Author Gerwig compares the character codes that have been offered. He contributes simplification, makes an outline for grades, treats of approach, means, sequence, development, measurement, sample lessons, definitions, a character creed and a select list of books that help.

I can't give you the price of the books. When I heard last they were being given away for the cost of postage, which I would estimate at six cents a volume.

LIBRARY AIDS

YOUR friend, the American Library Association, continues its timely output.[6] The titles of

[5] George W. Gerwig, editor, 'School Betterment Studies.'' Henry C. Frick Educational Commission, Pittsburgh. 40 to 80 pp.

[6] Edna A. Hester, ''Books for Junior Colleges,'' 194 pp., $3.25; Isadore Mudge, Doris Reed, Constance Winchell, ''Reference Books of 1930,'' 39 pp., 70 cents; Theresa Elmendorf, ''A Reader's List of Poetry and Poets,'' 78 pp., 75 cents; Committee on Work with Children, ''Children's Yearbook, No. 3,'' 80 pp., $1.35; Committee of College

the books as given in my footnote indicate their scope and purpose.

John Arthur Thomson, for over thirty years professor of natural history, University of Aberdeen, gives one of the simplest, clearest summaries of the evolutionary doctrine to be found in print, citing, as in all seventy volumes of the association's bright series, the few best books recommended to those who fain would go deeper into the theme.

"Booklist Books" is the title of a classified list of scientific, art, educational, travel, biographical and story-telling books of 1930, selected by librarians and requiring a designated majority vote to secure inclusion of each book.

The Teacher-Librarian Handbook is a short summary of essentials, from equipment to classified lists of books for the school shelves.

Douglas Waples, in the college book, summarizes the study of university students' reading.

Mr. C. P. Baker has in the same book a good hot article on the libraries of teachers colleges.

Miss Elmendorf's poetry book has a surprisingly long list of works on the joy and praise of poetry. She classifies the chosen poets and the anthologies, gives books on form, measures and rhythm, twenty pages of titles and appraisals of studies of chosen poets, and an arrangement of texts and studies by periods from the prehistoric days to now.

THE GREAT OBLIGATION CLARIFIED

Ginn and Company offer another radiant text[7] for junior and senior high schools' use in the social studies, Harold Rugg writing it. It is forty years since Thomas Balliet went around addressing schoolmasters on the duty of teaching sociology, economics and politics in the public schools. A hundred years earlier Franklin and a group of American statesmen had insisted that this was the main duty of schools in a republic. Rugg is the outstanding American to make this possible. His school series supplies the matter and manner. We are confronted, says Harold, with the duty of educating youth to become informed, thinking, participating, improving citizens. It is a difficult task, so hard as often to be neglected as beyond the capacity of common school-teachers. Is it? Let us try.

Ten years ago he has it attempted in mimeographed form. A year later he prints the lessons and gets a hundred and more schools experimenting on it. Printing again, he sees it in more than 300 schools, over 600,000 copies used in small towns, large ones and cities. Twenty-two researching investigations on matter and method, examination of 50,000 tests have guided the making of the series. Facts of civic situations, insists the author, must be beyond reproach. We will take ours from the findings of recognized authorities. The teaching must be real. We, therefore, scatter the use of dramatic episode through the text. Memorizing the words of an encyclopedic history gets us nowhere. The pupil must think. The very center of the course is the problem-solving activities of the work-book which, for each pupil, accompanies the volume. Rugg does not need to tell the teacher who has tried one that the work-book accompaniment is one of the greatest time-saving, satisfaction-giving blessings that have come into teaching in our generation. Its planned repetition, its clarification of ideas, its rescue of truth from far-off abstractions, getting it into the youngsters' cosmos, and its ever-ready record of achievement and progress have settled the work-book's indispensability.

Cure for Don't Know How

Laid out on the plan of established principles of learning, the truth of the surrounding world, its communities, neighborhoods, country, village, city, family, clubs, work, government, law, crime, newspapers, magazines, literature, art, public opinions, liberty, obligations, business, money, international relations and future are taken up with that animation and interest

and Reference Section, "Yearbook, No. 3," 114 pp., $2.00; Committee, "A Handbook for Teacher Librarians," 52 pp., 65 cents; Maud Van Buren, "Essentials of Library Administration," 72 pp., 65 cents; Samuel Ranck, "Library Heating and Ventilation," 10 pp., 55 cents; Committee, "Sixty Educational Books of 1930," 64 pp., 65 cents; Committee, "Recreational Reading for Young People," 59 pp., 50 cents. J. Arthur Thomson, "Reading with a Purpose: Evolution," 48 pp., 35 cents. Am. Library Association, Chicago.

[7] Harold Rugg, "Introduction to Problems of American Culture." Ginn and Company, Boston. 616 pp. $1.96.

that have marked this Rugg personality, no doubt from infancy, but, certainly, since we New Yorkers used to tell one another a dozen years ago that an hour's listening to this blond youngster was the best of mental and spiritual tonics.

One of the most respected of the Chicago high-school masters has said, "We want to train the citizen of to-morrow to the end expected by the statesmen who established the public-school system, but we don't know how." With this series in existence you can't say that any more. The successes and failures of our country, its present distress, the way democracy has slumped into the oligarchy of the bosses, the ways out proposed by thinking men are here, by word, by picture, by diagram, by statistical table, made as penetrative as any civic medicine could be. It is not a baby book. Like Carlyle, Rugg is "terribly in earnest." But he is fascinating in his directness. He will not say America is first, but she can be first in all the superb ideals the good old patriots dreamed. The key is the school. The less productive studies, much as teachers and some parents and many professors love them, must be kissed a fond farewell. For, to quote Walter Robinson Smith, William Bagley, Edward Sisson, Charlie Prosser, Thomas Briggs, Martin V. O'Shea, Lotus Coffman and fifty-eight other respectables whose names I will disclose, if asked, our society, for which education was established as the nurse and healer, is dreadfully sick, but would be well if the schools had done their duty.

Here is medicine, curative and preventive. Get it into the systems of your ninth-grade classes and older. Get all your teachers to study it. It is full of their every-day interests. And, ye managers of normal schools, training classes and teachers colleges, who have so long omitted from your courses the very core of public service, behold how the labor of clearing a path has been done here, and a very Rugg given you for your progressive feet.

ACCIDENT ARRESTER

A. S. BARNES AND COMPANY now publish an extra-curricular library, of which fifteen volumes are out, snug little books on thrift, commencement, home room, student publications, assembly, athletics, pupil participation, clubs, and so on. Ten more are promised. The one the publishers sent me[8] is by the executive secretary, Education Division, National Safety Council, Idabelle Stevenson, whom many a superintendent of city schools has called to help principals organize the new and urgent service. Miss Stevenson, by table, diagram and picture, works out the problem of reducing deaths due to accident. These have increased 30 per cent. in ten years. From 1922 to 1928, accidental deaths of adults increased 32 per cent., of children only one sixth of one per cent. Since 1924, St. Paul reduced accidents to children 50 per cent.; St. Louis, 48 per cent.; Detroit, 47 per cent. in five years after appointing a supervisor of safety teaching. Methods, student organization, patrols, accident reporting, publicity assemblies, campaigns, athletics, essential information, tests, lists of cities giving instruction, where to get belts, buttons, badges, etc., selected bibliography make this a very efficient and attractive manual.

UNUSUAL MIND BUILDER

WALKING west from the house I was born in, on the banks of the Huron, in Ypsilanti, you will come to the third house on the right. Here appeared Walter Boughton Pitkin, fourteen years after me. Tablet-placing societies will please jot this topography in their plan-book, for Walter has advantaged the world by a score of bright books—"The Twilight of the American Mind," "The Young Citizen," "The Psychology of Happiness," "The Psychology of Achievement," etc.; and I have Boswelled him for you.

As an editor on the *Herald-Tribune* and on the *Post,* both of New York, as a contributor to magazines, as a teacher of psychology and as a professor of journalism in Columbia for one year less than twenty, Walter ought to be able to assemble important prescriptions for the management of mind and to arrange them without the usual introductory husks that the writers of "power" books make you fuss with in hunting for the fruit.

In his "How We Learn,"[9] Walter catches me

[8] Idabelle Stevenson, ''Safety Education.'' A. S. Barnes and Company, New York. 157 pp. $1.00.

[9] Walter B. Pitkin, ''How We Learn. A Book for Young People with Emphasis upon the Art of Efficient Reading.'' McGraw Hill Book Company, New York. 263 pp. $1.60.

in the third paragraph of his preface, where he says, "Among Americans, learning is not a lost art; for them it must be a new one. How can they get it?" From here to page 263, which is the last in the book, I am captivated by a remarkably novel, searching, convincing succession of self-tests, personal searchings, generalizations of high probability and apt illustrations, set out by a psychologist turned journalist, who dare not be long-winded or uninteresting.

Every count shows that the geniuses whose flushes of success come without work are so few per thousand of us that your youngsters must depend on labor, and labor done in accordance with established principles, if Mary and John are to reach their mental maturity.

On reading, that is more than mere recognition of words, so much of advancement depends that the author comes back to it again and again. Those schools that carry oral reading beyond the danger point, so that their children get the habit of whispering, or moving the lips, or of hearing inwardly the sound of the words they read, cripple the mind of their graduates, often for life.

The book is addressed to youngsters of twelve years of age and up to twenty, but I can imagine no authentic person older than that who could fail to be attracted and benefited by it. Pitkin makes a point of great penetration into high-school policies when he shows that the natural aptitudes, the impulses of born musicians, artists, and so on, rarely come to any one. The interests we have mostly spring from favorable information. Just now, high-school boys want to be Lindberghs, the girls sigh to be Greta Garbos. The queries of vocational counselors as to what children wish to become gather hardly more than echoes of what the youngsters have heard. The lavish time and energy put by high school and college on athletics, dramatics and dances create an exaggerated interest in pursuits so unlikely to aid in successful careers that a committee of Chicago citizens, commenting on the schools, charged them with an over-supply of applicants for the stage, the ball field and the night club. Schools produce a woeful scarcity of young people desirous of doing the serious work of the world. If schools would study the everyday tasks which 97 per cent. of their children will undertake, if schools would feature the satisfaction which undoubtedly lie in these pursuits, we should have less national discontent.

Pitkin's classification of the different sorts of school mollycoddles inclines you to guess that he has taught many school boys and girls. His prescriptions for the mollycoddle's self-cure are stiff and sane. Uninteresting tasks should be regarded as obstacles to be surmounted, never as nuisances to be evaded.

There are many unusual but effective directions for making study productive and economical, for preparing for examinations, for writing a paper. The exercises, the tests, the "things to think about" are remarkably fresh and abundant.

When my mother attended college none of her professors gave the students any help on effective ways of working. My teachers never gave me any hints. In her day Todd's "Student's Manual" was bought and followed by many students. In my time a favorite was Hammerton's "Intellectual Life." Pitkin appeals to a common human curiosity to know the best ways of using one's mind. He gives new interest to the good old maxims of the scholar; he draws upon modern experimental psychology for many newer rules. Every high school has boys and girls likely to use the book as a guide to self-improvement. It is full of tips for the teacher who cares for solid success of the children. It is striking and different.

REVIVING THE NIGHTINGALE

Be glad that Rowena Keyes has prepared for school use Laura Richard's life of Florence Nightingale.[10] The author, a daughter of the famous Sam Howe, who fought with Byron for Greek independence, and afterward developed teaching of the deaf and rescued Laura Bridgeman, had for mother Julia Ward Howe, of immortal fame, author of the "Battle Hymn of the Republic." Laura Elizabeth, according to my memory, was a favorite writer for young folks when I began teaching, more than forty years ago. The Lady Rowena tells me more than ninety books have been written by this

[10] Laura E. Richards, ''Florence Nightingale, The Angel of the Crimea.'' D. Appleton and Company, New York. 183 pp. $1.00.

cheery daughter of New England, who is now living in Maine at the majestic age of eighty-one. The "Florence Nightingale" came out twenty-two years ago. It is one of the sprightliest, most wholesome and charming biographies in print. Its stories of the girlhood of the great sanitarian are full of sport, work, clothes, books, ambitions, and all set out in a sprightly style. Samuel Howe knew Miss Nightingale and urged her to follow her bênt to serve humanity in spite of the social prejudices in England against a woman's doing anything of a public nature. The amazement of the world at the appointment of a woman as superintendent of an army hospital in the field, the obstacles she encountered, the grit she showed, the triumph she won make a heroic story that will be of undying interest as long as boys and girls, generous men and women are alive.

FACING THE FACTS APPERTAINING TO TEACHER IMPROVEMENT

William Yeager's painstaking study[11] finds a gain of virile insistence by administrators upon better preparation of teachers and much timidity still responsible for keeping public schools from doing so well as their managers know how to make them function. Many training schools are lagging. Many teachers in service are like the baby whose falling out of bed was due, in her little sister's opinion, to going to sleep too near where she got in.

Mr. Yeager's book describes the shake-up of old bones begun by Commissioner Finegan, Governor Sproul and the Edmunds act, raising the requirements for state certification and requiring teachers in service to qualify before a given date. If ever there was an educational revival Pennsylvania had it. By September, 1927, the goal set by the Edmunds act, the first three types of school districts were notably advanced. In the fourth-class districts 60 per cent. of the teachers fulfilled requirements. Teacher shortage embarrassed the plan. Qualified married women were encouraged to teach. This has given the state an improvement in the sentiment which seeks the best teachers regardless of marital status. Backward districts retain bars against married women. Easy administration by some of Dr. Finegan's successors or other causes have impaired the success of the law. Observation of the workings of it has led many officers to wish all the qualifying courses to be taken in summer sessions. These facts and many others of vital importance are brought out in this study of a state which within the memory of the younger men was as backward educationally as any north of Mason and Dixon's line. Educators everywhere, whoever are of that annoying type who want the schools held up to a service which the country can afford, will gain much wisdom from the Yeager study.

HIGH-SCHOOL WRITERS

For the boy, says the oracular Emerson, learns more from his mates than from his teachers. Wherefore the hundred and thirty-three prize-winning essays, short stories, poems, reviews, editorials, news accounts, interviews and cartoons released by Quill and Scroll[12] will be devoured with as much appetite by your high-school boys and girls as they show when getting directions from the teacher of English. The winning schools and pupils are here listed. The comments by the eminent judges give teaching a new and valuable point of view.

CONDUCT TAUGHT AND PRACTICED

As sure as I am that you sit there with your eyes on this line am I that the prevalent wish of America for better demeanored men and women is headed toward practicality. Ernest Butterfield says that people are everywhere asking him what the schools are doing to improve character. Out in California Clarence Case remarks if the older generation fails to set up a moral code that children can tolerate, the result must be demoralization. Into the perplexity step a cooperating trio—Charters, Rice and Beck—with the new device for reaching all the children all the time, the workbook.[13]

[11] William Allison Yeager, "State Certification as a Factor in the Training of Elementary Teachers in Service." Kutztown Publishing Company, Kutztown, Pa. 353 pp. $2.00.

[12] H. A. Berens, editor, "National High School Awards, 1930–31. Best Creative Work." American Educational Press, Columbus, Ohio. 160 pp. $1.50.

[13] W. W. Charter, Mabel F. Rice, E. W. Beck. "Conduct Problems; Grade 4, Playing Fair; Grade 5, What Would You Do? Grade 6, Good Sportsmanship; Grade 7, What's the Right Thing

Told by the field scouts of the publisher that his "Teaching of Ideals" was in need of a tryout in the form of pupil activity, Professor Charters drafted Mr. Beck and Miss Rice as in daily contact with children and, therefore, able to furnish suitable vocabulary and to experiment with the scheme. So now come the direct instruction, reasoning and conduct exercises in accordance with the Charters book. The major importance of indirect instruction is recognized. It leaves wide gaps. This selection is made to supply the lack. To provide every-day situations, to create a desire for right action, to lead to pupil discussion, to discover why children go wrong, to translate knowledge into action are the aims of the course. Honesty, courtesy, reliability, fairness, thrift, punctuality and a selection of traits which, with their accompanying situations, occupy five pages of the teacher's manual, are the specific aims of the course. After the teacher has introduced the "case" and put the class in the frame of mind for identifying it, each with his own experience, the pupil reads the case in his work-book and writes the answer. The cases are stories, incidents, situations—good practice in silent reading—followed by the questions and blank lines for the answers.

It strikes me that some of my dear brothers whom I have heard at conventions vehemently orating against direct teaching of morals might do worse than introduce these books as reading and writing exercises.

Recalling vividly, after fifty years, the straight-from-the-shoulder talk of our teacher, Ypsilanti Joseph Estabrook, aimed directly at us young cubs, considering the salutary effect many of his old boys have attributed to his direct methods, I am for the Charters plan of honest, clear-eyed, unafraid discussion of moral problems. Bronson Alcott did wonders with it.

NEIGHBORLY

There are a few hundred good people incorporated under the name, Committee on Cultural Relations with Latin America, who, with noteworthy intelligence and tact, have been quietly going to Mexico and holding good-will conferences with teachers, artists, publicists, clergy, lawyers and various leaders. An outcome[14] of the fifth symposium is a handsome printing of the lectures there delivered by Moises Saenz, Ramon Beteta, Carlos Chabez, Rafael Ramirez and other Mexicans; by Mary Austin, Chester Lloyd Jones, Judge Florence Allen and other Americans, representative authorities in music, painting, letters, politics and education. All the addresses as here printed are in English, informative, progressive and remarkably good reading. Education in Mexico, religious and social problems, the anti-alcohol campaign, labor problems, Mexicans in the United States, relations with us are some of the timely topics discussed. The contents and spirit of the book make it of first rank value for school and college libraries and use. Mr. Herring's benedictionary chapter, "The Fine Art of Understanding," is one of the fairest persuasive presentations you will find anywhere. For this and for founding these annual get-together meetings in Mexico we vote him the degree of P. P.—Practical Patriot.

AS A MAN THINKETH

The zest which Joseph Jastrow, studying psychologist for fifty years, has put into his own life transfuses from his last book.[15] With a text from James Harvey Robinson, "We do not think enough about thinking," the sage of Madison launches into an intimate talk with you on patterns of thinking, cause and effect, instinct, intuition, reasoning, prejudice, prepossession, superstition, convictions, controversies and creative intelligence. It is a hygiene of thinking. Mind is a peculiar machine that grows or wanes in power, according to careful use or neglect. Training can give to thought point and edge. Practice doesn't make perfect, unless it be the right sort. Thinking expands by acquired interests. Beware of a senile fallacy that the old things are enough. In childhood we welcomed distraction. The trend of it in later years is to disaster.

INTERLUDE FOR REFRESHMENT

Too solid a menu of book reviews may be relieved by this helping of sherbet. Headmaster Vaughan of Rugby serves it.

to Do? Grade 8, Playing the Game.'' Each 71 pp. 40 cents. Teacher's Manual, 22 pp. 20 cents. The Macmillan Company, New York.

14 Hubert C. Herring, Katherine Terrill, editors, ''The Genius of Mexico,'' Committee on Cultural Relations with Latin America. 112 E. 19th Street, New York, N. Y. 334 pp. $2.50.

15 Joseph Jastrow, ''Effective Thinking.'' Simon and Schuster, New York. 271 pp. $2.50.

An Englishman, stranded in a small waiting room at a Scottish railway junction, with no fire and nothing to do but to study the numerous advertisements on the walls, lit his pipe. The porter came in and called attention to a sign on the wall, "No smoking allowed." "Yes, I see it," said the Englishman, and continued to smoke. The porter brought the station master, who called the smoker's attention to the notice.

"Well, what of it?" asked the Englishman.

"Aren't you going to mind it?"

"First," answered the smoker, "have you got on your spirella corsets?"

"I hae nae corsets. What for would I be wearing corsets?"

"Then don't be so keen to bother me. See that sign in your own station, 'Wear Spirella Corsets.' And you, an official, disobeying one command, prominently put up with the approval of your superiors, are making a fuss over me because I disregard another. Pooh, pooh, man, one would think you a schoolmaster."

The smoker went on smoking.

WORLD MANAGEMENT

In his presentation of the timely subject of international relations,[16] Professor Mower gives you the work of an orderly mind expert in selection, skilful in arrangement, and masterly in giving satisfaction to the general reader. Whether the theme is government in general or war or commerce, or any of the numerous details of common interest to nations, he gives enough of the history, the success, the failure, the theory, and the criticism appertaining to the project to leave you with a sense of adequate information on each point. This is a book of such present import, so conveniently arranged and indexed, that you may send high-school and college students to it again and again for the enrichment of the writing and speaking programs necessary in educational activities. Dr. Mower was one of the professors designated by the Carnegie Endowment for International Peace to study relations in Europe. The University of Vermont gave him an additional year by Sabbatical leave. He offers the volume as a text-book for college classes. Itself is a proof that every college man and woman should equip himself by a study of the inevitable problems here covered. If we may believe the researchers who investigate what people want to read about, the public libraries will find, here, satisfaction of a strongly felt want. The author knows how to write for easy reading.

After a crisp chapter on the origin and nature of international cooperation and government you are taken through the present situation and introduced to the acknowledged needs of improvement and future course. Diplomacy, international administrations, treaties, laws, arbitration, conciliation, past and present, are narrated as if by one who realizes that the general reader desires both animated story and solid fact. Dr. Mower satisfies one appetite by his power of interest and meets the other by extensive reference to source and authority.

With the investigators finding "the next war" a theme of high interest among American readers, you can well begin your incursion by mastering the twenty-six pages on "The Problem of War," competition in armaments, attempts at limitation.

There are 300 pages on "The League of Nations," its composition, legislation mandates, protection of minorities, health service, problems of opium traffic, prostitution, obscene publications, slavery, relief, military sanctions, labor adjustments and world court.

Old theory is confronted with the fact that the world of a century or two ago, when people could live pretty much on their own national resources and were kept out of government concerns by a régime that made relations with other realms a private and secret matter, has changed. Transportation, telegraph, radio, postal penetration, necessity of foreign raw materials, participation in government by masses of people, have made international cooperation an unescapable need. Individuals have found that team-work brings greater rewards than personal liberty can give. Hence governments have been developed. Individual states, unwilling to concede or compromise, have preferred to fight for what they want only to come out, victor and vanquished, worse off than before. By degrees, postal unions and other international organizations have saved mankind

[16] Edmund C. Mower, ''International Government.'' D. C. Heath and Company, New York. 736 pp. $4.00.

an appalling amount of waste. The emotional and unreasoned recourse to war is nearer dissolution than ever before. When reasonableness possesses a majority of the people of the great nations and is backed by a healthy determination, another of the stupidities of mankind will be pushed into the limbo. To give this push, as I read my Franklin, Jefferson, Mann, Bagley, Judd, Sisson and Rugg, public schools were established among us for which we have to pay, whether we wish or not. The Mower book is full of sustenance to build in you muscle to make your push more capable.

MANY ON ECONOMIC PROBLEMS

Beginning as pioneers where every man had to strike out for himself, America has kept enough of individualism to make it permeate business, law and politics with selfishness. So begins Dr. Daniel Kulp in his preface to the third year-book of the Educational Sociology Association.[17] Supply and demand in different occupations is treated by Harold Clark. President Green of the American Federation of Labor reviews the influence of workmen's organization in establishing our public-school system. The conditions of industry are rapidly changing. Schools must change too. They should pay more attention to the facts and problems of industry. Richard T. Ely looks to education to adjust the utilization of land. George Counts describes the major features of Russian education and the five-year plan. We may learn from the Soviets that the society which tries to plan its future has a tremendous advantage over one which leaves its future to fate. There are essays on economics in schools and colleges, at home and abroad.

A STATE OF DELIGHT

That large part of the salt of the earth who attended the record-breaking educational convention in Los Angeles this year will find Miss Richards' offering[18] a satisfying souvenir. Other teachers will see its value as a supplement to geography study because of its lively nature. It is a series of trips with children into every corner of this wonderful state. A wise and companionable grandfather hands out palatable portions of history, science and useful information with the flavor that is attractive to young folks and conducive to digestion.

ADVENTURE

Two bright boys of the Badger State, Theisen, assistant superintendent of Milwaukee schools, and Leonard, associate professor of English in the University of Wisconsin, utilize their researches on children's tastes by compiling a series of true tales.[19] Here are Dan'l Boone, Hamlin Garland, the Pony Express, Ida Tarbell, Lincoln, Joaquin Miller, Amy Lowell, animals, ships, trains, adventures, thrills and heroism beautifully bound and printed, larded with pictures. It is put out as a sixth reader, if you wish, or a supplementary or a library book or a regular "juvenile."

CHANGING CLOTHES

Your girls' classes, if you are up to date, don't spend so much time sewing as they did. They give more time to studying materials and design. You may well get the name for generosity and give outright to your classes the text-books on this line of work, for the next batch won't look at the stuffs and patterns of their predecessors. Dr. McGowan and Miss Waite offer an up-to-the-minute manual.[20]

How to buy, how to test, how to care for, how to mend, rayon, silk and all the rest, how to be stylish and preserve your health and beauty, are the contents of this trim little book.

MOTHERS

Archer Wallace, maker of books for boys, author of stories of grit, heroes of peace, etc., offers "Mothers of Famous Men,"[21] His biographical stories in the volume are of the mothers of St. Augustine, Wesley, Washington, Edward VII, Goethe, Benjamin West, J. Q. Adams, John B. Gough, Lincoln (also of his stepmother), Haldane, Gipsy Smith, Chantrey, Barrie, Booker Washington and John Ashworth.

[17] National Society for the Study of Educational Sociology,'' Education and Economics.'' Teachers College Press, Columbia University, New York. 68 pp. $1.50.

[18] Irmagarde Richards, ''Our California Home.'' Harr Wagner Publishing Company, San Francisco. 436 pp. $1.50.

[19] W. W. Theisen, Sterling A. Leonard, ''Real Life Stories, Heroic Deeds.'' The Macmillan Company, New York. 446 pp. 88 cents.

[20] Ellen Beers McGowan, Charlotte A. Waite, ''Textiles and Clothing.'' The Macmillan Company, New York. 344 pp. $1.32.

[21] Archer Wallace, ''Mothers of Famous Men.'' Richard R. Smith, New York. 105 pp. $1.00.

MORE SHAKESPEARE

NOT for an examination in grammar, philology, geography, or any such purpose, but for literary appreciation Dr. Herford is editing "The Arden Shakespeare."[22] Here are five plays with copious interpretative and critical notes, glossaries and literary appendices, all in one volume.

PROGRESS BY PERSUASION

THE last thing in the Presseys' new book[23] is one of the handiest conveniences for those of us who got out of the normal school too soon. It is a glossary of the new terms with which the later books on education abound. Starting with "ability" we are carried through the different kinds of quotients, ages, scores, medians, norms, correlations, percentiles and other words of the new language of the profession.

This book, a new edition of a work issued nine years ago when there were 300 standard tests on the market, comes at a time when 1,100 of them are available. Their use has become an accepted educational procedure. When my present boss, James McKeen Cattell, forty-one years ago, put out his recommendations for the scientific measurement of mental traits and capacities, when James Rice, seven years later, proposed that the worth of a teacher be estimated by measuring the advance of pupils, our big men in the school field assured us that these were fantastic absurdities due to brain infections contracted in Germany. The hope that all this would blow over has faded away. The school system or teacher resisting scientific testing and using the admitted imperfections of the scheme as a dam against the flood, has lost hope of immunity. The Presseys are largely responsible for the breakdown of prejudice against the new movement. They translated its literature into simple language. They stressed the saving of time and effort attainable by use of the improved devices; they kept the project within the realm of common sense.

This is the line of their contributions in the revised volume: what and why is a test; the need and methods of diagnosis; the tests suitable for teacher, supervisor and superintendent; the misuse of tests; the common sense of statistics; measurement of ability. Chapters are devoted to the standard tests in different elementary and high-school subjects, with appraisals of tests now on the market. A sane and persuasive chapter is devoted to how to make the tests worth while as a means of bettering the every-day work of the children and as a source of satisfaction to them and to the teacher in substituting progress known and demonstrable in place of a misty hope.

A MIRROR FOR YOU

I READ with real edification Dean Bankes' short summary[24] of what the psychologists know about you and me at three years of age, at five, eight, twelve, sixteen, twenty, twenty-five, forty, sixty, seventy-five and after. Bankes is a quiet, cheerful conversationalist, full of specific personal illustrations of what he is talking about. He has read a lot but he does not crow about it. It's a good book for parents and for teachers of all grades and especially for lazy old men.

SUPPLYING A DEARTH

Two Michigan women[25] note that the Starbuck-Shuttleworth study of children's reading shows a great scarcity of reading books touching the interests of very young children. What are their interests? From a series of tabulations of studies it is found that the dear old Froebellian pictures and plays of 1837 fail to charm American tots. From the high favorites of 1931 the ladies Read and Lee select grandfather's farm, locomotives, airplanes and boats. They make a delightful little primer about each, guided by Arthur Gates' word list. The big colored pictures, one for every lesson, I am sure would tickle my adored Froebel to pieces. Make no mistake; if you go into a classroom where their books are available the other teachers will gossip about your lingering in the kindergartner's room. If you think I am childishly excited over these gems, I'll have you know that Professor Patty Smith Hill says they are, for schools, an enlightening artistic delight.

[22] William Shakespeare, "Henry IV." "Midsummer Night's Dream," "Much Ado About Nothing," "Romeo and Juliet," "King Lear." D. C. Heath and Company, Boston. 1055 pp. $1.72.

[23] Sidney L. Pressey, Luella Cole Pressey, "Introduction to the Use of Standard Tests." World Book Company, Yonkers-on-Hudson. 266 pp. $1.80.

[24] Walter Joseph Bankes, "Your Complete Life." The Christopher Publishing House, Boston. 74 pp. $1.25.

[25] Helen S. Read, Eleanor Lee, "Social Science Readers." Charles Scribner's Sons. New York. Four books, 36 pp. 60 cents each.

SCHOOL AND SOCIETY

EDITED BY J. McKEEN CATTELL

WITH WHICH IS COMBINED THE

EDUCATIONAL REVIEW

EDITED BY WILLIAM McANDREW

Volume 34 | Saturday, October 10, 1931 | Number 876

THE EMERGENCE OF THE COLLEGE LIBRARY*

By Dr. LOUIS R. WILSON

LIBRARIAN OF THE UNIVERSITY OF NORTH CAROLINA

The purpose of this paper is threefold: (1) To comment briefly on the efforts made by American schools and colleges to redefine their educational objectives and procedures; (2) to review the studies which have been made of the status and functions of the college library and (3) to suggest ways and means by which the college library may be more effectively utilized in achieving the educational objectives of the modern American college.

I

For the past twenty-five years the American school and college (particularly the college) have undergone a continuous bombardment of criticism. From press and platform, classroom and office, both have been taken sharply to task for their seeming lack of purpose and effectiveness. They have been urged to reexamine their functions, to redefine their objectives and to perfect their procedures so as to guarantee a quality of training that will maintain an intelligent and vital democracy.

Fortunately for the school, it has been able and willing to submit its case to the experts in the major university schools of education and research foundations for diagnosis and prescription. Its entire procedure from the first grade to graduation from the high school has been investigated in the most minute detail. Its functions and objectives have been restudied and redefined, its curricula reorganized, its methods of instruction revised, its technique and measurements refined. School boards and administrators, state and national education associations, state departments of education, university schools of education, teachers colleges, summer schools, journals and graduate dissertations have allowed no aspect of its procedure to escape investigation and publication. The result is that the seven cardinal principles of education for the lower schools are as well defined and as generally known by the present generation as were the seven deadly sins in the Middle Ages. Not only are they known, but the school is consciously attempting to carry them into effect.

In consequence of this exact definition and statement of objectives, the place of the library in the school and the part it is expected to play are likewise clear. Courses on the purposes of the curriculum and the functions of the library for teach-

* Paper read before the American Library Association, New Haven, June, 1931.

ers and library workers, instruction in the use of materials for pupils, socialized recitations, individual assignments, project and problem procedures, the "Dalton Plan" and the "contract" technique place the library at the very center of the school and make of it the principal synthesizing instrument in the modern school educational process.

In the case of the college, self-examination has not been nearly so extensive. The college and the university, while quick to investigate the practices of the lower schools, have not shown an equal ambition to investigate themselves or to have their procedures investigated. Respect for tradition, and an insistence upon knowledge of subject and ability in research as the principal essentials to effective college performance have frequently stood as barriers against the search for knowledge of method and clarity of objectives. Only a few of the major universities have engaged in extensive experimentation or carried on systematic investigations of college and university methods of instruction, or have provided courses for training in methods of teaching at the college level. The University of Minnesota is one of the most notable examples. The difficulties in the situation have been further accentuated by the unprecedented increase in college enrolment during the past decade, the great expense involved in handling different groups within an institution in different ways, the absorption of the interest and time of deans in routine duties rather than the improvement of scholarship, and the lack of mutual understanding and cooperation on the part of colleges of liberal arts and schools of education in the solution of their common educational problems. On account of these conditions it naturally follows that the educational aims of the college and the part which the library should play in achieving them are less clear than they should be.

Nevertheless, significant studies have been made by the more competently staffed and adequately financed colleges and changes have been made with great benefit to the student bodies concerned. Books like President Wilkins' "The Changing College,"[1] Dean Hawkes' "College—What's the Use?"[2] Dean Kelly's "The American Arts College,"[3] Dean Johnston's "The Liberal College in Changing Society,"[4] Dr. Robert Kelly's "The Effective College";[5] honors courses such as those at Harvard and Swarthmore; courses in reflective thinking at Columbia and Chicago; the Wisconsin experimental college; deans of men and student advisers; freshman week and orientation courses everywhere; intelligence tests and college aptitude ratings for admission; and the sudden development of the junior college movement —all these represent aspects of this attempt at redefinition, and all have resulted in extensive modification and clarification of college objectives and procedures.

II

While the college library has received but slight consideration in these studies, it has received extensive and notable consideration by librarians and members of library school faculties in an effort to integrate it more effectively with the college program. "College and University Library Problems," by Works;[6] "Library Facilities of Teacher-Training Institutions," by Rosenlof;[7] "The Library in

1 Ernest H. Wilkins, "The Changing College," Chicago, 1927.

2 Herbert E. Hawkes, "College—What's the Use?" New York, 1927.

3 Frederick J. Kelly, "The American Arts College," New York, 1925.

4 John B. Johnston, "The Liberal College in Changing Society," New York, 1930.

5 Robert L. Kelly, Ed., "The Effective College," New York, 1928.

6 George A. Works, "College and University Library Problems," Chicago, 1927.

Land-Grant Colleges and Universities," by Brown;[8] "Budgets, Classification and Compensation Plans for University and College Libraries," by the American Library Association;[9] the Hilton[10] and Hester[11] book lists for the junior college and the Shaw[12] list for the senior college libraries; the study of reading interests, by Waples and Tyler;[13] the studies concerning standards in progress by the North Central[14] and Southern[15] Associations of Colleges and Secondary Schools; the statement by Reeves and Russell[16] of the new duties imposed upon the library by the new teaching procedures in the social sciences, and the projected book by Randall[17] growing out of the work of the Advisory Group on College Libraries of the Carnegie Corporation under the chairmanship of Dr. Bishop, all deal with the status of the library in the college of to-day. They pick up the work where it was left by the American Library Association Survey[18] and their value is apparent in the following particulars:

(1) In the first place, they have made available a general body of new, significant data. The Works[19] study treats of the financial support, resources for research, departmental collections, status of staff and other incidental matters of the libraries of eighteen major universities and colleges. The Rosenlof[20] investigation presents extensive data concerning books and periodicals, the training school library, the library staff and budget from libraries of 69 four-year teachers' colleges and 46 normal schools. The Brown[21] survey brings together data from 51 land-grant colleges and universities, covering functions of the library, requirements for good library services and methods for facilitating use, book collections, financial support and budgets. The Hilton[22] book list recommends 2,388 titles for 32 basic junior college courses, the titles being checked by 928 junior college instructors and 265 instructors connected with institutions of university grade. The Hester[23] list comprises 3,500 titles grouped according to academic courses most commonly offered. The Shaw[24] list contains 14,190 titles distributed over 24 major subjects, with books to support every subject presented in the arts college curricula. Its preparation involved the services of many of the most gifted instructors in American universities and colleges, and it has been checked by the libraries of more than 250 institutions.

7 G. W. Rosenlof, "Library Facilities of Teacher-Training Institutions," New York, 1929.

8 Charles H. Brown, "The Library in Land-Grant Colleges," *Office of Education Bulletin* (1930), No. 9, Vol. 1, pp. 609–713.

9 American Library Association, "Budgets, Classification and Compensation Plans for University and College Libraries," Chicago, 1929.

10 Eugene Hilton, "Junior College Booklist," *University of California Publications in Education*, Vol. 6, No. 1, pp. 1–84, Berkeley, 1930.

11 Edna A. Hester, "A Junior College Book List," Chicago, 1931.

12 Charles B. Shaw, "A List of Books for College Libraries," New York, 1930.

13 Douglas Waples and Ralph W. Tyler, "What People Want to Read About," Chicago, 1931.

14 Douglas Waples, "The North Central Association's Study of College Libraries," *College and Reference Library Yearbook*, No. 2, pp. 85–89, Chicago, 1930.

15 Association of Colleges and Secondary Schools of the Southern States, "Proceedings," 1930, pp. 280–281.

16 Floyd W. Reeves and John Dale Russell, "The Relation of the College Library to Recent Movements in Higher Education," *The Library Quarterly*, Vol. 1, No. 1, 1931, pp. 57–66.

17 Chapters in manuscript from a book in preparation by William M. Randall.

18 American Library Association, "A Survey of Libraries in the United States," 4 vols., Chicago, 1926–27.

19 Works, *op. cit.*

20 Rosenlof, *op. cit.*

21 Brown, *op. cit.*

22 Hilton, *op. cit.*

23 Hester, *op. cit.*

24 Shaw, *op. cit.*

The Carnegie Corporation Advisory Group on College Libraries has assembled returns, supplemented in many instances by data acquired through visits, from 200 institutions. The active participation of presidents, instructors and librarians has been secured in the answering of the questionnaire,[25] and has resulted in an emphasis on the importance of the library as a teaching instrument. Supplemented as the data in all these studies are by the bibliographies in the three numbers of the "College and Reference Library Yearbook,"[26] the problem of discovering the practice and procedure of the college library has been made far more simple than ever before.

(2) In the second place, these investigations have resulted in a restatement and clarification of the functions of the college library. There is fairly common agreement that its functions are as follows: (a) To furnish material for instruction to students in appropriate environment and through a personnel competent to serve as efficient liaison officers to connect instructor and student with library resources; (b) to develop general reading interests through open shelves, browsing rooms, attractive bookstores, book lists and a stimulating readers advisers' service; (c) to furnish new technical books and periodicals which enable the members of the faculty and library staff to keep abreast of their subjects; (d) to meet the needs of such members of the faculty as are engaged in productive investigation; (e) to continue book service to students after graduation; and (f) to make materials available to students involved in correspondence courses and extension classes.

25 Questionnaire prepared by the Advisory Group on College Libraries for the Carnegie Corporation of New York City.

26 American Library Association, "College and Reference Library Yearbook," Nos. 1, 2, 3, Chicago, 1929–31.

(3) A third result of these investigations is that greater exactness and objectivity have been given to standards and procedures essential to the performance of these functions.

(a) Dr. Randall,[27] in his visits to many of the 200-odd colleges applying for grants-in-aid from the Carnegie Corporation for their book collections, found that the college library is housed either very well or very badly—in the majority of cases, badly. Non-fireproof buildings have been erected as late as 1929. Of the stacks of 96 college libraries, 60 are crowded beyond their working capacities, or will be in ten years. One hundred and eighteen of 201 buildings have one seat for each 4.4 students. Space for administration and cataloguing has been so grossly neglected and so carelessly overlooked that proper performance of these duties is rendered extremely difficult. The data assembled in the chapter entitled, "Suggestions for Minimum College Library Standards" in the second "College and Reference Library Yearbook,"[28] plans of the more notable recent buildings contained in both the first and second Yearbooks,[29] and the eleven requirements recommended in Chapter V of the Brown[30] study set forth the requirements as to building, seating capacity, reading rooms for special groups, cubicles, etc., essential to the appropriate housing of the college book collection. Klauder and Wise contribute additional data in their volume on college architecture.[31] Drs. Randall and Gerould will add still further to the picture in the volumes which they now have in preparation on the

27 Letter from William M. Randall, April 17, 1931.

28 American Library Association, Nos. 1 and 2.

29 *Ibid.*

30 Brown, *op. cit.*

31 Charles Z. Klauder and Herbert C. Wise, "College Architecture in America," New York, 1929.

college library and college library buildings.

(b) These studies reveal the fact that college executives frequently know less about the duties of a librarian and the services he should render than of any other officer or teacher on the college staff. This is evidenced in a number of ways. The process through which the college goes in the selection of the librarian will serve well as an example. The selection of the head of an English department is a procedure with which the average college president is entirely familiar. Members of the department concerned and presidents, deans and acquaintances in other faculties are asked for recommendations. A thorough sifting goes on until a person is chosen whose scholarship, teaching ability, interest in investigation and general personal effectiveness are such as to make him suitable to the institution's needs. But not so in the case of the selection of the librarian. The probabilities are that the president and dean have had but slight acquaintance with librarians. Their contacts with the library staff, library schools and library extension agencies are limited. Their understanding of the functions which the library should perform and the way it should perform them is so hazy that a selection based upon knowledge of qualities desired in the appointee is exceedingly difficult. Frequently a librarian is secured fresh from library school and without experience in or special gift for integrating the library in the instructional program of the college. The salary paid is low, and the librarian, if called elsewhere at a larger salary, is replaced by a new recruit. Neither the importance of the selection nor the desirability of the retention of a thoroughly qualified librarian is sufficiently understood by the administration to result in an appointment which will insure the proper development of the library as an integral, vital part of the institution, or maintain its policies consistently over an extended period.

(c) Similarly, institutional policies concerning the librarian's rank, pay and vacation, his control of book collections and library personnel, and his participation in the selection of books and coordination of the objectives of the library with those of the instructional staff have hitherto lacked clarity and have often been left to casual decision. The professional qualifications of the library staff and its number in relation to enrolment and teaching staff have also lacked definition. Information concerning these matters is furnished in the aforementioned studies in sufficient detail to insure more intelligent procedure.

(d) Standards regarding adequate book and periodical collections have also received additional clarification. The Hilton[32] and Hester[33] lists for the junior college effectively ban the book shower as an appropriate means of meeting the requirement as to number of volumes owned by the library. Instead they emphasize the desirability of the careful selection of books for appropriate courses rather than large collections which bear no special relation to the curricula. Their use by the librarian and the teaching staff of the junior college will secure a higher degree of effectiveness in the selection of parallel readings for basic courses. The Shaw[34] list, developed along more extensive lines, performs an equally admirable service for the four-year college. The mere checking of these lists by instructors and members of the library staffs has resulted in a fine educational service to both groups. It has revealed the inadequacy of the collection of books and periodicals, and has indicated an orderly method of enriching the li-

[32] Hilton, *op. cit.*

[33] Hester, *op. cit.*

[34] Shaw, *op. cit.*

brary's total resources and insuring proper library support of each instructor's work.

(e) In like fashion, study by presidents and deans of the application blank for grants-in-aid from the Carnegie Corporation, with its queries concerning hours of service, special service to students and faculty, circulation within and without the library, honors courses, professional fitness of staff, has been a very illuminating exercise. It has left no doubt of the desirability of close integration between library and instructional staffs in creating a genuine library-mindedness on the part of the personnel of the arts college. Like the ancient Mosaic law, which the author of the book of Hebrews said had served as a teacher to the Israelites, the questionnaire has been a schoolmaster to the schoolmasters. It has given some college executives their first thoughtful lesson on the importance of the library in the college.

(f) The formulae for measuring the adequacy of financial support have also been more exactly stated. College executives have been given new yardsticks by which to determine this. The library should be thought of as a department, or rather as the equivalent of two departments, so far as support is concerned. It is urged that salary levels for the library staff, including the librarian, heads of departments and other members, should be equal to those for deans or heads of departments and the instructional staff. It has been convincingly shown that less than 7 per cent. of the total educational budget, or $20 per student, will not provide effective library service. Ten per cent. and $30 to $40 per student will be far better. Nor should the total library budget, providing adequately for personnel, maintenance and book and periodical collections, be thought of as something apart from the administrative, instructional and maintenance budget of the college, but as an integral part of the whole.

(4) The study by Waples and Tyler[35] on reading interests of adults breaks new ground for the publisher, bookseller and librarian, on the one hand, and the sociologist and psychologist, on the other. It presents the results of an extensive scientific investigation of the subjects which interest the minds of mature groups. Heretofore the college library collection has been built up upon the basis of the knowledge of the librarians and the instructor of the subject-matter of books. In the future the librarian and the instructor will be able to add to this knowledge the further knowledge of whether the books will appeal to the interest of the student or alumnus. In this highly important respect, the study contributes new criteria for the selection of the book collection and emphasizes the value of the library as a teaching instrument.

III

Valuable as these studies are on account of the data assembled and the specific recommendations made, they are additionally valuable for certain suggestions they offer and ideas they evoke. If, however, the college library is to make its full contribution to the college of to-morrow, it is essential that the suggestions and ideas called forth be acted upon by the following groups and in the following manner:

(1) The colleges must bring themselves to a further serious consideration of their objectives. They must submit themselves to the same sort of scientific investigation which they have insisted on applying, and with profit, to the lower schools. They will have to arrive at conclusions concerning educational issues by means of extensive experimentation and scientific evidence, instead of by decrees from the president or dean or the easy-going methods of faculty majority vote and committee compromise. This does not mean that

[35] Waples and Tyler, *op. cit.*

every state university will have to set up a "college within a college" as the Experimental College (now passing) at Wisconsin, nor that every institution will undertake honors courses, comprehensive examinations or other devices now being extensively employed to secure greater unity in educational purpose or closer application of students to the performance of intellectual tasks. But it does mean that administrative officers and faculty must recognize the necessity of knowing and being interested in students as well as in subject-matter and research. It means that they must discover the best methods of teaching the preparational, cultural and professional courses embraced within their curricula so that the objectives of the college may be most completely achieved. And certainly it means that they must understand and consciously determine the part which the library as an educational instrument is qualified to play in realizing college objectives. The relation of the library to the methods of instruction through lecture, laboratory, assigned readings, individual study, as they are employed singly or collectively, and the library's function in making these methods richly fruitful in the intellectual development of the student, must be discovered and understood by every teacher. These matters are far too important to be left, as they too generally have been, to hazy thinking or to chance

The idea must also be given up that the library is an adjunct, something added (like a department of home economics or journalism); that it is something, to quote Dr. Randall's[36] experience in talking with a number of presidents, which the college "was just going to do something about." It is not an adjunct. It is an integral element about which the whole college, if alive and alert, should be doing and is doing something to-day. It is, like the instructional staff, a teaching agency; and teaching in the best sense, as many secondary schools and library-minded colleges have discovered to their very great advantage, can not go on apart from it.

(2) The college administration must make adequate budgetary provision for such a teaching instrument. The idea of library support by means of fees is utterly untenable. A laboratory fee of $5 may take care of the expense of materials used in a given course in chemistry, but it will not pay the salaries of the departmental staff nor provide for effective departmental maintenance. Effective library service must be thought of in terms of administrative and instructional expense, and must be based, as are all essential divisions of the college, upon appropriations, income from endowments, tuition, fees and gifts, all combined. And it must not be the first of this fundamental educational trinity—administration, instructional staff, library—to feel a reduction in revenue when times are out of joint, as now, but it must be given its proportionate, well-considered share, as a matter of major importance.

(3) The library staff also has a part to play in the perfection of the college library. At present it is probably purchasing and organizing materials as effectively as it can under existing conditions. The Waples study should provide it with new and valuable criteria for the selection of books. But with more adequate support it must better understand the objectives of the college and function more effectively as a liaison agent between student and book collection in attaining them. As compared with the librarian, it is possible that the college register fills entirely too important a place in the mind of the student to-day. The registrar is too often

36 Letter from William M. Randall, April 17, 1931.

the only college officer who knows all the students by name and in turn is known by them. The unit of the college over which he presides is no side issue in their thought. The registrar is the official keeper of their credits—their educational attainment, their educational salvation! It is the librarian's privilege, however, and it might well be his ambition and that of his staff, to know the mind of the student and to help him enrich it. But he can do this only by contact and suggestion through an organization that not only selects and organizes books for use, but presents them to the student in an environment and in a manner that will contribute to the development of his personality and character, and lead him to intellectual mastery. To-day the library's task does not end with the collecting and preserving of books; it should go on to instruct the students in the best use of them. It must know how to use its materials as a teaching instrument. It must assume a positive teaching function. Instruction in the use of the library during freshman week, friendliness and helpfulness at the circulation desk, open shelves, browsing rooms, exhibits, all have their place in this scheme of things. But there must be something more. Student assistanceships in the library, courses about books by members of the staff, conferences with students by members of the staff qualified to advise on books of the day or books essential in optional attendance procedure, work for honors or comprehensive examinations, attractive bookshops within the library which stimulate book ownership should be added and other means steadily sought to increase the library's teaching effectiveness. Such an understanding of its functions and such an employment of its resources by the library staff will go far in laying the foundation in college of a kind of education which now only a few students take with them into life.

(4) The library school likewise has a duty to perform in relation to the teaching function of the library. Mr. Brown[37] has pointed it out in the case of the librarians of the land-grant colleges. He finds them lacking in knowledge of science. Dr. Works[38] discovered it in other institutions. He found that many instructors complained that librarians were lacking in knowledge of other subjects. It is apparent to any investigator that the college librarian frequently knows less than he should of the major subjects of the college curricula as well as of the purposes of the curricula and the best methods of coordinating the teaching objectives of the library with those of the instructional staff. Probably not much more can be accomplished within the one-year library training course than is now being done by way of providing instruction which will enable the librarian to integrate the library with other departments within the college. But a knowledge of the point of view of the scientific departments, an insight into the methods of investigation, a conception of the functions of the college which are to be performed through the combined effort of the library, the faculty and the administration, a knowledge of the student himself and the way in which books stimulate his mind and lead to the foundation of sound moral and social judgments are matters of fundamental importance to the librarian if he is to make the library the fine instrument it should be. These matters, as well as book selection and cataloguing, reference work and administration, should be emphasized somewhere in the librarian's training if he is to coordinate the fine educational influences of the library with the dynamic educational forces of the college teacher.

(5) A fifth and final obligation is one which rests especially upon the members

[37] Brown, *op. cit.*

[38] Works, *op. cit.*

of the College and Reference Section of the American Library Association. It is that of continuing and extending the sort of investigation begun by the American Library Survey, Works, Waples, Tyler, Randall, Rosenlof, Hilton, Brown, Shaw, Hester, the Advisory Group on College Libraries and others.[39] This obligation also rests upon the national associations and foundations devoted to the promotion of education. The advance attained in the school and the college has been attained in large measure by profound study of the underlying theories and principles of education, by extensive experimentation, and by careful analysis of educational technique and procedures. The synthesis of the school curricula was not achieved solely by the teacher in the classroom, harassed as she is by the details of the day. The research student and the investigator had to be called in before the seven cardinal principles of education could be nailed to the doorposts of the school and more skillfully devised techniques could be perfected for making them operative. The health and life-span of each of us here is preserved and increased, not so much by the medical practitioner, skilful and patient though he may be, but by the investigator toiling in his laboratory far removed from us in space and time, to whom the family doctor looks for new principles and new methods of protecting and prolonging life. To-day the body of data applicable to the college library, valuable as it is, is far too short of what it must be if college administrators, faculty and library staffs are to increase the power of the library as a revealing, synthesizing force upon the modern American college campus.

In the library of the American college of to-day, much is found that is disquieting. There are thoughtful observers who consider it the weakest link in the college chain. There are libraries that are housed in basements or in wooden huts of the wartime Y. M. C. A. type. Their equipment is meager and their atmosphere forbidding. Some of them are open for not more than thirty or forty hours a week, are insufficiently staffed, and are under the direction of librarians who have not been selected on the basis of general and professional training and special fitness for the positions they occupy. Some receive only 2 or 3 per cent. of the college's total educational budget. In others the collection of books and periodicals has been brought together with slight relation to the courses which they are supposed to support. Their variety and timeliness are not such as to broaden the vision or kindle the imagination of the students who, were they otherwise, might be stimulated by them. I know of one college in which honors courses were offered when it was spending only 2 per cent. of its total educational budget, or less than $8 per student, for library service. Its dean had worked out an elaborate paper set up for study in major fields, but he had not taken stock of his librarian and library resources to see that they properly reënforced and extended the work outlined. In this respect his planning might be compared to that of a quarterback who plans a brilliant end run without coordinating and utilizing his backfield in running interference and carrying the ball.

But, happily, this is only one side of the picture. There are other colleges that clearly reveal the emergence of the library as a well-coordinated, effectively employed teaching instrument. The building is planned with emphasis upon those features which are conducive to study—reading rooms conveniently located, offices for consultation with faculty advisers, open shelves, browsing rooms, cubicles in the

39 See earlier citations.

stack. Hours of service are adequate. Books and periodicals are available in sufficient variety and number. The staff understands the objectives of the college and coordinates its effort with that of the instructors, and the administration provides a budget commensurate with the services to be rendered. Librarians here and there, the Carnegie Corporation Advisory Group on College Libraries, members of library school staffs and of the College and Reference Section of the American Library Association, are increasingly subjecting the library to intensive study. In these and other ways the college library is steadily emerging as a major force in American education. It is evident that if the course now being pursued is pursued steadfastly, the influence which the college library can be made to exert in preparing students for effective participation in the affairs of life will be significantly multiplied.

INVENTION AND THE ENGLISH DICTIONARY[1]

By H. G. GOOD

OHIO STATE UNIVERSITY

Greek education was strictly Greek, an education in one language, and that, of course, the vernacular. Not so the Roman. The Latins for the first time in the history of education found it necessary to learn a foreign tongue and to teach it in their schools. As a consequence, the earliest lists of words in one language with their definitions in another were probably made by teachers in the Roman schools for boys who were studying Greek.

In or out of school the native language was learned by use and practice; but the acquisition of a foreign tongue like Greek in Rome or Latin in the later West and North was to be aided by a dictionary or glossary. When in the Middle Ages the vulgar languages had developed sufficiently and while Latin was still the universal language of scholarship it became the frequent practice to explain Latin words by their vulgar equivalents or, conversely, "the vernacular by Latin or what in the Middle Ages passed for Latin." A few of these English-Latin and Latin-English glossaries, to come to our own speech at once, will be mentioned a little later. In either form the purpose was to aid the study of the learned tongue and not that of the vulgar one which until about the end of the Middle Ages was not thought worthy the attention of a scholar nor to need teaching. Out of these bilingual and polyglot works, the dictionaries of the modern tongues have evolved. Medieval bilingual glossaries are the direct ancestors of our English dictionaries.

These glossaries were a product of the schools; and idealized schemes of the method of their construction have been made out somewhat as follows. A monastery or cathedral school having a number of glossed texts of Vergil, Orosius or other authors, in which the vulgar definitions had been interlined, the teacher, going straight down the margins, would write each hard Latin word and then its explanation, whether in easy Latin or in the popular tongue. Thus he produced a glossary of several pages which was valuable to any novice in reading the same author but useless for another author in which most of the unfamiliar words were wholly different. Now a second step involved the collection of the glosses from a number of authors, and these might be put

[1] This is the second of a short series of articles on the general topic, "Invention and the School." For the first see School and Society for June 20, 1931.

down in batches as they occurred in the sources or, more intelligently, might be rearranged according to some system into a single list. Later glossaries were made by combining previous collections perhaps without going back to any glossed authors at all or by merely adding the marginalia from one or more authors to earlier collections. At this point the alphabetic or some other principle of arrangement was invoked. Sometimes the words were arranged merely by initial letters into A-sections, B-sections and so on, or into AB-, AC-sections, that is, according to the order of the first two letters of the words. Only rarely was the alphabetic principle thus early extended beyond the first two letters, and the resulting arrangement was often faulty because of chaotic spelling. We have remaining to us a number of such glossaries, and from these the method of their compilation has been worked out by historical and comparative methods.

One of these glossaries is now in the library of Corpus Christi College, Cambridge, and it is hence called the Corpus Glossary. It contains about 8,500 items: Latin words arranged in an AB-order and defined usually by single Latin or Anglo-Saxon words. There is also a cognate Latin-English glossary, named EE by Henry Sweet because it is preserved in two manuscripts, one at Épinal and the other at Erfurt. The words in EE are arranged by initial letters only. Corpus and its cognates drew upon four sources which have been identified by W. M. Lindsay. Among the glosses for the Latin of the Corpus vocabulary there are about two thousand Anglo-Saxon words, the oldest English in existence and dating from the seventh century. A few of those most easily identified by the English reader of to-day are here given, as follows: *aeppel*(apple), *ald*(old), *braadponne*(frying-pan), *cuu*(cow), *faeder*(father), *feld*(field), *gaarleec* (garlic). With Corpus and EE may be compared a third glossary prepared in the monastery of St. Gall and now in the library of the University of Leyden. The Leyden Glossary is more primitive in its arrangement than Corpus or EE. It contains sections of glosses collected from individual authors and indicates the source from which each section was drawn as *De Eusebio, De Rufino,* and so forth. The construction of such a glossary demanded no rearrangement, merely the copying in the order of the marginalia from several books. Arrangement by initial letters would have been more difficult and that by the first two letters still more so. And this was a matter of importance when writing material was costly and the spelling irregular.

Two ways of arranging words in glossaries have now been mentioned; the order in which these words occur in some author or authors, resulting in collected glosses, is the first and most primitive; and a partially alphabetical order is the second. Two other ways of ordering words were also used. Vocabularies were formed by assembling those words which referred to the same subject, such as the farm, the house, the school or the practice of warfare and so on. This scheme led naturally to the "Colloquies" and phrase-books which were widely used in the school. Erasmus' "Colloquies" and Comenius' "Janua" and "Orbis Pictus" were ultimate results of this plan. These were practical teaching devices for which no one claimed any scientific value. It was quite otherwise with the fourth scheme to be mentioned which ordered words by roots and derivatives, the radical method. This was long and frequently used, and defended against the alphabetical arrangement. As late as the seventeenth century the radical method was employed in the first dictionary of the French Academy, which was planned in 1638 and issued in 1694. That was its last appearance, and in the second edition of the work which came out early in the eighteenth century the preface said: "The arrangement by roots is the most scientific, and the most instructive to the student, but it is not suited to the impatience of the French people and so the Academy has felt obliged to abandon it." This one time, at least, the Immortals reversed themselves at the behest of the French people, an event which almost constrains one to cite it as the beginning of the French Revolution.

Two or three of the vocabularies of the later medieval centuries, embodying either the alphabetical or the radical principle, should now be cited. Papias, a Lombard (fl. 1050), whose dictionary lasted far into the fifteenth century and was reprinted at Milan in 1746, used the alphabetical order; and John Balbi, who completed his "Catholicon" in 1286, a work which was printed at Mainz in 1460 and many times later, does likewise. Balbi felt it necessary to apologize for such an unscientific method, which he, like the French Academicians, regarded as a concession to the weakness of human nature. To the modern reader's surprise he goes into a long explanation of it as follows:

> I am going to treat of *amo* and *bibo*. I shall take *amo* before *bibo* because *a* is the first letter in *amo* and *b* is the first letter in *bibo;* and *a* is before *b* in the alphabet. Again I have to treat of *abeo* and *adeo*. I shall take *abeo* before *adeo* because *b* is the second letter in *abeo* and *d* is the second letter in *adeo;* and *b* is before *d* in the alphabet.

And so he proceeds. *Amatus* will come before *amor, imprudens* before *impudens.* Here in the thirteenth century we have the words completely alphabetized. In the same century Uguitio or Huguitio of Pisa compiled a Latin dictionary, of which the secondary title is "Dictionarium Etymologicum." Frequently recopied, its course was run before the invention of printing and it has never been put into type. As its subtitle declares, it used the radical system—and such etymologies! Under *capio* it treats *caput* and all its derivatives! It was one of the major drawbacks of all books of this class at that time that the true etymologies were not known. We have seen that the first issue of the French Academy's dictionary was the last great work to be carried out on this plan; but in the history of the evolution of the dictionary it is important to know that the present alphabetical arrangement is the survivor in a long struggle for existence between several arrangements.[2]

The curious titles used by the early dictionary-makers for their works have been frequently noticed in the literature of the subject. The "Promptorium Parvulorum" (1440), the storeroom for young pupils, was republished by the Early English Text Society in 1908, and the title-page of this issue names it "the first English-Latin dictionary." Among its sources were the works of Balbi and Uguitio and the "De Nominibus Utensilium" of Alexander Neccham (b. 1157). Neccham also wrote a "Reportorium Vocabulorum." Another English-Latin word-book is the "Catholicon Anglicum" (1483), the universal English remedy. "Catholicon" is a frequent term with this application. "Medulla Grammatices," "Expositour," "Nomenclator," "Ductor

[2] In the various writings of Henry Sweet, W. M. Lindsay and H. B. Wheatley, in the introductions to the appropriate volumes of the "Publications of the Early English Text Society," in Georg Goetz's monumental "Corpus Glossariorum Latinorum," further information on the invention of the dictionary may be found. The paragraph to which this note is attached is based upon a passage in P. S. Allen's "The Age of Erasmus," Oxford, 1914, pp. 42–52.

Vestibulum," "Thesaurus," are other examples of the names applied to early and later dictionaries. There is also the "Ortus Vocabulorum," the garden of words. *Ortus* is, of course, a beheaded form of *hortus*. After the discovery of America had sufficiently impressed the English mind it became common to name dictionaries, as Florio and Phillips did, the "Worlde," or the "New Worlde of Wordes." Phillips, the nephew and pupil of John Milton, used the latter title in 1678. And, to make an end, Peter Levins in the sixteenth century prepared a rhyming dictionary and called it the "Manipulus Vocabulorum," a handful of words. It is a collection of about 9,000 words, a considerable handful for its day, and has been reprinted by the Early English Text Society (1867).

Glossaries had a special and narrow purpose and use, but through printing and those national forces which created the modern literatures they led to the invention of the unilingual dictionaries of the modern tongues. The honor of having compiled the first English dictionary has been variously assigned, for it depends upon the definition of the word. Richard Huloet's "Abecedarium" (1552) explained English words by English words but added also Latin synonyms and French definitions. He dedicated it to the Bishop of Ely. "Some will condemn him," said Thomas Fuller in the "Worthies of England," "of indiscretion, in presenting so low a subject to so high a person, as if he would teach the greatest statesman in the land to spell aright." Robert Cawdrey compiled "A Table Alphabeticall Conteyning and Teaching the True Writing and Understanding of Hard Usuall English Words" (1604). A third competitor is Randle Cotgrave, who in 1611 issued his "A Bundle of Words." Those who think that none of these was sufficiently catholic to deserve the name of dictionary give the award to Dr. John Bullokar, who prepared (1616) "An English Expositour or Compleat Dictionary." Certainly Mulcaster, who lived in the generation immediately before Bullokar, thought that there existed no English dictionary deserving the name and had the vision to demand one. In his "Elementarie" he took advanced ground, asking for a completeness of vocabulary that was not attained for more than a century.

English dictionary-making, since the seventeenth century, has passed through three periods. The seventeenth century makers tried to collect the hard, the adopted and the less-known words that were in use, and to spell and define them. Cawdrey, who gathered what he called the "Hard Usuall" words, illustrates this, as do his immediate successors, Cockeram, Blount, Phillips, Coles and others. Many of these seventeenth-century dictionaries were compiled by schoolmasters, some of them in schools with the help of the pupils. As they grew in size they became too costly for school use and poorly adapted to school needs. Coote's "English Schoolmaster" (1590) was an attempt to overcome such difficulties and has a vocabulary with definitions, a catechism, an arithmetic and a spelling-list. Charles Hoole, famous teacher of the following century, wrote a similar miscellany. By and by "school dictionaries" were made by "abridging" larger works and leaving out all the hard words. In the same period spelling books were compiled by leaving out the easy words and retaining the polysyllables. A curiously inverted logic must have been responsible for both practices, for, certainly, schoolboys should be taught the meanings of words they do not know and the spellings of words they do know.

The eighteenth century begins a second period with a new ideal. Bailey, Johnson and their contemporaries, while they tried to provide a complete vocabulary, especially of the "literary" words, tried also to give laws to English speech, to refine, perfect and standardize it.

The third era opens with the second half of the nineteenth century when dictionary-makers learned to think of themselves as reporters of usage and as historians of the language and to take as their proper functions the portrayal of the whole language as it is and as it has come to be what it is. And this motive led to the great and recently completed Oxford or Historical Dictionary, certainly a far cry from Cawdrey's Table, and a much farther cry from the Leyden Glossary.

In such a simple and rapid story of the growth of the dictionary it has not been possible to say anything of the rise of comparative philology and its influence upon dictionary-making, nor of the encyclopedic tendency which has been so pronounced, nor of the nationalism implied in Noah Webster's title "An American Dictionary of the English Language," nor of the practice of illustrating usage and meanings by quotations and by cuts. Perhaps I should mention that the "Glossographia Anglicana Nova" (1707), "a dictionary interpreting such hard words as are at present used in the English tongue," with its woodcuts is supposed to represent the first attempt to illustrate an English dictionary and to support its definitions by that means.

EDUCATIONAL EVENTS

ECONOMY AND COST OF EDUCATION IN SCOTLAND

THE following joint manifesto has been issued by the National Union of Teachers and the Educational Institute of Scotland, as reported in the London *Times:*

In defining the attitude of teachers towards the proposals of the National Government for effecting economies in the education service the National Union of Teachers of England and Wales and the Educational Institute of Scotland, representing 165,000 teachers in Great Britain, take their stand on the principle of equality of sacrifice to which homage has so repeatedly been paid by the Prime Minister. As citizens, they will be prepared to meet the national emergency with public spirit and to bear their due share of the national burden distributed justly over the income of the whole nation, whether earned or unearned. In determining their contribution to the national sacrifice necessary to meet a financial crisis that is admittedly temporary, they demand that Parliament shall deal with them on the basis of their citizenship and not on the basis of reduction in their standard rates of salary as public servants merely because their earnings are easily accessible to the government.

They decline to accept the findings of the economy committee as an embodiment of the principle of equality of sacrifice and they protest against the action of the May committee in using the "Economy Report" as the instrument of a savage attack upon education and the professional position of teachers. The budgetary deficiency is estimated by the economy committee to be £120,000,000. That represents 3 per cent. of the national income. The application of the principle of equality of sacrifice can not possibly justify the proposal of the May committee to cut down the salaries of teachers by 20 per cent., to which would be added other demands which as citizens they would be compelled to meet. The recommendations of the committee were arrived at without the evidence of a single representative of the teachers being invited and on the basis of incomplete and inaccurate data. Teachers have not had a square deal from the May committee. They look for a square deal from the National Government.

If the National Government carry into effect the recommendations of the report they will cripple the schools of the nation and inflict grave injustice upon teachers. Staffs of schools will be depleted. Many teachers will be faced with the prospect of unemployment. Parents of the working and middle classes will find it difficult, or even impossible, to maintain their children in secondary schools if the school fees are heavily increased. The finances of education authorities will be deranged and additional burdens placed upon the ratepayers, while teachers deprived of one fifth of their income will in many cases find it impossible to meet their normal financial obligations.

It has been the proud boast of the schools of Great Britain that they have made a valuable contribution to the development of the character of the people and to the social security of the nation. It is the desire of the teachers of Great Britain to continue to make their contribution to orderly progress and social solidarity, but the performance of this important task will be made increasingly difficult, if not impossible, should the National Government impose upon the schools the crippling restrictions recommended in the "Economy Report," or inflict upon teachers so vindictive a reduction of their earnings.

Teachers claim to be dealt with by the National Government in accordance with the principles of justice and equity which the Prime Minister himself has enunciated, and the National Union of Teachers of England and Wales and the Educational Institute of Scotland will use every legitimate weapon at their command to secure such treatment for their members.

EXPENDITURES FOR EDUCATION IN NEW YORK CITY

Of all its expenditures for educational purposes, New York City devotes a larger percentage to the actual instruction of its children than any single one of the fifty-two American cities of 100,000 population or more included in the recent nation-wide survey made by the Federal Office of Education. New York City devotes 9.4 per cent. more to the actual instruction of its children than the average amount thus devoted by the same fifty-two cities.

New York City devotes 86 per cent. of its total educational expenditures to the actual instruction of its children. The average of the fifty-two cities whose costs were surveyed by the Federal Office of Education is 76.6 per cent. devoted to actual instruction. The city that comes nearest to New York in percentage of total educational expenditures devoted to instruction is Fort Worth, Texas, which devotes 85.4 per cent. to actual instruction. Included among the 52 cities in the survey, in addition to Fort Worth, are Chicago, which devotes 71.3 per cent. of its educational expenditures to actual instruction; Philadelphia, which devotes 77.6 per cent.; Los Angeles, 79.8 per cent.; St. Louis, 73.8 per cent.; Boston, 73.8 per cent.; Pittsburgh, 76 per cent., and Baltimore with a percentage of 81 per cent. These figures are based on a comparison of the tables made public by the Federal Office of Education last spring and the cost tables of the Board of Education made public last night in its annual financial and statistical report.

The cost of instruction is the amount spent for salaries of teachers and principals and for supplies, text-books, library books, etc. It represents what education would cost if there were nothing to be considered but the actual instruction of the child—if there were no need for heated and lighted buildings, no need for playgrounds or lunchrooms, and no need for a business or professional staff to administer the affairs of the school system. The cost of instruction does not include any of the money spent for administration, for the physical maintenance of the school plant or physical operation of the school plant, or for any of the auxiliary agencies, such as playgrounds, after-school athletics, recreation centers, etc. The cost of instruction represents solely and exclusively what it costs to teach the child—the teacher, the paper and pencil and the text-book. To this item—the cost of instruction—the figures show that New York City devotes a larger percentage than any one of the fifty-two cities included in the Federal Office's survey of the Office of Education, nearly 10 per cent. more than the average amount spent by the same fifty-two cities for the same item.

The annual financial and statistical report of the Board of Education of the City of New York shows also the per capita costs of education in this city. Because of local conditions and because many American cities arrive at their per capita cost figures in a manner different from that in which New York City arrives at her per capita cost figure, no comparison with the per capita costs of the fifty-two cities surveyed by the Federal Office of Education has been made. The comparisons made above of the varying percentages devoted to the cost of instruction are possible because the methods of computation and items included are virtually the same. The per capita cost of the day elementary and junior high schools in the City of New York based on average daily attendance of 815,515 pupils was $102.84 a year for the calendar year 1930, a slight increase over the previous year. The per capita cost of the day high schools, based on average daily attendance of 147,556, was $170.93 for the calendar year 1930—a considerable decrease from the previous year. This per capita cost may further decrease on account of a large increase in enrolment in day high schools.

SMALL RURAL HIGH SCHOOLS

The small rural high school trails far behind its big city sister high school in its contribution to education, according to a bulletin issued by the Federal Office of Education. More than 14,000 rural high schools of 250 enrolment or less were studied for the report, which found the spread of weak secondary schools in country regions actually delaying the progress toward better educational advantages in the United States.

Since the world war the idea of a high-school training for all the country's children has been so thoroughly "sold" to rural taxpayers that numerous small high schools have sprung up in sparsely settled regions—many with thirty to fifty pupils and with as few as two teachers. Many of these institutions, lacking any intelligent plan of what a rural high school should be, are very poor imitations of the great city schools with 100 times as many students and with elaborate equipment.

With a small teaching staff no teacher can be a specialist, as pointed out in the Office of Education study, "The Smallness of America's Rural High Schools," by Walter H. Gaumnitz, rural school specialist. He may be instructor in a dozen different subjects, in some of which he is poorly qualified; thus his pupils get a low grade of training. He is overworked, naturally. Since the city school attracts the better prepared teachers, with a promise of more pay and more leisure, the country high school usually gets the left-overs. The course of study also suffers, according to the bulletin. Modern secondary education has veered away from a rigid course in languages and mathematics. Social science, natural sciences and vocational training (stenography, bookkeeping, the trades, etc.) are now much in vogue. But the average small high school is deficient in science courses and is generally without any vocational work to offer.

Limited in funds and teaching force, it can stick only to type class organization and methods. Extra-curriculum work, sports, dramatics, the school paper, all of which play large and necessary rôles in city secondary school life as lessons, must often be omitted.

Remedies for the serious situation, as offered by the Federal Office of Education, are: First, the careful study by each state of its rural school situation; second, cooperation among all government and social agencies with a view to school consolidation, the conversion of some small senior high schools into junior high schools, and, third, the employment at good salaries of teachers who are experts in special subjects, to cover several schools in a district, or the wide use of correspondence courses under competent supervision.

THE CENTENNIAL CELEBRATION AT WESLEYAN UNIVERSITY

Internationally eminent men of many professions, including world-famous scholars and statesmen, men of letters and great financiers, will gather at Wesleyan University for the centennial celebration, which is to take place from October 10 to 12 with a program filled with events of wide interest and historical significance.

Prime Minister Richard B. Bennett, of Canada; Mr. Owen D. Young, originator of the famous reparations plan and chairman of the board of the General Electric Company, and Congressman Frederick M. Davenport, of New York, are among the prominent men in politics who will be present.

Robert Frost, the poet, and Kenneth M. Goode, editor, will be among the literary men. The famous scholars and scientific men scheduled to participate include Professor Willem De Sitter, of the University of Leyden, former president of the World Astronomical Union; President A. Lawrence Lowell, of Harvard University; President Nicholas Murray Butler, of Columbia University; Professor Ashley H. Thorndike, professor of English literature at Columbia University and author of numerous books; President Charles A. Plumley, of Norwich University; President Henry M. Wriston, of Lawrence College, and President Frederick C. Ferry, of Hamilton College.

Bishop Francis J. McConnell, president of the Federal Council of Churches of Christ in America; Bishop Herbert Welch, formerly president of Ohio Wesleyan University; Dr. George E. Vincent, former president of the Rockefeller Foundation; Judge John Clark, of New York; Mr. E. Kent Hubbard, of Middletown, Connecticut, president of the Connecticut Manufacturers' Association; Mr. Henry I. Harriman, Boston, president of the Boston Chamber of Commerce and prominent in the field of public utilities; Mr. Harold C. Grant, of Newark, New Jersey; Professor Arthur W. Browne, of Cornell University; Mr. Arthur B. Jennings, organist of St. Stephen's Church, Sewickley, Pennsylvania, and Mr. William B. Davis, supervisor of music in the schools of Middletown, Connecticut, will also take part in the program.

The festivities which will mark the conclusion of one hundred years of life and growth of the university will start with a soccer game between Brown University and Wesleyan University at ten o'clock on Saturday, October 10, and continue through to the centennial luncheon at noon on Monday. The centennial is expected to bring together more than a thousand graduates. The executive committee in charge is composed of: Mr. O. F. McCormick, of Philadelphia; Mr. G. W. Davison, of New York, N. Y.; President James L. McConaughy, of Wesleyan University; Professor Frank W. Nicolson; Mr. Henry I. Harriman, of Boston; Mr. E. M. Eldredge, of Brooklyn; Mr. W. B. Holton, Jr., of New York, and Professor Karl S. Van Dyke.

CHILD LABOR SUNDAY

CUTTING short children's schooling for work benefits no one, according to a statement issued by the National Child Labor Committee. It not only limits their education but may impair their health. The competition of children in industry, moreover, tends to depress wage rates, lower standards of living and aggravate unemployment. Even in the year 1930–31, with millions of adults unable to find work, in twenty-three states and some additional cities reporting to the U. S. Children's Bureau, permits were issued to 103,000 children fourteen and fifteen years of age to enter industry. If all states and all non-agricultural occupations were included, as well as renewals of permits to children under 16 who had been working over a year, the total number for the country would probably be 200,000 or more, with another 400,000 in agricultural employment.

Moreover, young workers are excessively liable to industrial accidents. A recent state report[1] tells, for instance, of Lorenzo, fourteen years of age, who was operating a leather-cutting foot-press in a shoe factory when he stepped on the wrong lever, caught both hands in the machine and fractured two fingers of his right hand; of Elbert, also fourteen years of age, working for the summer in a small town meat market, who was pushing meat into an electrically driven meat grinder when the fork caught, his left hand being drawn after it and so injured that it was necessary to amputate the first, second and third fingers, his thumb to the first joint and his little finger to the second joint; of Grace, who at the age of fourteen secured a job as a foot-press operator in a tin-can factory, and after ten minutes of work caught her hands in the machine, losing both index fingers.

Most children under sixteen are so immature and reckless, so easily fatigued and have such poor muscular coordination that no industrial employment, work in the vicinity of machines (even when they do not themselves operate them), nor employment in transportation are free from hazard. Thousands of fourteen- and fifteen-year-old children are injured in industry every year, some of them being killed or maimed for life. The only effective safeguard is to prohibit all industrial employment under sixteen years. Even for the boy or girl of sixteen and seventeen years, such occupations as oiling or cleaning machinery in motion, running elevators and operating dangerous or unguarded machinery are too hazardous. More than 2,000

[1] N. Y. State Department of Labor Special Bulletin No. 168.

minors under eighteen years of age receive industrial injuries each year in New York alone; another 2,000 in Massachusetts, and no less than 5,000 in Pennsylvania.

To prevent this costly toll of industrial accidents, burdensome to industry as well as to the injured children, laws must be enacted with the support of public opinion which will keep all children under sixteen years of age in school, and which will prohibit the employment of minors between sixteen and eighteen years of age in dangerous occupations. Such a course would serve the triple purpose of assuring to our young people a fully rounded education, safeguarding them against industrial injury and relieving the pressure of child competition in the employment market.

Child Labor Sunday, which will be observed for the twenty-fifth year on January 24, 1932, affords the opportunity to bring these facts before the people through churches and synagogues, schools, clubs and forums, to initiate programs of public education culminating in legislative enactments for the protection of children.

"ORIENTATION CONFERENCE" FOR FOREIGN FELLOWSHIP STUDENTS

THE annual International Student Conference of the Institute of International Education was held at the Storm King School, Cornwall-on-Hudson, New York, with 125 students, representing fifteen nationalities, in attendance. The purpose of the conference, which lasted for a week, is to more rapidly orient these newcomers from abroad to the changed régime of education, culture, business life and conditions in general which they are to encounter throughout the academic year as a result of their residence in an American institution of higher learning.

The Institute of International Education now administers approximately 400 fellowships annually, of which half are for Americans placed abroad, and the remainder for foreigners, chiefly from Europe and the countries of Latin America. Ninety American colleges and universities are participating in the exchange arrangements. Experience has proven that a very considerable portion of the three to five month period can be eliminated by a week of intimate conference proceedings.

Speakers are among the most distinguished that can be selected for the subjects covered, and in addition to the regular sessions of this nature a very fine entertainment program is made possible through the cooperation of various individuals of note who have caught the vision of the end for which the institute is striving. For example, during the past quarter of a century American students residing temporarily abroad, especially those who have been in Paris, have had frequent opportunity to hear gratis the best musicians at weekly meetings held under the auspices of the American Church, the American Cathedral and other similar organizations interested in serving the foreign student abroad. Among the great artists who have contributed their services at such concerts have been Madame Louise Homer, Madame Lillian Nordica, Madame Ellen Beach Yaw, Mr. Francis Rogers, Mr. Herbert Witherspoon and distinguished members of the French Grand Opera and the Opera Comique. This compliment to American youth abroad was richly reciprocated through the institute's conference of this year by Madame Myrna Sharlow, prima donna soprano of the Metropolitan Opera of New York, who gave a most delightful and entertaining song recital during one afternoon.

The spirit of the conference just concluded was well expressed by one of the German girls, who said, "I feel as I used to after mother and father had loaded me with presents at Christmas time and I went out to get them a little bit of needle work which symbolized my feelings toward them."

Prominent on this year's program were the following:

''Ted'' Coy, the famous Yale football captain and fullback, ''The Spirit of American Athletics''; Mr. R. J. Shortlidge, head master of the Storm King School, ''Welcome to Storm King''; Dr. Robert L. Kelly, executive secretary of the Association of American Colleges, ''Some Modern Student Migrations''; Mr. Charles D. Hurrey, general secretary of the Committee on Friendly Relations among Foreign Students, ''Student Pilgrims and International Friendship''; Dr. Wilbur K. Thomas, executive director of the Carl Schurz Memorial Foundation, ''Our Contribution to World Fellowship''; Professor Nelson P. Mead, of the department of history, College of the City of

New York, "The United States—Past and Present"; Mr. Adamantios Th. Polyzoides, editor of *Atlantis*, "An Athenian Looks at America"; Mr. Ed. R. Murrow, president of the National Student Federation of America, "America's Students"; Mr. Barclay Acheson, secretary of the Near East Foundation, "A Twentieth Century Conception of Philanthropy"; Major William A. Welch, chief engineer and general manager of the Palisades Interstate Park, "American Parks and Recreation"; Miss Anne Wiggin, secretary of the International Student Committee of the Y. W. C. A., "American Cooperation on Foreign Student Problems"; Mr. James S. Carson, of the Electric Bond and Share Company, "Some Observations on American Business and the American Business Man"; Dr. Edward H. Hume, vice-president of the New York Post-Graduate Medical School and Hospital, "Keeping Well"; Dr. Guy Edward Snider, of the department of foreign trade of the College of the City of New York, "American Policies in Foreign Trade"; Mr. Thomas W. Gerber, of the United Press Associations, "American Interest in World News"; Mr. F. Stuart Crawford, of the editorial staff of the *New York Herald-Tribune*, "The American Political Scene," and Dr. John H. Finley, associate editor of the *New York Times*, "Bon Voyage."

EDUCATIONAL NOTES AND NEWS

Dr. William Pearson Tolley was formally inaugurated into the presidency of Allegheny College on October 9. The inauguration of Dr. Tolley brought together a distinguished assemblage of college and university presidents, deans and professors. The Association of College Presidents of Pennsylvania attended in a body, and college and university representatives from most of the larger institutions of learning between New York and the Pacific Coast were also present.

Dr. Charles L. Wallace has been elected to succeed Dr. Edward P. Robertson as president of Wesley College at Grand Forks, North Dakota. He assumed his duties on October 1.

Dr. William Schoenfeld has been appointed dean of agriculture and director of the agricultural experiment station at Oregon State College, and Dr. H. V. Hoyt has accepted the position of dean of the school of commerce.

Professor James Voorhees Thompson has been appointed director of the new college of religious education and missions at Drew University.

The following promotions and new appointments have been made in the faculty of Bryn Mawr College: Dr. Mary H. Swindler, professor of classical archeology; Dr. Anna P. Wheeler, professor of mathematics and head of that department; Dr. Mary S. Gardiner, associate professor of biology; Dr. Ernest W. Blanchard, associate in biology; Dr. Jane Dewey, associate in physics; Dr. Paul Weiss, associate in philosophy; Dr. Eleanor L. Dulles, lecturer in economics; Mr. Edward M. H. Warburg, lecturer in the history of art; Dr. William W. Flexner, lecturer in mathematics, and Dr. Louise A. Holland, non-resident lecturer in Latin.

The faculty of the department of education of the University of Nebraska has been completed, with the appointment of Mr. L. Dale Coffman, Dr. S. M. Corey and Dr. John M. Matzen, who has become assistant professor of school administration. Dr. Matzen takes over the work of Dr. F. E. Henzlik, who is now dean of the teachers' college.

Professor Robert O. DeMond, professor of history at the State Teachers College at Buffalo, New York, has returned from a year's leave of absence spent in graduate study at Columbia University and Stanford University. Dr. Earl Cranston, who was acting head of the department of history during Mr. DeMond's absence, has accepted the position of assistant professor of history at Colgate University.

Mr. Daniel C. Murphy, of San Francisco, former state senator and at present a member of the San Francisco board of education, has been appointed a member of the state board of education, succeeding Mr. Charles Albert Adams, whose term has expired.

President B. H. Kroeze, of Jamestown College, has been reelected for a term of three years as a member of the commission on higher institutions of the North Central Association of Colleges and Secondary Schools.

Mr. Charles E. Dickey, superintendent of the schools of Allegheny County, Pennsylvania, has been reappointed by Governor Pinchot as a member of the state council of education.

Professor Friedrich von der Leyen, of the University of Cologne, will be Kuno Francke professor of German at Harvard University this year; Professor Pierre Martino, of the University of Algiers, will be exchange professor from France, and Sigurthur Nordal, of the University of Iceland, will be Charles Eliot Norton professor of poetry.

Marquis Piero Misciatteli, professor in the University of Siena, noted Dante scholar and authority on Italian art and literature, will lecture on Dante at the Casa Italiana, Columbia University, this fall.

The Reverend Toyohiko Kagawa, prominent Japanese theologian, has been engaged to give the Shaffer lectures at Yale University this year.

The University of California has appointed as the fourth occupant of the chair of Italian culture for the winter season the author and literary critic, Professor Giuseppe Antonio Borgese, of the University of Milan, according to the *Italy-America Bulletin.* The course which he will give covers the general history of literary criticism, with particular regard to Italy and the eighteenth and nineteenth centuries.

Dr. Marie Baum, lecturer in the institute of political and social science at the University of Heidelberg, will be the guest of Vassar College from October 14 to 21. During her stay she will give two general lectures, the first on Friday evening, October 16, on "The Family and the Social Structure," and the other in German on Monday, October 19.

The Kossovo Medal of the Royal Red Cross of Yugoslavia has been conferred on President Mary E. Woolley, of Mount Holyoke College, and Professor Jeannette Marks, head of the department of English literature and drama, in recognition of "the sympathetic and generous cooperation of Mount Holyoke College in a difficult international educational undertaking."

Mr. John Piersol McCaskey, editor emeritus of the *Pennsylvania School Journal,* observed the ninety-fourth anniversary of his birth on October 9 at his home in Lancaster, Pennsylvania. The *Pennsylvania School Journal* says: "The 65,000 readers of the *Journal* send cordial greetings to our Nestor, who, prior to 1921, made up every number of the *Journal* for 55 years."

Sir Frank Goldstone, who is retiring from the position of general secretary of the National Union of Teachers in England and Wales, completed a two months' tour of the United States on September 17 with a conference at the headquarters of the National Education Association in Washington and an address to the staff of the U. S. Office of Education. Sir Frank has recently been knighted by King George V for his meritorious services as an officer of the organized profession in his country. Eighty-five per cent. of the men eligible for membership in the National Union of Teachers belong to it.

Mrs. Josephine Corliss Preston, state superintendent of public instruction of Washington for sixteen years and president of the National Education Association during 1919–20, is lecturing at institutes and convention districts, in Pennsylvania.

Professor Clarence Manning, head of the Slavonic department of Columbia University, who has recently visited the universities of Cracow, Warsaw, Poznan, Lwow and Wilno, in Poland, referred during his talks in Warsaw to a project to establish chairs of the Polish language, history and literature in American universities.

Mr. Earl Dewey Myers, assistant professor in the school of social service administration of the University of Chicago, who returned to the university for the summer session, after holding a fellowship in Germany for the last two years while he has been studying the child welfare movement in Germany since the war, has gone to the Tulane School of Social Work.

Mrs. Alice M. Carmalt, who was a member of the board of education in Pittsburgh, one of the original appointees, and chairman of the committee of instruction from the date of its organization, died on September 3. She held positions on two faculties, the University of

Pittsburgh and the State Teachers College at Indiana.

Dr. Charles E. Crooks, for many years dean of Centre College, Danville, Kentucky, died on September 28, at the age of seventy-one years.

Dr. Ulrich von Wilamowitz-Moellendorff, professor of Greek at the University of Berlin and a noted classical philologist, died on October 1 at the age of eighty-two years.

Memorial services for David Starr Jordan were held at National Education Association headquarters on September 21. U. S. Commissioner of Education William John Cooper delivered the principal address, paying tribute to the great leader as educator, naturalist, writer and promoter of world peace.

A clinic of trained psychologists has been put at the service of the public schools of the state by the Pennsylvania State College through its school of education. The clinic was organized this fall by the addition of Dr. Robert G. Bernreuter, formerly of Stanford University, California, to the specialists already on the faculty. Dr. Bernreuter will conduct the necessary field work for the clinic. Other members will be Dr. William Lepley, clinical psychiatrist, Dr. Bruce V. Moore and Miss Mary Wyland, personnel and placement specialists, Mr. Herbert K. Baker, specialist in speech correction, and Dr. Joseph E. DeCamp, who will be consulted in cases of abnormalities.

Harvard University has awarded 300 fellowships and scholarships, carrying a total value of $216,145, to students in eight graduate schools of the university. Twenty-three of the awards are for travel abroad and six for research in the law school. Of the total, 182 go to men in the graduate school of Arts and Sciences, while law school students receive 43.

The annual conference of the faculties of the New York State Normal Schools and Teachers Colleges will convene on Monday morning, October 12, at the State Teachers College at Buffalo. The central theme of the conference will be "An Analysis of Curriculum Material." Mr. Benjamin Matteson, of the New Paltz State Normal School, is president of the organization. Mr. Charles C. Root, head of the department of education at the State Teachers College at Buffalo, has been responsible for most of the local arrangements. The Hotel Statler will be headquarters for the conference, although all meetings, except that on the evening of Monday, October 12, will be held at the State Teachers College. On this evening, the delegates will meet for a banquet, followed by an address by the Abbe Ernest Dimnet on "The Ideal View of Education." On Tuesday morning, October 13, Dr. Edgar W. Knight, professor of education at the University of North Carolina, will address the conference on "Teachers and Training."

The Harvard class of 1935 will be under the guidance of an expanded and improved advisory organization directed by Mr. Delmar Leighton, newly created dean of freshmen, according to the *Boston Evening Transcript*. Important changes were the appointment made last April of twelve faculty members as "associates of the freshmen" and the selection of eight instructors in freshman courses to reside in the yard. The "associates of the freshmen" will advise and consult with administrative officers on matters relating to the freshmen, especially on questions of instruction. They will also take occasional meals at the Union and thus come in contact with the first-year men. The group includes: Dr. L. B. R. Briggs, professor emeritus and former dean of Harvard College; Mr. R. S. Hillyer, assistant professor of English; Dr. Leigh Hoadley, professor of zoology; Dr. A. N. Holcombe, professor of government; Dr. F. W. C. Lieder, associate professor of German; Dr. K. F. Mather, professor of geology; Mr. L. S. Mayo, assistant dean of the graduate school of arts and sciences; Dr. R. B. Merriman, professor of history; Mr. Henry Pennypacker, chairman of the committee on admissions; Dr. F. W. Taussig, professor of economics; Professor R. DeC. Ward, professor of climatology and present chairman of the board of freshman adviser, and Dr. A. F. Whitten, associate professor of romance languages.

A tutorial system for freshman women at Northwestern University living in dormitories has been announced. The purpose of the new system is to adjust the first-year students to the work of the university as quickly as possible, and to help overcome some of the difficulties of instruction resulting from large classes. It is also hoped the experiment will raise the scholarship and decrease the mortality among the freshman "coeds." Ten tutors, all of them graduate students, will be present every night in Willard Hall, main dormitory for freshman women, during study hours. A student desiring assistance in any freshman subject will go to the tutor in that particular subject and receive as much help as she may need. The system will be entirely voluntary until midterm. After that, it will be compulsory for those students whose grades are low. Miss Vera MacLaren, a graduate student in the department of political science, has been placed in charge of the tutors. Installation of the tutorial system was made possible by the Northwestern University Foundation, which supplied the necessary funds.

Yale University will spend about $22,000,000 for new construction work in the next twelve months. The work probably will be maintained at the present rate, allowing for seasonal fluctuations, Mr. Farnam said. On August 31 there were 2,217 employed on university construction work. This force is to be maintained until weather conditions hamper outdoor work. Including those employed in maintenance, the total force is 3,049, with a monthly wage bill of about $500,000. The university has 1,321 on its teaching, administrative and secretarial staffs.

The formal dedication of Mira Hershey Hall, new residence hall for women on the campus of the University of California at Los Angeles, will take place on Tuesday, October 13. The regents will join in the ceremony, their regular October meeting having been scheduled to be held on that date. According to the plans made, President Robert Gordon Sproul will preside at the formal dedication, which will start at 11:30 A. M. The speakers will include Dr. Helen M. Laughlin, dean of women, and Dr. Ernest Carroll Moore, provost and vice-president of the university. Regent Margaret R. Sartori will unveil the tablet in memory of the late Miss Mira Hershey, the donor of the building through a provision in her will.

Birmingham-Southern College dedicated its new Stockham Woman's Building, which cost $75,000, on September 19. The chief address of the occasion was made by Dr. Kathryn McHale, director of the American Association of University Women. This is the seventh building added to the equipment of Birmingham-Southern College during the presidency of Dr. Guy E. Snavely, who has just completed his tenth year of service.

DISCUSSION

CONCERNING MARKS

There are times in the academic careers of all collegiate parasites when nothing would look so good to them as a respectable average. They may be willing to enjoy the prestige of a distinguished intellectual community without contributing to the sum total of the features that make it attractive, but when the time comes that their tenure is in the balance, nothing seems so desirable as a ticket of admission to the next semester. Others may pretend to resent the implication that they should absorb or acquire a certain amount of useful and cultural knowledge; but when the time comes to exchange their information for an academic passport that will admit them to all the rights and privileges of the social group to which they are pledged, they humble themselves and pay the price of sleepless nights and hectic days for enough useful information to make an otherwise barren blue book appear attractive to the instructor.

With other students respectable marks are as essential to their happiness as is food. Without them, they are in disgrace with themselves. Academic self-respect is a matter of habit. To fail would be to sin. They have always had creditable averages; they expect always to be among those with a substantial academic margin. To slump would be to break a record or to go bankrupt. Good marks are not so much an obsession as they are a foregone conclusion.

With still another class of students marks *per se* are the *summum bonum*. They do not resent the failure of a course to be rewarding so much as they do their inability to get an A out of it. Marks stand for departmental honors and Phi Beta Kappa keys. These are the crowning glories of four years of struggle. And so the cry is, "Give me marks or you do me to death."

In short, people with selfish, prudential, moral and semi-scholarly motives do, either habitually or periodically, have a craving for good marks. College faculties may resent these Gargantuan cries for "marks, Marks, MARKS"; they may say very idealistically that attainment and not marks is the important thing, and yet they must, so far as I can see, continue to translate attainment and failure into symbols on the basis of which students are sent home or tolerated or honored. Until someone appears with greater imagination than his predecessors have had, or until the temper of our mechanical civilization changes radically, ratings and gradings, even though they are human, will continue. Such an abject admission may seem as craven as it is inevitable unless we can make some higher use of this general, if sometimes perverted or camouflaged, desire for marks. Manifestly the "rod and sweetbread method" is ignoble.

With the real scholar, marks as such are a by-product. He is human of course, and enjoys marks of approbation as much as does any one else; but with him they are incidental rather than paramount. He works because he enjoys it. The satisfaction that comes with a sense of increasing power and amplitude is compensating. The titillation that he experiences when he receives his semester marks is mild compared to the afflatus which has already come to him with receding horizons and an enlarging imagination. His greatest exhilarations are not post-mortem but current. He lives as he works. He is not happy because he is not accused by unattempted and unattained assignments. He cannot be complaisant, however, when the land of promise is ahead; it confronts him and does not let him rest. He yearns to enter it and possess a part of it. With each forward movement he becomes aware of more fascinating mysteries. With every step he is conscious of new power. He becomes an intellectual prospector and is happy.

Is it not possible so to relate marks to our ideals as to make the former a more definite help to the latter? Do the students in our respective courses know in general what they must do in order to secure an "A"? Have we taken the pains to interpret the "A" to them with respect to each course? Have our prescriptions been such that if followed they would tend to produce the scholar?

A glance at the analysis of marks for the second semester of 1929–30 reveals some interesting facts. Thirteen out of thirty-six professors (more than one third) gave 50 per cent or more of their students "A's" and "B's." Five professors gave similar marks to 60 per cent. or more of their students, and one professor was fortunate enough to have 73 per cent. of his students similarly deserving. In the college as a whole 46 per cent. of all marks were "A's" and "B's." During the semester that has just passed (the first semester of 1930–31) fifteen out of forty professors (thirty-seven and one half per cent.) gave 50 per cent. or more of their students "A's" and "B's"; eight professors (20 per cent.) gave similar marks to 60 per cent. or more of their students; three professors gave the two highest marks to 70 per cent. or more of their students; and two professors gave "A's" and "B's" to the unprecedented number of 75 per cent. or more of their students.

Now I do not propose to conclude from this that our marks are too high. That is a question in itself. What interests me is this: We, as professors, indulge ourselves in a lot of regrets and laments over the deplorable state of scholarship in the student body. We look with envy toward certain eastern colleges where the spirit of learning seems to flourish more vigorously than it does with us. We pity ourselves for the mediocre run of students who come our way. We blame the materialistic Middle West from which we draw them. We commiserate with each other. In our less sanguine moods we dissertate at length upon the low ebb of intellectual endeavor among the undergraduates. We say that there are but few scholars in the whole lot. And then on the other hand we award almost as many "A's" and "B's" as we do all other marks put together. Objectively, it would seem that 46 per cent. of all our students must be unusual; actually we deny this.

May I insist once more that I am not meaning to suggest, let alone advocate, more rigid marking. The general faculty average, although not in accord with a suggested curve, has been remarkably constant over a period of years. Beginning with the first semester of 1925–26 the passing marks have been as follows in percentages:

A: 11, 7, 9, 10, 11, 15, 13, 13, 13, 14, 13.
B: 28, 31, 31, 32, 29, 31, 30, 33, 33, 35, 32.
C: 35, 36, 40, 46, 37, 35, 39, 37, 36, 37, 37.
D: 13, 11, 11, 12, 11, 13, 11, 12, 11, 9, 9.

In other words over a period of eleven semesters, 39, 38, 40, 42, 40, 46, 43, 46, 46, 49 and 45 per cent. of our marks have been A's and B's, and yet we decry the lack of attainment of our students.

Only two deductions are possible; either we have in our midst more students of genuine attainments than we are willing to recognize as such when we talk shop with each other; or we are rewarding with scholars' marks people who are in no wise scholarly.

Students desire good marks and teachers want scholars. Students get the marks, but teachers deny having the scholars. Does not this seem anomalous? Wherein lies the inconsistency? Can consistency come only with rigidity?

I venture to suggest that we may be at fault with respect to our expectations and interpretations. It is just possible that if our expectations coincided more nearly with our desires, and that if our awarding of marks were correlated more closely with actual attainment, we might find that our dreams would more nearly be realized.

The assignment sheets which one professor placed in the hands of every student in a given course on the first day that the class met, suggest what I have in mind. Herein the meaning of each mark is discriminatingly defined. At a glance it is obvious that an "A" will never come as a reward of mere assiduity or mere mechanical performance. A quality of mind, an attitude, and a distinguished accomplishment are the essentials. Neither desire or work or painstakingness or any other one thing will take the place of actual results—and the results must be scholarly ones. A "B" as outlined on these sheets, presupposes, as does the "A," an intelligent fulfillment of all the requirements of the course, but does not call for the originality, distinct ability, and individual insight that "A" work does; but is quite superior to the steady work of mediocre quality or the somewhat uneven, irregular or fragmentary work of a higher quality that might be rewarded with a "C."

Now this seems to be good pedagogy. It lets the student know definitely from the first what he must do in order to attain the highest marks, and is equally suggestive as to what the reward for average accomplishment must be. But it goes beyond mere definition. It says frankly that a premium is placed upon the one thing which above all else all college teachers wish to encourage.

We have adopted our own curve for the distribution of marks in large, typical classes. We have, for several semesters, published the percentages of each of our several marks given by each of our teachers. We have appointed committees to study the marking systems of other colleges, and have spent whole faculty meetings trying to find out what is wrong with our own. We have not found the perfect system, largely because it does not exist. We have not been satisfied with our own, partly for the reason that we have not applied it and worked it as thoroughly as we might.

Any new or fantastic or complicated or simplified system would have its defects. What we need to do is to be conscientious and constructive in applying the one that is ours already. To this end, these very simple and practical suggestions are made: (1) That before the beginning of next semester each professor define clearly for himself what are to be his requirements in each of his courses for the awarding of each of the several marks; (2) That at the beginning of the coming semester he be as frank and unequivocal as possible in outlining for his students what they must do and what qualities they must show if they are to receive other than average marks; (3) That he then make a special effort to teach and examine and guide his students with that vigor and exactness that begets respect and genuine scholarship.

A COLLEGE DEAN

SPECIAL CORRESPONDENCE

"A MODEST PROPOSAL"

I

IN the last seven years I have taught 2,000 students—in the West, the Middle West and now the East. Mr. Albert Jay Nock, in his article on "American Education" in the May number of the *Atlantic Monthly*, expresses the fervent belief that 90 per cent. of them should never have reached college. I do not know whether his information here is statistical or intuitive. It does not matter. The truth remains that Mr. Nock's indictment is altogether too provocative not to be pursued further.

The pages of my roll book are filled with arithmetical symbols evaluating the timber I am supposed to have hewn into shape. A number of "A's"; scores of "B's"; hundreds of "C's"; too few "D's"; and not enough "F's." What do they all mean? The following table is of interest:

Grade	No. of students	Percentage
A (93 to 100)	152	7½
B (83 to 92)	423	21
C (70 to 82)	861	43
D (60 to 69)	357	18
F (below 60)	193	9½
W (withdrew)	19	1
Total	2,005	100

These 2,000 grades, by the way, represent students from two well-known universities and a prominent teachers college in the country. Of the universities, one carries an enrolment well over 30,000; the other, over 15,000. The teachers college, I believe, has a registration of about 3,500. In other words, it is not unfair to assume that these are representative of America's better youth.

But before analyzing further these few statistics, let me assure the reader that I am not unmindful of the wholesale attack forever levelled against this system of grading which seems so smugly to reduce every student to an infallible $\frac{MV^2}{2}$ sort of formula. I am by no means unaware of the dangers of too literal construction upon these symbols *de convenance*.

In the absence of a more satisfactory medium of evaluation, however, it is the only tangible source of information that we have about our students. That the system has its multiform shortcomings no experienced educator would deny. But ideal standards require superior mentalities and fine characters, who, given all the freedom in the world, will take none. At present, "our educable fry" are not sufficiently hand-picked for these idyllic no-grade schemes so popular with "progressive" schools and other educational bedlams.

Of course, any one can say that grades mean nothing at all. I have yet to meet the failing student who, upon learning his fate, has not become supercilious about the matter and wagered with me that he actually knows as much as the boy whom I passed with an "A" or a "B" grade. It is to be remembered, however, that not every "F" student is a genius in an hostile environment. Nor is every Phi Beta Kappa an ineffectual dullard. Besides, it is not impossible for a teacher to use her intelligence in rendering a final estimate of a student. Not all of us are impersonal adding machines lacking in common sense and ordinary wit.

When I give a student an "A," he has generally convinced me that he is either brilliant or exceedingly accurate. The "B" student is usually a hard worker, a faithful retainer of knowledge and the possessor of an orderly mind. A student who receives his "C" in a course with me is almost invariably the type whose mental endowment is very ordinary, whose initiative is dangerously modest, who, as a matter of fact, is a well-meaning follower—never a leader. Before I record a "D" for a student I like to feel reasonably certain that the work is beyond his mental reach. And when I label a student "F," I am not unaware that he may be a genius or a high-grade moron.

II

Returning to our table, however, what is the story that it tells? Summarily speaking, these are the implications: That of the 2,000 students who made possible my salary for seven years, (1) about 72 per cent. (Mr. Nock modestly suggests 10 per cent.) should have been admitted to college, with a possible 60 per cent. receiving degrees; (2) 18 per cent. should have gone through the high school, the upper third of whom might also have received further training in technical or industrial institutes; (3) 10 per cent. should have been subjected to an elementary education only.

To be sure, these are no figures to please the eye of a fond parent. Then, too, there is this to remember: if we send one out of every four students away from college, we are necessarily retaining but three out of every four teachers. So we are. What of it? Too many college positions to-day are held by disappointed newspapermen, unsuccessful economists, middle-aged gridiron heroes, unpublishing novelists and misguided radio announcers. But that is another story.

To continue with our analysis, dangerously arbitrary as it must be, the question naturally arises as to why only 72 per cent. should be admitted to college when, presumably, an additional 18 per cent. are capable of doing passing work. The answer is simply this: the requirements of college courses are so pathetically modest that any student with reasonable intelligence and honest persistence could not help receiving an "A" or a "B," certainly a "C" for his efforts. Now, then, if his work nets him less than an average of 70, it is not unreasonable to suppose one of two things to be true: (1) either the student can not understand the language of higher education; or (2) he is not willing to put forth the effort necessary to achieve that understanding. In the first instance there is of course nothing to do. Wherever possible an ambitious "D" student should be enrolled in a trade or industrial school, where education is less ideational and more pragmatic. Here his native intelligence and honest labor would be capitalized to their fullest merits. Not only would he find himself more at home in this environment; he would actually emerge a happier, healthier individual.

In the second case, where the student presumably has an "A" or "B" mind and is satisfied with "D" work, the solution is perhaps more complicated. Personally, I put little stock in the student who babbles to me of "A" equipment and attributes his "D" results to impatience with detail or study or routine. The true college student is he whose personal pride and intellectual curiosity would not permit him to do less than the most he is capable of. It is therefore my honest opinion that the student who does "D" work and pretends to greater mental endowment does not belong in college. He does not possess the character discipline which distinguishes the superior mind from the typical dilettante. He is the type who should go into business; his confidence is unbounded; his optimism without a peer; indeed, by his very presumptuousness he has already embraced success. He does not need college any more than college needs him.

That this whole group of students whose grades run below 70 should have been permitted to enter college at all is most unfortunate. The fact is, these hundreds of young men and women have been given professional ideals and aspirations wholly incompatible with their mental capacities. They have been allowed to create for themselves hopes the fulfilment of which is as impossible as it is undesirable.

I have before me the final examination book of one of these students. He is a recent graduate of one of the largest state universities in the Middle West. His end runs brought his alma mater at least two football championships. He was the idol of his class, the darling of the alumni, the guest of the president of the university on more than one occasion—a consideration, by the way, of which few department heads could boast. But to return to our hero's examination book.

On the first page appears the following passionate if not eloquent appeal for mercy: "Cannidate for a degree this June! Senior!" Turning to the second page, where his answers begin, I read:

> The chief thing about Oscar Wild's plays was to many anagrams. He did not like sincerity so all his characters speak in these clever but unnecessary anagrams. His characters are all alike. He may know women but he certainly dont men.

I can see myself grading the paper of this "cannidate for a degree." I probably read it a second time. I graded as carefully as was humanly possible. The paper netted 68. The boy should have failed. He is illiterate. But his college decreed that he should pass on 65. He was even three points ahead! He should have been failed three years ago, when he was a freshman. Now that he was a senior, there was little I could do. The law was with him. He made his "D" and he is a college graduate now. He wears a solid gold football on his watch fob; he displays a fraternity pin on his bosom. Is there any doubt that Dwight Atwood was a success at college?

Or take his friend Roberts' examination book. On the flyleaf this memorandum greets me:

> Technicly I am only a first term soph. but due to extra work I can enter the law school next sept. if you pass me.

In the first question I learn that "the classical unities are time, space, and distance," and that "katharsis is when your characters are immoral." That isn't all. There are six more answers he has written. Whereupon in the "b" part of the third question he records the following oration on Montaigne's contribution to the essay:

> Originally people didn't want to think, so the essay developed last in literature. In fact the essay don't appear until Montague wrote his ribble books in the eighteen century.

This "technicly—first term soph" had planned to enter the law school that fall. It so happened that my grade prevented it. But that is a minor matter. He tried his luck in English 14 again—with some other teacher. He got his "D" and is probably a senior in the law school by this time.

III

The solution? Mr. Albert Jay Nock says it's quite simple. Merely cut adrift this mass of Atwoods and Roberts whose downward trend so threatens the prospects for American education.

But how shall we know the wheat from the chaff when we harvest our early autumn crop? That Mr. Nock does not answer for us. Are there, then, any special qualities which distinguish the desirable student from the non-qualifying applicant? In plain English, are there any telltale signs by which an intelligent parent—that is, one who can be unsentimental about his son or daughter—may determine whether or not his child is made of the stuff amenable to a higher education?

From observing my better students—those whom I should definitely label "college material"—I should say that a boy (or girl) does not belong in college:

(1) If he can not make a list of at least a dozen things that are wrong with him.
(2) If his general average is less than "C."
(3) If he can not write a simple passage of exposition without violating the elementary principles of composition.
(4) If he has an impatience with books and must literally torture himself to read.
(5) If he has any inclinations towards doing the minimum amount of work, towards "putting something over" on his teachers.
(6) If he deems himself superior to routine.
(7) If he can not take criticism.
(8) If his code of conduct does not include as much respect for others as for himself.
(9) If he is dishonest—mentally or actually.
(10) If he blames others too readily for his failings.
(11) If he can not be alone for twenty-four hours and be wholly interesting to himself.
(12) If he is not sufficiently curious to read at least a dozen good books in literature, science, and economics published through the year.
(13) If he looks upon education as a business proposition or as the ante-chamber to social success.
(14) If his intellectual needs do not grow from year to year.
(15) If he can not compete with the rest of the student body, but is eternally requiring special consideration.
(16) If he can not discipline himself to work full quota, even though he may know that the teacher will not check up on him.
(17) If he can not take part in a serious discussion without being bored, self-conscious or affected.
(18) If he can not stand to be wrong.
(19) If he does not "love all beauty, whether of nature or of art."

That is one angle of approach. To pretend that these qualifications are infallible would of course be absurd. Certainly no one or even all of these should be used as the sole measuring rod. Yet it seems to me that a college entrance examination (oral and written) designed to bring out some such facts about our students would prove no mean beginning towards determining their aptitude for college work. If, in addition, successful applicants were admitted to college for one year only, with the understanding that within that time they would, to use their own phrase, "either have to make good or make room," the problem of choosing the right "educable fry" would be well along the road to solution, and true culture would again become the mark of the college-bred.

L. Ruth Middlebrook

New York, N. Y.

QUOTATIONS

SCHOOL ENROLMENT IN SEPTEMBER, 1931

	Population	1930 Enrolment	1931 Enrolment	Per Cent. Increase or Decrease
California:				
Los Angeles	1,238,048	239,117	244,766	2.3
Riverside	29,696	5,866	6,294	6.8
Colorado:				
Denver	287,861	42,061	44,204	4.8
Illinois:				
Bloomington	30,930	4,530	4,548	0.4
Danville	36,765	7,628	7,760	1.7
Moline	32,236	5,277	5,316	0.7
Quincy	39,241	5,317	5,403	1.6
Rockford	85,864	13,803	13,889	0.6
Waukegan	33,499	6,324	6,361	0.6
Decatur	57,510	10,691	10,801	1.0
Indiana:				
East Chicago	54,784	8,961	9,323	3.8
Evansville	102,249	14,194	14,405	1.4
Fort Wayne	114,946	16,276	15,163	–6.7
Indianapolis	364,161	55,550	55,900	0.6
Kokomo	32,843	6,196	6,275	1.2
Michigan City	26,735	3,934	4,105	4.1
South Bend	104,193	16,704	16,883	1.1
Iowa:				
Burlington	26,755	4,541	4,673	2.1
Cedar Rapids	56,097	9,741	9,113	–6.4
Clinton	25,726	3,483	3,496	0.4
Sioux City	79,183	14,947	15,462	3.3
Waterloo	46,191	3,928	3,986	1.4
Massachusetts:				
Arlington	36,094	6,146	6,167	0.3
Beverly	25,086	4,517	4,597	1.7
Brockton	63,797	10,995	11,119	1.5
Chicopee	43,930	6,929	6,712	–3.1
Everett	48,424	9,085	9,110	0.2
Holyoke[1]	56,537	7,399	6,972	–5.7
New Bedford	112,597	17,601	17,632	0.2
Newton	65,276	10,294	10,716	3.9
Quincy	71,983	13,803	14,339	3.7
Springfield	149,900	28,337	28,772	1.6
Taunton	37,355	6,416	6,622	3.1
Michigan:				
Battle Creek	43,573	1,000	1,072	7.2
Flint	156,492	30,135	30,586	1.4
Jackson	55,187	7,421	7,399	–0.3
Kalamazoo	54,786	9,584	9,833	2.5
Muskegon	41,390	8,326	8,165	–1.9
Saginaw	80,715	14,198	15,114	6.7

[1] Elementary attendance not yet compulsory, due to prevalence of poliomyelitis.

	Population	1930 Enrolment	1931 Enrolment	Per Cent. Increase or Decrease
Minnesota:				
Duluth[2]	101,463	7,012	7,518	6.7
St. Paul	271,606	38,372	38,719	0.8
Missouri:				
Kansas City	399,746	61,866	62,355	0.8
St. Joseph	80,935	11,580	11,709	1.1
Springfield	57,527	10,929	11,032	0.9
New Jersey:				
Atlantic City	66,198	9,991	10,291	2.9
Montclair	42,017	7,481	7,603	1.6
New Brunswick	34,555	6,089	6,303	3.4
Orange	35,399	7,192	7,494	4.0
New York:				
Albany	127,412	14,137	13,566	–4.0
Jamestown	45,155	8,621	8,763	1.7
Niagara Falls	75,460	15,513	16,053	3.3
Rochester	328,132	50,450	51,244	1.5
Rome	32,338	5,297	5,498	3.6
North Carolina:				
Durham	52,037	10,152	10,068	–0.8
High Point	36,749	7,279	7,722	5.7
Winston-Salem	75,274	13,399	14,244	5.8
Ohio:				
Canton	104,906	20,589	20,934	1.6
Cincinnati	451,160	55,690	55,713	0.0
Circleville	7,369	1,477	1,598	7.0
Cleveland	900,429	142,925	143,197	0.2
" Heights	50,945	8,677	8,727	0.6
Columbus	290,564	41,576	42,008	1.0
Dayton	200,982	33,336	34,287	2.7
Hamilton	52,176	7,529	7,525	–0.0
Lakewood	70,509	10,799	10,652	–1.4
Lorain	44,512	8,237	8,314	0.9
Norwood	33,411	3,652	3,750	2.6
Springfield	68,743	11,570	11,798	1.8
Steubenville	35,422	6,094	6,188	1.6
Pennsylvania:				
Bethlehem	57,892	11,195	11,303	0.9
Chester	59,164	9,595	9,790	1.9
Johnstown	66,993	13,647	13,765	0.9
Lancaster	59,949	9,487	9,637	1.6
Lebanon	25,561	4,359	4,563	4.4
New Castle	48,674	10,595	10,870	2.5
Sharon	25,908	5,319	5,417	1.8
Williamsport	45,729	8,308	8,413	1.2
York	55,254	9,475	9,847	3.8

[2] High school only; elementary attendance erratic, due to poliomyelitis.

	Population	1930 Enrolment.	1931 Enrolment.	Per cent. Increase or Decrease
Texas:				
Port Arthur	50,902	7,309	6,968	–4.6
San Antonio	231,542	29,567	33,500	1.1
Wichita Falls	43,690	9,154	9,234	0.8
Utah:				
Ogden	40,272	10,325	10,743	3.8
Salt Lake City	140,267	29,967	31,139	3.7
Virginia:				
Newport News	34,417	6,609	6,986	5.1
Petersburg	28,564	6,032	6,080	0.6
Richmond	182,929	31,478	32,107	1.9
Washington:				
Seattle	365,583	58,716	60,532	3.0
West Virginia:				
Clarksburg	28,866	4,630	4,530	–2.2
Parkersburg	29,623	6,346	6,274	–1.1
Wisconsin:				
Milwaukee	578,249	74,677	77,828	4.1
Oshkosh	40,108	5,902	6,014	1.8
Racine	67,542	12,129	12,349	1.7
Superior	36,113	6,784	6,787	0.0
West Allis	34,671	6,563	6,766	3.0

—*The School Board Journal*

SOCIETIES AND MEETINGS

THE REGIONAL CONFERENCE ON SECONDARY EDUCATION

WITH a brilliant array of leading educators of the country in attendance, headed by Dr. William John Cooper, U. S. Commissioner of Education, the recent Regional Conference on Secondary Education, held on the campus at the Colorado State Teachers College, Greeley, Colorado, was fraught with considerable significance. While the U. S. Office of Education has been carrying on a nation-wide survey of secondary education, the people engaged in the three fields of articulation—the elementary school, the secondary school and the college—came together here for the first time in a group to discuss not only the survey but the problems as they have faced them. Much was revealed that will prove of tremendous value to the department and its aims through the survey.

The regional conference was called by the commissioner of education in cooperation with Dr. George Willard Frasier, president of the Colorado State Teachers College. The fact that it was held at a time when nearly 2,500 educators were in attendance at the summer school at the Colorado State Teachers College added materially to the importance of the sessions in that the discussions not only brought together more people vitally concerned into the discussions and opened up paths for the conductors of the survey, but it enabled large numbers of others interested in the subject to learn much that will undoubtedly prove of value.

In opening the conference, Dr. Cooper set forth at the beginning the purposes of the secondary educational survey under the direction of the U. S. Office of Education. He said:

The national survey of secondary education was authorized by the seventieth Congress as a 3-year program, to be conducted by the Department of the Interior through the United States Office of Education. The total amount authorized was \$225,000—\$50,000 for the first year, \$100,000 for the second year and \$75,000 for the third year. The survey began in July, 1929, and will close in June, 1932. The authorization for the survey states that it shall be "of the organization, administration, financing, and work of secondary schools and of their articulation with elementary and higher education."

According to Commissioner Cooper, there were four major fields for investigation and early in the year there was prepared an outline covering the subjects which it was proposed to investigate. Continuing, he said:

This outline in its tentative form was carefully scrutinized by a large number of persons, notably by members of the consultant group and the advisory committee already mentioned. As finally developed, the outline listed four major fields for investigation: The organization of schools and districts; the secondary school population and related problems; administrative and supervisory problems. There was no disposition to regard these as the only problems of secondary education needing investigation; a large number of others were considered. These four were selected as being important, unsolved, not about to be thoroughly investigated by other agencies, and still, as nearly as might be, susceptible of solution within the financial and time limitations of this survey.

The first approach in the effort to secure needed information was made to state departments of education; the next, to city school systems; the third, to individual secondary schools. The inquiry forms (numbered, respectively, 1, 2 and 3) addressed to these agencies aimed in each case to cover the whole field of the survey. Obviously it was not practicable to make these first inquiries sufficiently detailed to present an adequate picture of the practices; they could be and were merely first approaches. They were designed to give preliminary information, and to furnish important leads for later thorough inquiries.

From the standpoints of amount of money available, number of persons employed, and extent of investigations planned, this is undoubtedly the most significant research study of secondary education ever undertaken in the United States. Throughout it has been regarded as a cooperative undertaking. Request for the appropriation was a cooperative enterprise; the scope of the survey reflects a composite of opinion; the whole advisory system aims at pooling the best judgments available on secondary education; and, since the survey proceeds on the assumption that the most practicable solutions (as distinct from ideal solutions) to secondary school problems are to be found in the schools themselves, it becomes vital to its success that school administrators, teachers, and pupils, shall continue to cooperate with it, as they have in the past, by contributing of their time and experience."

The office of education is committed to a program which necessitates, first, keeping its studies on an objective basis, and second, leaving to volunteer agencies activities that might be considered as promotional or propaganda in character.

We should be negligent, however, if we fail to heed the requests for leadership in helping solve some of the serious problems which confront education in this period of rapid change. We are attempting to render this kind of assistance through conferences. To cite an instance: In December, 1929, we conferred with some half a hundred persons of various types of training, experience, and educational position. The 2-day discussion centered about the effects of the present industrial order on the American home.

One of the conclusions of the conference was that the Commissioner of Education should hold a series of regional home economics conferences. It does not appear to me that holding a meeting and making speeches is likely to make for much progress in solving a problem of such seriousness as the breakdown of the home. Yet we have not the resources in staff or funds to carry on the program of studies and we have reason to believe that conditions will vary sufficiently throughout our country to warrant different solutions.

The best procedure is to experiment, allowing each region to arrive at and try out its own solution. Accordingly, we are now attempting a series of regional conferences held in cooperation with higher institutions which have the facilities to guide and assist committees working in the field. The institutions have already invited us to participate in conferences of this kind on this particular problem—the University of Cincinnati and the State College of Agriculture and Mechanic Arts at Ames, Iowa. The conference at the latter institution was held November 10 and 11, 1930. Approximately 60 persons attended, many of whom participated actively in the discussion.

The half-day programs were built about themes attacking the general problem from the points of view of economics, sociology, and education. The committees which were appointed as a result of this meeting are now at work under the general direction of the faculties of the State College of Iowa and the State University of Iowa. It is the expectation that conferences of this kind may be stimulated in other parts of the country.

The program included discussions of the following subjects:

"The Present Student Population," led by Professor William L. Wrinkle, principal of Teachers College High School, Colorado State Teachers College.

"Individual Differences," led by Dr. H. H. Ryan, principal of the University High School at the University of Wisconsin.

"Vocational and Educational Guidance of High School Pupils," led by Mr. Paul Essert, director of instruction, Denver Public Schools.

"Current Theories and Their Effects on Secondary Education," led by Dr. William Chandler Bagley.

"The Survey of the Curriculum," led by Dr. A. K. Loomis, Denver Public Schools, and in charge of the curriculum study of the national survey.

"The Social Science Curriculum," led by Dr. Howard C. Hill, professor of the teaching of history, University of Chicago.

"The Sciences," led by Dr. W. L. Beauchamp, assistant professor of education, University of Chicago.

"The Curriculum and the Teacher," led by Dr. Earle Underwood Rugg, head of the Department of Education, Colorado State Teachers College.

"Articulation of Elementary and Secondary

Schools,'' led by Miss Elma A. Neal, assistant superintendent of schools, San Antonio, Texas.

''Articulation of the Secondary School and the College,'' led by Dr. George T. Avery, associate professor of psychology and education, Colorado Agricultural College.

''The Colorado State Teachers College Experiment in Articulation,'' led by Dr. Frederick L. Whitney, director of educational research, Colorado State Teachers College.

''Extra-Curricular Activities and Non-Athletic Interscholastic Contests,'' led by Mr. J. H. Risley, superintendent of schools, Pueblo, Colorado.

''Practices in the Selection of Teachers,'' led by Mr. D. M. Hibner, superintendent of schools at Ray, Arizona.

''Supervision of Instruction,'' led by Dr. A. L. Threlkeld, superintendent of schools at Denver, Colorado.

''Administration of the Secondary School,'' led by Dr. Jesse H. Newlon, director of the Lincoln School, Teachers College, Columbia University.

''Organization and Administration of Small High Schools,'' led by Dr. O. L. Troxel, professor of education, Colorado State Teachers College.

John H. Shaw

EDUCATIONAL RESEARCH AND STATISTICS

CHECKING READING CONTRACTS IN A COLLEGE COURSE

It is always interesting to hear about courses in which students are given opportunity for initiative and are allowed to follow their interests in a "natural" reading or study situation. This is an ideal to be striven for, but the ever-present requirement of a final mark brings up the grading problem which can not always be met so informally. This article describes one more attempt to give perfect freedom to students and at the same time to keep them in the straight and narrow path of meeting grading requirements.

The course in child care and training was chosen for the plan. Students selected their own lists of readings and used the scheduled class hour for reading, reporting on their readings, or for conferences with the instructor according to their wishes. Students reported orally, by check-tests, by outlines or in some other way suitable to the books they read.

The greatest difficulty was in evaluating the work of the various students closely enough to assign comparable grades. This problem was complicated by other factors. At Crescent students are expected to do work commensurate with their ability as nearly as that can be determined. This particular class in child care and training showed a wide range of reading abilities, both in speed and comprehension. This second factor necessitated special care on the part of the instructor to prevent the work of the poor readers from falling below a college level.

The plan of evaluating students' work in this course centered around four questions.

First: When each student was allowed to select her own list of books, how could the instructor make a comparable estimate of the average time and effort represented by each list? In order to meet this question she gave the class an approved list of twenty-four books on child care and training that had found favor with other classes in the same course. To each of these books was assigned a composite weight based on a scale of 1 to 4 according to difficulty and time needed for reading, as indicated by students in previous classes. This list of twenty-four books included six with 1 weight each, six with 2 weights each, six with 3 weights each and six with 4 weights each. Thus, the entire list ranged from easy to difficult and included a wide variety of subject-matter. This plan was intended to aid students in selecting equivalent lists of books.

Second: How could the instructor determine what would constitute reasonable minimum and maximum quantities and qualities of work to keep it on a satisfactory college level? There was no accurate way to answer this question. Therefore, the approximate amount and quality of work which had been accepted as inferior, yet of passing value in previous classes was decided upon as the minimum for any student in the course. By a similar method standards for average, superior and excellent work were fixed for the class. According to the Crescent College marking system, A indicates excellent work; B, superior work; C, average work;

D, inferior work; and F, failure. Hence, A, B, C and D contracts were adopted upon the basis of the composite weights assigned by previous classes in this subject. By comparison with class records of individual students in former classes, an A contract would require approximately a total weight of 18; a B contract, 17; a C contract, 16; and a D contract, 15. According to this plan a D contract would represent the minimum accepted and an A contract the maximum required of any student. Students selected any combination of books which interested them so long as the sum of the weights equaled the total required for the contract assumed by the individuals. For example, student H. B. selected for her A contract, nine books with weights of 1, 1, 1, 1, 2, 2, 3, 3, 4, respectively, totaling 18. Any combination from five to twelve books according to their weights could compose an A contract. Similar variation was possible in the B, C and D contracts.

Third: How should students' reading lists be made up to meet individual differences in speed and comprehension and in each case insure work commensurate with the individual's ability? Superior readers were required to take an A contract and other students were advised in their choices according to their ability to read. If consulted, the instructor gave short previews of various books and suggestions concerning the types of reports suitable in each case.

Fourth: How should the instructor estimate the quality of each student's work when completed? From the foregoing discussion it will be seen that a quantitative estimate was arrived at by the use of weights assigned to each book read. A qualitative estimate was made by applying the Crescent grade point system to each unit of work in the contracts. This point system assigns 4, 3, 2 or 1, grade points to each semester hour of A, B, C or D grade, respectively. Therefore, each report, quiz or problem completed by a student was credited to her contract record in two ways; namely, quantitatively in terms of weights and qualitatively in terms of grade points. The product of these two factors was the credit assigned to any given unit of the course and the sum of the credits of all units within a contract was the final credit given to the course for the individual student whose contract it was. According to this plan the various contracts would carry with them final credits as follows:

Contract	wt.	wt. × gr. points	Credit points
A	18	18 × 4	72
B	17	17 × 3	51
C	16	16 × 2	32
D	15	15 × 1	15

In terms of total grade points assigned to the four types of contracts, 72 or more credits were given a final letter grade of A; from 51 to 71, a letter of B; from 32 to 50, a letter grade of C; and from 15 to 31, a letter grade of D. Less than fifteen credit points was considered as failure. The selection of any one of the four contracts did not insure the normal grade letter which it represented, for the quality of work was more important than the quantity of the contracts. Inspection of the foregoing tabulation will show that A contracts could have a range of grade letters from D to A; B contracts, from D to B; C contracts, from D to B; D contracts, D to B. It happened that no student did any one quality of work throughout her contract. For example, one student's range of quality was from C to A on an A contract and her total was 58 credit points. This total was between 51 and 71, therefore, a grade letter of B was recorded for her in the course. In no case was a report accepted by the instructor if it were not satisfactory for the ability of that student. If a student desired to raise her record she was encouraged to do so by reading more than her contract called for and the credits thus earned were added to her record. This plan offered reward to the poor student for superior diligence.

This little game of grades proved interesting to both the instructor and her students and indirectly, if not directly, gave to the members of the class training in planning their own work and in exercising initiative in governing their own efforts. Students often came to the instructor for suggestions concerning methods of study and for further orientation on their reading. From an educational view-point the attitude and atmosphere of the class was very gratifying.

GRACE H. Y. GRIFFIN

CRESCENT COLLEGE,
EUREKA SPRINGS, ARK.

SCHOOL AND SOCIETY
EDITED BY J. McKEEN CATTELL
WITH WHICH IS COMBINED THE
EDUCATIONAL REVIEW
EDITED BY WILLIAM McANDREW

Volume 34 SATURDAY, OCTOBER 17, 1931 Number 877

THE FRENCH AND GERMAN ACADEMIC EXAMINATIONS AND DEGREES

By Professor M. J. DEMIASHKEVICH
GEORGE PEABODY COLLEGE FOR TEACHERS

I. THE ORIGINS

ANATOLE FRANCE in an *étude* found in the *Vie Littéraire* refers, in a few masterly lines, to the evening chats of students in the Garden of Luxembourg and under the stately trees of the Avenue d'Observatoire where the tumultuous citizens of the Latin Quarter "many times made over the world, arguing before an assembly of the stars and assisted by the silence of the deserted alleys."[1] It is fair to suppose that in their architectonic plans there were details relative to examinations and degrees. At least, the subject was likely to come up before the would-be reformers of the universe in their spring deliberations, at about the time when the approaching major examinations usually begin to take the ugly form of a disturbing reality even in the dreamiest heads among those enrolled in one Paris school or another. And it is certainly a venerable, if not always a pleasant, subject—it is undoubtedly older than the *Quartier Latin* itself.

Gabriel Compayré, the celebrated historian of education, advises those who disapprove of the multiplicity, if not of the very existence, of academic examinations and degrees that the criticism must be addressed to the medieval university administration. It was the medieval universities that invented college examinations and degrees. Greek antiquity was innocent of those shortcomings, guilty as it may have been of many others. To say nothing of Socrates, the Platonic Academy, nor the Aristotelian Lyceum, nor their successors in other Mediterranean countries granted any degrees. Rome, though much more awake to the rights and responsibilities of the state than were, on the whole, the Greek communities, did not do much in the way of state administration and supervision of education. A feeble beginning in that direction appears to have been made towards the end of the imperial régime, but it was, as the régime itself, without a future. Emperor Valentinian issued, in 399, an edict purporting to draw a distinction between the "sophists" of the time, that is to say, the ambulant professors of no competence and no value "who have no right to teach and who should be removed" and "masters who are respected by competent persons and should be differentiated from their deceitful rivals and permitted to pursue their calling."

The edict of Pope Honorius III, given

[1] V. III, p. 55.

in Rome in the year 1219, may be regarded as the beginning of the grievous institution of academic examinations. The edict established an examination for the degree of *licentia docendi, i.e.*, the license to teach. A further, and in a sense final, establishment of degrees dates from the regulation enacted by the University of Paris about 1231 and copied by the other continental universities. In accordance with this rule the degree of *licentia docendi* had to follow upon the baccalaureate, and the doctorate could not be obtained without the *licentia* as a prerequisite. Holders of the *licentia* were in some cases called *magistri* (masters), in distinction from *doctores*, holders of the higher degree. Yet, in some places, the terms *magistri* and *doctores* both were the denominations of holders of the higher degree, with this difference: *magistri* was the title of the university teachers of humanities (*magistri artium*) while *doctores* were instructors in the different branches of law (*doctores utriusque iuris*). Such, for instance, appears to have been the custom of the early German universities. After the Protestant Reformation the German Emperors arrogated to themselves the right of conferring the doctorate upon the recommendation of their *Pfalzgrafen,* the then equivalent of modern prime minister or imperial chancellor. The diplomas coming from the emperor's chancellery were decorated with the imperial seal (*bulla*). The beneficiaries were therefore called, in distinction from holders of regularly granted doctor's degrees (*doctores rite promoti*) *doctores bullati.* They were the forerunners of modern honorary doctors.

To attenuate the guilt of the medieval universities in the eyes of those of us who have to take their degrees, the pleading before those who already have theirs being scarcely necessary, it might be mentioned that the learned gentlemen of the time merely conformed, as it behooved their status, to the social usage of the era, when skilled vocations were organized in corporations or guilds, each of which was subdivided into three groups—apprentices, companions and masters. The baccalaureate, *licentia docendi,* and doctorate corresponded to the three divisions within the guilds. The promotion from one division to another was conditioned upon a certain quantity and quality of work, and the mastership was bestowed upon the presentation of a masterpiece to the committee of masters. Similarly, in order to become a *magister artium* or a *doctor iuris,* and thus to acquire the right to follow the profession of teaching it was made obligatory that the aspirant remain for a certain time on the benches of the school as a student and then pass a set examination given by persons competent to judge, in other words, the university teachers. The similarity between the guild situation and the university situation will show itself as a very close one if it will be recalled that the medieval academic degrees were at the same time professional diplomas or certificates.

The early medieval university customs relative to examinations and degrees seem to have been better preserved in France than in Germany.

II. The Present Situation in France

To begin with, the French universities grant, just as do the American universities and colleges of the university rank, all the three degrees which existed in the Middle Ages: (a) baccalaureate, (b) *licence,* which is the nearest continental approach to the American M.A. and M.S., and (c) doctorate. Furthermore, all the three degrees carry with them, as did the medieval degrees, certain vocational privileges, the smallest and least definite being those attached to the *baccalauréat.*

Baccalauréat (*diplôme de bachelier*), or

"*bachot*" as it is called in the familiar language, is granted on the basis of an examination given by special committees appointed by the minister of public instruction and fine arts. The committees are composed of the university and secondary school professors and sit twice a year, in June–July and October, at each of the French state universities. The nearest foreign equivalent of the French baccalaureate examination seems to be, on the procedure side, the English matriculation examination. The *baccalauréat* is taken in two parts. Normally, the first part is taken at the end of the junior year in the secondary school (*Première*) and the second part at the end of the senior year (*Philosophie-Mathématiques*). The examination consists of papers and oral interrogations in each subject on the examination program covering very largely the entire curriculum of the secondary school forms inclusive of the junior year or the *Première* for the first part of baccalaureate and that of the senior year for the second part. The examination may be repeated by the unsuccessful candidates. The number of trials is not limited, but each time the examination has to be taken *in toto*, irrespective of the previous success of the candidate in a given subject. The vast majority of candidates come from the public and regular private secondary schools, but under the law any person who is sixteen years of age is entitled to admission to the first part of the baccalaureate examination upon sending to the secretary of the academy[2] an application duly executed upon the legal form (*papier timbré*) bearing a stamp which represents a state tax. No candidate can be examined by his secondary school professor sitting on the committee.[3]

The value of the *diplôme de bachelier* is threefold. First, the baccalaureate is the state sanction of the completion of secon-

[2] Academy in this case means one of the seventeen regions into which France is divided for the purpose of educational administration.

[3] Types of topics in the French composition: On his return from England (1767), Jean-Jacques Rousseau has wandered for three years and then settled in Paris (1770), where he remained until death (1778). He lived modestly in a little apartment in the rue Platière persecuted by the curiosity of visitors. Often did he leave the town for long excursions on foot in the country around Paris. Bernardin de Saint-Pierre (1737–1814), who was introduced to Rousseau in June of 1772, accompanied him on some of the excursions, both being great lovers of nature. They admired the trees and flowers and "the peaceful solitary little valleys." Jean-Jacques herborised as at the time of his delightful stay in the island of Saint-Pierre. He talked willingly of his adventurous life and in these reminiscences, even the darkest days presented a moving charm while the happy occurrences, rare in the life of Rousseau, evoked in him a great joy. Jean-Jacques at times talked about education, literature and arts, or about social problems. Both grieved at the vanity of men which makes them desert the solid enjoyments of simple life in nature to seek corruptive and imaginary satisfactions in the pleasures of fashionable society. When the night was falling, the excursionists would take leave of each other, after having agreed that they would meet the next Sunday and Rousseau would return to his modest home, his serenity restored and almost happy. Drawing freely upon the indications given above, relate one of those excursions imagining a conversation between Jean-Jacques Rousseau and Bernardin de Saint-Pierre.

You have often come across the expressions such as "sweet" and "tender" Vergil. Already Horace in his "Satires" (I, x, v. 44) spoke of the "sweetness" and "elegance" of Vergil; Boileau, in his "Art Poétique" (II, v. 26) and Sainte-Beuve, in his "Pensées d'Août," also praised the "tenderness" of the writings of Vergil. Do you think, in the light of your knowledge of the work of the poet, that the characteristics attributed to him by Horace, Boileau, and Sainte-Beuve give an adequate idea of his genius?

You will imagine a dialogue between an uncle and his nephew talking in Paris around 1835. The uncle is a notary public and has remained entirely loyal, in his literary taste, to the traditions of classicism. The nephew is an ardent romanticist. He moves among the young writers and artists, and is infatuated with Lamartine, Hugo, Musset, and Gautier. Construct the dialogue in such a way as to make it possible for the dary education.[4] The secondary schools themselves, even the state schools, do not give any final examinations or issue graduation certificates.

Second, the *baccalauréat* is a passport for admission to the university, the university studies being on the graduate level, in American terminology. The *baccalauréat* diploma is also a legal document demanded as prerequisite at many civil service examinations. Admission to the higher technical schools (*les Grandes Ecoles*) military and civilian, and to the Superior Normal School (*Ecole Normale Supérieure*) is based on a highly competitive entrance examination given by each of those schools.

Third, the baccalaureate is very valuable socially—a title to respectability still imperative in case of young men of the middle and upper middle class and not superfluous in case of the young ladies. The rector of the Academy and University of Paris has very well said in his humorous address to the baccalaureate candidates at the October examination of 1929: "We all have gone through the mill. So will your children and grandchildren. The only Frenchmen who were not forced to take the baccalaureate examination were those who established the institution of the baccalaureate."[5] The failure to obtain the *bachot* is very much of a disgrace for the family of the young man and consequently a serious family concern.[6] Hence, the trade of private coaching of weaklings, and the efforts, apparently very seldom successful, to obtain the precious *bachot* by fraudulent methods. Hence, the suggestion offered by a somewhat cynical foreign visitor that every newborn Frenchman ought to receive from the state and have put into his cradle the baccalaureate diploma and the decoration of *Légion d'honneur*,[7] as such an arrangement would save much of the French national energy for more serious purposes.

Yet the French themselves appear to believe that the baccalaureate is a test of ability and stimulus to the display of the energy of French youth too valuable to be discarded or even facilitated. The educational career of a Frenchman is rich in the educational experiences known under the sinister name of examinations. Another foreign observer has remarked that the French could be properly divided into two groups: those who give examinations and those who take them. And they are determined to continue in that way. After the world war the wave of "easyism" was passing over Europe especially in the belligerent countries. It was probably an inevitable reaction to the tremendous concentration of energy necessitated by the war, and a device to make up for the years lost in fighting, by introducing short cuts. Among other social institutions, state examinations reflected the popular tendency, in a degree. The worst part of the war fatigue once overcome, the influential organs of the French press began the campaign for the stiffening or, to be exact, restiffening of the examinations.

reader to visualize the manners and the appearance of the persons of the dialogue, while following one of their conversations on literature inclusive of plays.

Does the "honest man" of the seventeenth century such as he is defined by La Rochefoucauld, Pascal, de Méré, possess qualities compatible with the needs of the contemporary society?

According to the celebrated formula of Fénélon ("Lettre à l'Académie") "the good historian is outside all time and all countries." To what extent, do you think, Michelet answers Fénélon's description of the good historian and if he does not, is he still a "good historian?"

[4] "La porte de sortie de l'enseignement secondaire."

[5] "Le Temps," November 17, 1929 (L'aimable Pédagogie).

[6] *Cf.* "Journal Officiel de la République Française," Débats parlementaires: Sénat, séance du 30 janvier 1930, p. 51, 54.

[7] Also in France a very valuable title to respectability sought arduously and sometimes through indirect methods.

The latest statistics published seem to bear out the contention of the Ministry that the standards of the baccalaureate are not being lowered.[8] The examinations not being competitive, it is interesting to note the percentage of failures. For the June session of 1929 the results of the baccalaureate examinations in the region of Paris were as follows:

First Part:

(a) Latin-Greek Section: registered 363; failed 182; postponed 22; passed 159.

(b) Latin-Modern Language Section: registered 2,055; failed 1,000; postponed 222; passed 833.

(c) Latin-Sciences Section: registered 655; failed 244; postponed 88; passed 333.

(d) Modern Language-Sciences Section: registered 1,758; failed 1,077; postponed 103; passed 578.[9]

The high percentage of failures in the baccalaureate examinations is partly accounted for by the virtual absence of promotion examinations in the French public secondary schools, to say nothing of the private, but undoubtedly the major cause lies in the rigidity of the baccalaureate standards.

Licence: It is the academic degree granted on the basis of examinations and certain requirements as to residence which differ from *faculté* to *faculté*. Generally speaking, residence at standard foreign higher institutions of learning is accepted, but not foreign credits. No candidate for the degree of *licence* can be excused from taking at a French state university all the examinations prescribed. The French state universities issue the following diplomas of the degree of *licence:*

(a) *Licence en droit* issued by the *facultés* of law. The requirements consist of the diploma of baccalaureate or its equivalent approved by the Ministry of Public Instruction; twelve trimesters of residence at a French university; satisfactory grades in the written and oral examinations taken at the end of each of the three prescribed years of residence and given twice a year: in June–July and October–November.[10]

(b) *Licence ès-sciences* issued by the *facultés* of sciences. The diploma of the *licence* in sciences is of two kinds: one conferring the right to teach mathematics and science in the state educational institutions on the secondary school level (*licence d'enseignement*) and the one not including that privilege (*licence libre*).[11] The latter is delivered on the basis of successful examination, written and oral (*certificats d'études supérieures*) in any three subjects taught at the *faculté*. Admission to these examinations is conditioned upon possession of the baccalaureate or its equivalent and three quarters of residence. Examinations are given semiannually: June–July and October–November. No candidate, without a special permission of the dean, may present himself for examinations for two certificates in one examination session. The diploma is granted automatically upon the presentation to the secretariat of the *faculté* of the three certificates. The degree of *licence ès-sciences*

[8] ''Journal Officiel,'' Débats parlementaires, 30 janvier 1930, p. 47.

[9] ''Revue Universitaire,'' July, 1930.

[10] At the end of the first year: Roman Law, Civil Law, Political Economy, General History of the French Law; at the end of the second year: Civil Law, Administrative Law, Penal Law, Political Economy, Roman Law. The success in the examination closing the second year and including as a prerequisite the success in the prescribed examinations of the first year entitles the candidate to the degree of Bachelor of Law, practically very seldom applied for. At the end of the third year: Civil Law, Commercial Law, Civil Process, Private International Law, Financial Legislation and any two other subjects chosen by the candidate from among the offerings of the *faculté* not included in the number of obligatory examination subjects.

[11] ''A free lance licence.''

in view of teaching is conditioned upon the completion of examinations in three subjects on the list of prescribed subjects for that kind of licence in sciences. For instance, the aspirants to teaching positions in the secondary schools are required to combine in their three certificates in the following manner: (1) Differential and integral calculus; rational mechanics (*mécanique rationelle*) and general physics or mathematics (but not general mathematics); (2) general physics; general chemistry; and rational mechanics (*mécanique rationelle*) or general mathematics or general physical and natural sciences (*sciences physiques et naturelles*); (3) zoology or general physiology; botany; geology. It may be noted that the *licence d'enseignement* which is not only an academic degree but also a professional diploma bestowing upon the beneficiary the eligibility for teaching positions in the state institutions on the secondary school level does not include among the requirements any training in the science of education.

(c) *Licence ès-lettres:* The present academic year will mark a very important turn in the history of the degree of licence in letters. Since 1920 and up to this year the *licence ès-lettres,* like the *licence ès-sciences,* has been of two kinds: *licence libre* and *licence d'enseignement.* The requirements for the former have been: the baccalaureate or an equivalent, four-semester residence and four certificates of higher studies (*certificats d'études supérieures*) attesting the passing of written and oral examinations in any four subjects taught at the *faculté* of letters. For the *licence d'enseignement* there have been required four certificates of higher studies, *i.e.,* the passing of written and oral examinations in four subjects to be taken in certain prescribed combinations. Again, no pedagogical subjects have been among the requirements. In view of the significance attributed by the French public to the humanities for the maintenance of an enlightened democracy at home and for the promotion of the French prestige abroad, much bitter criticism has been raised against the regulations on the licence in letters. The attack grew in volume and intensity as France was recovering from the war. The *licence libre,* obtainable on the basis of examinations in any four subjects offered at the *faculté,* was attacked as too easy and ridiculed as an amateurish enterprise: it was referred to in the press as the *licence d'amateur.* The *licence d'enseignement* was taken to task on the ground of omitting the French language and literature and the ancient languages from the requirements except in case of the future teachers of French, Latin and Greek. The offence in question was formulated in the press as licence in letters without letters. The Senate was aroused. The minister of public instruction was challenged in the plenary sittings of the Senate on March 12 and 13, 1931, and on the latter date a resolution was passed by the Senate prescribing the minister to reorganize the *licence ès-lettres* in the sense of abolishing the *licence libre* and making an examination in French, Latin and Greek obligatory for all aspirants to the teaching of humanities in the state institutions on the secondary school level. It is to be expected that the students entering the French universities next academic year will be placed under a new régime of the *licence ès-lettres.* No pedagogical studies have yet been made obligatory.

(d) *Diplôme d'études supérierues:* The next academic distinction sometimes sought after the license is the *diploma of superior studies* which has to be distinguished from the *certificates of higher studies* required for the *licence.* The diploma of superior studies is granted on the basis of a paper "of a superior order," defended before a committee, and an oral examination in problems announced to the candidate three months before the examination. No prerequisites are demanded, either with regard to age or degree or residence. The diploma may be sought only in certain groups of subjects established by the ministry of public instruction. For example, in the *facultés* of letters it is possible to obtain the diploma of superior studies in each of the following groups of subjects: (1) philosophy; (2) history and geography; (3) classical languages; (4) modern language and literature (German or English or Arabic or Italian or Spanish or Russian). The diplomas of the superior studies are of certain value for promotion in teaching positions and are also obtained by a number of holders of the degree of licence (*licenciés*) desirous of doing more advanced and highly specialized work in view of further degrees.

Doctorat: Two kinds of doctorate are conferred by *facultés* of the universities: *doctorat d'état* and *doctorat d'université*. The first is granted in the name of the French state, represented by the ministry of public instruction, and confers certain privileges in civil service and exercise of professions. No vocational rights or privileges are attached to the second, which is seldom sought by the French themselves: it is frankly considered as *Ersatz*-doctorate. The *doctorat d'université* is granted upon the presentation of a printed thesis of not necessarily considerable extent or originality. Two-year residence is required. As to the *doctorat d'état* the requirements for it differ somewhat from *faculté* to *faculté*.

(a) Doctorate in law (*doctorat en droit*) is conferred upon the defence of a printed thesis. The prerequisites are two diplomas of superior studies obtained from a *faculté* of law.

(b) Doctorate in medicine (*doctorat en médecine*) demands the fulfilment of the following requirements: the baccalaureate;[12] the certificates of higher studies in physics, chemistry and natural sciences issued by a *faculté* of sciences; five years of residence at the *faculté* of medicine of a French university; five comprehensive examinations at the end of each of the five years; three clinical examinations; presentation and defence of a thesis. The diploma of doctorate in medicine entitles the holder to the exercise of his profession in the entire French territory, home and colonial.

(c) Doctorate in sciences has four subdivisions: *doctorat ès-sciences mathématiques, doctorat ès-sciences physiques, doctorat ès-sciences naturelles* and *ingénieur-docteur*. The requirements are: the degree of licence (of the *licence d'enseignement* type, *i.e.*, based on examinations in prescribed groups of subjects) in sciences or an equivalent approved by the ministry of public instruction; the presentation and defence of two theses each containing original contributions, or one thesis and a discussion of problems assigned by the faculty council.

(d) Doctorate in letters (*doctorat ès-lettres*) is conditioned upon the following requirements: the licence or an equivalent; the presentation in print and defence of two theses; the larger one (*la grande thèse* or *thèse principale*) has to be a discussion or research of "unquestionable originality," while the smaller one (*la petite thèse* or *thèse supplémentaire*) "has to be an erudite contribution.[13]

[12] No equivalent is admitted.

[13] For example, in 1929–1930 there were accepted by the *faculté* of letters of the University of Paris the following doctorate theses (the smaller thesis is given first):

M. Régis Messac:

1. The French Influence upon the Work of Edgar Poe.
2. The Detective Story and Scientific Thought.

Mlle. Lasbordes:

1. The Poetry of Lamartine's Childhood Reminiscences.

Agrégation: It is at once an academic degree and a professional diploma of high value introduced by Napoleon, who was preoccupied with improvement of secondary and higher education in the post-revolution France. The word *agrégation* comes from the Latin *aggregatio.* One of the meanings of the word in French is *admission to a crowd, initiation into an association.* It is in this sense that the term *agrégation* is employed in the French educational terminology. *Agrégation* is the admission to the body of the *agrégés de l'université.* The members of that body are entitled to full professorship in the *lycée,* that is, in the higher type of the state secondary school and are eligible for university professorships. The moment the diploma is issued the holder is entitled to a position. If the ministry does not have it, the salary is paid anyway. In the case of the *agrégés* in medical subjects and of those of law the *agrégation* is a sure opening to university teaching. As a rule the French university teachers of letters and sciences hold both doctorate and *agrégation.* The diploma of *agrégé* is issued on the basis of a highly competitive examination national in scope given once a year in Paris by special committees appointed by the Minister of Public Instruction. Only candidates holding *licence* are admitted to the examination. The purpose of the examination is to test, besides the general culture of the candidate, his proficiency in a given subject. In view of the exceedingly eliminatory character of the examination, the diploma of *agrégé* is regarded as a certificate of ability and perseverance unequaled by any other diploma inclusive of the doctorate. Therefore, it has proved in many cases a passport to political advancement. Indeed, there hardly ever has been a French cabinet under the Third Republic that has not counted at least one *agrégé* among its members. The two latest cabinets in France, that of M. Steeg, appointed December 14, 1930, included two *agrégés:* the prime minister himself, who is an *agrégé* in philosophy, and M. Daladier, minister of labor, who is an *agrégé* in history (besides, the cabinet included three former university professors). The minister of public instruction in the Cabinet Steeg was M. Camille Chautemps, doctor of law. The Cabinet Laval now in office counts three *agrégés* among the ministers and almost gives the impression of being a realization, partial, to be sure, of the Platonic wish that the state be governed by philosophers: M. Charles Dumont, *agrégé de philosophie,* minister of the marine; M. Adolphe Landry, *agrégé de philosophie,* minister of labor; and M. Francois-Poncet, *agrégé* in German, undersecretary of national economy. The minister of public instruction in the present cabinet is M. Mario Roustan, doctor of letters.

The significance of the diploma of

2. The Poetic Creation.

M. André Basset:

1. The Geography of the Dialects of Kabyl.
2. The Verb in the Language of Berbers.

M. Ivan Shchukine:

1. The Indian Miniatures of the Epoch of the Great Moghols.
2. The Indian Painting of the Epoch of the Great Moghols.

M. René Taupin:

1. The American Interpretations of French Poetry.
2. The Influence of French Symbolism upon American Poetry 1910–1920.

M. Joseph Dagnau:

1. The Stroke of State and the Punitive Expedition to Gers (December 1851–December 1852).
2. Gers Under the Second Republic: the Conservative Reaction (1848–1851).

M. Anatole le Du:

1. The Symmetrical Repetition in the Alexandrinian Verse of Victor Hugo.
2. The Ternary Arrangement in the Prose of Victor Hugo (1818–1831).

(Revue Universitaire, April, 1930).

agrégation and the public respect for it becomes perfectly intelligible to a foreign observer after he has studied relevant statistics which are as simple as they are impressive. The latest statistics available advise the student in comparative education that, for instance, in the *agrégation* examination in history and geography, session of 1929, there registered for the examination 120 candidates; 109 appeared for the written examinations; 10 withdrew before the termination of the written examination; 43 were admitted to the orals; only 18 definitely passed.[14] In the *agrégation* in English in the session of 1929, 138 registered; 32 passed the written and were admitted to the oral examinations; 19 (nine ladies in the number) were admitted to the diploma.[15] In the *agrégation* in philosophy, session of 1930, 90 registered; 24 passed the written examinations and were admitted to the orals; 12 (inclusive of three ladies) were admitted to the diploma.[16] In the *agrégation* in German, session of 1930, 50 candidates registered; 20 were admitted to the orals; 12 (four ladies in the number) were admitted to the diploma.[17]

A brief course in the theory of education and a certain amount of observation and practice teaching in a secondary school are among the prerequisites of the *agrégation*.

III. THE GERMAN PRESENT-DAY SITUATION

The German academic situation with relation to degrees is a very simple one. To begin with, there is no baccalaureate in Germany. Its equivalent is furnished by the "certificate of maturity" (*Reifezeugnis*) issued by secondary schools on the basis of a leaving examination. The certificate of maturity entitles the holder to admission to any German higher institution of learning. Since the world war the leaving examination (*Abiturientenexamen* or *Reifeprüfung*) has been reformed. One of the features of the reform is that of making the examination easier. It is less comprehensive and decidedly less selective than the French baccalaureate. The examination is given at every public and private secondary school by a committee of instructors teaching in the senior form (*Oberprima*) and presided over, in the case of a private school, necessarily by a "representative of the State" (*Staats-*

14 "Revue Universitaire," May, 1930. The subjects of the written examinations were: Ancient History—"The Ionians of Asia Minor until the beginning of the Median Wars." Medieval History—"The Struggle between the Papacy and the Empire under the Pontificate of Alexander VII." Modern and Contemporary History—"The Foreign Policies of Italy under the reign of Humbert I and Victor-Emmanual III up to 1914." Geography—"The French Sahara: a study in physical and human geography."

15 *Ibid.*

16 *Ibid.* The topics of the three written examinations were: (1) Is it possible to assert the objectivity of truth as a subject of judgment and at the same time the liberty of judgment? (2) What is the substance of the notion of the will considered in the light of either the introspectivist psychology or objective psychology? (3) The relationship between the body and soul in the philosophy of Spinoza, Malebranche, and Leibniz. The oral examination consisted of translating and commenting on a Greek, a Latin, and a French original philosophical work indicated in the program (issued at the beginning of the academic year in which examination is taken) plus a sample lecture the topic of which is usually assigned to the candidate six hours before the examination and is prepared in the university library under supervision of special officers, but with the permission to use any books in the library. Among the topics assigned in the session of 1930 there were the following: Memory and imagination; The rôle of the imagination in the thinking process; To what extent and how can we know what is going on in the consciousness of other beings?; Psychology and Sociology; What is intuition; The idea of order; The idea of natural law; Being and becoming.

17 "Revue Universitaire," March, 1931.

vertreter) ordinarily a secondary school inspector (*Oberschulrat*), and in the public secondary schools, sometimes by the principal. Not all the subjects taught in the form are on the examination program. The Prussian regulations of July 22, 1926, recommend the secondary school authorities to limit the number of subjects to be put on the program of the leaving examination: *"Die Zahl der Prüffächer möglichst zu beschränken"* (O. 22.7.26; *Zentralblatt,* S. 283). The candidate is entitled to indicate the subject of his major interest and to present a thesis (*"eine grössere Hausarbeit"*). Besides, the failure in any given written or oral examination is not necessarily eliminatory. A kind of principle of indulgences operates: proficiency in one subject compensates for deficiency in another. Only if the failing mark falls upon the German language or upon a subject characteristic of a given type of secondary school, such as Latin or Greek in the Gymnasium, then the candidate has to gather three fourths favorable votes of his examiners in order not to be refused the certificate. The examination is treated *in toto,* and upon the termination of all written and oral examinations set forth by the program the committee meets, and deliberates upon each candidate and votes upon the general impression made by the candidate rather than upon the mathematical median of the grades he received. The examination may be repeated, not before the lapse of a year interval.

If the American B.A. and B.S. find their German correspondent in the certificate of maturity, there is no German correspondent to the M.S. or the M.A. unless it be *Lizentiat,* granted by the German theological schools and by them alone. The only degree the German higher institutions of learning can grant is the doctorate. In a sense Germany makes up, with its doctorate, for the scarcity of other degrees, because in her doctorate she offers a variety of choice of adjectives to be added to the title of doctor:

(1) *Doktor der Theologie* (*Dr. theol.*): Doctor of Divinity.

(2) *Doktor der Philosophie* (*Dr. phil.*): Doctor of Philosophy.

(3) *Doktor der Rechtswissenschaften* (*Dr. iur.*): Doctor of Law.

(4) *Doktor der Staatswissenschaften* (*Dr. rer.-pol.*): Doctor of Political Science.

(5) *Doktor der Wirtschaftswissenschaften* (*Dr. rer oec.*): Doctor of Economic Sciences.

(6) *Doktor der Naturwissenschaften* (*Dr. phil. nat.* or *Dr. rer. nat.*): Doctor of Natural Sciences.

(7) *Doktor der Medizin* (*Dr. med.*): Doctor of Medicine.

(8) *Doktor der Zahnheilkunde* (*Dr. med. den.*): Doctor of Dental Medicine.

(9) *Doktor der Tierheilkunde* (*Dr. med. vet.*): Doctor of Animal Medicine.

(10) *Doktor der Ingenieurwissenschaften* (*Dr.-Ing.*): Doctor-Engineer.

The doctorate is obtained upon the preparation and defence of a thesis and passing an oral examination in the major field or fields and in two minor fields. The examination is given by special committees appointed by the council of full professors of the *Fakultät* (*die engere Facultät*). The combinations of minors and majors differ slightly from university to university. The doctorate carries with itself a valuable social recognition: the importance of titles in Germany humorously pictured in the *Deutsche Kleinstädter* of *Kotzebue* has not become and is not likely soon to become an anachronism in the German life. Yet, the doctorate does not bestow any professional privileges. The right to exercise a profession in Germany, inclusive of teaching in the secondary schools, is conditioned upon the passing of a special examination (*Staatsprüfung*) given by special committees appointed by the government and operating under special laws.

EDUCATIONAL EVENTS

EDUCATION IN MOSCOW

FROM the primary school to the university, education in Moscow has felt the driving, quickening influence of the five-year plan, according to a correspondent of the New York *Sun*. A recent report of the Commissariat for Education indicates that the goal of universal primary education has been very nearly reached, over 90 per cent. of the children in the Soviet Union now receiving the minimum term of four years instruction which is now legally compulsory.

Quantitatively, this marks a distinct stride forward, if one considers that a few years ago about a third of the children in the Soviet Union were growing up without education. Before the war perhaps half the children in Russia were left uneducated.

Qualitatively, progress has perhaps not been so satisfactory. School buildings, as a rule, are now overcrowded; equipment, except in model experimental schools, leaves much to be desired; teachers are overworked and in some cases undertrained.

But at least two goals which Soviet educators have always set—universal primary education and elimination of illiteracy—are within hailing distance, and the material basis for effective universal education may become more solid with the passing of years.

Equally important, perhaps, with the introduction of general primary education is the creation of the so-called "polytechnical school." As a result of this process the Soviet primary school has become intensely practical and utilitarian in its methods of instruction.

Every town school is supposed to be attached to a factory; every country school to a state and collective farm. During one of the days of the five-day week the children go to the factory or farm, learn the use of machines and agricultural implements, and take part in such work as is suitable. These productive processes are closely linked up with their studies.

The old practice of teaching individual subjects in more or less water-tight compartments has been completely abandoned in Soviet schools. As a general rule a class is assigned some broad general subject for study: a street, perhaps, or a season of the year, or a town. In studying these subjects arithmetic, history, geography and other subjects are supposed to come in naturally, without being taught separately.

CHILD GUIDANCE IN LONDON

THE London County Council in May, 1928, accepted the offer of the Child Guidance Council to establish a child guidance clinic in London and to recognize it as an experiment for three years. The work of the clinic has been to give advice on children who do not seem to derive full benefit from the ordinary school curriculum or to respond to the ordinary methods of discipline. In every case the parents' consent has to be obtained.

The *London Times Educational Supplement* reports that the staff of the clinic consists of two doctors, two educational advisers (with teaching experience), six social workers, a part-time speech-training specialist, a secretary and clinical assistants. Nearly every child is submitted to a medical examination as a preliminary, and the parents seen by the doctor. In simple cases advice is given there and then. If necessary, a further examination is made by an educational adviser and detailed information of the child's behavior at school and at home is obtained from the school or from a social worker. In most cases no direct treatment is necessary, but in a few instances attempts are made to eliminate "phobias," etc., from the children's minds by simple conversations, but no psychoanalysis is employed. For physical treatment children are referred to the school medical officer or a suitable hospital. Most of the children treated have come at the instance of head teachers, school doctors, care committees and parents; a smaller number have been referred from juvenile courts, hospitals, private doctors, the Invalid Children's Association, etc. At first confined to Islington and St. Pancras, the institute now deals with children from other districts. Of the 325 referred to the clinic, 72 cases were closed, in 45 diagnostic service only was given, in 15 others fairly good or satisfactory results were obtained. Of the 174 still under treatment 22 children have become entirely normal, in 63 cases untoward symptoms have ceased or nearly ceased, in 39 considerable progress has been made. In 37 the change has been slight or nil. Many children are only attending for speech training or aid in backward subjects; this latter seems a course worthy of more extended exploration.

All authorities concerned, whether borough consultative committees of head teachers or care committees, are unanimous on the valuable results obtained. All emphasize likewise the supreme importance of the parents' cooperation and stress is laid by the Shoreditch local association on propaganda among the teachers to bring the clinic and its aims to their notice. Since the clinic was started, other clinics, those of the Jewish Health Organization and of the Maudsley Hospital, have been also recognized, and the next report to the council will deal with the valuable work of all three new organizations.

ILLITERACY IN VIRGINIA

The proportion of Virginia's population unable to read or write in 1930 was larger than the proportion for the entire country, and the progress made in the state toward eradicating illiteracy was less than the average for the entire nation, according to an analysis of Federal census returns just published by the University of Virginia and reported in an Associated Press dispatch to the *Baltimore Sun.*

The state was shown to rank fortieth among the states in illiteracy, and made less progress during the decade 1920–1930 than it did during the preceding decade. Moreover, the analysis says, the common explanation of a large extraneous racial element in the south does not apply so strongly in Virginia, since the Negro population is only slightly larger than for the nation at large, and the percentage of native whites is more than twice that of the entire country.

The minimum education program of the State Department of Education with an additional annual outlay of $2,000,000, would ultimately remedy this condition, in the opinion of Dr. Sydney B. Hall, state superintendent of public instruction. The census return demonstrated, he explained, that illiteracy in the state varied almost exactly with the amount of money spent on schools. The department now expends $6,500,000 annually.

Although six southern states rank lower than Virginia in literacy, they each have higher proportions of Negro population than does Virginia, while the other two, New Mexico and Arizona, have high percentages of Mexicans and Indians.

Eradication of Negro illiteracy has made marked progress in Virginia, however, the analysis shows, having been reduced from 30 per cent. in 1920 to 19.2 per cent. in 1930. The percentage of illiteracy among foreign-born whites, composing only 1 per cent. of the population, was so nearly in accord with the native-born that they were not separately listed.

The problem of illiteracy in Virginia is primarily a rural problem, especially intense where there is broken topography or a sparse population, the report says. The prevalence of illiteracy tapers from the open country to the larger cities, and for the larger cities, in most cases, illiteracy fell below 1 per cent. in 1930. The study pointed out that the cities through the agencies of public schools have had a marked advantage over the country in eradicating school-age illiteracy.

The state over the decade ending in 1930 reduced native white illiteracy in the age group of 10 to 20 years from 3.7 to 2.5 per cent. In urban territory this reduction was from 1 to 6 per cent. and in rural territory from 4.5 to 3.2 per cent.

In general, in Virginia native white illiteracy was found to be more prevalent in each region from east to west: Tidewater, 3.2 per cent.; Middle Virginia, 4.1 per cent.; Piedmont, 7.6; Valley, 6.2, and Mountain, 10.1 per cent.

The 1930 census demonstrated that eradication of illiteracy has been spotted and regional, and twenty-six counties showed actual increases in illiteracy from 1920 to 1930. Of this number four are in Tidewater, eight in Middle, eight in Piedmont and six in the Mountain division.

SCHOOL ATTENDANCE IN THE UNITED STATES

A general increase in school attendance in the United States during the last decade is shown by school attendance statistics for 1930 recently issued by the Census Bureau, and reported in the *U. S. Daily.*

The figures disclose that 26,849,639 children and young people between the ages of 5 and 20 years, or 69.9 per cent. of all members of this age group, were going to school when the count was made. Only 64.3 per cent. of this group were reported in school in 1920.

Although only 344,789 persons over 21 years of age were going to school in 1920, their number increased to 1,034,782 during the succeeding decade, as indicated by 1930 statistics.

In a classification of the population by age, sex, color and nativity, also just issued by the bureau, it is revealed that persons in this country under 19 years of age number 47,608,991 and make up about 38 per cent. of the whole population. The age group with the largest percentage of its members in school was the group of children from 7 to 13 years old. Ninety-five per cent. of this group were in school when the 1930 census was taken, as compared to 90 per cent. reported in school by the 1920 census.

Only 21 per cent. of young persons between the ages of 18 and 20 years were reported in school in the 1930 census, though this proportion is higher than the 14 per cent. reported in school during the previous period. The bureau's statement setting forth statistics on school attendance in the United States follows in part:

There were 38,387,032 persons from 5 to 20 years of age in the population of the United States on April 1, 1930, of which number 26,849,639, or 69.9 per cent., were returned as having attended school at some time since September 1, 1929. For males from 5 to 20 years of age, the percentage attending school was 70.2, and for females, 69.7.

The number of persons from 5 to 20 years of age returned in 1930 as attending school, 26,849,639, represents a gain of 5,475,663 since 1920, when the number so returned was 21,373,-976. The percentage attending school increased from 64.3 to 69.9 in the 10-year period.

Of the whole number of children 7 to 13 years of age, 95.3 per cent. were attending school; of those 14 and 15 years, 88.8 per cent.; of those 16 and 17 years, 57.3 per cent., and of those 18 to 20 years, 21.4 per cent. The number of persons 21 years of age and over reported in 1930 as attending school was 1,034,782, as compared with 344,789 in 1920.

Of the native whites of native parentage, 96.1 per cent. of those from 7 to 13 years old were attending school; 90 per cent. of those 14 and 15 years; 61 per cent. of those 16 and 17 years, and 24.4 per cent. of those from 18 to 20 years. For native whites of foreign or mixed parentage in these age groups, the percentages were, respectively, 98, 91.3, 54.4 and 19.3.

In the foreign-born white population, 97.5 per cent. of those from 7 to 13 years old were attending school; 92.6 per cent. of those 14 and 15: 52.3 per cent. of those 16 and 17, and 15.6 per cent. of those from 18 to 20 years.

THE FINE MATHEMATICAL HALL AT PRINCETON UNIVERSITY

The Henry Burchard Fine Mathematical Hall of Princeton University will be dedicated on Thursday, October 22, according to *The New York Times*. The building was erected in memory of Professor Fine, who organized the department of mathematics at Princeton University and was dean of the department of science there for nearly twenty years. The sum of $500,000 for its erection and an endowment of $150,000 for its maintenance were given to the university by the late Thomas D. Jones and his niece, Miss Gwethalyn Jones, of Chicago, shortly after the death of Dean Fine in 1928.

The new structure is located in the southeastern part of the campus, adjoining and connected with the Palmer Physical Laboratory. It is built of red brick and limestone and was designed by its architect, Charles Z. Klauder, of Philadelphia, in collegiate Gothic style to conform with neighboring buildings.

Mathematical formulae have been used as decorative motifs in the building. The ornamentation on some of the windows includes the Newtonian equations of gravitation, those of Einstein, two equations on the quantum theory, the five perfect solids and spheres, and the three conic sections. Over the fireplace in the common room is engraved in German a remark of Einstein, which, translated, means, "God is clever but not dishonest."

Two lectures on mathematical subjects will be given on the day of the dedication by former members of the department, Professor Gilbert Ames Bliss, of the University of Chicago, and Professor George David Birkhoff, of Harvard University. The exercises of dedication will be held in the afternoon in the library. At these Mr. Klauder, the architect, will present the keys of the building to President John Grier Hibben. Dr. Oswald Veblen, Henry B. Fine professor of mathematics, will set forth the ideas underlying the purposes of the building. Dean Luther P. Eisenhart will preside at the ceremonies, which will be attended by Miss Jones, trustees of the university, members of the faculty, relatives and friends of Dean Fine, including his daughter, Mrs. Bradford B. Locke, and his sister, Miss Margaret May Fine, both of Princeton, and former members of the Princeton department of mathematics. A reception in the common room will follow the ceremonies.

A NEW TEACHERS COLLEGE

A PLAN for a new type of teacher-training institution, to open in September of 1932, which will operate as an undergraduate unit at the college level, has been announced by Teachers College of Columbia University.

This new college is to be under the direction of Dr. Thomas Alexander, professor of education at Teachers College, and will attempt to demonstrate new methods in the selection and training of young men and women who are to become teachers in nursery, elementary and secondary schools. While preparing these young people for teaching positions the new unit, which will grant the bachelor of science and the master's degrees, will operate also as a demonstration college, in which graduate students in Teachers College may observe improved methods in teacher training.

In this respect the new college will be to the field of teacher training what the Lincoln and Horace Mann Schools of Teachers College are to the field of elementary and secondary education. As these schools attempt to create and demonstrate more effective procedures in elementary and secondary education, the new college will attempt to create and demonstrate improved procedures in the training of teachers for elementary, secondary and nursery schools.

Rigid methods of elimination will be used in the selection of students. High-school and college executives throughout America will be asked to cooperate in selecting those who show the richest promise of developing into highly competent teachers and educational leaders. Selection will be on the basis of good health, sound scholarship, desirable personal qualities and promise of unusual growth. The student body will not be restricted to local sections of the country but will be chosen from a wide geographical area.

This unusual care in creating the student body, to be limited the first year to one hundred men and one hundred women of outstanding ability and personality, will be taken because it is felt that mediocrity is to-day the curse of the teaching profession. Insistence that half the students be young men is based on the conviction that teaching should be a profession for men as well.

The duration of the period of study in the college will vary approximately from three to five years, according to the ability of the student, and will include at least one year spent in study and travel abroad. Students will be required to spend some time in actual work in industry and business so that when they become teachers they will have an adequate conception of the work of the world into which most pupils who graduate from our American schools must enter. One year of satisfactory teaching service in cooperating private and public school systems will be required before a degree is granted. Assurance of such cooperation has been obtained from a number of school systems.

It is stated that if the college is successful in achieving its purpose, it will not only develop teachers far superior to most of those of the present day, but its procedures will be adopted by teacher-training institutions throughout the nation to bring an educational reconstruction that, first and last, depends upon a new race of teachers.

With its emphasis upon quality rather than quantity the new college, in so far as it succeeds and becomes influential in creating such a race of teachers, should tend to reduce the present over-supply of teachers of mediocre ability and personality and make the teaching profession as attractive to American youth of superior ability and personality as those professions and callings in which only the superior person can achieve success that is measured by social usefulness as well as by financial remuneration.

THE JACOB COOPER GREEK PRIZE

ABOUT a year ago Mr. Drury W. Cooper informed the secretary of the College Entrance Examination Board that he wished to establish a Greek prize in memory of his father, Jacob

Cooper, who for many years was professor of Greek at Rutgers College. Mr. Cooper wrote that it seemed appropriate that in the year 1930, the centenary of his father's birth, a prize should be founded that would tend to promote more active interest and scholarship in the Greek language. According to his plan a prize of $1,000 would be paid each year to that candidate for admission to college who, on the basis of the board's examinations, appeared to be most proficient in Greek.

The following arrangement was made for the award of the prize in June, 1931:

(1) Among the answer books in three-year Greek written in ordinary course at the June, 1931, examination of the College Entrance Examination Board, the ten best papers will be selected.

(2) These ten papers will be submitted to a committee of three appointed by the American Philological Association, and the decision of a majority of these three shall carry the award.

(3) The committee on award shall have the power to reject all answer books as not coming in their judgment to the necessary standards of excellence.

(4) Upon being notified of the award the donor will remit the sum of $1,000 to a suitable person by whom the money shall be expended toward the payment of college tuition fees, room rent, living expenses, etc., from time to time as required during the freshman year of the successful candidate.

(5) The applications of all contestants for the Jacob Cooper Greek Prize must be submitted to and accepted by the committee on award or its representative in advance of the examination. The committee on award will be at liberty to adopt any regulations which in its opinion may be desirable in order to exclude candidates who have studied Greek for more than three years or candidates whose school records are unsatisfactory.

(6) If the successful candidate shall fail during his freshman year to maintain a satisfactory record in respect to scholastic standing or personal conduct he will forfeit his claim to any unpaid part of the prize.

The American Philological Association appointed the following committee to make the award: Professor A. M. Harmon, of Yale University, *chairman;* Professor R. J. Bonner, of the University of Chicago, and Dr. Richard M. Gummere, of the William Penn Charter School, Philadelphia, Pennsylvania.

The prize was won by Augustus Maverick Kelley, a member of the incoming freshman class of Harvard College. During the last two years Mr. Kelley has been a student at Phillips Exeter Academy, having previously attended the Browning School in New York City.

The following brief statement in regard to Jacob Cooper may be of interest to the readers of School and Society.

Born December 7, 1830, Jacob Cooper was graduated from Yale College with high honors in June, 1852, and licensed in the Presbyterian ministry in 1853. He received the degree of Ph.D. from the University of Berlin in 1854 and studied theology at Halle and Edinburgh in 1854 and 1855. He became professor of Greek at Centre College, Danville, Kentucky, in 1855. From 1866 to 1893 he was professor of Greek at Rutgers College and from 1893 to 1904 was professor of mental and moral philosophy at the same institution. He died on January 31, 1904.

EDUCATIONAL NOTES AND NEWS

Dr. A. Lawrence Lowell, president of Harvard University, received the honorary degree of doctor of laws at the centennial celebration at Wesleyan University. President James L. McConaughy, of Wesleyan University, in his citation said: "Under your guidance, America's oldest university has continued to be the leader of us all in broad-minded educational advancements; you are the foremost friend and adviser of the American college of liberal arts; Wesleyan honors herself by conferring upon you the honorary degree of doctor of laws."

Dr. Nicholas Murray Butler concluded his thirtieth year as acting president and president of Columbia University on October 8. He was made acting president on January 6, 1901. His election to the presidency followed on January 6, 1902.

President James Rowland Angell, of Yale University, has been made Officer of the Legion of Honor. The decoration of Chevalier of the Legion of Honor was conferred upon President Angell on behalf of the French government by

M. Paul Claudel, ambassador of France to the United States.

The Reverend Canon H. J. Cody, chancellor of the University of Toronto, has been appointed to the presidency of that institution. He will succeed Sir Robert Falconer, who will retire next June.

With the departure of Dr. Clarence A. Barbour, president of Brown University, who is going to the Far East as a member of the Laymen's Foreign Mission Inquiry, Dr. Albert D. Mead assumed his duties as acting president of the institution.

Dr. Ludwig E. Fuerbringer, member of the faculty of Concordia Theological Seminary at St. Louis, Missouri, for thirty-five years, has been offered the presidency of the institution.

A dispatch to the London *Times* states that Mr. Keenan, chief secretary and minister for education in Western Australia, has resigned.

Dr. Elijah Swift has been elected dean of the college of arts and sciences at the University of Vermont. He will succeed Professor George H. Perkins, who has resigned after thirty-three years of service. Professor Perkins, who has been connected with the university for sixty years, will continue to teach his class in anthropology.

The Reverend James A. Sullivan, member of the faculty of St. Francis College, Brooklyn, N. Y., for the past nine years, has been appointed dean of the institution.

Mrs. Clara M. Beyer has been appointed director of the industrial division of the Children's Bureau. She succeeds Miss Ellen N. Matthews, who resigned to pursue special studies here and abroad.

The Reverend Dr. Francis J. Haas, formerly a member of the faculty of the department of social sciences at Marquette University, has been appointed director of the National Catholic School of Social Sciences in Washington, D. C.

The election of Mr. Max Epstein to the board of trustees of the University of Chicago has been announced. In 1929 Mr. Epstein presented to the university $1,000,000 for an art building.

Miss Marie W. Wilson, formerly assistant dean of women at Miami University, at Oxford, Ohio, has been appointed to the position of assistant dean in charge of vocational and educational counselling at Syracuse University, and Miss Florence A. Partridge has been made assistant dean in charge of residence.

Dr. Eliot G. Mears, professor of geography and international trade at Stanford University, has been appointed director of the annual Institute of International Relations, which is to hold its eighth session at Riverside, California, from December 13 to 18. Three new members of the advisory board of the western conference on world conditions will be Dr. William B. Munro, a member of the executive council of the California Institute of Technology, Dr. David P. Barrows, of the University of California, and Mrs. George O. Robinson, of Pasadena.

Dr. George Alan Works, of the University of Chicago, has been selected by a subcommittee of the governor's commission on university consolidation of North Carolina to direct a technical survey into the details of combining the State University, State College and North Carolina College for Women, which will go under a single board of trustees on July 1, 1932.

The Reverend Paul H. Vieth has been appointed director of field work and associate professor of religious education in the Divinity School of Yale University. He succeeds Dr. H. Shelton Smith, director of field work for the past two years, who has resigned to be professor and head of the department of religious education in Duke University.

Mr. W. A. Robinson, formerly principal of the Austin High School of Knoxville, Tennessee, and prior to that inspector of Negro high schools in the department of public instruction of North Carolina, has been appointed principal of the Laboratory School of Atlanta University, Atlanta, Georgia.

Dr. Charles F. D. Belden, director of the Boston Public Library and former president of the American Library Association, has been elected an honorary fellow of the British Library Association by the council of the association.

Dr. Jacob Gould Schurman, formerly president of Cornell University, will be the principal speaker at the annual dinner of the Westchester County Historical Society at White Plains, New York, on October 28.

Dr. John Dewey, professor of philosophy at Columbia University, will give the second address in the series of radio lectures sponsored by the National Advisory Council on Radio in Education at 7:00 o'clock Eastern Standard Time, on Sunday, October 25, over WEAF and other stations of the National Broadcasting Company.

Dr. Walter Williams, president of the University of Missouri, has returned after a three months' tour of South America.

Dr. Thomas S. Gates, president of the University of Pennsylvania, delivered the address at the exercises at Lehigh University in memory of its founder, the late Judge Asa Packer, on October 7.

Mrs. Jessica Thompson Washburn, one of the first two women to be graduated by Stanford University and co-founder of the one-time Washburn Preparatory School at San Jose, California, died on October 11 at the age of seventy-two years.

Dr. James Graham, director of education for Leeds, England, died on September 26 at the age of sixty-two years.

The death is announced of Sir Gregory Foster, formerly provost of University College and vice-chancellor of the University of London, at the age of sixty-five years.

Lord Eustace Percy, formerly minister of education of Great Britain, has made a plea for the early establishment of a central institute of imperial education, where the results of experiments could be compared and conclusions disseminated. This policy-forming institution, he said, should emphatically be a university, not a state body, and there is no more suitable location than the University of London. A large number of other prominent education authorities supported the proposal.

Chancellor Carlos Chardon, of the University of Porto Rico, suspended 158 students from the university recently because they signed a public statement attacking the school administration for alleged discrimination against nationalist students in selecting the reception committee for the recent visit of the debating team from McGill University. All but 16 of the students were reinstated shortly afterward when they retracted the statement. The recalcitrant 16 issued a new proclamation, charging Chancellor Chardon with making the university an instrument of the American régime, "destructive to the sacred values of the Fatherland." One nationalist student was ejected from the campus for trying to incite a student strike.

Atlanta University, pioneer institution of higher learning for Negroes, located in Atlanta, Georgia, has been given one million dollars for new buildings and their maintenance. Five buildings are to be erected at an estimated cost of $625,000, including an administration hall, women's dormitory, men's dormitory, a residence for the president and a central heating plant. Forty thousand dollars will be expended in renovating existing classroom buildings, and $335,000 will be set aside as a building maintenance fund. The buildings will be located on a 60-acre campus which adjoins the campuses of the two undergraduate colleges affiliated with Atlanta University—Morehouse College for men and Spelman College for women. Atlanta University, which is coeducational, is a graduate school. More than 1,000 students were enrolled last year in the affiliated institutions.

Under provision of the will of the late John E. Good, of Denver, the University of Denver is given $100,000 to be known as the "Good Fund" for a building to be designated as a memorial to his parents. His executor and the trustees of the university are given discretion as to whether the fund shall be employed by itself or with other funds available for building.

The annual meeting of the Southern Conference on Education will be held at the University of North Carolina from November 5 to 7. The general theme will be "Education and the Economic Depression." The conference will be held in cooperation with the district meeting of the North Carolina Education Association. Speakers who have accepted invitations are: Dr. William L. Poteat, of Wake Forest College; Professor Thomas H. Briggs and Professor Paul Monroe, of Columbia University; Dr. Albert S. Cook, commissioner of education of Maryland; President Frank P. Graham, of the University of North Carolina; Dean J. J. Doster, of the University of Alabama; Mr. Sydney B. Hall, state superintendent of public instruction of Virginia; Mr. A. T. Allen, superintendent of public instruction of North Carolina; Mr. J. H. Hope, state superintendent of education of South Carolina; Mr. M. L. Duggan, superintendent of schools of Georgia; Mr. A. F. Harman, state superintendent of education of Alabama, and J. S. Richards, secretary of the Florida Education Association.

WITH the exception of a few special teachers, the entire teaching corps of the public schools of the Virgin Islands attended the summer school, which was held from July 6 to August 15. There were enrolled 144 teachers and candidates for teaching positions. The offerings consisted of both content and method courses. Under the latter was offered the psychology of the common branches, the teaching of arithmetic, the teaching of reading and English. As the majority of the summer students were elementary school teachers, the course in psychology of the common branches attracted the largest number. In connection with the teacher-training classes, a practice school of six years was maintained. It was conducted by native teachers and was used chiefly for observation purposes.

MERRILL HALL, the new home economics building at the University of Maine, named in honor of Dr. Leon S. Merrill, dean of the college of agriculture, was dedicated on October 10. The building is a three-story, red-brick structure of Georgian colonial architecture.

UNDER the supervision of Miss Elisabeth Morrow, daughter of the late U. S. Senator and Mrs. Dwight W. Morrow, the Nursery School of the Englewood Social Service Federation, Englewood, New Jersey, opened on October 4. Miss Ruth Fowler, who received her training for the work at the Child Educational Foundation, is in actual charge of the school, assisted by Miss Elizabeth Thatcher, a graduate of Smith College, and Miss Evelyn Bicknell, a graduate of Vassar College, both volunteer workers. Miss Edith Brown, director of the school last year, is serving as community worker. The same systems will be inaugurated by Miss Morrow as are in use at the Little School, a private day school for children from eighteen months to six years old, established by Miss Morrow last year. The Montessori system is applied to the younger children, and all receive the benefit of the latest advances in child hygiene.

THAT a very large proportion of students in the United States earn their way through college is indicated by recent studies of material collected for a survey of fifty-two land-grant colleges and universities. The Federal Office of Education reports that a careful check of returns from 34,589 alumni and former students shows that 24,952, or 72 per cent., were self-supporting wholly or in part while they attended college, and that 9,637, or 28 per cent., depended upon their parents to defray the cost of their higher education. The study showed that by far a greater proportion of the students pursuing courses in agriculture were self-supporting than in any other field of study, the percentage being 86. Next on the list were students in engineering and students preparing to become teachers. The proportion of students in arts and sciences who paid their way through college was 62 per cent.

THE public schools of Bessemer, Alabama, have entered into a three-year agreement with the College of Education of the University of Alabama to cooperate on a program of curriculum revision. The negotiations are made between the director of field studies of the college of education and the curricular supervisor of the Bessemer schools. According to the arrangements, the college of education furnishes three lecturers and incidental supervisory assistance, while the schools set aside the necessary time for the lecturers and conferences. The university furnishes professional service gratis and the public schools pay the expenses of transportation.

WITH the opening of the school year in September, a dental hygiene service was instituted in the Delaware public schools. It has been planned to divide the state into three sections, corresponding to the three counties, and it is hoped to have two dental hygienists in each county. They will examine the mouths of all the children in grades one through six and give each child needing it a card stating his need of dental attention. The children will be asked to have the necessary work done and to have their dentists sign the card, saying that the mouth of the child is in good condition. Statistics will be kept on a three-year plan. When the group now in the first grade has reached promotion time in the third grade, the conditions in the mouths will be noted and the results charted. When this group reaches the sixth grade, the mouths will again be examined and the results of six years of dental health education tabulated. The educational program will include a series of classroom lectures, to be given by the hygienists, it is said, and preschool clinics for prophylaxis will be conducted during the summer months.

RECENT legislation shows a trend toward placing greater responsibility upon the county as a unit in educational administration, according to the United States Office of Education. This responsibility has shifted from the district and not from the state. The county unit system for school administration has been fairly well developed in the following states: Alabama, Florida, Kentucky, Louisiana, Maryland, New Mexico, North Carolina, Tennessee, Virginia and Utah.

THE Americas' oldest institution of learning, the University of Mexico, will be closed or forced to remain in operation with only a skeleton organization and the discontinuance of many courses, unless its exhausted treasury is replenished, according to a dispatch to the *New York Sun*. In face of the prospect that the government will not be able to provide funds next year for the full budget, an appeal for contributions has been issued through the faculty and alumni. The University of Mexico was founded in 1551, thirty-two years after the Spanish conquest and ninety years before the establishment of Harvard University. After being conducted for centuries along conservative lines it was reorganized in 1910, that it might be in step with modern scholastic progress. The university recently was reorganized again with the object of making it wholly independent of government control.

THE first term of the new county school for boys at Dover, England, has opened. The school is modern, with about 25 acres of playing fields, and has a commanding view of the town, castle and the sea beyond the harbor. It accommodates 500 pupils in 15 classrooms, and in addition there are a hall, science and engineering laboratories, library, gymnasium and a dining room.

DISCUSSION

THE DISCUSSION TECHNIQUE. III

THE issues raised by Dr. Allen O. Hansen[1] regarding research article[2] on "The Discussion Technique" merit a response. The writers welcome the opportunity afforded to express their professional judgments upon these issues without the limitations imposed in the preparation of a research analysis.

Consideration of Professor Hansen's reply raises the question as to whether he had access to the stenographic report of the group discussion meeting led by Dr. Kilpatrick.[3] Our analysis was based upon an actual group meeting rather than our personal espousal of any discussion or "talk-fest." The discussion analyzed merits study by each teacher interested in developing proficiency in the discussion technique, both because stenographic reports of group discussions are difficult to secure and because we believe such study will reveal that the group discussion considered provided a real learning situation for adults as shown by their contributions, their acceptance of challenges to their beliefs or view-points, and the evidence of new S-R bonds being formed. Even those group members whose experience and positions naturally caused them to be most tenacious of old beliefs were challenged and seemed to become less sure that they were right with resulting increase in tolerance of new opinions and new facts.

Dr. Hansen questions the advantages of using

[1] SCHOOL AND SOCIETY, July 18, 1931, pp. 93–95.

[2] SCHOOL AND SOCIETY, May 23, 1931, pp. 704–708.

[3] Official Proceedings of the White House Conference on Child Health and Protection, Supplement, *United States Daily*, Sec. ii, Vol. v, No. 228, pp. 25–28, November 28, 1930.

the discussion techniques in the light of "the psychology of the learning process that underlies 'insuring changes in behavior.'" The important word in his query seems to be *behavior*. The behavior of an adult is influenced by his beliefs. The discussion technique provides the situation wherein the instructor has the opportunity to discover the peculiar beliefs and attitudes of the individual he instructs so that he may modify his curriculum offering—readings, lectures, the direction of the discussion—to bring the student into contact with the needed information whereby he may broaden his outlook and revise his previously held opinion.

The writers acknowledge their belief that learning which goes on during a discussion is more real, less academic than that which takes place during a lecture. During the discussion the individual responds to the facts and issues brought forward by the different members. These stimuli induce recollections from his past experience. He evaluates and makes judgments which are associated with those past experiences. Therefore, however poor or however worth-while his contributions may be, some real learning has gone on within him. This learning will be remembered much better and much longer than academic facts presented by a lecturer.

After all, when we consider the "curve of forgetting" should we be so much concerned about that cultural information which Professor Hansen stresses in the latter part of his article? How much of it is going to be remembered by the individuals listening to the well-informed lecturer? In most cases the lecture is composed of facts and more facts which to the listeners are academic. They have no connection with the real life of the individual student and are therefore little apt to be long remembered; just long enough to pass the examination. We submit that the real issue involves a case of real student growth through providing for participation *vs.* an accumulation of academic information which it is hoped may be stored up for future use. It reminds one of telling a youth in great detail exactly how to swim but not letting him go near the water until he finishes high school or, better yet, graduates from college.

The lecture method assumes that the instructor is informed regarding the beliefs of the members of the class, however numerous. It further assumes that the usual "canned" materials of the lecture will evoke in the students a uniform, desired educational outcome. If this outcome be the sitting through of a lesson period so that the lecturer may recast his typed lecture for final book form, the writers are willing to acknowledge the merit of the lecture as best advancing the interests of the instructor, if not of the students.

The value of the extent of an "interlude" as measured by the number of individuals involved without the need for the instructor to provide a restimulus is a quantity measure rather than a quality criterion. As an instructor becomes willing to concede that the sum total of knowledge held by the various mature members of his group may equal or exceed his own knowledge of the field, or as he places student growth through activity above listening, justification can be found for drawing the expressed view-points of as many students as possible into the class period.

Professor Hansen indicates that the use of the discussion method may "take the place of substantial scholarship and absolve . . . instructors from many rigorous labors." The writers hold that the opposite is true. Instructors using the discussion technique will be required to have a broader preparation and a keener insight in evaluating the problems and the contributions of the class members than if they merely put on a monologue or "lecture record" and broadcast without being required to revise their thinking and presentation by the questions and discussion of the group they address. In the discussion situation it becomes the duty of the instructor by leading questions to "guarantee that all factors and issues will be considered," to adroitly discipline the group members to secure warranted consideration to the view-points and problems presented. The leader will achieve success in educational development in so far as he manipulates the situation so as to lead the students to fully present and discuss the problems rather than by doing the major part of the presenting himself with the students sitting passive.

Professor Hansen indicates that discussions frequently take the group nowhere. We suggest trying the plan of outlining very carefully beforehand the subject for discussion and then going before the group to see if all the points listed are brought out during the discussion. In college classes under expert leaders students have frequently demonstrated that they were alive to the issues involved. Factual adherents who espouse the lecture technique will find the material, in most cases, is pretty well covered by a real discussion and moreover that it is presented in such a way that it becomes vitalized material and is more apt to be tied up with the student's past experience and therefore more apt to be remembered. This outcome may not result with a new group that has not been accustomed to the lecture method because such students are too used to remaining passive during the period.

Important data not covered can be brought in at a subsequent group meeting. The instructor, however, should reevaluate the worth of the material which has not been deemed important for consideration by the group members. In group discussion the instructor evaluates what has taken place and replans to meet the needs of each group, whereas the lecture instructor may outline his subject-matter months in advance to supposedly fit any or all groups.

The writers prefer to substitute for the "vast silence" desired by Professor Hansen at the end of lessons a silence period at the beginning. A dean of a recognized school of education uses this device to reveal to his students their own individual lack of information or of opinion and to encourage them to appreciate the very *acceptable* quantity of knowledge possessed by the sum total of the class members. The dean usually sets the stage in this fashion. "We are going to discuss three questions which I wish you to write down. Outline during the next five minutes briefs indicating your position on these questions. This will help you to prepare to participate in the discussion." At the end of five minutes the members are advised to compare notes with their neighbors. A Chinese bedlam school results. "Have you learned anything new?" the dean queries. Experienced educational workers in his classes achieve freedom of expression and discussion which vastly increases the value of the class period. The dean is afforded opportunities to contribute informally pertinent facts and observations.

The dean's group is composed of superintendents, principals, experienced teachers to whom a class period has been an accepted time for examination by the instructor rather than a time to learn something new—particularly from another student. Those who espouse the discussion technique hope to develop in the student a respect for his own intellect and the intellects of his fellow students. If a college professor is worthy of respect he should not fear to demonstrate his ability to survive in the give-and-take conditions inherent in the discussion situation. The oracles of Greece were well enough for their day, why should they be perpetuated exclusively in modern college and university education?

H. B. Smith
L. R. DeLong
Hunter College
Pennsylvania State College

A REJOINDER TO "INSTRUCTION IN OUR GRADUATE SCHOOLS—A PROTEST"

Under "Discussion," School and Society for July 11, appears an article which represents an entirely pessimistic view of graduate study, particularly that in literature. It seems to me the writer has overlooked the growing tendency of graduate schools to cease being hidebound.

The graduate school, like other parts of the American educational system, is at present a storm center of discussion. Perhaps more severe criticism comes from within than from without; certainly the former sort is more exact and constructive.

When graduate students advance the idea that a professor of English should dramatize the material assigned, so that members of the class may be entertained and thus brought to appreciate literature, I am always moved to inquire whether spoon-feeding of sugared morsels in the grades has pointed a way to the proper handling of students of advanced standing.

Usually a graduate faculty assumes that persons who aspire to a doctor's degree are not mere post-graduate students, but have some genuine and deep interest in the field in which they propose to work. These students should, by reason of maturity and former training, be able to derive increased zest through dint of doing their own tasks well. They should be prepared to carry out work on a graduate level, and to rely upon their professors for guidance rather than for the pampering that freshmen sometimes need.

The criticism of the graduate teacher as an individual would scarcely hold true in the case of universities who employ the same men for both undergraduate and graduate courses. In my own experience, the classes in literature which were richest in the personality of the teacher, in the sound philosophical interpretation of material, and in a broad view of life, came after my B.A. degree.

Graduate work should tend towards the development of critical taste and balanced judgment on the part of the student. He is encouraged to learn to think independently, but sanely.

If a student could welcome examinations as an opportunity to demonstrate work that has been well done rather than fear that they would reveal what has been poorly done, much of the strain and burden of graduate work would vanish. After all, examinations serve—but in a greater measure—the same purpose in graduate study that they do in honors courses or in ordinary undergraduate work: they give a motive for the collecting, organizing, and assimilating of related facts and ideas. Only on the foundation of sound knowledge can judgment rest securely; only on the possession of vaster learning than he can hope ever to impart to his pupils can a teacher work satisfactorily. Part of that fund of information which provides the possessor assurance and satisfaction may be derived from advanced study.

The ability to recognize facts and evaluate them, the vision to see ideas in their broader relationships, a certain depth of understanding and of tolerance—these may well be developed by means of advanced work. The situation is well summed up in the words of Professor Norman Foerster: "Our goal is not erudition but scholarship, the union of accuracy, thoroughness, culture, taste and critical judgment." He urges that in the School of Letters a graduate student strive for this well-rounded scholarship, and that he give "evidence of a special capacity for any one side: linguistic, historical, creative or critical."

Some desire the separation of graduate programs in education from those in other fields, and the giving of a special degree, a Ph.D. in education. Some believe that research and teaching should be distinct. I am in sympathy with the view voiced by Professor Walter R. Agard, of the University of Wisconsin, when he said:

> But I can not agree that research and general teaching should be, in most cases, divorced. Certainly the teacher who has lost his interest in investigation, who has allowed his devotion to teaching to dull his ''enquiring mind,'' can no longer hold the proper attention and respect of college students. And it is equally true that the scholar who limits himself exclusively to research will have courted intellectual anaemia, by cutting himself off from those most stimulating and vitalizing personal teaching contacts which make literature significant.

Another phase of graduate work is well presented by Professor Charles Bundy Wilson:

> If the scientist may declare ''at the foundation of material science is the belief that the universe is orderly,'' we may defend the assumption that at the foundation of literature is the belief that there is harmony in the world. It is the business of letters to discover and interpret man's place in this harmony. Through literature then it shall be one function of the Graduate College to encourage efforts towards this discovery and this interpretation of the meaning, the purpose, and the beauty of human life. Here is an opportunity for creative writing, which should be encouraged wherever there is even a suggestion of a gift or of an aptitude. Should not a School of Letters be among the first to offer such encouragement?

This year the University of Iowa has, I understand, adopted a plan by which creative writing of value may be accepted in the place of a dissertation of the traditional type. This procedure should answer the criticism that graduate work leaves no place for the functioning of the student's imagination. The working out of this new experiment will be interesting to watch.

June Jack

Kansas State Teachers College,
Emporia, Kansas

WHAT ABOUT TEACHING EXPERIENCE?

"We want a teacher with experience," has become a very common request from boards of education and superintendents of almost all types of schools from the one-teacher rural school to the large city system. Whereas formerly only the bigger towns required teaching experience of those people starting work in those towns, now it seems that the size of the school is not indicative of what will be required along that line.

The whole situation regarding the matter of experience raises several attendant problems that are serious in their significance to the field of school administration and teacher personnel. Among the more important of these problems are the following: (1) Where will beginning teachers be able to serve their apprenticeship? (2) Practice teaching *vs.* teaching experience; (3) Does teaching experience guarantee success? (4) Possible solutions to the problem. These questions will be discussed in the order they are listed above.

The wide-spread demand for teaching experience has likely grown out of the feeling that there exists a general over-supply of trained teachers, hence it is possible to take a pick of those who have had actual experience. Also, since there are plenty of teachers, school boards feel that they can secure one with experience at a salary formerly paid to an inexperienced teacher.

A few years ago the smaller towns served as apprenticeship centers for the larger cities. Newly trained teachers would begin their experience in the small systems and the more ambitious ones would work their way rapidly up to better positions. City superintendents would be on the alert for particularly successful small town teachers, visit their classrooms, and when the teachers qualified on the matter of experience they would be offered contracts by the city school board.

Now beginning teachers are having to start their experience elsewhere. Even persons with two years of teacher training are finding it difficult to locate themselves in town schools unless they can show a background of experience.

Very naturally the rural school presents itself as the last resort where new teachers can get a start. The largest share of the rural schools will still employ the teacher novice, although some of the better country sections are starting to demand experience. Each year there is something like a 50 per cent. turnover of rural teachers. Some move to other rural schools, some are married and many move into town positions, having proved unusually successful and having increased their training during their rural school apprenticeship. In any case the large turnover gives large opportunity annually for the beginning teacher to start his experience.

The rural school gives a beginning teacher a remarkable all-around experience. Here are presented all types of problems, including those of administration, such as the buying of supplies, organizing the curriculum and arranging the daily class schedule; those of supervision, such as the selection of the methods of teaching, checking of results, and seeking special project activities; those of discipline, such as programs of study, plans of punishment and penalty and keeping up the general morale; and those of community contacts, such as school programs, parent-teacher organizations, and others. The teacher must learn to know the nature of children of several age levels, and must have an adequate knowledge of subject-matter of every grade level. All this carries with it an intensive experience. One year in a rural school with its many grades seems to be equivalent to several years in a town or city position with but one or two grades. In the rural school one is faced with every possible situation all the way from problems of janitorial service to complicated questions of teaching method—and the teacher faces these problems alone. If she is successful it would seem the finest type of experience background for promotion to a better position. If this is the beginning teacher's last resort to get experience it presents itself as a good one. The novice teacher who can weather the storm on a rural school proposition is well started on the road to teaching success.

It would seem that no finer preparation

could be imagined than a few years' experience in a rural school, followed by specialized training to get ready for a more limited piece of work in a town graded school.

Will practice teaching ever serve as a substitute for actual teaching experience? This is a vital question and one that should be given considerable thought. Most school superintendents give very little weight to the success of a beginning teacher's cadet work, probably feeling that what the young person may do under the close supervision of the room critic teacher would be no indication of success in the actual field. As a matter of fact investigations that have been made at Natchitoches, Louisiana, Greeley, Colorado, and other places give evidence that there is a higher correlation between practice teaching and success in the field than between any other one factor and success, even including the all-important quality of scholarship. In other words, success in practice teaching would be a better measure of possible teaching success than high scholarship.

Practice teaching should prove very valuable in the beginning teacher's equipment. In the training school the cadet has a very good opportunity to become familiar with varying procedures in handling subject-matter. All types of planning and organization are used and ideas are passed around among the many practice people so that the alert student gains materially from the practice school contacts.

The one instance where practice work is not so strong as actual teaching is in connection with discipline or pupil control. Here the cadet teacher always knows that the room teacher or critic will come to his rescue in case of serious difficulty, hence the practice teacher does not meet up with natural teaching situations on that phase of school activity. Since the disciplinary side of the school work is so important, perhaps this would be one reason why practice teaching can not be substituted for actual experience.

Simply because a school board is able to secure an experienced teacher does not guarantee that such teacher is going to be successful in the new position. Conditions vary so much from one teaching situation to another that a teacher might be highly successful in one place but fail miserably in another. There are many such instances on record. Such a circumstance may be due to marked differences in the new environment, including the school patrons, or might be the result of conflicts or differences arising among teachers or between teachers and superintendents.

Then, too, there are countless numbers of poor teachers with plenty of experience who have spent but one year in any teaching position, having to move on because of some inefficiency in service. That kind of experience, even though plentiful, is worse than none at all. It would be well to investigate the experience background of every prospective teacher candidate, to make sure of the exact circumstances under which that experience was gained.

One would not deny the value of teaching experience. In the majority of cases it would be a proper index of what to expect of a teacher. On the other hand, when it means a transfer to new surroundings, under new supervision, there is some danger that the experienced teacher might not be as successful as she was in the former position.

Beginning teachers will always be necessary to take the places of the thousands who leave the ranks each year. Some such plans as the following might be used to provide the initial experience for starting teachers.

(a) The rural schools might be used as training centers for town teachers. As suggested above, no finer all-around experience could be had than this. Rural sections would be certain to object to such a plan, first, because it would force all novice teachers upon them and, second, because the plan would force the poorer teachers to stay in rural districts while the best ones would be picked out to go into the town positions. Only a more attractive salary schedule would keep the better teachers in the country communities.

(b) Practice teaching of a certain quality and quantity could be made the equivalent of one year of experience. Careful standards of what the practice work would need to be would have to be set up by schools looking for new teachers, but such a plan would be feasible. If the teacher wished credit for additional experience, further practice work could be put in.

(c) Towns and cities may need to adopt a

scheme whereby new and inexperienced teachers will be started in their systems on a probationary status. If they weather the storms of their first year or two of actual experience, they will be made permanent parts of the teaching force. Many cities already have plans similar to this, or substitute plans of other types.

Some provisions will need to be made to give the beginning teacher her initial experience, since schools will always require a certain number of starting teachers. The solution to the problem will be determined in part by the trends in teacher supply and demand. As it stands at present the teacher who has no experience is being forced to start in rural schools, and the better rural teachers are being taken into the towns and cities. What is needed is a more comprehensive idea of the value of certain kinds of experience, of practice teaching and of advanced training.

Walter W. Ludeman
Southern State Teachers College,
Springfield, South Dakota

QUOTATIONS

PROTESTING TOO MUCH

Many teachers throughout the country must be feeling that the extremely efficient organization which represents the majority of them is exceeding its mandate. The *Times* will not be accused of indifference to their interests or to the importance of their work, and so a word of warning from a friend will not be taken amiss. These hastily organized processions are a mistake unworthy of what the leaders of the National Union of Teachers frequently and rightly describe as a great profession; and the subsequent speeches and resolutions are of little, if any, value. Such resolutions are as easy to obtain as signatures to a petition; and both have as much effect on the government as "stroking the dome of St. Paul's to please the Dean and Chapter." No one of us likes to have our income reduced, and it is safe to say that every income is now in process of reduction. That process is at least the foundation of equality of sacrifice, which can only mean equal payments by all when we reach the Socialist paradise of equal incomes for all. Meanwhile the old rule stands that all taxation must be based on capacity to pay. In the teachers', as in other professions, there will be many hard cases; but in the teachers' profession, as in few others to-day, there are security of tenure, practically no unemployment, increased incomes since the war and good and regular holidays. More teachers in these days are probably taking the old advice "to count our blessings" than are shouting protests to the empty air.

Apart from either occupation there is a very useful and important piece of work in which teachers' representatives ought to help without delay. It will be recalled that the Burnham committees on salary scales were to have met last spring; but the teachers' panel refused to meet because the local authorities insisted, wrongly as was said at the time, that the teachers should come committed to reductions. No one can be expected to attend a round-table conference with his hands tied. Subsequent events have completely removed this obstacle, and the committees should meet at once. Their duty will be to decide how the reductions fixed by Parliament can be most fairly made. At one time it was thought that every salary would be automatically cut by 15 per cent.; but this is a complete mistake. What is to be reduced is the aggregate cost of salaries, and here the committees have an opportunity to adjust the many anomalies and discrepancies which have arisen since the scales were last fixed for a term of years. Such adjustments will be a real step towards that equality of sacrifice which is the ideal of us all.—*The London Times.*

EDUCATION AND LABOR

The proposal to raise the school-leaving age in Britain to fifteen years is meeting some opposition on the ground that by giving advanced education to a larger section of the community the country will ultimately find itself almost without a supply of unskilled labor. Which is another way of saying that a certain proportion of people should be kept in a semi-literate state in order that the menial jobs of life may be done.

Is there any real reason why the menial jobs

should be done by illiterate people—why a scavenger should not be as educated as, say, a bank clerk? It is true that we have come to associate education with a certain kind of employment and to regard a matriculation certificate mainly as a passport to the white-collar professions. But such an association entirely belies the real object of education.

People are educated—or should be—in order to get the fullest intellectual pleasures of life. But that need not unfit them for useful labor. Ruskin says of himself that he was a bad road-maker, but that was not because he was educated but because he was Ruskin. Gladstone, on the other hand, was an expert tree-feller. The truth seems to be that we need education to-day as never before, as a corrective to the ever-growing monotony of increasing factory production. Without education the modern factory worker runs the risk of having his soul mechanized out of existence. Far from preventing a man from doing menial jobs education should enable him to do them and at the same time take a lively interest in life.

As things are now, advanced education is still rare enough to have a material value on the labor market. When it becomes more universal it will have to be sought for its own sake alone. And perhaps by that time we will be living in a community whose members would be too interested in living to be over fussy about how they earned their livings.—*Winnipeg Tribune.*

REPORTS

COURSE-CRABBING: A STUDY OF AN EDUCATIONAL TABOO

A negative attitude to an intellectual spontaneity and to an academic vigor in the class-room and on the campus is the indirect result of an educational taboo directed against the practice of course-crabbing. According to a tradition, no one should attempt to "crab a course." It may be a long familiar one under various names at different universities. Its unique characteristics are of considerable interest to psychologists and critics of higher education. Apparently, the tradition against C-C[1] is due to an underlying primitive fear that somehow advantage will be taken of the personal equation in the ranking-system, that a student will try unfairly to boost a grade beyond the deserved rank by playing up to an instructor. This suggests that a combination of certain weaknesses inherent in the ranking-system with its subjective elements and in the lecture-system with its formal absence of human contacts is, for the most part, responsible for this practice of course-crabbing. This paper will treat of course-crabbing from the view-point of students and will present results of a study made at a certain university of students' notions of, attitudes to, and suggestions about C-C.

[1] C-C will be used here as an abbreviation for 'course-crabbing' or 'course-crabber.'

(1) A Professor's Description of C-C

An illustrated definition and a first-hand description of the C-C taboo in actual operation in the lecture-hall and in the class-room is contained in the following excerpts from a professor's letter to the college paper. The view-point is definitely at odds with the C-C taboo and is also critical of the practice of C-C.

I believe the hour has struck in which we must begin to fight the *Great Silence*. . . . *The Great Silence* is abroad in the land and its victims congregate in every class-room in our campus . . . in his daily routine the instructor encounters two species of students, the leprous Course-crabbers (diminished now almost to the vanishing point) and the victims of the *Great Silence*.

. . . bell tolls. It is eight o'clock. The instructor calls the roll; he may be somewhat surprised that so many students answer. . . . Cautiously, the instructor introduces the subject for the day and asks a discreet question of John Smith, who is rather a good student. He replies briefly with the truth in the matter and shuts up like a clam . . . the instructor . . . throws the subject open to class discussion. "Are there any questions?" Do the members of the class discuss it? They do not! There is ominous silence, for back in every brain is that little hammer rapping out: Course-crabber! Course-crabber! Course-crabber! . . . No other member of the class can be urged to run the gauntlet of social disapproval; and the instructor in order to rescue the session from the air of a Quaker meeting house is himself forced into a discussion of the various phases of the subject at hand. . . . Stimulating? For the instructors and students alike? Hardly! . . . Most instructors are willing and anxious to give time outside of class to explain difficult points to any student. But do the students avail themselves of this opportunity? Rarely; because the word will go abroad that they are course-crabbers; they are cowardly slaves to the tyranny which is devouring them.

This description is emotionally colored and pictures dramatically an inhibition of intellectual give-and-take in school.

(2) A Questionnaire Study of Students' Notions of Course-Crabbing

The main purpose of this paper is to make a composite picture of students' conceptions of course-crabbing. Is there a common notion of this practice prevalent among them? Is there a sentiment favorable or unfavorable to it? Is what the professor calls the "Great Silence" defended at all on logical grounds? To find answers to these questions the following quiz-form was designed and given to 140 students consisting of sophomores, juniors and seniors who were in six classes under three different instructors.

The information asked for is solely for scientific and pedagogic purposes. Please be frank and as constructive in your suggestions as possible. You are not asked to write your name so that the information can be perfectly confidential.

1. What do you understand by ''course-crabbing''?
2. What is your attitude to ''course-crabbing''?
3. What suggestions have you to make in regard to ''course-crabbing''?

Two of the classes, after completing the quiz, were also asked to state how often they crabbed courses. The various answers to these questions will be treated systematically.

(3) Question 1: What Do You Understand by Course-Crabbing?

In general, course-crabbing is looked upon by students as anything which is done by a student to make himself conspicuous in order to put him in a favorable light. The aim of C-C is to attract the instructor's attention, so as to get a higher rank. A list of thirteen items which, taken together, constitute students' notions of classroom C-C is given in Table I. Not every one has the same ideas of what C-C is all about. Some views are extremely bent in one direction, and some in another.

TABLE I

Classroom Course-Crabbing Items

1. Asking questions you are not really interested in.
2. Asking the instructor any questions at all.
3. Bluffing or talking one's way through the course.
4. Saying what one thinks the professor wants to be said.
5. Too much discussion by a student.
6. Doing most of the talking.
7. Giving no one else a chance to say a word.
8. Showing a make-believe interest in the course.
9. Volunteering answers to questions which have been carefully prepared and ''weighed'' and known to be correct.
10. Taking copious notes to appear industrious.
11. Apparently taking notes, actually writing a letter.
12. Sitting in a front seat and appearing attentive.
13. Always showing off in class.

As for C-C outside of classroom hours, the fourteen items in Table II indicate that the students believe that contacts outside of classroom with the instructor may lead to a higher rank and such contacts are to be considered C-C. as course-crabbing.

TABLE II

Outside of Classroom Course-Crabbing

1. Cultivating the good-will of the instructor.
2. Social contacts with the instructor.
3. Playing up to an instructor in conferences.
4. General conversation with instructor.
5. Frequent visits to instructor's office.
6. Discussion of technical points.
7. Attempts to ''blind'' the instructor by ''hook or crook.''
8. Seeking the instructor's advice on various matters.
9. Trying to impress the instructor that one's mentality is far above that of the class.
10. Telling him you need an A or B to make the ''Dean's List.''
11. Flattering or ''soft-soaping'' the instructor.
12. Playing up to his intellectual vanities.
13. Doing more work than one is supposed to.
14. Trying to make a favorable impression through the effect of one's personality, appearance or dress.

(4) Question 2: What is Your Attitude to "Course-Crabbing"?

In a previous section of this paper, the attitude of a professor to C-C was cited. It was rather antagonistic to the tradition against and to the practice of course-crabbing. That professor regards it as a great social and educational evil, calls its effects "The Great Silence" and refers to the "leprous course-crabbers." And as a matter of fact, this questionnaire shows that most students dislike a course-crabber. Of the three general attitudes found—traditional, middle-of-the-road and progressive—the most popular one is the traditional one with its dramatic taboo against intellectual and social contacts with an instructor.

A curious mixture of logic and emotion makes up the foundations of the traditional attitude. It regards the C-C as a poor sport, as one who deserves to be outlawed by the campus community, as worse than a cheater. Indeed, the morale of the other students is said to be upset by the C-C, who succeeds in boosting his rank. And some even regard the C-C situation as a "most deplorable one." So emphatically opposed are they to C-C, that they urge seriously a maximum reduction of any intellectual discussion or social contacts with instructors. This summarizes rather briefly most of the answers of the students who took this C-C quiz.

Not so popular as this attitude is the less reactionary one which holds that there is really very little course-crabbing. This middle-of-the-road attitude points out (1) C-C is overemphasized, (2) it gets one nowhere, (3) those who do all the complaining are in truth unsuccessful course-crabbers.

A constructive attitude, held by only a few, maintains that the practice of tradition and taboo against C-C can be overcome by initiation of improvements in the educational structure. An editorial commenting on the letter of the professor, cited above, indicates certain changes on the campus which would go a long way to over-balance the effects of the tradition against C-C. It is representative of this constructive attitude.

> . . . There are some reasons for this lackadaisical air; one of them doubtless is the size of the average class, another is the formality insisted upon by many instructors (typified by the seating of students alphabetically), and a third is the method of teaching by instruction rather than by permitting the students to learn by doing . . . solution seems to be achieved in some degree . . . where a new plan of study. . . . This puts responsibility on the student. The premium is put on the student's initiative rather than on the selling ability of the instructor.

(5) Attitudes of Those Who Crab Courses to C-C

Of special interest is an analysis of attitudes shown by those who said they crab courses sometimes. It will be recalled, in two classes, after completion of the questionnaire, students were asked to state whether and how often they crabbed courses. In fact, 25 per cent. in one class and 27.3 per cent. in the other class admitted to C-C. This may imply that the practice is rather a usual and frequent one. This implication is upset, however, by a study of the following statements made in answer to the second question, what is your attitude to course-crabbing. Twenty-three admitted to course-crabbing and the statements of seventeen of these individuals are here included.

1. I don't care, if they're clever enough to get by with it. . . . Every man for himself!
2. As a means to an end it works, but I don't feel that it leaves a healthy attitude in the class.
3. A gullible instructor gives as much heed to the course-crabber as to the honest student, while a hard-boiled instructor is apt to put down these attempts on the part of sincere students as course-crabbing.
4. A course-crabber is the very lowest kind of a sport I know. If you can't earn rank fairly and squarely, don't try to get it.
5. Any one who can do it—more power to them . . . if one can get a high mark by course-crabbing I think it is all right.
6. I believe that it is very difficult to tell course-crabbing. Much of that . . . classified as course-crabbing is an honest attempt to understand a subject.
7. A person who does it is taking an unfair advantage of both the teacher and the other students, and any one who does this deserves to get shunned and laughed at by the other students.
8. There are times when I believe that . . . is justified. If a teacher is in doubt about a student's grade it may be permissible. But, after all students come to college to learn things, not to get grades they don't deserve.

9. I truly give credit to a course-crabber if his methods are not too obvious. If a person does not study at all, and tries to course-crab, then he becomes quite obnoxious to me. It is quite unfair to the rest of the students to have a course-crabber in the class.

10. I think that course-crabbing, in its extreme use, is very unpleasant to every one concerned. But, I do not think that one should go out of one's way to be antagonistic to the instructor in order to make sure that one is not suspected of course-crabbing. I believe that one should be reasonably agreeable to one's instructor, and if one happens to feel that the instructor is the sort of person whom it would be interesting to know better—I think it is perfectly all right to go out of one's way in order to bring that about. Instructors are here for the purpose of giving us as much as they can, and this must not necessarily be text-book matter. Much is to be gained by knowing different personalities.

11. Course-crabbing should not be indulged in as a permanent means of passing a course.

12. I believe in coming into a class-room, receiving instructions and information, then passing out of the room.

13. Real course-crabbing. . . . I consider low and mean, but course-crabbing doesn't exist half as much as it is reputed to. Most of the instances . . . honest motive back of them, a desire for information or friendship.

14. I do not believe in crabbing the course for rank. I do believe students and teacher should be on a friendly basis, but students should not seek their instructor's friendship solely for the hope of getting higher grades. I believe the instructors are as much at fault as the students, however, as, they encourage them, as a rule.

15. If you can course-crab and get away with it, o. k. . . . Best thing is to know your stuff so that you don't *have* to course-crab.

16. I dislike course-crabbing very much, but think that sometimes real interest in a course is not given sufficient encouragement because of the *awful* fear of becoming a course-crabber. If I find that a course is not particularly important to me and that others are crabbing it and if the instructor falls for it, I try it too—I can't see working hard on a course which is not particularly valuable to me and then getting a poor grade on it, while others in the class do very little (if anything) and come through with maybe an A+. Professional crabber?

17. I think it is the bunk. . . . I am regarded as a course-crabber (and a good one) . . . if what I do is course-crabbing, I'm going to keep it up. The courses I have received an "A" in, I was extremely interested in, in fact, intrigued. . . . I have talked to the professors of these courses (unpardonable sin) but usually for the sake of finding out something. I find out what a professor is interested in, what special field he likes. . . .

Almost all these statements reveal a disgust with those who course-crab and point to the conclusion that there is hardly any actual course-crabbing. What there is consists of considerable fear that course-crabbing goes on constantly. This is just the point advanced in the opening paragraph of this paper that "the tradition against C-C is due to an underlying primitive fear that somehow advantage will be taken of the personal equation in the ranking system."

(6) Question 3: What suggestions have you to make in regard to "course-crabbing"?

Most students feel that course-crabbing is due to the nature of the system of college education. Answers to this question represent different views and suggestions: "a hard thing to stop and the way I can see is to start with a clean slate and kick the upperclassmen out and start with a new group of freshmen where they won't be able to learn about the tradition"; "course-crabbing will most likely always exist since some students are by nature go-getters anyway and it will exist as long as we have grades as the reward for scholarship. When colleges are run on a basis of 'scholarship for scholarship's sake,' then course-crabbing may eliminate itself"; "the only way to prevent course-crabbing is to have inaccessible professors and this is not possible—every-one must have prejudices." Quite a number feel that the instructor should discriminate between conscientious students and course-crabbers and that he must "give the C-C the air immediately," "warn pupil, flunk him, if he persists." Most of the constructive suggestions center about the wider use of objective examinations, frequent conferences between instructors and students, and more frequent and less rigid social contacts between them. As for the ranking-system, it is even suggested that the A B C letter-grading scale be abandoned, as in some graduate schools, and that more general "passed" or "failed" grades only be used. A marked dissatisfaction with the ordinary lecture system is also expressed by some who picture it as a machine-like affair in which students, as automatic machines, record impressions from an automatic loud-speaker. Consequently, it is suggested that the time devoted to formal lectures be cut down, more time be devoted to discussion, which should not be forced.

(7) SUMMARY

Course-crabbing is regarded by students as the practice of playing up to an instructor in order to boost the grade beyond the obtained rank. It is an unpopular practice. Hence, it leads to a number of inhibitions and restrictions of contacts between instructors and students. A wholesome intellectual attitude on the campus is negatively affected by the taboo against C-C. The tradition against C-C rests not so much upon concrete facts as upon a basic fear that someone is bound to seek unfairly for a higher rank. This is pointed to by an analysis of the statements of those who admitted to the practice. For offsetting the tradition against C-C, students suggest more objective methods in examinations, less time for formal lectures, more time for discussion, frequent conferences and social contacts between faculty and students.

NATHAN ISRAELI

UNIVERSITY OF MAINE

EDUCATIONAL RESEARCH AND STATISTICS

IMPROVING THE TRUE-FALSE EXAMINATION[1]

THE true-false test has frequently been condemned because of its unreliability and its supposed encouragement to guessing on the part of the student taking the test. To neutralize the effect of guessing, the right-minus-wrong (R − W) formula has been approved by a number of writers, who have varyingly recommended that the examinee either be or not be encouraged to guess the correct answer. The present writer has always been somewhat skeptical of the validity of the R − W formula. If for no other reason, the formula is somewhat invalidated because it seems to assume that every item wrongly judged is very likely to be a result of guessing. He has also disapproved of the formula because many students have the feeling, regardless of the actual validity of the formula, that their scores do not truly represent their actual achievement on a test. A zero score is almost incomprehensible by many of these students. The present writer, accordingly, set himself about two years ago to the task of improving the reliability of his own true-false tests by devising a set of directions designed to reduce guessing to a minimum and to permit the score on a test to be the number of items judged correctly by the student. During the

COEFFICIENTS OF RELIABILITY FOR CROSS-OUT TRUE-FALSE TESTS

Test	Method of scoring	
	Items right	R–W
1	.77	.45
2	.73	.59
3	.70	.63
4	.69	.66
5	.66	.71
6	.64	.21
7	.61	.40
8	.57	.33
9	.32	−.16
10	.84	.81
11	.80	.80
12	.87	.84
13	.82	.77
14	.81	.76
15	.15	.01
16	.76	.25
17	.69	.54
18	.77	.77
19	.75	.76
20	.76	.70
21	.67	.52
22	.47	.40
23	.75	.55
24	.63	.68
25	.56	.66
Av.	.67	.56
S.D.	.15	.25
r	Difference	$S.D._{Diff.}$[2]
.72	.11	.03

[1] The writer gratefully acknowledges his indebtedness to the following of his students, who did all the clerical and most of the statistical work involved in the study: Misses Mary Elizabeth Napier, Louise Culbreath, Margaret Lemon and Eugenia Callison.

[2] *Cf.* T. L. Kelley, ''Statistical Method,'' p. 182, The Macmillan Company, New York, N. Y., 1923.

time of this study the following directions have been used in giving twenty-three different true-false tests to students at Coker College and two true-false tests to students at the University of Georgia in the summer of 1930:

DIRECTIONS: If you think a statement is TRUE, write a plus sign in the blank printed before it. If you think a statement is FALSE, write a minus sign in the proper blank, and THEN DRAW A LINE through the word or the words that make the statement false.

OMITTED ITEMS will not be given any credit.

A BLANK CONTAINING BOTH A PLUS AND A MINUS SIGN will be scored as *wrong.*

TO GET CREDIT FOR JUDGING A FALSE ITEM you must draw a line through the word or the words that make it false.

YOUR SCORE WILL BE the number of items you judge correctly.

The above directions, it is evident, provide a cross-out method for indicating the reason for judging an item to be false.

For each of these tests the reliability (Spearman-Brown formula) was computed, both when the R – W formula was used and also when credit was allowed for each correctly judged item. The coefficients of reliability under each of these two conditions are presented in the accompanying table. The data there presented show an actual difference of .11 in favor of the coefficients of reliability when the student was allowed credit for every item judged correctly. Since this difference is 3.66 times its standard error, the chances are 9,999 in 10,000 that the difference is a true and not a chance one. (*Cf.* Garrett, "Statistics in Psychology and Education, Table X, p. 91.) Examination of the accompanying table will also show that in only four of the twenty-five cases was the reliability greater when the R – W method of scoring was used. The positive correlation (.72) between the two sets of coefficients, while not sufficiently high to be absolutely convincing, indicates that the cross-out device tends to be consistent in its effectiveness.

The results of the study incline the writer to feel reasonably justified in drawing the following conclusions:

(1) The R – W formula would be more reliable if the student is required to indicate the basis for judging an item to be false. Before devising the cross-out technique, the writer gave at Coker College twenty-one true-false tests, for which the directions were approximately those quoted below.

If you think a statement is TRUE, write a plus sign in the blank printed before it. If you think a statement is False, in whole or in part, write a minus sign in the blank printed before it. Your score will be the number of items right minus the number of items wrong. Any blank containing both a plus and a minus sign will be scored as wrong.

For purposes of a rough comparison the writer computed the average reliability of these tests. This average was found to be .44. The average reliability for the R – W formula when applied to the experimental tests was .56 (see accompanying table). It will be recalled that in the experimental tests the student used the cross-out method to indicate the basis of each item judged to be false.

(2) The R – W formula reduces reliability when the cross-out method of judging false items is used. In the experiment, the average reliability was reduced from .67 to .56.

(3) When the cross-out method is used reliability is higher when the student is given credit for the number of items he judges correctly according to the directions for the test.

(4) The cross-out method makes the reliability much greater than it would be if the R – W formula is used without it. In this study it raised the average reliability from .44 to .67.

(5) The teacher's judgment as to whether the proper basis of judging an item to be false has been indicated by the student affects the reliability when the cross-out method is used. In six of the twenty-five tests used in this study the scores of a large number of students were greatly modified by the teacher's judgment of the proper basis for judging an item to be false. In four of them the reliability was higher than it was when credit was given for judging correctly any false item for which any basis of falsity whatever was indicated by the student. In the other two tests the reliability was lowered when items were counted wrong because an unsatisfactory basis of falsity was indicated by the student. Reliabilities were raised from .59 to .69; .75 to .76; .13 to .15; .41 to .64. They were lowered from .81 to .70; from .69 to

.63. These figures must not be taken too seriously, but it is not unlikely that a teacher who has carefully constructed and analyzed true-false items can raise the reliability of tests by refusing credit for judging any false item for which a satisfactory basis of judgment is not indicated by the student. In any case, occasional and unanticipated application of this device should encourage sincere judgments by the students.

(6) The cross-out method probably reduces guessing to a minimum in judging true-false items. This conclusion is supported by the lower reliabilities when the R – W formula is used along with the cross-out method. Students themselves uniformly testify to their realization of this fact.

(7) The cross-out method has specific diagnostic value in determining the student's comprehension of the test items. Many students have said that they realize this fact.

(8) The cross-out method makes true-false tests a task of reasoning as well as of recall. Student opinion supports this conclusion. Moreover, the time consumed in taking tests by this method is uniformly greater because of the seriousness with which the students judge the items.

(9) There may be several ways of satisfactorily indicating a valid basis for judging an item to be false.

(10) Students prefer the cross-out method because it eliminates the R – W method of scoring. This preference is explained by their feeling that they get credit for all that they accomplish.

(11) The use of this kind of examination is an incentive to the teacher to have a critical knowledge of his subject. Without this knowledge he is incapable of correctly evaluating the basis of judgment indicated by the student.

(12) The reliability of short tests is greatly increased by the cross-out method.

(13) The reliability of long tests seems to be little affected by either method of scoring when the cross-out method is used in judging items. This fact may be evidence that the cross-out device is a stabilizer of reliability.

(14) When the cross-out method is used it is unnecessary for the test constructor to make the true and the false items equal in number. He makes each item true or false, accordingly as he thinks it will best test the student's knowledge. For this reason artificiality of wording can be greatly reduced and the student will have no reason to check over his test to see whether he has judged as many items false as true, a rather prevalent practice where students are accustomed to have an equal number of true and false items in their tests.

W. A. Barton, Jr.

Coker College

NEW BOOKS IN EDUCATION

Avery, Maurice W. *Latin Prose Literature.* Pp. xii + 400. Little, Brown. $2.40.

Bachman, Frank P. and others. *Public Schools of Nashville, Tennessee.* Pp. xiii + 373. Division of Surveys and Field Studies, George Peabody College for Teachers.

Bachrach, Jeanetta W. *Tales of Old.* Pp. 80. Illustrated by Charles W. Robinson. F. A. Owen. $.48.

Board of Education of the City of New York. *Annual Financial and Statistical Report for the Fiscal and Calendar Year 1930.* Pp. 184. Illustrated. Division of Statistics, Bureau of Finance, The Board.

Brownell, William A. and Lorena B. Stretch. *The Effect of Unfamiliar Settings on Problem-Solving.* Pp. 86. Duke University Press.

Carhart, Margaret S. and Selena P. Ingram. *Experiments in Corrective English.* Pp. vi + 183. Prentice-Hall. $1.00.

Cofer, David B. *Saint-Simonism in the Radicalism of Thomas Carlyle.* Pp. 68. English Publishing Company. $1.00.

Coffman, Ramon. *The Story of America.* Book V: *Founding the Republic.* Pp. 128. Illustrated. F. A. Owen. $.72.

Commission on English. Examining the Examination in English: A Report to the College Entrance Examination Board. Pp. xv + 295. Harvard University Press. $2.00.

Corwin, Walling and Mae J. Corwin. *The Science of Discovery and Invention:* Pp. xix + 735. 341 figures. *The Science of Plant and Animal Life:* Pp. xv + 592. 260 figures. *The Science of Human Living:* Pp. xiii + 464. Illustrated. Harr Wagner.

Crandall, Lee S. *Paradise Quest.* Pp. xvii + 226. Illustrated. Scribner's. $3.50.

Good, Carter V., Walter L. Collins and Chester A. Gregory. *Abstracts: Graduate Theses in Education.* Volume I. Pp. xxv + 396. Teachers College, University of Cincinnati.

Harvey, B. C. H. *Simple Lessons in Human Anatomy.* Pp. 434. 234 figures. American Medical Association.

Marshall, M. V. *Education as a Social Force.* Pp. xxix + 161. Harvard University Press. $1.00.

Swift, Edgar J. *The Jungle of the Mind.* Pp. 340. Scribner's. $2.50.

Travis, Lee E. *Speech Pathology.* Pp. xxxiv + 331. 70 figures. Appleton. $4.00.

SCHOOL AND SOCIETY

EDITED BY J. McKEEN CATTELL

WITH WHICH IS COMBINED THE

EDUCATIONAL REVIEW

EDITED BY WILLIAM McANDREW

Volume 34 SATURDAY, OCTOBER 24, 1931 Number 878

THE NEW ENGLAND COLLEGE[1]

By Dr. A. LAWRENCE LOWELL

PRESIDENT OF HARVARD UNIVERSITY

WHEN friends are met for the birthday of a notable fellow citizen it is customary to recite his achievements, but it is still better to consider what he has stood for, his aspirations and their meaning in the life of the community; and so when we assemble here to celebrate the anniversary of Wesleyan it is well to review the meaning, the aims, the objects and the deep significance of the institution.

The New England college stands for general education, which, in the absence of a better word we may call by the much abused term cultural, in contrast with vocational, training. This has been true from the beginning. No doubt a leading motive in founding Harvard—the oldest, and a common type of them all—was to train ministers of religion, otherwise Hebrew would hardly have been given so much prominence. But ministers were primarily men of general education, as understood in those days, rather than technical scholars in the present sense. Moreover, the students from the outset were by no means confined to such as looked forward to the church. Of the first class to graduate, five became ministers and four did not; one of the latter, with not too rigid a character, serving as ambassador under both Cromwell and Charles II. In fact, for eighty years the clergy had, on the average, a slight, but only a slight, preponderance in numbers. The college was, as New England colleges have always been, conducted for all youths seeking higher general education.

Now what do we mean by general or cultural, as distinguished from vocational or professional education? The difference is hard to define, because it is not clear cut. The two things are not mutually exclusive; they overlap, and yet the divergence is real and perceptible. We all recognize the difference between a lawyer and a jurist, between a physician and a biologist, an engineer and a physicist, a clergyman and a theologian. The difference is one of degree, based upon the mode of approaching the subject, whether as an art to be practiced or an intellectual region to be explored. The former is the professional, the latter the scholarly, approach. They are not inconsistent, for a man may be both, although that is uncommon; but they are different, and in most men produce a different attitude of mind.

This is merely an illustration. The distinction is not the same as that we are considering now, for a man may excel in pure science, jurisprudence, philosophy or

[1] Address delivered on October 12, 1931, at the Centennial Exercises of Wesleyan University, Middletown, Connecticut.

linguistics without being cultivated. He may know all about his own field and be ignorant and opaque to all beyond. That again is a matter of degree, not to be logically circumscribed but none the less significant. Let us not for a moment assume that either is more important than the other. Both are essential. The progress of knowledge and art is maintained by specialists—with or without general culture—and so is the efficient conduct of all human occupations; while largeness of view, breadth of understanding, expansion of sympathy is promoted by culture. Not only does the individual, whether a specialist or not, benefit by its possession, but the community profits if its intelligent citizens have a body of common knowledge. Most of this must, of course, be obtained through life, outside of formal instruction, by observation, reading and conversation; and one of the objects of general education is, by opening the mind, to enable men to do so. To put it in another way, the object of general education is resourcefulness, the development of the mental powers so that they can be used in any direction; that of vocational so that they can be used with the greatest effect in one direction. Both, let me repeat, are of the highest importance, and the college is concerned with the former.

The difference between general and vocational education lies not in the subject taught. To an omniscient intelligence, thought and knowledge in all their manifold branches must appear, not as a complex system with distinct compartments, but as a single whole where every part is interfused with all the rest; not as a patchwork, but a seamless texture; not like the heaven studded with stars, but as a sun resplendent with light. The object of a cultural education is a faint reflection of that light at an immeasurable distance. Any subject can be studied and taught in a cultural or a highly specialized vocational way, as Professor Goodwin in a Phi Beta Kappa address many years ago pointed out in the case of Greek. In fact classical philology, commonly regarded as the summit of instruction in the ancient languages, is often taught in a vocational way for the benefit of the future scholar rather than for that of the unprofessional reader of classic literature.

An example of the different approach came to my notice in college. William James, fresh from the medical school, gave a most interesting course on comparative anatomy and physiology, and found that he could pick out the men who intended to study medicine by their special attention to the fragments of human anatomy included therein. Those fragments would be insignificant when they came to study anatomy in the medical school, but they stored them away at the expense of the larger scientific aspects of James' teaching. This illustrates the difficulty of teaching a subject both to men who are taking it for a vocational object and those who are not. Either the former will get far less than they would in a professional school, or for the latter it will have little cultural value. Such a course is almost certain to fall between two stools and rest securely on neither. People often argue that if a subject can be either cultural or vocational both results may be obtained in a single course. The answer is that while it may be taught in either way there is little use in trying to teach it in both. Hence the best results are reached by having general education end before the vocational begins.

Almost every subject may be taught in a cultural way, indeed in a way to be in itself a broad general education. History, for instance, may include not only politics, wars, biography and the growth of states and institutions, as is usual, but also the progress of literature, philosophy, art and science. References to literature are more common; but how many teachers of English history allude, save in the most cursory way, if at all, to the work of Harvey, Newton, Jenner and Faraday, point out the scientific bearing thereof or the significance for the advance of civilization? Yet the theory of gravitation, for example, profoundly modified human thought, and the calculus, invented by Newton and Leibnitz, is probably the most important single intellectual tool acquired by man since the alphabet, Arabic notation and algebra.

One can see how other subjects could be taught in a highly comprehensive way, and many teachers do it so far as they can, but to carry it to the point of universal culture would require infinite time and omniscient instructors. The first of these can not be compressed within the period of adolescence, and the second do not exist. When the range of human knowledge was far less than it is now, to obtain it all may have been feasible; but a Casaubon has been impossible since his day, if it was not really so then. To know everything can be achieved only, as the squib about Benjamin Jowett put it, by claiming that what one does not know is not knowledge. A specialist sometimes comes near this by assuming in his teaching that things outside his field are unimportant to his students, and by striving to get their whole time for his own subject. In a professional or graduate school, where the object is not general but vocational education, this is proper; but in the college we can ask each instructor to remember that his department covers only a fraction of universal knowledge, and that the student should be learning other branches also.

With this caution in mind instruction can not practically go far afield of the special subject taught, and the student must get his general education from a few facets, each showing a limited point of view. Some one may object that this is asking him to do the trick of the man on the staff of the *Eatanswill Gazette* who for an editorial on Chinese metaphysics read in the "Encyclopedia Britannica" the articles on metaphysics and on China and combined the information. But this is not so, because the object is not a conspectus of all learning, but a broadening of the mind by acquaintance with different types of thought, an outlook beyond one's own vocation, an ability to see it in a larger than a technical light. That is what a liberal college is for.

We are faced then by the paradox that general culture must be imparted by the study of particular subjects taught by specialists; and we may also observe that a wide smattering of many things does not serve the purpose. It is apt to leave in the mind of the ordinary student a chaotic mass of vague generalizations—that such a one was a great man, or an event or idea a good thing—without giving him the power of accurate and refined analysis and discrimination. Unless a man has mastered some subject thoroughly he has not learned to know the difference between profound and superficial knowledge, either in himself or in others. This may not be so important for those who afterwards enter a professional school where they will learn one thing well, but it is essential for others, and saves them from a snare that entraps too many people in our day of a universal modicum of education.

General or cultural is the most difficult form of education because all higher learning is essentially a process of self-education, and depends on the active desire of the student to obtain it. He believes in the value of the tools of his vocation, and therefore his will to learn in a professional school may usually be assumed. Even if he studies there many things he will never use, he is told they are an essential part of his training, and he accepts them on faith. But he often fails to understand the object and meaning of a wider general education. He does not see its use to him. While he appreciates the specific knowledge required in his future career, the greatest tool of all, a brain trained to think freely and broadly, seems to him vague and intangible. He thinks, as most people do, in terms of knowledge, finds that much of it has been forgotten, and wonders what good it has been to him. A college graduate sometimes says he took in college courses in Greek and German and now can not read either, in philosophy and can not recall what was the special contribution of Descartes, several more in history and knows scarcely a date; and therefore suspects that the whole thing was a waste of time. Of such a one Professor Kittredge asks how many pounds of beef he has consumed since graduation and how much of them has remained in his system in the form they were eaten, for if any of them did he would be dead.

The very enlargement of knowledge has greatly increased the difficulty of a general education. Two hundred years ago it was believed to consist in a body of learning sufficient for the man of culture and not too large to be covered by an undergraduate. Hence there was a fixed curriculum for all, and it had two effects. Every well-educated man was presumed to be familiar with certain things within and outside of that curriculum. He was ashamed not to understand a Latin quotation, and, although not a part of formal instruction, he felt an obligation to read the classic works in the literature of his mother tongue. But when a growth in the range of knowledge rendered a rigid curriculum impossible, and forced the adoption of numerous electives, so that no man could cover any large part of the ground, there came to be no part of it a college graduate was ashamed not to know. One hears a student remark of some topic with which we expect him to be familiar, "No, I did not take a course on that subject."

Another result of the change has been a lessening of the spirit of competition. President Hadley pointed out how we have forgotten that a curriculum meant running a race. Under the fixed curriculum there was constant emulation, and much was expected of those who stood at the top. At Harvard, and I presume elsewhere, graduates, although not themselves of high rank, knew who the first scholars were in all the classes near their time; but after free electives came, there were, and could be, no first scholars. Yet the desire for competition springs eternal in the breast of youth, and it is noteworthy that the development of intercollegiate athletics is contemporaneous with the downfall of the fixed curriculum. While there are other causes for its growth the coincidence is by no means wholly accidental. Some people have thought scholarship might be helped by abolishing these athletic contests, but although these are no doubt now excessive, it is futile to attempt to encourage one good form of activity by suppressing another.

When the free elective system was introduced it was expected to result in greater eagerness for study by permitting each man to pursue the subject in which he was most interested; but while it was a great help to the earnest student who knew what he wanted to learn—commonly in a more or less vocational direction—it did not stimulate the indifferent. To some extent it had the opposite effect by fostering a search for courses that were deemed easy. Everywhere to-day it has been modified to compel the student to select a series of courses intelligently planned.

We have changed, or we should change, our ideas of a general or cultural education from the acquiring of a definite body of knowledge to a familiarity with the diverse phases of human thought, and especially to training the mind to deal accurately and seriously with the manifold complex ideas it will meet in life; and above all we must make the student see that the highest excellence he can attain in the work provided in college for that purpose is deeply worth while. Many years ago I was told this was impossible, that the serious devotion to study of the professional school could not be brought into the college. I did not, and I do not, believe it; and now that every college is striving for it, the results show how much can be done by systematic and persistent effort. In our various institutions we all have this as the same major problem, and therefore it is a pleasure to take part in the anniversary of one of our sisters who has called her sons and friends about her as she pauses for a day on her beneficent march.

To those who in the past hundred years have here fed the flame of learning when the fire around was burning low, to those who in better days have made the light stream forth, we bring our gratitude to-day. To those now here, or who will come hereafter, we bring in full measure joy for the opportunities that beckon from an ever-rising path.

TEACHER-TRAINING CURRICULA FOR DEVELOPMENT OF INTERNATIONAL UNDERSTANDING[1]

By Dean MILTON BENNION
UNIVERSITY OF UTAH

By way of preface, let it be noted that the most enlightened curricula alone may be very ineffective without appropriate character and personality on the part of the teacher's college faculty and students.

A first step, therefore, will be selection of faculty and development of a plan for selection of students. Prospective teachers who are merely seeking the shortest route to an occupation as a means of making a living will never transform the world, irrespective of the care with which institutions plan their curricula. The prospective teacher, to be effective, must put service to fellowmen above financial gain, must attack the teachers' problems with enthusiasm as well as with intelligence; and must himself exhibit the social qualities and attitudes that the school seeks to develop in the pupils. This is, of course, not altogether a matter of native endowment; experience in and out of school may contribute much toward developing a desirable teaching personality.

This experience should include wide and varied social contacts, either through travel or by reading, or better still, by both. The teacher-training curricula can at least make provision for the kind of reading that will contribute toward international understanding. Exactly what this shall be in any particular case will depend in part upon what the college grade student has done in the elementary and secondary schools. In any case the teachers college student can further develop his knowledge of world literature and extend his acquaintance with contemporary publications that will further his understanding and appreciation of the various races and nations of the world. This will call for greater emphasis upon world literature and geography, including the fundamental facts and principles of anthropology, than is now generally given in teacher-training

[1] Read before the Department of Preparation of Teachers, World Federation of Education Associations, Denver, Colorado, July 27, 1931.

institutions. While the study of technical English (grammar and composition) is essential, this study is wholly inadequate if not supplemented by studies in literature; not merely English and American literature, but the great masterpieces of the world.

We suggest, therefore, a course in world literature, coordinate with required courses in English. This course in world literature should not be restricted to western nations. The masterpieces of India and China may well be included with those of Palestine, Greece, Rome, France, Germany, Scandinavia, Russia, Italy and Spanish and English-speaking countries. The course should be truly cosmopolitan, and both historical and contemporary. To become acquainted with the masterpieces of the great nations of the world is a major contribution toward understanding and appreciating the peoples that produced them.

Of similar import is a study of the art and handicrafts of all nations. In this case, fortunately, translations are not necessary. Both art and handicrafts speak a universal language. Research in anthropology has revealed the fact that many primitive peoples attained marvelous skill in artistic expression. Knowledge of this fact tends to create a respect for primitive peoples that has thus far been too rare among people who call themselves civilized. There has, of course, been greater appreciation of the works of art of the great historic peoples. This appreciation should be systematically developed in the schools; not that all children of the future are to become artists, but that they may have a reasonable degree of artistic judgment, and may more fully realize the sources of artistic productions and the value of art as a part of the common social heritage.

Music, too, speaks a universal language, a language that may be understood by all normal people. Here again the schools can teach to all children appreciation of the contributions of all nations, both historical and contemporary, to the common social inheritance in music. Children should be made acquainted with the folk songs and the national anthems of the various nations, as well as with the great productions of classical music. While the majority of children may not have ability or opportunity themselves to reproduce the music of the great masters, practically all can with training, learn to appreciate it, and to participate in the singing of folk songs and national anthems. Such participation will doubtless contribute toward international understanding and goodwill.

We are not convinced that every teacher can become a successful leader in music. Most schools can, however, be departmentalized to the extent of having the music classes taught by one especially gifted and trained for the work. In some rural schools, on the other hand, the teacher must direct all studies and activities. Teachers in training for these schools should have both native ability and training in music. All teachers should have at least as much training in music as is desirable for all pupils of the elementary and secondary schools.

Closely allied to folk songs, and also speaking a universal language, are the games and rhythmic activities of historical and contemporary peoples. Many such activities are common to primitive and civilized man. This common interest of mankind in games is very strikingly illustrated in the motley crowds that attend college football games, public baseball, and other such substitutions of universal interest and enthusiasm for universal participation. Teachers in training should learn to know and to participate in a variety of games and rhythmic movements and to be able to lead children in these activities. In highly organized school systems physical education teachers may be provided who will be familiar with the many national games and folk dances. In this connection teachers of physical education may join with teachers of art and world literature in reproducing the plays, games, and costumes of foreign peoples. This may become a very effective means of developing sympathetic international understanding. It comes near to demonstrating the truth of St. Paul's pronouncement that "God hath made of one blood all the nations of the earth." At any rate they all participate freely in a native tendency to play, to imitate, and to engage in rhythmic movements.

Another very important, but much neglected subject in teacher-training institutions is human geography. This neglect is also characteristic of the senior high schools; thus the student enters the teachers college defective in this type of knowledge, which is far more important to the majority of teachers than is geometry. Yet fateful tradition impels the colleges to require for entrance the one, while it neither requires for entrance nor gives adequate instruction in the other. A generation ago geography was a common study in secondary schools and in normal schools having preparatory departments. This was, however, as a rule, physical geography or physiography. The human geography recently introduced as a college subject is generally restricted to the relation of man to his physical environment and the interaction between these two. This is, of course, basic and important as an aspect of geography, but it is primarily only the foundation upon which adequate education in human geography should be built. It should be followed by direct study of the races and nationalities of mankind and the influences of social environment. Objection may be raised on the ground that this would be carrying geography into the fields of anthropology and sociology. If this be a valid conclusion the remedy lies not in neglect of these topics or in parceling them out to different departments in a teachers college, but rather in renaming the course. Call it, if you will, an orientation course in race and national characteristics and relationships. The artificial divisions of the sciences should not be allowed to impede development of the most effective curricula.

There are contemporary publications in abundance from which may be selected suitable readings for such a course. It should be taught by a person who is equipped by wide social contacts and sympathetic understanding of races and nationalities, in addition to his academic training; such a teacher can make a major contribution toward teacher training for international understanding and good-will.

Somewhat closely allied to this course is one in social psychology, which is now given either by the department of psychology or by that of sociology. Here again the conflicting claims of the departments should not be permitted to impede progress. The course should be given by the teacher who can best realize the objectives. This course should not be very technical, not a laboratory science patterned after physics. It should be more human than highly technical, more practical than theoretical, more a treatment of human nature as a whole in its social relations than a detailed study of phases of human nature abstracted from their concrete setting.

One of the troublesome problems of the teachers college administrator is to secure to students the practical results of the work of scholars in all fields without overwhelming them with the technical terms and procedures with which the specialist is concerned, and in which the non-specialist student victim may become lost, if not paralyzed. If the student is to be the beneficiary rather than the victim he should have opportunity to learn, in as simple terms as the subject will permit, the most fundamental outcomes and pedagogical applications of the principles of the human sciences studied. This purpose should determine the nature of the course in social psychology and the department or the instructor who is to give it.

It should not be inferred that the so-called individual psychology, including the psychology of the learning process, is to be neglected. Such a study may be a highly desirable prerequisite to the course in social psychology as well as a very necessary part of the equipment of a teacher. There remains, however, the fact that a course in social psychology such as has been here indicated may contribute very greatly to the teacher's understanding of people by groups and in group relationships, thus enabling him more successfully to develop in pupils that international understanding that is basic to good-will and the peace of the world.

What has been said of social geography and social psychology is also true in large measure of other social studies. This is especially true of history. But here again, as a rule, college courses in history are in practice too highly specialized. All students in a teachers college can not specialize in history. The courses, however, are often constructed for those who do. Thus, under prevailing practice, the majority of teachers college students may receive somewhat intensive training in one period of history at the expense of appalling ignorance of other periods, and with no clear conception of the general course of history, and of the debt that the peoples of the later periods owe to their predecessors. The history of modern Europe can not mean what it should to the student without knowledge of the civilizations of Palestine, Greece, and Rome; these, in turn, need to be illuminated by knowledge of the earlier civilizations of the Orient. The history teacher may readily agree with this, but may disagree concerning the remedy here suggested.

History specialists, like specialists in science, have generally been more successful in analysis and abstraction of parts of reality for detailed study than they have been in synthesis and interpretation of the meaning of the whole. For purposes of either historical or scientific investigations abstractions from the whole are doubtless justified. Teachers in the elementary and secondary schools, however, need to have these abstractions brought together in their concrete relationships, and interpreted as to their meaning for life and social living. We suggest, therefore, that history courses for teachers college students be reorganized along the lines of what is now being undertaken in the course in world history in secondary schools, but upon a somewhat broader, as well as more intensive scale.

The required history in a teachers college should be primarily a history of civilization from its beginnings with primitive man, and should include all the nations and races that have contributed toward developing all the types of civilization extant. There is now no justification for omitting from such history courses China, Japan, and India; nor need there be, for the majority of teachers college students separate courses in European and American history, to say nothing of the omission from so-called American history courses, of practically all reference to American history other than that of the United States, except as this nation has quarreled with fellow American nations.

Europe, North and South America, and some parts of Asia, Africa, Australia, and many islands of the seas have contributed toward development of a common civilization which now belongs not to any one nation or group of nations, but to all mankind. To make clear and impressive this fact should be a major objective of the history courses in the teachers college.

Akin to history and of major importance in developing international understanding and appreciation is biography. If not offered in teachers colleges as a separate course it may be attached to either the course in world history or the course in world literature as directed reading for information and character appreciation. The biographies read should be of persons who have made the most outstanding contributions to human well-being, whether physical, intellectual or spiritual. Such reading brings to mind most effectively the debt of each nation to other nations. Every teacher should become qualified to direct the biographical readings of young people. It is a source of many character values, in addition to its possible contribution to international understanding.

Also closely akin to history is the course in international relations, now offered as an elective in some institutions. In such a course the most momentous social and political problems of this generation may be dealt with directly and specifically. This is not to underestimate the importance of domestic social and political problems; these, too, should be studied most earnestly. But what, at any time, may become of domestic institutions and practices, so long as they are subject to the hazards of international lawlessness? Yet current international problems and institutions are but little understood by the great mass of citizens; and may not soon be adequately understood unless development of such understanding is made a major function of the schools. The most momentous undertakings of far sighted humanitarians and statesmen fall short of realization because citizens of a boasted democracy act upon their prejudices; and partisan politicians, on partisan interests rather than upon knowledge and proper evaluation of facts and principles. A course in international relations for all teachers will be one step in the direction of bringing about better understanding and more intelligent action on the part of the nations who are, or ought to be, cooperating in the peaceful solution of world problems. Such a course will, to be sure, include thorough study of the League of Nations, the World Court, the Paris Pact and all other important institutions and measures for world cooperation for the common good of mankind.

International dependence can be very strikingly illustrated in classes in economics. The material advantages of friendly cooperation in international trade are manifest to any one familiar with economic geography; the social and spiritual benefits, too, should not be overlooked. Economics, as a secondary school study at any rate, is relinquishing the coldly financial point of view. It is concerned rather with the influence of economic factors upon the total life of men, individually, and collectively. When this point of view becomes generally established through education, tariff wars will be no more; thus one great barrier to international cooperation will be removed. Knowledge of the fundamental principles and more especially of the ethical aspects of economics should be part of the equipment of every teacher.

International relations is so much a matter of government actions that it would seem to be quite necessary that teachers should engage in a study that passes under the name comparative governments. Every teacher should, of course, have a good working knowledge of his own government; but it is also important that he should understand and appreciate the merits of other civic forms of organization and administration. He should also know the handicaps of peoples who have to struggle with backward and reactionary governments, and be able to sympathize with them in their efforts toward civic reforms.

Finally, we suggest for consideration another very important, though much neglected study for teachers; namely, social ethics. Ethical considerations enter into the solution of all social problems. These considerations are of primary importance in the affairs of family, church, and state; they are also foundational to law and its administration. This applies with equal force to international law and to the conduct of international affairs.

Ethics has most commonly been thought of as relating to personal conduct and relations obtaining between persons, as such. This type of ethics has its place; we are, however, here concerned primarily with the relation of the individual to social institutions and of these institutions to each other. The use of ethical concepts in the discussion of current social problems is so common as to make the use of these concepts, clear or otherwise, almost as common as is use of the mother tongue. Yet in teacher training and secondary school curricula the subject of ethics is almost as universally neglected as were courses in the mother tongue a few generations ago. The mother tongue they already know, let them study something else, seems then to have been the assumption. Educational experience, however, has led to a policy of attempts to improve upon imperfect knowledge and use of mother tongue through courses especially designed to overcome these imperfections; this without relaxing indirect and more general methods of linguistic improvement. So now it seems generally to be taken for granted that the individuals of the high school and the college know what is right and what is wrong and therefore need no instruction in ethics. It is quite true that they may know the most common moral precepts in the abstract; it is also true that they may fail woefully in their attempts to apply these precepts to the complex problems of modern social life. They may even fail to carry over these precepts into their relations to industry and business, to say nothing of their relations to the state and to mankind at large, on the one hand, and to the interrelations of institutions, nations, and races, on the other.

Some educators intensely interested in the ethical aspects of the social studies have assumed that these aspects will be sufficiently brought out in each of the social studies without provision for a course in ethics as such. This assumption, as we have just pointed out, is comparable to that of making no provision for instruction in the mother tongue on the ground that it may be adequately cared for incidentally. In the one case there is need for correct usage, in the other case, for right moral judgments, but to secure these educational results there is in both cases also need of direct instruction by one who is especially prepared to teach the more difficult and technical phase of these subjects.

Language composition and social ethics are furthermore alike in that each draws upon other subjects for content. As one should not write chiefly about grammar and composition; so in the study of social ethics one's major concern is not with moral judgments in the abstract, but with their applications in the concrete situations of social, political and economic life. Without these concrete applications of ethical theory the study would be barren.

Ethical standards had their beginnings in the small group, clan or tribe. These standards were not universally applied to persons without the group or between groups. In ancient times the obligation of Greek to barbarian was not the same as that of Greek to Greek; that of Jew to Gentile not the same as that of Jew to Jew. As to extension of recognized ethical codes to the relations between the larger units, such as independent states, we are even now struggling to secure such recognition and to establish corresponding practices in international affairs. This result can be attained only by systematic, strenuous, and unrelenting effort. It is but yesterday that "gentlemen" settled their questions of personal honor by dueling; and questions of vital interest, by lawless means. These practices have now been supplanted by systematic means of determining and administering justice. It will be a great epoch in the history of ethics and of mankind when dueling and lawlessness between nations may be supplanted by international justice, fairly and peacefully determined. Why neglect in the teacher-training institutions a most important means of hastening the process?

In case the teacher-training course is too brief to include adequate instruction in separate courses in all of the subjects here listed and others essential to the preparation of teachers, it is possible to include in the course in social ethics many of the most fundamental problems of sociology, economics, and civics, treated from the ethical point of view. The course may be so organized as to become an orientation course for the social studies. Such usage is especially valuable in teacher training institutions.[2]

In summary it may be said that as practically every aspect of school curricula may make some contribution to international understanding, so may every aspect of teacher training curricula help to qualify teachers for their part in the process; toward this end, however, some subjects are more effective than others. For this reason in the reconstruction of teacher-training curricula emphasis should be given to development of adequate courses in world literature, music, art (including handicrafts), recreation in physical activities, social geography, world history, international relations, social psychology and social ethics, including important aspects of civics, economics and sociology. Emphasis upon these studies in four or more years of study and professional training beyond high school may do much toward bringing about better international understanding and extension of justice and good-will to all mankind.[3]

EDUCATIONAL EVENTS

BRITISH EDUCATION IN 1930

The annual report of the British Board of Education for the year 1930 has been published. According to a summary in the London *Times,* the board states that further considerable progress has been made in the reorganization of schools in accordance with the principles of the Hadow Report. The total number of existing departments affected by schemes of reorganization during the year was 1,202, as compared with 1,103, 742 and 552 for the three preceding years, while the number of existing departments reorganized during the nine months ending December 31, 1930, already amounted to

[2] See "Orientation through Social Ethics," *Journal of Higher Education,* May, 1931.

[3] Graduate students and experienced teachers of senior college standing may well add to this program of studies a course in "Comparative Education."

942, as compared with 807 for the same period of the previous year. The great number of new schools opened during the year were organized on Hadow lines. A classification made after consideration of the age statistics furnished by school authorities showed that the number of senior departments had risen from 883 on March 31, 1929, with 209,899 pupils of 11 years of age and over, to 1,017 on March 31, 1930, with 238,681 pupils of 11 years of age or over. These departments contained on March 31, 1930, 15.3 per cent. of the total number of pupils in public elementary schools aged 11 and over, as compared with 12.6 per cent. on the same date in the previous year. The number of departments classified as junior had risen from 2,518 with 500,126 pupils to 3,212 with 665,999 pupils. Of these the majority for junior boys and about half of those for junior girls were restricted to pupils over the age of seven on admission.

The reorganization movement has extended to voluntary as well as to council schools, and on March 31, 1930, there were in voluntary schools 151 senior departments (114 Church of England, 29 Roman Catholic and eight others), and 1,330 junior departments (1,181 Church of England, 109 Roman Catholic and 40 others). Voluntary school managers usually endeavor to redistribute the children in their schools between a group of schools belonging to the same denomination, but this is not always practicable, and the board is glad to be able again to record that there have been several instances during the year under review in which a friendly cooperation between the managers and the local education authority has resulted in arrangements being made for pupils from a junior voluntary school to proceed to a council senior school, or *vice versa*. The number of schools on March 31, 1930, was 20,803, with 30,429 departments, as compared with 20,747 schools with 30,522 departments on the same date in the previous year. The year was again one of great building activity on the part of local education authorities, the approved capital expenditure amounting to £5,509,505, as compared with £4,298,909 and £3,859,614 for the two preceding years.

Progress continued to be made in the elimination of large classes. The total number of classes with over 50 pupils on the register fell from 10,883 on March 31, 1929, to 10,017 on March 31, 1930. There were on that date only 306 senior classes (limited to children over 11) with more than 50 pupils, as compared with 514 on March 31, 1929. In addition, the number of senior classes containing more than 40 but not more than 50 fell from 6,362 to 5,193. The total number of children on the register of public elementary schools maintained by local education authorities on March 31, 1930, was 5,527,113, as compared with 5,512,283 in the previous year. A considerable improvement is reported in the provision made for practical instruction in the case of pupils over 11, and in particular there has been an increase in the number of departments which make provision for this important subject on the school premises.

The number of secondary schools recognized by the board as eligible for grant continues to increase and on March 31, 1930, reached a total of 1,354, as compared with 1,341 in 1929. The number of pupils was 394,105, as compared with 386,933 in 1929. Of 66,741 pupils who left grant-aided secondary schools in 1929–30 after reaching the age of 14, 2,477 boys and 1,352 girls were known to have proceeded direct to universities. Of these 64.3 per cent. were ex-public elementary school pupils. For the previous year the corresponding figures were 2,336 boys and 1,302 girls out of 67,998. The increase in the number of students at continuation, technical and commercial schools still continues and particularly those attending evening courses.

EXPENDITURES ON MEDICAL INSPECTION IN THE SCHOOLS OF THE UNITED STATES

THE Federal Office of Education in studying the amount spent on medical inspection in the schools of the United States finds that the expenditures for medical, including dental, inspection in cities with a population of 100,000 or more average about 67 cents per child of the school census population.

The minimum expenditure is 7.7 cents and the maximum is $2.55. Where the expenditures are given separately, the comparative cost of dental work runs from one seventh of that for medical inspection to, in two cities, an excess over medical inspection. Probably in most of the cities there is considerable expenditure for treatment of dental defects.

For medical inspection in the group alone the average expenditure reported separately by 22 cities was 43 cents per child. For dental inspection in these same cities the expenditure was 17 cents per child. The medical and dental costs are probably mostly for salaries.

The expenditure for physical education was $1.21 per child as the average for the 18 cities of this group reporting. Probably this was chiefly for salaries of special teachers. The highest expenditure was $2.85 per child (school census) and the lowest 8 cents per child. It is quite probable that in the cities reporting very low expenditures most of the teaching is done by regular teachers.

Only three cities reported separately expenditures for "health education" and only seven for "nutrition work." For the latter the average cost was 6 cents per child. The average expenditure by six cities for "mental hygiene" (whatever this might include) was 9½ cents per child.

In reply to the question, "What official is in charge of all of your health work?" 23 superintendents (about one third) replied, "A director of health," or "director of hygiene"; four answered "The director of medical inspection"; one "The director of physical welfare"; one "The superintendent," and one "The assistant superintendent." The remaining cities of this group did not answer the question.

Turning to the group of cities with a population ranging from 30,000 to 100,000 the following facts were ascertained:

In the 56 cities furnishing data an average of 81 cents per child (school census) is paid for medical and dental inspection. The highest is $2.10 and the lowest 9 cents per child. In the same cities an average of $1.32 per child is paid for physical education, with a maximum of nearly $5 and a minimum of 14 cents.

Figures for the cost of health education were given by 13 cities (and in all but one separately for physical education). The average expenditure per pupil under this heading in these cities was 65 cents; the highest $1.78, and the lowest 11 cents. In the city spending the highest for "health education" the expenditures for "physical education" were $1.85 or approximately the same. In some cities these were five times as high as for "health education." In the 10 cities reporting expenditures for mental hygiene the average was 19 cents per child.

THE EDWARD S. HARKNESS LIBRARY AND SCHOOL OF LIBRARY SERVICE AT COLUMBIA UNIVERSITY

ACCORDING to *The New York Times* plans were filed on October 19 for the six-story Edward S. Harkness Library and School of Library Service to be built by Columbia University in 114th Street between Amsterdam Avenue and Broadway. James Gamble Rogers, the architect, estimated the cost of the building at $3,500,000.

The structure will be 107.10 feet high and will occupy a plot 264.8 by 167.4 feet, taking up a part of South Field. It will face the Low Memorial Library, long since outgrown, which in the future will be used to house special collections and manuscripts, an exhibition hall and offices of the president, secretary and trustees.

Excavations on the site are virtually completed, the contractors are expected to start construction without delay. The schedule calls for opening the structure for the fall session in 1933.

The design will be in harmony with the other buildings of the university group. The library's capacity at first will be 2,900,000 volumes, but stacks may be carried higher when needed to provide an ultimate capacity of 4,000,000 volumes, making the building one of the largest college library structures in the country. The Sterling Library at Yale has an ultimate capacity of about 5,000,000 volumes. The present Low Memorial Library, built thirty-five years ago, has a capacity of 750,000 volumes. Since the university's collection is almost double that total, the overflow and various special collections have been scattered about in seven or eight buildings.

A feature of the layout in the new building will be the concentration of the fifteen tiers of stacks, many of which will measure 154 by 80 feet, in the center of the library, leaving all outside space free for windows and reading quarters. The basement facilities will include a lecture room seating 300.

On the first floor will be the Columbia College reading room, eight seminar rooms and two reserved book rooms. The main reading room, which will measure 200 by 48 feet, with a ceiling height of more than 30 feet, will be on the north side of the second floor, overlooking South Field. On this floor also will be the administrative offices, periodical and reference rooms, cataloguing department and a browsing room. The browsing room, intended for leisure perusal of standard literature, will be equipped with eighty easy chairs and floor lamps.

Fourteen graduate reading and research rooms will be provided on the third floor, each for a different department of the university classes. The School of Library Service, now in old East Hall, will have expanded facilities on the fourth and fifth floors of the library. The sixth floor will be given over to stacks.

RESIDENTIAL COLLEGES OF YALE UNIVERSITY

DR. JAMES ROWLAND ANGELL, president of Yale University, has announced the names of three of the new colleges in the university's residential quadrangle plan. One of the colleges now remains to be named. Dr. Angell also announced the assignment of masters to the nine colleges.

The college which will include the Sterling Quadrangle on Elm Street, between High and York Streets, has been named Trumbull College, in honor of Jonathan Trumbull, Revolutionary patriot and Governor of Connecticut. The college now under construction at Elm and College Streets, on the site of the former Divinity School buildings, has been named Calhoun College, in honor of Senator John C. Calhoun, of South Carolina, who was graduated from Yale in 1804. The name of the other college, now being erected on the south side of Old Library Street, which will include Wheelock and Dickinson Halls, will be Jonathan Edwards College, in honor of Jonathan Edwards, theologian and metaphysician, who was graduated from Yale in 1720.

The masters assigned to the colleges follow:

Professor Alan C. Valentine, to Pierson.

Professor H. Emerson Tuttle, to John Davenport.

Professor Robert Dudley French, to Jonathan Edwards.

Dean Clarence Whittlesey Mendell, to Branford.

Professor Elliott Dunlap Smith, to Saybrook.

Professor Stanhope Bayne-Jones, to Trumbull.

Provost Charles Seymour, to Berkeley.

Professor Arnold Whitridge, to Calhoun.

Dean Charles H. Warren, of the Sheffield Scientific School, will be master of the unnamed college to be erected in Vanderbilt Square.

The university expects to inaugurate the "House Plan" in 1933, when there will be a total of eleven colleges. The entire program is being financed by Mr. Edward S. Harkness, who also provided funds for the Harvard "House Plan" which has been opened with seven houses.

The first two of the Yale colleges, Pierson and John Davenport, have been opened this fall and now are being occupied by members of the Class of '35. They are across York Street from the Memorial Quadrangle and occupy more than half a block. Designed along Colonial Georgian lines, their general plan consists of two large courts, each surrounded by connected buildings. Each has a building, still unfinished, for a dining room, commons and library.

SALARY INCREASES AT WESLEYAN UNIVERSITY

THE trustees of Wesleyan University, at the time of the centennial celebration, announced the inauguration of a new plan for professorial salaries. Establishment of the plan is made possible by the expected receipt by the college, during the year 1932, of the income of approximately a half million dollars. It is possible that the amount available in succeeding years will be greater. This annual grant to the college comes from Mrs. Charles L. Denison, of Saddle River, New Jersey, whose husband was a trustee for three years prior to his death. In his will, Mr. Denison left the college, subject to Mrs. Denison's use during her life, half of his estate, for endowment purposes; it is estimated that the ultimate gift will be considerably over a million dollars, the largest gift in Wesleyan's history. To inaugurate the plan, in which Mr. Denison took much interest, Mrs. Denison is assigning to Wesleyan part of the income of the estate.

By resolution of the board, the new plan recognizes a normal professorial salary, which shall apply to the professors on the Wesleyan faculty, numbering approximately thirty. Beyond that, all salary increases will be voted by the trustees, on a term basis—usually three years—the choice of men to receive the additional award being based on superiority in teaching, influence on undergraduates, eminence as a scholar, intellectual growth and service to the college and the community. The selection is made through the ratification by the board of the nominees submitted by the executive committee. The awards are payable in two semi-annual instalments; they do not apply during sabbatical leave.

The action taken in early October will result in additional compensation to six professors on the basis of $2,500 extra for a calendar year, and to eight professors on the basis of $1,250 extra. If funds are available in the future, the plan will be continued; and if the funds increase, and the board so decides, possibly an even larger number of men will be included in the plan.

The fundamental basis of this plan was announced by Willbur Fisk, the first president of Wesleyan, in his inaugural in September, 1831. He stated that he was not in favor of permanency of tenure, irrespective of the quality of a professor's service, and strongly advocated that the professors on the Wesleyan faculty should have differentiated salaries, based on superiority. Although there has been some slight differentiation in professorial salaries during the first century of Wesleyan's history, this plan, instituted in the hundred and first year, is really the first definite embodiment of Willbur Fisk's original proposal of a hundred years ago.

EDUCATION WEEK

THE National Education Association as a preface to its program for American Education Week states that the purpose of the 1931 program is to point to the significant accomplishments of the schools and to maintain and increase the support of public education in this country. The general theme is to be "What the Schools are Helping America to Achieve." The program proposed for the week is as follows:

MONDAY, NOVEMBER 9—Theme: *What the Schools are Helping America to Achieve in Economic Progress.* Show how education increases and refines human wants, making larger demands upon the products of industry and business. Show how schools help students select occupations for which they are best fitted because of their interests and abilities, and give training in vocations, helping industry and business effectively to staff and man large-scale operations. Point out the work of the schools in promoting ideals of honesty and ethics without which modern business could not be transacted. Show how the schools contribute to the stability of government without the protection of which business and industry could not operate.

TUESDAY, NOVEMBER 10—Theme: *What the Schools are Helping America to Achieve in Child Health and Protection.* The work of the White House Conference on Child Health and Protection, carried on under the direction of President Hoover and Secretary of the Interior Wilbur, has recently been completed. Many of its findings are now available for use in school and community. They constitute a great charter of the rights of American childhood to a fair start in life. They should be in every city and school library. This topic offers an opportunity to familiarize the community with the epoch-making recommendations of the White House Conference. (Have citizens inventory the child welfare provisions of the entire community in light of these recommendations.) Show what the schools do to protect children from poor health, exploitation and moral delinquency.

WEDNESDAY, NOVEMBER 11—Theme: *What the Schools are Helping America to Achieve in Citizenship and Loyalty to Law.* Visualize the schools as the great unifying force in American life. It is universal education which makes our widely separated people one in loyalty and devotion to the flag and the constitution. Show how our schools encourage youth to emulate the lives of our country's noblest characters; how they create a respect for our national aims, and inspire a sense of responsibility for personal right, conduct and observance of law. Point out the dependence of a democratic form of government upon enlightened citizens. Explain the work of the schools in teaching the privileges and duties of citizenship.

THURSDAY, NOVEMBER 12—Theme: *What the Schools are Helping America to Achieve in the Improvement of Rural Living.* Farm life faces a reconstruction that is as fundamental as the industrial revolution. These far-reaching readjustments call for the most capable leadership the nation can produce. Many of these leaders must come directly from the farm. Point out this challenge to the rural school to train farm youth for new needs and new conditions. Show what has already been done in spite of meager support. Agriculture is firmly based on the solid rock of human necessity. From the farm have come many of our great leaders in politics, business and the professions. Upon agriculture the whole world depends for food. Show why a fair start in life for the rural child should be of concern to every citizen.

Friday, November 13—Theme: *What the Schools are Helping America to Achieve through a Higher Level of Intellectual Life.* Point out the contribution the schools have made to the welfare of the nation in even the simplest and most common skills they teach—the ability to read and write. Education for all extends far beyond these fundamentals. American citizens have attained the highest average intellectual life ever enjoyed by any nation. Show what this means in increased enrichment of living and the general advance of civilization.

Saturday, November 14—Theme: *What the Schools are Helping America to Achieve through the Enrichment of Adult Life.* Since psychologists have shown that youth is not the only learning age, adults have applied themselves in increasing numbers to study and the development of new skills. Increased opportunities for adults in night schools, in colleges and libraries have been the result. Show the growing significance to individual happiness and national welfare of facilities which enable adults to spend their constantly expanding leisure time in these worthwhile ways. Survey the adult education opportunities of your community and point out ways in which they may be improved and extended.

Sunday, November 15—Theme: *What the schools are Helping America to Achieve through High Ideals of Character and Home Life.* Plan the cooperation of home and school and church in inspiring noble character based upon high ideals and wholesome habits. Ideals and habits grow largely out of the environment in which people live. It is the privilege of home and school and church to promote the clean and elevating activities of community life. The churches will usually take the lead in carrying out this program, which may well be the theme for an entire Sunday service.

The Division of Publications of the National Education Association, 1201 Sixteenth Street, Northwest, Washington, D. C., will send free to any teacher or school officer an outline of the program for American Education Week, with suggestions for carrying it out. The Division of Publications has prepared bulletins and posters to use locally during and previous to American Education Week. These may be obtained ready to use at the cost of publication and distribution, or they may be reproduced in school printshops or in other economical ways, and used in whatever way local committees find most effective.

EDUCATIONAL NOTES AND NEWS

Dr. Karl Tinsley Waugh, professor of psychology at Long Island University and previously dean of the College of Arts and Sciences of the University of Southern California, was elected to the presidency of Dickinson College on October 10. Dr. Waugh succeeds Dr. Mervin G. Filler, who died last March. He will assume his new duties about December 1.

Dr. Robert E. McConnell, who has been head of the department of education at the Washington State Normal School at Cheney, has been elected president of the Washington State Normal School at Ellensburg.

The Reverend Archimandrites Gerasimos Ellias has been chosen from among 250 ministers of the Greek Orthodox Church in the United States and Canada to become the head of the Hellenic Greek American College, which has been established in Gastonia, N. C.

Dr. Virginia C. Gildersleeve, dean of Barnard College, has been granted leave of absence for the present academic year. Miss Gertrude Vority Rich has been appointed to the position of assistant dean of the college.

Mrs. Rufus Jones, assistant to Miss Josephine P. Simrall, dean of women at the University of Cincinnati, has presented her resignation. She will be succeeded by Mrs. M. F. Little.

The following appointments to the faculty of Teachers College, Columbia University, have been announced: Dr. F. Ernest Johnson, Dr. Edmund deS. Brunner, Dr. Heber Harper, professors of education.

Four appointments of professorial rank have been made by the University of Maine. These appointments with the departments concerned are: Dr. Alfred C. Andrews, as assistant professor of Latin; Dr. George B. Fundenburg, as associate professor of French; Dr. Lillian M. Hatfield, as assistant professor of psychology, and Miss Helene Heye, as assistant professor of home economics.

New appointments have been made as follows to the Bowdoin College faculty: The Reverend Maurice Roy Ridley, of Balliol College, Oxford, England, will be the visiting professor of English literature and Ernst Christian Helmreich will be a new instructor in history and government. Rhinehart Launde Korgen will be instructor in mathematics. Frederick W. Pickard, of Wilmington, Delaware, one of the trustees, will again provide for a teaching fellow in French and also one in Spanish. Ivan de Tarnowsky, who has been selected as teaching fellow in French, is a graduate of the Lycée de Nice. The teaching fellow in Spanish is to be Argimiro Martinez, of Santiago, Chile.

Mr. Archibald Cameron has been appointed to the position of Regius professor of Greek in the University of Aberdeen, in the place of Professor John Harrower, LL.D, whose resignation took effect on September 30.

Mr. Thomas Malcolm Knox has been appointed lecturer in philosophy at Jesus College, Oxford.

Professor George W. Burns, assistant dean of the College of Engineering and Commerce, University of Cincinnati, has been elected president of the American Association of Cooperative Colleges.

Mr. Arthur K. Loomis, director of the department of curriculum of the Denver public schools since 1925, has taken up his work with the University of Chicago as director of the laboratory high school and associate professor of education. Mr. C. L. Cushman has been appointed to succeed Mr. Loomis as director of the department of curriculum.

Mr. George S. Palmer, chairman of the trustees of Connecticut College for the last ten years, tendered his resignation at the first board meeting of the year held at the college. He will continue to serve in the newly created office of honorary chairman. Mr. Harrison B. Freeman was elected new chairman of the board.

Dr. John L. Lamonte, of the University of Minnesota, has been appointed assistant professor of history at the College of Liberal Arts, University of Cincinnati.

Dr. Henry A. Jeep, professor of education at the State Teachers College, Mayville, South Dakota, has accepted a similar position at the Ball State Teachers College at Muncie, Indiana.

Professor Don May, son of the late President S. T. May, of the Dickinson State Teachers' College, North Dakota, who has served as superintendent of the Willow City schools for four years, has accepted a position as superintendent of the U. S. Indian School at Santa Fe, New Mexico.

Mr. Paul L. Essert has been appointed to a newly established position of supervisor of high school instruction in the Denver schools.

Dr. Harry M. Crooks, president of Alma College, has been elected moderator of the Presbyterian Church.

President Hoover received an honorary degree from the College of William and Mary as part of the sesquicentennial celebration at Yorktown, Virginia, on October 19.

The decoration of Officer of Public Instruction, of the French Government, has been conferred upon the Rev. Dr. Matthew L. I. Fortier, dean of the school of sociology at Fordham University. The award is in recognition of the school's work in cooperation with the Catholic Charities of New York.

Dr. George C. Wood, professor of education in the extension session of Hunter College, has left for San Francisco for an eight months' trip around the world. He will make a special study of teaching in Japan, China, India, France, Belgium and England.

Dr. Ernest L. Sabine, of the department of English of Ball State Teachers College, Muncie, Indiana, has returned after a year's leave of absence spent in London, where he has been engaged in research work under the auspices of the Rockefeller Foundation.

Dr. James Sullivan, who recently retired from the position of assistant commissioner for higher and professional education of New York State, died on October 9 at the age of fifty-eight years.

Mr. Walter L. Brown, formerly president of the American Library Association and for fifty-five years connected with the Buffalo Public Library, died on October 16, at the age of seventy-one years.

Dr. Henry Barrett Learned, professor of history at Stanford University, died on October 14, at the age of sixty-three years.

More than 500 teachers in elementary schools, superintendents, deans of teachers colleges and other educators are expected to attend a conference on the reorganization and revision of curricula for public schools to be held under the auspices of the school of education of Northwestern University on October 30 and 31. Among the principal speakers at the conference will be Herbert B. Bruner, of Columbia University; G. W. Willett, of the LaGrange High School; Will French, associate superintendent of public schools, Tulsa, Oklahoma; Dr. Leonard V. Koos, school of education, University of Chicago; Harold O. Rugg, Lincoln School, Teachers College, Columbia University, and John E. Stout, dean of the school of education of Northwestern University. The morning and evening of the first day of the conference will be devoted to general sessions. In the afternoon of the first day and all the second day, small groups will meet for round-table discussions of problems affecting public school curricula.

The tenth session of the International Child Welfare Association will be held at Lisbon, Portugal, from October 25 to 29.

The will of Charles H. Ditson, music publisher, bequeathed $100,000 each to Harvard, Yale, Columbia and Princeton Universities, to the New England Conservatory of Music in Boston, to the College of Music in Cincinnati, to the Ann Arbor School of Music, and to the Chicago Musical College.

The Latin-American Exchange Fellowships of the John Simon Guggenheim Foundation will be available to Porto Ricans for the first time in 1932. The island is to be included as a separate unit in the fellowship plan. The scholarships, the normal stipend for which is $2,500 a year, are also available to citizens of Argentina, Chile, Cuba and Mexico for work in the United States and to citizens of the United States for work in Latin America. It is expected that candidates will generally be graduates of universities or professional schools. Mr. Henry Allen Moe is secretary of the foundation.

Ten coordinated services are offered in the new health center dedicated in Cleveland on July 28, to function under the health and public welfare departments of the city. The center, formerly the Babies' and Children's Dispensary, now contains a tuberculosis clinic, an x-ray diagnostic clinic, infant welfare station, school health service, public health nursing service, housing and sanitation department, prevention of blindness department, supervision of boarding homes for children, babies' dispensary and maternity dispensary. Located in a congested district, it will serve about 100,000 persons, the health authorities have estimated. Western Reserve University will cooperate in all the services of the center.

A laboratory of child research has been established at Mooseheart, Illinois, the institution for dependent children of deceased members of the Loyal Order of Moose. The plans for the new laboratory were worked out by a conference of experts called together by Dr. E. A. Doll, present director of the research laboratory of the Training School at Vineland, New Jersey, which for 43 years has done notable work in training those "whose minds have not developed normally." In addition to the practical service which the new laboratory will offer in solving the behavior and school problems of the children of Mooseheart, it is believed that the population of 1,300 physically and mentally normal children of both sexes, ranging in age from infancy to that of high-school graduates, with an average stay at the institution of about eight years, will offer unusual opportunities for valuable contributions to the general problems of child research. Information in the form of medical, school and family records will be available to aid in the work. The new laboratory will have the assistance of an advisory council of nationally known scientists. Close cooperation with other research centers and with universities will be sought, and opportunities to use the laboratory's facilities will be accorded to interested and qualified persons. Fellowships consisting chiefly of maintenance will be offered to graduate students.

THREE thousand teachers, who will have to take a 15 per cent. pay cut under the British government's economy plan, marched through the streets of London recently to Kingsway Hall, where they passed a resolution protesting against the reduction. "This mass meeting of members of the National Union of Teachers and the London Teachers' Association protests emphatically against the government's indefensible proposals to reduce teachers' salaries," the resolution said. "It voices the bitter resentment of teachers that they should be selected as a special class for harsh and unjust treatment, and pledges itself to support the executive of the National Union of Teachers in strong determined measures to resist this penal and vindictive cut." Most of those who marched in the parade were young men. They carried small banners reading: "Schoolmasters protest" and "No cuts."

THE Board of Control of Mental Health Services, with the approval of the British Minister of Health, has, according to a report in the London *Times,* appointed the following to advise the board upon questions arising in connection with scientific and ancillary mental health services: Mr. L. G. Brock, *chairman;* Sir Hubert Bond, Mr. Robert Bruford, Mr. W. E. Lovsey, Mr. T. S. Good, Dr. Adeline Roberts, Mr. J. C. Grime, Professor J. Shaw Bolton and Mr. P. Barter, *secretary.* The mental treatment act, which came into operation on January 1, confers upon local authorities powers to provide for outpatient treatment and for the after-care of mental patients, and, subject to the approval of the board of control, to undertake or to contribute to research in regard to mental illness. The board of control has appointed the advisory committee to assist them in the consideration of schemes of research submitted for the board's approval, and in regard to such questions as the organization of social services in connection with outpatient treatment and after-care, on which local authorities may seek the board's guidance. On technical questions relating to research the advisory committee will have the expert advice of members of the Medical Research Council's committee on mental disorders.

THE *Museum News* reports that a standing commission on museums to act in a general advisory capacity has been appointed by the British Government. The commission is constituted as follows: Viscount D'Abernon, *chairman;* J. B. Beresford, of the treasury, *secretary;* Evan E. Charteris; Sir Richard Tetley Glazebrook; Lord Hanworth, the Earl of Harewood; Sir George MacDonald; Sir Henry A. Miers; Charles Reed Peers, and Sir Philip Sassoon, M.P. The functions of the commission are: (1) To advise generally on questions relative to the most effective development of the national institutions as a whole, and on any specific questions which may be referred to them from time to time; (2) to promote cooperation between the national institutions themselves, and between the national and provincial institutions; (3) to stimulate the generosity and direct the efforts of those who aspire to become public benefactors.

Izvestia, the official organ of the Soviet, states that a special university with one and two years' courses is to be opened in Leningrad for the foreign manual workers employed in the U.S.S.R.

A DISPATCH to the New York *Sun* states that the Chinese government has decided to subsidize schools of journalism in several government and private universities of China, beginning with the school year opening this month. The people's conference last spring recommended immediate action to improve Chinese newspapers. A department of journalism was established in St. John's University in Shanghai several years ago. The first school of journalism was established in Yenching University, a mission school in Peiping, a few years later. The success of these experiments has attracted official attention.

ACCORDING to the results of the physical examination performed by the school physicians in Tokyo last year, among 203,097 primary school children, 23,388 (23.02 per cent.) were in need of medical observation, which was a decrease of 0.16 per cent. in comparison with that of 1929. The number of children with carious teeth amounted to 182,175 (more than 17.9 per cent.).

WE learn from the *Journal of Education* that the adoption of a phonetic sign system is the latest step of the Chinese Ministry of Education in fighting illiteracy among the masses. With the masses engaged in fighting each other or trying to promote the spread of communism, the success of the venture is problematical, but that the idea is good seems to be the opinion of both Chinese and foreign educators. The system consists of forty phonetic signs and as a whole will resemble the alphabet system. The signs are not intended to take the place of Chinese characters, but are so arranged as to enable illiterate Chinese to read their own books and newspapers. All schools that remain under the Nanking stndard this fall will be forced to use the new system, and all industrial establishments have been ordered to give their workers instruction in it.

AN enrolment of 345 and a graduating class of twenty-two are reported by the New York *Times* for the Albanian Vocational School, which is supported by the American Junior Red Cross. The attendance was the best in the history of the institution. Eight of the graduates were from the mechanical and electrical courses, six from the agricultural courses, and eight from the normal course for teachers. To the faculty during the year were added three new teachers. The staff now numbers eighteen Albanians, two Americans, two Czechoslovaks, one German and one Russian. One of the school's former graduates is in charge of light and power equipment at Durazzo. Another directs the light plant at Valona, a city of 8,000 population. A third is taking advanced work in mechanics at Yeovil, England. Others are in positions of leadership in progressive agriculture. Junior members of the American Red Cross contributed to the establishment and support of the Albanian Vocational School as part of their program of international good-will and helpfulness to children of limited opportunity.

A DISPATCH to the *Christian Science Monitor* says that an order from the Ministry of Education states that in the future all foreign and minority schools must employ Turkish professors to teach Turkish pupils geography, history and civics, in the Turkish language. The order, which states that these subjects must be taught according to the general prospectus followed in all Turkish schools, comes only a month before reopening, with the result that these institutions are unable to cancel contracts already concluded with foreign professors for the next term. The Turkish authorities have every right to impose such restrictions, but the American ambassador intends to make a personal appeal to them for one year's postponement of the order to obviate financial loss, for which the American schools become liable.

DISCUSSION

SCHOOL NEWS FOR THE MAN WHO RUNS

ABOUT ten minutes, newspaper men hold, is the average life of an edition of a metropolitan daily. It is read under all sorts of handicaps in all conceivable—and in some inconceivable—places. Hastily readers turn its pages in crowded street-cars, in cafés filled with a medley of noises, in bus stations and on street corners. Even those who are fortunate enough to be able to linger over the evening edition at home in a comfortable chair are usually too tired to read anything that does not make a rather direct and vigorous appeal.

Newspaper men know this and have mastered the art of swift narration and of bringing into relief significant particulars of the apparently commonplace. The young reporter soon learns that he must write for "the man who runs," and that he must sense the element of strongest appeal in everything that he handles. It is his business to search the byways as well as the highways for any circumstance or incident that under his touch will hold the interest for a minute or two of the vast, always curious, newspaper-scanning world.

Of all the sources of news none has from day to day deeper and richer appeals than the public schools. That this fertile field has been little more than scratched is in the main due not so much to negligence as to partial or total inability of school people to recognize and to write such school news as is not perfectly obvious. It is vastly encouraging, however, to note that from year to year the big dailies are telling the public more about the children in the schools and the work of the schools. A large part of the credit must surely go to the newspaper editors, who, realizing the potential news values of the school, have appointed education editors and in some cases have given whole pages to school news. But school authorities, too, in many cities are meeting the papers half way by including on the staff a director of publicity, who is presumed to have both journalistic and educational training. His work, however, no matter how industrious and omnipresent he may become, can interpret adequately the schools and tap their multitudinous founts of interest only when the school executives and teachers train themselves to a better recognition and a more skilful handling of school news.

Given some training in writing news, as teachers in Cleveland are given it,[1] the vast majority of teachers would without doubt enter gladly into any concerted program directed toward telling the public everything of interest about the schools. Without that training they find themselves uncertain as to what constitutes news, and even when it is clearly recognized as news, they are bewildered and ineffectual in writing it so that its appealing features will be patent to others.

Every one has his own theories as to what constitutes news. Definitions are as numerous as they are varied. It is, however, rather generally agreed that for anything to be news it must interest a large group of people. Sometimes this interest is secured through what is known as straight news; sometimes it is reached and held through the emotions in a feature or human interest story. Straight news with appeal to the universal interest in preservation of life, in liberty, in famous names, the unusual, the unexpected, loss of life or property, the mysterious, the heroic, the pathetic, the great achievement, the great sacrifice fills the columns, interspersed here and there with feature stories which quicken the heart with generous emotions or entertain with humorous incident.

> This week over 20,000 young people are marching back to school.
>
> Movie-making is the unusual activity undertaken this semester by students of Lowry Junior High School.

These and a hundred other stories of the child in his school life greet the fathers and mothers of the city, of all America, every day and are read because, when correctly focused by the news writer, they are rich in elemental appeal. Farley[2] gathered approximately 2,000 school news stories and articles on every conceivable school topic. His study gives further impetus to the conviction that news waits everywhere in the school system. Yet a dull and formal account can kill the interest in any story. Witness the all-too-common reports of Parent-Teacher meetings. How does the experienced schoolman but inexperienced news-writer go about his story? Usually it gets under way in somewhat this fashion:

> The third regular meeting of the Florin district Parent-Teacher Association was held at the Noble school last night. The meeting was called to order. . . .

That is about as far as the average reader would get before abandoning the story for a gangster killing in the next column. But the story was not without interest. Here it is again with its opening sentence or lead written by a trained reporter:

> Instead of sitting in the corner and making up poetry about "Backward, turn backward, oh Time, in your flight, make me a child again, just for to-night," several hundred Detroit adults went ahead and looked after the matter themselves, Tuesday night. . . .

The reporter then carries the willing reader through a lively account of how the parents tried out the children's schedule in the children's rooms and seats.

Innovations in the curriculum, special projects, honors, programs, health—anything about the school may have its point of appeal if it can be written properly. The news may be timely, that is, about something that has just

[1] C. R. Miller and Fred. Charles, "Publicity and the Public School," Houghton Mifflin Company, New York, p. 154.

[2] B. M. Farley, "What to Tell the People about the Public Schools," Teachers College, Columbia University. Contributions to Education, 1929, p. 62*ff*.

happened or has just been announced. The value of such stories depends in large measure upon how soon they can be printed. There are many school news stories, on the other hand, which are as good in one edition of a paper as in another; they are timeless. Here, for example:

> Feeling that the world is badly in need of Spring songs, 50 pupils of grades 3 to 6 throughout the city compose songs, which they have sent to the directing supervisor of music.[3]

The charm and incidentally the news value of this story lie largely in the manner of expression. Those who believe that news, especially straight news, stories must be so packed that they have nothing of the whimsical, fanciful, startling would do well to read the papers more carefully. School news, more than crime, scandal or accident, has need of the adroit touch, the careful analysis of appeals. When the vital germ of news is obscured in a fog of pedagogical terms, as it too often is in reports of school officers to the press, one can not blame the reader for saying the next day, "I didn't notice it." The searchlight of the reporter's art must point surely and swiftly to something in the fact or incident that is bound up closely with man's life. If the language used is unfamiliar to the reader or the news account begins with a dull recording of unimportant details, the writer has lost his reader before he ever won him.

Let us for the sake of illustration take a situation which might conceivably arise in any school. The children of the school have been taught economy in all things and have been saving their pennies diligently. But winter has settled over the city, and two children, brother and sister, have decided to give all their savings, $20, to the teacher to buy shoes for the poor little children of the room who need them and can't buy them.

Too often this beautiful story would be allowed to escape a world that beneath its brusqueness has a deep vein of tenderness. What would better illustrate the character building of the school than this incident? The story is not difficult to write, and a picture of the two children might well be sent along as adding value for the newspapers. Here is how one reporter begins his story:

> Virginia and Frank Eaton, students at the Cooper school, believe that "Charity begins at home," in this case, the school room.
>
> Virginia, 10 years old, and Frank, 6, are the children of ——— ———. They had heard so much about the present hard times. . . .

The story goes on to tell of the decision, of bringing the money to the teacher, of how they had saved it, etc. This story is of the feature type, the value of which is not in its intrinsic news but in its emotional appeal. Such stories with human interest backgrounds find an unlimited field in education.

When teachers have learned through newspaper study and imitation or through special courses to be sensitive to the news values in the activities of the children and to interpret them in the light of basic appeals, the schools will inevitably enjoy more sympathetic relations with the public.

J. Erle Grinnell

Stanford University

[3] *Ibid.*, p. 66.

AFTER PLACEMENT—WHAT?

Occasionally one hears of a college which feels no responsibility for the placement of graduates who have made preparation within its walls for teaching positions. Recently a senior in such an institution told of efforts to find a position, without assistance. After writing eighty letters of application, she was elected to teach in a school where she stayed one year, although in work for which she was not really adapted. Such stories are rare, however, and we may assume that the practice is fairly well established in most of our colleges, of maintaining some systematic organization and procedure for placement of graduates who have made the proper preparation for the teaching profession.

Less common, however, is the practice of following up such beginners, with endeavors to readjust those who may prove to be improperly placed or at least to be making a poor start. Can we rightly say that we have fulfilled our moral obligation to these young people, when we have found for them their first "job"? Is it altogether their own responsibility thereafter whether they make mediocre or superior teachers—whether they survive or perish? Further than this, is it not possible that the college itself will profit by keeping in touch with them after such placement?

Intermountain Union is a college of liberal arts, a goodly proportion (about 60 per cent.) of whose graduates enter the teaching profession. For some years it has been the custom at Intermountain to carry on follow-up work of several types, and results secured have fully justified the time and trouble, in the minds of those who have had it in charge.

The appointment bureau, which is under the direction of the department of education, keeps a permanent file of credentials for all graduates requesting it, and from year to year alumni are calling for such service in increasing numbers. This part of the program is not unusual and needs no further mention except to note that it plays an important part in maintaining a friendly spirit toward the institution.

About the middle of the beginner's first year of teaching, a letter of inquiry is sent to the supervising principal or superintendent. This letter is worded somewhat as follows:

> Intermountain Union College is much interested to know whether our graduates are making good, and if not, in what respects they are falling short.
>
> Mr. A—— B—— is representing us in your school system and we should much appreciate a report from you as to his success, both as a teacher and as a member of your community. Such reports help us to decide what we need to do to train the next class of prospective teachers. Anything you say will be treated as strictly confidential.
>
> We thank you for your cooperation.

Executives have been most cordial and cooperative in their replies, and while they have expressed most hearty commendation of good work, in many cases they have described very frankly the difficulties encountered and the weaknesses shown by the teacher. One superintendent expressed his appreciation of the interest taken by the college as indicated by the inquiry, saying that it was new in his experience. These confidences are respected in every case, but if there is reason to think that conditions might be improved by kindly advice or assistance, request is made of the writer, for permission to correspond with the teacher concerned. In some instances, noticeable improvement has followed such proffers of help. Occasionally the trouble proves to be merely misunderstanding on the part of the novice of what is expected of him by his superior officer.

Analysis of the data obtained through these replies has shown that failures or difficulties of adjustment are due in general to two types of problems—those which may be said to involve the ethics of the teaching profession, and those of a disciplinary nature. Furthermore, violations of ethical principles often are responsible, directly or indirectly, for weakness in discipline. As a second result, therefore, of these inquiries, a unit of work has been developed in connection with the senior class in high-school methods. In this unit the students are made acquainted with a large number of situations involving ethical questions, from which they evolve a code which they are individually willing to accept as teachers. Other problems are presented as the unit on "management of young people" is studied, and both of these units have been modified each year by new information secured from those in the field. As a consequence, it has been possible to make the course in methods seem very real to those enrolled.

As the commencement season approaches, the department of education extends to each senior a cordial invitation to write for assistance of any kind which it is possible for the college to give, should he encounter difficulties in his new work. This has resulted in many calls for library books, bibliography, advice on questions of discipline, method, ethics, and all the other problems bound to be met by members of the profession. These calls for help receive prompt attention and have added to the reputation of the college for preparing good teachers, as well as proving a means of developing and holding a loyal alumni group. They have also served a purpose in the revision of the above mentioned course in methods, as they indicate the needs which should be met before graduation. This correspondence has been carried on under such pleasant relations, over a period of years, that many letters are now received which volunteer practical problems as material for the courses in education, even when no particular need for assistance is felt by the writer. This does much to keep the work of the department up to date and of personal interest to students.

Thus, while the follow-up work was inaugurated because of the conviction that the college should continue its interest in the student and service for him so long as he should be in need of it, both sides have derived so much value from the relations established that follow-up methods at Intermountain College bid fair to continue indefinitely and to increase in scope rather than to be restricted.

Ida M. Yates
Intermountain Union College,
Helena, Montana

QUOTATIONS

THE NEW YORK CITY SCHOOLS

The annual report of the City Superintendent of Schools is for the year ending July 31, 1930, and fills 843 pages. Valuable as the material is for purposes of record, it is regrettable that a summary could not have been prepared for the general public. As it is, not one person in a thousand outside of the system will be able to get a comprehensive view of the schools or to translate the statistics into human values, or to discern in what respects there is a change in general objective or in emphasis. Moreover, the period covered is so far past as to diminish interest on the part of the general reader. It would have greatly stimulated that interest if there could have appeared with the report a few pages to tell what progress had been made since July, 1930, toward answering some of the questions put in 1929 and 1930.

Among them were asked what is the most important aim of the schools, what forms of service they should render to the children and the public, and what unsatisfactory results will follow holding back from grade to grade large numbers of pupils because they do not reach fixed standards of attainment. One answer emerges. It is that the development of good character is the fundamental aim of our public schools. Imparting information and acquisition of skill are highly important aims, but not the most important. Yet teachers and supervisors have differing personal points of view which affect the promotion of pupils, with the result that retardation has become serious. A committee for studying it, as well as truancy and problems of personality and conduct, was appointed two years ago last June. Some progress has been made, but we must await the official report for another year.

Dr. O'Shea reiterates that they of the city system should be their own most severe critics and should not be deterred by fear or pride from ascertaining the facts in reference to their pupils. But he confesses that educators (in 1930) were not able to say with conviction just how satisfactory the results of instruction are in a given case. He should therefore be welcoming the aid of the State Education Department in determining standards of measurement; for nothing is more needed in the efficiency and economical administration of this greatest city department of education than a scientific basis for classification of pupils. When this has been determined, not only will the great wastage to which the 1930 report refers—loss of time on the part of the pupils, loss of money expended for instruction, dissatisfaction with school work, etc.,—be reduced or eliminated, but the best methods of advancement will be disclosed. The report is in itself the best support for the request made by the President of the Board of Education for an investigation of the city's efficiency in the schools by the State Education Department.—*The New York Times.*

UNEMPLOYMENT AND THE SCHOOL-LEAVING AGE

Where is the state government that is not concerned with the problem of unemployment, that is not deluged with schemes for its solution, that does not drip with oratory on the subject from the bleeding hearts of the people's representatives, executive or legislative? Yet constructive action is singularly slight. For example, we have the word of Courtenay Dinwiddie, general secretary of the National Child Labor Committee, that "in no single state has a law been passed this year raising even by a single year the age at which children are allowed to leave school for work, although bills for this purpose were introduced in the Legislatures of Illinois, Massachusetts, New York, Nevada, Pennsylvania and Texas."

Here is such an obvious step in the direction of reducing the competition for jobs and at the same time of benefiting the rising generation that one must pause in wonder at the inertia or worse which prevents its being taken. Every year sees something like 100,000 children under sixteen years of age enter the labor market. In present circumstances, whether they receive employment or not, the result is deplorable. Those who are able to connect with jobs do so by depriving their elders of employment opportunities; the rest—and in all likelihood they will constitute the majority this winter—join the army of the idle with all that this implies of discouragement, loss of morale and the temptation to follow evil counsel. From any point of view it would be far better if these children continued in school, receiving the extra training for their battle with life while relieving the vastly over-burdened labor market of their presence.

In a summary of child labor legislation during 1931 the National Child Labor Committee notes the fate of the various bills to accomplish this end. The Hofstadter-Moffat bill, which would have raised the age requirement of children leaving school for work from fourteen to fifteen years, was reported favorably in both houses of the New York Legislature; it was allowed to die. In Illinois a similar bill raising the limit from fourteen to sixteen years was tabled; it died. After the Massachusetts effort is the notation: "Failed; postponed to next annual session." The Nevada bill "died," the Pennsylvania bill "died," the Texas bill "passed Senate; died in House." This is surely a limp record for a live issue, but so typical of our political saviors that it would be funny if it were not tragic.—*The New York Herald-Tribune.*

REPORTS

LEGAL STATUS OF MARRIED WOMEN TEACHERS

IN view of the present depression and enforced economy on the part of school corporations, and their philanthropic concern that unemployment relief be extended as far as possible, there seems to be a decided trend toward discrimination against the married woman teacher. In a recent survey upon the subject of, "Board Rules Affecting the Status of Married Women Teachers in Ohio," Logan A. Waits[1] made the startling discovery that approximately 72 per cent. of 147 city boards have adopted policies discriminating against the employment of married women teachers; and of 1,833 rural boards, 264 have rules against employment of married women, and 343 have an understanding to that effect in the absence of explicit rules. There are 171 boards in Ohio requiring, by contract or by regulation, immediate resignation if the teacher marries. Waits further states, "There is no specific law found in the statutes of Ohio which makes marital status a cause for discrimination against public-school teachers, yet many Ohio boards of education do have rules against the employment of women teachers who are married and, apparently, *such rules are legal.*

[1] Logan A. Waits, ''Board Rules Affecting the Status of Married Women Teachers in Ohio,'' SCHOOL AND SOCIETY, 33: 867–871, June 27, 1931.

The preceding words are italicized in order to focus the attention of the reader upon the problem of this treatise. The mere fact that a custom is generally in vogue or is judicially smiled upon, does not create legality. It is the purpose of this study to ignore completely the question of capacities and teaching potentialities, to disregard the problem of economics and philanthropy or the existence of a spoils system in operation: but rather, to focus attention upon the legal side of the question only, to summarize existing studies upon the legal status of the married woman teacher, to review the statutes upon the subject, to clarify and harmonize certain court decisions, to note the effect of teacher tenure laws upon the problem, to indicate public sentiment for legislation discriminating against the employment of married women teachers, and, last of all, to clarify the effect of maternity or childbearing upon the teacher's tenure.

STATUTORY PROVISIONS

The situation in Ohio, discovered by Waits, if characteristic of the states as a whole, brings forth an unexplained inconsistency between the liberalness with which girls are educated and the extent to which they may profit by it. Brubacher says, "Two of the many constraining forces producing this situation are the possibilities of a woman's marriage and her consequent potential maternity."[2]

What is the voice of the state laws upon the question of marriage of female teachers? There is no voice. Not one of 50 separate school codes under the American flag mention the status of marriage, except where such wife or husband is the wife or husband of a board member, in which cases they are generally held not to be legally employed by the local board.[3] A review of the certification laws of the several states, reveals nowhere marriage as a bar to women's securing licenses or other proper credentials to teach.

At the last session of the California legislature, two radical and chaotic bills were proposed, curtailing the right of married women as public and civic employees. Assembly bill No. 378 proposed that no married woman whose husband is earning $150 monthly, or more, shall be eligible for civil service examinations.[4] The second bill struck directly at teachers and was a matter of much anxiety and editorial concern for some time. It was known as A. B. 1630, and was, "An act to prohibit the employment of married women by the state, city, city and county or county government,"[4] with subsequent provisions for its enforcement and penalties for violation. Needless to say, both of these bills never got past the committee; but the intensity which 1630 produced among the educators is best portrayed by the exact words of Albert M. Shaw, legislation reporter for the California Teachers Association, when reporting the outcome back to the association. He said,

> Truly, "in union there is strength." It has not been necessary for the married woman to carry on this battle against A. B. 1630 alone. All teachers, married or single, men and women have joined in the fight and have contributed time, effort and financial support in an adequate and fully satisfactory manner. . . . It now gives me much satisfaction to shout with you, "It's dead—very dead." And you had a very large part in assisting with its early but timely demise.[5]

At common law the married woman's rights to the fruits of her labor have been generally and securely established in the United States. The direct antithesis of this proposed legislation of California is found in the statutes of Michigan which is herewith quoted in part:

> Each and every married woman in the State of Michigan shall be absolutely entitled to have, hold, own, retain and enjoy any and all earnings acquired by any such married woman as the result of her personal efforts; and to sell or otherwise dispose of any and all such earnings and to make contracts in relation thereto to the same extent that any such married woman could have or do if unmarried.[6]

Upon the legal status of discriminatory statutes against the employment of married women, Judge Alonzo Bales, in a Madison circuit court (Indiana) decision, recently voiced the opinion that, "Had the legislature of Indiana declared in the teachers' tenure law that marriage should be the ground for dismissal of a public school teacher, such a law would have thereby been rendered unconstitutional."[7]

If the school codes are silent upon the subject, how then are the prevailing discriminatory rules legally justified? By the natural right of freedom of contract. Within the certification requirements set by the state, a board of education is free to hire whomsoever they please, and among several applicants the laws in no way attempt to dictate to the board whom they should choose. So it is generally conceded that the board may act under an arbitrary rule, at their pleasure, in employing whichever person they wish or refusing to employ likewise.

Higher Court Decisions

The test of the legality of the rule comes when boards attempt to dismiss a female employee on the charge of marriage. The first case to come before the courts was that of Grendon v. Board of Education of the City of

[2] John S. Brubacher, "The Judicial Status of Marriage and Maternity as an Obstacle to the Education of Women for Professional Careers in Public School Teaching," School and Society, 26: 428, Oct., 1927.

[3] John S. Singleton, "Married Women as Teachers Causes for Dismissal of Teachers in State Laws," pp. 54–56.

[4] A. F. Johnson, "Legislation and Women in Industry," *Los Angeles City Teachers Club Bulletin,* March 26, 1931, pp. 14–15.

[5] Albert M. Shaw, "Legislative News Letter," *Los Angeles School Journal,* 16: 16, March 16, 1931.

[6] "Authority of School Board to Employ Wife of One of Its Own Members," *El. Sch. Jr.,* 31: 411, Feb., 1931.

[7] Decision of Judges Bales on an Elwood School Case, Madison Circuit Court, Indiana.

New York, 1903, in which Mary L. Grendon was caused to tender her resignation under persuasion because of a rule making dismissal upon marrying automatic. The fact that she had tendered a resignation which was accepted and did not bring mandamus action for reinstatement until 1906 caused her reinstatement to be denied on the grounds of laches,[8] but the court ruled, "the regulation in question is subsequently illegal and void."[9]

In 1904, the Kate M. Murphy case, which later became a nation-wide precedent, established the following principle: The rule of the board declaring the position of a teacher marrying to be vacated, was held void as it was contrary to statute, since the statutes made provisions for the grounds for removal.[10] In this decision attention is brought to a fundamental principle which has generally been held, with but few adjudicated cases to the contrary. The principle is: that where the state law specifies causes for dismissal, local or subordinate units of control are without authority to enlarge upon the causes for dismissal or to change the manner in which the dismissal can be brought about. Quoting from the case of Kate Kennedy,[11] the following rule is typical of all court decisions (one excepted) in regard to marriage as an additional charge for dismissal. "The rules adopted by the board of education can not control the provisions of the statute and are immaterial in determining the statutory rights of a teacher."[11] Other cases where similar decisions were given are noted below.[12]

The one exception noted above was the Matter of Appeal of Conger v. Superintendent[13] which was determined under jurisdiction of the New York State Commissioner of Education in 1916. In Buffalo the city charter contained a blanket clause giving the local board power to make all rules necessary for administering the school, "not inconsistent with the laws of the state." The board was upheld, not upon the reasonableness of the rule, but upon a municipality's authority to set up statutory regulations in addition to those required by the state. As this is a controversial subject bearing upon governmental functions, very little weight is attached to the decision; furthermore, the trend of this decision was reversed by the Commissioner of Education in 1925 in the Matter of Appeal of Thomas.[14] An intermediate state tenure law, setting forth provision for dismissal, being the chief factor in reversing the precedent of the Conger case. There are other cases on record where the board was upheld in enforcing the rule against marriage, but in several which were typical of these decisions the element of fraud entered into the decision, whether the judge took cognizance of it as such or not. In one the lady signed her single name when in fact she was already married.[15] Furthermore if this Indiana case was even taken as establishing precedent, legalizing the dismissal of teachers for marriage, the present state tenure law has caused such precedent to be set aside by the lower courts[16] and a final decision is now pending in the appellate court.

The weight of the evidence quite firmly establishes the principle that, "where the legislature enumerates certain causes for the dismissal of teachers, the courts regard such enumeration as exhaustive. The theory is that the law-making power expressed its full intent."[17] That leaves just three states, New Jersey, Washington and Connecticut, in which dismissal for marriage might be upheld as a legal case, since their school statutes do not specify causes for dismissal.

Another subtle question in this relation is

[8] Undue delay.

[9] "Grendon v. Board of Edu. of the City of New York," 100 N. Y. S., 253.

[10] "People ex rel Murphy v. Maxwell," 177 N. Y., 494.

[11] "Kate Kennedy v. Board of Edu. of City and County of San Francisco," 82 Cal., 483.

[12] "People ex rel Peixotto v. Board of Edu. of the City of New York," 144 N. Y. S., 87.

"Blaire v. United States ex rel Hellman," 45 App. D. C., 353.

"Tompson v. Gibbs," 97, Tenn., 489.

"Jameson v. Board of Edu.," 74 W. Va., 389.

"Richards v. District School Board," 78 Oregon, 623.

[13] "Matter of Appeal of Conger v. Sup't.," 8 *State Dep't. Reports* 616; Sch. and Soc., 26: 430, Oct., 1927 N. Y.

[14] "Matter of Appeal of Thomas," 33 *State Dep't. Reports* 12; Sch. and Soc., 26: 431, Oct. 1927 N. Y.

[15] "Guilford School Twp. v. Roberts," 28 Ind. App., 355.

[16] Decision of Judge Bales on an Elwood School Case, Madison Circuit Court, Indiana.

[17] J. N. Edwards, "Marriage as a Legal Cause for Dismissal of Women Teachers," *Ed. Sch. Jr.*, 25: 69.

whether a clause in the signed contract is more binding in this respect than a rule of the board; and whether a contract containing an automatic clause of dismissal or resignation upon marriage, may be held enforceable either in whole or in part.

Since most contracts contain a clause directing the employee to rules of the board and requiring submission thereto, it matters little whether the clause is borne upon the face of the contract or not. Upon execution the adopted rules, in effect, become a part of the contract. "The law, however, constitutes a part of the contract, nullifying any written provision inconsistent therewith."[18] The board's authority to add, and the extent to which such provisions, as are here under consideration, are held enforceable, is well expressed in the following decision: "A reservation of the right to annul all contracts every fourth month stamped across the face of the contract with a school teacher for an indefinite term is not authorized by law and is void, and does not invest the school directors with power to dismiss the teacher arbitrarily without cause or trial and employ another for the unexpired scholastic year."[19]

More specifically, there are a large number of court decisions upon the question of restraint of marriage by contract. Where such clauses are the primary consideration to the contract, they have always been held void and invalidating the whole contract.[20] Others, where the clause abrogating the parties' natural right to marriage was merely incidentary to the principal consideration, have been held valid in all but the offending clause. The case of King v. King,[21] expressing the opinion of the Ohio courts on this question, although not a school decision, is almost analogous to the case of Fletcher v. Osborn,[22] in which the court ruled, "Where, however, the restraint upon marriage is a mere incident to the main object and purpose of the contract, the courts as a rule hold that the contract is not invalid in all of its terms, but only with respect to the promise not to marry." It would seem, therefore, that a promise in a teacher's contract restricting her right of marriage is void and without effect.

There remains one question yet to be settled before passing to the next topic. Does the acceptance of such a contract by a teacher estop her right to bring action against the enforcement of this provision? Of course the answer is "no"; and another Ohio case gives the answer regarding the binding power of illegal clauses in these words: "The acceptance of such an appointment does not estop him from attacking the validity of any act that may be in the statute book. He accepted the appointment subject to the valid and constitutional laws of the state only."[23]

Maternity as a Bar

Where the regulations of a school system provide for permanent tenure upon conditions, and grants leave of absence for cause, the question has arisen whether absence for the purpose of childbirth should deprive the married woman teacher of her right to be reinstated in her former position. In an attempt to settle this question once and for all, the case, People ex rel Peixotto v. Board of Education of the City of New York, was carried to the Supreme Court,[24] then to the Appellate Division, First Department,[25] to the final court of the Appellate Division,[26] and finally appealed to the State Commissioner of Education.[27]

The facts in summary are that Mrs. Bridget Peixotto presented a doctor's statement declaring her illness to be an affection of the ears, from which she was actually suffering, and made no statement in respect to her pregnancy. After three months' absence during which time a child was born to her, she presented herself

[18] H. R. Trusler, *Essentials of School Law*, p. 232.

[19] "Tompson v. Gibbs," 97 Tenn., 489.

[20] "Chalfant v. Payton *et al.*," 91 Ind., 202.
"White v. Equitable Nuptial Benefit Union," 76 Ala., 251.
"Mary Lowe v. Cornelius Doremus," 84 N. J. Law.

[21] "King v. King, Executor *et al.*," 63 O. S., 363.

[22] "Fletcher v. Osborn," 282 Ill., 142.

[23] "Hubbard v. State of Ohio," 65 Ohio State, 574.

[24] "People ex rel Peixotto v. Board of Edu.," 144 N. Y. S., 87.

[25] "People ex rel Peixotto v. Board of Edu.," 145 N. Y. S., 853.

[26] "People ex rel Peixotto v. Board of Edu.," 212 N. Y. S., 463.

[27] "Mrs. Bridget Peixotto Appeal to the State Superintendent of Education," Sch. and Soc., 26: 430, Oct., 1927.

for her original position. On being refused the right of reinstatement, she carried the case to the Supreme Court seeking mandamus action to secure her former status. In rendering his decision in favor of Mrs. Peixotto, Justice Seabury established some significant rules which were not altogether concurred with by the courts of appeals. They follow:

(1) Constitutional Law—The Legislature has no authority to remove the Court's power to review cases or place such power in other bodies.
(2) The Court may review decisions of the State Commissioner of Education in spite of legislation to the contrary.
(3) Mandamus lies to establish reinstatement.
(4) New York State statutes specify the causes for which dismissal can be made and no subordinate body can establish other arbitrary rules.
(5) A female teacher in New York City can not be removed for marriage.
(6) Greater New York charter provides for absence for serious personal illness and hence childbirth is a legal grounds for serious illness.[24]

Now it appears that Mrs. Peixotto had complied with all the requirements of the provisions to obtain leave of absence, except to secure permission from the superintendent, and on those grounds the board charged her with neglect of duty and discharged her after she had been successful in establishing mandamus on the first account.

In again appealing this decision she went directly to the courts and was twice denied appeal on the grounds that the board had acted within its jurisdiction and, since the law provided for appeal from the board's decision to the State Commissioner of Education, the Court had no power to review until the other means had been exhausted.[25, 26] Accordingly she appealed to the Commissioner of Education where she was again sustained in her right of tenure under the existing laws. The expressed opinion of the State Commissioner, Dr. John H. Finley, follows in part:

As this honorable board appears to hold married women teachers should end their services on maternity, this policy (which I can not believe sound in principle) can be made possible only through legislation making it lawful to discharge because of marriage of a teacher in service.[27]

The case of Kate Kennedy of California[28] also succeeded in establishing reinstatement after a protracted illness wherein the board tried to demote her in both salary and position.

The French government has met this problem squarely and has seen fit to clarify the legal status of married women teachers and the subsequent results of childbirth by legislation upon the subject. "Teaching by married women is not only accepted but special provision is made to have husband and wife teach in the same district."[29] Motherhood and marriage are further encouraged among women teachers by legislation of the following type: "A leave of absence for two months with full pay is allowed married women teachers, half before and half after the period of confinement. The teachers are not to be allowed to return to their teaching duties without a statement from a physician that they are able to do this without injury to their health. If not able to return within two months, an extension is accorded them under the same conditions for a term up to two months additional."[30] Until the American people and school boards assume a similar attitude, teaching will never be professionalized on the highest level as far as women are concerned.

TENURE LAWS AND MARRIAGE

Tenure laws are of such recency in most states that no authentic data is to be had upon the subject at present. An unpublished master's thesis by M. H. Strubble on the subject, "Legislation Affecting Teacher Tenure," reveals the fact that tenure laws are effectively in operation in many of the states and that fifteen have legislative provisions for permanency in tenure. In some, the tenure provisions are mandatory and in others merely directory. The significant part is, that in no tenure law is marriage made a disqualifying cause. Certainly the courts can not hold that the legislators have overlooked

[28] "Kate Kennedy v. Board of Edu. of the City and County of San Francisco," 82 Cal., 483.

[29] E. W. Anderson, "Columbia University Contributions to Education," No. 246, p. 118.

[30] "Le Livre des Instituteurs Administration Legislation et Jurisprudence de l'Enseignement Primaire," *Librarie H. L. Soudier.* E. W. Anderson, "Columbia Contributions," No. 246, p. 119.

the subject and failed to express their legislative intent. In fact, E. W. Anderson says, "Teachers under permanent tenure by statutory enactment are universally held to be protected from rules of local boards allowing termination of contract on account of marriage."[31]

In conclusion what can be said of the statement, that was first challenged in the beginning of this paper? Do restrictions against and in restraint of marriage of women teachers still appear to be legal? If teaching is to remain open as a profession to women, it is high time some one is doing something about the one hundred seventy-one boards of education in Ohio, and those of other states, who are abridging the teachers' natural rights by illegal rules and contractual provisions. "Courts do not notice illegal practices of their own motion; some one must bring them in proper form, to the proper judicial forum."[32] It is time professionally minded teachers defend themselves, testing the case in those states in which there is not already an established court ruling. Certainly, in the interest of right, something should be done to stop this prevalent "hi-jacking" by racketeer school boards.

Paul N. Garver
Ohio State University

EDUCATIONAL RESEARCH AND STATISTICS

DOES THE CHURCH COLLEGE DEVELOP CHARACTER?

Advocates of church college education stress the importance of Christian environment and influence in the development of the character of the student. In recent years heads of denominational colleges have eloquently advertized their educational wares as superior to those of the secular brand by virtue of their programs of religious education. The one slogan of all church college promotion has been, "A Christian College for Character."

It is very probably true that the religious program of the Christian college does constitute a factor in the development of good character in the lives of its students. The Christian college has various definite agencies designed for this specific purpose. These include generally the following: (1) Compulsory chapel attendance; (2) a required course in Bible; (3) a president outstanding as a religious leader; (4) a faculty of professed Christian ideals; (5) a student body recruited largely from Christian homes.

These are the peculiar assets of the Christian college. Granting that they are valuable, their real evaluation is yet an important problem to be investigated. Those in close association with the work of the Christian college for the most part have faith in its mission of character development, and yet they are at the same same time handicapped by a lack of specific information as to what the college is actually accomplishing in the lives of the students under its direction. For example, of the above-listed assets peculiar to the Christian college, who knows which are of the most importance? What agencies are actually most effective in moulding the lives of students, and what is the extent of their effectiveness? These are questions of paramount importance and it is expedient that progress be made in the direction of finding specific answers for them.

An attempt is made in this little article to suggest by an illustrated procedure one of the ways by which some information may be gained. The familiar device of the questionnaire is employed. This questionnaire in two parts was administered to a group of college freshmen who had been in attendance a little less than one regular session. The questionnaire follows:

Part A

Which have constituted the most influential character forming agencies in your life, that is, which have exerted the most influence to determine your actual present conduct? List in order of importance, in a column, giving the most important first:

1. *Home:* Parents, guardians, and members of family.
2. *Church:* Pastors, Sunday school teachers, professors of Bible, Bible study.

[31] E. W. Anderson, "Columbia University Contributions to Education," No. 246, p. 118.

[32] H. R. Trusler, "Essentials of School Law," p. 288.

3. *Associates:* Friends, business associates, schoolmates, social groups as fraternity, athletic squad.
4. *School:* School teachers and professors of secular subjects, courses of study.
5. *Experience:* Independent conclusions based upon your experiences and observations of life, travel, general reading, amusements, work.

Part B

Which to you have constituted the most influential character forming agencies of the college. List in a column in order of importance, with the most important first:

1. Instruction of professors of Bible subjects.
2. Instruction of professors of non-Bible subjects.
3. Character and personality of professors.
4. Chapel services and religious meetings of college groups.
5. Student associates, fraternities, athletic squads, dormitory life.

Abbreviations for ''Part B'' are as follows: 1, I.B.; 2, I.N.; 3, C.P.; 4, Chapel; 5, Associates.

Table I summarizes the results of Part A. The factors in order of weighted scores are listed in the first column. The values of the weighted scores in the second column are determined in each case by totalling the products of the frequencies of each rank by the assigned weights for each rank. Rank 1 is given a weight of 5; rank 2, a weight of 4; rank 3, a weight of 3; rank 4, a weight of 2; rank 5, a weight of 1. Thus, for example, the score for "Associates" of 295 equals the sum of 9×5 plus 37×4 plus 20×3 plus 15×2 plus 12×1.

TABLE I

Rankings of General Character Forming Agencies by 93 College Freshmen

Character forming agency	Weighted score	Rank 1	Rank 2	Rank 3	Rank 4	Rank 5
Home	416	61	19	9	4	0
Associates	295	9	37	20	15	12
Experience	261	16	13	21	23	20
Church	221	5	15	22	19	32
School	202	2	9	21	32	29

The following important facts are disclosed by the data of Table I:

Sixty-one out of 93 students (practically 2 out of 3) testify that the home is the most influential character forming agency in their lives. Thirty-seven out of 93 students (practically 2 out of 5) place the influence of associates of second importance. The five listed factors really constitute three primary agencies of character development. By grouping "Associates" and "Experience" under the single category "Life," and the factors "Church" and "School" under the category "Education," we see that "Home," "Life" and "Education" are the three social forces under consideration. Of these three the "Home" appears to be of greatest importance, the factor "Life" of intermediate importance, and the factor "Education" of relatively least importance. Of course, these terms should be used advisedly. For example, both "Home" and "Life" are educational factors. The term "Professional Education" would probably more accurately comprehend "Church" and "School."

Table II gives the weighted scores of the group of Table I separated by sexes. It is seen that there is no significant difference on the basis of sex.

TABLE II

Rankings of General Character Forming Agencies by Sexes

Character forming agency	39 women weighted score	54 men weighted score	93 total weighted score
Home	197	219	416
Associates	125	170	295
Experience	106	155	261
Church	95	126	221
School	82	120	202

Part B of the questionnaire was administered two days later than Part A. Part B was designed to test the relative effectiveness of the various character developing agencies of the college, and also to check in part the results of Part A of the questionaire.

Table III, constructed upon the same basis as Table I, summarizes the replies to Part B of the questionnaire. Abbreviations for the factors are employed as indicated in Part B of the questionnaire.

The following significant facts are disclosed by the data of Table III:

Forty-nine out of 84 students (practically 3

TABLE III

Rankings of the Character Forming Agencies of the College by 84 Freshmen

Character forming agency	Weighted score	Rank 1	Rank 2	Rank 3	Rank 4	Rank 5
Associates	329	49	10	6	7	12
C. P.	293	16	37	12	10	9
I. N.	232	5	14	34	18	13
I. B.	212	9	13	16	21	25
Chapel	194	5	10	16	28	25

out of 5) rank the influence of their associates in college higher than any of the other factors. Next in importance is the observed character and personality of their professors. It will be noted that these two factors come under the category "Life" used in the discussion of Table I. Also, "I. N.," "I. B." and "Chapel" very nicely come under the category "Education" used in the same discussion. The ranking of the social forces "Life" and "Education" is the same in both places. It is evident that these categories are at least partly disguised in the two questionnaires. The results of Table III seem to suggest that character is "taught by being caught" rather than "caught by being taught."

Table IV gives the weighted scores of the group of Table III separated by sexes. A most interesting difference between the men and the women is to be noted here. The women considered Bible instruction of slightly more influence in character development than non-Bible instruction, whereas the men placed non-Bible instruction before that of the Bible. However, in comparing the influence of Bible instruction with secular instruction it is to be noted that there was but one instructor of Bible to the three or four instructors in secular subjects. Moreover, the secular instruction may be considered as given with a view-point sympathetic to Christian principles.

TABLE IV

Rankings of the Character Forming Agencies of the Colleges by Sexes

Character forming agency	37 women weighted score	47 men weighted score	84 total weighted score
Associates	145	184	329
C. P.	130	163	293
I. N.	93	139	232
I. B.	99	113	212
Chapel	88	106	194

Conclusion

(1) The home is the most important social force in the development of character.

(2) Associations and experience are next in importance to the home in character development.

(3) Professional education, including the church and the school, is less effective than the home, associates and experience in the development of character.

(4) Student associates and example of faculty are more potent influences on the character of students than are secular instruction and religious education.

(5) More data are needed bearing on the relative effectiveness of various agencies having to do with the development of character.

C. A. Maney

Lexington, Ky.

NEW BOOKS IN EDUCATION

Department of Classroom Teachers, National Education Association. *Sixth Yearbook: The Economic Welfare of Teachers.* Pp. 244. The Department. $1.50.

Fraser, Chelsea. *The Model Aircraft Builder.* Pp. xi + 384. 199 illustrations. Thomas Y. Crowell. $2.50.

Fritz, Charles A. *The Method of Argument.* Pp. ix + 395. Prentice-Hall. $2.50.

Hart, Joseph K. *Creative Moments in Education.* Pp. xvi + 476 Holt. $3.00.

Hodgson, James G., editor. *Trends in University Education.* Pp. 163. H. K. Wilson. $.90.

Newmark, David. *A Study of a Class in the Philadelphia Normal School.* Pp. 150. 7 figures. Author.

Rose, William, editor. *An Outline of Modern Knowledge.* Pp. xv + 1103. Illustrated. Putnam's. $5.00.

Russell, Bertrand. *The Scientific Outlook.* Pp. x + 277. Norton. $3.00.

Smith, Clarence B. and Meredith C. Wilson. *The Agricultural Extension System of the United States.* Pp. x + 402. 23 figures. Wiley. $3.50.

Whitford, William G., editor. *Masks by Herbert R. Kniffin.* Pp. 135. 53 figures. Manual Arts Press, Peoria, Illinois. $3.00.

Worthington, Josephine and Catherine V. Matthews. *Our Clothing.* Pp. 256. Illustrated. F. A. Owen. $.96.

SCHOOL AND SOCIETY

EDITED BY J. McKEEN CATTELL

WITH WHICH IS COMBINED THE

EDUCATIONAL REVIEW

EDITED BY WILLIAM McANDREW

Volume 34 SATURDAY, OCTOBER 31, 1931 Number 879

SOME ASPECTS OF MODERN EDUCATION[1]

By Professor JOHN DEWEY

COLUMBIA UNIVERSITY

THE largest single army in the world, a legion of hope, industry, peace and intelligence, began about six weeks ago to mobilize its units for this year's campaign. Tots of four and five sought the kindergarten; boys and girls of from six years to the early teens thronged the elementary school; their older brothers and sisters went to the high school, the college, the technical and professional school.

This army forms a mighty host. There are thirty million children and youth in its ranks—as many as made up the entire population of this country within the lifetime of the oldest in my unseen audience. Two thirds of the number are in the elementary schools; four million lads and lassies are in high schools; colleges and other higher institutions take care of almost a million. This vast army is staffed and serviced by a corps of about a million administrators and teachers. More than a quarter of a million of young men and women are recruiting for future service in normal schools and teacher-training classes. The financial outlay is in proportion to the size of the task. We spend on education about $3,000,000,000 annually, drawn from taxes and the endowments due to private beneficence. The budgets of our municipalities devote, upon the whole, about one third of their total sum to the schools.

This is but the outside of the educational picture. In their work and achievements the schools represent the most important as well as the largest undertaking of the American nation. And their scope is constantly growing. Their rate of growth has been enormously speeded up since the world war. It used to be said that only one child in twenty succeeded in passing from the elementary school into the secondary, and only one in a hundred of the former number ever found his way to college. In the last few decades the absolute number has increased some sevenfold and the relative number, in comparison with increase in population, at least fivefold. We can search the history of the world in vain for any similar occurrence. For the first time in recorded history there is a promise that universal education will become a fact, and not a dream on paper.

Growth in the number of those who get beyond the merest elements of an educa-

[1] The second address in the "Men of America" series of radio lectures sponsored by the National Advisory Council on Radio in Education, given at 7:00 o'clock Eastern Standard Time, on Sunday, October 25, over WEAF and other stations of the National Broadcasting Company. The first of the "Men of America" lectures was delivered in May by Dr. Robert A. Millikan, on "Radio's Past and Future." Other lectures will be given during the coming winter.

tion is more than matched by expansion of educational facilities. The colleges have ceased to exist simply for the children of parents who had had themselves a classic training. Their scope is now as broad as all the activities of our modern complex society: schools of agriculture, all the branches of engineering, pharmacy, dentistry, business and commerce, journalism, etc. University extension reaches out to include the public that has been deprived of higher education. The high school was once mainly a preparatory school for those going to college; it is now itself a college for the people. In our larger cities, school buildings are often better and better equipped than were the universities of a generation ago.

If the older among you will think back to the elementary school of your childhood, you will recall a series of rooms whose sole equipment was rows of benches screwed to the floor, forbidding blackboards and thumbed text-books. These dreary structures are now being replaced with buildings in which there are gymnasia, libraries, pictures, statuary, assembly halls for music and dramatics, shops for wood work, rooms for cooking and sewing, often dental clinics and offices for medical inspection. In spite of cries of "fads and frills," the old curriculum of the "three R's" with a sparse smattering of history and geography, taught by rote from a single text-book, has given way to an enriched program. The ideal is that the whole boy and whole girl shall go to school and shall find there opportunities for the development of all the potentialities of a many-sided nature. Drill halls are becoming places in which children may live happily and may grow as they live. Let me cite one fact as typical of the situation. Investigations undertaken thirty years ago have been repeated lately, and have shown that the amount of reading matter covered by a pupil in a good elementary school is now eight or nine times as much as it used to be.

In addition to this internal enrichment there has been a great expansion outward. There is not a large city in which adult education is not being carried on; in some of the more progressive places, this work is as well organized as that for children and youth. Nursery schools are springing up at one end of the scale, balanced by parental education at the other. Handicapped, neglected and delinquent children are receiving systematic attention. Schools for the deaf and blind have been greatly increased; those for the crippled and the subnormal are largely a product of the last twenty years. There is a constantly growing number of towns and cities which have community centers which provide health and recreational facilities. It is noteworthy that about one fourth of the aims listed in the children's charter of the White House Conference have to do with safeguarding the physical development of the young. Recent developments in hygiene and medicine are making us realize that sound health is the basis of individual and national well-being, and the connections between schools and public-health agencies are drawing closer.

It would be foolish to assert that our educational expansion has always been well directed. On the contrary, it has frequently been attended with aimless dispersion and has led to superficiality. But when all allowances are made for mistakes and eccentricities, it still remains true that we now have and for the first time in history the physical and administrative basis for a truly universal education. For a universal education means not only one that extends its advantages to all, but one which meets the immense variety of social needs and of individual capacities and wants. Much remains to do even in the way of extension. Pre-school education, parental education, adult education generally are only in their early infancy. Much has been said and written about a plan of vocational guidance which will help individuals find the callings in which they can be of use to others while finding happiness in their work for themselves, but as yet the schools have actually accomplished almost nothing. The trend toward high school and college still leaves two thirds of our future citizenship with only the bare elements of intellectual preparation. Think of your own children of from twelve to fourteen, the degree of maturity they have reached, and call to mind the complex and difficult conditions of life and of making a living, and you will realize how far even in education we still come short of realizing the ideal of an equal start and an equal chance for all. Ignorance, lack of trained skill, are handicaps imposed on two boys and girls out of three. The evil is increased by the amount of child labor, even of a seasonal migratory sort, which our laws still permit.

Nevertheless, whatever our shortcomings, it is in education more than anywhere else that we have sincerely striven to carry into execution what James Truslow Adams has recently called "the great American dream": the vision of a larger and fuller life for the ordinary man, a life of widened freedom, of equal opportunity for each to make out of himself all that he is capable of becoming. Some have ridiculed the American faith in education; they have called it, derisively, a religion, and a religion which is a superstition. At bottom, however, there is no difference between faith in education and a generous faith in human nature. If the whole democratic enterprise to which our fathers committed the American people is a delusion, then—but then only—is our trust in education a superstitious mistake.

For a great idea lies behind the mobilization of this army of thirty million children and youth; a great ideal is at stake in the remarkable expansion our schools are undergoing. A hundred years ago, in the thirties and forties of the last century, the wiser of our ancestors began to realize that the democratic experiment was not one which was sure, automatically, to succeed. With one voice they cried that the enduring existence of republican institutions was dependent upon the spread of popular enlightenment, that popular education was the corner-stone of the Republic. As this idea was originally at the basis of the creation of the public-school system, so it has continued to be the fountainhead and inspiration of the expansion of the public-school system and its services.

The movement is an endless one; the need for expansion and alteration in education can never be ended, because the need can never be fully satisfied. It is the need of a human nature and of a society that are themselves in process of constant change. The most universal ambition of the average American parent, man and woman, has been that his boy and girl should have a better chance in life than the father and mother had. This desire, which has been the source of infinite self-sacrifice, inheres in our social system with its belief in the possibilities of the common man. It can only be carried into effect through ever-renewed improvement of our educational system.

Consequently I am here this evening to say that great as have been the changes in our educational system in the last hundred years, and especially in the last thirty, they are nevertheless slight in comparison with those which must be undertaken in the next generation. How can education stand still when society itself is rapidly changing under our very eyes? The sense of unsolved social problems is all about us. There are problems of crime, of regard for law, of capital, of labor, of unemployment, of stability and security, of family life, of war and peace, of international relations and cooperation—all on a larger scale than the world has ever seen before. Anticipation of continued and large-scale changes in education is, then, not so much a prophecy as it is a warning. Unless education prepares future citizens to deal effectively with these great questions, our civilization may collapse. It can not give this preparation unless it itself undergoes great transformations. H. G. Wells said, soon after the close of the war, that we were engaged in a race between education and catastrophe. Here in America, it might be truer to say that we are engaged in a race between a *mis*education which will bear no vital relation to the needs and conditions of the modern world and a possible education which will face the future and which will defer to the past and its traditions only as far as the past gives us aid in effectively facing the future.

The necessity of great educational change may be indicated by sketching the changes which life has undergone in the United States.

First, one hundred years ago, our life was agrarian and rural. Agrarian civilization has always when left to itself moved at such a slow pace that, to those who lived in it, it did not seem to change in any fundamental way. It is static, based on the traditions of the past, and accommodated to the course of nature. During the nineties of the last century, our society became definitely urban and industrial. It moves neither at the tempo of the ox-cart nor of the horse, but at that of electricity, the motor car and the airplane. Life has to adapt itself to the mechanical inventions which control the processes of nature rather than to the cycle of nature itself. Invention rather than routine and custom determines the course of events, and no one can say what further inventions are going to modify the course of living in the years that are before us. We do know that railway, telegraph, telephone, electric light, power, transportation, automobile, radio, airplane and their multitude of accessories have revolutionized our habits of work, of amusement, of communication and intercourse. Schools which have looked upon their task as that of preserving and transmitting the classic cultures of the past have fought shy of adopting into their own aims and methods enough of the new forces, the forces which determine our life, to fit individuals to cope with them. They may wreck us unless they are intelligently regulated and employed. Our mechanical devices and processes have got far ahead of our capacity to plan and to enjoy—ahead of our minds in short. The gaps between our machines and our ability to control them for human ends is widened because education has clung to old traditions and aims of culture in the face of the new industrial situation.

Secondly, there has been a revolution in the methods by which things get done. Our fathers worked by custom and the models laid down in the past. These models and procedures have been thrown into the scrap heap, not intentionally and deliberately, but none the less effectually. For science has dictated to men new ways of doing things based upon understanding of natural energy and the relations of cause and effect. Because of scientific advance, because of the methods it puts at our disposal, a single great industrial company creates devices by which the work can be done which would occupy our entire population, men, women, children and babes, if the work had to be done with the instruments and processes of even sixty years ago. It can not be said that our schools have begun to introduce scientific method into teaching to anything approaching the part which it plays in shaping our actual lives.

Thirdly, we have altered from a population with simple political problems to one with extremely difficult and complex issues. When the outlines of our school system were formed there was no great separation into rich and poor; there was free land; there were abundant unused and unappropriated natural resources. There was work and opportunity to get on for all. Then the aims of political democracy were easily understood, since they were in harmony with the conditions of soil and occupation. Now there are vast and concentrated aggregations of wealth; there are monopolies of power; great unemployment; a shutting down of doors of opportunity, a gulf between rich and poor, and no frontier to which the hard-put can migrate. In consequence, the problem of democracy is no longer chiefly governmental and political. It is industrial and financial—economic. It is infinitely ramified, and the threads which bind the social structure together are subtle and invisible. It would be absurd to hold educators responsible for our present depression, a depression which is obviously mental and moral as well as financial. But the depression is a warning that we live in an age in which education must take on new responsibilities and come to grips with realities which it has passed by as outside its province.

Fourthly, control of natural forces by means of machinery has brought to humanity the possibility of an amount of leisure from which the mass of men and women in the past were hopelessly shut out. At the same time, popular amusements and recreation have been seized upon as means of financial profit. The combination of these two facts has created what may be truly called a crisis in our national moral life. A new conception of the uses of leisure has to be created; boys and girls need to be instructed so that they can discriminate between the enjoyments that enrich and enlarge their lives and those which degrade and dissipate. The possibilities of artistic production and appreciation can no longer remain the privilege of a select class, but must become a universal possession. Otherwise the increase of leisure time may become a demoralizing agent on a vast scale.

Not all the social changes which are going on are good and beneficial. But it is claimed that these changes are here and must be faced, not ignored; education has the responsibility of developing types of mind and character that can direct these new forces toward good and that otherwise they will surely become forces of destruction and disintegration.

The sum of the matter is that at the present time education has no great directive aim. It grows, but it grows from specific pressure exerted here and there, not because of any large and inspiring social policy. It expands by piecemeal additions, not by the movement of a vital force within. The schools, like the nation, are in need of a central purpose which will create a new enthusiasm and devotion, and which will unify and guide all intellectual plans.

In earlier days there was an aim which worked throughout the whole system. Education was the key to individual success, to making one's way in life, to getting on and getting ahead. The aim corresponded with the realities of social life, for the national need was the material subjugation of a continent, the conquest of a wilderness. There was always a frontier just beyond, and the pioneer advanced to take possession of it. It was enough for the school to equip the individual with the tools of learning and to fire him with ambition and zeal to get on. His real education came in contact with others and in struggles with the forces of nature. The aim was individualistic, but it was also in harmony with the needs of the nation.

This earlier purpose has lost its vitality and its meaning. It survives, but operates as an oppressive handicap. As President Hoover said some time ago: ''We are passing from a period of extremely individualistic action to one of associational activity.''

Except for a favored few, there is no longer any unbounded opportunity for advancement open to individuals. We live in an epoch of combination, consolidation, concentration. Unless these combinations are used democratically for the common good, the result will be an increasing insecurity and oppression for the mass of men and women. Education must cultivate the social spirit and the power to act socially even more assiduously than it cultivated individual ambition for material success in the past. Competitive motives and methods must be abandoned for cooperative. Desire to work, for mutual advantage, with others must be made the controlling force in school administration and instruction. Instead of imbuing individuals with the idea that the goal is to sharpen their powers so they can get on personally, they must be trained in capacity for intelligent organization so that they can unite with others in a common struggle against poverty, disease, ignorance, credulity, low standards of appreciation and enjoyment. There must be a purpose and methods which will carry over the earlier ideals of political democracy into industry and finance.

Only in respect to methods of thought and judgment should the earlier individualistic aim be retained; *there* it should be intensified. Democracy will be a farce unless individuals are trained to think for themselves, to judge independently, to be critical, to be able to detect subtle propaganda and the motives which inspire it. Mass production and uniform regimentation have been growing in the degree in which individual opportunity has waned. The current must be reversed. The motto must be: "Learn to *act* with and for others while you learn to *think* and to judge for yourself."

The problem of educational reorganization is not one which it is easy to solve. But we are discovering that the problem of maintaining the democratic ideals of our founding fathers is not easy, either. The only way to attain the latter is by giving a social direction to our educational system. If the good will, the loyalty, the political faith and hope of the American people can be united with the affection which parents have for their children, and the union can be directed by the spirit of free scientific inquiry, there is no ground for fear of failure. When the ideals of democracy are made real in our entire educational system, they will be a reality once more in our national life.

THE BASES OF PERSONALITY ADJUSTMENT[1]

By Dr. IRA S. WILE

THE efforts of President Hoover to bring about world agreement for a moratorium should be effective in promoting international financial stability. It is doubtful, however, whether all the serious phases of present day depression can be remedied because, even though a tide of re-employment sets in, there will continue to be large numbers of persons whose employment problems will present even greater difficulties than at the present time. There will be, in fact, a larger number of absolute unemployables and a relatively larger number of unemployed than this country has ever known.

We may regard the problems of the unemployed in terms of world depression, seasonal unemployment, technological unemployment, over-crowding in industry, a

[1] Digest of an address given before the Association for Personality Training at the opening of its seminars on "Personality Difficulties of the Young Adult," at the Russell Sage Foundation Building, New York City, July 6, 1931.

rise in commercial standards of age for employment at the juvenile end of life, with a falling in the age of employability at the upper end of life. In addition there are problems of unemployment due to illness, accidents and dependent old age, dependent in part because of the ailments of the later decades of life and in part due to the fact of age itself.

It is important to consider how the problems of industry are to be met in terms of personal adjustment. There will always be unemployables and more than ever in the future with a five-day week and thirty to forty hours of work. There will be serious problems for the unemployed, because with a diminished number of actively engaged citizens, there will be greater competition for specific positions. It is because of this that the problems of personality will play a larger part in the hiring and firing of men than in the past. This is amply demonstrated by the keen interest of personnel departments throughout the country in the personality problems of their employees. There is further the full recognition of the value of saving men rather than scrapping them in industry, a desire to find out wherein a man lacks, and actually to make adjustments that will enable him to enlarge his personality in terms of temperament, emotions, application, industry and attitude so that he will fit into the scheme of things. Labor turn-over is a costly affair, in some industries amounting to more than $200 for each change. It is this financial value which makes the problems of personality training of primary significance to industry.

Personality, however, is not a problem of industry, *per se*. It includes and involves the reaction of human beings in and through living with other persons, beginning within the home, extending through the school and friendly organizations, as well as in the experiences in industry. It is obvious that personality with its reactions to human relationships must depend upon the essential factors inherent in the nature of the individual and in the past and present circumstances, conditions and events which constitute his environment. Some factors in personality are fixed and unchangeable, though most are alterable by intelligent efforts. One can not alter a blue or brown eye, but one can change physical elements as diabetes or nervous dyspepsia. There are, however, circumstances affecting personality which depend entirely upon the external factors. These are illustrated, for example, by the sense of security in one's job, the rate of one's wage, the attitudes of one's superiors and inferiors, the hours of labor, the pressure of machines, etc. It is patent that any service in modifying personality calls for an investigation of the man and the job and the man in the job.

Personality involves the totality of an individual. It is not merely the sum of his various parts and systems. One may speak in terms of his physical make-up, his intellectual capacities, his emotional system and his social reactions. If we were to add all of these together we should still not have the personality of the man, which is fabricated from the inter-workings and the dynamic potentials of his interacting being. His integrated personality reflects his esthetic possibilities, his spiritual aspirations and his capacity for manifesting various facets of his adapting nature under completely different conditions and circumstances. After all, the overt personality of a child at school is not identical with that exhibited on the playground, any more than the personality of his father is the same in church and at a baseball game or that of his mother at a ball and in the laundry.

The basis of personality adjustment involves, therefore, an inquiry into the basic changes involving possibilities of leverage upon the total personality. Are the changes to be voluntary or involuntary or are they to be subject to pressures? Do they call for immediate attention in the physical realm, the intellectual realm, or the emotional realm or the social realm? As a matter of fact the great majority of people are normal and adjustable. The problems of the personality adjustment which are increasing in significance in this age of heightened neuroses and mental disorders are confined more largely to the groups at the extremes. The very tall, the very short, the very bright, the very dull, the unemotional and the hyper-emotional, the self-seclusive, isolating type and the one who is so expansive that he is minding every one's business. When, however, one speaks of personality one should think in terms of the personality of the specific individual under discussion. Personality is scarcely generic; one does not speak of the personality of the Caucasians or of the Negroes or of the Mongolians. The personality to be adjusted is a personality but it is the personality of the individual who is to be aided.

There is no doubt in my mind that the bases of adjustment should be thrown back into the home and the school. Industry should not be charged with all of the responsibility which is now fastened upon it, particularly in the intellectual realm. Intelligence and achievement are primary concerns of schools, and the understanding of these phases of juvenile development should lead to intelligent vocational guidance, not guidance into specific industry, but broad guidance into lines of study and effort in which at least intellectual capacity will be adjusted and emotional satisfactions may be found. I say "maybe" because one can not tell the degree of satisfaction of an individual in a specific industrial career until he is placed therein, in contact with other workers. Many a man's adjustment has been disturbed by the promotion of a relative of the owner, by the demotion of a superior of kindly attitudes or by rasping competitive interaction within a department that is prejudicial to personal comfort and peace of mind.

People frequently talk of square pegs in round holes. One can not always find the exact square hole for each square peg, but there is a possibility at times of rounding the square peg so that it will fit some other form of hole. The process of personality adjustment does not carry with it the necessity of a hyperindividualism which means that the entire world must change to meet the demands of a single person. It still maintains a rational position that internal adaptations are requisite to satisfy the demands of an environment. But neither one goes on alone. The two are concomitant.

From an educational standpoint in this machine age there must be recognition of the interplay of social, economic, physical and even climatic factors. No one will deny that illness at home, low wages and a sense of insecurity in times of depression, the feeling of a loss of friendship or affection, the *affaire de coeur,* a poorly organized constitution, easy fatiguability, chronic illness, inadequate dietary, unhygienic home conditions and the like, all play their parts in diminishing comfort, satisfaction and capacity for adaptation. They help to mould personalities. A personality is affected by appearance, by strength, by a sense of orderliness, by state of health, by intellectual ability, by pleasure in industry, by industrial affiliations, by long hours, by monotony of process and sundry other factors found within and without the specific industrial plant.

Society is responsible for its units. Industry can absorb a certain measure of this responsibility but the school system should absorb still more. There is a crying need for a broader and deeper educational outlook. It is necessary that we continue to view the child at school as a potential industrial citizen in this age of machines. But he is more than that—he is a person and not a peg—a being, not a thing. There must be an organization of the industrial machinery so as to promote his social welfare but far more significant is the re-arrangement and re-constitution of our educational systems so that they take cognizance of the personality needs of our growing population. The problems of intelligence are not primarily and fundamentally responsibilities of business and industry. They still belong to the schools. There is need not merely for the development of vocational education and guidance in public school systems but there is a great opportunity for the development of adequate functional relationships between the schools and the homes and the homes and industry. There must be cooperation with a view to producing in the juvenile population persons capable of making adaptations to the stress and strains of life and not merely industrial life in a machine age.

There are innumerable gaps between our knowledge of what should be done and our practical performance in our school systems. A set curriculum at the present time is by no means fixed, even though it is being altered slowly. A plan of vocational guidance that is based merely upon intellectual capacity of children is bound to be a failure. High intelligence potentials do not carry with them the assurance of industrial success because our measures of intelligence at the present time give no insight as to industry, special ability, initiative, leadership, and the like. The problem of vocational guidance in so far as it is resident in the schools calls for a more definite knowledge of what is in the child and what the child is, in terms of his physical make-up, his intellectual power, his home and cultural background, his special abilities and capacities, his aptitudes and his interests. But it equally calls for an intelligent understanding of industry in terms of its aims and goals, its demands for employees, in terms of its strains, hours of labor and wages. It involves an understanding of the parent-sibling relationships, of the effects of under-guidance and over-guidance, over-protection, with some recognition of the useful spiritual and social factors in beauty, truth and religion. The entire child, therefore, is the matter of concern rather than merely a consideration of a part of his nature. Herein lies the opportunity for the educator as a coworker with industry.

We have not reached a time when dogmatism is advisable, nor when it is possible to lay down rules of thumb, nor general directions for personality adjustment. Inasmuch as the great mass of people possess normality, specific problems arise for those who are deviates from what is regarded as a norm, which varies under various conditions. The norm of personality for a man employed in a boiler factory is not identical with that involved for a statistician. In the last analysis personality changes are constant as a result of the interaction of the individual and his specific position. This becomes then a special province of industry and the educational system.

A highly efficient personnel department is conscious of the dynamic quality of its employees and appreciates the interaction of neurasthenia and high wages; neuroses and financial insecurity; inadequate stimulation and absence; lateness and enervating situations inherent in the complicated economics of homes, or arising from inadequate habits and determinative experiences during the processes of adolescent development.

There can be no doubt that personality adjustment involves manipulations of personality, whether the strings be pulled from within or from without; whether the environment be altered or the personal well-being modified by the use of endocrines, medicaments, a change of scene or psycho-analysis. There are no rules that can be applied as machine-like tests. Every personality is vital and individual —every industry and job is special and variable. And yet the two must find a common basis of service without hazard or destruction.

The educational factors in the home, school and industry must find a common ground wherein they can pool their knowledge and work out some scheme that will benefit those who need it. There is need for greater information concerning personality and its functions; and a far wider need for sufficient knowledge to enable men intelligently to analyze the personality of an individual and to synthesize it again into a more useful, effective, satisfying and happy form of personality. The initiative should be taken by educators working in and through the elementary schools and high schools. Industry should know much more of its employees from those whose prolonged stimuli should elicit the social responsiveness which is the foundation of justice, loyalty in industry and honesty, without which no personality can function in a democracy.

EDUCATIONAL EVENTS

EDUCATIONAL ENDOWMENT FOR SAMOA

Creation of a $200,000 foundation for the education of natives of American Samoa has been announced by Mr. and Mrs. William S. Barstow, of Great Neck, L. I., according to a wireless dispatch from Honolulu to *The New York Times*. The fund, which will be administered from Honolulu, is a memorial to their son, Frederic Duclos Barstow, who died there of pneumonia last May. It was his wish, after three visits to American Samoa, that something practical in education be done for the natives of that land.

A committee of five Honolulu men will be appointed as a board of directors. The spending of the income from the foundation will be regulated by the following proviso: "The objective of the educational fund shall be to develop leadership among the people of American Samoa in all the arts of living and of government under modern conditions, thus to facilitate the raising of that branch of the Polynesian race to its proper place in present-day life, this education to be in such practical and cultural pursuits, occupations and professions as the committee shall, from time to time, determine."

The foundation requires that once every five years one or more persons selected by the permanent committee shall visit American Samoa and report on the state of education there, making recommendations as to the most practical steps to be taken by the foundation in furthering its purposes. The expenditure of the income will be for school expenses, including teachers' salaries, erection of school buildings, education in hygiene and stimulation of research in Samoan culture.

In general the foundation plan will apply to Samoan youths of both sexes of whole or part Samoan blood, to whom American Samoa is home. The benefits, however, may be extended to those of more mature age in the discretion of the committee. If youths are sent abroad for education, Hawaii is to receive preference.

THE BRYN MAWR SUMMER SCHOOL

Because of the unemployment situation more applications than ever before were received for the Bryn Mawr summer school, according to the *Journal of Adult Education*. New York City alone sent in 80 applications, although the number of places allotted to the city is only 20. But a rapid withdrawal of applications took place in the week before the school opened, as students found they could not afford to risk the loss of work during the summer. There were finally enrolled for the eight-weeks course 99 students, who represented varied trades and national backgrounds. Garment workers and textile workers were in the majority. There were four students from Europe, a textile worker and a printer came from England, a garment worker from Denmark, and a metal worker from Sweden.

Unemployment, the most serious question facing industrial workers to-day, was chosen for the main theme of discussion this summer. By means of psychological tests, the school was divided into five units of instruction. Each unit based its study program on some aspect of the unemployment situation, relating to this general subject their work in English, science, history or psychology. International relations, the history of the labor movement, economic history, government and social reorganization were studied specifically in each unit. School forums on unemployment, the need for political action and types of community organizations served to correlate the program for the whole school. The faculty reported that the students on the whole maintained a high standard of work and achieved genuine progress.

The chief problem of the summer was found to be in the health department. In spite of preliminary medical examinations, many students showed serious conditions, due to fatigue and undernourishment. The intensive work of the health department proved successful in many cases, and the standard of health steadily improved. The whole situation seemed to reflect conditions in the industrial world, where unemployed workers are suffering from the effects of nervous strain and lack of sufficient food. The small fund for emergency medical cases allowed by the school was severely taxed. No funds are available for the necessary follow-up work demanded in the most serious cases.

Interesting events in the school this summer were a trip to the near-by steel mills; the trade party, dramatizing the unemployment situation in every trade; the international peace festival, unusually vivid and full of color, with its pageant of nations and program of folk songs and folk dances. Attempts at spontaneous labor drama on Saturday evenings brought forth unexpected talent, picturing for the whole school the experiences of individual students or of various trade groups.

The students have gone out from the school determined to apply what knowledge they may have gained this summer in their own industrial situations. Workers from each district of the country have met together to consider the next steps in an educational program for their own communities. The winter program includes plans for helping these former students to carry out their ideas for usefulness in the most effective way, cooperation with local groups for study classes, the preparation of suitable material for teachers and students, and an intensive publicity program in order to inform the public as to the needs of industrial workers in education.

PUBLIC SCHOOL APPROPRIATIONS IN FLORIDA

A SPECIAL dispatch to *The New York Times* states that, with the opening of her schools this fall, Florida began her most concerted effort toward the education of her youth in the history of the state. The drive is directed toward equal educational opportunities for all children, urban and rural, and follows the adoption by the 1931 Legislature of portions of recommendations made by a state educational survey commission, under whose direction an intensive study was conducted by field workers, headed by Dr. George D. Strayer, of Columbia University.

More than a score of specialists participated in the survey, and although the report of the commission, covering more than 700 printed pages and dealing with every phase of public educational work, was ready in 1929, the legislators did not get down to the recommendations until this year. Once their attention was directed to them, however, one legislative act alone more than justified the expenditure of $75,000 for the survey, according to Dr. I. E. Phillips, of Jacksonville, chairman of the commission. The General Education Board of New York contributed $25,000 to the survey fund.

That act provided for the teacher-unit basis of financing under which the people have been made to realize that school functioning is a state instead of a local problem. Under provisions of the act the state is paying, for the first time this session, 75 per cent. of the cost of operating the schools and the counties the remainder.

The act further specifies that the counties must send their children to school if they are to benefit by the new plan of distributing the funds. Ample funds have been provided, according to Mr. Phillips, for eight months' schooling for every child, white or Negro, an achievement never before realized in Florida. The scope of this advance is indicated by the fact that heretofore many of the smaller counties in Florida have operated schools for terms as short as six weeks annually.

Under the new act the wealthier counties are called upon to contribute to schooling in the weaker counties. The bulk of the revenue comes, incidentally, from the sale of license tags for automobiles, from which $6,000,000 goes annually to the schools.

While Florida already occupied, according to the survey, "a comparatively favored place among the southeastern states in the percentage of illiterates 10 years of age and over," the new plan is expected to place the state well out in the lead in this respect.

SUPERVISED CORRESPONDENCE COURSES FOR PUBLIC HIGH SCHOOLS

Use of supervised correspondence courses in small high schools is gaining considerable attention in various parts of the United States, according to the Federal Office of Education. As a result, students are being offered hundreds of courses which could not otherwise be made available. In addition to supplementing the regular work offered in the small high school, the variety of correspondence courses provides a specialized and high-grade type of instruction, despite the limitation of a small teaching staff. Such courses also make possible a better adjustment of studies to individual pupil needs.

Supervised correspondence courses, according to Mr. Walter H. Gaumnitz, rural school specialist of the Federal Office of Education, are offered by local high schools which make a contract with a reputable correspondence school, state or university extension service. The local school secures the lessons, provides periods in the regular school day for study, supervises the pupils' work and returns the lessons to the correspondence study center for a report on pupil accomplishment. The local school board pays for courses pursued.

A recent bulletin of the Office of Education, reporting a study of more than 14,000 rural high schools with an enrolment of 250 or less, pointed out that a multitude of small high schools have sprung up in the United States, some with only 30 to 50 pupils and as few as two teachers. In fact, reports show that 130 schools are attempting four years of high-school work with but one teacher. Many schools of this type have found correspondence courses helpful to both teachers and pupils.

Correspondence courses, designed mainly for high-school purposes, are offered by the Massachusetts State Department of Education, the University of Chicago, Columbia University, Indiana University, the University of Nebraska, the University of Minnesota, the University of Wisconsin, other state departments of education, university extension services and correspondence schools.

Successful pioneer experiments in this type of supervised study have been made by Superintendent S. C. Mitchell, of Benton Harbor, Michigan; Mr. C. M. Himel, Maine Township High School, Des Plaines, Illinois; Mr. H. F. Wooden, principal of the Ann J. Kellogg School, Battle Creek, Michigan; Mr. J. H. Hufford, principal of the high school, St. Charles, Illinois; Superintendent B. C. Berg, of Newton, Iowa, and by many other school officials, with the cooperation of state departments of education and university extension and correspondence school services.

PSYCHOLOGICAL TESTS FOR ART STUDENTS

To advance intellectual standards in the Woman's Art School of Cooper Union and to aid in selecting only young women of recognized artistic ability, psychological tests have been adopted as the sole basis of admission, it has been announced by the director, Austin Purves, Jr.

In the first of these tests, which were directed by Professor Carl C. Brigham, of Princeton

University, assisted by Professor W. G. Findley, of the psychology department of Cooper Union, and the art faculty, 155 young women were examined. Of these, 32 qualified, 42 failed and the remainder, characterized by Professor Brigham as "doubtful," will be reexamined next spring. The 32 young women who passed both the intelligence and the composition tests will be admitted to the school in the fall of 1932, the registration having been closed early in September for this year. The "doubtful" group will be given no priority over new applicants, who will be examined at the same time next spring.

The tests were of four types, including art judgment, composition, freehand drawing and a spatial relations test prepared by the New York College Entrance Examination Board. These tests were also given to students admitted to the Woman's Art School in September for comparative purposes. "The averages were good," Mr. Purves reported, "although there were some failures."

The psychology department agreed to give these tests as an experiment, according to Professor Findley, who worked with Professor Brigham in tabulating the results. To determine their value, however, these findings will be correlated with the work of the students after they are admitted to the school.

SUMMER SESSION OF THE UNIVERSITY OF HAWAII

Professor Thayne M. Livesay writes that since the beginning in 1927, summer sessions at the University of Hawaii, of which he is the director, have shown a steady growth in enrolment, reaching the total of 594 in 1931. A majority of the students came from the territory, but a total of 83 from outside sources, 77 from the mainland and 6 from the Orient, indicates that Hawaii is gaining recognition in other parts of the world. Of the students from the mainland 53 came as members of the tour organized by the University of Oregon, the second of such successful ventures.

To take care of the increased enrolment, a faculty of twenty-nine instructors gave a total of 39 courses in the following fields: agriculture, art, botany, economics, education, English, French, geography, geology, health education, history, household art, Oriental studies, physics, political science and psychology.

The 1931 summer session was strengthened by a number of visiting instructors, including Dr. John E. Corbally, assistant professor of education at the University of Washington; Dr. Leland H. Creer, assistant professor of history at the University of Washington; Dr. Thomas A. Jaggar, chief of the section of volcanology for the U. S. Geological Survey; Professor Linden A. Mander, associate professor of political science at the University of Washington; Dr. Mark A. May, professor of educational psychology at Yale University, and Dr. Philip S. Platt, director of Palama Settlement, Honolulu.

A unique feature of the 1931 session was a course in botany given at Kilauea Volcano by Mr. Theodore C. Zschokke, extension forester at the agricultural extension service of the University of Hawaii. It is hoped that this can be made a regular part of future summer sessions with a larger number of courses available.

The 1932 summer session, which will be held from June 29 to August 9, promises to be one long remembered in Hawaii because of a number of unusual features. In addition to the regular work as usually offered, there will be a school of Pacific affairs, and, during the last week in July, the meeting of the World Federation of Education Associations in Honolulu.

DEDICATION OF DWIGHT HALL AT YALE UNIVERSITY

A chapter in the history of two Yale institutions was written on October 23, when the university formally dedicated the new quarters of Dwight Hall in the Old Library. The exercises opened at 4 P. M. with an organ recital in Dwight Memorial Chapel. The dedication exercises were held at 8 P. M. in Dwight Hall, as the Old Library is now called. The opening address was made by Mr. William E. S. Griswold, of New York City, chairman of the alumni advisory board of Dwight Hall, who spoke for the alumni. Mr. Robert Brank Fulton, of Rockford, Illinois, president of Dwight Hall, spoke for the undergraduate body. Mr. Luther Tucker, of Mount Kisco, N. Y., secretary of Dwight Hall, represented the Student Christian Movement. Professor William Lyon Phelps, who was secretary of Dwight Hall in 1887, spoke for the faculty and former secretaries. President James Rowland Angell spoke for the university. The dedicatory prayer was offered by the Reverend Dr. George Stewart, secretary of Dwight Hall in 1915.

The simple dignity and charm of the Old Library, second oldest building at Yale, has been preserved for the enjoyment of future generations, and the University Christian Association has received a home worthy of its traditions. In 1842 Mr. Henry Austin received the commission to design the first separate library building for Yale College. Members of the class of 1880, desiring a coordination of Christian activity at Yale, organized the Christian Association Union.

As a graduate committee began to collect funds for the erection of a suitable building, Mr. Elbert B. Munroe, of Stamford, Connecticut, announced his intention of donating the building in memory of his wife's uncle, Mr. Frederick Marquand, whose plan to provide quarters for the association in honor of the elder President Dwight was thwarted by his death. The second President Dwight delivered the dedicatory address and received from Mr. Munroe the keys to the first Dwight Hall, just forty-five years ago. It was found necessary, in 1926, to demolish the old building, and the University Christian Association moved into Durfee Hall. Meanwhile it was agreed that the university would remodel the Old Library for the requirements of Dwight Hall as soon as Sterling Memorial Library was completed. Thus the destinies of two independent institutions at Yale were merged.

The building now embodies the conceptions of religion which the organization has developed. Central in the scheme is the Dwight Memorial Chapel, perpetuating the memories of two Yale presidents and Christian leaders, and symbolizing the attitude of devotional worship. An auditorium in the southern wing becomes the center for gatherings and lectures held every Wednesday evening, with the Liberal Club, the Chapel Committee, and the Round Table cooperating with Dwight Hall, in the presentation of social, economic, political and religious discussions by capable speakers. Occasional suppers may be served from a small kitchen adjoining the common room and auditorium. Here also will take place the Sunday afternoon teas.

The reading room on the first floor carries on the tradition of both institutions. In the north wing are housed the administrative offices and cabinet room, which will serve as a center for the associated activities, such as the New Haven Boys' Club and the Yale Hope Mission. On the second floor are living quarters for the graduate secretary and occasional guests, as well as discussion rooms, where small groups may meet. The Cosmopolitan Club occupies the second floor of the south wing.

EDUCATIONAL NOTES AND NEWS

Dr. Ellen Fitz Pendleton celebrated on October 19 her twentieth year as president of Wellesley College.

Dr. Ray Lyman Wilbur, on leave as president of Stanford University since 1929 to be Secretary of the Interior, was given a degree of doctor of laws, and Dr. Frederick G. Banting, of the University of Toronto, was made a doctor of science at the opening of the sixty-seventh annual convocation of the University of the State of New York on October 15.

Dr. Ralph D. Hetzel, president of the Pennsylvania State College, has been appointed chairman of the Greater Pennsylvania Council by Governor Pinchot.

Dr. Franklin W. Johnson, president of Colby College, was the speaker at the Founders' Day exercises at Wheaton College, Norton, Massachusetts, on October 17.

Dr. Harold Glenn Moulton, president of the Brookings Institution, Washington, D. C., lectured on the Manie Hooper Smith Foundation in Catherine Hooper Hall, Goucher College, on Friday evening, October 30. His subject was "The International Economic Situation."

Dr. Alexander C. Flick, state historian and director of the archives and history division of the state department of education of New York, was reelected corresponding secretary of the New York State Historical Association at the annual convention in Schenectady on September 26. Dr. Dixon Ryan Fox, of Columbia University, was reelected president. Among other officers elected were: Dr. Thomas E. Finegan, formerly deputy commissioner of education of New York, first vice-president; Dr. John H. Finley, formerly commissioner of education of New York, and Dr. James G. Riggs, principal of the New York State Normal School at Oswego, trustees.

MR. COMPTON MACKENZIE, the novelist, Scottish Nationalist candidate, was elected on October 25 to the position of Lord Rector of Glasgow University. The results of the polling were: Mr. Compton Mackenzie, Scottish Nationalist, 849 votes; Sir Robert Horne, Conservative, 762; Professor Gilbert Murray, Liberal, 581; Mr. Tom Johnson, former Lord Privy Seal in the Labor Government, 110, and Sir Oswald Mosley, leader of the New Party, 21.

MR. LEONARDO GUZMAN, minister of education of Chile, has resigned with the explanation that he is retiring for reasons of politics. It is reported that the university students' strike, now virtually solved, was a factor in his decision.

MR. EDWARD CORSI, director of the Council on Adult Education for the Foreign-born in New York City, has been made commissioner of immigration at Ellis Island by presidential appointment.

DR. DAVID SEGEL, of Long Beach, California, has been appointed to the position of specialist in educational tests and measurements in the research and educational division of the Federal Office of Education. The creation of this position was authorized by the last congress.

ON October 1, Mr. J. W. Bateman assumed active charge as head of the agricultural extension division of Louisiana State University, succeeding Mr. W. B. Mercier, who will be retained in an advisory capacity.

DR. JAMES I. WYER has accepted the chairmanship of the board of education for librarianship of the American Library Association, succeeding Dr. Louis Round Wilson, who has resigned. Dr. Wilson will remain a member of the board.

MR. ROY D. HUNTER was elected president of the board of trustees of the University of New Hampshire at their fall meeting. Mr. Hunter succeeds Mr. Dwight Hall, whose membership on the board was concluded last June.

DR. FREDERICK ARTHUR FORD has been appointed to fill the newly created office of dean of the Louisiana State Normal College.

MR. THEODORE L. KELLER has become instructor in the division of educational administration at the University of Pennsylvania.

DR. ROBERT MURRAY HAIG, who in recent years has been adviser on financial and economic affairs for various governments, has been appointed McVickar professor of political economy at Columbia University to succeed Professor Edwin R. A. Seligman. Professor Seligman, who retired last June, has been appointed professor emeritus in residence.

DR. WALTER TERENCE STACE, member of the governor's council and the legislative council of Ceylon, has been appointed lecturer in philosophy by the trustees of Princeton University.

MISS WILLIE WELCH, recently librarian at High Point, North Carolina, a graduate of the Atlanta Library School, has been appointed state school library supervisor for Alabama.

MR. PAUL NORTH RICE, librarian of the public library at Dayton, Ohio, has been granted leave of absence by the library in order to accept the position of executive assistant to the committee on cooperative cataloguing of the American Library Association for a period of two months.

DR. GEORGE F. ZOOK, president of the University of Akron, has resigned the secretaryship of the commission on higher institutions of the North Central Association of Colleges and Secondary Schools, a post which he has held since 1926 and in which he is succeeded by Dean George A. Works, of the University of Chicago, formerly of Cornell University. Dr. Zook has been named chairman of a committee to direct a five-year program for the revision of standards in accrediting higher institutions. The study thus undertaken is financed by a grant of $110,000 from the General Education Board and $25,000 by the North Central Association for the use of the committee on revision of standards.

MR. J. M. SEN, professor of psychology in

the David Hare Training College and inspector of schools in Bengal since 1927, will arrive in the United States the third week in January on a traveling fellowship from the University of Calcutta, to spend six months studying the working of our compulsory education acts, and also to what extent intelligence and other psychological tests are used in the United States for determining the qualification of children for promotion. Mr. Sen is a member of the Bengal Legislative Council and had a large share in drafting the rural primary education act of 1930. During his stay here, Mr. Sen will be available for lectures.

Dr. Edward Christian Glass, for fifty-four years superintendent of public schools at Lynchburg, Virginia, died on October 26 at the age of eighty-one years. He was one of the oldest school superintendents in the United States. Dr. Glass was one of twenty teachers named to staff the first free schools at Lynchburg, Virginia, in 1871, only one of whom, Mrs. Lucy B. Childs, now survives. He originated a normal school system in 1881, which was the forerunner of the present summer school of methods at the University of Virginia.

Mr. Frank W. James, a member of the board of education of Naples, New York, died recently. He was seventy-eight years old, and for forty consecutive years he had served on the board of education, the last twenty of which he was president.

Dr. Lee Wilson Thomas, director of the bureau of child hygiene of the health department of New York City, died on October 27. He was forty-five years of age.

The forty-fifth annual convention of the Association of Land-Grant Colleges and Universities will be held at the Stevens Hotel, Chicago, from November 16 to 18. As in previous years, representatives of the land-grant colleges and the Department of Agriculture will attend this convention, to discuss various questions relating to agricultural education, research and extension, including also engineering and home economics. The president of the association is Dr. G. W. Rightmire, president of the Ohio State University, Columbus, and the secretary-treasurer is Dean Thomas P. Cooper, of the Kentucky College of Agriculture and director of the Kentucky agricultural experiment station and extension service, Lexington. The chairman of the executive committee is Dr. R. A. Pearson, president of the University of Maryland, College Park, Maryland.

The U. S. commissioner of education, Dr. William John Cooper, has called a conference of educators of fourteen southern states to discuss problems relating to the improvement of instruction in rural schools, according to an announcement by the Alabama State Department of Education. The meeting is to be held in Montgomery, on December 14 and 15, and will bring together state and county supervisors, county superintendents, school principals and those engaged in teacher training in the states of Alabama, Arkansas, Florida, Georgia, Kentucky, Louisiana, Mississippi, North Carolina, Oklahoma, South Carolina, Tennessee, Texas, Virginia and West Virginia.

Appointment of a committee to make plans for an international celebration by Columbia University on January 27, 1932, of the one hundredth anniversary of the birth of C. L. Dodgson, or Lewis Carroll, author of "Alice in Wonderland," has been announced. The chairman is Dr. J. Enrique Zanetti, professor of chemistry. Other members are: Mr. Frederick Coykendall, trustee of the university and director of the Columbia University Press; Dr. Frank D. Fackenthal, secretary of the university; Mr. Roger Howson, librarian; Dr. David Eugene Smith, emeritus professor of mathematics, and Dr. Charles C. Williamson, director of libraries. Professor Harry M. Ayres, of the department of English, will deliver a lecture on Lewis Carroll at an evening ceremony. Other speakers will be announced later. There will be an exhibition in the Avery Library of Columbia University of Lewis Carroll's works, which, according to the announcement, will be the most complete ever held.

More than one hundred invited guests and members of the Council of the World Association for Adult Education met during the week of August 16 in Vienna to consider the business of the world association and to participate in two working conferences, one on the subject of "Adult Education in Relation to Unemployment" and a second on "Radio in Relation to Adult Education." Americans present who are regularly constituted members of the council of the world association were Mr. Spencer Miller, Jr., secretary of the Workers Education Bureau of America, and Mr. Morse A. Cartwright, director of the American Association for Adult Education. Also in attendance as substitute members of the council for this meeting were Mr. J. Walter Dietz, superintendent of industrial relations, Kearny Works, Western Electric Company, and Mr. Levering Tyson, director of the National Advisory Council on Radio in Education. Mr. Dietz and Mr. Miller both presented papers at the unemployment conference, and Mr. Tyson officiated as chairman and organizer of the radio conference.

To celebrate the one hundred and fiftieth anniversary of the founding of the faculty of fine arts of the University of Mexico, formerly the San Carlos Academy of Fine Arts, an exposition of "the industries of the human habitation" is being organized. It is being held from October 25 to November 30 at the National Theater of Mexico. In connection with the same event an exposition of fine arts, including architecture, painting, sculpture and engraving, is being arranged for the period from October 12 to November 30 at the National Theater.

The Polytechnic Institute of Brooklyn has initiated an evening course for alumni in applied psychology under the direction of Dr. Henry C. Link, continuing for one semester. The course is novel by reason of the fact that it is open to alumni only, and is given without charge and without credit. Preliminary inquiry brought forth the fact that the graduates of this engineering college were particularly interested in continuing their education in cultural rather than in technical subjects. In the present course every class from 1898 to 1931 is represented, and the registration totals 250 men.

The National Survey of School Finance has launched a nation-wide series of conferences, the first of which has just been held in St. Paul, Minnesota, destined to draw every state into direct cooperation with the Federal Office of Education in its study of public-school expenditures.

The British committee for the interchange of secondary women teachers has arranged 11 exchanges for the year, September, 1931, to July, 1932, between members of the staff of schools in Great Britain and the United States. This number represents an increase of 50 per cent. over the exchanges arranged during the last two years.

The new library building on the campus of the University of Kentucky, completed this fall at a cost of $400,000, was dedicated on October 23 with ceremonies on the mall which faces the structure. Dr. John H. Finley, associate editor of *The New York Times,* was the principal speaker. Governor Flem D. Sampson made the official presentation of the structure to the board of trustees of the university, and felicitations were extended to the university from the citizens of the state by Judge Samuel W. Wilson, of Lexington; from the American Library Association, by Mr. Edward A. Henry; from the Kentucky Library Association, by Mrs. Mary McClure Curry, and from the faculty of the university by Professor George K. Brady, of the English department. Dr. Frank L. McVey, president of the university, presided at the dedication exercises.

Lafayette College has received a gift of $50,000 from Israel P. Pardee as a memorial to his son, a trustee of the college, who died last year.

A memorial fund of $10,000 to be known as the Charles E. Merrill Fund, is given to Dartmouth College under the terms of the will of Sally Markoe Merrill, who died on October 11. The will stipulates that the income be used annually for such undergraduates as are deemed worthy by the proper authorities.

Among recent bequests to Cornell University are the following: According to the will of the late Jessica Tyler Austen, wife of Willard Austen, emeritus librarian, $1,000 has been made available to the university for a book fund for the department of American history. In the will of Charles Dipple, Jr., who died on May 20 at Minneapolis, Cornell was named residuary legatee of an estate valued at $75,000. Walter Platte Cook, of Buffalo, who died on August 4, left $50,000 to the university to be held as a fund to assist with loans worthy students in the college of law.

Plans are now being formed to make the U. S. Office of Education the repository of all facts and theories on education by radio. It is the aim of this division to collect any material or information dealing with broadcasting which is of educational nature, whether sponsored by private commercial stations or publicly controlled educational stations.

The quality of high-school instruction in Michigan is of a high average, according to a report from the University of Michigan, which shows that a majority of the schools, 601 in number, are on the accredited list of the university. Students of accredited schools, recommended by their principals, may enter the university without taking examinations. The report also shows that 210 of these schools with 119,627 students are also members of the North Central Association. The enrolment for all accredited schools is 161,875. These students are taught by 7,711 teachers, who commonly conduct five classes daily, 64 per cent. having less than 141 pupils each day, 11 per cent. from 141 to 150 pupils, 7 per cent. from 151 to 160, and 18 per cent. over 160. In the Michigan public schools of the North Central Association the average salary of 983 new teachers was $1,749, and the degrees they held were: Doctor, 2; master, 150; bachelor, 722; no degree, 109. Of all teachers in these high schools the largest number received their training at the University of Michigan, the next highest numbers being at the Michigan State Normal College and Michigan State College.

That 26.4 per cent. of the students in the universities and colleges of Canada are women is shown in a Dominion government report on higher education in Canada, for 1929–30, which is summarized in *The Christian Science Monitor*. If extramural students and students of evening classes, summer schools and other short courses are included, the percentage is increased to 29.2. The figures of university grade students for Ontario are 9,595 men and 4,639 women, showing a rapid increase, and in Quebec Province 8,791 men and 1,825 women. The University of Montreal has 5,494 students of university grade, 3,714 men. Students of university grade at the University of Toronto are 6,704, of which 4,277 are men.

DISCUSSION

HUMANIZING GRADES

This note is an attempt to apply to the teaching of an exact science, like chemistry, some of the points emphasized in Laurence R. Campbell's excellent paper, "So Pupils May Know."[1]

Far too many students credit—or discredit—their teachers with a kind of "I'll-give-you-any-grade-I-damn-please-and-you-can't-do-a-damn-thing-about-it" complex. When this state of equilibrium is reached grades become, from the student's view-point, as incalculable as acts of God—and as futile, as far as any educational value is concerned.

Most progressive teachers deplore the necessity of inflicting grades of any kind upon their students, but as long as it must be done every effort should be made to inject as many elements of helpfulness into the system as possible. The students should be able to take it for granted that the grading will be: (1) Fair; (2) impartial; (3) impersonal; (4) uniform; (5) entirely comprehensible to the student.

In handling a class of five hundred elementary chemistry students the writer has found the following procedure helpful to himself and his staff of assistants and encouraging to the students. At the outset of the course the system of grading is carefully explained. All grading is done on the basis of 100 per cent. for the *best* work. The proportion of marks which will be assigned, in the final grade, to each branch of the work—recitations, written quizzes, laboratory work and final examinations—is explicitly stated. In this course it is 25 per cent. for each branch. Every effort is made to give the system the *appearance,* as well as the reality, of absolute fairness. It is explained to the students that all their quiz and examination papers are marked by the whole staff of assistants, each assistant taking one question throughout the whole set of papers, thus elimi-

[1] School and Society, 32, p. 762.

nating, as far as possible, any personal bias on the part of any assistant.

The students are frankly told that their instructors make no claim to omniscience—that mistakes may occur, either in the totalling and averaging of numerical grades, or in judgment of evaluating the students' answers. Every quiz-paper, exercise, set of problems, and examination paper is returned to the students, plainly marked. While it is not possible for the instructors to write out the corrections of each mistake, some kind of mark indicating the location of the error is always put in. Students are asked, for their own protection, to keep all their papers until the end of the term, figure out their own grades, and bring back their papers to the clerk of the department if they think any mistake in calculation has been made. If any error is proved (there are a few) due correction is made, and put through the registrar's office, no matter what inconvenience may be involved. The student is never told that the grade has gone through and can not be changed.

Students are urged to study their returned papers and satisfy themselves of the fairness of the marking. If they are unable to do this, they are invited to take the paper to their individual instructors and discuss the matter with them. If the instructor feels that a mistake has been made, he takes the paper to the colleague of his who has marked the question (students are not told which instructor marks each question) and if the two agree, an adequate correction is made. If the instructors can not agree, the paper comes to the head of the department, who makes the final decision. If the student feels that he has not obtained justice from his instructor, he may appeal directly to the head of the department. In actual practice, this hardly ever occurs.

There is no doubt that this system, however mechanical, induces a considerable amount of genuine study. Students check over their errors carefully, look up the correct answers, and even consult other texts to find justification for statements or equations not found in the official course. Such study is far more fruitful than routine "boning" for a quiz. The knowledge that the grades they assign will be carefully scrutinized and compared also induces methodical, accurate marking on the part of the instructors.

Many teachers will feel that encouraging students to criticize their grades and "come back for points" must open the door to all manner of abuse. As a matter of fact, the proportion of papers which come back is not large—varying from 5 to 10 per cent. And in the vast majority of these the student's claim is found to be justified. The instructors and recorder make as many mistakes, on the average, as the students. Certain precautions against fraud have to be taken, and very occasionally a student is warned not to bring up obvious quibbles. In dubious cases, the student is always given the benefit of the doubt. The department would rather let an occasional student "get by" with something than give the impression of arbitrary unfairness.

No "snap" quizzes are given and no "trick" questions are used. All the questions in any quiz or examination are equally "weighted," for marking purposes. Assignments for study and laboratory work are made as accurate and explicit as possible. In the reviews which precede quizzes and examinations the classes are told exactly "what they will be held for." As far as possible, every chance for misunderstanding or "bad luck" is excluded.

Having established a sure foundation of fairness and a bedrock of minimum requirements which every student—even the average high-school graduate—can understand and upon which every student can absolutely depend, some attempt is made to clothe this admittedly mechanical skeleton of routine with a little intellectual flesh and blood. Students are told that their grades will depend upon the accuracy and excellence of their work rather than the amount they "get over." No attention is paid to the appearance—internal or external—of laboratory notebooks but grades are based upon the symmetry, compactness and efficiency of laboratory setups and the skill shown in manipulation. Every experiment—students are told—should be a work of art, worthy of being photographed as a model. "Synthetic" questions and problems, requiring the student to put together methods and pieces of information in various parts of the text, are frequently used. Problems are worked from first principles—not formulae—and are stated in various ways to test the students' intellectual grasp of the principles involved. Instructors are taught how to vary their class programs and diversify their work by giving demonstrations of practical applications, assigning simple qualitative and quantitative determinations, bringing in bits of history, referring to current chemical discoveries, etc. Ambitious students (of which there are a few) are assigned difficult experiments to demonstrate to the section, or given an occasional "project."

Probably no system of grading can be made ideal—certainly not in a class of five hundred students where the subject is difficult and unpopular and taken, for the most part, only as a subsidiary prerequisite to the student's main purpose. But the writer believes that a straightforward, explicit and scrupulously fair system of grading will go far to eliminate the heart-burnings and bitter disgruntlements that so often follow the giving out of term-grades. Of the several thousand students who have gone through the educational machine described above, the writer knows of no single one who has left the department feeling that he has not had a fair deal. And if the students' confidence and respect can be won at the outset, and maintained throughout the course, even the most mechanical system of grading can be so handled as to constitute a definite, positive, educational factor.

G. WAKEHAM
UNIVERSITY OF COLORADO

QUOTATIONS

SCHOOLS FOR THE JAPANESE AINU

WITH the opening of the school season in Hokkaido this autumn, another great forward step has been taken in educating the Ainu aborigines of this island to fit them to take their place in the modern world.

For more than a century the Japanese Government has been concerned with the problem of the Ainu settlers in Hokkaido, this last remnant of a great prehistoric race whom many believe to be the forefathers of the Japanese themselves. Like the American Indians, the Ainu have survived to this day but, retaining their primitive customs and tribal isolation, they have failed to take much part in the active life about them.

To remedy this situation the educational bureau in Hokkaido has decided that the time has now come to cease sending Ainu children to exclusive schools and hereafter Ainu and Japanese children are to be educated alike in the government schools of the island. As a start in this direction, three of the largest primary schools heretofore reserved for the Ainu have been closed this year and the pupils of these special institutions are mingling to-day on an equal basis with their Japanese neighbors.

The money appropriated for the running expenses of these Ainu schools will be used now for social service work in the tribal villages, while the buildings themselves have been converted into museums where Ainu relics are exhibited and Ainu handicrafts are offered for sale.

Another important step has been taken in promoting the higher education of Ainu children with the incorporation this year of the Batchelor Educational Institute, a privately financed enterprise for the purpose of bringing Ainu boys and girls of exceptional ability to the provincial capital here for advanced training.

The institute has been named in honor of Dr. John Batchelor, the English missionary scholar who has lived in Hokkaido and worked among the Ainu for the past 55 years. It was Dr. Batchelor who recorded the Ainu language in written form, studied the customs and folklore of the people, and used his influence at home and abroad to "give the Ainu boys and girls a chance to make a place for themselves" under present competitive conditions.

Dr. Batchelor's home in Sapporo now adjoins the dormitories of the institute which bears his name. There is room here for 12 students, although funds at present are sufficient for the education of only seven youths. All the money for the institute has been contributed by Japanese who sympathize with the plan to bring boys and girls from the isolation of the Ainu villages to Sapporo, where they may not only obtain advanced education but also mingle with the Japanese and obtain work among them.

To an Occidental, the Ainu and Japanese look much alike, especially nowadays when most of the aborigines wear kimonos and speak Japanese. There has also been much intermarriage between the two peoples and many Ainu families have adopted Japanese babies, so that it is difficult to determine exactly how many of the original settlers of Hokkaido still exist. The census taken in 1908 recorded 20,000 Ainu living in their native villages, but latest figures indicate that there are now not more than 15,000 descendants of the once warlike tribes which overran all of Japan centuries ago.

Relations between the Ainu and Japanese to-day are entirely friendly. None of the friction which sometimes mars conditions in Formosa or Korea appears to exist in the cold Hokkaido and attached to every Ainu village one finds Japanese teachers and scholars who are devoted to the amiable folk whose conditions they are seeking to improve. Near Obihiro, for instance, where in the far interior of Hokkaido the special Ainu primary school was abolished this year, Mr. Iwao Yoshida has acted as the school principal for 22 years. Although eligible for retirement now and able to return to his homeland in the south, Mr. Yoshida has decided to remain at Obihiro doing voluntary education work among the Ainu of his district.

Mr. Yoshida's practical experience in teaching confirms the special tests given to Ainu children in Sapporo, showing that the Ainu are in no way deficient in intelligence. The children's studies not only compare favorably with those of Japanese children of the same age, but many Ainu graduates have distinguished themselves in work undertaken in their adult years.

The Hokkaido provincial government has provided individual farms for each Ainu family to recompense them for the wide plains in which the men formerly hunted game. But as the people are not naturally agriculturally inclined, the Ainu are admittedly poor farmers, growing barely enough crops for their own needs. For this reason many Ainu boys are now being encouraged to take special advanced agricultural courses so they may assist in bringing the standard of farming in their villages to a higher level.

A convention of 50 delegates from Ainu tribes all over Hokkaido met in Sapporo last summer, coming here to attend the Colonial exhibition which was staged in the capital. These village chieftains assembled to discuss their mutual problems and to study advances in agricultural methods which they might apply in their own districts.

Like the people whom they represented, it was found that the delegates more than 60 years of age spoke no Japanese, while those less than 40 no longer could understand the tongue of their forefathers. It remained for the men of middle age, speaking half Ainu and half Japanese, to act as interpreters among their own people.

Addressing this mixed assembly, first in one language and then in the other, Dr. Batchelor urged that the Ainu organize "Bee Societies," not necessarily to go in for apiculture, but rather to "emulate the habits of the bee and so by industry and organization create honey" for themselves.

The eagerness with which the Ainu to-day are seeking to improve their conditions gives every promise, Dr. Batchelor declared, that although the race is fast disappearing, largely through intermarriage with the Japanese, the Ainu strain that is being carried on is one well worthy of preservation—Special correspondence from Sapporo, Japan, to *The Christian Science Monitor*.

REPORTS

THE CLASSICS AND THE MODERN MAGAZINE

"Faust" unread, "Tom Jones" forgotten, "Tartuffe" neglected, "The Iliad" discarded and "Pickwick Papers" ignored. Have these magic titles, which delighted our parents and grandparents, fallen into disuse before the onrush of modern publications? Have the classics lost their former authority and favor in the literary world? Or are these old favorites still the background of modern writings and vital to an intelligent understanding of them? Is contemporary literature bringing new angles of approach and different emphases to the older books?

Many people assert that the fiction which was

written prior to the latter decades of the nineteenth century is of no vital concern to our modern life and thought. They claim that the subject-matter is treated in a manner romantic and unreal; the elaborate plot is far-fetched and untrue to life; the slowness of action and the mass of detail is tiresome; the sentences are long and complicated; and the style is heavy and dull. The essays deal with a view of religious and moral life which has essentially changed; the systems of philosophy conceived prior to the scientific age appear narrow and circumscribed; the political and industrial discussions are remote and dull and the comments upon manners and customs are tiresome or stupid. The older poetry is said to give little pleasure, for it is too often either difficult to read and concerned with a heaven in which a materialistic world has little or no interest or is insipidly romantic or didactic.

The critics who object to the older literature argue that traditional usage still too largely determines both the substance and taste in literature as advocated by the departments of literature in the high schools and colleges and by the public library reading lists. Many of the scholars and laymen, who are not in sympathy with the wide-spread use of the classics, believe that "present social needs" are the best clues to the choice of reading matter, and advocate for the general reading public a more extensive perusal of the books and magazines which grapple with our present-day ideals and problems in a realistic manner. They contend that the reader's interests and his psychological aptitudes should largely determine his choice of reading material. Mr. Abraham Flexner, a foremost educator in America, believes that in literature study students' interests should provide the starting point (perhaps the finishing point also), and that it is damaging to good taste and wasteful of time to insist that they read the classics. "Reality" and "interest" would be his sole guides to the choice of materials and from these he would endeavor to develop and refine the students' tastes. As a criterion for determining the reality of material Mr. Flexner would include nothing which does not prove its worth here and now in terms of significant occurrence in every-day life.

A few years ago an effort was made to determine the objectives in the teaching of literature through the consensus of judgment of teachers and educators and as a result 1,500 aims were listed. Each of these goals, no doubt, has some claim, but it is obvious that they are not all of equal importance or very generally accepted. Practically all teachers agreed, however, that one aim of literature teaching is to prepare students to read good contemporary literature with pleasure and profit.

At first sight it would seem that in order to read twentieth century fiction, essays or poetry with pleasure and profit a knowledge of and interest in contemporary problems and life is all that is necessary. Even if historical or classical subject-matter is chosen, the penetrating intensity of modern scientific research is often turned upon it in such a way that it emerges clothed in present-day garb—*a la* Erskine's "The Private Life of Helen of Troy." Without doubt the trend of current reading and writing is away from the traditional and classical, and it is obvious that subject-matter which is pertinent to-day is absorbing the attention of most authors. Nevertheless, it would be interesting to analyze the general utilization of library materials as revealed in newspapers, magazines, library withdrawals and book sales to see what demand they make upon the reader. If the classics or references to them do not occur in sufficient amounts and frequencies in bodies of printed matter used outside of school then the case against them may be a legitimate one. If, on the other hand, a knowledge of the classics and traditionally esteemed literature is necessary as a background for an intelligent understanding of contemporary literature then the case asuumes an entirely different aspect.

As a check upon these possibilities the writer concluded that it would be interesting and possibly enlightening to apply some standard of measurement which might give a clue to the literary information essential if pleasure and profit is to be received from the reading of current literature. It was assumed that a high-grade magazine is a representative form of contemporary literature. A systematic inspection of such a publication would reveal the specific pieces of literature and the authors the contributors to the magazine take for granted that the reader knows both of present-day writings and of the earlier centuries. It would also show the classics which are functioning in twentieth century literature and whether such critics as Flexner are justified in their suspicion of them. The *Atlantic Monthly* was chosen as a sample of a good current magazine. Any other magazine of the same quality would have served the purpose equally well and, no doubt, with much the same results.

The magazines were carefully read, nothing being omitted except the advertisements, while reading attention was centered upon the allusions made to pieces of literature and authors in essays, short stories, poems, letters and the like. For example, if while reading a political or social essay some reference was made to Shakespeare's "Merchant of Venice," to Cervantes' "Don Quixote," or to Masefield's "A Window in Bye Street," the name of the author and his work thus referred to was noted. These allusions were later grouped under the various forms of literature, fiction, non-fiction, drama and poetry and classified according to the century or literary period in which a given work was produced. The frequencies of allusions were also recorded. Generally speaking, the more often a piece is referred to the more essential it is that the reader be familiar with it if he is to read intelligently. The editors assume that the books and authors thus referred to are sufficiently well known so that allusions to them open in the reader's mind wide vistas of related or comparative knowledge.

It was difficult to determine the amount of data necessary to make the results somewhat dependable and representative. Finally, it was decided to limit the study to two years' issues of the magazine, the twelve months of the year just prior to the outbreak of the world war and the twelve issues of a recent year. Evidently, two rather widely separated years would give a more representative picture of social practices and concerns than would two consecutive years. The war, too, might have had some effect upon the content and emphasis in the magazine contributions. A third or fourth sampling, perhaps 1903 or 1920, would have made the frequencies of reference a more reliable index of permanency of value of specific selections. This study does not in any way attempt to settle the dispute concerning the classics or to evaluate the relative merits of the pieces. The sampling of social usage in one magazine, even for the whole period of its existence, would be inadequate and would only touch the very edge of the problem. As has been stated before, the purpose was simply to use a tangible method for ascertaining what classics the better magazines allude to.

It was soon apparent that many allusions are shadowy and implicit, not clear and explicit; so that only a real literary scholar could hope to identify them. The writer's own pleasure, large though it was, was handicapped by having frequently to forego the connection between the theme and the allusion. Perhaps many readers suffer a similar deprivation. It is impossible to repair such gaps at the time of reading the magazine because the meaning of an allusion must be learned in context if it is to be informative. Therefore, it was practical to list only those which were explicitly given. The necessity of omitting a considerable number of references that could not be readily identified seems not to have affected the results adversely but only means that the actual number of books alluded to was considerably larger than was recorded. The allusions are undoubtedly of unequal significance. Some are vital to the meaning of the piece and others are purely ornamental. Citations of literature in the *Atlantic Monthly* were of two kinds, those to specific selections and references to authors. The latter are not of quite the same importance as the former. They do not enable one to identify definitely a book or poem, but nevertheless they are essential, for reference to an author often indicates his masterpiece, as in the case of Cervantes. The mention of his name serves the same end as an allusion to Don Quixote and a reference to Browning presupposes a general knowledge of his lyric poems.

These tabulations show that there are 2,693 references to selections and authors in twenty-four issues of the *Atlantic Monthly*. They represent a rich and varied choice from all the periods of literary history from Greek and Roman time to the present.

The books which have been written since the opening of the twentieth century are not rightly called classics, for they have not yet been evaluated nor have the worth-while been sifted from the trivial. Many of to-day's best sellers may eventually become classics, and if we are to believe the critics a large number of them have a lasting and enduring value. Only time can do this weeding out process, and so this period is passed over with only a few general comments. There are 348 allusions to twentieth century literature. These deal primarily with the strictly current books of the years studied in this survey. This would, no doubt, be true of the popular books mentioned in any magazine and is a phase to be expected in contemporary writings. Naturally, the latest thing in fiction, essay or poetry holds the popular attention and is the vogue of the moment.

It is somewhat easier to arrive at well-defined attitudes toward nineteenth century literature than toward twentieth century material, for they represent tested writings and their relative and lasting importance has been more nearly determined. References to authors and selections of the nineteenth century far outnumber all other periods with 770 allusions. Qualitatively the list is as significant as quantitatively. All the great novels of the past century are included. We find "A Tale of Two Cities," "Pickwick Papers," "Martin Chuzzlewit," "Henry Esmond," "The Newcomes," "Middlemarch," "Last of the Mohicans," "Lorna Doone," "Cranford" and "Ivanhoe" and most of the other English and American favorites. The *Atlantic Monthly* also assumes that the readers know the works of the continental writers, Balzac, Loti, Daudet, Tolstoy, Zola, Flaubert, Dostoyevsky, Hugo, De Maupassant and Bjornson.

The references to the non-fiction of the period are solid and heavy in quality and assume a rather comprehensive reading of forty-six specific selections and a knowledge of sixty-three writers. Emerson's "Essays," Thoreau's "Walden" and "Maine Woods," Carlyle's "Sartor Resartus" and "French Revolution," Ruskin's "Selections" (12 of them), Trollope's "Autobiography," and Darwin's "Origin of Species" are representative general works. Considerably emphasis is placed upon religious discussions, such as Arnold's "St. Paul and Protestantism," Cardinal Newman's "Apologia," Rénan's "Life of Jesus," and James' "Varieties of Religious Experience." Philosophical writings and philosophers receive much attention. Bergson's "Creative Evolution," Haeckel's "Natural History of Creation," Nietzsche's "Beyond Good and Evil" and "Thus Spake Zarathustra," and Spencer's "First Principles," are specifically mentioned and many other philosophers are alluded to. The fact that Durant's "Story of Philosophy" found such a responsive audience on a large scale in the United States seems to indicate that people are eager for this type of knowledge when it is presented in a sufficiently popular form for the layman to comprehend. However, diluted or straight, the contributors to the *Atlantic Monthly* expect their readers to be informed on philosophical theories.

Nineteenth century drama received small attention with only five plays listed—Oscar Wilde's "The Importance of Being Earnest," Rostand's "Cyrano De Bergerac," Pinero's "The Second Mrs. Tanqueray" and "Isis," and Ibsen's "Peer Gynt" and "Brand." Did the nineteenth century produce but few dramas which have become a part of our literary heritage?

The eighty-four references to nineteenth century poetry generously cover the principal English and American authors. All the qualities which are considered suitable for poetry during the romantic nineteenth century are adequately expressed: love, appreciation of nature, reflections upon life, chivalry and the like. Walt Whitman is almost the only poet listed who approached his material in the spirit or method of realism. It is surprising to note that the names of Bryant, Longfellow, Holmes, Whittier, Lowell and Poe do not figure largely in the *Atlantic Monthly* references. Probably they would in a larger survey. Goethe and his masterpiece "Faust" are alluded to twenty times, more than any other nineteenth century poet. Likewise, a larger survey might not proportionately exalt Goethe in present social utilization. "The Ancient Mariner," "Kubla Khan," "The Grasshopper and the Cricket," "The Thrush," "Prometheus Unbound," "To a Skylark," "Omar Khayyam," "Dante's Dream," "The Town and the Old Court Suburb," and many poems of Tennyson and Wordsworth should be so well known that the moment these magic titles or quotations from the poems themselves are seen the whole lovely word-pictures flash instantly into the reader's mind.

It would seem that eighteenth century literature is not of the same importance as are nineteenth century writings. References to this century are comparatively few in the *Atlantic Monthly* articles. Presumably, those pieces and authors which are referred to, however, have a certain permanency of value, and an intelligent reader should be familar with Defoe's "Robinson Crusoe," Goldmith's "Vicar of Wakefield," Swift's "Gulliver's Travels," Le Sage's "Gil Blas," Richardson's "Clarissa Harlowe" and "Pamela," Sterne's "Tristram Shandy" and "Sentimental Journey," Johnson's "Rasselas," Day's "Sanford and Merton," and the works of Marie Edgworth, Mrs. Hannah Moore, Fielding, Smollett and Walpole.

In the field of eighteenth century non-fiction a wider knowledge is essential for Gibbon's "Decline and Fall of the Roman Empire," Adam Smith's "Wealth of Nations," Lessing's "Education of the Human Race," Chateaubriand's "Genius of Christianity," Boswell's "Life of Johnson" and "A Tour of the Hebrides," Addison's "Spectator," Paine's "Age of Reason," Rousseau's "Emile" and "Social Contract" are mentioned several times. In fact twenty-five selections and ninety non-fiction writers are alluded to from three to eight times each. Some knowledge of the eighteenth century philosophers, Hume, Kant and Voltaire, are vital to the thorough understanding of contemporary literature.

The only eighteenth century dramatists whose works seem to function in modern writings are Goldsmith's "She Stoops to Conquer," Sheridan's "The Rivals," "The School for Scandal" and "The Critic," Voltaire's "Candide," and the dramas of Schiller, Wycherly and Von Kotzebue.

Burns' "Tam o' Shanter," "To a Mountain Daisy" and a "Cotter's Saturday Night" are the favorite eighteenth century poems. Cowper's "The Task," Hood's "Bridge of Sighs" and "Silence," Thomson's "The Seasons," Gray's "Elegy," "My Grave Lord Keeper," Goldsmith's "Deserted Village," and Pope's "Essay on Man" are cited and the names of Blake, Collins, Crabbe, Herbert, Lessing, Ramsay, Schiller and Shenstone are used by way of comparison and correlation.

Without doubt the sixteenth and seventeenth centuries which include the great Elizabethan period are salient in the history of literature, and presumably the reading public has at least a passing acquaintance with the works of such men as Shakespeare, Samuel Pepys, Francis Bacon, Bunyan, Cervantes and La Fontaine. In the realm of non-fiction appear the works and names of most of the Protestant reformers; the essays of Isaac Newton, John Locke and Francis Bacon; the Maxims of La Rochefoucauld; the diaries of Samuel Pepys and of Blaise Pascal; the philosophy of Spinoza, and the autobiography of Benvenuto Cellini. In fact, the contributors presume that the reader has some knowledge of sixteen selections and the works of thirty-nine non-fiction writers who lived in the sixteenth and seventeenth centuries.

As would be expected, references to Shakespeare's plays far outnumber all other works of this period. Each of his dramas is mentioned a score of times. The names of several other dramas appear, Corneille's "Polyeucte," Racine's "Phèdre" and "Mithridate," Dryden's "An Evening's Love" or "The Mock Astrologer," Ben Jonson's "Volpone" or "The Fox," Marlowe's "Tamburlaine," and Molière's "Tartuffe."

Milton's poems "Paradise Lost," "Paradise Regained," "On His Blindness," Spencer's "Faerie Queene," Samuel Butler's "Hudibras," and Tasso's "Jerusalem Delivered," are each referred to, but it is doubtful if these have a wide reading outside of schools and colleges. Jonson's "Drink to Me Only With Thine Eyes," the King James' version of the Bible, and Shakespeare's "Sonnets," no doubt, have a wider popular appeal, and references to them call forth a ready response in the minds of the readers.

Mention is made of fifty-five selections of literature produced during the fourteenth and fifteenth centuries. These include Erasmus's "The Praise of Folly," Boccaccio's "Eulogy of Rome," Froissart's "Chronicles," Thomas À Kempis' "Imitation of Christ," Malory's "Holy Grail," Rabelais' "Gargantua," Brandt's "The Ship of Fooles," Wycliffe's "Triologues," More's "Utopia," and the works of Caxton, Huss, Melanchthon, Petrarch, Luther, Machiavelli, and the poets, Archibald Douglas, William Dunbar, Sir David Lyndsay and François Villon. Undoubtedly, many of these are well known to the layman, for so general has the name and theme of More's book become that the word Utopia has almost ceased to be a proper name.

Even medieval literature figures largely in current magazines with eighty-four allusions. Chaucer appears to be the best known to the present-day writers. They make frequent mention of the man himself and his "Canterbury Tales," with special emphasis on "The Miller's Tale," "The Parson's Tale," "The Knight's Tale" and "The Nun Priest's Tale." Dante is often quoted, as are verses from the lovely English and Scottish ballads. The early folk-lore as recorded in "Chanson de Roland," "The Elder Edda," and the "Lays of the Minnesingers" form an integral part of the background for the enjoyment and understanding of present-day writings. The fulness of representation of the choicest selections of each century is most surprising, especially in a sampling of only one magazine over a period of two years. If the list becomes much longer the magazine reading public will demand an even more comprehensive selection of classics than is included in Eliot's Five Foot Shelf.

The reader can not be content with knowing something of medieval and modern European and American literature, but he must have pigeonholed in his mind a generous knowledge of Greek and Roman writings, for 225 references were made to the classical period. Homer's "Iliad" and "Odyssey" were mentioned many times in each issue of the magazines, as were Aristotle's "Ethics" and "Politics," but the contributors also demand that the readers be familiar with Theocritus' "Greek Anthology" and "Greek Prosody," Ovid's "Tristia," Aeschylus' "Orestes," Apuleius' "Asse of Gold," Aristophanes' "Lysistrata," and the works of thirty-five other authors. Likewise more than one hundred allusions were made to Greek and Roman mythological characters. A number of studies have shown that it is futile to use a dictionary or encyclopedia in trying to understand allusions to mythology; they must be learned in context to have any real meaning. The classical mythology is lovely and symbolic and should be so well learned in childhood that references to it open up a whole treasure gallery of stirring and dramatic pictures.

Recently, the Bible Guild raised the question whether there is a prejudice against quoting the Bible or using its phraseology in editorial writing. The discussion which ensued was to the effect that if there is a decline in the number of Biblical allusions it is because writers are not familiar with the Bible or because of the readers' ignorance of Biblical stories and characters, which seems "to be assuming a good deal of knowledge about the readers." Neither of these charges can be made against the men and women who write for the *Atlantic Monthly,* for 607 allusions to the Bible or quotations from it were made in two years' issues of that magazine. The number of references to the Old and New Testament was only surpassed by allusions to nineteenth century literature. An interesting disclosure is the fact that the Old Testament has only twenty allusions less than have the Gospels and the Letters. Genesis is the favorite Old Testament book, and Matthew is most often quoted from the New Testament. Post-war skepticisms and indifference to religious observations and practices seem not to have materially affected the literary use of Biblical references. There was only a slight decrease (50) in the number of references to the Bible in the post-war year from the ante-war year. Religious thought in America, if it can be judged by this sampling, is overwhelmingly Christian because less than fifty comments were made upon the other great religions of the world. The large number of allusions to Biblical literature suggests that if current literature is to be read with pleasure and profit the Bible must not be relegated to a dark, unused corner of the library but must stand on the library table beside Shakespeare, Jane Austen and the best seller of the month.

Not a mean order of classics! To be exact, reference was made to 725 specific selections of literature, the names of 425 writers and 607 Biblical quotations, making a grand total of 1,757 selections and authors. If to this is added the frequencies or duplications, the total amounts to 2,693 allusions to literature in twenty-four issues of one typical high-grade American magazine. A vast majority of these books are rightly called classics, books which have stood the test of time and the processes of elimination and have become the very warp and woof of our literature. They hold within their covers the joys and sorrows, the triumphs and failures, the loves and the hates, the hopes and the fears of mankind which are elemental and ageless. The facts presented here seem to prove rather conclusively that the classics still live in our literature and motivate it, and the reader of current literature loses a priceless share of the joy and beauty of reading if he does not possess this precious heritage. Apparently the critics who insist that "present social needs" should determine the choice of reading matter have failed to realize the important part the classics play in the fulfilment of that aim. The lovers of the old books are vindicated. Once more we may suffer with Faust, laugh at Tartuffe, thrill at the Iliad, and chuckle with Mr. Pickwick. Long live the classics!

MURIEL LEWIN GUBERLET
UNIVERSITY OF WASHINGTON

SOCIETIES AND MEETINGS

THE WORLD CONFERENCE ON EDUCATION AT DENVER

DR. CHARLES H. WILLIAMS, secretary of the World Federation of Education Associations, writes that the World Conference on Education held at Denver, Colorado, from July 27 to August 1, by the World Federation of Education Associations has been one of the most successful of international educational meetings. The paid registration numbered more than three thousand eight hundred. Twenty-nine countries had representatives present as follows: Alaska, Belgium, Bulgaria, Canada, Canal Zone, Chile, China, Czechoslovakia, Dominican Republic, England, Finland, France, Germany, Guatemala, Hawaii, India, Iraq, Ireland, Japan, Mexico, New Zealand, Northern Ireland, Palestine, Panama, Philippines, Scotland, Sweden, Syria and the United States. Attendance at the group conferences was open without charge to all persons, so the actual attendance was larger than indicated by the registration figures.

The program, which covered a wide range of general and special educational topics, proved highly satisfactory, the interest manifested being most gratifying. Especially significant was the large attendance at the sessions featuring speakers from several countries, thus attesting the rapid growth of the international view-point.

The presidents of many of the chief educational associations of the world were among the speakers, including Miss Florence M. Hale, National Education Association of the United States; Count Hirotaro Hayashi, Japanese Imperial Education Association; Harry Linville, American Federation of Teachers; R. B. Miller, Educational Institute of Scotland; Robert Neilly, Irish National Teachers Organization; Angus Roberts, National Union of Teachers of England and Wales; and P. Seshadri, All India Teachers Federation. Among the general secretaries of national organizations outside the United States appearing on the program were Sir Frank Goldstone, National Union of Teachers of England and Wales; Mr. Thomas Henderson, Educational Institute of Scotland; Dr. Masanori Oshima, Japanese Imperial Education Association; Mr. G. R. Parker, honorary secretary, Association of Assistant Masters in Secondary Schools of England and Wales, and Mrs. U. Gordon Wilson, Association of Assistant Mistresses in Secondary Schools of England and Wales.

One of the most attractive features of the conference was the exhibition of rapid transmission of dispatches to various parts of the world, messages being telegraphed from the platform at one of the general meetings and answers being received in a few minutes from many eminent educators in the United States, Europe, Asia and South America. The extensive education exhibits, both of books and of samples of educational work in various cities, were of excellent character and attracted numerous visitors.

Important resolutions were adopted carrying out the policies of the Herman-Jordan committees in the interest of world peace and calling upon teachers everywhere to assist in advancing the cause of education in the fields represented by the various sections of the conference. These resolutions will be printed and made available in a short time. The proceedings will also be published in the near future.

The accommodations offered by the city of Denver were excellent, and the entertainment provided by the teachers and citizens of Denver and Colorado was of outstanding character, affording much pleasure to all participating.

Officers for the next biennial period were elected as follows: *President,* Dr. Paul Monroe, of Columbia University, New York; *Vice-presidents,* Europe—Mr. Thomas Henderson, Edinburgh, Scotland; Asia—Dr. P. W. Kuo, Shanghai, China; America—Mr. Harry Charlesworth, Vancouver, Canada; *Secretary-General,* Dr. Augustus O. Thomas, Augusta, Maine; *Secretary,* Charles H. Williams, Columbia, Missouri, and *Treasurer,* Dr. E. A. Hardy, Toronto, Canada.

Members elected or re-elected on the board of directors were as follows: Miss Selma M. Borchardt, Washington, D. C.; Mr. Harry Charlesworth, Vancouver, Canada; Count Hirotaro Hayashi, Tokyo; Mr. Thomas Henderson, Edinburgh; Dr. P. W. Kuo, Shanghai; Mr. Thomas J. O'Connell, Dublin; Mr. G. R. Parker, London; Mr. Angus Roberts, London; Mr. P. Seshadri, Cawnpore, India; Dr. Otto Tacke, Stettin, Germany, and Miss Annie C. Woodward, Somerville, Massachusetts.

The time and place of the next World Conference were left to be determined later, though invitations were received from several countries. The holding of a regional conference in Honolulu, Hawaii, in the summer of 1932 was approved by the board of directors, the details of arrangements being left in the hands of the executive committee.

EDUCATIONAL RESEARCH AND STATISTICS

VALIDATION OF A STATE-WIDE EDUCATIONAL GUIDANCE PROGRAM FOR HIGH-SCHOOL SENIORS[1]

THE Arkansas Educational Guidance Survey was inaugurated by the University of Arkansas in April, 1930, as a guidance program for high-school seniors. Thirty-nine of the larger high schools, mainly of North Central Association ranking, participated in the survey. Over 2,300 seniors, or approximately 40 per cent. of Arkansas high-school graduates for 1930, took the tests and were sent advisory letters based on test results and information obtained from questionnaires. The tests were four in number, as outlined below. Each student took three tests—the American Council psychological examination, the English test and either the mathematics examination or the foreign language aptitude examination (in no case both), depending upon the probable nature of his curricular selection in case he should go to college. He also filled out a brief one-page questionnaire asking for information concerning his parentage, home address, paternal occupation, educational and vocational intentions and financial condition. The tests of the survey battery were: (1) The American Council psychological examination—a 60-minute test of mental ability; (2) a 50-minute English examination, consisting of a 60-item test of ability to detect errors in punctuation and grammar and a 45-item test of sentence sense or of ability to distinguish between basic types of word groupings; (3) a 65-minute mathematics examination —an aptitude and training test consisting of thirteen arithmetical examples, twenty-two examples in algebra and eleven algebraic problems requiring relatively little computation; (4) the foreign language aptitude examination of the Iowa Placement Examination series—a 45-minute test consisting of one section on grammatical usage, one on recognition of English equivalents for simple Esperanto words and two sections on Esperanto translations of various types.

The authors report reliability coefficients of .94 and .97, respectively, for the 1928 edition of the psychological examination and the foreign language examination, while the coefficients for the English and mathematics tests are, respectively, .87 and .89.

The purpose of this article is to show the relationships existing between the scores of these high-school seniors on the tests of the survey and the first term or semester scholastic success in college for those survey students who entered certain Arkansas institutions of higher learning. This report was made possible through the cooperation of 13 colleges and junior col-

[1] Research Paper No. 249, Journal Series, University of Arkansas.

leges of the state and their courtesy in supplying data concerning scholastic success of the survey students enrolling as freshmen in the autumn of 1930.

The validity of any guidance program depends upon the degree to which the adviser's predictions are borne out in the subsequent experience of the students. To determine the success of the Arkansas survey in this direction, the writer, as director of the program, conducted an investigation with the cooperation of three fourths of the colleges and junior colleges of the state intended to show the degree to which the survey tests predicted both general and specific scholastic success in college for survey participants. The Pearson "product-moment" method of correlation was used to determine the relationships between the following sets of variables: (1) Between percentile scores on the psychological examination and a grade point average (G.P.A.) or measure of general scholastic success for the first term or semester; (2) between percentile scores on the English test and term or semester grades in the basic freshman English course; (3) between percentile scores on the mathematics test and term or semester grades in the basic mathematics course; (4) between percentile scores on the foreign language examination and term or semester grades in all foreign language courses combined.

For the last three types of relationships mentioned above, the letter grade in the specific subject was used as the second variable. It was found by a comparison of reports from the various institutions that the grading standards all adhered closely to the "normal curve" method of grade distribution. All institutions used the A, B, C, D and F grades, while most had an intermediate E for conditions and an Inc. for unfinished courses. Deviation from the "normal curve" allotment of grades—A, 7 per cent.; B, 24 per cent.; C, 38 per cent.; D, 24 per cent.; E and F, 7 per cent.—was not sufficiently great in any school to warrant an attempt at equating grades, so those from the various institutions were accepted as directly comparable. The University of Arkansas has established an arbitrary system of weighting grades in the determination of grade point averages or measures of general scholastic success. The weights assigned to various letter grades are: A—6, B—4, C—2, D—0, E— -1 and F— -2. These weightings were used in obtaining the grade point averages for correlating with percentile scores on the psychological examination.

Table I presents a list of the schools from which final data were received and the correlation coefficients obtained between the sets of variables outlined above. Except for the psychological and English examinations, correlations were not run for less than ten cases. Therefore, comparatively few coefficients are listed for mathematics, due, in part, to the fact that the mathematics test was given to only about 40 per cent. of the original survey students. As foreign languages taken in college were somewhat varied and the numbers taking each language were relatively small, the correlations in this subject-matter field do not discriminate between languages or course advancement but are based on all foreign language courses at any level. A limitation similar to that in mathematics exists here, also, for only about 55 per cent. of the total survey participants took the foreign language test.

It should be understood that the numbers of students listed in Table I do not indicate the relative freshman enrolments of the various institutions, for in no case does the number of freshmen represented exceed half of the entire freshman class, and the percentages for the several schools fluctuate greatly.

Correlation coefficients obtained with the American Council psychological examination and grade point averages range from .17 to .81. Eight of the 12 coefficients are significantly high, as indicated by the starred items in the table. For the three term-basis schools combined and the ten semester-basis schools combined, the coefficients obtained are both .54 with both probable errors of small account. This degree of relationship is rather surprisingly high, for the usual range of correlation coefficients between scores on this examination at college entrance and first semester scholarship is from .40 to .50 or .55. The "r" for freshmen entering the University of Arkansas in September, 1929, was .47, a fairly representative figure. In general, relationships between test scores and scholastic success in college have been

TABLE I

CORRELATION COEFFICIENTS AND PROBABLE ERRORS: PERCENTILE SCORES ON SURVEY TESTS VERSUS SCHOLASTIC SUCCESS IN THE FIRST TERM OR SEMESTER OF ATTENDANCE AT ARKANSAS HIGHER EDUCATIONAL INSTITUTIONS

Institution	Psychological			English			Mathematics			For. Lang.[1]		
	No.	"r"	P.E.	No.	"r"	P.E.	No.	"r"	P.E.	No.	"r"	P.E.
Arkansas (Batesville)	22	.61*	.09	21	.40	.12	......	......	......	10	.75*	.10
Arkansas Teachers[2] (Conway)	27	.74*	.06	25	.77*	.06	......	......	......	......	......	......
John Brown (Siloam Springs)	10	.51	.17	9	.65*	.13	......	......	......	......	......	......
Central (Conway)	11	.81*	.07	11	.70*	.11	......	......	......	......	......	......
Crescent (Eureka Springs)	......	......	......	......	......	......	......	......	......	......	......	......
Ft. Smith Junior (Ft. Smith)	34	.38	.10	30	.75*	.05	......	......	......	14	.38	.15
Galloway Women's (Searcy)	29	.44*	.11	26	.68*	.07	......	......	......	23	.69*	.07
Henderson State[2] (Arkadelphia)	10	.50	.16	9	.68*	.12	......	......	......	......	......	......
Hendrix-Henderson (Conway)	23	.76*	.06	21	.80*	.05	......	......	......	10	.90*	.04
Little Rock Junior (Little Rock)	78	.54*	.05	73	.48*	.06	19	.59*	.10	26	.12	.13
Ouachita[2] (Arkadelphia)	14	.17	.18	12	.73*	.09	......	......	......	......	......	......
Texarkana Junior (Texarkana, Tex.)	21	.65*	.09	21	.70*	.08	......	......	......	......	......	......
University (Fayetteville)	148	.54*	.04	141	.65*	.03	47†	.64*	.06	35	.33	.14
							23	.50*	.11			
Term Basis	51	.54*	.07	46	.73*	.05	......	......	......	18	.36	.14
Semester Basis	378	.54*	.03	356	.60*	.02	114	.59*	.04	154	.41*	.05

[1] Correlations for the foreign languages based on all courses in modern or ancient foreign language.
[2] Schools organized on term basis; all others on semester plan.
* Coefficients more than four times their probable errors, so the relationships are unquestionably significant, *i.e.*, represent "true" positive correlation coefficients greater than zero.
† College algebra—47 cases; plane trigonometry—23 cases.

closer for college entrance tests than for high school testing.[1]

A range of coefficients from .40 to .80 indicates the predictive power of the English test. Eleven of the twelve coefficients are significant. Coefficients for combined term- and semester-basis schools of .73 and .60, respectively, are significantly high, and compare very favorably with comparable coefficients obtained for college entrance testing.

For mathematics the scattered correlations show rather high predictive power. All coefficients obtained are significant and compare favorably with college testing results.

[1] An investigation made by the writer at the University of Iowa furnishes some data bearing on this question. Reports of the investigation may be found in: J. R. Gerberich, "A Personnel Study of 10,000 Iowa High School Seniors," University of Iowa Studies in Education, Vol. v, No. 3, University of Iowa, Iowa City, 1930, 112 pp.; J. R. Gerberich and G. D. Stoddard, "A Personnel Survey of 10,000 Iowa High-School Seniors," SCHOOL AND SOCIETY, 30: 515–520, Oct. 12, 1929.

The fact that the correlation coefficients for the foreign languages are based upon all languages at any level of advancement is undoubtedly a strong factor tending toward understatement, in comparison with the relationships which would exist with properly equated variables. However, three of the six coefficients are significant and the combined semester-basis schools also show a significant relationship.

A second method of indicating the relationships between test scores and college scholastic success is utilized in Tables II, III and IV. Here are presented in tabular form the relationships between decile ranks on the psychological and English examinations and college scholarship. Similar tabulations are not given for the other subjects, because too few cases are available to justify this mode of presentation. However, it is reasonable to expect that these subjects would show the same trends as are brought out for English in Table IV, although probably to a less degree.

TABLE II

DECILE RANK ON THE PSYCHOLOGICAL EXAMINATION OF THE 1930 ARKANSAS EDUCATIONAL GUIDANCE SURVEY IN RELATION TO SCHOLASTIC SUCCESS FOR THE FIRST TERM OR SEMESTER OF 1930–31 AT ARKANSAS INSTITUTIONS OF HIGHER LEARNING

Decile	Number of cases	Grade Point Averages									Average G.P.A.
		− 2.00 to − 1.51	− 1.50 to − 0.51	− 0.50 to + 0.49	+ 0.50 to + 1.49	+ 1.50 to + 2.49	+ 2.50 to + 3.49	+ 3.50 to + 4.49	+ 4.50 to + 5.49	+ 5.50 to + 6.00	
		(F)	(E)	(D)	(D+) (C−)	(C)	(C+) (B−)	(B)	(B+) (A−)	(A)	
10	80				1	11	13	31	19	5	3.89
9	61			2	3	13	17	16	9	1	3.20
8	48		3	1	7	16	11	6	3	1	2.38
7	48		2	5	8	11	12	6	2	2	2.29
6	36			3	7	10	11	4	1		2.25
5	41	1	1	4	5	18	6	4	2		1.88
4	33	1	1	5	10	10	5			1	1.45
3	34	1	1	8	9	9	5		1		1.29
2	23		2	4	6	6	3	2			1.43
1	25	1	2	6	10	5	1				0.76
Total	429										

Table II shows the number of students from each decile of the psychological examination and their grade point averages for the first term or semester of college attendance. It is readily apparent that there is a strong tendency for students who scored high on the psychological examination to do well scholastically and for low-scoring students to make low grade point averages. This apparent relationship is probably not as great as the true relationship would be, for low-scoring students who were not doing satisfactory work and who dropped out of college early enough to avoid actual failure are not included in this tabulation. The average G.P.A. for students of the various deciles decreases consistently from the highest to the lowest decile, except in the case of next to the lowest decile, where the average G.P.A. exceeds that of the next higher decile.

TABLE III

PERCENTAGES OF SURVEY STUDENTS OF EACH DECILE ON THE PSYCHOLOGICAL EXAMINATION MAKING HIGH, AVERAGE AND LOW SCHOLASTIC RECORDS FOR THE FIRST TERM OR SEMESTER OF COLLEGE ATTENDANCE

Decile	Grade point averages		
	− 2.00 to + 0.49	+ 0.50 to + 3.49	+ 3.50 to + 6.00
	(F) to (D)	(D+) to (B−)	(B) to (A)
10	0	31	69
9	3	54	43
8	8	71	21
7	14	65	21
6	8	78	14
5	15	70	15
4	21	76	3
3	29	68	3
2	25	65	10
1	36	64	0

Number of cases 429

Table III presents a summary of the data from Table II, giving percentages of students from each decile making high, medium and low grade point averages. As is indicated by the data of this table, prediction of relatively high and relatively low or failing work is more definite than of standing near the middle of the group. For example, nearly seven out of ten students from the highest tenth of test scores make averages of B or higher, while no student from this group makes an average as low as D. At the other extreme, 36 per cent. of the students from the lowest decile make averages of D or lower. An average equivalent to a D is in many institutions below the scholastic standard a student must maintain for graduation and approaches perilously near the minimum standing required for continued attendance. Of this same group, 64 per cent. make grade point averages ranging from D+ to B–, while no student succeeds in achieving an average as high as B. The remaining percentages of the table are fairly consistent in showing an increase of low and failing grades from the highest to the lowest decile and an accompanying decrease in grade point averages equivalent to B or A standings.

TABLE IV

PERCENTAGES OF SURVEY STUDENTS OF EACH DECILE ON THE ENGLISH EXAMINATION MAKING HIGH, MEDIUM AND LOW GRADES IN THE FIRST TERM OR SEMESTER OF THE BASIC ENGLISH COURSE

Decile	Grade in basic English course		
	F and E	D and C	B and A
10	0	9	91
9	0	40	60
8	0	39	61
7	2	51	47
6	2	61	37
5	9	67	24
4	0	81	19
3	12	76	12
2	16	80	4
1	47	53	0

Number of cases 402

The data of Table IV present further evidence concerning the predictive power of the English examination. The percentages of students achieving various grades in the first term or semester of the basic English course are shown for each decile of the English examination. The degree of relationship shown by this table is especially evident in the upper three deciles, in which no pupil achieves lower than a D grade and well over six out of every ten students make A or B grades. Nine of every ten students of the highest decile make grades one or more letters above the average grade of C. Nearly half of the lowest decile students are conditioned or failed, while none makes as high as a B grade.

SUMMARY

A state-wide program of testing high-school seniors for purposes of educational guidance was inaugurated by the University of Arkansas in the spring of 1930. Twenty-three hundred students from 39 high schools took three tests each—the American Council psychological examination, an English test, and either a mathematics test or the foreign language aptitude examination.

During the school year 1930–31, with the cooperation of other Arkansas higher educational institutions, the survey students were followed through their first term or semester of college attendance to determine how satisfactorily the survey tests had predicted scholastic success in college. Correlation coefficients obtained between percentile scores on the psychological examination and a measure of general scholastic success were at least as high as comparable coefficients obtained with college entrance testing. Similar relationships between the three aptitude and training tests and scholastic success in those subjects showed the high-school testing to compare very favorably with prediction based upon college entrance testing.

J. R. GERBERICH

UNIVERSITY OF ARKANSAS

NEW BOOKS IN EDUCATION

Board of School Commissioners of Baltimore City: One Hundred and Second Annual Report; for the Scholastic Year Ending June 30, 1931. Pp. 191. Illustrated. The Board.

ELSON, WILLIAM H. and WILLIAM S. GRAY. *The Elson Basic Readers.* Book Five: Pp. 448. Illustrated. Book Six: Pp. 464. Illustrated. Scott, Foresman. $.84 each.

KEATINGE, M. W. *Comenius.* Pp. 255. McGraw-Hill. $2.00.

MCFEE, INEZ N. *How Our Government is Run.* Pp. xxi + 336. Illustrated. Thomas Y. Crowell. $2.50.

MARTIN, LILLIEN J. and CLARE DE GRUCHY. *Salvaging Old Age.* Pp. 175. Macmillan. $2.00.

MORRIS, ALTON C. and HERMAN E. SPIVEY. *Essentials of Correctness in the Use of English.* Pp. viii + 100. Prentice-Hall. $.80.

POKROVSKY, M. N. *History of Russia.* Pp. xiii + 383. International Publishers. $3.50.

SNEDDEN, DAVID. *Cultural Educations and Common Sense:* Pp. 324. Macmillan. $2.00. *American Secondary Schools in 1960:* Pp. 121. $1.50. *Towards Better Educations:* Pp. 427. $4.00. Teachers College Bureau of Publications, Columbia University.

SCHOOL AND SOCIETY

EDITED BY J. McKEEN CATTELL

WITH WHICH IS COMBINED THE

EDUCATIONAL REVIEW

EDITED BY WILLIAM McANDREW

Volume 34 SATURDAY, NOVEMBER 7, 1931 Number 880

IN DEFENSE OF SCHOLARSHIP[1]

By Professor WILLIAM LOUIS POTEAT

There appeared standing over my head a woman's form, whose countenance was full of majesty, whose eyes shone as with fire. Her clothing was wrought of the finest thread, woven with her own hands. On the border below was inwoven the symbol Pi (for Practical Philosophy), on that above was to be read Theta (for Theoretical Philosophy). In her right hand she carried books, in her left was a sceptre brandished.

—*Boethius, of Philosophy.*

TEN centuries are chronicled in the stones of Oxford. That long history has been made honorable by the noblest of achievements. By some strange secret, says Professor Gilbert Murray, it has preserved the power of training in its best men a habit of living for the things of the spirit, and the purpose to glorify God by the pursuit of knowledge. Of course, such an issue and fine fruit of university studies requires a favoring atmosphere in which to grow. It comes mainly by the contagion of fellowship, by association with persons who have attained this inward excellence and beauty, whether walking literally by our side or giving themselves to us with less reserve in the bright pages which are the transcript of their souls. Our guides to culture are men and books, which is to say, men: for Milton taught us that a good book is the precious life-blood of a master spirit embalmed and treasured up on purpose to a life beyond life. Accordingly, in Matthew Arnold's phrasing, culture is the fruit of acquainting ourselves with the best that has been known and said in the world.

Acquaintance with the best is scholarship, the fruit of it, ripening into refinement, elevation, sensitiveness, courage, and wisdom, is culture. This acquaintance with the best may be but a speaking acquaintance, able merely to recognize and locate against any future need of expansion. Or it may be ultimate and free and happy. It may vary also from field to field. But the scholar may be at home in every province of the intellectual realm, certainly able to read its symbols and interpret its significance. Gilbert Murray may be forgiven only a speaking acquaintance with the science of physics, provided he is not contemptuous of it. Shakespeare may be forgiven his little Latin and less Greek, provided he is respectful enough to those ancient cultures to dig into them for the materials of his art. Millikan might have been a professor of Greek but for the chance occurrence which turned him into physics. That wizard of mathematics so disrespectful of the cosmos as to upset it, so free with the stately law of gravitation as to bridle it, yet loves his Wagner and

[1] Phi Beta Kappa Address, Tulane University, June 8, 1931.

Bach. The Huxley or Romanes of biology allows his spirit wings in the aery architecture of the sonnet. And an English poet of the day writes,—

> I might have been a poet still,
> I might be singing carelessly,
> Had some one not come up one day
> And sown philosophy.

You picked men and women of this university have had here the privilege of fellowship with men of culture. They have walked with you through the literatures of the world and the laboratories of science. They have themselves followed the history of the human spirit and marked its triumphs. They have led you along that brightening path. They have themselves pressed resolutely into the mystery which envelops us on every hand, and they have asked you to share with them that holy adventure. They have seen the radiant and ordered beauty of our Father's house of many mansions, from whirling electrons to whirling universes of stars, and these four years they have been showing you about the place, like the interpreter of the old allegory. And you—they have seen you, shy and awkward, gaining by degrees confidence and ease of manner. They have seen that subtle sculptor, intelligence, rechiselling your countenance, your vagrant interests settling to a consistent purpose, your spirit shedding the fetters of selfishness, ideals organizing themselves in character, dreams becoming policies, your intellectual horizon widening, your attitude softening into catholicity; in short, boys and girls growing into men and women, alert, thoughtful, emancipated, self-controlled and happily at home in the world of men and things.

This is culture in process and result. It authenticates itself by what you are, not by what you have; by the way you feel, not by what you know; by the fellowships of your spirit, not by the work of your hands. It is inward wealth which accountants can not inventory, which time, the pilferer, can not reach. The secret of your power now and in mid career is there. And in after years when fortune still waits below the horizon, when friends fall away, when outside activities and interests steadily contract with the inevitableness of fate, these inner resources will guarantee your independence and refresh you as fountains in waste places where no water is.

People commonly think of institutions of learning as places where learning is kept in storage, and if you have money, you may journey to them and buy as much as you can carry away, as the sons of Jacob journeyed to Egypt to buy corn. But we know that the best service which such institutions can render us is to develop in us "the instincts of the gentleman and the horizon of the scholar," to discipline our rudeness into refinement and to transfigure our common clay with the love of learning. We must admit, however, that this ennobling discipline and enhanced quality of life are not consciously sought by the majority of the college population. Eighteen per cent. of our young people of college age are in college. And they present varied types. One has come up because it is nice to go to college; most nice people go. Another is driving a bargain for enhanced earning capacity. And there are the wise guys, they are so called, who seek a new thrill in the dissolute elements of life in a new situation. Every college has a chapter of the A. S. R. fraternity—the Amalgamated Sons of Rest, whose constitution has but two articles,—one announces the fraternity name, the other prohibits all work between meals. The prig appears also, the animal over-fed for its size. The vulgar snobs of sophistication are there strutting insolently in a lofty cynicism, contemptuous of ideals, of restraint, and the decent conventions of our ordered life. The idle rich committed without reservations to "having a good time." The children of the underprivileged who have understood the colleges to be places for elevating sons above the social rank of their fathers. The devotees of extra-curricular activities, with which studies are not allowed to interfere. And the saving salt of a sound and humble scholarship, which owns its indebtedness to the past and the gravity of its task in the blundering present, the true Phi Beta Kappas of college life.

Beside this rising tide of youth sweeping through our universities, colleges, and professional schools, there are twice as many students of home study courses directed by the universities. And at least one writer thinks that Sinclair Lewis, Mencken, and others of their ilk have made American business men "culture conscious," and bankers, real estate salesmen, auto mechanics and plumbers' assistants are neglecting their business to read poetry and philosophy, with the practical result of the wide-spread financial depression.

And yet with all this study in and out of educational institutions we remain an ignorant nation. Let me illustrate. A big publisher tells us that there are three or four thousand poets in the United States. Drop one thousand. We can spare them well. Say three thousand. Mr. Ogden Nash is one of these, "a new voice" in American poetry. Take a sample or two.

Like an art lover looking at the Mona Lisa in the Louvre
Is the New York Herald-Tribune looking at Herbert Hoover.

Or this,

Candy
Is dandy,
But liquor
Is quicker.

Or this,

The turtle lives 'twixt plated decks,
Which practically conceal its sex.
I think it clever of the turtle
In such a fix to be so fertile.

The volume of this sort of material is described as a best seller probably because, as Christopher Morley says, Nash's verses precisely click with the wave-length of 1931.

Mr. Mencken says of "Middletown," which he considers one of the most valuable documents ever concocted by American sociologists, that the record shows the normal American to be a man of almost unbelievable stupidities, well fed, well dressed, complacent and almost destitute of ideas. A few days ago I heard Professor Laski, of London, say: "We Europeans respect American power and appreciate American good will, but sometimes we have some doubt of American intelligence." See how we are duped by propaganda,—political, into acquiescence in the wicked and stupid ever-rising protective tariff; religious, the amazing fundamentalist movement, in which one thought now and again of a saying of Montaigne, "It is setting a high value on one's opinions to roast men on account of them." Think of the every morning meal, form and content, which the newspapers provide, as they say, at the public demand. And the low level of movie presentation. And the domination of all our life by the economic motive. On the front wall of a bus is a placard reading, "Smile, it pays." So a genial temper is commercialized. It is justified by its economic value. Its counterfeit is worth as much. An electric ventilating equipment advertisement reads, "Bad air is bad business." So health is commercialized. Scholarship itself is commercialized. Why take the trouble to grow your own? Rent or buy another's. Is it an essay or sermon or speech you require? The Speaker's Library will build it complete for your individual use on any subject for $3 per thousand words. And there is a bargain counter of sermons on Lot's Wife, The Unpardonable Sin, The Second Coming, Christian Socialism, etc. —any nine for $1, any twenty for $2. The more you buy the cheaper they come. The service is "strictly personal and confidential." So without peril of exposure you make the impression of scholarship with a small equipment—a little conscience and a little cash. And this trade in fake scholarship appears to prosper. I sympathize with Professor Harvey Robinson when he says, "There is something humiliating about this situation, which subordinates all the varied possibilities of life to its material prerequisites, much as if we were back again in a stage of impotent savagery scratching for roots and looking for berries and dead animals."

I challenge you, in all the horizon of our public life name me a man of great leadership. James Bryce said that the only thing remarkable about American presidents was that being so commonplace they should have climbed so high. That was written before Wilson's time. And the appearance of that scholar in politics so flatly contradicted the tradition of the office that it was the occasion of no little surprise and merrymaking. Similarly the practical politicians have been amused that a Yale professor has lately become Governor of Connecticut. It is a long time since Thomas Jefferson said that he would rather be known as the founder of the University of Virginia than as a president of the United States. And does it not seem necessary to provide somehow a kindergarten for the benefit of the United States Senate? It is so stupid, as well as shameful, to hesitate about adherence to the World Court and to keep our great country, in company with Russia and Mexico and Afghanistan, aloof from the organized intelligence and conscience of mankind. The trouble with us is that here political life is a business or profession, and men go into it for what they can get out of it. Contrast England, where only chairmen and secretaries of party associations make any money by political activities, and men of ability, learning and rank hold administrative posts, sit in Parliament, and pursue politics for the sake of fame, power, or excitement. It is no surprise, therefore, to find a Prime Minister President of the British Association for the Advancement of Science, or a Secretary of State for War write a treatise on Relativity and hold the Rectorship of Edinburgh University.

Extend your observation into the educational field itself. Push open college and university doors and look about you. Here is a college student writing a note to a young lady asking if he might call on her at four a.m., and admitting when he showed her reply that he did not know the difference between p.m. and a.m. A professor of Bible asked "What were the food, language, and dress of John the Baptist?" Ans.: "His food was that of other people, his language was elegant, and he was dressed in swaddling clothes." A professor asked freshmen for what certain persons and places were famous, and got these written replies. "Roosevelt was a great railroad man." "Darwin, his writings on the Underworld and Hades." "Martin Luther, for starting the Catholic Church." "David, for resisting temptation and being in the den of lions." "The Sermon on the Mount was preached by Moses about A. D. 40." "Athens, a great city in Rome where many unhappy occurrences took place in Biblical times." A student, assisted to find the Rhine River on the map, was asked in what direction it flowed. He replied that it flowed south. "In that case," said the professor, "the

Rhine would deluge Europe with the North Sea." "Professor," said the student, "you may be a learned man, but you can never convince me that river runs up hill, for we say *up north* and *down south.*"

Press, if you dare, into the faculty and look about you. Here is a Ph.D., the subject of whose thesis was "Family Bereavement." There is another whose thesis determined the bacterial content of cotton undershirts. And what sort of inspiration and guidance for aspiring youth could be found in a professor who won his doctorate on "A Photographic Study of Boiled Icing?" One professor is reported to have spent three years and $42,000 making a list of the miscellaneous things which a teacher has to do and the 83 personal traits which he must possess in order to do them. It is 83, understand, not 82. Such scraps of information, in and of themselves, have nothing to do with scholarship or culture. That is on another plane, where thought is active, the humane feelings play, and the vision of beauty lifts itself up before responsive eyes. A specialist is a man with one interest and no horizon.

And there is the curriculum. It is printed. Any man may look at it. I do not guarantee that he will understand it. Nothing in American life has developed faster, if you mean by development increase in complexity of structure. Indeed, the extended and varied program of education is probably the outgrowth and expression of the multiplied interests and activities of our new time. And we may go further and agree with Santayana that all studies are good—why else have universities? It is said, moreover, that a college of liberal arts will show itself vital by response to its environment; that it is but simple justice that it serve the community which maintains it. Accordingly, with this appeal and justification there has been a frontal invasion of the field of higher education by the mercenaries of vocationalism threatening the citadels of scholarship throughout the country. The expansion of American industry has tended to push profit-making into the primacy of human interests, and intellectual, aesthetic, and moral concerns, which ring no cash-register bells, have suffered some disparagement of their former prestige. Another factor of the situation has one eye on a big college enrollment and the other on the American policy of democracy in education—take all who offer, educable and ineducable. Of course, in order to keep what you catch, the ineducable must be provided for. They will make good in Banking and Business Administration, in Modern Salesmanship, in Real Estate, in Advanced Tailoring, Practical Poultry Raising, Home Economics, Elementary Millinery, and the Care of Lawns. And so, rather than cut the enrolment we cram the curriculum. In they go, these courses and a hundred others. Lowering of standards, increase of budget, and dissipation of energy, inevitably follow, and scholarship is betrayed in the house of its friends.

Who wonders that a university of ten thousand students can not find among its own alumni a man fit to be its president? That the clamor for intellectual leadership gets no answer? That, according to a foreign observer of experience and distinction, the few well educated persons he had met in America were all about sixty years old, and not one below that age impressed him as even respectably educated? Albert Jay Nock, to whom I am indebted for this observation, declares in the May *Atlantic* that, with relatively poor equipment and no better raw material or pedagogy than ours, French institutions turn out extremely well-educated men, and ours do not. He thinks that the trouble is that the American system from beginning to end is gauged to the run-of-mine American, rather than to the picked American, whereas the run-of-mine Frenchman gets no nearer the university than the adjacent wood-pile. Forty years ago this French policy obtained in America; run-of-mine aspirants could not make the grade.

An adult illiterate student in a big university wrote, "Modern dress is extreme and ought to be checked." I beg to insist that a check is demanded on the progressive variegation of this Joseph's-coat curriculum. I am not concerned with the garment's length, but with its screaming dissonant colors. I do not propose to lower it above and heighten it below. A distinguished North Carolina lady, beginning an address, said that a speech ought to be like a woman's dress, long enough to cover the subject and short enough to attract attention. Such proportions in the curriculum would please me,—long enough to cover the intellectual and moral riches of the race, short enough to win the capable and the responsive.

But our educational prophets are confused by our complex and changing civilization. Our universities, they say, are instruments for adjusting our young people to the bewildering life of the twentieth century, and must, therefore, provide a wide range of liberal and professional opportunities. Maybe so, but discriminate.

The road to scholarship does not always run through a college campus. Think of Burns and Darwin and Browning. Mr. Van Loon thinks that, until the American College shall have caught up with the times, his boys would have a better opportunity in the little boat of Jack Mulhaley, who does know lobsters and can talk of them with feeling. And Herman Melville, perhaps the brightest light in American literature, says, "A whale ship was my Yale College and my Harvard."

Discriminate further. The universities are not developing scholarship and enlarging the intellectual life when they teach tailors to cut and sew, farmers to keep bees and raise poultry, merchants to conduct a mail order business, landlords to rent and lease successfully, or salesmen to mislead people about their own desires. What have they done to the man? They have put a tool in his hand, but the man who wields the tool they have left alone.

Discriminate yet again, and this fog of "the new day in which we live" will lift and melt. It dreadfully needs to be remembered that what is new in our civilization is in the externals of it, the machinery of it. The fundamental interests and needs of human life remain the same. Let the conditions and apparatus of civilization be yet further improved and, if need be, become more complex, in order that these universal and timeless concerns of ours may be the better served. The sabbath was made for man, said the Master, not man for the sabbath. The institution justifies itself by the service which it renders. It has no meaning otherwise. I am my mind. I possess instruments. I have a fountain pen, an automobile, a radio, a microscope, a telescope. These are my tools in the service of my mind. Do they make me a better man than my Scotch grandfather, who had none of them? Do these things bewilder me or change the center of gravity of my life? I can live without them. Other men have lived without them. Plato did, and Jesus and Vergil and Dante and Shakespeare and Washington. What do I want with a fountain pen but to trace the intimate symbols of friendship? what with an automobile but to get home the sooner? what with a radio but to hear the rustle of the garments of beauty sweeping through the world? what with microscope and telescope but to extend the horizon of my soul? Let the new powers make more secure and ample the economic foundation of my life, but you must not expect me to live in the foundation. You will find me in the statelier sunlit mansion above it. I reassert my mastery in the midst of these marvels of modern science. I bow to no machine. I allow it no significance whatsoever except as it ministers to Personality, before whose sceptre the whole round of nature bows. *Mihi res, non me rebus.*

And so I decline to adjust myself to the new order. I adjust it to my needs. Our scientific civilization is not an end, but a means to an end. The eminent Britisher's definition suits me,—civilization is a condition of social life in which men have leisure for noble ends. And we are lost, if in our industries and the material means of existence we sink out of sight of these noble ends. We are lost, I tell you, professors, academicians, doctors, dons, Phi Beta Kappas, all lost in a common vulgarity,

> Through blackness void, as in a dying brain
> Where one by one the thoughts have flickered out,

if in the academic, economic, and social phases of our life we do not insist on the eternal supremacy of mind over things, and hold the guardians of our intellectual and spiritual inheritance, our colleges and universities, to their proper task of growing men and women to share this inheritance and pass it secure and enhanced to their successors.

Permit me to add a concluding word. What I have said of civilization is true of culture. However satisfying and charming it may be, culture is not an end in itself. The first motive which ought to impel us to study may be, as Montesquieu said, to augment the excellence of our nature and to make an intelligent being yet more intelligent, but it is not the last motive. An enriched and trained intelligence, a moral sense enlightened and disciplined, refinement of manners, tastes and feelings, generosity and tolerance of spirit are the badges of culture wherever they appear, and they adorn any life. But culture is not ornament. Somebody wrote lately of the brilliant Dean of St. Paul's that he wore his learning like a flower. No; learning is not a removable ornament. Removable beauty is not beauty. It is affectation. Culture is rather a certain quality of the tissue of the organism itself. It is not ornament, but equipment. And if pure learning is to survive as one of the purposes of universities, as Mr. Bertrand Russell says, it must be brought into the service of the community as a whole, and not merely provide refined delights for a few gentlemen of leisure. A barren intellectualism wants justification. And my word to you men and women of recognized capacity and distinction in this university must be Browning's, himself one of the great scholars of his time—

> Know, not for knowing's sake,
> But to become a star to men forever.

EDUCATIONAL EVENTS

A NEW SCHOOL IN GERMANY

SPECIAL correspondence of *The New York Times* from Luebeck, Germany, reports that in completeness of equipment and in attention to the problem of insuring plenty of sunlight in classrooms, the new primary school, Am Klosterhof, recently constructed by the town of Luebeck, ranks high. A product of close cooperation between educators and building experts, it was erected with spacious accommodations for 800 pupils at a cost of $250,000, which was $25,000 below the amount appropriated.

It is a low, elongated structure, built of brick, with so many windows that it is called the "school of glass." The classrooms—there are twenty-two—all face the sunny side of the building, so that they all receive sunlight the whole day long. The spaces between the windows are reduced to a minimum. Nor are there any dark corridors. On the inside walls of the rooms frosted glass lets ample light through.

The walls of the corridors are used for exhibits. Here are assembled under glass specimens of animals and birds used in nature study, as well as woodwork and drawings made by the pupils.

The window-sills are equipped with tile shelves so that the pupils can place flower-pots upon them, as is the custom in northern Germany. And in each classroom is a tiled wash basin, which serves as a reminder of the adjurations to keep clean.

As biology and physics are taught these young pupils, separate rooms for classes are provided where there are work tables equipped with gas jets and water taps. Here the pupils make simple experiments without leaving their seats. Individual microscopes are included in the laboratory equipment. Lessons in drawing and singing are given in a room with a large bow-window arrangement to provide plenty of light. Another large room has work benches and tools for carpentering.

An exercise room is provided, and beneath it is a gymnasium with shower baths and foot-baths where the pupils can wash after their games. These rooms are open for use outside of school hours as well as during school time, and so are separated from the rest of the school and have a separate entry. In this section of the building are an assembly hall with a stage on which plays can be presented, and also meeting rooms for parents and quarters for the use of district nurses and physicians. A large room on the ground floor serves as a milk kitchen, where warmed milk is provided for the children. This room likewise can serve as a meeting hall after school hours.

One room forms a planetarium where single stars or a representation of the entire heavens appears, at the will of the teacher. The planets can be made to move in their courses or to stand still. Cooperation of astronomers made it possible to erect this device at moderate cost. It is used by all the schools of the town. On the roof is a sort of metallic dome through which the sky may be studied. In addition to a play yard there are balconies and covered quarters where the children can play in wet weather.

THE CLOSING OF COUNTRY SCHOOLS IN AUSTRALIA

Vigorous opposition has arisen to proposed economy measures which would close small schools in remote sections of South Australia and place limitations upon high-school enrolments, according to *The Christian Science Monitor*. Alternative proposals were offered to the Cabinet and the Parliament when the matter came up for attention during a consideration of the budget in October.

An education committee, appointed six months ago by the government to investigate the policy and administration of the education department, in its report has suggested closing 154 country schools having an average attendance of less than 10 each, and intimates that 211 more, with an average of less than 15 each, might also be closed.

The students affected by the closing of 154 schools would number about 1,300, but an area of thousands of miles would be affected. If the 211 added schools were closed the total number of students affected would be about 4,000.

Mr. Malcolm M. McIntosh, member of Parliament, minister of education in the former Liberal Government, opposing the plan, has declared the state would save only £9,000 a year in a total national expenditure of £12,500,000 by closing 154 schools, and he showed that the area affected would extend to the extreme borders of the state in all directions.

The education committee, in its report, does not propose that the children shall be left without education, however. The government is preparing a plan which, by saving about £170,000 a year, may save the schools. But, if it does not, the committee suggests the development of correspondence study, subsidized schools and the employment of itinerant teachers. This latter proposal is criticized by Mr. McIntosh, who says:

> If an itinerant teacher inspected three schools a week his visits to each one would be about eighteen

months apart. What help would this be? There remains, then, the correspondence school. This is a most successful institution, and one is filled with admiration for its work. The system, however, imposes a very severe strain and sacrifice on the majority of the parents.

The proposal to close 154 country schools strikes at the basis of constructive rural statesmanship. Lacking roads and railways, these little communities have been content to center around the school, often built at their own expense, and used as a social meeting place. Some of the schools are conducted in portable departmental buildings. In many cases the ground was given and fenced, and the material carted and erected by the pioneers.

THE FRANKLIN INSTITUTE BUILDING

A STAFF correspondent of *The Christian Science Monitor* reports that excavation for the $7,500,000 Benjamin Franklin Memorial and Franklin Institute, which will be built on the Parkway, Philadelphia, is under way.

The whole of the building, which will be of Indiana limestone, will not be erected at the outset, but plans are so drawn that the portion now to be built will embrace the full elevation on Twentieth Street, including the main entrance façade of 365 feet, and also the full elevation on Winter Street, thus presenting, from the Parkway, the impression of the completed whole. The site faces Logan Square on the Parkway, between Twentieth and Twenty-first Streets.

In addition to the entrance hall, the Franklin Hall and the members' chamber, where the heroic statue of Franklin will be placed, there will be a museum of graphic arts where a display of the art of paper making, the literature of the Franklin Institute, the museum of railroad engineering, the museum of aeronautics, photography, transportation, power machinery, life-saving apparatus, chemical industries, electrical communications, etc., will be shown.

The Fels Planetarium and the astronomical observatory and astronomical historical museum will also be in the memorial. There will be 5,500,000 cubic feet in the part of the memorial to be erected at this time.

In order to prepare the exhibits for display in the memorial the Franklin Institute during the summer leased a building on Seventh Street, near the institute's present location, to house its staff, with a machine shop and other workrooms where the actual models may be constructed. This work is now in progress, and some of the exhibits already in possession of the institute have been made ready for viewing.

An interesting part of the location of the work rooms is that on this very spot stood the original mint, which was the first public building to be erected by the United States Government.

One of the first sets of exhibits which will be undertaken will be models of 28 famous bridges, beginning with one Julius Caesar constructed, vividly described in his "Gallic Wars," and coming down to one as near home as the Delaware River Bridge.

The famous Rittenhouse orrery will be loaned by the University of Pennsylvania for the Franklin Institute Museum. The orrery, constructed by David Rittenhouse, whose 200th anniversary will be observed in 1932, illustrates the movements of the sun, moon and planets. According to present plans the memorial building will be ready for occupancy by January 1, 1932. The architect is Mr. John T. Windrim.

EXPENDITURES OF THE PHILANTHROPIC FOUNDATIONS

How education fares at the hands of the country's philanthropic foundations is shown in a summary of a report of the Twentieth Century Fund of New York City, printed in *The New York Times*. Using figures submitted by the foundations themselves or other authentic statistics, the report shows—as part of its general study of the contributions of the foundations—the degree of interest which the various types of educational enterprises win, or are able to arouse, and what developments these students of our progress are seeking to foster.

More foundations—fifty-two of the 122 listed—are interested in education than in any other field. And only the field of medicine and public health ranks above it, taking 35.5 per cent. of the funds distributed, as against the 27 per cent. or $14,171,755, education receives. The other fields trail off rapidly, the physical sciences coming third with 9.2 per cent., and so on.

The field of education as a whole, also, is receiving more than first meets the eye. For, while there are twenty-nine fields of interest listed, ranging from medicine and public health to maintenance of cemeteries, the work in many of them is furthered at least in part by some amount of educational activity. Medical expenditures are a good example. Nearly half, or $8,396,932, went into education as against an almost equal amount into what is described as "social action," while the remainder went into research. Considered on this basis, education is easily the favored channel through which most of the work of the foundations is done, for 51.1 per cent. of the year's appropriations, or $26,810,262 went to it.

Within the field of general education, however, the amounts provided for particular activities vary enormously. Research is represented by a direct grant of only $367,730, or 2.8 per cent. of the appropriations.

By far the largest amount given to the colleges by any of the foundations was the appropriation of the General Education Board of $4,158,805, while other Rockefeller units—the Rockefeller Foundation and the Spelman Fund—gave $1,868,991 and $4,000, respectively, accounting for well over half of the appropriations in this field. The Carnegie Corporation, the largest single foundation reported, was only one of the medium-sized contributors, giving $162,600.

The pioneering which the foundations appear to be doing in higher education does not carry over into that other virgin field—from the standpoint of public finance—that of pre-school agencies. Only two foundations are listed as having made contributions in this direction, the total being $7,600. Nor is extensive concern shown for the training of teachers, a field to which nine foundations contributed $188,361.

Libraries rank high in the appropriations of the foundations, coming fourth in the educational list with total appropriation of $589,734. The field of adult education, of which so much is heard to-day, received $409,651, having interested eight organizations, while a special activity, such as handicrafts, received $19,000 from one, the Russell Sage Foundation. Industrial and vocational schools received $307,816.

THE AGE OF COLLEGE STUDENTS

A WIDE variation exists in the ages of college students. Although the general impression prevails that college students are young people of approximately the same age, recent information shows that the actual differences in their ages are very great. Facts concerning this question were collected in the survey of land-grant colleges and universities made by the Federal Office of Education. The land-grant group includes some of America's largest institutions of higher learning, such as the University of Wisconsin, Cornell University, the University of California, the University of Florida, the Texas Agricultural and Mechanical College, the Kansas State Agricultural College, the Mississippi Agricultural and Mechanical College, the University of Kentucky, the University of Maine and 41 other colleges and universities.

The study was based on the age of students at the time of entrance in college, as reported by 22,159 former students. According to the data gathered, 1 per cent. of the students were 15 years old or under when they entered college, while 4 per cent. were 16 years old. Fourteen per cent. of the total number began their college work at the age of 17 years. The greater number of these students entered the land-grant colleges in their early history, when entrance requirements were not so rigid.

Since most young people graduate from high school at the age of 18 or 19 years, the majority of students entered colleges at these ages, it was found. The proportion of college entrants at this age was 51 per cent. Returns showed that 12 per cent. started their college course at 20 years of age, and an additional 7 per cent. at 21 years. That a considerable number of older persons attend college is indicated by the large proportion over 21 years of age, which totalled 11 per cent. of the 22,159 students. In many instances the students were more than 35 years of age.

Students matriculating in college below the age of 16 years were in most cases young women who studied home economics or young men who pursued liberal arts courses. A great majority of the students in agriculture entered college at the later ages of 20 and 21 years. Of the older students, a very large proportion took courses in education and were school teachers who were attending college for the purpose of improving their training and keeping up with modern changes in school practices and methods.

MARRIED TEACHERS AND MULTIPLE POSITIONS IN THE NEW YORK CITY SCHOOLS

ACCORDING to the New York *Sun* efforts by the board of education to list the names of married teachers whose husbands also are in the service has aroused the opposition of the Teachers Union. In a letter sent to President Ryan, of the Board of Education, Dr. Henry R. Linville, president of the union, states that so long as a teacher serves efficiently in the classroom the board has no right to inquire into her home life, any more than into her religious or political views. However, the union endorses the board's multiple-job inquiry.

The protest of the Teachers Union reads in part as follows:

The union is amazed that the board of superintendents has even considered the matter of listing husbands and wives who are teaching in the New York public school system. Does the board not realize that the dismissal of a married woman teacher for any reason other than incompetence would be a violation of the legal provision under which married women teachers have held public school positions in New York City since 1914? The fact that the board of superintendents is yielding to the clamor of a small section of the public in preparing to list such teachers indicates that the board itself insists on considering these positions from the point of view of the philosophy of Tammany Hall as means of sustenance rather than as positions for efficient social service.

The union has already taken the position that no teacher should have more than two positions in a single year, a day school position and either an evening school or a summer school position, but not all three. Principals of day elementary, high, vocational or training schools can hardly carry even a second job and be expected to do both acceptably. By insisting that such principals confine their professional activities to one task the board of superintendents should be able to insure more leisurely thinking and constructive work going on in these most important positions.

In these, as in other situations, the number of positions held should be determined on the basis of the character of the work, the responsibility involved and on an adequate performance of the work.

IN HONOR OF DR. WINSHIP

DR. ALBERT E. WINSHIP, dean of educational journalists, now eighty-seven years of age, was honored last week at the headquarters of the National Education Association, before officers and representatives of the 220,000 members of the organization, by the presentation of an oil painting of himself, which will remain permanently in the offices of the secretary of the association. This is the first time in the history of the association, organized in 1857, that such an honor has been accorded.

The painting was presented by the artist, Mrs. Donna Wilson Crabtree, who painted the portrait as a recognition of Dr. Winship's long services to education. "My interest has been greater in painting his portrait than in any piece of work I have ever attempted to do," said Mrs. Crabtree in her brief presentation address. "Into these features I have tried to put the genial and alert expression and the inspiring personality which have for so many years characterized a great educational leader. Dr. Winship's life work is a permanent contribution to the development of the American schools. It is fitting that the profession preserve a permanent record as well of the personality of one of the nation's best-loved educators." Mrs. Crabtree's husband, J. W. Crabtree, has been secretary of the National Education Association since 1917.

Other addresses at the presentation ceremony included one by Miss Maria Machien, dean of women at the University of Porto Rico. A delegation of students from Teachers College, Columbia University, New York, headed by Dr. Winifred E. Bain, assistant professor of education, were present. Following the presentation, Dr. Winship went to the White House where, upon special invitation, he had lunch with President Hoover.

Dr. Winship, who has been editor of the *Journal of Education* since 1886, has known personally every United States commissioner of education and every president of the National Education Association. His speaking tours have taken him across the continent more than sixty times, and he has addressed educational and other meetings in nearly every large university and college in the nation. He is the author of "Jukes-Edwards," "Great American Educators," "Life of Horace Mann," "Educational Preparedness," "Famous Farmers" and other books. A native of Massachusetts, his home is in Boston.

EDUCATIONAL NOTES AND NEWS

DR. JEREMIAH E. BURKE, superintendent of the Boston public schools and president of Boston Teachers College, died on October 29 at the age of sixty-five years.

DR. FRANK PORTER GRAHAM will be inducted into office as president of the University of North Carolina on November 11. He was elected in June, 1930, to succeed Dr. Harry W. Chase, who had resigned to become president of the University of Illinois. More than 250 delegates from colleges and universities, learned societies and foundations are expected to attend.

DR. PHILIP M. BRETT, New York lawyer, who has been acting president of Rutgers University since October, 1930, will not accept permanently the presidency of the university. A petition urging Dr. Brett to continue as president had been forwarded to him with the signatures of 267 members of the faculty. In his reply Dr. Brett, who succeeded Dr. John Martin Thomas, pointed out that he had accepted the position only with the understanding that it would be temporary.

DR. WILLIAM JUDSON BOONE, president of the College of Idaho, has completed forty years as president of that institution. He is said to be the oldest college president in point of service in the United States at the present time.

A MARBLE bust of Miss Helen Keller by the German sculptor, Count Harrach, presented to the American Foundation for the Blind by its president, Mr. M. C. Migel, was unveiled on October 29. Dr. Otis J. Caldwell, of the Lincoln School at Teachers College, Columbia University, presented the bust, which was accepted by Dr. O. H. Burritt, principal of the Pennsylvania Institution for Instruction of the Blind.

DIRECTORS of the Tercentenary Conference of City and Town Committees have presented a silver coffee set to Professor Joseph H. Beale, professor of law at Harvard University, and a desk set to Mr. E. B. Mero, in recognition of their service during the tercentenary celebration in Massachusetts. Professor Beale was president of the conference and Mr. Mero was the executive secretary.

MR. G. ROWLAND COLLINS, assistant dean of the school of commerce, accounts and finance of New York University since 1927, has been appointed to the position of associate dean.

DR. ALINA M. LINDEGREN, for the past three years instructor in medieval history and modern European history at State Teachers College, Superior, Wisconsin, has been appointed to the foreign school systems branch of the Federal Office of Education as specialist in Western European school systems.

LUCIUS A. WHIPPLE, principal of the senior high school at Pawtucket, Rhode Island, has been named director of research and survey of the State Department of Education of Rhode Island.

DR. STANLEY HARCOURT PEPPARD, formerly of New York, has been appointed director of the bureau of mental hygiene of the state department of health of Connecticut. He succeeds Dr. James L. McCartney.

THE curators of the Oxford University Chest have offered Sir Arthur McWatters, secretary to the finance department of the Government of India, the post of secretary to the University Chest, and he has accepted. Sanction by convocation remains to be given. If the appointment is thus completed he will sail from India on December 12 and take up the appointment on January 1.

THE electors to the King Alfonso XIII professorship of Spanish studies at Oxford have elected Professor William James Entwistle, Stevenson professor of Spanish at the University of Glasgow, to the professorship as from January 1, 1932.

PROFESSOR ARTHUR B. MOEHLMAN, of the University of Michigan, will spend the second semester studying the public-school systems of the southwest, with headquarters at Tucson, Arizona.

SIR E. DENISON ROSS, head of the College of Oriental Studies of the University of London, arrived in New York on October 30. He will deliver lectures at Princeton and other eastern universities.

DR. JAMES SHELLEY, professor of education

at Canterbury College, New Zealand, is coming to America to lecture on "Communication and the Future of Civilization" at the eighth annual Institute of International Relations, which will meet at Riverside, California, from December 13 to 18.

MR. ARCHIE M. PALMER, associate secretary of the Association of American Colleges, was the speaker at the Cap and Gown Day exercises at Elmira College on October 24. The subject of his address was "The Liberal College."

DR. BENJAMIN STUYTES TERRY, a member of the original faculty at the University of Chicago, died on October 31 at the age of seventy-four years. He was widely known as a scholar of English history.

THE REVEREND DR. THOMAS CECIL FITZPATRICK, president of Queens College, Cambridge, died on October 29 at the age of seventy years.

THE committee on problems and plans in education of the American Council on Education assembled on November 1 at Briarcliff, N. Y. Dr. Samuel P. Capen, chancellor of the University of Buffalo, was chairman of the conference. Others attending were Professor Edward Thorndike, of Columbia University; Dean James E. Russell, of Teachers College of Columbia University; Dr. Charles Riborg Mann, director of the American Council on Education, Washington; Dean Charles H. Judd, of the University of Chicago; Dr. Beardsley Russell, of the University of Chicago, and Dr. Frederick P. Keppel, of the Carnegie Corporation, New York.

MORE than 200 school men were at the Pennsylvania State College on October 30 and 31 to consider means by which high schools and colleges of the state may be brought into closer harmony. Widening opportunity for the high-school graduate in college curricula and better guidance for the prospective applicant for higher education were advocated. Meetings were held under the auspices of Penn State College as the second annual Guidance and Personnel Conference of Secondary Schools and Colleges. The state department of public instruction, the state teachers colleges, public schools and private colleges were all represented. More than half of the sixty-seven counties in Pennsylvania sent representatives.

A LUNCHEON meeting of teachers of modern languages in and about New York City will be held under the auspices of the modern language section of the New York Society for the Experimental Study of Education on Saturday, November 14, at the Hotel Taft. Among the speakers will be Professor Harold A. Palmer, director of modern languages for the Government of Japan, and Dr. Stephen P. Duggan, director of the Institute of International Education. Discussion will be led by Dr. Hymen Alpern, first assistant in modern languages at De Witt Clinton High School, who is president of the association.

HAVERFORD COLLEGE observed the ninety-eighth anniversary of its founding on October 28, with Founders' Day exercises, which, while paying tribute to the group which nurtured Haverford through its infancy, looked ahead to the college's second century. Professor Rufus M. Jones, who has been connected with the college for forty-nine years, half of the life of the institution, and Dr. W. W. Comfort, president of the college, were the speakers at the Founders' Day convocation, attended by many descendants of the first students and original board of managers, by the alumni and others interested in the college.

OXFORD UNIVERSITY has accepted the challenge of Harvard University to the first international collegiate radio debate. Short-wave transmission will be used to carry the English and American teams' debate across the Atlantic for rebroadcasting in the United States. The National Broadcasting Company has invited the British Broadcasting Corporation to re-broadcast the debate in England.

THE corner-stone of the New York State Theodore Roosevelt Memorial at the American Museum of Natural History was laid by Governor Franklin D. Roosevelt on October 27.

AT the dedication of Merrill Hall at the University of Maine on October 10, the chief address was made by Professor Cora M. Winchell, of Teachers College, Columbia University, who spoke on "Extended Horizons in Home Economics." A portrait of Dean Leon S. Merrill, of the College of Agriculture, for whom the building was named, was unveiled.

THE corner-stone of the Atlanta University

Library, which is being erected with funds furnished by the General Education Board, was laid on Sunday, November 1. The ceremonies were witnessed by the faculty, students and friends of the university and its affiliated colleges, Spelman College for women and Morehouse College for men, as well as representatives of the other Negro institutions of higher learning in Atlanta which may enter into cooperative arrangements for the use of the library. The library, an imposing brick building conforming to the Georgian Colonial tradition, will provide stack room for 125,000 volumes, seats for 400 readers and facilities for seminar teaching. The cost of the construction and equipment of the building will be about $300,000. It will be ready for occupancy some time in the spring of 1932.

THE California Bureau of Juvenile Research, which formerly had headquarters at the Whittier State School, has moved to Los Angeles near the campus of the University of Southern California. This change of headquarters is in accordance with the program of the California State Department of Institutions, which has increased the scope of the work of the bureau to include clinical work in all institutions of the state in which there are children. This means that, in addition to having charge of the clinical work at the Whittier State School, the bureau will be available for consultant service to the California School for Girls at Ventura, Pacific Colony at Spadra and the Preston School of Industry at Ione. Being located near the University of Southern California will make possible the expansion of the program of research work carried on by graduate students. The bureau has been given a large increase in its appropriation for the coming biennium with which to carry on this expanded program.

COLUMBIA UNIVERSITY, with a capital endowment of $80,380,470, will spend $17,577,519 for educational purposes during 1931–32, according to budget figures announced by Mr. Frank D. Fackenthal, secretary of the university. The total resources of the university are estimated at $140,138,152. This includes the valuation of the sixty-four buildings which house it.

DURING the past twenty-nine years the number of books in the Princeton University Library has increased by 382,000 volumes, according to Mr. James Thayer Gerould, the librarian, in his annual reports on the library and on the Benjamin Strong Collection of Foreign Public Finance. The reports are for the year ending June 30 and deal with the book and document collections, new gifts and purchases, financial outlay and remarks on the work in general. In 1912 the number of books was approximately 280,000; in 1931 it is 662,000. Total expenditures on the library have increased from approximately $50,000 to over $190,000, and the amount spent annually on books, periodicals and binding from $10,000 to between $70,000 and $80,000.

NINETY-EIGHT of North Carolina's 100 counties will have a share in the $1,426,875 school equalization fund designed to lower local taxes in the operation of extended terms of two months beyond the state-supported six-months' term. Using the state school provisions as a standard, the State Board of Equalization estimated the cost of all extended terms at $4,415,-123. From this was deducted the $1,500,000 state fund voted by the 1931 Legislature, leaving $2,915,123 to be provided through local taxation.

THERE were enrolled last year in the colleges of the United States, 18,500 Negro students, 1,980 of whom received degrees, according to a statement by the commission on interracial cooperation, whose headquarters are at Atlanta, Georgia. Negro colleges in the South enrolled 16,437 of the total, while the remaining 2,063 were in 62 northern universities. Howard University, Washington, D. C., headed the list with 2,473 students and 222 graduates. Prairie View College, Texas, was second with 135 graduates in a total of 997 students; and Fisk University, Nashville, Tennessee, third with 101 graduates in an enrolment of 473.

A SCHOLARSHIP providing one year of research work in Europe or in this country is offered to advanced women graduate students by the Boston branch of the American Association of University Women, aided by the Radcliffe Alumni Association, the alumni clubs of colleges in the Boston district and private individuals. The scholarship is one of ten being made available for next year. The holder must be a graduate of an approved college, and must show evidence of being fully fitted to carry on the work she proposes to do.

THE University of Berlin has opened its foreign courses with a total enrolment of 300 students from abroad, eighty of whom are Americans. Forty countries are represented. Besides the beginners' courses, conducted by Professor Paul Curts, of Wesleyan University, there are courses in art, given in cooperation with the College of Fine Arts of New York University, and a teachers' course covering German education, conducted by Professor Ruth MacMurray, of Columbia University.

DISCUSSION

PUBLICATION

To write or not to write! That is the question that eternally dogs the step of the pedagogue who hopes that he can be at least a second lieutenant in his particular parade rather than a member of the rear rank. If he fails to appear in print he may be adjudged as having nothing to impart, whereas if he does his readers may be sure of it. Publication has become the coin and the capital of the academic realm and it is not to be wondered at that its virtues, like those of its monetary equivalent, should be often counterfeited. It is inevitable with published theses being demanded for higher degrees, and with higher degrees being required for higher positions, that a worthy requirement should lose a good deal of its original respectability.

The publication of new truths was intended as a means of advancing knowledge rather than individuals, but the forward progress of the impersonal drew, naturally enough, its creator in its wake. This is as it should be since few of us ever rise to a stature where we are willing to send our efforts forth anonymously. Nor perhaps should we do so even if we would. As the value of a car is vouched for by the integrity of its maker's name or as the honesty of metal is indicated by the Sterling stamp on its back, so the name of the writer is the hallmark that guarantees his production. And here it would seem we have the crux of the whole business.

The writer should feel sincerely that he has something to contribute. This may be a new scientific discovery, a new technique, a successful method of teaching or a new way of presenting a subject. He should know that either the subject or the treatment of his material is sufficiently new to be worthy of a bid for attention. An experienced teacher or investigator is sufficiently familiar with his field to know what is a real addition to knowledge along these lines. In the graduate schools, where most of the scientific apprentices are found, the senior men should be constantly on the watch for publishable material that is being produced by the younger men. The latter are usually both too experienced and too modest (a condition most of us soon get over) to prepare a paper without encouragement.

At this point I can not help injecting a remark or two concerning authorship. Occasionally we find a senior staff advisor who feels that his contributions to a paper written by his student is so great that he is justified in claiming joint authorship. Great though the labors of the teacher usually are on any of the early literary efforts of his students it has always seemed to me that in adding his name to the paper the older man subtracts at least fifty per cent. from the very rightful pride of creation that should belong to the student. This objection naturally does not hold in those cases of genuinely cooperative research where each does his own particular phase of the problem and the written account brings all phases together.

The seemingly wholesale encouragement to publish, that has just been advocated, may appear to lead to a clogging of our sources of publication. Our sources are, however, abundant and if reasonable care is exercised to see that the papers deal with fresh facts, carefully and briefly set down, I think there will never be much trouble. Brevity is something still to be learned by the majority of biological writers.

It has been pointed out that, although publication is the coin of the academic realm, this would not seem to be the deplorable condition that some seem to think, particularly those who are short of this medium of exchange. There are many things that may be said for publication, most of which apply directly to the writer. Preparing a paper for the printer clears the writer's mind through forcing him to think logically. The concentration demanded for the process of writing focuses the author's attention on the subject in a way not likely to occur otherwise. New problems will arise from this concentration as well as will loopholes appear in work already done. Through his struggle to express himself clearly in print the writer should gain in facility of description and this should be reflected in his teaching.

Despite the many and obvious abuses that publication has and may suffer, proper graduate training and editorial supervision will limit much of it. The printed contribution of merit gives definite evidence of the teacher's or scientist's advance in his chosen profession. And on top of this, publication gives to the writer confidence, a professional spirit, the feeling of authority, spurs him on to work, and, by no means least important, gives him the unbeatable "thrill of print."

My original statement that publication is intended for the advancement and dissemination of knowledge seems to have been largely forgotten in a discussion of the value of publication from the standpoint of the writer. The former is generally recognized and needs no discussion. We can not have action without a corresponding reaction, and I have merely intended to present the side of the value of publication from the standpoint of the individual who is responsible for it. We must not forget that ordinary men of all ages have needed concrete evidence of their deeds. His name in print over his first contribution is to the graduate student what spurs and accolade were to the newly created knight. Both were and are symbols of having arrived.

Robert T. Hance
Zoological Laboratory,
University of Pittsburgh

THE STUDY OF SPANISH

After reading Professor Seashore's indictment of the study of Spanish in the high schools, I felt that I must do as did Cortes of old, raise my banner and cry, "Santiago y Adelante," St. James and Foreward, in defense of Spanish.

May I state first of all that after studying Latin for eight years, Greek for seven, and French for two, I took up the study of Spanish some eighteen years ago. I have been studying that language ever since, and far from hanging my head in shame, I am proud to confess it. It has been always a source of pleasure.

The teaching of Spanish is my life work, but besides that I have seldom been away in the summer to resorts or for travel but that I have met people interested in the language. That community of interest has been an "open sesame" for many pleasant times and friendships that I would not have had otherwise.

I have spent many delightful hours also reading the literature. If, as Professor Seashore says, he has no quarrel with the literature, why should not one be prepared for his leisure hours then, by studying Spanish as well as French or German?

Professor Seashore says Spanish is such an easy language. Has he studied it? It is easy to get a smattering of it, but the Spanish language has such a wealth of idioms and vocabulary that the task of learning them is never finished. The use of the subjunctive is more difficult in Spanish than in French because in French you can usually "get by" with the infinitive, and in Spanish the sequence of tenses is more important. The translation too is not easy, as any one who has attempted to read Unamuno, Azorin and others can testify.

Professor Seashore takes exception to the fact that although Spanish is studied for commercial purposes, only about one per cent. of those who study it ever use it. Yet he says French and German are necessary in learned careers. Do more than one per cent. use French and German in this way when every article of note is translated into English immediately?

If more prominent men had taken an interest in the study of Spanish for commercial purposes I wonder whether the Prince of Wales would have walked away with fifty million dollars worth of orders for England? It was not too low a language for the Prince to learn, and if reports are true, he did not hang his head in shame because he knew it.

Then, too, we must look to the future. With

nineteen Central and South American Republics where Spanish is the native language is it too much to suppose that out of the years to come may emerge great literary lights from these countries?

In fact, rather than cast aspersions upon the study of Spanish, the great future of the language must give us pause.

LOUISE PERKINS

CINCINNATI, OHIO

QUOTATIONS

BIBLE READING IN PUBLIC SCHOOLS

THE Supreme Court of the United States refused, on October 19, to consider the challenged validity of the provision of the Constitution of the State of Washington prohibiting Bible reading and instruction in the public schools.

The court dismissed, for want of a substantial Federal question involved, the appeal in the case of Clithero, etc., *v.* Showalter, etc., No. 80, in which it was claimed that the prohibition is violative of rights guaranteed by the Federal Constitution and the Declaration of Independence.

The provision of the Washington State Constitution, as construed by the Supreme Court of Washington, affirmatively forbids religious worship, exercise or instruction in the public school system. The lower court, upholding the constitutional provision, denied the petition of the appellants, taxpayers and parents, for a writ of mandamus to compel the State Board of Education to arrange the curriculum of the public schools to provide for Bible reading and instruction.

In opposing consideration, counsel for the state had maintained that the Federal Constitution makes no provision to protect citizens in their religious liberties. This matter was said to be left to state constitutions and laws. There is also no guarantee in the Declaration of Independence, it was declared, "of the right of these appellants to have the Bible read and studied in the public schools."

The case was instituted, according to the petition for appeal, in the Washington Supreme Court to compel the State Board of Education to make provision for daily Bible instruction in the public schools. A petition incorporating this request was filed by George I. Clithero and 36 others with the board, September 9, 1930. On September 26, 1930, the board passed a motion that the petition be returned to Mr. Clithero, the board deciding that it "had no jurisdiction and no authority to make a decision of any kind upon the petition because it raised a constitutional question."

Construing this as a refusal to action, the petitioners asked the Supreme Court of the state to issue a writ of mandat, commanding the board to vacate its action, and to receive and grant the petition.

The state court ruled that Mr. Clithero and his associates could not maintain a suit to coerce action by a state officer or board unless they showed a pecuniary loss distinct from that suffered by the general public, its opinion shows.

The state court declared that the "questions presented have all been decided against relators' contentions in state *ex rel.* Dearle *v.* Frazier, 102 Wash. 369, 173 Pac. 35, where an elaborate argument was indulged in and our State Constitution was held to forbid everything that is here demanded."

In the petition for appeal to the Supreme Court of the United States, which forms part of the unprinted record in the office of the clerk, it is contended on the part of Mr. Clithero and the others that "a denial of the things demanded would be as a denial to petitioners of their rights and privileges guaranteed under the laws and Constitution of the United States."

Mr. Clithero and those with him are described in the record as "parents and school-age children of the State of Washington." A detailed list shows their ages to range from 6 years to 57 years.

The action of the Supreme Court was not unexpected and leaves the question of Bible reading and freedom of religion, guaranteed by all state constitutions, where it was before the case arose, Ward W. Keesecker, associate specialist in school legislation, stated orally at the Federal Office of Education on October 19.

The case was unique in that it represented for the first time an attempt to compel Bible reading, since other cases where Bible reading was involved, litigation was to restrain its reading on the grounds of an infringement of religious liberty, he said. Additional information on the question of Bible reading was made available as follows:

Bible reading in public schools is now expressly required by statute in 11 states and by order of the Board of Education in the District of Columbia. It is specifically permitted by law in five states, and is generally construed as lawful in 20 other states.

Bible reading in public schools is held lawful by Supreme Court decisions of 12 states. Of these, six are found in states whose laws either specifically require or specifically permit Bible reading, and six are found in states whose laws are silent on the subject.

In 12 states, Bible reading in the public schools is generally regarded unlawful. This view rests on four state court decisions, one state attorney general's opinion, one state superintendent's ruling, while the other six states exclude its reading either by general consent or implied prohibition. In these states where its reading is regarded adversely, Bible reading in public schools is generally construed as sectarian instruction or influence, or as an infringement of religious liberty and in conflict with the state constitutions.

No constitution or law of any state has specifically declared the Bible to be a sectarian book, nor has any state expressly prohibited its reading in the public schools. No law requiring Bible reading in public schools has ever been held unconstitutional by the courts. However, the Supreme Court of South Dakota in 1929 held a legislative enactment permitting Bible reading without comment to be in conflict with the constitution of that state.

The power to regulate Bible reading in the public schools of the state does not appear among the powers granted by the Constitution of the United States. The guarantees of religious liberty found in the first amendment to the Federal Constitution place a restraint on the Congress from enacting laws respecting an establishment of religion, or prohibiting the free exercise thereof, and this amendment can not be invoked by the states.

The states in which Bible reading has been upheld by state supreme court decisions are: Colorado, Georgia, Iowa, Kansas, Kentucky, Maine, Massachusetts, Michigan, Minnesota, Nebraska, Ohio and Texas.

The four states in which the highest court handed down adverse decisions are: Idaho, Louisiana, South Dakota and Wisconsin.—*United States Daily.*

SOCIETIES AND MEETINGS

CONFERENCE OF THE INTERNATIONAL STUDENT SERVICE

To seek a common ground for student action in the present world crisis, to bring together students of North America and those of other continents, and to help clarify the guiding principles of the university here and abroad, was the purpose of the tenth annual conference of International Student Service, held September 1st to 9th at Mount Holyoke College, South Hadley, Massachusetts, and attended by over two hundred students and leaders in university circles from thirty-nine countries.

Representatives of nearly every creed and shade of political belief, of nearly every country in Europe, of China, Japan, India, South Africa, Canada, Australia and Latin America, were included among the delegates, about ninety of whom were from this country, and one hundred and twenty-five from overseas. Among the American delegates were students and faculty members from about forty colleges.

The conference, first of its sort to be held in this country without religious or political sponsorship of any kind, found itself faced eventually by two major questions, two questions that dominated the student horizon in nearly every one of the thirty-nine countries the delegates represented. The first was the problem of university overcrowding, overproduction of graduates and the resultant unemployment that exists in the professions to-day. Nearly every one of the delegates testified to the alarming fact that the universities of his country were turning out a considerably greater number of candidates for the professions than our economic system can ever absorb, even in normal times.

The second issue was what Dr. Walter M. Kotschnig, general secretary of International Student Service, termed "the university's failure in the most vital respects in its function in social and international relationships. There has hardly ever been a time when the university has had so little influence on the political, economic and social life of the world as at present."

The speeches by prominent educators, European and American, which formed part of the conference program, were aimed at acquainting delegates with the broad facts of to-day's political, economic and university situation in America, Europe and Asia. The discussions that followed gave delegates from every country an opportunity to thresh out in open forum the bitterly contested issues—racial, political and economic—that divide Europe to-day; and resulted in concrete and striking plans for concerted student action for the future.

The conference was opened by Dr. Stanley K. Hornbeck, chief of the division of Far Eastern affairs of the United States State Department, who, on behalf of President Hoover, greeted the delegates in an address that went farther than any administration speech had gone previously in indicating abandonment of this government's policy of "isolation." The speech, which was considered an expression of an increased willingness on the part of the President to cooperate with Europe both politically and economically, created a stir in diplomatic circles.

Dr. Kotschnig, speaking the following day on "International Student Service and the University," declared that the tendency to overprofessionalization which characterizes higher education throughout the world to-day had cut the university off from society at the very moment when its contribution was most acutely needed. He asserted that the university was at present making no attempt to inculcate a sense of social responsibility in students, nor to combat the ignorance of international problems that led to militant nationalism on the one hand, and to "the sentimental internationalism, so prevalent in Anglo-Saxon countries, that refuses to recognize any differences between peoples" on the other. He called the latter attitude "as warped and as dangerous" as exaggerated nationalism.

Dr. Kotschnig declared that the university, by its failure to present concrete labor problems, by its aloofness, detachment and "intellectual snobbery" was serving to widen rather than bridge the growing gulf between classes that was threatening catastrophe to-day. By its overproduction of graduates, it is partially reponsible, he said, for "one of the most dangerous elements in the social unrest of to-day—the despair of those who after completing their studies can find no suitable posts." "Jobless graduates, and students faced with a prospect of two or three years of unemployment after graduation are turning in desperation to any sort of political extreme that promises complete reversal of existing conditions. In Germany over half the student body are Hitlerites; in Greece, a great proportion are Communists."

Dr. William Allan Neilson, president of Smith College, offering an "Analysis of American Civilization" later that day disputed the accepted notion that this country is inferior to Europe in culture because it is "young."

The European has a vague notion that we are inferior in culture because, he says, we are young. In what sense are we young? Politically, what republic is older? The German Empire is far newer than the United States of America politically. We are much older because we have come from people who have merely changed their country. Where did they come from? They came from your countries. So we are just as old as anybody. We are young then only in the particular combination in which we exist. . . .

It may be true that our country is uncultured, but I do not think we can excuse it by youth in any of the ordinary senses of the word. The objection, I believe, is made first because of the enormous size of our middle classes. You come to a country where an enormous proportion of the people are well off. It is not only that we have a great many ''new rich,'' but that we have a great many ''new well-off.'' But if you have in mind the elastic society we have here, with vast numbers rising from hand labor to wealth in several generations, you begin to see that the expectation with which foreigners come to investigate American society, the expectation of people having been brought up in comfortable surroundings, is not valid. Half of them have been brought up in very humble surroundings. If you took the same proportion of the population here which you would expect to find cultivated in Europe, the cultural level would be about equal, but the objector takes a much bigger slice of America and therefore finds the proportion lower.

Dr. Neilson found that a similar retort might be made to derogatory comparisons between American students and Europeans.

> We send to college ten times as many persons proportionally as any European country. If you take one in a thousand and send him to college in one country, and one in a hundred in another country, it is clear that the average level of ability in the second college will be much lower than the first.
>
> In universities in France and in other countries of Europe, men correspond, not to our university population, but to the top 10% of our university population. Why do we have the other 90%? Because of the efficiency of our educational institutions. If our colleges were made up of our top 10%, they would make a better showing to the world. But we are educating a grade of natural ability that is left in Europe to industrial occupations, to the minor clerical work which can be engaged in without higher training. We do it because we believe in education—it may be said naively and touchingly—but profoundly.

Dr. Henry Noble MacCracken, president of Vassar College, presented the "American Conception of the University," followed by the Abbé Joseph Gremaud, of the University of Fribourg, Switzerland, who set forth the European conception:

> The American university is a school for adolescents and adults. That is all. If the adults are ready for the highest levels of study and education, they can obtain instruction on those levels; if they are practically illiterate and can hardly read and write their own language, they can get instruction on that level in the same university. America being what it is, I find this an excellent thing.

America, according to Dr. MacCracken, is characterized by

> a vicarious passion for education. Our enthusiasm for education in this country is an enthusiasm for somebody else to have it.
>
> Our oldest universities, such as Harvard and Yale, were founded by the community to educate its ministers; our State universities, by parents who wanted their children to have a better education than they had; and our women's colleges for the most part by men who believed that women ought to be better educated.
>
> Higher education in this country is a product, not of the passion for learning of a group of students or professors, as in Europe, but of the community as a whole, who believe that education is a good thing for the public at large. The American student is studying, not as the result of his own nature, but through the will of the community. It is that situation that explains his parochialism and his passion for applying his knowledge long before he really knows what it is all about.

Abbé Gremaud found the European university characterized by "extreme specialization," which had led to its maintaining a "splendid isolation," just when the nation had the greatest need of its cooperation.

Claude W. Guillebaud, pro-proctor of the University of Cambridge in England, speaking on the "Power of the Past and the Realities of To-day," declared that the formation of a United States of Europe was an impossibility, cultural and traditional differences being, in his eyes, insuperable obstacles. "The family has broken up and not even a federal structure is in the least likely ever to unite the members again under a single roof. Even the more modest proposal of a European customs union would be met by most formidable difficulties."

Dr. Arnold Wolfers, director of the School of Politics in Berlin, and chairman of the conference, presented a masterly analysis of "The Crisis in the West," maintaining that "the present depression is more than one of those cyclical crises which have shaken the capitalistic world every seven or eight years" because it is an inescapable demonstration that the Western World has reached the limitations of every economic system within its choice. He saw no system which promised a cure-all, but declared that for the immediate future, only the help of America in lightening the burden of debts and reparations in the economic field and her "disinterested mediation" in the international field, would make economic recovery possible.

"In helping, America certainly will be helping herself, too, for she will be leading the way out of a crisis which is threatening the whole of Western civilization."

"The Crisis in the East" was presented by Dr. S. K. Datta, former member of the Indian parliament, and also a delegate to the London Round Table Conference. "The Asiatic countries believed, that the inner nexus of unity would be discovered in nationalism, whether cultural, economic or imperialistic. Nationalism has succeeded to a certain extent, but as we look into the future, it may be doubted whether it will continue to hold people together, especially under the stress of economic inequality."

Dr. John Hope, president of Atlanta University, spoke on "Negro Education in the United States," and Dr. Alain Locke, head of the philosophy department at Howard University, contributed a study of "The Negro in Art." The race problem in this country was presented by Miss Marion Cuthbert, former dean of women at Talladega College, Talladega, Ala., and the racial situation in Europe, was analyzed by James Parkes, author of "The Jew and His Neighbor," and head of the department of cultural cooperation of International Student Service. A spirited discussion, in which leaders of German, Austrian and Polish nationalist student organizations, and of Jewish student organizations here and abroad, participated, followed Mr. Parkes' speech. Mr. Parkes commented:

"This is the first time in the ten years of our history that the discussion of this topic has been carried on without tension and bitterness, and that our delegates have been able to hear without resentment points of view directly opposed to their own. Our conference this year marks tremendous progress."

The discussion resulted in a resolution to have International Student Service arrange a tour to Palestine for non-Jewish students during the coming year, before the next Jewish-anti-Semitic student conference, of which the organization has already held three. It is proposed to give Central and Eastern European students an opportunity to see the Jew in his own cultural background.

Other resolutions growing out of the conference included a decision to sponsor a conference of experts abroad in 1932, for the purpose of investigating the whole problem of university overcrowding, overproduction of graduates and unemployment in the professions. Professors, students and representatives of organizations of employers and employees will be among the delegates.

The crux of the university and professional overcrowding situation was seen to be the need for a saner appreciation on the part of public opinion of the intrinsic worth and dignity of manual labor and other forms of practical work, in contrast to the over-emphasis hitherto placed on purely intellectual occupations.

To combat American student indifference to, and ignorance of, international affairs, a problem which was a high point in the conference discussions, and which occasioned a bitter and despairing outburst on the part of the American undergraduates present, it was decided that the organization hold an annual seminar of a month in Russia for twenty picked American seniors and graduate students, to terminate by a conference with Russian students. Similar seminars will be held in Italy and Germany.

Plans were made in the final recommendations for a Balkan student conference next year; for the establishment of student self-help and rural social work movements in India, and possibly in China, similar to those the organization has sponsored in Wales, in Bulgaria, in Poland and in other European countries; for the granting of medical scholarships in European universities to South African students, who are frequently debarred from their own country's medical schools; and a proposal was made to organize, where possible, "University Weeks," during which an attempt would be made to bring before the university and the outside world "some of the most urgent problems of university education to-day."

Next year's conference of International Student Service will be held during the summer near Brno in Czechoslovakia.

HELENE BLANCHARD

SPECIAL CORRESPONDENCE

ELEMENTARY EDUCATION IN COLOMBIA

THE basis of the present school system in Colombia is the organic law, No. 39, promulgated in the year 1903, under the able minister of education Doctor Antonio Jose Uribe, probably ablest educational leader of Colombia, and under the presidency of Doctor Jose Manuel

Marroquín. However, this organic law is exceedingly general in character and lays down but the barest skeleton of the system. It consists of but 46 articles totalling not more than about 2,500 words.

According to the nature of Colombian legislative procedure it is supplemented by presidential decree amounting to more in this case than the legislative act. The decree, No. 491, of the year 1904, consists of 186 articles, or approximately 17,550 words. This decree outlines in detail the administration of the organic law and defines also, in quite lengthy detail, all meaning and terms of said law.

The law is further defined in regard to other certain specific details in decree No. 229 of the year 1905, decree No. 1601 of the year 1916, and decree No. 571 of the year 1926.

In addition, the educational system is guided continually by bulky bulletins issued monthly by the educational ministry of the government. These *revistas* or bulletins contain many treatises by well-known educators of the country besides suggestions of the educational ministry of the government. The uniformity with which these suggestions are carried out would vary as much as the individuality of the teachers and directors themselves.

Probably the most significant statement one could make about the educational system of Colombia, if approached in a comparative way to our school systems, would be to say that the Colombian educational system compares to the educational system of the U. S. as the government system of Colombia compares to the governmental system of the U. S. That is, if one who is familiar with our educational system should make a comparative study of the two governments he could deduce the main characteristics of the Colombian educational system. For instance, Colombian government is of the centralized type and Catholic. Likewise the Colombian educational system is very centralized and very catholic. The aforementioned type of federal law and decree serves to substantiate the first point while a literal translation of the first article of the organic law will substantiate the second point. It reads as follows: "Public instruction in Colombia will be organized and directed in accordance with the Catholic religion."

According to the above-mentioned laws and decrees public instruction is divided into primary, secondary, industrial and professional. Primary education is free but not compulsory. However, subsequently it is defined as compulsory by law, but, lacking means of enforcement, this law hardly changes it from its former status. Primary education is under the charge of the departments (corresponding to the states in the U. S.), secondary education is under the care of both the national and departmental governments and also the municipalities, the industrial and professional education is taken care of by the nation or the departments. General administration is in the hands of the executive power as they term their central executive department of government, whereas the immediate care of the schools is in charge of the departmental governors through directors or secretaries of public instruction.

Outside of public instruction there exist corresponding private schools. These play an important part especially in secondary education, as technical and commercial institutes, universities, etc.

Besides the above-mentioned, the civilizing of the aborigines is under the care of national government throughout the territories, that is the *intendencies* and *comisarias*.

Primary Schools

Article 6 of organic law says it is the obligation of the departments to establish primary schools to teach the elements, principally those which train for citizenship and prepare for agriculture, manufacturing and commerce. Primary education is generally thought of, depending on the locality, anything up to the first six years of education. Primary schools are divided into three kinds: (1) rural schools, (2) urban schools and (3) kindergartens.

Rural Schools (*escuelas rurales*) comprise by far the majority of all schools, for the majority of the population are country dwellers. However, municipalities may support rural schools and likewise private institutions. They are classed as rural schools more from the fact that they are the simplest and most elemental of the entire system.

These rural schools are divided into two

classes again, those of one sex and those called alternating. The former are found in districts of denser population where there are enough numbers to supply schools of separate sex. The alternating get their name from the fact that one school serves for each sex, alternating during the day; as, for instance, one sex in the morning and one in the afternoon, for periods of two hours each. They are found in more backward districts where the population is less dense, where, perhaps but some twenty pupils can be served.

Again either one of these two schools may be periodical or permanent according, as the law dictates, "to the necessities of the people, the resources of the departments or as local circumstances may require."

The curricula in these *escuelas rurales* or rural schools extends over three years and comprise the subjects of arithmetic, reading, writing, religion, a little geography, civic instruction, agriculture and the manual arts.

Urban Schools (*escuelas urbanas*). These schools are found in the municipal centers and localities of denser population. The ideal type, as described in the organic decree supplementary to the organic law, takes in a period of six years of study. The curricula include the following: Religion, reading, writing, arithmetic, drawing, geography, national history, natural history, Spanish grammar, physics, singing, gymnasium, civics, agriculture and domestic arts for the girls. The average age of attendance runs from six to fifteen years of age.

However, like many Latin-American institutions these urban schools seldom measure up to the ideal. Due to the poverty of the rank and file who patronize these schools, the children at the end of three or four years of schooling are forced to abandon their studies to aid their parents.

It thus results that the first four years of this plan comprises the ordinary type of this class of school. In the larger and more flourishing centers we find these four year primary urban schools supplemented by what are called *escuelas superiores* or Higher Schools. These are not to be confused with the High Schools of our land, for they are but elementary schools more like our Junior High Schools, although not representing as many years of study. They are attended by pupils desiring to prepare for their secondary education.

Most of the departments (states) have developed these urban schools gradually and in an evolutionary way. In most cases all such schools in one locality are under the administration of one director who is aided by subdirectors or sectional teachers. In some districts each school is administered as a distinct unit. Salaries range slightly higher than those in the rural schools, depending upon the locality.

Administration and teaching of primary instruction is controlled considerably by a more or less elaborate system of inspection evolving from the national government through the Ministry of Education. The directors of public instruction and national inspectors are the agents of this system in the various departments (states) and school territories.

The former, that is the directors of public instruction, are appointed by the governors of the departments (states) while the latter, that is, the national inspectors, are appointed by the executive power, that is the central authority. Subordinate to the above are the provincial inspectors. (A province is a subdivision of a department or state). These provincial inspectors do the real work of checking up, visiting the schools personally, giving varying amounts of directions, correcting irregularities, selecting the teaching personnel and in a general way inaugurate any new and useful improvements. Thus we can see that considerable control of the primary schools is exercised by successive steps from the central authority.

The several above-mentioned types of primary schools have their fiscal needs taken care of by local inspectors (*inspectores locales*) who are employed by the provinces (subdivisions of the states). This is an honorary position much like our local school boards. They generally work altruistically and industriously for the material needs of the schools. Ordinarily the parish priests perform this function.

Complementing the administrative machinery mentioned above, there exists in each municipality, councils of inspection (*juntas de inspeccion*) made up of the town mayor (*Alcalde*), the parish priest (*Parroco*), the president of the town council (*Presidente del Concejo*) and some outstanding citizen. This body in a great measure provides for the progress of the schools of its locality.

Speaking of the expenses of the three above-mentioned types of elementary education, it may be said that they are distributed between the national, departmental and municipal governments. The national government pays for the school materials as texts, etc. Also the national government takes entire charge of the schools and other institutions for civilizing of the aborigines in the *intendencias* and national territories. The departments pay for the teaching personnel and the municipalities furnish the school plant and equipment.

The source of income in 1923 was as follows: national government 4.8 per cent., departmental governments 65.9 per cent. and municipal governments 28 per cent. However, half of the 4.8 per cent. contributed by the national government is for use in the national territories.

There are no special sources of income set aside for school expenditures. Appropriations are taken from the public treasuries and likewise these amounts fluctuate according to fiscal circumstances of the governments.

In general, primary education has begun to make serious inroads against illiteracy. It is perhaps unfair to measure the quantity or quality of their education against that in the United States.

However, there is a tremendous spirit of hope and optimism in their general attitude toward education. The writer has visited some of these urban schools and associated in the company of the teaching personnel. The buildings are generally rented, most often of one room, the furniture often consists of benches and table desks, home-made. Slates are used and some paper. There are not many teaching aides. The text-books are good, often printed by the American Book Company and others of the U. S. The buildings are naturally quite open in the tropics. The general attitude of the pupils is noisy but busy.

Schools for the Aborigines are provided for the immense indigenous population of Colombia. The vast eastern sections and some central parts of Colombia, as the Choco, Tierradentro, Goajira, etc., are peopled by barely civilized Indians. Colombia is quite conscious of her duty to these native peoples but the Christianizing and educating of these peoples is an Herculean task. Sections are inaccessible, tribes are often at war with each other and offer in many cases a resentful attitude toward any intrusion. It is said some practice customs bordering on barbarity. This duty is however entrusted almost solely to Catholic missions. It is interesting to note that here in modern times is going on a process very similar to the Catholic mission system of the 16th, 17th and 18th centuries.

Industrial Schools are found in some departments and territories where in conjunction with the elements there is taught industrial education such as weaving of various kinds, agriculture, silk cultures and other manual arts. Plants of such type are only beginning really to develop but it is planned to develop such schools to greater extent.

H. C. Lanks

NEW BOOKS IN EDUCATION

Barr, A. S. *An Introduction to the Scientific Study of Classroom Supervision.* Pp. xv + 399. Appleton. $2.50.

Brubacher, John S., Editor. *Henry Barnard on Education.* Pp. x + 298. McGraw-Hill. $2.25.

Cole, Percival R. *A History of Educational Thought.* Pp. 316. Oxford University Press. $3.50.

Davis, Howard L. *The Young Man in Business.* Pp. xi + 172. Wiley. $2.00.

Dondo, Mathurin. *Modern French Course.* Pp. xiv + 546. Illustrated. Heath. $1.72.

Fraser, W. H., J. Squair and David H. Carnahan. *Standard French Grammar.* Pp. xiii + 621. Illustrated Heath. $1.76.

Hills, E. C. and Mathurin Dondo. *La France, son Histoire sa Civilisation.* Pp. viii + 290. Illustrated. Heath. $1.32.

Monash, Louis. *Know Your Child.* Pp. xiii + 246. McGraw-Hill. $2.00.

Moore, Bruce V. and George W. Hartmann. *Readings in Industrial Psychology.* Pp. xxxix + 560. Appleton. $5.00.

Morgan, B. Q., Max Griebsch and A. R. Hohlfeld. *Neues Deutsches Liederbuch.* Pp. 162. Heath. $1.56.

New York Commission on Ventilation. *School Ventilation: Principles and Practices.* Pp. viii + 75. Teachers College, Columbia University. $1.00.

Pittaro, John M. and Alexander Green. *Modern Spanish Grammar.* Pp. xviii + 532. Illustrated. Heath.

Rodriguez, P. Teodoro. *El Estatismo y la Educación Nacional en los Países Civilizados.* Pp. 573. Del Real Monasterio.

Taylor, J. Carey. *The Reliability of Quarterly Marks in the Seventh Grade of Junior High School.* Johns Hopkins Press. $1.15.

EDUCATIONAL REVIEW

Edited by WILLIAM McANDREW

EDITORIAL COMMENT

FEATURING FAIRHAVEN

When I was at Bridgewater one day in the spring, consorting with the entertainingly conservative schoolmasters whom Payson Smith assembles every now and then, three separate men incidentally remarked that if I wanted to see schools well run by a real master I should spend some time in Charlie Prior's bailiwicks, Fairhaven and Mattapoisett.

I have ventured to drag you along before this on pedagogical pilgrimages to Beveridgeton, which is Omaha; Morganburg, otherwise Antioch; Kellygrad, alias Binghamton; and Chewningopolis, or Evansville. I hope you will come on with me to the Priory, by which I mean the two beautiful towns on Buzzards Bay next eastward from Keithville, which the unenlightened call New Bedford.

Inlets of blue sea water curve through green meadows. You would not feel uneasy if your younger boys tried sailing in these sheltered coves, and, as for swimming—oh, boy! You walk over a handsome long bridge spanning water once alive with a hundred whaling ships. A handsome spire thrusts upwards out of a layer of glorious old trees. The charm is not spoiled by factories. It is a town of pretty homes, of churches and of such a comfortable sense of content that I should imagine the unique feature of Prior's work would get very little attention from the respectable burghers, who seem to me as calmly satisfied as most New England communities, resting on their storied past. Fairhaven, with its tablets, memorials and historical museum, reminds you that the Norsemen settled here five hundred years before Columbus. Here was born of Gudrid and Karlsefne the first white child of all America. Out of Fairhaven sailed Ezekiel Hopkins in the *Alfred,* on which John Paul Jones hoisted the first American flag to fly from a vessel. All this I read in the Fairhaven history book which Ruth Brocklebank, a teacher in the Rogers Grammar School, has written for the children to study. In it, the deeds that men have done for this old town are set down in enlivening stories. There is especial praise for Henry Rogers, oil magnate, born here of humble parentage and later bestowing churches, libraries, schools and parks upon his birthplace.

Charles Prior has been superintendent here for what must seem to a Chicagoan a phenomenally long time—fifteen years. Every summer, like most Massachusetts schoolmasters, he sees a migration of many of his experienced teachers, lured away by higher salaries. In New England one must begin again training the new ones into the ways of the departed.

Codified Experience

I like Prior's outlines of school ways found to work well. They are terse and crisp. One is in every teacher's possession. These summaries of experience tell you the time between opening and closing of school every day is a very precious period, paid for by the town, which is entitled to service well thought out and planned. Every exercise has to be guided by a definite purpose, not left to chance nor turned this way and that by incidents.

To make a plan will require of you, at first, much time, but professional work is planned work, with a clear purpose guiding it.

We hear much praise of personality, says the outline. Good! I like a pleasing personality in a doctor, but I want to know first that he is well up in professional skill.

It is well to create a pleasing atmosphere through your personality. The unanalytic may call you a good teacher but, if you have no clear idea of what you want, how to get it, and whether you really have got it or not, you are not a teacher, just a pleasing personality.

Prior makes no pretension to wit, scholarship, originality or eminent skill. During the whole day he said nothing of himself except as I coaxed it out of him. But in these outlines are bits of pure Priorism.

I noted one—"Some things to keep in mind when a supervisor visits you." It is a list of the points in teaching which impress an inspector favorably. Prior wants his teachers marked high. As he is one of the most frequent of supervisors to visit your class, what this standing announcement means is that he believes you are entitled to be seen at your best. The last thing in this list of what to keep in mind when your work is inspected is—"Your treatment of the supervisor on leaving." I used to get unsatisfactory marks from a late lamented superintendent of the New York schools. No Prior hinted to me that I should not have let my relief at the supervisor's departure show plainly. Would that I now were teaching! I would try this on the arriving inspector: "I have been hoping you would come. I am right glad to see you." Then, after half an hour of torture: "Must you go so early? I wish you might stay longer. Do come again soon."

Here are other things that struck me in the suggestion each teacher has from the Fairhaven superintendent: When a parent complains, guard your temper. If you lose it your effectiveness is gone. Don't exaggerate, don't protest. Let your facts be indisputable. Most parents are reasonable if skilfully treated. You should have your materials well in hand and in full amount.

A designated pupil, immediately a visitor comes in, should offer a chair and a book.

Each pupil should keep an assignment book and write carefully each assignment of lesson when given.

Each teacher is responsible for the success of her pupils.

When assigned to study periods you will not use the time for other work. Your best place is not the front of the room.

Better not have your children try a self-governing organization until you have found that you can govern them yourself.

Prior told me he is converted to pupil self-government as an indispensable school exercise for the coming civic duties of this generation, and that his best disciplinarians among the teachers are the ones who seem to throw the greatest responsibility on children to discuss and decide what proper conduct is.

Of course, he touches up the points of these standing suggestions by discussions with teachers in meetings.

His bulletins must take a great number of hours. But they seem to me worth many times the trouble they cost.

Montclair Bliss used to advocate a separate notebook for every teacher in which the inspector wrote comments after a visit and left the book with her. When he came back she gave him his notes as a cue to following up what he had said before. Prior's bulletins, omitting personal reference, recite especially good things he has observed on his rounds, even reproducing blackboard drawings used in some particularly good lesson. These paragraphs of specific reasons for his praise are an example of getting a school system to lift itself by its own bootstraps. The best poems written by the children are reproduced: "Fireflies," "What I Like," "The Baby," "Toys," "Games," anything you want. One girl, bless her unescapable femininity, had rhymed of her attempts to make her hair curl and concluded to "adjust myself to fate and be a good sport though my hair is straight."

Every school man I have known has his obsession. Prior's, on the day I visited him, was the dread of formalism. The salute to the flag is a beautiful ceremony. Repeated too often and without discussion of its meaning or questioning on what are you going to do about it or what have you done, it degenerates into only beautiful sound. Prior served overseas in the world war and noted the officials' opinion that too much use of the oath of allegiance creates indifference or even antipathy. The Fairhaven bulletins bristle with warnings that form grows deadening, abstract ideas get anesthetic. Things taught must be vivified and related to action. Get your feet on the ground often.

WHAT ARE YOU DOING FOR FAIRHAVEN

The thing that makes Fairhaven especially unique among schools known to me is the persistent urge for making school life a patriotic adventure. In all the halls and classrooms I saw pupils' colored posters, old and new: "Rake your leaves out of the gutter," "Pick up the litter in your own yard," "Help your mother," "A good citizen does something for his city; what have you done for Fairhaven?"

I happened into Elizabeth Hastings' classroom as her junior service league was in session. She was seated among the children and was as interested and uninterrupting as the visitors. A boy president was hearing reports of committees on civic help: progress in scrapbook making for the hospital, schemes for keeping the new school buildings spick and span, the latest suggestions in the matter of infantile paralysis, thrift campaign and the destruction of ragweed by the school children for the benefit of the sneezers of Fairhaven.

In each school building I noted large score cards in the main hall, recording the number of civic deeds done by pupils of different classes. Beginning thirteen years ago the Fairhaven teachers have experimented with the idea that boys and girl receiving education at the cost of the community should, while taking it, be giving something in return. It may not be much, but if encouraged and recognized, the civic spirit may develop into the habit of active citizenship. So says Mr. Prior.

By degrees, the scheme has developed into a regular feature of the school program. Each class is a Junior Improvement Association, a sort of understudy of the Fairhaven citizens' organization that looks after tree planting and other means of beautifying the city. The teachers found that the organization needs a moderate amount of money and that the handling of funds is good training for the citizen. You become a member of the society by reason of your enrolment in the school. But your enlisting as a paying member is entirely voluntary. In any case, you are frequently asked what you have done for Fairhaven that has done so much for you.

Prior says he has become convinced that so large a majority of human beings, other than him and me, are strengthened by recognition of one's good deeds that the schools find it desirable to record and reward the civic acts performed by the children. Ten hours of service for others gives you a handsome pin of blue, white and gold inscribed: "F.J.I.A. Civic Service." A hundred hours brings a certificate. For a hundred and fifty hours, a third of which have been given to service other than to the school, you get a civic diploma signed by your principal, superintendent and president of the board, certifying that you have made this preparation for a life of good citizenship in community, state and nation. At the top of it is this motto: "The Noblest Motive is the Public Good."

I saw a young matron wearing the pin. She said her diploma is framed and hanging in her home, more valued than her high-school sheepskin, which is still rolled up. You, as a psychologist and philosopher, can conjecture the deep reason why this is so. The one testifies to familiarity with the high-toned influences of quadratic equations, Latin prosody and the culture canonized by college entrance boards; the other credits relieving trees of caterpillars' nests, killing rats, putting ashes upon icy walks and doing work for people who can not afford to hire.

Second New-England Revolution

Mind you, this is in New England, where Tom Briggs' Harvard lecture is still a shocking memory of suggestion that the high schools of that region are wedded to a culture remote from civic duty. This is in New England, in which school-master Vinyard, in his book, says the fewest number of teachers know anything of citizenship training.

If any one has gone farther than Prior in stressing general welfare, let his name be shouted, and I'll take you on a pilgrimage to his school. On the day I was in Fairhaven, Prior told me the high-school students had voted to divide the profits of school athletic and other entertainments with the Fairhaven welfare fund.

You don't have to write to the Fairhaven superintendent for details of his scheme. He'll tell you the motive is the main thing. Realize your school is supported by the money of every day laborer and factory hand in your town who have no children at all. Realize that all the guff about class spirit and school loyalty is nine tenths selfishness at best. Get a bigger spirit than that! Let's put our town before our school. It has been paying for our education for many years. What have we done for it What can we do? Take a piece of chalk; stand in front of a class; ask the questions and write down the answers. You will get a list of services more valuable to your children than Prior's summary is, for it will be their own. Get your good writers to tell the newspapers about it. Get the service organized as well as spelling is, or geography. Cheer up the pupil officers and keep enough in the background to give them a sense of self-direction; but let them feel you know they are running the biggest thing in the school.

Lure them into studying your town's needs, physical and political.

Don't let Kilpatrick or Bagley mean you when they say American school children, pampered with delightful club life, with their athletics, dramatics and dancing parties, are vaccinated against catching the real spirit of cooperative conduct of an unselfish democracy.

BOOK REVIEWS

MONTHLY RATION

FROM the sixty-three new books offered by respected publishers this month I recommend the following twenty-four as aids to success in your big business.

NOW A FEARLESS CIVICS

LET me, for the reasons given, doff my hat to Edmonson, University of Michigan, and Dondineau, public schools of Detroit. In their book[1] they have pushed civics down into the junior high school where they reach more coming citizens. They have saturated the informational content with a virile flavor of obligation. They stimulate community knowledge with the desire to become intelligent participants in public welfare. They correct the selfish individualism of the older education by stressing the fact that your getting on involves the duty of doing your share in the world's work for the benefit of the world as much as of yourself. They present the machinery of government as incidental to these larger aims. They integrate occupations and a variety of often separated portions of social science with clarity and unity. They use language and examples suited to their clientage. They analyze the good citizen into qualities and acts largely belonging to boys and girls of the adolescent level. They enrich their book with cartoons and photographs of current interest. They make it a veritable workbook by many and thought-compelling problems. They tell you to use the actual elections in your community as occasions for parallel ones in your school, pupils scanning the papers for policies and qualifications of candidates, campaigning and voting for these in school. They do not abide by the absurd pussyfoot command to keep controversial subjects out of school. They put the task of discussion and conclusion on the pupils, relieving the teacher of the charge of offensive partisanship, a condemnation which might put a stop to practical and needed attention to citizenship problems. They show realization that public schools were recommended as civic and political trainers by those who established the United States, and were made a public charge not so much for aiding parents to get their children advantaged as to maintain and improve government by the people.

[1] James B. Edmonson, Arthur Dondineau, "Citizenship and Occupations through Problems." The Macmillan Company, New York. 759 pp. $1.80.

SCHOLARSHIP AS SERVICE

Two bulletins issued by the School of Education, Indiana University, you will find prime examples of research turned to present needs.[2, 3] They offer classified summaries of writings on good will, ideals, nationalism, international attitudes, individualism, politics, religion, human nature, group behavior, war and peace. They exemplify a superb application of scholarship to current needs. If you have periods of civic lassitude I recommend your using these books as anthologies, for doctrine, for edification and for a brace.

DEMOCRACY

THE epic story of man's wounds from the Frankenstein of machinery, the awakening of national conscience, the rise of the working people, the awakening of legislatures, the idea of a living wage, the growth of the unions, the effect of strikes, pensions, doles, socialism and contemporary events from 1900 are the subject of Professor Pipkin's history:[4] "Social Politics and Modern Democracies." Two old civilizations, French and English, are the main fields of study. The nature and effect of their ameliorative laws are presented. Their progress in putting their national life in the way of reason and justice in domestic policies and international relations is traced. At the beginning

[2] Henry Lester Smith, Levi McKinley Krueger, "Source Book, Psychology of Human Relationships, Individual and Social." 107 pp. 50 cents.

[3] Henry Lester Smith, Harold Littell, "Source Book, Philosophy of Human Relations, Individual and Collective." 326 pp. 75 cents.

Both by University Book Store, Bloomington, Indiana.

[4] Charles W. Pipkin, "Social Politics and Modern Democracies." The Macmillan Company, New York. Two Vols. 794 pp. $7.50.

of the nineteenth century the worker was alien from participation in the life of the community as a whole. His progress to responsible citizenship is what popular government means to-day. In a confusion of opinion as to the success or failure of democracy near at home, in a more or less vivid realization that when "the people" are mentioned it has to mean people over 90 per cent. of whom are laborers, the clearness with which Professor Pipkin brings out the fact that democracy must mean government by working people is striking. He abstains from argument and propaganda. His narrative is of movements and acts.

TONIC SOCIOLOGY

OUT of the dust clouds of the conflict of philosophers, metaphysicists, moralists and reformers, Clarence Case comes bringing a new sociology,[5] "trying to point out certain subprocesses which make up that more comprehensive process called social progress." Herbert Spencer's evolution as progress needs cleaning up. Mere adaptability to environment won't do. If the environment is bad, the fitting for it is anything but progress. Spengler's denial of consideration of thought of past or future to all but western civilization is an eloquent exaggeration. Egyptians, Hebrews, Greeks, Chinese disprove it. Lists of the marks of progress give us mostly preferences of the markers. Professor Perry's definition as "society's passage from good to more of the same" does not save "good" from the region of dispute. But with the Alexander-Bain style of dismissing hairsplitting as a preventive of starting on the journey, Mr. Case cuts the knots: "Let's assume we know what we mean by social progress, that it is an actual fact, that we can recognize it when it comes down the road, that we have the collective wisdom to direct the common life." When he gets into his stride, the professor climbs upon a pile of problems and selects old and new pieces of perplexity which he exhibits with a raciness and point irresistibly arresting. Read his "grown-up infantility" if you want piquancy and power. The history of peoples, even the most enlightened, has been a story of groping, still continuing. A wide-spread movement of thought proposes the deliberative establishment of a society of nations to reduce war and protect the rights of weaker groups. This would be a clear case of societal self direction. Yet the forces of greed, race-hatred and ignorance marshal forces against the project, either its principle or its particular form. A thousand reasons are adduced to show why it is impossible. The real reason is that mankind is too little above the level of racial infancy, and too afraid of the childish political partisanship that is in opposition.

What the human race requires is to be awakened to realize its condition. The feeble plaints of a few are not enough. There must be complete race consciousness.

Yet the most advanced societies of the present hold that progress is right and desirable, to such a degree that it is heresy to believe otherwise.

The world that suffered the last great war was infantile. Actually and inevitably, through no sort of accident, the stupidity of society produced it and is now, with consciousness of its horrible loss to victors and vanquished, saying that another is inevitable and soon to come. The average social infant says "We have always had wars, we always shall, so let's get ready."

The sickening orgy of nightriding sweeps over this country. An admirable young Iowa legislator, just home from the war, exhorts the legislature to pass a law making masked gatherings by day or night a felonious crime. He hopes to give his state an enviable position as the delirium spreads; astounding public indifference confronts him. Americans are politically degenerate.

Read Author Case on "flaming youth" and find him saying what you have wanted to think if you had not been bathed in newspaper and magazine hysteria.

As a propounder of salutary doctrine, discriminately opposing or approving the views of Compte, Spencer, Ward, Mrs. Besant, Garret, Cooley, Ross, Hobhouse, Leuba, Beard, Lloyd Morgan, Bertrand Russell, Lewis Terman, Richard Ely, Spengler, Sumner, Wallas and Whitehead; as a penetrating critic of the pretentions of intelligence testers; as a clarifier of eugenics, politics, legislation, education, religion and culture; as a stretcher of your brain and a stiffener of your spine, I recommend to you liberal doses of Case.

[5] Clarence Marsh Case, ''Social Process and Human Progress.'' Harcourt, Brace and Company, New York. 763 pp. $2.25.

YOU ARE THE CHARACTER COURSE

IF you have read President Sheldon Davis's "Self Improvement" and "Teacher's Relationships" you'll hurry into his new book.[6] I am a Davis addict. Of the Zanesville Davises, he was caught young by Missouri, where, with breaks for study in Columbia, Chicago, Leipzig and Berlin, he did almost all the grades of teaching and supervising there are, until Montana put him at the head of her State Normal College at Dillon.

The theme of his present text for teachers as are and as wish to be is this: It matters more what the pupils are gaining than what you do. But there's the curriculum. The conservative says it has been hurt by changes; the radical is worried because it hasn't changed enough. You can't change it much. While it is what it is your concern is to have it do the best for the children of which it is capable.

So goes Dr. Davis into it—reading, spelling, art, health, all the parts of it—and lays down what the successes have been shown to depend upon.

History need not be jingo stuff; nations, like folks, make mistakes and commit crimes. We have also deeds that make the school child thrill to the realization that this is his country and it is a glorious thing to help it along.

Character education and civics belong together. The old civics neglected obligations. You need to vitalize this study. But parents resent teaching children what to think rather than how to think. Your example is the most powerful influence on character development. You may not be the geography curriculum but you can not escape being the course of study in civics and character. Pupil self-government, with the right school spirit, is an effective preparation for the conditions of civic life. The spirit of it in simplified provisions can be utilized in the lowest grades. One mistake of moral teaching is assumption that invariable and quick reward comes from doing right. Open your eyes. The old schools knew better when they taught to do the just thing "though the heavens fall." Civics supplements history in that the one is past and the other concerned with real, unsolved, nearby problems of present and future. We must learn to teach it better.

[6] Sheldon Emmor Davis, "Teaching the Elementary Curriculum." The Macmillan Company, New York. 549 pp. $1.75.

SHORT ECONOMICS

HERE is a short illustrative treatise on economics[7] by an Englishman, John Marriott, former lecturer in political science at Oxford. In popular language is presented subsistence, costs, profits, money, agriculture, rents, ownership, wealth, value, capital, labor, wages, the industrial revolution, free trade, business, trade unions, cooperative buying, banks and speculation. The author does not allow his subject to be "the dull and dismal science." He writes with animation and simplicity. He gives other peoples credit for such conditions as he sees better than those in England. Fourteen per cent. of English farms are cultivated by their owners. In Denmark 80 per cent. are so worked. If you give a man absolute ownership of a bit of sandy desert he'll work like a slave to make it a smiling garden. If you put him on the same patch for you and pay him wages for his work, you will wait long for the smiling. It is a magnificent thing for a country to have its land cultivated by those who will get the most out of the soil. A prosperous agriculture is a nation's greatest asset.

Especially valuable is Professor Marriott's appraisal of trade unions.

DEWEY AND EDUCATIONAL CONFUSION

SEVEN secondary-school sagas are now in print: Harvard's Inglis Lectures by Leonard Koos, Paul Hanus, Abraham Flexner, Charles Judd, George Counts, Thomas Briggs and John Dewey.[8] This last lecturer finds education an uncertainty beyond any bewilderment of other times. No one is satisfied. Not only methods and results but ideals and aims are under fire. The address is so short and illuminating that it need not be mutilated here.

It offers a definite proposition for you to tackle. There must be a reorganization of subject-matter which will lead into the wide world of man and nature, of knowledge and of

[7] Sir John A. R. Marriott, "How England Lives." Oxford University Press, 114 5th Ave., New York. 142 pp. $1.00.

[8] John Dewey, "The Way Out of Educational Confusion." Harvard University Press, Cambridge. 41 pp. $1.00.

social interests and uses. The intelligence to bring this about is not lacking, but rather long-time patience and a will to cooperation and co-ordination. Refinement of existing practices, trying to make them "scientific" will only increase confusion. We must have an interrelation of subjects with one another and with social bearing and application.

Confusion is due to aimlessness.

Only new aims can inspire educational effort for clarity and unity.

A RESEARCHER SPEAKS TO TEACHERS

NOTABLY well informed, citing hundreds of investigations, cautious, encouraging, luring to standpoints where the footing is better, Director Whitney[9] sees teaching, with its frequent disregard of undeniable facts under its nose, clinging to disproved assumptions but in many instances moving along the road made safe by the laborious surveys and constructions of careful, unprejudiced enquirers. Education, in that it sets up objectives, is a philosophy. When it measures progress toward its aims by calm comparison of methods and results it employs the methods of science. What hinders these methods, asks our author. Conclusions, then investigation to find proof, rejection of facts pointing the wrong way. The amusing classical investigation started with a pious faith in the value of Latin and spent many good dollars proving that the teachers of Latin have faith in it. Mental discipline is a religion. Every teacher has his hobby, none I say have I, but all the hobbies smile at me; need a body cry?

Men no older than I recall Doctors of Medicine hilariously pooh-poohing the clinical thermometer, stethoscope, and "machine-shop medicine." Who does it now? Who made the change? Youngsters. Young assistants in the medical college, young practitioners in the field. Education is surely following the same course. No collegiate school of education dare hold up its head unless it has courses in research. Dr. Whitney is director of such studies in Colorado State Teachers College. He got the scientific slant as teacher and school superintendent. He has inoculated hundreds of young school workers with the serum of research and sent them out to spread it. I confess to prejudice in his favor created by his vigorous lambasting of the wild questionnaire habit some years ago. But, by the method of real research, I am attempting to correct my estimate of him by a critical examination of his output. His students, as I have met them, are wary of unsubstantiated claims; his other books are moderate and precise. His motive in writing this one, to suffuse with a confidence of justifiable sureness the good teaching that needs it, is a drive toward making the service into as real a profession as medicine is and by the same scientific road on which the healing art has been led. This is a handbook for intending teachers and for live ones in service and is a source book as well.

Whereas every large productive concern in the industrial world and all enterprising small ones, whereas chemistry, medicine, electricity, engineering and architecture are moving ahead by the study of their products and methods, whereas teaching is still lagging more than it has to, try the conversion of more of your staff to the belief that their art and their science needs to grow. This safe and scholarly book written for the amateur, is a piece of good fortune for you.

MITIGATED SUPERVISION

EFFECTIVE classroom supervision is the most important thing for a superintendent to provide after he has buildings, children and teachers. Only by classroom supervision can efficiency be maintained. This is the truth Milo Hillegas has been preaching to superintendents in a state system and, later, teaching to students in Teachers College, Columbia University. The number of teachers who persuade one another to the contrary view, the number of superintendents who coddle themselves into thinking that office-hours, letters, buildings and "being a business man" must have first place, the number of principals whose habits of busy idleness keep them away from the real works, must be known by the experienced professor. But he says nothing of them in his book.[10] Rather he presents supervision as an intensely interesting occupation, full of learning, perfecting, success and satisfaction, profitable, if well done, to

[9] Frederick Lamson Whitney, "Methods in Educational Research." D. Appleton and Company, New York. 335 pp. $2.25.

[10] Milo B. Hillegas, "The Elements of Classroom Supervision." Laidlaw Brothers, Chicago, 755 pp. $1.76.

teacher and supervisor alike, and really the indispensable necessity of teaching. The origin and nature of supervision, its difficulties and improved technique, its function in schools, make an admirable approach. Dr. Hillegas is happy as a conductor through it. From then on the treatment is sympathetic and firm, supported by quoted studies and tests. Considering a not uncommon aversion to being supervised, copies of this considerate book in the teachers' libraries would help cure the what's-he-after-now complex.

THE SUPERINTENDENT IN THE SMALLER TOWNS

THE temper of Superintendent Hunkins' book[11] on supervision of schools of smaller towns may be appreciated from passages like this: "Stand up against the temptation to show a weak-kneed policy in your supervision." "Progress won't come without leadership." "Beware of high-handed methods acclaimed by those who boast of how they handle their boards." "The board represents democracy's way." "The only really poor board is one that does not represent the people." "You are the main factor in getting the proper community regard for its schools." Adapting to the smaller and often impoverished school systems the forward-looking schemes of the better-off districts, Schoolmaster Hunkins goes cheerily into the selection and improvement of teachers, administration of finances, acquisition, care and upkeep of buildings and equipment, courses of study, grading and promotion, inspection, supervision and professional growth. His chapters on publicity are replete with effective suggestion. His insistence that supervision is teaching is convincingly elaborated. Where he finds a high authority illuminating a point, he quotes him. He keeps feet on the ground by references to his own mistakes and successes. It is a decidedly practical book imbued with high principles and a fine spirit for community service.

GIVING OUT THE LESSON

Now an entire book on "to-morrow you may take pages 140 to 148."[12] Director Carr, research division, National Education Association, and Counsellor Waage, Huntington Beach, California High School, write it. It is a good collaboration: researcher and practitioner. One confronts you with findings showing the expensive pupil failures due to sloppy outlining of work by teacher. The other makes easier the principal's and teacher's duty in providing that study and recitation follow the rule of all efficient productive work, that it is planned with care and foresight.

Chicago researches found a marked degree of skill in this duty shown by teachers whose work had been, previous to the study, rated as superior. Sixty-eight per cent. were highly efficient in this responsibility. Eight per cent. only of the ordinarily good teachers were superior in assigning lessons.

Here you have types of assignments described and calibrated, the times and length of them, their motivation, their follow-up and checking. Luring you through an interesting discussion of seventy pages, establishing their points by reports and by decisions of educational authorities, the Carr-Waage team cap the sheaf with thirteen assignment principles, observing which the guide of students on the road to success may save them from falling by the wayside.

STANDARDIZING THE MARKS

THE Duke of Buckingham, christened Burdette, whilom head researcher of Ohio State University, sometime accommodating neighbor when we two showed New York how to administer offices in the Board of Education Building, tells me I ought to study Dr. Charles Russell's guide calibrator,[13] tried and perfected in the Massachusetts State Normal School in Westfield and used in the public schools of that city. Very well. It is a compact, sliding, slit and column device of heavy bristol board dressed for easy cleaning. Like an interest table it saves the labor and avoids the errors of computation. Its use takes the ratings of children, for teachers' class book, home report cards and promotion, from the variation of teachers' notions at the time of making marks to a more objective standardized appraisal in accordance with modern statistical usage. Also, it is

[11] R. V. Hunkins, "The Superintendent at Work in Smaller Schools." D. C. Heath and Company, Boston. 401 pp. $2.00.

[12] William G. Carr, John Waage, "The Lesson Assignment." Stanford University Press, California. 98 pp. $1.50.

[13] Charles Russell, "Classroom Scaler and Grader." Ginn and Company, Boston. 12 forms. $2.00.

claimed it will save many dollars due to improperly designated repeaters.

Now, Charles, try one for rating the teachers and reduce to rationality one of the grossest absurdities of school administration.

MAKING A PRINCIPAL

A GREAT book,[14] raising the average of this year's output is the work of Professor W. C. Reavis, of the University of Chicago, and two of his pupils, principals of schools in that city. I know 'em all. You may take it from me that their work will be as profitable an investment as ever you made. What is the modern elementary school, its function, curriculum, organization, importance? The first 17 chapters, a convenient composite of hundreds of magazine articles, books, reports and visits freshened by the constructive criticism of a forward-looking faith give a standard and model for comparison with your own school. What makes this kind of institution? Why, you know the chief factor is the principal. The old saying (remark these three wise men), "As the master so the school," has become a truism, confirmed by surveys and accepted by proponents of better education.

A marked change of attitude of writing for educational advance is manifest. My authors abandon the mild suggestion of what you ought to do. Unhesitating, they tell you what you must.

You must meet professional demands. You must build on accepted requirements established by modern research. You must not waste public money and the lives of children by trial-and-error methods, by experience unsupported by professional study, by mere adherence to traditional routine assuming that teachers will teach and there's the end on't. The management of a school is a big task, it requires ability administrative, executive, directive, encouraging, educational.

With masterly care these three authors have listed the little things which eat up a principal's time and keep him from his most valuable use. They have shown how efficient masters dispose of these interferences. Even the way to improve the administration of bad-boy cases sent to the office by a harried teacher who is short of sleep. How often are your teachers thrown off the didactic track in the middle of a successful run by some sweet little maid bringing a notice from the office? Get a bulletin board and a set of boxes. Put your general notices on one and use the others for particular messages. How bored are your people by teachers' meetings? Probably it is all your meeting and not theirs. Study the constructive Reavis, Pierce, Stullken schemes and get the meetings so cooperative and valuable that you can tell your folks the affairs are purely voluntary with no roll-call and no need for anyone to explain why she didn't come.

Why should an elementary-school child be made to repeat a subject satisfactorily pursued because he has failed in others? Consult page 133. What is needed in every school after a bowing acquaintance is acquired between teachers and the curriculum? Ans. P. 155. Whence came, and how shall be broken, barriers set up by teachers against being supervised? Read the inestimable chapter on classroom teaching written with the sympathetic understanding of men whose memory of their own staff work is fresh. One reason why the supervised exhibit little white heat of enthusiasm for direction may be because they are not enough used to it. My authors say so. The principal puts supervision, his hardest task, last in his list of duties and fools himself into believing that his office work takes all his time. But the man who holds work, out in the works, his inviolate program and who, after it, does what office work he can, gets good teaching done and office work, too. Our authorial triumvirate leave no doubt of this.

Do you, as principal or superintendent, follow this formula: Commend the good, point out the unsatisfactory and make suggestions for improvement? All this hast thou done from thy youth up? Thou art nought. "To pass muster as efficient you must develop qualitative evaluation of classroom work and the use of scientific methods of diagnosis and treatment."

EMINENTLY ATTAINABLE

If I understand this it means what Inspector Dickinson told the hospital superintendents: "I mark you on the per cent. of successes and failures of your patients. After that I appraise

[14] William C. Reavis, Paul R. Pierce, Edward H. Stullken, "The Elementary School, Its Organization and Administration." University of Chicago Press. 571 pp. $3.00.

your method, equipment, etc., and tell you what you need."

The principal, to be worth his pay, I learn from this book, must be conversant with the improvements which have been made in the methods of measurements, must see that the teachers know the criteria and how to test. The principal may not depend on teachers' judgment as to the success of their own teaching. He must measure pupil progress. The primary purpose of this testing is not to get a basis of rating teachers but to provide for pupil benefit. It is not a casual duty to be done occasionally. It is a regular periodic system of preponderating importance.

So, so. This will give you an idea of the kind of bowl these three wise men venture in upon the sea of public education which is vexed with the rocks and shoals of opposition to change, indifference to mediocre service, ignorance of facts uncovered by research. Happy the hamlet that wants a school like the one outlined in this inspiring volume. She can have it. The making and conduct of it are eminently attainable if the right man is chosen and supported. What of the big systems where City Hall determines who shall fill administrative places, where board members in competition for the title of "Teachers' Friend" will block the use of any of the effective means with which this book abounds, where an underworld of soreheads raise a hullabaloo against the introduction of any reform that requires time and work?

Why, don't you know that, on an average, more than 10 per cent. of public school teachers have the innate drive toward progress and improvement? Eighty per cent. are galvanic and will respond to the electric waves of help and encouragement. Only 10 per cent. of the teachers in large cities are so infested with indolence or contention that they lay ties on the track. A superintendent with a term long enough can, from the records of two or three good schools, spur enough into superior work to run a fair chance of getting rid of a few incapable masters remaining. Public education's main clog is the lay board which, encouraged by backward principals and teachers, holds the new turns in school management to be wild creations of fool professors. An esteemed president of the Chicago board of education told me that half the school people don't know anything and what the other half know isn't so. Let us then make presents of this newest book to school board members, for it is so clear and convincing, withal, so surely to be realized, that it will give teaching a grand push ahead.

PROGRESS IN OUR DAY

THE whole of Columbia University's quarter century volume[15] is more than ordinarily easy and pleasant to read. The chapters are addresses delivered by Columbia professors during the celebration of the university's one hundred and seventy-fifth anniversary. Dixon Ryan Fox, in a brilliant introduction, makes us glad to be alive in this generation. Athwart it fell the shadow of the world relapse into war. How many brilliant young light-bearers were snuffed out in it will never be known. In the dreary days of reconstruction, especially in central Europe, learning was pathetically undernourished. Yet, despite the losses, one who reads these lectures will be impressed with the quantitative growth of scholarship. After all, most of the twenty-five years were marked by peace and progress. In America, although the number of colleges increased by less than 20 per cent., their teaching personnel trebled. American psychologists have increased seven fold since 1904. Research foundations have multiplied in number, resources and usefulness. Learning has increasingly adopted the method of the laboratory. Psychology has left the armchair. Education has become a science.

Curious to see how the younger Russell will jam the whole of education into the narrow space allotted to him, you turn to the address by William F., the dean of Teachers College. It is a stimulating review. In twenty-five years, the doctrine of mental discipline has suffered at the hands of research psychologists. They have accumulated evidence nearly disproving the doctrine. Its loss has put education into much bewilderment. The *table-d'hote* course of study is supplanted by an *a-la-carte* curriculum. Dewey has shown us how the mummified remains of thought injected into school children make them incapable of thinking. Mental discipline does not come from hard work nor

15 Eighteen Columbia Officers, "A Quarter Century of Learning." Columbia University Press, New York. 380 pp. $3.50.

special subjects, but only from emphasis on the pupil's own thinking.

The devisers of tests have given the school manager the equivalent of the thermometer, stethoscope, and other aids by which the doctor gets to his diagnosis. Standards, tests break school isolation. Arithmetic has been revolutionized by the researchers' demonstration that undirected practice does not make perfect. Slowness and inaccuracy do go hand in hand. You can not correct a defect by doing work over and over. Proper teaching consists in diagnosis, discovery of individual troubles, and the administration of a particular remedial drill.

The most spectacular advance has been made in the teaching of reading.

Formal discipline might have done for a monarchy. It concealed weaknesses of the masses. The brighter children got along in spite of the formality of their education. It is due to the psychologists that we no longer put the blame for failure on the children, but rather on the ignorance of the principals and teachers. In twenty-five years we have learned the need of readjusting education that it may do for all what good fortune did for the favored few.

The turning of education into a science has brought the possibility of encouraging further effort to serve the youth of college age, which is right in a democracy, rather than ruthlessly to exclude them, leaving with them a sense of despair and lack of hope.

You really must read Russell's survey, it is so broad, so sound and so confident.

You will enjoy, too, Professor Howard McBain's discourse on government, his reminder to you directors of education that man is the political animal. Politics lie at the core of his instincts. He was given the opportunity to perform his chore at the polls. His job has been relinquished to his political bosses. He has become a rubber stamp. But in all our units of government the merit system has been extended in these twenty-five years. But Americans are more interested in the slogans than in the realities of efficiency and economy. The margins of the unachieved are wide.

You will profit by Mitchell on economics, McIver on sociology, Smith on law, Woodworth on psychology, Hawkes on college administration, Ashley Thorndike on letters, Moore on classical studies, Boring on architecture, Wilson on biology, Darrach on medicine, Sherman on chemistry, Pegram on physics, Parsons on engineering, and Berkey on geology.

It is a stimulating book, comprehensive, popular and conversational.

THE WOMEN, GOD BLESS 'EM

A growing suspicion that women graduates are going at the large social and educational problems with eyes open and campaigns carefully planned is confirmed by reading an account of their first fifty years of organized service.[16]

How seventeen young alumnae, meeting in Boston, determined that there should be an association of all college women "for practical educational work," how they spread their conviction that the woman graduate owes a large debt to the country and the world, how they combatted the doctrine that the average girl hasn't the strength to endure the hard work required of the college boy, how they pushed athletic games for women, how they fought the cheap "female colleges," how they organized branches everywhere, how they set up scholarships for women and engaged in social, political and educational research, how they advanced the study and care of pre-school children, how they opened the vocations for women, served in the world war, got into post-war replacement, watched educational legislation, promoted international peace and educated women voters, is told modestly and simply with the plain intent to show how much more there is to do and how plain the duty of college women is to keep on doing it.

If you live in a city where the men's university club is essentially a comfort and pleasure house for its members, an easy-going resort free from civic obligations, a place of banquets, reunions and rah-rahs for the team, you must be amazed and, maybe, shamed, by the superb earnestness of this huge college association concerned with solid issues of the day. Extension classes, adult education, health, family success, history textbooks, international understanding, tenure and pension for teachers, a federal secretary of education, child labor, students' aid, legislation and politics, carefully studied and attacked or aided under a constitution that checks wild and hasty action—these make a rec-

[16] Marion Talbot, Lois Rosenberry, "History of the American Association of University Women." Houghton Mifflin Company, Boston. 479 pp. $4.00.

ord of solid service unique among educational associations.

It is a book to be commended to men.

AWAKENERS

BARNEY ROBERTS, schoolmaster who had to leave New York and get into the high and dry country, got a job as track-walker through an Arizona canyon. Before and after the passage of trains he made his excursions up and back through the two-mile gorge, looking for any portion of the scenery that might have been jarred loose. He had an almost five-foot library in his cabin. He told me that on night shifts he found that books for him could be put into out of two classes; awakeners or other kinds.

A favorite pair,[17] Frasier and Armentrout, offer a new collaboration. They have collected a hundred and eighty-five crisp discourses of a hundred and twenty-five noteworthy persons from Adams, Elizabeth, educational consultant for the girl scouts, to Woody, Thomas, school expert. Although intended as a supplementary reader and study book for classes in institutions that train teachers, it will be especially valuable as an eye-opener for people already in school service. For it is a fresh survey of the field of education, administration, measuring, learning, curriculum revision and professional needs. For the awakening of school men to recognition of an old duty in danger of smothering among the newer fashions, the compilers arrange in a chapter upon school functions in a democracy, extracts from Boyd Bode, T. E. Miller, W. H. P. Faunce, Touton and Struthers, George Strayer, E. E. Lindsay, Katherine Hodgson, Mary Brown, Laura Cairnes, and David Weglein's admirable Baltimore Bulletins. You will find here 562 classified pages of very up-to-date observations.

INTEGRATING EDUCATION

DIRECTOR DOUGHTON, State Teachers College, Mansfield, Pennsylvania, deploring the scrappy nature of the reading done by intending teachers, has for three years been experimenting with outlines to integrate this sort of unrelated study. His Syllabus[18] is now printed and available. It is based on integrating everything commonly taken up in teacher courses. It does it by questions, classified according to relations.

PSYCHOLOGIST LOOKS AT PSYCHOLOGISTS

WITHOUT praise or blame, Columbia Professor Woodworth summarizes the leading schools of to-day's psychology.[19] Here you have the new psychologies of the nineteenth and twentieth centuries. Watson exhibits his brand of behaviorism; the Russians, theirs. Rebellious Gestalt cuts loose from the orthodox as behaviorism had done but comes to a different end. Freud proposes double personality, puts new emphasis on the unconscious complexes and pushes psychoanalysis. Adler preaches his individualistic proposition. Jung brings out his introverts and outward lookers, McDonald strives for purposivism.

If the three thousand psychologists were assembled on a field for a joust, a large majority would seek a part of the ground not preempted under the banners of the hardiest fighters. Author Woodworth enumerates well-known students who would be found in this multitude. They refuse to swallow the medicine offered by any of the schools. Every positive result they seize.

My guess: Professor Woodworth will give you a better understanding of the theories of modern psychologists than you get from reading their own books.

WHAT STUDENTS ARE

NOTABLY significant among the efforts of colleges to adjust their offering to the needs and capacities of those who seek it is a great study of student attitudes made of all the enrolment of Syracuse University.[20] With singular directness it gathers, summarizes and puts to working plans, students' reasons for coming to college and remaining, the bearing of college activities on students' ideals, why acquaintance with a professor is desired, what studies are satisfactory, cribbing, academic freedom, types of students most admired, desire for advice, choice of voca-

[17] George Willard Frasier, Winfield Dockery Armentrout, "Introduction to the Literature of Education." Scott, Foresman and Company, Chicago. 562 pp. $2.00.

[18] Isaac Doughton, "Syllabus: Philosophy of Education," published by the author, Mansfield, Pa. 108 pp. $1.25.

[19] Robert S. Woodworth, "Contemporary Psychology." The Ronald Press, 15 East 26th Street, New York. 232 pp. $2.50.

[20] Daniel Katz, Floyd Henry Allport, Margaret Babcock Jeness, William E. Mosher, "Students' Attitudes." The Craftsman Press, Syracuse. 408 pp. $3.50.

tions, attitudes toward fraternities, snobbishness, supervision of morals, coeducation, double moral standard, religious ideas. Merely to list these subjects is to interest teacher, administrator and sociologist. To call the book a mine of valuable human facts would imply a wealth of raw material. But here you have sorting, measuring, judgment and working hypotheses modestly and cautiously discussed in the spirit of unemotional science. The generous employment of results of attitude studies, earlier and elsewhere, gives the book an expansive application.

EDUCATIONAL PSYCHOLOGY

IF psychologists delight in controversy, why should it be denied to their students? I shall not attempt to indoctrinate you with any of the disputed theories, nor try to reconcile conflicting claims. With some such resolve William Trow, University of Michigan, launches a new venture.[21] Motivation, emotion, adjustment, measurement, methods of learning and the scientific method, social learning and character education, are handled in an awakening manner.

Unquestioned convictions inherited from an earlier day are outmoded by the change in the world of youth and in himself. The daily press, with unexampled vigor, calls attention to the need of a civic conscience. Home has lost an alarming amount of influence. A greater load is on the school. It must understand the nature of the humanity it serves. This is the underlying thought.

POCKET CYCLOPEDIA OF HEALTH

MAY I call your attention to a beautiful tribute to a superb woman?[22] Emma Dolfinger was a science teacher in the Louisville Girls High School. She studied medicine and sanitation in the New York College of Physicians and Surgeons and elsewhere. She returned to Louisville and built up its health-education program. I remember her, a beautiful creature, queenly in appearance, of distinct nobility of face, keenly curious towards new ventures in education, intensely admired by women and men and unspoiled by it. She came back to New York in 1922 and became director of the Division of Health Education of the American Child Health Association. She died four years ago.

Seven women and two men, serving as a committee, many friends and admirers, assisted the work of two indefatigable compilers who have produced, as Silver, Burdett and Company have printed, an unusually beautiful book. It is on Bible paper so thin, yet impervious, that 568 pages in perfectly legible type make a book less than three quarters of an inch thick. Its end papers are Emma Dolfinger's own bookplate designed by her: trees, a lake, lofty mountains and the confident aspiration: "auf allen gipfeln ist Ruh."

It is a veritable pocket cyclopedia of health anecdotes, discoveries, narrations, facts and summaries, on child welfare, food, nutrition, prevention of communicable disease, air, clothing, heredity, mental hygiene, safety, first aid and so on.

From about five hundred books, reports and articles in medical journals, the compilers chose the matter, giving play to their singularly human appetite for the odd and picturesque, so that you pass through short spicy paragraphs on laughter, oxygen, "Sauntering is hard work," "How many are pigeon-toed?" "After-effects of athletics," through statistics, recipes and cautions—everything you need in becoming an authority. I perused it, being, unhappily, no longer in charge of a school, as entertaining reading. You can use it as a manual, for it has thirteen pages of modern bibliography and twenty-six of as good a quick-fire index as you ever saw. Ladies and gentlemen, contributors, committee, Doctors Broadhurst and Lerrigo, you are hereby cited for conceiving a fitting memorial for an inestimable public benefactor and for giving it unique value to teachers and parents.

EARS TO HEAR

RADIO, remarks Peter Dykema, restores to man the ears which printing did much to take away. The beautiful first year-book[23] of the Institute for Education by Radio contains the papers and discussions of American and Euro-

[21] William Clark Trow, ''Educational Psychology.'' Houghton Mifflin Company, Boston. 504 pp. $2.80.

[22] Jean Broadhurst, Marion Olive Lerrigo, ''Health Horizons. A Memorial to Emma Dolfinger from her Friends.'' Silver, Burdett and Company, New York. 568 pp. $3.00.

[23] Josephine H. MacLatchy, Editor, ''Education on the Air.'' Ohio State University Press, Columbus. 400 pp. $3.00.

pean broadcasters and educators. You will learn from it what, in a ten-days' session in Columbus, they reported on the status of education by wave-lengths at home and abroad, how it should be administered in elementary, high and university schools. How music, literature, current events, politics, sciences, health and happiness is broadcasted and how the disseminators are trained. Inevitably the speakers include much warm comment on the untouched duties of education. Mrs. Jessie Allen Charters notes the amazing opportunity of reaching millions of homes by the new invention and the pitiful dearth of expert instructors who are available to tell the mothers what they are eager to know. Husband Charters warns against counting on the radio, as circus, to take the place of all of elementary schooling. When experiment determines what the radio can do better than the teacher, *in propria persona,* we may turn on the dial. In the midst of the wealth of material we miss Joy Morgan. One must be sorry he was unable to be present. He has some distinctive lines needed in the rigging of the new ship.

ANTHOLOGY

"OLD MAN RAIN, at the window pane, knocks and fumbles and knocks again." Read and re-read poetry aloud to children, says Mrs. Stokes,[24] you can't, by talking about it, analyzing it or making it a task, get anywhere. Poetry is made for delight or some other exercise of the emotions, not for the mathematical part of the brain. So here are two hundred short poems that children like. Shakespeare, Tennyson, Wordsworth and other Olympians dance along with Rose Fyleman, Vachel Lindsay, Sara Teasdale and the moderns.

GRAMMAR AS A GOLDEN MEAN

MR. TRESSLER has cleverly christened his book,[25] "Grammar in Action." By this he means, you have guessed, grammar for use rather than as the older schoolmasters used to value it, as a field for disputation. If you have any of the old pedagogic blood in you, you will want to challenge Author Tressler on his opening definition, "A sentence is a group of words expressing a complete thought." Our village schoolmaster holds to the fuller definition by Gould Brown, "A sentence is an assemblage of words, making complete sense and always containing a nominative and a verb." The Maxwellians will make you more definite yet: "A sentence is a group of words used as a statement, a question, a command, or an entreaty." George Curme's monumental treatise gives you this: "A sentence is a word or group of words, expressing a thought or feeling in such form and manner as to convey the meaning intended." The writer of a grammar may easily be halted on the very threshold by the hair-splitters. Brother Tressler is practical enough to jump over all the philosophic obstacles by answering in the Scottish manner of Alexander Bain, "A sentence is a sentence." Do you remember the story Laertius tells of the irritating Diogenes tripping Plato on many occasions? When the great analyst had evolved the definition of man as a two-legged animal without feathers, Diogenes threw a plucked fowl into the circle and cried, "Behold, Plato's man!" As a result Plato used to add, "with broad, flat nails."

Grammarian Tressler has the right idea: if you enjoy quibbling, go to it among yourselves. Don't inflict it upon children. It means complication and confusion. In grammar, as in morals, the best answer often is, "either or both." The book recognizes that we have reached a middle ground between the barren acres of formal grammar and the battlefield of the denouncers of everything save usage drills. The boy who grows up in an atmosphere of correct and elegant English speaks and writes well without study. But to-day's teacher does not find these fortunates in numbers that count for much. Wherefore, with an abundance of fresh and interesting modern matter, Mr. Tressler offers a rich array of short searching exercises along with the authoritative laws that good writers and speakers observe. Diagramming, springing from and aiding analytic thought, correction of common errors, are abundant. In his exercises "for getting better sentences" the author's interest in promoting more varied, brighter and handsomer speech has worked out a remarkably constructive scheme. Other happy elements are the use of pictures and an appendix with answers to all his questions.

24 Anne Stokes, "The Open Door to Poetry." Charles Scribner's Sons, New York. 304 pp. $1.00.

25 J. C. Tressler, "Grammar in Action." D. C. Heath and Company, Boston. 404 pp. $1.28.

SCHOOL AND SOCIETY

EDITED BY J. McKEEN CATTELL

WITH WHICH IS COMBINED THE

EDUCATIONAL REVIEW

EDITED BY WILLIAM McANDREW

Volume 34 — Saturday, November 14, 1931 — Number 881

THE INFLUENCE OF THE ECONOMIC DEPRESSION ON STUDENT LIFE AT THE UNIVERSITY OF MICHIGAN

By Dr. ROBERT C. ANGELL

ASSOCIATE PROFESSOR OF SOCIOLOGY, UNIVERSITY OF MICHIGAN

THAT the depression has had widely ramified effects upon student life was indicated by the results of a study made by my class in "The Sociology of Student Life" last spring. In gathering the data the class members took carefully prepared blanks to a random sample[1] of students to be filled out, secured statistics from university and other sources, conducted investigations into student organizations and activities, and interviewed business men, landladies and university officials.

School or College	Sex	Aimed at No.	Aimed at Per cent.	Reached No.	Reached Per cent.
Literary	M	148	4.7	109	3.4
Literary	F	81	4.8	48	2.8
Engineering	M	69	4.7	49	3.3
Medical	M	28	4.7	19	3.1
Law	M	25	4.5	20	3.6
Education	F	13	4.8	13	4.8
Graduate	F	16	4.6	8	2.3
Unclassified				7	
		380	4.7	273	3.4

[1] The sample actually reached was considerably smaller than the sample aimed at: The sample was made up of students who were in college during both the years 1929–30 and 1930–31. The blank was designed to compare the first semesters of these two years, the assumption being that the depression had intervened. The random character of the sample was assured by taking, for instance, the first man in the medical school on every fifth page of the student directory who was in school the year before. Each student in the sample was called upon by a member of the class (or a member of Professor Copeland's class in economic statistics, who assisted us). The class member presented a letter of introduction explaining the purpose of the inquiry and the students filled out the blank anonymously, either with the class member's help or without. In the latter case the blank was mailed back. We received 284 returns—96 short of the quota. One hundred and sixty were returned by class members and 124 came by mail. Only 273 blanks were complete and consistent enough to be used.

(1) UNIVERSITY POPULATION

There were 9,431 resident students on November 1, 1930, as compared with 9,688 on November 1, 1929. This drop of 257, or $2\frac{2}{3}$ per cent., is probably largely attributable to the depression. That there was some tendency for enrolment to be larger than it otherwise would have been because of lack of jobs was shown by the fact that 13 of our random sample of 273 would have stayed home in September, 1930, if they could have found jobs. The corresponding number in 1929 was 7.

Accompanying the decline in university enrolment was an increase in the enrolment of Michigan junior colleges from 1,814 to 2,241, or about 23 per cent. This is probably in part due to students staying at home, where expenses were less, instead of coming to Ann Arbor to college. Eight of our 273 were kept from attending a school more expensive than Michigan by the depression.

Withdrawals for financial reasons up to March 1 for the two years were as follows:

	1929–30	1930–31
Men	104	106
Women	8	24
Total	112	130
"To accept jobs"	52	28
No jobs in sight	60	102
Total	112	130

It seems likely that the withdrawals in 1930–31 represented a greater proportion of drastic necessity, since many more of those of the previous year might have been to accept lucrative positions where there was no great hardship. The large increase in the withdrawals among women may reflect a smaller number of opportunities for self-supporting work as compared with the men and, perhaps, less willingness to undergo real hardship to stay in college.

(2) STUDENT INCOME

The income, including work for board and room, available for the needs of the first semester 1930–31 averaged:

All (242/273)[2]	$472.40
Working students (80/83)	452.50
Non-working students (162/190)	481.48
Literary men (103/109)	484.95
Literary women (38/48)	464.47
Engineering men (48/49)	460.42
Law men (16/20)	487.50
Medical men (14/19)	485.71
Education women (9/13)	505.55
Graduate women (8/8)	400.00

A remarkable similarity by schools and colleges is here indicated, especially if the small, unreliable groups are omitted. The difference between the working and non-working students would be expected.

As compared with the year previous this income averaged slightly less.

More income 1930–31 than 1929–30	By $101 or more	12	
	" $25 to $100	33	45
Approximately same income (less than $25 change)		132	132
Less income 1930–31 than 1929–30	By $26 to 75	20	
	" $76 " 100	24	
	" $101 " 150	10	
	" $151 " 200	4	
	" $201 or more	9	67
No answer			29
Total			273

Thus we find 22 more persons having smaller incomes than persons having larger incomes this year, in spite of the fact that as a student progresses through college both his needs for money and his income tend to increase. It is significant here that the number of those paying their tuitions in instalments rose only slightly from 352 in 1928–29 to 357 in 1929–30 and then jumped to 561 in 1930–31.

The women seem to have suffered slightly less in income than the men. The non-working students have suffered more often than the working students, perhaps because among the non-workers were 19 who worked the year before and who wanted work this year but were unable to find a job.

	Percentages		
	More income 1930–31	Same income	Less income 1930–31
Men (187/203)	17.1	55.6	27.3
Women (57/70)	22.8	49.1	28.1
Working students (79/83)	25.3	45.6	29.1
Non-working students (156/190)	15.4	58.3	26.3

The sources of income were as follows:

[2] In this, as in all questions, some did not answer. The number replying and the number in the class are therefore given.

	Percentages	
	1930–31	1929–30
Allowance	59.8	62.1
Work during the semester	13.1	13.6
Savings from summer work	11.5	12.9
Non-university loans	7.1	4.4
University loans and scholarships	2.0	1.6
Other sources	6.1	4.7
	99.6	99.3

Since the 1930–31 income was slightly less, there was considerable shrinkage in allowance and income from work, both during the summer and the semester in question; while there were gains in loans and income from unnamed sources.

Of the 251 who gave the information, the median amount of allowance was $64.30 per month. Of this number, 59 received no allowance this year, while only 40 received none last year. There were 55 who received less this year as compared with 31 who received more, in spite of the usual tendency for allowances to become larger as one proceeds through college. Only 74 received reduced allowance this year, despite the fact that 156 families were adversely affected by the depression. The figures on this question follow:

No effect	91
Adversely affected	92
Severely affected	64
More income since depression	7
No answer	19
	273

Evidently one of the last places where families economize is on their children's college expenses.

Was the total income from working during the semester less because of fewer working, or of fewer hours apiece, or a lower wage scale, or all three? The university employment figures indicate a decrease in work. The number of requests for students coming to the bureau from employers fell from 3,445 in 1928–29 to 2,703 in 1929–30, and again to 2,429 in 1930–31. Most of this decrease was due to the sharp falling off in requests for students to do odd jobs.

Among the workers in our sample the mean number of hours a week employed was also slightly less this year—21.2 hours, as compared with 22.7. There was only slight evidence of a lowered rate of remuneration—12 out of 61 replying having received less, 7 more and 44 the same.

Not only were there fewer working, but our sample showed more desirous of work but unable to find it—19 as contrasted with 9. Also 22 of the workers desired more work this year, as compared with only 11 in 1929–30. The university employment figures give little support to this theory, there being actually fewer requests for work this year (1,252) than last (1,298). The difference may perhaps be accounted for by the decrease in enrolment.

Among the new activities or "rackets," for earning money discovered on the campus were: Comely coeds selling coupon books gotten up by local merchants and guaranteed to save the purchaser $200; a varsity swimming star earning $150 or more by selling corduroy trousers after he had started the fashion; a new student magazine published for income as well as for intellectual interest; a student making $5 a week as a representative of a big fish concern selling to local restaurants and fraternities; dormitory girls giving finger waves for 35 cents to their more prosperous friends; a boy trying without marked success to sell ink by the pint; foreign students peddling novelties characteristic of their native lands, such as Oriental cigarette cases; a student whose father has invented a patented window cleaner selling it from door to door; a senior jobbing a humorous book called "A Job for Seniors" to drug stores; a boy selling stones originally worth 5 cents for $1 after he had carved persons' signatures on them; two students taxiing couples to dances in a disreputable hack drawn by a similar horse.

Fewer students could get summer jobs in 1930, though more wanted them; those who did get work worked on the average almost twice as long, but the savings which could be applied to college expenses were slightly smaller. The reasons for this latter fact were probably lower wages and greater family need for the student's earnings. The figures are as follows:

	1930	1929
Worked during the summer	186	195
Average hours per day × weeks worked	80.8	41.0
Desired more summer work	68	18
Percentage of workers saving nothing for college expenses	31.7	27.7
Average savings of all who saved	$197.70	$202.30

Sixty of our sample tried to borrow from non-university sources this year, of whom 57 were successful as compared with 26 and 25 the year before. Also, among those who borrowed both years the loans this year were larger. The median loan this year was $230.50 and the mean $307.90. Fraternities, sororities and student religious organizations all reported a greatly increased number of applicants for loans this year and the early exhaustion of their loan funds.

Only a small proportion of our sample received pecuniary help from the university in the way of loans or scholarships either year, but the increase applying for such help is significant. Five applied and received help in 1929–30, while 18 applied and 11 received help in 1930–31. During the first semester of 1930–31, 545 students received loans from the university amounting to $76,187.25, an average of $139.79. This number of loans was much greater than normal; indeed, the requests for assistance were just about double this year.

Grave doubt was thrown on the reality of the apparent increased income "from other sources" by internal inconsistencies in the replies; in any event the amount involved is unimportant.

(3) STUDENT CONSUMPTION

On the blank each student was asked to indicate whether he put more, the same, or less money into certain items, like clothes, rent, etc., this year than he did the year before, and also whether he actually consumed more, the same or less of these items. Thus we were able incidentally to discover how the depression had affected values. In our sample expenditures as a whole proba-

	Indices[3] of		
	Expenditure	Consumption	Value
Savings	−.02		
Room rent	+.10	+.13	+.03
Meals	−.04	+.11	+.15
Clothes	−.23	+.03	+.26
Laundry and cleaning	−.11	−.03	+.08
Text-books and university supplies	+.09	+.10	+.01
Movies and other shows	−.20	−.11	+.09
Sodas, sandwiches between meals, teas, etc.	−.29	−.22	+.07
Dances	−.06	−.04	+.02
Canoeing, horseback riding, etc.	−.22	−.21	+.01
Taxies	−.10	−.04	+.06
Traveling expenses	−.19	−.12	+.07
Organization dues and fees	+.19	+.22	+.03
Hair cuts and hair dressing	−.08	−.03	+.05
Doctors' and dentists' services	+.01	+.04	+.03
Insurance	+.09	+.12	+.03
Contributions to church and charity	−.07	−.05	+.02
Liquor	−.04	+.04	+.08
Non-required books and magazines	+.004	+.06	+.06
Other hobbies	−.08	.00	+.08

[3] If all who checked a particular item spent more on it or consumed more of it this year than last the index would be +1.00.

bly[4] decreased, while the standard of living went up, since the main items in the preceding table all show increased consumption.

The savings item is inconclusive. The Ann Arbor banks report a 10 per cent. increase in student depositors. Perhaps this means that they exercise greater care with the money that they do have.

The figures for room rent may seem surprising, in the face of general reduction in room prices, greater economy among girls in selecting rooms, according to the dean of women, and the fact that 16 of the 85 students in the sample personally adversely affected by the depression were living in less desirable locations to save money. When the figures from the sample are broken down by schools and sex, however, the reason appears.

Indices of expenditure	
Literary men	.00
Literary women	+.19
Engineering men	−.09
Law men	+.47
Medical men	+.33
Education women	+.09
Graduate women	+.75

The women and the professional students account for the increase, and this is probably because the women's dormitories raised their charges this year and because professional students tend to move into more expensive quarters than they occupied in their pre-professional courses.

Our sample indicates reduced expenditure for meals but increased consumption. The evidence from other sources confirms the former but would seem to throw some doubt on the latter. Menu prices have been reduced 10 to 15 per cent. according to restaurant operators, but there seems to have been some tendency for students to cut out "extras" in the way of sundaes, etc. Students have been getting all they can for their money, it being noticeable that they order regular dinners at a fixed price rather than *à la carte*. The fraternities and sororities report that fewer meals have been eaten out of the houses by their members and thus paid for twice. Of the 85 adversely affected above mentioned, 20 said that they were eating less to save money, three of them to the extent of impairing their health. Fourteen of the 85 were receiving more food from home this year.

The greatest savings in dollars this past year have perhaps been on clothes. The merchants say that although students have been buying almost as many suits, shirts and neckties as usual they have been getting the same quality for at least 10 per cent. less. The shoe merchants feel that sales of shoes have fallen off 20 per cent. It has been noticed that shoes brought in for repair have been in much poorer condition and that students have been buying the cheapest grades of shoes which they would not consider before. Sixty-seven of the 85 adversely affected said that they were trading at cheaper stores to save money.

The figures on laundry and cleaning are confirmed by business men who think there has been a 15 per cent. decline. They notice that students have been wearing old clothes more than formerly. Twenty of the 85 were sending their laundry home more this year.

Text-books and university supplies show an increase. With each successive year on the campus, especially as students enter professional schools, more of an outlay on these items is required. The book stores report the sale of text-books unchanged.

The indicated decreased attendance at movies and other shows is probably accurate, but the students were wrong in believ-

[4] The figures do not prove this, since the items represent nothing like equal shares of the student budget.

ing that they received more for their money, since admission charges have not changed.

Of the 85 adversely affected 84 were cutting down on their amusements, and it is probable that much of this was on shows, since dances show but a slight decrease. Other things to suffer were pool and billiard halls and bowling alleys. The Michigan Union's facilities in these fields were used much less than the year before, while the commercial places reported a 35 to 40 per cent. drop in business. The university skating rink attracted more skaters (paid admissions) than the year before, but there was a deficit in 1931 in place of the profit of 1930 because much less was spent on skate-sharpening, checking and other incidentals. Students also bought fewer extra tickets for football games in the fall of 1930.

The reduced expenditure for, and consumption of, sodas, sandwiches between meals, tea, etc., corresponds fairly well to the testimony of the dispensers. The soda bar at the Michigan Union and the tearoom at the Michigan League, for instance, both showed marked decrease in income. Fraternities reported that their members were doing less eating between meals.

There was not much falling off in attendance at dances this year, according to all the data available. For instance, the Frosh Frolic and the Pan Hellenic Ball sold more tickets than the year before, and the regular weekly dances were well attended.

There is a strong indication that the students who were pressed for money economized on traveling expenses. Eighty-four of the 85 reported that they were going home less often, or taking pleasure trips less, or hitch-hiking more.

Organization dues and fees show an increase probably because of the financial pressure on many organizations, and also perhaps because dues naturally increase as the student goes through college. Twenty-six of the 85 said they had refrained from joining organizations because they could not afford them. Of course some of this occurs in a normal year.

Barber shop proprietors were emphatic in portraying the decrease of business this year, so that probably our figures do not indicate the extent of the economizing in this field. Some felt business had fallen off 40 per cent., saying that there had been a 60 per cent. decline in shaves and that students were allowing their hair to grow much longer before having it cut. There has been a sharp decrease in "extras," such as tonics, washes, etc.

There seems no very good reason for the increase in the case of doctors' and dentists' services, since the Health Service reports a sharp increase in the use of their free facilities this year, without any epidemic to account for such an increase. The university dental clinic reports more students applying for service than could be handled. For the first time this year many students requested the Health Service that they be allowed to pay for eyeglasses in instalments. Also more requested the Health Service to arrange for non-emergency surgical operations at the low rates available to students. Twenty-one of our 85 felt that the situation was seriously interfering with their recreation, exercise or rest.

The decline registered in contributions for church purposes is confirmed by most of the student religious groups. Not only have ordinary collections fallen off, but these organizations have been unable to raise as much for student loans as usual, though there has been a greatly increased need.

Our sample indicates slightly more liquor consumed this year, though slightly less paid for it. Lower prices are current, but it is doubtful whether there was actually more consumed this year. The fraternities sampled felt that there had been a decrease in drinking. It is perhaps significant that only 52 of the 203 men failed to admit expenditure for this item.

Non-required books and magazines show no decline in the figures from our sample, but this is almost certainly not representative, according to bookstore owners. It may be true that students are reading as much, but they are buying the cheaper dollar editions.

We did not have a category for gifts or for small personal accessories like fountain pens, cigarette lighters, pipes, etc. All these items have been bought much less. Gifts average 65 per cent. of the former amount, and merchants say that students are buying smaller boxes of candy, smaller bunches of flowers and more inexpensive brands of cosmetics, tooth paste, etc. The whole situation seems to indicate that students are being less extravagant, more certain of getting their money's worth. Confirming this, the fraternities and sororities report a decrease in luxuries among their members and more borrowing of articles.

For comparative purposes we have the following table showing the indices for women as compared to men and for working students as compared to non-working students.

The women spent comparatively more this year on room rent and organization dues, less on meals and clothes, movies, sodas and hair dressing. They were better bargain hunters than the men in regard to clothes, and hair dressing (beauty parlors cut prices this year), but poorer ones relative to meals and traveling expenses. Working students economized relatively more than the non-workers this year on room rent, meals and text-books and spent relatively more on clothes, dances, organization dues and hair cuts. On the chief items of room, meals and clothes the working students received slightly better values.

	Indices					
	Women as compared to men			Workers as compared to non-workers		
	Expend.	Cons.	Value	Expend.	Cons.	Value
Savings	+.21			-.10		
Room rent	+.18	+.19	+.01	-.07	-.02	+.05
Meals	-.08	-.13	-.05	-.08	-.03	+.05
Clothes	-.06	-.02	+.04	+.12	+.14	+.02
Laundry and cleaning	.00	-.10	-.10	+.03	+.06	+.03
Text-books, etc.	+.05	+.03	-.02	-.08	+.02	+.10
Movies and other shows	-.15	-.01	+.14	+.04	-.01	-.05
Sodas, sandwiches, teas	-.13	-.08	+.05	+.04	-.04	-.08
Dances	.00	+.01	+.01	+.16	+.12	-.04
Canoeing, horseback riding	+.14	+.09	-.05	+.03	+.07	+.04
Taxies	-.16	-.09	+.07	-.12	-.11	+.01
Traveling expenses	+.08	-.10	-.18	-.03	+.02	+.05
Organization dues and fees	+.15	+.23	+.08	+.09	-.01	-.10
Hair cuts and hair dressing	-.22	-.10	+.12	+.12	+.09	-.03
Doctors' and dentists' services	-.07	-.03	+.04	.00	+.10	+.10
Insurance	-.07	-.14	-.07	+.06	+.06	.00
Church and charity	-.10	-.03	+.07	-.01	+.07	+.08
Liquor	+.04	+.04	.00	+.03	+.14	+.11
Non-required books, etc.	-.15	-.03	+.12	+.05	+.11	+.06
Other hobbies	-.13	-.08	+.05	+.04	+.06	+.02

(4) MENTAL AND MORAL FACTORS

Most landladies and merchants found students only slightly less prompt in settling their accounts this year.

The effect of the depression upon the mental health of the students has as yet been slight, according to the psychiatrist at the Health Service, though it was more noticeable the second semester than the first. This year the economic situation often made matters more serious where mental health was already impaired by other factors, but it was rarely a primary cause. Among the 85 adversely affected, 53 were worried or depressed. To reconcile these two sets of evidence it must be assumed that most of the worries were not of a very serious character.

Of this group of 85, 26 felt that the situation had hurt their friendships, though seven felt it had brought them closer to their fellows. Forty of them more carefully budgeted their time, though four believed that they were less careful (perhaps because of broken morale).

Among the 164 in our sample who had never done self-supporting work in college, 30 felt that the depression had made their attitude toward the working students more sympathetic, while two felt the opposite.

The assistant to the dean of students thought that the depression was responsible for the decrease in the violations of the automobile ban this year because students had less money to spend on escapades. There were fewer disciplinary cases of all kinds this year.

The depression seems to have improved the academic work of students. Comparison of records made by 100 seniors in the first semester with the same individuals' work as sophomores, using the first semester's work in the sophomore and senior years of 100 members of the class of 1929 as a control, shows the following honor-point-hour ratios.

	Class of 1929	Class of 1931
Sophomore	1.49	1.48
Senior	1.62	1.65
Improvement	.13	.17

This possible indication of a more serious attitude this year is confirmed in various ways. Fewer students were asked to withdraw in February of this year than usual and more got off probation. Within our sample the effects were as follows: 12 of the 85 adversely affected took lighter academic schedules in order to help meet the situation; 30 of the total 273 reported that they were taking their academic career more seriously than before (though two were taking it less seriously) and 13 said that they were more interested in their courses (taking things seriously need not, after all, be equivalent to interest); four were taking more courses and 22 were receiving higher grades because of their interest or seriousness; three, however, reported that they were receiving lower grades because of the strain.

With regard to their more general adjustment to life 103 said that the depression had affected their point of view on economic issues, 46 claimed that the depression had given them new intellectual interests, and 63 believed their philosophy of life had been affected.

(5) Student Organizations

Fourteen fraternities and five sororities taken at random showed in general a problem of decreasing revenue: (1) More individuals have had to turn down bids for pecuniary reasons, and membership was therefore smaller; (2) more members have had to work for their board and so were no longer eating in the houses; and (3) residents of Ann Arbor were eating more often at their own homes. House bills were not being paid quite so promptly, nor were alumni so able as formerly to help with redecorating and repairs. Fraternities and sororities cut down in the following ways: (1) Reduction in number of parties and in cost of favors, flowers, etc.; (2) redecorating done only when absolutely essential; (3) fewer out-of-town banquets and fewer members sent to fraternity conventions. Despite these savings and the lower cost of food, house bills have been generally higher.

Campus activities have been affected both as to participation and revenue. Twenty-seven of the 85 adversely affected reported that they were participating in campus activities less on that account; and this is borne out by other evidence gathered. In the matter of revenue those organizations suffered most which depend on the general public, while those dependent primarily on student support fared better.

There was a marked drop in the number of men trying out for the varsity athletic teams this year—275 as compared to 313 in 1929–30. However, there has been no noticeable tendency on the part of the candidates to skip practice or to spend less time on their training.

Since athletic revenue is dependent on football receipts, and since the latter vary with the caliber of the teams and where the games are played, it is difficult to be sure how much effect the depression had in decreasing football revenue this year. It is my personal opinion that it made a difference of about $50,000, but that is only the rankest sort of guess.

Intramural athletics have flourished among the men this year, as have those among women. Activities of this kind are very inexpensive.

The student publications suffered considerably through loss of both advertising and circulation. *The Daily* had a $1,485 decrease in income from circulation and a $2,185 decrease from advertising, but by economizing on production costs it was able to show a small profit. Much the same conditions prevailed with *The Michiganensian* and *Gargoyle*. The profits of the three publications were the smallest in many years.

The number of students working on the publications also declined, but *The Daily* staff was the chief loser. *The Daily* work takes more time and can not be carried very well by individuals who have part-time jobs. The editors felt that, as a result of the greater load of other work, the staffs were made up more largely of those with a professional interest this year.

Musical and dramatic organizations have suffered little or no decline in student interest but have found it difficult to sell tickets for their performances and concerts, so that their programs have been curtailed somewhat. The two dramatic organizations upon which we secured information have also been affected. Both organizations put on one less show this year.

The four forensic societies found that their memberships remained about the same this year and that dues were only a little harder to collect, so that on the whole the depression has not affected them much. The Oratorical Association, which presents a series of prominent speakers every year, had an unusually successful season, probably because there was a fine group of speakers.

EDUCATIONAL EVENTS

STUDENT UNREST IN BALKAN UNIVERSITIES

According to a special cable to *The New York Times* under date of November 6, twenty casualties were reported at Warsaw University in a fight between Jewish and Nationalist students. The Jewish group organized a defense force, which was attacked by the Nationalist Student Corporation, and several students were taken to hospitals. More than 100 windows were smashed in university buildings, mainly on the premises of the Jewish Brotherhood. The Jewish students were driven out of the university grounds and the struggle was continued in Warsaw's main thoroughfare until the police intervened. The dean of the university, Professor Lukasiewicz, is reported to have said that the university would not open and students would not be admitted to the grounds until order was restored. Cracow University and the University of Lwow have been reopened.

It is also reported in *The New York Times* that demonstrations against the dictatorship by students of Belgrade University, in connection with the forthcoming elections, which started on November 5, culminated on November 6 in serious disorders, in the course of which more than one hundred students were arrested. The university was temporarily closed on November 5. The Belgrade press has been forbidden to report the disorders. Owing to the recent distribution in the streets of Belgrade of leaflets by the government party, which the students considered insulting to members of the former opposition, especially M. Davidovitch, several groups of students recently occupied balconies and doorways of a students' club and began to demonstrate for free elections and a Parliamentary régime. The police, who promptly surrounded the club, were greeted with showers of stones and blocks of wood. Three students caught outside the club were arrested.

The second day a delegation of one hundred students visited the prefect of police demanding the release of those arrested, which was refused. When it was learned at the university that forty more arrests had been made, furious demonstrations against the régime began. Passersby looked on sympathetically, but did not dare to support the students openly. The students informed the rector of the university that unless those arrested were released by 6 P. M. the students would start street demonstrations against the régime. The rector obtained the temporary release of all except two of the students, who had been sentenced to fourteen days' imprisonment because of being armed with revolvers. In the evening there were renewed demonstrations, with the students throwing anti-government leaflets from the club windows. Police surrounded the building again, making one hundred arrests. Stones, coal and other missiles were thrown at them. At midnight large forces of police were stationed around the university, the students remaining blockaded within. An Associated Press dispatch on November 9 says that on that day the police closed the Polytechnic and Agricultural High Schools, as well as the university.

EDUCATIONAL APPOINTMENTS IN THE INDIAN SERVICE

Nearly 800 educational positions in Indian territory of the United States have been filled during the past year, according to Dr. W. Carson Ryan, Jr., education director of the Indian Bureau in the U. S. Department of the Interior.

Appointments included superintendents of schools, principals, visiting teachers, home-economics teachers, heads of departments of home economics, girls' advisers, directors of boys' activities, teachers of physical training, teachers of fine arts and elementary instructors. Of 614 elementary teachers now in the employment of the Indian Office 100 are new appointees.

Four Indian reservations have been placed under the jurisdiction of experienced school men. Dr. Joe Jennings will act as superintendent of education in Pine Ridge Reservation, South Dakota, where there are nearly 8,000 Indians and 27 Indian schools. He was formerly county educational superintendent in Tennessee, a high-school inspector in Nashville and director of extension in the State Teachers College at Livingston, Alabama.

Turtle Mountain Reservation, North Dakota, has been placed under the superintendency of Dr. J. Arthur Anderson, who has filled various teaching and administrative positions throughout the state of Minnesota. He recently received his doctor's degree from the University of Minnesota. In this reservation is the largest development of consolidated schools in the entire Indian territory. No Indian home is more than a mile away from an Indian consolidated school.

The third superintendent, Mr. Richard N. Tisinger, a graduate of Virginia Polytechnic Institute and Cornell University, directs the educational work in the Pima-Papago Reservations. He was a county superintendent of Richmond, Virginia, schools and has had wide experience as a foreign missionary. For three years he taught in the Reformed Church Mission College in China and later was on the research staff of the rural social organization department at Cornell University.

Mr. Carl H. Skinner, superintendent of schools for seven years in Fairview, Nortonville and Ashland, Kansas, and for three years in St. Paul, Nebraska, has been appointed superintendent of the U. S. Indian School at Phoenix, Arizona. He received his bachelor of arts degree from Teachers College, Emporia, Kansas, and just completed his work for a doctor's degree at Leland Stanford University in California.

Another forward movement in Indian education has been the appointment of George C. Wells, secretary of the state board of education in Oklahoma, to the position of state supervisor of Indian education in that state. This is the first real step toward cooperation between federal and state government, where progress will be directed in close cooperation with state offices.

CHILD WELFARE IN NEW YORK CITY

The *Brooklyn Daily Eagle* states that within the next twelve months the Board of Child Welfare of New York City will expend $11,000,000 to keep minor children of the city's dependent mothers in their own homes, rather than in institutions. It is the largest sum ever appropriated by the Board of Estimate for this work. It represents a 60 per cent. increase over last year's $7,000,000 appropriation, which was a record high up to that time. It is a sum 36 times larger than the amount expended in 1916, when the Child Welfare Board was established.

Calls upon the board's funds have increased more sharply than ever before in the organization's history, according to Mr. John T. Egan, executive secretary. In October a total of $840,000 was given out to needy mothers.

Without this aid they would have had to place their children in institutions. A total of 20,000 families and 35,000 children are now being cared for by the board. Its average monthly allowance for each of its youthful wards is $20 and its maximum allowance is $30.

The board as an organization is not concerned with mothers, except as they are responsible for the children. Its allowances are granted to them as "board money" for the minor youngsters, who might otherwise have to go into institutions. It was established by state law on the theory that it would be cheaper for the city of New York as well as other municipalities to keep children in their parents' homes than to maintain them in institutions; cheaper not only from a standpoint of immediate expenditure but also from a standpoint of remote returns.

The Child Welfare Board has no connection with the Department of Public Works nor with any other of the city's organizations to help the poor. It holds at least two unique records. It is one of the few, if not the only, city board which serves absolutely gratis. Only the executive secretary and his staff are paid. Their total salaries and incidental administrative expenses constitute the board's second record. They amount to less than 4 per cent. of the entire funds allotted for the work.

Mothers' allowances under the law are not dispensed without discrimination. A mother must prove herself to be dependent before she can claim benefits. She must be a widow or the wife of an insane, an imprisoned or a permanently incapacitated husband. Even these restrictions are further limited. A mother may not claim funds from the board if her husband is in prison, unless he has been sent there for five years or more; if her husband is ill, she may not claim a benefit unless he is permanently hospitalized.

Certain citizenship and residence requirements are also laid down by the board to prevent colonization in and around New York by indigent mothers. At present women applicants must be either citizens or aliens of at least five years' residence and with at least one child born in this country. There are also state residence requirements. Even in the face of these restrictions the number of applicants eligible for and receiving municipal aid is increasing rapidly.

REGISTRATION STATISTICS AT CORNELL UNIVERSITY

The enrolment and distribution of students at Cornell University have not been adversely affected by business conditions, according to official registration figures.

Students from 47 states, five territories and dependencies and 43 foreign countries are present on the campus this year. The national distribution of students has not decreased because of prevailing economic conditions, for the figures show that 35 per cent. of the total enrolment, or 1,981 students, come from outside New York State.

There was an increase of 411 students at Cornell University this year, 3,904 coming from New York State to make up the record total of 5,923 at Ithaca. The enrolment at the Medical College in New York was practically the same as last year, with 213 students.

The large percentage of students from New York State is directly attributable to the presence on the Cornell campus of the state colleges of agriculture, home economics and veterinary medicine, all of which attract the bulk of their students from within the state. In addition to this there are awarded annually 600 New York State scholarships for Cornell University.

President Livingston Farrand and Dr. E. F. Bradford, director of admissions, have both expressed their gratification at the national and international character of the student population. It has been pointed out that there are over 500 colleges in the United States whose total enrolment is less than the number of students at Cornell University coming from outside the state of New York. An increase in the number of students from Southern states and from the Southwest are noted particularly this year.

Among the foreign students the Chinese again lead, with an enrolment of 53, with the Canadian delegation of 41 in second place. Last year 24 Canadian students were enrolled. Of special interest in the foreign representation this year are the 16 students from Russia. Ten of them are here on scholarships from the Soviet Republic and are engaged in technical studies.

Next to New York State students, who number 3,904, come Pennsylvania with 376, New Jersey with 351, Ohio with 178, Massachusetts with 111, Connecticut with 88, and Illinois with 85. Far-away California has 31 students on the campus this year.

Of the foreign students, next to the 53 Chinese and the 41 Canadians come Russia with 16 students, England, India and Japan with 7 each, and South Africa with 6. Other nations represented in the Cornell student body are as follows: Abyssinia, Albania, Armenia, Australia, Barbados, Belgium, Brazil, Bulgaria, Costa Rica, Cuba, Denmark, Ecuador, Egypt, Germany, Greece, Hungary, Iraq, Italy, Java, Korea, Latvia, Mexico, Palestine, Panama, Paraguay, Persia, Peru, Poland, Scotland, Siam, Spain, Sweden, Syria, Transjordan, Turkey, Venezuela. United States territories and dependencies represented at Cornell are Alaska, Canal Zone, Hawaii, the Philippines and Porto Rico.

THE SMITH COLLEGE ENDOWMENT FUND

SMITH COLLEGE will seek an additional endowment fund of $1,500,000 from outside friends, it has been announced by the trustees of the college. This increase will be applied directly to scholarships, thus releasing funds needed for buildings and equipment. The alumnae are engaged through the alumnae fund in raising an annual amount for faculty salaries.

The trustees expect to concentrate their efforts for the next few years on securing this sum, which will absorb at least $75,000 of the amount that is being taken annually from current funds, Mrs. George B. Ford, vice-president of the trustees, said. The present endowment fund is $6,000,000.

For the last few years the trustees have voted $100,000 annually for scholarships, in addition to the help given for fellowships, students' aid, self-help bureau, cooperative houses and emergency funds. But this is not enough to meet the present emergency. Therefore the trustees have increased this amount this year to $130,000. The annual income from scholarship endowments is $20,500, plus $5,700 from alumnae clubs.

There are 2,039 students enrolled at the college. One sixth of them are on scholarships. They include 78 seniors, 86 juniors, 82 sophomores and 93 freshmen, a total of 339.

The college offers free tuition amounting to $19,150 to students living in Northampton and Hatfield, the birthplace of Sophia Smith, founder of Smith College; $5,000 to foreign students, of whom there are seventeen; $8,000 in fellowships; $1,000 in residence scholarships; $2,300 in music scholarships, and $1,500 in prizes. The college has also increased its low-cost housing facilities and emergency aid.

The money voted by the trustees for scholarships would normally have gone into buildings and equipment if the need for scholarships had not been so urgent, said President William Allan Neilson. "I constantly insist on the value to the college itself of the type of girl to whom we give scholarships," he declared. "They are, intellectually and in point of character, to a very large extent, the backbone of the college."

President Neilson and the trustees feel that the immediate needs of the students must outweigh everything else. The endowment income for scholarships at Smith is, the trustees believe, the lowest of any college of its rating.

EDUCATIONAL NOTES AND NEWS

DR. ROBERT ENLOW O'BRIAN was formally inducted into the presidency of Morningside College, Sioux City, Iowa, at ceremonies held on Saturday morning, October 24.

DR. ELMER ELLSWORTH BROWN celebrated his twentieth year as chancellor of New York University on November 9. During this period the student body increased from 4,175 to 31,523 and faculty members from 225 to more than 1,700.

PROFESSOR HENRY FAIRFIELD OSBORN, director of the American Museum of Natural History, Dr. Walter Bradford Cannon, professor of physiology at the Harvard University Medical School, and Professor Maurice Ansiaux, of the University of Brussels, received honorary degrees from the University of Paris at a special ceremony held at the Sorbonne on November 7.

DR. FRANK P. GRAVES, president of the University of the State of New York and state commissioner of education, was the dedicatory speaker at the opening of the Pennsylvania education building in Harrisburg, erected at a cost of $5,000,000.

THE Alumnae Kindergarten Association of Hunter College, New York City, gave a testimonial luncheon to Professor Helen Graham Coles at the Hotel Astor on November 7, in commemoration of her thirty years of service in the kindergarten department of the college.

MR. PRETOR W. CHANDLER, who retires this year from the chairmanship of the council of the London Society for Teaching and Training the Blind, with which he has been associated for twenty-five years, and Mrs. Chandler have been presented with a mounted silver bowl.

DR. EDGAR C. HIGBIE, president of the Eastern State Teachers College, Madison, South Dakota, since 1921, has accepted the presidency of the Wilson Teachers College, Washington, D. C.

DR. SAMUEL NEWTON SPRING, professor of silviculture in the department of forestry at Cornell University, has been appointed assistant dean of the New York State College of Forestry at Syracuse University. Professor Spring will assume his duties as assistant dean and director of instruction for both the college and the New York State Ranger School early in 1932.

DR. HENRY ALDEN SHAW has been appointed assistant professor of mental hygiene at the Harvard University Medical School. He has been associated with the school since 1925 as assistant in hygiene and psychiatrist.

DR. HARRY M. JOHNSON has assumed the direction of the department of psychology and education in the graduate school of the American University. Dr. Johnson was formerly at the Mellon Institute and the University of Pittsburgh.

PROFESSOR W. N. MEDLICOTT, of the staff of the University College of Swansea, South Wales, will be acting professor of history at the University of Texas for the present academic year.

PROFESSOR DWIGHT C. BAKER, for several years university examiner of the University of California, has been elected dean of the Junior College, Modesto, California, to succeed Mr. C. S. Morris.

THE curators of the Bodleian Library at the University of Oxford have elected Mr. Herbert Henry Edmund Craster, fellow of All Souls College, to be librarian.

DR. JOHN M. GLENN, general director of the Russell Sage Foundation since its inception twenty-four years ago, has resigned that post, but will continue to serve as one of the trustees of the foundation. Mr. Shelby M. Harrison, director of the department of surveys and exhibits of the foundation since 1912 and vice-general director in recent years, has succeeded Mr. Glenn as general director.

Because of the proposed expansion of the work of the international committee of the Y. M. C. A., Dr. John R. Mott, for sixteen years its general secretary, has signified his intention of resigning. The post has been offered to Mr. Francis S. Harmon, editor and publisher of the *American*, Hattiesburg, Mississippi. Dr. Mott will retain his position as president of the World Alliance of Young Men's Christian Associations, with headquarters in Geneva.

As Dr. Frederick L. Gamage enters into his twenty-fifth year as head master of Pawling School and his fiftieth year in the education of boys in New York State he has relinquished part of his executive duties to his son, Frederick L. Gamage, Jr., who has been appointed acting head master. Dr. Gamage will continue as head master and acting chaplain with general oversight of school affairs.

Dr. Abram Simon was elected president and Mrs. Marion Wade Doyle vice-president of the District of Columbia Board of Education at an organization meeting on November 4. Dr. Simon, rabbi of the Washington Hebrew Congregation, served as president of the board during a previous term as member. Mrs. Doyle is the wife of Dean Henry Grattan Doyle, of George Washington University. The board had been without a president since the resignation of Dr. Henry Barrett Learned, followed by his sudden death at Stanford University, where he had gone to teach history.

Dean F. W. Shipley, of Washington University, St. Louis, was elected president of the Association of Urban Universities at the recent meeting of the association in Toledo.

Professor Harvey A. Wooster, head of the department of economics of Oberlin College, has been appointed director of a new commission on the stabilization of employment for the state of Massachusetts, and has been granted a year's leave of absence from Oberlin.

Dr. Harley L. Lutz, professor of public finance at Princeton University, has been named a financial consultant in the government's national survey of school finance. The survey, which began on July 1, will require four years and will cost approximately $350,000.

Dr. Marie Schleuter-Hermkes, of Berlin, was the guest of the Boston branch of the American Association of University Women at a luncheon given on November 6 at the College Club, Boston. Dr. Hermkes is at present lecturer in the Akademie für Soziale und Paedagogische Frauenarbeit in Berlin. Her subject was "The Place of Woman in the Intellectual Life of Germany." Dr. Fannie Fern Andrews, chairman of the international relations committee of the Boston branch, presided.

Professor W. J. Hinton, director of studies at the Institute of Bankers, London, and formerly professor of political economy at the University of Hongkong, has been invited to give a course of lectures on Far Eastern economic conditions at the University of Hawaii in the summer of 1932. Professor Hinton expects to spend some time in the United States on his way to Hawaii.

Mr. Edwin E. Embree, president of the Julius Rosenwald Fund, Chicago, was one of the principal speakers at the Conference of Southern Educators, held recently at the University of North Carolina.

Dr. Frederick P. Keppel, president of the Carnegie Corporation, was the principal speaker at the Mount Holyoke Founder's Day ceremonies on November 6. The occasion commemorated the ninety-fourth anniversary of Mount Holyoke College.

Dr. Peng-Chun Chang, professor of philosophy at Nankai University, Tientsin, visiting professor at the University of Chicago and formerly secretary of the Chinese Education Commission to the United States, spoke in Boston on November 8 on "The Sprit of Chinese Philosophy—a Challenge to Modernism."

Dr. George H. Bridgman, who was for twenty-nine years until his retirement in 1912 president of Hamline University, St. Paul, Minnesota, died on November 4 at the age of ninety years. Dr. Bridgman was principal of Genessee Wesleyan Seminary in Lima, New York, for ten years before going to Hamline University.

Professor Henry M. Tyler, who became the first dean of the faculty of Smith College and who was for more than thirty-five years head of its department of Greek, died on November

3. Dr. Tyler went to Smith College in January, 1877, and was eighty-eight years old when he died.

THE REVEREND DR. CHARLES T. HOCK, dean of the Bloomfield College and Theological Seminary, Bloomfield, New Jersey, died on November 7 at the age of sixty-one years.

THE death is announced of Miss Juliette Derricotte, dean of women at Fisk University in Nashville, and a member of the National Board of the Y. W. C. A. since the biennial convention in 1930. Miss Derricotte was the second Negro woman to be elected to the board.

MISS HARRIET SAWYER, executive secretary of the Associate Alumnae of Vassar College, died on November 3 at the age of forty-seven years. Miss Sawyer was the chief organizer of the war service fund that financed the Vassar unit in France in 1918. She led in raising the college's emergency fund of $300,000 in 1919 and the $3,000,000 salary endowment fund in 1921.

DR. MYRON J. MICHAEL, superintendent of schools at Kingston, N. Y., for the last twenty-one years, died on November 6 at the age of eighty years.

THE sixth conference on rural school supervision in the Southern states, sponsored by the U. S. Office of Education, has been called by Commissioner William John Cooper, to be held in cooperation with the Alabama state department of education at Montgomery, Alabama, on December 14 and 15. In addition to representatives of the Office of Education and a number of education officials from Alabama, conference speakers will include Dr. Lois Coffey Mossman, Teachers College, Columbia University; Dr. H. L. Donovan, president, Eastern Kentucky State Teachers College, Richmond, Kentucky; Mr. William McKinley Robinson, director of rural education, Western State Teachers College, Kalamazoo, Michigan; Dr. Frank P. Bachman, George Peabody College for Teachers, Nashville, Tennessee; Mr. M. E. Moffitt, Mississippi state department of education, and Howard Dawson, Arkansas state department of education. State and county superintendents of schools, state and county rural school supervisors, principals of rural schools and representatives of state teachers colleges are expected to attend the conference. Each of the scheduled sessions will be devoted to consideration of important aspects of rural school supervision in the Southern states. Progressive education in the supervision of public elementary schools, administrative problems related to supervision, extension of the professional interests of teachers and other subjects will be discussed.

PRESIDENT FRANK PARKER DAY, of Union University, addressed on November 2 the tutorial students and members of the faculty of Colgate University at a banquet given in honor of the trustees at the Colgate Inn. His topic was "Honors and Tutorial Work." Following the adoption last year by the Colgate faculty of the plan for tutorial work proposed by Dean C. H. Thurber, by which a student may carry three fifths of his total load by the tutorial-seminar plan throughout his junior and senior years, fifty students were admitted to this group for the current year. These students are ordinarily excused from routine attendance at classes in their field of concentration but meet their tutors regularly once or twice a week for extended sessions. The following departments have tutorial students: Biology, economics, English, geology, German, philosophy and psychology, while others are making provisions for the work for next year.

HEADS of departments of education in South Dakota colleges met at State College on October 23 and 24 to study the matter of qualifications for admission to departments of education and the general problem of teacher-training courses in colleges. Mrs. Mabel Trooien, of the state department of public instruction, was appointed chairman of a committee to make a further study of these matters during the coming year. Other members of the committee are Dr. Hyde, of Dakota Wesleyan University, and Dr. L. M. Hrudka, of South Dakota State College. Others in attendance at the meetings were Mr. and Mrs. J. M. McAllister, of the Northern Normal and Industrial School at Aberdeen; Professor W. P. Hieronymus, of Augustana College; Mr. W. P. Knox and Mr. Russell Thomas, of Sioux Falls College; Miss Caroline Waltner, of Freeman Junior College, and Miss Catherine Klein and Professor C. R. Wiseman, of South Dakota State College.

The twelfth annual meeting of the Associated School Boards and Trustees of the State of New York was held on October 12 and 13 in Syracuse, N. Y. Among those who addressed the meeting were the following department representatives: Commissioner of Education Frank P. Graves; Dr. Lewis A. Wilson, assistant commissioner for vocational and extension education; Mr. Charles A. Brind, of the law division; Miss Treva E. Kauffman, supervisor of home economics; Miss Helen Hay Heyl, of the rural education bureau.

An exhibit on methods, materials and devices for teaching English to the adult foreign-born opened at the Russell Sage Foundation on November 6. It will continue until Saturday, November 14, daily from 3 to 9 P. M., and on Saturdays from 10 A. M. to 6 P. M. The exhibition was prepared by the Council on Adult Education for the Foreign Born, of which Dr. John H. Finley is chairman, and the Adult Education Bureau of the New York State Department of Education. Miss Caroline A. Whipple is representing the State Education Department as technical supervisor of the exhibition. The exhibition includes 300 text-books and supplementary readers, over 100 charts on lesson plans and teaching devices, reports and teaching material from twenty cities and states, special material on naturalization and allied subjects. Subject-matter and visual material for use with adults who have acquired a working knowledge of English is emphasized.

The combined faculties of Boston University and every employee of the institution have accepted a five per cent. cut in salaries for the remaining three fourths of the school year, it has been announced by President Daniel L. Marsh, whose own salary is likewise affected. The university council recommended the cuts, which were approved by the executive committee of the trustees. The announcement stated that the action was deemed advisable to save the university from a possible deficit without some extraordinary economy. The cuts are accepted with the understanding that at the end of the fiscal year, circumstances warranting, the old salaries will be restored.

DISCUSSION

HUMANITY REINFORCED

"Power," wrote Mr. Wiggam recently, "is in the hands of those who have no knowledge; knowledge is in the hands of those who have no power." This seesaw state of affairs is no new thing; it is as old as the Egyptian slave-driver or the stone-carved records of Ur. The bonus tyranny in Congress, the prohibition and law enforcement problem as analyzed by the Wickersham Commission, and the "knock-knock in the name of Beelzebub" that echoes all over our educational premises—these are indications that habits and statutes established by the march of a mass-production civilization and by men whose whiphand was derived therefrom, are most difficult to overthrow or to replace by the calm and constructive thinking of people with ideas and reason.

We need not be pessimistic on the subject. To one who heeds the throb of our American life, we are on the eve of a great awakening. Now that preparedness debates are growing stale, individual voices concerned with the economic, intellectual and spiritual welfare of our country are being raised, with gratifying variety of emphasis and view-point. And perhaps nothing is more significant than the ever-recurring debates on this subject: "What material and method of study in our secondary schools, both public and private, will produce the best citizen of the future?"

Just as there is no panacea for prohibition problems, or for the civic and legal complications that puzzle the well-wisher for America, so there is no panacea for education. The home plays more of a part in the drama than does the school. No water rises higher than its source. Coal-mining towns send to daily classes children who thrive in terms of coal; children of Palm Beach millionaires think in terms of Dusenberg motor-cars; children of the Intelligentsia reflect the talk at the dinner-tables of their elders. The school must stand on its own legs, and struggle against or cooperate with the *milieu* from which its pupil material is derived. The school-teacher is therefore one of those who has the knowledge but not the power, as far as his or her direct influence and operation in the later life of the pupil is concerned. Our only hope of effectively dealing with this later world of cross-currents and inconsistencies is the inculcation in boys and girls of a thorough and honest way of thinking, based on the best traditions of the past and inspired with a vision of its application to the future. Novelty in itself is nothing. The past in itself is valueless. The reintegration of the old in terms of the new is what science itself is based on, and what this very mass-productive civilization of ours lives by. Therefore, we must fight the undesirable things and promote good causes by the same principle—cumulative progress.

The latest group of critics, mostly representatives of education departments in our large universities, would scrap practically all the traditional subjects offered heretofore in secondary curricula. They talk internationalism and understanding with other nations, and yet they make such astounding statements as: "Better English does not come from studying other languages. It is usually hurt by such study. You must make it an aim and see that better English comes. The days of fights for language when hot air was the only weapon are gone. The experimenters have given you solid shot in the form of results piled up by standardized tests."[1] Here is a view-point that not only expresses reluctance to understand a French boy's medium for conveying thought, but applies the very principle of mass production which the critic decries in our American life. The major premise is wrong on two fundamental counts. In the same publication comes another electric shock (p. 339): "Teachers who have spent time and money preparing to teach Latin, Algebra, French, German and standard school subjects are a hindrance. Gentlemen who have money invested in text-books are an obstacle." The suggested substitutes for these so-called outworn topics are, according to Mr. Edward Reisner, "those programs of social and political improvements which are discoverable." In other words, our children should, in Soviet groups, spend all their time in immature theoretical speculation on the government of their country, studying from multitudinous new pamphlets and text-books made up with scissors and paste by these very educationists in overwhelming masses, and leave school without a knowledge of mathematics, physics, languages and "pure" English: being consequently unable to think hard uphill on an abstract problem of number and proportion, or to know the laws of the universe that surrounds them, or to correspond with a friend in Grenoble, or to diagnose between "Death Comes to the Archbishop" and a tabloid front-page. A mind which, at the age of eighteen, fares forth into an arena of law-rectifying, bonus-restraint and prohibition-control will be helpless if it has been taught that intellectual mastery comes by hit-or-miss discussion of current events. In such a case Mr. Wiggam's epigram will become still more pointed, and a class will rise up in America which possesses no knowledge, and no power either.

This mass-mind which has neither any use for traditions nor a rational stock-in-trade with which to plan the future is not confined to the United States. In spite of M. Georges Duhamel's defense of the European progressive-conservative, the continental himself is feeling the attrition of mechanistic forces—and these forces are not necessarily of American manufacture. The *London Times Literary Supplement* (August 27, 1931) calls our attention to a Spanish book—"La Rebelión de las Masas," by José Ortega y Gasset, recently published in Madrid. It is an analysis of the European "Mass-Man" of the twentieth century, who has no roots in the past. The Renaissance Man was rooted in the Middle Ages; the medieval man was rooted in Rome; but the "Mass-Man" gets his ideas, like his products, ready-made; and soon the present will cease to supply him, because he has no past and no mental savings for the future. Pleasure is his god; his cult is mediocrity, a car and a comfortable house. And he follows a uniformity imposed by those who pull the strings in dictation of his manners and ideas. His very vitality, according to Señor Ortega y Gasset, is using itself up for his own destruction. Such is the result of mechanistic and utilitarian ways of living. And such is the end of men who live by the evanescent inspiration of the present only, or the poverty of future hopes which have no basic foundation.

No such debate as that between Huxley and Matthew Arnold is now in order; for both science and the classics have their place in any sound program of thought and study. The liberal-vocational clash died a natural death

[1] SCHOOL AND SOCIETY, September 5, 1931, page 343.

about ten years ago. And the striking trends in American life are enough in themselves to put out of court the proposals of the educational "Methodists" for scrapping both the humanities and the mathematico-scientific branches of learning. Their two commandments of experiment and testing, with the admission that "transfer" *does* take place from one field to another, amuse one greatly; since in order to test, one must have some real material other than guess-work, and in order to experiment one needs cumulative evidence gathered from past science and literature.

Examples of the revivifying power of the classics are so numerous that one instance alone need be mentioned. The whole concept of the American state—which the educationist would nullify into current "Problems of Democracy"—is based on the classical ideas of Greece and Rome as investigated by Franklin, Jefferson and John Adams in the formation of our New Republic of 1776 and 1787. They search for data from Livy, Plato, the Stoics, Roman Institutes (The Law of Nature and of Nations), Thucydides, Cicero and Demosthenes. A brief reading of Mr. Becker's work on the "Declaration of Independence" will show this indebtedness; and if the reader wishes to seek farther, the original works of these three fathers of our Constitution will give ample material. This was a political tradition; and if one wishes a view of the literary awakening, Emerson and his New England Platonism are obvious to the seeker. Every time that great waves of pioneer thought have rolled along and over the people, the humanities have played a part.

Some contemporary testimony is also in order. Among American poets with a real message and an inspired way of delivering it is Robinson Jeffers, of California, whose cosmic view of mind and soul has done away with the magical element, and who, in the opinion of Mr. Lehman, has joined Shakespeare, Lucretius and Omar Khayyam in his ability to write without the dictation of presences and powers. Jeffers makes nature neutral and not sentimental: he "breaks out of humanity" into the infinite cosmos of development which Professor Millikan reaches in science. His is the Greek idea—a return to Hellenism; and when he reaches a stage of inspiration which will include humanity at its highest cosmic point, he will speak the words for which American poetry has been waiting. The magnificent philosophical duet between Electra and Orestes in "The Tower beyond Tragedy," gives us the contrast between an *ad hoc* personal interpretation of the universe and the spirit of human inquiry which, like Shelley's "Alastor," takes the firmament as its province. It is here that the souls of youth love to wander.

In religion we have had enough of dogma. We are reaching out into an identification of man with his universe which has acknowledged connections with ancient Stoicism. Our "micromania," as Dr. Felix Adler has termed it—is ceasing to be so acute; and the belittling of the human soul, characteristic of the "miserable sinner" motif from flagellating medievalism, is something which has no appeal to the modern young person who is searching for a real adjustment between intellect and emotion. Dean Inge combines a Platonic underlier of serenity with the indispensable *élan* of the Christian message. Thus, without our realizing it, the Platonic and Stoic themes of idealism and patience unite with the long line of saintly followers of the Galilean to offer us a spiritual prop upon which so many lean without acknowledgment.

The Spanish Southwest in Willa Cather, the impressive output of biography, the foundation of such publications as "American Literature" in North Carolina, the architecture of classic simplicity which goes back to the *cella* of the ancient temple, the archaeological hook-ups between Wall Street business men and the excavations of the Athenian Agora—these are all indications of a return to tradition for purposes of future development. And, in more mundane affairs, the international and diplomatic developments which indicate growing sympathy with the languages and ideas of Europe make such mastery of the past even more necessary than it was when our Jefferson and Franklin and Adams built up a new country on the foundations of ancient republics and empires.

The civic-social system of study which men like Professors Rugg and Goodwin Watson advocate is very good; but it must be based on knowledge of the past. Otherwise, there will be still less of a policy in our democracy twenty years from now. The economic courses in our schools and colleges are the only agencies that have resisted the "racket" theory in government. But there must be more than moralizing over our public affairs—in the face of political and industrial mass production.

For such a reason the French and Latin and algebra and science must be retained, modified and improved in order to turn out persons who can think their way through their problems. I do not find fault with the fact that civics should be studied, but only with the method. We must fight formalism in future planning as well as in past institutions. The knight-priest system of Spain fell because it was nothing but ancient; the mass-product will perish because it has no roots in the past from which to repeat itself. The American conception of a new world, based on the soundest elements of the old, won the admiration of critics who compared it with the Athens and Rome upon which it improved. Facts and ideas win over impressions and emotions. *Humanity* is the primary thing; and it must be cumulative. Hence the need of solid and satisfying subjects of study which will enable us to guard and guide it.

McAndrew's hymn (Kipling) is as applicable in 1931, amid all the repercussions of the National Education Association, as in 1893:

We're creeping on wi' each new rig—less weight
and larger power:
There'll be the loco-boiler next, an' thirty miles
an hour!
Thirty an' more. What I ha' seen since ocean-
steam began
Leaves me na' doot for the machine: but what
about the man?

Richard M. Gummere
William Penn Charter School,
Philadelphia, Pa.

SPECIAL CORRESPONDENCE

A STUDENT VIEWS THE YALE EXPERIMENT IN THE GRADUATE STUDY OF EDUCATION

The Yale plan for the graduate study of education has a history of only one year and consequently, perhaps, no one should either extol it too highly or condemn it too severely. More years must pass, demonstrating the success of the venture, before other universities, in any considerable number, will be able to afford, either from the point of view of its educational expediency or its finance, to borrow in a significant degree from the plan adopted by Yale. However, since every university offering graduate work in education has opportunities to make changes in its curricular offering to a greater or less extent, more should be known of the Yale plan. It has much to offer. Furthermore, the spirit which emanates from the situation in mind can not be considered educationally unwise or financially prohibitive. The spirit of the Yale plan, if it could be assimilated by conventionally organized graduate work in education, would be of great value. This consideration, combined with a wide-spread interest in the plan encountered at every turn while off the New Haven campus, has led to the writing of this post-view of a year's work as a student under the plan at Yale.

It is the purpose to present in very brief form a description of the plan as seen through the eyes of one member of the student group, for the plan can not be separated from the students participating in it. Furthermore, the advantages and disadvantages of the plan apparent to the writer will be presented frankly. The reader is asked to remember that this is an individual evaluation for which the student writing it is responsible, although naturally his point of view has been affected by association with his fellow students. The plan itself is favorable to the intimate association of students regarding experiences through which they are passing.

The plan requires roughly three years of work for the Doctor of Philosophy degree. The first year, or approximately so, is devoted to the general seminar. Through the general seminar it is hoped to give each student a comprehensive view of the entire field of education. The seminar was composed of twenty-five students and seven faculty members and met, as a rule, two two-hour periods per week. At this seminar students and faculty were encouraged to present any problems which were confronting them. The students usually took the lead in presenting and attacking problems. The seminar was truly the debating association and clearing, or better, the clarifying house for the students. A varying degree of the control of this seminar was exercised by the faculty, but the major control was at all times in the hands of the students. Enthusiasts of student control may be assured that this degree of control by the faculty was not a wolf—that is, conventionally organized education—in sheep's clothing. Faculty control resembled the control exercised by the highest type of social worker who is busily engaged studying cases and accumulating data on individuals at all times, and who, when it is most desirable for the individual, is co-active in the achievement of the desired end. There was no faculty domination, but rather less faculty control than the students requested. The extent of faculty control varied, it being the aim of the faculty to have it sufficient only to cause the learning process, in the largest number of cases possible, to operate with maximum efficiency.

Certain distinctive features of the general seminar were as follows:

(1) Very frequently small groups of students met voluntarily, after a general seminar meeting, to continue the discussion of a problem to which no more time could profitably be devoted by all members of the seminar. The individuals composing these groups varied widely. With initiative completely in the hands of the students, the member or members of the faculty best prepared to guide in the discernment of all sides of the problem in question were invited and attended the session. Seminar rooms were provided for this purpose and no time limits existed.

(2) Sections were organized for any group of students, no matter how small the number, who desired specific factual instruction in any of the so-called fields of education. This was particularly desirable in a field such as educational statistics, for it is an especially difficult subject for a student to master from books.

(3) Visits were made to schools of varying types when seminar discussions indicated that they were desirable as an aid in giving concreteness to the discussion.

(4) Men who are recognized authorities in education were frequently brought to Yale to speak to, and to discuss with the members of the general seminar problems which had arisen in the seminar discussion and which came within the limits of, or pertained to the specialization of the educational leader in question.

(5) Students were able to indicate mastery of educational materials and problems through examinations, conferences with faculty members, participation in seminar discussions, propounding stimulating questions for seminar meetings, submitting papers on any educational subjects, preparing objective examinations in some phase of education, *et cetera*. Whether a student used any or all or none of these means was his problem. He realized very probably, however, that the evaluation of himself by the faculty could not be satisfactorily made if he showed no activity through any of the aforementioned or other methods.

(6) The faculty members were available at almost any time for conferences in regard to any problem the student had in mind. A student in conference with any member of the faculty was made to feel that the faculty member was really interested in giving his time to the student. The professors at Yale were concerned not only with writing books and carrying on research work, for they recognized the desirability of an intimate relationship with the students. This did not involve an under-estimation of the value of books and research. This faculty attitude made it exceedingly improbable that any student would feel that the faculty members would consider the university a splendid place in which to spend their time if no students were in evidence.

The second stage of the plan, which occupies in most cases the second year, or an approximation thereof, is devoted to a mastery of the field of specialization of the student. During this year it is hoped that most students will meet a vital and challenging problem, which in its attempted solution will constitute the third stage and third year, namely, the preparation of the dissertation. In the discussion which follows, the last two stages of the plan will not be considered because the first stage is the only one tried out as yet in a significant measure, the plan having been in operation only one year.

In making the comparison between the first stage of the plan and conventional graduate work in education, the writer asks that it be understood that this plan is not favored as a panacea for all or even any of the ills of graduate work in education. It should be borne in mind that unquestionably the plan could be worked more successfully at Yale than at any other institution, for Yale admits only fifty graduate students in education in any one year, and selects these principally on the criterion of ability to pursue successfully the work as it is there organized.

The outstanding disadvantage of the plan appeared to be its indefiniteness during the early part of the first year at Yale. No one knew what specific materials had to be learned in order to meet the requirements. What facts should be memorized? Examinations were not required. If examinations were elected, what knowledges would they test? For a time the consideration of these questions kept some students in a quandary. After a short time, however, they gave up this apparition of traditional course work to which they, as students, previously had been subjected, and decided that truly the faculty meant it when they said they were looking for individual intellectual growth and maturation, qualities which neither essay nor objective examinations could satisfactorily measure, but which would have to be evaluated, both objectively and subjectively, as evaluations occur when one is on the job of living. When the above conclusion was arrived at, the stage was prepared for learning to occur in an estimable sense, as a scanning of the advantages of the plan which follow will show it did.

Other adverse criticisms of the first stage of the plan which have been heard very frequently are that it lacks required examinations and specified common essentials which every student must learn or rather memorize. The strength of these criticisms wanes in the light of the advantages of the plan, which are as follows:

(1) There are no particular sets of facts to be memorized by all students. The student does not end the year feeling that he now has the solution to this or that problem fixed and absolute. The learning or the memorization of facts is probably not as great immediately as in the case of the student in the conventional course. A short time ago a so-called creative course in graduate work in education was observed in which the professor graded entirely on the basis of eight hundred objective questions which tested how well the students had memorized the facts recorded in a particular book. That book was all a student had to memorize; he did not have to learn it—for the questions were all in the identical clothes in which they appeared when he met them previously—to make a grade approaching perfection. Truly the course was not creative and in no sense gave returns in learning, unless learning is merely storing up facts, commensurate with the effort required. Perchance the professor was a believer in formal discipline. If not, whatever the cause of this condition was, the type of learning situation in question demonstrates well what is not happening at Yale. In passing, note that a belief in facts and their teaching is held and that it is understood how basic they are to the intelligent solution of problems, but that the Yale plan of securing them is preferred, given conditions as they existed at Yale.

(2) There are no required examinations. It may well be asked which of the following is more life-like, which is therefore not only the more wholesome living of life but also the better preparation for later life: a series of courses and examinations similar to the one previously mentioned, or a few students and faculty members gathered together cooperatively learning and evaluating, and having multiple opportunities for coming to know each other's qualities and for estimating each other's abilities? In the latter case, each faculty member daily evaluates each of the students, noting what he is reading, what problems are interesting him, what part he takes in discussions, and in general just what desirable things he is achieving. Tests were developed to aid the instructor who was under conditions which made an evaluation approaching fairness impossible otherwise. Yale has overcome conditions making examinations a necessity and thus sagaciously dispenses with them. The writer prefers to be evaluated as he will be evaluated in life, not by one examination or many of the traditional type, but by the daily impressions which he leaves. The writer is willing to accept a man as rated by the faculty, each member of which knows him well, rather than as rated by an examination which as yet is a poor substitute for life as an evaluating

agent. To the ardent follower of John Dewey, who recently chided the writer for his fervor in this matter, it is in order to quote, "The Child and the Curriculum":

> The child is the starting point, the center, and the end. His development, his growth is the ideal. It alone furnishes the standard. To the growth of the child all studies are subservient; they are instruments valued as they serve the needs of growth. Personality, character is more than subject-matter. Not knowledge or information, but self-realization, is the goal. Literally, we must take our stand with the child and our departure from him. It is he, not the subject-matter, which determines both the quality and quantity of learning.

In the light of the different original nervous systems, the different environments the graduate students have encountered, and the different environments by which they are going to be challenged in the future, and in the light of the above quotation, can a disciple of Dewey sincerely state that he would prefer the traditional system of examinations to the life-like system of evaluation employed by Yale?

(3) The habit of reading books and men is developed. No longer are pages 69–104 read for Monday's recitation. A book is read or skimmed and the author's view-point, particularly if he is a leader, is sought not only in this book, but in all of his books. There is a mass of material and, of course, not nearly all can be read that the student should like to read, but the evaluating of it and searching for that which is worth while is just what the schoolman in every case will have to do in life if he is to keep in step and advance. Such abilities should be developed in the graduate school where guidance exists. This is much more to be preferred than the prescription of certain pages of books. The student, who has advantage of opportunities such as Yale offers, upon the conferring of his Doctor of Philosophy degree, should be in no danger of being thrown out into a world so large and confusing as to be almost meaningless to him. Traditional education is confronted with this danger and as an evidence of it, it may be noted that the educator is frequently confronted by a serious problem, namely, that a great number of his well-trained teachers and supervisors frequently do little of that which is expected of them in actual field service. Are they not in a rowboat without oars on a rapidly flowing stream? It is to be doubted that any one who is in intimate touch with our public schools will challenge this as being a fact.

(4) The student spends his time on materials he has not previously covered. A student in almost any college of education, graduate or undergraduate, will vouch that much time is inefficiently spent as a result of duplication in courses. The duplication has been eliminated at Yale.

(5) The student comes to know the professors and gets a glimpse of them in their entirety, not only as teacher to student, but as man to man. Although student participation is very valuable in seminar discussions, the student profits much in hearing faculty members sincerely battle over some problems. It shows the student so conclusively that education is not all settled, scientifically determined, an impression one might easily gain while being passively indoctrinated by many professors.

(6) It brings the students face to face with vital problems and forces them by discussion to take a point of view, as they must in practical situations, and to carry it logically through. This experience benefits each student by establishing for him, as an individual, a sound, defensible, basic philosophy.

(7) A very desirable condition at Yale is that each new group enrolling has it in its own hands to determine in very considerable measure what its course will be. The faculty does not permit absolute student control as has been pointed out before, but the plan demands a very considerable amount of student control compared to the traditional situation. The exercise of such control permits learning that is extremely worth while and that in general can not be obtained through courses. The thought of having a year in which one must determine the materials to be studied is most challenging and invigorating.

This constitutes a post-view of a year's study at Yale. When more of the progressive educational philosophy being taught is applied to the actual life situation in our public schools I can only believe that Yale as now organized in the Graduate Department of Education will be regarded as conservative because of her failure to have a greater sharing of control by the students. These students will share in control in life very shortly; why not permit the practice of sharing in control where it is not so expensive or dangerous from the point of view of the number of persons involved and where expert hands are eager to guide?

THEODORE L. RELLER
UNIVERSITY OF PENNSYLVANIA

QUOTATIONS

THE EFFECT OF INDUSTRY ON BRITISH EDUCATION

SPEAKING last week at the opening of the new School of Economics and Commerce at Dundee, Sir Josiah Stamp scouted the idea that a successful scheme of higher education in economics and commerce requires a less advanced foundation of general knowledge than other callings such as law, medicine, teaching and the church. On the contrary, real success in the field of economics and commerce made greater demands upon the non-specialized general school education, since economics is compounded of a knowledge of mathematics, history, geography, modern languages and English, and, indeed, all subjects in the school curriculum except the advanced stage of classics. Indeed, this apparent exception is no exception, since a thorough training in advanced classics has been proved in more than one instance to have led to capacity to succeed in the world of physical science. Though Sir Josiah Stamp makes no special plea for the study of advanced classics, except as a basis for modern languages, he pleads for thoroughness in the ordinary school curriculum as a basis for that training for commerce which has become essential for the future of the British Empire. In the sixteenth century, when the nobility and gentry of England scorned commerce, Venice at the height of her commercial power recruited her merchants from the highest and noblest families in the state. The Queen of the Adriatic knew what she was about. There was no snobbery in her outlook. She wanted character and brains for commerce, and she found them in a class whose motto was *Noblesse oblige*. Into comparatively recent times, at any rate into late Victorian times, the Elizabethan prejudice against commerce (definitely noted by Richard Mulcaster) was still visible in England. The fighting services, the church, the bar and teaching at the universities and in the schools were the respective goals of innumerable families who scorned, on the ground of their "gentility," the Mercantile Marine and the mercantile houses of London, Glasgow, Manchester, Liverpool, Bombay and Calcutta. The openings extended with the creation of the competitive Civil Services for England and India, but the gentry of England did not follow the example of Venice, whose best blood did not scorn the Counter and the Bagman's bag.

The stream of economic change that has followed the discoveries of Faraday and Clerk Maxwell has at least altered all that; and today youth is asking on every side to be trained on the Venetian pattern and to see what part *Noblesse oblige* has to play in the developments of English commerce, English industries and English science. The present generation hopes to live dangerously and not to be tied to the safer worlds of the civil and fighting services, the bar, the church and the teaching profession. The signs of the times are quite clear. Much of the intellect of the schools is no longer tied to the professions. It is indeed with great difficulty that sufficient men are to be found for the church, the teaching profession and the practising bar. It is now no longer a question of men of caliber but of men at all. There is indeed a real fear that the teaching profession will become a woman's profession. In the public elementary schools in London there were in 1929–30 12,497 women teachers out of a total of 18,070. In the county council areas out of 70,601 teachers 53,921 were women, in boroughs and urban district areas, out of 25,181 teachers 18,164 were women, while in the county borough areas, out of 54,186 teachers 40,214 were women. Here is one of the signs of the times. Men more and more are trying to enter the fields of commerce and economics, and all that the new generation asks is that they should be properly trained, trained with thoroughness in a non-specialized school education.

At this very juncture, in a momentary interlude between his exertions in a general election which has, as its main goal, the safe-guarding of English finance, economics and commerce, Mr. Baldwin has been discoursing on the significance of the old grammar schools as homes of piety and true learning. He was opening the new buildings of a grammar school at Wolverley, in Worcestershire, founded in 1620 by William Sebright, town clerk of the city of London, a school with an essentially mercantile source. Piety he defined as that gift of reverence for all things that are good; the gift of performing your duty primarily to those among whom you live and through them to your country and the world, your duty to God and man. This sense of duty, coupled with the encouragement of true learning, was and is at the root of all education, both ancient and modern. These two educational functions are inseparably interwoven, though the scope of true learning advances side by side with the advance of scholarship in every field. But thoroughness is the basic note of true learning. As Mr. Baldwin said last week: "True knowledge covers a very wide field. It means knowledge of yourself, which is not common, and implies knowledge of your own ignorance, which is not common." The grammar schools of the country form a continuous tradition of learning far back into early Saxon times, and they persisted in their work amidst all the troubles of all the centuries. Mr. Baldwin said that he liked to think of the grammar schools also as a link between all classes in the country; sons of country gentlemen, yeomen, and farmers sitting together and forming that knowledge of each other and of the country which was part of the binding force that made the unity of the nation before we became industrialized.

The process of industrialization and the processes of science applied to agriculture have all been taken into account by the governors of grammar schools and by the modern board of education and by pious donors in the last fifty years, and to-day the work of giving a thorough modern education is consistent with the old ideals of the grammar schools. Piety and true learning can flourish to-day as never before in this country if students are taught to understand that their lives can be lived as well and as usefully in business and industry as in the more intellectual professions.—*The London Times Educational Supplement.*

SOCIETIES AND MEETINGS

THE COLLEGE ENTRANCE EXAMINATION BOARD

THE first definite step toward a new form of testing to supplement school records was taken by the College Entrance Examination Board at its 1931 annual meeting, held on October 28 at Columbia University. The board passed resolutions approving "the general proposal to establish a series of validating examinations," agreed to offer such examinations "as soon as the funds necessary for their conduct are assured," and authorized a committee "to investigate ways and means of securing funds."

The proposed new system would not replace the subject examinations which the board has conducted since 1900, now required of all candidates by five colleges for men and five colleges for women. It would be a device rather for institutions which at present use the board examinations only in the case of candidates who do not qualify for admission upon school certificate. To these institutions the board would offer facilities for supplementing the school record by a form of test differing from the examinations of subject-matter in specific courses.

Two interesting features mark the project for these validating examinations, as presented to the board by Professor Adam Leroy Jones, of Columbia University, chairman of the commission, and as amplified in the report of Professor Carl E. Brigham, of Princeton University, associate secretary of the board. The examinations would be designed to validate school marks in English, in mathematics and in modern foreign languages upon the principles and techniques followed in the scholastic aptitude test—a test developed by a commission of psychologists headed by Professor Brigham. The examinations would be given to seniors in secondary schools; not in June, as are the subject examinations of the board, but "in January or February, possibly on a Friday and Saturday," thus permitting completion of the admission procedure before the close of the school and college year.

Professor Brigham pointed out as an additional advantage that the early examinations would enable the colleges "in consultation with the schools still in session to make up advanced sections for especially promising freshmen or to offer them direct admission to certain sophomore courses in which the high level of their school work and attainment would seem to guarantee success."

For the preparation of validating tests in English and in mathematics the commission on the scholastic aptitude test already has abundant material. "In the modern languages the board could take over types of tests evolved by the American and Canadian Committees on Modern Languages and by the Pennsylvania Study. Eventually it might be possible to standardize aural tests by means of the radio and phonograph. At present no tests have been developed in Latin."

It has been suggested also by Professor Brigham that, in addition to the special examination in English, the new arrangement should call for the writing of an essay by the candidate on a comprehensive subject. "These essays would represent the work of several months on the part of the candidate. They would be certified by the head of the school. The essays would not be marked or rated by the College Entrance Examination Board, but forwarded to the college to which the candidate is seeking admission."

The board voted to ask representatives of secondary school associations to bring the validating examination proposal before their associations.

REPORT OF SECRETARY FISKE

In his annual report Secretary Thomas S. Fiske referred to the total of 22,741 candidates taking board examinations in 1931 as a trifle higher than totals for 1927, 1928 and 1929, but as 737 below 1930. If conditions continue as they have been, a decline of perhaps 500 next year may be expected. Dr. Fiske pointed out that, for the first time in many years, the disbursements of the board, $257,183, exceeded the receipts, $256,966. The expenses of the board, per candidate, were $11.31 for 1931, as compared with $10.65 in 1930 and $11.09 in 1929. Each candidate pays an examination fee of $10. It was brought out in the report of Dr. Wilson Farrand as custodian that the board has investments of $113,575 which have fallen off somewhat but not markedly from purchase prices.

For the conduct of his office and for the 1932 examinations Secretary Fiske was authorized, under the direction of the executive committee, to expend $225,000 "or so much thereof as may be necessary," with an allowance of $10 for every candidate in excess of 22,250. An authorization of $22,000 was made for the preparation and scoring of the 1932 scholastic aptitude test, and $3,000 for the expenses of committees and commissions of the board.

DEFINITION OF LANGUAGE REQUIREMENTS

Professor Robert N. Corwin, of Yale, chairman of the committee of review, spoke in praise of the "careful and painstaking work" done by the commission on English headed by Chairman Charles Swain Thomas, of Harvard. The complete report of the commission has recently been published under the title "Examining the Examination in English" in the series Harvard Studies in Education. The following teachers in schools and colleges have been appointed a commission to recommend requirements in English: Chairman, Professor Harrison R. Steeves, Columbia University; Professor Ralph P. Boas, Wheaton College; Professor Jack R. Crawford, Yale University; Dr. Wilson Farrand, Newark Academy, Newark, N. J.; Miss Carolyn M. Gerrish, Girls' Latin School, Boston; Professor Henry B. Huntington, Brown University; Professor Charles N. Kennedy, Princeton University; Dr. John A. Lester, Hill School, Pottstown; Mr. Charles N. Raymond, Lawrenceville School, Lawrenceville, N. J.; Professor Alice D. Snyder, Vassar College; Miss Katharine Taylor, Shady Hill School, Cambridge, Mass.; Professor Charles Swain Thomas, Harvard University.

Following comment by Professor Corwin on the report of the commission on the requirements in the modern foreign languages, a resolution was passed authorizing the distribution of the report and inviting suggestions and criticisms from teachers and associations interested.

Because of the small numbers taking the board examinations in two subjects, the meeting voted, upon motion of Professor Corwin, to discontinue after 1932 examinations in "Mathematics c d, plane and solid geometry, minor requirement" and "Italian B, third year Italian."

Action on Examination Ratings

Reporting for the committee on examination ratings, Chairman Farrand said that "the reading of examination books by the 770 readers of the board last June was conducted with the usual admirable efficiency." He reported action by the committee on three matters. Hereafter readers are not to re-read books which are rated high by the first reader. "The rule that no marks should be given between 55 and 60 is abrogated." The number of readers of the comprehensive English books will be reduced from 170 to about 100, those readers being retained who have proved most efficient; provision is to be made also for promising younger readers.

Upon motion of Dr. Farrand, the board voted that "the writing of comments by readers on new plan books be hereafter omitted."

Professor Adam Leroy Jones reported on the "examination to test competence in the use of the English language," which was given last April at a score of centers in Europe, Asia and South America. The two centers where considerable numbers took the examinations were Brussels, with 17 candidates, and Moscow, with 83 candidates. The latter were young Soviets desiring to come to American engineering schools for the training they need in U. S. S. R. construction work. Professor Jones said that the examination had proved an excellent test, according to the experience with entering foreign students at Columbia and other institutions.

In the absence of the chairman of the board, President Pendleton, of Wellesley, and of the vice-chairman, Vice-President McClelland, of the University of Pennsylvania, the acting chairman at the meeting was President Ferry, of Hamilton College.

Officers were elected for 1931–32 as follows:

Chairman: President Ellen F. Pendleton, Wellesley College. *Vice-chairman:* Vice-president George W. McClelland, University of Pennsylvania. *Other members of the executive committee:* Dr. Mather A. Abbott, Lawrenceville, N. J.; Professor Robert N. Corwin, Yale University; President Frederick C. Ferry, Hamilton College; Dean Radcliffe Heermance, Princeton University; Dr. Clement C. Hyde, Hartford, Conn.; President Marion E. Park, Bryn Mawr College; Mr. Henry Pennypacker, Harvard University. *Custodian:* Dr. Wilson Farrand, Newark, N. J. *Secretary and treasurer:* Professor Thomas S. Fiske, Columbia University. *Associate secretary:* Professor Carl C. Brigham, Princeton University.

Raymond Walters

Swarthmore College

EDUCATIONAL RESEARCH AND STATISTICS

AN ANALYSIS OF SCHOLASTIC APTITUDE OF FRESHMEN IN SOME PRIVATE COLLEGES IN MINNESOTA[1]

The scholastic graveyard of college freshmen has grown so large in the past two decades that the administrative caretakers are faced with a perplexing problem. The solution of this problem is not found in an increase of burial grounds but rather in a decrease of the death rate. Many suggestions for reducing this mortality have been proposed, one of the more hopeful of which is the guidance use of psychological tests in combination with high-school scholarship. It is an established fact that very few college freshmen who rank in the lower third of their high-school class are able to do satisfactory college work; research studies establishing this fact are so well known that they need not be reviewed here. When these facts are understood by high-school seniors and their parents, a reduction will follow both in the number of low-aptitude students who enroll in college and in the mortality rate.

The present study was undertaken at the request of the Association of Minnesota Colleges, the purpose being to determine:

(1) Whether the state-wide testing and guidance program for high-school seniors results in the encouragement of high-aptitude students and the discouragement of low-aptitude seniors in their intention to enroll in college.

(2) Whether the prognostic use of psychological test ratings and high-school scholarship ratings is justified.

All colleges of the association were asked to

[1] The author is indebted to Dean J. B. Johnston, Professor D. G. Paterson and to Mr. F. S. Beers for assistance in the preparation of this report.

furnish data regarding the college aptitude rating (average of high-school rank and test rank), high-school scholarship percentile rank, college ability test percentile rank, and fall quarter or first semester grades of all freshmen enrolled in September, 1929. A total of 1,010 freshmen for whom the above data were available are included in this study. Because of the fact that a number of the colleges gave no test to those Minnesota freshmen who are not reached by the spring testing program, and that for some freshmen no high-school scholarship rank was available, a large number of cases could not be used. Of this total of 1,010 freshmen, 637 had been tested in the spring of 1929 and 373 additional students were tested by the individual colleges in September (151 of these freshmen were graduates of Minnesota high schools and 222 came from schools outside the state).

College scholarship was computed uniformly for all colleges by means of honor points assigned to letter grades:

A: 3 honor points per credit hour.
B: 2 honor points per credit hour.
C: 1 honor point per credit hour.
D: No honor points per credit hour.
F: Minus one honor point per credit hour.

These 1,010 freshmen were divided into three groups, which, for the sake of clarity, will be designated by the following symbols:

SM: Spring-tested freshmen from Minnesota high schools.

FM: Fall-tested freshmen from Minnesota high schools.

FNM: Fall-tested freshmen from non-Minnesota high schools.

The total number of honor points earned was divided by the total number of credit hours carried to obtain the honor point ratio. This honor point ratio was used as a measure of the student's scholastic achievement in college. Since this ratio is a measure of relative achievement, *i.e.*, quality of work in relation to amount, the ratios of students from colleges where the semester is the unit for credit hours may be combined with the ratios of students from colleges where the quarter system is used. It is obvious, however, that differences in standards of grading in the various colleges introduce errors which are concealed in a general statement of quality of scholarship.

TABLE I

COMPARISON OF SPRING AND FALL-TESTED FRESHMEN IN COLLEGE SCHOLARSHIP AND COLLEGE APTITUDE RATING

	Spring-tested freshmen from Minnesota high schools	Fall-tested freshmen from Minnesota high schools	Fall-tested freshmen from non-Minnesota high schools
Total number	**637**	**151**	**222**
No. earning "C" or higher average grades	362	78	131
Per cent. earning "C" or higher grades	56.8	51.7	59.0

A comparison of the spring and fall-tested freshmen regarding college scholarship is made in Table I. Fifty-six and eight tenths per cent. of the SM freshmen received average grades of C, as compared with 51.7 per cent. of the FM freshmen, and 59.0 per cent. of the FNM freshmen. As concerns the number of students receiving C, or satisfactory grades, the FNM group is largest, the SM group next in number and the FM group smallest. In all three groups over half of the freshmen received at least average grades, C or higher. Later tables of data indicate that these large percentages are due to the fact that an unusually large number of students very low in college aptitude rating were given C grades. This fact supports the previous implication about differences between the colleges in standards of grading, course content, and the like.

When these three groups of college freshmen are compared in Table II with respect to college aptitude rating, we find 5.8 per cent. of the SM group above 91 percentile in college aptitude rating, but only 1.9 per cent. of the FM group and 6.3 per cent. of the FNM group.[2] On the other hand, there are 4.7 per cent. of the first group with C.A.R. of 10 or less, 4.6 per cent.

[2] In the remainder of this paper College Aptitude Rating will be designated as C.A.R., High School Scholarship Percentile Rank as H.S.R., and College Aptitude Test Percentile Rank as C.A.T.

TABLE II
COMPARISON OF SPRING AND FALL-TESTED COLLEGE FRESHMEN IN COLLEGE APTITUDE RATING

College aptitude rating	Spring-tested freshmen		Fall-tested freshmen from Minnesota high schools		Fall-tested freshmen from non-Minnesota high schools	
	No.	Per cent.	No.	Per cent.	No.	Per cent.
91–100	37	5.8	3	1.9	14	6.3
81–90	47	7.4	11	7.3	20	9.0
71–80	66	10.4	14	9.4	23	10.4
61–70	79	12.4	9	5.9	33	14.9
51–60	83	13.0	18	11.9	39	17.6
41–50	91	14.3	24	15.9	28	12.6
31–40	88	13.8	26	17.2	29	13.1
21–30	68	10.7	20	13.3	19	8.5
11–20	48	7.5	19	12.6	13	5.8
1–10	30	4.7	7	4.6	4	1.8
Totals	**637**	**100.0**	**151**	**100.0**	**222**	**100.0**
Average C.A.R.		51.05		45.40		55.05
Standard deviation		24.40		23.00		22.55

of the second group, and 1.8 per cent. of the third group. If the use of C.A.R. by high-school teachers and others in the state-wide guidance program of high-school seniors has been effective, we may expect to find a large percentage of high-aptitude students from Minnesota high schools enrolled in college and a small percentage of low-aptitude freshmen. Since the fall-tested freshmen probably have not been subjected to such a guidance program, then we may expect a lower percentage of high-aptitude freshmen and a higher one of low-aptitude students enrolled in college. In other words, does the guidance use of psychological test ratings and high-school scholarship result in the encouragement of potentially "good" students and the discouragement of "poor" students in their college intentions? It does to the extent that we find more high-aptitude freshmen among the SM group than in the FM group. But the number of low-aptitude students is approximately the same for the two groups. We find that the guidance program was successful in persuading a larger percentage of high-aptitude students to go to college, but that it had little deterring effect upon the potentially "poor" college freshmen, since there are 4.7 per cent. of the SM and 4.6 per cent. of the FM freshmen in the first decile of college aptitude rating. But if the number of students of the three groups in the second (11–20) and third (21–30) deciles be compared, we see that the FM freshmen are greater in number and are, therefore, a very unsatisfactory group as regards college aptitude rating. These same differences in number and percentage are present when these three groups are compared with respect to H.S.R. and C.A.T. This evidence bears out what high-school teachers and college administrators have reported on numerous occasions, namely, that it is less difficult to persuade potentially "good" high-school seniors to go to college than it is to dissuade poor students. When we consider the C.A.R. of freshmen who have graduated from non-Minnesota high schools, we find evidence of a highly desirable selection. There are 6.3 per cent. of these freshmen above 91 percentile in C.A.R. and only 1.8 per cent. below a percentile rank of 10. Some selective factors have operated to make the group of non-Minnesota freshmen a potentially higher group as regards college scholarship. We find similar percentages when an approximate upper third of these groups is compared with an approximate lower third in college aptitude rating. This evidence further indicates that the guidance use of combined ratings in college ability test and high-school scholarship increases the number of high-aptitude students who enroll in college, but does not decrease the number enrolling in college. It is also apparent that the enrollment in college of applicants from other states is an efficient method of culling out the scholastic husks from the kernels of the crop of high-school seniors. It is difficult to understand why this is true, unless the potentially poor students tend to select colleges that are situated near their homes.

The average C.A.R. for each of the three groups is given at the bottom of Table II. The FNM group is highest with an average of 55.05 (± 22.55). The FM group has an average of 45.40 (± 23.00) which is the lowest for the three groups; the SM group has an average of 51.05 (± 24.40). We see, therefore, that the groups fall in the same order of aptitude rating

TABLE III

COMPARISON OF THE SCHOLASTIC ACHIEVEMENT OF SPRING AND FALL-TESTED COLLEGE FRESHMEN WITH REGARD TO COLLEGE APTITUDE RATING

College aptitude rating	Spring-tested freshmen from Minnesota high schools			Fall-tested freshmen from Minnesota high schools			Fall-tested freshmen from non-Minnesota high schools		
	No.	No. with C or higher average grades		No.	No. with C or higher average grades		No.	No. with C or higher average grades	
			Per cent.			Per cent.			Per cent.
96–100......	20	20	97.3	1	1	100.0	5	5	100.0
91– 95......	17	16		2	2		9	9	
86– 90......	25	25		8	7		6	6	
81– 85......	22	19	93.5	3	2	82.4	14	14	97.1
76– 80......	31	29		6	5		14	13	
71– 75......	35	25		8	8		9	8	
66– 70......	43	33		1	0		18	15	
61– 65......	36	26	72.1	8	3	65.7	15	10	70.4
56– 60......	40	29		11	7		23	13	
51– 55......	43	29		7	5		16	11	
46– 50......	40	22		13	8		12	9	
41– 45......	51	26	48.9	11	6	55.3	16	5	40.5
36– 40......	42	17		14	7		14	3	
31– 35......	46	18	36.2	12	7	33.3	15	4	25.0
26– 30......	45	15		12	1		13	3	
21– 25......	23	4		8	3		7	1	
16– 20......	27	4		13	5		9	1	
11– 15......	21	3	12.9	6	0	26.5	4	1	13.0
6– 10......	16	1		4	1		3	0	
1– 5......	14	1		3	0		1	0	
Total	637	362	(56.8)	151	78	(51.7)	222	131	(59.0)

Ninety-seven and three tenths per cent. of the SM group with a C.A.R. of 91 or higher earned C averages or higher grades as compared with 100 per cent. of the FM and FNM groups.

as of college scholarship. The FNM freshmen are superior both in aptitude and in scholastic achievement; the FM freshmen are least satisfactory in aptitude and scholarship.

College freshmen from non-Minnesota high schools resemble the SM freshmen in the relationship between C.A.R. and scholarship. That is, a large percentage of the high-aptitude students and a small percentage of low-aptitude freshmen earn satisfactory college grades. The percentage of FM freshmen is less on each level of aptitude except for the 36–50 percentiles and the 1–25 percentiles. The threshold dividing potentially satisfactory from unsatisfactory students has been set by Dean Johnston, for University of Minnesota freshmen, at 26 percentile rank, in C.A.R., when men and women are considered together. Applying this threshold to SM and FM freshmen, we find that 12.9 per cent. of the former and 26.5 per cent. of the latter group, below this threshold, get C or higher grades. A larger percentage of FM freshmen do satisfactory college work, as compared with SM freshmen of similar aptitude. The low-aptitude freshmen who were tested in the fall earned better college grades than did those of the spring group who were low in aptitude. It is difficult to explain why the nine fall-tested Minnesota freshmen below 26 in C.A.R. received grades of C or better. Four of these nine freshmen were in one college, four in another, and the ninth student in a third college. The large number may be due to some difference in course content or grading standards of these three colleges.

From a comparison of these three groups of

freshmen, we may conclude that FNM freshmen are superior to the other two groups, both in college aptitude rating and in college scholarship. The SM freshmen are next in order, and the FM group are lowest in aptitude and in scholarship. This latter group has an unusually large number of low-aptitude freshmen who do satisfactory college work.

Relative Effectiveness of Devices in Predicting College Scholarship

The last section of this report deals with an analysis of the relative efficiency of the college aptitude rating, high school scholarship rank, and college ability test as devices for discovering students most likely to do satisfactory scholastic work and also for discovering those likely to do unsatisfactory or less than C grade work in college. Such an analysis for freshmen in private colleges is not expected to yield results identical with those obtained by Dean Johnston for University of Minnesota students because of possible differences in severity and accuracy of grading systems, differences in scholastic motivation, and other factors affecting achievement. Dean Johnston's most recent report of his research in the prediction of college scholarship is found in the pamphlet issued to the 1930 freshmen applicants at the University of Minnesota and entitled, "Who Should Go To College?" (University of Minnesota Press).

First we shall compare the efficiency of C.A.R., H.S.R. and C.A.T. in predicting achievement of freshmen of high aptitude. Table IV gives the percentage of students of various aptitude levels who do C grade work or better in their freshman year in college, as compared with the total number of students at that level of aptitude. Ninety-eight and one tenth per cent. of the freshmen in the upper decile (91 to 100 inclusive) in C.A.R. do satisfactory scholastic work as compared with 94.5 per cent. and 85.9 per cent. for H.S.R. and C.A.T., respectively. In other words, for purposes of predicting satisfactory scholarship of students high in aptitude, C.A.R. is more efficient than either of the other two devices. We also see that C.A.R. is superior to H.S.R. in predicting satisfactory achievement of students between the 76th and 90th percentile ranks, the percentages being 93.0 and 77.5 of students earning C or higher average grades. C.A.T. is the least efficient of the three devices for predicting satisfactory scholarship of students on all levels of aptitude.

This same tendency for C.A.T. to be least satisfactory in the prediction of scholarship is revealed by the coefficients of correlation between these three devices and H.P.R. (see bottom row of Table IV). The coefficient for C.A.T. is +.64, for H.S.R. +.65, and +.42 for C.A.T. These coefficients are of similar magnitude to those found between these same three predictive devices and H.P.R. for University of Minnesota freshmen in the College of Science, Literature and the Arts, with the exception that C.A.R. was higher than H.S.R.

Next, mention should be made of the fact that there are marked differences among the individual colleges both in the aptitude ratings of their students and in the relationship between these ratings and scholarship. Some colleges have enrolled a large percentage of low-aptitude freshmen. Furthermore, it seems to be easier for low-aptitude freshmen to earn C grades in certain colleges than in others. There was a total of 158 freshmen below 26 in C.A.R.; 108 of these 158 were enrolled in one of three particular colleges. Twenty-five received C average or higher grades; sixteen of these 25 students were enrolled in the same three colleges referred to above. These three colleges are responsible for giving C grades to more than two thirds of the low-aptitude students who were scholastically successful.

H.S.R. is slightly superior to C.A.R. and very much more efficient than C.A.T. in predicting the college scholarship of low-aptitude freshmen. Of the students who were below 26 percentile rank in C.A.R., 15.8 per cent. received C or higher average grades. The corresponding percentages for H.S.R. and C.A.T. are 17.1 and 40.2, respectively. By the use of either of the first two devices, it is possible to identify, with fair accuracy, those students below a certain rank who will do less than C, or unsatisfactory, college work. For this group such a prediction would be accurate in 84.2 per cent. of the cases by use of C.A.R. and in 82.9 per cent. of the cases for H.S.R. If C.A.T. were used alone in the prediction of satisfactory college scholarship, the prediction would be correct in only 59.8 per cent. of the cases.

TABLE IV

The Relative Efficiency of College Aptitude Rating, High School Scholarship and College Ability Test in Predicting College Scholarship

Percentile Rank	College aptitude rating of freshmen in Minnesota colleges 1929			High-school scholarship percentile rank of freshmen in Minnesota colleges 1929			College ability test percentile rank of freshmen in Minnesota colleges 1929		
	Total no.	No. with C or higher average grades		Total no.	No. with C or higher average grades		Total no.	No. with C or higher average grades	
			Per cent.			Per cent.			Per cent.
96–100	26	26	98.1	123	116	94.5	31	29	85.9
91– 95	28	27		61	58		40	32	
86– 90	39	38		68	56		25	21	
81– 85	39	35	93.0	87	70	77.5	20	15	81.5
76– 80	51	47		56	43		36	30	
71– 75	52	41		45	32		46	32	
66– 70	62	48		55	33		32	23	
61– 65	59	39	70.6	46	21	56.4	39	27	67.4
56– 60	74	49		51	33		52	36	
51– 55	66	45		30	9		49	29	
46– 50	65	39		64	24		42	26	
41– 45	78	37	47.9	36	12	36.8	45	26	59.9
36– 40	70	27		36	14		55	33	
31– 35	73	29	36.6	40	6	24.5	43	24	51.9
26– 30	70	19		54	17		59	29	
21– 25	37	8		42	8		53	29	
16– 20	49	10		35	11		70	33	
11– 15	31	4	15.8	25	2	17.1	87	33	40.2
6– 10	23	2		30	3		92	37	
1– 5	18	1		26	3		94	27	
Total	1,010	571		1,010	571		1,010	571	
Correlation with college scholarship (H.P.R.)					r = +.64		r = +.65	r = +.42	

Dean Johnston found that only 1.1 per cent. of University of Minnesota freshmen, below a rank of 26 in C.A.R., received satisfactory grades. The corresponding percentage may be due to the variable difficulty of freshmen courses or other similar factors. For instance, one student in one of the colleges who had a college aptitude rating of only 4, received an honor point ratio of 1.13 because of an A grade in freehand drawing; had it not been for this A grade he would have earned less than the C average predicted by his C.A.R. But another possible interpretation of these percentages is that students of low aptitude in the private colleges profit to such an extent from individualized instruction that they are scholastically motivated beyond what is ordinarily expected of students of corresponding aptitude. This has been the contention of certain educators for many years, but unfortunately such an interpretation of these data is questionable. Still another possible reason for the large number of low-aptitude freshmen in the Minnesota colleges who earned C average or higher grades, is the differences in grading standards of the courses in the several institutions.

We may conclude from an inspection of the data in Table IV that C.A.R. is the most effective of the three devices in the prediction of satisfactory college scholarship of high-aptitude students. But H.S.R. is almost as efficient as C.A.R. in predicting the college scholarship of low-aptitude students. A tentative conclusion from this fact is that in the character of their work some colleges are more nearly like high schools than are others. It is shown above that some colleges gave satisfactory standing to a larger number of low-rating students than did others.

Although H.S.R. and C.A.T. differ in the efficiency of prediction, yet it has been found advisable to use both devices, since some of the small high schools and most of those outside the state fail to supply the colleges with an applicant's scholarship rank. Furthermore averaging H.S.R. and C.A.T. enables one to rectify discrepancies between the two. Some students who do well in high school receive low rankings in the test because of reading difficulties, misunderstanding directions, emotional disturbances or low verbal ability. Averaging these two ranks, in part at least, reduces the serious consequences of an accidentally low test rank. C.A.T. also provides a satisfactory universal yardstick by means of which students from different high schools and colleges may be compared with each other in intellectual capacity. Because of differences in content, standards of grading and other factors, high-school scholarship is not as satisfactory a means of comparison. C.A.T., furthermore, enables college administrators to locate the potentially superior college freshmen and to encourage them to go to college; and, as indicated in the next section it is useful in predicting superior scholarship for high-aptitude freshmen.

Predicting Superior Scholarship

We have seen that C.A.R. is of value in predicting that 84.2 per cent. of freshmen with a C.A.R. of 25 or less receive lower than C grades and also that 98.1 per cent. of students above 75 in C.A.R. will receive satisfactory grades. To what extent will this same predictive device enable us to predict A and B grades? Are we able to select students who do superior scholastic work?

We can answer this question by making a tabulation of C.A.R. and grades in addition to that given in Table IV. We find that there are 183 freshmen with college aptitude rating between 76 and 100. Eighty-five, or 46.4 per cent., of these high-aptitude students received an average grade of B or A. Forty-seven of these 85 superior students were registered in one of two particular colleges; they also contributed over half of the superior students. These two colleges also contributed about half of the low-aptitude students who received satisfactory grades. Table IV shows that 173, or 94.5 per cent., of these same 183 superior students received C or higher grades. There are 394 freshmen who have high-school scholarship ranks above 76. One hundred and twenty-four, or 31.3 per cent., of these students received A or B average grades. Of the 152 students above the 76 percentile in college ability test 58, or 38.2 per cent., earned A or B averages. We conclude that C.A.R. and H.S.R. are not as efficient in predicting superior scholarship of superior students as in predicting that low-aptitude students will do unsatisfactory work. But the fact that less than half of the superior students earn high grades shows that these students are not sufficiently motivated to make full use of their academic ability. In other words, these three devices are satisfactory instruments for culling out the husks from the kernels, but college administrators and teachers must develop more efficient ways of turning out a palatable scholastic product.

Summarizing the findings of this investigation, we may say: (1) The three groups are arranged in this order of their aptitude for college work: fall-tested non-Minnesota high-school graduates, spring-tested Minnesota seniors, and fall-tested Minnesota seniors; (2) The order of college achievement for these three groups is the same; (3) For the prediction of satisfactory college scholarship of low-aptitude students, H.S.R. and C.A.R. are almost equally efficient, and C.A.T. least effective; (4) For the prediction of superior scholarship of high-aptitude college freshmen, C.A.R. is most efficient, C.A.T. next and H. S. R. least satisfactory.

Edmund G. Williamson
University of Minnesota

NEW BOOKS IN EDUCATION

Anthony, Alfred W., Editor. *Philanthropy for the Future.* Pp. 148. Federal Council of the Churches of Christ in America.

Gauss, Marianne. *Book of the Woods.* Pp. xiv + 269. Illustrated. Laidlaw. $1.50.

Lie, Haakon. *Ekorn.* Pp. ix + 150. Illustrated. Laidlaw. $2.00.

Wynne, May. *The Masked Rider.* Pp. ix + 256. Illustrated. Laidlaw. $1.50.

SCHOOL AND SOCIETY

EDITED BY J. McKEEN CATTELL
WITH WHICH IS COMBINED THE
EDUCATIONAL REVIEW
EDITED BY WILLIAM McANDREW

Volume 34 SATURDAY, NOVEMBER 21, 1931 Number 882

POET TAGORE'S UNIVERSITY

By RAMANANDA CHATTERJEE
CALCUTTA, INDIA

RABINDRANATH TAGORE'S UNIVERSITY, known as Visva-Bharati or "World-University," was at first a small school which he founded thirty years ago in Santiniketan, the "Home of Peace."

But why should a poet have established a school for children? Many a time has he told the story.

When he was young, he was sent to school like other boys. His life at school was miserable and absolutely intolerable to him. When he grew up he could clearly understand what it was that hurt him so deeply to attend his school. He had his natural love for life, for nature, and for his surroundings, where he had his dear ones; and to be snatched away from these natural surroundings with which he had all his deeper life of relationship, and to be sent every day for many hours as an exile to the school, to the class with its bare white walls and its stare of dead eyes, frightened him. When he was once inside those walls, he did not feel natural. It was a fragment torn away from life, and this caused him intense misery, because he was uprooted from his own world and sent to surroundings which were dead and unsympathetic, disharmonious and monotonously dull.

It was not possible for the mind of a child to be able to receive anything in those cheerless surroundings, in the environment of dead routine. And the teachers were like living gramophones, repeating the same lessons day by day in a dull manner. His mind refused to accept anything from them. And then there were some teachers who were utterly unsympathetic, and did not understand at all the sensitive soul of a young boy, and tried to punish him for the mistakes he made. Such teachers in their stupidity did not know how to teach, how to impart education to a living mind. And because they failed, they punished their victim. And this was how the boy Tagore suffered when he was thirteen years old. And then he left school, and, in spite of all the efforts of his guardians, he refused to go to school again.

Thus it was the intense misery of his school days which led him in the years of his mature manhood to found a school in natural surroundings where the children would have joy and freedom. He had very profound sympathy for children. And he was also very certain about his knowledge of their psychology. He felt that he could help them more than the ordinary teachers. And I can say from personal knowledge that he is a very able, skilful and inspiring teacher. He can draw out from the minds of children what is there—perhaps in an inchoate form.

In India too much importance is attached to examinations, which the students must pass in order to get some clerical or other job to make a living. The education given in the ordinary schools and colleges takes little count of India's true history, India's past tradition and her civilization. But Tagore wants to give Indian boys and girls an education which is based upon the best that there is in the Indian civilization and tradition, builds them up through and into the soul of India to take hold of India and build the India of the future that all true Indians wish to see. For it should be remembered that, centuries ago, India achieved a soul. This she did pre-eminently in the *Tapovanas* or "Forest Sanctuaries" of her ancient sages and saints. These forest homes of ancient India have always had a special appeal to his mind. He wanted to make his school, in spirit and in externals, as much like these ancient forest homes as modern conditions would permit.

For this purpose, he chose a beautiful place on an upland 100 miles west of Calcutta, far away from the turmoil and contamination of town life. He himself in his young days was brought up in that town, and all the time he had a sort of homesickness for the open country where his heart, his soul, could have its true freedom. He knew that the mind had its own hunger for the ministrations of Mother Nature. And so he selected this spot where the sky is unobstructed to the verge of the horizon. There the mind could have its fearless freedom to create its own dreams, and the seasons could come with all their colors and movements and beauty into the very heart of the homes of men. And there he got a few children around him and taught them. He was their companion. He sang to them. He composed musical pieces, operas and plays, and they took part in the performances. He recited to them the Indian epics. Though it has now been admitted by competent educationists that Tagore has a very penetrating insight into the very best educational theory, people did not at that time have confidence in a poet for bringing up their children and educating them. And so he had only about five or six students to begin with.

His idea was that education should be a part of life itself, and must not be detached from it and be made into something abstract. And so when he brought these children around him, he allowed them to live a complete life. They had perfect freedom to do what they wished—as much liberty as was possible for him to give them. He tried to arouse their interest in all things, in nature's beauty and the surrounding villages, and also in literature. He tried to educate them through play-acting, through listening to music in a natural manner, and not merely by class-teaching.

They knew when the poet was engaged in writing a drama, and they took an intense interest as it went on and developed, and in the process of their rehearsals they acquired a real taste for literature more than they could through formal lessons in grammar and class-teaching. And this was his method. He knew the children's mind. Their sub-conscious mind is more active than the conscious one, and therefore, the important thing is to surround them with all kinds of activities which could stimulate their minds and gradually arouse their interest.

Thus an atmosphere was created, and what was important, this atmosphere provided the students with a natural impulse to live in harmony with it. When Tagore had only a few students, it was easier to feel this. But as the number grew, it became more and more expensive for the poet to carry on the school in his own way. The tradition of India is that it was the responsibility of the teacher to give education to those who came to him to be taught; and in days past—and even at present in some of the old style Sanskrit seminaries—students used to have free tuition and also free lodging in their teacher's house, in recognition of the fact that the teacher, too, in his boyhood and youth had had similar free education. And the poet also began like that, in keeping with the ancient tradition of the country;—he provided his students with free tuition, board and lodging and other necessaries out of his own resources. But he could not maintain the old tradition that it is the duty and the privilege of the teacher to impart education to his students, and that an educational institution is not a shop where one can buy things with money. So gradually his school has, in some directions, taken the shape of an ordinary school.

But the poet still tried to have certain things in his school which are ordinarily lacking in schools recognized by the government education department. His teachers shared the common life with the boys—it was a community life. In the sports and festivals the teachers and the students fully cooperated with one another. This is still true to a great extent.

The idea of a university for higher studies and research was a later development. One object which the poet has in view may be stated in his own words.

> The East, for its own sake and for the sake of the world, must not remain unrevealed. The deepest source of all calamities in history is misunderstanding. For where we do not understand, we can never be just. Being strongly impressed with the need and the responsibility which every individual to-day must realize according to his power, I have formed the nucleus of an International University in India, as one of the best means of promoting mutual understanding between the East and the West. This institution, according to the plan I have in the mind, invites students from the West and the Far East to study the different systems of Indian philosophy, literature, art and music in their proper environment, encouraging them to carry on research work in collaboration with the scholars already engaged in this task.

Accordingly savants from America, England, Norway, France, Czechoslovakia, China, Japan, Hungary, etc., have already visited and worked in this university, and some of them are still at work there. Some foreign students also have come from distant countries. In addition to conserving and teaching what is best in the Indian civilization, Tagore takes whatever good the West has to offer and uses it in an Indian setting for Indian purposes. When Indian civilization is spoken of, it is to be understood that the university seeks to promote the study of Hindu, Jain, Buddhist, Islamic, Sikh, Christian, and other cultures.

As the object of this university is to study the mind of man in its realization of different aspects of truth from diverse points of view, it seeks to touch life at all points. For the realization of spiritual truth, there are collective prayers and hymn-singing and periods of individual meditation every day, and weekly collective worship of the supreme spirit and a sermon in the *Mandir* or temple, conducted by the poet or some senior professor. There are no images and no image-worship here.

In the school and college departments of the institution all ordinary subjects of study are taught. Some science teaching is included. The poet intends to extend the teaching of science as resources expand. As far as practicable, the students are taught through the medium of their vernacular, which is not the case with departmentally recognized institutions. In response to public needs and desires, students are taken through public examination courses; but there are additional courses intended to give them a liberal education.

The institution is residential. Santiniketan is a hamlet which owes its origin and existence to the university. It is at a distance of about two miles from the nearest town, but has its own post and telegraph office, telephone, motor bus, electric light, cooperative stores, bank and other modern facilities.

From the infant department right up to the highest research class, the institution is co-educational. The number of girls has been steadily increasing. Boys and girls have separate dormitories and playgrounds. They have a common life as regards festivals, and meetings for lectures, speeches, recitation of poems composed by them, story-telling, reading of essays, singing, etc. There are frequent picnics in the neighboring woods and riverside in which boys and girls take part. Once a year in winter there are long excursions to some place of interest, during which the boys do some of the rough work and the girls cooking, etc. They take tents and some provisions with them.

Among the teachers and professors there are both men and women. The poet desires to have more women among the staff. One woman graduate teaches Sanskrit in all the college classes containing both young men and young women and is in addition in charge of the infant department.

Santiniketan has made a name for games, both Indian and Western. There are various kinds of athletic exercises. An expert teacher of Jiujitsu has been brought out from Japan to teach that art to students of all ages. Under his instruction some girls and young women and some boys and young men have become proficient in it.

Classes are usually held in the open, under the leafy branches of trees, in whose groves the Ashram is set. There are no classrooms. The beauty of nature is ever before the students. There is an atmosphere of peace and meditation. "In such surroundings," writes the poet, "the ancient forest-dwellers of India realized the spirit of harmony with the Universe." This spirit is induced in every aspect of his Ashram.

No side of human culture is neglected here. This school is one of the greatest centers of truly creative work in the art of painting in India to-day. Students come from different parts of India and the world to study in it. Various useful arts and crafts are also taught.

The music section embodies the ideal of a new school of Indian music initiated by the poet by writing the music for his own songs. Both vocal and instrumental music are taught.

In Bengal, dancing had come to be looked upon as disreputable for girls and women of respectable families. Holding the right view that dancing is a part of culture, Tagore has had many of the girl students taught graceful rhythmic movement and some of them have become expert in it, as he himself is.

The poet has written many plays fit to be acted by his students. They are suited to different seasons and moods. During the seasonal festivals in Santiniketan, there is music, dancing, decoration with the flowers of the season, and the acting of some of these plays. The poet being himself a great actor, the students also can act well under his guidance and training.

Tree-planting and ceremonial ploughing are parts of the "Festival of the Rains." On this occasion, in addition to the other features, the poet sometimes reads an appropriate story specially composed for the purpose. There is sometimes a sort of masque during this festival, in which the five Indian mythological elements of Fire, Air, Earth, Water and Sky appear in fancy costumes. On the boundary wall of a field used for the ploughing ceremony, there is a long fresco representing different agricultural operations.

Visva-Bharati has a useful library. It differs from other university libraries in India in that it contains a larger collection of German, French and Italian books and learned societies' journals. These books were presented by the governments of Germany, France and Italy. King Fuad of Egypt has presented a choice selection of Arabic books. There are many old Sanskrit manuscripts in this library. It is housed in a two-storied building, of which the upper story contains fine frescoes on the walls of the verandahs.

In the research department of this university, literary and philosophical researches are carried on. In ancient times many Sanskrit works were translated into Tibetan and Chinese. The Sanskrit originals of many of these Chinese and Tibetan translations are no longer extant. In the Visva-Bharati research department the work of retranslation into Sanskrit of these Tibetan and Chinese translations is going on. The library contains a collection of Tibetan manuscripts, including the Tibetan Encyclopaedia, and a collection of Chinese works. The courses of studies include French, German, Tibetan, Chinese, Persian, Sanskrit, Pali and Arabic, in addition to Bengali and English.

There is self-government among the students here. They elect their own captains and judges and settle their own disputes. If any student does anything wrong, he is tried by the students' court. There is no invigilation at examinations.

This university does not observe any distinctons of caste and creed. Students of all castes may, and most of them do, dine together. The kitchen arrangements are under the charge of the lady superintendent of the women's hostel. Periodically cooking and serving for the day are done by the students themselves, the men students drawing water and doing other similar work, and the women students preparing the vegetables for cooking and washing the dishes.

Feeling keenly the divorce of the existing educational system from our every-day life, the poet wanted to lay the foundations of education on the firm basis of the life of the people. As the vast majority of the people of India—and specially of Bengal—live in villages, our true national life has always been rural. For the re-constitution and improvement of this village life the poet has established the Institute of Rural Reconstruction in connection with his university. Its need will be evident from what the poet writes:

> "At one time our villages were in intimate contact with the manifold culture of India. They were cherished and served by all capable persons with the best that their minds produced. To-day the villages are fatally neglected. They are fast degenerating into serfdom, compelled to offer to the ungrateful towns cheerless and unintelligent labour for work carried on in an unhealthy and impoverished environment. The object of our Institute is to bring back life in its completeness into the villages, making them self-reliant and self-respectful, acquainted with the cultural tradition of their own country and competent to make efficient use of modern resources for the improvement of their physical, intellectual and economic condition."

The institute has adopted the policy that regeneration of the village must take place in all aspects of village life and along lines which the villager himself, once taught, will be encouraged to pursue of his own desire and with his own resources. There is in this institute an experimental agricultural farm for demonstrating modern methods to classes of villagers; a sericultural farm for re-introducing silk culture into the district by training village young men; a School of Arts and Crafts giving instruction to villagers in spinning, weaving, dyeing, carpentry, tanning, poultry-keeping, etc.; an adult and elementary school; and the central organization of a system of rural banks with over 220 branches to give help to agricultural and industrial enterprises among the peasants. The institute has a meteorological observatory. Social workers from the institute live in the surrounding villages and organize cooperative societies among the villagers. These societies engage in many kinds of communal help, such as rural banks, communal irrigation, elementary schools, medical relief and public health work. They render aid in such emergencies as famine and epidemics. During popular fairs and festivals, when thousands of pilgrims congregate, the staff and students of Visva-Bharati work day and night to make and maintain hygienic and sanitary arrangements. Every year there is a training camp for teaching village work. There are troops of village boys for doing such work.

The district in which the university is situated was once very healthy and prosperous. Decay set in about 50 years ago. Owing to the efforts of the workers and students, the university has been able, in some measure, to obtain the whole-hearted confidence and cooperation of the villagers. Already the good results are beginning to be manifest. Dr. Harry G. Timbres, an American medical man, reports that "In the villages organized under the Institute of Rural Reconstruction the incidence of malaria is becoming less each year, the peasants are moving back into these villages, and the general economic level is rising."

Apart from this institute, the boys and girls of Santiniketan have their own society for village welfare work. They have founded a school for giving elementary general and technical education in a neighboring village; they undertake the nursing of sick villagers; they make roads and drains for the villagers; and engage in other kinds of beneficent work as occasion requires. In all these activities, they receive cooperation and help from the villagers themselves.

WHAT AM I REALLY DOING?

By Professor H. W. FARWELL
COLUMBIA UNIVERSITY

SOME months ago I was interested in reading Dr. Tildsley's report on the science teaching in New York City high schools. Several points were made on which further comment might have been offered, but after attempting to make some of those comments, I laid them aside as being perhaps of so little worth that they would serve only for my own amusement. Recently, however, some discussions have indicated that possibly those matters were of interest to others, and I have ventured to recast my thoughts in a more general form.

Criticism is a valuable tool but an ugly weapon. If it can be used in the proper constructive spirit it is of the greatest service, but it should not cut where it is not intended to cut. A survey of science teaching, properly conducted, should be welcomed by all those involved. Yet it ought not to be entirely a matter of occasional inquiry from already overloaded administrators. It seems that every physics teacher ought to do a little inquiring himself. Let him answer at not too long intervals. "What do I think that I am doing?" And then "What am I really doing?" In general the answers are not identical, and it is possible that some teachers actually do not know the answer to the first query, much less that to the second.

To show what I mean two illustrations will suffice. One is an old story, the other quite recent, but they belong in the same book. A certain high-school teacher asked to see a special piece of apparatus used in the physics laboratory for college freshmen. After inspecting carefully, he expressed himself as satisfied, and then asked, "What accuracy do you require with this?" My answer was that we did not require any particular accuracy. Evidently he felt that his question was misunderstood, for he said, "In using this apparatus what per cent. error is your limit?" Again I said that we did not have a limit.

Then came the deluge, "To think that I have lived to see such a day! In an institution of this magnitude, and you have no requirements in precision! Why did I ever come into this building?"

It was necessary to interrupt him to ask, "How long have you been teaching physics?" "Twelve years." "And haven't you learned in that time that whatever arbitrary precision limit you set up for your pupils, they will see to it that by some means or other they come inside your limit; that if you won't accept a report with an error as great as one per cent. you will always get results which conform?" "I never thought about that." "Now it is my turn to be shocked, only I shall probably stay shocked. What you have been doing amounts to little else than putting a premium on dishonesty. Personally I prefer to have the student feel that the most important thing is to report exactly what he finds."

The other illustration needs no comment. I shall merely reproduce verbatim a page from a laboratory notebook submitted in fulfilment of a college admission requirement.

EXPERIMENT 42

Electroplating

Apparatus:—Cell, connecting wires: copper sulphate solution large steel wire nails: glass beaker.

Method:—We scoured the nails thoroughly with sandpaper and washed them off with clean water. We wound around the head of each a half dozen turns of copper wire from which the insulation had been stripped. We connected one nail with the plus terminal of the battery and another with the minus. We dipped the nails into the solution of copper sulphate and observed what took place on each nail. After the battery had been sending current for about ten minutes we took out the nails and examined them. We washed and dryed them and tried the effect of rubbing each of them with an eraser.

We changed the connections of the nails to battery so that the one that was connected to the plus will now be connected to the minus, and the one that was attached to the minus to the plus. We dipped the nails into the solution and observed what took place.

Conclusion:—The Cu of the solution was set free at the cathode and the SO_4 at the anode. The copper ion in the copper sulphate goes in the same direction as the current in the solution. The oxygen goes in the opposite direction. The copper ions are charged with a plus current.

Experiences of this sort make one very meek indeed, and, if he is honest with himself, wish with Bobbie Burns that some power would gie us a giftie. "What are we really doing?" In the first case the teacher seemed at least to think that he was inculcating an appreciation of the necessity and value of precise measurement, and I know from bitter experience that over-emphasis on precision and arbitrary limits (frequently unjustified by the apparatus supplied) lead to no such end. I don't know what the second teacher thought he was doing, though I'll guess that he had the idea that he was meeting the requirements of the College Entrance Examination Board. I have, however, a definite notion about what he actually was doing. If these were characteristic illustrations of physics teaching it would be easy to answer the objection that science teaching has accomplished nothing in the way of raising the level of general intelligence. We could say simply, "We haven't been teaching science."

Of course I am well aware that the cases mentioned are quite extreme, but I feel sure that unless the teacher has recently put himself and his work under honest scrutiny he is apt to provide samples, perhaps not so ridiculous, for the benefit of the official investigator.

The two illustrations may also serve to raise a question about the value of laboratory work in general. One may say without fear of serious contradiction that in the two schools concerned the laboratory work in physics was practically of no value whatever, and actually did considerable damage. There is such a wide range in what is called laboratory practice that detailed criticism is of no point here, but it may be said in general that the best of laboratories loses ground the minute that its procedure is so uniform that it can all be put into cold type. Years ago a very careful observer said to me, "Keep your laboratory manual always in temporary form."

However, that is not the whole of this particular story. There seems to be a fairly wide-spread feeling that the laboratory work in the high schools could be made much better were it not for the rigid requirements of the College Entrance Examination Board or the Board of Regents or some other board. I have had experience with various boards over a considerable number of years, have prepared many entrance examinations, and I have yet to see anywhere any statement that the student "must do such and such experiments in a thus and so fashion." There is need enough of supervision and guidance—alas, that it is so—but if there is any real head of an educational system who wouldn't welcome the efforts of a live competent teacher to keep his laboratory program free from the microbe that produces dry rot that fact ought to be published.

I wonder sometimes if teachers of physics in high schools realize that in many colleges the students who have had no physics in high school are placed in the same class with those who have, and that in many cases the evidence seems to indicate that those with no previous course do the better work. On the other hand, I wonder just as often why those colleges will credit one student with an entrance unit in physics and then treat him as though he did not have it. Somewhere there is a strange inconsistency, and it does not appear that the high schools are entirely in the wrong.

One of the criticisms is that the average student who comes to college with an entrance unit in physics has quite the wrong idea of the subject, partly due at least to the presentation of the material as a "book" subject. The text-book is the court of last resort, and the experimental side is all too often lost in a maze of formulas. This situation is not improved by the incorporation in algebra courses of the "physics formulas."

To go further with the matter let us suppose that one presents the argument that so far as physics is concerned the average teacher of mathematics is doing more harm than good. In support of this argument are numerous points. For example, a colleague in social science says, "I wish I had an easy subject like physics, all that you need to do is to memorize a rather limited number of formulas, and there you are." Again most of the students who come into physics classes after having been given "enriched" courses in mathematics seem to have acquired entirely the wrong idea of the mathematical aspect of the subject. "We were told that this was the formula which the physicist used for such and such."

Further, many teachers of physics are so taken with the beauty of mathematical rigor that all phenomena are to them merely occurrences in obedience to laws laid down by Boyle, Newton and others. The experimental side of the subject is slighted or completely overlooked. The results of human effort in measurement are regarded in the same light as are the numbers adopted by the mathematician. They are complete, fixed and definite. Yet it is a matter of common knowledge that more and more are the limitations of measurement becoming evident and that processes which have been treated as simple are in fact quite complex.

These objections are not raised for the purpose of proposing to present physics without mathematics. That is an impossibility, the quantitative aspect of physics is the real joy of the subject. Kelvin expressed that idea many years ago. But certainly physics should not be taught as being the slave of mathematics. The first question which comes up is naturally, "What happens?" That being answered, there are numerous other questions crowding in, and if in order to answer them mathematics is called upon to aid in expressing ideas, such appeal does not put the phenomena under control of the logarithm table.

Another point on which much can be said has reference to the much-discussed "Keeping up to date." Teachers of physics all over the country, occupied as they are with much routine and many classes, find not too much time for deep study of new developments, and to date there seems not to have been any too generous an attitude on the part of somebody to see that what little time they have can be used to best advantage. The debatable ground here lies around what is meant by "keeping up to date," and in the backyard of "somebody."

In many instances keeping up to date is absolutely out of the question; any effort of the sort is merely sham and pretense, and leads only to a breeding of superficiality which is worse than ignorance. One would hardly recommend to an average high-school boy for his graduation essay the topic "Relativity." Keeping alive is important, but to pretend that one is really conversant with last night's discoveries when it is not the case is to be worse than ridiculous.

At the risk of being considered at least ridiculous I would suggest in the first place that the high-school teacher with a background of not more than one year of college work in physics certainly doesn't make much of an impression when he drops casually into a college professor's office and says in effect: "For five years I haven't looked at anything outside of the text I am using. Tell me in a few short snappy phrases what has been happening." The necessary preparation for teaching certainly includes a sufficient study of fundamentals to enable the student to recognize applications when they present themselves, and it ought to be enough to permit the individual to go ahead by himself a long distance. To be specific I will state my opinion that no one should consider himself properly grounded in the fundamentals of physics before he has carefully studied analytical mechanics.

The methods by which the average high-school teacher can keep alive are various, but they are not all as good as they ought to be. "Somebody" is not looking out for that situation. It might be that if an altruistic soul took it upon himself to do for this great body of teachers the sort of thing that Dr. Karl Darrow does for the Bell Telephone Laboratories the situation would be cleared decidedly. Yet it is not obvious that this is the best solution, since such a plan is stimulated from the outside. The finest periodical for publication of results of physical research is the *Physical Review,* supported by the physicists themselves. If it is not satisfactory to the majority, that is their own fault. By analogy, the identification of "somebody" is more or less apparent.

On the whole the proper methods of stimulating teachers are already in operation, but, as it seems to me, generally at very low efficiency. Individual action may not be able to effect much change, but group action certainly could accomplish a great deal. It is doubtful if we need more writing of the "popular" type, but we do need better writing, and popular articles by authoritative workers ought to be made more available. Yet publishers would surely hear a sound made by a group as large as the body of physics teachers of the United States.

Perhaps the answer to this point is that at present there is no way in which those teachers can make a collected noise. Yet there are all over the country organizations of science teachers with more or less regular meetings. To be sure at some of those meetings the most important business seems to be the reading of the minutes of the last meeting. It ought to be possible to make every one of these groups a unit in a general organization which could then make a forward move for the benefit of all.

This point about material for reading is highly important, yet frankly I feel that some of the teachers of physics are not exactly using great judgment in the matter. For example, every year I get numerous requests from teachers as well as from students for reading lists, and at the same time they must know as well as I do that practically every general text in college physics published in the last ten years has a wealth of references to general and special topics.

The articles appearing in the new "Reviews of Modern Physics" ought to attract attention from high-school teachers, not that they should be expected to master all of every article, but at least that they should be able to recognize authority and try to distinguish between good opinion and poor opinion. There is some excellent material issued from the Bureau of Standards as well as from other laboratories which ought to help in keeping the experimental side of physics from being completely lost. However, this is not the place to propose a reading list, only to suggest a suitable means of keeping a live list in view.

In this connection there seems to be a reasonable doubt about the desirability of some of the efforts which have been made in the direction of following the interest of the younger students. Some high-school teachers have advocated giving up the classical physics courses and substituting radio courses, "because after all that's what the boys want." Perhaps it is even more necessary than ever to look over the whole situation and try to find out what is the real job to be done. If the job is to give the student a background of science, on which he may lay out in later years such further detail as his interest and opportunity may warrant, the procedure is somewhat different from that designed to train specialists in the art of picking up any given broadcasting station from any given point.

There is then plenty of need for self-inquiry, and if this serves its purpose it seems not to matter so much whether official surveys are made or not. But without criticism of some sort it is quite easy for any one to get into a "so-so" state, and perhaps to remain there without realizing that such is really the case.

As a final remark it is perhaps unkind to say that for many teachers of physics the best way of keeping alive is to study if not less pedagogy at least more physics. Twice within one recent week have I been faced with a variety of the question as to how much moisture "the air can hold," and frequently with an entirely erroneous concept of Newton's Third Law of Motion. The list would be fairly long if made complete, yet I am not here considering the statements made to me by students.

Lest the intent of this article be misunderstood, I am quite willing to admit that I am frequently wrong and undoubtedly make my full share of blunders, oft-times adverse criticism sends shivers up my spine, and in general I seem to react about the same way that any normal human reacts. Yet when all is said, there is a situation in elementary science (physics as bad as the rest), which most of us feel should be improved. Instead of saying, "Somebody ought to do something about it," I have made a poor attempt to offer a grain of constructive criticism in the spirit of a teacher who has recently uncovered some of his own shortcomings.

EDUCATIONAL EVENTS

ATHENS COLLEGE

A DISPATCH to *The New York Sun* states that the Greek government has passed a law which exempts Greek boys from other countries who are enrolled as students in Athens College from military service. Greeks in all parts of the world are anxious to send their sons to Greece to attend school so that they may learn the language and become familiar with the country of their ancestors.

Since Athens College was founded in 1925 boys have come from the United States, England, Egypt, South Africa, Indo China and other countries to study there, but the number has been limited because many such boys have been subject to military service.

Appreciating the opportunity offered by the Athens College, the Greek government gave serious consideration to means of facilitating the coming of boys of Greek parentage to Athens for the purpose of study, and enacted a law exempting them from military service as follows:

> Children of Greeks domiciled abroad who desire to study in public or private schools in Greece may return to their families without hindrance, and with no restriction as to the performance of their military obligations.

Consular authorities have been advised to furnish those eligible with a card of identity specifically mentioning this scholastic condition, which can be presented to the authorities when necessary.

Such boys are required to be enrolled in a school within a period of three months after their arrival in Greece. Their annual enrolment and their regular studies will be certified on the identification card by and upon the responsibility of the principal of the school.

Upon the termination of their studies, or in case of interruption, they must leave for abroad within a period of three months, leaving their cards at the enrolment bureau of the war ministry, which will furnish them with a departure permit. Any one who belongs to a class serving under the colors and who fails to conform to these requirements, will be required to complete his military obligations.

The course at Athens College has been lengthened by one year, with a reduction of class periods each year, reduction of material to be studied each year, rearrangement of the courses on the basis of the capabilities of students of various ages, increase in time allotted to study, laboratory work and recreation.

This reorganization was approved by the governing boards and by the ministry of education and the ministry of national economy, as Athens College is looked upon as a laboratory in which educational methods can be tested and proved before they are assimilated by the public school system of Greece.

SALARY REDUCTIONS IN WALES

THE London *Times Educational Supplement* states that the Carmarthenshire education committee have decided to reduce the salaries of their teachers by a uniform reduction of 10 per cent. This, together with other reductions, will save the county over £2,000. As a result of requests from a deputation representing the school managers of the county, the committee have decided to consider what additional duties can be added to the work of the local managers so that they may be encouraged to take a keener interest in the schools. Among other matters the local managers would like to be able to appoint all assistant teachers subject to confirmation by the county authority, and to be given extended powers in the care and administration of the schools. The powers of the Carmarthenshire managers have been considerably curtailed, and unless more responsibility is given, lack of local interest will in time interfere with the efficiency of the schools.

The Swansea education authority expects to gain over £3,000 by the 10 per cent. reduction which it is proposed to make in the salaries of the teachers. The reduction in grants so far as elementary education is concerned will involve a slight loss; on the other hand, the reduction in the salaries of the secondary teachers more than makes up for this loss. It was reported that the Burnham committee will meet soon to draft the conditions of a new scale of salaries which is to come into operation in March next. The education committee have agreed to make a grant of £200 in aid of the work of the joint committee for the promotion of educational facilities in the coal fields of South Wales and Monmouthshire. This committee has already done remarkable work in the South Wales coal field. The workmen's institutes and libraries in the valleys have been surveyed, and in many instances the stocks of books have been replenished. Courses of lectures in conjunction with the Workers' Educational Association have been organized, and through the National Council of Music classes, concerts and music clubs have been arranged. Under the present scheme the Carnegie United Kingdom Trustees are contributing a sum in aid of the work, provided the local authorities, such as Monmouthshire, Carmarthenshire, Merthyr, the Rhondda, Swansea and others contribute proportionate amounts. Most of the local authorities have agreed to subscribe, and there is every hope that the work will continue. The senate of the University College, Swansea, is also organizing regular daily courses for the unemployed in the district, and it is proposed to organize a number of musical festivals on the model of the Three Valleys Festival.

Unemployment in South Wales is still increasing and the burden falls heavily upon the young boy or girl between the ages of 14 and 16 years. Last month the "live" register for boys and girls in Cardiff stood at 1,100, the highest ever recorded by the Juvenile Employment Bureau. The usual efforts are made to induce the boys and girls to remain at school. At the end of last term it was found that 850 boys and girls were qualified to leave. Of these 226 had returned to school in the following term. But they soon leave either to take or to look for jobs before the term is out. Last term 191 (116 boys and 75 girls) had remained at school, after eight weeks 141 (72 boys and 69 girls) were still at school, and in the fourteenth week of the term there were 123 (60 boys and 63 girls).

EDUCATION IN THE PROVINCE OF SASKATCHEWAN

To carry education to children in remote settlements where adequate schools are difficult to maintain, the provisional government of the Province of Saskatchewan, Canada, has developed the use of correspondence courses until this year it has an enrolment of nearly 10,000, according to a statement made by Mr. J. T. M. Anderson, minister of education, who sponsored the plan which has been summarized in *The New York Times*. To the lessons given by printed instructions also has been added this year a series of half-hour radio talks five days a week.

The population of this wheat-producing province is more than 70 per cent. rural, living in widely scattered settlements. The correspondence school was organized in 1925. Included among those now enrolled are children whose homes are situated outside organized school districts, crippled and ailing children whose disability prevents them from attending school, adults who are anxious to acquire the rudiments of an education but whose age prevents them from attending grade school, and returned soldiers whose education was interrupted by war service.

The courses for the first eight public-school grades are prepared by professional teachers. There is no charge for tuition and readers are supplied free of charge to the six junior grades. Approximately 6,000 students are taking high-school courses. Some of these are studying entirely at home and others are supplementing the work of the rural courses they attend. The high-school courses are organized by university specialists and follow the course of study prescribed by the department of education. A year's work in each subject is divided into about twenty lessons, each of which requires about two weeks' study. In most cases small tuition fees are charged for high-school courses, but due to the prevailing economic situation the government has waived fees in certain cases.

The supplementary radio broadcasts are made possible by the cooperation of the broadcasting stations in the province and the provincial government department of telephones, which has arranged the necessary hook-ups. Radio lessons are being given in English, history, science, Latin, French and German. The talks also deal with the difficulties of the pupils and answer questions that are daily reaching the school from both pupils and teachers.

Questionnaires as to the value of the broadcasts, the most interesting subjects and suggestions they may have to offer are being sent to the pupils.

NEW BUILDINGS AT ATLANTA UNIVERSITY

It is reported in *The New York Times* that on the sixty-acre campus of Atlanta University, which is situated on the highest point of land in the Southern metropolis, there are under construction, or soon to be constructed, buildings costing in the neighborhood of $1,000,000. These include an administration building, men's and women's dormitories, a dining hall and a residence for the president, all of which have been made possible by the gift of $1,000,000 from an anonymous donor.

They include also a library which has been provided by the General Education Board and for which the corner-stone has just been laid. Under the terms of the grant the library is to be available not only to the students of the university and affiliated colleges, but to the other Negro institutions of higher learning in Atlanta—Morris Brown College, Clark University and Gammon Theological Seminary—which may enter into cooperative arrangements with Atlanta University for the use of the library.

Thus, according to President John Hope, there is being developed in the very heart of the South a Negro university that will conform to the highest standards of scholarship. For more than sixty years the university has trained men and women for professional careers, largely as teachers and school and college executives. Recently its effectiveness has been increased by its affiliation with two neighboring institutions, Morehouse College for men, which was founded in 1867 and has become the largest college for Negro men in the country, and Spelman College for women, established in 1881 and named for the parents of Mrs. John D. Rockefeller, Sr., who were among its earliest patrons. Each of the three institutions retains its corporate identity, but close cooperation in all matters is assured.

The development, according to a statement from the college, reflects a change that is taking place in the life of the Negro in the South. The statement says:

> Slowly, perhaps, but inevitably, Negroes are assuming control of their own economic, social and educational life. In increasing numbers they are engaging in business, entering the professions and taking full charge of their schools and social welfare agencies. In the changing Negro college, accordingly, where once the emphasis was on training in agriculture, domestic science and the trades, the students to-day are preparing to become business men, lawyers, physicians, social workers, librarians and, of course, teachers and ministers.
>
> There is abundant opportunity, to be sure, for Negro youth to become trained farmers, artisans and domestics. Every Southern state maintains an agricultural and mechanical college for Negroes; in many privately endowed or church-supported colleges work in shop and field is offered. The noteworthy fact, however, is that the life of the artisan is no longer the chief goal of the Negro boy or girl who goes beyond the grade school; increasingly they seek fields of larger usefulness, and in business and professional careers they are finding such opportunities.

LIBERAL ARTS COLLEGE BROADCAST

President Hoover and spokesmen of the liberal arts colleges of America participated in a nation-wide "college night" radio program broadcast on Saturday, November 14, from 9:00 to 9:30 P. M., Eastern Standard Time, over an NBC–WEAF network.

Other speakers were Dr. John H. Finley, associate editor of *The New York Times;* Dr. A. N. Ward, chairman of the Liberal Arts College Movement; Dr. C. R. Mann, director of the American Council on Education, and Dr. Robert L. Kelly, executive secretary of the Association of American Colleges.

The coast-to-coast program was dedicated to the liberal arts colleges and their contributions to the educational, social and economic life of the country. Local broadcasts under auspices of individual colleges preceded and followed the national half hour. Alumni groups throughout the country met to hear the programs.

President Hoover, delivering the principal address from the White House, was the final speaker. Dr. Finley, talking from the NBC New York studios, introduced the speakers who, with the exception of the President and Dr. Mann, addressed the nation from New York.

"This national broadcast is a concerted effort to interpret the needs, aims and achievements of the college," according to an announcement made by Albert St. Peter, executive secretary. "It seeks to strengthen the appreciation of the public for the contributions the liberal arts college has made to American civilization and to enlist the sympathetic cooperation and support of the people."

Nine regional directors organized the local rallies. They included:

President Daniel L. Marsh, Boston University, for Connecticut, Maine, Massachusetts, New Hampshire, Rhode Island and Vermont.

President George L. Omwake, Ursinus College, for Delaware, District of Columbia, Maryland, New Jersey, New York and Pennsylvania.

President Rees E. Tulloss, Wittenberg College, for Illinois, Indiana, Iowa, Kansas, Michigan, Missouri, Nebraska and Ohio.

President W. J. McGlothlin, Furman University, for Florida, North Carolina, South Carolina, Virginia and West Virginia.

President Guy E. Snavely, Birmingham-Southern College, for Alabama, Georgia, Kentucky, Louisiana, Mississippi and Tennessee.

President E. McS. Waits, Texas Christian University, for Arkansas, Oklahoma and Texas.

President D. J. Cowling, Carleton College, for Minnesota, North Dakota, South Dakota and Wisconsin.

Chancellor F. M. Hunter, University of Denver, for Colorado, Idaho, Montana, New Mexico, Utah and Wyoming.

President Charles K. Edmunds, Pomona College, for Arizona, California, Oregon and Washington.

The programs were arranged under the auspices of the Liberal Arts College Movement, the Association of American Colleges and the American Council on Education.

THE YALE-IN-CHINA TWENTY-FIFTH ANNIVERSARY

THE twenty-fifth anniversary of the opening of Yale-in-China at Changsha was celebrated at Yale University on November 16. On November 16, 1906, the Collegiate School of Yale-in-China was opened in a rented building in the heart of the city of Changsha. In 1914 a permanent site for Yale-in-China was purchased on high open ground outside the city, and the campus now includes a hospital, a chapel, a science hall, quarters for the medical school, dormitories, recitation buildings and faculty residences. In all, there are thirty buildings on forty-two acres of land which belong to the institution.

The trustees, the founders and faculty, and the alumni of Yale-in-China, as well as the alumni of Yale University, were represented at the exercises. Addresses were given by Dr. Arthur B. Dayton, chairman of the Board of Trustees; Dr. Anson Phelps Stokes, canon of Washington Cathedral, former chairman of the Board of Trustees; Ying Kai Shih, proctor of the Middle School at Yale-in-China, and a graduate in the class of 1924; and by the Rev. Elmore M. McKee, former chaplain of Yale University, now rector of Trinity Church, Buffalo, N. Y. The benediction was pronounced by Dean Luther A. Weigle, of the Yale Divinity School.

It was in 1902 that Yale-in-China was organized in New Haven by a group of Yale alumni, and Lawrence Thurston sent out to China as its first representative. A year later the authorities of Hunan Province invited the Yale Mission to Changsha to undertake the work of providing an institution of higher education for the province. In 1904 the first representative of Yale-in-China, Mr. Brownell Gage and Mrs. Gage, reached Changsha with Professor and Mrs. Harlan P. Beach, to make a survey of the situation. The following year Mr. Gage and Mr. Warren Seabury took up their residence in Changsha, and Dr. Edward H. Hume reached China. In the fall of 1906 William J. Hail joined the staff, and on November 16 of that year the Collegiate School was opened with an enrolment of twenty-two students. In 1908 the temporary hospital was opened for service to the community. Two years later Dr. F. C. Yen, first American trained Chinese on the staff, came to assist in the medical work. The first class was graduated from the Collegiate School in 1912 and two years later the College of Yale-in-China was opened, and the Hunan-Yale plan for cooperation in medical education was formed. The first buildings on the present campus were completed in 1916; in 1918 the Hunan-Yale Hospital was finished, and in the following year Yale-in-China was given power to grant degrees by the Connecticut Legislature.

From 1919 to the winter of 1927 Yale-in-China saw steady growth in all departments, with increasing support from friends in China and America. In January, 1927, a serious outbreak occurred in Changsha, which resulted in the evacuation of all foreigners from the city. The work at Yali (as the Chinese call Yale) had to be given up for the most part for over a year, but the campus, left in charge of faithful members of the Chinese staff, remained unharmed.

In the fall of 1928 work was resumed on the Yale-in-China campus with the opening of the Yali Union Middle School, organized under a cooperative agreement between Yale-in-China and four other mission boards. A little later, with the active assistance of Chinese in the province, the hospital and Medical School were reopened and the Nursing School was reorganized. Since Yali could not undertake alone the financial responsibility of senior college work, it was decided to transfer this part of the work to Central China College at Wuchang, one hundred miles from Changsha. Under the present agreement, Yale-in-China supports the department of sciences in the college at Wuchang, of which Dr. Francis Wei is president. Dr. Paul Kwei, formerly at Yali, is dean of the school of sciences.

EDUCATIONAL NOTES AND NEWS

DR. CHARLES F. THWING, president emeritus of Western Reserve University, celebrated his seventy-eighth birthday on November 10.

DR. FRANK PORTER GRAHAM was installed as president of the University of North Carolina on November 11. He succeeded Dr. Harry W. Chase, now president of the University of Illinois.

DR. HOMER PRICE RAINEY, formerly president of Franklin College, Franklin, Indiana, was installed as president of Bucknell University on November 13.

DR. RALPH C. HUTCHISON, for thirty-three years dean of the American College at Teheran, Persia, has been elected president of Washington and Jefferson College. He succeeds Dr. S. S. Baker, who has resigned.

DR. WILLIAM S. LADD, formerly of the College of Physicians and Surgeons of Columbia University, has been appointed associate dean and assistant professor of medicine.

MR. PATRICK T. CAMPBELL has been named superintendent of schools in Boston, to succeed the late Jeremiah Burke. Mr. Edward J. Muldoon, master of the Bigelow district, South Boston, is the new assistant superintendent.

DR. WILLIAM WARNER BISHOP, librarian of the University of Michigan, was elected to the presidency of the International Federation of Library Associations, at the recent meeting at Cheltenham, England. Dr. Bishop attended the meeting as chairman of the committee on international relations of the American Library Association.

DR. JOHN R. CHILDS has been appointed assistant professor of education at Teachers College, Columbia University. Eleanor M. Witmer has been made librarian of Teachers College and assistant professor of education, and Edgar Wallace Knight is visiting professor of education.

PROFESSOR FRANK L. MARTIN, dean of the University of Missouri School of Journalism, has been granted a year's leave of absence to permit an exchange of professorships with Yenching University, China.

A PROTEST over the arrest of Dr. Carlos de la Torre, seventy-six-year-old dean of science at Havana University, has begun to take form. Individual friends have appealed to the State Department at Washington for information concerning his imprisonment.

GOVERNOR WILBUR L. CROSS of Connecticut will head the National Institute of Arts and Letters during the coming year.

DR. L. P. JACKS, principal of Manchester

College, Oxford, England, spoke on "Education and Leisure" at the Horace Mann School on November 17.

Professor Frederick J. E. Woodbridge, of Columbia University, opened his courses in philosophy as visiting Roosevelt professor at Berlin University with an inaugural address delivered on November 11.

Dr. Howard E. Wilson, of the Harvard Graduate School of Education, lectured on "Recent Trends in Education" on November 13 at the fall meeting of the Massachusetts Society for the University Education of Women.

Dr. A. Monroe Stowe, professor of education at Randolph-Macon Woman's College, addressed a meeting of high-school principals and teachers at the annual convention of the northwestern district of the North Carolina Education Association.

Professor L. A. Pechstein, dean of the Teachers College, University of Cincinnati, gave three addresses before the Indiana State Teachers Association, South Bend, Indiana, on October 9 and 10. He addressed three divisions of the Kansas State Teachers Association at meetings in Chanute, Manhattan and Lawrence, from November 5 to 7.

Dr. Edward Kennard Rand, professor of Latin at Harvard University, gave the first lecture under the Ichabod Spencer Foundation on "Libraries of the Middle Ages" at Union College on November 21.

Sir Harold V. Mackintosh, president of the World Sunday School Association, has arrived from England to attend the annual meeting of the organization in New York.

The Reverend Dr. Herbert Armitage James, president of St. John's College, Oxford, died on November 15 at the age of eighty-seven years. He was the head of St. John's College for twenty-two years, and had previously served for thirty-four years in the public schools.

James Frederick Hopkins, director of art education in Massachusetts from 1912 to 1920, and twice delegate to the International Congress of Art Education, died on November 12 at the age of sixty-three years.

Mr. William Alanson Borden, organizer of more than four hundred public libraries in India, died on November 16. He was seventy-eight years old. He was in India from 1910 to 1913.

Professor Frank E. Seavey, of the English department of Tufts College Engineering School, died on November 13, after being struck by an automobile. He taught at Tufts College for twenty-three years.

Dean Richmond Austin Rasco, of the University of Miami Law School, died on November 16. He was sixty years old.

Memorial services for the late Dr. Sidney E. Mezes, formerly president of the College of the City of New York, who died on September 11, were held on November 9 in the great hall of the college. President Frederick B. Robinson and former President John H. Finley gave addresses.

Yale University will receive $1,931,810 by the will of the late Chauncey M. Depew, Jr.

Mrs. Emily Fawcet left in her will a bequest of twenty thousand pounds to the University of Leeds, to endow a chair of theology there, the choice of the professor being left to the university authorities or a committee appointed by them.

A tentative budget of $1,000,000 for the school relief fund during the coming winter and spring has been adopted at a meeting of the school superintendents of New York City. The fund, which will be raised by monthly contribution pledges from teachers, principals and other employees of the Board of Education in all branches of the school system, will be used to provide food, milk, clothing and other necessaries for children in the public schools whose families are in financial difficulties.

The Board of Education of Philadelphia has ratified its school budget, with a deduction of $500,000 for teachers' salaries. A six and one-half per cent. decrease has been made in the salary of every teacher and official in the public-school system of Baltimore.

Cornell University is commemorating the hundredth anniversary of the birth of its first librarian, Daniel W. Fiske, by a special display of some of the valuable books given by him to the university. In addition to the book collection Mr. Fiske provided a fund of more than $500,000 for the library.

AMONG the speakers at the meeting in Elmira of the New York State Association of Deans are: Dr. Herbert E. Hawkes, dean of Columbia College, on "Can a Dean be an Influential Factor in the Character and Development of Students?"; Dr. Riverda H. Jordan, director of the school of education, Cornell University, on "Guidance Program in the High School"; Dr. Esther Lloyd-Jones, assistant professor of education, Teachers College, Columbia University, on "Factors that Make for Growth during College"; Miss Adele Bildersee, dean of Brooklyn College, on "Loans, Scholarships and Fellowships." Mrs. Meta Steinhausen, dean of girls, Washington Junior High School, Rochester, leads the discussion on "The Social Program of the High School as a Laboratory for the Development of Social Attitudes and Techniques." Professor Sarah M. Sturtevant, of Teachers College, is president of the association.

THE new building of the Museum of the City of New York at Fifth Avenue between 103d and 104th Streets will be opened to the public on January 11, the 174th anniversary of the birth of Alexander Hamilton. Although the new museum building has been completed for nearly a year, it has been opened only two days during last December for inspection by subscribers and guests. The new building was constructed at a cost of $1,500,000 on land donated by the City of New York.

THE new $182,000 Memorial Hall at the University of North Carolina was recently dedicated in connection with the celebration of the institution's 138th birthday. It was formally accepted by Mr. John Sprunt Hill, of Durham, chairman of the building committee of the board of trustees. Governor O. Max Gardner delivered the presentation address. Occupying the site on which its predecessor was erected in 1830, the building is rectangular in shape—157 feet long, and 104 feet wide. Its design is classic and harmonizes with the antebellum buildings scattered around the campus.

IN commemoration of the 100th anniversary of the death of Goethe, the Carl Schurz Memorial Foundation, Inc., has announced an essay contest open to all undergraduates at colleges and universities throughout the United States. Cash prizes, amounting to almost $1,000, are announced. The first prize for an English essay is $200 and a similar first prize is offered for the best essay written in German. The choice of subjects and the rules of the contest are given on a poster which is being distributed to colleges and universities. Essays, limited to 5,000 words, must be submitted to the headquarters of the foundation, Philadelphia, not later than September 15, 1932.

ACCORDING to *The New York Times,* a new scientific laboratory for the study of paintings was opened at the Louvre on October 14. It is the gift of Professor B. Maraini, of the faculty of medicine of the University of Buenos Aires, and Dr. Fernade Perez, Argentine ambassador to Rome. The equipment of the laboratory enables direct examination of the paint, reveals the technique and progress of the artists' work, shows where repairs were made and bares imitations. Aside from x-ray, photographing the paintings at a direct angle from the side with the aid of 1,000-candlepower reflectors brings out each stroke like a relief map and even shows the fingerprints the old masters caused by smoothing the paint with their fingers. Dr. Perez has studied photographically by this method 2,000 paintings of Italian masters, and these photographs are part of the gift to the Louvre. The inauguration of the laboratory was under the auspices of the Ecole des Beaux Arts. Comparative studies of primitives and moderns is made possible and the Perez method offers opportunity to art students to study the masters' methods and color values, indicating the durability of the colors' various bases. The laboratory is regarded as the finest existing in this line.

RICHARD J. LIBBY, of the department of education of the State of Maine, has contributed to the *U. S. Daily* details concerning the progress in rural education in Maine. The latest tabulation of the state department of education shows that of the 135,000 pupils enrolled in the elementary schools nearly 77,000, or 56.08 per cent., are in the rural schools. A considerable portion of this group is enrolled in the 1,781 one-room schools which are scattered over the state and in the 1,343 schools in the buildings of two or more rooms, most of which are in villages of less than 2,500 population. Most of the children enrolled in the rural schools attend school from ten to twenty days less each year than those enrolled in the urban schools, for while no urban school system maintains a school year of less than thirty-six weeks, many of the smaller towns provide a shorter school year, and many, nearly one hundred, are obliged to accept the minimum of thirty-two weeks. While only thirty-six persons without previous experience as teachers were employed last year in the fifty-two cities and towns listed as urban, more than five hundred were engaged in teaching in the rural areas.

THE New Mexico workmen's compensation law applies to state educational institutions, according to an opinion rendered by Assistant Attorney General Frank Patton. While the law does not specifically require such institutions to secure compensation under the act, Mr. Patton recommended that for the sake of protection, adequate insurance should be carried.

A STUDY by the federal Office of Education shows that the average American boy or girl of 1931 receives two more years of schooling than the average boy or girl of 1914; that he is one of a class of 30 pupils, while his father's 1910 class had 34 pupils; that his chances of going to high school, which were but 1 in 10 in 1900, are now fifty-fifty, and his chances of going to college are 1 in 6.

THE total enrolment at Northwestern University for the first semester of this year is 11,812. This is a decrease of more than 600 from that of the same period last year. Most of the decrease is accounted for in the evening classes of the school of commerce. Last year in the first semester, 5,277 were enrolled, while this year the registration dropped to 4,700, a decrease of 577. There was also a decrease of 40 in the law school, due largely to more rigid entrance requirements. The medical school and the dental school have an enrolment of approximately the same as last year, while the McKinlock campus division of the college of liberal arts reported an increase of 45. On the Evanston campus, the school of speech, the school of education, the school of commerce and the school of engineering showed increases varying from 10 to 30. There was a decrease of 30 in the school of music, 10 in the college of liberal arts and 4 in the school of journalism.

THE enrolment in the ten Boston University schools and colleges for the present academic year is 12,396 students, a shrinkage of only 481 from last year's record figures. Registration in five Boston University departments showed increases. Five others had fewer students than they had in 1930. The greatest increase in graduate students is found in the Graduate School of Arts and Sciences, where 572 students are now enrolled, 49 more than last year. The greatest increase in undergraduate students is at the College of Business Administration, where Dean Everett W. Lord's report shows a total of 3,614, showing an increase of 239. The school of education, which enrolls undergraduaate and graduate students, notes an increase of ten students in the departmental total of 3,300, which makes it second in size to the college of business administration. The latter department also includes the Sargent School of Physical Education in Cambridge.

THE board of trustees of Wesleyan University have approved the suggestion made by the alumni council and the faculty that there be established five or six informal alumni visiting committees, the purpose of which is to acquaint interested alumni with the work of definite departments of the college. Committees will be organized and invited to visit the campus, meet with the faculty members of the department, learn of their problems, and, in any way they can, assist the department in its work. It is expected that the committees will be asked to report to the board of trustees at the mid-winter meeting in 1933. Committees probably will be organized for the following departments: Classics, economics, music, psychology, Romance languages and possibly art.

THE student body at the New York State Teachers College includes during the present year 45 holders of New York State scholarships gained by high standings on the regents' examination. This number is considerably larger than for any year during which the college has been on the list of eligible institutions. Last year the number totalled 33, the year before 28. The fourth year class has 11 such scholarship holders; 8 are juniors, 7 sophomores and 19 freshmen. The winning of the scholarship carries with it the award of $100 in cash for a four-year period, all recipients of the scholarship being required to state when they accept it that they expect to finish the four-year college course.

THE U. S. Office of Education, through its specialist in the education of Negroes, arranged a radio program to be broadcast over a nation-wide hook-up during American Education Week, which began on November 9. A similar program was broadcast last year, at which time the principal address was made by Dr. Ray Lyman Wilbur. This year's observance was planned as formerly in cooperation with the National Education Association, which has taken the lead in sponsoring the observance of American Education Week with a view to stimulating greater interest and activity in the solution of some of the important educational problems confronting the nation. Likewise the special broadcast on Negro education was designed to assist in focusing the attention of the people on some of the more acute problems in this field. The main address was given by Dr. Julius Klein, assistant secretary of commerce. Other features of the program were an address by President H. Councill Trenholm, of the Alabama State Teachers College at Montgomery, who is also president of the National Association of Teachers in Colored Schools; and Dr. Ambrose Caliver, specialist in the education of Negroes, U. S. Office of Education. Music for the occasion was furnished by the Howard University Glee Club, under the direction of Professor Roy W. Tibbs. Mr. G. C. Wilkinson, first assistant superintendent of schools of the District of Columbia, acted as master of ceremonies.

REEDUCATION of unemployed persons who have been trying to work at unsuitable jobs is one of the primary aims of the Minnesota Unemployment Research Institute, centralized at the University of Minnesota, which has begun to publish through the press of that university an account of its organization and findings. Four thousand unemployed men and women are registered under this project, which is directed by Dean R. A. Stevenson, of the school of business administration. A complete record of each case is made, these records including not only details concerning the registrant's occupational history, but also his physical and mental assets and liabilities, vocational interests, trade skill proficiency and personality traits. Retraining is then recommended for those who appear to need it. This program enlists the services of sociologists, physicians, psychologists, employers of various types of labor and the economists and business experts of the university. Descriptions and results of the work accomplished under the survey will be published at intervals during the next two years.

DISCUSSION

VARSITY FOOTBALL

HIGHER education in the United States to-day is in turmoil, if not in chaos, and in this period of self-scrutiny and change nothing needs concentrated thought and profound wisdom more than the problem of conducting intercollegiate sport. But where are the institution heads who dare to face that problem or who are doing more than showing their dismay or taking to the cyclone cellar, hoping that the storm may soon be over? The storm is surely brewing unless all signs fail. The undergraduate himself is becoming interested in the situation, and with the energy and enthusiasm of youth the problem will be carried through to some more worthy and satisfactory solution. The wise college head to-day is, in my judgment, the man who with courage and discernment resolutely faces this problem and in the light of modern educational psychology and the biological and social sciences attempts to arrive at a solution that will make his sports program appropriate to and worthy of an educational institution.

It may have been both possible and wise for medieval scholasticism to ignore and even to suppress the instinctive urge of youth to physical activity, although even in those days vigorous protestants against such suppression were not lacking. But in the light of modern scientific thought, it is almost inconceivable that keen educational leaders have so universally failed to realize the potentialities for leadership training, citizenship and outstanding personality which are inherent in competitive sports properly selected and wisely administered.

The minds of our educational leaders are so jammed with traditional academic impedimenta, their eyes are so blinded by the glamor of the big stadium crowds and their courage so dissipated by the tremendous power of the present day set-up that they are completely dismayed. Here and there a president calls for a special commission to study and report on further rules and regulations, or for some slight modifications pointing to the deflation of the present system, but few, if any, heads of colleges have dared to make a constructive approach to the problem. No one has asked himself and his faculty the question, "How can we set up a system that will retain the admitted values of a highly competitive sports program, weave them into the product which the institution is turning out, and thus justify them as a worthwhile experience in the education of young men?"

If we honestly and ardently believe in competitive sports as a powerful influence in the training of young men, how shall we go about building a procedure to get the most out of this influence? How shall we best make sports fit into the educational program? How can we make them worthy of an educational institution? Surely a rational educational procedure would be to take one and all who were interested in this type of sports training and give them the best instruction and the safest and happiest experience in playing the game so long as it returns dividends in social training, personal attitudes, joyous recreation and consequent health.

Quite certainly we should not select out those already the best performers and center our efforts upon them—the characteristic procedure of the present set-up. And just as certainly we should have no thought of putting these students into a circus to entertain others. And surely there would be no thought of exploiting groups of our students as performers for the sake of making money. Most assuredly none of these things will suffice, for we are building a sports system with one great objective, education in the broadest and most modern sense of that word. This means education for complete living. We are interested in sports as tools in the making of manhood. We are intent upon focusing with all possible force innate tendencies to activity, emulation, satisfaction in achievement and love of glory of the young men in our colleges to the end that they may become happier and more useful citizens.

In the urge to play, in the love of competitive sport, in the boundless enthusiasm, in the tireless vigor of the American youth, our educational institutions have at hand a limitless source of power waiting only to be harnessed; a Niagara, resistless and almost infinite in its potentialities, at present running wild and unutilized, but which with direction and control is capable of astounding results in education. My plea is for our college leaders to approach this problem from this point of view. Let them exclude from their thought the present system which has evolved in spite of rules, edicts and gentlemen's agreements; let them take this power for good and attempt to fit it into the educational program of their institutions in such a way as to make it most effective in the training of the participants and most appropriate for educational institutions. This new approach will bring out some startling revelations. It can have only one result. The present system of selecting and developing the representative team must go, for it violates every principle of pedagogy. It smacks of the prize ring and the circus and not of the university. It exploits and aggrandizes the "few chosen" and ignores the many who would like to be "called."

With the development of a new varsity system educationally justifiable, the evils which are to-day so generally deplored would be dissipated like mists before the rising sun. Where is the far-visioned, courageous university head who will summon the conclave out of which a new era in intercollegiate competition may emerge?

A COLLEGE DIRECTOR OF ATHLETICS

IN DEFENSE OF PARENTS

THERE are few teachers who have not, at some time or other in the long course of their struggles with obdurate young minds and untamed youthful emotions, felt some resentment toward the attitudes of parents. Occasionally the complaint has been against some rather "nebby" mother or father, but more frequently the grievance has been over the apparently slight and inadequate attention and real companionship parents give their offspring. Very often the cry is that parents are too generous in shifting the child burden onto the school.

We who know parents largely as the jealous yet seemingly thoughtless and unreasoning protectors of the youth in our classrooms will find some real food for reflection in contemplating the problem of the average American parent from the standpoint of the time requirements levied upon modern mothers and fathers. If we consider the time demanded by all the widespread activities that legitimately fall into the average parent's day we are likely to wonder if, after all, we can rightfully expect more than that the student should be dispatched to us in the morning and given a place to study and sleep at night.

Modern life has become so complicated and the duties bearing down on a really conscientious American are so heavy it seems probable that no parent can be expected to function as an ever-present and eternally watchful companion to sons and daughters. Possibly teachers have failed to enlarge their own conceptions of their duties sufficiently to see their extended rôle under the changed conditions of present-day living.

Consider the economic and social duties pressed down upon the average parent. Primarily, there is the proposition of providing a home and subsistence for the family. Forthwith we recognize a slice of time out of every parent's day that may vary from eight to ten or twelve hours. Put with this the other major time requirement—eight hours for sleep and rest—and we see at least sixteen out of every twenty-four hours belonging to the parent taken away from the child. Mark down another two hours for meals, time which we can not say is given exclusively to the children, and we leave mothers and fathers only six hours available for their functioning as parents, granting there are no competing factors coveting this residual time.

Unfortunately for the teacher who would have the parent do more of the child's training, other obligations than parenthood must be met out of these half dozen hours. Political leaders assert that our American citizen is appallingly unacquainted with the political life and problems of his country and that we shall have little improvement in the quality of our democracy until there is a more general and profound knowledge on the part of the public. Such a knowledge on the part of citizens in a nation whose condition and standing embrace factors world-wide in scope and very technical in nature would dictate that our American parents spend a minimum of an hour a day reading newspapers and magazines. Put this hour into the parent's time budget and we leave but five hours for the child.

A reminder often comes from the pulpit that Christians give all too little time to their church. Tithing, both in time and money, has been recommended for church members. Active, day-by-day Christianity has been urged in place of Sabbath morning pew polishing. Say that the church gets an average of thirty minutes of the parent's day and the child's share has been reduced to four and a half hours.

No family can live strictly unto itself. Social activities of a very justifiable and valuable nature should be allowed a daily hour of the parent's time. Too, each married couple should have some time together, alone, free from all intrusions, free even from the presence of their children. Now, make allowances for time to go back and forth from work, time for the mother to do her shopping and neighborly deeds of helpfulness, time for attending lectures, concerts, time for physical recreation and exercise, and what time is left? Consider too that the probability of what spare time a parent might have coinciding with time when children should not be sleeping or studying is slight.

Why, one could almost argue that married couples should not beget children on the grounds that they will have no time to do the thousand and one things parents are supposed to do in person for their offspring. It is rather difficult to deny that the teacher has infinitely more time and opportunity for work with the child than does the child's parent. All of which means nothing that most good teachers do not ordinarily recognize. Be that as it may, the thought of the time limitations imposed on parents might stand the teacher in good stead when the next occasion for deploring parental neglect arises.

WILLIAM E. SLATER

SPECIAL CORRESPONDENCE

MORE RIGID ENTRANCE REQUIREMENTS FOR TEACHER-TRAINING INSTITUTIONS

A GREAT deal is heard to-day about the entrance standards which general colleges and universities are setting up for the purpose of selecting from the throngs of high-school graduates requesting admittance those students which seem to offer the greatest promise of benefiting from collegiate training. This sifting and selecting is necessary if credits and degrees from such institutions are to continue to be recognized as badges earned for advanced study. In fact, so far has the popularization of higher education progressed in this country and so common have college degrees become that even now the possessor of a college diploma does not necessarily receive any special advantage in the work-a-day world. This condition may be as it should be, but however the individual may argue, the trend of the times is for colleges and universities of standing to carefully select only the most promising of their applicants.

Many professional schools, especially colleges of engineering, antedate the general colleges in setting up rigid standards for admission. This was only natural as many of the professions require, for successful pursuit, special abilities in addition to general ability.

In general, teacher-training institutions have been slow to set up selective entrance requirements on the basis of either the general or the special ability of the applicants. Most teacher-training institutions to-day accept, with minor reservations relating to the physical health or the moral standing of the applicants, all graduates of recognized high schools. Leaders in teacher-training, however, are recognizing that this condition can not go on or teacher-training institutions will be placed in the unfortunate position of having to take the material excluded from other professional schools and colleges of liberal arts.

A more worthy motive, however, than self-protection is at the base of this new attitude in teacher-training. Teaching, and especially the teaching of children, is being recognized as a profession; it is coming into a new dignity, or rather, its ancient dignity is being restored. Society has been educated to the value of the child, the school and the curriculum. Public education in this country is demanding and meeting increasingly higher standards. These standards can not be maintained unless idealistic, practical and gifted youth is challenged by the privileges and opportunities of educational service and leadership.

How, in this age which has been so dazzled by the glitter of money-making careers, can the profession of teaching be made attractive to the superior graduates of our high schools? There are probably a number of answers to this question, but certainly a long step forward will be taken when the profession is dignified by having its personnel a highly selected group.

Why have students considered it such a privilege to attend our national schools of military training, Annapolis and West Point? Surely the graduates of these institutions receive only ordinary incomes! True, but the personnel of these schools has been carefully selected. Not only must the student be chosen on his merits, but in addition he must be able to stand the pace. His diploma means not only that he has received a very fine general and special training, but a unique education in that the government has chosen him from many applicants to hold a particular position. The writer firmly believes that the same psychology which attracts students to our national, non-tuitional military colleges can be made to operate toward the attracting of a superior quality of students to our state supported teacher-training institutions. When the state, as is the condition in New York, limits the number of teachers trained to the requirements in the field, when it gives these teachers the best training available in order to meet the increasing standards in public education, and when it chooses its material from the best material graduating from the high schools, entrance into a teacher-training institution will then become a recognition of merit and graduation the possibility of holding a very much desired position.

The New York State Teachers College at Buffalo is one of the, as yet, relatively few teacher-training institutions in eastern United States which is subjecting its applicants to matriculation examinations for the purpose of choosing the most desirable students. The very fact that the State of New York limits the number of teachers in training to the requirements in the field should operate toward the employing of a selective policy in all the state teacher-training institutions. However, a non-tuitional college located in a large city, as is the case with Buffalo, has a certain advantage in the fact that large numbers of resident students will seek entrance. Present economic conditions have strengthened this position, for while Buffalo supports a good university and several Catholic colleges, these, especially the university, are supported by high tuitional costs.

For the year 1930–31, the first year in which the State Teachers College at Buffalo made a scientific study of its selective policy, applications for admission were considered only from candidates who made an average of 75 or better on the State Regents' Examinations. This is ten points higher than the minimum of 65 required for high-school graduation. During that year the Director of Research Studies administered a number of examinations to the freshman body for the purpose of discovering what measures could be obtained on applicants which would most closely predict their college scholarship. The variables chosen for study that year were: (1) high-school achievement as measured by the Sones-Harry High School Achievement Test, (2) reading ability as measured by Section V of the Ohio State University Psychological Test, (3) general intelligence as measured by the Ohio State University Psychological Test in its entirety, (4) personality as measured by the Thurstone Personality Schedule, and (5) Regents' Averages. The highest predictive measure of scholarship, as it existed at the end of the first semester, was found by combining in a formula the Regents' Average with the reading section (Test V) of the Ohio State University Psychological Test. As a result of this study it was recommended that applicants for admission the following year be given the Ohio State University Psychological Test, the Thurstone Personality Schedule and at least one other personality test. This recommendation has been acted upon and the freshmen students for this year have been selected on the basis of a combination of their averages on the Regents' Examinations and their reading ability. Although in the 1930–31 study little relationship was found between either personality and scholarship or personality and intelligence, the Director of Research Studies feels that personality factors are definitely related to successful teaching, and therefore that as many objective measures of personality as possible should be obtained, these to be analyzed for their relationship with the students' general success in college, their success in practice teaching and their success later in the teaching field.

A study of the measures obtained on the two freshmen classes yield the following comparisons with norms for college freshmen.

The 1930–31 freshman class ranked as follows. (1) The median on the Sones-Harry High School Achievement Test was 223. No norms have been worked out for this test as a whole, but it was found that the median score for each of the four sections of this test was significantly higher than the norms for graduating high-school seniors. (2) The median reading score was 62, higher than the norm of 53. (3) The intelligence score median was 220 which is considerably above the norm of 182, established on this examination by entering freshmen in colleges distributed over the country as a whole. (4) The median personality score was 44.75, higher than a median of 33.40 (worked out by the writer for the freshmen at the University of Chicago). However, since the higher figures on personality represent the more poorly adjusted individuals, the significance of these figures is reversed. No data are available at present to explain the divergence between our freshmen and the freshmen at the University of Chicago on this personality measure. The median of the Regents' Averages was 80.68 which is high when consideration is given to the fact that the minimum for high-school graduation is 65, and that there was a piling up of applicants with Regents' Averages around 75, since that was the minimum for college entrance and no other selective process was employed for the year 1930–31. Considering all these measures, last year's testing program indicated that the students at Buffalo State Teachers College ranked in academic ability considerably above the average for college freshmen.

This year many more students with Regents' Averages above 90 applied than last year, and practically the entire group selected has Regents' Averages above last year's median score of 80.68. The median of the Regents' Averages for the 1931–32 selected group is 84.08, for the Ohio State University Psychological Test is 221, and for the reading test is 65.44. Comparing these figures with the medians and norms given above, it is evident that the State Teachers College at Buffalo has a right to be increasingly proud of the quality of students who are seeking and obtaining admittance to the privileges of the institution.

Prospective students and citizens of Buffalo, through personal correspondence and newspaper publicity, have had this selective program quite definitely presented to them and there is considerable evidence that in Buffalo it is coming to be considered a recognition of high merit to be selected to attend the State Teachers College. The administrators of the college are proceeding on the assumption that the profession of teaching offers unique advantages and opportunities for leadership, and therefore that admittance to a teacher-training institution should challenge the best material graduating from the high schools.

OSCAR E. HERTZBERG
STATE TEACHERS COLLEGE,
BUFFALO, N. Y.

QUOTATIONS

THE LIBERAL ARTS COLLEGES

I AM glad to express appreciation of the service of the liberal arts college, that is, the small college. I do this the more freely because of the more than 600 such institutions in our land. Most of them have little, if any, endowment or state support. In these times of trends toward larger units, the difficulties of the unsupported small college multiply, which makes their successful operations less hopeful, and in many cases a desperate struggle.

The important place which these institutions hold in our system of education renders their support of the utmost importance. Whatever be the magnificent services of the larger and highly specialized universities, the liberal arts college places an emphasis upon personal contacts of teacher and student which render them a vital part of our educational system.

A primary purpose of education is a product of high character and noble ideals, which regard moral and spiritual qualities superior to mere material things, without which any purely economic system would collapse.

Throughout our history these colleges have been and are now the seed beds of leadership. They have contributed a large part to the presence in our land of nearly 2,000,000 college trained men and women. Theirs is a great honor roll of men and women in our nation. The finest traditions of our country are rooted in their associations and their inspiration.

The disadvantage of the small college is obvious. The dramatic element in education does not play a great part in its activities. It must remain content with the character of service it renders to the individual man and woman to the public weal. In the last analysis the chief service to higher education in our country must rest not alone with the few highly endowed universities, but, in large degree, with the more than 600 smaller colleges for whose future welfare I am now speaking.

It is through them that each state and section must maintain ample cultural opportunities for the youth within reasonable distance from their homes and in circumstances fitted to the needs of each community and its people.

That service for the youth is a guarantee of equality of cultural opportunities and a bulwark for the spiritual life of the generation in which our children will have to live, a service which I sincerely commend.—*Address on the liberal arts colleges given by President Hoover over the radio on November 14.*

REPORTS

THE COLLEGE ADMINISTRATOR GOES TO SCHOOL

DURING recent years the summer sessions conducted on college and university campuses have provided an immeasurable stimulus to the professional growth of college faculties, and a steadily increasing number of college administrators and teachers have been taking advantage of the opportunities for in-service improvement offered during the long vacation period.

Whereas a decade ago the principal groups served in summer sessions were undergraduate students, many of them making up scholastic deficiencies, now the predominating group is composed of teachers and other professional men and women who are unable to attend courses during the academic year.

Not only do faculty members and graduate students planning to enter the college teaching profession seek subject-matter courses in their chosen fields, but they also demand professional courses designed to improve their teaching technique and to provide them with a broad conception of the college enterprise. College administrators also seek opportunities for the study and discussion of problems in the field of higher education. In response to this demand professional courses dealing with problems in the field of college administration and college teaching are to be found listed in nearly forty university and college catalogues.

The summer vacation seems to be the most popular time for conducting these professional courses on high education. Not only are college administrators and college teachers more likely to be able to attend courses then, but there is also better opportunity for enlisting the services of specialists and experienced workers in the field to direct the work of these groups during the summer months.

Twenty-six institutions offered courses on various aspects of college administration and college teaching during the past summer. Included in the group were the Universities of California, Chicago, Cincinnati, Colorado, Iowa, Kentucky, Michigan, Minnesota, Missouri, Nebraska, Oklahoma, Pittsburgh, Southern California, Washington and Wisconsin; Duke, Indiana, New York, Northwestern, Ohio State, Stanford and Western Reserve Universities; Colorado State Teachers College, George Peabody College for Teachers, Iowa State College of Agriculture and Mechanic Arts and Teachers College of Columbia University.

The regular teaching staffs of these institutions were augmented by a number of specialists and experienced workers in the college administrative and teaching fields. Among those giving their services last summer were a number of college presidents, including Frank L. McVey, of the University of Kentucky, George F. Zook, of the University of Akron, Homer P. Rainey, of Bucknell University, and Wendell S. Brooks, of Intermountain Union College; former presidents Clarence C. Little, of the University of Michigan, George A. Works, of the Connecticut Agricultural College, and A. M. Stowe, of the University of the City of Toledo; Vice-President C. S. Yoakum, of the University of Michigan; and a number of presidents of teachers colleges. Deans H. D. Sheldon, of the University of Oregon, Shelton Phelps, of George Peabody College, H. L. Smith, of Indiana University, Charles E. Friley, of the Agricultural and Mechanical College of Texas, and A. J. Brumbaugh, of the University of Chicago, also conducted courses this past summer, as did Registrars Ezra L. Gillis, of the University of Kentucky, and J. R. Robinson, of George Peabody College, and many other experienced survey and research workers in the field of higher education.

While the offerings at most of the institutions were limited to a single course or two on selected phases of the field, there were to be found more comprehensive and varied programs available at several institutions, particularly at the University of Chicago, Teachers College of Columbia University, the University of Michigan, Ohio State University and the University of Pittsburgh. Basic or general courses on the organization and administration of the American college and university, as well as specific problems of instruction and of the professional duties of the various administrative officers were offered at these five institutions. General courses were also given at the University of Colorado, Indiana University, the University of Kentucky, the University of Minnesota, New York University, Duke University and Western Reserve University.

The courses offered at the University of Chicago included "The Organization and Administration of Colleges and Universities," "Problems of College Instruction," "Financial Administration of Higher Institutions," "Professional Duties of Deans and Registrars," "The Administration of Student Personnel in Higher Institutions," "The Junior College, Its Organization and Administration," "The Organization and Administration of Teacher Training Institutions" and "Problems of Instruction in Teacher Training Institutions." In addition to this sequence of courses, an institute for administrative officers of higher institutions was held at the University on July 8, 9 and 10, to which officers of such institutions were invited. The central theme of the institute this summer was "Recent Trends in American College Education."

The variety and scope of the courses on the organization and administration of higher education, which have now been offered at Teachers College of Columbia University for the past eight years, have been steadily increasing. During that period opportunity has been offered for the study and discussion of a wide range of problems in the field of higher education to some 540 instructors, administrative officers and others interested in higher educational institutions. The positions they hold indicate the types of college officials who have taken advantage of these courses. Included in the group who have studied at this particular institution are 45 college presidents, 66 deans, 30 registrars, six deans of men, 19 deans of women, 36 heads of departments, 128 college professors and instructors, four directors of research, three directors of personnel, five assistants to presidents, four librarians, two treasurers, two business managers, and a number of others in various college or other educational positions.

The summer offerings at Teachers College this year included two "Basic Courses for Instructors and Administrators in High Educational Institutions," a course on "Problems of College Instruction," one on "Student Personnel Work," one on "Publicity and Public Relations," one on "Finance and Business Operation," and a series of eight two-week unit courses on special problems in higher education. The unit courses were devoted to such topics as the investment of institutional funds; accounting for institutional funds; tests, measurements and rating scales; admission and classification of students; registration and student records; the college curriculum; the work of the dean of the faculty; and vocational guidance in colleges. A number of related courses were also available, including those dealing with problems of teacher training, guidance, the junior college and the teaching of special subjects.

Five courses in the field of higher education were offered last summer at the University of Michigan. One of these courses was on the "History of Higher Education in the United States." In another, entitled "Current Problems in Higher Education," and directed by Vice-President Yoakum, the following general topics were discussed in their present bearings on educational policy: (1) selection, assignment, counseling and supervision of students; (2) trends in curricula, teaching, faculty personnel; (3) tendencies in college and university organizations and administration. Two courses were given in the field of personnel problems in colleges, one a seminar designed for an intensive study of special problems in connection with personnel and guidance departments of high schools and colleges and the other a less advanced course involving a study of traits associated with successful and unsuccessful students. There was also offered a course on "The Teaching of English in College," which consisted of analysis and discussion of the problems of teaching the elementary or introductory courses in English composition, language and literature.

A number of general courses for the training of college teachers and administrators are offered at Ohio State University in the departments of principles and practice of education, of psychology, and of school administration, both during the regular school year and in the summer quarters. Several of these are given by Arthur J. Klein, who was, until the fall of 1930, chief of the division of higher education in the U. S. Office of Education, but is now a member of the permanent staff of the university. Among the offerings available during the 1931 summer quarter were courses on "The Administration of Colleges and Universities," "Financial Administration in Higher Education," "College Teaching," "The Junior College Curriculum," "Administration of the Junior College," and "Seminar in Administration of Higher Education." Two courses on "Psychological Problems of Deans of Women" and one on "Research Problems of the Dean of Women" were also given, as well as courses on "Psychological Problems in Higher Education," "Professionalized Subject-Matter Courses in Teacher Training Institutions" and "Administration of Teacher Training Institutions."

For research in higher education generally and for the study of its own problems in that field, the University of Pittsburgh established in 1927 a division of research in higher education. Out of this division there has developed a department of higher education in the Graduate School of Education which since September, 1928, has offered, both during the regular year and in summer session, courses in this field for students desiring to pursue such study for university credit. The members of the staff of the division and others, appointed from the general faculty conduct the courses.

Four summer courses in higher education were announced by the department of higher education this year. The discussion in the course on "College and University Administration" was directed particularly to the junior college years and their particular problems. Courses were also given on "Educational Personnel Methods in College and University" and on "Office Organization and Record Forms," as well as the "Major Course for Deans of Women." A conference for the discussion of both internal and external problems of the junior college was held at the university on July 16 and 17.

Basic or general courses were offered under various titles at eight other institutions. At the University of Colorado, President Brooks, of Intermountain Union College, gave a course on "Problems in Higher Education," in which the history of the college in the United States was traced, including the development of its curriculum, the functions of its officers and its expansion to the university type, as an introduction to a survey of present conditions. Dean H. L. Smith offered a course at Indiana University entitled "Thesis Work in the Field of Higher Education," while a "Seminar in Higher Education" was given at the State University of Iowa.

President McVey gave a course on "The Administration of Higher Education" at the University of Kentucky which dealt with problems relating to the organization and administration of universities, colleges and teacher training institutions, financial problems of higher institutions, and professional duties of registrars, deans and business managers. During the first term of the University of Minnesota summer session, President Rainey, of Bucknell University, offered a course on "Problems of College Education." A "Seminar in University and College Administration," including a critical study of types of organization and administrative practices found in American universities and colleges, was announced at New York University. At Duke University a study of current college problems and of experimental efforts being made toward their solution was incorporated in the course on "American College Problems," directed by A. M. Stowe. A general course entitled "Research in Higher Education" was offered at Western Reserve University.

Considerable attention was given to questions of college instruction and its improvement in the courses offered this past summer, both in the basic courses and also in specific courses on this subject which were conducted at a number of institutions. Dean Sheldon, of the University of Oregon, held a "Seminar in the Improvement of College Teaching" at Stanford University. "Introduction to College Teaching" was the title of a course given at the University of Southern California. A course on "Methods of Teaching College Subjects," with special reference to the use of motivated problems in presenting technical subjects, was offered at the Iowa State College. At the University of Missouri a course on "College Teaching Methods" was announced.

"The Improvement of Teaching in Colleges and Universities" was the subject of a course given at New York University. At the University of Cincinnati Carter V. Good announced a course on "Problems of Teaching in Higher Education," covering the current literature in the field, status of students and teachers, objectives and standards, curriculum, psychology of learning, classroom method, measurement and guidance, reorganization and adjustment, and research. Dean Phelps gave a course on "College Teaching" at George Peabody College for Teachers in which was included the visitation of college classes and directed teaching.

Reference has already been made to the courses on "Problems of College Instruction" at the University of Chicago and at Teachers College of Columbia University. Courses on training school problems in the professional education of teachers, intended primarily for those concerned with teacher training institutions, were offered at the Universities of Chicago, Minnesota and Wisconsin, the Colorado State Teachers College, Teachers College of Columbia University and George Peabody College for Teachers. These courses included the consideration both of administrative and of instructional problems.

Courses of particular value to those concerned with or interested in the office of the college registrar were offered at the Universities of Chicago and Kentucky, at George Peabody College for Teachers and at Teachers College. The course at the University of Chicago was given by Dean Charles E. Friley, of the Agricultural and Mechanical College of Texas, who has for a number of years been making intensive studies of the professional duties of deans and registrars. The "dean of college registrars," Ezra L. Gillis, offered two courses at the University of Kentucky this summer, one on "Problems in the Registrar's Field of Administration" and the other on "Technique and Professional Work of the Registrar." At George Peabody College for Teachers, J. R. Robinson, the registrar of that institution, has for a number of years now been offering a general course on "The College Registrar." The Teachers College offering included two of the series of two-week unit courses on special problems in higher education previously referred to, one on the admission and classification of students and the other on registration and student records.

Special courses on the financial and business administration of higher institutions were offered at the University of Chicago and at Teachers College. Among the topics treated in these courses were the organization of financial and business offices, accounting, budgeting and reporting procedure, cost analyses, management and investment of endowment and other trust funds, the financing of supplementary business activities, purchasing and supply management, plant operation and maintenance, and the administration of student fees, scholarships and loan funds. Messrs. Russell, Reeves and Works were in charge of the course at the University of Chicago, while Messrs. Evenden, O'Rear and Hungate, the latter auditor of Teachers College, conducted the Teachers College course.

Thomas E. Benner, the former chancellor of the University of Porto Rico and recently elected dean of the School of Education at the University of Illinois, gave a course on "Publicity and Public Relations" at Teachers College, in which attention was directed to such topics as the institutional organization for publicity and public relations, publicity and publications, student recruiting, financial campaigns, alumni and alumni work, abstracting, news clipping and other services. A course on "Vocational Guidance in Colleges" was offered at the same institution by Harry D. Kitson, in which methods of gathering information about occupations in which college students engage, methods of imparting this information, techniques of analyzing and counseling with individuals were among the areas covered.

Instruction in the work of deans of men, deans of women and other college personnel officers, was announced among the offerings at the Universities of Chicago, Iowa, Michigan, Pittsburgh and Southern California, New York University and Teachers College of Columbia University. Such topics were included as the meaning and scope of personnel work, the selection and admission of college students, their orientation into the college environment, educational guidance and vocational counseling, extra-curriculum activities, student discipline and student government, placement and part-time employment, the moral and religious life of students, health service records and reports, and the administrative organization of personnel. Attention was also given to the study of objective data and experimental investigations bearing on these topics.

The following institutions offered specific courses on the junior college last summer: the Universities of California, Chicago, Iowa, Missouri, Nebraska, Oklahoma, Southern California, and Washington; Duke, New York, Northwestern, Ohio State and Stanford Universities; George Peabody College for Teachers, and Teachers College of Columbia University. These courses were intended both for administrators and instructors in junior colleges and for those interested in learning about this important educational movement. The genesis and development of the junior college, its purpose, objectives, curriculum and administration, and its articulation with the high school and the senior college and university were the usual content of these courses. In several instances the approach was made from the secondary school angle. At Teachers College three distinct courses on the junior college were given: one a general course, one on curriculum and instructional practices, and one on problems of administration. Under the direction of Walter C. Eells, editor of *The Junior College Journal*, Stanford University also offered a group of related courses on the various aspects of the junior college work. Superintendents of schools, principals and directors of junior colleges, as well as professors of secondary education, were among those conducting summer offerings in this field.

Special libraries in the field of higher education have been established at a number of institutions as valuable by-products of the instructional side of these professional courses. Bibliographies on the different phases of college administration have been compiled. Significant research studies have been made, and publications, including Ph.D. dissertations, have resulted. At several institutions the students in the courses, as well as the staff, have been afforded opportunity to participate in surveys of individual colleges, of groups of colleges, and of entire state systems of education.

In 1930 a total of twenty institutions announced summer courses on the professional study of problems of higher education. Although three of these—the Universities of Alabama, Idaho and Texas—did not offer such courses this past summer the number of institutions was augmented by nine new ones, bringing to twenty-six the total number of institutions offering such summer courses this year. The individual course offerings have also been expanded materially both in number and in scope, and in addition to these specific professional courses there are offered many courses on the history, principles and philosophy of education and in particular subject-matter fields which are of value and of interest to college teachers and administrators.

Archie M. Palmer
The Association of American Colleges,
New York, N. Y.

EDUCATIONAL RESEARCH AND STATISTICS

KNOWLEDGE OF SOCIAL USAGE IN JUNIOR AND SENIOR HIGH SCHOOLS

Knowledge of social usage is often a factor in happiness and success. Many moments of adolescent unhappiness are due to unintentional discourtesy on the part of the adolescent or to rude treatment by some one else. Part of the unnecessary adolescent "storm and stress" is doubtless due to lack of knowledge of the approved behavior in certain social situations. Knowing the proper thing to do promotes calm and confidence. Accordingly, good manners which appear somewhat superficial and trivial may be an important factor in adolescent adjustment and an aid to good mental hygiene.

A person is seldom embarrassed by possessing good manners, but is frequently handicapped by a lack of knowledge of the correct way to act in certain social situations.

Courtesy, like moral behavior, may be interfered with by three things: (1) lack of knowledge of the approved way to act in a particular situation, (2) indifference, thoughtlessness, failure to reflect upon the best course of action, and (3) deliberate refusal to be courteous when the courteous conduct is clearly recognized. The second cause of discourtesy is undoubtedly the most common, but the first should not be neglected.

A test of knowledge of social usage designed for junior and senior high schools should be of value not only in discovering the pupils' lack of knowledge but also in reminding them of rules of courteous conduct which they know but do not always practise. A simple test of this kind was devised and given to 1,614 pupils in four senior and two junior high schools. Table I shows the distribution of pupils by grades and schools. Some of the results of this test will be given in this article.

The Test

The test consists of 110 statements, selected from standard books of etiquette and adapted to the experience and vocabulary of high-school pupils. The following are three examples:

TABLE I

School	Number of Cases: 7th Grade	8th Grade	9th Grade	10th Grade	11th Grade	12th Grade	Total
Senior High Schools							
I. Located in large city, foreign-born parents. No systematic instruction in courtesy	0	0	84	293	159	218	754
II. Located in another large city and similar to I.	0	0	22	8	30	42	102
III. Similar to II.	0	0	59	0	22	102	183
IV. Located in an attractive suburb of a large city. Only girls were included. Majority of parents, American born. Instruction in courtesy in connection with Girls' Organization	0	0	0	63	49	34	146
Junior High Schools							
V. Located in small city. Majority of parents foreign-born. No systematic instruction	73	64	71	0	0	0	208
VI. Located in small town, about half of parents foreign-born. Systematic instruction given in seventh grade	107	0	114	0	0	0	221
Total	180	64	350	364	260	396	1,614

. . . . Knives are placed on the left side of the plate.

. . . . A boy walks next to the curb when walking with a girl.

. . . . In introducing a man to a woman, one always presents the man to the woman, as, for example, "Miss Jones, have you met Mr. Smith?

The test can be given in a thirty-minute period, and is very easily and quickly scored.

Relation of Knowledge of Social Usage to Grade

There is an increase in the mean score from 68.6 in the seventh grade to 87.9 in the twelfth grade. Moreover, there is a small but consistent increase in mean score from grade to grade in each of the six schools. The same tendency to improve in knowledge of social usage is indicated by the increase in range from 26–98 in the seventh grade to 48–110 in the twelfth grade. This increase is in schools having no systematic instruction in good manners in grades eight to twelve.

Relation of Knowledge of Social Usage to Age

The progression in knowledge of social usage from the younger to the older pupils is not so clear as is the improvement from the seventh to the twelfth grade. The mean score of the 24 eleven-year-olds in three different schools is 74.3, and of 21 pupils nineteen years old, 81.3. The mean scores of pupils from eleven to nineteen years of age are as follows:

11 years	74.3	16 years	83.8
12 years	70.8	17 years	85.3
13 years	77.1	18 years	86.9
14 years	77.6	19 years	81.3
15 years	82.8		

A study of the age averages within each grade shows a tendency for the scores to increase up to a certain age, and to decrease in the case of the over-age pupils.

The correlation between age and score in each grade shows another interesting relationship. The coefficients of correlation between age and total score in each grade are as follows:

Seventh grade	$-.11 \pm .05$
Eighth grade	$-.36 \pm .07$
Ninth grade	$-.31 \pm .05$
Tenth grade	$+.27 \pm .05$
Eleventh grade	$+.03 \pm .06$
Twelfth grade	$+.03 \pm .06$

It will be noted that in the eighth and ninth

grades there is a negative correlation between age and score large enough to be significant; in the tenth grade, there is a small but significant positive correlation. In the eleventh and twelfth grade no relationship is evident. One possible explanation of the lack of negative relationship in the upper grades is that a keen interest in social usage may have overcome to some extent the handicap of lower intelligence on the part of the over-age pupils. That this interest may be greater in the case of girls than in the case of boys is suggested by the fact that in the tenth grade, in which the correlation was significantly positive, there was a larger proportion of girls than in the other grades. There seem to be two factors at work—general intelligence and social maturity. The lack of social maturity on the part of the under-age pupils tends to prevent their obtaining a score commensurate with their general intelligence; while the lower intelligence of the over-age pupils tends to counteract their advantage in social maturity. It would be interesting to study the extent to which instruction in social usage could overcome the handicap apparently due to low intelligence.

Relation of Knowledge of Social Usage to I.Q.

Intelligence quotients derived from scores made on the Otis self-administering test were obtained from one school, and Pearson's coefficients of correlation between I.Q. and scores on the test of social usage were computed for grades seven, eight, and nine.

The coefficient of correlation in the seventh grade (67 cases) was $.44 \pm .07$; in the eighth grade (60 cases), $.51 \pm .06$; in the ninth grade (68 cases), $.33 \pm .07$; and for the combined grades (195 cases), $.36 \pm .07$. The coefficients of correlation for the seventh and eighth grades are about the same as those found between intelligence and the George Washington test of social intelligence, and suggest that general intelligence is an important factor in knowledge of social usage. In the ninth grade, however, the correlation is decidedly lower, and differs so much from the seventh and eighth grades that it alters the expected result for the combined 195 cases. The scatter diagram of the ninth grade shows the majority of scores bunched in the high-social-usage-low-I.Q. quarter.

Relation of Knowledge of Social Usage to Occupation of Father

It would seem as though knowledge of social usage should be more closely related than other forms of school achievement to the home background of pupils. One indication of home background is given by the occupation of the father. The range and mean score on the test of social usage was obtained for each occupation. No consistent or striking differences were found among the occupations on adjacent parts of the scale, but there was a tendency in each school, as well as in the total cases, for the mean scores to increase in a fluctuating way from the unskilled labor to the professional group. The mean score of children of day laborers is strikingly low, although there were a few very high scores in this group. The children of physicians, preachers, lawyers, technical, mechanical and mining engineers, college teachers, and educational administrators, though few in number, made consistently high scores on the test.

When the occupations were thrown into three groups—(1) unskilled labor, (2) skilled labor and business, and (3) professions—the differences, as may be seen in Table II, became marked. Aldrich[1] found a similar situation with regard to general intelligence. No specific occupational group was found to be consistently higher than any other group, but there was "a substantial difference when the cases were grouped as labor and non-labor classes."

Relation of Knowledge of Social Usage to Participation in Extra-Curricular Activities

The pupil who engages in extra-curricular activities does not necessarily make a high score on the test of social usage, although in general the pupils obtaining the highest scores belong to two or more clubs and hold offices more frequently than those having the lowest scores. Thirty-seven pupils in one school belonging to only one club obtained a mean score of 87.8; 11 belonging to two clubs and holding one office, a mean score of 92.18; eight belonging to four clubs, a mean score of 94.4; two belonging to five clubs, a mean score of 88.0; and seven

[1] Julien C. Aldrich, "The Intelligence of High School Pupils," *The School Review*, xxxv (November, 1927), 699–706.

belonging to five clubs and holding two offices, a mean score of 89.7. A similar lack of consistent relationship between membership in clubs and score on the test of social usage was also found in the other schools.

TABLE II
MEAN SCORES ACCORDING TO THREE OCCUPATIONAL GROUPS

Type of occupation	Number of cases	Lowest score	Mean	Highest score
Unskilled labor	152	26	54.6	84
Skilled labor and small business	1,121	26	79.0	108
Professional work and big business	100	64	90.5	110

SUMMARY

A test of knowledge of social usage which has been given to 1,614 junior and senior high school pupils has shown:

(1) An increase in mean scores from the seventh to the twelfth grade.

(2) A less marked increase in mean scores from 11 to 19 years of age, and an indication of the influence of low intelligence upon the growth in knowledge of social usage in the case of the over-age pupils in each grade.

(3) A relationship in grades seven and eight between the scores on the test of social usage and general intelligence similar to the relationship frequently found between the George Washington Test of Social Intelligence and general intelligence, but a decidedly lower correlation in the ninth grade. The number of cases was too small to warrant any general conclusion, but suggests an interesting topic for further study.

(4) A significant difference in favor of the professional group, in the mean scores of the three vocational groupings—unskilled labor, skilled labor and small business, and professions and big business.

(5) No consistent tendency for the pupil who engages in many extra-curricular activities to obtain a higher score than the pupil who engages in few.

(6) A common body of knowledge of social usage possessed by more than 95 per cent. of the pupils.

(7) Common misconceptions regarding certain technical rules of etiquette and general principles underlying true politeness.

A test of social usage of this kind should be useful in arousing the pupil's interest in courtesy; in measuring the results of incidental and systematic instruction in social usage; and in discovering deficiencies in knowledge of social usage in the case of individuals and groups.

RUTH STRANG

TEACHERS COLLEGE,
COLUMBIA UNIVERSITY

NEW BOOKS IN EDUCATION

BALTIMORE DEPARTMENT OF EDUCATION. *Geography Course of Study for Grades Four, Five and Six.* Pp. 326. Illustrated. *History Course of Study for Grades Four, Five and Six.* Pp. 262. Department of Education.

BOWYER, VERNON L. and others, Editors. *Sixth Yearbook. Character Education.* Pp. x + 292. Chicago Principals' Club.

COIT, MARJORIE C., Editor. *Projects in Science and Nature Study.* Pp. 63. Illustrated. American Museum of Natural History.

COSS, JOHN J. and others. *Five College Plans.* Pp. 115. Columbia University Press. $1.00.

FLICK, ALEXANDER C. *The Papers of Sir William Johnson.* Pp. xiii + 1160. Illustrated. Division of Archives and History. Vol. VII. University of the State of New York.

GRAY, WILLIAM S., Editor. *Recent Trends in American Education.* Pp. ix + 253. University of Chicago Press. $2.00.

HENMON, V. A. C. and F. O. HOLT. *Report on the Administration of Scholastic Aptitude Tests to 34,000 High School Seniors in Wisconsin in 1929 and 1930.* Pp. 104. University of Wisconsin.

HOFFMAN, U. J. *Modernized Teaching in Rural Schools.* Pp. 143. Illustrated. F. A. Owen.

HOUSE, HOMER C. and SUSAN E. HARMON. *Descriptive English Grammar.* Pp. viii + 366. Prentice-Hall. $1.85.

MARSHALL, DAVID T. *Recollections of Edison.* Pp. 117. Illustrated. Christopher Publishing House. $1.75.

MILLARD, THOMAS F. *The End of Exterritoriality in China.* Pp. 278. The A.B.C. Press. Shanghai.

MORGAN, DANIEL E. *When the World Went Mad.* Pp. 163. Christopher Publishing House. $1.75.

QUIGLEY, SAMUEL. *The Integration of Teaching.* Pp. v + 198. Edwards Brothers. $2.00.

TAYLOR, J. CAREY. *The Reliability of Quarterly Marks in the Seventh Grade of Junior High School, together with the Value of Certain Standard Tests in Predicting Them.* Pp. x + 54. Johns Hopkins Press. $1.15.

THOMSON, J. EARLE. *Our Pacific Possessions.* Pp. xii + 264. Illustrated. Charles Scribner's Sons. $0.90.

WHITE HOUSE CONFERENCE ON CHILD HEALTH AND PROTECTION. *Nursery Education.* Pp. xxi + 187. Illustrated. Century Company. $2.00.

SCHOOL AND SOCIETY

EDITED BY J. McKEEN CATTELL

WITH WHICH IS COMBINED THE

EDUCATIONAL REVIEW

EDITED BY WILLIAM McANDREW

Volume 34 SATURDAY, NOVEMBER 28, 1931 Number 883

MEDIOCRITY AND THE COLLEGE

By President WILLIAM MATHER LEWIS

LAFAYETTE COLLEGE

WHAT does America need most? A good five-cent cigar, said Vice-President Marshall; thrift, suggests Calvin Coolidge; the repeal of the 18th Amendment, cries the thirsty patriot; an old-time revival, affirms the evangelist. Thus the answers come, according to the desires of the individuals who make them.

Truly, what the nation most needs, at this perplexing moment in its history, is relief from the policy of mediocrity which has prevailed within our borders for, lo, these many years. Most of our present difficulties are due to incapacity in our governmental, financial, social, educational and spiritual leadership.

Is it easy to name five real statesmen in the present federal organization, five outstanding governors of states, five truly able and incorruptible mayors? What financial authorities have exhibited any evidence of ability to lead us out of the wilderness of depression during the last two years? To whom shall we look with confidence in connection with the increasingly critical industrial situation? Can one readily call to mind many who see our great problems of education in the large and who really present a program that answers the need of the times? Is the church giving its adherents vital and impelling leadership?

We have ridiculed the highbrow and extolled the regular fellow. We have averaged everything down to the plane of the majority in this great republic. And now we reap the consequences. When tranquillity prevails in our international affairs and prosperity pours its golden treasure into our laps, we are the wonders of the world! But let the war clouds gather or depression come upon us and what a lot of rabbits we are! Hopeless confusion of thought, childish panic, mob reactions, with no voice of authority rising above the clamor to steady and to calm. Perhaps this is a somewhat exaggerated statement. Here and there, if we listen keenly, we do hear the still, small voice of wisdom. It does not come from the regular fellow but from the despised highbrow. The high-powered salesman, who has been the idol of the American market place, suddenly becomes silent and turns imploring eyes toward the theorist whom he ridiculed in former days.

Mediocrity is the word which epitomizes our apparent national ideal. We believe so thoroughly that all men are created equal that we attempt to keep them so throughout their lives. And as a result we have in high places what Lord Bryce thought the President's Cabinet to be—a first-class group of second-class men. The cult of mediocrity finds a fine breeding place in our educational system. Here the slogan seems to be: "A little for every one, not much for any one." If the moron and his parents demand the privileges of the high school, the college and the graduate school, they must be provided. For is not this a free country with equal opportunity for all? If the brilliant youth cries out for the chance to expand his intellectual life according to his capacity, does he get it? No, indeed; our schools are for all the children of all the people, not for the privileged few. And so from our high schools and universities, committed to the policy of quantity production, there pour forth annually hundreds of thousands of vehicles with attractive bodies but with very little under the hood. One must search among them for a very long time before he finds a high-powered machine tuned to go over the long road with speed and safety.

And still the remedy for mediocrity in the educational process is simple, if we would but apply it. There are perhaps only two outstanding elements which must be considered in a truly effective educational program. One of these has to do with the evaluation of individual capacity; the other with the development of such capacity and the encouragement of independent intellectual achievement. The great weakness in American education is that we submit all students to the same schooling process, giving no consideration to individual capacity. There are students admitted to college who have what may be termed 60 per cent. minds, others with 70 per cent. minds, and still others with 90 per cent. minds. In a few of our better institutions an attempt is made to recognize these obvious differences by sectioning classes, placing the slow together in one group, the average in a second, and the exceptional in a third. But in general we call upon all the students to produce the same results, starting them off with an equal amount of credit and demanding that all attain an average of, let us say, 70 per cent.

Under this system we are succeeding fairly well in educating the youth with the 60 per cent. mind because we are requiring him to do 70 per cent. work. In other words, we force him to "stretch his mind," and this is the essence of real education. But the student with the 90 per cent. mind who is likewise required to do 70 per cent. work does not stretch his mind. With no incentive for outstanding achievement he becomes content with mediocre attainment and leaves college with a mind less alert than upon the day of entrance. And he becomes the congressman who would rather talk about than study a problem of government, the bank official who conceals ignorance with profundity, the clergyman who preaches to empty pews. We complain that the college student is lazy, that he is satisfied with a "gentleman's grade," that he devotes his attention to everything but his intellectual interests. Is the fault all his? Can not part of the blame be laid at the door of our college system, where marks are made a fetish, where 50 per cent. is a failure, 59 per cent. a condition, 60 per cent. passing and so on.

A common campus expression is that this or that student got his plane geometry *off* last year, or will get Chemistry I *off* this semester. What a revelation of academic ideals this statement is! Seemingly, we attend college to get something off rather than to get something on; to endure a disagreeable task in order that we may add one semester credit to our academic stature. And when enough has been gotten off, when, in other words, the student is denuded, a philanthropic faculty covers him with a sheepskin.

It is high time that we abandon this conception of education and turn our attention to stretching 90 per cent. minds; that we forget for the time our parrot-like slogan of equal opportunity for all and honestly make the effort to secure outstanding accomplishment from outstanding people. It is our clear duty to provide the student with every opportunity for independent and creative intellectual activity. To do this we must see to it that freshmen and sophomores have the best teaching the institution provides. This arrangement is quite the reverse of that in vogue in our present educational system from kindergarten to graduate school. In elementary and secondary schools we place the youngest pupils under the guidance of the youngest and most inexperienced teachers. When these teachers show any ability we promote them to higher grades and fill their places with other amateurs.

Likewise in college the average freshman who had just received the best instruction the secondary school provides is placed at the tender mercies of some untried instructor fresh from the graduate school, who has yet to prove whether or not he has the slightest teaching ability. Many times this young doctor of philosophy looks upon his teaching as a necessary though unwelcome step toward the research position upon which his heart is set. And in many instances, the ineffectiveness of his instruction is known neither to department head nor the president because of the academic tradition that a man's classroom is his castle. The theory seems to be that it is better policy to deaden the intellectual interests of fifty students than to embarrass one teacher by observing him in action as he faces his class. These things go far to explain the blasé attitude which the average freshman soon assumes toward his academic work and the over-emphasis which he places on certain extra-curricular activities. Obviously, the main object of education is to teach the individual how to think. Only those can do this who themselves have learned how to make intelligent use of their mental faculties and who have assumed a thoughtful attitude toward life's problems. Here and there, those in charge of educational units have appreciated the soundness of this reasoning, have given the youngest pupils the benefit of seasoned instruction and have secured amazing results. Thus it becomes evident that the love of thinking, the reflective attitude so much needed in American life, will only become general when we reverse our present procedure and place our best teachers in charge of those young students whose minds are plastic. Then college juniors and seniors will be much more capable of reading for honors than they are to-day, because they will have been taught how to control their mental machinery. If good teaching can not be maintained throughout the four years of undergraduate life, if there are not enough good teachers to direct all the courses, the effect of dull and aimless instruction will be far less detrimental to upper-classmen than to under-classmen because the former can go rejoicing on their independent, intellectual way.

Another generally neglected incentive to the maximum development of intellectual capacity is concentration. Monday morning our college student has French at nine o'clock, geology at ten and calculus at eleven. The geology professor, in order to drive anything home, must get the student's mind away from French at the earliest possible moment. And the instructor in calculus must make him quickly forget that there are such subjects in the world as French and geology. The student who is reading for honors escapes some of this erasure process through freedom to concentrate on one subject. But most undergraduates have little opportunity really to ascertain where their true interest lies, to fan some latent spark into a blaze of intellectual enthusiasm. Some day faculties will turn their attention to providing at least one week of concentration during the year for each subject in each student's schedule. The program makers tell us that this is impossible. However, most of the significant advances in the world have been connected with doing the impossible, so this need discourage no one who really wishes to help students find themselves. In the week which the freshman devoted to chemistry or history or political sciences, he might discover the major interest of his life. Many men do not find that interest until they stumble upon it in middle life; may go through life and never find it.

One sometimes becomes pessimistic relative to the rapidity with which these and other essential reforms can be worked out in existing American colleges and universities. Many institutions are making earnest and promising efforts to meet the needs of this challenging time. But they are hindered by tradition, by academic inertia, by barnacles on the curriculum, and a hundred other obstacles. The best of our universities will ultimately come to a state of greater usefulness than at present. But they need better models to follow, better experiments to observe than are now available.

There are enough college and university facilities in America to-day to take care of every qualified student who seeks higher education. The general opinion that the colleges have been swamped with seekers after truth, during the last ten years, is not quite accurate. Many have been flooded with applications for admission, but a very great number of these have come from young people who should stop their formal education at the end of their secondary school careers; who are seekers not for truth but for the recreation and the social prestige which college life is supposed to give. There are indeed enough colleges in the United States but not enough kinds of colleges. And one that does not exist at present and that would go far to help existing institutions find themselves would have but a short life.

There was a great deal of sense in the suggestion of Julius Rosenwald that money for an institution of higher learning should be given not as permanent endowment but for use over a brief period of years. The experimental college in which could be worked out the wisest methods of giving the exceptional student his chance would be organized in agreement with that thought.

Let some one give five million dollars for the founding of such a college with the understanding that it would live for ten years only. The first step in realizing the plan would be for a temporary board of trustees, made up of the soundest educational thinkers in the country, to gather together a small group of outstanding teachers and scholars to make up the faculty. These men would be paid salaries of from $20,000 to $25,000 a year so that they would suffer no material loss in giving up their present permanent berths and accepting positions which would last but ten years. Then there would gather around these teachers a group of not more than a hundred or a hundred and fifty students, scholars in the making—a group not interested in fraternities or winning teams—who would come to sit at the feet of inspiring masters as did the youth of Abelard's day. These students would be chosen not on the basis of secondary school credits nor entrance examinations but through a careful study of their intellectual life history.

The organization of this college would be exceedingly simple. There would be no president, because there would be no endowments to be secured; no alumni to be harangued; no necessity for profound pronouncements on this, that and the other public issue. There would be no dean, for this group of students, having their minds on something engrossing, would be but mildly interested in appropriating stop signs, battling with the police and oversleeping the nine o'clock hour. No registrar would be required, for admission records would cease to be sacred and college achievement would not be measured by a credit yardstick at the end of each semester. All that would be required in the way of administrative personnel would be the chairman of the faculty and a business manager.

Professor Laski, in a recent criticism of American universities, states that "in no country can the buildings and equipment of universities compare with those of America. . . . Yet something is wanting in the American university for which no material splendor can compensate." Truly, we are running wild on extravagance of construction on the American campus. Beautiful college buildings have a great influence in the esthetic education of the student. But what beneficial effect displays of wealth and luxury in college buildings have upon college youth is problematical. Said a sensible student, showing a guest about his dormitory, equipped like a metropolitan club, "Yes, it's fine, but how will I feel when I move out into a hall bedroom?" In our experimental college there will be no capital investment in campus and elaborate buildings. An empty apartment house of moderate size might serve perfectly, or an estate on the edge of the city. All that would be necessary would be accommodations for lecture halls; plain laboratories and attractive living quarters where teachers and students would have the opportunity of mingling in the happy relationships of a group of men interested in the same pursuits. This social grouping would mean much in the life of those who participated, stressing as it would the finer social and intellectual values, a thing well-nigh impossible where the life is less continuous and the associations of teacher and student less constant and intimate.

Aside from the simple housing which has been suggested, little in the way of physical equipment would be necessary. There would be no great libraries or scientific collections to build up, only books and appliances for immediate use. For this college would be in some great center such as New York, Boston, Philadelphia, Washington or Chicago, where splendid libraries and museums are available. Here professors and students would also have at hand the best in American architecture, in the drama and in music. Great industrial organizations would provide opportunities for research. Laboratories for social studies would be found in the teeming life of the city.

But what about opportunities for play? question those whose conception of American college life centers in the stadium. The student in the experimental college would have in the urban environment every possible recreational advantage. Within a short radius of the college he would find public golf courses and golf clubs and likewise facilities for tennis. Clubs where he could enjoy swimming and squash would be open to him. If on Saturday afternoon in the fall he wished to see a football game, he would have the choice of several good intercollegiate matches. And in the spring various college and professional baseball teams would offer him a choice of diversion. There would be a choice of athletic activities suiting the student's desire to be a spectator or a participant. And there would be no grind of training nor any serious emphasis which would take toll of the intellectual program. Here would be a fine demonstration of sport for sport's sake.

In this college professors and students would strive for attainment along whatever lines seemed good to them, unhampered by the limitations of a conventional curriculum. Theories would be tested and assertions challenged. The search for truth would be pushed by those who could distinguish between evidence and propaganda. There would develop a well-founded determination to hold fast to that which is good and an equally fearless desire to discard outworn formulae and dogmas in the light of new discoveries and new social demands. And out of it all would come knowledge not now available, as to the most effective ways of stretching the best minds to the end that real competence might take the place of haphazard mediocrity in the leadership in the affairs of men.

Then when tradition begins to assert itself, when demand for organization begins to be felt, as it always is in America, when convention begins to supersede initiative, the ten years will be over and the institution will pass out of the picture, leaving those who enjoyed its privileges inestimably enriched and institutions of learning everywhere benefitted by the results of its pioneering in the intellectual field. And it is not too much to believe that after the unscrambling of this college, there would arise a demand for another institution on the ten-year plan—yes, for several to serve the needs of that increasing number which is crying out for something which they find difficult to secure in most long-established institutions.

Such a college may never exist. Mediocrity may have such a hold on those who control the means for enterprises in higher education that they will have no interest in making the experiment possible. They may have the feeling of one to whom I sketched this picture and who wrote; "That may sound extremely sensible. But it wouldn't be college. And who wants anything to do with young persons who have no interest in 'anything but intellectual achievement'?" Well, there are a few who would welcome such association, who would find joy in being thrown with just that type of youth. A world full of them might be a bit stuffy, and a nation with no colleges other than the type which I have pictured would have many unfilled educational needs. But doesn't America need to-day at least one laboratory where brain power can be weighed and developed intensively, where the things of the mind are honestly made the things of paramount importance, where mediocrity gives way to superior achievement? What does America need most?

COOPERATING IN ECONOMY[1]

By Dr. THOMAS H. BRIGGS

PROFESSOR OF EDUCATION, TEACHERS COLLEGE, COLUMBIA UNIVERSITY

FROM the vantage point of the present it seems a great pity that the democratic project of universal and advanced education at public expense could not have had a sounder basis than sentiment and a better planning. It can hardly be questioned now that the fundamental reason why society furnishes education and legally compels attendance at schools is that it may perpetuate and improve the ideals that determine the conduct of men and women in a democracy. Stated in another way, the state—that is, organized society—provides education in order that it may be made a better place in which to live and a better place in which to make a living. There is no other reason that justifies society in taking taxes out of every pocket to furnish education for every child.

Having accepted this principle because it is irrefutable, we are forced to the conclusion that because it was not clearly understood in the formative days of the public school, it has largely been disregarded in the direction and development of the educative program. The fetish is so strong, in the profession as well as among

[1] Extract from an address delivered at the Southern Conference on Education, The University of North Carolina, November 5, 1931.

the general public, that tradition has to a tragic extent determined the curriculum and the methods of its presentation. Even those whose position in society should make them leaders toward a new light have been the most stubborn defenders of the traditional because they did not clearly understand the criteria by which values should be measured. If the purpose of public education is to make every individual better able and better disposed to contribute to the betterment of society, then a large part of the popular school program is resulting in lamentable wastes of public funds and in prostitution of the labors of large numbers of pupils. The most common curricula can be shown to have little relation to societal welfare. If the individual is to better society, he must first be bettered himself. The same program is not suited to all individuals, and fortunately society has need of many different kinds of members. If secondary and higher education is to pay dividends on the great investment that is being made, it is doubtful if one now in five receives such profit from the studies that he pursues as to enable him to contribute better to the happiness and the welfare of society.

The economic depression has now begun to cause people to question where money can be saved; and inasmuch as the appropriation for education constitutes the largest single item in the public budget, it is but natural that responsible officers should prune the most flourishing tree. Unfortunately in seeking to effect economies, which are to a large extent made necessary by reckless expenditures in other branches of government, the public is generally using no long-sighted policy. The business man, who during prosperity was in a fair way to become our national hero, is, in cooperating with the politician, forgetting sound principles of economics in his effort to curtail expenditures regardless of consequences. Insurance for the future is more necessary than luxuries and even than some accustomed comforts in the present.

Some communities and even entire states have cut the salaries of all teachers regardless of their competence or of their needs. Economies should not begin with teachers; the last to profit from prosperity should not be the first to feel the pinch of depression. Salaries must be kept at such a level that not only will competent teachers be retained with morale high enough for efficient work but also that promising young men and women will be attracted to prepare themselves for the profession. When readjustment of teachers' salaries is necessary, horizontal reductions for all are neither good business nor good sociology. When used, they are an admission of incompetence on the part of those in authority to determine who are the best teachers or of a lack of faith in the public to support a schedule that assigns pay in proportion to effective work. From a sociological point of view, it is entirely proper to discriminate between two teachers of equal competence in favor of the one with greater family obligations. But the schools should never be a means of charity: whatever needs a teacher may have, he should be retained and assigned only because of ability and zeal to do required educational work. When those in authority look through the needy but incompetent individual to the more important present and future needs of the thirty children to be educated, they can gain courage to do their duty to society, which provides other agencies of charity.

A few communities in their efforts to reduce expenditures are dismissing or retiring teachers on the higher levels of salary schedules, those who have proved their competence and their efficiency, replacing them with others of less experience and of doubtful promise, sometimes of those who are glad or fortunate to receive any remuneration whatever for professional service. This is, of course, penny wise and pound foolish. The pinch of poverty is not yet so keen that it is necessary for us to eat bad eggs.

Sometimes in our devotion to professional tenure we lose sight of the fact that in staffing the rapidly growing number of schools we have accepted many as teachers who are not and never can be significantly competent. Some are limited by nature; others by training and attitude. Necessary economies provide a rare opportunity to weed out such people. If administrators are incompetent or reluctant to do this, they themselves should be replaced by others who feel their professional responsibility and have both judgment and courage to perform a manifest duty. One important economy is to make the public money buy as much as possible.

Another means of false economy is the reduction or omission of expenditures for increasing the efficiency of the schools, expenditures for an enlarged and enriched curriculum, medical inspection, health promotion, provisions for maladjusted pupils, and the like. Such activities have been slowly added in the schools because by the most careful and convincing study of facts they have been found necessary. They are abundantly justified by the principle of sound investment, that public money should be so laid out that the largest and most important dividends may be returned to society. They can not be abandoned without the most serious consequences.

To the layman, and even to the schoolman of narrow vision, some of these activities may seem "fads" and "frills." But as a matter of fact they are the essentials. In devotion to the fetish of education men and women often forget to define what education is. Traditional subjects and traditional details of other subjects are identified in their minds with education, and in consequence they fail to consider what returns they make to society for the great investment in the schools. As we are all pragmatists to-day, we should begin our thinking with the postulate that nothing is important that does not make a difference. If foreign languages, higher mathematics, grammar, and history make such differences in boys and girls that they are happier and better citizens, then these subjects are justifiable. They do make such differences in a small fraction of the school population. But the fact is obvious to any informed and fair-minded judge that for the great majority of pupils who are required, encouraged or permitted to take these subjects at public expense (it is doubtful if many parents would actually pay for them out of their own pockets) the results are altogether insignificant and in many cases actually maleficent. One place for true economy is in those subjects or topics, new or old, that do not make an ultimate difference for the social good.

Another means of economy that is being used is the shortening of the school year. This may be wise. We do not know just what length of school year or week is best. But before acquiescing in a policy for which nothing has been argued except expediency it would be wise to consider several neglected phases of the matter. If the education that is offered does not materially affect the pupils for good or for bad, the amount of it is immaterial. It would just as well be abolished altogether. But if it is beneficent or can be made so, then the more the better. Any shortening of the year is a direct harm not only to the children but also to society that is making the investment. If the educational programs of two communities or states are equally good, those of the one that provides a seven-month year for seven or eleven years can not be expected to compete with those that have nine months of opportunity for eight or twelve years. The mathematics is perfectly simple: the ratios of opportunity are 49 : 72 and 77 : 108—or, roughly, 7 to 10. One group has an all but insuperable handicap. Then, too, we must ask what boys and girls are doing in the months that schools are not in session. With the rapidly increasing urbanization of even our most rural states it must be recognized that there are fewer and fewer opportunities for systematic home chores, for parental oversight and for the development of steady habits of responsibility by means of assigned obligations. On the other hand, modern civilization has brought a rapidly increasing number of opportunities for amusements, diversions and temptations that have large possibilities, especially in the case of older boys and girls, for evil. With the tragic number of unemployed adults, industry has to-day no need for youth. Every one employed tends to displace an adult. It can fairly be questioned if boys and girls are not better off in the wholesome influence of the schools, even if they were learning nothing of permanent value, than freed from all restraint other than that which can be given by the busy modern parent.

A final means that has been used to secure economy is a reduction of supervision. Under the most ideal conditions imaginable supervision would still be a necessity and a wise investment. Conditions are not ideal in our schools: in the best systems teachers vary incredibly in ability, preparation, devotion and consequent effectiveness; courses of study are only beginning to get enrichment and application to life from directed concerted action; and coordination is obviously impossible without a coordinator. In the poorer schools conditions are far worse. Supervisors are found an economic necessity in all industrial plants that must pay dividends. In our schools they are not a luxury but an insurance. Doubtless there are poor supervisors, as there are poor teachers. True economy would result from replacing rather than eliminating them. If a supervisor can coordinate the work of a faculty, direct its activities toward sensible goals, and improve each teacher only 10 per cent. (which is a modest enough estimate) he would easily earn his salary. The large number of beginning teachers and of transfers in our schools emphasizes the need of supervisors. If I had the entire responsibility of directing any unit of education, with due regard to economy and assured achievement, I should unhesitatingly increase the number and the quality of the supervisors.

Economies in school expenditures, as in all other activities, are undoubtedly necessary. This is a time neither for selfishness nor narrow vision. As citizens as well as professional educators we must cooperate. It is our challenge to exert ourselves to the utmost to see that economies are wise and not short-sightedly foolish, that the future welfare of society is assured through the best possible education of the children. Unless the professional educator busies himself to cut the budget where the least harm results, the public without his knowledge of the facts and without his vision will continue to cut it to the lasting harm of the advance of education and of social welfare.

How can the professional educator serve in this crisis?

First, with his intimate knowledge of the costs of education and with criteria emanating from his experience he can voluntarily eliminate items and cut what can be spared with least harm to education. It is only natural that in some phases of our work we have expanded farther than necessary. So have other men, in their private as well as in their business activities. We all recognize some luxuries that are proper in prosperity but improper in depression. It is a civic as well as a professional duty to begin economies by paring down these luxuries in order to retain and improve the essentials. It will be a professional accomplishment of high order to confine reductions to them.

Second, the professional educator can apply the findings of educational research to budgeting, administration, classification of pupils, determining class size, prognosis, the reduction of failures through the proper placement of pupils, individual attention and better teaching, guidance, the elimination of incompetent teachers, elimination of unjustifiable subject-matter, restriction of unwise elections of pupils, and so on. Not all advances in education cost additional money. If the administrator is properly trained and competent in his job, he will know better than any one else, certainly better than the laymen who determine the total of the budget, where economies may be effected by efficiency. More than this, he should continuously inform the public of conditions, of the reasons for proposed changes, and of the results achieved. Ordinarily the public trusts too much to inaccurate reports by pupils, the dissatisfied ones being most active, or to casual conversations, usually with complaining parents. Frequent publicity reports to the patrons and stockholders in the great investment of education are a part of sensible business administration. If the public had more real information about the schools, education would not be so embarrassed as it now is.

Third, the professional educator can check up current practices by sound educational principles and act on the consequent conclusions. We undoubtedly have more items of sound and generally accepted educational philosophy than have been put into practice. Here is an opportunity and an obligation. What we want to do in improving education, certainly on the secondary school level, probably would cost no more than is wasted now in doing what we know we should not do. Educational advance might well begin with the elimination of dead wood in the curriculum and the forbidding of pupils to continue at public expense studies for which they have manifested no competence. Such economies can not be made arbitrarily, but they are possible when justified by a principle or a policy to the acceptance of which the public has been educated. The one principle that education is a public investment to perpetuate its ideals and to promote its interests, to make the supporting community a better place in which to live and in which to make a living would, even if liberally applied, revolutionize the practice of our schools and effect significant economies.

The chief obstacle to economies that would result from a sensible reform of the curriculum practices lies, of course, in the fact that education, especially above the elementary grades, has become a fetish. The public has an unreasoning belief in the efficacy of traditional subjects, regardless of unproved and unprovable beneficent results on individuals. The fact that a few men and women have mastered them and found them useful has led them to think that democracy, in the name of which many sins are committed, requires all pupils to have the same diet. As well have one menu or one type and size of clothing for all. Any detailed proposal for economic reform of the curriculum would undoubtedly disturb the vocal minority who wish their children to follow the fetish, but at the same time it would, after proper preparation through publicity, tremendously please those who pay the taxes and expect some obvious return from the societal investment. Any sound proposal for reform can show by common-sense principles what is essential and what is merely luxurious. If the public is willing to provide funds for the latter, it assumes the responsibility. But if retrenchment is necessary, it is quite possible that the economic depression will provide such an opportunity for curriculum reform as every sensible and informed educator knows is long overdue.

Fourth, the professional educator can at this time prepare a forward-looking comprehensive plan for the education of the children of his community. It may not be a perfect plan, but it will be better than none. It will be a tentative goal and guide. Hand-to-mouth procedure should be a relic of the past, an advertisement of incompetence. It was never creditable to any educator who claimed to be professional and competent. By this comprehensive plan for social betterment, the best that he with all possible professional assistance can honestly make, every educational practice should be examined, and by it every proposed change should justify itself. Probably not in this generation has the need of such a plan been so great or a hospitable consideration of the public been so likely. If the plan is sound, it can be understood by John Citizen. If it is to have effective support, it must be.

Fifth, the professional educator can by his activities convince the public that teachers are citizens as well as public servants. They should make their influence felt in determining public policies, especially those affecting education; they can and should exert themselves to show the importance of education as contrasted with other public activities; they can and should support its rights against those of road-building, policing the country, protecting it from fires, collecting garbage and cleaning the streets. The divorce of education from politics, for which we have fought so long and on the whole so successfully, is proper. But it has also resulted in too much of a divorce of educators from politics, which is improper. The politicians probably know more workers in every other community service than in education, know them and look out for their interests, partly through friendships and partly through respect for their votes. As a result they are too frequently more interested in other civic departments than they are in the schools. They are supported by many selfish patrons of private schools. Of course teachers should not become obligated to politicians and should not tolerate any influence by them on appointments, promotions, and policies. But that is not saying that the profession should abandon its rights and, let us emphasize, its duty to work actively to influence public opinion to support the right kind of education as liberally as it deserves. Teachers should never become civic eunuchs.

This is a dangerous and easily misunderstood topic. But this is a dangerous time for education. In this period of economic depression the professional educator, whatever his position, must be active to influence the public to maintain all the essential activities of the schools. To do this he must first of all clean house, cooperating in economy by saving wherever there has been waste. He must have and he must popularize a program for promoting a better type of education. He must be not only ready but also active to justify before the public the necessary expenditures for what is of most worth. He must rally all possible influences to gain the support of an informed and an interested citizenry. And he must, at least for the time being, subordinate his personal and selfish interests. If physicians in their conventions spent their time in discussing fees instead of fits and fevers, as Arnold Tompkins used to say, they would become discredited. In our conventions, then, we must concentrate on the meaning of education and on the means of making it effective. We must cooperate in economy that it may not be foolish, short-sighted and socially harmful. The truest economy will begin in making every educational activity return the largest dividends on the great social investment in the schools.

I have faith in the land that gave me birth. Fated to work elsewhere, I have been jealous of those who have actively and directly contributed to its great achievements. Its steady and at times marvelous advance has made me thrill with pride. I have admired the honesty with which in this period of economic depression, the seriousness of which I appreciate, it has laid aside pretense and sought to get down to the bedrock facts that it may build again substantially. But I know that it can build only with education. As in economics, so in education it must get down to the bedrock of facts and with the tentative blueprints of the whole structure build with the principles of common sense and social idealism. Education is no benevolence and no charity. It is the only instrument that society has to perpetuate and to improve the democracy to which we are devoted. The depression offers a rare opportunity for leadership, nowhere more needed than in education. The time is ripe. While cooperating in economy, at the same time be audacious to lead. The future of society is in the hands of the schoolmaster of to-day.

EDUCATIONAL EVENTS

TEN MILLION CHINESE IN SCHOOL

TEN million children, men and women in China are now attending schools of all grades from primary to and through the university in that country. This statement was made by E. H. Cressy, secretary of the Committee for Christian Colleges in China, in a recent address to the staff of the Office of Education. Mr. Cressy has been in educational work in China for some twenty years.

He says that each year the school enrolment in China increases, and the standard of instruction offered steadily improves. Children are commonly admitted to the four-year primary school at the age of six. These schools are financed and managed by the counties, and, as an illustration of the encouraging progress that is being made, the fact is cited that by about 1925 a program including the establishment of short-cut normal schools and universal education through the first four years was well under way in 49 of the 60 counties of the province of Kiangsu.

Up to about 1910 Chinese women and girls rarely attended school, and as late as 1915 only one government high school for girls had been established, although there were a considerable number of girls' normal schools of high school grade. The first mission girls' school had been founded in 1844, but up to 1900 educating women and girls was opposed in China so that the school authorities found it difficult to get any pupils for the school.

Physical training, athletics and other extra-curricular activities are now finding their way into the regular school programs in China, and have been instrumental in developing greater activity and alertness among the students.

In an endeavor to decide on an effective working program of adult education to reduce illiteracy, more than one hundred specialists in one county are now carrying on extensive study and experimentation.

Thirty-five mission boards in various countries finance the program of Christian education in China, which includes about 20 institutions of college and university rank. These universities enroll more than 4,500 students majoring in professional or semi-professional lines, with definite vocational objectives. Hospitals and churches, also financed by the mission boards, cooperate in educating the Chinese.

SCIENCE FAIR FOR CHILDREN

A SPECIAL feature of this year's American Institute Children's Science Fair, to be held from December 3 to 9 at the American Museum of Natural History, New York City, is the arrangement of model and special exhibits by science organizations. These exhibits will be non-competitive and are intended to serve as guides in similar work by the youthful scientist. The organizations to be represented are:

New York City Department of Health, a model illustrating the rules of health which a child should follow during a twenty-four hour cycle.

Conservation Department of the State of New York, a special forestry exhibit.

New York Botanical Garden, unusual food-producing trees, such as the cinnamon, banana tree, etc.

Brooklyn Botanic Garden, conditions necessary for plant growth.

New York Museum of Science and Industry, two visitor-operated models, one a color wheel, the other showing the generation of a color spectrum.

Newtown High School, a special agricultural exhibit.

Garden Club of America, conservation of wild flowers and birds.

American Society for the Prevention of Cruelty to Animals, three models—one of a rabbit hutch, one a goldfish aquarium and one a canary cage.

National Association of Audubon Societies, bird conservation exhibit.

This is the Fourth Children's Science Fair to be held by the American Institute. As in previous years, the American Museum of Natural History and School Nature League are cooperating with the institute in the holding of the fair. The Board of Education has given official recognition to the fair and lends its support by arranging for school attendance.

The purpose of the fair is "to focus attention on the sciences and to foster a scientific interest in agriculture, gardening, nature study and conservation." Entry classes call for exhibits by New York City children, not over 18 years old, in many fields of science—biology, chemistry, physics, astronomy, geology, agriculture, nature study and conservation.

LECTURES OF THE COUNCIL ON RADIO

AT the end of the first five broadcasts in the series of thirty lectures on psychology and economics sponsored by the National Advisory Council on Radio in Education, and broadcast over a nation-wide network by the National Broadcasting Company, the council reports the results. Committees, appointed by the American Economics Association and the American Psychological Association at the instigation of the council, have helped to plan the lectures and to prepare printed material to accompany them.

With the idea of promoting further study and reading on the subjects of the lectures, the council arranged that their publishers, the University of Chicago Press, should print the addresses so that they might be obtained by listeners directly after each broadcast. Other publications printed by the University of Chicage Press for listeners were prepared under the direction of the committees. Dr. Walter V. Bingham and Dr. Henry E. Garrett prepared for the committee on psychology a listener's notebook, "Psychology To-day." The second notebook prepared by Dr. Bingham and Dr. John E. Anderson on "Child Development" has just been issued. Each notebook summarizes the separate address on the particular subject and gives supplementary information, pictures, diagrams, questions for discussion groups, and has a bibliography.

The secretary of the Committee on Economics, Mr. Felix Morley, of the Brookings Institution in Washington, D. C., prepared a reading guide, consisting of a digest of the lectures and a carefully compiled bibliography, to accompany the economic series. The University of Chicago Press announces that the distribution of the lectures, notebooks and the reading guide has reached 50,000 copies.

This printed material is being used to supplement the radio lectures in a number of colleges and universities by both the resident and extension departments. The Division of University Extension of the State of Massachusetts is offering the lectures on psychology together with printed material as a course and will give credit to students who pass a satisfactory examination on it. The University of Iowa has not only recommended the programs to the students and to the faculty of the university, but it has also distributed copies of the program to other educational institutions throughout the state, to the press and to interested individuals. At the University of Nebraska, the lectures are discussed in the graduate seminar and in classes of elementary psychology. Five hundred students of psychology at George Washington University are listening to the broadcasts. At Skidmore College, the president has set aside a special radio room so that the students can hear the broadcasts undisturbed. Among other institutions where students are listening regularly to the lectures and using the printed material are George Peabody College, the University of Minnesota, Stanford University, Columbia University, New York University, the Ohio State University, and Western Reserve

University, as well as many junior colleges in the middle west and far west. In some of the southern colleges an effort is being made to measure the actual amount of information obtained by listeners. In general, most of the institutions are using the "Listener's Notebooks" and the printed addresses in connection with introductory courses in place of part of the required reading.

The American Library Association is cooperating with the council by sending notices to librarians asking them to supply their readers with the printed material and the books recommended in the bibliographies of the "Reading Guide" and the "Notebooks." Many libraries have responded to the association's appeal and have purchased large quantities of the printed material.

Word has come from various parts of the country that groups, large and small, are listening to the lectures regularly. Parent-teacher groups, women's clubs, members of the American Association of University Women, are among those who have sent word that they listen to the lectures every Saturday evening.

Plans are being considered for making transcriptions of the talks for use by non-network stations. By means of these transcriptions it would be possible to put the lectures on the air during school hours.

GRADUATE FELLOWSHIPS OF THE AMERICAN ASSOCIATION OF UNIVERSITY WOMEN

THE American Association of University Women awards annually from ten to thirteen graduate fellowships "to encourage women to devote themselves to scientific work and scholarly pursuits." Six of these fellowships are memorials raised by groups of college women to honor women who have played a part in the educational history of America: the Alice Freeman Palmer Fellowship, the Julia C. G. Piatt Fellowship, the Rose Sidgwick Fellowship, and the Mary Pemberton Nourse Fellowship. The association also awards the Sarah Berliner Fellowship established by Dr. Emil Berliner in memory of his mother, and the fellowship offered by the Alpha Xi Delta Sorority. Fellowships established by the Association are: the A. A. U. W. European Fellowship (established in 1890), the International Fellowship, the Latin-American Fellowship, the Margaret E. Maltby Fellowship. The Boston Alumnae Fellowship, which is awarded by the association, was raised by the Boston Branch and alumnae associations of the near-by colleges. The Northwest Central Section also supports a fellowship.

The number of fellowships awarded varies from year to year, as several are biennial and one triennial. The stipends range from $1,000 to $2,000, the majority being for $1,500. Of the fellowships administered by the association, three are for foreign students, one for an American woman to study abroad, one for scientific research, one for advanced work in public health, two for advanced work by women who intend to make teaching their profession, two for advanced work in the field of the social sciences, three for advanced work in any field. In general, it is the policy to make awards to women who have already made some progress in their graduate studies, and who offer promise of distinction in their fields.

The association is now engaged in a campaign to raise a fund of a million dollars for the endowment of additional fellowships. Of this sum $160,000 has already been secured.

Applications for further information should be addressed to the American Association of University Women, 1634 Eye Street, N. W., Washington, D. C.

THE CHICAGO MEETING OF THE AMERICAN ASSOCIATION OF UNIVERSITY PROFESSORS

REPRESENTATIVES from the faculties of colleges and universities in all parts of the country will attend the eighteenth annual meeting of the American Association of University Professors at the Stevens Hotel, Chicago, on November 27 and 28, according to the official announcement of the association. Some of the more urgent problems of the academic profession will be discussed at the various sessions. One of the most vital questions featured on the program will be a comprehensive survey of college teaching with a view to possible improvement. For this important purpose the association has recently been granted $20,000 by the Carnegie Foundation and Corporation for the systematic investigation of present conditions and standards of instruction and for the formulation of higher standards of efficiency.

Addresses will be delivered by Professor Leslie B. Rogers, of the University of Southern California, president of the National Society of College Teachers of Education, and by Professor C. H. Judd, of the University of Chicago, who will represent the same organization. President R. M. Hutchins, of the University of Chicago, will speak at the annual dinner, and President Walter Dill Scott, of Northwestern University, and Professor Alzada Comstock, of Mount Holyoke College, at the luncheon on Saturday. The address of the retiring president of the organization, Professor W. B. Munro, of the California Institute of Technology, will be delivered at the Saturday morning session.

The report of the committee on academic freedom and tenure, to be presented by the chairman, Professor S. A. Mitchell, of the University of Virginia, will be received with special interest because of the wide-spread unsettled conditions in the faculties of universities at the present time. Professor W. W. Cook, of the Johns Hopkins University, will speak on the association's current study of the prevailing conditions of tenure.

In his report as general secretary, Professor H. W. Tyler will speak of the gratifying growth of membership, which is now over 11,000, and also of the increase in the number of institutional chapters, which has reached nearly 200.

THE TENTH ANNIVERSARY OF PRESIDENT RUFUS B. VON KLEINSMID, OF THE UNIVERSITY OF SOUTHERN CALIFORNIA

Trustees, alumni, faculty and friends of the University of Southern California, as well as representatives of national and local educational institutions and civic organizations, are joining in a testimonial of respect, gratitude and affection at an anniversary banquet on December 12, honoring President Rufus B. von KleinSmid upon the completion of the first ten years of his administration. Delegations of students representing the twenty schools and colleges of S. C. will also pay homage to Dr. KleinSmid at the honor function, to be held at the Los Angeles Biltmore.

Mr. John G. Bullock is chairman of the honorary committee of citizens. Mr. George I. Cochran, president of the board of trustees of the University of Southern California, is honorary toastmaster. Mr. Asa V. Call, president of the General Alumni Association of S. C., is chairman of the alumni committee. Dr. Frank C. Touton, vice-president of the university and dean of the College of Letters, Arts and Sciences, represents the faculty and administration. Plans have been formulated at headquarters of the Alumni Association, of which Mr. Frank Hadlock is executive secretary.

Dr. Walter Dill Scott, president of Northwestern University (alma mater of Dr. von KleinSmid) will go from Chicago to be a speaker at the event in honor of his former student. Dr. Scott was appointed professor of psychology at Northwestern in 1901, and President von KleinSmid is a member of the class of '05. Fred I. Kent, chairman of the board of trustees of New York University, and director of the division of foreign exchange of the Federal Reserve Board, also is to speak at the testimonial dinner. Governor James Rolph, Jr., Dr. Robert A. Millikan, of the California Institute of Technology; President Robert E. Swain, of Stanford University; President Robert Gordon Sproul, of the University of California; President Homer L. Shantz, of the University of Arizona (where Dr. von KleinSmid was president from 1914 to 1921), and President G. Bromley Oxnam (Southern California alumnus), of DePauw University (where Dr. von KleinSmid was professor from 1905 to 1914), are to attend.

Since 1921 the University of Southern California has almost tripled in student enrolment, the faculty has about doubled, seven schools and colleges have been added, and seven new buildings have been erected. The schools of medicine, engineering, philosophy, merchandising and public administration; University College (evening adult education division), and Los Angeles University of International Relations (affiliated) have been established during the past ten years, as well as a department of journalism, a physics-optics refraction laboratory, a legal aid clinic, and chairs of musical composition and aviation.

INSTALLATION OF PRESIDENT GRAHAM AT THE UNIVERSITY OF NORTH CAROLINA

Dr. Frank Porter Graham, for some years a member of the history department of the

University of North Carolina, was installed on November 11 as the eleventh president of the university. The exercises took place on a special stage in the stadium and were attended by many thousands of alumni and friends from all parts of the state. There were faculty or alumni delegates from about 160 colleges, universities and learned and professional societies, including the twenty-nine member institutions of the Association of American Universities, whose annual meeting followed the inauguration.

In his inaugural address, which will be printed in School and Society, President Graham had an introductory section on world conditions with reference to Armistice Day, and he then discussed educational conditions in America and in North Carolina.

Greetings were delivered as follows: For American universities and learned societies, by Dean J. C. McLennan, of the University of Toronto; for colleges and universities of the South, by President F. L. McVey, of the University of Kentucky; for colleges and universities of North Carolina, by President W. L. Lingle, of Davidson College; for the public schools of North Carolina, by Superintendent A. T. Allen; for the alumni of the university, by Kemp D. Battle, class of 1909; for the student body, by Robert M. Albright, class of 1932; for the faculty, by Professor Henry V. Wilson. Governor O. Max Gardner presided.

At the lunch following the inauguration the presiding officer was the Honorable Josephus Daniels. Short talks were given by President Walter Dill Scott, of Northwestern University, who praised the scholars and scientific men developed in the North Carolina faculty, and by President James R. Angell, of Yale, who eulogized the University of North Carolina as a shining example of what the state university may accomplish.

At the inaugural dinner to delegates, guests and faculty on the evening of November 11, the toastmaster was President Harry Woodburn Chase, of the University of Illinois, formerly president of the University of North Carolina.

TRIBUTE TO THE LATE DR. JAMES SULLIVAN

A resolution expressing appreciation of the distinguished service of the late Dr. James Sullivan and extending sympathy in his death was adopted by the Board of Regents of the University of the State of New York at its meeting on October 15. The resolution was proposed by Regent Roland B. Woodward, of Rochester, and reads as follows:

On May 21, 1931, by reason of long-continued ill health, Dr. James Sullivan was obliged to tender his resignation as assistant commissioner for higher and professional education. The regents accepted his resignation with genuine regret and expressed at that time their deep appreciation of his distinguished service and their heartiest good wishes for his enjoyment of the leisure he so richly deserved. He was a patient and philosophic sufferer and he bore his great affliction with rare courage. For a time his extraordinary will made it seem as if he might be restored to comfortable health. He was stricken again, however, on October 6 and died on October 8 without regaining consciousness.

Dr. Sullivan was a man of very unusual mold. He had fine scholarly training and instincts and was an active and even an intense intellectual force throughout his life. He served every cause which aroused his interest unsparingly and with a high level of disinterested devotion. He was a discriminating and an exacting scholar and he had small sympathy for shallow thinking or timid conduct. His rugged, outspoken character, his courageous independence of mind and his acute critical sense gave him distinction among educated men everywhere.

The regents are proud of the contribution the example of his useful and forceful life makes to the general store of American ideals and good citizenship. They record anew their appreciation of his career as teacher, scholar, historian and professional leader, and extend to his family their profound sympathy in the common loss of one who left a rich inheritance of character and accomplishment to his day and generation.

EDUCATIONAL NOTES AND NEWS

Lowell House, Harvard University, will give a dinner to President A. Lawrence Lowell, on December 13, his seventy-fifth birthday. When a report, ascribed to a "close friend," that Mr. Lowell would retire soon was recently printed in the daily press, he authorized the following announcement: "President Lowell has no intention of resigning at the conclusion of the current academic year."

DR. NICHOLAS MURRAY BUTLER, president of Columbia University, will celebrate his seventieth birthday on April 2, 1932. Next year will also mark the fiftieth anniversary of his graduation from Columbia College and the thirtieth anniversary of his presidency.

THE honorary degree of doctor of laws was conferred upon Dr. Frank P. Graves at the diamond jubilee celebration of Niagara University on October 12. In conferring the degree President John J. O'Byrne said: "To an educator among educators, a graduate of Columbia, holding degrees innumerable, earned and honorary, from colleges and universities many, and author of well-known books, an honored member of honorary societies, a professor, dean, vice-president, president, of several colleges and universities, educator, alumnus, trustee, a man of broad liberal education, with added culture from his environmental and parental influence, exceptional and cordial relationships with schools and colleges, a man of national reputation, his knowledge of educational problems extensive, his administrative ability unquestioned, a commissioner of education and president of the University of the State of New York, Niagara University pays homage where homage is due and to-day confers the doctorate of laws on Frank Pierrepont Graves." Following the conferring of the degree Commissioner Graves gave an address in which he paid tribute to the Vincentian Fathers, who seventy-five years ago founded the university.

THE Town Hall Club's 1931 Gold Medal for "accomplishment of lasting merit" was presented to Miss Martha McChesney Berry, founder of the Berry School for Mountain Children in Georgia, at a dinner of the club on November 19. The medal, which was awarded last May, was presented by Mr. Francis H. Sisson, president of the club. Mrs. John Henry Hammond, president of the Association of Berry Pilgrims, an organization for the support of the school, and the Reverend Dr. Robert E. Speer, who were the chief speakers, traced the development of the school from its foundation in an old log cabin in 1902. It now has a student body of about 1,000. Miss Berry's name will be inscribed on a plaque in the club.

THE Leslie Dana Gold Medal, which is awarded annually for "outstanding achievements in the prevention of blindness and the conservation of vision," was presented at St. Louis on November 20 to Edward M. Van Cleve, of New York City, principal of the New York Institute for the Education of the Blind. Mr. Van Cleve was selected for this honor by the National Society for the Prevention of Blindness in cooperation with the St. Louis Society for the Blind, through which the medal is offered by Mr. Leslie Dana. Mr. Van Cleve played a leading part in the formation, in 1915, of the National Society for the Prevention of Blindness, for which the Russell Sage Foundation was sponsor, and he became its first managing director.

A UNIQUE record in teaching was recognized recently in connection with the installation of Dr. Charles Albert Anderson as president of Tusculum College, when two professors were honored because of a combined record of one hundred and two years of teaching in the college. Dr. Landon Carter Haynes has been professor of mathematics for fifty-five years, and Dr. Thomas S. Rankin has been professor of ancient languages for forty-seven years, the latter retiring from active teaching this year.

PROFESSOR FREDERIC W. SCHLUTZ, of the University of Chicago, who arrived in Havana on November 16, on the following evening received a diploma as a corresponding member of the Cuban Pediatric Society in honor of his achievements in the field of physical culture for children.

DR. A. R. BRUBACHER, president of the New York State College for Teachers at Albany, New York, was the guest of honor and speaker on November 19 at the Boston University School of Education.

DR. GEORGE H. LOCKE, the chief librarian of the Public Libraries of Toronto and formerly professor of education in the University of Chicago, has been honored by the Library Association of Great Britain and Ireland by having conferred on him an honorary fellowship in that association.

DR. WILLIAM ALLAN NEILSON, president of Smith College, was elected chairman of the trustees of the Carnegie Foundation for the Advancement of Teaching at the annual meeting of the board on November 17. Dr. Livingston Farrand, president of Cornell University, was elected vice-chairman and Dr. Josiah Penniman, provost of the University of Pennsylvania, was re-elected secretary.

MR. AUGUST HECKSCHER, of New York, and Mr. Martin J. Insull, of Chicago, have been elected to the board of trustees of Cornell University.

LEAVE of absence has been granted to President Frank Aydelotte, of Swarthmore College, starting at the end of January, to go to Mexico and continue his study of the Latin-American countries. Later he will represent the United States at the Pan-American Conference at Havana, and will then go to Germany to study the development of universities there. Professor John A. Miller will be acting president in Dr. Aydelotte's absence.

DURING the absence of Professor Henry W. Holmes, dean of the Graduate School of Education of Harvard University, who is on leave until January 1, Professor Walter F. Dearborn is acting as dean of the school.

THE New York alumnae of Western College, at Oxford, Ohio, gave a luncheon on November 21 to Dr. Ralph K. Hickok, recently elected president of the college and formerly head of the department of religious education at Wells College.

REPRESENTATIVES of thirty colleges attended the inauguration of the Reverend Dr. Herman Brezing as president of Wagner College on November 18.

DR. WALTER L. COLLINS, director of graduate work in Teachers College, University of Cincinnati, has been elected president of Wilmington College, Ohio.

DR. GEORGE EVERETT WALK, dean of the Teachers College at Temple University, was elected president of the Pennsylvania State Teachers College at Shippensburg at a meeting of the trustees on November 10.

MR. ROBERT H. HALLOWELL has been elected president of the corporation of the Perkins Institution and Massachusetts School for the Blind, at Watertown.

A CHANGE in the administration of the College of Agriculture of the University of New Hampshire has been announced, creating a new office of associate dean and director of resident instruction. Dr. M. Gale Eastman has been appointed to the position. Dean Frederick W. Taylor will center his attention on the direction and supervision of business and management problems under the title of dean and superintendent of commercial departments.

MR. DAVID J. HAYKIN, of Washington, D. C., has been appointed chief of the division of documents at the Library of Congress. He will begin work on January 1, 1932, after resigning his present position with the American Library Association.

DR. IPATIEFF, member of the Russian Academy of Science and professor in the Russian Artillery Academy and the University of Leningrad, will be visiting professor in the department of chemistry at Northwestern University.

THE following members of the faculty of the University of Michigan have been granted leaves of absence for the second semester of the current academic year: Professor Edson R. Sunderland, who expects to travel in Europe and study the various systems of court procedure; Professor Henry F. Adams, who intends to visit psychological laboratories in the various countries of Europe; Professor Russell A. Dodge, who wishes to take some advanced work in hydraulics at Columbia University; Professor Norman L. Willey, who will visit the Scandinavian countries, especially Norway, Germany and Lithuania; Professor Warren E. Blake, who wishes to devote his uninterrupted efforts to certain research work in which he is interested and which is nearly ready for publication; Professor Philip E. Bursley, who will spend the period in study and travel; Professor R. K. McAlpine, who will study with Professor Baxter at Harvard University, and Professor Christian N. Wenger, for travel and research in comparative literature in England and Germany.

DR. JAMES B. PRATT, professor of philosophy at Williams College, has sailed for Java and the Orient, *en route* to India, where he will teach for three months in Tagore's School. In the spring he will go to Italy.

The death is announced at the age of sixty-seven years of Henry B. Dewey, formerly superintendent of public instruction for the State of Washington.

Dr. William J. Bickett, for the last eleven years superintendent of Trenton, New Jersey, schools, died on November 18 at the age of fifty-two years.

According to an Associated Press dispatch W. W. McConnell, superintendent of the Winfield, Kansas, schools, was found shot to death on the high-school campus on the night of November 18 under circumstances which led officers to believe that he had been murdered.

Dr. George Guille, president of the William Jennings Bryan Memorial University, Dayton, Tennessee, died on November 19 at the age of fifty-eight years.

Professor Isaac Franklin Russell, formerly chief justice of the Court of Special Sessions, New York City, and the oldest professor in point of seniority at New York University, where he had taught law since 1881, died on November 21 at the age of seventy-four years.

The death is announced of Mr. James Alexander Richey, late educational commissioner with the Government of India, at the age of fifty-seven years.

The twelfth annual conference of the Progressive Education Association will be held in Baltimore, from February 18 to 20, 1932, with the Emerson Hotel as headquarters. The speakers so far announced include Dr. George S. Counts, Dr. Hughes Mearns, Dr. Fannie Dunn, Marion E. Miller, Dr. Lois Hayden Meek, Dr. Thomas Alexander, Mr. Ralph M. Pearson and others. The sessions will all relate to the present status of education in the problem of social reconstruction. As before, the chief feature of the conference will be a series of group discussions with leaders, exhibits of school materials, and well-planned programs. New topics have been added. The conference promises a large attendance both because of many new features and the opportunity to attend the sessions of the National Education Association in Washington the week following, and the events of the Washington Bi-Centennial.

The annual report of the president of Howard University shows that the total enrolment of the university for the year 1930–1931 was 2,380 students from 39 states (including the District of Columbia) and 16 foreign countries. At the June commencement 307 men and women received degrees in 9 schools and colleges. The president reports far-reaching improvements in instruction as a result of an addition of 63 new members to the teaching staff of the university; a steady increase in the libraries of law, medicine, dentistry and the natural and social sciences, through gifts from private educational foundations; the upward revision of entrance requirements in the Colleges of Medicine and Law; the admittance of the School of Law to accredited rating by the American Bar Association and its registration by the State of New York; reorganization and marked progress in the pre-clinical and clinical divisions of the College of Medicine; the steady growth of graduate work; the completion of three new dormitories for women; the reorganization of system and the establishment of a budget director in the office of the secretary-treasurer.

A decision rendered by Superior Judge Fred G. Remann makes the College of Puget Sound the recipient of a bequest of $150,000 from the estate of the late Leonard Howarth, of Tacoma. The court held that the College of Puget Sound was legally entitled to the Howarth bequest after evidence was brought forward to show that the college was not entirely self-supporting and therefore fulfilled the conditions of the will which designated the fund for a charitable institution. $100,000 of the fund will be used to pay the mortgage on Science Hall, which is to be renamed the Leonard Howarth Hall of Science, and the remaining $50,000 will be devoted to scholarships. The securing of the bequest enables the college to match the $125,000 offer of the Rockefeller Foundation, which, with the Howarth fund, will increase the endowment of the college to about two million dollars.

Cornell University fraternities will be permitted, under certain restrictions, to build houses on ground owned by the university and now reserved for the housing of men students, under a plan approved by the board of trustees. The decision follows a comprehensive survey of the housing of men students and makes it possible for fraternities to obtain sites in close proximity to the campus. The entire university tract has not been made available for this use. The land to the west of the campus, recently acquired by the university and known as the Franklin Cornell property, is the section now opened to fraternity building.

School attendance among all age groups has increased in the 93 cities having a population of 100,000 or more, according to statistics compiled by the Bureau of the Census. The number of persons 21 years old or over attending school shows especial increase and doubled in some cities between 1920 and 1930. In 1920 only one city reported 98 per cent. of its children between the ages of 7 and 13 in school, while in 1930 31 cities returned such a percentage, according to the statement.

A raise in pay for Russia's school teachers has been voted by the Council of the People's Commissars. Effective on January 1, according to an Associated Press dispatch, primary teachers' salaries will be raised from $35 to $45 a month, and the salaries of those in the higher grades from $50 to $65. The teachers also have been promoted to the first category of food privileges, on equal footing with the "workers."

DISCUSSION

THE MARKET FOR SCHOLARLY AND COMPETENT TEACHERS

Articles by Dr. Malcolm W. Wallace and H. G. Langdon in School and Society for August 22, 1931, provoked a train of thought. Dr. Wallace states that many scholarly and competent teachers are usually to be found working under impossible conditions in our larger cities.

It may be contended that I am conceited to class myself as a scholarly and competent teacher. I worked in a very large city under ideal conditions for eight years and under bad conditions which gradually grew worse for eight more years. This city permits teachers to retire on pensions when they have taught twenty-five years, though they may be only forty-five years of age. Some of them have the appearance of thirty, and a few are men. Many of these persons have deep reasons for dissatisfaction.

In addition to large classes and noisy classrooms situated on boulevards where decent class discussion is impossible, many teachers never teach their college majors. I had taught economics for ten years, but it was handed to an individual who had done three years of post-graduate work in Greek. This instructor had found teaching classics much less pleasant than handling social science, and an accommodating principal supplied the desired program assignment.

In this city teachers who remain at work until they are sixty-five years of age receive pensions of $1,800 to $2,000 a year. I can live decently upon the $800 a year I receive, plus some returns on savings. I know that with a capital of $2,000 a person who can amuse himself with a garden, chickens and some writing or tutoring need not starve, if $1,000 to $1,200 is expended for a house and lot. Plumbing, electricity, gas and certain other comforts can be installed for a few hundred dollars additional. A car is not needed, since buses will take you to the larger cities, where library facilities are available, for one dollar per year. These living conditions are possible in towns of one thousand and under. People like me deserve no sympathy, and time is never heavy on my hands.

Am I a scholarly person? I made Phi Beta Kappa when I graduated from college. When I had my oral examination for a master's degree the head of the department encouraged me to work for a doctorate. I have done about three years of post-graduate work in social science at a leading university. My grades may be too high to be healthy, but I have never been in a hospital. I have never sat up until midnight to do school work of any kind. Perhaps that is the road to success.

Am I a competent teacher? I have been guilty of changing jobs, but my salary has constantly increased. I was invited to take a college assistantship five years after attaining my bachelor's degree. I had done no graduate work at the time. My salary as a high-school teacher was very good and the professor who made the offer had given one woman assistant a very raw deal when she was no longer young and handsome. A few years later I was indulging in a course in American history at summer school. The professor recommended me for a position in agricultural college of his state. I was not a candidate for a position and knew nothing about the matter until the head of the department wrote me. I was then teaching in a normal school, but I would have accepted the position. The president of the agricultural college told the head of the department, "Get a man, even though he never taught a day in his life."

I had eight years of glorious teaching in the city where conditions are now well-nigh impossible, with a principal who permitted me to to carry out my own ideas. At the end of the day I could go over to the university for a seminar. The man died, the school changed its racial complexion and I was offered two other positions, one in a junior college.

A year ago I went to a vocational adviser at a great university. "What are the opportunities for mature persons with my educational preparation?"

"For persons who must write forty as their age there has been a slight improvement, but conditions are still much worse than they should be."

If I insisted upon returning to work in the great city, which now pays me $800 a year for no service whatever, I could do so, provided I exerted myself to secure strong political backing. I know the game, and the exertion would not be great. I doubt whether I will choose to do so, because teaching conditions are well-nigh impossible and there is no prospect of improvement. The city needs to employ at least 50 per cent. more teachers than it now has on the staff. Teachers available for employment have better educational preparation than 25 per cent. of of the instructors now at work. The requirements of the North Central Association of Colleges and Secondary Schools in regard to class size and teacher qualifications are persistently violated. The slogan of a professional teachers' organization is "Observe North Central Requirements."

For variety I attended summer school this season. In vocational guidance I took twenty-five psychological tests. Some of them were a bore. I do not know my I.Q., despite the orgy of tests. For my own pleasure I have studied taxation the last five years. The professor who taught public finance told me that he feared that I was getting nothing out of it, but I learned something about the tax laws of this state. The professor of the junior college course was relatively young and peppy. He considered me something of a nuisance, but we were friends at parting.

I know that there are teachers, male and female, who desperately need jobs at high salaries because they have expensive families to support. Some folks are in debt and must be taken care of. But it is also true that application blanks of mature individuals with scholarship and teaching experience merely clutter up the files of appointment bureaus, for no college presidents will consider such persons for places on their faculties. There is constant and persistent complaint that good teachers are hard to find, but scholarly and competent women teachers are at work under impossible conditions in the larger cities, and the person who dares to leave must plan to find other occupation than teaching.

AN EXPERIMENTEE

FIRST GRADERS' RELIGIOUS IDEAS

IDEAS are dynamic, as they lie back of every good and bad action. Children begin very early to have ideas, some of which urge their possessor on to immediate action, while others lie dormant and pass through a ripening process in the very grooves of character until at later date they crop out in the form of ideals, complexes, phobias, prejudices and the like. It can be safely said that the first years of a child's life lay the foundations of his future character as well as his emotional outlook on life and the part he will play in society for good or bad. Plato with his admirable foresight made provision for this belief, which is now beyond the realm of theory. The late G.

Stanley Hall, Maria Montessori, the Freudian School, the Behaviorists and Psychiatrists and students of child nature consider these early years as the foundational period in a person's life.

If education is to yield desirable effects, it has to be put on a sympathetic but scientific and not a mechanistic basis, with the teacher as an observing student of human nature. Although an intelligent teacher could treat religious problems with fairness and justice, yet the responsibility of influencing and guiding children's ways of thinking is that of the parents and of adult society, for they are the main sources of good or bad ideas handed down to the oncoming generation.

The first-grade pupils in the Ohio University Training School provided striking examples of what the writer has just stated. It was shortly before Christmas when teacher and thirty boys and girls, mostly from good homes, sat in a friendly circle to express their ideas and incidentally better their oral English. A student teacher was appointed to record the proceedings verbatim.

The experiment, which was to find out the children's religious ideas, started with a question asked by the teacher: "Something is going to happen in December, boys and girls." To which all eagerly shouted out, "Christmas." Then each proceeded to review his or her experiences in the following lines (each statement represents an individual):

On Christmas I have some little bells down home and they tinkle.

When bells tinkle, Santa Claus and witches are coming.

My biggest brothers when they were little boys, Santa brought them Irish mails. They asked if they wanted an Irish Mail and they said, ''Yes, sir, Yes, sir, Yes, sir,'' three times.

I like Christmas, you get a whole lot of things, dolls, bananas, candies.

We put snow on the Christmas tree and many presents.

Last year I got things for Christmas that I could make windmills out of.

Santa brought me a doll and it fell off the couch and broke.

Santa brought me an electric train and it would run forward and backward, and a wagon and bicycle and a monkey with electric light inside of it.

Last year I got a sleepy doll and its eyes got broken and it was blind, I have to wait for next Christmas to get another.

At this point, the teacher made an attempt to draw her pupils' attention to the homeless children living in an institution close by the town. After a promise to bring them toys that were to be discarded at Christmas time, they eagerly went on recalling their past experiences and putting in their orders. Up to this point, the One for whom Christmas was supposed to be celebrated was not even mentioned.

One of them continued:

Last Christmas I got a tricycle and the next year I got a mama doll.

Teacher: Why do you like Christmas?

Because Santa Claus brings us candy and toys.

Because we get good things to eat. Mother makes pies and cookies.

'Cause we get shoes and coats.

Because we have roast chicken and trees.

Santa Claus brings us suckers and ice cream.

He brings us trains and books to read.

He comes every year through the chimney.

I like Christmas because daddy always gets me a box of candy and some toys and mother gives me handkerchiefs.

Because I got a really big piano on Christmas.

Because the Lord was born in a stable. I like to hear the bells ring.

Santa brought me a truck and Mother got a fur coat.

I like Christmas because Santa has brought me a wagon and a new brown suit.

Santa will bring me a baby brother.

Santa brings us oranges, apples and grapes.

We get sleds and apples and bananas.

We have a good dinner and cranberries and ice cream.

Santa is going to bring me a doll that will sleep and talk, wink and blink, and say ''Mama'' and cry and sleep. Then she is going to walk too.

I like Christmas because Santa takes our money and brings us stuff.

Last year I had a bank half full of money and after Christmas night I couldn't find any money in it. I asked my mother but she just laughed.

Santa must have taken the money because he has to get presents with it.

Because we get baby caps and doll babies and then I get a doll that talks and walks. I always get more than other children.

I know a good way to pay Santa: Put a note up on the mantle and put the money right by it.

I know how to pay Santa: Get him to leave his hat and then put the money in his hat and then Santa will come and take his hat away.

I don't pay Santa, I just hang my stockings up and he puts things in it.

When Christmas comes my cousin has so many toys that he has to take a wagon and pull them away.

Here the teacher made a strong attempt to direct their thoughts to the religious phase of the celebration and received the following interesting expressions:

Jesus was born on Christmas day.

We get a calendar with Jesus picture on it. Jesus has a long beard.

In our bed room there is a picture with three crosses in it. Men hang from it and I get scared.

I like Christmas because Jesus is our brother and Mary is our mother and Jesus is our father, mother and uncle too.

Mama said Mary was a bad woman and Jesus was good and Mary cried hard and Jesus made her good again.

One day I was out playing and some cows were coming along and one came up and hooked a little boy.

Jesus got killed to keep us from getting killed.

We have two fathers and two mothers: One is Jesus and one is our really father, one is our mother and one is Mary.

Jesus loves us and makes us rich.

Once Jesus got killed and he got alive again and then he died again.

He got hung on the cross and he had nails put right in his hands and feet.

They put nails through God's head too.

The Jews did it; they are bad.

God gives us everything if we are good. When we are bad he takes it away and punishes us.

He puts us in dark and hot holes.

He helps us so we don't get killed from anything.

They put God in the hole and then put a big stone over it. Over the stone there was a bird singing and Jesus grew up to be God.

He came from heaven and sat in Mary's lap. He is now in heaven where the clouds sail.

The wicked Jews made blood come out of his hands and feet.

They put a sword into his side.

We have a picture in our home and a man fell down before the picture and said, "God, Oh God, help me out," and God helped him out.

We have a picture of Jesus and He was walking on the water with a big ship in front of him and many fishes in the boat.

Roughly speaking, these youngsters had gathered from Christmas and their religious training the following main ideas: (1) Christmas was an occasion to appease their acquisitive tendencies to the pitch of greediness. They were, without exception, strong on *getting*. The idea of *giving* had hardly won a place in their consciousness. (2) The general notion (in most cases final) was that the Jews were bad. (3) Ideas of killing, getting killed, bloodshed and other morbid notions closely allied to their religious impressions were predominant. (4) That God was a hard and cruel taskmaster ready to punish the disobedient and reward the submissive—in other words, the good.

In the light of the foregoing contributions we can not help thinking of the fact that there is a strong sadistic and imitative tendency in primitive and modern man. That the chaotic religious state in which the young find themselves is far from desirable, no one will deny. Is it not time to stop erecting even progressive or up-to-date structures on dangerous and weak foundations? Regardless of external detrimental conditions, teachers and schools have been subject to pressure from outside and unjustly held responsible for all the waywardness of youth. But by the time the children come to school, their character traits are formed; then why place all the burden of reconditioning conduct on the school? The constructive work of the school will have to start with parents and society.

Hilda A. Freeman
New Mexico State Teachers College

SPECIAL CORRESPONDENCE

THE AUSTIN FOUNDATION AT NORTHWESTERN UNIVERSITY

In the fall of 1929, Northwestern University began a unique experiment in education. This was the training of a small group of carefully selected young men for executive positions in large business and industrial enterprises. These men were recipients of scholarships provided by the late Frederick C. Austin, a wealthy retired Chicago manufacturer.

Mr. Austin was convinced that in future generations the greatest form of organized human activity will be business. He was of the opinion that consolidations will go forward in every phase of business, but that such organizations will be successful only to the extent that competent leaders are trained for the more important executive positions. While colleges and universities have specialized in training men in the arts and sciences, he said, the business world has been allowed to go it blind in training its executives.

Technical training is needed as much in preparing men for the various fields of business, in his opinion, as in the professions; and it was his desire that all his holdings should go toward a new movement in education for developing not only the executive abilities of youth, but also to train them in the science of leadership.

In pursuance of this, Mr. Austin deeded to the university property in the loop district of Chicago valued at several million dollars. The income from this property was to provide scholarships for "male persons of the Caucasian race, without reference to nationality, religion or wealth, for the purpose of fitting the recipient to attain proficiency in business and industrial pursuits, having specially in mind the fitting of such persons for executive positions in large business and industrial enterprises."

Mr. Austin, under the agreement, retained the income during his lifetime; but as he was eager to see the program put into partial operation at once, that he might share in the work of establishing the foundation and planning its future, he provided for ten new scholarships each year. Thirty Austin scholars are now on the campus, and next year there will be forty.

The work of selecting the Austin scholars, of guiding them through their years of training, and of obtaining for them after graduation suitable openings in the business field, was turned over to the department of personnel of the university, of which Dr. Delton T. Howard is director.

It is specified that Austin scholars must enter Northwestern University as freshmen, with no advanced standing credits, except such as may be earned in the high school. All applicants must be in the upper tenth of their high-school classes in scholarship ability. They are given mental alertness tests and are examined in English composition.

Since the object of the scholarship is to train men for managerial work, qualifications other than scholarship are emphasized. Stress is laid upon such qualities as leadership, originality, public speaking, physical health and development, popularity and character.

When and where have they been leaders? What have they done that exhibits originality? Have they actually made public addresses, are they actually able to say what they mean in a clear and incisive manner? Who has trusted them with responsibility and why? What evidence of popularity or general esteem can actually be cited? These are some of the questions for which answers are sought.

Many applications are received each year. The process of sorting out the most promising candidates is an interesting one. Large rating sheets are prepared. The student is given a grade on each of the traits which it is desired to consider. These grades are assigned various weights in accordance with their importance. When the total scores are computed some twenty or thirty men are found ranking highest. This special group is then investigated more thoroughly. Personal interviews are obtained. Additional information is called for. Special clues are followed up. Finally, ten men are selected to be Austin appointees.

The question often is raised whether a boy interested in engineering, journalism, chemical engineering or some other form of technical training is eligible for an Austin scholarship. But the answer is fairly simple, providing the governing principle is kept in mind. The Austin scholarship is designed for men who expect to enter the business world to do extensive work. It is not designed to provide technical training to fit men for particular professions.

The student may take many courses in journalism, engineering, chemistry or accounting, if he so desires. Modern business involves many sciences and techniques. But the student must, in any event, follow those courses of study that will give him an understanding of modern business and fit him for executive work.

There is no fixed course of study for Austin

scholars. A special board of advisers has been created. This board has general oversight of their studies. The college of liberal arts has permitted the board to set aside the regular requirements and to register the Austin scholars in such courses of study as seem best fitted to their individual needs.

In general, the Austin scholars carry very substantial programs. The departure from general regulation has seemed an advantage in several instances. Certain special courses of study have been created. In no instance, however, has the university assigned special funds for this purpose.

The Austin scholars live together in a dormitory, under the supervision of a proctor. A new dormitory for their special use is now being built on the campus and will be ready for occupancy next fall. The scholars are not permitted to join fraternities. They are encouraged to participate in campus affairs, especially in those which have distinct values in the way of social and leadership training. Nearly all the scholars do some sort of remunerative work to help pay a part of their educational expenses.

It should be understood that we stand at the beginning of what promises to be a most unusual experiment in education. At some future time the Austin Foundation will support a large number of students. Austin scholars will be setting a pace that average students will find it difficult to follow. The faculty will have modified many courses and programs as a result of their presence on the campus. The project will touch campus life and tradition, will change many things in the classroom and will affect administrative policies. A huge program remains to be worked out. What has been done so far—and it is considerable—is only a part of what must be done eventually.

The Austin scholars on the campus now are not great geniuses. They are not supermen, nor are they overpowering in personal presence. They are more notable for sanity than brilliance. They know how to work, but they also know how to play. The freak has no place in the Austin program.

The Austin scholarships pay at present $650 a year, with the probability of a fifth year abroad at $1,500 for travel and study. It is probable that this is the best undergraduate scholarship now offered by any university. It pays well and it carries with it many special privileges.

The attachment of the Austin scholars to the university will be direct and constant. Our placement service will aid the men in finding suitable jobs after graduation, and the foundation will never be out of touch with them thereafter. It is an inspiring program, once its possibilities are apprehended. We sincerely hope that it will develop into the really great enterprise that it is capable of becoming.

WALTER DILL SCOTT

OFFICE OF THE PRESIDENT

QUOTATIONS

FEDERAL RELATIONS TO SCHOOLS

THE National Advisory Committee on Education concerning the relation of the Federal Government to education is to be commended for the emphasis which it has given to local autonomy and responsibility. Incidentally, this means "working away from recent tendencies toward centralization in Washington of powers over the purposes and processes in education," both in legislation and in administration. This is sound doctrine. It is to be hoped that the "working away" from centralizing influences will be begun immediately.

It should lead to abandoning federal grants based on conditions imposed upon the states. Such appropriations have been made for "special forms of education of interest to special groups of people." Whatever may have been said for this course in the past to help in setting up types of training which the states were slow to undertake, it has no longer that justification. It is suggested by the committee that unconditional subventions might be made, but they should be for education in general and only after thorough studies. Grants might be made for a definite and limited period in helping the states to eliminate illiteracy—a purpose basic to citizenship. But even in so vital a matter, the greatest care should be taken not to weaken the sense of state and local responsibility.

With the findings of the first section of Part I of the admirable report (embracing senior education in states, education in territories and outlying possessions, training of government personnel, research and information and international relations) there is substantial accord on the part of the members of the committee and will be by the public. But when one comes to the proposed governmental organization there is seeming inconsistency in setting up, in name at least, a more highly centralized machinery than now exists. Chiefly in order to give the government "a spokesman for the American spirit and method in education," it is recommended by a large majority of the committee (38 to 11) that there should be a Secretary of Education having, it is to be inferred, though it is not specifically so stated, a place in the President's Cabinet. But the principle of non-centralization leads to the restriction that his department would have "no legal or financial power and no regulatory or executive authority, direct or indirect, explicit or implied, by which it may control the social purposes and specific processes of education." With such reservations a secretary would be a secretary only in name. Would it not be best that the coordination of the purely federal agencies of education and research should be carried on under the Commissioner of Education, adequately supported within the Department of the Interior? The educational authority of a political officer and spokesman clothed with the title of "secretary" and without power is not likely to be superior to that of a commissioner who is known as an educational leader. A Secretary of Education with full powers would not be welcomed by a democracy that wishes to keep its schools close to the community and the home.—*The New York Times.*

A YES AND NO REPORT

HAVING spent $100,000 and two years' time in the study of American education, an able national committee submits its report to President Hoover. One imagines that a document of this character must have some important things to say about education. Unfortunately, however, the summaries published to-day do not convey that impression. In two columns of news-print no comment can be found regarding education itself. No statement, either general or particular, is offered concerning the current position of public and private schooling throughout this broad land, its major trends, its strength or its weakness.

The official summary, on the other hand, deals exclusively with a problem of educational administration. It is, to be sure, a very great problem, for it concerns nothing less than the policy and power of the Federal Government in relation to the power and duty of each of the separate states to deal with education in its own way. On this score, a large majority of the committee is strongly in favor of sharp restraint upon the growing tendency of the Federal Government to exert direct pressure upon the course of education in the various states. It would have the work of the central government restricted solely to informative and fact-finding functions. The desirability of keeping the federal administration as far removed as possible from any rôle of active control over the course of educational affairs in the several states has always seemed to us very clear and important. We still regard it so.

The majority of the president's committee, holding this view, has recommended a means of supporting local school autonomy, which on its face is a paradox. In order to cut down interferential educational control on the part of the Federal Government, forty-three of fifty-one members have voted in favor of the creation of a Federal Department of Education, its head to hold, of course, a place in the cabinet. The argument of the majority runs as follows:

> The lack of such an official spokesman for education, competent and influentially situated in the government, has been one of the conditions, and a major condition, which has permitted us to drift into our present dilemma where a nation, by tradition and experience opposed to the federalized administration of education, has in fact developed a pluralized federal control of education in the states through various federal agencies, which are not even coordinated in their efforts. This drift toward centralized federal controls is attested by the effects of enabling acts, land and money grants with a restricted education purpose, and approvals and vetoes of state plans, all sanctioned by law and department rulings.

Now there is, of course, a serious logic in the committee's position. If the Federal Government's bureau of education should be raised to the dignity and strength of a federal department, with a chief of its own in the cabinet, and if an iron-willed man can be found for that office who will ruthlessly cut down every existing federal control over state policy in the schools, and steadily resist every tendency of his department to seek new power, then surely the future will work out in the way the committee desires, that is—if the new secretary lives forever. But who can say that the practical political experience of this nation justifies any such anticipation? On the contrary, has not the whole history of the Federal Government shown an opposite tendency? The head of a great department is always trying to make his department greater, both in authority and in the number of office-holders within it. That, we are bound to say, would almost inevitably be the result of an adoption of this committee's recommendation. A federal department of education would increase Washington's direct control over education in the states, not diminish it.—*The Boston Evening Transcript*.

A SECRETARY OF EDUCATION?

FURTHER proof that an idea often has even greater persistence than the persons who promote it is to be found in the annual return of the proposal for a Secretary of Education in the Cabinet of the President of the United States. It now appears as the major recommendation of Mr. Hoover's National Advisory Committee on Education.

Many who read of this recommendation a few days ago are still surprised that it should be made by this particular committee. The members were chosen by the Secretary of the Interior, who has spoken against a federal department of education. A number of them were believed to have affiliations that would lead them to hush such a proposition. Notwithstanding all this, the proposal has come again boldly into the limelight.

The first recommendation for a Secretary of Education came in 1918 from the spokesmen of the public schools, the members of the National Education Association. Since then a long list of national bodies have one by one become its strong supporters. With each session of Congress a new bill has been framed, and an effort made to improve the wording each time so that objections would be met and the intent of the plan be made unmistakably clear.

There is significance in the fact that Mr. Hoover's committee, after two years of study, has made this recommendation within a report that is thoroughly devoted to state control. Apparently the committee, voting 43 to 8, has little fear that the bill as now worded would open a way for federal encroachment upon a state's management of its own schools. It is on this phase of the proposal that there has been the most apprehension. The promoters of the new seat in the cabinet have tried to recognize the reasons for this apprehension and to show that they want only a department that is purely a research center and a clearing house for constructive educational information.

Mr. Hoover's advisory committee, composed of fifty-one prominent educators, presents the opinion that it is on account of the lack of a department of education that the states are today in many financial snarls with the Federal Government. There are, for instance, certain grants made by the National Government to the individual states for specific phases of education, resulting in unfortunate political, social and financial consequences. The committee goes on to point out various wasteful duplications in the services of the different agencies dealing with the states.

Public school educators long have wanted to give to education as a whole a certain official dignity which they believe can be conferred by the admission of a Secretary of Education to the President's Cabinet. It must be remembered, however, that to merit a seat in this council an official must head a department which has some authoritative part in national administration, and therefore some definite contribution to make to public policy.

The duties and powers outlined by the committee hardly seem to justify such a post. A mere bureau can disseminate information, as does the present Commissioner of Education, or carry on research, as do the Bureau of Standards or the Bureau of Animal Industry. To assemble under one head the administration of the various forms of federal financial aid to education would confer some executive responsibility. Then to add the functions of Indian education, and possibly agricultural extension service, would round out a department.

But the committee opposes federal supervision of fiscal aid to the states, such as that for vocational education, urging that these subventions be continued as outright gifts without strings. With every respect for efforts to avoid bureaucracy, it must be said that this is unthinkable. There must be some national standards and some enforcement of them. A Secretary of Education with no authority would be a poor spokesman for the schools. He must be more than a figurehead. Some balance must be struck between provincialism and centralization. Then the persistence of those who wish to see education represented in the President's Cabinet undoubtedly will be rewarded.—*Christian Science Monitor.*

REPORTS

REPORT OF THE NATIONAL ADVISORY COMMITTEE ON EDUCATION[1]

Far-reaching recommendations concerning the policies and the activities of the Federal Government with regard to the education of the American people have been submitted to President Hoover by his National Advisory Committee on Education in its final report made public on November 16.

The greatest emphasis in the report is placed on conserving local autonomy and local responsibility by working, both in legislation and in administration, away from recent tendencies toward centralization in Washington of powers over the purposes and processes of education.

To that end the committee advocates abandonment both of federal appropriations to the states, for special forms of education of interest to special groups of people, and of the practice of requiring that federal appropriations be matched by the states. A continuance of federal subventions to the states in support of education is endorsed provided that each state is left free to use the money as state authorities consider to be for the best interests of the people of the state and without direction from Washington. Periodic audits by the Treasury Department, supplemented by regular and detailed public reports on how the money is used, constitute, in the opinion of the committee, an adequate check on proper expenditure of federal funds.

The committee was given the task in May, 1929, of making a chart by which to guide the course of federal relations to education.

The problem was found to involve questions reaching into literally every phase of federal administrative activity.

The report treats of the difficulties of education in territories, outlying possessions and in special federal areas; in teaching of the Indians and other indigenous peoples; in training of governmental personnel; in proper federal research and information services; and in international intellectual relations. In each of these matters, conditions are described as found and recommendations made as to how they may be bettered. Among these is a recommendation for setting up a "federal headquarters for education" which would serve both as a center of cooperation for the educational work of all federal agencies and as a reliable source of comprehensive, accurate data on education for all concerned.

By a vote of 45 to 6 the committee endorsed these recommendations as to policies and procedures, as set forth in the 90 pages which constitute the first section of the report.

In the 10 pages that constitute the second section of the report, the committee by a vote of 38 to 11 endorsed the recommendation that the federal headquarters for education take the form of a government department, with a secretary of education at its head. Its functions would be limited to research and information service that would foster cooperation with and among the states on educational matters. It would also act as a center of cooperation through which the now conflicting federal educational activities might be coordinated under one guiding policy.

As a nucleus for the Department of Education, as recommended in this report, the committee suggests the Office of Education now located in the Department of the Interior. The existing federal subsidies for vocational education would be retained, but some of their limita-

[1] Abstract sent by Dr. C. R. Mann, chairman of the committee.

tions removed through amendment of the Smith-Hughes Act of 1917, by repealing those provisions that require state matching of federal funds and federal approval of state plans and standards and that give Washington officials power to withhold funds. This done, the Federal Board for Vocational Education would be abolished and its remaining activities would become a major division in the proposed department.

Educational activities instrumental to proper administration of some other primary function of the Federal Government would be left under jurisdiction of the department responsible for that primary function; such as Indian education under the Office of Indian Affairs in the Department of the Interior; agricultural extension in the Department of Agriculture; military training in the War and Navy Departments, etc.

Coordination would be achieved, however, through the establishment of an Interdepartmental Council on Education, to work with the secretary of education in the department.

The committee emphasize that powers of the department recommended must not be such as to encourage centralization of authority in Washington at the expense of state autonomy. As stated in the report, it would "have no legal or financial power and no regulatory or executive authority, direct or indirect, explicit or implied, by which it may control the social purposes and specific processes of education." This limitation of powers is a return to the original federal policy in this matter and necessitates a complete reversal of the tendency exhibited in much recent federal legislation to build up a centralized control of the purposes and processes of education in the Federal Government.

The report was approved by the final vote of 43 to 8 on the report as a whole.

The committee comprised 51 men and women prominent in education, business and other activities. Their names and addresses may be found on pages 124–6 of the report. The roll call giving the vote of the committee on the first section is on page 89; that on the second section is on page 99. The final vote on the report as a whole is recorded on page 100.

Two minority reports are attached. In one Messrs. G. Johnson and Pace take the position that a federal department is unnecessary and a centralizing menace.

In the other Messrs. Davis, M. Johnson and Moton urge that an exception to the policy of no federal grants for special forms of education of interest to particular groups of people be made in the case of Negro education.

The committee recommends continuing and thoroughgoing studies designed to provide the data needed for guiding the improvement of education in the states. The most important of these would deal with tax systems, distribution of national income, living costs, public expenditures for educational institutions, etc. This study is essential to a readjustment of present specialized federal subventions.

The findings and recommendations of the committee are supported by four hundred and forty-six pages of basic facts which constitute Part II of the report. These consist of excerpts from the statutes, statistical tables and other data designed to help the reader secure an adequate picture of present conditions.

The studies of the committee were made possible by a grant of $100,000 by the Julius Rosenwald Fund and were carried out under the direction of Henry Suzzallo, former president of the University of Washington at Seattle and now president of the Carnegie Foundation for the Advancement of Teaching.

Copies of the report and of the volume of basic data may be secured without charge from the office of the committee, 744 Jackson Place, Washington, D. C.

SOCIETIES AND MEETINGS

THE ASSOCIATION OF AMERICAN UNIVERSITIES

Assembling at the University of North Carolina immediately after the inauguration of President Graham, representatives of the twenty-nine institutions composing the Association of American Universities held their thirty-third annual conference from November 12 to 14. They heard addresses at the general sessions delivered by four widely known educational thinkers, took part in conferences of deans on problems of graduate schools, and, at the final business session, voted to add ten colleges and technical schools to the approved list of the association.

The speakers at the first general session of November 13 were Dr. Abraham Flexner, who read a paper on "The Graduate School in the United States," and Dean Roscoe Pound, of the Harvard Law School, whose subject was "The Opportunities for Developing Research in the Field of Jurisprudence." At the afternoon session of November 13, President Robert M. Hutchins, of the University of Chicago, presented a paper, "Graduate Study and the Chicago Plan," and President H. M. Tory, of the Canadian National Research Council, discussed "The National Research Council and its Relations with Canadian Universities."

At the deans' conferences ten-minute and five-minute papers were read at the afternoon and evening sessions of November 12 as follows: "Master's Degrees in American Universities," Dean Edgar S. Furniss, of Yale; Dean Arthur H. Daniels, of Illinois, and Dean Charles S. Slichter, of Wisconsin. "Residence Requirements for Master's and Doctor's Degrees," Dean E. B. Stouffer, of Kansas; Dean W. J. Robbins, of Missouri (paper read by Professor Walter Miller); Dean John C. Metcalf, of Virginia, and Dean William McPherson, of Ohio State. "Problems of the Part-Time Teacher-Graduate Student and the Status of the Research Assistant as a Part-Time Graduate Student," Dean W. W. Pierson, Jr., of North Carolina; Dean G. Carl Huber, of Michigan; Dean F. K. Richtmyer, of Cornell, and Dean Carl L. Alsberg, of Stanford. "The Number and Variety of Graduate Courses in Education," Dean Fernandus Payne, of Indiana; Dean Carl E. Seashore, of Iowa, Dean Elton J. Moulton, of Northwestern, and Dean Henry W. Harper, of Texas. "The Possibility of Linking Professional Education in Law, Medicine and the Engineering Sciences to the General Educational Program of the Graduate School," Director Louis B. Wilson, of Minnesota; Dean Henry G. Gale, of Chicago; Dean George H. Chase, of Harvard, and Dean H. Lamar Crosby, of Pennsylvania. "The New Ph.D. Degree in England and France," Dean Augustus Trowbridge, of Princeton; President Wallace W. Atwood, of Clark; Dean J. C. McLennan, of Toronto, and Dean Roy J. Deferrari, of Catholic University of America. There were informal discussions of other topics.

At the business session on Saturday morning, November 14, Professor Adam Leroy Jones, of Columbia, presented the recommendation of the committee on classification of universities and colleges by which, upon unanimous vote, the following institutions were added to the approved list of the association:

Baldwin-Wallace College
Bradley Polytechnic Institute (technological list)
Carroll College
Colorado State School of Mines (technological list)
Georgia School of Technology (technological list)
Marquette University
Michigan State College (technological list)
New Jersey College for Women
Shorter College
University of West Virginia

Reports of other standing committees were presented by chairmen as follows: Dean Gordon J. Laing, of Chicago; Dean Charles B. Lipman, of California, and Dean G. Carl Huber, of Michigan; and reports of special committees as follows: Academic and Higher Degrees, Dr. A. O. Leuschner, of California; Classification of Oriental Universities, Dean Lipman, of California; Training of Graduate Students for College Teaching, Dean Fernandus Payne, of Indiana.

The guests of the association at this meeting were the following: President William P. Few, Duke University; Dr. Abraham Flexner, Institute for Advanced Study; Dean William H. Glasson, Duke University; Dean R. G. D. Richardson, Brown University; Dean Reed Smith, University of South Carolina; Dean Roswell P. Stephens, University of Georgia; President H. M. Tory, Canadian National Research Council; Dean Raymond Walters, Swarthmore College.

The social events of the program included a visit to Duke University at Durham, with a tour of the campus and luncheon as guests of Duke; an informal dinner and a formal dinner at the Carolina Inn, and attendance at a folk play presented by the Carolina Playmakers at the Playmakers' Theatre, Chapel Hill.

R. W.

EDUCATIONAL RESEARCH AND STATISTICS

EQUALITY OF OPPORTUNITY IN COLLEGES AS DETERMINED BY PER CAPITA COSTS

During recent years much has been said about equality of opportunity for children in the public schools. In arriving at comparisons we have used such items as the months or years of training teachers have received, the length of the school year and the cost per pupil. No consideration has been taken of the quality of the training the teachers have received. This is a factor which should be specifically used in arriving at the equality of educational opportunity of children.

It is true that a perfect evaluation of the quality of the training which teachers have received can not be made. Many elements should enter into such a study. Undoubtedly one index of the quality of teachers trained is the amount of money spent by the teacher-training institutions. If we accept public school per-pupil cost as an index of educational advantages we must accept cost per-teacher trained as an item in the quality of training. Therefore the cost of training a teacher becomes an index of the quality of educational opportunity for children.

But the compilation of reliable data as to teacher-training costs is not easily made and not entirely reliable. Unit cost studies can not be used because they are not available. Student clock hour costs are too detailed for comparative purposes. In making this study it was found necessary to use the student-year cost basis. The total student number was arrived at by use of an index of attendance.

Reports of the state departments of public instruction for three central-western states for 1928–1929 were studied. Current educational costs for the year were computed where they were not specifically stated. In computing the cost total expenditures, less debt service, and capital outlay were used. In other words, current educational expense included instruction, administration and library. In some institutions this total may have included minor repairs. No recognition was made of items of depreciation because this did not show in reports. Further, the practice of adding a depreciation cost is not generally used and not universally accepted.

The indices of attendance were arrived at by adding one fourth of the number of summer-school students to the total number for the regular year. Some colleges had three six-week spring and summer sessions. Others had a twelve-, nine- or six-week summer session. The greater number had a twelve-weeks' term. The number of students enrolled for the summer terms other than twelve weeks was about equally divided between institutions with the longest and shortest terms. Approximately 90 per cent. of summer students attended twelve-weeks' sessions. The plan used seems therefore to be reliable as a measure of student-year load at the various institutions. Per-capita costs were arrived at by dividing the current education cost for the year by the index of attendance.

Eighteen private and church colleges and ten state institutions which train teachers were studied. Most of the private and church colleges were not teachers colleges, but great numbers of their graduates enter teaching. The ten state institutions include three state universities, the remaining seven were state teachers colleges, two in each of two states, three in the third state.

Table I shows per-capita costs for the eighteen non-state colleges. In this table "F" indicates the average cost of the seven teachers colleges, inserted here by way of comparison. The range in Table I is from $81 per-capita cost for one year in institution "A" to $662 per capita cost for one year in institution "T." Both of these schools are located in the same state. The average for these eighteen institutions is $190, the median $257.

The size of the institution has little to do with average costs. In institution "A" the index of attendance was 579 students, while in "C" it was 2,127 students. In "I" 1,700 students, "K" 462 students, "P" 924 students, in "S" 240 students and in "T" 415 students.

Table II indicates the per-capita costs for a year in the state institutions. The range is from $132 in "$A^1$" to $600 in "$J^1$." The average is $336 and the median is $215. In each state institution the index of attendance is over 1,000, so comparisons are of no value, although the range was from 1,500 to over 10,000 students.

Equality of Opportunity in Colleges as Determined by Per-Capita Costs

TABLE I

Per-Capita Costs, Private Colleges, 1928–29

Institution	Cost per student	Institution	Cost per student
A	$ 81	L	$271
B	131	M	294
C	146	N	323
D	155	O	376
E	164	P	377
F	165	Q	382
G	217	R	386
H	243	S	451
I	244	T	660
J	245	Median	257
K	268	Average	190

TABLE II

Per-Capita Costs, State Institutions, 1928–29

Institution	Cost per student	Institution	Cost per student
A′	$132	G′	$288
B′	155	H′	360
C′	161	I′	522
D′	193	J′	600
E′	216	Median	215
F′	218	Average	336

TABLE III

Per-Capita Costs, State and Private Institutions, by States, 1928–29

Private institutions in states:	Average per capita cost	Private institutions in states:	Average per capita cost
U	$130	X	$315
V	245	Y	435
W	305	Z	550

Table III gives averages of non-state and state institutions by states. "U," "V," "W," indicate averages for private institutions in the three states, "X," "Y," "Z," averages for state institutions. The range of averages by groups "U" to "Z" is from $130 per student year (per-capita cost) to $550 per student year.

The writer recognizes that there are elements which enter into this study, making it unreliable in detail. However, comparison of cost data with other studies indicates a close resemblance. The reports of costs for 1927–1928 in U. S. Bulletin No. 38 (1929) compares closely for the institutions studied. Studies by Kelly, Arnett, Stevens and Elliot, Reeves and Russell, and Lindsay and Holland, all indicate average costs closely resembling the data presented in this paper.

Conclusions are too obvious to need enumeration. Summaries will enable the reader to draw his own.

In one of the states studied the non-state institutions train fully half of the teachers trained in that state. This is the state in which schools "A" and "T" (Table I) are located.

The average for state teachers colleges, $145, is lower than the average of non-state colleges, $190. But the average for all state institutions, including these state teachers colleges, is $336. Undoubtedly the state universities which do graduate work and carry on expensive off-campus professional schools, extension work, etc., should not be included in the study.

Shall we expect equality of educational opportunity for boys and girls in public schools so long as we have such glaring inequalities in cost of instruction in the colleges which train the teachers of these boys and girls?[1]

Homer L. Humke

Evansville College

NEW BOOKS IN EDUCATION

Fargues, Marie. *La Redáction chez les Petits.* Pp. 168. Juvisy, Seine-et-Oise, France.

National Education Association. *Proceedings of the Sixty-ninth Annual Meeting, 1931.* Volume 69. Pp. 1200. National Education Association, Washington.

U. S. Department of the Interior. *List of Educational Research Studies in City School Systems, No. 2.* Prepared in the Library Division by Edith A. Wright. Pp. 71. Office of Education, Washington.

[1] It may not be significant, but it is intensely interesting to note that the report on the American Council Psychological Tests for 1930 assigns the following median scores to freshmen in institutions included in this study as follows: C 108; G 123; H 136; R 130; S 137; T 145; E[1] 120; H[1] 129; J[1] 165. Question: Do higher instruction costs attract more intelligent freshmen?

SCHOOL AND SOCIETY

EDITED BY J. McKEEN CATTELL

WITH WHICH IS COMBINED THE

EDUCATIONAL REVIEW

EDITED BY WILLIAM McANDREW

Volume 34 SATURDAY, DECEMBER 5, 1931 Number 884

DIRECTIVE AIMS IN EDUCATION

By Professor DAVID SNEDDEN

TEACHERS COLLEGE, COLUMBIA UNIVERSITY

The sum of the matter is that at the present time education has no great directive aim. It grows, but it grows from specific pressure exerted here and there, not because of any large and inspiring social policy. It expands by piecemeal additions, not by the movement of a vital force within. The schools, like the nation, are in need of a central purpose which will create a new enthusiasm and devotion, and which will unify and guide all intellectual plans.

In earlier days there was an aim which worked throughout the whole system. Education was the key to individual success, to making one's way in life, to getting on and getting ahead. The aim corresponded with the realities of social life, for the national need was the material subjugation of a continent, the conquest of a wilderness. There was always a frontier just beyond, and the pioneer advanced to take possession of it. It was enough for the school to equip the individual with the tools of learning and to fire him with ambition and zeal to get on. His real education came in contact with others and in struggles with the forces of nature. The aim was individualistic, but it was also in harmony with the needs of the nation.

This earlier purpose has lost its vitality and its meaning. It survives, but operates as an oppressive handicap.[1]

I

As the present writer sees it, Dr. Dewey has in the above words very cogently stated the conditions which give rise to large proportions of the baffling problems of present-day American public and private educations.

In certain quantitative respects American public school and university educations have, as he indicates, now achieved "bignesses" and dynamic qualities similar to those others in city buildings, automobile construction, wheat harvesting and advertising which cause foreigners to marvel at American energy and resourcefulness. We count by millions the pupils in our secondary schools, and by hundreds of thousands those in our universities. Our national and state associations of educators hold stupendous meetings. Funds now raised for support of public schools now reach some three thousand million dollars per year.

But expectations of intelligent lay citizens for certain kinds of tangible results from these extensive and expensive systems of educations seem yet to be unfulfilled. Nation-wide literacy we have nearly realized. Nation-wide improvements of health have likewise been achieved, partly owing doubtless to hygienic enlightenments diffused through schools. Beyond those things—what? What effects on widely operative qualities of morality, civism, toleration, refinement of manners, sumptuary standards, personal cultures? Thoughtful citizens have their doubts—

[1] From John Dewey, "Some Aspects of Modern Education," SCHOOL AND SOCIETY, Oct. 31, 1931.

and educators of sensitive insight, convinced that outcomes of our vast educational enterprises are far from satisfactory, can as yet offer only confused and excessively aspirational counsels as to what should next be done.

All progressive Americans, realizing that nearly all our states, their local communities and their families are burdening themselves to the limit for larger *quantities* of schooling, now aspire intensely after improved *qualities* in the educations provided through schools and universities. These progressives can readily imagine societies like ours but with much less crime, vulgarity, family breakdown, poverty, vocational incompetency, civic lassitude, immorality or private greed. They can think of wider distributions and finer qualities of reading tastes, political idealisms, personal honors, social tolerations and economic efficiencies as being the fruits of really functional educations. Why can not America, for its extraordinarily generous outlays, get more of these good things?

II

Our education has now no great directive aim, says Dr. Dewey. That criticism is undoubtedly correct and fair—as any moderately keen reader of journals of opinion and treatises on educational theory during recent years can confidently testify.

And Dr. Dewey is no less correct when he asserts that though our education grows "it expands (and improves) only by piecemeal additions." A recent mail brought to the writer a fourteen page "Survey of Curriculum Activities of City and State School Systems," summarizing reports from more than one hundred city and state agencies of constructive work in public school education. Growth, or at least change, is much in evidence in these enthusiastic reports—but, in Dr. Dewey's words, it is growth due to "specific pressure exerted here and there," and one searches the survey in vain for evidence of any critical study of the more basic values to be sought through application of the "educational plans and specifications" which curricula surely are if they are anything. "Opportunism is in the saddle and rides our educators," clearly. And, sad to confess, in the rich soils and jungle growths of American wealth, ambitions, economic specializations, expansions of political controls, wealth-getting preoccupations, and popular philosophies, opportunism too frequently bears malodorous fruits in a thousand faddisms, coterie-fostered panaceas, exploitive charlatanries and even state-wide corruptions.

III

". . . . education has the responsibility of developing types of mind and character that can direct these new forces (urbanization and industrialization of America, scientific procedures in all productive work, political complexification, increase of leisure) toward good (ends)," says Dr. Dewey in the same article.

But this implies for education not one but a multitude of coordinated tasks which in all probability will preclude any simple formulation of "a directive aim" of such education. Certainly none of the one-sentence formulations, and still less the "slogan" formulations so abundantly popularized during the latest four decades, have proven of any considerable "directive" value—whether they were child-centered or adult-centered, whether they pointed towards more individualization or more socialization. One recalls the western institute orator of a few years ago who reiterated with such resounding effect "the purpose of education is to take children from where they are to where they ought to be!"

One or both of two weaknesses seem to the writer to characterize all these recent inclusive formulations of "the aim of education.'' First, they not only ignore, but by subtle implication they seem to deny, those inevitable divisions and coordinations of processes through which every superior activity in civilized societies is being made effective to-day. Second, they carry no clear implications that the final tests of *all* human valuations and of means taken to achieve them are to be determined by actual functionings. A few analogies may help to explicitness at this point.

The searcher after philosophical ''simples'' asks: What is *the* purpose of medicine? of government? of travel? He wishes short one-sentence answers to such queries as: What is food? Who is the good citizen? How shall men be saved? He imagines that he can find solutions to ''*the* rural problem,'' ''*the* problem of unemployment,'' ''*the* problem of personality adjustment!''

Even large proportions of laymen are now able to think discretely and effectively about the hundreds of distinctive curative and preventive purposes of the hundreds of distinctive medicines now available—though they increasingly prefer to leave to expert specialists the specification of particular means to critically diagnosed ends if optimum functionings are to be assured.

The first four ''purposes of government'' stated in the preamble to the Constitution of the United States were politically simple and of ancient historical derivation; but how endless have been the complications resulting from efforts to develop functional means of realizing the countless demands every year being made under the last two!

Let us for a moment press the analogy of foods, dietetic proportionings and vitality functionings. The scientist in these fields now knows that there can be no simple answer (of any tangible reality or significance) to such an empty query as ''what is the purpose (or 'the aim') of food.'' He knows that no one simple formula can be devised which will prove directive in choices and adaptations of foodstuffs to babies or out-working adults or corpulent office-holders. His researches turn ever more realistically to particular components of diet, particular proportionings and coordinations among them for well-diagnosed case-types of needs, and, finally, towards daily determinations of the actual functionings of the recommended means and methods.

It is submitted that ''a science of educational values,'' analogous in many respects to a science of dietetic values, can presently be developed which will really give American educations not a simple ''great directive aim,'' but rather a series or ensemble of ''great directive aims,'' each one capable of such realistic determination as clearly to open the way to researches after optimum means and methods of realizing it, and, no less important, the combination of purposes being also realistic enough to permit of extended researches to discover optimum coordinations of expected functionings of means and methods for varying social situations or on behalf of varying classes of affected personnel.

IV

As tentative suggestions of procedures whereby thinking and experimentation could presently be pushed in these problems, let us here consider one illustrative proposal.

Each reader is asked first to turn the flashlight of his understanding upon certain well-matured and, as approvable local opinion judges, fairly successful, personalities—the reader's own probably among them.

Now over-simplified thinking has heretofore tried to think of ''the career'' of each of these personalities. Let us rather think of the several ''careers'' of each one—including his economic-production (or wealth-getting or vocational success) career, his family-rearing career, his civic-participation career, his religious-affiliation career, and the like. We might even profitably consider such differentiations as his health-sustaining career, his wise-use-of-leisure career, his sleeping career, his adult self-culturing career, and others.

It has become in recent years a commonplace of anthropological inquiry that under those primitive social conditions where simple divisions of functions within social groups had become long stabilized—and, above all, for the recent millennia of a dominating land tillage economy—the coordinations of the above careers towards wholesome "integrations of personality" commonly took place without drastic disturbance.

But it has become no less clear to the present-day mental hygienists that under those "civilized" conditions manifested perhaps in their most advanced forms in the modern suburbanite, the above "careers" tend increasingly to specialize for each individual—not only as to times and seasons of optimum exercise, but as to material paraphernalia and human co-workers wherewith they are to be discharged.

Like all other specializations in organic nature, these extended specializations of function of our suburbanites increase many classes of the goods of life. But a variety of heavy costs must also be paid for them, often by the individual himself, and, perhaps even more often, though less tangibly, by those of his fellows whom his effective social coordinations of effort should have enriched.

Keeping to our figurative distribution of careers, each one of us is even painfully familiar with cases where a man's work career has been pursued at the damaging expense of his family-rearing, his self-culturing and his health-sustaining careers. We know, too, of cases where excessive devotion to "use of leisure" careers have greatly injured wealth-getting careers. And how many American suburbanites are to-day half-way meeting the normal obligations of their civic-participation careers?

V

Now it is here contended that a well-developed "science of educational values," applicable at ages ten to twenty, could, through working on foundations suggested by the above analysis, accomplish at least as much relatively as our present-day science of dietetic values in preventing personality and local group maladjustments due to excess, deficiency or defective coordination of these "career" components.

Dr. Dewey, as quoted above, holds that in earlier days our school educations were guided by the relatively simple and forthright aim of helping each person to make his way in life, to succeed, to "get on"—always, it is implied, in individualistic and economic senses.

Let us grant all that, and then let educators of to-day, following the examples of dietitians who recommend that prospering peoples eat more fruit and less meat, give their babies more milk and less coffee, and especially compensate for missing vitamins, study optimum amounts and combinations of "careers" essential for wholesome personal living in part and for wholesome family and political and fellowship living in part.

Why should not students of educational values hold to that excellent ideal "success in life" or "a successful life," but insist always on taking it inclusively so as to embrace such component and increasingly purposefully harmonized "successes" as "success (between twenty and thirty) in getting well-started on a vocational career, success (between twenty-five and fifty) in rearing a fine family, success (after twenty-one, especially) in sharing in the furtherance of superior local and federal political life, and all other species of success?"

EDUCATIONAL EVENTS

CLOSING OF NORMAL SCHOOLS IN PRUSSIA

ACCORDING to a copyright dispatch from the Berlin correspondent of the *New York Evening Post,* the state of Prussia, responsible for the education of over two thirds of Germany, has given notice that all normal schools in the state are to be closed. Students now in the schools will be allowed to concentrate in one or more schools this year and next. The action has been taken partly to relieve pressure on the finances during the present crisis. Fundamentally, however, it represents the decision of the educational authorities that further teacher training in Germany is merely treachery to candidates for teaching posts.

The normal schools will remain closed for a period of at least three years. The reason for the Prussian Government's decision is simple. There are in Prussia 20,000 fully trained teachers with experience who are unable to find any place in the school system, not as the result of any weakness of their own, but because of the few posts available.

Prussia's teachers are in general men. The blow that has struck them is the same that has broken up the fashion of living of most of the so-called intellectual class. Nowhere is there place for them. To a much greater extent than is the case with American school teachers, they are research scholars. Each hopes for the time when he will be able to publish his commentary on a commentary, or some other work that will establish his reputation as a scholar.

Besides the scholars Germany is flooded with would-be artists, designers and architects. The surplus of candidates for academic, higher scientific, literary, editorial and like posts is greater because of bad business, but under any circumstances there would have been too many of them.

In the struggle to overcome disappointment and find a place in the post-war life, women are doing better than men. In lists of new professions invented by energetic, jobless intellectuals which have recently been compiled by the press, the greater number were the creations of women. The educated woman has also had the courage to descend on the German restaurant. Going has not been hard for her here when she made up her mind.

In general the unfortunate male of the species intellectual has been less willing to compromise.

TEACHING BY MOVING PICTURES IN ENGLAND

THE use of films for purposes of teaching history in elementary and secondary schools has been subjected to a test during the last three years, and a report based on the experiments, now issued by the Historical Association, indicates that the method has been found an improvement on the ordinary system of teaching history. The report has been compiled by Miss Frances Consitt. Assistance in financing the inquiry was given by the Carnegie United Kingdom Trust. According to an abstract in the London *Times,* the report in its conclusions announces that a remarkable change in attitude was noticed among the teachers who took part in the inquiry and saw the results obtained in follow-up lessons. The particular advantages obtained by film teaching are stated as follows:

(*a*) It gives life to the past, as nothing else does, by portraying life in movement and giving a background with full detail; (*b*) it arouses interest that stimulates the children to further mental effort. This is shown in their readiness to ask questions, in the desire for books, and in other forms of self-activity. It has been found to be a fallacy that the historical teaching film encourages mental passivity. The interest aroused seems to be permanent; (*c*) it stimulates imagination: the children realize the past, gain some sympathetic insight into the lives and feelings of the men and women of the past, and get a fuller and clearer picture of their environment. Thus they can the better imaginatively reconstruct for themselves other scenes of the same period; (*d*) it helps children to assimilate. They gain both in grip and atmosphere; (*e*) it helps children to remember. This is gathered from the results of delayed tests; (*f*) it forces children to find their own words to express opinions and describe scenes, and not merely to borrow those of the teacher or textbook; (*g*) it presents a point of view to the children in addition to that of the teacher and the textbook; (*h*) it affords pleasure to the children, not merely because it is a change from the ordinary routine, and hence it tends to lead children both to enjoy history more and to desire a better type of film.

The investigation showed that though children below the age of nine derive less advantage from the film than from oral lessons, the film is particularly valuable in the senior schools and even in the secondary schools, despite their academic bias. One experiment only was made in a training college, but it produced striking results, and it is concluded that for the non-specialist type of history teachers the historical teaching film might be of the greatest value. Many backward children profited notably by the method, whereas some children, usually near the top of the class, did less well under the film method than in the ordinary lesson. A few experiments with Latin classes seemed to show that interest in learning the language could be increased by a film which made real and living the peoples of another civilization and gave significance to what often seemed otherwise to be a matter of mere words.

THE ANNUAL REPORT OF THE OFFICE OF EDUCATION

LAUNCHING of the National Survey of School Finance, steady progress in the National Surveys of Secondary Education and Teacher Preparation, appointment of three new education specialists, continued research in all fields of education, and transfer of the Alaska medical and educational service to the Office of Indian Affairs, constituted the most significant work of the Federal Office of Education during the past year, according to the annual report of Wm. John Cooper, U. S. Commissioner of Education, just submitted to the Secretary of the Interior.

The National Survey of Secondary Education marked the end of its second year of progress, and the National Survey of Teacher Preparation was one year old in July when the National Survey of School Finance, a four-year study, was launched. All three nation-wide studies are now bringing to the Federal Office of Education data never before collected.

Recently appointed Office of Education specialists are: Dr. Frederick J. Kelly, chief, Division of Colleges and Professional Schools; Dr. Cline M. Koon, specialist in education by radio; Dr. Alina M. Lindegren, specialist in Western European school systems, and Dr. David Segel, specialist in educational tests and measurements.

During the year the Office of Education made a public school survey in Buffalo, New York, began another in Youngstown, Ohio, and is now cooperating in a third in the State of Mississippi. A survey was also made of home economics education in the junior and senior high schools of Montclair, New Jersey, of the school building situation in Warwick, Rhode Island, and of the Park View School, Washington, D. C.

With the Department of Agriculture, the office is now cooperating in a social and economic survey of the Southern Appalachian Mountain Region. It is concentrating on the educational phase of this study. It is also aiding Pennsylvania in formulating its 10-year state educational program. During the year the office also made a survey of Oregon and Arkansas higher education, and cooperated in the rural survey of Vermont.

Regional conferences on homemaking, parent education, rural school supervision, school building problems, higher education and radio problems were sponsored during the year.

The research and investigation division under Miss Bess Goodykoontz, assistant commissioner of education, completed more than fifty studies during the 1931 fiscal year, these studies covering many fields of educational interest and activity. They were addressed to school executives, teachers, curriculum workers, supervisors, parents, research workers, college students and to the general reading public.

Educational movements in Alaska and Mexico were studied, and the foreign schools division made comprehensive reports of education in Belgium, the national ministries of education and secondary education in Norway.

Transfer of the Alaska medical and educational service to the Office of Indian Affairs relieves the Office of Education of any administrative responsibilities for schools. It is now primarily an establishment for educational research and the dissemination of data on education.

THE SCHOOLS AND UNEMPLOYMENT

WHAT are the public schools in the 48 states doing to help improve the unemployment situation? "If the 1930 ratio per cent. of school attendance to population for persons 16 and 17 years of age had remained the same as for 1920, more than 671,000 young people now attending school would be out of school and would be potential competitors with the adult group for employment," according to a statement made by Dr. Maris M. Proffitt, consultant and specialist in guidance and industrial education in the Federal Office of Education.

"The holding powers of the schools over this potential wage-earning group increased from 42.9 per cent. in 1920 to 57.3 per cent. in 1930," Dr. Proffitt says, basing his conclusions on 1930 census reports of population and school attendance. "In 1920 the percentage of urban population attending school was 39.2. In 1930 there were 60.5 per cent. of urban residents (16 and 17 years of age) in school. The percentage of the rural population attending school in 1920 was 46.1, and in 1930 it was 53.9."

Increases in school attendance are not always the direct result of population increases, statistics show. Dr. Proffitt explains that in some of the states there was an absolute decrease in the rural population of this age group, but the school attendance increased, nevertheless. "Illinois, for example, had a rural population of 16 and 17 year old boys and girls in 1920 of 80,459, which had decreased in 1930 to 77,874, yet the rural school attendance of this age group increased from 34,911 in 1920 to 42,211 in 1930. In Minnesota the rural population of this age numbered 55,582 in 1920 and only 54,806 in 1930. Rural school attendance climbed from 21,654 in 1920 to 26,482 in 1930."

California leads all other states in the percentage of increase with 27.4 per cent. more boys and girls 16 and 17 years of age attending school in 1930 than in 1920.

"Among the factors contributing to increased school attendance during the past 10 years of the 16 and 17 year old population group, with the consequent result of eliminating them as potential competitors with adults for employment," Dr. Proffitt says, "are the increase in the amount and character of vocational training offered in the public schools; the increased age for compulsory school attendance and better enforcement of attendance laws; increase in age at which youth is accepted into employment, mainly because of increased need for technically trained and skilled workers; the increasing use of power machinery, which tends to eliminate unskilled labor and the growing recognition by students, parents and employers of the practical value of the educational training offered in the upper years of the public-school curriculum."

EDUCATION OF THE DEAF

THE annual report of the Columbia Institution for the Deaf, given out by the Department of the Interior and summarized in *The U. S. Daily,* shows that during the fiscal year ended June 30, 1931, there were under instruction in the advanced department of the institution, known as Gallaudet College, 78 men and 54 women, a total of 132, representing 35 states, the District of Columbia and Canada. In the primary department of the institution, known as the Kendall School, there were under instruction 41 boys and 29 girls, a total of 68, 64 of whom were admitted as beneficiaries of the District of Columbia.

Good health prevailed throughout the year, although an unusual number of surgical cases were taken care of. All these operations were successful. There were no contagious diseases at all among the college students, and almost none among the pupils of the Kendall School.

Courses in business practice for the girls of the college department, and in architectural drawing for the boys of the college, were put into operation with much success. Two young women of the college had the opportunity of studying photographic negative retouching through the cooperation of one of the photographers of Washington. One of the boys of the Kendall School was also given the opportunity of learning machine shoe repairing.

On February 5, the alumni of the college presented to the board of directors the sum of $50,000 toward a memorial building to be erected in honor of Dr. Edward Miner Gallaudet. The presentation of the gift took place during a special convocation held in the chapel of the institution to celebrate the anniversary of the birthday of Dr. Gallaudet. The Secretary of the Interior, the Honorable Ray Lyman Wilbur, delivered the address on this occasion, and Dr. Knight Dunlap, of the Johns Hopkins University, was given the honorary degree of doctor of humane letters at the close of the convocation.

From a questionnaire sent out to the graduates and ex-students of the institution it was found that teaching and printing lead the list of occupations of the deaf. From the replies to this questionnaire it was found that the average salary of the deaf is $150 per month. A large majority own their own homes, and over half of those replying own and drive their own cars.

THE FINANCES OF YALE UNIVERSITY

YALE UNIVERSITY has an endowment of $93,795,551, according to the annual report of George Parmly Day, treasurer. This represents an increase of almost 350 per cent. over ten years ago, when Dr. James Rowland Angell assumed the presidency, and of 800 per cent. over the amount of the fund twenty years ago, when Arthur Twining Hadley was president. The figures, which are as of June 30, the close of the university's fiscal year, show that the endowment fund increased almost $11,000,000 during the year, as compared with an increase of more than $12,000,000 the previous year.

Despite this great endowment fund, the university may have to curtail its educational program this year because of the general movement for reduction of dividends which, according to the report, "will materially affect the current resources of the university."

It is stated that in three months since the close of the fiscal year substantial losses have been suffered in the amount of dividends paid on some of its holdings of stocks, so that at the opening of the new year the university is faced with the necessity of curtailing its educational program and at the same time of being more dependent than heretofore on gifts to income for carrying on the work which can not be abandoned or deferred.

The market value of the stock and bond holdings as of June 30, were $62,381,114, as compared with a book value of $71,615,652, or a decline of about 13 per cent. from cost. This compares with a 17 per cent. decline from cost on June 30, 1921, and a 9 per cent. premium above cost on June 30, 1929.

The total investments of the university as of June 30, 1931, amounted to $92,697,798, of which bonds amounting to $25,746,814 comprise 27 per cent. of the total list and yielded 5.13 per cent.; stocks of $45,868,838 equal about 50 per cent. of the total, yielding an income of 5.16 per cent. The income on mortgage notes was at the rate of 5.48 per cent., subscription and collateral notes 5.16 per cent. and real estate 2.85 per cent. The average rate of all investments was 4.96 per cent. as compared with 5.18 per cent. in the previous year.

INVESTIGATION OF COLLEGE TEACHING BY THE AMERICAN ASSOCIATION OF UNIVERSITY PROFESSORS

A COMPREHENSIVE investigation of teaching in the colleges and universities of the United States under the direction of the American Association of University Professors has been made possible by a grant of $20,000 from the Carnegie Corporation and Foundation.

The investigation will include a systematic examination of the actual conditions of instruction with a view to setting up principles of discrimination between good and bad teaching. It will seek to find methods of promoting effective teaching both among those now engaged in the profession and of those young instructors who are preparing to enter it.

The plans already outlined according to Professor William B. Munro, president of the association, include the appointment of a full-time field agent who will visit a considerable number of American colleges and universities which have been conducting experiments along the line of improved teaching methods. The committee which is to have general charge of the investigation has not yet been appointed, but it is understood that it will include nine well-known educators chosen from the various fields of collegiate instruction. The survey will utilize the work of various agencies which have been investigating the methods of instruction in English, history, mathematics and other individual subjects.

Officers of the association pointed out the great significance of the fact that the official organization of the college professors of America is undertaking this searching examination of the standards and efficiency of its own members. It proves, they said, the deep interest of college teachers not only in the protection of academic freedom and tenure, but in the improvement of professorial efficiency in every respect. The results of the investigation will be sent to the eleven thousand college professors who now constitute the association's membership.

EDUCATIONAL NOTES AND NEWS

DR. KENNETH GORDON MATHESON, president of the Drexel Institute, Philadelphia, since 1922 and of the Georgia School of Technology for seventeen years previously, died on November 28 in his sixty-eighth year.

PRESIDENT LOTUS D. COFFMAN, of the University of Minnesota, is making an educational survey of schools and universities in New Zealand and Austria for the Carnegie Corporation. In addition to the survey, President Coffman will serve as visiting professor of the Endowment for International Peace. He will deliver a series of lectures on educational administration at the University of the Philippines at Manila.

DR. WILLIAM J. COOPER, U. S. Commissioner of Education, and Professor Edward L. Thorndike, of Teachers College, Columbia University, have been appointed visiting professors at the Johns Hopkins University.

DR. AYMER J. HAMILTON was recently elected president of the State Teachers College at Chico, to succeed President R. D. Lindquist. Dr. Hamilton served as president of the California Elementary Teachers Association for three years.

DR. LEONARD W. RILEY was recently made president emeritus of Linfield College, Oregon, after serving for twenty-five years. Dr. Elam J. Anderson, present head of the American School in Shanghai, China, has been elected successor to Dr. Riley. He will take up his position on August 1, 1932, and until that time Dr. W. R. Frerichs, who is acting president, will continue to serve.

DR. CONWAY BOATMAN, who was elected last May to succeed Dr. William Fielder as president of John H. Snead Seminary, Boaz, Ala., has been formally inducted into office. Bishop H. Lester Smith presided at the ceremonies.

MR. JOHN WAGNER, JR., civil engineer, industrial agent of the Reading Company, has been elected president of the Wagner Free Institute of Science, succeeding his father, Mr. Samuel T. Wagner, who died on August 7.

MR. MILTON EDWARD LORD, director of the library of the University of Iowa, has been appointed to succeed the late Charles F. D. Belden as director of the Boston Public Library.

A PORTRAIT of President Mary E. Woolley, of Mount Holyoke College, painted by Leon Gordon, will be on exhibition at the Milch Galleries, New York City, in a group of paintings of "America's Twelve Greatest Women."

DR. HEINRICH LUEDERS, rector of the University of Berlin, gave a reception on November 21 at Harnack House, the center of the university's faculty activities, in honor of Professor Frederick J. E. Woodbridge, of Columbia University, now Roosevelt professor of philosophy at the university. The reception was attended by representatives of the ministry of education and other distinguished guests.

THE city authorities of Heidelberg have given the name Schurman Street to a part of the former low Neckarstrasse in honor of former American Ambassador Schurman, who raised funds for the new buildings of the Heidelberg University.

IN recognition of their twenty-five years of service as members of the faculty of Marshall College, West Virginia, a dinner honoring Miss Frances Burgess, Professor E. E. Myers and Professor W. H. Franklin was held on October 12 at Huntington. All three of the honor guests are heads of departments in the faculty of the Teachers College—Mr. Myers in art; Miss Burgess in geography, and Mr. Franklin in English.

DEAN L. A. PECHSTEIN, of the Teachers College of the University of Cincinnati, and Miss Anna Logan, formerly assistant superintendent of the Cincinnati schools, were the guests of honor at a tea recently given by the Cincinnati Teachers Association.

Mr. Raymond S. Jewett, of Mount Vernon, was re-elected president of the Associated School Boards and Trustees of the State of New York at the closing session of the annual meeting held in October in Syracuse. Dr. Frank Quackenbush, of Northport, was re-elected treasurer, and Mr. W. A. Clifford executive secretary. Vice-presidents elected at the meeting are: George R. Stephens, Lancaster; Guy W. Cheney, Corning; William F. Seber, Troy; James H. Anderson, New Rochelle; Harold L. Fuess, Waterville, and G. Burchard Smith, Freeport. Edward Villars, of Carthage, who has retired from the Carthage Board of Education after thirty-nine years' service, is succeeded on the executive committee by Dr. James T. Ivory, of Binghamton.

At the thirty-sixth annual meeting of the National Association of State Universities, held at the Stevens Hotel, Chicago, on November 18 and 19, the following officers were elected for the coming year: President Walter E. Clark, University of Nevada, *president;* President Walter Hullihen, University of Delaware, *vice-president;* President George H. Denny, University of Alabama, and President Herman G. James, University of South Dakota, *members of the executive committee.* President A. H. Upham, of Miami University, was elected *secretary-treasurer* for the fifth consecutive year. Pennsylvania State College was admitted to membership in the association.

Mr. O. H. Bennett has been elected president of the Southwestern Ohio Teachers Association.

At a recent meeting of the Board of Regents of the State of New York Dr. Arthur L. Janes, principal of Flushing High School, was reappointed a member of the State Examinations Board; Superintendent W. Howard Pillsbury, superintendent of schools at Schenectady, was appointed to succeed Superintendent Ernest C. Hartwell, of Buffalo, and President Henry T. Moore, of Skidmore College, to succeed Dr. Henry Noble MacCracken, of Vassar College. The appointments are for terms of five years.

With the closing of the Berea Secondary Normal School Mr. Ira D. Shaw has been appointed associate professor of education in Berea College, Kentucky.

Dr. T. Howard Winters has been named acting professor of education at Bethany College, West Virginia, to fill the vacancy caused by the death of Dr. H. T. McKinney. Dr. Winters has been engaged in educational work for a number of years as high school teacher, principal, superintendent, state supervisor and college professor.

Miss Kathryn E. Maxfield, of New York City, recently research secretary for the White House Conference on Child Health and Protection in preparation of the report on the visually handicapped child, will join the staff of Perkins Institution for the Blind beginning with the next school year. She will be director of personnel and research, a new position at Perkins. Miss Maxfield is now supervisor of educational research of the American Foundation for the Blind.

Dr. Harvey J. Howard has been appointed director of the department for prevention of blindness of the Missouri Commission for the Blind. He succeeds Dr. Meyer Wiener, who recently resigned.

Professor George H. Blakeslee, of Clark University, an authority on Far Eastern affairs, has been summoned to Washington to act as an adviser to the Department of State during the present Manchurian crisis. Professor Blakeslee was a member of three conferences of the Institute of Pacific Relations at Honolulu in 1925 and 1927 and at Kyoto, Japan, in 1929.

Professor C. W. Savage, of Oberlin College, has been appointed a member of a special legislative committee named by the Ohio State Council of Physical Education to consider ways and means of meeting the crisis created by the last state legislature in abolishing the position of state supervisor of physical education.

Dr. Arthur H. Buffinton, assistant professor of history at Williams College, will be in England this winter, with headquarters in London; he will study certain phases of eighteenth century history at the British Museum and in the Public Records Office.

Arthur Bridgman Clark, retiring professor of education in the graphic arts department of Stanford University, left recently for a tour of

Europe. While there he will study painting, sculpture and architecture.

PROFESSOR FRANCIS D. CURTIS has leave of absence from the department of education of the University of Michigan.

MISS JANE ADDAMS, of Hull House, will give an address at 11 A. M. on December 5 before the Central Council of Childhood Education. Mrs. Dorothy E. Willy, of the Chicago Normal College, will speak at the luncheon on "Experiences in the Unification of College Theory and Training School Practice."

DR. HENRY SUZZALLO, president of the Carnegie Foundation for the Advancement of Teaching, was the principal speaker at the meeting in New York City on November 27 of the Interfraternity Conference.

DR. FREDERICK B. ROBINSON, president of the College of the City of New York, and Dr. J. H. Cousins, Irish poet and special lecturer at the college, were the principal speakers at the seventy-eighth annual dinner of the college, which was held on November 14. Dr. Cousins was the guest of honor and spoke on the "Renaissance in Modern India."

PROFESSOR FLETCHER HARPER SWIFT, of the School of Education, University of California at Berkeley, delivered a series of addresses on public school finance at the annual meeting of the Idaho Education Association in Boise from November 26 to 28.

PROFESSOR L. P. JACKS, of Manchester College, Oxford, England, spoke recently on "Education for Leisure" before the New York University School of Education under the auspices of the National Recreation Association.

THE inaugural lecture of the new chair in psychology at the University of Edinburgh was delivered on October 20 by Professor James Drever, the first occupant of the chair.

DR. OSCAR I. WOODLEY, president of Marshall College, Huntington, West Virginia, from 1915 to 1918, died on November 24. He was sixty-eight years old. After retiring as president of Marshall College in 1918 he became secretary of the Florida Educational Association and editor of its journal.

THE death is announced at the age of fifty-eight years of George O. James, dean of the College of Liberal Arts of Washington University, St. Louis, and a member of the faculty for twenty-eight years.

DR. GEORGE W. MYERS, for nearly thirty years professor of teaching of mathematics and astronomy in the College of Education of the University of Chicago, died on November 23 at the age of sixty-six years.

DR. JOHN J. HATTSTAEDT, founder and president for the last forty-six years of the American Conservatory of Music in Chicago, died on November 30 at the age of seventy-nine years.

DR. HENRY TURNER BAILEY, dean of the Cleveland School of Art for twelve years, a director and lecturer of the Cleveland Museum of Art for many years, and from 1903 to 1917 editor of *The School of Arts Magazine,* died suddenly on November 26 in his sixty-sixth year.

THE death is announced of the Reverend Dr. H. A. James, president of St. John's College, Oxford, at the age of eighty-seven years. Dr. James had been the successful head master of three leading public schools and head master-elect of a fourth, besides officiating during an interval of some three years as dean of a cathedral. He was for twenty-two years the head of Oxford College.

THE Carnegie Corporation has given to Lafayette College the sum of $150,000 to endow the college librarianship of the institution. The next step in the plans for the Lafayette library is the enlargement of its physical facilities. For some time the need has been felt for larger reading rooms, more stack space and general library equipment. This improvement is one of the main objectives of the Centennial Building and Endowment Campaign now being carried on.

WILLIAM FELLOWES MORGAN, chairman of the board of trustees of Wells College, Aurora, N. Y., has announced a gift of $25,000 from Myron C. Taylor, a trustee, and one of $50,000 from the Carnegie Corporation toward the administration building fund. These gifts bring the total contributions up to $497,277, leaving $27,723 to be raised by December 31 to complete the fund required for the building to provide administrative offices, classrooms and an auditorium large enough to seat the entire student body. Construction will begin at the earliest possible date in the spring.

A BUDGET for the public schools of Denver of $6,242,149 for the year 1932 was formally approved by the Board of Education at a special meeting. This sum is $605,066 less than the budget of 1931 and $465,960 less than the actual expenditures for the year 1931, expenditures for November being estimated. The major item affected by the cut in the budget is that of capital outlay. New building projects and alterations to old buildings have been postponed. Reductions in expenses of general control, educational supplies and text-books, and a number of economies affected by internal reorganization are other factors involved in making the decreased budget possible.

THE *Journal of Educational Research* reports that beginning with the present quarter the department of education of the University of Chicago is giving a new type of advanced research course. Instead of registering students for any research problem in which they are interested, each instructor has announced the problem on which he will be working constructively during the quarter in which the course is given. For example, W. C. Reavis is carrying on intensive research concerning "The Committee Organization of Boards of Education"; G. T. Buswell has organized critical experiments on the constancy of eye movement habits and the relation of pheneloscope records of rhythm and pronunciation in reading to photographic records of eye movement; K. J. Holzinger is carrying on advanced study in statistics with special application to the problem of the factor theories of mental abilities, and W. S. Gray is engaged on a series of critical studies and investigations of the nature of the reading activities required in studying secondary-school subjects. The students who register for these and other similar courses will participate with the instructor in the various steps and stages of the studies which he is pursuing.

A SERIES of tours of Russia is being arranged for the summer of 1932 by Mrs. Lindsay Patterson, author and newspaper woman, who is now in Russia studying travel conditions and arranging itineraries, and Roy H. Mackay, who has been conducting Russian tours for the past several years. A special tour for those who wish to make a study of political, social and economic conditions in Russia and their international significance, will be given under the personal direction of Dr. John Barrett, former United States Minister to Siam, Argentina, Panama and Colombia, and one time (1907–1920) director general of the Pan-American Union at Washington. University credit may be secured for the completion of this trip. Those who propose to go to Russia during the coming summer are urged to submit a brief summary of their plans early in the year so that individuals of similar interests may be grouped in small parties to follow itineraries of their own choosing. Communications should be addressed to Roy H. Mackay, New York University, Washington Square, New York City.

A UNITED PRESS dispatch from Mexico City dated November 28 reads as follows: "The fate of the several score of school teachers who were arrested last Sunday at San Luis Potosi was disclosed to-day through private advices to the newspaper 'La Prensa.' The reports said that the teachers were working as peons (laborers) at the Las Palomas ranch, near San Luis Potosi, which is owned by General Saturnini Cedillo, former Secretary of Agriculture. The general, the report said, 'intends to punish the teachers for their activities as strikers.' Teachers' organizations protested further to the government against the holding of the teachers by force, especially as General Cedillo now holds no official post in the government. Those arrested had been protesting non-payment of salaries."

DISCUSSION

A NEW MATHEMATICAL ENCYCLOPEDIA

A HUNDRED years ago a mathematical dictionary or a mathematical encyclopedia could be prepared with a comparatively small amount of work, but the last fifty years have witnessed such great advances in various fields of mathematics, including the elementary parts thereof, that the preparation of an encyclopedia even of elementary mathematics now attracts wide attention on the part of those interested in school mathematics. It is more than twenty years ago that a number of Italian mathematicians decided to undertake the preparation of such a work and recently the first volume thereof, covering the subject of analysis in a little over a thousand pages, was published in two parts under the title "Enciclopedia delle Matematiche Elementari," by Ulrico Hoepli, Milan, Italy.

The details of such a work are naturally of interest only to the mathematical specialist, but various questions relating thereto may be of interest also to those who aim to keep in touch with changes relating to the modern educational subjects. One such question relates to the concept of elementary mathematics on the part of leading modern mathematicians. This is partly answered by the fact that in the present encyclopedia the twenty main headings of analysis with the number of pages devoted thereto are as follows: Logic (75), general arithmetic (126), practical arithmetic (52), theory of numbers and indeterminate analysis (66), progressions (17), logarithms (42), mechanical calculus (28), combinatory calculus (9), elements of the theory of groups (51), determinants (30), linear equations (13), linear substitutions and linear, bilinear, and quadratic forms (28), rational functions of one or more variables (37), general properties of algebraic equations (59), equations of the second, third, fourth degree and other particular algebraic equations, systems of algebraic equations of elementary type (57), methods for the discussion of problems of the second degree and a sketch of some of the third degree (63), limits, series, continued fractions and infinite products (45), elements of infinitesimal analysis (101), relations between the theory of aggregates and elementary mathematics (11), analytic functions from an elementary view (29).

Fifty years ago few mathematicians would have been so bold as to predict that in 1931 an encyclopedia of elementary mathematics would devote fifty-one pages to the theory of algebraic groups, especially in Italy, since the Italians have contributed comparatively little towards the development of this subject, as may be seen from the extensive references contained in the present work. The amount of space devoted to algebraic groups in this work seems to be in line with a statement made by Simon Newcomb in 1893 before the American Mathematical Society as follows: "The mathematics of the twenty-first century may be very different from our own; perhaps the schoolboy will begin algebra with the theory of substitution groups as he might now but for inherited habits. But it does not follow that our posterity will solve many problems which we have attacked in vain, or invent an algorithm more powerful than the calculus." We do not mean to predict that this suggested change in the teaching of elementary algebra in our schools is about to be realized but merely to point out that the Italian work under consideration points in the same direction.

The fact that there is now no modern mathematical dictionary or encyclopedia in the English language should be of general educational interest in view of the important place occupied by mathematics among the school subjects. In this respect the German language is now the most fortunate, since there is not only a large mathematical encyclopedia in this language which has been almost completed, but there is also therein a modern encyclopedia of elementary mathematics, and a mathematical dictionary has been announced but not yet published. The publication of the large French mathematical encyclopedia was discontinued as a result of the world war. In fact, the great delay in the publication of the work under consideration has been attributed to the same cause. The remaining two volumes thereof are to be devoted to geometry and to applications, history and the teaching of mathematics. It is to be hoped that the success of this work may inspire similar efforts in English, since the wide use of this language would greatly enhance the usefulness of such a work. Fortunately a considerable part of the mathematical language is universal and hence it is a comparatively easy matter to learn to use mathematical works which appear in an unfamiliar language.

It should not be assumed that the term "elementary mathematics" is always used with the broad meaning given to it in the encyclopedia under consideration. The fact that this use of the term is not unique results from the almost equally advanced significance given to it in the well-known German encyclopedia of elementary mathematics by Weber and Wellstein. The latter work devotes much less space than the present one to historical questions and to elementary arithmetic. In fact, the numerous references to early developments which appear in the present work make it very useful to those who are interested in tracing mathematical developments to their sources. The wealth of material which thus becomes available to the student of elementary mathematics should greatly enrich the lives of those who teach this subject in our schools, and is much more inspiring than the view that the development of elementary mathematics was practically completed in 1700.

G. A. MILLER
UNIVERSITY OF ILLINOIS

ORGANIZED EDUCATION AND THE EIGHTEENTH AMENDMENT

I AM respectful of the view of the conscientious proponent of the Eighteenth Amendment and its enforcement act. In my personal habits, I am temperate almost to the degree of teetotalism. In fact, I am not here concerned with prohibition as an issue at all. I wish to point out the anomalous position of organized American education because it illustrates the pattern of thought of American school people.

The majority of the individual members making up the Wickersham commission voted for a revision of the Eighteenth Amendment. The *Literary Digest* poll of over six million Americans showed a substantial majority in favor of repeal or revision. Eminent Americans, such as the late Dwight Morrow, Nicholas Murray Butler, and Newton Baker, are dissatisfied with the present method of handling the manufacture and sale of liquor. More recently, the United States Bar, the American Medical Association, and the American Federation of Labor have favored repeal or modification. The American Legion Convention at Detroit passed a resolution urging Congress to submit the question of prohibition to the several states for settlement by referendum.

But American school officers assembled in convention voted almost unanimously in favor of the *status quo* and rudely resisted open discussion of the question. Are teachers and other school officers actually unanimous in their support of the Eighteenth Amendment? Or are teachers who conscientiously question the value of prohibition too timid to voice their opposition on the platform or in print?

What if the Eighteenth Amendment should be modified? Will the educational profession play a part in determining what form modification shall take or will organized American education continue to limit its social planning to the drafting of resolutions? Will it expect these resolutions to be accepted sheepishly?

If there is a minority opinion with respect to prohibition, why crush it? Why not put the minority to work studying modification? Let its report be aired. Let it be defeated. It could then, at least, be said that school officers encourage critical thought. And, perchance, should modification of the enforcement act or repeal of the Eighteenth Amendment come, it could at least be said that not all school men were quiescent.

HENRY HARAP
SCHOOL OF EDUCATION,
WESTERN RESERVE UNIVERSITY

QUOTATIONS

EDUCATIONAL PROGRAMS IN RADIO BROADCASTING

COMMERCIALISM is the heart of broadcasting in the United States. Competition is responsible for the high type of our programs. Government control in this country would involve enormous expense, and would be altogether impractical.

The situation in England is not at all like that in the United States. The country is so small that a very few radio stations may cover its entire area. The expense of covering this small area is trivial compared to that which would be incurred if government control were attempted in the United States.

Should the Government of the United States

try to control radio broadcasting here, the expense would run high into the millions. The government either would have to buy enough of the existing stations to cover the United States' area, or would have to junk existing stations and build new ones. Either procedure would cost millions of dollars. Then, there would be the cost of keeping these stations in operation without sponsored programs.

In England a comparatively small number of stations serve its entire listening public. In the United States, many stations would be required, if this country's millions of listeners were served adequately.

As to education, it is conceded generally that there are not enough programs of that nature broadcast in this country. Why? Because the listening public is the judge: they say what they desire, and apparently they do not wish for education. The public is the final censor. No commercial station will continue to broadcast any type of program to which listeners do not respond favorably.

Programs in the United States largely are sponsored by advertisers. Obviously, the advertisers are eager to give listeners what they desire. If they craved educational programs, advertisers would supply them. But, apparently, they don't care for this type of broadcast.

What has education contributed to radio? Not one thing. What has commercialism contributed? Everything; the life blood of the industry.

Commercial stations would buy educational programs almost without limit, if educators would make their programs of enough interest to the public to attract listeners as do popular programs of to-day. Large broadcasting systems vie with each other to buy the services of outstanding artists. They would compete just as zealously for educational programs if educators would make such broadcasts interesting enough.

Consider the situation as it would be if broadcasting were government-controlled in the United States. After expending millions of dollars for maintenance of stations, hiring station operators, providing power, etc., what would be left for employing talent for programs? Would the public be served even approximately as well as they are now? Without competition among stations and advertisers, could the government afford to pay hundreds of thousands of dollars to give the public programs featuring nationally and internationally known artists in every field?

The listening public of America, accustomed to programs of the highest type of entertainment, would not listen to programs the government might be able to afford if they had control of broadcasting.

A report recently received at the commission tells of the inefficiency of station operation in Europe. It points out that there are from 10 to 30 minutes of silence between parts of programs. It says programs are not efficiently arranged. That situation, remember, exists in countries many of which are of relatively small areas, where the expense of government control would not nearly approach that in the United States.

Would such broadcasting management be accepted by the listening public in this country? When broadcasting is government-controlled, listeners get not what they want, but what they should have.

What percentage of England's population listens to educational programs? In the United States, millions of persons listen daily and nightly. They are being entertained. When an educational program is interspersed, they keep on listening. If educational programs could be brought up to the high interest-point of popular programs, they would be received in an equally welcome spirit by American listeners.

Commercial stations are glad to give time to educational institutions, when these institutions have enough money to pay for their programs. No stations, though, will give time to an educational institution as a regular practice, when the station can make money from sponsored commercial programs.

When educators make their programs interesting enough, commercial firms will sponsor them, and broadcasting chains will compete for the privilege of broadcasting them. Until then, however, programs will continue much as they are at present.

The public is the sole judge. Stations give them what they wish for. If educators can show stations that the public wants their programs, educational broadcasts will have a prominent place on the programs of every station in the United States.

The United States system of broadcasting is exactly the same as that of England, except that in this country commercialism is the dictator, while in Britain the rule is vested in government.—Commissioner Harold A. Lafount, of the Federal Radio Commission, in the *United States Daily*.

REPORTS

RECOMMENDATIONS OF THE NATIONAL ADVISORY COMMITTEE ON EDUCATION[1]

FEDERAL RELATIONS TO EDUCATION IN THE STATES

(1) CONTINUE SPECIAL AID NOW IN FORCE. For at least five years and until the results of the finance surveys recommended in Number 4 below are adequate to provide a sound plan for an equitable and economical method of federal financial assistance to the states, continue the special appropriations now in force for the purpose of aiding agricultural education and research, rural extension for adults, vocational education, and similar educational enterprises, but leave the states free to expend such monies for the specific purposes designated without the requirement for matching of monies and without federal authority to approve or reject state plans.

(2) AMEND LAWS. Amend those existing laws which give or tend to give the Federal Government and its agencies power to interfere with the autonomy of the states in matters of education. These amendments should repeal all provisions that require the states and their local communities to match federal funds or that grant power to the federal agencies to approve or reject state educational plans, to prescribe the standards controlling instruction, or otherwise to supervise and direct educational or research activities within the states.

The foregoing discussion does not relate to federal research activities in fields other than education save as these affect the autonomy of the states in the conduct of their educational affairs.

(3) RESTRICT LEGISLATION. Enact no additional laws that grant federal financial aid to the states in support of special types of education or that increase existing federal grants for such special purposes as are already aided.

(4) STUDY FINANCES. In line with the study of school finance recently begun by the Office of Education, make further and continuing studies of tax systems, distribution of national income, living costs, public expenditures for eleemosynary institutions, bonded indebtedness, federal aid to states for purposes other than education, and of such other features of the situation as may be necessary to understand the total economic, political and fiscal organization of which the school system is a part. Such facts in particular should be sought as will reveal how far and by what methods the people are justified in using the federal tax system to supplement state and local taxes in support of public education in the states in order to insure meeting fully the national responsibility for education.

Similar studies should also be made at once to answer two questions: First: How far shall the Federal Government properly grant funds either to the states in support of specially designated institutions or directly to particular institutions? Secondly: What are the right uses of the remainder of the public domain in the states for the uses of education?

(5) AID EDUCATION GENERALLY. Make all future grants to states as grants in aid of education in general, expendable by each state for any or all educational purposes as the state itself may direct. Such grants should be made only after thorough educational and financial studies have shown to the satisfaction of the appropriating power that such federal aid is justified. Such grants should in no case be flat grants of an equal amount for each state, but should be apportioned to the states on the basis of adequate educational and financial studies. Such grants should be made for a definite and not an inconclusive period, and be subject to review at the close of every ten-year census period, when needed readjustments may be made to meet changed conditions. The only restriction placed by federal legislation on such educational grants should be the provision that every state, when it accepts the grant, agrees to make each year to the federal headquarters for education a full report on all questions on which the federal headquarters for education may require information concerning the manner in which the state has used the grant.

(6) RESTRICT AUDITS. Restrict the audits of the Federal Government to those made by the Treasury Department merely to determine whether or not monies granted have been spent for

[1] From the committee's report, an abstract of which was printed in the issue of SCHOOL AND SOCIETY for last week.

general or special educational purposes as defined in the several federal acts of appropriation, without making audit an indirect method of controlling or determining educational standards and processes.

(7) LIMIT EMERGENCY AID. Emergency grants made by the Federal Government to meet some special and transient crisis involving the use of education should be restricted to financial aid to investigate the problem, to disseminate the needed information and to promote cooperation among all the states and local communities. A new federal agency may be created for this temporary purpose if the needs are such as to necessitate this, but financial grants to such a new agency should be made for a strictly limited period, and not renewed.

(8) CREATE ADEQUATE FEDERAL HEADQUARTERS. Create an adequate federal headquarters for educational research and information, so organized as to serve both as a reliable source of comprehensive, correlated, and accurate information regarding national aspects of education for all concerned in the states, territories and outlying possessions, and as a cooperating center for all federal agencies with respect to the educational aspects of their work.

(9) INCREASE APPROPRIATIONS. Increase the federal appropriations for educational research and information service by the Office of Education, by the Federal Board for Vocational Education, by the Extension Service and the Office of Experiment Stations in the Department of Agriculture, and by other offices or bureaus of the Federal Government primarily concerned with the stimulation and improvement of various types of education in the states; and provide ample facilities to these offices for supplying to all concerned the results of research and statistical studies through publications and conferences.

INDIANS AND OTHER INDIGENOUS PEOPLES

(1) ESTABLISH PLANNING DIVISION. Establish in the Bureau of Indian Affairs a planning and development division, freed from administrative responsibility, which shall be concerned only with basic investigations, ethnological studies, planning and the accurate checking of results. This division should be responsible for developing a new-type school center suitable for the education of peoples with different cultural backgrounds.

(2) HAVE PERMANENT CONFERENCE. Create a special subcommittee of the Interdepartmental Council for Education to consider all problems arising in connection with the development of primitive and native peoples under jurisdiction of different Departments of the Federal Government with direct or indirect responsibility. This subcommittee shall consist of representatives, specially concerned and delegated by the secretaries or heads of departments having direction of: (a) The Division of planning and Development (Bureau of Indian Affairs—Department of Interior); (b) The Office of Island Governments (Department of the Navy); (c) The Bureau of Insular Affairs (Department of War); (d) The Bureau of American Ethnology (Smithsonian Institution).

This subcommittee should be privileged to requisition studies on special problems needing solution. The chief services which should be utilized in gaining basic information required for more effective administration, and usually requiring research and investigation, should be the Division of Planning and Development in the Bureau of Indian Affairs (new) and the Bureau of American Ethnology (old).

(3) GRADUALLY DELEGATE MANAGEMENT. Delegate the actual management of Indian affairs, now highly centralized, to local officials as much as possible and as rapidly as a new and retrained personnel is available.

(4) ALASKAN NATIVES. Transfer responsibility for the Alaskan natives now vested in the Bureau of Indian Affairs to the Territory of Alaska, as soon as that Territory is willing and able to take this over.

(5) PROVIDE BEST PERSONNEL. Provide special facilities and financial support, on recommendation of the Planning and Development Division of the Bureau of Indian Affairs, for the proper recruiting, training, and retraining of personnel for this service.

A trained personnel is the strategic point for all improvement in the Indian Bureau, particularly in the reform of a service which has been largely inferior because underpaid, and where a rather complete change of view and procedure is contemplated. No amount of new legislation, reorganization of staff, or adoption of new policy will succeed without a double program involving: Better recruitment of an ably trained personnel; and, the continuous improvement of personnel in service.

EDUCATION IN THE TERRITORIES AND OUTLYING POSSESSIONS

(1) RELY UPON EDUCATION. Continue to emphasize educational means as an instrument of health, social and political welfare in the life of our politically dependent peoples, and lay a new emphasis on the use of education in fostering their economic security.

(2) FORMULATE COMPREHENSIVE POLICY. Formulate a more comprehensive and unified federal

policy in education, equally just to all outlying possessions in consideration of their needs and suitable for future guidance of federal cooperation both financial and intellectual.

(3) EMPLOY EDUCATIONAL ADVISERS. Maintain in each department concerned with education in the territories and outlying possessions an educational adviser trained and experienced in the techniques of modern educational practice.

(4) PROVIDE CONFERENCE. Until the political responsibility for all the territories and outlying possessions is focused within some one federal department or agency, provide for cooperation and coordination of the work of the various departments now concerned through a subcommittee of the Interdepartmental Council for Education specially appointed to consider education in the outlying areas and on which each educational adviser concerned shall have a seat.

(5) PROVIDE FOR RESEARCH. Provide at once for a competent and continuing study by the Federal Office of Education of the problems involved in the education of politically dependent peoples within our territories and outlying possessions.

RESEARCH AND INFORMATION SERVICE

(1) DEVELOP THE SERVICES. Develop the Federal Government's research and information services with increasing emphasis on comprehensive research and on the diffusion of information that is pertinent to the decision of critical national issues.

(2) EXPAND IN EDUCATION. Continue to expand the federal research and information service in the field of education until it meets adequately the needs of the American people for intellectual assistance in all phases of education, including the educational aspects of health, recreation, and other community activities that vitally affect physical, mental and moral growth.

(3) COORDINATE ACTIVITIES. In the interest of efficiency, economy, and continuity of policy, organize as a subcommittee of the Interdepartmental Council for Education an interdepartmental conference on educational research and information services in education.

(4) CONFER ADEQUATE STATUS. Give the general headquarters for education in the Federal Government a status and influence within the governmental organization that will permit it to present forcibly both to Congress and to the President the scientific and other professional facts which are pertinent and crucial in determining the policies of the Federal Government with regard to education.

INTERNATIONAL INTELLECTUAL RELATIONS

(1) ENCOURAGE INTERNATIONAL COOPERATION. Develop and extend our intellectual and educational cooperations in the international field, particularly throughout the western hemisphere where our neighborly responsibilities are large.

(2) SELECT APPROPRIATE COMMISSIONS. Appoint as members of commissions sent abroad to represent the United States only men and women who are especially equipped both by training and by experience to make clear the purpose and operation of our educational systems, the nature of our institutions, and the cultural characteristics of the American people.

(3) STUDY FOREIGN EDUCATION. Empower the federal headquarters for education, in cooperation with the Interdepartmental Council for Education, and the Foreign Service of the Department of State, to gather and publish such information concerning foreign educational theory and practice as is of significance to American education.

(4) COORDINATE VISA MACHINERY. Establish closer cooperation between the Departments of State and of Labor in such manner as to insure closer coordination in the administration of passport visas.

DEPARTMENT OF EDUCATION

WE THEREFORE RECOMMEND: That a Department of Education with a Secretary of Education at its head be established in the Federal Government, in accordance with the following specifications.

NUCLEUS. The nucleus for an appropriate organization of a Department of Education now exists in the United States Office of Education of the Department of the Interior. This was originally established as a Department of Education in 1867, for the purpose, as stated in the act, "of collecting such statistics and facts as shall show the condition and progress of education in the several states and territories, and of diffusing such information respecting the organization and management of schools and school systems, and methods of teaching, as shall aid the people of the United States in the establishment and maintenance of efficient school systems, and otherwise promote the cause of education throughout the country." Its present policy with regard to the conduct of national inquiries is in harmony with the policies and procedures recommended by this committee.

CONCENTRATION. Transfer the Office of Education and all pertaining thereto to the Department of Education and establish it as a major division of that department under direction of an assistant secretary of education.

Amend the Smith-Hughes Act of 1917 and all acts subsequent thereto dealing with vocational education by repealing those provisions that require state matching of federal funds and federal approval of state plans and standards and that give federal officials authority to withhold funds; abolish the Federal Board for Vocational Education, transfer its remaining functions and its staff to the Department of Education and establish the staff as a major division of that department under direction of an assistant secretary of education. These changes relieve that staff from its present obligation to ascertain and certify to federal officials whether federally aided schools are or are not complying with the provisions of federal acts. These changes also concentrate the energies of that staff on cooperative studies and experiments designed to produce that fusion of humanistic and vocational training which is so sorely needed to promote the liberal and practical education of the American people in the several pursuits and professions in life.

Other existing federal activities, which have as their chief function educational investigation and information service and which are now operating in harmony with the policies and procedures recommended, such as the studies of physical growth of children now carried on in the Public Health Service, should also be transferred to the Department of Education.

No regulatory or executive responsibilities should be vested in the Department of Education through these transfers. Should it prove desirable to transfer to the Department of Education any federal office that now has regulatory or executive responsibilities or that has authority to withhold federal funds to secure compliance with federal acts, such powers shall be removed from that office, as in the case of the Federal Board for Vocational Education, before making the transfer.

DISTRIBUTION. Leave those federal educational activities which are instrumental or incidental to proper administration of some other primary function of the Federal Government under jurisdiction of the department which is responsible for that primary function. This applies to such activities as Indian education in the Bureau of Indian Affairs, agricultural extension for adults in the Department of Agriculture, military training in the Departments of War and Navy, schooling in federal areas and in outlying possessions under the department primarily concerned, and training of its own personnel in each of the government departments.

COORDINATION. Establish an Interdepartmental Council on Education, as already recommended, to coordinate the policies and procedures of these dispersed federal educational activities. Designate the Secretary of Education chairman of this Interdepartmental Council and constitute the executive heads of every federal office intimately concerned as members. When properly organized, such an Interdepartmental Council will hold regular stated meetings to consider general federal educational policies and procedures and will appoint a number of sub-committees or sub-conferences to consider special problems of interest to limited groups. Such a council will initiate investigations but its findings will be wholly advisory. Each department or independent establishment will be free to adopt such portions of the recommendations of this council as the head of the department desires to have adopted. Such a council will be authorized to use the facilities and personnel under jurisdiction of its various members to carry on its work.

SCOPE. The combined facilities of the present Office of Education and of the Federal Board for Vocational Education are inadequate to render the intellectual assistance which our recommendations require. Their recent inquiries and surveys, while constantly giving useful and accurate information much needed by the American people, do not cover some of the most important fields of federal responsibility for education. The Department of Education, when properly established, will have sufficient financial support to enable it to collect and publish critical data and pertinent information on all significant phases of education. Some of the more important phases now needing this service are education in the outlying possessions and in foreign countries; education of the physically, mentally, and socially handicapped; education of government personnel under the various departments; education on governmental areas; and the educational aspects of clinics, playgrounds, parks, libraries, museums, motion pictures, radio and other similar environmental activities that are such powerful influences in molding the spirit and character of American youth.

STAFF. Under this plan the Secretary of Education will aid the President, the heads of departments, and Congress in consideration of educational problems. He will plan and organize the national research and information service of the department in such manner that all phases of the work are conducted in harmony with the policies and procedures recommended in this report. He will contribute constructively to development of the leadership which American education needs for its coordination and intelligent advance.

The assistant secretaries will direct the technical work of the department, supervise its publications and their distribution, and maintain cooperative professional relations with other educational institutions.

The head of each subordinate office will have a rank and a salary that should make it possible to secure the services of thoroughly competent men and women.

Such a Department of Education will also be authorized to recruit for the transient period of an inquiry the best educational ability available in the country. Often such talent is permanently associated with the public school systems, voluntary agencies and scholarly institutions on private foundation rather than with the Federal Government itself. The use of such men avoids the necessity of maintaining in the federal employ a large permanent staff at high cost. The department will also have ample funds to establish advisory boards consisting of leading citizens and to conduct regional conferences wherever these may be necessary for effective enlightenment of the people through discussion.

FUNCTIONS. The Department of Education as here recommended will perform those functions that were assigned to the Department of Education when established in 1867. It will collect "such statistics and facts as shall show the condition and progress of education in the several states and territories," and will diffuse "such information respecting the organization and management of schools and school systems, and methods of teaching, as shall aid the people of the United States in the establishment and maintenance of efficient school systems, and will otherwise promote the cause of education throughout the country."

POWERS. The Department of Education as here recommended will have no legal or financial power and no regulatory or executive authority, direct or indirect, explicit or implied, by which it may control the social purposes and specific processes of education. This limitation of powers necessitates a complete reversal of the tendency exhibited in much recent federal legislation to build up a centralized control of the purposes and processes of education in the Federal Government.

SOCIETIES AND MEETINGS

EDUCATIONAL CONFERENCES OF INDIAN SERVICE SUPERINTENDENTS

FOUR regional conferences of superintendents of Indian agencies and schools, primarily dealing with educational matters, were held during October at Bismarck, North Dakota; Spokane, Washington; Winslow, Arizona, and Oklahoma City, Oklahoma.

The Bismarck conference, attended by 24 reservation and school superintendents from the states of Michigan, Wisconsin, North Dakota, South Dakota, Wyoming and eastern Montana, was held on October 12 and 13; the Spokane conference, at which 20 superintendents from Oregon, Washington, Nevada, Idaho, Utah, western Montana and northern California were present, took place on October 15 and 16; a group of 27 superintendents, mostly from Arizona and New Mexico, gathered at Winslow for the conference at that point on October 21 and 22, and the Oklahoma conference, held on October 26 and 27, brought together 20 Indian Service superintendents from Oklahoma, Iowa, Kansas, Mississippi, Nebraska and North Carolina.

The conferences were entirely of a discussion type, with no set speeches. One session was usually given over to questions of general administration with particular reference to Indian schools, and another to personnel, with the three intervening sessions devoted to the aims and problems of the various branches of the educational program, including: (a) Trade and industrial training; (b) home economics; (c) emphasis in the primary, intermediate and secondary grades; (d) character-building and leisure-time programs for boys and girls; (e) public-school relationships. Some of the special questions discussed were: What changes are necessary this year in Indian education in view of the difficult industrial and economic conditions? What should be the distribution of authority and responsibility between agency and school superintendents? What should be the program for vocational education in Indian schools? How can we cooperate more effectively with state and local school systems? How should the Indian schools help meet community needs?

Members of the headquarters staff of the

Indian Office at Washington who attended the conferences included Robert T. Lansdale, assistant to the commissioner of Indian affairs; W. Carson Ryan, Jr., director of education for the Indian Service; Rose K. Brandt, supervisor of elementary education; John H. Holst and George F. Miller, supervisors of secondary education; Samuel H. Thompson, supervisor in charge of public school relations; Edna Groves, supervisor of home economics; James Arentson, supervisor of trade and industrial training, and A. C. Cooley, director of extension for the Indian Service. Accompanying the Washington staff in the capacity of special consultants were Joseph McCaskill and Paul Gordon, of the Brookings Institution.

Among those in attendance at the conferences were the three newly designated superintendents of education on Indian reservation: Superintendent Joe Jennings, of Pine Ridge, South Dakota; Superintendent J. Arthur Anderson, of the combined Turtle Mountain-Fort Totten Agencies, North Dakota, and Superintendent R. M. Tisinger, of the Pima-Papago jurisdictions, Tucson, Arizona; the first state supervisor of Indian education to be appointed, George C. Wells, of Oklahoma, and the four recently selected heads of large Indian boarding schools —Robert D. Baldwin, Haskell Institute, Lawrence, Kansas; B. J. Brophy, Flandreau Indian School, South Dakota; Carl H. Skinner, Phoenix Indian School, Phoenix, Arizona, and Herman Bogard, Genoa Indian School, Genoa, Nebraska.

W. CARSON RYAN, JR.

EDUCATIONAL RESEARCH AND STATISTICS

HIGH SCHOOL AVERAGE VERSUS HIGH SCHOOL CLASS RANK AS A MEANS OF PREDICTING COLLEGE GRADES

AN important criterion in predicting the probable success of applicants for admission to college is the quality of work done in high school. As a statement of this quality we commonly use the average high-school grade or the rank in the class. If all schools were of the same size, had truly unselected student bodies and used the same grading system, and if all high-school faculties had the same grading standards there might be, except for chance factors, a one-to-one correspondence between average grades and ranks. However, these conditions, as the data below indicate, are far from being fulfilled.

To get some idea as to the relative value of the two criteria for predicting first and second semester grades, coefficients of correlation were collected from freshman classes entering the College of Liberal Arts of Northwestern University. For each correlation all students for whom data were available were considered.

Table I shows the coefficients of correlation (Pearson's r) obtained between high-school average and average quality of work during the first and second semesters. (To equate the high-school averages for the different grading systems the relative position of each student's average in respect to passing and a perfect grade was taken). The unweighted mean of these coefficients is .455.

TABLE I

SHOWING THE CORRELATION BETWEEN HIGH SCHOOL AVERAGE AND COLLEGE GRADES. PROBABLE ERRORS RANGE BETWEEN .03 AND .05

Subjects	1st semester		2nd semester	
	r	N	r	N
1919 Men	.443	238	.486	207
1919 Women	.452	278	.473	256
1923 Men	.366	168	.422	135
1923 Women	.418	274	.422	243
1925 Men	.518	238	.438	203
1925 Women	.536	359	.489	319
Unweighted mean	.455		.455	

In Table II we have the r's for the high-school class rank and college grades. (Only exact ranks, such as 20th in a class of 116, were used and these were expressed in .2 sigma intervals, assuming that the grades of the high-school classes fell under a normal curve). The unweighted mean of these coefficients is .510.

Information concerning high-school average comes from earlier classes than do the data

TABLE II

SHOWING THE CORRELATION BETWEEN HIGH SCHOOL CLASS RANK AND COLLEGE GRADES. PROBABLE ERRORS BETWEEN .03 AND .04

Subjects	1st semester		2nd semester	
	r	N	r	N
1925 Men	.519	233	.492	208
1925 Women	.570	292	.528	261
1927 Men	.431	253	.509	230
1927 Women	.499	303	.529	282
Unweighted mean	.505		.514	

concerning high-school rank. It is only in the 1925 group that we have a chance for fairly direct comparison, and even here the two groups of men and of women are not entirely, although almost, identical. Disregarding these two factors making for something less than an ideal comparison, high-school rank is indicated as being slightly more closely related to college marks of the first and second semesters than is high-school average.

Among the entering freshmen of 1930 it was found that there were 351 men and 275 women for whom we had for each information concerning rank, average and college grades. The coefficients for each pair of these variables are shown in Table III. Here also are the r's for high-school rank and average for the men and women who entered in 1925.

TABLE III

PROBABLE ERRORS OF THESE COEFFICIENTS ARE FROM .02 TO .05

Subjects	Items correlated	r
351 men of 1930	Rank and average	.768
	Average & 1st Sem. grades	.584
	Rank and " " "	.448
275 women of 1930	Rank and average	.732
	Average & 1st Sem. grades	.590
	Rank and " " "	.316
195 men of 1925	Rank and average	.852
290 women of 1925	" " "	.810

The data of Table III indicate that high-school averages were more closely related to 1st semester grades than was high-school rank. It will also be noted that rank and averages were much less closely related in 1930 than in 1925.

The apparent advantage shown in Tables I and II of high-school rank over average for indicating college grades seems here to be disproved. There are, however, additional facts not shown in the tables of coefficients of correlation which may serve to explain this apparent discrepancy. Although the total number of freshmen did not change much from year to year, there was a great increase in the number of applicants. Since high-school class rank, not average, was used to grant admission without entrance examinations, the range of high-school ranks shortened somewhat faster than the range of averages. (This shrinking of range of ranks during recent years was due in small part to the fact that some students were ranked as being somewhere in the upper half when they had relatively low high-school averages.) Had both high-school ranks and averages been used in selecting applicants it is likely that the relationship between these two variables would not have dropped so much between 1925 and 1930 nor would high-school average probably have been so superior to rank in 1930 in predicting college grades.

In conclusion, these data do not indicate a convincing superiority of high-school rank over average, or of average over rank, for selecting freshmen who will make good grades in college. However, the relatively low (about .80) correlation between these two measures of high-school achievement indicates that both, instead of either one alone, may be used to advantage.

EDWARD L. CLARK

NORTHWESTERN UNIVERSITY

NEW BOOKS IN EDUCATION

CHAVE, ERNEST J. *Supervision of Religious Education.* Pp. xv + 352. University of Chicago Press. $2.50.

CLARK, BERTHA. *The House on the Hill.* Illustrated by Gertrude H. Howe. Pp. 142. Little, Brown. $.75.

DINWIDDIE, COURTENAY. *Child Health and the Community Fund, New York.* $1.00.

EDMONSON, JAMES B. and others. *Secondary School Administration.* Pp. 483. Illustrated. Macmillan. $2.25.

NEWMARK, DAVID. *Educational Plays of Modern Days.* Pp. 106. Badger.

EDUCATIONAL REVIEW

Edited by WILLIAM McANDREW

SURCEASE OF CODDLING

THE autumn conventions of the state teachers associations are over. The mayors have made their addresses of welcome and gone back to common councils. The chief magistrate of Dayton, Ohio, may be taken as a type of what honest men in these troubled times said to the other meetings. He offered no sympathy to hard-working, conscientious educators. Our luck in having any employment at all offsets the good old *confectio pomorum* the welcomers used to ladle out. On the contrary, Mayor McDonald reminded us that the country is nearer the break-up of democracy than at any time in his memory. A bewildered and unintelligent citizenry, untrained in economic and political affairs, indicates a need for an educational program more directly pertinent to democracy than the brand the schools are giving to the public.

BREVIARY FOR THESE TIMES

A book of daily offices to be read in the closet by those of major orders in the brotherhood of schoolmasters may be compiled from the addresses, sermons and editorials of this present. Truly, as the Preacher said of old, there is a time to cast away stones, and a time to gather stones together, and the fool foldeth his hands.

These sayings, the first of 224, gathered in a village library in three days, and all of them of the same tenor, the words not of chronic fault-finders, but of respectable men and women who are students of large affairs, are only a sample. If you live in a large town where books are easier got at you could gather many more. They seem to indicate that you'll have to start something soon.

1. OUR DEMOCRACY THREATENED. Our future depends more than ever before on how we train our youth. The problems America faces are more serious than those that confronted our early settlers. Unseen forces threaten the nation's existence. WILLIAM JOHN COOPER, U. S. Commissioner of Education. In Macmillan's News Review. October, 1931.

2. SCHOOLS ON THE WRONG TRACK. Unless education gives up promoting selfishness and turns to preparing future citizens to deal effectively with the problems of crime, law observance, capital, labor, unemployment, war and peace, political dishonesty, our civilization may, indeed, collapse. JOHN DEWEY. Radio address. Oct. 26, 1931.

3. EDUCATION MUST BE POLITICAL. Our inspiration for education must arise from the American conception of government and of citizenship under it. PRESIDENT EMERITUS WM. O. THOMPSON, Ohio. Address to National Education Association. 1930.

4. OUR CIVIC DISEASES. The trouble with America is cynicism, apathy, despair, laziness, cowardice and greed. NORMAN THOMAS. Radio Broadcast. Nov. 2. 1931.

5. A NATION BETRAYED. The racketeering principle runs through our political systems. Investigations come and go. The betrayal of the community continues. We'll have mass meetings and forget. Politics must be taught as a ceaseless duty of the people organized for self-protection. NEW YORK HERALD-TRIBUNE. Editorial, Nov. 2, 1931.

6. VIGILANCE. Only by steady supervision and frequent investigations can government be kept clean. The founders of the nation knew this and pleaded for eternal vigilance. The people must be brought, by education, back to this fundamental fact. The public is apathetic. It has not been trained. PROFESSOR JOSEPH McGOLDRICK, Columbia University. New York Herald-Tribune. Oct. 17, 1931.

7. YOUR SCHOOLS ARE NOT UP. This is the climax—the challenge of democracy to American education. We are not making the kind of schools the twentieth century requires. We have not brought the challenge up to the same level that the teaching of present school courses have reached. Do you think you can do it? PROFESSOR CARROLL D. CHAMP-

LIN, Pennsylvania State College. Address to the teachers of Binghamton. 1931.

8. EVASION. No one contradicts Dr. Bagley's word that public schools must be maintained to be the nurse and physician of good government. What sort of a nurse or physician abstains from the study of diseases? How do you explain that the periodicals for schools, covering current events, omit all mention of the disclosures of political corruption of which the daily papers give extended notice? RICHARD WELLING. National Self-government Committee. 1931.

9. OSTRICH CIVICS. Most of the schools known to me teach the children that we have the best government in the world. All the statisticians tell us we have the worst crime and political corruption. The generals of Napoleon III told him he had a perfect army. It crumpled as soon as it met the trained troops of Von Moltke. WALTER A. WATSON, Philadelphia. Address to teachers. 1931.

10. A CHALLENGE TO YOU. Not in years has the principle of good government been so vitally involved as now. The situation is a direct challenge. EDITORIAL, NEW YORK HERALD–TRIBUNE. Nov. 3, 1931.

11. SCHOOL A BULWARK OF CORRUPTION. To the extent that education is engendering a spirit of futility toward efficient democracy it is a bulwark of governmental corruption. DR. WILLIAM BRADLEY OTIS. College of the City of New York. 1931.

12. SCHOOLS FOR SELFISHNESS. The almighty dollar, said Washington Irving in 1836, is the great object of the universal devotion throughout our land. Almost a hundred years later, we are regarded by the rest of the world as too individually selfish to devote ourselves to the common good. Training for selfish pleasure and profit is the daily exercise of our schools. HARRISON K. OLDS. Boston. 1931.

13. POLITICAL ANESTHETIC. To the boy or girl who is thinking or reasoning, the schools, for the most part, cry "halt." SUPT. WILLIS A. SUTTON. Atlanta. 1930.

14. EDUCATION'S TASK. It is plain enough that the education of citizens must be a survey of government at the points where it touches the rights of the people; to cultivate the courage requisite in pointing out abuses and in testifying about them; to sift complaints and present them; to help correct the wrongs that are discovered; to destroy the appalling lethargy and indifference of the community; to create an army to fight for fair dealing and honest government. Dr. EDWARD T. DEVINE. New York Committee of One Thousand. 1891.

15. DOCTORS OF DEMOCRACY. I can not see that any of the claims of culture, leisure, health, home-membership, vocational skill, college preparation or other schoolmastery aims can honestly be considered by any teacher so real a duty as the training of the generation to right the tragic evils of our democracy. Nothing short of a recasting of our educational system will do. The schools were set up to keep democracy hale. Democracy is sick. We can not dodge the issue. JOHN O. CHEWNING, Superintendent of Schools, Evansville, Indiana. Address at Los Angeles. 1931.

16. A PATTERN FOR YOU. No diploma shall issue to any person unless and until his record shows him, in knowledge and conduct, giving promise of being a worthy citizen. Rule of BOARD OF EDUCATION, EVANSVILLE, INDIANA. 1931.

17. AND NOW THE LAW. The people of the state of Michigan enact: In all high schools a one-semester course, five recitations a week, shall stress the rights and responsibilities of citizens. No diploma shall be issued to any student not satisfactorily completing said course. Act 148. MICHIGAN LEGISLATURE. 1931.

18. TEETH IN IT. In all normal schools a course of four term-hours shall be given in civics. In all colleges receiving public funds a six-hour course shall be given. Recommendation for graduation of a student not satisfactorily covering the course shall be deemed a misdemeanor. Act 148, laws of 1931. MICHIGAN LEGISLATURE.

19. NEED A FIGHTING SPIRIT. The main not the incidental duty of the American public school is training better citizens than we now have. This can not be done by abstract, academic, safe and harmless study of the anatomy of government. It must be a recognition of the corruption of our times and the cultivation of a fighting spirit to get and maintain the ideals vital in the aims of the founders. JOHN J. MAHONEY, Director, Harvard-Boston University extension courses.

20. THE DEMOCRACY CONCEIVED BY THE FOUNDERS IS VERY FAR FROM ACHIEVEMENT. This nation is dedicated to the achievement of the democratic ideal. We are engaged in the process of creating a democracy which shall vindicate the principle of self-government. We are very far from having achieved it. A corrupt political organization may seize the treasury of your city and use the government for self enrichment while the poor are plundered. Organized civil government may do this. It may be so powerful that it would take unlimited money and a quarter of a century to match it. SAMUEL SEABURY. Address: Hobart College. June 8, 1931.

21. NEGLECT OF DUTY. Such a wave of criminality as is now upon us would be impossible if the schools had done their civic duty. WALTER ROBINSON SMITH. The Nation's Schools. Sept., 1930.

22. SAD FAILURE. Our education is one of the sad failures of our history. The education America needs is so different from what we have that it would have to be called by another name. JAMES HARVEY ROBINSON. The Nation's Schools. Sept., 1930.

23. EDUCATORS INDIFFERENT. Educators are singularly indifferent to the needs of the times. Our teachers should be the quickest to respond to the call of democracy. We have not taken it seriously. We have entrusted our government to petty politicians and bosses. So long as we cling to traditional education we shall not solve the problem of a new democracy. The times demand a new education, pledged to justice for all. We are called to higher things. JAMES EARL RUSSELL, Dean, Teachers College, N. Y. "The Trend in American Education." 1922.

24. EDUCATION'S TRAITOROUS POLICY. American school children are vaccinated against thinking on economic and political problems. It is a traitorous policy and sells us out to the past. To hold on to the ways of old individualistic pioneers keeps us from working together. The thinking of teachers needs remoulding. WILLIAM HEARD KILPATRICK. As reported in N. Y. Herald-Tribune. July 10, 1931.

25. CIVIC FAILURE OF SCHOOLS. Our educational systems are fitted only for an outworn philosophy. The Seabury investigation shows the failure of the schools' teaching of "civics" to the present generation of citizens. One can graduate from a splendid college program as now maintained and still be morally a menace to society, and politically a grafter. PROFESSOR GOODWIN WATSON. As reported in the N. Y. Times. July 18, 1931.

26. DEMOCRACY THREATENED. A blow is being struck, a threat is being made, against the cardinal principles on which our government rests. Every one in the country must answer the call. MAX D. STEUER, N. Y. Attorney. Reported in N. Y. Times. July 26, 1931.

27. CIVIC INDIFFERENCE. A little preliminary knowledge, a little downright love of honest men on the part of citizens, would save us from scandal. We should have citizens intelligent enough to prevent election of dubious men. REV. JAMES SHEERIN. Address St. Ann's Episcopal Church. Reported in N. Y. Herald-Tribune. Aug. 10, 1931.

28. MORE PROSPEROUS AND MORE CRIMINAL THAN ANY OTHER NATION. Education has not addressed itself to American social and political problems. The average American has more wealth than any one in the world and commits more crimes. The native-born in proportion to their numbers rate worst; negroes, next; the foreign-born citizen has the cleanest record in our courts. PROFESSOR ANN BREWINGTON, U. of Chicago. At

Nat. Education Assn., Los Angeles. July, 1931.

29. EDUCATION SUPINE BEFORE CORRUPTION. Education is hindered because its purposes are not clear. It is going nowhere because it isn't sure of the larger objectives it should seek. At present, people do not seem to believe in the possibilities of political health and efficiency. We are supine before the organized forces of corruption and personal advantage. PROF. EDWD. H. REISNER. "Science and Faith in Education." N. Y. Times. July 20, 1931.

30. POLITICAL DISHONESTY GROWING MORE PREVALENT. The serious criminality of our countrymen has been growing steadily. No matter what method of calculation you apply you find robbery, murder, and political dishonesty more prevalent here than in any other country. PROFESSOR WILLIAM BENNETT MUNROE. "American Government To-day." 1931.

31. HAVE FAILED TO MAKE THIS A GOVERNMENT BY THE PEOPLE. If schools fail in teaching citizens that it is a duty to vote we are not a government of the people. Fifty per cent. of qualified voters do not vote. PAUL McNUTT. National Education Convention. 1929.

BEST OF THE NEW BOOKS

EDUCATIONAL DEMOCRAT

FROM James Ross's[1] case-studies, comments, dreams, parables, poems and answers to college presidents, to Henry Ford, Thomas Briggs, Henry Pritchett and others, here are samples.

American school boards are uniformly honest. Not many of them play politics, either party or personal. They are elected by the people of the community who know them. No better plan exists. No better plan is thinkable.

Tenure of the good teacher is sure enough. For every worthy one who has lost her job a thousand failures have been kept on, not worth their salt.

The young thing, fresh from college, getting a thousand dollars just for being in the way, is a burden the schools have to bear. Some of them are "rescued" from teaching, others grow more sour every year and as cold as the artificial eggs on which they sit, hatching nothing, and drawing the salary of a real teacher.

America's expectation of getting an adequate teaching force without adequate pay has failed.

If I had more money I couldn't help teaching better.

No intelligence test ever told what a student will do, led by a teacher of intelligence, sympathy, hope and encouragement.

A measuring worm can hump himself all over you, but he never brings you anything.

[1] James Ross, "The Heart of Democracy: The American Public School." James-Ross Press. Sandusky, Ohio, 263 pp. $2.10.

The most characteristic thing in all America is the school building, but the most pressing demand is for better teaching.

Hundreds of thousands of children never get a good teacher.

The most important fact in all the world is that there are millions of American youths destined to become idle, muttering, dangerous men and women, unless we give them better training than we are giving now.

If their powers of thought are not developed and directed upward they will develop downward and mutter. Muttering is dangerous.

The distress of the masses is removable only by the intelligence of the masses.

The colleges are trying to exclude from education the only people who can solve this problem.

Why should education craven slink? Let the intelligentsia, whose cry has been "Education for leadership," come out and furnish some leading.

Do we still have a United States Commissioner of Education? What's the matter? Has some one sewed up the bureau? If so, for heaven's sake, let some one kick the bag open!

Education, the hope of the world, can't help if the highest work of its bureau is receiving, filing and publishing statistics. Robots could do that.

American democracy is the hope of the world. The public school is the heart of democracy.

The teacher is the heart of the school. Get busy.

DR. SNEDDEN PRICKS SOME BUBBLES

Opening this book[2] anywhere you will at once know you are in the presence of Dr. Snedden. He is unlike, singular, Missourian, uninfatuated, suspicious of slogans, penetrative, particular, vigilant, insists that you know whither you are going before he consents to come along. Too many of you are centering on methods without consideration of worth-while aims or purposes. He will subscribe to none of your general methods, because every aim must have a specific way of hitting the mark. To use all these particular techniques is not going to be so complex as you fear, for when aims have been selected and analyzed, when reliable estimates have been made of the means for realizing them with different types of learners, the task is going to be far simpler than you think. The weakness of educational philosophy is to leave aims in a limbo of abstractions and emotional mist.

It is now of more moment to be less interested in how John learns than in what he will do with his learnings later. What are learnings for? Why should John learn Latin? Will it enable him to safeguard his health, make him moral, enable him to keep from being a burden on society? In what ways and degrees will John, by the study of Latin, render that civic political service to his community which is paying for his education, for community protection against dishonest government? Will his learning of Latin better serve these functions than would other learnings which could have been achieved with the time and energy given to the study of Latin?

Regarding other common studies, curriculum, methods, policies, the unmesmerized David asks his searching questions. The child-centered school, the project method, the activity doctrine, the intelligence tests, socialization, training the gifted, teaching the handicapped, chasing the changing civilization, child guidance, vocational training, creative education, bunk about democracy, individualism, motivation, morals integration, orientation, progressive education, play—all get the Snedden x-rays here.

You get a unique collection of the creeds of Dewey, Kilpatrick, Bode, Bonser, Counts, Ellwood, Gwinn, Jennings, Newlon, Porter, Pearson, Rugg, Shumaker, Rusk, Russell, Thorndike, Trabue, Yeomans and other present-day apostles. Each quotation is followed by a gripping of the sound kernel if there is any and by a puff of breath blowing away a surprising amount of unneeded chaff. There is no rudeness in it. Our doctor is as gentle and courteous in his phlyarotomy as the genial surgeon who cuts out your appendix and assures you, now you will be better.

Keeping Feet on the Ground

"These assertions," says Dr. Snedden, after quoting a brilliant passage of a present-day educator, "are not, so far as I am aware, supported by any evidence anywhere." To others he answers, "incomplete and misleading" or "a perplexing ambiguity" or "bewildering" or "good but—" and so on, inviting the various enthusiasts to put their feet on the ground and answer a few questions.

The whole delightful book reminds one of the prayer meeting in which the brethren, filled with "the power," made their testimony.

"I've been travellin' to the kingdom of heaven on a grand steamboat fifteen miles an hour!"

"I've been goin' to glory on an express train, forty miles an hour!"

A hard-headed Snedden-like woman got up and testified, "I've been trudgin' on in de ways of de Lord on foot. Seems to me some o' these fast goin' travellers better take care they don't bust their bilers."

Why so much fuss, asks the professor, over making the child-centered school like the child-life outside? If the school has any excuse for its expensive existence it would seem as though it should give the worth-while things not likely to be had in the child-world outside.

The reason the young girl teaching the kindergarten is not interfered with is because legislatures, school boards and executives don't know what kindergartens are for.

Do the promoters of the progressive schools have any conception of where they are really going, or what outcomes are expected?

[2] David Snedden, "Towards Better Educations." Bureau of Publications, Teachers College, New York. 427 pp. $4.00.

We are smothered with pious generalizations. When we try to give them concrete application we are baffled.

It seems hard for the idealists to realize the difference between work and play. Each fulfils a mission, but to make play of those selections of the world's work that are for contingent, extrinsic or derived values, to give them the play quality of seeking immediate satisfaction oblivious to remote ends, is a wicked waste.

The learnings of the children can be left to develop naturally like the grasses or shrubs of the wilderness, or they can be controlled and guided toward civilized human ends like domesticated grains and fruits.

What are the proper functional values of the studies in our high schools? The question at once elicits answers of faith or belief, according to the answerer's acquired prepossessions. That's all. Millions of Chinese have faith in the healing virtues of fossils.

As to high-school training for leadership, those who freely use the phrase are in reality lending themselves to the soporific effects of mythical conceptions deriving from medieval habits of mind.

So runs this critical examination of a variety of current problems of coordinating purposes and methods in education. It is full of meat and spice. Like a guide coming upon a troop of travelers who have lost their way this unemotional writer urges to make up your mind what your goal is, whether you really have justification in going there, and then to watch your step.

THE CLASSIC HORN-BLOWER

Mixing into all sorts of Roman society, attending weddings, funerals and sessions of the senate, tripping to Athens, to scattered country villas, conversing with every one of prominence in the decaying republic, Gaston Delayen[3] takes you with him into an intimate but discriminating acquaintance with the chief of Latin orators.

Not from lack of moral precepts aplenty did the often wobbly great man fall into contemptibilities. The oracle told him at the beginning of his career that he must make his own conscience, and not the opinion of the populace, the guide of his life. In a period of unbridled indulgence, Cicero was no whit behind the fashion in composing essays on morals.

Winning prizes in his oratorical contests at Athens, Cicero, on his return asked Cato how those triumphs had impressed the Romans.

What a stab the old man gave him by asking, "What, Cicero, have you been away?"

Rarely has any great man so often reminded his beneficiaries of the things he has done for them. He was unendurable with conceit. The voluminous correspondence of his which has been preserved reveals that Cicero really believed himself the center of events, that the universe revolved around his personality, that everything taking place in the Roman world and even in the realm of nature manifested itself solely to confirm or destroy the glory of his consulship. The excessive praise bestowed on himself in and out of season, says Plutarch, and his constant boasting, which wounded all who heard him, had won him the envy and hatred of many. He certainly did not practice the precepts of Confucius that we should never speak good or ill of ourselves—good, for no one will believe us; ill, for we will be believed too readily. Poor old misser! He couldn't guess who would be on top in the bloody and bewildering mess of Roman politics. Victim of frequent terrors he would retreat to some out-of-the-way place, passing whole days in weeping, reproaching himself with having lived too long, and speaking of nothing but suicide.

But he had scarcely ever felt pity. He was too much a Roman to grieve over other people's troubles.

In the trial of Milo, the great orator who in the Catiline affair had never shown fear was seized with a panic that paralyzed all his faculties. The listeners booed and hissed him. The ushers restored some sort of order. He drivelled a long defense. The judges yawned. The power of the great orator was gone.

In the struggle between Caesar and Pompey, Cicero knew not which side to take. He guessed wrong and declared for Pompey.

Mean and Manly

Toward his first wife Terentia, he was as wobbly as in politics. After a period of fulsome praise he repudiated her on uncredited

[3] Gaston Delayen, "Cicero," Translated from the French by Farrell Symons. E. P. Dutton and Company, New York. 303 pp. $4.00.

charges and, at sixty-one, married his secretary, a young girl of both beauty and fortune.

Even in the Roman riot of repudiations, divorces and remarriages, the old man's conduct was sharply criticized and cited in ridicule of his numerous moral maxims. "To do wrong of any kind," he was fond of quoting Metellus, "is characteristic of the evil-minded; to do good when there is no danger indicates the common person; but to do good when it is dangerous marks the real man."

He had eulogized Brutus; he changed to Caesar and made him the object of public admiration, while consoling himself by excusing flattery on the ground of safety first. But in case of Antony he guessed wrong again and got himself listed among the proscribed. Hiding in the woods, he was caught by the hired assassins and, saying calmly to them, "I am not ignorant that I was born to die," he yielded his life to their swords.

Lawyer Delayen's biography, embellished with confirmatory quotations, awarded the Montyon prize by the French Academy, lauded by President Poincaré, has the rare vitality that projects you into the time and scenes of its story. You become an intimate of the noted Roman. His acquaintances are yours. Mr. Symons's translation is smooth, flowing, natural and vivacious. The book will hold you on every page.

The contrast between this biography and the one-sided laudations of the school editions of Cicero is startling. For two hundred years the American schoolmaster has been painting the heroic side of three Latin writers—Caesar, Cicero and Vergil. Admiration needs sturdy propping for American boys and girls who spend more time upon these Romans than is given to any other three men of history. My neighbor, who teaches Latin in the high school, tells me that the development of attitudes, interests, motives, ideals and appreciations is an ultimate aim of this study, now that the terrible testers have discredited the old claim of mental discipline and better command of English. Lord, what attitudes, interests, motives, ideals and appreciations can an American get out of these three creatures of a corrupt and selfish society, cruel, unscrupulous, pleasure-loving, libidinous and predatory? Then speaks Kilpatrick: "Education has vaccinated itself against thinking and traitorously sold out to the past."

MASTERLY TELLING

TACITUS, says Greek Professor Woodhouse, of the University of Sydney, Australia, had his real heart in psychology and ethics. His dominant interest in the human spirit made him akin to the greatest of the Greeks from Homer down. He is compact of poetry. His histories are the delight and despair of all generations. With much thought and love Professor Woodhouse translates the third book of the histories.[4] With old and dignified words, with a flowing style of distinct beauty, with a pictorial skill in narration that paints the old scenes with lifelike movement and color, the translator follows his classic author through the march of the Danube legions to Rome to depose the glutton emperor Vitellius. Page by page, the Latin text is faced with the English rendition, the whole done into a volume singularly pleasing to hand and eye.

KNOWLEDGE UNITS

To epitomize history, science and literature, Barnes and Noble are bringing out books at a hundred and forty pages or so as aids to review and in preparation for examinations. The first of this series[5] of college outline books analyzes history by means of paragraphs supplied with catch headings, the whole period divided into chapters, each beginning with a block of selected dates. A full index makes reference easy.

NO WOOL OVER THESE EYES

THE lessons of the past more than its mere facts, what Aristotle makes us think rather than what he thought, are of importance, begins Dr. Messenger, dean of Idaho University's school of education, offering a new review of schooling.[6] It is a book for a one-term course in teacher training and for use in reading circles. Education, up to the Middle Ages, is described

[4] W. J. Woodhouse, ''The Fight for an Empire.'' Angus and Robinson, Publishers to the University of Sydney, Australia. 173 pp. $1.50.

[5] Henry Wilson Littlefield, ''Europe 1500–1848.'' Barnes and Noble, 76 Fifth Avenue, New York. 142 pp. 75 cents.

[6] J. Franklin Messenger, ''An Interpretative History of Education.'' Thomas Y. Crowell Company, New York. 387 pp. $2.00.

with emphasis on aim, content and method. As leaders begin to emerge, Dean Messenger revives such of their work as bears on present problems. He confirms their theories by present instances. Part III reviews the beginning of American education from which he draws entertainment, inspiration and warning. "We have come," says the dean, "to the point where we must recognize that education is not a charity but a vastly important provision of the country to preserve and perfect democracy."

Forward-looking statesmen, after the revolution, stressed this manfully, but schools went on using, as they are still prone to do, the same text-books, and holding the old prerevolutionary aims. Schools lag behind human needs. The text-books get no farther along than the date of publication. School tends to put teachinto a static state of mind. The saving factor of education is that it is not confined to school. Insisting upon changes parallel with the nation's life, Dr. Messenger cites the work of Mason, Sheldon, Parkes, Payne, Harris, Hall, Eliot, Russell and Hanus, each ahead of his time and opposed. He dips into all the distinctive movements and tells us we are not doing nearly so well as we know how. The hopeful sign is the jolting of many teachers out of dogmatism and complacency. Our present bugaboo is scientific style. A mathematical formula looks impressive and seems to throw validity upon trivialities or absurdities. The method of research is often more emphasized than the result of it. The norm becomes a fetish; ideals, for that they can't be measured, are taboo. The curse of education has been the relapse into formalism. The normal curves will git you if you don't watch out.

OLD MASTERS

DR. REISNER'S series of education classics, coming from the press of the McGraw-Hill Book Company, will include studies of Comenius, Locke, eighteenth-century French liberals, Pestalozzi, Mann, Barnard, Francis Parker and Loyola. Women educators, Benjamin Franklin, are already out. Dr. Eby[7] selects pertinent educational writings of Luther, Melanchthon, Bugenhagen, Calvin, Knox and the Anabaptists.

The author's design is to facilitate the use of source material in history-of-education courses. He selects from the writings of his worthies such things as by similarity or contrast aid breadth of view and contribute professional scholarship for teachers of to-day. For example, the sturdy Luther exhorts: "If labor is irksome to the schoolmaster, as we often see, dismiss him and get another who will not shrink from duty.

WOMEN WHO WON

WILLYSTINE GOODSELL introduces you to three interesting women.[8] She shows you handsome and charming Mrs. Emma Willard avoiding the old-fashioned terror in disciplining her girls. Emma wouldn't harden the youngster's defense reaction by blame. She disarmed her by praising good qualities and then suggesting that the misdeameanor in question was not at all consistent with the rest of so fine a girl. You will enjoy the cleverness of the young woman apostle of fair play in education. She knew that public appeal from a platform would give her the name of blue stocking and ruin her chances of getting endowments for girls' schools. She wrote appealing speeches for delivery by ministers, lawyers and platform spellbinders. She trained the teachers for her successive schools. She set up a normal school in Athens for the nation newly escaping from the Turkish yoke. She threw herself into the school-betterment campaign of Henry Barnard in Connecticut.

Author Goodsell makes the story of Mrs. Willard, of Catherine Beecher and of Mary Lyon lively and engaging. She amplifies each with short, typical selections from the educational writings of her heroines.

LEARNING TO WALK

FOR facts and principles in guiding the physical growth and mental development of very young children, the University of Minnesota selects 25 infants and studies them from birth during two years.[9] The first volume resulting from this study considers sitting, standing,

[7] Frederick Eby, ''Early Protestant Educators.'' McGraw-Hill Book Company, New York. 312 pp. $2.25.

[8] Willystine Goodsell, ''Pioneers of Women's Education in the United States.'' McGraw-Hill Book Company, New York. 311 pp. $2.25.

[9] Mary M. Shirley, ''The First Two Years.'' Vol. I. University of Minnesota Press, Minneapolis. 227 pp. $2.00.

creeping, walking and baby play. Measurements, charts, photographs, summaries, conclusions, put a wealth of accurate detail into convenient form.

KNOWS YOUTH

PROFESSOR BOLTON taps us teachers on the shoulder, remarking, "In all your hurry and crowding subject upon subject, better think of the fact that knowing your boy is as necessary as knowing your books." His study[10] of the means of developing youth physically, mentally and for service to the world draws upon the accepted conclusions of experimenting educators and is tempered by a sane judgment of how far the school can go into certain fields.

For instance, Dr. Bolton advises, don't call morality teaching by that name. There's a prejudice against it, a hook-up with disputed religious doctrines. Call your morality and character-teaching "training for citizenship." There's no outspoken prejudice against that. The trend of the book through presentations of the characterics of adolescence, its physical and mental traits, its emotions, imitations and intelligence, is toward the paramount objectives of high-school education, chief of which is character, that is, morality, citizenship. His long chapter, "Youth and Crime," is a clarion for immediate awakening of the high-school managers on the road to everywhere except toward the goal originally set by the men who made education a state concern. The most of the high-school and college curriculum presents knowledge as intellectual facts. To reach character we must teach with an evident stress on human values and general, not individual, welfare. The highly attractive study of mathematics has no inherent morality, nor has science, nor art, nor music, nor athletics, nor extra-curriculars, nor manual training. But all great literature attempts to bias one toward higher and nobler striving. History as chronology, names, dates, events, is naught. Rich ethical values are possible in history if taught with the proper motive. Civics certainly has helped little. Memorizing the constitution, knowing the machinery of democracy, can result in as clever masters of corruption as now give the United States unenviable precedence among bad governments. Discussion of rights and wrongs around us, judgments upon civic morality, an enlightened political conscience, the will to make politics purer must be the aim of civics. But actual participation in public welfare, now, while accepting the real sacrifice and generosity of every citizen whose earnings support the schools, is necessary. A growing spirit of democracy in the schools has brought both successful and disappointing experiments in self-government. In its failure the cause does not lie in the idea but in unintelligent guidance or neglect. Without pupil participation in the management of the school community a real understanding of our American system is impossible.

This gives you an idea of Brother Bolton's temper. He is ahead, but not at all beyond being caught up with. He is sympathetic with youth, schools and teachers. He is undisappointed, though experienced, and is full of a well-nourished confidence for the realization of the goal he sets before the schools.

DIRECT ACTION

ARTIST SINDELAR took me for dinner to the Salmagundi Club, where unfrozen gentlemen sit at a common mess table. Something turned the talk toward school. Sindelar expressed himself with deep regret, "If only they had told me when I was in school what it was all about!"

It was surprising how many of these educated diners expressed the same regret. They and many a man of forty years would praise the Laidlaws for their orientation primer prepared by Doctors Hill and Mosher for immediate consumption by junior-high-school students.[11]

Among very attractive pictures and test exercises that get under the skin is a wealth of persuasive text on the present indispensability of life and work purposes and planning, the kind of leisure that counts, the offerings of high schools, the extra-curriculars, and how to study. Then follow short and catchy chapters on the separate studies that make up the usual high-school courses. Superintendents who organize recruiting campaigns with intent to give the community more citizens who have taken

10 Frederick Elmer Bolton, ''Adolescent Education.'' The Macmillan Company, New York. 506 pp. $3.00.

11 Clyde M. Hill, Raymond D. Mosher, ''Making the Most of High School.'' Laidlaw Brothers, Chicago. 288 pp. 96 cents.

full benefit of its educational opportunities will find large help here.

HOME HAPPINESS

Professor Mary Matthews' treatise[12] on domestic felicity has come into its second edition already. It is full of happy pictures. Besides much upon the preparation of food and selection and care of clothing, it includes entertaining in the home, the picnic luncheon, the care of an invalid, candy making, care of the baby, the preschool child, and so on. It is a book for beginners and covers an entire course. It makes me realize how the world do move. In 1902 my then lord and master, Superintendent Maxwell, reprimanded me because one of our Washington Irving High School publications depicted gymnasium girls in knickerbockers. The frontispiece of this book, written in Purdue University and published in prudish Boston, is a photograph of a bevy of girls in trousers, right outdoors!

TEACHING THE GROWN-UPS

Brooklyn, city of churches, homes and schools, remains distinctive in spite of thirty years and more absorption into a greater metropolis. Old New York became Manhattan. But Brooklyn never lost her good name. Her cooperative civic service is distinguished. Her adventure in adult education blossoms in a book.[13] It contains the study of the adult population, its interests, aspirations and educational needs, training for commerce and industry, vacational guidance, culture, parental information, social and political knowledge, clubs and unions. What Brooklyn here writes down as the result of her conference on adult education is applicable to other cities and towns.

THE WORKER EDUCATING HIMSELF

Discussion, remarks Marius Hansome, quoting and approving Walter Bagehot, breaks down the yoke of fixed custom, tends to give a premium to intelligence, undermines prejudice, promotes tolerance toward experiment: the essentials to a democratic civilization. In a stately volume[14] Dr. Hansome reviews the educational aims and accomplishments of working men and women and others who see the vital necessity of social literacy for all mankind. Apart from the high informative value of this text, never so needed as now, its consolidation of this later advance with the whole body of human improvement is masterly. Dr. Hansome is lecturer on sociology at Columbia University, student of workers' education abroad, delegate to world conferences, and intimate of Giddings, McIver, Lindsay and Ross. Without truculence or complaint, broad-minded, confident and determined, he reviews the cooperative political, cultural and altruistic emphasis of present workers' institutions, discussing their problems and mapping their future.

LIBRARY INFORMATION

The school's silent partner continues its active assistance. The American Library Association's contribution this month is two books.[15] One is a list of twentieth century French books, recommended for American libraries. The titles are grouped according to departments of knowledge. There are frequent appraisals.

The school library yearbook has a compilation of laws and standards for school libraries, departmental rulings summarized by states, accounts of training agencies, a special report on high-school service, a buxom bibliography, directories of school libraries and of members of the school library branch of the national association.

VIRILE SPEECH

Chairman Kane's first book on speech[16] is a jump into self-activity for the student and as snappy a succession of exercises as a live sergeant would wish to give to make his squad good and fit. Get your paper and pencil. Sit down, alone, undisturbed. Set down your skills or abilities; on the other side write your faults. Don't know any? Ask your father, mother, sister, brother, relatives, friends, enemies, teachers. Diagnosis, my boy! That's what medicine,

[12] Mary Lockwood Matthews, "Elementary Home Economics." Little, Brown and Company, Boston. 623 pp. $1.50.

[13] Frank Lorimer, Editor, "The Making of Adult Minds in a Metropolitan Area." The Macmillan Company, New York. 245 pp.

[14] Marius Hansome, "World Workers' Educational Movements." Columbia University Press, New York. 594 pp. $5.00.

[15] Charles Cestre and others, "French Books for American Libraries." 53 pp. 65 cents. Education Committee, "Fourth Yearbook for School Libraries." 277 pp. $2.50. American Library Association, Chicago.

[16] Edwin A. Kane, "Your Speech." Doubleday, Doran and Company, Garden City, New York. 141 pp. 80 cents.

engineering, business, teaching, every productive process, banks on nowadays.

In this way Author Kane starts. He pushes in some of the newest, most business-like requirements you have seen in any text-book. He sounds like the managing editor who knows what he wants and how to say so. The tools, the surrounding interferences, the cost and cure of carelessness, remembering names, telephoning, tests, courtesy, writing messages, muscular motion, the conscious eye, labor-saving devices, the critical ear, attention, are some of the topics surprising in a book on speech but driven by craftsman Kane so snugly into the structure of his teaching that you see they are indispensable, especially when he caps them with quotations from the good and great. On every page is the "chore," which is a direct command to do what the page has demonstrated should be done. Without padding, with the air of one whose fifteen years of teaching oral English have taught him what's what, Master Kane has done here a very virile piece of work.

HANDSOME ENGLISH

WE designate Dr. Blanche Colton Williams, head of the department of English, Hunter College, New York, our official selector of material for general reading. She has the many-sided taste essential for such a post. You will agree when you get her Book of Essays[17] introducing high-school and college students to complete samples of the best of English literature during three hundred years. Poe on composition, A. Huxley on Holland, Bradford on biography, Bacon on friendship, Dunsany on nowadays, thirty-five masterpieces, old and new, and the collector's breezy introduction are done into a book soothing to the hand and eye.

HONEST DEBATING

Now comes a book on debating[18] that doesn't evade the Wilsonian, Rooseveltian abhorrence of school exercises that allow students to attempt making the worse appear the better reason. Carl Miller insists that sincerity and a high ideal of honor are too important, in the citizenry schools must aim at, to allow a boy or girl to argue on a side in which he does not believe. With the development of integrity as one of the aims of school debating the author writes his manual with this and the following other objectives of practice: influencing others to true belief, accuracy, reliability, breadth, interest in public questions, politics, civic betterment, personal value to society, toleration and good citizenship in general. Instructor Miller, scorning appeals to prejudice, passion, class spirit and cheap tricks, sets out to teach you to argue like a gentleman. With text, illustrations and working projects, he covers practically and entertainingly the principles and good usages of public argument.

DRAMA EVEN IN THE COUNTRY

WHAT particularly appeals in Mary Russell's book,[19] quite apart from her finished and lucid treatment of the essentials of learning, rehearsal, make-up, lighting, scenery and related matters, is her penetration into the large value of dramatic participation by common folks. Especially sympathetic is Lady Mary for the people in the country. They have the race-old craving for self-expression. They are lured to the city in search of recreation. The rural church and school may have a great happiness in putting into drama the best ideas, both religious and secular. The spirit of refinement, artistry and cheer, with which Miss Russell lists church and school plays, pageants, children's service and anniversary festivals, the workable schemes for accessories and the entire performance, make her book remarkably valuable.

WHY SLEEP IN ENGLISH CLASSES?

PROFESSOR ROBERT CRAWFORD[20] asks and answers questions that have vexed college and high-school students for half a century. Why is writing English so dull a task? It ought to be one of the brightest games in the world. School makes it a drudgery. When experienced writers serve as judges in college literary contests they are amazed at the monotonous similarity of the products and at the far-off themes selected. One judge protested, "I'd rather read what this young chap thinks of his father than how the boy regards Byron."

[17] Blanche Colton Williams, "A Book of Essays." D. C. Heath and Company, New York. 388 pp. $2.00.

[18] Carl G. Miller, "Argumentation and Debate." Charles Scribner's Sons, New York. 230 pp. $1.20.

[19] Mary M. Russell, "Producing Your Own Plays." Richard R. Smith, 60 Fifth Avenue, New York. 139 pp. $2.00.

[20] Robert P. Crawford, "The Magazine Article." McGraw-Hill Book Company, New York. 340 pp. $3.00.

When I worked in the Washington Irving High School our young hopefuls were lured into a prize contest producing essays on Robert Fulton. The excellent English department of the school took charge. We received a small share of the awards. Later, another newspaper set Lincoln as the theme of a similar project. We relieved the hard-worked English teachers of responsibility this time. We used our assembly periods as occasions for informal discussions of the great emancipator. When these youngsters warmed up to telling the truth about what they thought interesting, the academic crust of English teaching melted off and some surprising conclusions came out. Nobody should anywhere write, "Abraham Lincoln was born"; no fact should be given except as the writer made it illustrate a meaning; no one should attempt directly to instruct the reader, but always to interest him. These beliefs, mind you, were evolved by children aged fourteen to eighteen and, for the time, free of academic traditions. We skimmed the cream of the contest prizes and were rewarded by an enthusiastic editorial praising the wonderful Washington-Irving English staff.

Dr. Crawford is appalled at the astonishingly little evidence that the students of to-day are pushed into the pressing problems of the world and trained to use the observant, critical and understanding eye which their training is supposed to give.

Readers of Allen Oscar Hansen's "American Education in the Eighteenth Century" will, by this lament, be reminded of the efforts of Franklin, Jefferson and a group of other statesmen, to get a system of public education aiming at what Dr. Crawford finds lacking: political, civic, social intelligence and ability. The scholarship which the present author finds criticized by broad thinkers as isolated from present needs could hardly be more vigorously decried than it was by Dr. Rush, Governor Sullivan, and Supreme Court Justice Chipman, in 1789. "It is worthless for a democracy," cried Noah Webster. "We need," said Chipman, "to break the scholastic tradition and to educate for civic progress." These worthies insisted that most of the teachers for the public be drawn from those expert in economics, government and politics.

Dr. Crawford finds the American magazine the most efficient medium for availing society of the aid of educational institutions; it is read by millions; it is not hurried into the inaccuracies of the newspaper; it is perused with greater leisure.

Dr. Crawford studies hundreds of magazines, finds the essence of acceptability in their stuff, quotes their editors to back up his thesis that a thorough master of the art of writing gets nowhere unless what he has to say fills the present need. The book is itself an example of the principles advocated: intensely interesting, timely, direct, concrete, illustrative and "snappy." He puts the horse before the cart. He has given his "how to write" a stimulating dose of "why" and "what."

SENDING STORIES HOME[21]

Every week during Lent the First Congregational Church of Hyde Park, Massachusetts, sends into every home having children under twelve years old three mimeographed bedtime stories. Some tales are tried-and-true favorites; some are new, written with the thought of present needs and mindful of the habits and hungers of children. The pastor asks the parents to tell one story each night, letting the children retell and dramatize it next night. In the week-day school of the church or in the Sunday school or in the junior church, the stories are retold and talked about.

Margaret Eggleston has selected fifty of these and printed them in an attractive volume. She has supplied a topical index, indicating what tales are conducive to courtesy, dependability, helpfulness, generosity, loyalty, obedience, and so forth. "Perhaps," remarks Author Eggleston, "the bedtime hour is the most precious of the day for the mother. When the story has been told, its uplifting thought may quietly glide into the child's mind and push out the less desirable impressions of the day. It may do its subconscious work while the little one is asleep."

When a child says, "tell me a story," whether he is three or thirteen, why not give him something with good healthy nourishment in it? There is enough cynicism, selfishness and barbarity in the literature of the day to make it worth while to offer what is designed to build a stout moral fiber.

So here are tales of newsboys, chickens, dogs,

[21] Margaret W. Eggleston, ''Fifty Stories for the Bedtime Hour.'' Richard R. Smith, New York. 149 pp. $1.50.

birthday parties, the sea, the Bible stories and doings of good-hearted people, of whom the world has many yet.

You can do a good turn for your friends who have children by recommending this collection. The teachers who are always looking for fresh material of this sort will welcome this assortment.

GENERAL SCIENCE WORK BOOK

To guide the learning process so that every pupil may work at his full capacity, Ralph Watkins, professor of education, and Ralph Bedell, teacher of general science, have made an individual workbook.[22] Besides the working exercises the authors intersperse summaries of facts and principles to be remembered.

SCIENCE FOR CHILDREN

THE actual course in science given to children in the fourth grade of the University of Chicago's elementary school is in print.[23]

Science, there, is to lead to observation, attitude, acquaintance with the method of science, and to develop study habits. A preliminary chapter for the teacher explains experimentation, reading, games, trips, construction, gardening, making notes and is followed by the lessons given.

EVERY-DAY PHYSICS

COVERING the first 49 experiments recommended by the college entrance board, adding many new tests of every-day appliances, Dr. Carleton Lynde's manual[24] covers the six main divisions of school physics, shows how to test gas and oil ranges, various refrigerating devices and electric household articles. With crisp illsutrations, forms of reports and needed advice to the young experimenter, the book is a neat and attractive directory.

BETTER BUSINESS

AFTER nine years of service, Lyon's book on business[25] appears in its third edition. During these years the civic obligations of the business man have been more widely recognized. Service clubs have perfumed commerce with high social principles. More than technical skill is aimed at by the school classes. Author Lyon built his book on the theory that business is public service.

What is business? What does it say it wants? How does it fit into the functions of education in a democracy? What is its culture? These questions are answered at length. The approach to curriculum making is discussed. There are surveyed the agencies which educate for business the work of high schools and junior colleges, continuation schools, evening schools and the training and supervision of business teachers. The author is not satisfied: he radiates reform and supplies definite means.

GETTING AND KEEPING JOBS

AN abundance of big-brother advice marks Edward Gallagher's talks to boys and girls on getting on.[26] Happy-go-lucky days for America are played out. Free land, boundless opportunity, are gone. A higher degree of will, brains and persistence is necessary than when your fathers were boys. Gallagher's essay, intended for classroom use, stresses self-study of aptitudes, correction of the childish hopes of being a bareback rider or a movie star, knowledge of the requirements of different occupations, the inevitable dependence on sterling character, attention to school duties, continued investigation of demand and supply and the satisfaction of doing your best.

EDUCATION OF AN ENGINEER

CONSIDERING the general run of boys, every high school is likely to have a good many who will find an electrical and mechanical engineer's own story[27] full of interest and profit. William Emmet, familiarly known in the world of dynamos, steam engines and electrical power of all sorts, sets down the things he has seen and done, the interesting people he has met from his boyhood days to the present. Often he wished he had a higher quality of brains than he thought he possessed. As he found himself

22 Ralph K. Watkins, Ralph C. Bedell, "Learning and Test Activities in General Science." The Macmillan Company, New York. 184 pp. 60 cents.

23 Bertha M. Parker, "Introductory Course in Science for Intermediate Grades." University of Chicago Press. 129 pp. $1.25.

24 Carleton John Lynde, "A Laboratory Course in Everyday Physics." The Macmillan Company, New York. 205 pp. $1.00.

25 Leverett S. Lyon, "Education for Business." University of Chicago Press. 586 pp. $3.50.

26 Edward J. Gallagher, "Vocational Guidance and Success." The Bruce Publishing Company, Milwaukee. 201 pp. $1.20.

27 William LeRoy Emmet, "Autobiography of an Engineer." Fort Orange Press, Albany, New York. 213 pp. $2.00.

getting farther along than the makers of brilliant class records he came to believe that the necessity of working harder with a moderate grade of intelligence is better for a man than to be endowed with brilliant mentality. As experience widens the philosophic Emmet grows surer of this and at times boasts that he has an an ordinary mind and is glad of it. Europe, with all its much praised education, is behind America in scientific and machine progress. Mr. Emmet finds that the old-world depends too much on learned doctors and fails to consider the possibilities of the man of little education. The aim of the average European is to be somebody. The average American expects to do something. We comb the ranks of the uneducated thousands to find men with native ability to design labor-saving machines. We make it easy for any of them to acquire an influence greater than that of the less able and more learned doctor whom custom places on a pedestal. "I am a doctor," continues the democratic William, "but no one calls me that. I'm glad of it. I'd sooner be called 'Bill' than 'Doctor.' "

In the United States Naval Academy he studied the stiff mathematics required. After spending a lifetime in engineering operations of the most complicated kind, never failing to get the exact quantitative information for everything he undertook to do, he seldom used anything beyond the simplest slide-rule arithmetic. Higher mathematics he has found of prime value in other men. He has employed experts to make calculations. But only those who constantly have the higher mathematics at their fingers' ends can use it without waste of time. Few people whose minds are occupied with complicated and difficult affairs can keep a good mathematical facility. It is necessarily an ability for specialists. "I once read," he says, "an article by a distinguished English mathematician who had associated with engineers and had never known a good one who personally used anything but the simplest mathematics."

All through Engineer Emmet's book are flashes of comment on education. They appeal to the school man as coming direct from the outside world. They are spoken by a keen observer who has no axe to grind. He continually tells you that he is an ordinary working man who has made good by personal investigation of alleged facts and by following an experiment to a conclusion. How he fared at Annapolis and in the navy, how he went at low wages into the groping ranks of electric-power developer, how corrections and improvements had to be sneaked in without the knowledge of doubting Thomases higher up, how the author pushed the steam turbine as a substitute for the reciprocating engine and promoted electric drive for big ships, how he got into the project of power from mercury vapor, how it will save fuel costs—these and a fascinating succession of adventures, sports, studies and contacts with well-known men are set down in a plain conversational style in refreshing contrast to some of the biographies with the overdone polish of the professional writer. It's a good book for schoolboys and schoolmasters.

FESTIVALS WITHOUT MONEY

Adelaide Linnell, who at Mankato makes musicians of the Minnesotans, is a cheery missionary for the schools in the hard-up region. She writes[28] of festivals in schools where discouragement from lack of funds chills the teacher's hope of artistic recreation. Miss Linnell finds uncommon talent in the common people and inspires the ordinary teacher to bring it out. Festivals built on children's own ideas and experiences, festivals centered upon legends, on history, on nursery tales, festivals of goodwill, are her theme. She makes it enticing. She gives it realization by means of numerous plays and pageants completely outlined.

CARDINAL NEWMAN

Two American publishers have recently brought out John Henry Newman's "Idea of a University." The Cambridge University Press supplies a new edition[29] for England. Editor Yardley gives a spirited account of the rebellion against old university methods of the Benthamite campaigns, and prepares the reader for the place of Newman in educational reform.

MORE THAN A THOUSAND JOYS

The index to children's plays, for which schools and churches have the American Library Association to thank, has come out in a

[28] Adelaide Linnell, "The School Festival." Charles Scribner's Sons, New York. 124 pp. $1.25.

[29] May Yardley, editor, "Select Discourse from Newman's Idea of a University." University Press, Cambridge, England. The Macmillan Company, New York. 164 pp. $1.00.

third revised, enlarged edition.[30] Compiler Hyatt, who has expanded the list first made by Alice Hazeltine, has made available an indispensable reference book for the school library. First come four pages on books on play productions; then, costuming, puppet shows, folk-dances and singing plays; then, a great list of plays, 164 pages, each selection described as to its story, its number of characters and so forth. There is, also, a grouping of titles suitable to anniversaries and holidays, and to special drives, as health, safety, thrift, etc.; a long list of plays for eight or less characters, one of plays for nine or more, and a list for large casts. These library folks know how to make indexes. You can locate, here, a play by author or by subject, and can find enough about it to give you a decision as to using it or not.

THE WHOLE JUNIOR COLLEGE

Six years have passed since Leonard Koos, in "The Junior College Movement," gave a comprehensive view of that particular field. Walter Eells,[31] editor of the *Junior College Journal,* than whom, etc., begins his handsome compendium with the note that since 1925 the number of junior colleges has more than doubled. Before '25 no university gave a course for junior college instructors and administrators. In 1930 twenty universities gave such courses. This year more are organizing them. I find in Professor Eells' work a judicious, fortified, unperplexed, keen, far-sighted presentation of the reasons for this type of college, its historical development, its present status, a classification, functions appraised, physical plant, curriculum, administration, instruction, finance, publicity and catalogues, standard tests, student activities, and other particulars. His six critical chapters leading up to the future of the junior college make an essay of distinctive power. If this book should get into the hands of the powerful opponents of the junior college, who are blocking the progress of it in certain communities, its advocacy of the plan in general may be offset by the stiff requirements set up for teaching of college grade. The faculty will do well to get it first. It will help set the house in order and disprove the charge that they are not maintaining any sort of college at all.

30 Aeola L. Hyatt, "Index to Children's Plays." American Library Association, Chicago. 214 pp. $2.50.

31 Walter Crosby Eells, "The Junior College." Houghton Mifflin Company, Boston. 883 pp. $4.00.

MORE RADIO

The National Advisory Council's Information Book No. 5[32] is a report of a committee on engineering developments covering telephone broadcasting, television, wired radio, talkies in school and home, and allied matters.

DAILY EXERCISES FOR SUPERINTENDENTS

When George Kyte put out his "How to Supervise," I ventured to tell you that his references to the backwardness of the superintendency was worth all the guff about the dignity of it that has flavored much of the educational literature of the past. The professor's new work[33] might be called "Exercises in Harmony," or "Tuning up Your School System." It is, to be in style, a workbook. The author, in the University of Michigan, has classes of superintendents with experience. He has quizzed them on their supervisory troubles. The typical cases are collected and arranged here in the style of "What would you do when—?" A general procedure for all problems is suggested: get a clear-cut understanding of the difficulty; analyze it; think of previous ways out of similar troubles; read up; plan; apply. With selected references to available books each problem is put as a moot. Initial organization; steering the supervisors; directing projects, drills, appreciation lessons, etc.; revising courses, dividing into groups; treatment of the progressive and of the hold-back teachers are put in such form as to make you feel like a superintendent on the spot.

Now, George, your service to public education will not be complete until you gather from these schoolmen pupils of yours, and put into a similar book, the most bothersome of all superintendent's problems: how to steer the school board into paths of righteousness and how to keep it on the straight and narrow way. Nobody knows better than you how hard it is to organize and supervise a school system when

32 Levering Tyson, editor, "Present and Impending Application of Radio and Allied Arts to Education." National Advisory Council on Radio in Education. 60 E. 42nd Street, New York. 94 pp.

33 George C. Kyte, "Problems in School Supervision." Houghton Mifflin Company, Boston. 214 pp. $1.60.

your bosses are perpetually itching to finger the pie. Before half an hour's conversation with any superintendent, some of the most irritating and weird interferences with orderly management are mentioned in such detail and with so familiar earmarks that an organizer like you can find their common denominators and the specific medicines that are indicated for treatment.

Want some chapter headings?

What a school board knows.
Teaching it education.
Curbing "the teachers' friend."
Board relatives in the schools.
The job distributer.
The burrower.
The treasury watch-dog.
The gossip receptacle.
The mayor's yes-men.
The lady member.
The backwash.

Oh, come, professor, there's so much adventure in all this that if you keep complaint out of it, but treat it with the detachment of a true scientist endowed with a scent for humor, you'll make a best seller and tone up the whole profession.

MEANS BUSINESS

FOR simplicity, directness, construction from actual usages of large, prominent firms, for playing up the old familiar grammar teaching in new situations, for accepting new and effective changes in correspondence and advertising, for selection of exercises to correct errors reported as common, you will like "The Business Man's English."[34] It is a well-done workable text.

LIFE AND MONEY SAVER

EVERYBODY knows, says Dr. Cubberley, introducing Dr. Scheidemann's work,[35] that we are wasting much money because we do not sufficiently specialize teaching to fit the thousands of children who are realizing but a small percentage of their educational possibilities. What marks the inferior and the gifted children? What should be done for them is discussed by the author, a psychologist and teacher, enriching her exposition by copious examples from history, biography and life.

DRAWING FOR LITTLE CHILDREN

THREE envelopes, each with forty-eight rectangles of white paper[36] on which are crisp simple drawings, increasing in detail, make a course based on study of what very young children wish to draw. Boys, girls, animals, flowers, trees, Indians, automobiles and so on make a fascinating set.

MANDATE

SCHOOL people, because of long acquaintance with Fannie Fern Andrews, as speaker and writer on citizenship and patriotism in schools, will expect from any book by her a practical idealism presented in engaging style. Two brilliant volumes,[37] illustrated with beautifully clear, full page photographs, describing present Palestine, enhance her reputation. One of the oldest, most recent, strangest and greatest problems of history, as James Shotwell calls it, is covered in attractive detail.

Written with first-hand knowledge of the land and its administrators, documented with scrupulous and scholarly care, supplied with a wealth of picturesque incident, it is a revelation that has been verified, chapter by chapter, by scholars and statesmen.

A mandate is an American concept. President Wilson put it into the state system of the world, an idealistic substitute for a colony conducted mostly for the benefit of a sovereign country. He planned it as a bulwark against the exploitation of weaker peoples, a frontier of democracy in unfamiliar places, a temporary aid to enable a people to achieve self-government, an improvement on the earlier scheme of fair-minded Americans defining our attitude toward neighboring republics on our continent and its adjacent islands. Carrying the reader with her on her travels through Palestine, pointing out, as we advance, the romance and history of city, river, mountain and plain, the author describes the geography, resources, life, personalities, religions, government, politics, dissensions, perplexities and hopes of the most famous land in history.

[34] Wallace Bartholomew, Floyd Hurlbut, "The Business Man's English, Written and Spoken." The Macmillan Company, New York, 350 pp. $1.20.

[35] Norma V. Scheidemann, "Psychology of Exceptional Children." Houghton Mifflin Company, Boston. 520 pp. $3.25.

[36] Jessie M. Todd, "Learning to Draw." The University of Chicago Press. Three sets of 48 plates each, 35 cents per set.

[37] Fannie Fern Andrews, "The Holy Land Under Mandate." Houghton Mifflin Company, Boston. 797 pp. $10.00.

SCHOOL AND SOCIETY

EDITED BY J. McKEEN CATTELL

WITH WHICH IS COMBINED THE

EDUCATIONAL REVIEW

EDITED BY WILLIAM McANDREW

Volume 34 SATURDAY, DECEMBER 12, 1931 Number 885

STATISTICS OF REGISTRATION IN AMERICAN UNIVERSITIES AND COLLEGES, 1931

By DEAN RAYMOND WALTERS

SWARTHMORE COLLEGE

COLLEGIATE attendance this year, despite adverse economic conditions, more than maintains the previous highest enrolment record (that of 1930), as shown in reports received from 444 approved universities and colleges in all parts of the United States for November 1, 1931. The increase is about six tenths of one per cent., the total of 599,124 full-time students being 3,721 more than last year. This advance is small, of course, compared with the sharp upward surge of the post-war years and it may be that the plateau predicted for collegiate education has been reached. It is, in any event, a plateau nearly twelve per cent. higher than that of the prosperous period five years ago as revealed in comparative figures supplied by 420 of these institutions for November 1, 1926.

Analysis of the current reports reveals several interesting and significant points. In the first place, it has been found that while the total of full-time students, both men and women, is 3,721 or .62 per cent. greater than a year ago the total of women in 286 liberal arts colleges and departments is 2,044 fewer than a year ago, or a decrease of 1.6 per cent. This means that where families have felt the financial pinch some of them have continued their sons at college and have kept their daughters at home.

A second point is that the falling off in attendance this year is in the group of the

1931 AND 1930 GROUP COMPARISONS
Totals of Full-time Enrolment

Size of group	No. +	No. –	1931 Full-time	1930 Full-time
3,000 and up	25*	24	293,084	293,193
1,000 to 3,000	59*	41	171,102	167,212
500 to 1,000	62*	48	75,955	75,666
Up to 500	90†	88	58,983	59,332
Totals	236	201	599,124	595,403

* One additional institution had the same enrolment both years.

† Four additional institutions had the same enrolment both years.

1931 AND 1926 GROUP COMPARISONS
Totals of Full-time Enrolment

Size of group	No. +	No. –	1931 Full-time	1926 Full-time
3,000 and up	39	9	292,008	254,533
1,000 to 3,000	70	29	168,068	152,106
500 to 1,000	71	36	74,802	70,052
Up to 500	96	70	54,484	52,847
Totals	276	144	589,362	529,538

largest universities and in the group of the smallest colleges. The fifty institutions having enrolments of 3,000 and upward—which usually record great gains—are almost equally divided, with 25 increases, 24 decreases, and one unchanged; and the total enrolment for the group, 293,084, is 109 less than on November 1, 1930. The little colleges—those with student bodies under five hundred—have a trifle larger number of gains—90 reporting increases, 88 reporting decreases, four precisely the same enrolment, and a total for all of 58,983 students as compared with 59,332.

It is in the two middle brackets that increases are indicated. The group with enrolments ranging from 1,000 to 3,000 shows 59 increases and 41 decreases, with 171,102 students as against 167,212 last year. The group with enrolments from 500 up to 1,000 has 62 increases and 48 decreases, and its total is 75,955, or 289 more than a year ago.

As to regional areas analysis reveals that New England is first in enrolment gains over last year, with 22 institutions reporting increases and 9 decreases. Other regional summaries are as follows: Middle Atlantic States, 61 institutions report increases, 41 decreases; Southern States, 49 increases, 40 decreases; North Central States, 68 increases, 69 decreases (with 30 of the decreases in colleges having less than 500 students); West Central States, 8 increases, 12 decreases; Southwestern States, 20 increases, 13 decreases; Northwestern States, 6 increases, 8 decreases; California, 7 increases, 5 decreases.

A further point manifest in the reports is increased attendance in non-professional graduate schools and in courses in education, which one registrar summed up by writing: "Many students are attending graduate school or a teachers college during the depression to continue their education while waiting for a job."

This study does not include junior colleges. It is possible that, as in Michigan, the increase in attendance at the state universities has been diminished by students spending two years at their home junior college before transferring for the two upper years, or discontinuing their higher education. Nevertheless attendance has continued steadily upward at the state universities in California and in Texas, states where the number of junior colleges is largest. The junior colleges doubtless reduce somewhat the attendance at liberal arts colleges. However, other studies have shown that, from 1929 to 1930, the rate of increased attendance in junior colleges was lower than that of the present approved list of higher institutions from 1929 to 1930.

The grand totals of 444 institutions for November 1, including part-time students and the summer session of 1931, are 926,611, a decrease of 5,417, or one half of one per cent., compared with the same totals for 1930.

Tabulations are given herewith showing full-time enrolments according to groups for 1931 and 1930 and for 1931 and 1926.

Table I gives a list of the twenty-five largest institutions of those considered in this series.

The ten largest liberal arts enrolments are reported by the following: University of California (at Berkeley and at Los Angeles), 10,650; Minnesota, 4,473; New York University, 4,403; College of the City of New York, 4,328; Michigan, 3,996; Wisconsin, 3,919; Illinois, 3,635; Columbia, 3,402; Texas, 3,349; Harvard, 3,266.

The five largest enrolments of men undergraduates in liberal arts colleges or departments are: California, 4,881; College of the City of New York, 4,328; Harvard, 3,266; New York University, 2,962; Minnesota, 2,554.

As to women undergraduates, the size order in coeducational universities for the five largest colleges is: California, 5,769; Minnesota, 1,919; Wisconsin, 1,616; Illinois, 1,609; Michigan, 1,454.

The ten largest colleges for women are: Hunter, 4,456; Smith, 1,932; Florida State College for Women, 1,660; North Carolina College for Women, 1,652; Winthrop, 1,620; Wellesley, 1,551; Simmons, 1,516; Texas State College for Women, 1,334; Georgia State College for Women, 1,180, 1,142.

The five technological institutions or departments reporting the largest engineering and chemistry enrolments are: Purdue University, 2,801; Massachusetts Institute of Technology, 2,653; Minnesota, 1,989; Illinois, 1,812; California, 1,646.

Among law schools the five largest are: Harvard, 1,595; New York University, 1,220; Fordham, 1,071; Columbia, 561; Michigan, 515.

The ten largest medical schools are reported as follows: Northwestern, 746; Pennsylvania, 667; Minnesota, 649; Illinois, 592; Chicago, 524; Michigan, 520; Harvard, 517; New York University, 479; Tulane, 459; Temple University, 448.

The five largest non-professional graduate schools are as follows: Columbia, 2,871; California, 2,234; Chicago, 1,338; Wisconsin, 1,224; Pittsburgh, 1,210. There is no clear-cut differentiation between full-time and part-time students in the reports of certain graduate schools; the enrolments are listed as interpreted by the individual institutions.

In numbers of students in commerce and finance, the largest schools are as follows: New York University, 2,238; Pennsylvania, 2,082; Boston University, 1,992; Ohio State, 1,893; Illinois, 1,869; University of Washington, 1,153; Harvard (graduate), 1,096.

Among dental schools the largest is that of Temple University, with 528; New York University has 494; Northwestern is third in size, with 473; the University of Pennsylvania has 355; the University of Southern California is fifth, with 351.

Teachers College, Columbia University, continues to have the largest enrolment in students in education, with a total of 5,694. The University of California is second, with 2,467, of whom 1,712 are in the Teachers College at Los Angeles. Ohio State reports 1,816; New York University, 1,621, and Minnesota, 1,612. Table III includes the enrolment of numerous normal schools and colleges which are on the various approved lists.

In the number of divinity students, the University of Chicago advanced to the numerical top, with 262. Boston University has 245 and the Yale Divinity School has 218 students.

Among forestry schools, that of Syracuse University, with 401 students, is largest. The University of Missouri leads in the number of journalism students, 345. Northwestern continues to have the greatest number of music students among the universities, the enrolment in music being 261. With 711 students, Illinois has the largest registration in pharmacy.

The part-time and extension figures in Table I suggest the measure, more fully indicated in Table III, in which the urban universities and the state universities have extended their educational offerings. The part-time reports are in general for collegiate work available for secondary school teachers and business and industrial employees in late afternoon, evening and Saturday classes.

The 1931 summer-school attendance was in many instances larger than that of 1930. The five largest summer sessions were at these universities: Columbia, 14,016; California, 7,294; Minnesota, 6,210; Wisconsin, 5,088; Chicago, 4,957.

Table I gives figures in detail of universities which have been included for some years in statistical articles in *Science* and, later, SCHOOL AND SOCIETY. Table III

TABLE I

	California	Chicago	Cincinnati	Columbia	Cornell	Harvard	Illinois	Indiana	Iowa	Johns Hopkins	Kansas	Michigan	Minnesota
College men	4881	1614	551	2396	1334	3266	2026	1362	1298	425	1302	2542	2554
College women	5769	1293	547	1006	629	...	1609	898	1041	...	862	1454	1919
Engineering	1646	...	1633	248	1178	294	1812	...	401	367	597	1390	1989
Law	462	339	148	561	154	1595	226	150	210	...	122	515	253
Medicine	293	524	306	418	239	517	592	437	379	282	280	520	649
Non-Prof. Graduate	2234	1338	130	2871	955	1043	1295	321	420	349	347	1394	1449
Agriculture	576	...	...	...	881	...	658	...	...	...	...	...	900
Architecture	160	...	*	124	170	72	411	...	...	...	*	255	...
Art	155	...	301	...	19	...	59	9	...	...	*	...	...
Commerce	1278	229	...	433	...	1096	1869	208	360	103	148	121	427
Dentistry	156	...	...	241	...	130	122	168	173	...	...	231	238
Divinity	...	262	...	...	...	47	...	...	...	...	...	...	...
Education	2467	*	161	5694	673	342	874	383	*	18	79	328	1612
Forestry	120	...	...	...	123	...	...	...	...	...	...	53	...
Journalism	...	...	...	156	...	...	89	128	*	...	...	...	...
Music	54	...	...	...	...	...	151	73	102	...	233	188	...
Pharmacy	286	...	...	564	...	...	711	...	94	...	51	64	161
Other courses	19	200	309	501	788	124	168	181	235	108	82	253	603
Deduct duplicates	2214	373	...	104	1007	...	520	137	135	...	137	143	215
Total	**18342**	**5426**	**4086**	**15109**	**6136**	**8526**	**12152**	**4181**	**4578**	**1652**	**3966**	**9165**	**12539**
Part-time	...	2237	6445	5553	...	...	...	91	894	3219	117	...	...
Summer session	7294	4957	1272	14016	2440	2486	3088	2121	3493	1446	1902	4329	6210
Deduct duplicates	2457	1672	...	2700	...	...	1301	730	1059	650	650	1558	2400
Gd. tot., Nov. 1, '31	**23179**	**10948**	**11803**	**31978**	**8576**	**11012**	**13939**	**5663**	**7906**	**6317**	**5335**	**11936**	**16349**
Gd. tot., Nov. 1, '26	**24756**	**12833**	**8335**	**30562**	**7604**	**10463**	**13089**	**5244**	**7178**	**4553**	**5086**	**12313**	**10711**
Gd. tot., Nov. 1, '21	**17909**	**12576**	**4890**	**26006**	...	**8080**	**10198**	**3659**	**5760**	**3683**	**4265**	**10527**	**5725**
Exten. courses	9064	5889	1124	8000	...	950	66	6224	1228	...	1740	1836	8670
Teaching staff	1733	829	590	1900	943	1725	1263	316	...	675	239	815	...
Administrative staff	53	74	19	75	13	...	71	31	...	7	19	75	...

* Included elsewhere.

supplies a less detailed report upon students and teachers of additional institutions. In recent years, the institutions considered were those on the list approved by the Association of American Universities. Because of economic conditions it was thought that a wider range would be useful and all colleges and universities on the list of the American Council on Education were asked to supply their enrolment figures. Table III, therefore, includes institutions approved by national and regional organizations as follows: New England Association of Colleges and Preparatory Schools; Association of Colleges and Secondary Schools of the Middle States and Maryland; North Central Association of Colleges and Secondary Schools; Association of Colleges and Secondary Schools of the Southern States; Northwest Association of Secondary and Higher Schools.

The names of three state institutions of Mississippi are not printed in Table III inasmuch as they were removed in 1930 from the approved lists by the national and regional associations because of polit-

TABLE I—(*Concluded*)

Missouri	Nebraska	Northwestern	Ohio State	Pennsylvania	Pittsburgh	Princeton	Stanford	Syracuse	Texas	Tulane	University of Washington	Virginia	Washington University	Western Reserve	Wisconsin	Yale
987	934	1245	1484	1018	1308	2041	3019	852	1865	562	776	1529	687	1163	2303	1658
484	658	1281	604	39	538	...	500	630	1484	493	1105	3	647	902	1616	...
353	647	304	1533	387	810	238	350	377	902	283	932	170	406	...	1245	630
131	159	363	277	443	378	...	221	114	284	149	239	253	120	218	279	318
90	338	746	356	667	265	...	186	193	325	459	...	240	332	290	317	195
279	242	442	1277	525	1210	242	...	250	294	149	635	218	344	119	1224	846
386	527	...	886	...	...	...	...	78	...	...	...	...	...	...	616	...
...	56	...	73	264	...	...	...	65	*	47	567	*	106	67	...	96
...	195	...	...	47	...	...	16	450	...	157	...	52	160	*	*	142
172	670	495	1893	2082	721	...	73	817	264	214	1153	227	251	*	250	...
...	101	473	201	355	284	...	...	...	...	...	...	...	210	144	*	...
...	...	...	...	...	...	...	...	...	...	...	...	...	...	...	*	218
306	1043	327	1816	621	870	...	118	206	142	*	171	77	...	412	760	*
...	...	...	...	...	...	...	...	401	...	...	121	...	...	...	*	41
345	169	92	...	...	...	...	44	104	*	*	50	...	...	*	121	...
97	185	261	*	27	...	...	...	*	...	32	...	...	...	*	126	113
...	62	...	143	...	230	...	...	...	79	13	120	...	...	104	65	...
...	116	314	340	490	13	...	2511	573	132	117	1055	...	249	698	111	214
62	690	...	192	14	13	...	3519	...	...	96	...	281	29	370	268	78
3568	**5412**	**6343**	**10691**	**6951**	**6614**	**2521**	**3519**	**5110**	**5771**	**2579**	**6924**	**2488**	**3483**	**3747**	**8765**	**5239**
425	536	5469	107	5176	4414	...	...	313	564	631	...	46	240	5519	...	30
2291	2713	2592	4845	2162	4007	124	1135	2287	4170	1178	3686	2374	1050	1803	5088	29
576	700	1012	1746	1125	1843	124	1135	...	1400	...	499	543	338	223	1272	7
5708	**7961**	**13392**	**14021**	**13164**	**13192**	**2521**	**3519**	**7710**	**9105**	**4388**	**10111**	**4365**	**4435**	**10846**	**12581**	**5815**
5461	**8654**	**10225**	**11139**	**14081**	**9449**	**2511**	**4065**	**6711**	**7067**	**3671**	**9161**	**4208**	**4251**	**5300**	**11914**	**5583**
4234	**5841**	**7523**	**8195**	**14030**	**7568**	**2253**	**3843**	**5183**	**6236**	**3478**	**6065**	**4096**	**3099**	**3588**	**10507**	**4041**
2904	4207	...	...	1726	1392	...	...	1474	2118	...	6697	1133	2553	...	12974	439
...	366	800	851	1448	831	315	563	641	409	424	456	260	454	685	586	697
...	30	...	12	116	59	27	84	25	30	28	24	21	24	29	38	82

ical interference in these institutions. For the completeness of this record their November 1 enrolments have been obtained. They are as follows: University of Mississippi: 918 full-time and 1,180 grand-total students; 64 teachers. Mississippi Agricultural and Mechanical College: 1,134 full-time and grand-total students; 97 teachers. Mississippi State College for Women; 920 full-time and 932 grand-total students; 87 teachers. These enrolments are included in the opening summaries.

Following the differentiation introduced in this series in 1920, Tables I, II and III are arranged to bring out clearly the enrolment of full-time and of part-time undergraduates. The full-time student is defined for this series as a student who has completed a high-school course and is devoting substantially his full time to study during the collegiate year. The student whose main time and attention are given to some other employment and who takes college and university courses in late afternoon, evening and Saturday classes is listed as a part-time student. The grand-total figures for 1931 include full-time students, part-time students and summer school students of 1931, but do not include extension and correspondence students, who are, however, recorded in Table I.

The thirty universities having statistics in detail in Table I are those to which this annual study was restricted for many years. The following paragraphs explain statistics given in the table and give additional information including, for comparison, the full-time enrolment at each university five years ago:

As usual the report of the recorder of the faculties covers students in the University of California at Los Angeles as well as the University of California at Berkeley. The full-time total of 18,342 marks an increase, as compared with last year, of above 7 per cent., distributed rather uniformly throughout the several stations of the university. Despite the enforcement of new and supposedly more rigid entrance requirements (see SCHOOL AND SOCIETY, November 29, 1930), the number of high-school graduates going directly to the university has been larger than the number so entering in 1930. The customary increase of about 10 per cent. in graduate student enrolment at Berkeley is apparent again this year. In the College of Letters and Science at Berkeley the total enrolment is 6,281; in the College of Letters and Science at Los Angeles the enrolment is 4,369. Of the 2,467 students listed in Table I under education, 1,712 are in the Teachers College, U. C. L. A.; 719 are in the non-professional graduate school and 36 are included also in liberal arts. The summer enrolment of 1931 includes the following: Intersession (Berkeley), 1,735; summer session (Berkeley), 3,743; summer session (Los Angeles), 2,361; total, with duplicates deducted, 7,294. The teaching staff is reported as 1,733, a considerable increase over last year. Full-time students 1931, 18,342; in 1926, 17,101.

The beginning of the new plan of study for undergraduates at the University of Chicago this fall is accompanied by a somewhat lessened attendance. That this decrease is due to economic conditions seems to be indicated by the diminished number of part-time students and by the smaller enrolment in law, in medicine and in graduate courses. The total November 1 registration is 5,426, as compared with 5,679 a year ago. In Table I, the figure of 200 for other courses means students in the graduate schools of social service administration and of library science. Education at Chicago is now a department of arts, literature and science. Full-time 1931 students, 5,426; in 1926, 5,694.

The University of Cincinnati total of 4,086 full-time students is 65 larger than

TABLE II

University	Full-time students	Rank	All resident students	Rank
California	18,342	1	23,179	4
Columbia	15,109	2	31,978	1
Minnesota	12,539	3	16,349	5
Illinois	12,152	4	13,939	7
New York U.	11,857	5	28,662	2
Ohio State	10,691	6	14,021	6
Michigan	9,165	7	11,936	14
Wisconsin	8,765	8	12,581	12
Harvard	8,526	9	11,012	15
Pennsylvania	6,951	10	13,164	11
U. of Wash.	6,924	11	10,111	18
Pittsburgh	6,614	12	13,192	10
C. C. of N. Y.	6,398	13	26,005	3
Northwestern	6,343	14	13,392	9
Cornell	6,136	15	8,576	21
Boston U.	6,106	16	11,001	16
Temple U.	5,913	17	9,283	19
Texas	5,771	18	9,105	20
Nebraska	5,412	19	7,961	23
Yale	5,239	20	5,815	......
Syracuse	5,110	21	7,710	25
Oklahoma	4,975	22	6,655	......
S. U. of Iowa	4,578	23	7,906	24
Hunter C.	4,456	24	12,161	13
U. of S. Cal.	4,446	25	13,837	8
Fordham	4,430	......	8,229	22
Western Reserve	3,747	......	10,846	17

TABLE III

Institution	Students Full-time	Students All residents	Teaching Staff
Adelphi	524	524	48
Agnes Scott	465	475	48
A. & M. College of Tex.	2,197	2,859	194
Alabama C.	791	1,167	89
Alabama Polytechnic Inst.	1,888	3,072	143
Albion	665	665	50
Albright	367	409	29
Alfred U.	484	584	46
Allegheny	588	650	44
Alma	253	272	22
American U. (C.A.L.)	342	406	34
Amherst	644	644	71
Antioch	576	586	62
Arizona State T. C.	867	867	49
Armour I. of T.	820	896	80
Ashland	301	741	22
Augustana, Ill.	475	666	32
Augustana, S. D.	352	467	35
Baker U.	322	374	34
Baldwin-Wallace	455	534	47
Ball State T. C.	1,215	1,328	64
Bates	710	1,020	39
Battle Creek	381	561	32
Baylor C. for Women	592	905	45
Baylor U.	1,035	1,625	86
Beloit	531	546	43
Berea	560	720	41
Bethany	345	348	30
Birmingham-South.	864	1,362	68
Blue Mountain	231	511	26
Boston C.	2,096	2,390	130
Boston U.	6,106	11,001	463
Bowdoin	568	568	54
Bradley Polytech. In.	716	1,054	50
Brigham Young U.	1,102	1,723	84
Brown U.	2,159	2,159	163
Bryn Mawr	447	490	82
Bucknell U.	1,107	1,407	73
Butler U.	1,597	2,353	104
Calif. Inst. Tech.	699	718	100
Calvin	354	354	20
Canisius C.	953	1,195	60
Capital U.	516	592	68
Carleton	846	865	58
Carnegie Tech.	2,547	4,246	294
Carroll	460	567	25
Carthage	252	282	26
Case S.	759	842	78
Catawba	342	567	27
Catholic U.	1,175	2,232	138
Centenary	513	1,020	47
Central C.	563	714	38
Central S. T. C.	969	2,217	84
Centre	379	379	30
Citadel	635	635	41
Clark U.	325	580	40
Clemson Agr. C.	1,227	1,427	100
Coe	728	959	70
Coker	146	147	25
Colby	610	610	41
Colgate U.	1,007	1,007	85
C. of Charleston	300	334	21
C. City of Detroit	2,662	9,523	238
C. City of N. Y.	6,398	26,005	850
C. of the Holy Cross.	1,070	1,070	70
C. of Idaho	368	446	27
C. of Mt. St. Vincent	518	518	43
C. of New Rochelle	796	826	58
C. of Notre Dame of Md.	128	254	19
C. of the Ozarks	300	660	30
C. of the Pacific	555	855	72
C. of Puget Sound	563	1,035	44
C. of Sacred Heart	207	418	34
C. of St. Catherine	408	643	48
C. of St. Elizabeth	312	427	35
C. of St. Rose	225	225	22
C. of St. Teresa	371	721	33
C. of St. Thomas	590	610	45
C. of Wooster	864	919	71
Colorado Ag. C.	1,319	2,251	110
Colorado C.	596	654	54
Colorado S. of Mines	568	727	48
Columbia College, Ia.	353	782	24
Columbia U.	15,109	31,978	1,900
Concord S. T. C.	561	1,219	26
Concordia	410	415	38
Connecticut Agri.	584	591	75
Connecticut C. for W.	565	578	54
Converse	346	348	35
Cornell C. of Ia.	561	642	41
Cornell U.	6,136	8,576	943
Creighton U.	1,819	2,571	216
Dartmouth	2,375	2,375	256
Davidson	641	733	38
Denison U.	778	786	65
DePauw U.	1,579	1,683	109
Dickinson	550	555	38
Doane	194	200	23
Dominican	197	463	45
Drake U.	1,228	1,781	98
Drexel Inst.	1,560	1,713	109
Drury	307	320	..
Duke U.	2,658	4,344	295
D'Youville	219	219	23
Earlham	472	502	40
Elmira	501	510	57
Elon	238	256	22
Emory and Henry	336	559	17
Emory U.	1,178	1,811	232
Erskine	289	289	17
Eureka	229	231	21
Evansville C.	352	562	24
Florida S. C. for W.	1,660	2,377	120
Fordham U.	4,430	8,229	384
Franklin C. of Ind.	273	291	22
Franklin & Marshall	711	711	43
Friends U.	333	433	40
Furman U.	416	1,152	28
Geneva	727	1,418	50
George Peabody C. for T.	528	3,399	93
Georgetown U.	2,633	2,649	371
George Wash'ton U.	1,793	7,983	411
Georgia S. of Tech.	2,224	2,224	153
Georgia S. C. for W.	1,180	1,964	84
Georgia S. W.'s Coll.	291	503	26
Georgian Court C.	165	243	24
Gettysburg	580	580	45
Good Counsel C.	150	150	22
Goucher	804	806	84
Greensboro	205	207	31
Grinnell	661	687	64
Grove City C.	654	769	41
Guilford	295	326	22
Gustavus Adolphus	391	394	27
Hamilton	448	448	43
Hampden-Sydney	301	301	16
Hanover	305	305	18
Harvard U.	8,526	11,012	1,725
Hastings	578	866	47
Haverford	310	310	39
Heidelberg	335	335	35
Hendrix-Henderson	280	343	28
Hillsdale	316	386	34
Hiram	358	479	27
Hobart	319	319	38
Holy Cross	1,070	1,070	69
Hood	459	462	46
Hope	470	470	23
Howard U.	1,662	2,022	269
Hunter	4,456	12,161	618
Illinois C.	385	395	25
Illinois S. Normal U.	1,513	3,795	132
Illinois S. T. C. East.	701	701	65
Illinois S. T. C. Nor.	729	1,346	63
Illinois Wesleyan	474	488	46
Immaculata	170	415	36
Incarnate Word	304	565	34
Indiana S. T. C.	1,723	4,046	79
Indiana U.	4,181	5,663	316
Internat'l. Y.M.C.A.	541	709	44
Ia. State A. & M.	3,982	4,974	376
Ia. State T. C.	2,037	4,252	164
James Millikin	390	390	35

TABLE III—(*Continued*)

Institution	Students Full-time	Students All residents	Teaching Staff
Jamestown	331	433	28
John Carroll U.	317	759	60
Johns Hopkins U.	1,652	6,317	675
Judson	210	210	29
Juniata	498	667	41
Kalamazoo	384	384	24
Kansas S. C. Agri.	2,897	3,605	323
Kansas S. T. C., Emporia	1,173	2,750	100
Kansas S. T. C., Pittsburg	1,248	3,073	119
Kenyon	227	227	29
Keuka	202	202	28
Knox	610	633	43
LaCrosse S. T. C., Wis.	818	818	49
Lafayette	994	994	99
Lake Forest	387	391	28
LaSalle C.	180	276	24
Lawrence	823	980	77
Lebanon Valley	385	513	30
Lehigh U.	1,476	1,689	157
Lenoir-Rhyne	302	762	19
Lewis Inst.	1,241	2,056	117
Limestone	254	442	20
Lincoln U.	337	337	23
Lindenwood	396	399	43
Linfield	296	345	23
Loretto Heights	125	189	19
Louisiana State U.	2,927	3,721	177
Loyola U. (Chicago)	5,445	6,889	489
Loyola U. (New Orleans)	603	1,685	127
Luther	268	268	23
Lynchburg	237	262	21
Macalester	521	521	39
McKendree C.	258	309	22
MacMurray C.	418	421	35
Manhattan	936	936	61
Marietta	346	354	32
Marquette U.	2,480	3,656	362
Marshall	1,574	3,170	105
Marygrove	425	1,004	61
Marymount	273	273	40
Maryville	767	772	34
Marywood	346	805	58
Massachusetts State C.	870	1,025	109
Massachusetts I. of T.	3,188	3,188	439
Mercer U.	377	837	35
Meredith	387	387	40
Miami U.	2,332	3,153	189
Michigan C. of M. & Tech.	599	888	65
Michigan S. C. of Ag. & Apld. Sc.	3,240	3,835	301
Michigan S. Norm.	2,114	4,061	195
Michigan S. T. C., Northern	717	717	58
Middlebury	655	1,189	57
Mills	505	515	81
Millsaps	443	553	25
Mississippi C.	380	594	17
Missouri S. T. C., Northeast	648	1,591	57
Missouri S. T. C., Southeast	620	1,546	32
Missouri S. T. C., Southwest	1,368	3,073	67
Missouri Valley	271	341	25
Monmouth	519	553	40
Montana State C.	1,025	1,085	81
Moravian	143	143	16
Morgan	512	846	32
Mount Holyoke	991	1,019	119
Mount Mary	230	500	36
Mount St. Joseph	195	427	32
Mount St. Mary's	463	463	..
Mount Union	505	602	33
Muhlenberg	455	918	32
Municipal U. of Wichita	1,187	2,014	77
Muskingum	677	1,490	50
Nazareth-Rochester	141	246	20
Nebraska Wesle'n U.	474	667	40
Newcomb	617	651	67
New Mexico C. of A. & M. Arts	465	676	48
N. Mexico S. T. C.	121	642	34
N. Y. State C. for T.	1,241	2,542	89
New York U.	11,857	28,662	1,563
Niagara U.	460	460	46
N. Carolina C. for W.	1,652	2,391	122
N. Carolina State C. of Agri. & Engin.	1,790	2,175	142
North Central	498	518	41
North Dakota Ag. C.	1,451	1,766	124
Northwestern U.	6,343	13,392	800
Oberlin	1,607	1,688	163
Occidental	603	631	59
Ohio State U.	10,691	14,021	851
Ohio U.	2,458	2,541	228
Ohio Wesleyan U.	1,641	1,663	141
Oklahoma A. & M.	3,058	4,235	29
Oklahoma C. for W.	821	834	53
Oregon State Ag. C.	3,022	4,474	260
Ottawa U.	238	290	20
Otterbein	332	394	36
Ouachita	244	248	24
Our Lady of the Lake	201	846	35
Pacific U.	269	280	21
Park	527	527	39
Parsons	250	389	28
Penn	254	338	26
Pennsyl'a C. for W.	273	276	32
Penn. State	4,548	4,857	..
Poly. Tech. Inst. of Brooklyn	525	2,475	48
Pomona	734	855	82
Presbyterian	295	299	17
Princeton U.	2,521	2,521	315
Purdue U.	4,388	5,031	331
Radcliffe	748	855	..
Randolph-Macon M.	284	284	16
Randolph-Macon W.	642	642	69
Reed	373	402	34
Rensselaer Poly. In.	1,642	1,642	138
Rhode Island State	777	777	53
Rice Inst.	1,362	1,451	98
Ripon	407	438	34
Roanoke	314	447	22
Rockford	345	387	39
Rollins	428	450	64
Rosary	274	678	34
Rose Poly. Inst.	333	333	27
Rosemont C.	175	175	28
Russell Sage	432	445	45
Rutgers U.	2,879	4,599	290
St. Ambrose	254	398	21
St. Benedict's	290	568	28
St. Bonaventure's	685	921	44
St. John's (Ann.)	291	296	28
St. John's (Bklyn.)	4,996	5,899	165
St. Joseph's (Em'b.)	178	361	31
St. Joseph C. for W.	326	326	36
St. Louis U.	3,484	4,676	594
St. Law. U. (C.L.S.)	683	908	52
St. Mary's (Ind.)	292	441	44
St. Mary's (Cal.)	624	675	35
St. M.'s-of-the-Woods	240	1,171	36
St. Olaf	878	884	59
St. Thomas	781	975	38
St. Vincent	341	342	39
Salem	269	269	37
Scripps (W.)	190	190	23
Seton Hill	270	449	40
Shorter	190	190	26
Shurtleff	265	323	18
Simmons C.	1,516	1,779	153
Simpson	525	670	43
Skidmore	674	749	72
Smith	1,932	2,086	225
S. Dak. S. S. of M.	359	367	24
S. Illinois Norm. U.	1,340	1,371	97
Southw. Louisiana I.	878	906	60
Southwestern U.	389	430	30

TABLE III—(*Concluded*)

Institution	Students Full-time	Students All residents	Teaching Staff
Springhill	210	210	21
Stanford U.	3,519	3,519	563
State C. of Wash.	3,213	3,896	230
Sterling	127	230	21
Stevens. Int. of T.	502	503	57
Susquehanna U.	301	531	44
Swarthmore	566	568	74
Sweet Briar	467	467	41
Syracuse U.	5,110	7,710	641
Tarkio	188	194	24
Temple U.	5,913	9,283	728
Texas S. C. for W.	1,334	2,076	130
Texas Tech. C.	1,767	3,033	127
Thiel	256	368	31
Transylvania	275	481	26
Trinity C. (Hartfd.)	426	426	38
Trinity C. (Wash.)	359	389	46
Tufts	1,966	1,966	473
Tulane U.	2,579	4,388	424
Tusculum	262	263	18
Union	842	842	82
U. S. Military Acad.	1,256	1,256	147
U. of Akron	1,080	1,537	80
U. of Alabama			
U. of Arizona	1,784	2,400	171
U. of Arkansas	1,563	2,383	141
U. of Buffalo	1,641	3,893	428
U. of California	18,342	23,179	1,733
U. of Chattanooga	456	774	26
U. of Chicago	5,426	10,948	829
U. of Cincinnati	4,086	11,803	590
U. City of Toledo	1,654	2,680	107
U. of Colorado	3,280	6,646	358
U. of Delaware	743	1,186	84
U. of Denver	1,474	3,426	169
U. of Detroit	1,913	3,172	144
U. of Dubuque	170	317	25
U. of Florida	2,435	3,917	169
U. of Hawaii	1,342	2,116	19
U. of Idaho	1,880	2,326	152
U. of Illinois	12,152	13,939	1,263
U. of Iowa	4,578	7,906	..
U. of Kansas	3,966	5,335	239
U. of Kentucky	3,160	4,630	254
U. of Louisville	1,494	2,237	264
U. of Maine	1,682	2,122	167
U. of Maryland	3,061	3,992	500
U. of Michigan	9,165	11,936	815
U. of Minnesota	12,539	16,349	..
U. of Missouri	3,568	5,708	313
U. of Montana	1,446	2,064	90
U. of Nebraska	5,412	7,961	366
U. of Nevada	881	1,050	69
U. of N. Hampshire	1,650	1,953	149
U. of New Mexico	860	1,561	67
U. of N. Carolina	2,825	4,467	216
U. of N. Dakota	1,762	2,326	132
U. of Notre Dame	3,172	4,107	210
U. of Oklahoma	4,975	6,655	311
U. of Oregon	2,940	4,563	226
U. of Penna.	6,951	13,164	1,448
U. of Pittsburgh	6,614	13,192	831
U. of Redlands	564	602	50
U. of Richmond	927	1,119	65
U. of Rochester	1,261	2,051	130
U. of the South	248	248	28
U. of S. Carolina	1,517	1,995	98
U. of S. Dakota	791	1,121	90
U. of South. Calif.	4,446	13,837	550
U. of Tennessee	3,290	5,299	224
U. of Texas	5,771	9,105	409
U. of Tulsa	663	1,111	55
U. of Utah	3,117	3,772	182
U. of Vermont	1,263	2,120	200
U. of Virginia	2,488	4,365	260
U. of Washington	6,924	10,111	456
U. of Wisconsin	8,765	12,581	586
U. of Wyoming	1,171	2,143	121
Ursinus	455	455	36
Utah State Ag.	1,323	1,693	89
Valparaiso	550	708	47
Vanderbilt U.	1,410	1,410	392
Vassar	1,142	1,142	156
Villanova	1,117	1,620	51
Va. Military Inst.	710	710	55
Va. Poly. Inst.	1,575	1,984	114
Wabash	380	380	31
Wake Forest	737	1,020	37
Washburn	717	931	74
Washington C.	264	266	23
Washington U.	3,483	4,435	454
Wash. & Jefferson	447	643	33
Washington & Lee	864	864	58
Webster C. for W.	151	156	35
Wellesley	1,551	1,559	162
Wells	259	260	39
Wesleyan C.	297	299	28
Wesleyan U.	598	637	64
Western C. for W.	368	368	38
Western Maryland	461	593	47
Western Reserve U.	3,747	10,846	685
Western S. C. of Col.	256	625	36
Western S.T.C., Mich.	1,990	3,875	204
Westminster (Mo.)	294	294	18
Westminster (Pa.)	504	528	33
West Va. State C.	611	1,040	56
West Va. U.	2,586	2,861	240
West Va. Wesleyan	369	620	28
Wheaton (Ill.)	619	734	39
Wheaton (Mass.)	453	453	55
Whitman	460	468	40
Whittier	443	472	35
Williamette U.	616	707	40
William & Mary	1,604	1,877	72
Williams	809	809	84
William Jewell	424	566	24
William Smith	121	121	40
Wilson	450	450	45
Winthrop	1,620	2,065	157
Wisconsin S. T. C. (Oshkosh)	647	1,173	48
Wittenberg	800	1,269	82
Wofford	332	586	25
Woman's C. of Ala.	318	385	41
Worcester Poly. Inst.	648	704	74
Xavier	428	736	41
Yale U.	5,239	5,815	697
Yankton	332	418	..
TOTALS	596,152	923,383	....

that of 1930. Because of 329 more in the part-time enrolment, the grand total of 11,803 represents a gain of 414. The liberal arts college has more men and more women; medicine, education and graduate courses likewise have an increased attendance. The engineering enrolment of 1,633 is 22 fewer than a year ago. In Table I, the entry for art means applied arts, including architecture; the total for other courses includes 181 in household administration and 128 in nursing and health. The teaching staff of 590 is precisely what it was a year ago. Full-time students 1931, 4,086; in 1926, 3,254.

The 15,000 mark is topped this year at Columbia. The figures for November 1 show full-time attendance in all schools of the university of 15,109, which is 266 larger than in 1930. There is a decrease in the number of part-time students and full-time students in university extension classes (the reports are 5,553 as compared with 7,214 last year) so that, despite a gain of 129 in the 1931 summer session, the grand total of resident students of 31,978, is 1,166 below that of 1930. The estimated teaching staff of 1,900 is larger than that of 1930. As to non-resident students in university extension, the estimates are 2,000 for extra-mural courses (with or without academic credit) and 600 for special courses (without academic credit); to which may be added about 8,000 taking home study courses without academic credit.

In Table I the liberal arts total includes 1,780 men in Columbia College; 1,006 women in Barnard College; 283 men in Seth Low Junior College, Brooklyn; 211 university undergraduates (men and women); and 122 men in Saint Stephen's College at Annandale. The figure for dentistry includes oral hygiene. Teachers College students in education and practical arts are covered in the education total of 5,694, which is 157 more than last year. The term other courses in Table I takes in 254 students in library service, 199 unclassified, and 48 in optometry. Full-time students 1931, 15,109; in 1926, 12,519.

The increase of 411 in the Cornell University full-time enrolment of 6,136 is accounted for by gains in graduate students (173 more than last year), in liberal arts, in agriculture (a gain of 144) and in forestry. There are slight decreases in law, architecture and education. The total for other courses in Table I is made up of 405 in home economics, 194 in veterinary medicine, and 189 in the hotel course. The teaching staff of 943 is 52 larger than in 1930. Full-time students 1931, 6,136; in 1926, 5,471.

In most schools Harvard has more students this year than last; the total of 8,526 is 84 greater. There are 26 more in liberal arts, 34 more in engineering, 22 more in the graduate school of business administration, 11 more in dentistry and 59 more in the graduate school of education. The remaining schools have about the same or slightly fewer students. In the figures for other courses in Table I are included 52 in landscape architecture, 43 specials, 24 in public health and 5 in city planning. The teaching staff numbers 1,725. The statistics for Harvard do not include Radcliffe, which is separately reported in Table III. Full-time students 1931, 8,526; in 1926, 7,983.

A decrease of nearly 300 women in liberal arts and a decrease of 264 men in the college of commerce are the chief items in lessened enrolment at the University of Illinois, which is 12,152 as compared with 12,709 in 1930. The apparent losses in registration in the colleges of engineering and of agriculture are due to a transfer of architecture and architectural engineering, formerly recorded under agriculture, to a newly organized college of fine and applied arts. This new college has 254 students in architecture, 157 in architectural engineering, 151 in music, 62 in landscape architecture and 59 in art. Of the 1,812 students listed under engineering in Table I, 463 are taking chemistry and chemical engineering, and they are included also in liberal arts and sciences, the proper deduction for duplicates being made in the table. There are increases at Illinois this year in graduate students, in medicine, in pharmacy; and an increase in the teaching staff from 1,187 in 1930 to 1,263 in 1931. Full-time students 1931, 12,152; in 1926, 11,810.

Indiana University's full-time total of 4,181 is 21 larger than that of a year ago; the grand total of 5,663 is 115 larger. There are slight increases in law, non-professional graduate study, business, dentistry and education, and slight decreases in the other departments. The term other courses in Table I here means nurses training. Full-time students 1931, 4,181; in 1926, 4,064.

Graduate study is the one field at the State University of Iowa which has more students this year than last—420 as compared with 329. The 1921 summer school enrolment was 3,493 or 169 greater than in 1930. In Table I, the students listed under other courses are in nursing. The part-time enrolment is made up of 524 graduate students, 316 in liberal arts, 2 in commerce, 6 in medicine, 15 in engineering, 7 in law and 5 in music. Full-time students 1931, 4,578; in 1926, 4,901.

The figures reported for Johns Hopkins reverse the general tendency. There are fewer graduate students (349 as compared with 366 in 1930) and the increase of total full-time enrolment from 1,578 to 1,652 is owing to gains of men in liberal arts, in engineering, in medicine, in business and in hygiene and public health. Due to a larger summer session, the grand total is 6,317 this year, or 343 more students than last year. The teaching staff is 675, an increase of 15 over 1930. Full-time students 1931, 1,652; in 1926, 1,499.

At the University of Kansas the graduate enrolment of 347 is 71 larger than last year, but practically all the undergraduate figures are somewhat lower, so that the full-time total of 3,966 is 209 less than in 1930. The teaching staff shows a reduction from 250 last year to 239. In Table I the total of 597 for engineering includes students in architecture. The enrolment of 233 reported under the heading of music includes music and art students in the school of fine arts. Full-time students 1931, 3,966; in 1926, 3,964.

For the decrease in numbers at the University of Michigan (9,165 this year as compared with 9,431 in 1930 and 9,597 in 1926), Dr. Robert C. Angell, associate professor of sociology, gives a partial explanation in the enrolment increase of Michigan junior colleges, which was 23 per cent. from 1929 to 1930. Students stay at these home institutions where expenses are lower than at Ann Arbor. There are increases at the University of Michigan this year in the graduate school, in business administration and in forestry. In Table I, the total of 253 under other courses includes 243 in nursing and 10 in oral hygiene. The teaching staff numbers 815; in 1930 it was 833.

At the University of Minnesota the November 1 enrolment is 12,539, or 49 more than a year ago. There are more students in graduate study (1,449 as compared with the 1930 figures of 1,138) and more in business administration, dental hygiene and education. The deduction for duplications in summer session and present enrolment is estimated as 2,400 on the basis of duplications last year. In Table I, the figure for engineering includes other technological fields as follows: chemistry 420; mines and metallurgy 159. Students in forestry and home economics are included in the report for agriculture. The figure for other courses embraces these fields: Nursing 476, dental hygiene 66, university college 45, unassigned 16. The extension total of 8,670 includes 4,974 extension, 1,137 sub-collegiate and 2,559 correspondence. Full-time students 1931, 12,539; in 1926, 10,796.

A gain of 37 students in agriculture is the marked feature of the University of Missouri report. The totals of 136 graduate students in 1930 is more than doubled in the present enrolment of 279. There are 73 more students in journalism and 18 more in medicine. In the liberal arts and other undergraduate courses there are decreases, both for men and for women. Full-time students 1931, 3,568; in 1926, 3,908.

At the University of Nebraska there are small increases in law, medicine, graduate study, architecture and music, but these are exceeded by decreases in most of the undergraduate courses. The full-time total is accordingly 383 under that of 1930. In Table I, the total under art includes 138 in fine arts, dramatics, etc. The 116 students designated under other courses are students in nursing. The deduction for summer session duplications is estimated. All the 2,355 students in collegiate extension are doing work which counts toward a degree. Full-time 1931 students, 5,412; in 1926, 5,930.

The full-time total at Northwestern University, 6,343, is precisely 50 larger than last year. The report reveals small increases in graduate students, in engineering, business, education and speech courses, with small decreases in liberal arts, law, medicine, dentistry, journalism and music courses, and also in part-time attendance. The 314 listed in Table I for other courses are students in speech. Full-time students 1931, 6,343; in 1926, 4,916.

Substantially the same as last year is the 1931 total of 10,691 full-time students at Ohio State University. This is due pretty largely to an increase of 173 in the graduate enrolment; there are slight decreases in most of the undergraduate courses. In the education department, however, the total of 1,816 (including 51 working for degrees in both arts and education) is 183 larger than in 1930. Under other courses in Table I are included students in applied optics, veterinary medicine and nursing. The teaching staff of 851 is 46 under that reported for 1930. Full-time students 1931, 10,691; in 1926, 9,209.

A decrease of about 8 per cent. in the attendance at the Wharton School—oldest school of commerce and finance in the United States—is the largest factor in the lessened enrolment of the University of Pennsylvania. There are small decreases also in liberal arts, in law, in graduate study, in architecture, in education and in music, with increases in engineering and chemistry, in medicine, in art and in other courses which, in Table I, are veterinary medicine, 131; nurses training schools, 307, and oral hygiene, 52. The summer school of 1931 has 92 students more than that of 1930. In Table I, the engineering totals include 69 civil, 102 electrical, 107 mechanical, 27 chemical engineering and 34 in chemistry. In the figures for medicine embrace 500 in the school of medicine and 167 in the graduate school of medicine. There are 252 in architecture and 12 in landscape architecture. The commerce total is made up of 2,006 in the Wharton School and 76 in the graduate course in business administration. The education total of 621 includes 24 graduate students. Full-time students 1931, 6,951; in 1926, 7,845.

Law and medicine have small increases, and the number of students in education remains precisely the same; in other schools at the University of Pittsburgh there are small decreases. The full-time total is 469 less than in 1930. The 1931 summer session was nearly 500 larger than that of 1930, so that the grand total figures are not greatly diminished. In Table I the report for engineering includes 119 students in mines. The 13 students listed under other courses are in "retail training." Full-time students 1931, 6,614; in 1926, 5,555.

Following a definite policy of limitation of numbers, Princeton has kept its liberal arts enrolment to precisely the 1930 figures of 2,041. More students were taken in engineering (238 as compared with 203 enrolled a year ago) and there is a small increase in the Princeton Graduate School. Full-time students 1931, 2,521; in 1926, 2,511.

With the enrolment of women held strictly to the limit of 500, Stanford University has a total of 3,519 students, which is 57 less than in 1930. All the departments listed in Table I have more students than a year ago, except the schools grouped under the term other courses, which are biological sciences, hygiene and physical education, letters, physical sciences and social sciences and the lower division. Full-time students 1931, 3,519; in 1926, 3,303.

With more students in all except four departments, Syracuse University this year has a total of 5,110, as compared with 5,053 last year. Because of an increase of over 500 in the summer school attendance of 1931, the grand total is brought up to 7,710 as compared with 7,065 in 1930. In Table I the term other courses here means 167 students in home economics, 160 in nursing, 101 in the library school and 52 forest rangers. Full-time students 1931, 5,110; in 1926, 5,148.

An increase of 286 in the full-time enrolment at the University of Texas is due to gains in liberal arts, for both men and women, in engineering, in education and in nursing. In Table I, the 132 students listed under other courses are students in nursing. Students taking architecture are included in the total for engineering, and those taking journalism are included in the liberal arts total. The deduction of 1,400 for summer session and "long session" attendance is an estimated figure. The report shows a teaching staff of 409 as compared with 422 in 1930. Full-time students 1931, 5,771; in 1926, 4,841.

Decreases in liberal arts men, in medicine, architecture, art and music at the Tulane University of Louisiana are more than offset by increases in liberal arts women, in engineering, in law, in non-professional graduate study, in commerce and in pharmacy, so that the full-time total for 1931 is 2,579, as compared with 2,551 a year ago. There are 121 fewer part-time students, and as there was only a small rise in summer school attendance, the grand total of 4,388 is 75 under that of November 1, 1930. In Table I the term other courses takes in 81 who are doing short-time review work in the graduate school of medicine and 36 doing social work, a professional course. Full-time students 1931, 2,579; in 1926, 2,318.

At the University of Washington, Seattle, the full-time total of 6,924 is 444 lower than in 1930, due to decreases in liberal arts enrolment, in engineering, law, education, journalism and in the colleges of science and of the fine arts. Due to a larger summer session than in 1930 (3,686 as compared with 3,272) the grand total is only 86 under that reported for last year. In Table I the engineering figures of 932 include 57 students in mines. Under the heading art are listed 567 students in the college of fine arts, which embraces architecture, music, painting, sculpture and design. The heading other courses takes in 1,027 students in the college of science and 28 in library science. The teaching staff is given as 456, or ten lower than in 1930. Full-time students 1931, 6,924; in 1926, 6,851.

Small gains in engineering, medicine, graduate study, business and education outweigh losses in law and courses in art and architecture at the University of Virginia, with the result of an increase of 77 over last year in the November 1 total of 2,488. In Table I, the entry for art includes students in architecture. The registrar writes that, "in addition to the above, there are 164 in the hospital nurses' training school." Full-time 1931 students, 2,488; in 1926, 2,101.

Washington University, at St. Louis, reports an enrolment of 3,483 full-time students, a grand total of 4,435 and a teaching staff of 454, as compared with corresponding figures for 1930 of 3,445 full-time students, 4,383 grand total and 436 teachers. There are gains in six departments and losses in five. The term other courses in Table I in this instance means students in nursing. Full-time students 1931, 3,483; in 1926, 3,354.

An increase of 174 students at Western Reserve University is accounted for by gains in full-time men in Cleveland College and of women in Adelbert College and small increases also in medicine, in graduate study, in dentistry, in pharmacy, in nursing and in the school of applied social sciences. The part-time enrolment in Cleveland College is less than last year. The 1931 summer session had fewer students than in 1930. By other courses in Table I are meant 325 students in the school of applied social sciences, 271 in nursing, and 102 in the library course. The teaching staff of 685 is 15 below that of 1930. Full-time students 1931, 3,747; in 1926, 2,791.

The present attendance of 8,765 students in all the schools of the University of Wisconsin is 636 fewer than last year. The decrease was greatest in the number of women, which is 1,616 as compared with 2,043 in 1930. There are small increases in medicine, in agriculture, in education, in journalism and in graduate study. The summer session figures of 5,088 were 83 below those of 1930. The teaching staff is reported as 586; a year ago it was 623. In Table I the other courses total includes 69 graduate nurses and 42 in library science. Full-time students 1931, 8,765; in 1926, 8,220.

Yale University reports a slight decrease in the number of students and a decided increase in the number of teachers. The figures show that there are 5,239 students as compared with 5,272 last year and 507 full-time and 190 part-time members of the teaching staff, as compared with 492 full-time and 175 part-time teachers in 1930. The 846 students in the freshman year, a separate unit, are included in Table I under other courses, a category that here takes in also 114 students in drama and 100 in nursing. This separate accounting of freshmen must be reckoned with in considering the enrolments for Yale College (recorded under liberal arts in Table I and for the Sheffield Scientific School, recorded under engineering). Students in education at Yale are included in the graduate study total. Full-time enrolment 1931, 5,239; in 1926, 5,015.

FREDERICK GORDON BONSER: PIONEER IN ECONOMIC EDUCATION FOR CHILDREN

By Professor HENRY HARAP

WESTERN RESERVE UNIVERSITY

WRITING in *Harpers* about two years ago, the celebrated British biologist, J. B. S. Haldane, discussed the neglect of the skilled manual worker in history and concluded his essay thus: "Historians have inevitably thought in terms of words. . . . They have not been manual workers, and have seldom realized that man's hands are as important as and more specifically human than his mouth. . . . When I look at history I see it as Man's attempt to solve the practical problem of living. The men who did most to solve it were not those who thought about it, or talked about it, or impressed their contemporaries, but those who silently and efficiently got on with their work."

I recall this quotation because it expresses Mr. Bonser's view of the social studies, but on rereading it I find there is also, in this excerpt, the suggestion of the character of the man whose contribution to economic education I am about to review.

The present economic depression has intensified a latent interest in education having to do with securing and maintaining a living in an industrial society. It is significant that more than twenty years ago Mr. Bonser had the foresight to formulate a comprehensive school program pertaining to the production and consumption of goods. His lasting contribution to education will be his clarification and propagation of a plan of economic education for the American school.

He espoused the cause of industrial arts because it afforded a direct and basic means of bridging the gap between a generally accepted subject of study and the realities of modern civilization. The industrial arts gave the pupil intimate contact with the materials, processes and products of industry. It only remained to expand it to take in the factors which naturally related to it, namely, health, economy, art and social responsibility. Almost from the beginning, his conception of industrial arts involved the esthetic and social impulses and activities of children.

On the suggestion of the elder Dean Russell, Mr. Bonser undertook in 1910 to put his theories to the test in a public school especially set aside for that purpose. The curriculum of the school was organized around the fundamental needs of food, clothing, shelter, utensils, records and tools. In the first two grades the material was introduced under the subject of social and industrial life. In the remaining four grades it was designated industrial arts for boys and household arts for girls. Geography, history, arithmetic, nature study, fine arts and hygiene were retained as subjects but were so constituted as to form many points of contact with industrial arts, the core of the curriculum. Although informational content was not neglected, the emphasis was laid upon the economic elements in the immediate and remote environment.

Based upon his experience in developing the Speyer School Curriculum and upon a decade of ripening thought, Mr. Bonser published in 1920 "The Elementary School Curriculum," which has for its setting the practical activities involved in the production and use of food, clothing, shelter, utensils, records and tools. Although a chapter is devoted to each of the formal subjects he repeatedly reverts to the basic economic goods and processes as points of departure in the several formal subjects. Following the work on the elementary school curriculum, Mr. Bonser in collaboration with Mrs. Mossman again took up the practical or industrial arts, this time elaborating his subject in a single complete volume entitled "Industrial Arts for Elementary Schools." Again, he conceived industrial arts in its broadest implications. Indeed, the subject from its inception was never merely utilitarian; he always emphasized the ethical and esthetic aspects of the daily activities involved in fabricating and using material goods. In his second work he was careful to incorporate this in his definition of the industrial arts: "A study of the changes made by man in the forms of materials to increase their values, *and of the problems of life related to these changes.*"

By this time he had become an adherent of the project method and pointed out that the industrial arts offered a means of bringing all the subjects together in child-centered situations in which they were directly usable. It is significant that the project curricula developed at about this time incorporated much of the content of economic life from the major fields of food, clothing, shelter and tools. One of the very first accounts of such curricula was published in 1921 by Miss Margaret Wells, who had served her apprenticeship under Mr. Bonser at the Speyer School when he and his associates formulated the curriculum based on social and industrial activities. The work of each grade was related to a basic project such as "playing store" and embodied much of the content of commodities of every-day living. Another experiment, applying the industrial arts as formulated by Mr. Bonser, was made by Miss J. B. Welling and Miss C. W. Calkins in the public schools of Grand Rapids, Michigan. The social and industrial studies were made the general background for the work of the first six grades. In each grade they were introduced in a different historical setting and social radius; thus progressing from primitive to modern times; and from the family to the world.

In more recent years Mr. Bonser had been stressing the activities of consumption. The study of the intrinsic value of the products of industry should yield economy in the selection of materials and intelligent thrift in purchasing and using them. He was impressed by popular ignorance of economic values and habits of extravagance, and became convinced that it was profoundly important to offer training in the selection and care of material goods with expenditure that is neither extravagant nor niggardly. Furthermore, he advocated the development of good taste to correct the tendency toward the gaudy, the bizarre and the fantastic. But perhaps more than anything else he stressed social understanding of consumer and producer.

Writing with particular reference to the junior high school he maintained that consumer values should be stressed within narrower fields and with more exact knowledge of technical processes, especially for exploratory purposes. Industrial arts should develop social appreciations with emphasis upon current industrial problems. He showed how units of work might be designed to typify various industries while they simultaneously furnished the equipment for effective consumption. The building trades might be introduced by projects in the building of an animal house or perhaps a small housing enterprise. This would raise questions as to design, materials and methods in the construction of dwellings. These, in turn, might require the observation of houses under construction; consultation of building contractors and supply houses, and the examination of house plans and specifications. A study of the durability, fabrication and cost of materials for the construction of walls, floors, ceilings, roofs, windows, doors, paints and hardware might follow. Undoubtedly the elements of repair and upkeep would be discussed and would require investigation in treatises on building materials. Growing out of the study of dwellings, the pupil might become interested in office buildings, libraries, churches, cathedrals, palaces, and the like. Summarizing his discussion he reviewed the various goals of the industrial arts but concluded that "achieving consumer value is the most important and inclusive purpose of all."

It is impossible to ascertain the number of school systems influenced by Mr. Bonser's program of industrial arts. He was consultant in course-of-study building and in surveys; he was the principal adviser for many research studies; and he taught thousands of students. His lucid and practical published works were widely read. The courses of study in which he had a share in constructing were extensively circulated and drawn upon. The result is that to-day there is hardly a school in the country which does not include some activities pertaining to food, clothing, shelter and tools. He found manual arts a narrow and mechanical subject and transformed it into an economic study rich in esthetic, constructive and social activities of children.

EDUCATIONAL EVENTS

GOVERNANCE OF STUDENTS IN PRUSSIAN UNIVERSITIES

ACCORDING to a wireless dispatch to the *New York Times,* the German Ministry of Education has drafted a new disciplinary law for the governance of students of all universities and technical and other colleges in Prussia to supersede the antiquated statute in force since 1879 and to furnish a more up-to-date and efficient instrument for academic discipline. The preamble of the law says its object is to "maintain order, morals and honor among students and to protect the freedom of teaching and learning."

Under the new law proceedings against an offending student may be instituted at the instance of the university rector or the Ministry of Education, the university's counselor acting as a preliminary examiner and prosecuting attorney. The trial court is the full university senate or a disciplinary committee appointed by it for three years, which must be composed of the rector and not fewer than four professors, and the accused student may be defended at his trial by a professor. Appeal from the disciplinary court's verdict lies with a newly created appeal board constituted of a representative of the Ministry of Education and two professors, of whom one must be drawn from the university at which the trial took place, while the other must be a member of the law faculty of Berlin University—every such professor under the German system being eligible to a regular justiceship.

Confinement in a university prison, long a dead letter—in some universities victuals are stored in what used to be "karzer"—is formally abolished and the penalties prescribed range from a formal reprimand and loss of credit for the current semester's attendance to expulsion and, in the worst cases, exclusion from all higher institutions of learning.

The law stipulates that "the status of a student implies no exemption from the provisions of public and civil law" and it directs the institution of disciplinary proceedings "when students commit acts endangering the order and decencies of academic life or obstruct the freedom of teaching and learning; when they violate their own or fellow-students' honor; when they recklessly run into debt or conduct themselves in a manner opposed to the purpose of their attendance at the institution."

EDUCATION IN THE TRANSVAAL

IN the annual report of the Transvaal Education Department for 1930, Mr. N. M. Hoogenhout, director of education, states, according to the *Times Educational Supplement,* that unfortunately the year 1930 can not be characterized as one of progress or even normal development. Early in the year the Executive Committee decided to suspend for an indefinite period the granting of vacation leave to teachers; staffs during the year were considerably reduced by the abolition of posts which could not be regarded as absolutely essential; experience gained in other provinces ceased to be recognized in determining initial salaries; certain allowances were discontinued, with the proviso that those teachers who were then in permanent employment were allowed to retain them; and the provision of books, school material, and equipment was drastically curtailed.

The recommendations of the Education Committee appointed in 1928 to report on the question of the possibility of extending the limit of compulsory school age for Transvaal children occupied the attention and time of the department, but it was found impossible to proceed with the plan, on account of lack of funds, lack of suitable accommodation, and the unwillingness of certain sections of the public to give up the least portion of what they considered to be their rights or vested interests on behalf of the general good. In the Witwatersrand area especially there was strong opposition to the scheme. It is promised that the question will be reconsidered during the coming year.

During the year there was a slight increase in the number of schools, and the number of pupils rose from 207,702 to 216,326. The number of teachers on the staff of the department at the end of the year was 5,605, as compared with 5,623 in the year 1929, and the average rate of salary paid to European teachers at the end of 1930 was £375 9s., as against £374 15s. 11d. at the end of 1929. In the section dealing with native education the director notes that it is extremely difficult to obtain any reliable figures in regard to the number of native children of school-going age. An estimate, however, based on the 1921 Census gives 332,000 native children between the ages of seven and 14, inclusive. For the last term of 1930 the enrolment in the schools and institutions registered and subsidized by the department was 72,800, a figure representing nearly 22 per cent. Commenting on these figures, it is stated that not only are the great majority of native children growing up without any schooling, but those that do attend school do not get much chance owing to insufficient staffing. Statistics show in one case 85 pupils per teacher; in another, 112 pupils per teacher; in a third, 84; and in a fourth, 88. In addition, it is stated that there are several cases on record of a woman assistant teacher having to handle classes of 100 or more juniors. Buildings costing £72,162 for secondary and £66,475 for primary education were completed during the year, and works in progress comprise £29,468 for secondary and £3,560 for primary education. The total expendiutre on education for the year 1930 was £3,139,515 5s. 11d., as against £3,146,393 16s. 7d. for the previous year.

ENROLMENT IN VOCATIONAL SCHOOLS

The annual report of the Federal Board of Vocational Education states that enrolment in vocational schools in the United States giving courses in agriculture, trade and industrial subjects, and home economics increased approximately 61,000 during the past year. The 1931 enrolment amounts to 1,125,000 as compared with 1,064,000 reported for 1930. Included in the 1931 figures is the enrolment in agricultural schools of 237,000, in trade and industrial schools of 602,000 and in home economics schools of 285,000.

Unemployment has evidently played a part in the increased enrolment in trade and industrial day and evening schools. This indicates that those who are out of employment are spending some of their leisure getting instruction which will help them when they return to work.

It was inevitable that under the economic conditions which have existed during the year the board should take cognizance of the relation of vocational education to unemployment. A bulletin entitled "Vocational Training and Unemployment," has been issued which shows what can be done to train unemployed persons for jobs actually available, and to retrain those who because of changing conditions in processes and machinery have been thrown out of work. Following the board's recommendations many states have worked out special courses for these groups and have sought by providing training in short units to aid as quickly as possible those who need intensive courses. For this purpose "opportunity" schools have been set up in a number of states and are filling a real need. These courses are given in schools, plants, or in any other place convenient for the workers concerned.

The board has during the past year opened up several new avenues of education for special groups. Outstanding among these are the new courses developed for city fire department employees. An investigation of the possibilities of such courses was carried out by staff members in cooperation with the International Association of Fire Chiefs. As a result a number of cities already have in operation or are planning to inaugurate training programs for firemen.

At present an analysis is being made of occupations in the paper and pulp industry with a view to recommending and setting up courses of training for the workers.

In order to reach all groups of workers the vocational courses are operated in day, part-time and evening schools. Adult workers, employed during the day, took advantage of the courses open to them in evening vocational schools in 1931 to the number of 397,000. Trade and industrial workers contributed 176,000, farmers 87,000 and housewives 134,000.

A summary of the program of vocational rehabilitation of civilians disabled through accident or disease, which under the terms of the national vocational rehabilitation act is also promoted by the Federal Board for Vocational Education, shows that notwithstanding the depressed condition of business in 1931 the number of rehabilitations increased over the preceding year by 13 per cent. The criterion of rehabilitation for a particular person is placement in a suitable job. During the year, 5,192 persons were rehabilitated by this standard. To this number should be added 869 persons who were trained and placed in jobs for which they had been fitted, but who were still being followed up on June 30, 1931, and consequently are not included in the above total as rehabilitated. The total of these two groups is 6,061. Persons who were trained for but not placed in employment because industry in 1931 was not operating at its normal capacity numbered 2,455. Thus the total number of disabled persons rendered fit for employment during the year 1931 was 8,516.

Since the board's last report was issued vocational education has by Act of Congress been extended to the Island of Porto Rico, and the program is now rapidly being organized there. The report contains the usual statistics covering the vocational education and vocational rehabilitation programs carried on by the 48 States and Hawaii.

COLLEGE COURSE IN RADIO AT THE UNIVERSITY OF WISCONSIN

THERE has been a long-felt want in the radio field for a school of recognized standing to give a complete, comprehensive, well balanced course in radio communication, to be complete within itself and capable of being finished within a reasonable time. Realizing this need the Extension Division of the University of Wisconsin in Milwaukee is giving such a course to fit students for advanced places in radio activities. This is a new type of college training of a semi-professional nature with the object of training young men for positions existing in a field between the skilled craftsman and the trained professional engineer.

All trades and professions are now demanding that the men participating in them shall be thoroughly trained in the theory and fundamentals of the trade or profession in question. The ever expanding science of radio is possibly more exacting in this than any other because of the extremely technical nature of the subject and of the enormous responsibilities upon the shoulders of an operator. A few years ago a man could be a fairly good operator or technician without any particular training, but today if a man expects to succeed in this field he must be thoroughly grounded in the theory and practical applications of the fundamental principles of radio communication. The question has been to the serious-minded person, "Where can I secure such an education without taking a regular degree in engineering?"

The course given in Milwaukee is not an experiment, for it has grown out of auxiliary courses given during the past six years and is planned as a definite preparation for the actual problems met in practice. The work given is substantially of collegiate grade, requiring only a high-school education or the equivalent for entrance. The training is very intensive, requiring the entire time of a student for two semesters. The entire day is occupied from eight until four thirty with lectures, class work and laboratory experiments, and special problems and assignments to be completed after class hours. This same course may be taken in evening classes over a period of two years or by correspondence.

The principal course of a complete training in radio communication is strengthened by supplementary subjects which assure a thorough understanding of the various phases of the theory and practical applications of receiving and transmitting circuits. These correlated subjects include elementary electricity, high frequency currents, thermionic vacuum tubes, and laboratory work which is divided into three parts: (1) actual experiments, (2) design of apparatus and circuits and (3) adequate drill in International Morse Code. The entire list of studies is completed more easily because of a study of technical mathematics as applied to electricity and technical English, which pertains to the writing of reports and experiments. The satisfactory completion of the course qualifies a student for the government examination for a second class commercial operator's license, or he may enter many of the allied branches of the radio industry.

STATE INVESTIGATION OF THE NEW YORK SCHOOLS

AFTER a conference held on December 7 with an advisory commission of educators and other citizens at the headquarters of the State Department of Education at the state office building, Commissioner Frank P. Graves announced he would undertake at once an investigation of the school system of New York with particular reference to the efficiency of teaching methods and the administrative supervisory policy of the

Board of Education, the Board of Superintendents, and the Board of Examiners.

The inquiry will be started with a preliminary fund of $2,500 collected by the State Board of Regents from its present and former members. At the next session of the Legislature the Education Department will seek an appropriation of $50,000. If this is not forthcoming, the investigators will go as far as they can with the help received from the state and city education departments. Each department has assigned a group of assistants to serve on the investigation commission.

Without additional funds it will be next to impossible to give the tests for instructional efficiency the commission has in mind.

Dr. Graves emphasized that it was not his purpose to go into charges of corruption or graft in the appointment and promotion of teachers or the handling of the funds of the department. But if evidence of irregularities comes to the attention of the investigators it will not be ignored.

"Ours is to be a constructive inquiry," said Dr. Graves. "We want to see wherein our educational methods are weak and to strengthen them in accordance with our findings."

Dr. Graves first was asked last May by Dr. George Ryan, president of the Board of Education, to undertake the investigation. Dr. Ryan's request was the Board of Education's answer to charges by Alan Fox, of the National Republican Club, that of 8,000 graduates of the elementary schools of the city, only 30 per cent. were able to pass the tests in arithmetic given by the State Department of Education for seventh and eighth grade pupils.

When the request of Dr. Ryan was received at Albany, Dr. Graves objected that an inquiry such as that desired would tax the facilities of his department to the utmost and would occasion expenses which his department had no funds to meet.

The members of the advisory committee who conferred with Dr. Graves were Professor John H. Withers, dean, College of Education, New York University; Dr. Frank E. Spaulding, professor of school administration, Graduate School, Yale University; Dr. William F. Russell, dean, Teachers College, Columbia University; Dr. Herbert S. Weet, superintendent of schools, Rochester; Mr. Henry W. Taft, lawyer, of 40 Wall Street, and Mr. Robert E. Simon, vice-president United Parents Association, 654 Madison Avenue.

In a statement issued after the meeting with the advisory commission, Dr. Graves described the aims of the investigation as threefold:

First, a study of the organization and the administrative supervisory policy of the central authority of the school system, namely—the Board of Education, the Board of Superintendents, the Board of Examiners, the district superintendents and those other services directly responsible to the central office.

Second, a study of selected schools in which an intensive study will be made of the pupils and their achievements, of the curriculum and methods of teaching, of the teaching and supervisory staff, of the building or school organization, of the administration and supervision, of the relationships of the school to the community which it serves and to the central office.

Third, a testing program focusing on the upper elementary and lower secondary levels for the purpose of determining pupil achievement and as an aid in interpreting the instructional service.

Dr. Graves will be in direct charge of the inquiry, assisted by Dr. George M. Wiley, Dr. J. Cayce Morrison and Dr. Lewis A. Wilson, assistant state commissioners, and Harold G. Campbell, John E. Wade and William E. Grady, associate superintendents of the City Department of Education.

The number of schools inspected will depend upon the funds available.

VOLUME IN HONOR OF PROFESSOR LIGHTNER WITMER

DR. LIGHTNER WITMER, professor of psychology at the University of Pennsylvania and director of the Psychological Clinic, was the recipient of a volume entitled "Clinical Psychology—Studies in Honor of Lightner Witmer—Commemorating the Thirty-Fifth Anniversary of the Founding of the First Psychological Clinic," before a special meeting of the faculty of the college on December 11. Dr. Paul H. Musser, dean of the faculty, called upon Dr. Robert A. Brotemarkle, editor of the volume, who, after reading the dedication page, explained the contents of the book and expressed the pleasure and privilege enjoyed by the contributors in honoring their former teacher and colleague. Dr. Edwin B. Twitmyer, professor of psychology, assistant director of the psychological clinic and chairman of the department of psychology, extended to Dr. Witmer the congratulations of the department of psychology and the staff of the psychological clinic. Dr. Twitmyer's remarks were based upon his memories of his student days with Dr. Witmer, and as a departmental colleague for forty years. Dr. Josiah H. Penniman, provost in charge of research, made the commemorative address, in which he spoke most highly of the "man and his work." His remarks were of an intimate nature growing out of an acquaintanceship of college student days continued as academic colleagues "during the whole of his career." President Thomas S. Gates, on behalf of the university, then presented the Commemorative Volume to Dr. Witmer as Founder of the first psychological clinic.

The presentation volume was an embossed leather-bound copy of the edition published by the University of Pennsylvania Press. The press has announced a limited edition of 250 copies autographed by Dr. Witmer, and will later issue a text-book edition of the work.

The editor in his introduction states: "This volume is the enthusiastic expression of the personal affection and scientific appreciation of Lightner Witmer. Written by a group of his former students, colleagues and friends, it gives voice to the gratitude of all whom he has served in the founding and motivating of clinical psychology. . . .

"The historical significance of the volume is indicated by the recording of the founding and development of the Psychological Clinic—the first psychological clinic in the world. This is the work of Dr. Samuel W. Fernberger, professor of psychology, a recognized authority on the history of psychology in America. The historical value of the volume is greatly enriched by the biographical sketch written by Dr. Joseph Collins, a warm personal friend and counselor in the neurological backgrounds of Witmer's scientific labors.

"The scientific significance of the volume is indicated by the scope of development in the relationships of a new profession—that of clinical psychologist."

The volume contains the contributions of twenty-five writers all of whom were former students of Dr. Witmer and recipients of the degree of doctor of philosophy in psychology from the University of Pennsylvania during the years 1900–1931.

EDUCATIONAL NOTES AND NEWS

DR. JOHN A. COUSENS, president of Tufts College, was elected president of the New England Association of Colleges and Secondary Schools at the concluding session on December 5 of the forty-ninth annual meeting of the association. Other officers elected were: William E. Wing and Otis E. Randall, vice-presidents; George S. Miller, Tufts College, secretary-treasurer. President Edward M. Lewis, of the New Hampshire State University, was elected to the executive committee, and Wilfred Ringer, principal of the Brookline High School, was elected to the standing committee on public secondary schools.

DR. JOSEPH E. ROMER, of Peabody College, Nashville, was on December 4 elected president of the Association of Colleges and Secondary Schools of the Southern States at the meeting in Montgomery, Alabama. He succeeds Mr. C. A. Brown, associate superintendent of schools at Birmingham. Other officers elected by the association are Dr. O. C. Carmichael, president of Alabama College for Women, *first vice-president;* Miss Juliet Poynter, Shelbyville, Ky., *second vice-president,* and Dr. Guy E. Snavely, president of Birmingham-Southern College, *secretary-treasurer.*

MR. C. J. BREWER, director of teacher training in the Eau Claire State Teachers College, has been elected president of the Wisconsin Teachers Association. He has served as rural school teacher, county superintendent, high-school teacher and principal and city superintendent. Professor A. E. Whealdon, a member of the faculty of the Superior State Teachers College, was elected *first vice-president;* J. B.

Layde, superintendent of the West Depere schools, *second vice-president*, and Miss Anna Ryss, superintendent of Winnebago county schools, *third vice-president*.

DR. WILLIAM P. DEARING, president of Oakland City College, Indiana, has been elected president of the Indiana State Teachers' Association.

DR. S. P. NANNINGA, dean of the College of Education at the University of New Mexico, was elected by the State Education Association at the recent convention at Santa Fe president for 1932. Mr. Vernon O. Tolle, for the past two years superintendent of schools at Lordsburg, was elected vice-president.

BROTHER CORNELIUS, president of Manhattan College, was elected president of the Association of Colleges and Universities of the State of New York at the recent annual meeting.

E. BOYD MORROW, head master of Gilman Country School, has been elected president of the recently organized association of private schools of Baltimore and the vicinity.

DR. HENRY NORRIS RUSSELL, professor of astronomy at Princeton University and director of the Princeton Observatory, was elected president of the American Philosophical Society at its meeting on December 4.

DR. ROBERT A. MILLIKAN, of the California Institute of Technology, made the principal address at the dedication on December 5 at Hendrix College, a Methodist institution at Conway, Arkansas, of a science building, erected with funds supplied by the Rockefeller Foundation.

DR. ROY M. MCCUSKEY was installed as president of West Virginia Wesleyan College on November 21. Dr. McCuskey, who was elected president of West Virginia Wesleyan last June, succeeds Dr. Homer E. Wark.

UPON recommendation of the board of visitors of the Fredonia State Normal School, New York, L. R. Gregory has been named principal to succeed Dr. Herman Cooper, who has accepted a position in the State Education Department.

PROFESSOR NORMAN LEHMER, of the department of mathematics of the University of California, has been appointed visiting professor at the University of Pennsylvania for the summer session of 1933.

DR. FRANK MANKIEWICZ, of the Bryant High School, New York City, has been appointed associate professor in the School of Education of the College of the City of New York. A testimonial dinner in his honor will be given to him by his associates on February 6.

M. B. KECK, principal of the schools of Clear Lake, Wisconsin, for the past six years, has resigned, to accept a position in the schools of Minneapolis. Mr. C. L. Johnson, formerly of Withee, will succeed Mr. Keck in January.

MR. BURT W. REED has been appointed assistant superintendent of the Los Angeles, California, schools. In 1911 he became principal of the first junior high school established in Los Angeles.

PROFESSOR GRANT SHOWERMAN, of the University of Wisconsin, will be director of the tenth summer session of the American Academy in Rome School of Classical Studies, which will be in session from July 4 to August 12, 1932.

MISS JULIA C. LATHROP, formerly chief of the U. S. Children's Bureau, has submitted her resignation as an assessor-member of the advisory committee on child welfare of the League of Nations. Miss Lathrop was appointed in 1926 as a result of a request made by the League Council to the president of the National Conference of Social Work in the United States. In her letter of resignation Miss Lathrop said that "her interest will not be lessened by her resignation and that she hopes to serve the purposes of the committee in any way possible."

THE University of Michigan has been presented with the bust of Dr. Cyrenus Garritt Darling, professor emeritus of oral surgery. The ceremony was held at his home, the presentation being made by Dr. Frederick Novy, professor of bacteriology, who spoke for the donors. The bust was accepted for the university by Dr. Alexander Grant Ruthven.

DR. JAMES R. ANGELL, president of Yale University, lectured recently on "The Days of William James" at the New School for Social Research, New York City.

DR. JAMES T. SHOTWELL, director of the division of economics and history of the Carnegie

Endowment for International Peace, is giving a series of lectures at the University of Vermont. Dr. Shotwell returned recently from an extended trip to Europe where he studied various phases of the present international situation.

THE general subject of psychology will be given especial consideration during the coming summer session at the University of California at Los Angeles, according to an announcement by Dean Gordon S. Watkins. Dr. Shepherd Ivory Franz, chairman of the department of psychology, will offer two courses, as will Dr. Clarence Truman Gray, professor of educational psychology, of the University of Texas.

PROFESSOR WILLIAM M. PROCTOR, of Stanford University, gave five addresses before the Utah State Teachers Association at Salt Lake City on October 16 and 17. He also represented the national officers of Phi Delta Kappa in installing a new Alumnus Chapter of the National Honor Fraternity at Salt Lake City. Some twenty members were received into the new chapter.

DR. J. CAYCE MORRISON, New York State Assistant Commissioner for Elementary Education, and Dr. J. E. Butterworth, director of the Graduate School of Education at Cornell University, were the principal speakers at the annual convention of the State Association of District Superintendents meeting at Syracuse, New York, on December 4.

THE death is announced of Professor Frederick M. Warren, professor emeritus of modern languages at Yale University, in his seventy-third year.

PROFESSOR GEORGE HERBERT LAMSON, JR., dean of the division of arts and sciences in the Connecticut Agricultural College at Storrs, died suddenly on December 4.

CHARLES A. GREATHOUSE, who was state superintendent of public instruction of Indiana for three terms, died on November 5 at the age of 62.

DR. ALBERT LEONARD, superintendent of the public schools of New Rochelle for the last twenty-five years, died on December 5. He was seventy-three years old and had retired from office on November 21. The Board of Education of New Rochelle has renamed the Central Junior High School after Mr. Leonard.

DR. HENRY H. BRINKERHOFF, director of medical inspection in Jersey City schools, died on December 5 at the age of sixty-seven years. For many years Dr. Brinkerhoff was a member of the Jersey City Board of Health, a post he relinquished to take charge of the school inspection.

THE $5,000 memorial fund that is being raised in the memory of James M. Edsall, late district superintendent of schools in Brooklyn, New York, has reached the half-way mark. The fund will be used to provide vacations for "needy and deserving" children.

THE cornerstone of the new building of the New York State College of Forestry, at Syracuse, named in honor of Louis Marshall, was laid on December 4. Participating in the ceremony were former Governor Alfred E. Smith, Dr. Frank Pierrepont Graves, president of the University of the State of New York, Dean Hugh P. Baker, of the State College of Forestry, and Dr. Charles W. Flint, chancellor of Syracuse University.

THE Oriental Institute on the campus of the University of Chicago, built at a cost of $1,500,000, was formally opened and dedicated on December 4. Dr. James H. Breasted, director of the institute, made the principal address.

THE *Journal* of the American Medical Association reports that the Ann J. Kellogg School was formally dedicated in Battle Creek, on November 24. Presentation of the building was made by Dr. Stuart Pritchard, director of the W. K. Kellogg Foundation, and the speech of acceptance was made by W. G. Coburn, superintendent of schools. The guest speakers included Honorable Wilber M. Brucker, governor of Michigan; Dr. Alexander G. Ruthven, president of the University of Michigan, Ann Arbor; Dr. Harry E. Barnard, director, White House Conference on Child Health and Protection; Honorable Webster H. Pearce, superintendent of public instruction, and Dr. Charles Scott Berry, director of special education in the Ohio State University. The Ann J. Kellogg School is a special institution designed and equipped to meet the individual needs of all types of children, and its program provides for normal free association of the handicapped with the normal children. The school's objectives embody the aims set forth by the recent White House Conference on Child Health and Protection. The state contributes financial aid for the education of certain types of handicapped children, and the W. K. Kellogg Foundation furnishes professional service and helps finance additional expenses. The school was made possible by the board of education and Dr. W. K. Kellogg. It is named and dedicated in memory of Dr. Kellogg's mother, who was a pioneer teacher in Michigan.

THE eighth annual Junior-High-School Conference will be held at New York University on March 18 and 19, 1932. The central theme will be: "Improving Junior-High-School Instruction." Two general sessions on Friday evening and Saturday morning will be followed by some thirty round tables related to the central topic. This conference is a cooperative arrangement, with an advisory committee of thirty-six representative educators distributed throughout the eastern states. In 1931, upwards of 2,000 attended the conference. With seven round tables and thirty speakers in 1925, it has expanded to include thirty-one round tables and one hundred and thirty-four speakers for 1931.

IN November an exhibit of thirty-six maps of Omaha and seven charts portraying social conditions in the city was held by the department of sociology of the Municipal University of Omaha. The display was prepared by the department over a period of several years. Information was given on the following subjects: juvenile delinquency, playgrounds and parks, infant mortality, child welfare agencies, recreation, domestic relations, mothers' pensions, poverty, character-building agencies, churches, mobility, immigrant areas, second generation immigrants, Negro population and other subjects pertaining to Omaha as a whole. A special feature was a series of eighteen maps portraying in detail the conditions in Ward Seven, which includes the packing house area.

IT was stated in the issue of SCHOOL AND SOCIETY for November 21 that the Board of Education of Philadelphia had ratified its school budget, "with a deduction of $500,000 for teachers' salaries." Dr. Edwin C. Broome, superintendent of the Philadelphia schools, writes: "It is true that we did suffer a cut in the total salary item of five hundred thousand dollars, but that is a very small percentage in an item which in itself amounts to twenty millions and we expect to meet it by various economies other than reduction of individual salaries. The salaries of the teachers and of the entire force in Philadelphia will not be reduced. In fact the scheduled increases will be given as heretofore for 1932. Our budget making that possible has been passed."

AN Associated Press dispatch dated November 30 reads as follows: "Fifty of Chicago's wealthiest business men have come to the support of 23,000 city employees with a pledge to insure imperiled salaries. Their aid was enlisted by Mayor Anton J. Cermak, who told them the city was "broke" and many payless pay days were in prospect for school teachers, policemen and even himself unless something was done. The program adopted was to sell within the next few months $30,000,000 worth of 1930 tax anticipation warrants to provide funds for payrolls and other expenses. A campaign patterned after the "Liberty Loan" drives of war-time was planned to sell the certificates. Among those who would be financially aided by the plan are 18,000 school teachers and other Board of Education employees whose salaries are in arrears since last May." On December 7 the first official report was issued showing that $830,000 in cash and $1,710,225 in pledges had been received.

THE observance of Education Week in the United States of America was shared in Turkey, where, at Constantinople Woman's College, a series of meetings was held. Naturally emphasis was placed on education and its needs in Turkey. Addresses were made as follows: "The Program of the Turkish Ministry of Education," by Dean Eleanor I. Burns; "New Trends in College Education," by Dr. Marion Talbot, who is now directing the college; "What the Lower Schools are Doing to Help Turkey Achieve a High Order of Citizenship and Loyalty to Law," by Shemsettin Bey, state inspector of foreign schools. Two Turkish members of the faculty of the college who have studied in the United States also took part in the program. Miss Fazile Shevket, M.A., Mt. Holyoke College, spoke on "What Education may help Turkey to Achieve in Child Health and Protection," and Sahire Mouhtar, Ph.D., Cornell University, spoke on "What Education is Helping Turkey to Achieve through the Enrichment of Adult Life." Dean Burns recently spent a few days in Angora in conference with the Ministry of Education concerning methods of cooperating with the government in its educational program and the adjustments in the college curriculum necessarily involved.

DISCUSSION

THE EDUCATIONAL CONFERENCE —TO WHAT END?

THE recent Detroit meeting of the Department of Superintendence of the National Education Association leaves one with much material for pause. The educational leadership in America was presumably adequately represented. The addresses were often verbal combats upon trivial or debatable points and, in many instances, dull, wordy platitudes or evasive gestures. Despite the sensational arguments, conventionalize and follow the leader seems to be the present trend in American education. This fact is well illustrated by the terminology employed successively and repeatedly by those who read papers or delivered set speeches.

THE CHILD-CENTERED SCHOOL

"The child's needs" is one of the modern educator's pet phrases. The child nevertheless is often employed as an instrument to obtain professional recognition or advancement. Indeed, in many instances the child's interests and purposes are not ascertained or utilized to any appreciable degree. The teacher in some schools makes "his" pupils work, and he even attempts to make them play. Only recently a father complained to one of the writers, stating that his small daughter was being forced daily to go through a routine performance that was labeled "organized play," a part of an activity program in a *progressive* school. Upon awakening one morning, this child glanced through the window and observed gleefully a pouring rain. The father reports that the child exclaimed, "Oh, goody! We won't have to play to-day."

Although the administrator of this school boasted loudly of his "activity program," he was obviously not concerned greatly with the needs of the individual child; the curriculum was devised to conform to the "system."

THE ACTIVITY PROGRAM IN COLLEGES

Colleges and universities to-day presumably serve students, and they are ostensibly devised for no other purpose. The curriculum reveals that the system is first, the student second, perhaps third (after the alumni).

The present-day exploitation of the college athlete is a vicious practice. Originally adopted as means of recreation for the student players, college athletics to-day are made to serve as advertising devices for the schools. Although the educational institution was founded for furthering the welfare of the student, by a curious turn of affairs, it often employs the student as an instrument for the furtherance of the assumed needs of the institution.

Not only in athletics does one observe the opportunist, but also in various other activities presumably educative in nature. The current practice has been described tersely by a recent contributor to SCHOOL AND SOCIETY.

> Who has not read scores of articles about "The Honor System at Siwash," "The Reorganization at Jerkwater," and "The Point System at Podunk"? New schemes of administrative organization, new methods of instruction, new intra-curricular or extra-curricular activities, since they do not lend themselves to immediate and exact measurement, may be seized upon as ready-to-hand vehicles of favorable publicity for the institution.[1]

All plans serve to bring their administrators conspicuously to the attention of the public; most of the schemes are presented to a credulous public before they have been evaluated or even carefully conceived. When evaluation is attempted, it is often superficial and highly subjective in character. This is true not only of the verbal attempts at justification by campus opportunists; it characterizes also the administrators of many elementary and secondary schools.

For example, in public address one school administrator cited as a measure of the efficiency of "his" system the number of lecture "calls" that he had lately received. Thus, the success of "his" school system and the success of his

[1] R. Façade, "Acid in the Literature of Education," SCHOOL AND SOCIETY, 34, 401–403, 1931.

lecturing were to him about the same product. Obviously, his data proved nothing except that by advertising his school system he had also advertised himself.

THE CHILD'S "FELT NEEDS"

That the demand for activity programs is great was clearly demonstrated by the orations delivered last year in Detroit. The following expressions were found over and over again in *The Gist,* a publication which presents daily summaries of the papers or the orations delivered at the meetings of the Department of Superintendence of the National Education Association.

The child's needs.
The child's real needs.
The child's specific needs.
The child's practical needs.
The child's present needs.
The child's future needs.
The child's immediate needs.
The child's ultimate needs.
The child's vocational needs.
The child's educational needs.

Do the foregoing expressions have clear-cut meaning? Can it be that these phrases which are so glibly employed in public are often compensatory devices which develop because the administrator has utilized children as stepping-stones to professional recognition? It will be of interest to examine the effect upon the school of the educational opportunist's activities. The attitude which results in the teachers when the school is employed for the administrator's professional advancement frequently is directly opposed to the children's interests and certainly to their needs.

THE AUTHORITARIAN ATTITUDE

From the typical teacher's point of view[2] the model pupil is the one who does not interfere seriously with the school's routine. Wickman has discovered that the classroom teacher and the mental hygienist differ markedly in their estimates of the desirability (or undesirability) of various behavior traits.[3] For example, the mental hygienist considers traits such as recessiveness, a tendency to withdrawal, shyness, sensitiveness, etc., to be symptomatic of maladjustment. The teacher, however, rarely regards the excessively timid child as "a problem," probably because the timid child is unlikely to interfere with the teacher's plan and the administrative machinery.

In view of the foregoing, one would naturally anticipate that the school administrator's ideal of a "good" teacher would differ from that of the educational philosopher. This suspicion is supported in part by the Charters-Waples continuum of the qualities which administrators wish teachers to possess. These investigators found that administrative officers usually want to employ teachers who are neat, attractive, considerate, adaptive, cooperative and enthusiastic—administrators care much less apparently about qualities such as originality, open-mindedness and progressiveness.[4]

Rare indeed is the prominent school administrator who resists the temptation (and the temptation must indeed be a strong one) to manage the school as if it were a vested interest. Hence it is that the Charters-Waples job analysis as a means for the improvement of teaching is much more likely to appeal to the school administrator than to the educational philosopher or to the enlightened teacher.

Try as he may, it is difficult for any successful school executive to avoid managing "his" school system as though it were his private enterprise. This authoritarian attitude is one that is easily understood. The powerful individual usually wants nothing to challenge his authority—not because such a challenge might really injure the welfare of the school, but because a challenge might interfere with his personal comfort—and advancement. To him, his personal welfare and the welfare of the school become one.

THE OPPORTUNIST'S MECCA

Any one who within recent years has attended an educational conference should be fully cognizant of the present-day trend. Personal prestige, community prestige, institutional prestige, regional prestige, but above all professional

[2] Particularly the teacher who follows meekly the progressive administrator's dicta.

[3] E. K. Wickman, "Children's Behavior and Teachers' Attitudes," (pp. 42–43). New York: D. Appleton and Co., 1928.

[4] F. G. Bonser, "Qualities Desired in Teachers by Administrators," SCHOOL AND SOCIETY, 31, 260–262, 1930.

advancement—it is precisely these that are fostered by the so-called educational conference.

More than one speaker will be found who regards participation in the program as "an opportunity" to get before the educational public. Always there will be a few speakers who manifest thinly veiled indifference for—even contempt for—their audience. Too bad that the audiences are more polite (or more timid)! These speakers may address their audiences after making an eleventh-hour preparation—occasionally with no preparation whatsoever. They may deliver for the nth time an address that has been delivered so often that it has long since become threadbare. Occasionally the paper or the address is one that has previously appeared, word for word, in print. And the same speaker appears again and again during the meeting. This latter fact would meet with whole-hearted approval if ability and respect for the audience were always among the criteria determining the selection of speakers. Unfortunately, a flair for personal publicity is too often the apparent criterion.

An editorial in *The Journal of Educational Method* has described aptly the type of "general program" that is all too often provided at meetings of state teachers' associations. The description applies also to some of the national meetings that the writers have attended.

> The general program is devoted, not to education but to entertainment or occasionally to politics. Pleasant speakers who can ramble on in a humorous or striking sort of way about everything in general and about nothing in particular have the call. . . .
>
> The great day—or night—comes. The celebrity appears, flanked by an orchestra, a band, a quartet, or a chorus on one side and a local political light on the other. The crowd is vast. It is there expecting to be thrilled. The celebrity obliges. He opens the throttle wide. He uses superlatives, striking epigrammatic phrases, ironic humor; he tears to pieces, paints roseate pictures, runs the gamut of emotions. The audience goes out *ohing* and *ahing* and there has been done to advance sound educational practices in the state—just exactly nothing.[5]

In addition to the general meetings one may attend the meetings of the smaller professional groups. These often bear a close resemblance to the ancient jousting tournament. The hope and the promise of a sensational "oratorical scrap" suffices to draw a large audience. For some time prior to the hour appointed for the meeting, the hall where such a combat is anticipated is usually well filled. The affair promises to be interesting; the atmosphere is a bit tense. Since the general points of view of the several speakers are well known, the oratorical sallies are likely to bring quick responses from the audience.

It must be confessed that, like most types of combat, an oratorical clash is likely to be interesting. But what have these forensic demonstrations to do with education? Certainly, something remains to be desired when "the best meeting" of an educational conference is merely one at which some gifted orator once more demonstrates forensic prowess by attacking nothing more than a straw man. It is true, of course, as has been stated by E. G. Boring, that controversy may be a method of science.[6] But surely no one would assert that Don Quixote's tilting at windmills was a boon to science.

PAUL A. WITTY
NORTHWESTERN UNIVERSITY
HARVEY C. LEHMAN
OHIO UNIVERSITY

A TEACHERS' CONVENTION—DIARY OF A PARTICIPANT

October 21. "THE —— section of the —— State Teachers' Association will meet in two weeks. I have been notified to-day that I am to discuss. . . . Wrote at once to ask where the meeting is to be held, what group is to be the audience, and how much time is to be allotted to me."

October 23. "Have not had a reply to my questions about the meeting. Hope it comes to-day; for the next day or two will be the only possible time I can use between now and the association date; and I do want to plan my discussion to fit the audience and the amount of time."

October 24. "Reply received to-day: 'You are to have from twenty to twenty-five minutes.'

5 "Editorially Speaking," *The Journal of Educational Method*, 7, 157–158, 1928.

6 E. G. Boring, "The Psychology of Controversy," *Psychological Review*, 36, 97–121, 1929.

It is good that I am to have that much time; for the ideas they have asked for are rather new to that audience. If they had wanted me to use but twelve or fifteen minutes I could merely have described practices or I could only have explained facts giving rise to the practices; but I couldn't have done both. Being allotted twenty to twenty-five minutes I'll use exactly twenty-two minutes and shall first explain the facts that give rise to the practices and afterward describe the practices fully enough so that teachers can see how they may be used."

October 26. "I cancelled everything else yesterday and the day before and worked out the ideas I want to put into that discussion. I have divided the time between developing the background of facts that determine the practices and illustrating how the practices are carried out. I have tested a dozen times or more to see how long it will take to give the complete discussion; for I do dislike to infringe on the time allotted to some other discussion or to fail to complete my own. That couldn't possibly be necessary with this, for it comes easily into twenty-two minutes.

"That will be a bad meeting place for this group. It is so large and the acoustics so poor that when I have been there I could not hear public addresses unless I was favorably located. Oh yes, that will be all right; for I remember now that the last time I spoke there microphones had been installed and I had no difficulty in making myself heard."

November 6. "The meeting is just over. The program had been extended to include six numbers, five of them unrelated in theme. An untimed pageant by scores of young school children, who could neither be seen nor heard by hundreds of persons in the audience, opened the session. All microphones had been removed from the hall since last night's session. To-day, against the uproar of running children in the adjacent corridors and of workmen in the rear, unaided voices had to carry on the discussions. The chairman, frantic to get the program over with in time for the ball game, rose when I had been speaking seven minutes. Without explaining that he was cutting my time without forewarning me, he took on the manner of one calling down a garrulous speaker and authoritatively announced, 'Five minutes for you to finish!' Should I have wasted part of those five minutes in justly stating my situation, since any attempt to crowd in the remainder of the discussion was bound not only to be void of benefit to the listening teachers but also bound to make my presentation of the topic ridiculous since the plan could not be changed so abruptly? Well, maybe, but I did meekly submit to the false implications and try to salvage as much as possible, in fragments. . . If I had teachers whose efforts were as ill-planned and badly executed, as largely futile and as expensively wasteful as some convention efforts they wouldn't be recommended for continued tenure. . . . Yet, this program must have been a success; for it did close in time for the game."

November 7. "The convention is over and I'm reflecting about it. My personal expense bill while attending the convention was $15. (I was guest for several meals and for transportation home and made no purchases in stores.) It is likely that it cost each of the 8,000 teachers proclaimed to have been in attendance at this section alone as much as I spent. For this total amount of $120,000 spent in just this one year by the teachers themselves for necessary expenses in attending the convention they could easily have engaged for themselves the full-time help of the finest educational expert on the program, *for the remainder of his life* and could have compensated him better than he ever will be compensated, too—enough better so that he could actually give his most expert help to them. Or, for the amount paid by themselves for necessary expenses in attending this convention just this one year the teachers of this section of the state could secure for themselves the whole-year help of *each of forty* of the very finest supervisors of instruction in the United States. . . But why be so impractical in my reflections? The hotels were filled to overflowing. One department of one store reported the sale of two hundred coats of one make. There were two mighty football crowds. 'A great educational convention has just closed.'"

Olive Gray
Extension Division,
University of Kansas

SPECIAL CORRESPONDENCE

THE PURPOSES OF THE SCHOOL OF BUSINESS

DESPITE its being the latest professional school established, in many universities, the school of business or commerce frequently has one of the largest undergraduate enrolments on the campus. Pointing to this attainment in numbers as unmistakable evidence of success, the faculty has found it easy so far to go along uncritically without developing any very clear statement of purposes or aims.

So general has been the acceptance of this pseudo-pragmatic test of our work that the Association of Collegiate Schools of Business has not done as much as it ought to do in studying the progressive needs of American business or the field performance of former students in relation to the component elements of the curriculum. Just what subjects are really necessary and the extent of time that should be devoted to each are matters concerning which there has been wide difference of opinion between the advocates of courses in general methods and theory and the advocates of practical descriptive courses. How much business law, for example, should be taught to the student in the university school of business? What should be the fundamental common requirements in accounting, statistics or economic geography, and what elements in each of these subjects are basic have not as yet been determined.

If the graduates of our schools of business, however, are to receive the training which will help some of them at least to rise above the ranks and assume positions of responsibility in an advanced business order, these questions will have to receive further attention. Whether business institutions will come to follow as their guide the wise opportunism of such a statesman as Edmund Burke or some more rigidly methodical philosophy, still our students must learn how to live in and help manage a relative world where facts change and relationships are moving forward.

Feeling the necessity for some statement objectifying and setting forth its own general policy, the faculty of the School of Business Administration in the University of Buffalo recently drew up the following paragraphs. While not committing themselves as to the future developments that may be made in the light of increased experience and further investigation of the problem, the members of the faculty have accepted this composite statement as a beginning upon which to develop a sounder institution.

The course leading to the degree, Bachelor of Science in Business Administration, is designed to train students for successful performance not only in business but also as effective and understanding members of our modern industrial society. While the School recognizes, of course, a primary vocational or professional interest among its undergraduates, it does not believe that satisfying accomplishments in business can or should be obtained at the sacrifice of well-rounded development. It is for this reason that the student is provided with generous access to the opportunities for the study of the wide range of liberal subjects offered by the faculty of the College of Arts and Sciences.

The more specialized professional training within the School of Business aims particularly to provide the student with an intelligent comprehension of the characteristics and functioning of the modern economic order, especially as these are made manifest in the world of business, and with a sound technique for the recognition and solution of the problems arising in that world. Modern business is a structure of gigantic proportions. With the extension of division of labor, the perfection of methods of communication and transportation, and the growth of every sort of large-scale enterprise, the individual participant in affairs, no matter how apparently great or modest his function, has progressively assumed a position of profound interdependence. His own behavior is affected by the acts of numerous other persons, and his decisions, in turn, influence many others. To perform his duties wisely and successfully he must, consequently, understand his place in a vast and complicated organization, anticipate the more remote consequences of what he contemplates doing, and possess the ability to weigh opposing considerations and to arrive at definite and rational decisions.

To develop these abilities the School of Business Administration aims to provide students with a general acquaintance with such basic business functions as finance, production, marketing, management, accounting, etc.; a thorough training in economic principles, and in statistical and other methods of scientifically assembling, interpreting, and expressing business facts; and to cultivate in students, so far as possible, those qualities which will later enable them to assume and successfully maintain positions of executive responsibility. Vocational guidance, as well as assistance, is offered to students, but narrow specialization of study is not permitted. The experience of Collegiate Schools of Business has shown that only a small proportion of students ultimately pursue those business branches in which they have been allowed to specialize. Moreover, it is accepted that what this School ought to provide is general background and broad principles: detailed knowledge of special fields will be much more easily and effectively gained when the graduate enters upon the specific tasks of the position which he will later assume. The School does not pretend, then, to provide what is wholly a substitute for practical experience. It does, however, believe that it gives to its students a general point of view and a technique which practical experience seldom provides yet which are essential for fullest success. The school further believes that its graduates as a consequence of their training, may reasonably expect to spend less time in routine work than would otherwise be necessary before being given some responsibility. It also believes that its students will be helped later to live lives that are personally satisfying and socially useful.

Here, then, is a nucleus of thought embodying a tentative point of view. It will, of course, be tested, refined, modified and adapted to meet as well as possible the unforeseen needs that may arise, but it is presented as a type of effort to which the school of business faculties should be especially urged to devote their best abilities.

C. S. Marsh,
Dean

University of Buffalo

QUOTATIONS

EDUCATION IN THE FEDERAL GOVERNMENT

The question has often been asked of late: How should the Federal Government be concerned with educational activities?

Many answers have been given, depending, first, upon what particular domains of educational responsibility one happened to be thinking of at the moment, and, second, upon the working philosophy or prejudices of the person passing judgment.

Thus most people think exclusively of the relation of the Federal Government to the people of the states in the matter of education, which is historically an indirect and cooperative one.

In giving answer, such persons usually overlook completely the fact that there are numerous educational activities for which the Federal Government has a direct and final responsibility, as in educating children in federal districts outside the jurisdiction of the states, Indians on reservations and other wards of the Federal Government, the peoples of the territories and outlying possessions, and those in the service of the Federal Government.

Again there are those whose social and political philosophy commits them to a belief in the increasing necessity of federal participation in all social affairs, economic and educational. Opposed to them are those who believe educational centralization on the federal level of political control is contrary to all that is natural and historic in the American situation and destructive of the essential characteristics of a democratic system of education.

For about a century and a half the Federal Government has been evolving, in this matter of participation in education, and the result has been a confused and often inconsistent policy which has fallen short of desirable results.

Now, for the first time in American history, the Chief Executive of the United States has, through the appointment of a National Advisory Committee on Education, attempted to see the educational work of the government as a whole, and to view it in terms both of the folkways of our people and of the changing necessities of the American situation.

The report of that committee is now the possession of the American people. To the extent that citizens read and comprehend the facts, generalizations and procedures recommended, we shall have that sustaining public opinion which will move the Federal Government toward the gradual adoption of an effective plan and a fruitful policy in matters of education.

A secretary in the cabinet is recommended to

meet an urgent need in the Federal Government. But the public must be warned that the officer recommended is unlike any provided in previous suggested legislation.

He is a secretary without administrative portfolio. He is merely advisory, and is left deprived of coercive authority. His influence is that of intellectual assistance, based on fact-finding and experience reported.

His business is to see the sound interests of American education as a whole, playing a fundamental rôle in American civilization, rather than in terms of special phases already intrenched in the Federal Government with financial and supervisory powers which force compliance by the states.

For these specialized ministries of education with administrative control, the proposal is made to reduce their centralized control and to add an advisory secretary without more power than scientifically determined facts will bring to an intellectual leadership so placed in the government that its counsels will at least be heard at the seat of government.—*Henry Suzzallo, President, Carnegie Foundation for the Advancement of Teaching, Member of the National Advisory Committee on Education, in The New York American.*

EDUCATIONAL RESEARCH AND STATISTICS

UNDERGRADUATES IN A GROUP OF EVANGELICAL CHRISTIAN COLLEGES[1]

THE purpose of this study was to determine four things: (1) The general backgrounds of the students before entering these colleges; (2) the purposes and aims of the students; (3) the habits, attitudes and opinions of the students; and (4) the chief unmet needs of the students.

The methods of the study were: A careful study of the literature of these schools; a visit to each of the schools for interviews with the students, and observance of the student-life; study of the college records; and two questionnaire forms.

The chief results of the study are given under three headings: (1) Student backgrounds; (2) the purposes and aims of the students; and (3) the habits, attitudes and opinions of the students.

The backgrounds of the students were found to be very definitely religious, with both parents of devout religious habits in most cases, and with at least one parent devout in the other cases. The students have engaged in a wide variety of church and religious activities, and very few non-religious activities. They attended church very regularly, and the mean age for declaring their acceptance of the Christian faith was 12.25 years, for all students—the girls being from one to three years in advance of the boys. The economic level of the homes was not sufficient to provide many cultural opportunities. The parents are chiefly of the skilled-labor class, farmers or ministers. The average income of the parents is higher than the average of all employed heads of homes in the United States. The students ranked, mostly, in the upper or middle thirds of their high-school graduating class; and they entered into few extra-curricular activities (40.6 per cent. engaged in none). The mean size of the high-school graduating classes was 101 persons. The chief forms of diversion were religious meetings and athletic contests. Most of the students read the newspapers quite regularly. The average number of books read was 2.31 books the last year before entering college.

The aims and purposes of the students changed during high school, and later seemed to return to childhood ambitions. The religious purpose is dominant; 39.9 per cent. expect to enter Christian service; and 25.6 per cent. expect to engage in teaching. The commercial field does not attract many. The chief reason why the students entered these particular colleges were: "The religious atmosphere," "low cost" and "family desire." More than 90 per cent. of the students named the religious motive. Most of the students would be in college elsewhere if these colleges did not exist. About two thirds of the students say they expect to graduate where now enrolled. Those who will not graduate are leaving chiefly because of lack of courses which only a university could give. Four fifths

[1] Abstract of a study used as a doctor's dissertation at Yale University, School of Education, 1931.

of the students say they would choose the same college if starting over.

The habits of the students show a definite increase in religious devotion after entering college in all aspects except church attendance, which declines. Many not professing to be Christians at entrance now profess Christ. The health of most of the students is probably adequate, but about 15 per cent. are definitely "physically unfit," while at the same time carrying full college curricular loads and heavy student-labor for self-support. The health habits of the students seem to be poorly established, and there is a poor system of checking up on student-health at most of the colleges. Most of the students enter into some form of extra-curricular activity. Athletics, literary societies and debate clubs rank highest. Religious organizations of some sort include nearly all students. The students read very little of world news or fiction, and their recreations turn from the non-religious type to religious and cultural types, as rated by these schools. Self-support is popular. Less than one third of the students are wholly supported by parents or friends. Some are carrying excessive programs of work and curricular studies, with no college regulations to prohibit such. The average number of hours per week for self-help is 15.2 for those who are at all self-supporting. The aspect of these colleges which is causing the greatest amount of dissatisfaction to students is "athletics." Only one school has intercollegiate contests. "Social life" and "strict rules" come next as disappointments. "Friendliness" is the outstanding point of pleasure to new students when they arrive; "Christian spirit" and "faculty-student relations" follow as pleasing features. The courses regarded as strongest and weakest were different for each college. About one fourth of the students have wanted to leave school. The reasons were chiefly lack of courses and "rules too strict." The students regard their college work superior to their high-school work in most cases. They like to attend chapel, but think it monotonous. They think the social life is very poor, and suggest "more formal affairs." They do not feel that they are receiving sufficient social training to prepare them for life's social demands. They are also much dissatisfied with the physical education departments. 87.5 per cent. say they enjoy their college work; the others are indifferent.

Definite problems for these colleges were seen to exist with reference to the following: Regulation of student-work; development of social life; and providing of more social experiences; more careful check on student-health; making the chapel services more interesting; developing more regular church-attendance; providing more and better training in the physical education departments; cooperation between the colleges of the group for the division of labor regarding the courses or departments outside the liberal arts college; unification of the religious conceptions of the students and determination of the future attitude of these schools regarding intercollegiate athletics.

The participating colleges were: Houghton College, Houghton, New York, James Luckey, president; Asbury College, Wilmore, Kentucky, L. R. Akers, president; Taylor University, Upland, Indiana, John Paul, president; John Fletcher College, University Park, Iowa, Joseph Owen, president; Eastern University, Philadelphia, Pennsylvania, Charles Ball, president; Wheaton College, Wheaton, Illinois, James Oliver Buswell, president.

JOHN HARVEY FURBAY

NEW BOOKS IN EDUCATION

ALBERTY, H. B. and V. T. THAYER. *Supervision in the Secondary School.* Pp. 479. Heath. $2.00.

BADANES, SAUL. *A Child's Third Number Book.* Part Two. Pp. 139. Illustrated. Macmillan. $.64.

HOWES, RAYMOND F. *Debating.* Pp. 192. Heath. $1.00.

JOHNSON, ERWIN L. *Latin Words of Common English.* Pp. 335. Heath. $2.00.

MASON, JOSEPHINE D. and GERTRUDE E. O'BRIEN. *A Practical Reader for Adults.* Pp. xvii + 155. Heath. $1.00.

MAXEY, CHESTER C. *You and Your Government.* Pp. 605. 114 illustrations. Heath. $1.76.

TYSON, LEVERING, Editor. *Radio and Education.* Pp. viii + 271. University of Chicago Press.

U. S. DEPARTMENT OF THE INTERIOR, OFFICE OF EDUCATION. Bulletin 13. *Bibliography of Research Studies in Education: 1929–30.* Prepared in the Library Division by Edith A. Wright. Pp. xii + 475. Superintendent of Documents. $.85.

WHITE HOUSE CONFERENCE. *Nursery Education: Section III, Education and Training.* F. J. Kelly, chairman. Pp. xxi + 187. Century. $2.00.

SCHOOL AND SOCIETY

EDITED BY J. McKEEN CATTELL

WITH WHICH IS COMBINED THE

EDUCATIONAL REVIEW

EDITED BY WILLIAM McANDREW

Volume 34 SATURDAY, DECEMBER 19, 1931 Number 886

THE UNIVERSITY TO-DAY[1]

By Dr. FRANK PORTER GRAHAM

PRESIDENT OF THE UNIVERSITY OF NORTH CAROLINA

INTRODUCTION

THE local occasion which brings us together is submerged in the international occasion which focuses to-day the thought of the world upon the coming of the peace. A university is so dynamic in its life that no occasion, however local or however international, is outside the range of its radiation. The campus and the world interact upon each other with generative and regenerative power. A university is more than intellectually dynamic, it is vitally organic with the life streams of the culture of the ages and the present hopes of the people. With a rootage as deep as the race and as wide as the world, the university grows in local soil for the finding of truth for all mankind and for the development of youth in whom are gathered both the local and international hopes of mankind.

A modern university is such a vital and manifold institution, has been so integrated into the structure of western civilization, unbroken in their interconnection since the twelfth century, is so intimately a part of the context of every real problem of the modern world, that any life strand found at hand anywhere running through the life of the world enters into the texture of the modern university. We may work out from that strand into the complex life of the university and back again into the tangled life of the world.

ARMISTICE DAY AND THE UNIVERSITY

This is November 11, 1931, the fourteenth Armistice Day. As we, in Chapel Hill, go back to the armistice hour of that first day we find as the minute hand moved close to the hour, a young man, not long from the classrooms and playing fields of this university, was struck down at the head of his men and lay dying as the armistice hour struck the peace for a war-wrecked world. He was one of the tens of thousands of college men killed where danger stretched its farthest front, one of the ten millions of the fittest men on earth killed in four years of war. Greater than the gigantic figures of death, disease and physical destruction is the uncountable loss of creative intellectual and spiritual power. All gone the training, the potential discoveries, inventions, literature, ideas and dreams of youth done to death. Disillusionment to those who killed them! With all the heroism and idealism of the war, came also moral and spiritual damages suffered far from the battlefront by millions caught in the awful backwash of the war and the wreckage of the values of human life and personality. Upon the

[1] Inaugural address given at Chapel Hill, November 11, 1931.

back of those who fought the war and whose work sustains a broken and bewildered world is now loaded the crushing costs of the war to be paid by them, their children and their children's children.

To-day, as the sun makes its way across the world to the armistice hour, the peoples of Europe and America become still and silent as they remember their dead and the peace that came. It ties us to all mankind as we listen to the deep stillness of the millions in their silent commemorative aspiration for peace. Here in this beautiful Kenan Memorial Stadium we were silent and joined in the stillness of the peoples in a spiritual fellowship of the hope for peace on earth and good will toward men everywhere. We would be untrue to the spirit of this university, which has ever given and will ever give her life and her youth to every call that comes to the idealism and heroism of youth, if we did not link the purpose of this day to the purpose of this university and schools everywhere.

The colleges and universities, by virtue of their humane purpose and the very nature of their social being, have the responsibility of helping to build a world in which the call to the idealism and heroism of youth shall never again be a call to war. It is their function to make realistically intelligent and morally heroic the aspirations and work of mankind toward a warless world, vivid with the unfolding possibilities of cooperative work and play, valorous with the adventures of physical and social mastery and beautiful with the artistry of the human spirit.

A. The College

To these high ends stands the university. At the center of the university is the college of liberal arts. In these recent decades the college of liberal arts, as a result of its own incoherence, the advance of the junior college, and the encroachments of the professional and vocational schools, has been subjected to a severe defensive reexamination as to its place in the scheme of higher education. Several fundamental and dramatic experiments are now under way, involving both the personalities of the experimenters and the function of the college. Scores of other experiments involving the purpose of the college in general and the curriculum and teaching methods in particular give a various and cumulative content to what has been called "a movement" for the college of liberal arts. The history of the college of liberal arts, whether as the denominational college which heroically blazed the trail for all the others, or as the privately endowed independent college, or as the central college of the modern university, private or state, gives solid ground for such reinvigoration of the college of arts and sciences. The college of arts and sciences, the foundation college for the professional and graduate schools and service province of them all, has a kingdom of its own and a purpose within its own high nature. This purpose, toward which it has in various forms been groping for centuries, is the development of the more complete human being, a unified victorious personality, increasingly equipped to understand himself and the world in which he is to play his useful and cooperative part. The struggle of the college to find its place and purpose has helped both to reflect and shape the spirit of the age. Any sound reconsideration of the curriculum of the college should be from the threefold approach of historical experience, the unchanging values of the whole human personality, and the needs of the changing times.

(1) *The Background of the Curriculum:* Amid its medieval origins the liberal arts were subordinated to the ecclesiastical ends of preparation for the next world. With the Renaissance, despite all its vivid implications in the affairs of this world, its recovery of old ideas, its discoveries of a

new world and a new way to an old world, a new earth and the new heavens, yet the widening interests of the universities centered largely in the ancient learning as containing all learning. Learning for the next world gave way in part to learning from the classic past. The scientific revolution of the seventeenth, eighteenth and nineteenth centuries brought the minds of the men of the universities from their absorption in the next world and their preoccupations with the ancient culture to a concern for the present and the mastery of this earth and the forces of nature. It came to be thought that the human intellect, with its new sciences, could go beyond the learning of the ancients and bring heaven to earth now, whether in the New Atlantis or in New Worlds for Old.

In these three periods of cultural history —scholastic, humanistic and scientific— we find curricular adjustments in slow response to the intellectual emphasis of the age. In the medieval university, though the secular process was under way, we still found in this stronghold of scholasticism scorn of the body and this world. Incidentally, it may be said that physical education is yet to break through the scholastic doors and get into the curriculum of this university and many American universities of the twentieth century. During the Renaissance the revived classics had a difficult time winning a place in the curriculum and there are those to-day who would throw them out altogether. With the rise of the new science, the scholastics and the humanists, who became dominant in the universities, combined to delay the recognition of science on a basis of curricular equality with the humanities. But there can be no mistaking the masterful tones of science to-day in the universities and in the world. In response to the increasing complexity of modern society there arose in turn the new group of social sciences. The humanities and the natural sciences gave questioning admission to the newer social sciences. Paleontology and anthropology are not yet in the curriculum of this university and many other universities. This questioning is a valid process, but more and more the new social sciences will prove their saving value in this complex and baffling age.

(2) *The Body as Basic to the Whole Personality:* In so far as the curriculum failed to meet the physical needs of youth in the medieval university and the esthetic and spiritual needs of youth in modern America, it was, and is, incomplete in meeting the needs of the whole human being. The ideal of the liberal college is to develop the whole personality. It is the high witness of the race from the ideal of the Greek philosophers to the findings of the modern psychologists and biologists that youthful training should be based on the unity of the human being. William James said that every experience involves the neural mechanism. Professor Conklin from his Princeton and Woods Hole biological laboratories says, "More and more science is recognizing the unity of the entire organism; structure and function, body and mind, are parts of one living whole." Neglect of the body, then, is a neglect of an instrument of thought and feeling. The whole personality participates for better or worse in every physical or mental or emotional expression of the human being. Damage to the body cuts down the intellectual and emotional capacities. Deficiencies in the training of the physical senses short-circuit much of the beauty and glory of the world. Resiliency of the body brings resiliency of the mind. Generous energies make for the liberal spirit. Yet the college would miss its purpose in exalting the physical and athletic to the subordination of the intellectual and spiritual. Athletics should be a means on the way to something higher. Physical education, with its courses in physiology

and hygiene, its gymnasium, playing fields, intramural sports and the promotion of both indoor and outdoor volunteer play, would constitute the wholesome groundwork of both the general physical well-being and college sports. The varsity teams would then be the democratic and natural but the none-the-less crowned products of a community participation in athletics. The college would then work through the body, through sports and sportsmanship, hardihood, courage and fair play, to a higher human code, and to the imaginative release of the human spirit through sport into the building of a more beautiful personality.

(3) *Intellectual Content and Training:* With the recognition of the indispensable values of the body, the college of liberal arts can then justly and more successfully insist on that excellence in intellectual training which is one of its basic concerns. The body will be better equipped and more alert to respond to a trained mind. This basic need for trained minds recurringly raises the question as to what are the best subjects for intellectual discipline and excellence. This question takes us, as we have noticed, into the historical midst of the fifteenth and sixteenth century struggle as to the comparative intellectual and spiritual values of the sacred and secular learning and the seventeenth, eighteenth and nineteenth century battle of the classics and the sciences. It also takes us into the midst of the nineteenth century rivalry between the ancient and modern languages and between the elective system and required courses once considered essential for formal discipline. It finds us now in the very center of the twentieth century pull between the humanities, natural sciences and older social sciences, on one side, and the newer social sciences, on the other.

In these days, when we hear, on one side, that the liberal arts college in the university should be abolished and university work be made immediately professional and vocational or of senior college and graduate grade, and, on the other side, that the liberal arts education should be divorced not only from any specific connection with the professions and vocations but should include no subject that has any utilitarian value, it is well for us not to be dogmatic, but to try to keep our historical perspective and preserve our cultural balance. Well on in the nineteenth century we hear James Russell Lowell say that a university should be a place where nothing useful is taught and Ezra Cornell say that a university should be a place where any student could study anything he wanted to know. As we listen to the dead masters of the arts and sciences speaking on the subject of the content, distribution and values of the liberal courses, Francis Bacon, Milton, Goethe, Cardinal Newman, John Stuart Mill, Huxley, Charles W. Eliot, Gilman, Harper, James R. Angell, Benjamin Ide Wheeler, Charles R. Van Hise, David Starr Jordan and Edwin A. Alderman, or the living teachers, thinkers and experimenters in the field of a liberal education, we may dare to adapt their liberal view to modern developments and sum them up essentially in saying that a liberal education should include those matters every human being should know, as a human organism, as an intelligent citizen and as a spiritual personality, about himself, his body, his mind and his emotions; the race, its origin and historical development; the economic and political structure of society and its human implications; some languages, the essence of the great literatures, arts, philosophies and religions of mankind, with some limitations on the breadth of the distribution of courses and some provision for the depth of concentration in the field of a special interest. The physical and mathematical sciences, the biological sciences, the social sciences and the humanities constitute the main divisions in America's most daring and dramatic curricular adventure. Many American colleges are now working out the values of some such curriculum. It is important that we do not merely imitate. We can, as we tentatively explore the curriculum, keep our minds open to these welcome experiments out of which are to come values, we believe, for all our colleges and universities.

In the mastery of these liberal subjects, if reenforced by master teachers with laboratories, observatory, library, music hall, theater, studio, galleries, museum and the world of nature, will come limitless opportunities for mental discipline and student self-education in exactness in observation, relentless analysis, logical organization of materials and ideas, clear exposition, appreciation of truth, beauty and moral heroism, and practice in expressing in various art forms more beautifully what is deep in the mind and soul of youth.

(4) *The Campus:* Supplementing the classroom, the library and the laboratory is the campus. Sometimes, unfortunately, the campus and its activities supplant the classroom, the library and the laboratory. Sometimes they doubtless partly serve to make up for the lack of imaginative vitality and the opportunity to participate creatively in the learning process. These activities are vivid with personalities and the warm currents of youthful life, with opportunities of leadership and cooperation, and challenging with problems of freedom and self-government. The campus should not supplant or merely supplement, but can, with well-balanced activities and wise and sympathetic guidance, organically reenforce the purpose of the college to develop the whole human being, the integrated view and the creative life.

(5) *The Integrated View and Spiritual Values:* Above campus activities, curriculum and content, above intellectual power itself, is the spirit of culture, the integrated view, the understanding mind that sees in deep perspective and in wide relation. There is no magic in the liberal arts course to make the liberal mind. A student may master the words and syntax of a language and miss the majesty and beauty of the literature. He may work daily in the stacks and miss the decisive significance of the library as the reservoir of the race from which the streams of history gather momentum and direction. He may make an efficient routine of work in the laboratory and fail to realize that in quiet laboratories work the scholars who are blazing now the obscure trails which are to become the highways of the world's life. He may, with his microscope, identify the particles of an electron and miss the personality next to him in the laboratory. He may, with his telescope, get a sense of the sweep of the universe and may fail to develop the imaginative sympathy that senses for him the struggles and sweep of mankind through history. He may learn historical facts and miss the influence of the moral heroism of Socrates or a Wilson or the spiritual beauty of Saint Francis or a Florence Nightingale. He may discover or dig out facts and have no sense of humility or opportunity in the presence of the implications of the discovery of truth for mankind. The teacher's opportunity comes in the opportunity to help the student develop not only mental discipline, mastery of content, and intellectual excellence, but also an attitude of mind, an intelligent response to heroic situations and an appreciative assimilation into the core of his own character the nobility in the lives of those whom he meets in books and in life. The liberal education would give both depth and breadth to the mind and would embrace in its deepening processes of integration the spiritual values of human personality.

This integrated view includes within its

range not only the unity of the courses and groups of courses which constitute the content of the liberal arts and sciences, but also the unity of the race and more and more the unity of the universe. Departments of knowledge, despite elaborate separation, overlap and merge into other departments. Conklin says, for example, that psychology and education are branches of biology because they are all studies of living things. Then, for example, physics is geological, biological and chemical in nature. Astronomical and mathematical physics, with its seventeenth century universe of a fixed reference frame, and immutable laws of nature which God himself respected, carried over its influence and contributed to the political conception of a constitution of fundamental law and the inalienable rights of man which the king, himself, with his divine rights had to respect. The mechanical conception of the universe, reenforced by a mechanical civilization, went over into the preconception of a mechanically self-balancing economic system operating automatically according to immutable economic laws. There is the trace of this mechanical influence as a strand in the weaving of the classical economics of the nineteenth century, the behavioristic psychology of the twentieth century, and varying forms of the mechanistic philosophy in the last two centuries. Biology, with its theory of evolution, reenforced the preconceptions of a free competitive society and the philosophy of war. Thus we see from these fragmentary and often fugitive bits of influences the deep interrelation of physics, mathematics, biology, psychology, economic and political theories and a philosophy of life. The integrated view of the many strands and influences that go into the making of our lives and our philosophy that can come from the new curriculum of the college is essential not only to a student's better understanding of himself and the most acute problems of the modern age, but is essential also to a view of the universe.

We listen to a great American physicist as he traces the steps in the gradual integration of the six formerly rigorously separated branches of physics on the way to becoming one great whole. The professor of theoretical physics in the University of Berlin recently writes that the study of philosophy, once in scientific disrepute, is coming back with a new meaning and a wider power. Professor Planck points out that, as scientific research by its conquest of the world of sense "simplifies the world picture of physics, the structure of the physical world moves further and further away from the world of sense." What Professor Planck points out as the increasing simplification of the world picture becomes the basis for a more integrated view of the universe. We deeply need the values in the integrated view of the great philosophers. The scientist and philosopher are approaching a more respectful meeting in the presence of the mystery of life and the universe. Haldane moves from matter to mechanism to life to personality to spirituality. Personality, as an evolutionary achievement, reveals the spiritual quality of the materialistic process. From physics we go into metaphysics. Matter becomes energy, and energy brings us to the borderland of a universe, seen and unseen, the reverberations of whose moral sovereignty are in the inner man in answer to the intuitions and aspirations of the human spirit.

As in life, so in college subjects, ideas and processes can not be kept in separate departments. We should in college, if for no other reason than convenience, have departments of subjects but not compartments of knowledge. The very fluidity of ideas and the organic nature of life processes make it necessary that in our very respect for specialization and the value of departments we should from time to time reexamine the curriculum. Let us welcome the scores of experiments under way all over America and not adopt any of them by way of imitation but adapt what is good as we venture on our own account according to our own needs. In no other way than by the integrated view can we understand the wider implications of the specialized knowledge. Only with the whole view can we build up correlative social control of the new forces and mechanisms let loose upon the world by specialized knowledge with the power to destroy or rebuild the structure of the modern world.

These are the high stakes for which the college would play its part. Its conception of the unity of learning, the unity of life and the unity of the universe makes for a sense of the spiritual potentiality of the total personality. This integrated view makes for a sense of the spiritual essence of civilization, even in its gathered fragments transmitted more and more from age to age with the possibility of being transformed into the Kingdom of God according to the pattern of Him who was the master teacher of the inner way of the integrated life.

B. The Professional Schools

In the building of the civilization of the kingdom, we need not only the specialized knowledge and the integrated way of life but also specialized ways of making a living. The college is based on the idea of Jesus that man does not live by bread alone; but we must remember that the first petition in the Lord's Prayer is "Give us this day our daily bread." Youth to play a significant part in the world's life needs a specialized skill, a vocation, a profession. The vocational and professional schools came in America largely outside the universities on account of the gaps in the university structure. This specialized skill in law, medicine, pharmacy, agriculture, engineering, education, business, journalism and public administration and welfare was learned by the apprentice on the job. But as the professions and vocations became more complex, proprietary schools of law, medicine, pharmacy and business arose to meet a real life need. Schools of religion have a rightful place in the modern university. The school of religion at Duke University has high potential value to the whole South. In time the joint processes of the specialization and integration of knowledge in all the fields resulted in the incorporation of all professional schools and some high-grade vocational schools within the framework of the university.

The university needs the professional schools with their specialized knowledge, equipment and skill, their high standards of scholarship, their spirit of work, thoroughness and excellence. The professional schools, assimilated into the organic structure of the university, need the university with its wide variety of skills, interests and contacts, its general resources and wholeness of view. Consider the reciprocal contributions of Osler, Welch and Hopkins, the Pound group and Harvard, the Russell group and Columbia, Shailer Mathews and Chicago.

The professional schools, while raising the standards of specialized scholarship, need to be concerned more and more with the liberal cultural equipment of the master. The teacher in the professional school is in a strategic position to preserve and carry forward the liberal culture and the general view. He can bring to a focus on the most highly technical problem all the historical, economic, social, psychological, political or philosophic influences which converge upon it with implicating power. In the law schools there is the beginning of the recognition of the value of the liberal reenforcement of the most highly technical knowledge. For example, a professor who received his liberal arts training in a Southern university, his doctorate in economics in the Middle West, is teaching torts in the law school of an Eastern university. Another, who has the liberal arts degree, the doctorate of philosophy in economics and politics, and two law degrees, is, despite his youth, already a productive scholar and able teacher of law. A new professor of pharmacy in this university has a liberal training as the foundation of, and doctorate of philosophy on top of, his special scientific training. Without falsely making a fetish of degrees, this liberal training is basic to a wholesome attitude of mind in professional training. Some of the most scholarly and liberally cultured minds in America are in schools of engineering, commerce, agriculture and education. Many who have never seen a college have a spirit of the rarest culture distilled from nature, books and life. These men have been careful not to set method over against content or vocation over against liberal learning. With a view to the cultural and human implications of the most specialized knowledge, they find themselves in the midst of work and culture, surging life and the difficult, but at times thrilling, processes of rebuilding a world.

A teacher in an East Carolina city communicated the flame within his heart to women and to men who transformed communities, became teachers, superintendents of schools and presidents of several Southern colleges and universities. A permanently crippled but youthful ex-Confederate, no longer master of slaves but master of botany and chemistry, scientifically remade old plantations, built mills, endowed a college and became the source of hope to people over a wide area. A later youth trained culturally in the South and vocationally in the North brought back into the Southern Piedmont a kit of tools and a youthful dream for a venturesome part in refounding the structure of our Southern civilization. A young lawyer in a public religious meeting, standing up for freedom of scientific inquiry against the tides that rolled in upon him, stood unmoved in the tumult, steadfast in the strength of science, history, the humanities and the religion of Jesus which mustered to his almost lonely side. Many business men in these hard times are draining their reserves and are taking their losses standing up in order that people may have work and food. Editors, with courage for opprobrium and financial loss, have fought the fight of the inarticulate peoples and of despised minorities. Physicians daily minister to the bodies, minds and spirits of men. Rabbis, priests and preachers come out of lonely vigils to sustain the sympathies, courage and faith of men in cruel times. To farmers, lawyers, doctors, pharmacists, teachers, journalists, business men, scientific engineers, social engineers, statesmen and ministers of religion; to them with the depth of a specialized mastery and the breadth of an imaginative mind, there open opportunities as wide as the needs of the people.

(To be concluded)

DAVID STARR JORDAN

By MARVIN L. DARSIE

UNIVERSITY OF CALIFORNIA AT LOS ANGELES

THOSE who were privileged to know David Starr Jordan realize that in all respects he was gigantic; in his massive physical frame, his comprehensive reaching mind, his many-sided interest in life, and his influence upon men and affairs. Because he was gigantic, because he achieved greatly in many fields, it is impossible for one of ordinary stature to attempt an adequate evaluation of his life. I can only give my impressions of a man who for nearly twenty-five years I have been proud to call prophet and leader.

The keynote of his life may be found in the foreword to his wonderful autobiography, "The Days of a Man." "The record is objective—simply the story of what one man did and saw in the world about him, being always eager to know the Cosmos as it is, and never unduly distressed at his inability to 'remold it nearer to the heart's desire.' " This "eagerness to know the Cosmos as it is" dominated his life from early student days to the final hours among the great oaks of his beloved home on the Stanford campus.

He graduated from Cornell in 1872. The next seven years were passed in minor teaching appointments and incessant field study and research. Especially memorable was the summer spent with Agassiz, perhaps the greatest teacher America has known. It seems likely that the choice of his major field of research, ichthyology, as well as his philosophy of higher education based on independent research were due in large part to the contagious enthusiasm of the great Swiss naturalist.

Doctor Jordan's major career began with his appointment as Professor of Natural History at the University of Indiana in 1879. In the same year he spent several months as a member of the Federal Fish Commission, the first of a long series of scientific services to the nation. Shortly he began laying the foundations for his monumental work, "The Fishes of North and Middle America," a magnificent achievement not completed until 1900.

In 1885, at the age of thirty-four, he was invited to become president of the University of Indiana. With many misgivings he accepted the new responsibility. His heart had been set on research, and he had looked forward ultimately to a post with one of the great museums or research foundations, such as the Smithsonian Institute. It was one of the minor tragedies of his life that twenty-one years later the secretaryship of the Smithsonian was offered him, the invitation reaching his hands on the morning that Stanford University was partly demolished by the great earthquake of 1906. Again he felt that administrative responsibilities claimed his undivided loyalty and the offer was regretfully declined.

In accepting the presidency of Indiana, he resolved that however onerous might be the duties of the office, he would abandon neither teaching nor research. He was one of the few men to make such a vow and keep it. Throughout the long period of epoch making university administration, he taught and lectured regularly, and was almost continuously engaged in original investigation. The two fields do not easily harmonize, and he often told with a chuckle how he was compelled to abandon his resolution to know every Stanford freshman by name because "every time he remembered the name of a freshman, he forgot the name of a fish."

The last quarter of the nineteenth century saw emergence of the true American university from the traditional college of earlier days. The new type of institution was largely the result of the vigorous, constructive thought of five men, Eliot at Harvard, White at Cornell, Gilman at the Johns Hopkins, Angell at Michigan and Jordan at Indiana and Stanford. Of the five, Jordan was by no means least. He often quoted with relish Agassiz's statement that "Harvard was no university: it was only a respectable high school, teaching the dregs of knowledge." The true university he felt should be composed of a group of eager students working independently under the guidance of men who were themselves keen investigators. It must be constantly in touch with the living present and not greatly concerned with the shadowy past. Under his guidance and inspiration Indiana, and later, Stanford, became outstanding centers of research and constructive thought. He believed that the absolutely free elective system established by Eliot at Harvard did not sufficiently provide for the thorough mastery of a field of knowledge. To meet this need he set up a plan of major fields of study, wherein at the junior level, a student chose a major professor and thereafter mastered a field, working hand in hand with the scholar of his choice. This system in one form or another has since become general in the more advanced American institutions of higher learning. Dr. Jordan's notion of the ideal university is eloquently expressed in his own words.

> The university should be the great refuge hut on the ultimate boundaries of knowledge from which daily and weekly, adventurous bands set forth on voyages of discovery. As the shoreless sea of the unknown meets us on every side, the same house of refuge and supply will serve for a thousand different exploring parties moving out in every direction into the infinite ocean. After countless ages of education and scientific progress, the true university will still stand on the verge, its walls still washed by the same unending sea, the boundless ocean of possible human knowledge.

It is especially interesting to note that Dr. Jordan's entry into the field of world affairs was through the medium of his eminence in biological studies. In 1896 he was appointed by President Cleveland as head of a joint high commission of investigation of the fur seal problem in Bering Sea. Unchecked destruction of the herds by American, British, Russian and Japanese hunters was rapidly leading to the extermination of the whole species. The successful adjustment of the delicate and complex problems involved in this international issue seems to have established Dr. Jordan's profound faith in joint arbitration as a means of settling international disputes.

The Spanish-American war of 1898 led to the important series of studies dealing with the dysgenic effects of modern warfare. War does not result in the selection of the fittest. Rather are the best and bravest the first to fall, leaving the propagation of the race to cowards and physical weaklings. This thesis was reiterated during the Boer war, and throughout the tragic days leading to the major disaster of 1914. Dr. Jordan was often accused of being a "Pacifist," and came close to martyrdom during the hysteria of 1917. Actually, he stood throughout as a prophet of humanity, almost the one serene, gigantic figure in a time of world madness.

My first personal contact with Dr. Jordan was in 1911, when on the occasion of his return from his second visit to Japan, he talked of his experiences. He told of his cordial reception by young Japanese men who had been students at Stanford; of his visits to fish markets and conversations with fishermen; of his earnest talk with Viscount Shibusawa and his reception at the Imperial Court. I had long admired him as scientist and world leader. Now I was impressed both by his innate simplicity and his personal force. His bigness and a certain "shagginess" seemed to embody primordial energy. I realized how infinitely more potent are friendship and common intellectual interests than the most subtle diplomacy in building up international cordiality and good will.

Ten years later I was in his home at one of the Thursday evening gatherings which became a Stanford institution. The stormy days of the war were past. Dr. Jordan seemed to have become physically vaster—greyer—wholly patriarchal. During the evening he was asked what he thought to be the major contribution of the Anglo-Saxon race to civilization. His surprising answer was "the ideal of romantic love." I caught a glimpse for the first time of the tender, almost mystic element in his character so well known to his intimate friends, so hidden from the public at large. Later as I read "The Days of a Man" I realized that he was both a seer and a poet of rare insight and charm. In the early nineties he and Mrs. Jordan spent some time at Mazatlan. His response to the quiet beauty of those days is told with profound feeling in the verses entitled "Sinaloa."

I dream of gray rocks rising rough and sheer
Above the trembling azure of the sea;
Of long green lines of waves that listlessly
Break in slow foam, then slip away in fear—
Or hide themselves in rock pools, crystal clear.

Behind us lies the town in slumber deep,
And all unrestless—as to thee and me
Man and his strivings now had ceased to be,
Or by some spell were bound in endless sleep,
Leaving us only on enchanted ground,
Alone together, where there comes no sound
Save the slow pulse-throb of the tropic sea
In the white moonlight beating steadily.

Perchance, dear heart, it may be thou and I,
In some far azure of infinity,
Shall find together an enchanted shore
Where Life and Death and Time shall be no more,
Leaving Love only, and Eternity.
For Love shall last, though all else pass away,
The harsh taskmaster that we call Today,
Till each concession Time from Life has wrung
Like outworn garments from the Soul be flung,
And it shall stand with back no longer bent,
Slave to the lash of its environment!
Then this great earth we know shall shrink at last
To some bare Isla Blanca of the past—
A rock unnoted in the boundless sea
Whose solemn pulse-beat marks Eternity.

The last time I saw Dr. Jordan was some five years later. I was attending a football game in the Stanford Bowl. As he came unobtrusively through one of the lower tunnels, those near him spontaneously rose to their feet. Presently a wave of rising figures swept the stadium, thousands standing in silent respect till the grand old warrior for humanity was in his seat. The years had set their seal upon him, but his head was erect and his gaze still outward.

As the shadows closed about him in the final peaceful years at Stanford, Dr. Jordan realized what few men are privileged to experience: the certainty that his spirit was already among the cloud of witnesses impelling the eager young to new conquests; the assurance that his achievements were imperishably woven into the rich fabric of our civilization.

The final call came as he had foreseen it would in the exquisite epitaph to himself written nearly thirty years earlier.

A darkening sky and a whitening sea,
    And the wind in the palm trees tall;
Soon or late comes a call for me,
Down from the mountains or up from the sea,
    Then let me lie where I fall.

And a friend may write—for friends there be,
    On a stone from the gray sea wall,
"Jungle and town and reef and sea—
I loved God's Earth and His Earth loved me,
    Taken for all in all."

EDUCATIONAL EVENTS

RIOTS OF CHINESE STUDENTS

ACCORDING to dispatches to the New York *Times,* about 30,000 students at Shanghai on December 9 tied up the municipal administration, caused the dismissal of Chen Chi-tsang, chief of police; disarmed policemen and troops; smashed the Kuomintang party headquarters, and interfered with railroad service. Five thousand of the students, forming fifteen groups, overcame the armed guards of the municipal headquarters building. Then, in complete control, they presented a series of demands to General Chang Chun, mayor of the Chinese city section of Shanghai. The mayor yielded to their demand that the chief of police be dismissed for "failure to maintain order," and he also agreed to order the arrest of Pao Teh-chuang, a leader of the Kuomintang party.

The Nanking Minister of Education issued instructions to the presidents of all schools urging them to restrain students from flocking to Nanking and to make efforts to prevent the agitation. He advised the distribution of copies of General Chiang Kai-shek's statement denying the creation of a neutral zone in the Chinchow region or that direct negotiations with Japan were proceeding. When railroad authorities refused to grant students free train rides to Nanking, a party of three hundred started walking toward the national capital along the railway tracks. But they got only five miles from Shanghai.

Rowdy scenes continued in Nanking, where the authorities showed the utmost leniency and forbearance in order to avoid serious incidents. The Foreign Office was deserted. Roving bands of students caught the guards unawares and stoned the building, breaking windows. Most of the business of the government was conducted in secluded parts of the city.

Then, after three days of student demonstrations, the Nanking State Council replied on December 11 with an ultimatum flatly rejecting all students demands. The council refused to permit interference in foreign affairs and refuses to supply arms and ammunition, which the students had demanded in order that they might proceed to the front.

In handing its reply to a student leader the State Council defied the threat of the youths to continue their strike, but at present there is no trouble owing to a diminution in the original firebrand enthusiasm. The capital, however, continues overrun by more than 50,000 students, several thousand having arrived from Peiping and Tientsin to demand an interview with General Chiang Kai-shek, which was refused.

Railway service is functioning normally after three days of interruptions, and the situation is quieter in Shanghai. The students have been temporarily appeased by the Nanking Government ordering General Chen Ming-chu, the garrison commander, to investigate the recent disturbance which was followed by the allegedly illegal arrest of a Peiping student.

Both the National Government and students have requested General Chang Chun, Mayor of Shanghai, to continue in office instead of resigning. The Kuomintang party's anger against the student unruliness is manifested in a strong statement denouncing the students' activities and their attempts to "browbeat" Kuomintang officials.

This statement follows the raiding of the Shanghai Kuomintang headquarters and reports to the effect that students have also raided the Hangchow Kuomintang headquarters, wrecking the building. The students continued their strike, but the demonstrations were milder.

HEALTH OF THE ENGLISH SCHOOL CHILD

IN his annual report on the health of the school child, as summarized in the *Journal* of the American Medical Association, Sir George H. Newman, principal medical officer to the ministry of health, says that school medical officers should conceive the primary object of medical inspection to be the answer to the question "Is this child developing according to the plan which nature has mapped out for him?" This is a difficult question, for it does not depend on averages of height, weight, alertness or mental attainment, but on an estimate of the whole individual, who may be naturally short or tall, fat or lean, lethargic or alert, bright or stupid, and never intended by nature to be otherwise. What has to be determined is not whether he is below the average in any respect but whether he is below the standard which nature has set for him. To answer this, the medical officer must be able to vizualize each child in a state of normal health and to estimate in what respect he falls short. The defect most frequently encountered in medical examination is related to vision; next come enlarged tonsils and adenoids, skin diseases and malnutrition. Only one per cent. of the children now suffer from malnutrition. A great improvement has taken place. The better dress of the children is both a cause and an effect. No self-respecting school girl would now accept an accusation of uncleanliness without shame. There has been a revolution in cleanliness and dress, which has been conducive to health. The improvement in nutrition has been brought about partly by supplementary school feeding and partly by general care of the child at home and at school. When the school medical service began in 1907 there was approximately 10 per cent. of malnutrition in the London schools. During 1930 in London, excluding special schools, 4,760,004 milk meals and 776,192 cod-liver-oil meals were given on the advice of physicians, the cost being recovered from the parents in non-necessitous cases.

The introduction of the open-air school for debilitated children has been of great service but more sunlight and open air are required for every child, sick or well. The principles of the open air school must be applied to the normal child. Progress in this respect is shown by the fact that 80 per cent. of the building plans submitted to the board of education include proposals for throwing open to the outside air whole portions of class rooms and for admission of more sunlight than was formerly deemed necessary.

SCHOOL SAVINGS

THE annual national report on school savings banking issued by the Savings Division of the American Bankers Association, says: "School savings during the year closing on June 30, 1931, had its greatest test and demonstrated its possible service." W. Espey Albig, deputy manager of the association in charge of the division, writes further: "In 14,628 schools throughout the country 4,482,634 children deposited $26,783,610. Eighteen more schools have school savings than last year, the number of children utilizing school savings is 115,097 smaller and money deposited less by $2,329,453."

Mr. Albig points out that these figures show that the number of schools, as compared with last year, where savings may be deposited by children and they may have instruction in the meaning and use of money, has increased, while the number of pupils depositing decreased by only .025 per cent. and deposits by only 8 per cent., despite wide-spread unemployment. He continues:

That for two years school savings have faced adverse conditions and yet continue to enlist interest and enter new territory evidences the soundness of the idea of giving children a working knowledge of what money is, the part it plays in everyday life and the machinery by which it is conserved and utilized in the best manner for the good of the child or the family.

During the past two years the utilitarian value of school savings has been appreciated, bringing out that during the school year 1928–1929, 37 per cent. of the money deposited remained as a balance at the end of the year, a year later the balances decreased to 26 per cent., while the past year showed a balance of $2,342,888, or 9 per cent. of the amount deposited during the year.

During the past two years casual withdrawals have been supplemented with increasing frequency by withdrawals to afford succor to families whose income has been reduced or else rendered negligible. Pupils of districts which, since the inauguration of school savings, have increased bank balances year after year are now withdrawing not only the deposits made this year, but also a part of those made in previous years.

Despite the pessimistic atmosphere which settled like a cloud over this country, deposits per pupil averaged only 5.7 per cent. below that of the preceding year. The withdrawals of five and a quarter million dollars more than last year, mostly by pupils who were in attendance both years, marks the extent to which school savings came to supplement the family earnings.

EDUCATIONAL NEEDS OF THE YOUTHFUL UNEMPLOYED

DR. FRANK P. GRAVES, New York State Commissioner of Education, has issued the following statement to superintendents of schools:

Despite the fact that the public schools of the state have to-day the largest enrolment in their history, there are many thousands of youths who are neither employed nor attending school. This is not as it should be. For the most part their efforts to secure work are certain to be fruitless and they are wasting time which might better be spent in preparing themselves for future social, civic and economic responsibilities. Moreover, at a time like this such jobs as are available should be given to heads of families and to those who have dependents. For these reasons I am urging the local school authorities to do everything possible to secure the return to school of young people who have not attained their majority.

That this recommended attendance may be productive of the greatest amount of good, both to individuals and to society in general, I suggest that care be taken to meet the real educational needs of those we are seeking to serve. This may be accomplished through wise guidance and suitable training. Each boy and girl who seeks to return to school should have the counsel and advice of the strongest and most experienced teachers in the school system to the end that pupil interests, powers and capacities may be properly evaluated and a rational educational program planned in each case. I regard the guidance phase of this proposed endeavor as being of the highest importance.

Many of these youths will require special training. The regular curriculum may not include the kind of courses which will best meet their needs. It may be necessary to organize special academic, commercial, industrial, homemaking or other classes. Our schools have strong teaching staffs and excellent facilities. All our educational resources should be put to use in this work.

Your local employers at some future time will be calling for the services of members of this group. The schools can then aid effectively in placement. In some communities this can be done in cooperation with existing agencies, in others the teachers must perform the function. If our work in guidance and training has been well done, placement should be easy. The return of general prosperity will find our young people better equipped to take up their duties.

It is to be hoped that all civic, social and economic agencies in the state will assist the school authorities in whatever endeavors may be made to bring back to school those boys and girls who are now idle and whose potentialities for future usefulness can be greatly increased by more education and training.

THE NEW BUILDING OF THE TEACHERS COLLEGE AT THE UNIVERSITY OF CINCINNATI

THE University of Cincinnati is engaged in a building program covering several years, in the course of which approximately five million dollars, provided by municipal bond issues and private sources, will be spent for improvements and additions to the university plant. The most recent building to be completed is that of the Teachers College, funds for which were secured by a bond issue voted in 1927. On Sunday, October 25, a memorial vesper service signalized the opening of this new structure.

In keeping with a campus plan worked out under the direction of President Herman Schneider, the Teachers College building is constructed in Georgian style, and is located between the administration building and the new university library. It comprises five stories, and houses all of the units of work for which the college is responsible.

Four major divisions comprise a memorial given by the friends of Miss Annie Laws (1855–1927), a prominent Cincinnati educator, to perpetuate her memory. The first of these is a beautiful assembly room in eighteenth century style, seating four hundred and fifty persons. Two units of the memorial are planned primarily for the training of teachers of little children. The physical activities room houses training in plays, rhythms, dramatic games and festivals. Adjoining this is the manual activities room, a workshop center for training in industrial, applied and fine arts work. Completing the memorial is an exceptionally beautiful reception room furnished in the style of the late colonial period. This room and an adjoining dining room provide for social events under the auspices of the college and its student organizations.

The administrative offices provide quarters for the dean and five directors, of graduate, undergraduate, extension, student teaching and placement divisions, respectively. Separate suites of ten offices each for men and women faculty members are supplemented by faculty rest rooms. Laboratory facilities are provided for educational psychology, including the comparative psychology of learning, for clinical work in psychology and school subjects, and for public-school art, public-school music and school administration, in addition to the facilities for the training of teachers of young children. Other features include a faculty room, a study room for students and two seminar rooms, in addition to nineteen classrooms of various sizes, and provisions for lockers for one thousand students.

The university library (opened in 1930), which immediately adjoins the Teachers College building, includes a special graduate education reading room, with desk space for seventy-two students, and a special librarian in charge. It also includes stack cubicles for research workers and an education seminar room, in addition to the services of reference librarians, periodical and general reserve rooms, and the general reading rooms, which are available to the entire university. No practice teaching is done in the Teachers College building. Practice teaching centers are maintained in public schools throughout Cincinnati and in suburban towns. Two near-by elementary schools are designated as special observation and experimental schools for the use of the Teachers College.

For the present semester the Teachers College has a registration on the campus of 1,088 students, including 388 graduate students and 376 teachers in service. Away from the campus there is an extension registration for the semester of 1,036. Registration in the Teachers College for the summer session of 1931 numbered 1,603 students. Two hundred thirty-eight degrees were granted by the Teachers College in June, 1931, the largest number for any college or group of colleges within the University of Cincinnati. Dr. L. A. Pechstein is now serving his tenth year as dean of the college.

SELF-SUPPORTING STUDENTS AT THE UNIVERSITY OF WISCONSIN

EARNING as well as studying their way to a university degree, nearly three fifths, or 59 per cent., of all students attending the University of Wisconsin this semester are either wholly or partially self-supporting, according to figures released recently by Miss Annie B. Kirch, University statistician.

Based on replies to a question asked when the students registered in September, the figures show the degree of self-support of students at the present time by college, school, rank and sex. That the figures present a true estimate of the number of students who are earning part or all their expenses is indicated by the fact that of the total number enrolled, 8,765, only 876 or slightly less than 10 per cent. failed to indicate the degree of their self-support.

The figures show that a total of 1,810 students, or 23 per cent. of the entire student body, are wholly self-supporting; that 1,138 students, or 14 per cent., are more than half self-supporting; while 1,713 students, or 22 per cent., are less than half self-supporting.

A total of 3,228 students, or 41 per cent. of the entire student body, do not earn any part of their living. Of this total, 1,798 are women and 1,430 are men.

Exactly 64 per cent. of the 2,818 women are not self-supporting, while these figures are reversed for the men, only 28 per cent. of whom are not earning any part of their living. On the other hand, 3,641 or 72 per cent. of the total of 5,071 men are either wholly or partially self-supporting, while only 1,020 or 36 per cent. of the total number of women are earning either part or all their living.

Of the number of those entirely self-supporting, 418 were women while 1,392 were men; of those over half self-supporting, 228 were women while 910 were men, and of those less than half self-supporting, 374 were women, while 1,339 were men.

While first-year men outnumbered the men in all other classes who are wholly or partially supporting themselves, the first year women were able to gain less support for themselves than the more experienced sophomore, junior, or senior class members. 186 first year women either entirely or partly supported themselves during their first year, while 721 first year men were either entirely self-supporting, or partly so.

TENURE OF OFFICE AT GOUCHER COLLEGE

ACCORDING to a statement made by President David A. Robertson, Goucher College Trustees, at their meeting held in Baltimore, December 7, 1931, made Goucher College an example of the best modern practice in regard to tenure of office of members of the faculty and organization of the college faculty.

The Board of Trustees revised its by-laws so that they now include provision for cooperation of the departments with the president in selection of members of the teaching staff. Teachers hereafter will receive, before March 1, letters of reappointment or non-appointment covering salary, rank and period of appointment. After three years of service a teacher's term of appointment becomes indeterminate, that is to say, with the presumption of permanency. Hereafter, there will be a Committee on Dismissals elected by the members of the faculty themselves. Any teacher whose dismissal is under consideration will have the right to a hearing before this committee and the president. The report of this committee and that of the president, if it be at variance with that of the committee, will be considered by the Board of Trustees before final action is taken.

The foregoing recommendations were made after a year of study. The Board of Trustees unanimously adopted the recommendations of the faculty, gratified by the cooperation of members of the faculty and confident of an even greater amount of good will through the formulation of the foregoing procedure.

Hitherto, in Goucher College only those of full professorial rank and such others as were designated by the president had the right to vote on educational policy. Hereafter, all members of the instructional staff of the rank of professor, associate professor, assistant professor and instructor will be members of the faculty. Instructors who have served less than three years in Goucher College will not have the right to vote. In addition to the general faculty thus set up, there will be a president's council made up of the president, the dean, and additional administrative officers designated by the president not to exceed three, and nine members of the teaching staff, of whom three may be elected by the college faculty. Those members elected by the faculty will serve for three years, one being elected each year. The president will appoint his members yearly.

CELEBRATIONS IN HONOR OF PRESIDENT NICHOLAS MURRAY BUTLER

IT is stated in the *Columbia Alumni News* that preparations by the Alumni Federation of Columbia University to honor President Nicholas Murray Butler during the coming few months, are rapidly nearing completion. President Butler is this year observing three anniversaries, his fiftieth anniversary of graduation, his thirtieth anniversary as president and his seventieth birthday. The federation's plans include:

(1) A huge Butler dinner on Alumni Day as part of the annual "Round the World Columbia Night" program. The largest hotel ballroom in New York has been reserved to accommodate up to two thousand Alumni. William Fellowes Morgan, '80, '84-Mines, one of the earliest alumni trustees of Columbia, has accepted appointment as chairman and toastmaster and two of the three speakers will be Chief Judge Benjamin N. Cardozo, '89, '91A.M., '92L., '15Hon., of the Court of Appeals, and John Erskine, '00, '01A.M., '03Ph.D., '29Hon.

(2) Alumni hope ways can be devised and, if necessary, statutes amended so that Columbia for the first time can confer a supreme honorary degree on President Butler, who holds no Columbia honorary degrees, although he has them from more than a score of other universities in America and foreign countries.

(3) Alumni are almost unanimous in feeling that the new library on South Field, generously given to Columbia this year by Edward S. Harkness, '28Hon., should be named the "Nicholas Murray Butler Library."

(4) Alumni feel that the Columbia Alumni Fund could this year be a method whereby Columbia men could show their appreciation. It is suggested the fund this year be known as the "Butler Fund" and that the proceeds go to President Butler for whatever university uses he decides are the most suitable.

(5) Alumni feel that the proposed federation nine-day cruise to Nova Scotia, Newfoundland and Labrador on a chartered trans-Atlantic liner next August should appropriately be called "The Butler Cruise." Tentative plans call for having President Butler on board so that he, along with several internationally known Columbia professors, could be the leader of afternoon round-table discussions on current events.

EDUCATIONAL NOTES AND NEWS

THE Nobel peace prize was awarded at Oslo on December 10 to Dr. Nicholas Murray Butler, president of Columbia University, and Miss Jane Addams. Neither Dr. Butler nor Miss Addams was present, Mr. Hoffman Phillips, American minister to Norway, representing them at the ceremony. Three German scientific men received on the same day at Stockholm the 1931 Nobel prizes in chemistry and medicine. The chemistry award was divided between Dr. Carl Bosch and Dr. Friedrich Bergius for their work in chemical industry. Professor Otto Warburg received the prize in medicine for his studies in respiration. The 1931 prize in literature was posthumously awarded to the late poet and secretary of the Swedish Academy, Erik Axel Karlfeldt. The poet's widow and three small children were present at the ceremony.

DR. ROBERT C. CLOTHIER, dean of men at the University of Pittsburgh, was elected president of the Rutgers University at a meeting of the board of trustees on December 15.

FOR reasons of health Dr. Vernon Kellogg has resigned the permanent secretaryship of the National Research Council and has been elected secretary emeritus. During the war, Dr. Kellogg served as a leading member of President

Hoover's staff in Belgium and at home. For more than 25 years prior to the war he was professor of entomology at Stanford University. He is the author of numerous books on biology and other subjects. Under his administration, the National Research Council, which is a part of the National Academy of Sciences, with offices in the beautiful building opposite Lincoln Memorial in Washington, has served to coordinate and encourage research in various science fields, and the system of National Research Fellowships was inaugurated.

ROBERT FROST, professor of English at Amherst College, New England poet and twice winner of the Pulitzer prize for poetry, has won the first $1,000 award of the National Institute of Arts and Letters.

IT is announced by the principal of the University of London that as the result of a consensus of opinion among representative graduates of the university the Earl of Athlone has consented to be nominated as chancellor.

AT the convocation of the University of Oxford on November 23, the vice-chancellor, the master of Pembroke, presiding, the honorary degree of D.Litt. was conferred on Professor Graham Wallas and on Mr. W. W. Vaughan, lately head master of Rugby. On December 1 the degree was conferred on Professor Paul Fournier, of the University of Paris.

A TESTIMONIAL dinner was given on December 12 to Dr. R. B. von KleinSmid, president of the University of Southern California, marking his tenth anniversary as president of the university.

THE fiftieth annual dinner meeting of the New York Association of the Alumni of the Phillips Exeter Academy was held on December 10 in honor of Dr. Lewis Perry, principal of the academy for the last seventeen years.

THE Atlanta Public School Teachers Association recently gave a dinner in honor of Mr. W. W. Gaines, retiring president of the Board of Education.

MR. HOWARD L. RAWDON, who has been superintendent of the Oberlin public schools for over twenty-five years, was elected vice-president of the Northeastern Ohio Teachers Association at its recent meeting in Cleveland.

SUPERINTENDENT H. O. SAXVIK, of Bismarck, has been elected president of the North Dakota Education Association for the ensuing year. Mr. Saxvik was recently presented with life membership in the National Education Association by the teachers of his staff.

MR. H. P. HARDING, superintendent of Charlotte city schools, was elected chairman of the South Piedmont district of the North Carolina Education Association on October 31. Mr. Harding was the first president of the organization and was reelected over his protest.

DR. EDWARD KENNARD RAND, professor of Latin at Harvard University since 1908, has been elected to the Pope professorship of Latin to succeed the late Clifford Herschel Moore. Mr. Thomas Stearns Eliot will be the first American to hold the Charles Eliot Norton professorship of poetry.

MR. FRANCIS N. BALCH has been appointed associate professor of business law at the Harvard Graduate School of Business Administration.

MRS. IRENE TAYLOR HEINEMAN has been appointed assistant state superintendent of public instruction for California with headquarters in Los Angeles.

MR. OLE R. SANDE, of Moorhead Teachers College, has been appointed assistant director of the rural education division of the Minnesota State Department of Education.

PROFESSOR FRED ENGELHARDT, of the University of Minnesota, has been selected as one of the members of the staff engaged to conduct a comprehensive survey of the public schools of Chicago. His work will be in connection with the study of school buildings and the business administration of the school system.

PROFESSOR JESSE S. REEVES, University of Michigan, has been elected to membership in the American Institute of International Law. Professor Reeves, who is the William W. Cook professor of American Institutions in the university, takes the place of Mr. Robert Lansing among the members of the institute from the United States.

Dr. Sidney L. Pressey, professor of educational psychology at the Ohio State University, has received a grant from the National Research Council for a study of emotional attitudes and interests among certain tribes of American Indians.

Dr. E. N. Farriss, of Cornell University, is making a survey of school types for the National Education Association.

Mr. John S. Galbraith, assistant professor of Greek and Latin at Williams College, will be on leave of absence during the second semester of the current academic year.

An appreciation of the late Charles F. D. Belden, for fourteen years director of the Boston Public Library, was published in the October issue of *More Books*, a monthly bulletin issued by the trustees of the library.

Professor Carveth Read, professor emeritus of philosophy and comparative psychology at the University of London, died on December 8 at the age of eighty-three years.

By the will of the late Edward Bement, of New York City, Yale University is bequeathed $50,000 for the university library and $5,000 for the alumni fund and $5,000, the income to be used for the annual award of three prizes to be known as the Montaigne prizes.

By the will of W. K. Bixby, of St. Louis, who died on October 29, the City Art Museum, St. Louis, receives $80,000 and art works valued at $60,000. Mr. Bixby also left to the Artists Guild of St. Louis $1,500 for its building fund, $2,000 for endowment and $3,000 for prizes.

The Bennett School of Liberal and Applied Arts, Milbrook, New York, will benefit from the estate of the late Baron W. Gage, by the forgiveness of a $212,405 debt.

Phi Beta Kappa, the college honor society founded in 1776 at the College of William and Mary in Virginia and now having chapters in one hundred and twenty-six American colleges and a living membership of over 63,000, announces the appearance in January, 1932, of a new quarterly, *The American Scholar*. This periodical is designed not only for members of Phi Beta Kappa but for all who have general intellectual interests. The editor is William Allison Shimer, Ph.D., formerly a professor of philosophy at the Ohio State University, the consulting editor is Clark Sutherland Northup, professor of English at Cornell University, and the editorial board consists of Ada Louise Comstock, John Erskine, John Huston Finley, Christian Gauss, Will David Howe, Adam Leroy Jones, William Allan Neilson, Harry Allen Overstreet, J. Herman Randall, Jr., and Frederick J. E. Woodbridge. The first number will contain articles by Frank Aydelotte, John W. Davis, John Erskine, John Finley, Dorothy Canfield Fisher and Owen D. Young, and a poem by Odell Shepard.

President A. Lawrence Lowell, of Harvard University, has notified President Albert Britt, of Knox College, that because of the death during the summer of Dean Moore, chairman of the Harvard Exchange Committee, and also because of the temporary demand on the Harvard faculty for men to fill the residence and tutorial positions created by the new house plan, it will not be possible to send out any exchange professors during the present academic year. The Harvard Exchange was established in 1911. In that year Harvard sent a professor to five colleges of the Middle West—Knox, Beloit, Carleton, Colorado and Grinnell. In return each of the five was entitled to send one of its instructors to Harvard for half a year. Pomona College was added to the list of colleges in 1920 and since then every year two Harvard professors have visited three colleges each, spending four weeks at each college and offering courses for which credit is given.

Final results of the election of American Rhodes Scholars were announced on December 13 by Dr. Frank Aydelotte, president of Swarthmore College, American secretary to the Rhodes Trustees. Complete returns show 32 scholars elected of whom four were students at Harvard University, and 2 were graduate students at the same institution. There were two students of the University of Michigan and two of the United States Military Academy. No other college or university had more than one. There were 584 candidates for 32 appointments throughout the country. This is the largest competition in the history of the Rhodes Scholarships. This year's election is the second to be held under the new plan, by which the country is divided into 8 districts of six states each. There is a competition in every state every year. Each state selects two candidates to appear before the district committee and from the twelve men so nominated, each district committee selects four to represent their states at Oxford.

THE Germanistic Society of America is again offering a fellowship of the value of $1,500 for American students who contemplate studying some phase of German civilization at a German university. This fellowship is administered by the Institute of International Education under the auspices of its American German Student Exchange. It is open to both men and women who at the time of making application have pursued advanced studies in one or more of the following aspects of German civilization: architecture, art, history and government, literature and language, and philosophy. Applications must be filed at the Institute of International Education on or before January 15. The usual German fellowships are available under the auspices of the American German Student Exchange. These fellowships are open to seniors as well as to graduate students. The closing date for the filing of applications is also January 15.

AT a recent meeting of the Education Committee of the London County Council the committee accepted the offer of the court of the University of London to forego certain maintenance grants and to postpone claims to certain capital grants from the council in the financial years 1931–32 and 1932–33. The sub-committee also reported that the governing bodies of technical institutions aided by the council had submitted revised estimates of income and expenditure for the session 1931–32. Consequently the sub-committee recommended reductions in the council's maintenance and equipment grants for the current session. These reductions would bring the grants to within the amounts provided in the revised estimates. The savings amounted to £39,549 for the financial year and £51,865 for the session. Of these amounts £23,410 and £31,152, respectively, represented the reduction in teachers' salaries. The general purposes sub-committee recommended that the estimates of expenditure for 1931–32 be further reduced from £12,252,850 (as revised) to £11,812,130. This revision, it stated, was due to the 10 per cent. reduction in teachers' salaries, the offer of the University of London, and reductions in other votes. Mrs. E. M. Lowe, a member of the council, said that the Labor members could not view with approval the tremendous reduction which had been made in the education services of the council.

A REPORT to the London County Council Education Committee states that the number of children attending school was 685,004, a decrease of 32,913 over the number for 1929. In 1915 there were 898,439 children. It is estimated that 15,000 of the decrease during the last two years is due to the falling birth-rate and 18,000 to migration outside the area. Greenwich is the only district that shows an increase. This is due to the new housing estates at Downham and Charlton Park. The heaviest falls in child population have occurred in Wandsworth, Camberwell, Southwark, Poplar, the City and Stepney, and Chelsea; 98.9 per cent. of the children of compulsory school age (those over five) are under instruction. Only 830 children in London were certified as "ineducable"; 43.3 per cent. of the children between three and five years of age were being sent to school.

A LIBRARY of British Empire films has been formed by the Empire Marketing Board and the first catalogue, containing the names of over 130 films, has been issued. Schools in all parts of the country are now receiving regularly short films of life and work oversea. These have been catalogued under countries, and practically every school in the United Kingdom will receive a catalogue. Mr. John Grierson, the board's film officer, recently visited Canada and brought back much material from the Canadian Government Motion Picture Bureau. There is now a particularly good selection of Canadian films, ranging from pictures of production—the felling of lumber, harvesting of apples and catching of salmon—to fighting forest fires with seaplanes, camping in the Rockies and other aspects of life in the Empire. Films of how people live and how the Empire's food is raised in other Dominions and in several of the Colonies are included in the catalogue. Over 2,000,000 people, of whom about half were schoolchildren, have now attended the Imperial Institute cinema at Kensington, where the Empire Marketing Board films are shown continuously. One of these pictures is described as a "dramatized lesson in economic history," and shows, in a series of swift, vivid flashes, the development of the North American prairies. Another is a one-reel version of *Drifters,* a film epic of the North Sea.

DISCUSSION

THE NATIONAL EDUCATION ASSOCIATION AND THE EIGHTEENTH AMENDMENT

HENRY HARAP in SCHOOL AND SOCIETY for December 5, page 758, has a short statement in which he clearly implies that Superintendent Kealey, of Hoboken, did not have a chance to be heard at Detroit. This is hardly fair to President Norman R. Crozier who presided over that meeting and who insisted on a full hearing in spite of the fact that Mr. Kealey in his point of view does not represent one per cent. of the profession, and the additional fact that he had distributed his material widely to the newspapers before presenting it to the resolutions committee. Mr. Harap mentions a few organizations which seem to favor repeal. Are these not organizations that have always been wet? Does he not forget that the following great groups which deal with human life in its normal course are unwavering in their support of the Eighteenth Amendment?

The Homes, as represented by such groups as The National Congress of Parents and Teachers; The General Federation of Women's Clubs; The Women's Christian Temperance Union.
The Schools, as represented by such groups as the Representative Assembly of the National Education Association; the Department of Superintendence; the Department of Elementary School Principals; Various State Associations.
The Churches.
The Leaders of Organized Business and Industry.
Agriculture, as represented by such groups as The Grange.

Does not America have enough confusion now without creating more? Does it not have a right to expect that its teachers, who have a better opportunity to observe the entire population than any one else, would be a stabilizing force? Can our educational leaders maintain their professional leadership if they abdicate their civic leadership? Will not our effort to be scientific in education discredit itself if in the pursuit of the petty accuracies we overlook that larger science which is inherent in the experience and common sense of ordinary people? In his admirable book, "A Sociological Philosophy of Education," Dr. Ross Finney points out that:

> When numerous new and difficult social problems are to be solved is just the time when disintegration of the moral ideals is most dangerous. . . . The more profoundly one studies economic theory the more clearly he sees that morality is one of the two ultimate determinants of the production, distribution, and consumption of wealth. The other is intelligence. . . . A laboring man or a laboring class can never be very productive without certain old-fashioned virtues.

I have been a close student of the Eighteenth Amendment for a number of years and it is my best judgment that under the new director of prohibition, Colonel Amos W. W. Woodcock, there has been more progress during the last year than in all the years before. This is a good time to keep the ship steady.

JOY ELMER MORGAN, *Editor*
OFFICE OF THE JOURNAL OF THE NATIONAL EDUCATION ASSOCIATION

BONUSES FOR PETS

THE announcement in SCHOOL AND SOCIETY for October 24, 1931, of a new plan for salary increases at Wesleyan University suggests certain objections which are of a hypothetical nature, inasmuch as the writer is a stranger to Wesleyan and has never suffered from administrative discrimination.

Normally it is the president who determines the worth of a professor's services, at least in his own mind. His personal opinions have but little effect under a system in which permanence in tenure prevails and where there is a fixed schedule by which salaries are determined. But the Wesleyan plan apparently makes tenure impermanent and, in one way or another, places upon the shoulders of the president the duty of rewarding professors for "superiority in teaching, influence on undergraduates, eminence as a scholar, intellectual growth and service to the college and the community." This is a weight of responsibility which any thoughtful president should hesitate to bear.

In the first place, if due diligence and common sense be used in the choosing of professors, there is but little danger of much incompetence among the members of a university faculty. Consequently, the selection of a few for financial reward is likely to cause bitterness and discouragement among the individuals not recognized.

Furthermore, many extraneous circumstances may be accepted, consciously or unconsciously, as qualifying a professor under the terms of reward noted above. In brief, the president's likes and dislikes will enter into the choosing.

Some presidents appreciate a man who stands up for his own convictions, and some do not—especially if such convictions run counter to those held by a rather pompous executive. Some gentlemen prefer sycophants. A president may reward social qualities possessed by the professor or his wife; or he may not. A professor, popular among his students, may or may not be deemed superior. A professor who "stands in" with the trustees is almost sure to please the president. A man's personality may pass for excellence with one president, and not with another. Membership in the proper fraternal or religious group may sway the executive. Publication of books, which no one reads, may pass as scholarship. The acquisition of a doctorate may qualify a professor on the basis of intellectual growth, when the only elements involved in obtaining the degree may have been nerve and ability to clip and copy. Surely a professor who can arrange for a call to another institution at increased pay would be selected as an eminent person, and would be temporarily rewarded by a bonus. Service to the community might include purging a city ward of dirty politics; and obviously it might not. It might inconvenience the college administration! In which event a disservice would have been rendered to the college.

By and large, it appears that such a plan as that in force at Wesleyan is intended to force or allow the president to get rid of the professors whom he dislikes by neglecting them. With the use of sufficient discrimination, this should allow any administration to build up a loyal following in the upper ranks of the staff. And the next administration can begin all over again, exchanging old favorites for new. Thus, in time, the tables will turn against the favored few; and they may tarry along on the faculty—neglected—or retire.

Permanence of tenure and a rigid salary schedule are the only safeguards of instructors who are paid so little as to make it impossible for them, even during the years of relative plenty, to save up a competency for their later years. Executives enjoy no tenure; but they receive considerable financial compensation for the lack of it. The inconsiderable addition to the salaries of the fortunate ones at Wesleyan will eventually prove to be no satisfactory offset to the loss of tenure and a rigid salary schedule. The plan plays into the hands of the dictator whom it establishes on the university throne.

Charles Roger Hicks
University of Nevada

REPORTS

THE ORIGIN AND WORK OF THE EDUCATIONAL RECORDS BUREAU

The Educational Records Bureau was recently incorporated and chartered by the Regents of New York State as a non-profit-making service and research agency for schools and colleges. The board of directors includes three representatives of each of three school groups, namely, the colleges, the independent schools and the public high schools. The personnel of the board at present includes the following: Professor W. W. Charters, of Ohio State University, Professor A. B. Crawford, of Yale University, Dean H. E. Hawkes, of Columbia University, Dr. E. R. Smith, of the Beaver Country Day School, Dr. John A. Lester, of the Hill School, Dr. William L. W. Field, of the Milton Academy, Professor A. B. Meredith, of New York University, formerly commissioner of education for Connecticut, Dr. James N. Rule, superintendent of public instruction in Pennsylvania, and Dr. John L. Tildsley, district superintendent of schools, New York City. The board of directors is assisted by several active committees, among which are the committee on tests and the advisory committee for independent schools.

The bureau began its work during the winter of 1927-28, with an active membership of four independent schools. Membership has grown rapidly; there are now about 216 member schools. The numbers of schools participating in the annual spring achievement test programs have been as follows: 1928, 32; 1929, 76; 1930, 98; 1931, 114. In addition, many other member schools give intelligence and achievement tests at other times during the fall and winter.

Two of the unique and significant services which the bureau is now rendering are concerned primarily with the problems (a) of securing accurate and comparable measurements of the abilities and defined achievement of students, and (b) of keeping permanent and authentic records of these measurements on a cumulative basis for each individual student whose test papers come to the bureau.

The first of these services involves keeping an up-to-date collection of available standardized tests, for all the elementary and secondary school grades; studying the relative merits of the various tests available in each field; advising with the schools on concerted testing programs with a view to securing agreement on the use of the best tests in large numbers of schools, thus increasing both the validity and comparability of the measurements made (in the schools concerned); scoring the tests accurately under expert supervision; checking and interpreting the results under uniform and standard conditions; reporting the results to the schools uniformly in standard terminology and units in such a way as to facilitate individual diagnosis of students, and their classification in the light of public school norms and of general independent school norms as well as of local or individual independent school norms, cooperating with individual schools in administering and scoring standardized tests used as secondary school entrance examinations; and making special studies of various sorts by special arrangement with individual schools and groups of schools.

The second service involves putting the test results on the permanent cumulative educational record of each student whose test papers are scored by the bureau. The form used for this record is a modification of the cumulative educational record folder of the American Council of Education, which was described in detail in the "Educational Record" for July, 1928, and which has been adopted by large numbers of secondary schools and colleges. The keeping of such authentic records, in comparable units, by a disinterested bureau, has already proved to be of considerable value to the schools. The comparability of these records is assured because all tests are scored and the results tabulated in terms of norms that have real significance. Such achievement records have an especial value in case of transfer of pupils from school to school or from school to college. They are less subject to the uncertainty and unreliability of individual school records that tend to vary with the varying standards of schools. Records such as these, kept over a period of years, tend to mitigate the ever-present unreliability of a single examination result, and present a *moving* picture of the amount and rate of growth of the student as well as his status at any one time.

The Educational Records Bureau is committed to the belief that teachers and counsellors must know the student before they can teach him well, or guide him wisely. Reliable measures of scholastic aptitude and reliable measures of achievement are indispensable if the student is to be directed into those fields of educational or vocational endeavor for which he is best adapted. The college student does not suddenly become "college material" at graduation from preparatory school. If a boy is ever a college type of mind, he is such from birth, and the differential needs of college youths at the age of six, or ten, or twelve, are as great as, if not greater than, they are at the age of sixteen or twenty. An earlier identification of college students will be a boon to student, parent, preparatory school and college alike. The cumulative records of the bureau will be instrumental in such identification.

The work of this bureau is looked upon with

great interest by many educational groups, especially by the associations and committees whose special province is educational guidance and personnel work. The Central Committee on Personal Procedures of the American Council on Education, and the Division of Educational Enquiry of the Carnegie Foundation have cooperated in furthering the work of the bureau, which closely parallels one major aspect of the Carnegie Foundation's Pennsylvania study, and is also in effect a pioneer effort to carry out one of the major recommendations of the central committee. More recently it has become apparent that the bureau can make a unique contribution to the Cooperative Test Service, organized by the central committee and financed by the General Education Board, and definite cooperative relations have already been established which will go far in the direction of realizing some of the fundamental prerequisites of constructive educational guidance.

BEN D. WOOD

BUREAU OF COLLEGIATE
EDUCATIONAL RESEARCH,
COLUMBIA COLLEGE

SOCIETIES AND MEETINGS

THE MIDDLE STATES ASSOCIATION OF COLLEGES AND SECONDARY SCHOOLS

THE Association of Colleges and Secondary Schools of the Middle States and Maryland, founded in 1886, celebrated its forty-fifth birthday by changing its name. The new name adopted, as President Murray Bartlett explained, "for the convenience of brevity," is the Middle States Association of Colleges and Secondary Schools.

The great majority of the 450 institutions holding membership were represented by a total of about twice as many delegates at the forty-fifth annual convention held at Haddon Hall, Atlantic City, on November 27, followed on November 28 by sessions of eight auxiliary associations and conferences of administrative officers and teachers of English, modern foreign languages, history, mathematics and science.

The curriculum was the general topic at the morning and afternoon meetings of the association on November 27, with papers by Superintendent James N. Rule, of the Pennsylvania State Department of Education; by Principal Lewis Perry, of Phillips Exeter Academy, and by Dean Herbert E. Hawkes, of Columbia College; and the same topic was continued at the morning session of November 28 at the Round Table Conference for College and School Administrators in reports by Dr. John Lester, of Hill School; by President David A. Robertson, of Goucher College, and by Dean Julian Park, of the University of Buffalo.

Touching upon continuity in the curriculum was the proposal discussed by President William Mather Lewis, of Lafayette College, at the association banquet, to ask the Federal Commission on Education for a survey of "the relationship of schools and colleges, particularly as it applies to preparation for college and college entrance."

THE CURRICULUM—FOUR ESSENTIAL STEPS

"Four essential steps in true education: exploration, choice, continuity, mastery" were considered in the paper of Superintendent Rule at the opening session. He began by saying that "the one thing sacred in school and college administration is the personality of the individual student, to the end that it may be conserved and integrated in terms of its highest possibilities." The curriculum should be thought of as "a suggestive grouping of subjects to insure a certain desirable continuity and concentration of effort, but subject always to desirable modifications of emphasis and content to meet known needs and demonstrated abilities of individual students."

Dealing with the first essential step, Dr. Rule declared that exploration, which has become associated with the junior high school, should in fact be "a step upward and forward every day if possible" for the individual into an appreciation of "the facts and forces constituting *his* environment."

Choice involves a variety of curricular offerings and of extra-curricular activities as well, Dr. Rule continued. "The subject labels of courses of study have come to mean in fact about as many different things as there are teachers. This is as it should be if the teacher is to fulfil her function of helping individual girls and boys learn at a rate and with a depth and a width appropriate to each one." Individualized instruction, the speaker thought, is "indispensable to a meaningful choice by and for the individual of materials for him most significant."

The third step, continuity, "which we also call concentration, should not be taken too early, since thereby the range of a pupil's interests may be permanently restricted." The problem as to when to take the second and third steps is an individual one.

"The needle, however, that points and directs one to the true education is mastery." Of this fourth step, Superintendent Rule said that, "without it, one simply does not arrive at the true North of educational effort."

How "we are trying in Pennsylvania in a practical way to provide the steps to a true education" was then recited by Dr. Rule in his report of a project recently begun with pupils of high scholastic ability in certain centers in connection with the Pennsylvania Study. He quoted at length from Progress Report IV of the Pennsylvania Study recently published by the Carnegie Foundation for the Advancement of Teaching.

CURRICULUM IN SCHOOL AND COLLEGE

Speaking upon the topic of choice and continuity of curriculum in school, Principal Perry devoted himself to the specific program now begun at the Phillips Exeter Academy under the gift of an unnamed benefactor who "had in mind an ideal, the application of a Christian ideal—the importance, the value of the individual mind, the *one* rather than the *ninety-and-nine*." The first step at Exeter, in fulfilment of this ideal, has been to provide a conference room instead of a recitation room.

> The furnishing of the room is symbolic: a large table, often round, with chairs for an instructor and ten or twelve students. Where the instructor sits may be the head of the table; but the center of interest easily changes at any moment to the place where any boy happens to be talking. There are blackboards, maps, and all necessary devices for teaching; but there are also books, pictures, everything that would contribute to making the room have the atmosphere of a study rather than that of a formal classroom. An element by no means negligible is that the table, chairs, lights, and all the furnishings are chosen as much for beauty as for use.

Principal Perry quoted the testimony of an Exeter teacher that "sitting in a group about a table instead of in formal rows of seats has abolished almost completely the stiff duality which used to obtain between instructor and class. * * * The boy and the teacher pursue a cooperative enterprise; they are in business together—trustees, directors of a corporation sitting around a common table." The conference method has results "different in quality rather than in quantity; in kind rather than in degree."

Under the new program at Exeter, there has been an increase of ten instructors, and "we expect to have in time a staff of 75 for our school of 650 boys."

> Just as the conference plan of instruction will prepare a boy for meeting the new conditions in college instruction—the preceptorial, the tutorial system, the honors group, etc.—so the system of advisers and the new arrangement of our dormitories will be a sort of preparation for the new House and College plans in Harvard, Yale and other colleges.
>
> As a preparatory school, then, Exeter will try to prepare its students to do college work. As a secondary school in the educational process, it is hoped that important conclusions will be reached here regarding the effect of the relative size of sections on individuals. The conference method of teaching will be here tried out under most favorable conditions. The distribution of students into sections according to abilities and attainments and especially the attention paid to boys who can go farther and deeper into a subject than the normal boy may offer some solution to the important problem of wastage in American education.

Principal Perry added, in closing, that "of course there is no one of these things that is really new," and that "what is significant perhaps is the completeness with which these experiments are being made."

Dean Hawkes began his presentation of "choice and continuity in the collegiate Curriculum" with a historical reference to the days when liberal arts college was "highly standardized and amounted to about the same thing whether it was in one place or another." To-day there is a wide divergence in the character of colleges, which furnishes the first choice to be made. "After the institution has been selected there must be a choice between the various opportunities offered by the chosen institution. Who is to decide this matter?" Dean Hawkes gave this answer:

> The kind of choice that a student must make runs the best chance of being entered upon wisely if it results from a conference between an adviser who knows the institution, who knows something about boys in general and this boy in particular, but who is willing to assume that the youth who presents himself is an individual in his own right and should be responsible for his own choice. The principal function of the adviser is not to make choices for the student but to give the boy the information on the basis of which he can make choices for himself.

In discussing the criteria for choices, Dean Hawkes stressed the point of view which takes into account the student rather than the subject-matter of the curriculum. "Unfortunately most of our educational institutions are so geared as to take care only of those who have keenness in book-brightness, without any consideration of mechanical brightness or social brightness. If a boy does not fit into our scheme we ought to recognize the fact but not to condemn the youth."

As to the criticism of the American college that so many of its students have no goal in sight, Dean Hawkes declared that "academic work must not merely *be* worthwhile, but it must be related to the student's ambitions and interests so intimately that it will *seem* to the boy to be worthwhile while he is doing it." The speaker made it plain, however, that he would not emphasize knowing the student to the exclusion of giving proper weight to various items of knowledge. He gave, in closing, a generalized statement of "several procedures which bear the common name of honors work." The fundamental idea is the attempt "to stimulate the student to select a field of interest and then to give him an opportunity with the help of appropriate teachers or tutors to cultivate it continuously for at least a couple of years."

EXPERIMENTS IN CURRICULUM CONTINUITY

Dr. Lester began the morning conference of November 28 for college and school administrators. He said in part:

> We must admit that the tools, skills and opportunities for effective exploration are not yet available, and in the independent secondary schools, even when exploration has revealed them, present conditions curtail the indicated choices. Newton, von Humboldt, Davy, Wagner, Hume, Huxley, Spencer, Darwin and numbers of others who have profoundly influenced our thinking did so rather in face of their early schooling than because of it. A school like Oundle in England has successfully experimented with means of salvaging for the benefit of society the possibilities of the one-sided boy. While the good school will attempt continuity up to reasonable mastery, for certain persons and groups of persons, in language, science, mathematics, and the representative and musical arts, yet continuity in establishing understanding and attitude in respect to the urgent social and international problems which will condition living through the next twenty years is necessary for all of them. For the control of warfare, and the understanding of the economic, social and racial questions which underlie that control must be accomplished by the generation now in our secondary schools.

In his report on "Acceleration of Gifted Students in Baltimore," President Robertson began with a review of "the interesting record of service to pupils of superior ability" which the Baltimore public schools have attained for more than twenty years. This included the work of three so-called preparatory schools and later the junior high schools. "For nearly thirty years the Baltimore Polytechnic Institute, which is a boys' technical high school, has offered, in four years, a curriculum which is substantially that of a four-year high school and of the first year of an engineering school. Standards have been high, as indicated by the success of those students in securing and justifying admission to the sophomore class at Massachusetts Institute of Technology, Cornell University Engineering School, and the engineering courses at Lehigh University." Since 1926 Baltimore City College, which is a boys' high school, has afforded a curriculum of five years' work to be completed in four. Johns Hopkins has accepted some of these students with advanced standing.

President Robertson then gave an account of the way in which Goucher College is proceeding to provide similar arrangements for graduates of the Eastern and Western High Schools for girls and of Forest Park High School, for girls and boys. Written tests are to be available in each subject for which advanced credit is sought. Goucher is cooperating by conferences in which the objectives in the freshman courses are made clear and by reserving books in the college library for the use of the Baltimore accelerated group.

Dean Park outlined how, with the assistance of a subsidy from the General Education Board, the University of Buffalo has this year inaugurated a project which "aims at making more consecutive and continuous the educational progress of those high-school students who intend to enter the university." The objective of the cooperation between the high-school and university authorities in Buffalo is "to discover whether there are not ways heretofore untried in which the work of the high schools may be more closely linked up with that done in the college, with resulting benefits to superior students who avail themselves of the opportunities afforded by the two institutions. Many of these students will be fitted for the B.A. degree in three years." Dean Park told of three studies now in progress bearing upon the problem: two in the East High School relating to English and one in the office of the university registrar.

President Lewis, in his address at the annual dinner of the association, declared that "we must inspire in youth a vision of education as a continuous and continuing process; must make the transition from school to college a normal and orderly procedure." In support of his thesis that "better methods of college selection and of college entrance must be devised," Dr. Lewis cited opinions of a number of school and of college administrators and referred to the proposed validating examinations of the College Entrance Examination Board, the work of the Educational Records Bureau and the cooperative test service of the American Council on Education. His recommendation, passed by the Middle States Association and shortly to come before other regional associations, was:

That the Federal Commission of Education be requested to appoint a commission, made up of representative high school principals and teachers, head masters and masters of independent schools, faculty members and administrative officers of colleges and universities, to survey the entire field of the relationship of schools and colleges, particularly as it applies to preparation for college and college entrance. Such a commission should be given all the time necessary to make an exhaustive survey and ultimately to present their findings and recommendations.

At the dinner, greetings were presented from the North Central Association by Professor B. L. Swartley, of Ohio State University, and from the Southern Association by Professor M. E. Ligon, of the University of Kentucky.

Business Meeting

Resolutions passed at the business session included changing the name of the association; provision that after September 1, 1933, a place on the accredited lists of the association shall require membership in the association; and provision that "any membership institution not accredited through the appropriate commission shall be designated as an associate member."

Dr. Carl V. Brigham, associate secretary of the College Entrance Examination Board, addressed the association briefly on the proposed validating examinations of the board (reported in School and Society for November 14, 1931).

Dr. Adam Leroy Jones, chairman of the commission on higher institutions, reported for the commission that the following four-year colleges have been placed on the accredited list: Loyola College, Baltimore; Mercyhurst College, Erie; Wagner Memorial Lutheran College, Staten Island, and the Engineering School of Villanova College. The association instructed the commission to make a further study of the junior college and to define standards preparatory to forming an accredited list. A proposal to prepare an accredited list of teachers colleges was referred to the commission.

Reporting for the commission on accredited schools, Dr. E. D. Grizzell told of the acceptance of 53 new schools, bringing the total on the accredited list to 606.

Dr. Wilson Farrand, for the nominating committee, presented the following nominees who were unanimously elected as officers of the association for 1931–32:

President: Richard Mott Gummere, William Penn Charter School.

Vice-Presidents: President Henry Noble MacCracken, Vassar College; Head Master Boyd Edwards, Marcersburg Academy; Dean Mabel S. Douglass, New Jersey College for Women; Dean Winifred J. Robinson, Women's College, University of Delaware; Superintendent Frank W. Ballou, Washington, D. C.

Treasurer: Stanley R. Yarnall, Germantown Friends School.

Secretary: Vice-President George William McClelland, University of Pennsylvania.

Executive Committee: Officers, and President Murray Bartlett, Hobart College; Registrar W. J. O'Connor, Georgetown University; Head Mistress Elizabeth Forest Johnson, Baldwin School; Principal C. H. Threlkeld, South Orange.

To Commission on Accredited Schools: Assistant Commissioner George M. Wiley, Albany; Principal L. Gertrude Angell, Buffalo Seminary; Principal W. A. Wetzel, Trenton High School.

To Commission on Higher Institutions: Professor Adam Leroy Jones, Columbia University; Deputy Commissioner H. H. Horner, Albany; Head Master Wilson Farrand, Newark Academy; Registrar R. N. Dempster, Johns Hopkins University.

The sessions of the association were in charge of President Bartlett and Secretary McClelland.

AUXILIARY ASSOCIATIONS

At the third annual meeting of the Eastern Association of College Deans and Advisers of Men, addresses were given by Dr. Robert A. Brotemarkle, of the University of Pennsylvania; Dean A. R. Warnock, of the Pennsylvania State College; Dean Herbert E. Hawkes, of Columbia College, and the presidential address by Dean Fraser Metzger, of Rutgers University.

Speakers scheduled for the meeting of the Association of Modern Language Teachers of the Middle States and Maryland included Professor Eunice R. Goddard and Louise Seibert, of Goucher College; Professor E. C. Byam, of the University of Delaware; Professor R. B. Roulston, of Johns Hopkins University, and Dr. L. A. Roux, of Newark Academy.

At the general and group meetings of the college conference on English in the central Atlantic States the speakers included Miss Louisa McCrady, former secretary for appointments at Harvard; President D. A. Robertson, of Goucher College; Professor Donald L. Clark, of Columbia University, and Dr. R. M. Gummere, of the Penn Charter School. A paper written by President Frank P. Day, of Union College, was read in his absence.

The program of the Association of History Teachers of the Middle States and Maryland was scheduled to include these speakers: Professor C. M. Gill, of New York University; Professor Ella Lonn, of Goucher College; Mrs. Helen Goss Thomas, Teachers School of Science, Boston; Professor Anna Lane Lingelbach, of Temple University, and Professor Florian Znaniecki, of the University of Poznan, Poland, visiting professor at Teachers College, Columbia University.

Dr. Howard Hawkes Mitchell, of the University of Pennsylvania, read a paper and Dr. Fletcher Durrell led the discussion at the meeting of the Association of Teachers of Mathematics of the Middle States and Maryland.

At the eleventh annual meeting of the Association of Science Teachers of the Middle States and Maryland, the scheduled speakers were: Dr. Homer W. Le Sourd, of Milton Academy; Miss Ann Shumaker, editor of *Progressive Education;* Dr. J. M. Jameson, of Girard College, and Dr. W. P. Montague, of Columbia University.

At the meeting of the Association of Collegiate Registrars of the Middle States and Maryland an address was delivered by Dr. William S. Learned, of the Carnegie Foundation, introduced by Dean C. M. McConn, of Lehigh University.

RAYMOND WALTERS

SWARTHMORE COLLEGE

QUOTATIONS

CHICAGO'S SCHOOL-ADMINISTRATION DEBACLE

THERE is probably no chapter in the history of city school administration more singular and at the same time more distressing than that which has been written this year by the City of Chicago. For months the system has been insolvent. The teachers have had no salary between April and October. The scrip which has been issued by the board of education, running in figures of millions, issued in payment of its obligations, has proved of doubtful value.

The situation can not be attributed to the business depression. Nearly all of the larger cities are in excellent condition as far as their school treasuries are concerned. There have been some nominal salary cuts but, on the whole, the schools have been conducted with their customary momentum and efficiency. Every financial obligation has been met.

Nor can it be claimed that the Chicago Board of Education is entirely to blame for the distressing situation which confronts it. Its financial affairs were so interwoven with the municipal government, which proceeded along reckless lines that it was bound to plunge the school interests into its own failures and shortcomings.

The Chicago situation, as far as this applies to the school system, is in part attributable to a defective method of setting up the administrative machinery. The board of education was created upon the basis of political expediency, made subservient to the dictates of the party in control, and subject to the whims and caprices of its leaders. These leaders had friends to reward and enemies to punish. The school administrators became an integral part of the political organization. It had to stand or fall with that body. Thus, when the city administration went into bankruptcy the school system went down in the crash.

But the causes for the debacle go deeper. The root of the evil lies in a defective system of taxation, loosely administered. The property holdings in the State of Illinois are undervalued on the assessment rolls by several billion dollars. The discrepancy becomes most glaring when the United States census figures are compared with the local tax rolls. What applies to the State of Illinois, as a whole, applies even in a stronger degree to the city of Chicago.

The bright spot in a dark picture must be found in the fact that the teachers of the Chicago schools have worked along, under the most trying conditions, bravely and efficiently. Superintendent Bogan has led an army of 14,000 schoolroom workers with tact, skill and professional leadership. They stuck to the ship with an admirable loyalty and with a determination to render service whether their pay checks came or not.

In comment upon a distressing situation, it must be said that the school system of Chicago can not be placed upon a sound financial basis until the tax laws have been properly amended and an efficient, honest and fearless administration of the laws is assured.—*The School Board Journal.*

THE BIBLE AT OXFORD

The University of Oxford debates to-day a proposal to abolish the examination in Holy Scripture. The oral element in it was abolished early this year. It has long been part of the "first public examination" and, save that certain exemptions have been admitted, it has been an obligatory test for every undergraduate. In its present form it has few, if any, defenders. The miracle is that "Divvers"—it would be affectation not to use the name by which several generations have known it—has survived into our own day. It has been an almost pointless and certainly perfunctory diversion in the academic career. The candidate who had by heart the topography of St. Paul's journeys and a few cognate details might count himself fairly safe. What Divinity Moderations mainly demanded from the examinee was a capacity for speedy and relevant cramming, and not too much even of that.

The debate to-day will, none the less, make it clear why the examination has stood so long. Unanimity ends with the question what, if anything, should take its place. What form of substitute should be chosen and to what end? Where should its place lie in the curriculum? Should the reformed examination be optional or compulsory? These are the questions that will underlie to-day's discussion. Outside the university there will be no wish to dogmatize on the details, but there will be many besides Oxford men to watch the course of events curiously and a little anxiously. The practice of the university largely settles the practice of the public and secondary schools. It would be no service to English teaching if the university henceforth required from its undergraduates no knowledge of a book which is, to say the least of it, a fundamental document for civilization, especially for Anglo-Saxon civilization, and for the English language. Oxford would be much the less Oxford and much the less English if its scholarship were to lack the greatest of all "texts" and if its humanism were permitted to ignore its own sources.—*The London Times.*

EDUCATIONAL RESEARCH AND STATISTICS

CAN COLLEGE FRESHMEN IN THE LOWEST TENTH IN READING BE AIDED SCHOLASTICALLY?

THIS paper presents some experimental findings as possible answers to the following questions: First, how much does the clinical analysis and treatment of the reading inadequacies of freshmen in the lowest tenth in reading ability aid them scholastically? As a collateral problem, results are given to show the scholastic success of a comparable group of students without remedial aid. Second, which students benefit most from this training? Third, is the clinical or the class method of training more efficient in remedying the difficulties of the lowest tenth in reading?

The training group consisted of a random sampling of forty-two freshmen from the year 1930–31 who scored in the lowest tenth in comprehension on the Iowa Silent Reading Examination. Their scholastic improvement with training was evaluated in terms of the achievement of a control group consisting of the 95 freshmen men from the year before who scored in the lowest tenth in reading ability. Both groups were equal in intelligence as measured by the University of Iowa Qualifying Examination. It should be kept in mind that this is a study of poor readers. Although intelligence is related to reading many of these students were intellectually capable of doing successful college work, but were hindered by a specific difficulty, reading.

The remedial work was organized on a clinical basis so as to deal with each student individually. This method was used because a person who is still a poor reader when he reaches college has failed to respond to group methods of instruction, and so must have his individual difficulties analyzed and treated. The analysis sought all possible factors causing the difficulty. This included an evaluation of intellectual ability, emotional stability, sensory difficulties and eye movement, perceptual and comprehension habits. The developmental, medical, social and school histories were scrutinized in an attempt to find the genesis of the difficulty. All the factors found were treated when possible. The students were also taught better methods of reading and where to use them, such as how to handle books, the organization of material, reading for the general idea, reading to answer questions, skimming, increasing their rate, etc. A clinician[1] held half-hour training periods twice a week for about eight weeks with each student. The length of training was dependent upon the progress made. In addition to these training periods every effort was made to have the students practice outside on their lessons. All participation was voluntary and most of the students were cooperative, particularly after they had noted some progress. Tests were given again after the training was completed to note the gains made.

Marked gains were made in reading ability. The training group raised its ranking in comprehension from the 5th to the 29th centile, or an average gain of 24 centiles. In rate they increased from the 27th to the 70th centile, or an average gain of 43 centiles. However, the vast gains actually made by these poor readers are not adequately indicated by centile ranks. For instance, one student doubled his comprehension score, but his centile rank increased only 11 points. However, since centile ranks are easily understandable they are used here.

In turn marked gains were made in scholastic success. Even though training was not started until the middle of the first semester there was an 18 per cent. increase in grade point average over the control croup. That the gain in grades was due to the gain in comprehension is further brought out by the fact that 80 per cent. of those making above average

[1] Three graduate students, D. B. Lindsley, P. G. Murphy and F. P. Robinson, handled the students on half-time appointments.

gains in comprehension exceeded the group grade point average. Also, the mortality during the freshman year of the lowest tenth in reading was reduced from 25 per cent. in the control group to 17 per cent. in the training group. The fourteen fortnightly delinquency reports, or warnings of failing work, made a good measure of scholastic improvement, since there was an average of five reports before training started and nine afterwards. After training started there was a steady decrease in the number received. During the period from the time training started until the end of the school year, the training group received 39 per cent. fewer delinquencies than the control group. Therefore, training in reading can be considered a scholastic aid to those freshmen in the lowest tenth in reading.

The value of this training is further enhanced by showing the scholastic success, or rather the scholastic failure, of the lowest tenth in reading who received no such training. That is, the value of clinical training in reading is not only one of increasing efficiency in school but also one of "saving" these students from the scholastic failure which the following statistics demonstrate is the probable fate of the poor reader in college. About 68 per cent. of the freshman class usually return as sophomores, but only 44 per cent. of the lowest tenth in reading returned. Further, the lowest tenth in reading ranked at the 17th centile in grade point average the first semester; and the second semester, even though many of the poorest students were eliminated, they ranked only at the 21st centile. If reading were unrelated to school success an average centile rank of 50 could be expected in grades, but this group, due to its poor reading ability, was only able to make about a "D" average (A B, C, D, scale) which is far below the graduation requirements.

The progressive increase in the number of delinquencies received by the control group in comparison with the whole freshman class shows clearly that the lowest tenth in reading is unable to succeed in college. This is shown in Table I, which summarizes the distribution of the 11,593 delinquencies given.

Column one gives the date of the report, column two the percentage of all delinquencies that were given in the university which were received by the freshman class and column three gives the percentage of the total number of freshmen delinquencies received by the lowest tenth in reading. The large percentage at first going to the freshman class and the steady decrease thereafter indicates an early ferreting out of their difficulties to which they soon make adjustments. On the other hand, the lowest tenth in reading received more and more delinquencies as the semester progressed. There is actually a 31 per cent. increase in the average number received during the last half of the semester over the first half in comparison with the number received by the whole freshman class. This would seem to indicate an inability of the lowest tenth in reading to do college work with a consequent increase in the amount of failing work as their lack of ability is discovered. No constant trends are shown the second semester. This is because students have made their adjustments; and, since the poor students are known from the semester before, they are given delinquencies from the first. However, the lowest tenth in reading still receives more than its share of the delinquencies. (Variation here is due to chance and to a faculty habit of not giving upperclass delinquencies each time but regularly at wider intervals.)

The general conclusion can be drawn, then, that students in the lowest tenth in reading without training do not succeed in college, for most of them are eliminated and the others continue as very poor students. On the other hand, the results from clinical training indicate that many of these can be aided scholastically and to

TABLE I

First Term			Second Term		
Date	Per cent. to fresh. class	Per cent. fresh. to lowest tenth	Date	Per cent. to fresh. class	Per cent. fresh. to lowest tenth
10/12	73	13	2/22	53	19
10/26	69	16	3/8	48	20
11/9	65	17	3/22	64	12
11/23	43	17	4/5	59	18
12/6	57	19	4/19	48	13
12/20	29	27	5/3	59	22
1/18	35	21	5/17	63	10

such an extent that many of them will be scholastically "saved." However, there are great individual variations in the amount of improvement made. It is of importance, then, to find what factors make certain students better risks for training, so that remedial efforts can be administered on the most fertile ground. This, the second question, was studied to find the rôle of intelligence and cooperation in making for improvement.

To find the rôle of intelligence, both the training and the control groups were divided into two subgroups: Training and Control Groups I were composed of those students in the lowest tenth in intelligence as well as in reading, and Training and Control Groups II of those above the lowest tenth in intelligence. (Training I, N = 25, Reading 4.2 percentile, Intelligence 5.7 percentile; Training II, N = 17, Reading 6.2 percentile, Intelligence 28.3 percentile; Control I, N = 67, Reading 6.3 percentile, Intelligence 5.2 percentile; Control II, N = 28, Reading 8.3 percentile, Intelligence 27.0 percentile.) Since the sampling is not adequate in some cases the results are only indicative of the causative factors. The gains made by the two training groups are summarized in Table II.

TABLE II

	Percentiles gain in comprehension	Percentiles gain in rate	Per cent. decrease in delinquencies	Per cent. increase in grades
Training I	17.4	41.3	30.6	6.0
Training II	33.8	45.4	49.7	22.0

The gains in comprehension and rate are in terms of a retest, while the improvement in delinquencies and grades is in comparison to the control group. It is evident that intelligence is highly related to improvement, except in the case of rate of reading. The actual gain in grades of Training I over Control I may be larger than indicated; for although compared with a control group equal in reading ability and intelligence, Training I received 35 per cent. more delinquencies for the period before training than Control I. This would indicate an inferior group due to some undetermined cause.

However, many students, in Training I who did not have the advantage of superior intelligence made marked gains. In fact, many students in Training I made as great gains in comprehension and grades as the students in Training II. Fifty-seven per cent. of those in Training I who ranked above average in comprehension gain exceeded the average comprehension gain of Training II. Twenty-five per cent. of the grades of the Training I students who were above average in comprehension gain exceeded the grade average of Training II. This shows that intelligence is not the only factor that affects improvements.

Cooperation, as measured by the number of clinical appointments missed, was a factor in this overlapping. Although this is not a refined measure, it is an objective measure. Those below average in comprehension gain missed 32 per cent. more meetings than those above average. Those below average in grades missed twice as many meetings as those above average. At this level cooperation and intelligence are not related ($r = .04$).

This would indicate that intelligence, or ability to learn a mental skill, and cooperation, or desire to improve in a mental skill, are two independent factors affecting improvement. A person of low ability can improve if he tries, although not as much as some one of better ability who also cooperates.

Whether it is worth while to work with all freshmen who are poor readers irrespective of the above factors is a matter of administrative policy. That is, if facilities for remedial aid are adequate, all poor readers can gain something from this training, but if the facilities are limited it is worth much more to aid those who will benefit most by it. The first criterion of selection should be cooperation. Those who do not try gain very little, but improvement can be noted in all students who apply the recommended techniques to their work. Students not willing to work can soon be weeded out to make room for those who are willing. The necessity of paying a tutoring fee might aid in this elimination. However, the burden of gaining cooperation rests upon the clinician, since most students will work diligently as soon as they note some improvement. Of these students who cooperate those who have the requisite intellectual ability to do college work respond the best to remedial work. Students in this select group are well worth the effort of training, for without remedial aid they are very apt to be eliminated, but with training many of them can carry on college work at a high enough level to graduate. These students can easily be selected on the basis of standardized intelligence and reading tests. It is suggested that poor readers for training be selected from among those willing to cooperate in order from the upper intellectual levels downwards until the remedial quota is filled.

Whether these students should be given training by a clinical or a class method is a question of efficiency. Several studies using a class method have reported gains in reading ability and college grades. Some of these have been with sophomore and upperclassmen and so are not considered here, since very poor readers are usually eliminated before reaching these levels. Pressey,[2] working with freshmen in the lowest quarter in reading ability and with probation students, found improvement in reading ability and grades but concludes it is not worth while to work with students below the 25th percentile in intelligence. Remmers and Stalnaker[3] give further corroboration to this conclusion. They gave training to seven freshman volunteers in the lowest quarter in intelligence and found only 25 per cent. improvement in reading the book used and no transfer even to other reading tests. Eurich,[4] using a group method with freshmen, found no gain in reading or grades with training in vocabulary and paragraph comprehension. The general conclusion can be drawn, then, that a class technique will usually give some gain with superior students, but will not materially aid students low in intelligence. The relationship of the amount of gain to intellectual ability was corroborated in this study, but more efficient gains were made with the clinical technique. The average intelligence of the training group ranked only at the 15th percentile, and 76 per cent. were in the lowest quarter in intelligence, the group abandoned by Pressey. Yet this group made marked gains in scholastic success as indicated before in this paper. The value of a clinical over a class method lies in the better analysis of the causative factors to be eliminated, in the more efficient application of the remedial techniques and in the better rapport possible. Also the clinical method allows training to be started at any time and finished whenever its value for that student is ended. The conclusion is drawn, then, that for specific reading difficulties a clinical method is better. However, for the average college student a "How to Study" class is sufficient since it is not a matter of keeping him in school but one of improved efficiency. Also, the average reader has no glaring reading defects that demand individual analysis and treatment.

CONCLUSIONS

(1) The lowest tenth in reading after clinical treatment of their difficulties showed marked improvement in reading ability and school success.

(2) The lowest tenth in reading without training can be considered scholastic failures since most of them are eliminated the first year and those remaining continue as very poor students.

(3) Intelligence and cooperation, two independent factors, determine the amount of gain with training. For the best results, students who are willing to work should be selected in order from those with the highest intelligence downward until the remedial quota is filled.

(4) A clinical method is more efficient than a class method and should be used in remedying specific reading difficulties.

F. P. ROBINSON
STATE UNIVERSITY OF IOWA

[2] L. C. Pressey, "The Permanent Effect of Training in Methods of Study on College Success." SCHOOL AND SOCIETY, 28, 1928, 403–4; "Training College Freshmen to Read," *Ohio College Assoc. Bull.* No. 55, 1929.

[3] H. H. Remmers and J. M. Stalnaker, "An Experiment in Remedial Reading Exercises at the College Level." SCHOOL AND SOCIETY, 28, 797–800. 1928.

[4] A. C. Eurich, "Reading Disabilities of College Students." University of Minnesota, doctorate thesis, 1929.

NEW BOOKS IN EDUCATION

HOFSTEAD, JOHN A. *American Educators of Norwegian Origin: A Biographical Dictionary.* Pp. 316. Augsburg, Minneapolis.

KILZER, LOUIS R. *Supervised Study.* Pp. xi + 332. Professional and Technical Press. $3.25.

KIRKPATRICK, J. E. *Academic Organization and Control.* Pp. xxiii + 246. Antioch Press. $3.00.

TYSON, LEVERING, editor. *Radio and Education.* Pp. viii + 271. University of Chicago Press. $3.00.

SCHOOL AND SOCIETY

EDITED BY J. McKEEN CATTELL

WITH WHICH IS COMBINED THE

EDUCATIONAL REVIEW

EDITED BY WILLIAM McANDREW

Volume 34 SATURDAY, DECEMBER 26, 1931 Number 887

FIRST THINGS IN EDUCATION[1]

By Professor WILLIAM H. KILPATRICK

TEACHERS COLLEGE, COLUMBIA UNIVERSITY

THE title as announced is meant to include those factors or elements in education which stand strategically first, such that if these be well conceived other things follow in due order. Obviously the list I propose is my own, another would choose differently. Still I dare hope for a certain measure of approval from forward looking educators.

In making such a presentation I suffer a certain embarrassment. In education, as elsewhere, most had rather hear about new and better ways of getting things already desired than to be summoned to new objects of regard. I swim then against the current of your thinking from the start. For I call you to reconsider the things to which you now give educational allegiance; and many, I know, preferring the old will not hear my words or, hearing, will not harken.

An outline of what I shall say may make it easier to follow the argument. My discussion in brief is as follows:

(1) That our times emphatically demand of education a new social outlook.

(2) That applied intelligence in matters of public concern is accordingly needed, possibly as never before.

(3) That effectual intelligence as thus demanded is, in spite of current views, more a matter of acquisition and learning than it is of original native ability; and that the chief conscious task in education is to help build such appropriate effectual intelligence.

(4) That we can in general hope for the up-building of such effectual intelligence by and in the learner only as the like intelligence is present and active in the teacher and not simply limited to the administrator or "expert."

(5) That the schools need to see their work in new light, that curriculum and method need to be remade and extended in conformity with the foregoing considerations.

(1) THE NEED FOR A NEW SOCIAL OUTLOOK AND EMPHASIS

Our situation, carefully considered, is very serious. To begin with the most obvious, we are economically in a bad way. To my mind, however, the worst features of the economic situation are not those on the surface. In great probability we shall before very long get over the present depression and many will then once more think that all is well. A truer view of the present situation is like a mother's attitude toward high temperature in her child. A single instance of high temperature fol-

[1] Read before the Pennsylvania Education Congress, Harrisburg, Nov. 5, 1931.

lowed by a speedy decline and no further bad symptoms she may soon forget, but recurrent high fever she can not disregard. The child may seem well just now, but the recurrence means some deep seated trouble which must be found and got rid of. In the present case, to increase our anxiety, the fevers seem to grow more powerful, the disturbing cause seems to increase.

As we look into our situation we certainly find some growing factors. Each decade shows a decreasing proportion of people working in financial independence and a larger proportion who depend on wages, salaries, and corporation dividends. Till recently in this country the majority lived on relatively self-supporting farms. With increasing industrialization the people of our country as individuals are more and more dependent on economic forces beyond their immediate control. The time was when it was a man's own fault if he was long out of work. This is no longer true, as very many now well know. Similarly, too, trade is more and more dependent on world conditions. War, once a minor incident, becomes now a very real threat to civilization itself. In these regards we all hang together. No one stands alone.

Furthermore, while these things are so, a larger proportion of our people are educated than ever before and the means of spreading ideas are incomparably greater. Not only are newspapers and books more numerous and more accessible, but moving pictures and radio give entirely new access to the public eye and ear. Propaganda and combined mass action are thus easier than ever known before. Demagogic appeal is more easily made. In spite of the fact that great wealth may for a while control such publicity agencies, we must still believe that injustices on a large scale are now more easily brought before the bar of reason than ever before in history. Changes are more easily made.

Accompanying all these changes is one further change of attitude. The old "rugged individualism" is more and more being weighed in the balance and increasingly found wanting. Consider for example "the Swope plan." When a great industry recognizes that employment insurance as well as the maintenance of good wages is a proper charge upon industry and indeed nothing but financial wisdom, we are moving far away—as indeed we must—from the original pioneer notion of individual efforts, free contract, each man for himself alone. We see increasingly that we do in fact all hang together. The attitude grows—and the facts demand it—that we are indeed all in one boat. The cause of one is the cause of us all. In a true sense all support all and the fact does not operate as many have wished to think only in a one-way direction. "All support all" must somehow work in both directions.

While these facts have thus brought us to see more clearly the corporate fortune of us all, certain other tendencies have acted to build destructive anti-social attitudes which threaten perhaps the very foundations of social order. I refer especially to a growing proportion of people who refuse to draw the line between legitimate earnings based on service and a great variety of "hold-up" methods, both legal and illegal. Look at the army of people who tried to grow rich from the stock market before October 1929. They were trying to get from others money for themselves without rendering any service in return. Consider also business mergers from which fortunes are often made for no adequate service to society. Consider misleading advertising. All of these are legal, so to say. Then look at illegal efforts: the graft and corruption in financial and political life, the army of bootleggers, racketeering of all sorts, the gangs of thieves. The significance of all this is that we have, working at the very heart of our social and economic structure, a powerful education to teach young men and women, coming into the actual life of affairs, that wealth and service have no necessary connection and need have none. In fact to many, possibly to most, it seems that the quickest and surest way, if not the only way, to large wealth lies along a road divorced from any conception of service or even of social morality. Business is business, these say, and can not allow any weak or humane notions to interfere with its success.

Our society is thus at war with itself. On the one hand all the really vital processes make inherently for a growing social inter-dependence. On the other hand the actual management of business educates, ruthlessly and all but inevitably, against the moral habits and attitudes necessary to take care of our more corporate society. We may talk, idly, of a hoped for moral and religious education from schools and churches, but our economic system is a more powerful educator, and it increasingly educates for suicidal selfishness. If we do not like to think of these things we may shut our eyes to them—and many do—but the corruption at the vitals of society goes on none the less.

There is so much to be said here that one is at a loss to choose. Consider the bad workings of this ill-ordered economic system of ours. We raise so much wheat and cotton that it is seriously proposed to destroy a part in order to boost prices, yet we have bread lines and millions cannot buy food and clothing. Our factories and mines, if worked to capacity, would produce more than our present system can dispose of. Yet millions lack. Clearly production and distribution are not working in harmony. Our plan of affairs exactly and simply lacks intelligence.

And unless we change things the prospect is to get worse. We can and probably shall raise still more wheat and cotton. We can make better factories that need few or no workers and so increase unemployment. And to make matters still worse, our ways of living and thinking have changed so much that our former political and moral and religious conceptions no longer hold as once they did. We are trying to run 20th century industrial America on ideas built in pioneer days and some even in the middle ages. Meanwhile science, comparative religion, and higher criticism, acting in company with an increasingly industrialized society, make it practically certain that we shall never go back to those older outlooks. The only way to the future lies forward. We must review and revise many of our fundamental conceptions.

Nor have we yet seen the whole picture. The new industrial order has brought us comforts and even luxuries. But what about happiness? Are people happier? As we look either within ourselves or about us, we are forced to admit that many, many among us are not only not happy but are often deeply troubled. They have lost the former outlooks, the old satisfactions and have found nothing adequate to replace them. During our debauch of wealth there has been a mad quest for thrills. But a life of thrills defeats itself. It wears out. It will not satisfy. Man needs something better. For myself, I believe that man must have a faith which he can accept and a cause for which he gives himself. But the faith and the cause must be such as can stand before the bar of reason. No other can now satisfy. It is a hard saying, but we must hear it.

Let us, however, return to our economic situation, which I for one believe is the crux of our present difficulties. Our failure to coordinate production and distribution is critical. We hear, accordingly, of social planning and many are studying Russia's five-year plan. It appears plain that we must somehow put intelligent planning into our otherwise anarchic economy. But what plan shall we advocate? What plan would work with us? For myself, I do not know the answer to these questions, but of this much I am sure, our country will never go the Russian way. Whatever we do, we must work out for ourselves—using suggestions, yes, but work it out for ourselves, to fit us and our situation.

(2) THE NEED FOR APPLIED INTELLIGENCE IN OUR PRESENT SITUATION

As we face the situation indicated above, it becomes increasingly clear that we must *think,* and, apparently, as never before. Without deepseated reconstruction of thought and institutions we must expect things to get worse. Our system works badly and inherently so. The old social, moral and religious sanctions increasingly lose hold. The selfish possibilities in our economic and political system educate our people increasingly in a selfish indifference to the common good. Our schools in comparison are but puny affairs, their moral teaching distressingly impotent. People are easier got at by demagogic propaganda. And the future is even more than ever unknown.

What then shall we do? What is our hope? I can think of only one defensible course. We must have, as never before, widespread fundamental and critical thinking about our economic and social order. We must find and locate the weak spots. We must devise better ways. The many existing agencies must unite to foster study of these matters. New agencies must be devised. As never before we must think.

Let no one deceive you with professed alternatives of Mussolini or Lenin. Thinking is our bottom hope. There is no other final resource. Force, however well meant, if not obedient to defensible thought is but danger and tyranny. We can not trust it. And to continue as we are is simply to think badly. We must think and act accordingly.

But some among us will fear widespread public thinking. They hope to manage without it. In their hearts they mistrust man and thought. But I say to you it is not thinking that we have to fear. Rather is it the absence of thinking, that people will act without thinking. Or that people will think hastily and so badly and be led demagogically, and so again act badly. Our only safe alternative to chance and drift is better and more wide-spread thinking. In saying this I am but going back to the fathers. This was the original foundation of our democracy.

(3) EFFECTUAL INTELLIGENCE

Here some will ask and very sincerely: Can we trust the people to think? Has not science, through psychology, shown that the majority are but children? That only the few can think?

I answer emphatically, that science has not shown any such thing. Some scientists have indeed said so, but they have not shown it. For it is not true. On the contrary, I dare assert that just as we can not in the long run trust any alternative but thinking, so we can not in the long run trust any body to decide but the people at large.

Let us look back at the facts. As regards original ability to think, native intelligence, there is indeed a distribution curve. At the top a few geniuses, at the bottom an analogous number of idiots and feeble-minded, next to the geniuses a larger number of able, next to the bottom a larger number of dull and stupid, in the middle the large majority. But, except a small number at the bottom, all do think. The higher up the line the better quality of thinking, but all along it is a matter of degree. So much for original, native ability.

But in effectual intelligence there is another factor equally important, if not in fact more significant. We are, as everybody knows, more effectually intelligent where we are better acquainted. In other words, what we have learned is the stuff that we think with. Ask Einstein about relativity and he is a genius. Ask him about Pennsylvania politics and he is—in present effectual intelligence—inferior to any ward politician. And in this effectual intelligence we mostly learn from others. Strip Einstein of what he has learned from others and he would at the time be less intelligent about relativity, even than you or I. Any pronouncement from him on the subject would be exactly worthless. In a century from now college A.B.'s will think of relativity as naturally as you and I now find it difficult. The more we learn about anything, if only we keep checking up what we learn against others, the more effectually intelligent we shall become. In this way Presbyterian Scotland grew in a century or two to be astonishingly intelligent in theology, more so—I believe—than any other like group of people in the history of the world. In the same way, Germany became literary, and Italy musical. In Roman days Italy was not musical, while Germany and Scotland were barbarian, utterly indifferent to letters or systems of theology. These things in time they learned.

Here, then, is where education gets into thinking in relation to the urgent needs of our civilization. Elementary school, high school, college, adult education, as they face our civilization, must accept it as their dominating concern and task to help build appropriate effectual intelligence to deal with our threatening problems.

Note here that "adult education" is put in line along with the schools more commonly thought of. The time has now come when we can no longer expect our youth in some twenty odd years to learn enough to last them through life. Of course they never did so learn and now we know it. As life itself unfolds novelly, so education is and must be an ever continuing process. We must give up the fiction of "getting an education" as if it were got once and for all. Such an idea is a hurtful and fantastic untruth.

Note also the term "appropriate," in the phrase "appropriate effectual intelligence." There is no such thing as becoming intelligent in all matters. We can be reliably intelligent only as we are intelligently informed. If our schools are to help solve our urgent social problems, then must our young people work with those problems, not indeed in the same form as will their elders, but in the form and degree suited to youth and youthful experience. And if they or their elders are to develop "effectual intelligence," they must *think* as opposed to merely re-peating or re-hashing other people's thoughts. We shall utilize other people's thoughts but not first memorize them. To accept without thinking is to vaccinate against thinking. And our people, young and old, must think about our social, moral and economic situation, each age the part that properly does or might concern it. Let us have done, once and for all, with the refusal to let our young people think till we, their elders, have safely indoctrinated them against questioning. (This again never worked except badly, and now it must be stopped). No, it is the really controversial that we shall wish them to study—again each age according to what it faces. We must so manage that our young people and our older people become increasingly able and disposed to criticize existing social arrangements, for it is a very thorough-going reconstruction that lies ahead of us. I know that many will be pained at what I am saying. But the time has passed for easy going complacency. It is a condition and not a theory that confronts. We must control our machine or it will engulf us. And open-minded and critical thinking is our only safe reliance. Anything less is but faith in our evil present, reliance on our present evil system.

(4) THE NEED FOR THINKING TEACHERS

If now this kind of thinking, or any other worthy the name, is to go on in school or in adult education, our teachers must be thinking teachers, capable of thinking about these problems and anxious to help bring a better day to the world. Note that I am not proposing to hand out a system to be propagandized through our schools. Exactly the contrary. I am trying to get a generation better ready than we have been to find for themselves an adequate system. For myself, I do not think the schools can or should make up a system and teach it authoritatively to helpless children. Our school men are not equipped to devise an adequate system, and were they so able they ought not—in my opinion—to do it. My notion of education is quite different. I think the business of the schools is to help make people more promisingly intelligent than otherwise they would be, by helping them learn to face matters which actually confront them. As our young people grow older and come more and more fully to face life's problems, it is our task to help them as a continuing process to learn by facing actual problems and situations better how to face problematic situations. And by facing a problematic situation I mean doing something about it, doing the appropriate thing as best they can come to see it. And our business is to help our pupils at each successive stage according to the needs of that stage. Our aim is that they shall increasingly learn how to think and act adequately. Not necessarily what we think is adequate, but rather what a new and intelligent and impartial view as best they can get it shall promise as adequate. We propose to get them increasingly ready to think for themselves, in the end even, if need be, in opposition to what we, their parents and teachers have hitherto thought. For their responsibility is theirs. They must learn to face the problems of their day and generation.

That our pupils may learn increasingly so to think, we must have teachers who can then think and this means that as teachers they must have the opportunity and encouragement to think. In particular here, I mean to combat the idea—all too frequent —that experts at the top can and should do the thinking for a whole school system and hand it down for docile and obedient teachers to execute. People who thus as a matter of docility and obedience execute the thinking of others can not and will not teach young people to think. Thinking can not be put up in tin cans or orders and directions and handed out in this fashion. It is the everlasting condemnation of a certain theory of "scientific" education that it has allied itself with any such psychologically false and democratically vicious system of educational administration. Such a science and such an administration do but offer themselves as allies and outposts against intelligent action in behalf of the public good. They ally themselves with the selfish vested interests who propose to hold the schools and the many for the advantage of the privileged few.

But some of you will begin to say that teachers can not be expected to think, that too many are young, inexperienced, thoughtless. The picture is now only too true, and we can not ignore the facts. But we need not be content with any existing state of affairs. We can work for and not against a better condition of affairs. Normal schools must cease to be mere "training" schools (hateful term,—we "train" dogs, but we "educate" intelligent people). Our normal schools and teachers colleges must seriously mean to turn out thinking teachers. As matters stand, I venture to say that most such schools do not now seriously make any such effort. And many school superintendents prefer the docile and trained kind of teacher output—they are more easily controlled. To all this I can only repeat what has been said above, and ask if we are going to shut our eyes to what confronts us. In fact, far off as the end may be, we have not done what is right until we expect a teacher to be as well selected and as well educated as a doctor. For my part I hold that teaching is if anything more important than medicine. We must at least go forward as far and as fast as we can in the right direction. And school administration must increasingly see that its chief task is in fact educational and not business efficiency, that administration and all other educational machinery are but means to help learning and teaching go on best, and that so far as concerns school education, the chief work is done at the point of pupil-teacher contact and at that point must be concentrated the highest active intelligence that we can by any means summon. As the teacher is intelligent so may we hope the pupils to become.

(5) WHAT SHALL THE SCHOOLS DO?

At length we come to the work of the schools. I wish I might state outright a specific school program, but the matter is too complicated. We look ahead to a new and better kind of working and living. The schools of that day will have a different task and be run accordingly along different lines. We who now live must work to change what now is into those better things. While we can not with certainty plant for the future, we must have some conception of what to work for.

As I see it, the coming day will find us thinking more in terms of life—life as something good to live and how to make it better—rather than as now in terms of getting money. Economic programs must be made in the light of total consequences to life of all concerned. Shared thinking must become the rule, shared decisions made as far as possible by all affected by the decision. This is essential democracy and must be extended to all aspects of life. Business will be run not simply or primarily for profits but for life. The beauty of a factory plant for example will be considered as bearing on the lives of the people who work there. Any division of labor will be considered as bearing on the happiness attending the work, for happiness in and through work is as true a constituent of the good life as is the product turned out by the work, possibly a more necessary constituent. In a way which I have not time to develop, happiness comes peculiarly through work which is in its process educative—the broadening of view, the deepening of insight, the sensing of bearing, and shared contriving accordingly for the good of all concerned.

We look then forward to a day when labor and professions will be closer together, continuous in fact, when all labor shall be so managed and viewed in such manifold relations to life that to labor will be a shared enterprise in living and in contriving to make life better. In that day to work will be to think and to grow.

As we approximate such a state of affairs we shall begin to see that children should begin early to share in the responsible thinking and doing connected with such enterprises. What we once had and have lost will come back: children will share with their elders in the significant activities of life. The older the child the more actual and responsible the sharing. In this way life will again become educative in a manner and degree now denied us. Schools will cease to be isolated from life, probably cease to be as self-contained and self-bounded as now they are, and merge themselves more into the shared community activities. The change of attitude will be colossal. The initiative and the interested purposeful activity which we have often sought in vain under present school conditions will then come almost automatically.

Lest I seem to you to be dreaming, let me hasten to say that I have seen such in Russia and to a lesser degree in China.

The Russian plan we shall not, I hope, adopt; but the Russian schools that I saw had a social purpose and enthusiasm which I envy for ours. School life was knit to purposeful economic and social life in a way that gave it new spirit and interest. Young children and older fairly beamed with enthusiasm and eagerness for the cause.

What then for us now? We must, I think, work along two related lines. We must join schooling as significantly to life about us as ever we can manage. In season and out, the social motive must be used, social connections must be sought, individual and group endeavor at things significant for actual out-of-school life must be encouraged whenever possible. I do not mean that we are to impose socially useful tasks, not that. We must work that such shall increasingly come from the children's own demands. In the degree that we can succeed at such things, in like degree will the best aims of modern education be served.

The second related line is to get our pupils at once working at the thinking aspects of social and group life so that they may grow in appropriate open-mindedness, in critical mindedness, in social intelligence and in social interest. If this be begun early and continued with increasing seriousness and maturity, we can hope in a reasonable time to bring up a generation able and disposed to face our social situation with clear eyes, stout hearts and stable intelligent minds.

We shall not succeed well at either of these lines unless we can on the one hand be more willing than now to deal with controversial problems and situations, and on the other hand see that our present preoccupation with subject-matter course of study requirements is futile and mis-educative. And I am under no illusion as to the oppositions we shall encounter. This great State of Pennsylvania, so goodly in so many ways, holds among its citizens many who would stoutly oppose. Here and elsewhere not a few will shout for Diana of the Ephesians, while others will mock. All such, however, will be but signs that we are approaching vital matters, clear proof of life in educational thought and endeavor.

My topic said "first things." Some of you may think I have forgot the plural. The social program is not all. What constitutes the good life and the disposition to bring it to all is a second. And the building of integrated personalities, stout-hearted individual characters, is a third. But these three are not separate. If any one be sought in sufficiently wide setting the other two will be cared for.

As matters at present stand, I believe my insistence on a social program for education is the emphasis now most needed. The water is stirring even at this moment. People are thinking possibly as never before. The times demand it. I have chosen this occasion as a fitting one in which to announce what is now for me the chief demand on American education.

THE UNIVERSITY TO-DAY

By Dr. FRANK PORTER GRAHAM

PRESIDENT OF THE UNIVERSITY OF NORTH CAROLINA

C. The Graduate School

But a group of professional schools around the college do not make a university. Without a graduate school there can be no university. Postgraduate courses do not make a graduate school. The American Association of Universities, essentially an association of graduate schools, founded in

1900 by Presidents Eliot, Gilman and Harper in the interest of excellence in graduate research, holds as one of its present requirements for membership that a university be equipped in faculty, laboratories, general library and special source materials to give the degree of doctor of philosophy in five departments. However adequate be the laboratories and supplies, departmental libraries and source materials, carrells, seminar rooms and all the valuable facilities for thorough research, without great scholars the whole apparatus of research may become as so much sounding brass. There can be no great graduate school and no great university without great teachers. A good part of a lifetime given by day and by night on scant resources to the deep exploration of a field is the price of the scholarship of the master. No smattering and no sham; only thoroughness and excellence among the masters. Several groups of these masters, distinguished in different fields, prevent unchecked specialization in any one field. These various groups of eminent scholars, seekers for truth and teachers, by the very interrelation of fields, intellectual interchange and coordination on the level of graduate excellence, are integrated into the university. The university guidance of graduate work should make impossible research in ultra-scholastic and utilitarian trivialities, but at the same time should not by a routine uniformity or traditional control cramp the vigorous and autonomous life of schools and departments. Tradition and routine should give way to excellence. The quality of the college, the professional schools and the whole university is renewed from and advanced by the excellence of the graduate school. The college of arts and sciences is the youthful heart of the university, the professional schools are its skilful arms, and the graduate school is its crowning glory.

(1) *Research and Teaching:* The two particular functions of the graduate school are to train students in research and to prepare students to teach. The two functions, though separate in their techniques, reenforce each other in the unity of the graduate purpose for the advancement of knowledge and the well-being of the race. In some universities three fourths of the graduate students become teachers. A great teacher, without publication of his researches, is sometimes an apparently unrecognized gift of God to his generation. Yet research is a resource of the teacher. There is a sense of reverent humility in him who has to dig in the sources for his own facts and ideas. There is often a contagious enthusiasm communicated to the students by the teacher who comes fresh from the mine bringing the ore in the hands that dug it out. Research on the part of the teacher in the humanities and sciences deepens the content and insight of the teacher and makes available fresh resources for other teachers; develops the scholarly research spirit in many students, and thus widens the association and interchange of teachers and scholars around the earth who, by their patient discovery and teaching of truth, are doing their hopeful bit toward the gradual making of a better world.

(2) *Research on its Own Account:* Research, apart from teaching, has values on its own account. It was James Madison's patient and thorough researches into the structure of the ancient, Western European and colonial governments that enabled him, as a practical statesman in the critical period, to guide the framing of the constitution of the United States. Hertz, the German research scholar, standing on the pure researches of the English professor, Clerk Maxwell, discovered the idea out of which Marconi, the Italian, invented the mechanism for wireless telegraphy. The researches and hypotheses of Copernicus, Galileo and Kepler helped to make possible

the theory of gravitation which came from the integrating mind of Isaac Newton, or as President Walter Dill Scott calls him, Professor Newton of Cambridge University. The American Professor Michelson, by his researches, helped to prepare the way for the new revolutionary theory of the German Professor Einstein.

(3) *The Utility of Scientific Research:* If we were to recapitulate with President Scott the list of the names of the men whose researches in pure science have not only explored the far reaches of the universe and the inside of the atom but also discovered the scientific principles on which is erected the technological structure of our modern industrial civilization, we would call, for the most part, the names of college professors and quiet relentless seekers for truth in university laboratories. He has estimated that college and university research make possible in a normal time the production of more wealth in America in one year than has been spent on all the colleges and universities since John Harvard founded the college under the elms in Cambridge. It was also estimated that the results of college and university research in the pure sciences as the basis for sanitary and hydraulic engineering, personal health and public health save in America the lives of one million people a year.

(4) *The Graduate School and Organized Research:* In the complicated modern world, it was inevitable that research should be organized in institutes, councils and big industries. Mr. Vernon Kellogg has pointed out that the research organizations are dependent on the colleges and universities for manning and recruiting their staffs. The graduate school is par excellence the training ground for research, organized and unorganized. In graduate research there is no immediate profit motive, and the student has the unadulterated scientific freedom necessary for training in research. Deeply specialized as is research it should for that very reason keep its connection with all divisions of graduate work and never narrow its special eye to the wider implications of the smallest bit of truth found in the laboratory or library stacks or tentatively guessed on a walk about the campus or in some lonely nook in the woods or where you will. In the meagerly equipped laboratories of this university before the twentieth century and since, the researches of unpretentious scholars in the natural sciences have been recognized for their value to learning and mankind by scholars on four continents.

(5) *Research in the Social Sciences:* The social sciences, of course, are lagging behind the natural sciences. For the most part they have risen in recent times. Scholars in the social sciences have a tremendous task to bring their researches up to the needs of the times. Individuals in graduate schools and organizations here and there are doing heroic work, with civilization itself as the stakes of social mastery. On account of the complicated nature of our social structure, institutes for research in the social sciences are being organized mainly and naturally within the universities, as, for example, The Institute of Human Relations at Yale. The Institute for Research in the Social Sciences is an indispensable reenforcement of the graduate resources and impulses of this university in the unexplored fields of the social sciences. Together with the pioneer department of rural social-economics, the departments of economics, education, history, sociology, psychology and the law school, it is making realistic studies and significant contributions to the better understanding of the human and social implications of our economic, political and legal structure. The institute has had considerable regard for interracial relations with all their problems of human injustice and unequal opportunity in the present

South. These researches in interracial relations are based on the human attitude that, with all our racial solidarities and wisely pragmatic expedients of social separation, especially here in the South, the two great races have fundamentally a common destiny in building a nobler civilization and that, if we go up, we go up together. The University Press has made these researches available for the people of the South and has carried forward an intellectual exchange with scholars and institutions over the world. Five of the books from this Press have made the League of Nations list for international intellectual cooperation.

(a) *Research, Integrated Thinking and War:* Scholars, colleges, universities and research agencies all over the world need to join their intellectual and spiritual resources in research and make specialized and integrated studies of the problems whose social consequences reach around the world and down the ages. The world war and the world economic depression have taken their toll in human lives, human well-being and happiness beyond measurement or imagination. Wars and depression throw their cruel and sinister shadows across the homes of the people on all the continents of this earth. We, who, in our scientific pride, consider that we have mastered the earth, stand baffled in the midst of these two mighty foes of every locality and all mankind. The very fact of recurring wars and recurring depressions raises a question as to the quality of our education and the sincerity of our religion. The people in a world in which such depressions and wars can recur are not yet intellectual and spiritual in the control of their institutions. The nature of the war and the depression illustrate the complex structure of life and the world. They make necessary greater depths in specialization and a new integration of old and new knowledge in all fields for a better understanding of the problems and the processes of solution. The explanation that war is caused by economic interests is too simple to be true to the complex nature of human beings and human society. The human being carries around as part of his structure and heritage biological, psychological, anthropological, historical, economic, political, philosophical and spiritual equipment. Human society is as complex as the human life implicated in its framework. Wars may come from springs deep in the structure of human beings or deep in the structure of human society or both. It is the heroic task of biology, psychology and all the social sciences to try to light up the origins of war and work out its social control and abolition. On the surface it is clear that science and technology have with power engines, ocean lanes, rails, cables, concrete roads, farms, factories, stores and banks flung across the earth the mechanical framework of a mighty economic structure. A pistol shot in remote Serajevo or a stock market crash in Wall Street causes repercussions around the world. A Slavic student, in killing a German archduke, precipitated national antagonisms, imperial ambitions, economic rivalries, and released human passions and the dynamic energies of the peoples of two hemispheres which caused two million American soldiers to cross an ocean and left ten million dead on the battlefields of three continents. Press a trigger in a village or press a button in an office and you may release forces that involve the nations and civilization. This interdependent world economic structure has thrust through the national boundaries which would hedge it about. We should out of regard for the values of nationality not set nationalism over against mankind but rather work through the nations and all available international organizations for the preservation of the nations and the salvation of the human race. The social scientist is up against an almost impenetrable jungle in many regions of knowledge. He finds himself on the fringe of the wilderness in an internationally lawless world. From the pure research in colleges and universities have come the scientific findings and ideas which became the technological basis of modern civilization. From the colleges and universities must come the research and thinking which will become the basis for a more intelligent understanding, guidance and control of the processes out of which come wars and depressions.

(b) *Research, Integrated Thinking and the Depression:* Research and integrated thinking are desperately needed now to be brought to bear on the great depression. The rhythm of life and business, the high and low swing of the business cycle, unregulated over-production, the hangover of handicraft ideas with their controls in the age of the power engine, the dislocation of agriculture and the sickness of the coal and cotton industries, the placing of pecuniary considerations above the industrial and the industrial above the human and spiritual, destructive competition, the breakdown in the system and ethics of distribution and consumption, prohibitive tariffs, ultra-nationalistic politics in an interdependent economic world, the great fear and insecurity of the people, armaments, reparations and international debts, unemployment, hunger amid plenty, the misery and despair of the millions everywhere, demand the most realistic consideration and high thinking of business men, statesmen and scholars in the universities. Nothing less than an international enlistment of the most specially and liberally equipped minds and the most spiritually resourced personalities is needed against the darkness of this hour.

The colleges and universities stand strategic at the crossroads of a recurring transition in the history of modern times. They have, to our tragic cost, equipped us with only fragmentary views of human beings and human society. The universities are often slow to meet the needs of the age. In the transition from medieval to modern times, with its focus of forces involving the disintegration of the feudal order, the commercial revolution and the religious revolt, the universities tardily admitted to curricular equality the revived ancient learning which was the intellectual ferment of it all. Close to the beginning of the last century the Western world stood in the presence of the steam-power revolution. The universities were slow to give cultural equality to the new sciences which, in their own laboratories, were to rediscover and conquer the earth, and refound the technological basis of modern society. Modern democracies stand face to face to-day with communist and fascist dictatorships. The people of the Western world, already in the midst of the social challenge of the electrical and gas power revolutions, find themselves overwhelmed with three other great influences—the consequences of the world war, the world moral confusion and the world economic depression. The stakes are too great and catastrophic developments are too swift for the universities to stand aside or wait upon tradition for their course or vested interests for their cue. America, through the colleges and universities, must learn to be true to her inner Americanism of freedom of the mind and equality of opportunity for all people.

What the classics meant intellectually in Renaissance times and what the natural sciences have meant technologically in the industrial age, suggest something of what the social sciences in the twentieth century can mean humanly in the making of a nobler America and more beautiful world in which men and women can do their day's work and dream dreams for their children. Scholars of the first rank in all nations enlisted in high research can lay out the groundwork for the better cooperation of the nations in international diplomacy, disarmament, finance, commerce, culture, in scientific and social mastery, and catch the imagination and heroism of youth in the high adventures of the human spirit for the saving of the nations and the succor of the peoples of the earth who ask for the chance to earn their daily bread.

D. THE UNIVERSITY AND THE PEOPLE

(1) *The Extension Division:* It is the function of the state university not only to find its bits of truth and teach the truth gathered from scholars everywhere, but to carry the truth to the people that they may take it into their lives and help to make it prevail in the world of affairs. It is the ideal of the University Extension Division to make the resources of the universities, the discoveries of science and the finding of the social scientists available for the people of the commonwealth. The members of the general faculty, the special faculty, the special library, special lectures, courses in class and by correspondence, bureaus, institutes, interscholastic activities involving athletics, debates, classics, plays and playwriting, and in an independent and far-reaching way the general library and the Library School all serve to carry or send the university to the people. The public schools, teachers, men's civic clubs, professional associations, women's clubs and associations, and people in towns, on farms, and in remote mountain coves, all tap the life that is here. The universities should set their faces like flint against what is clearly trivial, merely current or only novel. Yet the American state university should not, from a fear to assert its own soul against what in its life would be a new Toryism of exclusive culture, high tuition and intellectual stratification, be misled into a mere imitation of European traditions and institutions. The state university comes from the people and should go out to the people. The intellectual life of the university should be quickened by contact and interchange with the people. They have a common destiny in the adventure of building a better commonwealth. The state university can not, as the university of the people, be an institution of a class, whether based on section, blood, money, creed, or intellectual background. Deep injustice anywhere in the commonwealth leaves its psychic scars upon university life; the well-being of the people makes more radiant the life of the state university. The state university can never lose the common touch without treason to its own nature and without drying up the springs from which flow the living waters of its own life. The state university is the university of all the people. It takes no side, but democracy and justice are on the side where it belongs. The university is organic with the life of the people, and the currents of its life would flow back into the life of the people with transforming excellence and creative power. There should be no lowering of standards in the extension process. Its standards and opportunities shall be second to none and open to all to the end that we build a commonwealth in which shall be preserved democracy without vulgarity and excellence without arrogance.

(2) *The Schools of the People:* The public schools are now and will increasingly be the community center of university extension and adult education. The university will not only extend and share its life with the public schools and the people, but university men, as citizens, if true to the traditions of this university made by men who can fight no more, Murphey, Yancey, Wiley, Vance, Alderman, McIver and Aycock, will fight for the schools of the people.

The university is resourced in the public schools, and the public schools are resourced in the university. They go up or down together. Now is the time, in the midst of depression, unemployment and educational defeatism, for the extension division and the public schools to envisage and lay out the plans for a future all-inclusive educational program in the communities for the continuous education of all the people as a way to use wisely the advancing leisure, to substitute cultural content for merely mechanical contacts, natural creative play for artificial and empty excitement, and to lay the intellectual groundwork for a more general and intelligent understanding of and participation in the affairs of the world and its opportunities for a larger mastery of human destiny. Land to the west for more than two hundred years helped to keep open and free our American life. The land is closed, but the schools are open and will help to make us free. Along the converging roads of the public schools, adult education and university excellence, lies one hope of our American democracy struggling for a higher mastery. We can not, in these critical times which test in our budgets what we really believe in, cut the schools and pinch our way out. With the inclusive and continuous education of all our people we must socially invest, we must develop and build, we must create our way out from depression into a higher prosperity and from poverty into a nobler power.

E. The Freedom of the University

Along with culture and democracy, must go freedom. Without freedom there can be neither true culture nor real democracy. Without freedom there can be no university. Freedom in a university runs a various course and has a wide meaning. It means the freedom of students with their growing sense of responsibility and student citizenship to govern themselves in campus affairs, and the right of lawful assembly and free discussions by any students of any issues and views whatever. This campus freedom carries with it a high moral responsibility. For the faculty, freedom means the right of the faculty to control the curriculum, scholastic standards, and especially matters pertaining to intellectual excellence; to teach and speak freely, not as propagandists, but as scholars and seekers for the truth with a clear sense of responsibility for the truth and a deep sense of the teacher's part in the development of the whole youthful personality; to organize their own independent association for discussion and statement of views, and as a basic part of the university's life help shape university policies by votes, representation, advice, and, may we hope, a larger sharing in the life of the people of the state. For the administrative head freedom means to take full responsibility in his own sphere and make decisions in the long run view of all the circumstances, to express views, without illusion as to their influence but with some sense of fairness, humility and tolerance, on those issues that concern the whole people, asking no quarter and fearing no special interest. Freedom of the trustees means the freedom to receive endowments for this meagerly endowed university from any honest sources without fear or favor or strings attached beyond an honorable responsibility, and the freedom to make the institution within the limits of their responsibility to the people and its own high nature an autonomous institution in its administration, faculty, standards, admissions, excellence and the budget which is basic to them all.

Freedom of the university means the freedom to study not only the biological implications of the physical structure of a fish but also the human implications of the economic structure of society. It means freedom from the prejudices of section, race or creed; it means a free compassion of her sons for all people in need of justice and brotherhood. It means the freedom of the liberated spirit to understand sympathetically those who misunderstand freedom and would strike it down. It means the freedom for consideration of the plight of unorganized and inarticulate peoples in an unorganized world in which powerful combinations and high-pressure lobbies work their special will on the general life. In the university should be found the free voice not only for the unvoiced millions but also for the unpopular and even the hated minorities. Its platform should never be an agency of partisan propaganda but should ever be a fair forum of free opinion. Freedom should never mean a loss of the sense of lawful and moral responsibility to the trustees and the people from whom the university came and to whom her life returns manifold.

But this freedom of the university should not be mistaken for approval of those who are merely sophisticated or who superficially exploit either the passing currents or great human causes or who fundamentally debase the deep human passions and poison the springs from which flow the waters of life. Such an abuse of freedom has the scorn of scholars whose intellectual integrity and wholesome life are the source of freedom. True freedom of self-expression is not the sort that leads to self-exploitation or to self-exhaustion but rather leads to the self-realization of the whole personality for the good life. No abuse of freedom should cause us to strike down freedom of speech or publication, which are the fresh resources of a free religion and a free state.

Finally freedom of the university means freedom of the scholar to find and report the truth honestly without interference by the university, the state or any interests whatever. If a scholar be enlisted by the state for research on a mooted issue, though such scholarly and independent report may be imputed to the university as an institution by powerful lobbies opposed to the report, the university will stand by the right of the state to enlist the scholar and the freedom of the scholar to make the report, whatever be the consequences. The real destruction of the university would come from the university administration's interference or any other interference with the report. Without such freedom of research we would have no university and no democracy.

These conceptions of the various forms of the freedom of the university are stated for the sake of fairness. The only recourse for changing such conceptions is to change the university administration. This is not said defiantly but in all friendliness and simply as a matter of openness and clearness. It is said with no personal concern, for it is our faith that whatever the administration, the freedom of the university, gathering momentum across a century, and the democracy of the people, sometimes sleeping but never dead, will rise in majesty to reassert the intellectual integrity and the moral autonomy of the University of North Carolina.

This integrity, democracy and freedom of the university comes out of its own nature. The idea and structure of the university evolve through the centuries under the impact of social needs and youthful hopes. The college and the campus, the professional schools, the graduate school, the library and laboratories, playhouse and music hall, the institute of research and the press, the library school and the democratic extension of the university's life throughout the commonwealth, are all gradually and organically being integrated into the idea and structure of this university of the people. In such a free university we will learn to see in every significant situation, personal, local, national or international, the composing elements, whether geographic, biological, psychological, historical, economic, social, political, intellectual or spiritual, or all. This organic university, with its humanities, natural sciences and social sciences, has the rootage of its growth in the experience of the race, the aspirations of the human personality and the needs of a changing age. Out of the very organic structure and quality of the university issue its democracy and its freedom.

Conclusion

Roll Call of Presidents and Muster of Sons: Out of the past come figures, living and dead, to stand by us in this inaugural hour in these woods where Davie, the founder, stood under the poplar and raised the standard of a people's hope. The lives of the presidents reassure us all with their spiritual presence and power: Caldwell, the first president, in whose administration for the first time in America a modern language was given curricular equality with an ancient language and the first observatory was established in an American college and whose communicated social passion sent Murphey to lay the foundation of the state's public schools, and Morehead to build railways to bind the East and West in bonds of iron; Swain, in whose time the university advanced to a high leadership in the South, and who, in the closing war days and reconstruction, was a conciliatory spirit in an age of hate; Battle, dauntless father of the reopening of the university, deviser of a separate group of graduate courses in the curriculum fifty years ago, and founder of the first university summer school in America, whose gay kindliness will ever pervade this place and whose noble spirit still walks in these woods; Winston, lying stricken in this village to-day, a casualty of the life militant, champion of religious freedom and educational democracy who synthesized the classical and the scientific, the cultural and vocational in his own varied and brilliant life; Alderman, lately and deeply lamented, who in his last days with something of a premonition of the end returned in filial memories to alma mater, her sons and her scenes, where his eloquence long stirred the creative imagination of the people of a commonwealth and caught the ear of the people of the nation; Venable, with his passion for soundness of scholarship and integrity of life, the symbol of the group of scientific scholars whose research and teaching won recognition among the scholars of the world, with us still in modest retirement these later years, gathering flowers from his garden for his friends in the village where he once gathered truth from test tubes for all mankind; Graham, major prophet of university extension and interpreter of culture and democracy to the people, his name memorialized in a students' building on the campus whose ideals he helped to create and whose life he passionately extended all over the state as he identified a democratic state university with the life of the people whose sustaining power has returned a hundredfold since his going; and Chase, under whose leadership came the greatest material expansion and intellectual advance, whose administration gathered up the momentum and values of the past, added high values of his own and worked a synthesis of all, champion of the freedom of scientific inquiry in testing times, genial leader and friend, now president of Illinois but always at home in Chapel Hill. These chieftains of the university and the hosts of her sons always muster in spiritual power in every hour of her need. Into the soul of the place has entered the spirit of an heroic woman, symbol of all the mothers and women whose hopes and prayers have wrought mightily under these oaks.

With the university to-day stand all the state and denominational schools, colleges and the neighbor university. Not in antagonism but in all friendliness and rivalry in excellence we would work in this region and build here together one of the great intellectual and spiritual centers of the world.

Chapel Hill: Here in Chapel Hill among a friendly folk, this old university, the first state university to open its doors, stands on a hill set in the midst of beautiful forests under skies that give their color and their charm to the life of youth gathered here. Traditions grow here with the ivy on the historic buildings and the moss on the ancient oaks. Friendships form here for the human pilgrimage. There is music in the air of the place. To the artist's touch flowers grow beautifully from the soil and plays come simply from the life of the people. Above the traffic of the hour church spires reach toward the life of the spirit. Into this life, with its ideals, failures and high courage, comes youth with his body and his mind, his hopes and his dreams. Scholars muster here the intellectual and spiritual resources of the race for the development of the whole personality of the poorest boy and would make the University of North Carolina a stronghold of learning with outposts of research along all the frontiers of the world. Great teachers on this hill kindle the fires that burn for him and light up the heavens of the commonwealth with the hopes of light and liberty for all mankind.

EDUCATIONAL EVENTS

THE CHILDREN'S GALLERY IN THE LONDON SCIENCE MUSEUM

THE new Children's Gallery in the basement of the Science Museum has now been opened. The general aim of the gallery (as described in the London *Times*) is to illustrate as simply as possible the development of applied science and its influence upon material and social progress, and it will thus provide a general elementary introduction to the museum collections. Models and figures of men and animals, painted backgrounds of natural scenery, and special systems of lighting have been introduced wherever possible to bring the objects into the child's immediate focus of interest, while a larger proportion of the objects than in any of the main galleries can be worked by pressing a button or turning a handle.

The initial exhibition falls into four main groups—a series of working models showing the conversion of energy, a succession of dioramas illustrating the historical evolution of transport, a smaller series of modeled scenes to demonstrate how lighting has evolved, and three life-size tableaux, in which effigies of men at work display the simple handicrafts of the potter, the flint-knapper, and the nail-maker. These three crafts are to be further illustrated by films of men practising them at the present day.

The working models which demonstrate the conversion of energy are each set in a miniature landscape. Thus the visitor sees the raising of water from a stream by the Archimedean screw in modern Egypt, and the same process conducted by animal power in a Moroccan scene, where a camel works a chain of pots. An undershot water-mill shows a relatively primitive method of using water itself as a source of power, and a Cambridgeshire post-windmill, reproduced upon a miniature scale, revolves in an artificial breeze to show wind-power. The series ends for the present with a reproduction of the steam power-plant introduced by Watt, but in another corner of the gallery a kindred group of exhibits shows the lifting and lowering of things by pulley and tackle, by a windlass, by levers and jacks, and by an electric traveling crane.

This group of objects forms a convenient transition for the mind to the series of nine large dioramas showing the evolution of transport. In these Mr. Roussell and his fellow-artists have exhibited the greatest skill in combining several distinct but contemporary developments in one comprehensive scene. Thus, in one, the Cro-magnon cave man is shown dragging a dead animal home upon his back, while a family of his companions are being pushed on logs across a shallow stream. In another a Neolithic man is seen more at ease with his sledge, while others of his tribe venture across the lake, which is their home, in a dug-out canoe. Animal transport is seen at its simplest in yak-teams crossing a pass in Northern China; the introduction of rollers appears in an Ancient Egyptian scene, where the sail, too, is first shown in the spoon-shaped vessels of the Nile. A brewer's dray of Roman times is seen being loaded from a merchantman, with a war-galley in the distance. A medieval scene displays packhorses, a rough cart and a rude ship under the lee of a castle. From this the visitor is introduced after a glance at the better carts and ships of the Elizabethan period to the simultaneous developments of the eighteenth century—the balloon, the stage-coach, and the specialized ocean-going merchantman and man-of-war. Finally there is a most lively meeting a century ago of railway train and paddle-steamer, steam-coach, velocipede, airship and fast mail-coach. The very poise of the figures suggests the increase in speed and frequency of communication which accompanied the full flow of the industrial revolution.

As companions to these in the center of the room are a group of horse-vehicles outside a miniature Victorian livery-stable, a set of miscellaneous means of transport from the sledge to the motor-lorry, and a row of tiny popular craft in a tank, illustrating the evolution of the modern dinghy from the log on which the cave-man straddled. Another case, set well away from the walls, shows the different methods of measuring time, from the Egyptian water-clock, the hour-glass, and King Alfred's candles, down to the pendulum clock.

Opposite the big dioramas, against the other long wall of the gallery, are primitive implements of flint and reindeer's antler. Then comes an aeroplane which rises in a wind-tunnel when the propeller and the wind itself are set in motion. This is followed by the tiny set scenes which trace illumination historically from the firebrands of primitive man to the Neon lamps and concealed electric lighting of a modern studio. Roman soldiers can be seen dicing upon Hadrian's Wall to the light of an oil lamp; Prince Arthur is shown in his prison lit by a tallow dip, and the Victorian colza lamp, the fish-tail gas burner, the arc-lamp, and the modern electric filament light up, at the pressing of a button, scences contemporary with their discovery.

Against the end wall are a series of transparencies showing the stages in the development of astronomy, medicine and human flight. All the exhibits are set low enough for the average child to see without standing on tip-toe, and the gallery is completely undecorated, so that the exhibits alone will attract attention. One isolated working model which will delight many youthful visitors is a thermometer which they can raise by frictional heat if they work hard enough upon a wheel.

SCHOOL ATTENDANCE IN THE IRISH FREE STATE

THE report issued by the Free State Education Department contains educational statistics for the school year 1929–30.

According to a summary given in the London *Times Educational Supplement,* tables show that between 1924 and 1930 there was an increase of 6,045 in the average number of pupils on the primary school rolls, and an increase of 58,353, or 9.9 per cent., in the average attendance. The average attendance of those pupils to whom the School Attendance Act applied was naturally somewhat higher; in 1929–30 the percentage was 84.8. In some areas it was much higher. In Waterford City it was 90.3, in Westmeath it was 86.7, in Meath 86.6, in Cork City and in County Carlow 86.4, in Dublin City 86.1, and in County Dublin and Louth 86. In no area was the percentage below 81.4. Attention is drawn to the sudden drop in numbers beyond the fifth standard. In the higher standards there has been an increase in recent years, but the difference between fifth and sixth standard numbers is still too great; in 1929–30 there were 49,319 fifth-standard pupils, and only 29,658 pupils of the sixth. But it is too soon to expect the full effects of the Attendance Act; the normal period of schooling, it is remarked, being eight years, and the act having been only four years in operation, one must wait for a few years before one can fairly pronounce judgment.

The rise in the qualifications of training college candidates means that the majority of entrants now-a-days have had a secondary education. In 1921 not quite one fourth of the entrants had had a secondary education, but in 1930 two thirds of the entrants were students who had done the full secondary course. In that year 30.3 per cent. of the entrants were preparatory college students, 34.4 per cent. were pupil teachers, 14.2 were university graduates and untrained assistants, and 21.1 per cent. were Easter scholarship candidates. The scholarship examination has been abolished, and the leaving certificate examination (the leaving examination for secondary schools) has taken its place, or has practically done so, for candidates for training college entrance are required to pass an oral and practical test at Easter as well as the leaving certificate examination in June. When the preparatory college scheme is complete it is expected that 670 students (600 Roman Catholics and 70 Protestants) will be preparing along secondary lines for admission to the training colleges.

REGIONAL CONFERENCE OF THE WORLD FEDERATION OF EDUCATION ASSOCIATIONS

THE Regional Conference of the World Federation of Education Associations will be held under the presidency of Dr. Paul Monroe, from July 25 to 30, 1932, at Honolulu, Hawaii. The conference will relate to all countries in the Pacific and will deal with such subjects as the dual language problem, modern educational problems in the Oriental setting, vocational education, health education and adult education.

The following statement has been given out by the federation:

The Pacific area at the present time is one of the most interesting and important sections of the world in economic, social and educational life. The United States is especially interested in the development of amicable, cooperative relations and of racial and international understanding with the groups this conference will represent. No area of the world is making more rapid cultural progress than the Asiatic-Pacific people. No place in all the world offers such an interesting and fascinating location for conferences of this nature as the Hawaiian Islands themselves. These islands represent a great human laboratory wherein is being worked out life problems of a complex social character but on a limited scale. Here are found all of the oriental strains of blood, intermingled with the occidental. People are living together in an enchanted land, working side by side without the prejudices and social distinctions which characterize such associations in other lands.

The group of islands with Honolulu as the capital, form a territory of the United States which eventually may apply for statehood. These islands are sometimes called "The Paradise of the Pacific," sometimes "The Crossroads of the Pacific," and other intriguing names. The islands lie in the midst of the Pacific, 2,200 miles southwest of San Francisco and Los Angeles, and between the Tropic of Cancer and the Equator, yet one is surprised to discover that he is not much nearer to Yokohama than to Seattle. The islands lie directly in the path of the trade winds which modify the climate and produce an even temperature the year around. The golden sunshine, the hedges of tropical plants, some of which are always in bloom, the fine homes sequestered in tropical foliage, and the friendly and industrious people, make these islands a valuable and enchanting part of the United States.

The islands are volcanic and are really the peaks of volcanoes thrown up from the bed of the sea. Lying in the path of the trade winds produces on one side of a small island a heavy rainfall with dense foliage, while on the other side, only a few miles away, is a semi-desert area. The islands are rich in agricultural products, the chief of which are sugar-cane and pineapples.

The educational system is modern in its organization, instruction and material equipment. School health, industrial forms of education, visual instruction and progressive types of education characterize the system.

American teachers who desire to attend the National Education Association meeting at Atlantic City, will have ample time to reach Hawaii before the Federation meeting begins. The total cost of round trip carfare and steamship, including meals, Pullman and the ten days' stay on the islands, will be about $450 from Atlantic coast points, with corresponding reductions for points west. Besides a fascinating educational experience, it will be a delightful travel experience which will enrich the life of the teacher. From time to time, as the program develops, more information will be given out. For information concerning the program, write to the President, Dr. Paul Monroe, 525 West 120th Street, New York City. For matters pertaining to travel, accommodations and general arrangements, write to the Secretary-General, 1201 Sixteenth Street, Washington, D. C.

SAVINGS OF NEW YORK CITY CHILDREN

IN spite of the depression, 238,325 new school savings accounts were opened by pupils in the City of New York in the past school year, bringing the number of open active accounts to more than 696,738. These figures, released by the National Association of Mutual Savings Banks, were said to indicate a broad interest on the part of the children, as more than one half of the total enrolment of 1,200,000 pupils are now regular savers. There was a gain of 25,707 new accounts over the previous year. A total of 42,140 new interest-bearing accounts of $5 or more were opened, also a gain over the previous year.

The total received by the 505 school banks cooperating in the movement last year was $2,762,614. In addition, there was $1,790,000 in "school trust accounts," deposits too small to be transferred to regular bank accounts. Cash transferred from the school banks to regular interest-bearing accounts in mutual savings banks in the same period amounted to $1,700,605.

Withdrawals were remarkably low. It was estimated that 61 per cent. of the total amount withdrawn was immediately transferred to regular interest-bearing accounts in mutual savings banks, while a considerable part of the remainder was withdrawn by children graduated from elementary schools. It is believed that a large portion of this sum was redeposited when such pupils entered high school or continuation school.

School savings in New York City is a voluntary activity. Of the 600 schools in the city, 505 have school banks, including 54 high schools out of 62. Forty-four mutual savings banks are depositories for the funds, with 38 of the banks operating systems in which no clerical or financial responsibility devolves upon the teacher or the pupil.

TRADE TRAINING FOR SMALL TOWNS

PRACTICAL plans for providing trade preparatory training for boys and girls in small towns and cities to fit them for wage-earning employment, are discussed in a publication issued by the Federal Board for Vocational Education under the title, "Trade Preparatory Training for Small Cities and Rural Communities."

As evidence of the diversity of the types of courses which it is possible to set up in small communities, the board lists six of these. They include general industrial courses, which are organized to give training in a variety of occupations; cooperative part-time courses, in which students alternate between regular employment and instruction in schools; unit courses in county or state trade schools which are designed to give training in many or all phases of the work of a single trade, and serve a number of communities instead of only one; apprentice courses in which apprentices in various industries are trained in plants or are sent to a central school for intensive training; dull season courses for workers in "seasonal" trades; and industrial arts courses which deal with industrial equipment and materials.

The general industrial and the cooperative part-time courses, according to the Federal Board for Vocational Education, are best adapted to the employment and industrial conditions obtaining in most small towns or cities. The general industrial course trains for some specific occupation and is intended primarily for those who are still in school, and the part-time cooperative course is for those already employed who can devote part of their working hours to school instruction.

General industrial courses offer opportunity for training in such trades as automobile mechanics, electricity, machine shop practice, bricklaying, plumbing, house wiring and carpentry, or combinations of these trades. For instance, courses in such allied occupations as automobile mechanics, electricity and machine shop practice or in sheet-metal work, plumbing, and house wiring might very appropriately be combined.

As an example of a combination course which has proved effective that offered in building construction in Lees Summit, Missouri, is cited. Students in this course receive instruction in carpentry, millwork, sheet-metal work and house wiring. Practical work in construction or remodeling residences, garages and other buildings in the town or near-by community includes the carpentry, wiring, sheet metal and concreting jobs incident to such work.

In the cooperative part-time type of courses are included those which train for a single trade, those which train for store and office practice and those which train for a variety of occupations.

Special attention is directed by the board to the plan followed in some states, notably Connecticut, New Jersey, Kentucky and North Dakota, of maintaining county or state trade schools where boys and girls from a number of communities may receive vocational training in industrial occupations. This plan applies particularly to sections where the need for workers in any one town is small and would not warrant organizing classes for a single town.

"It must not be forgotten," according to the Federal Board for Vocational Education, "that the vocational training needs of prospective industrial workers in small towns are as imperative as those living in the larger industrial centers. While the local demand in the smaller towns for additional workers in any one trade is not as great in the small towns as in the large ones, there are in practically every small community a number of desirable occupations for which some new workers are needed each year. The local employers prefer to employ and do employ local boys and girls whenever possible, but they feel the need for some plan of education which will help these young people to prepare for work that is to be done."

THE NEW PRESIDENT OF RUTGERS UNIVERSITY

Mr. Robert C. Clothier, dean of men at the University of Pittsburgh, who was elected president of Rutgers University at a meeting of the board of trustees on December 14, will take office on March 1. He succeeds Dr. John M. Thomas, who resigned in October, 1930, to become vice-president of the National Life Insurance Company at Montpelier, Vermont.

Since Dr. Thomas's resignation the position has been filled by Dr. Philip M. Brett, a member of the board of trustees and a graduate of Rutgers in the class of 1892. Dr. Brett, a New York lawyer, has accepted no remuneration for his work and has refused requests by the board of trustees to accept the presidency.

Dean Clothier was born in Philadelphia on January 8, 1885. He attended Haverford School at Haverford, Pennsylvania, and was graduated in 1908 with the degree of Bachelor of Literature from Princeton. There he studied under Woodrow Wilson, Henry Van Dyke and Harry B. Garfield. He was active in campus affairs, being a member of the senior council and editor-in-chief of *The Daily Princetonian.*

He went into newspaper work for a year and then joined the Curtis Publishing Company of Philadelphia, finally becoming employment manager. During the last year of the war he was in Europe studying the personnel procedures of the British and French armies as a member of the War Department's committee on classification of personnel. Later he was commissioned a Lieutenant-Colonel on the General Staff.

Dean Clothier joined Dr. Walter D. Scott, J. B. Hopkins and others in organizing the Scott Company, consultants in industrial personnel, after the war. In 1923 he went back to Haverford School as assistant head master and in 1928–1929 served as acting head master.

In 1929 the University of Pittsburgh called him to be dean of men, where he has carried out a program of promoting relationships between students and faculty members. He believes that education is interested not only in the student's knowledge of certain subjects but also in making him use his capacities for growth in intellect, character and social responsibility.

EDUCATIONAL NOTES AND NEWS

A dinner in honor of Dr. F. B. Dyer, who retires this month from the Cincinnati School Board, was given on December 11. The Hon. George E. Mills was toastmaster, and speeches were made as follows: "Correlation in Education," by Dr. Frederick C. Hicks; "From One Board Member to Another," by Hon. William J. Schroder; "To Our Children's Friend," by Mrs. Guy Mallon; "The Office of Superintendent," by Edward D. Roberts; "To Our Friend and Fellow Teacher," by E. D. Lyon; "Response," by Dr. Frank B. Dyer. Dr. Dyer was from 1912 to 1918 superintendent of the Boston schools.

A portrait of Professor John W. Cunliffe, director emeritus of the Pulitzer School of

Journalism at Columbia University, was unveiled at the school on December 17. The presentation speech was made by Mr. Joseph L. Jones, foreign editor of the United Press, an alumnus. Professor Ashley H. Thorndike made an address, and President Nicholas Murray Butler accepted the portrait for the university.

THE Penrose Medal of the Geological Society of America, given for outstanding service in the advancement of geological science, has been awarded to Dr. William Morris Davis, professor emeritus of geology of Harvard University. The presentation will be made on December 30 at the annual dinner of the society to be held in Tulsa in connection with the forty-fourth annual meeting.

A dinner has been given in honor of Professor Winterton C. Curtis, who has completed thirty years' service in the zoology department at the University of Missouri. The speakers were Dr. F. H. Woods, Dr. Lewis Stadler and President Walter Williams, of the University of Missouri; Colonel Lloyd E. Thatcher, of the Branham-Hughes Military Academy, and Father Alphonse M. Schwitalla, of St. Louis University. It was announced that a fund of $2,100 had been raised to establish a graduate scholarship in zoology for summer study at marine laboratories.

THE *Harvard Alumni Bulletin* remarks editorially that it is an unusual, perhaps a unique, circumstance that there are in Harvard University to-day two Plummer professors of Christian morals, *emeriti,* and also two Boylston professors of rhetoric and oratory, *emeriti.* Francis Greenwood Peabody, '69, A.M. and S.T.B. '72, S.T.D. '09, is the older of the two Plummer professors; he was Parkman professor of theology from 1881 to 1886, and Plummer professor from 1886 until 1913. Professor Peabody's successor was Edward Caldwell Moore, S.T.D., who was Parkman professor from 1901 to 1929 and Plummer professor from 1915 to 1929. Willard Learoyd Sperry, D.D., dean of the Theological School, is now Plummer professor. LeBaron Russell Briggs, '75, A.M., '82, LL.D., '00, was Boylston professor from 1904 to 1925; most Harvard graduates know him even better as dean of Harvard College from 1891 to 1902 and dean of the Faculty of Arts and Sciences from 1902 to 1925. Charles T. Copeland, '82, Litt.D., was Boylston professor from 1925 to 1928. That chair is now vacant.

DR. ROBERT T. CRANE, professor of political science in the University of Michigan, has been appointed permanent secretary of the Social Science Research Council with headquarters at 230 Park Avenue, New York. Dr. Crane succeeds Dr. Robert S. Lynd, who has resigned to become professor of sociology in Columbia University. Upon the retirement as president on February 1, 1932, of Professor Robert S. Woodworth, of Columbia University, Dr. Crane will become executive head of the council. He was one of the organizers of the council in 1923, and has since remained constantly associated with its work as a member of the committee on problems and policy and through active service on other committees. Professor Arthur M. Schlesinger, of Harvard University, has been reelected chairman and Professor William F. Ogburn, of the University of Chicago, vice-chairman. Dr. R. H. Coates, Dominion statistician for Canada, succeeds Dean Henry M. Bates, of the University of Michigan, as secretary. Dr. Isaiah Bowman, director of the American Geographical Society, becomes treasurer in place of Professor Wesley C. Mitchell, of Columbia, who has been named visiting professor in economics at Oxford University, England. Professor Mitchell has served as a member of the executive committee and of the committee on problems and policies and as chairman of the council.

DR. ARTHUR C. CHRISTIE, president of the Medical Society of the District of Columbia, has been elected president of the board of trustees of the American University at Washington.

MR. W. HOWARD PILLSBURY, superintendent of schools at Schenectady, was elected president of the New York State Teachers Association at the recent annual meeting of the house of delegates in Utica. He succeeds Carlos S. Blood, superintendent of schools of the third supervisory district of St. Lawrence County.

PROFESSOR A. B. LAMB, of Harvard University, has been elected president of the American Chemical Society for 1933. The president for 1932 is Dr. L. V. Redman, vice-president and director of research of the Bakelite Corporation, who succeeds Professor Moses Gomberg, of the University of Michigan, on January 1.

To fill the vacancy caused by the death of Dr. James Sullivan, the New York State Board of Education has appointed Dr. Avery W. Skinner, director of the examinations and inspections division of the department, a member of the committee on geographic names.

MR. B. C. VAN INGEN, principal of the Kingston, New York, High School, has been appointed superintendent of schools in that city to succeed the late Dr. Myron J. Michael. Mr. Van Ingen has been a member of the faculty of the Kingston High School for the past ten years.

MRS. JENNIE T. JENNINGS, who for the past twelve years has been assistant librarian, was appointed in September librarian of the St. Paul Public Library, to succeed Mr. Webster Wheelock, whose death occurred on April 1. Mrs. Jennings was formerly head cataloguer at the Cornell University Library. She had also served as cataloguer at Randolph-Macon Woman's College, Virginia, and as a reference librarian at the Iowa State College Library.

THE REV. WILLIAM MCKIBBEN, president emeritus of Lane Theological Seminary, Cincinnati, died on December 20, at the age of 81 years.

MR. HENRY MARTIN BRADFORD, of Nova Scotia, formerly head master of King's Collegiate School, at Windsor, Nova Scotia, and of St. Andrew's School, at Annapolis Royal, died on December 16, at the age of 65 years.

THE death is announced, at the age of ninety-one years, of Dr. Gustav Le Bon, professor of psychology and allied sciences at the University of Paris.

A SUIT was filed last spring against Miami University by Miss Jean West, of Portsmouth, Ohio. She had been notified by the university that she could not return to her classes because she had failed in her work. Miss West took her case to Common Pleas Court, where Judge J. D. Barnes, of Sydney, enjoined the university from dismissing her. Dr. A. H. Upham, president of the university, appealed and the Circuit Court reversed Judge Barnes's ruling on the ground that it was unfair to let a pupil who fell below standard retard others.

AN Associated Press dispatch reports that Professor Elisha Kent Kane, of the University of Tennessee, who was acquitted last week at Hampton, Virginia, of a charge of drowning his wife, has formally resigned as head of the department of Romance languages. His resignation, Dean J. D. Hoskins said, "relieved the University of Tennessee in a delicate situation." Professor Kane resigned first last September following his arrest. The announcement was, however, withheld for fear it would prejudice his case. He is reported to have said he had been treated "fairly and squarely by the university" and held the "deepest gratitude toward the administration and faculty for their support."

MR. JOHN J. GORMAN, of Chicago, former Representative in Congress, who as corporation counsel of Chicago conducted former Mayor Thompson's investigation of charges of British propaganda in history text-books, was disbarred by the Supreme Court on December 17 for not conforming to standards of the legal profession. The disbarment action, started by the Chicago Bar Association, was based on Mr. Gorman's prosecution of Mayor Thompson's suit for dismissal of Mr. William McAndrew, then superintendent of schools. Mayor Thompson charged that he was a "paid agent of the British crown" and permitted the use of text-books steeped in propaganda for King George. Mr. Gorman in his conduct of the case referred especially to Professor David Saville Muzzey, of Columbia University, whom he called a "propagandist," and his text-book, which he asserted was "unfit for use in public schools." Professor Muzzey filed a libel suit, but dropped the action when Mr. Gorman formally apologized.

ACCORDING to an Associated Press dispatch from Rome under date of December 18, several of Italy's most prominent educators are included in the list of eleven university professors who have sacrificed their positions by refusing to take the oath of allegiance to Fascism. The oath is required in addition to the usual oath of loyalty to the King and Royal Family. Four of the debarred are professors at the University of Rome, three at Turin, and one each at Bologna, Pavia, Perugia and Milan. They include former Premier Vittorio Orlando, professor of law, and Senator Vito Volterra, professor of mathematics at Rome.

Dr. Henry Suzzallo, president of the Carnegie Foundation for the Advancement of Teaching, will have charge of a California educational survey to be conducted by the foundation. The purpose of the survey is to study higher education in California and to help to formulate policies for the next year. Special emphasis is to be laid on determining whether or not regional four-year colleges should be established in the state.

On December 26 the program for the radio lectures on economics and psychology sponsored by the National Advisory Council on Radio in Education, and broadcast by the National Broadcasting Company, will be a summary of the first ten lectures in the series. Dr. Henry C. Link, of the Psychological Corporation, will summarize the lectures on psychology and point out their significance to young people who are planning their careers. Dr. Leverett S. Lyon, of the Brookings Institution, Washington, D. C., will summarize and comment upon the lectures on economics. On January 2, Dr. Robert M. Hutchins, president of the University of Chicago, will deliver an address as an introduction to the coming twenty lectures in the series. Dr. Walter V. Bingham, chairman of the committee on psychology, will give in detail the program for the coming lectures on psychology, and Mr. Felix Morley, executive secretary of the committee on economics, will speak for economics.

Rather than risk a decline in educational standards because of a budget cut of $1,080,000, 3,000 public school teachers and employees of the Board of Education of Rochester, New York, have signed over a month's salary to help the board meet expenses. To escape legal difficulties, the gift was made as an offer to work free of charge for 10 per cent. of the 1932 school year. The saving to the board by the voluntary offer is estimated at $590,000. The teachers also signed a pledge approving legal action to enforce the offer in case of defaults. Most of them are protected by state law against enforced reductions.

A public appeal for funds has been made for members of the faculty of the Atlantic University, at Virginia Beach, who have not received any salary this fall. Many of them are described as almost destitute and without food for their families. Dr. William Moseley Brown, anti-Smith candidate for Governor of Virginia in 1929, is president of the university. A petition for receivership for the university has been filed by Dr. Holly E. Cunningham, lecturer in philosophy, and M. L. Taylor, comptroller, who were dropped by the university on December 10. The school, in its second year, has been in financial difficulties since the Blumenthal Bros., New York brokers, who were instrumental in founding it, withdrew their support.

DISCUSSION

SHOULD DEPRECIATION BE ACCOUNTED FOR IN PUBLIC SCHOOL BUILDINGS?

In some states school boards are forbidden by law to set up reserves for depreciation over a long period of time. The theory is that taxation should represent only sums immediately needed for public service or public improvement. Some tax experts and public economists hold that a building erected for the future should be paid for by the generations which will enjoy its facilities. However, laws can be changed and the minds of tax experts may necessarily undergo some modification, and our present generation in the midst of a depression is paying back money borrowed in more prosperous times.

One of the most perplexing of all problems confronting the school executive in smaller cities is the housing problem. There seem to be many factors which unite to make this a serious handicap when reconstructing the school to meet new educational needs. Old buildings wear out and become obsolescent. Population grows and old buildings become crowded. Some buildings burn down or are destroyed by other forces of nature. The social concept of education is changing so rapidly that many boards of education lag behind in keeping the buildings up-to-date. This is made more acute by the inexperience and brief tenure of their school administrators. School boards seldom make any allowances in the budget for depreciation. Expenditures made for repair and maintenance tend to offset, to a degree at least, depreciation due to wear and tear, but they can not completely balance such losses nor furnish funds for replacing a building by the time it must be abandoned.

The real problem is a financial one. The brief tenure of school executives, who naturally do not have opportunity to put their plans into operation, and deferred maintenance programs on the part of boards of education only aid and hasten the acuteness of the financial difficulties. Much literature is available on building programs, surveys and building finance, in issuing bonds, in constructing type A and type B buildings, but not so much is available for the executive who is confronted with demands for immediate expansion, where the bonded indebtedness and where the mill levy for all school purposes are already up to the maximum limit established by law.

The meeting of bond payments when due is quite generally met, yet the issuance of the old type of term bond seems to be passed. The serial type which is replacing it has favor because of difficulties encountered when term bonds are due for payment. Sinking funds have not been properly handled. Many times bonds have been sold to counties, who ask only the payment of annual interest from year to year, thus causing payments into sinking funds to lapse. In cases of scores of South Dakota school districts, these sinking funds when established have been placed on deposit in banks, which subsequently closed, incurring losses in many instances up to 100 per cent. Other places keep their indebtedness up to the limit by issuing warrants and buying these warrants back with sinking funds. Boards of education in making levies too often fail to take into consideration emergencies and losses due to a small percentage of unpaid taxes. This deficit is met in the next year's levy, but without foresight is quite apt to develop into a financial lag.

These difficulties have to do with the paying for buildings already constructed and with the retiring of bonded indebtedness. Depreciation constitutes another financial difficulty. As a result, many old buildings are being used for school purposes which are inadequate in the light of new educational procedure, many which are beyond remodeling and repair, and many which should be abandoned. It seems that the idea of letting the future pay for the present in the matter of school buildings is a predominant one, and we must turn to the industrial world, with its well-established "depreciation funds" to learn how we can lay foundations for meeting future financial difficulties in matters of replacement.

There is no cut-and-dried way of determining the rate of depreciation of school buildings. The rate depends upon the kind of building erected in the first place. A modern fire-proof, reenforced concrete, brick or stone, steel-framed type of building will not depreciate as fast as a cheaper building. The materials which go into the building to make it fireproof will also be resistant to other forces of depreciation such as wear and tear, the weather and other agencies. The amount and rate of depreciation depends upon wear and tear, and the rate of this agency depends upon the community. In some communities there will be twice the rate there will in others, at least in internal structure. The rate of wear and tear may be twice as great during one period as in another within the same community. This will in part be due to school management, to type of pupils and to the janitor force. The rate of wear and tear and of physical decay of school buildings will depend upon climatic conditions, such as sudden changes of temperature and extremes of heat and cold. Rainfall, wind and hailstorms aid the climatic forces in bringing about physical decay. One needs to see the old, poorly constructed Spanish Missions of the Southwest to learn that the dry climate will prolong the life of a building. The rate of depreciation depends upon deferred maintenance and upon neglect, since a neglected building depreciates more rapidly than one which is repaired at regular intervals. Inadequacy depends upon the growth of population and upon changes in educational practice. Where population growth is great, extensions and new buildings are necessary. The character of the population growth may have an influence upon whether a new building is possible, since growth in school population might not mean a corresponding growth in assessed valuation.

The school executive in figuring the rate of depreciation of a school plant should not only consider the first cost, but what it would cost to replace the building at the time of proposed abandonment. A building built in 1913 could not be replaced for the same amount of money it took to build it, unless there is a decided falling off in building costs. He can not as a rule consider a great deal if any scrap value. For an old car, there is some resale value and it can be driven away, but in most cases it will cost as much to tear down an abandoned school building as the material would be worth, unless the building was a cheap all-wood structure. At any rate the scrap value would amount to little if one took into consideration the errors made in estimating the life of the building. Maintenance and repair in school administration is a neglected field. There are no depreciation rates on school buildings available. A building begins to depreciate as soon as it is built. Neither the causes of depreciation nor the parts most likely to depreciate have been scientifically studied. Much of the wear and tear could be kept to a minimum if the teachers, pupils and principals could be organized to carry on maintenance.

It has been established by the manufacturers in computing standard depreciation rates for factories that a brick and steel building with concrete floors depreciates annually at the rate of about 2½ per cent. on the original cost, brick and wood about 3 per cent. The problem confronting the school executive is to determine whether school buildings decay faster or slower and how much it will cost to replace them. After this is done, some systematic way of computing the depreciation and of handling a depreciation reserve fund should be attempted by the board of education. It has been a common practice among schools to charge the cost of replacing capital, which had depreciated in any way, to operating expenses for the year in which replacements were made. It can readily be demonstrated and seen that this method does not represent the facts. Depreciation accumulates year after year and is not justly chargeable to current operating expense, current capital outlay or current maintenance.

In working out some plan for calculating depreciation we might also turn to the business world. The following have been used:

(A) A fixed proportion of the original value
(B) A fixed percentage of reduced balances
(C) An annuity system
(D) A sinking fund
(E) An annual revaluation

In computing depreciation under the plan known as the proportion of original value, the difference between the original cost and scrap value, if any scrap value, is divided by the estimated number of years the building will be used before abandonment. An amount is then established which will be subtracted annually from the value of the plant. This method has been called the straight-line method of determining depreciation. The quotient in this case represents the amount to be charged off each year as depreciation.

In the case of computing depreciation by a fixed percentage of reduced values, a certain per cent. is taken annually from the value as established during the preceding year. It is not taken from the original cost. The heaviest reduction in value occurs during the first years of a building's existence, and the slight reductions occur annually in old buildings.

By the annuity system the gross charges in respect to depreciation are constant, but the credits to revenue, due to interest, diminish from year to year as the value of the asset decreases. Revaluation probably is not advisable in the case of school buildings.

The sinking fund is not the most widely used in business, because capital invested in one's own business earns a far greater amount of interest than can be realized by outside investment in the sinking fund. This fund, however, is perhaps the most scientific and most adaptable to school buildings, if properly invested. It is simply a method which allows for a sum of money to be set aside each year out of the school fund. With the interest on such a fund compounded at regular periods, the board of education would have on hand by the time a building must be abandoned enough to replace it.

With all these phases of the problem considered, it seems to the writer than the determination of depreciation as an element of cost in school buildings should be given some thought at this time. Particularly is it true in places where crop failures, depressed income and deflated values cause serious taxation problems. What well-meaning man would buy a farm with no intention of ever paying for it, mortgaging the lives of his sons and daughters for many years to come? It simply wouldn't be good business.

HARRY R. WOODWARD
HOT SPRINGS PUBLIC SCHOOLS,
SOUTH DAKOTA

WANTED: A MORAL EQUIVALENT FOR THE CLASSICS

WILLIAM JAMES told us that the world needs a moral equivalent for war. The conscience and common sense of the world can no longer tolerate war, and yet there is good in war, or at least in some of the preparation, organization and cooperation which usually accompany it. We are told that military drill provides discipline of mind and body and that as the recruit becomes a soldier he replaces softness, inaccuracy and timidity with strength, precision and courage. The development of these latter qualities, it is suggested, is partial compensation for the wastes of war.

Perhaps we need a moral equivalent for Latin and Greek, and for other of the formal disciplines which have so largely disappeared from our curricula. Like war, these studies had come to us from the past. Like war, they were charged with being wasters of time and energy. They were accused of getting in the way of social progress by taking the place which would otherwise be given to the study of science, social organization, esthetics and religion. And yet, there was good in these formidable and exacting studies of an older day. The art of warfare and the art of teaching the classics have this in common—both have a long history. These are trades in which man has had long experience and in which he has arrived at effective methods. These are fields of effort in which accuracy, thoroughness and tenacity of purpse are needed for success.

It is better for men to continue war than to become soft, selfish and cowardly. It is better to require year after year of the ancient languages than to turn out of our schools slovenly thinkers and moral slackers; and, whatever is believed about the possibility of the transfer of mental training, there is but little doubt that from the faithful study of the classics there came certain moral values, such as the habit of thorough work.

The classics are almost gone from our schools and colleges and we have had time to look about and view the result of what we thought would be educational progress. Are we satisfied with that which has replaced the old curriculum with its philosophy of drill and discipline? Many of us who do not at all regret the passing of the old type of education feel that in our present-day courses of study (and this is particularly true of the curricula of our secondary schools, liberal arts colleges and teachers' colleges) much that has replaced the classics is too general and descriptive. To too great an extent, mere reading has replaced study, and careless generalizations have taken the place of analytical thinking. Too many courses to-day are not much more than reading circles and too many classes are mere discussion groups.

But James reminded us that in modern industrial society there is much to call out the virtues presumed to be developed in camp and battlefield. May we not find in the studies closely related to the problems of modern life opportunities for the developing of those qualities traditionally supposed to come from the pursuit of the old curriculum? We do not need military drill in order to develop manhood and we do not need to laboriously plow the sands of the ancient languages in order to develop accuracy and clear thinking. But we do need to so organize the new courses of study that they will require exact definitions, objective treatment and clear analysis. We need courses in literature, philosophy, natural science and social science as well planned and as well taught as those which have been replaced. When we have brought about these changes, we shall have gone far toward providing a moral equivalent for the study of the classics.

J. S. CLELAND
MONMOUTH COLLEGE,
ILLINOIS

SPECIAL CORRESPONDENCE

NEW STATUTES OF THE UNIVERSITY OF ILLINOIS

THE University of Illinois recently has adopted a new series of statutes governing its internal administration. These statutes were drawn by a committee appointed last winter and were submitted by it to the University Senate,[1] which discussed them in a number of weekly meetings held last spring. After modifying them somewhat, the senate sent them to the board of trustees, which gave to them final approval this fall. These statutes define the powers and duties of various officers and administrative and educational groups, and are aimed to adjust the working machinery of the university to present conditions. The former statutes of the university occasionally were incomplete and did not always precisely define the function of these agencies. The new statutes knit together the various interests concerned.

Further, they eliminate what had been a dual jurisdiction over matters of educational policy on the part of the senate and another body, called the council of administration. The senate was vested with legislative powers over educational matters, but the council of administration, which was composed of the president and the deans, had authority to legislate in the interim between senate meetings. Under the new statutes the council becomes advisory to the president and is given no legislative authority. The senate, which is composed of all full professors and officers of corresponding rank, alone is given jurisdiction on questions of general educational policy. In carrying out its functions, the senate acts through committees which it elects after they have been nominated to it by a committee on committees. The latter committee is elected by ballot by and from the members of the senate, as are also three senate representatives who sit on the president's council.

The new statutes tend to decentralize the organization of the university and to place a larger measure of autonomy in the various colleges and departments of the university. Under them the colleges and schools are given independence over their curricula and proceedings, but provision is made that matters involving general university policy must be submitted to the senate. The intent is to allow the various units a greater freedom for experimentation, for variation and for individual treatment of students. Provision is made for a senate committee on educational policy for the consideration of such matters affecting the colleges as are of general educational concern. The relation of a college to the university, under the new measures, may be compared to that of a state to the federal government; as large a measure of freedom is given as is consistent with holding together the general structure in a unitary fashion.

The statutes remove student discipline from the jurisdiction of the old council of administration and place it with a committee of the senate. They provide that the dean of men and the dean of women shall be advisers for men and women students respectively and that their duties shall not be regulative. They designate that the functions performed by those deans shall include personnel work, vocational direction and guidance in problems involving intellectual, emotional and social adjustments.

The statutes assure faculty participation in the determination of questions of policy where such questions touch the educational program of the university. The aim is to secure this result through a scheme under which the various administrative officers are given councils or advisory committees. The faculties of the various colleges consist of all members of the teaching staff. Each faculty selects an executive committee which is designated for consultation by the dean in matters affecting the policy of the college, including the budget. These committees are advisory, not legislative. The provision is for consultation, not decision. Provision is further made that departments within the college may be organized either with heads or chairmen. Any department which decides to change its existing form of organization may make its wishes known to the president on this

[1] The senate is the general faculty of the University of Illinois consisting of the full professors, the president, provost, deans and other general administrative officials.

point for consideration. Heads or chairmen are appointed by the president, comparisons between the two being in the greater measure of faculty participation through committees in departments organized with chairmen.

The University of Illinois is a very large institution. Because of its size it is easy for the members of the faculty to lose a sense of responsibility for what goes on in the university. The statutes aim to decentralize administration and to distribute responsibility without at the same time blocking the possibilities of freedom and effective action. The new measures are, of course, experimental, but the university feels that it is taking a step in a promising direction.

H. W. CHASE

QUOTATIONS

CRITICISM OF YOUTH

IT is well-established practice that an older generation pretty constantly has fault to find with the youth of its time. From one point of view, this may be no more than a natural expression of dissatisfaction with a changing environment or of unwillingness or inability to adapt oneself to it. From another, it may be a sound and just criticism based upon the failure of youth either to aim at or to achieve fine and high standards of character and of intellectual life and interest. It is not always easy for the older generation to understand youth, and youth, in turn, is frequently impatient of what it regards as the stiff and harsh judgments of those who are no longer young. The elementary fact never to be forgotten is that all sound conduct and all high intellectual endeavor have certain characteristics in common, no matter when or where in human history or at what age they manifest themselves, and that these have also as many different forms of expression as there are peoples and nations and inheritances and environments and stages of life. The common denominator of excellence should always be present, but the numerator of individual mind and character will be infinitely varied. If the common denominator be at hand, no fault need be found with the numerator by those who live under other climes, at other times, or in very different environments, or who are of an older generation.

That there has been for some years past a steady decline in the practice of good manners is, unhappily, indisputable. Carelessness and inconsiderateness in dress, in speech, and in personal habits have become all too common, not among the younger generation alone by any means, but also on the part of their elders. It is not easy to find satisfactory reasons for such changes as these, or to fix upon the cause which would explain why it is that distinction and correctness of speech, of appearance and of manner are no longer esteemed as they once were. Unconcern for standards of excellence and over-concern for the quick satisfaction of one's own immediate personal conveniences and desires have combined to undermine that very desirable respect for age, for accomplishment, for excellence, and for high standards which have long marked, and should always mark, the cultivated gentleman. Probably the anti-philosophies and the pseudo-psychologies which are so widely diffused just now, and which are having such deplorable effects upon the instruction offered and training given, particularly in the elementary and secondary schools, have, consciously or unconsciously, played a large part in effecting these changes. Doubtless the careless and unconventional dress and the careless and unconventional speech of teachers and older persons have been seized upon as examples not unworthy of imitation. Whatever the causes may be, their results are deplorable, and there is need of a constant and strong emphasis on those personal habits which manifest themselves in good manners.

The virtually complete abdication of the family as a primary and controlling factor in education, together with the substantial collapse of the educational influence of the Protestant churches, have combined to put upon the school a burden and a responsibility which it can not bear and should not be asked to bear. Education has its beginning in the family, and it is merely to give formal instruction as part of the educational process that the school has been brought into existence. In no sense can the school be asked to bear the whole burden of that educational process. The moment that family influence and oversight disappear and the church, on one ground or another, allows itself to be pushed aside, there is nothing left of the formal educational process but the school, which is, and always must be, limited in its scope and partial in its influence. The cynical observer who is responsible for the statement that the school has become probably the least injurious influence to which youth is now exposed, no doubt presented an extreme point of view, but it is one which increasingly finds expression. The truth is that the school draws upon itself criticism, not so much by reason of what it fails to offer or accomplish in its own proper sphere, but by reason of its inability and incapacity to do the work of the school, the family and the church combined. If the family can not and will not meet that responsibility which belongs to it, and if the church continues to fail in its educational duty, nothing will be more certain than the gradual disappearance from society of those traits and influences in education which it is the business of the family and the church to foster and to strengthen.—*Dr. Nicholas Murray Butler in the Report of the President of Columbia University for 1931.*

THE ECONOMIC SITUATION AND THE SCHOOLS

Not a school door in Bledsoe County, Tennessee, has opened this winter, according to educational leaders in that state, who predict that one third of the schools of Tennessee will not be able to continue their term after the Christmas holidays. This curtailment of educational opportunity is one instance of hundreds of cases of reduced school services discovered in a country-wide survey of the effect of the depression on the welfare of children.

Decreased financial support of the schools comes at a time when they are overburdened with extra responsibilities due to the very circumstances that have reduced school funds. Enrolments in educational institutions particularly high schools and colleges where operation costs are greatest, have increased rapidly as the number of unemployed persons has mounted.

Graduates who had intended to enter vocations have discovered no vacancies in their chosen occupation. Many of them have reentered their schools to take post-graduate courses. Hundreds of thousands of high-school students who would normally have dropped out before graduation are remaining in school because there is nothing else for them to do.

President Hoover's Commission on Unemployment has urged students to remain in school as a means of relieving unemployment. The National Education Association has endorsed this recommendation because of the desirability of keeping those who would otherwise be idle engaged in better fitting themselves for the prosperity to which the nation looks forward. The result has been overflowing school buildings and greatly crowded classes. It is not unusual for one teacher to have more than fifty pupils in a class and some teachers have reported as many as eighty in one class.

The crisis in education has affected rural and city communities somewhat differently according to the National Education Association. Terms are more frequently cut in rural schools, or schools are closed altogether, due to meagerness of support which many rural schools receive. Even in times of prosperity the amount of this support is only a fraction of the amount spent annually per child for education in urban communities. With thousands of farmers unable to pay their taxes, the appropriation for education has become pitifully small in many rural districts. It is reported that some rural teachers are conducting their schools in return for room and board, a practice common in pioneer days, but long ago abandoned.

Teachers in city schools are finding it necessary to participate in many kinds of welfare work in which they do not normally engage. In all the larger cities teachers have subscribed liberally to the Community Chest and other welfare funds. In addition they are carrying out special welfare projects for which, on account of their positions, they are best fitted. Among these projects are the distribution of clothes and food to needy children and the preparation of warm meals at school for children who come hungry. Some cities have drastically cut school budgets.

Added responsibilities and decreased financial support combine to threaten the breakdown of the school systems of some states. The National Education Association urges citizens to choose carefully the public enterprises which they support during the crisis with a view to averting the sacrifice of children. Educators are urged to employ the greatest economy in school management and to hold the gains which the schools have made in effectiveness of instruction and physical care of children.—*Press Bulletin of the National Education Association.*

EDUCATIONAL RESEARCH AND STATISTICS

WHO CONTROLS THE LIBERAL ARTS COLLEGE?

FOR a period of three hundred years American society has used the privately owned college as a means of providing education on the higher educational level. That it should continue to do so is the contention of those who are seeking to secure more adequate financial support for the liberal arts colleges. Immediately the question arises whether the institutions in question are controlled by agencies other than those that have been organized for the primary purpose of providing higher education. An attempt has been made to arrive at a partial answer by visiting twenty colleges, chosen at random, in Iowa, Minnesota, Michigan, Wisconsin and Illinois. The data gathered in this way have been supplemented by information secured by correspondence with 160 additional colleges scattered throughout the country. It is a reasonable inference that the situation in these 180 colleges is typical of the privately owned colleges of the country.

SELF-PERPETUATING BOARDS OF TRUSTEES

The owning and controlling body of the college is in all cases the board of trustees. If this board is a self-perpetuating organization or has a majority of memberships that are self-perpetuating, no external organization can exercise direct control over the affairs of the institution. Of the twenty schools visited, only 10 per cent. have boards that are *wholly* self-perpetuating, but in 60 per cent. more a *majority* of the trustees are elected by the board itself. Fifty-nine per cent. (318) of the total number of trustees (538) attained office by the nomination and vote of their colleagues. This represents more than twice as many as hold office by any other suffrage.

EX-OFFICIO TRUSTEES

A small number of trustees hold their trust by virtue of some other office to which they have been elected or appointed. This is the case in 40 per cent. of the colleges, but in no case do *ex-officio* trustees exceed three in number. In every board that provides for *ex-officio* membership, the president of the college is a trustee in accordance with this provision. In two cases the offices which imply college trusteeships are offices in official boards of the church denominations to which the institutions belong. All others are administrative officers of the college. Less than 4 per cent. (19) of all trustees attain office in this manner.

TRUSTEES NOMINATED AND ELECTED BY CHURCH

In one of the twenty schools under consideration all the trustees are nominated and elected by the church. Some members of the board are nominated and elected by some church body in half of these institutions, but in only 30 per cent. of the colleges do they constitute a majority of the trustees. Of the 538 trustees only 27 per cent. (145) are nominated and elected in this way. The trustees elected by the church are second in number, and consequently in authority, to the self-perpetuating memberships on the boards of these colleges.

ALUMNI TRUSTEES

The alumni constitute a comparatively new agency in the control of their alma mater. Sixty per cent. of the colleges visited have alumni representatives on their boards, but in only one third of these are the trustees actually elected by the alumni organization. Of the total number (538), 4 per cent. (22) are elected and 10 per cent. (55) are nominated by this agency. The matter of alumni representation on the board was referred to the larger group of colleges and was found characteristic of 50 per cent. (89) of the 180 institutions involved. The distribution is not uniform among schools of various types nor throughout all sections of the country. It is more common in women's than in men's or coeducational colleges. In the North Atlantic section it characterizes 73 per cent. of the institutions cooperating in the investigation in contrast to 20 per cent. of those in the South Central section.

TABLE I

DISTRIBUTION ACCORDING TO TYPE AND GEOGRAPHICAL LOCATION OF COLLEGES WHICH HAVE ALUMNI REPRESENTATION ON THEIR BOARDS OF TRUSTEES

Type	North Atlantic	South Atlantic	North Central	South Central	Mountain	Pacific	Total	Per cent.
Men's	8	2	1				11	50
Women's	9	4	2	1			16	60
Coeducational	7	4	41	4	1	5	62	47
Total	24	10	44	5	1	5	89	
Per cent.	73	34	55	20	33	45		50

SUMMARY

The agencies which determine the membership of the liberal arts college boards of trustees are: the board itself, the church, the alumni and *ex-officio* membership. To get a clearer understanding of the extent to which these agencies exercise control over the twenty colleges visited, we may construct a composite institution. Such a school would have a board of twenty-seven trustees. Sixteen of these would be elected by the board itself, seven by some church body, three by the alumni, and one would be an *ex-officio* member. Seventy per cent. of these representative colleges are controlled by boards that have a majority of self-perpetuating memberships, and 30 per cent. by boards that have a majority elected by the church.

TABLE II

NUMBER AND PER CENT. OF COLLEGES IN WHICH TRUSTEES ARE NOMINATED BY VARIOUS AGENCIES AND THE NUMBER AND PER CENT. OF TRUSTEES NOMINATED BY THESE AGENCIES

Agencies nominating trustees	Number of colleges	Per cent.	Number of trustees	Per cent.
The board of trustees	18	90	318	59
The church	10	50	145	27
The alumni	12	60	55	10
Ex-officio	8	40	19	4

We conclude that the exercise of control divides the liberal arts colleges into two groups. The colleges of the first group are controlled by boards organized for the purpose of conducting institutions of higher learning *per se*, and they may look to private foundations and the general public for their support. The colleges of the second group are distinctly church colleges and must look to their constituency for support. We infer, with reasonable assurance of approximating the truth, that the former outnumber the latter in the ratio of seven to three.

CONCLUSIONS

(1) Fully two thirds of the private liberal arts colleges of the country are not dominated by any ecclesiastical organization.

(2) The boards of trustees in 60 per cent. of these colleges are self-perpetuating to the extent that the majority of the trusteeships are filled by a vote of the board.

(3) The alumni are becoming a factor in the control of these colleges by reason of the fact that they have representation on half of the boards of trustees. Among the older colleges the proportion is increased to three fourths.

(4) Ecclesiastical authority exercises control in about one third of the institutions which constitute the subject of this study.

IRWIN J. LUBBERS

CARROLL COLLEGE

NEW BOOKS IN EDUCATION

EBAUGH, CAMERON D. *The National System of Education in Mexico.* Pp. ix + 149. Johns Hopkins Press. $2.00.

HANS, NICHOLAS. *History of Russian Educational Policy (1701–1917).* Pp. xiii + 255. P. S. King, London. 10s. 6d.

LOTI, PIERRE. *Pêcheur D'Island.* Pp. xi + 137 + 42. Illustrated. Allyn & Bacon. $.80.

MORRIS, ALTON C. and HERMAN E. SPIVEY. *Essentials of Correctness in the Use of English.* Pp. viii + 102. Prentice-Hall. $.80.

PARKER, BERYL. *The Austrian Educational Institutes.* Pp. 184. Illustrated. New York University Book Shop.